MW01442371

The Story of Panama

THE STORY OF PANAMA

HEARINGS ON THE RAINEY RESOLUTION

BEFORE THE

COMMITTEE ON FOREIGN AFFAIRS

OF THE

HOUSE OF REPRESENTATIVES

COMMITTEE ON FOREIGN AFFAIRS

[Committee room, gallery floor, west corridor. Telephone 230. Meets on call.]

HENRY D. FLOOD, Virginia, *Chairman*.
JOHN N. GARNER, Texas.
WILLIAM G. SHARP, Ohio.
CYRUS CLINE, Indiana.
JEFFERSON M. LEVY, New York.
JAMES M. CURLEY, Massachusetts.
JOHN CHARLES LINTHICUM, Maryland.
ROBERT E. DIFENDERFER, Pennsylvania.
W. S. GOODWIN, Arkansas.
CHARLES M. STEDMAN, North Carolina.
EDWARD W. TOWNSEND, New Jersey.
B. P. HARRISON, Mississippi.
CHARLES BENNETT SMITH, New York.
WILLIAM B. MCKINLEY, Illinois.
HENRY A. COOPER, Wisconsin.
IRA W. WOOD, New Jersey.
RICHARD BARTHOLDT, Missouri.
GEORGE W. FAIRCHILD, New York.
N. E. KENDALL, Iowa.
J. HAMPTON MOORE, Pennsylvania.

FRANK S. CISNA, *Clerk*.

WASHINGTON
GOVERNMENT PRINTING OFFICE
1913

THE STORY OF PANAMA.

COMMITTEE ON FOREIGN AFFAIRS,
HOUSE OF REPRESENTATIVES,
Washington, D. C., February 19, 1913.

STATEMENT OF MR. FRANK D. PAVEY.

The CHAIRMAN. Mr. Pavey, you may proceed.

Mr. PAVEY. Mr. Chairman, in the way of slightly qualifying myself as a witness, I wish to say I held the official position of counsel of the legation of Panama from the 10th of November, 1903, to the 14th of February, 1905, when I tendered my resignation. My active work during that period was only during the period of four months, when Philippe Bunau-Varilla was minister of Panama accredited to the Government at Washington, and after his resignation and the appointment of his successor, although I had some relations with him, there was no very active work for me to do, and yet I continued officially to be the counsel of the legation until February 14, 1905, when I resigned, and soon afterwards Mr. William Nelson Cromwell was appointed as my successor to that position.

Prior to November 10, 1903, I had been an intimate personal friend of Philippe Bunau-Varilla for a period of more than four years, and had been one of his advisers and counsel in the United States in connection with the campaign in favor of Panama which he conducted in the United States. In the examination of the testimony which has been taken already before the committee under the Rainey resolution in regard to the revolution in Panama, I find that only one witness, I think, has been examined, and that was Mr. Hall, and his testimony to a very large extent is a résumé in his own language of material which was obtained by the World in an investigation which it made to defend itself against a libel suit brought by the Government, and the other document upon which he particularly relies for his facts is what he has designated as a plea for fees filed by Mr. Cromwell before the Board of Arbitration in Paris, which was examining into the question of the payment of his fees as counsel of the New Panama Canal Co. I draw attention to that fact to show that his sources of information were for all practical purposes from such sources as the plea for fees filed by Mr. Cromwell with the board of arbitration in regard to his fees in Paris.

Now, it is not surprising in the presentation of an account, a long, detailed account of his services extending over six or seven years, that Mr. Cromwell should have at least put the best foot foremost and attributed the result as much as possible to his own efforts. It was also perfectly natural that he should not give any notice or any credit to any other influences that were at work in the United States in favor of Panama at that time. It is also natural that even if he had been actuated by no motives other than to arrive at the exact truth, it is natural that a man who began his investigation with that as a basis would be very likely to acquire the idea that Mr. Cromwell was the sole source of activity in favor of Panama in this country during the four or five years prior to the revolution of Panama and the recognition of the Republic of Panama; and that once he had come to believe that, then he might in the very best of faith attribute to that fact results which were not at all due to that fact.

Now, that has been the case with Mr. Hall. I am not discussing the question whether he was acting in good faith or in bad faith in his conclusions, or whether he was trying to make out a case for the World when he made the investigation or not, but that fact appears so conspicuously in numerous places that I will cite only one to show to what extent it leads him in his statements.

On page 317 he states:

Dr. Amador's cables "disappointed" and "hope" were written the first after Mr. Cromwell had told him he would have nothing to do with the revolution, the second after information had been conveyed to him that if he would remain quiet in New York he would receive help from another quarter. Help did come from another quarter. Summoned in haste from Paris, Philippe Bunau-Varilla, one of the New Panama Canal Co., who had been instrumental in getting Mr. Cromwell reappointed as counsel, arrived in New York on September 23, 1903, some two weeks after Dr. Amador had sent his cable "disappointed" to the Isthmus, or just in time for Mr. Cromwell, who was anxious to get under cover after Dr. Herran's warning, to cable to Paris and have Bunau-Varilla take the first steamer across.

Unfortunately I do not have the cable that I believe Mr. Cromwell sent to the New Panama Canal Co. to have Mr. Bunau-Varilla sent over here, but that cable is also among the archives of the New Panama Canal Co., which are the property of the United States, and which are still in France, kept in the vaults there.

I cite that to show that, whether in good faith or bad faith, his belief in Mr. Cromwell as the sole influence and sole force that produced any activity in the United States in regard to Panama carries him to the point of stating, as he does there, that "unfortunately, I do not have the cable that I believe Mr. Cromwell sent," but it is in the archives. That was the state of mind of this man. I cite that as a precise illustration of the point I want to make, that there were two distinct and independent forces working in this country in favor of Panama for some years before the revolution of Panama. One was the New Panama Canal Co., with Mr. Cromwell as its representative, and the other was Philippe Bunau-Varilla, as an individual. Philippe Bunau-Varilla had been formerly chief engineer, along about 1885 or 1886, of the old Panama Canal Co., but he had become inimical to the management of the New Panama Canal Co., for what reasons in detail I do not know; but I do know of my own knowledge that that lack of cordiality and sympathy existed to a very great extent, and that it was in existence as early as 1898 or 1899, when I first met Mr. Bunau-Varilla.

Mr. SHARP. May I interrupt you there?

Mr. PAVEY. Certainly.

Mr. SHARP. I have heard you refer to the New Panama Canal Co. What organization was that?

Mr. PAVEY. What in English we commonly designate as the old company was I think merely called the Panama Canal Co., and that was the De Lesseps company, organized to take over the concession granted in 1878, and it continued in active existence until about 1894, when it fell into financial embarrassment, and then a different company was organized, called the New Panama Canal Co., as we translate it in English, and in French "La Compagnie Nouvelle du Canal de Panama."

Mr. SHARP. What connection, if any, as a stockholder or adviser or counsel of that company did Mr. Cromwell have?

Mr. PAVEY. He became counsel of that company, according to his own statement in his brief for his fees, in January, 1896. He had, according to this record, been counsel for the Panama Railroad Co. prior to that time, and the Panama Railroad Co. was owned by the New Panama Canal Co.

Mr. Bunau-Varilla was a stockholder in the New Panama Canal Co., but what amount of stock he had I can not state myself, although it is not at all a secret. It has been made public in some of these investigations of the Panama affair. I mention that fact in order not to appear to claim he had no connection with the company; but he had no connection as an officer or a director or a representative in this country or an agent in this country, because of the entire lack of cordiality and friendly relations which existed between them.

That first came to my attention, and his position in the matter first came to my attention in 1898 or 1899. At that time I was in Paris and met Mr. Bunau-Varilla for the first time; and he did to me what he was seeking to do to every American whom he could meet. He learned of my presence in Paris through a mutual friend, and insisted that before I left Paris that this man should bring me to his house to dinner. Dinner with him meant half past eight, and after dinner we settled down in his library, and he never let go of an American victim when he got one in that library until he thought he had converted him; and the first time I dined in his house I stayed until 2 o'clock the next morning, listening to his picturesque and fascinating argument in favor of Panama as against Nicaragua.

He found me in one sense a valuable victim, if I may use that phrase, because I had had very considerable knowledge of Nicaragua, as I had been a clerk in the office of the counsel of that country during its period of most prosperity, and was friendly with Mr. Warner and Mr. Hitchcock, of the Fifth Avenue Hotel; and he, learning that fact, made a special effort to convert me to the cause of Panama, which I am frank to confess he did. He was doing that with every American whom he could meet. I can mention a Mr. Schmidlapp, of Cincinnati; Mr. Herrick, present Ambassador to France; and I can also mention Mr. Loomis, former Assistant Secretary of State, and there were many others. Now, he was doing that in the firm belief that sooner or later the United States would come to adopt the Panama Canal route, and he was contributing his efforts in that direction.

Mr. SHARP. He was a promoter to that extent, was he not?

Mr. PAVEY. Yes.

Mr. KENDALL. How old a man is Mr. Bunau-Varilla?

Mr. PAVEY. Under 55. I should think he was between 52 and 55 years of age.

Mr. KENDALL. A man of prestige in France, is he?

Mr. PAVEY. Of very great prestige in his profession, and so far as I know his only activity has been in his profession. He has built railroads in Spain and has built railroads in the Kongo, and has been interested in enterprises in South America of different characters, although I do not know about that. He related to me at one time the way he came to go to Panama. His imagination was fired when he was a student at the Ecole de Polytechnique by a lecture which Mr. De Lesseps delivered there, and as a young man he then resolved when he got out of school he would go into the service of the Panama Canal Co. if he could. He did that and became chief engineer at a very early age, and it has become a fetish with him—perhaps I should not use the word "fetish," as it is not quite respectful—but an ideal, just as the Nicaraguan canal was an ideal that no amount of facts or arguments could move the late Senator Morgan from his opinion in favor of the Nicaraguan Canal, and that has been true of Mr. Bunau-Varilla.

My knowledge in regard to this lack of friendly relations with the New Panama Canal Co. first came to my attention in 1899, when I was in Paris again, and renewed my acquaintance with Mr. Bunau-Varilla by calls upon him. He came to see me and told me a fact that I was not particularly interested in, that a subcommittee of the Isthmian Canal Commission was then in Paris investigating the affairs of the Panama Canal Co., with a view to including that knowledge in its report, and that he wanted to meet the members of that subcommittee, but that he could not meet them through the New Panama Canal Co.: that there would be no introduction he could ever have to them from that source, and asked me if I could arrange it. I called upon Prof. Burr and Mr. Morrison, who were the two members there at that time, and made arrangements so they took lunch with me, and I brought about the acquaintance in that way. Mr. Bunau-Varilla then set himself to convert them, as engineers, by going over all the details of the engineering features of the canal, just as he had done with me in less technical language.

I remember in 1899 my telling him that he might talk to all the Americans he met in Paris, but he could not talk to them fast enough to overcome the public opinion which existed in the United States in favor of Nicaragua; that at that time there was only one opinion in the United States, and that was that there was merely a hole in Panama, into which a lot of French money had been sunk, and that no canal would ever be possible there, and that the sentiment in favor of Nicaragua would have to be overcome as a matter of public opinion before there could be any expectation that the Government of the United States would adopt that route.

Mr. Sharp. I would like to ask you in that connection, since you appear to be very familiar with the history that led up to the adoption of the Panama route, as a matter of fact should not the late Senator Hanna have more credit for changing that sentiment and for the decision to go to Panama than any other American citizen?

Mr. Pavey. That is absolutely true. Mr. Bunau-Varilla himself gives Senator Hanna credit for that result. He takes this credit to himself, which I think he is entitled to take—he was introduced to Senator Hanna by Mr. Herrick for the express purpose of giving Senator Hanna the benefit of his knowledge on the subject. I was just about to state that I had urged him to come to this country and make public addresses on the subject before chambers of commerce and other organizations, and he spoke English well enough to do that.

Mr. Herrick and Mr. Schmidlapp secured for him invitations to come to Cincinnati and Cleveland for that purpose, and he came to this country and went to Cincinnati and Cleveland and made addresses on the subject.

Subsequently I arranged it for him to be invited to speak before the Chamber of Commerce in New York City, and with those three meetings as a start he continued for a year and a half prior to the passage of the Spooner bill to do work of that character. He was in the United States a great deal of the time, but of course went back to Paris for a part of the time, but he was over here a great deal. I think he came here first in the fall of 1900 and continued that sort of work during 1900 and 1901, and then to some extent continued it down to the passage of the so-called Spooner bill in 1902. During all of that time he was acting absolutely independent of the New Panama Canal Co. and of Mr. Cromwell, and he continued to do so down to the time of his resignation as minister of Panama, after the ratification of the treaty in February, 1904.

Of course Mr. Cromwell was engaged in a great deal of activity in regard to Panama, and according to this record, which I have no doubt is substantially correct on that point, Dr. Amador came to the United States with the hope of securing the support of Mr. Cromwell, and through Mr. Cromwell the support of the Government of the United States, to a project for a revolution in Panama. All parties seem to agree that that was his object in coming to this country, and that he believed he had or would have the support of Mr. Cromwell and the officials of the Panama Railroad Co. in coming here for that purpose. It also appears from the record that he had after he got here some reason to believe that he was going to have that support; but as some knowledge of his plans came to the attention of Dr. Herran, the representative of Colombia, Dr. Herran wrote a letter of warning to Mr. Cromwell as to the consequences that would come to his company if any aid or comfort were given to the enemy in that shape. The record shows that Mr. Cromwell then turned his back upon Dr. Amador. Mr. Hall undertakes to maintain that this turning of his back upon Dr. Amador was only a ruse on the part of Mr. Cromwell in order to shield himself and his company from responsibility, and then in order to connect up what took place afterwards he had to invent his belief in this cablegram to have Bunau-Varilla come over here at the instigation of Mr. Cromwell, because it is necessary for him to do that to connect his first statement up with the things that subsequently happened.

Mr. Sharp. Do you deny that there was any such cablegram or any such invitation?

Mr. Pavey. No such cablegram or invitation was sent. Mr. Bunau-Varilla came here for personal reasons. At that particular moment he came for personal reasons of a domestic character, but he had intended to come a little bit later. He merely came a little sooner than he had otherwise intended, because he was in the habit of coming here two or three times a year for the express purpose of following the course of the Panama Canal question in this country and doing what he could to secure the adoption of the Panama Canal route by the United States.

Mr. SHARP. As a matter of fact, they had a large investment there that they simply wanted to get rid of, and naturally they were impelled by those motives to want the Panama route selected over the Nicaraguan route; is not that the plain truth?

Mr. PAVEY. That is perfectly true.

Mr. SHARP. And the same motives would guide anybody else in wanting to dispose of property when they saw their efforts must only end in failure if they let a new project get under way?

Mr. PAVEY. That is perfectly true; but the point I am making is that whatever Bunau-Varilla did, he did not do it at the instigation of the Panama Canal Co. or at the invitation of Mr. Cromwell or in cooperation with either one of them, because he was not in cooperation with either one of them at that time.

Now, having arrived here with no definite purpose in his mind, he found this situation: He had known Dr. Amador on the Isthmus. He learned through a Mr. Lindo, who was the banker for Dr. Amador when he was here, that Dr. Amador was in New York, and Mr. Lindo sent word to Dr. Amador and Mr. Bunau-Varilla telephoned to Dr. Amador, and in that way they got together. He learned from Dr. Amador what had taken place, which I have described, in regard to the encouragement he had received to come here, and then the fact that Mr. Cromwell had turned his back upon him, and then Mr. Bunau-Varilla himself took up with Dr. Amador, without any relation with Mr. Cromwell or without any relations with the Panama Canal Co., the whole question of the situation on the Isthmus of Panama, and he himself conceived and worked out the plans for the revolution.

The documents which Mr. Hall says were drawn in Mr. Cromwell's office were not drawn in Mr. Cromwell's office. They were drawn in the Waldorf-Astoria Hotel, under the direction of Mr. Bunau-Varilla, and so far as they were written in Spanish they were copied, letter by letter, by an English stenographer, who knew no Spanish, in order that there should not be any possibility of a knowledge of them leaking out. The whole project of the Panama Canal revolution as it was carried out was conceived by Mr. Bunau-Varilla in cooperation with Dr. Amador between the 23d day of September and the 18th day of November, when the treaty was finally signed, and between the 23d day of September and the 15th of October, when Mr. Cromwell went to Paris, undoubtedly upon the business of the company, but with no knowledge of what was going on between Dr. Amador and Mr. Bunau-Varilla. The transactions were entirely free from even the influence of Mr. Cromwell during that period, and Mr. Cromwell never reappeared upon the scene until he landed in New York on the 17th of November, 1903, the same day that the two new Panama commissioners arrived here, and he then renewed his relations with them, and they came to Washington the next day, on the 18th, arriving here at 9 or 10 o'clock in the evening, and the treaty was signed here at 6.40 on the evening of that same day by Mr. Bunau-Varilla.

During all that period from September 22, the exact day upon which Mr. Bunau-Varilla arrived here, until the 19th or 20th of November, Mr. Cromwell and Mr. Bunau-Varilla never saw each other.

Mr. KENDALL. Nor communicated with each other?

Mr. PAVEY. Nor communicated with each other at all. I have laid stress upon that for this purpose: The whole purpose of the record so far is to try to create and fasten upon the United States a responsibility in regard to the revolution of Panama, based upon the activities of Mr. Cromwell prior to and about that time. Now, the revolution of Panama happened, by reason of the circumstances which I have related, to be a separate and distinct affair during that period from September 22 to November 18, when the treaty was signed here in Washington; and no investigation will ever bring results that are accurate and true unless the errors in the record in that respect are corrected.

My object in asking for this hearing was particularly to make this statement and then to ask that there be printed in the record a statement by Mr. Bunau-Varilla on that subject. I have a typewritten copy of the statement here, which was submitted to the committee last spring under circumstances which I will relate, and that has been revised and printed, so that any typographical errors are pretty well eliminated. The origin of that statement was this: I think about the middle of last March Mr. Bunau-Varilla received copies of these hearings in Paris. He at once saw the many fallacies that existed in the facts and conclusions as well, based upon this erroneous conception in regard to the responsibility of Mr. Cromwell for things for which he was not responsible, and he cabled to me to ascertain whether the committee would receive a statement from him. I communicated with your then chairman, Mr. Sulzer, and also saw him in New York, as my letter passed him on the way. Mr. Sulzer said to me he would like very much to have Mr. Bunau-Varilla come over here as a witness, and requested me to use my good offices to bring that about. I did not deem it a matter that required cabling, and took my time about it, perhaps, and wrote a long letter of explanation in accordance with the suggestions of Mr. Sulzer to arrange to get him to come over here as a witness.

As Mr. Bunau-Varilla did not hear from me in response to his cable, and having some anxiety lest the Congress might be going to adjourn or the committee terminate its hearings, he prepared a statement and sent it direct to the Speaker of the House of Representatives, to be given to the committee, as I understand it was, and also sent me a copy, with the request I transmit it direct to Mr. Sulzer, which I did, and also to arrange with Mr. Sulzer to have it made a part of the record. As this statement arrived about the same time that my letter went over there asking him to appear as a witness, of course Mr. Sulzer took no action in regard to the statement, because he still clung to the idea that I could arrange to get Mr. Bunau-Varilla over here as a witness; and in accordance with my promise to Mr. Sulzer I made the best effort possible to bring about that result. I continued those efforts until it was approaching the time of adjournment in August, when Mr. Sulzer wrote me that there would not be a report made before the adjournment, and perhaps the arrangement could be made for this winter. When I was in Paris in September I went over the subject very thoroughly with Mr. Bunau-Varilla, and in some ways he was very anxious to come before the committee, but circumstances of a very serious domestic character—I mean illness in his family—and his very great preoccupation in other business matters that he has been working out, made it most inconvenient for him to try to make the trip at any time, and for that reason we have been unable to get him to come over here.

When I saw it was too late to think of having him come over, I decided to take up again the question of having this printed as a part of the record. The value of the document lies in the fact that it points out a number of very important errors in the record which to my mind are logically due to this erroneous conception in the minds of the men who made up that report as to the sole activity of Mr. Cromwell in the matter, and to the false idea they have that Mr. Bunau-Varilla was acting as a part of his organization, when as a matter of fact it was an independent activity, and no responsibility can attach to the revolution of Panama, as it was finally planned and executed, by reason of anything which Mr. Cromwell did, with the bare exception that he was, perhaps we will say, responsible for Dr. Amador being in New York in September. Now, with that statement I am perfectly willing to go into any greater details, but I promised to be brief, and that covers the principal purpose of my visit here.

Mr. KENDALL. Is this statement substantially the same statement Mr. Bunau-Varilla sent to various members of the committee last summer?

Mr. PAVEY. It is the same statement. I would like to make this suggestion, that there is just one error I have discovered in that copy in going over it, although it is corrected subsequently, but on page 65 the words "October, 1903," should be "November, 1903," although, as I say, it is really corrected at the bottom of the page.

The CHAIRMAN. You ask now, Mr. Pavey, to be allowed to file this as a part of your statement?

Mr. PAVEY. Yes, sir.

The CHAIRMAN. The printed statement will be included in the record.

STATEMENT ON BEHALF OF HISTORICAL TRUTH.

[By Philippe Bunau-Varilla, former chief engineer of the Panama Canal Co. (1885-86); former minister plenipotentiary of Panama to the United States (1903-4); officer of the Legion of Honor, etc. For the information of the Committee on Foreign Affairs of the House of Representatives. (Rainey resolution.)]

PARIS, *March 29, 1912.*

The Hon. CHAMP CLARK,
Speaker of the House of Representatives, Washington, D. C.

SIR: The hearings before the Committee of Foreign Affairs on the Rainey resolution have brought forward a so-called Story of Panama, which has been printed as a congressional document and distributed.

This "Story," outside of various imaginary and misleading facts enunciated by its author, is mainly based on the assertions of a plea written in 1907 in order to try, without success, to obtain from a court of arbitration a high fee of $800,000 for services said to have been rendered to the New Panama Canal Co., and which said company denied.

This plea is a tissue of erroneous and misleading assertions. The definition of its character is sufficiently given by him who wrote it when he says in it that the remuneration he asks is in part for having been "in a position to influence a considerable number of public men in political life" through the relations at the same time "intimate and susceptible of being used to advantage" in which his firm pretends to have been placed "with men possessing influence and power."

In this plea the House of Representatives is described as made powerless to vote a law which its majority enthusiastically supports and desires to pass. In this plea the actions of statesmen of the first rank, such as Secretary Hay and Senator Hanna, are described as those of passive mechanisms commanded by a subtle and exterior mind.

The gigantic work of the union of the oceans begun for the glory and utility of mankind by a French company is going to reach its apotheosis, thanks to the generous efforts of the people of the United States.

Will the story of its transmission from the French owners to the Government of America be written by taking as its base an unfaithful document dictated by a sordid interest?

If this document were true there would be a deep veil of shame on the memories of great American citizens, which ought to be on the contrary worshipped as those of men inspired by the most lofty ideals and served by a powerful intelligence, as those of men who have filled one of the noble pages of the history of their country.

If this document were true it would show the legislative power of the United States to be at the disposal of mercenary influences in questions of the highest gravity, and not, as it is, inspired by the sincere desire of serving the great interests of the Nation to the best of its ability.

This question is infinitely above any division of parties; it concerns the honor of the United States—one might say the honor of all free nations having representative governments.

I have thought that this monument of deceit should not be left in the congressional documentation without placing at its side another. document demonstrating its untruthfulness, and thereby vindicating the honor of those who have been the real forces which have determined the adoption of the Panama route by the United States.

The United States have not to blush of the history of the adoption of the Panama Canal, any more than France has to blush of the history of its conception and creation, if in both cases the history is written disinterestedly, sincerely, and faithfully.

I know what terrible disorders fictitious stories about Panama have created in France because the necessary jet of light has not been thrown on their mendacity.

I have thought it to be my duty to prevent the dissemination of the offensive fictions inserted in the so-called Story of Panama presented before a committee of Congress, and I have prepared for the Committee on Foreign Affairs of the House of Representatives a statement on behalf of historical truth. You will find it inclosed.

I allow myself, Mr. Speaker, to address it to this committee, through you as the head of the House of Representatives, with the respectful request, if the committee deems it justified, to insert it next to the Story of Panama in order to redress its misleading and deceitful errors.

Very respectfully, P. Bunau-Varilla.

In writing this statement I attach to it the same moral authority and legal responsibility as if it were made under oath.

The so-called Story of Panama as told in the hearings before the Committee on Foreign Affairs of the House of Representatives by Mr. Henry H. Hall is a fiction. This fiction is composed of true facts and documents mixed with fabricated assertions and fanciful documents. It does not differ from similar productions so often read in the public press and due to imaginative journalism.

My purpose is to demonstrate this statement by documentary evidence. I think it is my duty to do it, because said fiction has gained access to congressional documentation and should not be left there unexposed.

A STANDARD SAMPLE OF MR. HALL'S FABRICATED ASSERTIONS.

Before going seriatim into the study of the elements of that imaginary story I may be allowed to exhibit a standard example of the methods employed for fabricating it. I am selecting this sample because it is the only one of Mr. Hall's statements which has been widely reported by the press.

Mr. Hall (pp. 414–415) first reproduces a cablegram of the Secretary of State, Mr. Hay, to the American consul in Panama. It reads:

Washington, *November 5, 1903.*

American Consul General.
Panama:

I send for your information and guidance in the execution of the instructions cabled to you to-day the text of a telegram dispatched this day to the United States minister at Bogota:

"The people of the Isthmus having by an apparently unanimous movement dissolved their political connection with the Republic of Colombia and resumed their independence * * * He (the President of the United States) holds that he is bound not merely by treaty obligations but by the interest of civilization, to see that the peaceable traffic of the world across the Isthmus of Panama shall not longer be disturbed by constant succession of unnecessary and wasteful civil wars."

Hay.

Then after giving two other cablegrams referring to the appointment of Philippe Bunau-Varilla as envoy extraordinary of Panama to Washington, Mr. Hall says:

"Now I think there is a good place to point out a remarkable coincidence. We have the State Department telegraphing to its agent in Bogota on the 6th of November this dispatch, beginning:

"'The people of Panama having by an apparently unanimous consent,' and ending 'constant succession of unnecessary and wasteful civil wars,' The same day or rather the next morning, not from Washington, but in New York, Mr. Philippe Bunau-Varilla wrote to the State Department announcing that he was appointed as minister plenipotentiary of the Republic of Panama to the United States, and his letter reads:

"NEW YORK, *November 7, 1903.*

"His Excellency JOHN HAY,

"*Secretary of State, Washington:*

"I have the privilege and honor of notifying you that * * * It (the United States) has rescued it (Panama) from the barbarism of unnecessary and wasteful civil wars to consecrate it to the destiny assigned to it by Providence, the service of humanity, and the progress of civilization.

"PHILIPPE BUNAU-VARILLA.

"There you have Bunau-Varilla using the very words unnecessary and wasteful civil wars used a few hours previously by Secretary Hay in his dispatch to the American minister at Bogota, and the coincidence is almost as remarkable as," etc.

On page 419 Mr. Hall comes back on the same point and says:

"You will recall how in that communication to the State Department Bunau-Varilla made use of the same words, 'unnecessary and wasteful civil wars,' which Mr. Hay also made use of in a confidential dispatch to the American minister in Bogota."

In a few words Mr. Hall thus demonstrates to his own satisfaction that the same hand has traced the Secretary of State's confidential dispatch and the Panama minister's notification. Therefore, according to Mr. Hall, Mr. Bunau-Varilla is a puppet of straw handled by the American Government.

Who would doubt such obvious facts brought forth by a man who describes himself as a man who "has employed whatsoever of ability he possesses" and "the experience gained in more than 20 years of active newspaper work"; who has "endeavored fairly and impartially to place the truth before the Committee on Foreign Affairs as he saw it in the documents gathered by the World"; as a man who "firmly believes that righteousness alone exalteth a nation"; as a man who thinks that "with nations even more than with individuals honesty is the best policy"; as a man who "speaks in the name of Truth, Justice, and Honor." (All quotations from p. 471, Story of Panama.[1])

Who would doubt the assertions on points of facts made by a man who insists "that he has really confined himself, as the committee is aware, solely to documents and statements that could be substantiated" (p. 461).

Evidently nobody can refuse to give credence to such a proof brought forward by such a man.

However, all that he asserts on this point is a fiction, to say the least.

Even the almighty power of Truth, Justice, and Honor can not enable Mr. Hall to substantiate that a document, which he copies on page 414 with the date November 5, 1903, has been made on the day just before another document of which he gives a copy bearing the date November 7. Even the combined efforts of Truth, Justice, and Honor can not make the miracle of placing the morning of the 7th on the day following the 5th of November. (See p. 414 date of Mr. Hay's dispatch 5th of November, and p. 415, date of Mr. Bunau-Varilla's notification 7th of November.)

The three divinities above named even associated with the 20 years of journalism of Mr. Hall will also find it difficult to enable the writer of the "Story" to substantiate that a document is confidential when it is published by all the newspapers of the United States on the day following its date and preceding that of the other document, which borrows an expression in the first one.

This is precisely the case of the message of Mr. Hay bearing the date of the 5th November and which Mr. Hall terms confidential. All the evening newspapers of New York published on the 6th Mr. Hay's dispatch ending by "unnecessary and wasteful civil wars." All the morning newspapers of the 7th repeated it.

Now, is it possible that the so many endeavors of Mr. Hall, all the ability he possesses, all the experience he has gathered in 20 years' journalism, should have resulted in allowing his imagination to fabricate simply a fiction?

---

[1] Whenever I shall afterwards quote a page without further designation it must be understood that it is taken from the Story of Panama, hearings on the Rainey resolution before the Committee of Foreign Affairs of the House of Representatives Jan. 26 to Feb. 20, 1912.

It seems impossible, but it is so.

The simple truth is that having read in the evening papers of the 6th of November, 1903, Mr. Hay's dispatch of the 5th, I thought it courteous to employ his own expression "unnecessary and wasteful civil wars" in my communication of the day following. If it was confidential when I read it I was sharing the confidence with 80,000,000 people.

This is a very correct sample of the method by which the Story of Panama has been fabricated.

It was not unnecessary to expose this method at the start. We shall find its consequences everywhere. When a fact does not please the writer of the "story," it is either turned upside down or entirely replaced by another one. The substitute is furnished by imagination and solemnly presented as warranted by proofs and documents above the most severe suspicion.

Let us now turn to the base of the "story," that is the plea for fees made by Mr. Cromwell before the court of arbitration. Let us examine its impartiality first, its veracity afterwards.

What is the impartiality of Mr. Cromwell's plea for fees?

To judge this question it is necessary to know first for what kind of professional activities Mr. Cromwell demanded a high fee. Mr. Cromwell, besides the legal profession, practices another one. What is Mr. Cromwell's profession (outside of the legal one)? He will himself answer the question in the plea for fees. On page 96 it reads:

"In the course of a very active and very extended professional career * * * the firm Sullivan & Cromwell had found itself placed in intimate relations, susceptible of being used to advantage with men possessing influence and power * * * they (the members of the firm) have also come to know and be in a position to influence a considerable number of public men in political life * * * It is not suggested that the remuneration should be based upon this consideration alone."

Any commentary seems perfectly superfluous. Whether this clear definition of the kind of activities for which the fees are asked is in harmony with the ethics of the legal profession in America, it is not for me but for the Bar Association of New York to answer. But the question is not there. It was necessary to recall the clear definition given of Mr. Cromwell's profession by himself to understand that a plea for fees on account of such services can not possibly be impartial.

Human nature tends always to exaggerate in a man's mind the results of his efforts.

If the aim of the effort is to influence public men in political life, vanity only will lead any man to think that his influence has been greater than it really was. An active go-between will easily think he is the author of the messages he has to carry. But if he claims a fee for having exercised such influence the appetite for money adds itself to the appetite for vanity and the result is an extraordinary exaggeration of the facts presented by the claimant.

One might say that the more proper will be the methods by which the influence is exercised, the greater will be the exaggeration.

I think it is unnecessary to state that the great American citizens who had to treat this national question were infinitely above any improper consideration. Therefore, for both reasons above stated, the influence said to have been exercised over them was grossly and enormously exaggerated, if not entirely imagined by the man who wants a remuneration for it. It is the eternal story of the tail which sustains that it is wagging the dog.

A plea for fees written under these conditions of mind can not be impartial.

It is, therefore, an unfit base for writing the story of any great event.

However, if not impartial, it could keep the relation of events within the boundaries of verity. Let us examine if this is the case.

WHAT IS THE VERACITY OF MR. CROMWELL'S PLEA FOR FEES?

Suspicions were raised in the committee about a lack of veracity of Mr. Cromwell's assertions as exhibited by Mr. Hall in his presentation of extracts of the plea for fees.

On page 144 the following can be read:

"Mr. Kendall. That is what Mr. Cromwell says in his report to these employees of his?

"Mr. Hall. Yes, sir.

"Mr. Kendall. He was trying to get his $800,000 fee?

"Mr. Hall. We must presume he was telling the truth.

"Mr. Kendall. His purpose was to convince them how difficult it had been for him to accomplish the results he did?

"Mr. Hall. I suppose so, sir."

It seems that contrary to Mr. Hall's opinion in a plea for fees referring to an influence supposed to have been exercised over public men in political life the presumption is an exaggeration of that supposed influence, if not much more than exaggeration. Further, on page 291, the same doubt is raised about the veracity of Mr. Cromwell's plea for fees.

"Mr. GARNER. In behalf of Mr. Hay, who is deceased, would it not be assumed that Mr. Cromwell was making statements that could not be sustained by facts in order to secure a fee from the French company? In other words, to use a harsh term, it is not possible that Mr. Cromwell is lying about the matter of what Mr. Hay did?

"Mr. HALL. Quite possible.

"The CHAIRMAN. He certainly was trying to get a big fee."

Mr. Hall, who, as we will see later on, will attribute to Mr. Cromwell's plea for fees the value of a document under oath was evidently for a moment taken by surprise. Candidly, he admits that Mr. Cromwell may be, as Mr. Garner says, lying. This is a spontaneous and perfectly fair acknowledgement of what the document may be. If the Story of Panama is based upon such a doubtful document, what is it? But Mr. Hall will later on try to strengthen his base of action, and on page 293 the following dialogue takes place:

"Mr. KENDALL. These statements of Mr. Cromwell involving Mr. Hay, as Judge Difenderfer inquires, were not under oath, they were simply incorporated in his brief filed with that board.

"Mr. HALL. This is his brief. The point I was making was not in any way, shape or form a reflection upon the late Secretary of State, but in justice to Mr. Cromwell it is inconceivable that a man of Mr. Cromwell's standing at the New York bar should in a brief presented to arbitrators in a matter of this kind make statements which he would not be ready to substantiate under oath."

The same effort of Mr. Hall to strengthen the weak authority of the base of his "story" is further renewed on page 457.

"Mr. FLOOD. The accomplishments of Mr. Cromwell in getting officials to change their position on this question are based on his own testimony?

"Mr. HALL. On his own testimony, sir. The many assertions he makes affecting Secretary of State Hay, who is dead, and Senator Hanna, who is dead, are matters which rest on his own authority. It is improbable, of course, knowing that the company was in possession of all his correspondence and of all his accounts, that he would put forward statements he could not substantiate. Having made weekly and monthly reports to them covering a period of six years and having received their replies and acknowledgments, it is hardly to be believed that he could deliberately add into this brief anything he had not reported to the company at the time. Also, Mr. Cromwell's standing at the bar in New York is a very high one, and it would mean his disbarment if he were to present in an arbitration for remuneration for professional services facts which were not true. Of course, I have accorded the weight of testimony to Mr. Cromwell's own written assertions."

In trying to defend the shaky base of his "story" Mr. Hall thus represents Mr. Cromwell as acting under the formal and rigid supervision and checking of his employers, the company.

At this moment Mr. Hall unfortunately forgets that he has been obliged to disqualify the employers of Mr Cromwell for the necessities of his "story." These necessities have compelled him to attribute to Mr. Cromwell a universal power in all directions. On page 328 he had said of the president of the New Panama Co.:

"The president of the Credit Lyonnais was Marius Bo, also the president of the New Panama Canal Co. and Cromwell's chief instrument in France in its manipulation."

In spite of his endeavors to "fairly and impartially place the truth before the committee" (p. 471), Mr. Hall will find some difficulties in reconciling contradictory facts. He can not very well, in spite of his solemn declaration that (p. 461) "he confines himself solely to documents and statements that could be substantiated," demonstrate that the same Bo, who is a tool in the hands of Cromwell, on page 328, becomes a severe and incorruptible comptroller on page 457.

Let us in passing say that Mr. Bo never was in his life nor ever will be president of the Credit Lyonnais. In spite of his 20 years' journalism, Mr. Hall ignores that by giving without any semblance of reason to Mr. Bo the leadership of one of the greatest banks in the world, he again allows his imagination to create a wholly erroneous and misleading fact.

Mr. Bo is in reality a director of the Credit Lyonnais; this is the true fact. It does not mean much for Mr. Hall's "story." He immediately fabricates another fact instead, and Mr. Bo. the tool of Mr. Cromwell at one place, his severe comptroller at another, is fabricated president of the great banking institution by Mr. Hall's fancy for the sake of the "story."

After having established what spontaneous suspicions of untruthfulness the plea for fees raised in the committee, let us try to look into this question of veracity.

Of course, when a man is dead, his secretary can always pretend that the secretary was dictating the letters and not his master. That is practically what the members of the committee above named suspected when they listened to Mr. Cromwell's contentions for getting a high fee. It is difficult to establish the untruthfulness of the statement as regards men who are dead. To be sure, it is most unlikely that men of the mental greatness of Hay or Hanna ever were handled like straw puppets. However, if it can be demonstrated by documental evidence that in all places where documents speak alone the plea for fees presents facts untruthfully, the hesitation will cease. The suspicions of the members of the committee will be vindicated. The lack of veracity of the offensive assertions cast on the great memories of Hay and Hanna must be then considered as established. It is indeed obvious that if the plea for fees absolutely disfigures facts when they can be reconstituted by public documents, one will be sure that the facts relating to dead men's attitudes or actions will be still more adulterated if not entirely fabricated.

In probing thus the veracity of the plea for fees we shall choose as examples a series of facts. These facts are chosen not only because they can be reconstituted by public documents, but also because they are placed at the origin of critical periods.

Thus it will be established that the lack of veracity so demonstrated is not exceptional, but systematic; that there is a very high probability that it is the spirit pervading the whole document.

The first critical period in the relations between the New Panama Canal Co. and Mr. Cromwell is the beginning of Mr. Cromwell's activities in their behalf in 1896. The second one is the entrance of the Panama Canal into the list of solutions proposed to America. This entrance entirely depended upon the success or failure of the Nicaragua bill in the session ending March 4, 1899. A third one is the period during which Mr. Cromwell was dismissed from the service of the canal company—July, 1901, to January, 1902. A fourth one is from the presentation of the Spooner bill to its adoption (January-June, 1902). A fifth one is the period from the signing of the Hay-Bunau-Varilla treaty (November, 1903) till its ratification (February, 1904).

Of course there are many other critical periods, but as the facts can not be exhibited without introducing as evidence exclusively public documents I shall leave them aside. The lack of veracity of the plea for fees will be amply established by the five examples herein stated.

FIRST DEMONSTRATION OF AN ABSOLUTE LACK OF VERACITY ON A GIVEN POINT IN MESSRS. SULLIVAN AND CROMWELL'S PLEA FOR FEES.

On page 164 the plea for fees begins the description of Mr. Cromwell's activities on behalf of the company as follows:

"Thus, when we were intrusted with the affair in January,[1] 1896, we found ourselves face to face with a general and almost unanimous opinion in the United States in favor of the Nicaragua Canal * * *. We ascertained also that * * * bills were pending in Congress before the Senate and the House with a view to the adoption of the Nicaragua route * * * and that Congress had authorized the appointment of a special commission to again survey and report on the feasibility of this route, and the commission was then engaged in this work."

Then comes a chapter entitled: "January-December, 1896. Recapitulation of work done in 1896." It contains the following sentence: "Between January and June, 1896, Mr. Cromwell and Mr. Curtis made alternative stays in Washington for the purpose. They devoted themselves actively to the case * * * had interviews with number of Senators and Representatives. * * * Mr. Cromwell also had frequent interviews with Col. Ludlow in regard to investigations by his commission and urged upon (presented to him) the superior advantages of Panama. As a result of this exposition the Ludlow commission in its subsequent (ultérieur)[2] report made very favorable references to the Panama route."

Further on page 165 we find another chapter entitled: "Result: There was no legislation for Nicaragua that year 1896."

---

[1] The word "January" which translates the word "Janvier" existing in the original text has been omitted in the translation given by Mr. Hall. I reestablish it.

[2] In the original text the adjective used before the word "report" is "ultérieur," which means subsequent. In the translation given by Mr. Hall it is expressed by "supplementary," which has quite a different meaning. The French word "ultérieur" is in the said translation put into parenthesis to show the hesitation about the proper use of "supplementary" by which it is wrongly translated. The real meaning of "postérieur" there, which is "subsequent," has been reestablished in the extract I give.

It begins thus: "The reports of the Senate and House committee on the subject of the Nicaragua Canal bills were favorable to those measures but the arguments we had disseminated and the opposition we had created were sufficient to form an important minority which refused to join the other members of the committee and no Nicaragua bill was passed at this session which closed in the month of June."

The following chapter of the plea for fees is entitled: "December, 1896, to March 1897. Attack and defeat of the Nicaragua legislation." It ends thus: "In spite of the vigorous and almost successful efforts of the Nicaragua party, their bills had not reached a vote when the closure of Congress came on March 4, 1897, and we can say in all justice that our constant care, our serious opposition, and our varied efforts had contributed in a somewhat considerable degree to this result."

The innocent reader of the plea for fees being under the influence of the statement laid down at the outset that the firm Sullivan & Cromwell "had come to know and be in a position to influence a considerable number of public men in political life" (p. 161) will see in the failure of the Nicaragua bills in 1896 and 1897, if thus explained, a manifestation of that "influence over public men in political life." If he neglects the moral side of such a demand he will think the remuneration asked for this influence (p. 161) is well earned.

But if he turns to the public documents he will immediately think he has been grossly deceived.

The facts presented to him are disfigured either by transposition of dates or by the elimination in the list of the events of those which really determined the consequent facts.

It is very much like the history of France written by a celebrated Jesuit, called Loriquet, and taught in certain schools after the downfall of Napoleon the First. According to the Larousse Encyclopedia, this is how Loriquet worked: "He imagined the accommodation of facts according to his fancy. He falsified truth with audacity in order to present it in a light favorable to his doctrine."

The plea for fees distinctly and clearly says that in January, 1896, when Mr. Cromwell begins his work he ascertains that the Ludlow Commission is then engaged in the work of surveying and reporting on the easibility of the Nicaragua route.

The plea for fees distinctly and clearly says that between January and June, 1896, Mr. Cromwell had frequent interviews with Col. Ludlow. It further says that as a result of this exposition the Ludlow Commission afterwards made a report with very favorable references to the Panama route.

Now let us turn to the facts. When Mr. Cromwell entered the service of the company in January, 1896, the Ludlow Commission was not surveying and reporting, as it is stated with audacity in the plea for fees. It had gone since more than two months out of existence. Its report can not have been influenced by Mr. Cromwell's interviews with Col. Ludlow, which are said by Mr. Cromwell to have taken place between January and June, 1896, because the report of this eminent Engineer officer had been signed and transmitted to the President more than two months before January, 1896.

The apparent tranquillity with which facts are falsified in the plea for fees by transportation of dates is so amazing that I do not think it sufficient to give the authority of a parliamentary document only. I shall quote two entirely independent ones.

The first one is the Senate Document No. 54, Fifty-seventh Congress, first session. It contains the report of the Isthmian Canal Commission, 1899–1901. Among the signers of this report are the former members of the Nicaragua Canal Commission, which was formed in 1897 to prosecute the explorations recommended by the Ludlow report. On page 58, under the heading "Nicaragua Canal Board," the following can be read:

"The bill * * * was approved March 2, 1895. The President appointed Lieut. Col. William Ludlow, Corps of Engineers, United States Army; Civil Engineer M. T. Endicott, United States Navy; and Alfred Noble, civil engineer. * * * The appointments were made April 25, and the members of the board proceeded early in the following month to Nicaragua, and, after their examination there, completed their work in time to make their report by the 1st of November, as required by law. This report was printed during the first session of the Fifty-fourth Congress as House Document No. 279."

This statement is final. However, as I said previously, I thought necessary to call another witness of the falsifications of dates and facts by the plea for fees on this point which I am examining now.

In the Senate Document No. 1417, Fifty-fifth Congress, third session, can be found a "Chronological statement as to the Maritime Canal Co. of Nicaragua," by Senator Morgan. On pages 8 and 9 the following can be read:

"April 25, 1895, Secretary Gresham notified Lieut. Col. William Ludlow, United States Army, Civil Engineer M. T. Endicott, and Mr. Alfred Noble that they had been appointed a board of engineers to survey and examine the Nicaragua Canal route and to report on the same to the President on or before November 1, 1895 (H. Doc. No. 279, 54th Congress, 1st sess., p. 11):

"May 7, 1895. Board of engineers sail from Mobile for their inspection of the canal route.

"May 13, 1895. The board of engineers arrived at Greytown.

"May 21, 1895. The board of engineers left Greytown for inspection of the canal route.

"June 24, 1895. The board of engineers arrived at New York.

"October 31, 1895. The board of engineers submitted their report to the President. (H. Doc. No. 279, 54th Cong., 1st sess.)"

Nothing further is said in the chronology except for the transmission to Congress of the report which had been submitted to the President on the 31st of October previous. The board had then completed their task before the 1st of November, 1895, as the law required for the date of the report. There could be, there was no other action of the board after that.

With these two independent and corroborative documentary statements all doubt is removed. The plea for fees cynically displaces the events, so as to make appear as a consequence of Mr. Cromwell's activities what is materially anterior to their beginning.

But it does not limit itself to displace the real date of Ludlow's report; it withdraws any allusion to its contents as regards Nicaragua.

Any man will understand why, when he has read on pages 58 and 59 of the Isthmian Canal Commission's report, already quoted above (S. Doc. 54, 57th Cong, 1st sess.), the following summing up:

"The Nicaragua Canal Board found it impracticable within the time fixed in the law and with the limited means appropriated for the accomplishment of its work to make a full and thorough examination of the route and obtain the necessary data for the formation of a final project of a canal, and in the report a recommendation was included that there be further explorations and observations, so as to collect the information and data regarded as essential to the comprehension of the fundamental features of the canal problem, which should decide the final location and cost of work.

"In accordance with the views of the board there was included in the sundry civil appropriation act which was approved June 4, 1897, an appropriation to continue the surveys. * * *"

The law according to which the Ludlow Board was formed (see same p. 58 of the Isthmian Canal Commission's report above quoted) "was adopted in the Senate for the purpose of ascertaining the feasibility, permanence, and cost of the construction and completion of the canal through Nicaragua." It is therefore obvious that the declaration of the board as to the necessity of further explorations for ascertaining certain essential data before answering the question made by the legislator as to the feasibility and cost absolutely paralyzed any attempt of passing the Nicaragua bill through Congress before such explorations were made.

The exhibition in the plea for fees of the conclusion arrived at by the Ludlow Board would have made obviously futile and ridiculous all the talk inserted in the plea for fees referring to the imaginary victories won by Mr. Cromwell in the battles against the defenders of the Nicaragua bill in Congress during that period. The titles which the plea for fees places upon this inflated and imaginary stuff—"Recapitulation of work done in 1896—Result no legislation for Nicaragua that year.—1896-1897. Attack and defeat of the Nicaragua legislation"—would have been obviously shown to sum up a pure fiction.

The plea for fees after disfiguring the history by materially tampering with the dates is thus shown further to disfigure it by withholding and keeping concealed the essential fact which dominates all the situation, and this fact is the opinion of the Ludlow Board as expressed in their report signed before the beginning of Mr. Cromwell's activities.

I do not think there may be found anywhere a more flagrant and obvious disfiguration of truth.

These facts demonstrate:

First. The lack of veracity of Mr. Cromwell's plea for fees when it says that in 1896, when he began his work, the Ludlow Board was then engaged in the work of surveying and preparing their report. They had made their report before November, 1895, prior to any of his activities.

Second. The lack of veracity of Mr. Cromwell's plea for fees when it withholds in his description of events the findings of said report of the Ludlow Board, and thereby conceals from the reader's eye the paralyzing action this report had on all Nicaragua legislation in 1896 and the first part of 1897 until the appropriation for new explorations were made according to its recommendations.

Third. The lack of veracity of Mr. Cromwell's plea for fees when he substitutes the imaginary cause of his efforts to the real one which is the report of the Ludlow Board.

The consequence of this demonstration is that a document found to be so absolutely deficient in veracity as to material facts registered by official documents is the most unfit base for writing the history of Panama. This opinion will be further confirmed by the other examples I shall give of this lack of veracity.

SECOND DEMONSTRATION OF AN ABSOLUTE LACK OF VERACITY ON A GIVEN POINT IN MESSRS. SULLIVAN & CROMWELL'S PLEA FOR FEES.

In the autumn 1898 and in the winter of 1898–1899 the adoption of Nicaragua by the Congress of the United States seemed highly probable. The session, however, ended without seeing passed by the House the Nicaragua bill already voted by the Senate. Why did this extraordinary fact take place? What determined the stoppage of the Nicaragua bill in the House when nearly the unanimity of members were for a canal at Nicaragua?

Here is the explanation given by the plea for fees. On page 179 of the Story of Panama can be found the chapter of the plea for fees entitled, "A vote for Nicaragua is prevented in the House." It begins by the sentence "As a result of the support we gave to this plan, the efforts of the Nicaragua party failed, and this party seeing itself incapable despite its efforts to bring its bill to a vote, etc."

What is the force of this party which is, according to the plea for fees, incapable of bringing its bill to a vote on account of Mr. Cromwell's supposed support to another plan? The plea for fees describes this party on page 178 under the title, "The situation in the House is favorable to Nicaragua." It says: "An enthusiastic and large majority of the House was openly pledged to Nicaragua. The result of a vote in the House was absolutely certain if a vote were taken."

Who were the leaders of that Nicaragua party the plea for fees tells us on page 176 under the title "December, 1898–March 4, 1899, session of Congress." It speaks in the following terms: "Two bills were pending before Congress, one in each House, and they were backed by the official recommendation of the President in his message, and the Maritime Canal Co., with its officials and shareholders, nearly all important figures in politics, was ready in its own interests to furnish anything that might be lacking, if anything was lacking, to the zeal of the ever-active partisans of Nicaragua in Congress led by Senator Morgan in the Senate and Representative Hepburn in the House."

On page 178 the plea for fees further speaks of the two leaders of the common cause of Nicaragua: "Mr. Hepburn was the most earnest and most able champion of Nicaragua in the House, he having ability, power, and vigor on a par [in the original text, correspondant, which means corresponding] with the capable leader of this cause in the Senate, Senator Morgan."

I may be allowed to make a third quotation of the plea for fees, to show distinctly what it pretends the attitude of Representative Hepburn was and what efforts he was ready to make in association with Senator Morgan for promoting the passage of the Nicaragua bill, efforts which the plea for fees pretends to have been baffled by Mr. Cromwell's activities. On page 165 of the Story of Panama we read this passage of the plea for fees: "The chairman of this committee was Senator Morgan, whose stubbornness in favor of Nicaragua was only equaled by his continued efforts in favor of this project * * *. In the House of Representatives everything bearing upon the canal was first sent to the Committee on Interstate Commerce. The chairman of this committee was Mr. Hepburn, a man whose entire energy and every attainment was devoted to the success of the Nicaragua bill in Congress."

There we have a graphic description of the situation: Two most able leaders working for the same cause, followed by enthusiastic majorities in each House, have deposited the necessary bill. The plea for fees describes the success of the bill in the Senate on page 178 and we can read in the headline, "The Nicaragua bill is passed in the Senate almost unanimously," and further down that it was speedily passed by a vote of 48 to 6 on January 21, 1899, and was at once sent to the House.

Then we witness, according to the plea for fees, a most unique spectacle sufficiently described by the above extract. It is that of an enthusiastic and large majority in the House led by a most earnest and most able champion of Nicaragua and becoming absolutely incapable of arriving to vote the bill which has already passed the Senate. How can such an extraordinary fact take place? The plea for fees modestly answers: "It was the result of the support we gave to another plan" (p. 179), and the other plan as well as the support to it is said to be Mr. Cromwell's. If that were true, Mr. Cromwell's activities undoubtedly would justify any fees he claims for the influence which the plea for fees pretends his firm had over public men in political life. It is not only the influence on one man, either Mr. Hay or Mr. Hanna, it is the influence over a whole body of legislators, over a majority enthusiastically devoted to the bill which Mr. Cromwell fights. In spite of the number of its members and of their enthusiasm the majority is held at bay by Mr. Cromwell's only power, according to the plea for fees.

Fortunately for the historical truth, a House of Representatives does not die as a man. It does not carry away to the grave the memory of facts. Its memory is permanent; it lies in its records.

Let us look at the records of the House on this point. What do we see in the report of February 13, 1899 (55th Cong., 3d sess., H. Rept. No. 2104), made by Mr. Hepburn and entitled: "Maritime Canal Co. of Nicaragua." We must expect to see in this document, if we believe the plea for fees, an energetic effort made by the most able leader of Nicaragua in the House in order to complete there the work done by the capable leader of Nicaragua in the Senate, whose power and vigor corresponded to his own. We must find the application of Mr. Hepburn's entire energy devoted to this Nicaragua bill in Congress. We must also find in this document a trace of the backing which Maritime Canal Co. is ready to give, according to the plea for fees, as we have seen.

This is what we must expect if the plea for fees is truthful.

We have there fair and correct occasion of testing again the veracity of the document chosen as the base of the Story of Panama by Mr. Hall. If the test fails for the third time, it shows that the so-called document is fanciful and does not deserve the slightest credence.

We find that the test fails entirely. Far from recommending the adoption of the Senate bill for Nicaragua, the report is simultaneously aggressive against the bill itself and the Maritime Canal Co. Instead of the backing of the company it deserves its ferocious enmity.

On page 3 of the report of Mr. Hepburn the following can be read:

"The Senate bill, for which your committee recommended a substitute, proposes to amend the charter of the Maritime Canal Co., and then reorganizes the company by appointment of a majority of the board of directors by the President of the United States, and then uses that corporation as its agent for constructing and operating the canal. This corporation is created by the United States. It is a creature of the Government. After creating it the Government proposes by the Senate bill to inject itself into the corporation, and thus masquerading it proposes to do a work that it is in every way capable of doing in its own proper person. For what purpose should the Government thus convert itself into a corporation? * * * It becomes a person, artificial person, and takes the position of equality with citizens. As a corporation it may be sued in its own courts and may be fined for contempt by its own judicial servants."

The report thus continues severely attacking the Senate bill and the Maritime Canal Co. of Nicaragua.

There we find the real reason of the impossibility for the Senate bill to open its way through the House.

There the bill finds a lion in the path. It is not Mr. Cromwell's support of another plan. Such an obstacle at first glance appears as unlikely as it would be dishonorable for an enthusiastic majority of any parliament, if it were true.

The real lion in the path is precisely Col. Hepburn.

His entire energy, far from being devoted to the success of the Nicaragua bill in Congress (see p. 165), as is the fictitious assertion of the plea for fees, is in reality devoted on the contrary to the annihilation in the House of the bill as the Senate sent it. He is for a Nicaragua Canal built directly by the Government when the other leader, Mr. Morgan, with his Senate followers, is for a Nicaragua Canal built by a company. The internal strife is intense. Mr. Hepburn calls a masquerade the Morgan proposition and refuses to pass such a bill through the House.

There is the insurmountable obstacle, the memory of which is engraved in the public documents, and which the Senate bill met on its way through the House.

This capital fact is carefully concealed in the plea for fees. Not only is there no trace of it, but assertions to the contrary are inserted in it. It is done with an amazing audacity, as has been found in the preceding case, where the obvious tampering of the date of Ludlow's report and a similar suppression of the findings of his report were demonstrated.

As to Mr. Cromwell's supposed idea which the plea for fees says has thwarted the efforts of Mr. Hepburn and of his enthusiastic majority (p. 180), the truth is much more simple.

In face of the deadlock created by the inimical and irreconcilable attitude of the two leaders of either faction of the Nicaragua party, something had to be done before the end of the session.

What was done was the creation of a new commission for studying for the last time all the solutions of the isthmian problem. It was in line with the letter written some months before, on the 18th of November, 1898, by the president of the New Panama Canal Co. to the President of the United States. It was in line with the thought of all the people who knew the superiority of Panama over Nicaragua. They were a very small number in those days, but the publication I had made in 1892 (Panama, P. Bunau Varilla; Mason, editeur) had contributed to enlighten their minds. Among them was the eminent man who honored me by his deep and sincere friendship from 1886 till the day of his death in 1911, John Bigelow, who was termed the "grand old man of America" or "the first citizen of New York." Another was Lieut. Commander Baker, United States Navy, who was detailed at the Paris Exposition of 1900. He became my friend during the years he spent in Paris to prepare the exposition, and at the same time an enthusiastic supporter of Panama. Both these friends of mine spent the winter of 1898-99 in Washington and pressed upon those whom they met in high political circles that Panama was, contrary to the general opinion, worth being examined before selecting finally Nicaragua.

Mr. John Bigelow, who had been the ambassador to France sent by Lincoln, had in these remote days, as secretary of legation in Paris, Col. John Hay, who had been before the assassination of Lincoln the President's personal secretary. He had kept ever since the most cordial relations with his brilliant former subordinate.

On the 1st of December, 1898, when the arrival in Washington of the delegates of the New Panama Canal Co. bearing the letter of the 18th of November was announced, Mr. John Bigelow wrote me a letter, from which I extract the following:

"I have no special interest in either enterprise (Panama or Nicaragua).

"You have satisfied me that nature anticipated our old friend de Lesseps, in providing for a waterway across this continent at the Isthmus (of Panama), and nowhere else. * * *

"About two weeks ago [1] I wrote to Mr. Hay, our Secretary of State, recommending—as he would be consulted about the President's annual message at the opening of Congress—that the President should say what he thought fit about the importance of a transcontinental waterway, but not to commit himself to the Nicaragua route until he had taken the same measures to investigate the Panama route that he had taken to investigate the Nicaraguan."

It is this idea expressed by Mr. John Bigelow to Mr. Hay before even the new Panama Canal Co. had made the first step toward the American government which matured some months afterwards. The suggestion was followed when it became visible that the session was going to end before anything could be done for Nicaragua. This paralysis was created by the Morgan and the Hepburn factions dividing the Nicaragua party as we have seen.

This gives the true explanation of the decision taken at the end of the session and which the plea for fees explains by a chapter (p. 180) entitled as follows: "We obtain the passage of a bill appointing a new commission to examine the Panama route and report thereon, as also on the other canal routes (Mar. 3, 1899), and by this means we prevent the final passage of the Nicaragua bill."

We know that the last assertion is absolutely fictitious; we know that it is due to the stubbornness of both Morgan and Hepburn. We know also that the plea for fees has carefully withheld any reference to the fight between two irreconcilable enemies and presented them as associating their common efforts for the passage of the Nicaragua bill.

No clearer adulteration of facts established by official documentation could be imagined.

These facts related with the second important point demonstrate:

First. The lack of veracity of Messrs. Sullivan and Cromwell's plea for fees when it speaks of Mr. Hepburn as of "a man whose entire energy and every attainment was devoted to the success of the Nicaragua bill in Congress" (p. 165) and conceals the real fact that he was stubbornly opposed to the passage through the House of the Nicaragua Senate bill devised by Mr. Morgan.

Second. The lack of veracity of Messrs. Sullivan and Cromwell's plea for fees when it describes, on page 176, Senator Morgan, Representative Hepburn with their respective following and the Maritime Canal of Nicaragua as working with enthusiasm for a common cause at a time when the deepest division existing between them separated their party into two warring factions. The lack of veracity consists in the deceitful system of speaking of their common aim, which was a canal at Nicaragua, and of withholding any reference to the war waging on the question of its construction. Hepburn

[1] The letter to Mr. Hay was therefore written before the letter of the President of the New Panama Canal Co. in Paris to the President of the United States in Washington.

wished a law ordering it to be made by the United States and Morgan by the Maritime Canal Co.

Third. The lack of veracity of Messrs. Sullivan and Cromwell's plea for fees when it conceals the aggressive report of Mr. Hepburn February 13, 1899, against the Morgan bill and the Maritime Canal Co. as set forth in House Report No. 2104, Fifty-fifth Congress, third session, which forms an insurmountable obstacle to the passage of the Morgan Nicaragua bill.

The lack of veracity consisting in concealing this report is explained by the fictitious claim of the plea for fees that the obstacle to the passage of the Morgan bill through the House was Mr. Cromwell's activities thus expressed: "As a result of the support we gave to this plan the efforts of the Nicaragua party failed and this party being incapable to bring its bill to a vote, etc. * * *" (p. 179).

The consequence of this demonstration is exactly the same as that of the one referring to the first point. It shows again that a document found to be so absolutely deficient in veracity as to material facts registered by official documents is the most unfit base for writing the history of Panama. This will be further confirmed by the other examples I shall give of this lack of veracity.

THIRD DEMONSTRATION OF AN ABSOLUTE LACK OF VERACITY ON A GIVEN POINT IN MESSRS. SULLIVAN & CROMWELL'S PLEA FOR FEES.

The point I am going to examine is that of Mr. Cromwell's dismissal from the company's service.

It is a good point to probe the veracity of the plea for fees. If it is truthful it will state the fact in a few words. It will exhibit how afterwards on Mr. Hanna's request he was taken back again in spite of the company's reluctance.

Let us see how the plea of fees translates the fact. On page 196 there is a heading telling the story in these terms: "July 1, 1901, January 27, 1902—Our instructions are to cease all activity." Under this heading one can read: "For the period from July 1, 1901, to January 22, 1902, we have no responsibility as during that period the company for reasons it deemed sufficient ordered the cessation of all activity in the United States and took over the management of the affair, relieving us of all responsibility during that period."

On page 198 we further see under the heading "1902—January 27, resumption of our activities," we read what follows: "The above résumé shows only too clearly that the situation of the cause of Panama at this moment was in truth dangerous and desperate. In these circumstances the company cabled to Mr. Cromwell asking him to resume his former connection and activity as general counsel of the company in charge of the matter."

Who would think after reading such a relation of events that Mr. Cromwell ever was dismissed from the service and taken back thanks to the influence of his friend Mr. Edward Simmons over Senator Hanna? The reader believes that Mr. Cromwell simply received instructions to take the attitude of silent expectation, and that the company in despair when their situation became desperate cabled him to be active again.

This is the most complete disfiguration of facts which could be produced.

In fact, Mr. Cromwell was politely dismissed from the service by the following letter:

[Translations.]

PARIS, *June 19, 1901.*

DEAR SIR: We have the honor of informing you that in the meeting of June 14 last our committees have esteemed that in the actual situation there was a necessity for the company to manage directly all their business in the United States without the employment of any intermediate agent. It has, therefore, been decided that your situation as counsel of the company in the United States would come to an end on the date of June 30 next.

We address you the thanks of the company to the care you have taken of their business.

Please, etc. HUTIN.

There is a positive lack of veracity in translating such a letter by: Our instructions are to cease all activity.

There is an equal and obvious lack of veracity in stating also that, the situation being desperate, the company cabled to Mr. Cromwell to resume this activity which he had been, as he says, instructed to suspend.

At the end of January, 1902, for the first time the victory of Panama was dawning and rendered at last material by an extremely weighty fact. The most important event in its American history next to its final adoption by purchase had taken place. The unanimous recommendation of the Panama route by the Isthmian Canal Commission had been made on the 18th of January, 1902.

We have learned to know how the plea for fees changes dates, and conceals important events to adjust facts to its theories, but we have not yet seen qualified as a desperate thing the most happy and felicitous victory won on the technical field. It is this victory, which might have been considered as final, which the plea for fees considers as creating such a desperate condition that the company must look for Mr. Cromwell's activities to be liberated from the terrible condition into which it has fallen.

It is equally fictitious to state that the company took the initiative of appealing to him.

After the unanimous recommendation by the commission, Senator Hanna requested me to do him the service of urging the company to take again Mr. Cromwell.

"It is not because I care at all for him," said the Senator, "but my old banker, Edward Simmons, presses me to obtain that for his friend. You know it is difficult," added the Senator, "to refuse something to a man who has been your banker for 30 years. At any rate the company wants a lawyer to discuss the legal questions of Panama. Why not Cromwell? He is one of the best lawyers in New York and knows the question when another would have much to learn."

I answered: "I have never seen Mr. Cromwell. I know he has been dismissed by the company, but I do not know why, because the company and myself never were friends and I know their affairs by their public aspect. But you are the only hope of Panama. Whatever you want should be done. Though I have no direct connection with the company, I may get friends to inform them of your desire and if they are intelligent enough to understand that they must do it, they will do it."

On leaving Senator Hanna I stopped at the Raleigh, Mr. Cromwell's hotel, for some information. He was not there. I left a card. A short time after he came to see me at the New Willard and engaged in a conversation of terrible length rather in the form of a monologue.

I asked him if he was willing to accept that his fees would be determined sovereignly by the company, supposing it would be a good recommendation.

Finally I sent, immediately after he had gone, at 2 a. m. on the 23d of January, 1902, a cablegram to Mrs. Bunau-Varilla, in Paris, requesting her to inform a certain Mr. Dolot of the wish of Senator Hanna. This Mr. Dolot was the intimate friend of an important member of the board of directors, Mr. Terrier. They refused to listen to the suggestion. Seeing no result, and Senator Hanna growing impatient, I cabled again through the same channel, on the 26th of January, requesting Mrs. Bunau-Varilla to urge again my recommendation and also to inform my brother, Maurice, proprietor of the greater part and directing editor of the Matin. He acted personally on the board and carried their decision the following day in favor of the reinstatement of Mr. Cromwell.

The demonstration that the reinstatement of Mr. Cromwell was not desired by, but forced upon the company, is shown by the exchange of telegrams which can be found on pages 121 and 122, between Mr. Cromwell and myself:

WASHINGTON, *January 27, 1902—10 a. m.*

CROMWELL,
Care Sullivan & Cromwell,
49 Wall Street, New York.

Your affair was settled this morning Paris according to my recommendation which I had to renew yesterday with great force. Felicitation.

BUNAU VARILLA.

To which Mr. Cromwell answered:

NEW YORK, *January 27, 1901.*
(Received 2.15 p. m.)

NEW WILLARD,
Washington, D. C.

Many thanks for your kind message. When will confirmation be received? * * *

WILLIAM NELSON CROMWELL.

But the lack of veracity of the plea for fees in what regards the origin of the reinstatement is also obviously demonstrated by the almost insulting condition attached to the reinstatement in the cablegram and in the letter sent by the company for that purpose.

If it had been an initiative of the company looking for a saviour in a desperate condition, as the plea of fees asserts, another form, that of a polite request, would have been chosen.

A first telegram says without further advice to Mr. Cromwell:

"You will receive through Lampre, after translation, telegram reinstating you as general counsel Compagnie nouvelle and containing instructions."

This is not the way a lawyer of high standing is treated when he is requested to assume again a case which has been taken away from him seven months before.

The other telegram still more shows the irritation and the reluctance of the company.

It is absolutely equivalent to an insult. At the third line it contains a standing condition incompatible with the dignity of a lawyer:

"You to be reinstated in your position as general counsel of Compagnie Nouvelle de Panama; rely on your cooperation to conclude matter sale property; you better than anyone can show title Compagnie Nouvelle de Panama to property and incontestible right she has to sell them. But we require most expressly that no donations be made now or later, nor promises be made to anyone whomsoever which might bind[1] the Compagnie Nouvelle de Panama."

In order to make more precise the insulting signification of donations and promises, the company, in the letter confirming the cablegram, says (p. 122), after reciting the task she gives to the counsel: "But it must be clearly understood, and on this point we shall surely be in accord with you, that these results must be sought only by the most legitimate means; that is to say, that in no case could we recourse to methods as dangerous as they are unlawful, which consist principally in gifts or promises of whatsoever nature they may be, and that the same[2] reserve must scrupulously be observed by every person acting for us or in our name."

* * * * * * *

The use of such a language and the mention of such an insulting condition in writing to an eminent lawyer the services of which are asked for would be inconceivable. It is so much more inconceivable when said lawyer has been four years and a half in your service. To say that clearly means: "I reinstate you, but under the condition that you will not resort to these illegal and dangerous methods, called in plainer words corruption."

That is not the language anybody uses when he asks for a service. It is the language which may be used toward a man whom you know to be pressing himself into a place and who is therefore ready to accept any language used and any condition expressed, even those which would be inacceptable for a man of some standing.

These facts clearly demonstrate:

1. The lack of veracity of the plea for fees when it translates the dismissal of Mr. Cromwell by "our instructions are to cease all activity."

2. The lack of veracity of the plea for fees, when it minimizes the importance of the event of the first order for the company, which took place before the reinstatement of Mr. Cromwell and which is the unanimous recommendation by the Isthmian Canal Commission of the Panama route, and when the plea for fees says with incredible audacity that after such a signal victory the situation is desperate.

3. The lack of veracity of the plea for fees when after depicting as a desperate condition the brilliant victory won while Mr. Cromwell is not at the service of the company, it says that the company appeals to him. The telegrams exchanged, as well as the letter sent by the company, shows that it was with great reluctance that the company yielded to the pressure I indirectly exerted upon it to meet the wishes of Senator Hanna.

The consequence of this demonstration is the same as those of the demonstrated lack of veracity in the first and second point. There we have seen the plea for fees, tampering with dates and withholding the mention of real, important facts in order to give a fictitious prominence to imaginary services. Here we see the same systematic lack of veracity simply covering a wound of vanity.

FOURTH DEMONSTRATION OF AN ABSOLUTE LACK OF VERACITY ON A GIVEN POINT IN MESSRS. SULLIVAN AND CROMWELL'S PLEA FOR FEES.

We are going to speak of the Spooner law, of its inception and consequences.

In answer to the telegram reinstating him, Mr. Cromwell sends a message to the company, which can be found on page 200.

"I acknowledge receipt of your cable of 27 reinstating me. * * * I have inspired a new bill adopting our project and leaving to the decision of the President all ques-

---

[1] In the translation given on page 122 "bind" is erroneously written "find."

[2] Same is erroneously omitted in the translation of page 122.

tions relating to titles and to the new treaty to be concluded with Colombia with discretionary power to choose the other route if the President is not successful in obtaining a satisfactory title and treaty for our route."

This is the summing up of the so-called Spooner bill.

In his first cablegram to the company, Mr. Cromwell says he has inspired it. Is it true? Do we find there a new example of the method which characterizes the plea for fees and of which I have shown striking examples? Is it a new manifestation of the method of concealing the determinant facts, of changing the dates, in order to suit a fanciful account of events?

Fortunately for the historical truth, we have the statement of Senator Spooner before the Senate on this point.

The allegation of Mr. Cromwell, though contained in a purely confidential dispatch which has been dragged to light by a succession of unforeseen events, early filtrated in the public. Senator Morgan makes in the Senate allusions to it. Mr. Spooner, if he was not the author of it, could very well have said that it resulted from an exchange of ideas with different persons. There would have been no dishonor for him to do that nor would it have minimized his right to give his name to a bill that he had introduced into the Senate. What did he say about it? We find it in the Congressional Record. (Vol. 35, No. 145, 57th Cong., 1st sess., p. 7180, first column.) We reproduce the dialogue between Senator Morgan and Senator Spooner; but for its intelligence it must be noted that the Spooner proposition being an amendment to the House bill, the Spooner bill is called there "amendment."

"Mr. SPOONER (answering to Senator Morgan). If the Senator will allow me, as he uses my name and says I will not offer the amendment, does he mean that I am not the author of it?

"Mr. MORGAN. I am satisfied the Senator wrote it.

"Mr. SPOONER. And that the Senator was the author of it.

"Mr. MORGAN. Of course.

"Mr. SPOONER. And not only wrote it but devised it."

There was no reason whatever, if Mr. Cromwell inspired the Spooner law, for Senator Spooner to disgrace himself on the floor of the Senate by emphatically stating a thing he knows to be untrue, by emphatically stating that he has devised the bill, which in a confidential telegram Mr. Cromwell says he has inspired.

Mr. Spooner never has been accused, and therefore still less convicted, of making knowingly a false statement. The preceding study of Mr. Cromwell's plea for fees demonstrates on the contrary striking lacks of veracity in the latter one's written self eulogy. There should be on that account no hesitation between the assertions of the two men. Something must be added to indicate where the truth is. Mr. Hall asserts on page 294 that Mr. Cromwell flatfootedly told he inspired the Spooner amendment and that Mr. Spooner flatfootedly denied it on the floor of the Senate.

Mr. Spooner publicly and emphatically asserted that he had devised the amendment in response to an insinuation that he had not.

Mr. Cromwell has wired in a confidential dispatch to the company that he had inspired it. This dispatch being linked with his reinstatement must be brought to light before the arbitrators. It is time for Mr. Cromwell to reassert the authorship of the bill if he fathered it. Mr. Spooner has taken a strong position in the Senate and is not dead. If Mr. Cromwell has said the truth, he is bound to be behind his statement. If he has not, he will drop it in his plea for fees. This is the test of veracity of the plea for fees on this point.

The test fails again as it has always failed wherever we have probed the veracity of this document.

In his description of his activities in this important affair, which is the introduction of the Panama Canal into the laws of the United States, here is what he says on page 202, under the heading: "We encourage the passage of a law authorizing the purchase of the Panama Canal on certain conditions * * *."

It goes without saying that, unless the Senate and the Government of the United States had fallen in 1902 into a state of incurable imbecility, there was no necessity of the encouragement of Mr. Cromwell to pass a bill embodying the final report of the Isthmian Canal Commission. This bill had to come under one form or another. The question is, Who gave it the form of the Spooner bill?

The plea for fees does not dare to repeat in its description of Mr. Cromwell's activities in that period what he has cabled to the company in Paris after the flat-footed denial of Mr. Spooner in the Senate. Here is what the plea for fees says when it comes to this particular point: "These conferences (with Senator Spooner and Senator Hanna) resulted in Senator Spooner preparing and introducing in the Senate a bill for the adoption of the Panama route."

Therefore, far from reproducing and maintaining the assertion of his telegram, the plea for fees recognizes for Mr. Spooner the paternity of the bill.

It settles the whole question; it is equivalent to a confession of guilt.

This new test of veractiy shows the statements made to the company by Mr. Cromwell to have the same spirit which we find pervading every point of the plea for fees if examined with caution and method and placed next to documents as we have seen.

THE CONSEQUENCES OF THE INTRODUCTION OF THE SPOONER BILL.

I shall not follow in details the description the plea for fees gives of Mr. Cromwell's activities in that period.

It is concentrated in this heading, which we find on page 215: "Great struggle in the Senate on the occasion of the vote which was to decide the selection of Nicaragua or of Panama, our preparations to assure the adoption of the minority report favorable to Panama and our success."

It is further expressed by this modest conclusion to be read on page 218:

"Thus our long fight in the Senate has been won for Panama."

It is a proper time to remember that the fight was engaged on a technical field and that perhaps engineers and not a lawyer might have had some part to play in the demonstration of the superiority of one route over the other.

It is extremely distasteful to me to enter upon this subject, because during all the period from inception to the vote of the Spooner bill I was in America devoting my efforts and my knowledge to the victory of Panama. The documents I produced, the arguments I gave, were said to have some influence on the final result. I was qualified to speak, being the former chief engineer of the Panama Canal during the most active part of its existence, and having more published and publicly spoken about the subject than anybody living.

The plea for fees does not pronounce once my name. It acts in relation to what I did as we saw it has acted in relation to the report of Col. Ludlow of October 31, 1895, in relation with the report of Representative Hepburn of February 13, 1899.

If anything could lead me to believe I had a preponderant action in the events, it would be such silence which is even observed for the treaty of November 18, 1903, which is usually designated, except in the plea for fees, by the name of the signers, the Hay Bunau-Varilla treaty.

However, I may be mistaken. The demonstrated fact that Mr. Cromwell's plea for fees systematically withholds and conceals very important events and substitutes trifling ones for the interest of the plea for fees, does not carry the consequence that all he neglects is of importance.

In order to know which is true, I may be allowed to quote two authoritative statements. They will show if any reference to my acts has been withheld in the plea for fees because they were too important or because they were too unimportant for the plea for fees.

One is by the Sun.

This great New York paper, which had followed with a remarkable intensity and accuracy all the phases of the fight, published on the 19th of March, 1903, an article entitled the "Battle of the routes," from which I extract the following:

"The Senate's nearly unanimous vote for the canal treaty and for the canal by way of Panama may properly be placed in contrast with the previous expression of legislative sentiment as to the preferable route for the waterway.

"January 9, 1902. The Hepburn bill for a Nicaragua Canal passed the House of Representatives amid great applause by a vote of 308 to 2.

"March 17, 1903. The Colombian treaty for a Panama Canal was ratified by the Senate by a vote of 73 to 3.

"This remarkable change of policy and of national opinion indicated by these two votes has occurred within fifteen months. * * *

"Many persons, forces, influences, circumstances and accidents have contributed to the fortunate result. If we were asked to catalogue some of the principal factors we should promptly mention President Roosevelt, Secretary Hay, the Hon. Marcus Alonso Hanna, Senator Spooner's genius for doing the right thing at the right time, the monitory eruption of Montombo and the last but not least the former chief engineer of the French work on the Isthmus, Mr. Philippe Bunau-Varilla, who throughout the negotiations has typified the good sense and good faith of the Paris shareholders and has likewise illustrated in his own person a sort of resourceful energy which some people are accustomed to regard as peculiarly American."

Another statement was made by a man of considerable technical eminence, George S. Morison. He was then the greatest of American engineers and had been by far the most prominent personality in the very select body which was the Isthmian Canal Commission of 1899–1901.

In the Volume XXV, No. 1, February, 1903, of the Bulletin of the American Geographical Society can be found the text of a lecture made by George S. Morison in

December, 1902, before the same society. On page 37 the celebrated engineer expresses himself thus, speaking of Lake Bohio: "It will be a beautiful body of water and in it will be an island of about 400 acres, which I have proposed to call the Island of Bunau-Varilla in honor of the brilliant Frenchman who has never despaired of the completion of the Panama Canal and to whose untiring energy we owe much."

This what the Sun and Mr. Morison said after the battle of the routes. They were both independent and conscious witnesses. The Story of Panama (pages 120 and 593) speaks of Morison as of the friend of Cromwell. Why did he not mention his name if really his part in the success had any prominence? Why did the Sun forget the name of Cromwell among the great factors of success if it was really a factor at all? Does not the plea for fees say that Mr. Cromwell had influence on the press (p. 161)? The fact that the press was silent is extremely significant at this juncture.

I may be excused to quote an extract of a personal letter written to me from Cleveland by the intimate friend of Senator Hanna, Col. Myron T. Herrick, who afterwards became Governor of Ohio and has been recently appointed ambassador of the United States to France. It was written on the 12th of July, 1902, say 14 days after the Spooner law was approved (June 28, 1902). Here is the end of Col. Myron T. Herrick's letter to me:

"Your success in Washington gave us great delight. We spent the fourth at the Hannas and you were mentioned many times. Senator Hanna is, of course, greatly pleased with your success and spoke in the highest terms of you.

"I know that you will excuse this rather informal letter.

"Sincerely yours,

"MYRON T. HERRICK."

I take the liberty of mentioning this letter because it is much more a tribute to Hanna than to myself. This great and generous mind spoke of this historical battle he had won by his admirable will and power as of a success of his collaborator not as of a success of his own.

This allows us to size up the moral elevation of the Senator to whom America is indebted for the selection of Panama.

It is somewhat refreshing to consider it when we have been obliged to bring to light all the adulterations of truth, the tampering of dates, the falsifications of the history of the events with which the plea for fees is filled.

It gives a comforting and happy feeling to see in its true light the real moral face of Hanna after looking at it as it is represented in the plea for fees in conjunction with that of this noble type of the American citizen and thinker, John Hay. Both are depicted as stupid straw puppets either writing under the dictation of Mr. Cromwell or learning the speeches he prepares in order to repeat them in the Senate.

The facts demonstrate:

First. The lack of veracity of the plea for fees in what regards the origin of the Spooner law. It was devised by Senator Spooner and not at all inspired as Mr. Cromwell had written in a confidential telegram of which he was powerless after the emphatic statement of Spooner to confirm the contents in the description of his activities as given by the plea for fees.

Second. The lack of veracity of the plea for fees in concealing certain technical interventions of essential importance during the battle in the Senate on the Spooner bill. This lack of veracity results from the concealment of an essential fact contributing powerfully to determine the results. It is established by the testimonies of the Sun, of George S. Morison, of Senator Hanna, through Col. Myron T. Herrick, his most intimate friend.[1]

This adulteration of truth through omission of facts is entirely in line with the one already demonstrated in the case of Ludlow's and Hepburn's reports, and is shown thereby to be a complete system in the plea for fees.

The consequence of this demonstration of systematic lack of veracity shows an extraordinary persistence in the disfiguration of events. It could be continued on an infinity of points but it is necessary to set a limit if we try to show the truth without too much straining the patience of the reader.

---

[1] Since writing this "Statement," I have received an important book in which the claim of Mr. Cromwell that he converted Senator Hanna to the cause of Panama finds its complete refutation. This book is, Marcus Alonzo Hanna—His Life and Work, by Herbert Croly.

The author expresses the opinion that the selection of Panama by the Senate "constituted the most conspicuous single illustration of Senator Hanna's personal prestige" (p. 385). The importance of his influence on that event causes the author to give a corresponding importance to the true determination of the original of his conversion.

From this history, for which "all of his (Senator Hanna's) political and business associates were asked to contribute full and careful statements covering these phases of his career with which they were familiar" (p. V), I make the following extracts (p. 3817);

"Just when Senator Hanna became convinced that the Government would be making a grave mistake, in case the Nicaraguan route was adopted, I am not sure, but a visit, which M. Philippe Bunau-Varilla

It is to be sure necessary for the dignity of the American Congress, as well as for the respect due to the memories of Hay and Hanna, to establish that the plea for fees does not deserve any credit, that it is a wholly untruthful document. But the untruthfulness is an epidemic plague. When it is diagnosed with certainty in four or five places in a document, one may be sure it is present everywhere. It is therefore superfluous to extend indefinitely the proofs of untruthfulness.

I could therefore limit myself to the demonstrations already made which establish that a document so soiled by repeated lack of veracity is unworthy of any consideration and must be exposed when it has by the fortuitous course of events reached the congressional documentation.

I shall, however, treat a fifth point where facts can be detected which are of greater moment than the ones we have seen.

They prove on the part of men in close intimacy with Mr. Cromwell attempts of the gravest nature which would be, if instigated by him, treasonable acts either from the representative of the New Panama Canal Co. or from a citizen of the United States. In stating them we sincerely wish Mr. Cromwell will clearly establish they have been done against his instructions and contrary to his will.

Before going into them I wish to say that previous to the revolution I am convinced Mr. Cromwell served sincerely the cause of Panama. He acted as a diligent messenger between the men who controlled the situation. His material activity was great, and on that account he deserved the thankfulness of all those who, for different reasons, had the victory of Panama at heart. It is to be greatly lamented that he has not been satisfied with the expression in the plea for fees of the useful but subordinate part he had to play. He forgot that in a great thing like this there is glory for all those who play a part, even if, as was the case, it is secondary. It was impossible without tampering with facts to unduly increase Mr. Cromwell's share. He had the weakness to yield to the tempatation. It could not be done without such injury to facts as well as to the memory of great citizens that justice had to be done.

HOW I BECAME CONNECTED WITH AMADOR AND HOW SOME IMPORTANT FACTS RESULTED THEREFROM.

Before going into the demonstration of the lack of veracity on a fifth point I must give a short exposé of the circumstances, purely accidental, which brought me to the United States in September, 1903, and of some facts which resulted from that.

I intended to come some time in November before the opening of Congress in order to follow the development of the Panama affairs as a result of the rejection of the Hay-Herran treaty by the Senate of Colombia.

A personal question brought me there earlier.

In the course of the summer my wife and myself had had the pleasure of welcoming in our home in Paris our dear friends, Mr. John Bigelow and his daughter, Miss Bigelow. My young son was then afflicted with the hay fever. As nothing could remedy his condition, Miss Bigelow, when her sojourn with her father at our home came to an end, proposed to my wife to take the boy with her to America. She hoped that the sea voyage and the coolness of the Maine seaside resort, where she intended to go, would improve his condition. My wife with great reluctance accepted, for the sake of the health of her dear child, the first separation from him, which the friendly proposal entailed.

The condition she put to her acceptance was that she would go and join him in America not later than September. I accepted and said I would go later in November.

When September came my wife engaged accordingly staterooms for herself and her young daughter, but asked the steamship company to reserve a room in case I should decide to accompany her at the last moment.

She pressed me very much to do so. I thought that after all I could go and return immediately afterwards to settle my business and then join my family for a longer stay a couple of months later.

---

made to the United States early in 1901, had something to do with it. M. Bunau-Varilla had been chief engineer in charge of the work undertaken by the old French company and was peculiarly qualified both by his standing in his profession and by his practical experience in the work of construction at Panama to pass an authoritative opinion upon the comparative advantages of the two routes. He had been induced to come to the United States by a group of Cincinnati business men, whom he met by accident in Paris during the exposition of 1900, and whom he had convinced of the superiority of Panama. The visit was made for the purpose of addressing various commercial associations in the United States on behalf of Panama, and wherever he spoke he left behind him a trail of converts. Among them was Colonel Myron T. Herrick, whose interest was so much aroused that he made a point of introducing M. Bunau-Varilla to Senator Hanna. A series of interviews followed, which had much to do with Mr. Hanna's decision to make a fight on behalf of Panama. This decision had been reached by the Senator before the Canal Commission finally reported in favor of Panama."

I do state upon my word of honor, as everything which is in this paper, that no hint or indication came to me from any quarter whatever which prompted me to go then, outside of the cause I just described. When I left Paris I was convinced that I would be back within three weeks, leaving my family enjoying the delightful hospitality of the Bigelows at Highland Falls on Hudson.

Immediately after I arrived in New York, Amador, knowing of my arrival by a Mr. Lindo, to whom I had paid a flying visit during the day, twice called on me on the 23d of September, 1903, at 9 and at 9.25 p. m., at the Waldorf-Astoria. I was not there. He came back the following day and I received him. He was in a state of intense fury and despair. He told me that he and his friends on the isthmus in the course of a year had sent a man named Capt. Beers, an employee of the Panama Railroad, to see Mr. Drake, vice president of the company, and inquire through him if Mr. Cromwell could obtain for a revolution a positive support in money and in military force from the American Government. He told me that this question, which to me seemed childish, was answered encouragingly both by Mr. Drake and by Mr. Cromwell, who received Beers and promised everything to him. He further said that, in order to comprobate the results of Beers's mission, and to enter into activity if they were true, his friends had delegated him to see Mr. Hay personally through Mr. Cromwell. He told me that, having thus come to carry out that plan, he had been first very cordially received by Mr. Cromwell and by Mr. Drake, who was Mr. Cromwell's confidential man in the intrigue and corresponded with Beers about it. He told me that after this excellent reception, when he was expecting to go and see Secretary Hay with Mr. Cromwell, the latter one had suddenly turned his back upon him.

He considered that as an odious betrayal, exposing himself as well as his friends to be shot and their properties to be confiscated when Colombia would know of it.

He spoke to me of the letter of Arango, the translation of which can be found on page 649, as well as on page 317, and the original on page 316.

Here is the first part of the translation of this important letter, reproduced from page 649:

PANAMA, *September 14, 1903.*

MY DEAR FRIEND: As to-morrow, Tuesday, the *Seguranca* should arrive at Colon (sailed from New York September 8), I trust that during the day we shall receive your expected letter which will give us the explanation of your discouraging telegram: "Disappointed; await letters." Since then we have received the cable saying "Hope," and nothing more; so that we are in a position of fearful expectancy, as we are ignorant of what happened to you over there and of the reasons for the profound silence which Mr. Cromwell maintains.

Tired of so much incertitude, we decided to send the following cables to that gentleman; they are as yet unanswered, but which we trust he will give attention and reply to within two or three days:

On September 10, in cipher:

"Confidential. Regret Capt. Beers's letters and cables are not replied. Opportunity now excellent to secure success, provided United States promptly recognizes our independence under conditions with our agent there, who is fully authorized to contract for us. Should Congress [1] concede contract,[2] though improbable, will be through fear of our attitude. Congress [1] controlled by enemies of contract. Answer by wire in cipher through Beers. Tell our agent [3] that to use all discretion possible must send his cables through Beers, not to use Brandon again.—Arango."

On the 12th of September, also in cipher:

"Our position being critical, we must have immediate answer to act promptly or abandon business."

The recommendation made to you in the first cable set out above not to use Brandon is because your cable "Disappointed" was made *quasi public* and I suspect that the other one also has been known to several persons, which doubtless comes from the cable having been known to young Brandon and by him communicated to Gustav Leeman, who must have divulged it, but be that as it may, it is better for you to communicate through Capt. Beers even using Arias's or Boyd's cipher. * * *

....

....

J. A. ARANGO.

---

[1] Arango speaks there of the Colombian Congress then in session at Bogota.
[2] Contract means here the Hay-Herran treaty.
[3] Amador.

This letter showed that Mr. Cromwell was no more answering telegrams from the Isthmus and that indiscretions had been committed in the transmission of Amador's cables. Therefore he recommended the use of Capt. Beers, the confidential man on the Isthmus of both Cromwell and of the revolutionists, the same man who had first been sent to New York to obtain through Mr. Drake and Mr. Cromwell the support of the American Government. He was incensed that Mr. Cromwell had not even told him to be on his guard when Mr. Cromwell had been notified to do so by the cablegram inserted in the letter and dated September 10. He was in an indescribable state of fury to have been thus wickedly exposed, by want of a word of information from Mr. Cromwell as to the danger of seeing his communications thus made public and his friends thereby exposed to the death penalty for conspiracy.

He made it plain to me that if such a thing should take place he would consider it a duty to give up his life if necessary in order to revenge his friends on the man whose betrayal in his mind would have been the cause of their fate.

This is how I began again my connection with Amador in 1903. I had not seen him since many years. But I knew him well, he having been an employee as physician of the canal or of the railroad company when I was at the head of the Panama Canal on the Isthmus in 1886.

When he first began to tell me his lamentable story he tried to withhold the name of Cromwell. I interrupted him and said: "Why do you not name Mr. Cromwell? He is the only man in the United States who speaks as if he disposed of the Government and of the Congress. But that is only talk. It is childish to have believed it. There you are now with your imprudence."

I was, however, amazed that Mr. Cromwell, being a lawyer and the direct representative of the New Panama Canal Co., should have engaged in the whole business. It meant, if discovered, the confiscation of the whole property of the canal by Colombia.

I thought of what would be the irritation of the directors of the New Panama Canal Co. if they had suspected their representative's reprehensible action.

They were all men of high standing, directors of great banking institutions, men of weight and some men of wealth, and placing the care of their responsibility above all considerations. If the canal property had been lost by the fault of their representative they would certainly have been held materially responsible. The French law would have there recognized the gross error which entails the personal responsibility of directors. It would have been committed by them in intrusting such a responsible situation exclusively to a man capable of doing without their knowledge such an illegal and dangerous thing.

Amador saw in Cromwell's reversed attitude a betrayal of the worst nature. From the point of view of the victory of Panama and its completion by the United States, I saw in Mr. Cromwell's first encouraging the revolutionists a betrayal of his duty to his employers and in turning suddenly his back upon them, an act which was going to lead to the discovery of the conspiracy and subsequently to the confiscation by Colombia of the canal, thereby entailing the final adoption of the Nicaragua Canal by the United States according to the Spooner law.

The story of Mr. Cromwell's encouragement of the revolutionists and then of his abandoning them coldbloodedly to their fate was told in detail by Mr. José Augustin Arango in a pamphlet entitled "Datos historicos para la Independencia del Istmo." It bears the date of the 28th of November, 1905, and was published in Panama. Mr. Cromwell is designated by the words "La persona respectable (the respectable person). His name, however, is now made public by the publication in the "Story of Panama" (p. 649) of the letter sent by the same Arango to Señor Amador on September 14, 1903.

It is perfectly accurate in all the details I know except for a trifling detail. Señor Arango, on page 10 of his pamphlet, says that after having cabled the word "Disappointed" on account of the reversal of attitude of "La persona respectable" Amador cabled "Hopes" as soon as he had met me.

There is a slight confusion about the cable "Hopes." Mr. Arango had already received it when he wrote the letter of September 14, as he speaks of it there. I left France on the 16th of September only, and as I was two days before still uncertain whether I should go to the United States with my family or not his cable could not refer to me.

This cablegram had no reference to me, but people, not knowing on the Isthmus the exact date of my meeting Amador, have believed it referred to me on account of the rapid succession of events and of their superposition when seen from a distance.

In fact, the ardent hope of poor old Amador was to see Mr. Hay. He had left Panama with this aim in view. Cromwell had promised him to introduce him himself, and Amador believed victory would be near if he saw Hay. Cromwell very likely learned that Mr. Hay would not tolerate Amador's visit, and this is why, being incapable of fulfilling his promises, he turned his back on Amador.

Some days afterward Amador requested and received from Mr. Gudger a letter of introduction for Secretary Hay. This fact became known through the inquiry of the World, and reference to it can be found there (on p. 651). The perspective of obtaining an admittance into the office of the Secretary which Cromwell had been unable to fulfill fanned the hopes of the old man, and in his joy he cabled "Hopes" to his friends.

But it was before even I decided to go to America. However, Amador, who never made use of this letter, probably did not care to show he had been sending the cablegram "Hopes" on such a slight prospect of success, and left his friends in an error which had no serious consequences.

People believed it referred to me because the date of my intervention followed closely, and this is certainly why Arango made this only slight bona fide error in writing the "Historic dates" for the "History of the Independence of the Isthmus."

I return now to the rapid sketch I purpose to make of what I knew of Mr. Cromwell's activities from the 23d of September, 1903, to the day of the ratification of the so-called Hay-Bunau-Varilla treaty by the Senate of the United States on the 23d of February, 1904.

I never saw the shadow of Mr. Cromwell during all this period until after he returned from France on the 17th of November, 1903. He came to pay me a visit on the 19th at the New Willard Hotel.[1] The treaty had been signed on the previous day, and I never saw him afterwards, except the day of the ratification of the Hay-Bunau-Varilla treaty on the 23d of February, 1904, when I met him in the lobbies of the New Willard Hotel when I was going out of the lift.

When I heard, in October, 1903, that Mr. Cromwell had left for Paris, as he was unaware of the cause of Amador's stay in the United States, I thought he was seeking on the other side of the water a protection against the threats of the infuriated man if Colombia should come to discover the conspiracy initiated with him.

Nothing surprised me more when, on the eve of the signature of the canal treaty, the delegates of the Panama Government arrived in New York on the 17th November, and conferred with Cromwell. The delegation was headed by Amador and formed by him, Mr. Boyd, and Mr. Carlos Arosemena. I could not go to New York to meet them, being too busy in Washington. They undoubtedly were very much hurt in their new dignity by my absence.

Mr. Carlos Arosemena, who immediately after became my secretary of legation and some years after minister of Panama, himself told me the reason. He said he was responsible for the reconciliation. Having been met on the wharf by Mr. Cromwell's agent, Mr. Farnham, the delegates were urged by him to wait for Mr. Cromwell, who was returning from France some hours after. Amador refused to have anything to do with Mr. Cromwell. But Mr. Arosemena placated him on the ground that a man never must be sentenced without a hearing. He added: "Do not make an enemy of Cromwell, he may greatly harm us." The meeting took place. Cromwell excused himself by saying he had been frightened by Dr. Herran, the acting minister of Colombia. The danger was passed, the passion it had created had dwindled in Amador's mind. He remained. Cromwell reconquered him. To make his conquest still more sure he kept the delegates another day.

Never had Mr. Cromwell served more happily the cause of Panama without knowing it. While he was engaged in bringing the Panama delegates back under his influence, I was at work in Washington. Amador's great concealed ambition was to sign the canal treaty, and thus transmit his name to posterity. I knew this ambition, and I feared its interference in this supremely delicate moment when the fate of the Panama Canal was hanging in the balance.

When Amador arrived with Boyd on the 18th, about 10 p. m., at Washington, the first happy news I gave the delegation was that the treaty had been signed at 6.40 p. m., and that the Republic of Panama was placed under the guaranty of the United States.

Amador nearly swooned on the platform of the station when he heard me.

The better part of his mind regained, however, the power over him. On the following day when I read the treaty, his conscience of good old physician was awakened. He only said: "There will be no more yellow fever on the Isthmus, at last," and he declared that he would sustain the treaty, which it had been his great ambition to sign.

This short sketch was necessary for the comprehension of what follows. It will enable the reader to better understand when he knows, first, that my arrival in New York was absolutely accidental on the 22d of September, 1903; second, that when I

[1] Mr. Cromwell's visit was on the 20th of November if it was not on the 19th.

arrived I had not the slightest precise hint as to a revolution being started, though the press dispatches made probable that the state of discontent on the Isthmus would burst out at the first instance; third, that Mr. Cromwell was absolutely kept in strict ignorance of what was happening between Amador and myself; fourth, that the leaders of the movement, Amador, Arango, and others, considered Mr. Cromwell as having betrayed them, as is shown by the letter of Arango of the 14th of September, 1903 (p. 649). Therefore they did not take him a second time into their confidence until he succeeded after the victory, due to other influences, in obtaining his pardon and in making his peace with them on November 17, 1903.

Mr. Cromwell was kept absolutely ignornat of everything until then. Of course, he was infinitely displeased to have been in France or on sea when these important and decisive events were being prepared. He could not say as he did under any pretense whatever of the Spooner bill that he had inspired the Hay-Bunau-Varilla treaty nor that he made the establishment of the new Republic a success.

This short sketch of events being established and the state of mind of Mr. Cromwell being known, let us see what happened with the ratification of the Hay-Bunau-Varilla treaty, and let us proceed to the

FIFTH DEMONSTRATION OF AN ABSOLUTE LACK OF VERACITY IN MESSRS. SULLIVAN AND CROMWELL'S PLEA FOR FEES, SHOWING, IF FINALLY CORROBORATED, MOST REPREHENSIBLE ACTS OF A TREASONABLE CHARACTER, COMMITTED BY MEN CLOSE TO MR. CROMWELL, WHO USED HIS NAME AS THEIR AUTHORITY.

On page 239 of the Story of Panama we can read the following sentence in the plea for fees:

"We were relied upon to devote ourselves to the ratification of the treaty between the United States and Panama as we had already done for the Hay-Herran treaty, and we devoted ourselves to this task during the six following weeks."

The plea for fees observes a delicate care in not mentioning by whom Mr. Cromwell was relied upon to obtain the ratification. Was it the ratification at Panama? The provisional government had only to depend on themselves for it. Was it the ratification by the United States? It was the matter of the Republican Senators who had approved the Hay-Bunau-Varilla treaty before it was signed on the 18th of November, 1903.

However, if Mr. Cromwell had been willing to help, he undoubtedly would have come to the Panama legation and given me information.

As I said before, I never saw him but once, and that was on the day following the signature of the treaty.

To judge the varacity of the above statement, let us look into the facts.

I had the most serious reasons to believe that Colombia was intriguing on the Isthmus to prepare a counter revolution. The best way for it was to prepare the minds there to the idea that the treaty I had signed had been made without any regard to the Panama patriotism by a foreigner.

I had to foresee the loose or fiery talk which so often brings the Spanish-Americans out of their senses when the great words of honor and patriotism are handled in order to deceive them. The only measure I could take to prevent any possible reversal of public opinion was to have the treaty ratified as rapidly as possible after its arrival and to have it returned immediately to me.

The provisional government assented to an immediate ratification.

I had only to provide for the means of transporting it back.

Unfortunately the steamer on the regular schedule of the Panama Railroad for the line Colon-New York was leaving at noon when the steamer bringing the treaty was scheduled to arrive in the morning. The time was insufficient even for reading the treaty.

Very often, for the slightest reasons, the time of departure of the steamers was postponed for a few hours.

It was usual and nothing of any importance could result from the postponement of the departure for 24 hours.

I did not doubt that a simple request to the Panama Railroad, as the owner of the steamers, would be immediately satisfied. The quasi totality of the shares of the Panama Railroad being the property of the canal company, its agents had for immediate duty toward the principal shareholder of their company as well as citizens of the United States to satisfy my demand, which was made in the interest of a ratification which it was the interest of the canal company and of the United States to help. Mr. Cromwell was then the real head of the Panama Railroad. He was the general representative in America of the canal company. The vice-president of the railroad was Mr. Drake, the confidential man of Mr. Cromwell.

On page 645 of the Story of Panama this fact known to everybody of the close and intimate relations of Mr. Drake with Mr. Cromwell is thus set forth in the compilation of facts by Earl Harding (Exhibit K):

"Judge Gudger declares that neither he nor Mr. Cromwell discussed the revolutionary situation. On the other hand Prescott was talking nothing but revolution to Vice President Drake. He knew Capt. Beers's [1] cables to Cromwell were transmitted through Drake, so he freely discussed the plans."

Though there are several and extremely grave errors in Mr. Earl Harding's compilation of facts what he says there must be believed as a fact. Very likely it is extracted from testimony and is completely in harmony with everything known and testified to under oath during the World's inquiry on the Isthmus. There is scarcely any doubt that what Mr. Drake did was with the consent of Mr. Cromwell.

For these various reasons I expected that my demand for detention of the *Yucatan*, the steamer leaving in the morning of the day of the arrival of the treaty in Colon, would be immediately satisfied. It was refused.

It was an act made so obviously with the intention of detaining the treaty unduly that it so much more raised my suspicion about a conspiracy toward the rejection of the treaty by Panama.

I immediately requested my government to ratify the treaty as soon as received and to put it into the hands of the United States consul general on the Isthmus.

I parried thus the suspected efforts toward the same movement which lost the Hay-Herran treaty in Bogota—first enthusiasm, then coldness, then hatred.

Very likely the easily inflammable matter which is public opinion in contact with tropical oratory might have put the provisional Government in an impossible state if I had let the things go.

However I was so much struck by the inadmissible attitude of the Panama Railroad that I thought necessary to keep it on record.

On the 3d of December, 1903, I sent an official letter to the Secretary of State. It denounced the strange attitude of the officers of the Panama Railroad.

It gives the text of my telegram sent from Washington on the 28th of November, 1903, at 2.45 p. m., to the president of the Panama Railroad requesting the detention of the *Yucatan* with the view of "getting back duly ratified the canal treaty." It shows how I left on the same day from Washington for New York and waited there the 29th and the first part of the 30th without receiving an answer. I reproduce hereafter a part of this letter in order to show what happened in the rest of the 30th of November and on the 1st of December:

"Having received no advice until 3 o'clock I tried several times to get Mr. Drake, vice president of the company, by telephone, but without success, and finally went to his office about 4 o'clock. To my great surprise I learned from him that not even the slightest move had been made to comply with my request. Mr. Drake tried to demonstrate to me that it was something of great difficulty, that such a decision could not be taken without the approval of a committee, whose usual date of meeting was the following day. Finally he agreed that as soon as possible he would see the president, Mr. Simmons, and Mr. Cromwell, both of whom were indisposed and remained in their houses. I expressly stated to Mr. Drake that I was ready to take officially the pledge to reimburse the company for any material losses that such delay might cause from any point of view, and to facilitate the question of delay I stated that perhaps 24 hours would be sufficient, instead of 36 hours, which I had previously determined. We finally separated with the express pledge on his part to send me a telegram to the Waldorf-Astoria the same afternoon or early in the evening as soon as the decision would be taken. I left Mr. Drake, in spite of the excessive courtesy he displayed, without the slightest doubt about the intentions of his company, and I immediately went to the next telegraph office to inform the Department of State of the situation and to request the help of the American authority in Colon. Owing to the advanced hour of the day and not knowing whether you had yet come back to Washington, Mr. Secretary, I addressed to Hon. Francis B. Loomis, Assistant Secretary of State, the following telegram at 4.10 p. m., November 30:

"'I find here unexpected reluctance on the part of the Panama Railroad Co. to delay 24 hours departure of steamer *Yucatan* in order to bring back treaty duly ratified. I telegraphed my Government to employ all means available to detain ship time necessary even if Panama Railroad does not send express orders. I would respectfully request you to give similar instructions to the American authorities at Colon.'

[1] Capt. Beers is an employee of the Panama Railroad who was chosen by the revolutionists to go to the United States in order to know if they could find a support there. He went to his superior officers, Drake and Cromwell.

"An hour later, fearing that my previous dispatch would seem incomplete to the State Department, I wired again to Mr. Loomis, Assistant Secretary of State, the following additional dispatch:

"'I beg to inform you that the *City of Washington*, carrying treaty, is expected to arrive at Colon at 9 a. m. to-morrow (Tuesday), and that the *Yucatan* is scheduled to leave same port at noon. I requested the Panama Railroad Co., to whom these ships belong, to defer departure *Yucatan* 24 hours after arrival *City of Washington*.'

"About the same time I had sent to the Minister of Foreign Affairs of the Republic of Panama the corresponding suggestions.

"I received the answer from the State Department at 9 p. m.:

"'Have wired your suggestion to Admiral Walker.'

"From the Panama Railroad, in spite of the express assurances given to me by Mr. Drake of sending me a message in the afternoon or early in the evening, nothing came, neither that evening nor the following morning, and only at 12.15 p. m., after the scheduled sailing time of the *Yucatan* from Colon, the following telegram was delivered for me at the Waldorf Astoria:

"'New York, *December 1, 1903*.

"'P. Bunau-Varilla, *Minister*,
"'*Waldorf-Astoria, New York*.

"'Replying to your telegram of 28th ultimo and interview with Vice President Drake yesterday, the decision has been reached that it will be inexpedient to comply with your request.

"'J. Edward Simmons,
"'*President Panama Railroad Co.*'

"About half an hour after I met Mr. Drake on board the steamer *Seguranca*, where I had been to take leave of the delegation of the Panama Government. He tried to explain to me in behalf of the president of the company the signification of the word 'inexpedient.' I paid but little attention to what he had to say.

"The attitude of this company under such grave circumstances I fail to explain from any logical point of view. The interests of the Republic of Panama, as expressed by the only official authority having the right to speak in their behalf in this country, and the obvious interest of the New Panama Canal Co., of which the Panama Railroad is a property, should have led anybody, I think, to find it expedient to comply with my request.

"I do not care to allude to a third and more important kind of interest for American citizens. I have no quality to speak about it, but it seems to me that the directors of any corporation, the world over, when they have to take a decision bearing on a question of national policy, invariably guide their action after the convenience of their Government has been respectfully and tactfully consulted."

The Department of State acknowledged receipt of my letter of complaint on the 9th of December, 1903, in the following terms:

Department of State,
Washington, December 9, 1903.

Sir: I have the honor to acknowledge receipt of your note of 3d instant stating that the Panama Railroad Co. had declined to detain the steamship *Yucatan* long enough to receive the ratification by your Government of the canal treaty.

Accept, sir, the renewed assurance of my highest consideration.

Francis B. Loomis,
Acting Secretary.

But since then the inquiry made by the World has brought out a document of capital importance. It is necessary to restrain one's indignation not to qualify it as it deserves. It explains the inconceivable attitude of the officers of the Panama Railroad, as set forth in the official letter of which I just gave extracts and which must be filed in the State Department. And this document is signed by an American citizen, who says he has the support of Mr. Cromwell.

It is a cablegram reproduced on page 428 of the Story of Panama, dated November 30, 1903, 6.10 p. m.

It must be borne in mind that, according to my letter to the State Department, my conversation with Mr. Drake took place the same day between 3 and 4.10 p. m., and that he saw me the following day and tried to explain to me that Mr. Edward Simmons had found it "inexpedient" to detain the *Yucatan*.

The cablegram is signed by Mr. Drake, who, as my letter to the State Department shows, had promised me a couple of hours before to see immediately Mr. Cromwell and to inform me in the afternoon or early in the evening of the decision taken about the detention of the *Yucatan*, requested by me on account of a great public interest.

It is addressed to Beers, his agent on the Isthmus for political questions and the former intermediary agent between Mr. Cromwell and the revolutionists; to the very same man to whom Mr. Arango recommends Mr. Amador to send his cables in his letter of September 14, 1903; to the very same man who Mr. Amador told me at his first visit had been sent to see Drake and Cromwell in order to get help to start a revolution.

This telegram, if true, entails a crushing responsibility on him who signed it and at the same time on him who is said in it to give his support to it. If this telegram is a forgery, why have not yet the two persons interested raised a cry of indignation when it was made public on the 16th of February, 1912, before a committee of Congress and printed since in the Government Printing Office?

NEW YORK, *November 30, 1903—6.10 p. m.*

BEERS, *Panama:*

Several cables urging immediate appointment of Pablo Arosemena[1] have been sent to the Junta (provisional government) since Friday. We are surprised that action has not taken place and suppose it is only because minister of the Republic of Panama is trying to disturb the Junta by cabling that there is great danger that Washington will make a trade with Reyes and withdraw warships and urge his retention because of his alleged influence with President Roosevelt and Senators. This is absolutely without foundation. Mr. Cromwell has direct assurances from President Roosevelt, Secretary Hay, Senator Hanna, and other Senators that there is not the slightest danger of this. Evidently the minister's pretense of influence is grossly exaggerated. We have the fullest support of Mr. Cromwell and his friends who have carried every victory for us for past six years. Junta evidently does not know that objection exists in Washington to the minister of Panama, because he is not a Panaman but a foreigner, and initially has displeased influential Senators regarding character of former treaty. He is recklessly involving Republic of Panama in financial and other complications that will use up important part of indemnity. Delegates here are powerless to prevent all this, as minister of Republic of Panama uses his position of minister to go over their heads. He is sacrificing the Republic's interests and may at any moment commit Republic of Panama to portion of the debts of Colombia, same as he signed a treaty omitting many points of advantage to Republic of Panama, and which would have been granted readily, without waiting for delegates, who were to his knowledge within two hours of arrival. With discretion inform Junta and cable me immediately synopsis of situation and when will Junta appoint Pablo Arosemena. Answer to-day if possible.

DRAKE.

This denunciation, ridiculous in fact as much as perfidious in intention, would only regard me if the treaty had been ratified then. It would not be worth mentioning if I had been alone interested. But its importance is capital if we think that the treaty was to arrive on the following day in Colon, and that, owing to the refusal of detaining the *Yucatan*, it was likely to remain eight days on the Isthmus subject to criticisms and discussions.

As the telegram distinctly said that a more advantageous treaty would have been readily granted to Panama it was the most explicit incitation to respect the treaty. The odious misrepresentations as to the character of the man who had signed it on behalf of Panama, with the request for his immediate recall, was another way of rendering its ratification impossible. Had the provisional government yielded to this double pressure the treaty would undoubtedly have been rejected. Panama would have witnessed the same course of events which Bogota had with the Hay-Herran treaty.

If this telegram is not a forgery it shows an act from an officer of the Panama Railroad, an American citizen, against the acts of the American Government in a foreign country. It is a traitor's work against the interests of his employers, the New Panama Canal Co., the owners of the stock of the Panama Railroad, and a traitor's work against the interests and the policy of the United States, whose diplomatic efforts in a foreign country it tried to thwart.

If the document is true it is the demonstration of something grave. I sincerely hope that Mr. Drake will exonerate himself in demonstrating that the telegram in question is a forgery. I hope he will show that he did not send it while according to his promises he was consulting with Mr. Cromwell about the detention of the *Yucatan*. The fact in any case will remain that the *Yucatan* sailed against my pressing requests, and this one fact would be sufficient to establish the lack of veracity of the plea for fees.

It is inconceivable that Mr. Cromwell should not have been consulted on this excessively important subject by Mr. Drake, his confidential man, between the

[1] To the place of minister plenipotentiary I filled then in Washington.

arrival of my telegram on the 28th of November and the refusal of my request on the 1st of December, 1903. If Mr. Drake can not show the telegram to be a forgery it is also obvious that he did not send it without Mr. Cromwell's consent and approval.

It seems, therefore, established beyond doubt that, contrary to what the plea for fees asserts, Mr. Cromwell's activities were not exerted in favor of the ratification by Panama.

Were Mr. Cromwell's activities exerted toward the ratification of the Hay-Bunau-Varilla treaty by the United States Senate?

During the months of November, December, 1903, and January, 1904, many speeches were pronounced in the Senate in order to prevent the ratification, but not one could exhibit a fault in the Hay-Bunau-Varilla treaty against the interests of the United States.

As the enemies of the treaty seemed to be powerless to obtain the rejection of a convention, which its own fiercest adversaries proclaimed to be the best one ever offered to the Senate for ratification, a new system of warfare began.

One of the two signers was proclaimed to be an adventurer and a scoundrel, whose character was such that it was the duty of the Senate to reject the treaty on account of the supposed infamy of one of its authors.

This campaign began with an article of the World entitled "Panama revolution a stock gambler's plan to make millions," and was followed three days after by a series of scurrilous articles in the Evening Post.

The World's article appeared on Sunday, January 17, 1904, and occupied on the top of the front page six columns out of eight of the paper. It was a whole cloth fabricated story of a syndicate of which I was said to be the head in order to speculate on the difference in value of the Panama securities before and after the revolution. The hundred thousand dollars which I advanced to the new Republic after it was formed were said to have been furnished by this syndicate.

This wicked invention was mixed with very precise details about the inception of the revolution.

Fortunately for me, being devoted since many years to the resurrection of the great work of Panama and to its vindication, I had made it a law for me to avoid the interference with my efforts of anything in the form of material interests. I had subscribed in the formation of the new company $110,000 in 1894, because it was at this time a necessity to create it in order to avoid the cancellation of the Panama concession by Colombia. I was bearer then (in 1894) of a certain number of bonds the value of which was at the time I received them less than $15,000 and which had been transferred to me in settlement of accounts by a third party. Since 1894 I had not made for my interest[1] any single purchase of any Panama securities, either directly or indirectly, either personally or as associate with any syndicate. The same reserve had been observed by all the members of my family as far as I can know.

This strong base of my actions made me very indifferent to this abominable invention.

A curious fact struck me as well as the persons who knew about the incidents before the revolution. The details of events preceding the revolution were very precise and accurate; only one name of those mixed with it was absent; it was that of Mr. Cromwell. The lack of reference to him pointed toward the origin of this paper.

I instructed my lawyers, Messrs. Pavey & Moore, to institute legal proceedings in order to know from where the paper had come.

As the World had shown that it was not of bad faith by soon dropping the whole story, I decided to drop also the legal proceedings.

The question remained: "Who had instigated the article?" The general rumor in Washington pointed in the same direction. An officer general of the Navy, well posted in canal matters, affirmed to me that he knew the name and he pronounced it before me.

The direction from which it came is now well known. We find it on page 680 of the "Story of Panama:" "The facts were brought to the World by Jonas Whitley of

---

[1] I made in the fall of 1901 a purchase of $20,000 Panama securities, but it was not for my interest.

Here is how it came. After a luncheon at the Cafe Anglais with prominent men of affairs, the question of Panama came up. In spite of the recommendation by the Isthmian Canal Commission of the Nicaragua Canal, I maintained that Panama would finally win. One of my friends, Mr. Albert Dehaynin, a witty and caustic man, said: "Bunau-Varilla is the defender of the lost cause. He is the "Kruger of Panama." This allusion to the fruitless endeavors of the President of the Transvaal piqued me. "Now, Dehaynin," I said, "you understand as a banker only figures and market quotations. I am going to buy for $20,000 Panama bonds; you will see in a few years if I am a Kruger of Panama or not. But as I have decided not to derive any profit from my endeavors, if I am not a Kruger the profit will be either for remunerating the legal work or the employees who have faithfully served me or for paying for publicity for making the truth known. If I am a Kruger, I shall be penalized by the loss."

I acted later as I said: not 1 farthing of this went to my credit. There is still to-day $4,000 in the hands of the bank who purchased and sold the securities: Ferdinand Meyer & Co., now S. Grunberg & Co. I intend to devote it to the publication of the real and complete History of Panama since its inception.

Mr. Cromwell's staff of press agents and the World holds a receipt for $100 for the 'tip.'

"Mr. Whitley did not mention Mr. Cromwell as the instigator nor did he tell the most incriminating circumstances concerning the complicity of the Roosevelt administration."

This statement is made under the signature of Mr. Earl Harding, a staff correspondent of the World.

But I have another statement which confirms it.

The article of January 17 had an aim. This aim was outlined on the day following in the World by calling attention to the Senate's action expressed in these words printed in large capitals: "Action by the Senate to follow Panama exposé."

I opposed to this article only this answer: "So long as I shall not get from the World the identity of the scoundrel who furnished it this article I shall not receive anybody coming to me on behalf of the World." I maintained constantly this attitude until I received in Paris on the 18th of July, 1909, from Mr. John Douglas Lindsay, of the firm of Nicoll, Anable, Lindsay & Fuller, a letter of information from Mr. Don C. Seitz, assistant vice president of the World.

It said: "You can accept my word that the article about which you desired information came directly from the office of William Nelson Cromwell, to our editors through the medium of Jonas Whitley, his press agent, who is closely associated with Roger L. Farnham, Mr. Cromwell's general representative in such matters. Both Mr. Farnham and Mr. Whitley were employees of the World before going into the pay of Mr. Cromwell who, up to the time of his canal performances had not participated in public affairs, but was regarded as an extraordinarily keen lawyer, and statements of whom were apt to find easy credence."

These are the facts referring to this dangerous period when the fate of the great enterprise was hanging in the balance. The lack of ratification of the Hay-Bunau-Varilla treaty either by Panama or by the Senate of the United States would have on the eve of a presidential election surely meant the death of the Panama Canal and the adoption of the Nicaragua route.

Has Mr. Cromwell been the victim of a decision taken only by Mr. Drake and Mr. Simmons, against his will and consent, to refuse the detention of the *Yucatan*, so important for the certainty of the ratification? Has he inspired this decision? It is not my part to decide on this point.

Has Mr. Cromwell been the victim of an intrigue against me made by Mr. Drake alone in New York in sending the telegram of the 30th of November, 6.10 p. m., to Beers on the Isthmus, with the statement that a much better treaty would have been readily granted? Has Capt. Beers concealed from Mr. Cromwell this telegram when he came afterwards to New York and stayed for a long time near me at the New Willard, Washington, as is shown in Mr. Earl Harding's compilation of facts (p. 680)? "February 9, 1904, Capt. Beers sailed for Panama after having held his daily conferences with Mr. Cromwell where he was maintained at the New Willard Hotel at Mr. Cromwell's expense." Has Mr. Cromwell inspired this telegram to his agent, Drake?

It is not my part to decide on this point. Has Mr. Cromwell again been the victim for the third time of Mr. Jonas Whitley, his press agent, when the latter communicated to the World the offensive and wholly fabricated invention about the supposed cause of my efforts on behalf of Panama? It was plainly an effort to impress the Senate in order to obtain the rejection of the treaty on account of its supposed infamous origin. Has Mr. Cromwell been the victim of his agent, Whitley, again a third time? Or has he inspired the article?

For the third time I repeat:

It is not my part to decide on this point.

I have only to probe the veracity of the plea for fees. I mentioned the essential facts recited above with the sincere hope that Mr. Cromwell will demonstrate that he has been on three different occasions the victim of his agent or his agent the victim of a forgery in the second case.

But when these obstructions were placed in the path of the ratification, what was the duty of anybody devoting his efforts to this ratification?

It was to come and see me and to offer me his influence over the press if he had some, as Mr. Cromwell said he had, and thus help me to defeat the efforts of those who were trying to dishonor me with a view of killing the treaty.

Never once Mr. Cromwell came to see me, though he often was in Washington in the very same hotel where I lived, the New Willard, he having abandoned the Raleigh, his former hotel.

I can therefore state that there is a positive and demonstrated lack of veracity in the plea for fees when it says (p. 239 of the Story of Panama):

"We were relied upon to devote ourselves to the ratification of the treaty between the United States and Panama * * * and we devoted ourselves to this task during the six following weeks."

I shall not go any further because as I said the demonstration of the lack of veracity of the "plea for fees" if all points were examined would require a whole book.

It is unnecessary when a document is thus shown on five points, not specially chosen, to be tampering with dates and to be withholding the facts which govern the results. It is shown to be absolutely lacking in veracity.

It is therefore shown to be absolutely unfit to be taken as a basic and principal element for writing the story of a great event.

THE PERSONAL ADDITIONS OF MR. HALL TO THE FICTIONS INSERTED IN THE PLEA FOR FEES.

It is obvious that the plea for fees has had on Mr. Hall's mind a capital influence. It has conquered his whole mind. He is an obvious example of a curious kind of hypnotism which makes him believe in events that do not exist, to facts that a slight effort toward verification would instantly annihilate.

His admiration for the author of the plea for fees is without limit. Speaking of Mr. Cromwell, he says (p. 94), "The man whose masterful mind, whetted on the grindstone of corporation cunning, conceived and carried out the rape of the isthmus." On page 103: "Nothing seemed able to resist the influences combined in its favor (the Nicaragua Canal). Mr. Cromwell, however, proved himself equal to the task," etc.

We know that he is working under a delusion created by the fictions of the plea for fees. We know that Mr. Cromwell did not carry the rape of the isthmus, if there ever was such a thing. He had gone to France and abandoned the conspirators to their fate when the revolution took place without his knowledge. We know, also, that these extraordinary influences which Mr. Cromwell is said by his plea for fees to have overcome did not exist, and that Representative Hepburn, and not Mr. Cromwell, defeated the Morgan Nicaragua bill in the House.

No wonder, then, if Mr. Hall has been, in spite of his excellent intention, erring deeply in many cases. It is because he has taken to the foot of the letter the assertions of a document which deserves no credit whatever.

He thought it to be equivalent to a testimony under oath when it was just the reverse.

We are going to point out some of Mr. Hall's grave, erroneous, and misleading statements. They are taken as examples, but as we have said about the plea for fees they are not the only ones.

We have already seen him place on the 6th a document which bears and which he copied with the date of the 5th of November, 1903. We have seen him declare to be confidential a document which was published by all the papers of the United States on the evening of the 6th and on the morning of the 7th. Let us now look at some other errors of the same kind.

Point A.—On page 319, Mr. Hall asserts:

"Mr. Cromwell alone and Mr. Bunau-Varilla and Dr. Amador in company, had all made trips to Washington, and on October 15 Mr. Cromwell, all arrangements having been made, left for Paris to confer with the directors of the New Panama Canal Co."

I have already said, and I repeat, that since my arrival on the 22d of September, 1903, to New York till a day after the Hay-Bunau-Varilla treaty was signed (Nov. 18, 1903), I never saw Mr. Cromwell once. I did not see him afterwards till I met him accidentally in the lobbies of the New Willard when I was going out of the lift. It was the day of the ratification of the treaty. (Feb. 23, 1904.)

I further do state that I never went to Washington with Dr. Amador, nor that I even projected to undertake such a voyage. I believe he neither went alone nor with Mr. Cromwell. It is when he was expecting to do this trip with him that Mr. Cromwell turned his back upon him. He, of course, in that period never could meet Mr. Cromwell any more. He was then in an intense state of fury against the man who he thought had betrayed him.

To speak of a voyage in common in that period is purely a fictitious statement without any basis whatever.

Point B.—On page 324, Mr. Hall says:

"One hundred thousand dollars was telegraphed over by the Credit Lyonnais for account of the New Panama Canal Co. to Heidelbach, Ickelheimer & Co., and credited to Bunau-Varilla."

He further says, on page 327: "On October 26, three days after Mr. Cromwell's arrival in Paris, the Credit Lyonnais by cable to Heidelbach, Ickelheimer & Co., of New York, opened in favor of Bunau-Varilla a credit of $100,000. The president of the Credit Lyonnais was Marius Bô, also president of the New Panama Canal Co. and Cromwell's chief instrument in its manipulations."

It is a material fabrication and a most misleading one to say that the New Panama Canal Co. had anything whatever to do with or even knew I had ordered to send me $100,000 to New York, care of Heidelbach, Ickelheimer & Co.

It is most reprehensible to thus juxtapose names and to thus give color to a false and fictitious statement.

Never, as I said, was Mr. Marius Bô president of the Credit Lyonnais. The president then was Mr. Germain, the founder of that great institution. He died in 1905; his successor died since. Never for a moment was there a question of offering the presidency to Mr. Marius Bô.

The Crédit Lyonnais is an enormous banking institution with a great number of branch offices all over the country counting its clients by tens of thousands. I am one of them. It constitutes a vertiable ineptitude to establish a relation between the transfer of money I made through my banker, the Crèdit Lyonnais, and the fact that Mr. Marius Bô was at the same time a director of the Crédit Lyonnais and president of the New Panama Canal Co. Every day thousands and thousands of such operations are made and none reaches the ears of the directors nor of the president of the Crédit Lyonnais.

I feel somewhat ashamed to have to state such truisms, but it is necessary to show that the spirit pervading the plea for fees is so similar to that pervading Mr. Hall's statements that it seems to be made under the same general influence. Now I must come to the facts.

When Amador had reached the decision of shaking the tyranny of Colombia I undertook, if he carried out the plan of the liberation of the Isthmus, to help the first steps of the new Republic by providing her with some money if established and as soon as established.

My first idea was to get the money from some banking house in New York for account of the new republic. After Amador had left I began to think that in doing so I would have to accept a heavy brokerage for borrowing said sum on account of the risk attached to it. I thought also that nothing would interfere, if not the bankers themselves at least some employees of theirs were to speculate on the probability of the event. I saw that I was going to engage myself in a path where calumny would be free to impute to me the responsibility of such disgusting and dishonorable speculations. I saw only one way to do away with these difficulties. It was to furnish the money myself.

Then came the question of the method how to have the money quickly at my disposal in New York. I used always when in the States for my ordinary provisions of money in New York the bank of Heidelbach, Ickelheimer & Co.

I was used, when I needed money, to telegraph for it to branch office B of the Crédit Lyonnais, and give the order to telegraph to Heidelbach, Ickelheimer & Co. to place the same sum at my disposal in New York.

I thought that they being used to these cable transfers they would transfer also without difficulty a much larger sum than those I used ordinarily.

The method of transmission once settled I had next to provide the branch office B of the Crédit Lyonnais with the necessary amount of money to cover the telegraphic transfer to New York of $100,000.

I had then two banks holding securities in safeguard for me, the firm Balser & Co., of Brussels, and another branch office of the Crédit Lyonnais, the branch office A. S. of the Champs Élysées.

I prepared in the evening of Wednesday, the 21st of October, 1903, two cablegrams to these banks asking each of them if it could loan me immediately 250,000 francs on my securities deposited in its care, and in such case to remit it immediately to Agency B of the Credit Lyonnais, Paris.

Both these telegrams were deposited at the telegraph office at 1 o'clock a. m. Thursday, the 22d of October, 1903.

I copy them both:

[Translation.]

BALSER,

7 rue d'Arenberg, Bruxelles.

Could you make me an advance 250,000 francs ($50,000) on the securities which you hold in deposit for me, and remit immediately money to Branch Office B, Credit Lyonnais. Answer me Waldorf-Astoria, New York.

PHILIPPE VARILLA.

[Translation.]

AGENCE (Branch Office) CREDIT LYONNAIS,
55 Champs Elysées, Paris.

Can you make me an advance 250,000 francs on the securities you hold in deposit for me and remit immediately money to Branch Office B, Credit Lyonnais. Answer me Waldorf-Astoria, New York.

VARILLA.

I went to bed after sending these telegrams, and the same day, October 22, 1903, I was awakened at 8 o'clock a. m. by the page bringing the first answer.

[Translation.]

PHILIPPE VARILLA,
Waldorf-Astoria, New York.

We consent advance 250,000 on securities deposited for three months, unless we agree for prolongation. We are remitting Credit Lyonnais Branch Office B.

BALSER.

OCTOBER 22, 1903—6.36 A. M.

The second came at 11.10 a. m. from the Credit Lyonnais:

[Translation.]

BUNAU-VARILLA,
Waldorf-Astoria, N. Y.

We are in accord for 250,000 francs which we transfer to your account Branch Office B. Letter follows.

CREDIONNAIS.

Nothing remained but to give the order of transfer to New York to Branch Office B. I waited three days, so that the regular exchange of letters could be made and I cabled:

AGENCE (BRANCH OFFICE) B, CREDIT LYONNAIS,
Place Bourse, Paris:

First, you must have received 500,000 francs from Balser and from Branch Office A. S. Second, inform Heidelbach, Ickelheimer to give me against drafts emitted by me all sums I may want up to the limit of 500,000 francs, as it is done for letters credence. Third, answer me at Waldorf-Astoria, New York.

PHILIPPE BUNAU-VARILLA.

This dispatch was sent from Highland Falls on Hudson on Sunday, 25th of October, 1902, at 6.30 p. m.

The following day before noon the answer came. It is dated October 26, 11.38.

BUNAU-VARILLA, PHILIPPE,
Waldorf-Astoria, New York:

For crediting we are making necessary transfers by cable; please confirm instructions by letter.

CREDIONNAIS.

This is the whole story of the origin of the $100,000 with which I financed the first days of the new Republic. If it had succumbed, I would have lost this money. I thought that by incurring this risk I would be protected from all blame whatever may happen. But I was mistaken. The first theory made public was that on the 17th of January, 1904, in the article brought by Mr. Jonas Whitley, Mr. Cromwell's press agent, to the World. It says that this sum was furnished by a syndicate of low speculators, of which I was the head and inspirator. The last theory as told by Mr. Hall, again of the staff of the World, is that it was given me by the New Panama Canal Co. according to the orders of Mr. Cromwell, who arrived in Paris, if Mr. Hall is truthful on this point, three days before the 26th of October. As it has been seen, my dispatches were written in the evening of the 21st and sent at 1 o'clock in the morning of the 22d of October.

Point C.—Speaking of the loan made by the Bowling Green Trust of another $100,000, guaranteed by Mr. Cromwell's securities, Mr. Hall always confounds the dates and mixes up the whole affair. On page 461 we see, in answer to Mr. Cline, asking if Mr. Cromwell advanced some money to these parties prior to the revolution, Mr. Hall answers, after speaking, as I said in the previous point: "There was also a loan of $100,000 from the Bowling Green Trust Co. secured, as I shall show you later, by securities deposited by Mr. Cromwell."

Also, on page 401, Mr. Hall says that the money of which Amador spoke to Gen. Tovar, on the day following the revolution, was furnished—$100,000 by the Credit Lyonnais for the French Canal Co. and $100,000 by the Bowling Green Trust Co.—on the securities deposited by Mr. Cromwell.

All that is pure invention, as to dates and facts. We know the history of the $100,000, which was my own money. In repeating this same false statement about its origin, Mr. Hall does not make it less false. About the loan of the Bowling Green Trust Co., it was made after Mr. Cromwell had been able to make his reconciliation with Amador and the delegates when they arrived on the 17th of November, 1903, in New York.

The day following, the treaty giving the guarantee of the United States was signed. After that there was no risk of any great importance. Whatever was to be the fate of the ratification of the treaty, Panama could not be abandoned by the United States. If it had reverted to Colombia, it would have been peacefully done and the sums advanced would have been thus protected. It is for this reason that on November 25, and not before the revolution of the 3d of November, Amador and Boyd signed an agreement with the Bowling Green Trust Co. This is stated by Mr. Hall himself on page 427, but he does not remark it. If it was secured, as it is said, with securities deposited by Mr. Cromwell, the risk was infinitesimal then. It is a whole alteration of the truth of events to confound this loan made after the treaty was signed with money advanced at the very start of the Republic. Gen. Tovar can not have heard Amador speaking on the 4th of November of money resulting from an agreement which was signed on the 25th following. This seems obvious for anybody but not for Mr. Hall.

To displace, as Mr. Hall does, the date of this loan gives an absolutely fictitious part to Mr. Cromwell's situation when the revolution burst out.

Point D.—Mr. Hall is under the sort of hypnotic influence created by the belief in the plea for fees which seem as well as to have extended itself to Mr. Earl Harding in his so-called "statement of facts," in various important points. Mr .Hall is disposed to think Mr. Cromwell had an extraordinary power not only on men but on the future. He speaks of "Cromwellian piece of diplomacy" (p. 276); of "Hay-Cromwell instructions" (p. 289); of the "Cromwell-Hay" draft of treaty (p. 268); of the President of the Credit Lyonnais being Cromwell's chief instrument in France (p. 328); of Cromwell's masterful mind which conceived and carried out the rape of the Isthmus (p. 94). He says that Mr. Cromwell conceived and with the assistance of Mr. Roosevelt carried out the rape of the Isthmus and the establishment there of this little republic.

We have seen how Mr. Cromwell must be held as completely innocent of having carried out what Mr. Hall calls the rape of the Isthmus. It remains to show that he was also completely innocent of the conception of it.

In order to demonstrate his theory Mr. Hall, on pp. 296–297, quotes an article of the World which was published on the 14th of June, 1903, and wired from Washington in the evening of the 13th. Mr. Hall pretends the substance of this article foreseeing the revolution was brought to the World by Mr. Roger L. Farnham, the press agent of Mr. Cromwell, after a long conference at the White House between the latter gentleman and Mr. Roosevelt.

Mr. Hall sees there the undeniable proof that the 13th of June, 1903, was the day of the famous conception in Mr. Cromwell's masterful mind of the Panama revolution. Mr. Hall in his enthusiasm for Mr. Cromwell's master mind not only gives him the credit of the conception but also of the supernatural foresight of deciding then that the revolution would take place on the 3d of November following. Of course all of that is pure fiction.

At noon in Paris on the 13th of June, 1903, a cablegram was forwarded by me to President Marroquin in Bogota via New York. It was then 7 o'clock a. m. in New York. The message therefore passed over the American wires between seven and eight in the morning of the 13th of June.

It was made public by the Sun of June 27, 1903. Though I had not requested its publication I did not make a mystery of it. I copy it from the Sun:

PARIS, *June 13, 1903.*

MARROQUIN, *President Republic, Bogota:*

Beg to submit respectfully following:

1. One must admit as a fundamental principle the only person that may build the Panama Canal now is the United States, and that neither European Governments nor private financiers would dare to fight either against the Monroe doctrine or American treasury for building Panama Canal, in case Americans return to Nicaragua, if Congress (Colombian) does not ratify treaty.

2. It results from this evident principle that failure of ratification only opens two ways:

Either construction of Nicaragua Canal and absolute loss to Colombia of the incalculable advantages resulting from construction on her territory of the great artery of universal commerce, or construction of Panama Canal after secession and declaration of independence of the Isthmus of Panama under protection of the United States, as it has happened with Cuba.

3. I hope that your elevated patriotic policy will save your country from the two precipices where would perish either the prosperity or the integrity of Colombia and whither would lead the advices of blinded people or of evildoers who wish to reject treaty or to modify it, which would amount to the same thing.

PHILIPPE BUNAU-VARILLA.

As I said, I made no mystery of this cablegram, which I sent in clear language. It is a striking thing that having passed through the United States in the morning of the 13th an article was prepared exactly on the same line by Mr. Cromwell on the evening of the same day.

It may have been telegraphed from Paris by some person who knew of it; it may have filtered through the infidelity of some employee of the telegraph company when it passed through the United States.

There may be only a simple coincidence. At any rate, whatever may be the reality, the facts show that the paternity of the conception can not be attributed to the masterful mind of Mr. Hall's hero.

I had already at the end of the preceding year made a very forcible allusion to the secession in another cable to President Marroquin. It was then in order to break Mr. Concha's resistance to a canal treaty. A few days after sending this message to President Marroquin Mr. Concha left the legation of Colombia and was substituted by Mr. Herran, who signed the Hay-Herran treaty.

Here is the text of this important cablegram sent to President Marroquin by me on November 23, 1902, at 8.50 a. m., from New York:

MARROQUIN, *President Republic, Bogota:*

Extremely perilous situation justifies my submitting following considerations:

Suspension of signature of treaty Panama Canal on the eve of meeting of Congress has only three issues equally damaging for the vital interest of Colombia.

Either the final selection of Nicaragua as the Spooner law orders;

Or the loss of all the way conquered and indefinite prorogation if at the end of next February, when actual Congress ends, everything is not voted and settled;

Or the creation of international events of the highest gravity, of which might result that the canal be made at Panama against Colombia instead of being made with her amicably.

Only hope is decisive radical action of the supreme Government of Republic.

BUNAU-VARILA,
Waldorf-Astoria.

If the conception of the Panama revolution can be found anywhere, it is in this telegram sent one year minus 20 days before it burst out. It was not at all by Mr. Cromwell on the evening of the 13th of June, 1903.

But the knowledge of all these facts is in possession of all those who were personally interested. It has found its vivid expression in the cablegram which President Obaldia sent me when his predecessor Anador died, after having been the founder and the first president of the new Republic.

I had sent the following telegram from Paris to Mr. Obaldia, the president of the Panama Republic, on May 3, 1909:

"OBALDIA, *President Republic Panama:*

"At the moment of the death of your illustrious predecessor I wish to express to your Excellency how much I share the sorrow of the Republic which Amador has so much contributed to establish. His name will remain forever associated with the work of the free union of the two great oceans of the earth, a thing which, if it had not been for the foundation of the Republic of Panama, would have remained a mere chimera.

"My mind goes back with emotion to the tragic instant of September, 1903, when Amador betrayed and abandoned came to entrust to me his despair and when we have undertaken together the liberation of the Isthmus which was the basis of the realization of the 'Straits of Panama.'

"His heroic patriotism led to successful issue the revolution of the 3d of November. The murder of oppression has unchained progress.

"BUNAU-VARILLA."

I received on May 13, 1909, the noble expression of the sentiments of the people of Panama by the President of their Republic. It was published by the Paris Herald of May 15, 1909. It reads:

PHILIPPE BUNAU-VARILLA, *Paris:*

I am thankful for the share you take in the grief caused by the death of President Amador. The remembrances you recall have deeply moved the public sentiment. It is a page of our history. Our people will keep forever engraved your fruitful services and put in preeminent place the name of Amador and your own. The national gratitude gives them the title of Benefactors of Panama.

OBALDIA.

These sentiments based on facts intimately known on the Panama side may be put next to a similar expression of sentiments based on facts known on the American side. On May 12, 1904, say more than two months after I had ceased to be minister at Washington and I had returned to my home in Paris, Secretary Hay wrote me:

"It is not often given to any man to render such a service to two countries and to the civilized world as you have done."

Such public manifestations very easily break the threads of the spiders of fiction.

The impartial man easily finds where the truth is in spite of the efforts of imagination excited by fanciful theories.

Point E.—Mr. Hall seems to take a special pleasure in giving me a perfectly fictitious part as to my relations with the New Panama Canal Co. He calls me, on page 423: "The French Panama Canal minister." On page 317, he represents me as summoned in haste from Paris in order to comfort Mr. Amador.

Mr. Hall says: "Just in time for Mr. Cromwell * * * to cable to Paris and have Bunau-Varilla take the first steamer across." Mr. Hall adds: "Unfortunately I do not have the cable that I believe Mr. Cromwell sent to the New Panama Canal Co. to have Bunau-Varilla sent over here, but that cable is also among the archives of the New Panama Canal Co., which are the property of the United States and which are still in France, kept in the vaults there."

This is the most injurious statement for me. The dispatch which Mr. Hall only believes to exist but the place of which he distinctly knows with precision is in line with his other fictitious assertions. It has the same degree of veracity as his assertion that a document published on the 6th of November in all the newspapers is confidential. It has the same degree of veracity as his assertion that Marius Bô was President of the Credit Lyonnais when he never was. It has the same degree of veracity as his assertion that on the 4th of November, 1903, Amador had spoken of money advanced by the Bowling Green Trust Co., when the agreement with that trust company was made on the 25th following. It has the same degree of veracity as the statement that the New Panama Canal Co. sent me $100,000 for financing the revolution, when by the documents reproduced I have shown this sum to have been sent from my own money without anybody's cooperation.

I say and repeat that my position toward the New Panama Canal Co. has always been inimical, because I strongly blamed their weak policy which has led to the loss of the Panama Canal. There was neither cordiality nor any relation between us.

CONCLUSION.

After showing that the Story of Panama is based upon a document, Mr. Cromwell's plea for fees, entirely devoid of veracity, I have shown the additions of Mr. Hall to be strictly in conformity with the spirit of the plea for fees, so that they seem to be written by the same hand.

It would be without end if I were to show all the imaginary facts told by Mr. Hall. The statement he attributes falsely to me, according to which I have said to Mr. Don C. Seitz that Mr. Cromwell had made a contribution of $60,000 to the election fund in 1900, is also a pure fiction (p. 112). I never thought, and therefore never said, such a thing. In 1902 when Mr. Cromwell came to see me for his reinstatement, I asked him if there was an account pending with the company. "No," said he, "only a trifling matter of one or two thousand dollars. That's all."

If he had a claim of such magnitude he would have told me then.

It would be tiresome to follow every error into the labyrinth of imaginary statements of Mr. Hall. It would also be below my disdain to castigate some personal misstatements about myself. It might lead to the belief that I am writing this in a personal intention. A scurrilous attack more or less does not trouble me.

It is a penalty men have to pay when they work for great things. My compensation is to have brought back Panama to life. It is a sufficient reward for me and it makes me forget the powerless attacks directed against me in this long struggle for truth.

We must set a limit to such a study, and say in conclusion that the statements of Mr. Hall on all the important points must be considered as having the same value as the plea for fees.

Therefore the basic and principal element of the Story of Panama, as told by Mr. Hall, the plea for fees, as well as his personal additions, form a whole which is entirely devoid of the stable foundation in truth necessary for writing the Story of Panama. The whole thing brought before the Committee on Foreign Affairs must be considered as a fiction. This fiction is formed by true facts associated with wholly imaginary ones, the mass being combined with adulterated accounts of events so as to fit the fancy of the writer. It is entirely unworthy of the hospitality it has received in the congressional documentation.

P. BUNAU-VARILLA.

PARIS, *March 29, 1912.*
53 Avenue d'Iéna.

By direction of the chairman, the following letter is included in the record:

PAVEY & MOORE,
ATTORNEYS AND COUNSELLORS AT LAW,
New York, February 21, 1913.

Hon. HENRY D. FLOOD,
Chairman of the Committee on Foreign Affairs,
House of Representatives, Washington, D. C.

DEAR SIR: In my testimony before the Committee on Foreign Affairs on February 19, 1913, in reference to the revolution in Panama, I stated that at the request of your former chairman, Mr. Sulzer, I had made efforts by correspondence and by personal interviews with Mr. Philippe Bunau-Varilla in Paris in September to arrange for his appearance before the committee as a witness, and that he had been unable to come to this country for that purpose. You can imagine the surprise with which I learned upon my return to New York that Mr. Bunau-Varilla had arrived in New York on the morning of the 19th about 10 o'clock, and that at the very time I was testifying in Washington he was seeking me in New York. This coincidence was due to the following circumstances:

Mr. Bunau-Varilla left Paris on the 21st of January for Mexico, where he has large interests in petroleum lands. He had no intention of coming to New York, and I did not know that he was going to Mexico. Before he arrived in Mexico the revolution had broken out and he considered it unsafe to enter that country. He went to Los Angeles to meet some of his associates in the petroleum enterprise and waited there in the hope that order in Mexico would be sufficiently restored for him to carry out his project of visiting their property in Mexico. The continued disturbance in Mexico made any such trip dangerous and impossible. Before leaving Paris he had made definite engagements which compelled him to be there at the end of February. He remained in Los Angeles until he had just time to catch the Steamship Provence, which sailed from New York on the 20th of this month. His decision to come through New York on his return was taken at the last moment.

I did not know that he was in this country. He did not know the question of Panama was still under investigation by the committee. There had been no communication between him and me on that subject since our last interview in Paris in September, when he had given a definite decision that he would not be able to come to this country this winter.

It had been agreed between us that I should endeavor to secure the correction of the fundamental error which ran through the entire investigation. That fundamental error was that the New Panama Canal Company and Mr. Cromwell were the sole source of all activity in regard to the Panama Canal in this country prior to its adoption by the United States. It was desirable that it should clearly appear on the records of your investigation that the activity of Mr. Bunau-Varilla in the matter was wholly independent of the initiative of Mr. Cromwell or the New Panama Canal Comp ny. With that point made clear, there can be a correct determination as to where the responsibility for the revolution in Panama rests.

It was impossible for Mr. Bunau-Varilla to delay his departure for Paris, and he is of the opinion that my testimony has corrected the fundamental error which has colored the previous presentation of facts. If Mr. Rainey wishes further details as to the participation of Mr. Bunau-Varilla in the accomplishment of the independence of Panama, Mr. Bunau-Varilla will furnish him as complete information as possible on all such questions.

Mr. Bunau-Varilla begged me to express to the committee his regret that due to my lack of knowledge of his movements and his lack of knowledge of the continuance of the investigation, that I should have been put in the position of testifying to his inability to come to this country when he was actually in the country.

Mr. Prentice joins with me in this expression of our regret that by reason of our lack of information as to Mr. Bunau-Varilla's whereabouts the committee may have received an incorrect impression. In order that our position on this point ma be made clear on the record, we respectfully request that this letter be printed as part of my testimony.

I have the honor to be, yours, very truly,

FRANK D. PAVEY.

THE STORY OF PANAMA.

No. 1.

HEARINGS ON THE RAINEY RESOLUTION BEFORE THE COMMITTEE ON FOREIGN AFFAIRS OF THE HOUSE OF REPRESENTATIVES.

JANUARY 26 AND FEBRUARY 9, 1912.

THE STORY OF PANAMA.

COMMITTEE ON FOREIGN AFFAIRS,
HOUSE OF REPRESENTATIVES,
January 26, 1912.

Mr. SULZER (chairman). Gentlemen of the committee, we will take up this morning Mr. Rainey's resolution relating to Panama.

The resolution reads as follows:

[H. Res. 32. Sixty-second Congress, first session.]

Whereas a former President of the United States has declared that he "took" Panama from the Republic of Colombia without consulting Congress; and

Whereas the Republic of Colombia has ever since petitioned this country to submit to The Hague tribunal the legal and equitable question whether such taking was in accordance with or in violation of the treaty then existing between the two countries, and also whether such taking was in accordance with or in violation of the well-established principles of the law of nations; and

Whereas the Government of the United States professes its desire to submit all international controversies to arbitration and has conducted treaties with many other nations agreeing to submit all legal questions to arbitration, but has steadily refused arbitration to the Republic of Colombia: Therefore be it

Resolved, That the Committee on Foreign Affairs of the House of Representatives be, and the same hereby is, directed to inquire into the same; send for books, papers, and documents; summon witnesses; take testimony; and report the same, with its opinion and conclusions thereon, to this House with all convenient speed.

Mr. Rainey, you can proceed.

Mr. RAINEY. Mr. Chairman, the hearing the committee has so kindly accorded me is on House resolution 32, of the first session of the present Congress, which I introduced on the 16th day of last April.

At the present time before this committee it is my purpose to make out, if I can, a prima facie case, and I think when we get through presenting the evidence to the committee you will agree that we have made out something more than a prima facie case.

Now, in the first place, it might be important for the committee to know just what the propositions of Colombia are in this matter in order to show you the things Colombia could not ask for under her own proposition.

On October 21, 1905, the Colombian minister at Washington presented to our State Department a recapitulation of the events which preceded the alleged revolution on the Isthmus of Panama and asked for arbitration, and in a subsequent note on April 6, 1906, he had this to say in a letter to our State Department:

I note the fact that in your communication (Secretary Root's) it is stated for the first time on behalf of your Government that the United States espoused the cause of Panama, the language being:

"Nor are we willing to permit any arbitrator to determine the political policy of the United States in following its sense of right and justice by espousing the cause of this weak people against the stronger Government of Colombia, which had so long held them in lawful subjection."

I must say that the question between Colombia and the United States is not whether Panama was justly entitled to assert independence, but whether the United States was under obligation by treaty or by principles of international law, not to do the things which it is admitted were done by the United States after the declaration of Panama's independence was made.

If the acts of the United States were lawful and right this loss must fall upon Colombia. If, on the other hand, this loss was wrongfully occasioned by acts of the United States done in violation of the provisions of the treaty by which the United States has obligated itself or in violation of principles of international law to which the United States has assented, then the United States is lawfully bound to compensate Colombia for the damage thus done to her.

In order to facilitate a decision by the Government of the United States in case it can not yet see that it is lawfully bound to compensate Colombia, I propose, on behalf of Colombia, that the United States and Colombia forthwith enter into a convention for the purpose of securing an impartial judgment upon the following strictly legal questions:

1. Did the treaty of 1846 obligate the United States to maintain the sovereignty of Colombia over the Isthmus of Panama against menace or attack from any foreign power and against internal disturbances that might jeopardize said sovereignty?

2. Did the treaty of 1846 obligate the United States to refrain from taking steps which would hinder Colombia in maintaining her sovereignty over Panama by suppressing rebellion, revolution, secession, or internal disorder?

3. Did the treaty of 1846 grant to the United States the right to take those steps which it is admitted were taken by the United States to prevent the landing of troops in Panama and the suppression of the rebellion?

4. Did the treaty of 1846 leave the United States free lawfully to take the steps which it is admitted by the United States were taken as regards Panama?

5. Did these acts of the United States which it is admitted were taken prevent Colombia from taking the steps necessary to suppress the rebellion and to maintain her sovereignty over the Isthmus?

6. Were the admitted acts of the United States in respect to Panama in violation of principles of international law which have been recognized by the United States as binding upon nations in their dealings with each other?

7. What damage, if any, has been occasioned to Colombia by acts of the United States, which are admitted by the United States, and which may be adjudged as having been in violation of obligations imposed upon the United States by the treaty of 1846 or by principles of international law to which the United States has assented?

The CHAIRMAN. The treaty of 1846 was in force at the time of the establishment of the Panama Republic?

Mr. RAINEY. Yes, sir. It was in force at the time, and the treaty of 1846 contained the provision which I will read now to the committee. The committee is familiar, of course, with these things and with much of the evidence which I propose to produce this morning. What I now want to do, in order to assist the committee, is to assemble the available evidence on this question so that it may be presented together. Now, it exists in a great many different places and it is a difficult matter to find it.

The treaty of 1846 contained this provision:

The United States guarantees positively and efficaciously to New Granada, by the present stipulation, the perfect neutrality of the before-mentioned Isthmus, with the view that the free transit from one to the other sea may not be interrupted or embarrassed in any future time while this treaty exists; and in consequence, the United States also guarantees in the same manner the rights of sovereignty and property which New Granada has and possesses over said territory.

That the treaty which was in full force on the 3d day of November, 1903, when the revolution occurred. Two days afterwards our State Department directed our representative on the Isthmus to enter into relations with the Republic of Panama. On the 18th day of November—less than two weeks—about two weeks after the revolution on the Isthmus, we entered into a treaty with Panama, the very first section of which reads as follows:

The United States guarantees and will maintain the independence of the Republic of Panama.

There was in force on the 3d day of November and on the 18th day of November, between the United States and New Granada, now Colombia, a treaty by which the United States guaranteed to Colombia the rights of sovereignty and of property which Colombia had on the Isthmus of Panama. Without the consent of Colombia and against her protest, and she has been protesting ever since, the United States at the same time with this treaty in full force guaranteed to the new Republic of Panama its independence as against the sovereignty of Colombia, which we guaranteed to protect.

Mr. SHARP. What date did the United States guarantee the independence of the Republic of Panama?

Mr. RAINEY. The treaty was concluded on the 18th day of November, 1903. It was ratified by the Senate on the 23d day of February, 1904. It was ratified by the President on the 25th day of February, 1904; ratifications were exchanged on the same day; and it was proclaimed on the 26th day of February, 1904.

Mr. SHARP. In regard to the protests to which you referred a moment ago, of the United States of Colombia against the United States recognition of the Republic of Panama, how recently have those formal protests been made?

Mr. RAINEY. They have been continued until the present moment.

Mr. SHARP. In what form?

Mr. RAINEY. Various letters between the representatives of Colombia and our State Department and, last of all, perhaps, a protest of the representative of Colombia here against the speech made by President Roosevelt out on the Pacific coast in which he admitted that he "took Panama"; and he said in effect there were two courses for him to pursue, either to do as had been done—I am not quoting him exactly—or submit a state document to Congress, which Congress would be debating yet. But he said, "I took the Isthmus, and while the debate goes on now the work on the canal goes on also." The letter I have mentioned is a most vigorous protest made by Colombia against the taking of the Isthmus.

Mr. SHARP. What date was that—not to be exact, but within the past year?

Mr. RAINEY. Yes, sir; within the past year. It was, I think, last April.

Mr. SHARP. Now further. What remedy or reparation——

Mr. RAINEY. I might also say with reference to the present minister from Colombia, who has been here only a short time, that one of his first acts was to protest again to the State Department, again asking for an arbitration of this question.

Mr. SHARP. The Republic of Panama has now been in existence and for many years recognized by this country, which, of course, doesn't make it all right; I don't claim that it does, but having been inexistence for anumber of years, having formed a Government and exercised governmental functions, what remedy or reparation at this time does the United States of Colombia expect to secure, either by the adoption of this resolution or any other form of procedure?

Mr. RAINEY. Certainly not the return of her territory. Certainly not the abandonment of any of our property on the zone. Colombia is still demanding that we submit the matter to arbitration with a view of ascertaining whether there has been a violation of the law of nations, and if there has been such violation, then the question comes up as to how much damages she is entitled to receive.

Mr. SHARP. For which a money compensation ought to settle?

Mr. RAINEY. A money compensation is all. That is all we can do.

Mr. SHARP. I thought so, at this time.

Mr. RAINEY. It is so late. The Republic of Panama has been recognized by many of the great nations of the world. We can not destroy that recognition if we want to do so. The question can only be a question of indemnity.

Mr. SHARP. The Government of Panama is recognized everywhere now? No nation is withholding recognition on account of the question of its establishment?

Mr. RAINEY. No, sir; not at all. They are all recognizing the independence of Panama. There is no question about it now. It is established forever. The only nation that could ever interfere with it would be this Nation itself, if we ever should conclude to annex Panama. I hope we never will.

Mr. SHARP. Perhaps I ought to keep this in mind. What, if any, consideration or reparation has ever been made by the United States Government to the United States of Colombia for recognizing or aiding in the establishment of this independence of Panama?

Mr. RAINEY. None whatever except that a little over a year ago three treaties were negotiated here in this country. Under our contract with Panama, we were to pay her $10,000,000 for her relinquishment of her sovereignty on the Canal Zone, and then we agreed to pay her——

Mr. SHARP. Pay who?

Mr. RAINEY. Panama. We agreed to pay her, commencing in 1913, $250,000 a year, and there is still in controversy the question as to the ownership of certain of the Panama Canal shares of the French company in Paris amounting to a considerable sum of money. The treaties we negotiated here between this country and Panama, between this country and Colombia, and between Colombia and Panama provide that, commencing with 1913, if I remember now, we should pay, not to Panama but to Colombia, for a term of years this $250,000 rental; and these treaties also provided for the payment to Colombia of $10,000,000 by the United States upon relinquishment by that country of her rights of sovereignty over certain little islands.

Mr. KENDALL. What was that proposition? I understand the terms of it. Was it a bill introduced?

Mr. RAINEY. No, sir; three treaties were negotiated by the United States by which our State Department virtually conceded the claims of Colombia and endeavored to satisfy them by making this arrangement between the three nations; the $250,000 per year that we commence to pay Panama in 1913 under these proposed treaties was to be paid, not to Panama but to Colombia.

Mr. CLINE. Did Colombia participate in that agreement?

Mr. RAINEY. Her representative here did, and the representative of the Republic of Panama participated, and we participated in these treaties here; they were immed tified by Panama. I think Colombia refused to ra

Mr. KENDALL. The Colombi wed it?

Mr. RAINEY. They refused Panama is the only one of the three Govern treaties. The refusal of Colombia to ratify naction in our Senate.

Mr. FOSTER. Will you perm irst, while the original arrangement was t 1913 to pay $250,000, under the new ar arlier than that. We have already appropriat last year, as long as the money had not been taken n't appropriate the money.

Second, that the $250,000, was the arrangement between Panama and Colombia for the amount that Panama really owed Colombia as her part of the national debt, and so on.

Mr. RAINEY. You are right about that—and the $250,000 is the rental we agreed to pay Panama per year for the use by us of the Canal Zone.

Mr. FOSTER. Between us and Panama?

Mr. RAINEY. Yes.

Mr. FOSTER. And we agreed to pay it over to Colombia instead of pay it to Panama?

Mr. RAINEY. Yes.

Mr. FOSTER. And Panama agreed to that because of her share of the outstanding national debt?

Mr. RAINEY. Yes; that was the consideration.

Mr. KENDALL. That was in discharge of obligations existing between Panama and Colombia?

Mr. RAINEY. Yes, sir.

Mr. CLINE. In satisfaction of any damages?

Mr. RAINEY. The willingness of our State Department to enter into those treaties shows that this department recognized Colombia's claims, although we do not admit it in these treaties. The origin of the $250,000 proposition is this: The Panama Railway & Steamship Co., a New Jersey corporation, agreed to pay Colombia $250,000 rental a year for a right of way across the Isthmus of Panama, and they continued that payment until the independence of Panama. At the time when the independence occurred and for some 13 years prior to that time the Panama Canal Co., first the old and then the new company, owned a controlling interest in the railroad, and these French companies paid the rental.

Now we own the railroad, and this amount heretofore paid as rental for the railroad right of way we are paying now to Panama as rental for the Canal Zone, and by these three treaties we were to pay it, not to Panama, but to Colombia.

Mr. SHARP. The ostensible purpose, and perhaps the sole purpose, in this Government recognizing the independence of Panama against the protests of the United States of Colombia was to facilitate the building and construction of this canal, was it not; so as to secure rights to cross the Isthmus and go ahead and build the canal?

Mr. RAINEY. I think that was it; yes, sir.

Mr. KENDALL. The acknowledgment of the independence occurred on the 18th of November by this Government?

Mr. RAINEY. Yes, sir.

Mr. KENDALL. Recognition, I mean?

Mr. RAINEY. No; the recognition of Panama occurred immediately after the revolution.

Mr. KENDALL. That was the 4th, then?

Mr. RAINEY. Yes, sir; or perhaps it was the 6th when our State Department cabled to our representative to recognize the de facto government. The 6th day of November we commenced to recognize the representatives of the new Panama Republic.

Mr. KENDALL. Prior to that time for a number of years there had been negotiations between the United States and Colombia looking to Colombia relinquishing a strip across there for canal purposes?

Mr. RAINEY. That, among other things. Yes, sir.

Mr. KENDALL. Do you remember the amount of money we had tendered her for the surrender of her sovereignty there?

Mr. RAINEY. I think we tendered $10,000,000; something like that.

Mr. KENDALL. $20,000,000 at one time?

Mr. RAINEY. Perhaps we did.

Mr. KENDALL. Colombia refused?

Mr. RAINEY. No; Colombia at no time demanded larger payments from the United States. That is an impression that has been spread abroad in this country, but you will find when this evidence is all in that at no time did Colombia expect the United States to pay more than $40,000,000 for the canal. What she was claiming was a larger interest herself in the $40,000,000, or any amount that we were going to pay the French companies. In 1904 the charter she had given the French company, and all legal extensions of it, expired. This charter provided that the General Assembly of Colombia must approve any act of the President of Colombia in extending the charter. This charter expired in 1904, and the President of Colombia extended it himself, without any authority from the General Assembly, for 10 years. The position of Colombia was that in 1904 all this property would revert to Colombia. She has always denied the legality of the extension made after 1904 by the President of Colombia; and her position was that, in view of the fact that by its very terms the contract would soon expire, and when it did expire all the work the French company had done on the Isthmus would revert to her, that she ought to get a share of the $40,000,000, the consideration we proposed to pay the French companies. There was at no time any demand on her part that the United States increase its expenditures. As far back as 1869 a treaty was proposed between this country and Colombia by which Colombia agreed to everything we wanted her to agree to in the matter of a canal across the Isthmus. That treaty we never ratified.

Mr. CLINE. Is it your contention that the United States exercised undue haste in the recognition of the Republic of Panama before its status was established and that President Roosevelt did so for the purpose of promoting and handling the Panama Canal?

Mr. RAINEY. It is my contention that the representatives of this Government made possible the revolution on the Isthmus of Panama. That had it not been for the interference of this Government a successful revolution could not possibly have occurred, and I contend that this Government violated the treaty of 1846. I will be able to produce evidence to show that the declaration of independence which was promulgated in Panama on the 3d day of November, 1903, was prepared right here in New York City and carried down there—prepared in the office of Wilson Nelson Cromwell. I will show you that our State Department was cognizant of the fact that a revolution was to occur on the 3d day of November, 1903, and that in this country, months before that revolution occurred, there was an agreement as to the date it was to occur, and at this time we most solemnly pledged by the treaty of 1846 to maintain the sovereignty of Colombia on the Isthmus of Panama. Our State Department was a party to the agreement that a revolution should occur on that date—the 3d day of November, 1903—and that day was selected for the reason the papers of the United States would be filled with election news on that day and would not give much attention to news from the Isthmus of Panama.

My contention is that the part we played for months prior to the revolution in promoting that revolution in this country is a stain upon the history of this Government—such a stain as has never been placed upon it before. At this time, when we are preparing for the opening of this great canal, which everybody is in favor of, across the Isthmus of Panama—we are even building the lighthouses to-day to guide ships through the canal from sea to sea—at a time when we are contributing so much to all the nations, we can contribute a little something to the Republic of Colombia if we violated our treaty with her.

What better thing can we do, at a time we expect this canal to revolutionize the commerce of the world, than to make reparation to Colombia for the wrong we have done her, if we have done her any wrong. We expended $100,000,000 to free Cuba; we recently returned to China $12,000,000, which we did not think we were entitled to retain; therefore, in view of our recent career in matters of this kind, I contend—and I am asking the committee to take this position, if I succeed by evidence in sustaining the statements I have made—I contend that we should at this time give Colombia her day in court. In this way we may square ourselves with the nations of the world; in this way we may become a "gentleamn among the nations"—I use a term coined, I think, by William Nelson Cromwell himself—in this way we may wipe out this stain upon the diplomatic history of our country.

A MEMBER. Don't you think our intrigue in abetting this revolution constitutes the blackest page in the history of our international diplomacy?

Mr. RAINEY. I think so. That is what I want to talk to this committee about. We expect to produce evidence that will convince the committee, and in my statement of the case now I propose simply to tell the committee what evidence we can produce. I am not going to enter into any criticism or abuse of anybody, but I want to outline in this opening the evidence that we can present to this committee, and I want to assure the committee that we will be able to present to them the evidence I say we can present.

Mr. SHARP. Broadly stating it then, your views would be that our Government took the position that in its desire to build that canal the end justified the means?

Mr. RAINEY. They did a great wrong.

Mr. SHARP. The end justified the wrong?

Mr. RAINEY. I think that is the view our Government took of it.

Mr. LEVY. Do you consider that amount of money paid—$10,000,000—excessive? Why should we pay $10,000,000?

Mr. RAINEY. I do not want to discuss that, because it has nothing to do with the question I present.

Mr. LEVY. Some of it, or a portion of it, is invested in the United States?

Mr. RAINEY. $6,000,000 of it is supposed to be invested here, and it is believed to be invested in New York real estate; the only man who knows that is William Nelson Cromwell.

Mr. GOODWIN. Your position, then, is not exactly as was Portia's, who said that in order to do a great right, do a little wrong? But that the attitude of the administration at that time was that inasmuch as the election was on it was prompted to pull off this political stunt, and in doing so committed an irreparable injury?

Mr. RAINEY. My position is this: That even if in doing something that may prove of great commercial advantage to this country we committed a wrong upon a little republic that can not resist us except in The Hague tribunal, we ought to go with them to The Hague. They can not resist us by resorting to a clash of armored vessels on the seas and great armies upon the land; can not challenge us as to that sort of arbitration; they can only ask us to settle this in The Hague tribunal, and we can not in honor deny this reasonable request. My position is that if I can produce evidence——

Mr. LEVY. You claim this $40,000,000 paid was paid for a franchise that we had no use for?

Mr. RAINEY. I am not questioning the canal title at all. That has been settled so long that it is a closed incident.

Mr. LEVY. The only question is the excessiveness of the payments by the department?

Mr. RAINEY. I do not want to discuss the question as to whether it was excessive or not. I don't care whether it was or not. But in referring to the amount we paid to the French company, I referred to it only incidentally in my endeavor to show what Colombia's position was, and the procrastination with which she is unjustly charged simply grew out of her desire to get more of the $40,000,000. Her position was this, and it is a legal position that any country ought to take, or that any individual would take: In 1904 the French property, for which we paid $40,000,000, absolutely reverted to Colombia, and, therefore, she was waiting until the expiration of that time when it would all belong to her, and when we would be compelled to buy it all from her. That is the position we would have taken in this matter or any other matter, and Colombia took exactly the proper position. She wasn't demanding a larger indemnity from the United States. All that she was insisting upon was that she was entitled to more of the compensation we were willing to pay.

Mr. LEVY. If that company was defaulting and had virtually nothing and we paid them $40,000,000?

Mr. RAINEY. The French company had defaulted for many years and had not completed one-third of this work, and so under the original contract it was forfeited long before they opened negotiations with us.

Mr. CLINE. If the contention of Colombia was correct the French company eliminated all of their interest in the matter.

Mr. RAINEY. Yes. If the contentions of Colombia were correct, all the rights of the French company would expire in 1904.

Mr. CLINE. So whatever indemnity was fair should have been paid to Colombia?

Mr. RAINEY. That was her position, although she did not demand it all because the negotiations occurred prior to 1904, so she was asking for more of it for herself. After 1904 she would probably have asked for all of it, as she would have had a right to do.

Mr. SHARP. Does any of your evidence tend to show here, Mr. Rainey, what proportion of that $40,000,000 was actually paid over to the French?

Mr. RAINEY. I don't want to go into that, because that doesn't help out this international question. If there is a scandal there I don't want to uncover it. I don't want to bring up in this investigation this sort of a disgrace nor stir up that kind of a thing. I simply want to present on the highest plane possible before this committee, the most important committee, I think, of the National Congress, the international question, and if anything comes out during the progress of this investigation with reference to the distribution of the $40,000,000 it will come out as a mere incident of the real investigation. I do not expect to ask that that question be investigated by this committee. My resolution does not ask this committee to investigate that question.

Now, our convention of 1846 with Colombia was the most friendly convention we ever entered into with any power.

The CHAIRMAN. Will you insert that treaty in full in the hearings?

Mr. RAINEY. Yes; but fearing the committee will not read all of it, I want to read Article I of the treaty and call attention to the conditions existing at that time which made it important for us to negotiate this treaty.

> There shall be a firm, perfect, and inviolable peace and sincere friendship between the United States of America and the Republic of New Granada (now Colombia) in all the extent of their possessions and territory, and between their citizens, respectively, without distinction of persons or places.

At that time we were preparing to settle up the western coast, and it was important for us to have with Colombia a treaty of friendship, so that our citizens could go across the Isthmus.

Article IV of the same treaty:

> If any one or more of the citizens of either party shall infringe any of the articles of this treaty, such citizens shall be held personally responsible for the same, and the harmony and good correspondence between the two nations shall not be interrupted thereby, each party engaging in no way to protect the offender or sanction such violation.

To show how gross has been our violations of our treaty with Colombia I want to read what Secretary Seward said in a communication to the United States minister at Bogota on April 30, 1866, and I want to show what construction we placed upon this treaty up to the very time we fomented this revolution in the United States. Secretary Seward said in 1866:

> The United States desires nothing else, nothing better, and nothing more in regard to the State of Colombia than the enjoyment, on their part, of complete and absolute sovereignty and independence. If those great interests shall ever be assailed by any power at home or abroad, the United States will be ready, cooperating with the Government and their ally, to maintain and defend them.

The United States did keep the treaty in this particular, and the United States did, later on, on more than one occasion, send troops to the Isthmus of Panama for the purpose of preserving the sovereignty of Colombia on the Isthmus when it was in danger.

On the 9th of October, 1866, Mr. Seward wrote to the minister down there:

> The United States has always abstained from any connection with questions of internal revolutions in the State of Panama * * * and will continue to maintain a perfect neutrality in such domestic controversies.

Again, in May, 1856, President Pierce said:

> We concluded, in the first place, a treaty of peace, amity, navigation, and commerce with the Republic of New Granada, among the conditions of which was a stipulation on the part of New Granada guaranteeing to the United States the right of way or transit across that part of the Isthmus which lies in the territory of New Granada in consideration of which the United States guaranteed in respect of the same territory the rights of sovereignty and property of New Granada.

President Buchanan, in April, 1860, compared the language of the treaty of 1846 with that of the treaties with the Republic of Honduras, and said:

> In one respect it goes further than any of its successors, because it not only guarantees the neutrality of the route itself, but the rights and sovereignty and property of New Granada over the entire Province of Panama.

Again, in 1880, President Hayes, in December of that year, spoke of—

> The treaty obligations subsisting between the United States and Colombia, by which we guarantee the neutrality of the transit and the sovereignty and property of Colombia in the Isthmus.

President Arthur, in December, 1881, said:

> This Government has not been unmindful of the solemn obligation imposed upon it by its pact in 1846 with Colombia as the independent and sovereign mistress of the territory crossed by the canal and has sought to render them effective by fresh engagements with the Colombian Republic looking to their practical execution.

Mr. SHARP. What called out these expressions from the Presidents?

Mr. RAINEY. Various controversies between the Spanish-American Republics. They were statements of our position with reference to Colombia and with reference to the other Republics.

Mr. SHARP. Has it anything to do with the French Panama Canal scheme?

Mr. RAINEY. No, sir; nothing at all. The Salgar-Weise contract was not entered into until 1878.

Mr. SHARP. You are quoting now from Arthur and Hayes, and I wondered whether it was with reference to that Panama Canal scheme.

Mr. RAINEY. No; these messages referred principally to the Panama Railway Co., which was a New Jersey corporation, and these references grew out of certain other controversies. I am not going into detail as to the other matters which brought about these statements of our policy, but I simply put in the record these statements in order to show what our policy has been from 1846 down to the time we recognized——

Mr. SHARP. I just wanted to see whether this had any bearing on the French ownership there.

Mr. RAINEY. I do not offer these declarations for that purpose, but simply for the purpose of showing our construction of the treaty of

1846—it being, of course, the only construction that can be put upon it by any person who understands the English language.

Mr. SHARP. On the face of it I should think there ought to be no controversy as to that.

Mr. RAINEY. There ought to be none. I am showing by putting in the record these excerpts that there were a number of subsequent official statements as to our relations with Colombia under this convention, which made the treaty so plain that its meaning could not be misunderstood either in Colombia or anywhere in the world.

Mr. LEVY. I believe it was under that the United States was the only power to land troops.

Mr. RAINEY. I think you are right.

Mr. LEVY. We protected even the French at one time by sending our own troops.

Mr. RAINEY. Yes, sir.

Mr. LEVY. The French couldn't do it?

Mr. RAINEY. No; they couldn't do it; we did it by virtue of the treaty of 1846 and by virtue of the clause in the treaty in which we agreed to maintain the sovereignty of Colombia on the Isthmus.

Mr. SHARP. That is practically a confirmation of the Monroe doctrine in that respect.

Mr. RAINEY. Yes; we protected the French; that is, we had a right to protect them under this treaty. They were operating under a contract which they had with Colombia, and in order to maintain our agreement with Colombia it was necessary for us to land troops, even though by doing so we protected the French, and we did.

In 1885 President Cleveland said:

> Emergencies growing out of civil war in the United States of Colombia demanded of the Government at the beginning of this administration the employment of armed forces to fulfill its guaranties under the thirty-fifth article of the treaty of 1846 in order to keep the transit open across the Isthmus of Panama. Desirous of exercising only the powers expressly reserved to us by the treaty, and mindful of the rights of Colombia, the forces sent to the Isthmus were instructed to confine their action to "positively and efficaciously" preventing the transit and its accessories from being "interrupted or embarrassed." The execution of this delicate and responsible task necessarily involved police control where the local authority was temporarily powerless, but always in aid of the sovereignty of Colombia.

The CHAIRMAN. Mr. Rainey, as I understand it, you contend that if it hadn't been for the interference of the Government of the United States the Government of Colombia would have been able to put down the insurrection in Panama?

Mr. RAINEY. Yes, sir; there is no doubt about that. Colombia had sent to Colon 500 picked troops, comparing favorably with the troops that can be mustered by any nation in the world. There were only 500 of them, but they were sufficient to preserve her sovereignty on the Isthmus of Panama if they had been permitted by this Government to do so.

Mr. GARNER. I didn't have the privilege of hearing the first portion of your argument, but from the resolution I judge that your position is that the United States Government outraged Colombia in taking forcibly from her a strip of territory now utilized for the canal.

Mr. RAINEY. No. In violating her treaty obligations by making possible a successful revolution against the sovereignty of Colombia on the Isthmus.

Mr. GARNER. So that we might get some of that territory. What was the object of assisting the revolution unless we intended to benefit by it?

Mr. RAINEY. That was the apparent object of it, of course.

Mr. GARNER. Then the object of the interference by the United States was to get possession of that strip of territory across the Isthmus?

Mr. RAINEY. Of course, that was the object.

A MEMBER. His idea is that this committee ought to go into an examination of the question to determine what offense we have given and what we can do toward placing ourselves in status quo, as it were, and what reparation we should make.

Mr. RAINEY. What I am asking is this: That this committee go into this question now for the purpose of ascertaining whether there is an issue between this country and Colombia that ought to be tried by the only competent court that can try an issue of this kind, The Hague tribunal; if there is an issue, then I contend we ought to let The Hague tribunal pass upon the question as to whether we have wronged Colombia.

Mr. GARNER. In other words, the United States does not expect to do anything but give Colombia an opportunity to get what she claims from the United States?

The CHAIRMAN. Yes, as I look at it, Colombia wants her day in court.

Mr. GARNER. I understand. Her day in court. You are acting for Colombia, as it were?

Mr. RAINEY. No I am not acting for Colombia.

The CHAIRMAN. We should do justice to all.

Mr. GARNER. Your position is this: That we refuse to go to this Hague court for fear that Colombia will get the better of the contention there, you insisting that we shall give Colombia this opportunity. Your position, then, is the attitude of an advocate for Colombia's rights.

Mr. RAINEY. I don't admit that. If my friend had been here during my argument as far as it has progressed he would have understood that is not my position at all.

Mr. GARNER. What good is to be accomplished by the United States—what resolution, what legislation is to come from it?

Mr. RAINEY. The good to be accomplished is this: We give to a weaker Republic which can not oppose us in any other place in the world except in The Hague tribunal the opportunity to meet us there. We give them their day in court. We prove ourselves to be in touch with the modern spirit of progress among all the nations, which is in favor of arbitration.

Mr. GARNER. Indeed I agree with you, Mr. Rainey. But I was just coming to that. Your contention is that this Nation through its Executive has refused to give Colombia its days in court at The Hague. And you and the American Congress will say to the world by passing this resolution that we insist that Colombia shall have her day in court?

Mr. RAINEY. That is it exactly.

Mr. GARNER. Then we would be in the position of contending that our Executive has not given Colombia a fair show and the American Congress as its advocate has said that it shall have a day in court?

Mr. RAINEY. No; I wouldn't take that position. I take this position: I insist that The Hague shall pass upon the question as to whether this Government has given Colombia under the treaty of 1846 the recognition it was bound by the law of nations to give Colombia. I will present all of these questions——

Mr. DIFENDERFER. Do I understand that the United States of Colombia had granted to this French company a right to build a canal there?

Mr. RAINEY. Yes, sir.

Mr. DIFENDERFER. When did that right terminate?

Mr. RAINEY. It was granted to the company in 1878. They were allowed three years within which to perfect their plans and make their surveys and then two years in which to commence work. They commenced work along about 1880 or 1881. That company collapsed in 1888 and the new French canal company was formed and operated under the old contract. Colombia granted certain extensions. The original contract and all the legitimate extensions expired in 1904.

Mr. DIFENDERFER. And our Government took advantage of the situation at that particular time, on the 3d day of November, 1904; was that it?

Mr. RAINEY. That was in 1903.

Mr. DIFENDERFER. 1903?

Mr. RAINEY. Yes, sir. That was election time in the United States; that was the reason the date was selected.

Mr. KENDALL. I think the date wasn't selected that the news might be entirely excluded, but that it might be immersed in the election returns and not be noticed.

Mr. RAINEY. It was selected because a revolution on that day was less likely to attract attention in the United States.

Mr. KENDALL. That is the way I understood you. Brother Goodwin suggests that it was done as a matter of political profit to influence the election that year.

Mr. RAINEY. No. Now, having in mind what I have just said, I want to place in parallel columns something else. Having in mind the extracts that I have read from the treaty of 1846 and these numerous extracts I have read from state papers showing how we always construed this treaty almost down to date—showing how we have recognized and defended the sovereignty of Colombia on the Isthmus of Panama—I want to read the confession of the man who was responsible for it all and who admits in this confession that he violated this contract.

Here is Mr. Roosevelt's confession made in a speech delivered before the students of the University of California at Berkeley, Cal., on March 23, 1911. I quote now from his speech on that occasion:

> I am interested in the Panama Canal because I started it. If I had followed traditional conservative methods I should have submitted a dignified state paper of probably 200 pages to the Congress and the debate would have been going on yet. But I took the Canal Zone and let Congress debate, and while the debate goes the canal does also.

That is the confession and it shows how it was done. This is a carefully worded speech, evidently prepared in advance. If you will examine the wording carefully you will find it to be a most careful and deliberate statement. It was made before an intelligent audience composed of students of the university—the great university of that State.

Now, on November 6, 1903, three days after the alleged revolution, our State Department cabled this to the American consul general at Panama and said——

Mr. KENDALL. Who was Secretary of State then?

Mr. RAINEY. I think Mr. Loomis sent the telegram, but Mr. Hay was Secretary of State.

Here is the telegram:

> The people of Panama have by an apparently unanimous movement dissolved their political connections with the Republic of Colombia, and resumed their independence. When you are satisfied that a de facto government, republican in form, and without substantial opposition from its own people, has been established in the State of Panama, you will enter into relations with it as the responsible Government of the territory and look to it for all due action to protect the persons and property of citizens of the United States and to keep open the Isthmian transit in accordance with the obligations of existing treaties governing the relations of the United States to that territory.

Mr. SHARP. To whom was that sent?

Mr. RAINEY. To the American consul general at Panama, and it was sent 72 hours after the revolution, and 48 hours after the proclamation of the declaration of independence of Panama. The declaration of independence was prepared in New York.

Mr. SHARP. Will you read again the first few lines?

Mr. RAINEY. The first few lines are important, if true.

> The people of Panama have by an apparently unanimous movement dissolved their political connection with the Republic of Colombia and resumed their independence. When you are satisfied that a de facto government, republican in form, and without substantial opposition from its own people, has been established in the State of Panama, you will enter into relations with it.

If that is true, it is an important statement. I claim it is untrue. The people of Panama, by an apparently unanimous movement, did not accomplish their independence. On the 3d day of November, in the morning, when the revolution occurred, we will show you that no man knew anything about it except the revolutionists on the Isthmus of Panama—just a few of them, not over 10 or 12 of them—and the officers of the Panama Railroad & Steamship Co., who were under the control of William Nelson Cromwell, of New York, and the State Department officials in Washington. No one knew it was going to occur when it did occur except those I have mentioned and some of the Colombian generals in Panama, who had been bribed to betray their country and to turn over their troops to the new Republic as soon as it was formed.

Mr. SHARP. Before that revolution was generally known, or at least was recognized, or at least that country was recognized as a new Republic, isn't it a fact that our Government had warships situated or stationed on both sides?

Mr. RAINEY. Yes, sir. The warships arrived on the very day of the revolution. That is the question I am going into now.

Mr. HARRISON. Were those revolutionists natives of Panama or citizens of the United States?

Mr. RAINEY. They were natives there, most of them. I don't know where the officers of the Panama Railroad claimed their residence; I think most of them claimed their residence up here. At that time among the revolutionists were Col. Shaler, who was general superintendent of the railroad; Mr. Prescott, who was his assistant;

Mr. Arango, who was land agent down there for the railroad and who was also a local attorney in Panama; Dr. Amador, who was the physician for the railroad; and Capt. Biers, who was the American freight agent of the railroad on the Isthmus. Those were the railroad officials who were on the Isthmus—all the important railroad officials. All of them aided the revolution and assisted in planning for it.

Mr. KENDALL. Were there any troops turned over by the revolutionists?

Mr. RAINEY. I think these gentlemen, except Arango and Amador, might be United States citizens. The Colombian garrison espoused the cause of the revolution. They were bribed to do it. The commander was paid two days afterwards $25,000 in silver for doing so, and he is living now on the Isthmus of Panama engaged in the cattle business and is being paid $400 every month in silver, a pension by the Panama Government.

At that time in Panama there was only one company of troops loyal to Colombia, and there was only one general they couldn't bribe. Our railroad officials down there couldn't bribe him, and he with his company—this loyal company—was sent away just a few days before the time for the revolution, to repel a fake invasion from Nicaragua. They went into the jungles of Panama to stop a force that wasn't coming at all. The mistake Gov. Abaldio made was this: He telegraphed to his Government or wrote them a formal letter advising them that the sovereignty of Colombia in the Isthmus of Panama was threatened by an army from Nicaragua. This so frightened Colombia—they were so anxious to preserve their sovereignty—that they sent some gunboats out not for the purpose of suppressing the revolution, but for the purpose of assisting in repelling an invasion supposed to have come from Nicaragua. As soon as the governor of Panama, appointed by the President of Colombia, received the information from his Government that they were sending him troops to help in repelling that invasion, he sent back word that there was no invasion—don't send the troops. At that time the loyal officer and his company were out 100 miles or so in the jungle, where they could offer no opposition to the proposed revolution. Colombia acted so promptly in an effort to preserve her sovereignty that, when this second communication reached the Government, they had already sent two gunboats to Panama and they got there just before the revolution started.

Mr. DIFENDERFER. Were any of these men you have mentioned there in the pay of the United States Government?

Mr. RAINEY. No; they were in the pay of the Panama Railroad & Steamship Co., which was a New Jersey corporation—the controlling interest of which at this time was owned by the new French canal company. They were in the pay of that corporation, and the representative of that corporation in New York was William Nelson Cromwell. They belonged to him. He was the revolutionist who promoted and made possible the revolution on the Isthmus of Panama. At that time he was a shareholder in the railroad and he was its general counsel in the United States, and when the old Panama canal company, just before its dissolution, acquired control of the Panama Railroad Co. by buying a majority of the stock they annexed, unfortunately for this Government, William Nelson Cromwell, of New York, the most dangerous man this country has produced since the days of Aaron Burr—a professional revolutionist—and, we will be able to show you, one of the most accomplished lobbyists this country has ever produced.

Mr. DIFENDERFER. When did the Panama Railroad pass into the possession of the American Government?

Mr. RAINEY. When we bought the property and the franchises from the French companies.

A MEMBER. Your position is that William Nelson Cromwell, through whom we purchased the properties of the French companies in Panama, brought about this revolution for two purposes—the United States in order to get the territory to construct a canal, and the old French company to sell out property that was comparatively valueless to them. Is that your understanding of it? That Mr. Cromwell and his associates were the prime movers in bringing about this revolution?

Mr. RAINEY. Yes, sir.

A MEMBER. They were aided by the Executive of this Nation, the Executive having in view the getting of this territory in order to construct the Panama Canal?

Mr. RAINEY. Yes, sir. And the object primarily being of Mr. Cromwell and his associates—the object primarily being to get $40,000,000, or whatever we would pay, for the French company and keep Colombia from getting it?

A MEMBER. They were working for money and we—I mean the American officials—were working for territory?

Mr. RAINEY. They were working also for the French company to get them the entire $40,000,000. That was all Cromwell was working for, and we assisted him in that scheme. In effect, what we did was to assist Mr. Cromwell in beating Colombia out of the large part of the $40,000,000 that she ought to have had. We could have acquired all the rights we wanted by giving Colombia a little more of the $40,000,000 than we were willing she should have. The fight our officials made here was not for the purpose of getting the canal across the Isthmus—we could always do that if we wanted to; but I contend that the fight on the part of this Government was to see that this corrupt French company, which was composed almost entirely of penalized stockholders, except a few small shareholders who held a small part of the stock, get the $40,000,000. By "penalized stockholders" I mean stockholders who had stolen from the old company and who were compelled to take stock in the new company to an amount of stock equal in value to the sums they had stolen in order to keep from going to the penitentiary.

A MEMBER. Do you believe the French company got all that money?

Mr. RAINEY. I don't want to discuss that.

Mr. COOPER. You think that Roosevelt and John Hay got most of it? Is that your position?

Mr. RAINEY. On the contrary, I am convinced that they did not. On behalf of these gentlemen, I deny that.

Mr. COOPER. I am glad to hear that.

Mr. GOODWIN. Your position is that an investigation of this matter would reveal the fact that Mr. Cromwell and his associates got up this revolution for the purpose of selling out to the United States?

Mr. RAINEY. Yes, sir.

Mr. GOODWIN. And getting a larger share of what the United States would pay for that canal than they otherwise could get?

Mr. RAINEY. Yes, sir.

Mr. GOODWIN. And that our Government through its officials assisted him in order to put money in the pockets of the French rather than pay it to the Republic of Colombia?

Mr. RAINEY. Yes, sir.

Mr. COOPER. But what did you mean a moment ago when you spoke of the fight being to get Colombia a larger share out of the $10,000,000, or something like that?

Mr. RAINEY. She was trying to get more than that——

Mr. COOPER. The understanding was at one time——

Mr. RAINEY. She wanted more of the amount than we were willing to pay.

Mr. FOSTER. It was in the treaty.

Mr. COOPER. It is so long since I have read it. Have you heard that when she had an opportunity she refused to accept the $10,000,000 because a lot of the money from the transcontinental railroads got busy with her supreme legislature and stopped that?

Mr. RAINEY. I haven't heard that.

Mr. COOPER. I have.

Mr. RAINEY. But I know what the records down there show.

Mr. COOPER. They had agreed to accept the $10,000,000 and when they had the opportunity to take it they made up their minds that they didn't want it. I have had prominent men connected with some of these transcontinental railroads speak to me of the dreadful nuisance of the Panama Canal. I have heard the rumors—I have and I think Members of the House have—that money was sent from this country to prevent Colombia from taking that $10,000,000 and letting us build that canal, and that thereupon there was a substantial unanimity among the people of Panama who thought upon the subject at all that they should get rid of Colombia as soon as possible and let the United States build that canal, and that alone was the trouble.

Mr. RAINEY. The rumors you heard I think I heard too, but I can call some facts to your attention which will show there could be absolutely nothing in those rumors.

William Nelson Cromwell, who was promoting the sale of the Panama Canal Co. to the United States and who was responsible for the revolution, was one of the attorneys for the Harriman Lines, or, to speak more accurately, was the attorney for the Harriman Steamship Co., operating on the Pacific coast from San Francisco down to Panama. He would not have permitted the company he represented, if he could help it, to send any money to Colombia to prevent the very sale he was trying to accomplish.

Mr. COOPER. As a matter of fact they always have been opposed to the construction of this canal.

Mr. RAINEY. Yes; I think they are opposed to the construction of all canals. I think they are opposed to the construction of this canal across the Isthmus and are opposed to the railroad across the Isthmus farther up. Naturally you would expect them to oppose it; but the Hay-Herran treaty was unpopular in Colombia from the start, from the time it was entered into here by Dr. Herran at the instance of William Nelson Cromwell. It was at once repudiated in Colombia, and speeches were made on the floor of the National House immediately after the news reached there, and before any transcontinental money could have gotten there at all speeches were made denouncing Dr. Herran as a traitor to his country and threatening him with execution when he returned home. The President of Colombia—the man whom the railways would have approached first of all, because our evidence will show that he might have been approached—stated afterwards that the halter would have been a proper recompense to Dr. Herran for entering into that treaty.

Mr. Goodwin. Isn't it a fact that there was a great difference—a great drop in the bonds of the Panama company at the time we expected to cross over the Nicaragua route, at which time those bonds were low—at ebb tide—when we switched from the Nicaragua to the Panama route? And then the bonds were certainly inflated and rose to high tide. At that time we bought those bonds on the crest of the wave.

Mr. Rainey. I think you are right.

Mr. Goodwin. That was paying two prices for the Panama company as compared with the time when we could have had them for half that price?

Mr. Rainey. We could have made better terms with Colombia if we had let the contract expire.

Mr. Levy. The fact is that the only satisfaction we got for the $10,000,000 was the control of the Panama Railroad, and wasn't it generally supposed that we also paid in that $10,000,000 sufficient for all claims that they might have against us for their profits or their proportion of the rental for tha railroad instead of giving them now $250,000 a year in addition?

Mr. Rainey. Those contentions were made of course at that time. But those contentions are not important in the present controversy. It isn't important what assets we got from the Panama Canal Co. It isn't important whether or not the railroads sent a corruption fund to Colombia to keep her from ratifying this agreement. The important thing, and the only thing I want to present is, not whether the railroads have been corrupt; not whether Colombia has been corrupt; but the sole question is whether we have stultified ourselves, that is all. We do not care how many persons were bribed in Colombia. We do not care what amount of money the railroads contributed for bribery in Colombia, if they contributed money for such purpose. The question is how can we do justice to ourselves and resume the position we ought to occupy among the 22 Republics of the Western World.

Mr. Cooper. You want us to resume the high position held among the nations of the Western world? Has there ever been a time in the history of this Republic when the position was as cordial as it is at the present moment? Has the friendship for us ever been as great as it is at this hour?

Mr. Rainey. I am not aware that the friendships have ever been particularly close between the United States and the Latin Republics on the south of us, except perhaps Mexico. But no matter how close it is at the present time, it wouldn't do our trade any harm to have it closer. The trade we ought to have with the Latin Republics is going to other nations. To-day, in the plazas of the more important cities of the Spanish American Republics, as they sit there in the evenings, you will find, if you listen, that they refer to the United States as the "great hog of the north."

Mr. LEGARE. Do you think it would do any good to have that arbitrated and have it decided that we are the great hog of the north, and have robbed them? Do you think it would do any good to have that given to the nations of the world?

Mr. RAINEY. I don't want to anticipate what the Hague tribunal might do. I certainly would not say that. No court—certainly not the highest court in the world—would make use of any expression like that.

Mr. LEGARE. I was only expressing your own language.

Mr. RAINEY. It will not do any harm to correct the impression they have of us and to cultivate more friendly relations with them.

I am simply contending that we ought to ask and insist that the court of The Hague pass upon this legal international question between these two Republics of the Western World, just the same as if they were equal in size. We have already treaties with 12 nations by which we agree to arbitrate legal questions; we have no arbitration treaty with Colombia.

Mr. LEGARE. What evidence have we that Colombia has agreed to submit these differences to The Hague tribunal?

Mr. RAINEY. I read it into the record here.

Mr. LEVY. Wouldn't you think it better if we admitted it—if we come to the conclusion that Colombia had been treated badly—instead of referring it to The Hague tribunal, we have a commission appointed to settle that? Wouldn't it be rather unfair for us to go before The Hague tribunal? They might give $100,000,000 in damages.

Mr. RAINEY. I certainly would not take the position that I was afraid to go into court for the reason that the verdict against me might be excessive; and I do not think, as a Nation, we can take that position.

Mr. LEVY. Wouldn't it be better for us to come to a conclusion, and then, if we had treated them wrongfully, refer it to a commission, to settle?

Mr. RAINEY. I don't think so. There is only one tribunal in the world that can settle questions between nations, and Colombia is a nation, although she is a small one. There is only one other way to settle questions between nations, and that is the way which results in the meeting of navies in awful clash upon the seas and the contending armies upon the land. Of course, Colombia can not meet us in that way. The only thing she can do is to go to The Hague, and that is the only thing we can do in justice to ourselves in dealing with a weaker nation.

Mr. LEGARE. Don't you think it would look better to the Latin Republics and the rest of the world if we should look into the case—if we should look into these questions ourselves—and, after a thorough investigation, if we are convinced that we have committed a wrong, to make the proper amends without submitting them? Wouldn't that look more magnanimous and just?

Mr. RAINEY. No, sir; I am not asking the Government of the United States to go to that extent. I am not even asking the Government of the United States to admit that they are wrong. I am only asking this committee, when you have reviewed this evidence, to say whether or not there is an issue between this country and Colombia. A commission which might be selected I imagine would either be a commission in favor of this country or in favor of Colombia. At the present time, when we are endeavoring to enact arbitration treaties, and particularly at the present time, when Norway and Sweden have set the pace for the world and have gone into an arbitration treaty which provides not only for arbitration, but for compulsory arbitration, of questions involving national honor, vital interests, and national independence, we should not refuse to arbitrate this question at the present time, when we are about to enter into arbitration treaties with England and with France, when there are 63 peace societies in the United States, when there are 600 active peace organizations in the world, all working for international peace and for arbitration, I don't think we can afford to insist that The Hague tribunal shall not be permitted to arbitrate this question. We can not say that we propose to arbitrate this ourselves by a commission of our own selection.

Mr. LEGARE. Don't you think there would be some question involving this big ditch that we are also interested in?

Mr. RAINEY. That is absolutely impossible, as I have already shown.

Mr. LEGARE. If we came by that strip of land wrongfully, if we have taken it wrongfully, there is a possibility that they might want to so decide?

Mr. RAINEY. Not the slightest. I have already discussed that question. It is an absolutely incomprehensible position—an absolutely impossible position—to be taken by the court, in view of the fact that the nations of the world have now recognized the independence of Panama and in view of the demands made upon this Nation by Colombia herself. This limits the extent of any recovery which can be had against the United States to a mere money indemnity.

Mr. FOSTER. Didn't you miss the third method by which international difficulties might be settled, the ordinary channels of diplomacy, and wasn't that the thought that your good friend Mr. Legare had in mind, that first the two nations should undertake to settle this?

Mr. RAINEY. The ordinary channels of diplomacy have failed. The ordinary channels of diplomacy have brought about the present deplorable situation.

Mr. FOSTER. Colombia has done something, but we haven't done anything.

Mr. RAINEY. We do not show any symptoms of doing anything.

Mr. FOSTER. Supposing the committee should ask that instead of, first of all, before referring it—I am not anticipating anything of the kind—but if there is a real difference there, shouldn't we undertake to adjust it between ourselves? Shouldn't the Government be urged to adjust it first of all?

Mr. RAINEY. The Government has refused to do that. President Taft told the minister from Colombia, Mr. Borda, I think, that we could not think of arbitrating this matter because our national honor is involved, and all efforts on the part of Colombia to accomplish anything through a diplomatic source have failed.

The CHAIRMAN. Why is our national honor involved?

Mr. RAINEY. Well, that was the position taken by President Taft; the position, however, taken by him in New York recently was that questions of national honor ought to be arbitrated. Mr. Taft's opinions as to arbitrating questions of national honor during the past year have undergone a radical change.

Mr. COOPER. You think the administration of this Government on this particular subject has been guilty of conduct any more reprehensible than that of Thomas Jefferson when he ratified the Louisiana Purchase, after acknowledging that there was no constitutional authority for it but the welfare of the Republic demanded it, and so consented to take it?

Mr. RAINEY. I think this question is hardly to be compared with that.

Mr. LEVY. That is a different state of affairs.

Mr. KENDALL. Let me ask you this question——

Mr. COOPER. He had no constitutional authority. He asked for an amendment, but before an amendment was drawn he ratified it. In great public emergencies we take territory.

My understanding of this whole problem was this: That a treaty had been entered into by which Colombia agreed to take $10,000,000 and let the canal go through Panama territory. The Panama people knew that nothing else conceivable was more for their prosperity by so enhancing and increasing it as the construction of the Panama Canal. The people wanted it, and all of them, to a man—and the women and children, if they thought of it at all. The treaty was made. They agreed to accept $10,000,000, and everybody thought the Panama Canal was to go through. Everything was arranged, and suddenly they refused to take $10,000,000. Charges were made that money had gone down there from this country by people directly interested in that canal and that they had prevented it for generations.

Mr. RAINEY. That statement isn't in accordance with the facts.

Mr. COOPER. So it is said, at least; and I know they lobbied against it and talked against it.

Mr. RAINEY. If you will read the treaty of 1869 you will find that you are mistaken about that. Your understanding is not correct in that particular. Colombia was willing to give us anything we wanted.

Mr. COOPER. I presided over the House as Chairman for two days when we were trying to put through the bill letting the canal go through the Nicaraguan route. It passed the House. As the matter came up there were rumors that there were lobbyists interested in the Nicaraguan project—interested in the transcontinental railways—bitterly opposing that bill. Men came to me when I was presiding in the chair and mentioned the fact that men were lobbying, and that they were then lobbying, on the floor of the House. Through my personal knowledge of this, this statement is true against the Nicaraguan canal, this is true.

Mr. RAINEY. Right in this connection, I might call your attention to the fact that William Nelson Cromwell, on the floor of the Senate, was denounced openly as the lobbyist who was opposing the Nicaragua route.

Mr. SHARP. William Nelson Cromwell refused to appear before the committee and refused to answer questions.

Mr. COOPER. I am speaking of what took place in the House of Representatives.

Now, then, they had agreed to take $10,000,000. All of them wanted the canal.

Mr. RAINEY. When you say "they," what do you mean?

Mr. COOPER. All the people.

Mr. RAINEY. I deny that.

Mr. COOPER. Well, practically all.

Mr. RAINEY. No.

Mr. COOPER. There was nothing that could help Panama like the construction of the canal. It has made it one of the pleasantest places in the world, and is going to make it a prosperous community forever. After this had all been agreed upon they refused suddenly to take $10,000,000, and these charges were made that American money had stopped them from taking it. My understanding was that there was great indignation among the people of Panama because they were going to lose the canal, and they immediately became so indignant that they ratified a program and decided to organize to get away from Colombia.

Mr. RAINEY. You are using the identical argument used by Mr. Cromwell.

Mr. COOPER. I never exchanged a word with Mr. Cromwell and never read his testimony. I am stating what I have heard since I have been in the House of Representatives, which is 20 years.

Mr. RAINEY. I have heard the same rumors, but I am able now, through the evidence I will produce, to trace these rumors back to their source and locate them all as emanating from Mr. Cromwell and his associates. Even if all you have stated is true it would not constitute a valid reason why we should refuse to submit this question to The Hague tribunal.

Mr. COOPER. My idea was confirmed somewhat by my experience as chairman of the committee. I was in my office one day and a man came in and introduced himself and told of his relationship with a very prominent official of one of the transcontinental railroads, looked about the room and noticed the frescoes on the wall, and spoke about them, and finally he spoke of the Panama Canal. This was about 1907 or 1908—1906, I judge. He claimed from an engineering standpoint that it never could be successfully completed. We couldn't get it built for less than $700,000,000. It was ridiculous on the face of it to think of it.

Mr. SHARP. Was that the Panama Canal?

Mr. COOPER. Yes; and that it ought to be stopped.

Mr. RAINEY. That may be.

Mr. COOPER. It only goes to show the feeling on the part of those men to the construction of the Panama Canal.

Mr. RAINEY. What difference does that make—the feeling against the construction of the canal? Does that make it necessary for this country to violate a solemn treaty because somebody here is opposed to the building of a canal?

Mr. LEVY. Mr. Cooper, don't you think you are unfair in your parallel with Thomas Jefferson? The French had sold Louisiana to the United States. Congress was in session. He was afraid that Great Britain would interfere. It was so serious at the time that he had to determine it. It was a different state of affairs.

Mr. COOPER. I admire Thomas Jefferson and have often spoken of the magnificent part—of the magnificent thing he did in taking the Louisiana Purchase.

Mr. SHARP. In assuming that there was any connection between the opposition of the parties concerned, referring to Mr. Cooper's statement that the railroads were all combined, isn't it also a fact the chief opposition to that canal came from William Nelson Cromwell, who was largely instrumental in choosing the Panama Canal?

Mr. RAINEY. There was no objection to the Nicaragua Canal until——

Mr. COOPER. I want to say that the thing that defeated the Nicaragua Canal was a speech I heard Mark Hanna make in the Senate. He had his charts up on the wall, and he had the earthquake territory marked, showing that there had been frequent earthquakes and shocks along the line of that proposed canal, and he said that as a practical man, while he wanted the canal, he was utterly opposed to constructing it in a territory that had such frequent earthquake shocks. In my judgment, that was one of the things more than any other that influenced the passage of the Spooner bill through the Senate for the Panama Canal.

Mr. RAINEY. The gentleman is absolutely correct.

A MEMBER. This being granted that the railroads were opposed to the Nicaraguan route, were they less hostile to the Panama route?

Mr. RAINEY. Yes; less hostile perhaps because it was farther away, and therefore less important as a competing trade route.

A MEMBER. Would it interrupt you for the committee to rise and meet again and you continue?

Mr. RAINEY. Not at all. I am starting now with the presentation of the facts. No statement that I have made or will make will be based upon rumors.

Mr. GOODWIN. A moment ago I asked you—it being granted that the railroads were opposed to the Nicaraguan route—whether or not also they were at any time less hostile to the Panama route, and you said that they were possibly less hostile to the Panama route; then, would it not follow, as a logical conclusion, inasmuch as the railroads were opposed to a canal, doesn't it follow that Cromwell was more powerful than all the railroads in the country?

Mr. RAINEY. I am afraid the conclusion reached is almost inevitable.

The CHAIRMAN. The committee will now take a recess.

COMMITTEE ON FOREIGN AFFAIRS,
HOUSE OF REPRESENTATIVES,
Washington, D. C., Friday, February 9, 1912.

The committee met at 10.30 o'clock a. m., pursuant to recess.

Hon. William Sulzer (chairman) presiding.

The CHAIRMAN. The committee will come to order, and Mr. Rainey will resume his argument.

STATEMENT OF HON. HENRY T. RAINEY, OF ILLINOIS—Continued.

Mr. RAINEY. Mr. Chairman and gentlemen of the committee, I realize that what this committee wants this morning is not oratory but production of proof, so I am going to proceed but a few minutes with my own statement and then present some evidence. Later on I may ask the indulgence of the committee to address it again and attempt to assemble and bring to the attention of the committee in regular order the evidence that will soon be presented.

When I was last before your committee I called attention to the position the United States now occupies in connection with the treaties this Government has entered into; that is, first, the position of guaranteeing the sovereignty of the Republic of Colombia on the Isthmus of Panama, and, second, the other position of guaranteeing the sovereignty of the Republic of Panama over the same territory.

Until 1900 the movement in favor of the Panama route for an isthmian canal had gained no headway in the United States at all. The Republican platform of 1896 contained this plank with reference to the Nicaragua route:

> The Nicaragua Canal should be built, owned, and operated by the United States; and by the purchase of the Danish Islands we should secure a proper and much-needed naval station in the West Indies.

Such was the declaration by the Republican Party in convention assembled in favor of the Nicaragua route.

On the 16th day of May, 1900, Senator Hanna's committee, the Senate Committee on Interoceanic Canals, made a report (see Report 1337, Fifty-sixth Congress, first session) severely criticizing William Nelson Cromwell and the lobby he was maintaining here in Washington in favor of the Panama Canal; criticizing his methods. It was a bitter arraignment; one of the most severe arraignments ever heard in the Senate. But what next do we see? Not long afterwards Senator Hanna is found supporting Mr. Cromwell's Panama route, but not until after the meeting of the Republican national convention in the year 1900.

In the year 1900 the Democratic platform contained this declaration:

> FOR THE NICARAGUAN CANAL.
>
> We favor the immediate construction, ownership, and control of the Nicaraguan Canal by the United States, and we denounce the insincerity of the plank in the Republican platform for an isthmian canal in face of the failure of the Republican majority on this subject to pass such a bill in Congress.

The Republican convention had already met; and on the 20th day of June, 1900, just a month and four days after the arraignment of William Nelson Cromwell by Senator Hanna's committee, they inserted this plank in their platform:

ISTHMIAN CANAL AND NEW MARKETS.

We favor the construction, ownership, control, and protection of an isthmian canal by the Government of the United States. * * *

And this section goes on to tell about new markets needed. This was the first step taken in favor of Mr. Cromwell's scheme, and was brought about by a donation of $60,000 made by Mr. Cromwell to the Republican campaign fund in that year. From that time on we find Senator Hanna supporting the schemes of Mr. Cromwell, and the report favoring the Panama route presented in the Senate later on by Senator Hanna was really prepared by Mr. Cromwell. The speech that Senator Hanna made on the floor of the Senate, which has been referred to here by the gentleman from Wisconsin, Mr. Cooper, as the speech elucidated by maps of the earthquake belt, and which really influenced the Senate and House and the country in favor of the Panama route, was prepared by Mr. Cromwell, as we will be able to show.

From that time on the conspiracy proceeds. I do not propose at this time to discuss the various telegrams; the orders, some of which have been published in the public press, though not all of them, by any means; telegrams to the commanders of our naval vessels directing them to appear at the pyschological moment on each side of the Isthmus; the meeting of conspirators months before the alleged revolution in Panama at the house of Arrias and other places on the Isthmus; meetings participated in by officers of the railroad company down there and a Colombian general who was afterwards bribed; culminating finally in the visit of Capt. Biers to this country to arrange with the State Department as to the details of the proposed revolution on the Isthmus of Panama. Still later on there was the visit by Dr. Amador to the United States, the codes he took back with him, and the code that Capt. Biers brought up with him to this country, all furnish the most damaging evidence. Finally, Dr. Amador, the first President of Panama, returned to the Isthmus of Panama, taking with him the flag for the new Republic prepared by Madam Bunau-Varilla in New York—not the flag afterwards adopted, however—and also taking with him the declaration of independence of the Republic of Panama. Just two days before he sailed Dr. Amador sent to his son, a surgeon in the United States Army, a letter, which I propose now to read. This letter carefully outlines the proposed revolution on the Isthmus and the attitude to be taken in the November following by our Government. This letter shows that our Government proposed to do just what he says it had already agreed to do, or it makes of Dr. Amador the greatest prophet the world has produced in the last 2,000 years. Just before Dr. Amador was ready to sail for the Isthmus, anxious to have his son prominent in the proposed revolution and get a part of the spoils, he wrote him this letter:

New York, *October 18, 1903.*

Dear Little Son: I received your telegram that you are not coming as they have refused you permission; also received your letter of the 17th. If the wreath does not come they will send it from the *Endicott* by the next steamer.

The reason for your coming was for you to meet Bunau-Varilla, to whom I have spoken of you. He says that if all turns out well you shall have a good place on the medical commission, which is the first that will begin work; that my name is in Hay's office and that certainly nothing will be refused you.

The plan seems to me good. A portion of the Isthmus declares itself independent, and that portion the United States will not allow any Colombian forces to attack. An assembly is called, and this gives authority to a minister to be appointed by the new Government in order to make a treaty without need of ratification by that assembly. The treaty being approved by both parties, the new Republic remains under the protection of the United States, and to it are added the other districts of the Isthmus which do not already form part of the new Republic, and these also remain under the protection of the United States.

The movement will be delayed a few days—we want to have here the minister who is going to be named so that once the movement is made he can be appointed by cable and take up the treaty. In 30 days everything will be concluded.

We have some resources on the movement being made, and already this has been arranged with a bank.

As soon as everything is arranged I will tell B.-V. to look out for you. He says if you do not wish to go he will look out for a position for you in New York. He is a man of great influence.

A thousand embraces to Pepe, and my remembrances to Jennie and Mr. Smith.

Your affectionate father,

AMADOR.

The CHAIRMAN. Mr. Rainey, what does the "B.-V." in the concluding portion of the letter refer to?

Mr. RAINEY. Bunau-Varilla.

The CHAIRMAN. He was interested in matters down there?

Mr. RAINEY. Yes, sir; he was a stockholder in the new French canal company, and was the first representative in the United States of the new Government in Panama. He was the first minister of the Republic of Panama. Through him came $100,000 from the French canal company which was used on the Isthmus of Panama in assisting in bringing about this revolution, though of course they had other moneys besides this. I think I forgot to say that $60,000 campaign fund donated by Mr. William Nelson Cromwell in 1900 to the Republican Party, and which influenced this declaration in the platform of that year by which the party changed position from an advocate of the Nicaragua route to an advocate of an isthmian canal, came directly from the Panama Canal company in Paris, and Mr. Cromwell charged it up there as a part of his necessary expenses.

Mr. SHARP. Mr. Rainey, I came in late, and although you may have explained about this campaign fund in my absence, I would like to ask something about it. Will you state what evidence you have of that donation of $60,000 to the Republican campaign fund?

Mr. RAINEY. Yes; we will produce that later. I am finishing up my statement now, so that we may get into the evidence at once.

Mr. KENDALL. Is Dr. Amador now living?

Mr. RAINEY. No; he is not.

Mr. KENDALL. Is the son, to whom that letter is addressed, living?

Mr. RAINEY. Yes; he is living.

Mr. KENDALL. Have you the original letter?

Mr. RAINEY. We will produce a photograph of it in a moment, when we begin the introduction of the evidence, and the original is in existence and can be examined.

After the revolution was over, and after the United States had recognized the temporary Government on the Isthmus of Panama, Dr. Amador sent this telegram to Mr. Prescott, the gentleman I have referred to before and who was connected with the Panama Railroad Co. as one of its officials:

NOVEMBER 7, 1903.

H. G. PRESCOTT, *Colon*:

The chief conspirator congratulates his first aid-de-camp for the manner that he behaved during the conspiration.

DR. AMADOR.

The CHAIRMAN. To whom is that telegram addressed?

Mr. RAINEY. It is addressed to H. G. Prescott, Colon.

Mr. TOWNSEND. Was he an official of the Panama Railroad Co.?

Mr. RAINEY. Yes, sir; he was an official of the railroad company, and prevented the movement of troops across the Isthmus.

Mr. SHARP. I did not quite get the purport of that telegram; will you read it again? [The telegram was read.] To whom was that telegram sent?

Mr. RAINEY. It was sent by Dr. Amador to H. G. Prescott, Colon, the latter, among other services, having prevented the movement of troops across the Isthmus.

Mr. KENDALL. You propose to submit proof to substantiate the charge that Mr. Cromwell contributed $60,000 to the Republican campaign fund?

Mr. RAINEY. Yes, sir; we will submit proof of that. In conclusion for the present, I wish to state that when I introduced this resolution (H. Res. 32, 62d Cong., 1st sess.) the New York World kindly placed before me the evidence it had collected in the preparation of its defense in the suit for criminal libel instituted by the Government of the United States against that paper, and they agreed to produce before this committee so much of that evidence as is relevant to the inquiry this committee is now undertaking under my resolution. At my request the chairman of this committee, in order to make unnecessary the issuing of a subpœna, addressed a letter to the New York World asking them to produce this evidence.

I now present to the committee Mr. Henry N. Hall, of the New York World staff, and ask the committee to listen to him while he produces the evidence to which I have referred.

Before taking my seat I wish to ask permission to insert in the record the treaty of 1846 with New Granada—now the Republic of Colombia—and the treaty of 1903 with the Republic of Panama; as well as an article published in the last issue of the North American Review on the Panama Canal question entitled, "A chapter of national dishonor."

The CHAIRMAN. If there is no objection the permission asked will be granted. [A pause.] The Chair hears none and it is granted.

Mr. FLOOD. I did not have the pleasure of hearing you at the other hearing. As I understand, Mr. Rainey, you have made a statement of the case and are now going to produce the evidence?

Mr. RAINEY. That is correct. I now present Mr. Hall, of the New York World staff.

[See Hearing No. 2 for Mr. Hall's remarks.]

[By Leander T. Chamberlain, in the North American Review, February, 1912.]

A CHAPTER OF NATIONAL DISHONOR.

In a recent public statement ex-President Roosevelt declares:

"It must be a matter of pride to every honest American proud of the good name of his country, that the acquisition of the [Panama] canal in all its details was as free from scandal as the public acts of George Washington or Abraham Lincoln.

"The interests of the American people demanded that I should act exactly as I did act.

"Every action taken was not merely proper, but was carried out in accordance with the highest, finest, and nicest standards of public and governmental ethics.

"The [1903] orders to the American naval officers were to maintain free and uninterrupted transit across the Isthmus and, with that purpose, to prevent the landing of armed forces with hostile intent at any point within 50 miles of Panama. These orders were precisely such as had been issued again and again in preceding years, 1900, 1901, and 1902, for instance.

"Every man who at any stage has opposed or condemned the action actually taken in acquiring the right to dig the canal has really been the opponent of any and every effort that could ever have been made to dig the canal.

"Not only was the course followed as regards Panama right in every detail and at every point, but there could have been no variation from this course except for the worse. We not only did what was technically justifiable, but what we did was demanded by every ethical consideration, national and international.

"We did harm to no one, save as harm is done to a bandit by a policeman who deprives him of his chance for blackmail.

"The United States has many honorable chapters in its history, but no more honorable chapter than that which tells of the way in which our right to dig the Panama Canal was secured, and that of the manner in which the work has been carried out."

In an address previously delivered at the "Charter Day" exercises of the University of California, Mr. Roosevelt proudly declared that the securing of that "right" was his personal act. As reported, he then said:

"I am interested in the Panama Canal because I started it. If I had followed traditional, conservative methods, I would have submitted a dignified paper of probably 200 pages to Congress, and the debate on it would have been going on yet; but I took the Canal Zone and let Congress debate; and while the debate goes on the canal does also"

And previous to that California address, in his famous message to Congress of January 4, 1904, President Roosevelt wrote:

"When this Government submitted to Colombia the Hay-Herran treaty (January 22, 1903), it was already settled that the canal should be built. The time for delay, the time for permitting any Government of antisocial spirit and of imperfect development to bar the work was past.

"I have not denied, nor do I wish to deny, etiher the validity or the propriety of the general rule that a new State should not be recognized as independent till it has shown its ability to maintain its independence.

"But like the principle from which it is deduced, the rule is subject to exceptions; and there are in my opinion clear and imperative reasons why a departure from it was justified and even required in the present instance. These reasons embrace, first, our treaty rights; second, our national interests and safety; and third, the interests of collective civilization.

"The United States in intervening, with or without Colombia's consent, for protection of the transit, has disclaimed any duty to defend the Colombian Government against domestic insurrection or against the erection of an independent government on the Isthmus of Panama.

"That our position as the mandatory of civilization has been by no means misconceived is shown by the promptitude with which the powers have, one after another, followed our lead in recognizing Panama as an independent State."

It will be more than worth while to examine in the light of ethical principle and international law, of recorded fact and diplomatic precedent, of national honor and treaty pledge, these several statements, in which personal boasting, sweeping assertion, and a perfervid invoking of high morality are so interwoven. To present individual character in its due disclosure will be something; but to see to it that history is not belied, and that the requirements of justice are not travestied, will be far more.

Certain fundamental considerations must be taken into account in any worthy discussion of the conduct of governments. First, that diplomacy now stands committed to "the extending of the empire of law and the strengthening of an appreciation of public justice." Second, that "international jurisprudence is based on the moral law and embodies the consensus of civilized peoples with regard to their reciprocal rights and duties." Third, that "all nations stand on an equality of rights—the old and the new, the large and the small, monarchies and republics." It is, accordingly, in view of these considerations, that the Panama embroglio of 1903 is to be judged.

As one of the parties to that imbroglio was the United States of Colombia (formerly New Granada), there is needed a brief statement of Colombia's history. The United States of Colombia, afterwards the Republic of Colombia, was fully established in 1863. Her constitution was patterned on that of the United States of America. Her area, previous to the dismemberment of 1903, was hardly less than 500,000 square miles, or more than twice the area of Spain and Portugal combined. Her population was at least 4,000,000, or approximately twice that of Norway. Bordering on both the Atlantic Ocean and the Pacific, her coast line was more than a thousand miles, bountifully provided with convenient bays and excellent harbors. Extensive and varied mineral products were elements in her material wealth. But the rarest of her properties, the gem of her domain, was the Province of Panama, northernmost of her possessions, at the extreme north of the southern continent. Included in that province was the Itahmus of Panama, narrowest barrier between the two oceans. As the American continents were discovered in the search for a westward passage from Europe to Asia, so, through the centuries subsequent to that discovery, the Isthmus of Panama was regaredd as the likeliest route for an interoceanic canal.

In 1855 an isthmian railroad was completed along a course substantially the same as must be taken by a waterway. In 1881 a French company undertook the construction of a canal, both railroad and canal having been neutralized. The original construction company failed, and a New Panama Co. was formed to take over the existing canal rights and obligations and to complete the undertaking. But the new company also proved unequal to the task, and as early as 1897 it was realized that no private resources would be adequate and that no Government save that of the United States was wholly competent. It was understood that the United States was willing to proceed upon certain conditions.

But meantime, even antedating the establishing of the United States of Colombia, a treaty had been entered into between the United States of America and the Government of that same country, to wit, the Republic of New Granada. It was entitled "A treaty of peace, amity, navigation, and commerce." It was negotiated by the respective administrations on December 12, 1846, and was ratified and proclaimed in June, 1848. The preamble reads:

"The United States of North America and the Republic of New Granada in South America, desiring to make lasting and firm the friendship and good understanding which happily exist between both nations, have resolved to fix in a manner clear, distinct, and positive the rules which shall in the future be religiously observed between each other by means of a treaty, or general convention of peace and friendship, commerce, and navigation.

* * * * * * *

"ARTICLE I. There shall be a perfect, firm, and inviolable peace and sincere friendship between the United States of America and the Republic of New Granada in all the extent of their possessions and territories and between their citizens, respectively, without distinction of person or places.

* * * * * * *

"ART. XXXV. The United States of America and the Republic of New Granada, desiring to make as endurable as possible the relations which are to be established between the two parties by virtue of this treaty, have declared solemnly and do agree to the following points:

"First.

* * * * * * *

"In order to secure to themselves the tranquil and constant enjoyment of these advantages, and as an especial compensation for the said advantages and for the favors they have acquired by Articles IV, V, and VI of this treaty (articles which secure to the United States reciprocal privileges of importation and tonnage dues, and equal customs duties) the United States guarantee positively and efficaciously to New Granada, by the present stipulation, the perfect neutrality of the before-mentioned Isthmus, with the view that the free transit from the one to the other sea may not be interrupted or embarrassed in a future time while this treaty exists; and in consequence the United States also guarantee in the same manner the rights of sovereignty and property which New Granada has and possesses over the said territory.

"Second. The present treaty shall remain in full force and vigor for the term of 20 years from the day of the exchange of ratifications.

* * * * * * *

"Third. Notwithstanding the foregoing, if neither party notifies to the other its intention of re-forming any of or all the articles of this treaty 12 months before the expiration of the 20 years specified above, the said treaty shall continue binding on both parties beyond the said 20 years, until 12 months from the time that one of the parties notifies its intention of proceeding to a reform.

* * * * * * *

"Sixth. Any special or remarkable advantages that the one or the other power may enjoy from the foregoing stipulations are and ought to be always understood in virtue and in compensation of the obligations they have just contracted, and which have been specified in the first number of this article."

Such is the solemn treaty of 1846; a treaty "to make lasting and firm the friendship and good understanding which happily exists between the United States and New Granada" (now Colombia), whose stipulations were to be "religiously observed";

a treaty decreeing "a perfect, firm, and inviolable peace and sincere friendship" between the two nations; a treaty in which, as compensation for specified "advantages and favors," the United States "positively and efficaciously" guaranteed to New Granada "the perfect neutrality of the Isthmus" and, in the same manner, "the rights of sovereignty and property which New Granada has and possesses over the said territory"; a treaty terminal on 12 months' notice. The practical interpretation and application of the treaty are plain.

Under date of February 10, 1847, only two months after the initiation of the treaty, President Polk, in a special message to the Senate, said:

"There does not appear any other effectual means of securing to all nations the advantages of this important passage, but the guaranty of great commercial powers that the Isthmus shall be neutral territory. * * *

"The guaranty of the sovereignty of New Granada over the Isthmus is a natural consequence of this neutrality. * * * New Granada would not yield this province that is might become a neutral State; and if she should, it is not sufficiently populous or wealthy to establish or maintain an independent sovereignty. But a civil government must exist there to protect the works which shall be constructed. New Granada is not a power which will excite the jealousy of any nation."

The neutrality guaranteed to New Granada undoubtedly referred to foreign nations only. It was against interference by an outside government, interference which might among other evil results, interrupt the transit from the one to the other sea. Similarly the guaranty of New Granada's "rights of sovereignty and property" was the primary reference to an invasion by a foreign power which might imperil the isthmian transit. And since the paramount issue in the case of both the neutrality and sovereignty which the United States guaranteed was the safeguarding of the transit, there was a valid implication that the United States, on due occasion and especially at New Granada's request, would give aid against transit interference from any source whatever, whether foreign or domestic.

The direct authority, however, to be cited by the United States as warrant for the aid actually given to New Granada (now Colombia) in the maintenance of free isthmain transit, as also the clear ground of the duty of the United States to render such aid, is in the fact that by the treaty of 1846 New Granada distinctly pledged herself to keep the said transit inviolate for the free use of the Government and citizens of the United States.

"The Government of New Granada guarantees to the Government of the United States that the right of way or transit across the Isthmus of Panama upon any modes of transportation which now exist, or that may be hereafter constructed, shall be open and free to the Government and citizens of the United States, and for the transportation of any articles of lawful commerce belonging to the citizens of the United States."

That guaranty by New Granada, in a treaty of "peace, amity, navigation, and commerce," a treaty "to make lasting and firm the friendship and good understanding" of the two nations, established a relation between the United States and New Granada in which mutual aid became not only rightful but also assured. Henceforth it was to be implicitly relied upon that if the weaker nation was temporarily incapable of a perfect fulfillment if its guaranty, the stronger nation would, upon request, lend assistance. In New Granada's guaranty, acknowledged by the United States as an "advantage and favor" received, is the original and sufficing basis for the right and obligation of helpful interference by the United States in the emergency of transit interruption. A corroborative, complementary basis also exists in the avowed motive and purpose of the counter guaranty by the United States of New Granada's neutrality and sovereignty—"with the view that the free transit from the one to the other sea may not be interrupted or embarrassed in a future time while this treaty exists." Yet the prime basis lies in New Granada's pledge which the United States gratefully accepted.

But beyond the bounds of such reciprocal right and obligation the United States might not go. In emergencies other than the disturbance of interoceanic transit, or peril to the persons and possessions of Americans, there might be no intervention in the affairs of New Granada (now Colombia). By the law of nations and the terms of the treaty itself, Colombia as the successor of New Granada was the sovereign peer of the United States. Save for the main purpose of protecting free transit and thus safeguarding her own interests in such transit, the United States might no more land her forces on Colombia's soil, or even threaten such landing, than she might land her forces, or threaten to land them, on the soil of Russia or Japan.

Nor is even this the full measure of the restraint which the Executive of the United States was bound to recognize and respect. It has been conceded that the guaranteed neutrality and sovereignty had reference to foreign powers. But it is to be borne in mind that in guaranteeing Colombia's neutrality and sovereignty as against foreign powers the United States distinctly decreed and surpassingly emphasized her own exclusion from acts of evasion. She determinately erected an impassible barrier against her own interference with Colombia's independent authority. And this in the simple fact that she herself was a "foreign nation." The treaty inhibition affected her first of all. She virtually named herself in the guaranty; and the guarantor, being thus included in the inhibition, was, beyond all others, forbidden to violate its terms. Otherwise it were as if the guardian of a dependent child should record his oath and give his bond to defend his charge against all unlawful acts, and then should himself expropriate his ward's possessions and assume dictatorial control. It were as if an officer of the law, sworn to uphold the citizen's rights and to lay violent hands on no man save by statutory warrant and command, should wantonly assail the helpless and ruthlessly strike down the unoffending. Being a nation foreign to Colombia, the United States, in her "positive and efficacious" guaranty, freely placed herself under supreme restraint.

With the civil wars of Colombia the United States had no concern, save as they harmfully affected the persons or possessions of American citizens or interrupted or endangered isthmian transit and traffic. Yet on November 6, 1903, Colombia was informed that "the President holds that he is bound to see that the peaceable traffic of the world across the Isthmus of Panama shall not longer be disturbed by a constant succession of unnecessary and wasteful civil wars."

The official records are open. Those records will either uphold the presidential assertion or they will prove it to be wild and inexcusable. Let it be seen to what extent from the establishing of the United States of Colombia in 1863 to the Panama imbroglio of 1903, isthmian transit was so disturbed that the interference of the United States was required.

In March, 1865, our Panama consul was apprehensive of harm from local lawlessness, and a few marines guarded the consul and other citizens for 13 hours. In May, 1873, a small force of marines and sailors protected the persons and property of American citizens in Panama for 15 days. In September of the same year a similar service was rendered for 16 days. In January, 1885, 12 marines guarded property in Colon for 13½ hours. Later in the same year isthmian transit was seriously interrupted and forces were landed for 56 days. Toward the close of 1901 protection of transit was required for 14 days. In the autumn of 1902 transit was guarded for 62 days.

Thus during full 40 years United States forces were employed in only seven instances and for a total period of 164 days. In each case the forces were employed with Colombia's approval. In no case was there fighting, the mere precautionary measures being sufficient. In no case did the force exceed 824 men. Moreover, in four out of the seven instances there was no "interruption of transit," only an apprehension of peril to persons and property. In fine, isthmian transit was interrupted in only three instances in the 40 years of Colombia's history, and for only 132 days.

Yet the President officially represented that isthmian transit had been disturbed almost incessantly for many years; that interruption was the chronic condition. A constant disturbing cause bringing about a virtually constant disturbance. In the comparison, the increase of Fallstaff's men in buckram—"eleven grown out of two"—was accuracy itself, three reduplicated into an implied constant succession. What of the author of such assertions? It would appear that he then took for his motto, Throw mud vigorously, some of it will stick—Asperge fortiter, aliquid adhærebit. That was on November 6, 1903.

Meantime, on June 25, 1902, the President gave his approval to the act commonly called the Spooner Act, looking toward the construction of an isthmian canal. That act embodied the decision of the United States in favor of the Panama route. It authorized the President to acquire, if possible, at a cost not to exceed a certain sum, "the rights, privileges, franchises, concessions," and all other assets of the new Panama company; and to obtain from Colombia on such terms as he considered to be fair, perpetual control (nor cession) for canal purposes of a strip of land from ocean to ocean not less than 6 wiles mide, such control to include the emergent defense of the canal, the instituting of needful legal tribunals, and the making and enforcing of the requisite police and sanitary regulations. The act also provided that if, from the Canal Company and the Colombian Government, the President was unable to obtain satisfactory terms within a reasonable time, the route known as the "Nicaragua route" should be adopted.

After the passage of the Spooner Act, the Colombian administration—not Colombia in propria persona, but only the Colombian administration—initiated negotiations in favor and furtherance of the Panama route. Those negotations led, on January 22, 1903, to the well-known "Hay-Herran convention." In that convention Colombia was to give to the United States jurisdiction over the desired strip of land and to concede the right to construct and operate a canal for the period of one hundred years renewable at the option of the United States for periods of a similar duration. The convention reaffirmed Article XXXV of the treaty of 1846, and explicitly provided that only in exceptional circumstances, on account of unforseen or imminent danger to the canal, railways, or other works, or to the lives and property of the persons engaged upon them, should the United States employ its armed forces, without previously obtaining the consent of Colombia; and that as soon as sufficient Colombian forces should arrive, those of the United States should be withdrawn. But the Hay-Herran convention being simply an agreement between the respective administrations, was necessarily dependent for its vital force upon its ratification by the respective Senates. It was expressly stipulated that—

"The convention, when signed by the contracting parties, shall be ratified in conformity with the laws of the respective countries."

The Washington administration has urged that any two governments, in initiating a treaty, "bind themselves, pending its ratification, not only to oppose its consummation, but also to do nothing in contravention of its terms." That is true of governments in the limited sense of the executive, the administration, but it does not apply to the attitude and act of a nation's congress; and in the final event the ratifying power is to proceed in accordance with its own reasoning and conviction, no matter what administrations may have stipulated or done. Furthermore, as the Canal company could, in no case, transfer its rights and possessions, without the consent of Colombia, the first article of the Hay-Herran convention provides:

"The Government of Columbia authorizes the New Panama Canal Co. to sell and transfer to the United States its rights, privileges, properties, and concessions, as well as the Panama Railroad and all the shares or parts of the shares of that company."

Of course, that and the other provisions of the administrational agreement were to come before the Colombian Senate for consideration; and that senate, like any other independent legislature, was bound to take full cognizance of the matter, and freely discuss all offered amendments. Yet even before the Colombian Senate convened, the American minister to Colombia, on April 24, 1903, addressed the follwing note to the Colombian minister of foreign relations:

"I am directed to inform your excellency, if the point should be raised, that everything relative to this matter is included in the convention recently signed between Colombia and the United States, and that, furthermore, any modification would be violative of the Spooner Act and therefore inadmissible."

Again, and still in advance of the session of the Colombian Senate, the minister of foreign relations was advised that—

"If Colombia should now reject the treaty or unduly delay its ratification, the friendly feeling between the two countries would be so seriously compromised that action might be taken by the Congress next winter which every friend of Colombia would regret."

And after the Colombian Senate was in session, on August 5, 1903, further warning was sent through the Colombian minister of foreign relations, to the effect that apparently the force of the notes of April 24 and June 13 had not been duly appreciated as "the final expression of the opinion or intentions" of the Washington Government. The warning proceeded:

"If Colombia desires to maintain the friendly relations which at present exist between the two countries, and at the same time to secure for herself the extraordinary advantages that are to be produced for her * * * the present treaty will have to be ratified exactly in its present form, without amendment whatsoever."

Yet the Hay-Herran instrument itself provided that "the convention, when signed by the contracting parties, shall be ratified in conformity with the laws of the respective countries." Assuredly. Else the mere Executive, the mere administration, would have full and final authority in matters involving the nation's vital interests—to a fatal usurpation of the power of the Congress. The Senate of the United States has again and again amended, and rejected, treaties which had been duly negotiated by the administration. Still, the Washington administration peremptorily forbade Colombia's Senate either to amend or reject.

Was this attempted coercion "not only technically justifiable, but demanded by every ethical consideration, national and international"? Was it "as free from scandal as the public acts of George Washington and Abraham Lincoln"? In utmost soberness of inquiry, did any civilized representative of superior power ever indulge in browbeating so pitiable and so pitiless? Can such cowardly disrespect be matched in the annals of treaty-making nations? And that, on the part of the Executive of a great Republic which professed to do justice and to love mercy, and against a nation helpless, yet standing in a relation of acknowledged equality of sovereignty and independence. A nation at whose hands we had confessedly received important "advantages and favors." A nation to which we were bound by an inviolable treaty of "peace and amity," of "friendship and good understanding," a treaty whose stipulations were to be "religiously observed." That nation coolly informed that if, in the exercise of her indisputable prerogative, she followed what might be her patriotic judgment, she should suffer a retribution whereat the ears of them that heard should tingle.

What must be the character and culture of the President who proudly affirms that such was his highest conception of what was "demanded by every ethical consideration," and should be "a matter of pride to every honest American."?

After long and vehement debate, and postponement to an extra session, the American Senate, on March 17, 1903, ratified the treaty. After long and earnest debate, the Colombian Senate, on August 12, 1903, despite the President's unveiled threat, refused ratification, and adjourned on October 31.

It is to be distinctly observed at this point that, while there was no stipulation for the absolute cession to the United States of the Canal Zone, there was to be perpetual occupancy and jurisdiction—periods of 100 years, with the option of renewal by the United States, but no option of rejection by Colombia—the construction of vast and permanent works, the right to safeguard those works, along with police and sanitary control. The constitutional authorities in the Colombian Senate held that such a grant, although less than absolute cession, was contrary to the nation's organic law. They regarded it as, so far forth, a surrender of national sovereignty, notwithstanding the statement that "the United States freely acknowledges and recognizes this sovereignty [of Colombia] and disavows any intention to impair it in any way whatever." Would the constitutional authorities in the Senate of the United States be likely to hold otherwise in case it was proposed to grant to a foreign power a similarly endless occupancy and jurisdiction of a part of our national domain? Would they admit that their discussion of that issue might fairly be regarded as factious and deceitful? Yet, as has been pointed out, it was proposed in the deliberations of the Colombian Senate so to amend the constitution that the apprehended legal objection should be removed.

As for the considerations which prompted the adverse action of the Colombian Senate, it may be said that in any case they were properly beyond our official animadversion or even official discussion. High-minded diplomacy usually holds in courteous respect the motives which may have inspired the legislative act of a sovereign nation. Yet in addressing Colombia our administration ascribed to her the basest of motives. The mere opinion of our minister to Colombia was cited as showing that the Senate's discussions were prolonged and the ratification finally rejected, with the sordid view of holding up the construction of an isthmian waterway, and thus being the better able to exact terms from the United States. Further, what was only a report of the Colombian Senate's "committee on the Panama Canal" was officially quoted as proof of that accusatory opinion. The following statement was published in a rejoinder to Colombia's minister plenipotentiary in Washington:

"By a report of the majority of the Panama Canal committee, read in the Colombian Senate on the 14th of October last, it was recommended that a bill which had been introduced to authorize the Government to enter upon new negotiations should be indefinitely postponed. The reason for this recommendation is disclosed in the same report. * * * By a treaty concluded April 4, 1893, the original concession to the Panama Canal Co. was extended until December 31, 1904. The report of the Colombian Senate's committee affirms that the aspect of the question would be entirely changed in consequence of the fact that when a year later the Colombian Congress should meet in ordinary session the extension of 1893 would have expired and every concession with it. In that case * * * the Republic would become the possessor or owner, without any need of a previous judicial decision and without any indemnity, of the canal itself and of the adjuncts which belong to it; and would not only be able to contract without any impediments, but would be in more clear, more definite, and more advantageous possession both legally and materially."

The administration's official statement continues:

"This program if not expressly, was at least tacitly adopted by the Colombian Congress. * * * It was a scheme to which this Government could not possibly become a party."

And that, although the Colombian Senate was a national legislature and had acted within its sovereign rights.

Is it conceivable that the President would have cast such innuendoes and accusations in the face of Great Britain or Germany or France? Would he have tolerated such open affront on the part of any other nation? To ask the questions is to answer them. The physical weakness of Colombia should have been her triple protection. Toward helplessness power should have felt itself bound by a chivalrous noblesse oblige. It is safe to say that never in the previous history of civilized diplomacy was there such a public official characterization by one nation of another nation's motives for legislative action. Therein the President's conduct was audaciously wrong.

At this point the President vainly seeks his vindication by a reference to practical results. He says:

"Be it remembered that unless I had acted exactly as I did act there would now be no Panama Canal. * * * Every man who at any stage has opposed or condemned the action actually taken in acquiring the right to dig the canal has really been the opponent of any and every effort that could ever have been made to dig the canal."

Here is a veritable "Daniel come to judgment." The great Burke professed his inability to draw a valid indictment against the people of a whole nation; but this self-eulogizer finds no difficulty in denouncing the innumerable critics of his Panama action under the one base category of those wishing to deprive the world forever of a waterway from the one to the other sea. No matter how many the dissidents, nor how worthy their reputation and achievements, nor how earnestly explicit their declaration that they yielded to none in their desire for interoceanic navigation, they are charged with hostility to any Panama Canal whatever.

How insensate the President's charge. As if those who were confident that Colombia would appreciate decent treatment and would agree to amended but still reasonable terms were thus confident without a vestige of reason. He himself had already declared:

"Colombia, after having rejected the treaty in spite of our protests and warning when it was in her power to accept it, has since shown the utmost eagerness to accept the same treaty if only the status quo could be restored."

He had, furthermore, and for his own purposes, quoted a Colombian high official as affirming, on November 6, 1903—the very day on which the Panama insurgents were recognized as having established a new nation—in a note to the American minister at Bogota, that on certain conditions—

"The Colombian Government will declare martial law and, by virtue of vested constitutional authority when public order is disturbed, will approve by decree the ratification of the canal treaty as signed; or, if the Government of the United States prefers, will call extra session of Congress, with new and friendly members, next May to approve the treaty."

The American minister at Bogota adds, "There is a great reaction in favor of the treaty." On January 6, 1904, Colombia's minister plenipotentiary at Washington officially declared:

"The necessity of the canal is so well recognized in Colombia that it was proposed in the discussion in the Senate to amend the constitution in order to remove [what Colombia regarded as] the constitutional difficulties, and the minister of foreign relations, after the sessions of Congress were closed, directed the chargé d'affaires to advise the Washington Government that the Government of Colombia was ready to enter into renewed negotiations for a canal convention."

He further averred that the fact of the rejection of the Hay-Herran convention—"does not mean that we have been opposed, nor that we are opposed, to the realization of the greatest undertaking of the kind which the past and future centuries have seen or will see. * * * I have been directed to declare to your Government that Colombia, earnestly wishing that the work of the canal be carried into effect, not only because it suits her interests, but also that of the commerce of the world, is disposed to enter into arrangements that would secure for the United States the execution and ownership of the said work. * * * The charge made against the Government of Colombia that it proposes to cancel the concession of the French company vanishes as soon as it is known that under the latest concession granted by Colombia the said concession would not lapse until the year 1910."

Who can doubt that if the President had curbed his angry impatience and withheld his irritating, insolent threats Columbia's Senate would have acceded to terms rightly advantageous to both countries? Who disbelieves that if, as was our acknowledged perfect right, we had invoked the third point of Article XXXV of the treaty of 1846, to wit—

"The said treaty shall be binding on both parties until 12 months from the time that one of the parties notifies its intention of proceeding to a reform"—

Columbia would have been duly impressed with the gravity of her situation, and have earnestly striven to come to terms with her indispensable ally? Accordingly, it is pure hardihood for the President to affirm "Unless I had acted exactly as I did act there would now be no canal." It is simple slander, silly slander, when he says, "Every man who at any stage has opposed or condemned the action actually taken in acquiring the right to dig the canal has really been the opponent of any and every effort that could ever have been made to dig the canal." His critics asked that the right to dig the canal might be acquired by lawful means. Being enthusiastically in favor of an interoceanic waterway, they only demanded that "a decent respect for the opinions of mankind," a substantial regard for international law and treaty obligations should guide the acts of the Washington administration. It certainly is not too much to suppose that if their protests had been heeded we should now have a canal whose title would be wholly free from stain and whose advantages might be enjoyed with complete self-respect.

In this chapter of national dishonor there are still other transactions to be considered.

The President, according to his published admission, was aware as early as August, 1903, that the secession of the Province of Panama was secretly fomented. He has openly declared that, toward the end of October, the attempt "appeared to be an imminent probability." In his message to Congress of January 4, 1904, he said:

"In view of these facts I directed the Navy Department to issue instructions such as would insure our having ships within easy reach of the Isthmus in the event of need arising. * * * On November 2 the following instructions were sent to the commanders of the *Boston*, *Nashville*, and *Dixie*: 'Maintain free and uninterrupted transit. * * * Prevent landing of any armed force, either Government or insurgent, within 50 miles of Panama.' "

That is, in time of profound peace between Colombia and the United States; while the treaty of "peace and amity, of friendship and good understanding," was in undisturbed force; while it was still written, "There shall be a perfect, firm, and inviolable peace and sincere friendship;" while the neutrality and sovereignty of Colombia were solemnly and gratefully guaranteed by the United States as against interference by foreign powers, and therefore against interference by the United States herself; while isthmian transit was absolutely free from interruption; while there was no slightest overt act on the part of the would-be seceders; and while Colombia's acquiescence had not been so much as requested, Colombia was forcefully forbidden to land her own troops within 50 miles of the city of Panama, where, if anywhere, the secession would be attempted. In other words, the success of the revolt, whenever it might occur, was resistlessly decreed. When the President of the United States issued the "50-mile order" of November 2, 1903, he virtually declared war against the very nation of which the United States was the sworn ally and to which the United States was united by obligations admittedly paramount. He bound Colombia hand and foot and delivered her over to her domestic foes.

Yet the President, in his floundering attempts at self-defense, declares that—

"These orders were precisely such as had been issued again and again in preceding years—1900, 1901, and 1902, for instance."

But no identity, nor even resemblance, appears when the orders of those preceding years are brought into comparison. Here is the record. On July 25, 1900, our consul at Panama was thus instructed:

"You are directed to protest against any act of hostility which may involve or imperil the safe and peaceful transit of persons or property across the Isthmus of Panama. The bombardment of Panama would have this effect, and the United States must insist upon the neutrality of the Isthmus as guaranteed by the treaty."

Here was simply a protest in advance of possible harm. It was merely a warning of Colombia that she would pursue a certain course upon her own responsibility, and that the United States would interfere if free transit was interrupted. On November 20, 1901, this telegram was sent to our Panama consul:

"Notify all parties molesting or interfering with free transit across the Isthmus that such interference must cease, and that the United States will prevent the interruption of traffic upon the railroad. Consult with captain of the *Iowa*, who will be instructed to land marines if necessary for the protection of the railroad in accordance with the treaty rights and obligations of the United States."

That order went no further than to demand that interruption of transit should cease, and to provide means, in case of necessity, for enforcing the demand. On September 12, 1902, the commander of the *Ranger*, then at Panama, was notified:

"The United States guarantees perfect neutrality of Isthmus, and that a free transit from sea to sea be not interrupted or embarrassed. * * * Any transportation of troops which might contravene these provisions of treaty should not be sanctioned by you, nor should use of road be permitted which might convert the line of transit into theater of hostility."

Here, again, was a merely admonitory order sent to forestall any use of the transit line which would destroy its legitimate function by making it, unnecessarily, the scene of armed conflict.

Thus the official record shows that, so far from countenancing the "50-mile order," the asserted precedents clearly condemned it. In direct refutation of the President's declaration is the fact that the previous orders were: First, in accordance with Colombia's understanding and wish; second, that they sought, in authorized ways, to safeguard Isthmian transit from critically impending or actual interruption; third, that they constituted no assault upon either the supreme jurisdiction or the supremely free action of Colombia. The 50-mile order grossly offended in all these respects. It was known to be infinitely abhorrent to Colombia as a sovereign nation; it had prime reference to an apprehended political insurrection against Colombia's territorial integrity and national control, with only consequential reference to a possible transit interruption; it laid essentially violent hands on Colombia's sovereignty; it forcibly prevented Colombia from taking precautionary measures; it was a virtual declaration of war. Colombia was suddenly, peremptorily restrained from the free disposition of her own troops on her own soil. The venerable treaty whose stipulations were to be "religiously observed" was, so far forth, flung aside as vacuous and its covenants trampled in the dust.

The President's search for justifying precedents was foredoomed to failure. There was a vast improbability that the history of the United States would furnish any analogy of such despotism. The President should have known beforehand—doubtless he did know—that the outrage was wholly novel, conspicuous in its infamous isolation. An unoffending ally fettered and gyved, in forecast of her instinctive movement for self-preservation. The President's act was truly monumental. It was altogether and characteristically his own.

Imagine that when the Confederate forces threatened Washington, a nation whose strength outmeasured ours as ours outmeasured Colombia's had forbidden our Government to send troops within 50 miles of the endangered capital. Imagine that the dictating nation was bound to us by treaty pledges of "inviolable peace and sincere friendship." Imagine that our Government had guaranteed that nation, to the effect that its legation in Washington should not be imperiled. Yet that when we thought to safeguard the capital from secession's deadly attack—all legations being then unmolested, and it being by no means sure that, even if there was armed conflict, any legation would be injured—our overawing ally forcibly prevented our proposed defensive action, thus handing us over to our assailants; making our disruption a certainty, foregone and absolute. What in that case, would have been our feeling and judgment? What would have been the verdict of the civilized world? Would it have been conceded by us, or by anybody, that the interdict was other than atrocious? On the very face of it, and in its very nature, the peremptory ban would appear as unspeakably abusive.

But the President tells us that he then knew, and now knows, no standard of public and governmental ethics "higher, or finer, or nicer." Perhaps he is entitled to the plea.

The "50-mile order," however, was destined to be outdone. On the succeeding day, November 3, 1903, the following order was sent to the commander of the *Nashville* at Colon:

"In the interests of peace make every effort to prevent Government troops at Colon from proceeding to Panama. The transit of the Isthmus must be kept open and order maintained."

The President's repressive determination was not to be balked. As yet, our Panama consul had forwarded only the news of what he called an "uprising" in that one city. Yet the President issued an order preventing Columbia from moving her own troops, via her own railway, from her own Colon to her own Panama. So far as concerned their freedom to go to the scene of danger, Colombia's troops were reconcentadoed and manacled. Let it still be borne in mind that there was no interruption of transit by either loyalist or insurgent. Let it be taken into account that the President himself, under the pretense of maintaining peace and order when peace and order perfectly prevailed, violently interrupted free transit, absolutely closing it to the forces of sovereign Colombia, a treaty-bound ally of the United States.

In self-exculpation, the President has declared that—

"The theory that the treaty obliged the Government of the United States to protect Colombia against domestic insurrection or its consequences finds no support in the record, and is in its nature inadmissible."

Well said. But, conversely, the treaty did obligate the Government of the United States not to take sides against Colombia in any conflict she might have with the agents of domestic insurrection. In both its letter and spirit the treaty did bind the President of the United States not to predoom an ally to defeat in the face of attempted dismemberment. The treaty did make it inevitable that such crushing hostility should forever appear as gratuitous perfidy.

What the Washington Government should have done in place of the cruel "50-mile order" and the still more cruel repression of the following day, was to respect Colombia's right to a perfectly free moving of her troops, whether overland or by sea, or by her Isthmian railway; at the same time notifying Colombia that any interruption by her of Isthmian transit, if not absolutely necessary to her self-protection, would be prevented by American forces. But the President, in a deliberate, calculating forecast of the Panama insurrection, joined forces with the seceders and conquered Colombia in the interest of secession.

The true quality of the President's procedure will be the more clearly perceived through a moment's consideration of what, in such a crisis, Colombia herself might rightfully have done. Colombia had the indisputable right to defend herself against disruption. In case of actual civil war or its perceived imminence, especially civil war involving territorial integrity, any nation may take such measures, within the recognized rules of warfare, as that nation may deem needful. The right of self-preservation is elemental. It inheres not only in national sovereignty, but also in national existence. Not even treaty stipulations can be set up in contravention of it. Accordingly, Colombia, if threatened by secession, might herself, were it in the imperative interests of self-preservation, close Isthmian transit to all except her own troops. Or she might close it to all except herself and the United States. Or she might impose special conditions to which everybody using the transit must temporarily conform. In other phrase, Colombia, if vitally assailed might take supreme control of all the resources within her domain. Her inherent sovereignty, whether guaranteed or not, would give her a right paramount to the rights of even her allies. In fine, in the emergency of self-preservation the control of Isthmian transit was completely Colombia's. In that case, the President of the United States was authorized to do no more than to see to it that Colombia's interruption, or closure, of transit was neither wantonly imposed nor unreasonably prolonged. Only on proof of such wantonness or unreasonableness would there be just cause of offense. To hold otherwise would be to hold that, in our own Civil War, foreign nations might justly complain because our blockade of an insurgent coast rendered nugatory, for the time being, their long-standing right to navigate our ports and rivers.

Let, then, the 50-mile order of November 2, 1903, and the still severer interdict of the following day be judged in the light of those first principles.

No doubt, upon the bombardment of Panama and the threatened violence to Americans in Colon, United States troops were rightly landed to protect American citizens and their possessions. Such precautions are sanctioned by humane considerations and by universal precedent concerning a government's duty to protect its unoffending people. But that has nothing whatever to do with the President's forbidding Colombia so much as to attempt her self-defense. For the 50-mile order, and for the preventing of Colombia from moving her troops which were already within the 50-mile limit, modern history offers no counterpart and international law no sanction. It was sheer usurpation. Yet the author of that sheer usurpation emphatically avers that so far as his acquaintance with diplomacy and international law extends, or his education in the first principles of national sovereignty has advanced, his course was superlatively right. His words are:

"Not only was the course followed as regards Panama right in every detail, but there could have been no variation from that course except for the worse. We not only did what was technically justifiable, but we did what was demanded by every ethical consideration, national and international."

He vehemently declares that he did as well as he knew how. To believe it would be a relief.

In the final act of the drama, events move with accelerated swiftness. As we have seen, on November 2, 1903, in time of profound peace between Colombia and the United States, while there was no slightest interruption of transit, the President's amazing 50-mile order was issued. On the evening of November 3, at 6 o'clock, the émeute which the President had anticipated took place in the city of Panama, the chief promoters being "the fire department." The less than 200 Government soldiers were "persuaded" to join the movement. The few Government officials were taken prisoners. "Four hundred Colombian soldiers landed at Colon." This was received in Washington at 9.50 p. m. of November 3. One hour and twenty-eight minutes later—viz., at 11.18—word was returned directing the commander of the *Nashville* to "make every effort to prevent Government troops at Colon from proceeding to Panama." That is, in 88 minutes from receipt of notice of an "uprising"—it was so named in the dispatch—in the one city of Panama, the President transcended his 50-mile order of the previous day, and embargoed Colombia's troops that were already within the 50-mile limit. The next day, November 4, at 9.50 in the morning came the consular assurance, "The troops will not be moved. * * * [Colombian] gunboat *Bogota* threatens to bombard city to-day." At 2 minutes past noon of that same November 4, a telegram was sent directing that the *Bogota* cease the "wanton shelling of Panama." It was significantly added, "We shall have a naval force at Panama in two days."

At 7.10 p. m. of that same November 4, a telegram from the Panama consul announced that a proclamation of independence had been issued by the insurgents, and that three persons had been deputed to draw up a form of government. During the following day, November 5, the interchange of telegrams respecting the details of the situation was frequent and urgent. On November 6, at 12.51, the following Government message was sent to our Panama consul:

"The people of Panama have by an apparently unanimous movement dissolved their connection with the Republic of Columbia and resumed their independence. When you are satisfied that a de facto government, republican in form and without substantial opposition from its own people, has been established in the State of Panama, you will enter into relations with it as the responsible Government of the territory."

A mere consul authorized to acknowledge a new nation, as soon as he thinks that a republican form of government has been put in operation. And then, "to make assurrance doubly sure," 1 hour and 54 minutes later, at 2.45 p. m., for the consul's guidance "in the execution of the instructions" just cabled to him, the transmission of a copy of a telegram already sent to the United States minister at Bogota:

"The people of Panama * * * having adopted a government of their own, republican in form, with which the Government of the United States of America has entered into relations, the President of the United States * * * most earnestly commends to the Governments of Colombia and Panama the peaceful and equitable settlement of all questions at issue between them. He holds that he is bound not only by treaty obligations, but by the interests of civilization, to see that the peaceable traffic of the world across the Isthmus of Panama shall not longer be distributed by a constant succession of unnecessary and wasteful civil wars."

[We have already traced the record. Interruption from any and all causes, in the 40 years of Colombian history, of only 164 days.] Had the President wholly forgotten his Latin: Mendacem memorem esse oportet?

Thus at 12.51, midday, November 6, 1903, the President recognized the new nation, the Republic of Panama. From the November 2 of the 50-mile order, 4 days. From the 7.10 p. m. of November 4, when announcement came that a proclamation of independence had been issued by the insurgents, 1 day, 17 hours, and 41 minutes.

Beyond peradventure, civilized diplomacy affords no analogy of that recognition of the Republic of Panama. Under a treaty specifically guaranteeing, as against all foreign nations, Colombia's "rights of sovereignty and property" over the identical territory in question, and also that territory's efficacious "neutrality," a treaty whose stipulations were to be "religiously observed," the President of the guaranteeing Nation, itself unavoidably included in the treaty's provisions, forcibly disabled Colombia from taking the slightest precautionary measure against secession, continued and expended his hostilities, and then, in 1 day, 17 hours, and 41 minutes from the issuance in the one city of Panama of an insurgent proclamation of independence, recognized a new sovereignty. A popular uprising, at a single point, of less than one-tenth of the population of the Province of Panama; no revolutionary committee representing the other five districts of the Province; no formulated statement of grievances; no congress, no army, no navy, no courts of justice, no financial stability, evidently unable to withstand the forces of the parent country; yet an admission to the great sisterhood of nations. Admitted in less time than measures two revolutions of the earth on its axis. It is ample cause for thankfulness that the annals of civilization are sullied by no sustaining precedent.

In a note to Mr. Seward, Secretary of State, to Mr. Adams, American minister at the court of St. James, in 1861, he said:

"We freely admit that a nation may, and even ought to, recognize a new State which has absolutely and beyond question effected its independence and permanently established its sovereignty; and that a recognition in such case affords no just cause of offense to the Government of the country from which the new State has detached itself. On the other hand, we insist that a nation that recognizes a revolutionary State with a view to aid its effecting its sovereignty and independence commits a great wrong against the nation whose integrity is thus invaded, and makes itself responsible for a just and ample redress. * * * To recognize the independence of a new State, and so favor, possibly determine, its admission into the family of nations, is the highest possible exercise of sovereign power, because it affects in any case the welfare of two nations and often the peace of the world. In the European system this power is now seldom attempted to be exercised without invoking a consultation or congress of nations. That system has not been extended to this continent. But there is even a greater necessity for prudence in such cases in regard to American States than in regard to the nations of Europe. * * * Seen in the light of this principle, the several nations of the earth constitute one great federal republic."

There spoke the informed conviction of a real statesman, and therein appear the immemorial practice of honorable governments.

Suppose that when we were at the threshold of our last domestic struggle, as soon as those disaffected had declared their scheme, Great Britain had decided that the dismembering purpose was already accomplished; and, when the second 24 hours was scarce more than half over, had accorded the revolted States the full prerogative of independent sovereignty. Our patriotic indignation would have known no bounds. Like jealous love it could not have been quenched by many waters nor drowned by floods. The flame of our anger would have "burned to the lowest hell." Life, fortune, sacred honor would have been freely cast into the sacrificial balance. Amazed resentment, "hors'd upon the sightless couriers of the air, would have blown the horrid deed in every eye."

The President naively refers to Panama's secession as but a "resuming of her independence." Such is the phrase in his telegram of recognition. In his message to Congress, of January 4, 1904, he says:

"A third possibility was that the people of the Isthmus who had formerly constituted an independent State, and who resently were united to Colombia only by a loose tie of federal relationship, might take the protection of their own vital interests into their own hands, reassert their former rights, and declare their independence on just grounds."

But in no proper sense of the term was Panama ever an "independent State;" nor was it by a "recent and loose tie of federal relationship" that Panama was united to Colombia. In 1840 the Provinces of Panama and Veragua seceded from New Granada; but so brief and futile as the separation that history simply records the departure and return. In 1857 Panama, availing herself of a new provision of the central constitution, assumed such quasi-independence as was consistent with a federal connection with the central Government—precisely that and not one whit more. Even that quasi-independence under a federal relationship lasted only four years. In 1863 Colombia became successor to New Granada, with Panama as an integral part of the new Government. From 1886 to 1903 the Province of Panama was as absolutely identified with Colombia as Massachusetts with the United States. Not at all the President's loose tie of federal relationship of comparatively recent origin, but a scarcely interrupted integral relationship of almost a half a century, and a final absolute identity of nearly a score of years.

To return, the President says:

"I have not denied, nor do I wish to deny, either the validity or the propriety of the general rule that a new State should not be recognized as independent till it has shown its ability to maintain its independence. * * * But, like the principle from which it is deduced, the rule is subject to exceptions; and there are, in my opinion, clear and important reasons why a departure from it was justified and even required in the present instance. These reasons embrace, first, our treaty rights; second, our national interests and safety; and, third, the interests of collective civilization."

Could there be a more decisive disclosure of the President's personality and development than his invocation of "exceptions to a principle"? Could there be a more significant revelation of his attainments in moral science? It had been taken for granted that a "principle," whether a law of nature or a standard of conduct, was fundamental, having continuous and uniform force, and that exceptions could exist in only the applications of the principle. For instance, veracity as a principle is "good faith between those within the bonds of good faith." In the relation of speech to fact there are said to be permissible variations. It is affirmed that speech need not conform to reality when one is conversing with the wholly insane or with those whose manifestly malign intent puts them beyond the pale of mutual obligation. Would the author of the Panama policy claim for himself not only exceptions in the practical modes of veracious speech, but also exceptions in the rule itself? In view of the President's acts and utterances as related to the Panama imbroglio of 1903, one might be at least half pardoned for so thinking. The clear terms, the induvitable intent, the time-honored interpretation of the treaty of 1846 he haughtily set aside, substituting therefor his egotistic sic volo, sic jubeo, stet pro ratione voluntas—"I took the Canal Zone."

But there is a second ardent appeal, and this time to our own "national interests and safety." That also is revelatory of the appellant. Was it perceived by others than the President, at 12.51 midday of November 6, 1903, that our national welfare, even to the verge of national peril, was hinged on the immediate construction of an Isthmian canal? According to the statistics of population and pro rata wealth, of production and trade, of education and religion, we were fairly prosperous and making commendable progress. We were at peace with all nations. Domestic insurrection was not apprehended. It was thought by some that we were already in need of the ancient admonition, "The pride of thine heart hath deceived thee, O thou that dwellest in the clefts of the rock, that holdest the height of the hill." During the years in which the successful digging of the canal has been going on, has it been generally fel that we were trembling in the world-power balance, timidly awaiting deliverence? When the canal is finally opened, will our national well-being be suddenly and completely assured? Yet the self-hypnotized Executive who ways, "I took the Canal Zone," "I am interested in the canal because I started it," asks us to condone his betrayal of a trustful ally, on the patriotic ground that our own national safety was at stake, and that there was no warrant for another instant's delay. National well-being is not thus secured. He who "has established His throne in the heavens and whose kingdom ruleth over all" acquits none who work iniquity and are unrepentant. The Persians have the proverb, "When even one wronged child cries in the dark, the throne of God rocks from side to side."

It remains that we consider the President's excuse of "a mandate of collective civilization." Herein the "mandatory" of progressive humanity rises far above mere patriotic zeal. He sees, as through the mists of apocalyptic vision, an indeterminate and indeterminable something which he calls "collective civilization." He appears to have been in such trance as befell the man of the land of Uz—

"Now a thing was secretly brought to me,
And mine ear received a whisper thereof;
Then a spirit passed before my face;
It stood still, but I could not discern
The appearance thereof."

It will ever be regretted that the user of the phrase "collective civilization" did not attempt to define it. Is it possible that he adumbrated the slow accretion of human betterments through political and social organization; the fair evolutions of art and literature; the consummate achievements of liberty under law; the infinitely precious fruitage of religious aspiration? May he have dimly seen the endless procession of those who had gone by the crimson path of martyrdom to receive earth's undying gratitude and heaven's unending acclaim? May he, by proleptic realization have felt what Wordsworth calls "incommunicable ecstacies" as he dreamed of the progress yet to be made, the felicities yet to be won? Let us endeavor thus to suppose. But even so, how could he think that from such high source there had come to him alone the mandate which conferred autocratic power? In what hour of rapt meditation did he hear the voice which bade him move unhestitatingly, unshrinkingly to the goal of his desire? In connection with what celestial sign did he read the words "In hoc signo vinces"? "Collective civilization," whatever it may mean, if issuing any kind of mandates, issues mandates utterly at variance with the self-will which "took" the Canal Zone while treaties gasped, and diplomacy stood bewildered, and international jurisprudence averted her astonished sight. It were a moral fatuity, on the very face of it, to imagine that the greatest good of the greatest number could possibly be subserved by flouting good faith and reckoning Providence as a co-conspirator against essential justice. Yet the self-appointed protagonist of imperial efficiency still declares:

"We did harm to no one, save as harm is done to a bandit by a policeman who deprives him of his chance for blackmail."

The verdict of history reads: "The policeman himself turned bandit. In the name of equity and under the guise of friendship he smote the innocent and plundered the defenseless."

He who hurried with "Tarquin's ravishing strides" to make irrevocable Colombia's dismemberment still argues that his "position as the mandatory of civilization" was fully recognized by the powers, as witness "the promptitude with which, one after another," they followed his lead "in recognizing Panama as an independent State." Therein he again takes to himself the sole responsibility, and therein he is in perfect accord with the facts. He adopted the child before it was born. He midwifed its birth. He certified, for what the certificate was worth, that the child was not a bastard. He safeguarded its puny, puling infancy. He lifted it, cradle and all, to the seats of the mighty. He gained for it world-wide recognition. Consequently he might not divest himself of responsibility, even though he would. But the powers, in following his lead, did not thereby approve his act. Their course was not only perfunctory, but also virtually compulsory. They could scarcely do aught else than "recognize" the new nation on whose political status the President of the United States had set his official, though tarnished, seal.

Finally, the restless, strenuous "doer of things," the seizer of the Canal Zone, asserts his worthiness of the unfading laurel. He triumphantly declares:

"The United States has many honorable chapters in its history, but no more honorable chapter than that which tells of the way in which the right to dig the Panama Canal was secured and of the manner in which the work itself has been carried out."

The raid on defenseless Colombia, in the interest of a swift indomitable construction of an Isthmian waterway, made to vie with the heroic settlement of a new continent, in the interest of civil and religious freedom. The "50-mile order" and its congener of the following day, foredooming a "guaranteed" ally to defeat by secession, ranked with the proclamation which gave freedom to enslaved millions. The coddled Panama "uprising," insured in advance, set in the illustrious category of Lexington and Bunker Hill, Valley Forge, and Yorktown. The recognition of a new sovereignty, after 1 day, 17 hours, and 41 minutes of pampered, flimsy independence, favorably compared with an independence which was won by years of ceaseless conflict and the sacrifice of treasures untold. Such a treacherous rending of one of their number as has awakened dismay and distrust in all southern republics put on a par with that reconstruction of a northern union which has heartened the friends of democracy in all parts of the world.

Is it possible that there should be condonation of the President's "taking" of the Canal Zone, because inwoven with the plottings of self-centered ambition there was the hastening of a national and international good? Therein is also is there "an exception to the principle" that right is right, sacred, and eternal? Is the end to sanctify the means? Then Ahab's rape of Naboth's vineyard was well, provided he took it for a public park. Then the rich man's seizure of the poor man's one ewe lamb was fair, if therewith he enlarged his feast for the hungry. Then Judas Iscariot may be acquitted with applause, if only he was a thief in order to pay his honest debts, and a traitor that he might quiet disturbance and strengthen "law and order" in the land.

Here let the chapter of national dishonor close its record. Let the final verdict be rendered as required by the law and the facts. Let the prime actor in that national dishonor take his place as determined by that same law and those same facts. Fiat justitia.

Meantime, the treatment of Colombia demands that "just and ample redress" of which Mr. Seward spoke. Our national honor was dragged in the mire. It ought to be rescued from its disgrace. With propriety we might repair to The Hague tribunal, humbly bespeaking such penalty as that high court might declare to be right. Until reparative action is somehow taken, the national reproach abides. Save as we, nationally, make the amende honorable, "great Neptune's ocean" will not remove the stain. The "damned spot" will still persist. There is grim satisfaction in the poet's words:

> "Yea, though we sinned and our rulers went from righteousness;
> Deep in all dishonor though we stained our garment's hem;
> Oh, be not dismayed,
> Though we stumbled and we strayed;
> We were led by evil counselors—the Lord shall deal with them."

Yet the satisfaction is mingled with pity for those same evil counselors, as we recall the inspired declaration:

"And in covetousness shall they with feigned words make merchandise of you; whose sentence now from of old lingereth not, and their destruction slumbereth not."

TREATY BETWEEN THE UNITED STATES OF AMERICA AND THE REPUBLIC OF NEW GRANADA.

[Concluded and signed at Bogota Dec. 12, 1846. Ratification advised by the Senate June 3, 1848. Ratified by the President of the United States June 10, 1848. Ratifications exchanged at Washington June 10, 1848. Proclaimed by the President of the United States June 12, 1848.]

A proclamation by the President of the United States of America.

Whereas a general treaty of peace, amity, navigation, and commerce between the United States of America and the Republic of New Granada, together with an additional article thereto, was concluded and signed at the city of Bogota by the plenipotentiaries of the two countries on the 12th day of December, 1846, which treaty and additional article are hereunto annexed.

And whereas the said treaty and additional article have been duly ratified on both parts, and the respective ratifications of the same were exchanged at Washington on the 10th day of June, 1848, by James Buchanan, Secretary of State of the United States of America, and Gen. Pedro Alcantara Herran, envoy extraordinary and minister plenipotentiary of the Republic of New Granada, on the part of their respective Governments:

Now, therefore, be it known that I, James K. Polk, President of the United States of America, have caused the said treaty and additional article to be made public, to the end that the same may be observed and fulfilled with good faith by the United States and the citizens thereof.

In testimony whereof I have hereunto set my hand and caused the seal of the United States to be affixed.

Done at the city of Washington this 12th day of June, in the year of our Lord 1848, and in the seventy-second year of the Independence of the United States.

[SEAL.] JAMES K. POLK.

By the President:
JAMES BUCHANAN,
Secretary of State.

A GENERAL TREATY OF PEACE, AMITY, NAVIGATION, AND COMMERCE BETWEEN THE UNITED STATES OF AMERICA AND THE REPUBLIC OF NEW GRANADA.

The United States of North America and the Republic of New Granada in South America, desiring to make lasting and firm the friendship and good understanding which happily exists between both nations, have resolved to fix in a manner clear, distinct, and positive the rules which shall in future be religiously observed between each other by means of a treaty or general convention of peace and friendship, commerce, and navigation.

For this desirable object the President of the United States of America has conferred full powers on Benjamin A. Bidlack, a citizen of the said States and their chargé d'affaires in Bogota, and the President of the Republic of New Granada has conferred similar and equal powers upon Manuel Maria Mallarino, secretary of state and foreign relations, who, after having exchanged their said full powers in due form, have agreed to the following articles:

ARTICLE I. There shall be a perfect, firm, and inviolable peace and sincere friendship between the United States of America and the Republic of New Granada in all the extent of their possessions and territories and between their citizens, respectively, without distinction of persons or places.

ART. II. The United States of America and the Republic of New Granada, desiring to live in peace and harmony with all the nations of the earth, by means of a policy frank and equally friendly with all, engage mutually not to grant any particular favor to other nations in respect of commerce and navigation which shall not immediately become common to the other party, who shall enjoy the same freely if the concession was freely made, or on allowing the same compensation if the concession was conditional.

ART. III. The two high contracting parties, being likewise desirous of placing the commerce and navigation of their respective countries on the liberal basis of perfect equality and reciprocity, mutually agree that the citizens of each may frequent all the coasts and countries of the other and reside and trade there in all kinds of produce, manufactures, and merchandise, and that they shall enjoy all the rights, privileges, and exemptions in navigation and commerce which the native citizens do or shall enjoy, submitting themselves to the laws, decrees, and usages there established to which native citizens are subjected. But it is understood that this article does not include the coasting trade of either country, the regulation of which is reserved by the parties, respectively, according to their own separate laws.

ART. IV. They likewise agree that whatever kind of produce, manufacture, or merchandise of any foreign country can be, from time to time, lawfully imported into the United States in their own vessels may be also imported in vessels of the Republic of New Granada; and that no higher or other duties upon the tonnage of the vessel and her cargo shall be levied and collected whether the importation be made in vessels of the one country or of the other. And in like manner that whatever kind of produce, manufactures, or merchandise of any foreign country can be from time to time lawfully imported into the Republic of New Granada in its own vessels may be also imported in vessels of the United States; and that no higher or other duties upon the tonnage of the vessel and her cargo shall be levied or collected whether the importation be made in vessels of the one country or the other.

And they further agree that whatever may be lawfully exported or reexported from the one country in its own vessels to any foreign country may in like manner be exported or reexported in the vessels of the other country. And the same bounties, duties, and drawbacks shall be allowed and collected whether such exportation or reexportation be made in vessels of the United States or of the Republic of New Granada.

ART. V. No higher or other duties shall be imposed on the importation into the United States of any articles the produce or manufacture of the Republic of New Granada and no higher or other duties shall be imposed on the importation into the Republic of New Granada of any articles the produce or manufactures of the United States than are or shall be payable on the like articles being the produce or manufactures of any other foreign country; nor shall any higher or other duties or charges be imposed in either of the two countries on the exportation of any articles to the United States or to the Republic of New Granada, respectively, than such as are payable on the exportation of the like articles to any other foreign country, nor shall any prohibition be imposed on the exportation or importation of any articles the produce or manufactures of the United States or of the Republic of New Granada to or from the territories of the United States or to or from the territories of the Republic of New Granada which shall not equally extend to all other nations.

ART. VI. In a order to prevent the possibility of any misunderstanding it is hereby declared that the stipulations contained in the three preceding articles are to their full extent applicable to the vessels of the United States and their cargoes arriving in the ports of New Granada and reciprocally to the vessels of the said Republic of New Granada and their cargoes arriving in the ports of the United States, whether they proceed from the ports of the country to which they respectively belong or from the ports of any other foreign country; and in either case no discriminating duty shall be imposed or collected in the ports of either country on said vessels or their cargoes whether the same shall be of native or foreign produce or manufacture.

ART. VII. It is likewise agreed that it shall be wholly free for all merchants, commanders of ships, and other citizens of both countries to manage, by themselves or agents, their own business in all the ports and places subject to the jurisdiction of each other, as well with respect to the consignments and sale of their goods and merchandise by wholesale or retail, as with respect to the loading, unloading, and sending off their ships, they being, in all these cases, to be treated as citizens of the country in which they reside, or at least to be placed on an equality with the subjects or citizens of the most-favored nation.

ART. VIII. The citizens of neither of the contracting parties shall be liable to any embargo, nor be detained with their vessels, cargoes, merchandise, or effects for any military expedition, nor for any public or private purpose whatever, without allowing to those interested an equitable and sufficient indemnification.

ART. IX. Whenever the citizens of either of the contracting parties shall be forced to seek refuge or asylum, in the rivers, bays, ports, or dominions of the other with their vessels, whether merchant or of war, public or private, through stress of weather, pursuit of pirates or enemies, or want of provisions or water, they shall be received and treated with humanity, giving to them all favor and protection for repairing their ships, procuring provisions, and placing themselves in a situation to continue their voyage, without obstacle or hindrance of any kind or the payment of port fees or any charges other than pilotage, except such vessels continue in port longer than 48 hours counting from the time they cast anchor in port.

ART. X. All the ships, merchandise, and effects belonging to the citizens of one of the contracting parties, which may be captured by pirates, whether within the limits of its jurisdiction or on the high seas, and may be carried or found in the rivers, roads, bays, ports, or dominions of the other, shall be delivered up to the owners, they proving in due and proper form their rights, before the competent tribunals; it being well understood that the claim shall be made within the term of one year by the parties themselves, their attorneys, or agents of their respective Governments.

ART. XI. When any vessel belonging to the citizens of either of the contracting parties shall be wrecked or foundered or shall suffer any damage on the coasts, or within the dominions of the other, there shall be given to them all assistance and protection, in the same manner which is usual and customary with the vessels of the nation where the damage happens; permitting them to unload the said vessel, if necessary, of its merchandise and effects, without exacting for it any duty, impost, or contribution whatever, unless they may be destined for consumption or sale in the country of the port where they may have been disembarked.

ART. XII. The citizens of each of the contracting parties shall have power to dispose of their personal goods or real estate within the jurisdiction of the other, by sale, donation, testament, or otherwise, and their representatives being citizens of the other party, shall succeed to their said personal goods or real estate, whether by testament of ab intestato, and they may take possession thereof, either by themselves or others acting for them, and dispose of the same at their will, paying such dues only as the inhabitants of the country, wherein said goods are, shall be subject to pay in like cases.

ART. XIII. Both contracting parties promise and engage formally to give their special protection to the persons and property of the citizens of each other, of all occupations, who may be in the territories subject to the jurisdiction of one or the other, transient or dwelling therein, leaving open and free to them the tribunals of justice for their judicial recourse, on the same terms which are usual and customary with the natives or citizens of the country; for which purpose they may either appear in proper person or employ in the prosecution or defense of their rights such advocates, solicitors, notaries, agents, and factors as they may judge proper in all their trials at law; and such citizens or agents shall have free opportunity to be present at the decisions or sentences of the tribunals, in all cases which may concern them, and likewise at the taking of all examinations and evidences which may be exhibited in the said trials.

ART. XIV. The citizens of the United States residing in the territories of the Republic of New Granada, shall enjoy the most perfect and entire security of conscience, without being annoyed, prevented, or disturbed on account of their religious belief. Neither shall they be annoyed, molested, or disturbed on the proper exercise of their religion in private houses or in the chapels or places of worship appointed for that purpose, provided that in so doing they observe the decorum due to divine worship, and the respect due to the laws, usages, and customs of the country. Liberty shall also be granted to bury the citizens of the United States who may die in the territories of the Republic of New Granada in convenient and adequate places to be appointed and established by themselves for that purposes, with the knowledge of the local authorities, or in such other places of sepuluture as may be chosen by the friends of the deceased; nor shall the funerals or sepulchers of the dead be disturbed in anywise nor upon any account.

In like manner the citizens of New Granada shall enjoy, within the Government and Territories of the United States, a perfect and unrestrained liberty of consequence and of exercising their religion, publicly or privately, within their own dwelling houses, or in the chapels and places of worship appointed for that purpose, agreeably to the laws, usages, and customs of the United States.

ART. XV. It shall be lawful for the citizens of the United States of America and of the Republic of New Granada to sail with their ships, with all manner of liberty and security, no distinction being made who are the proprietors of the merchandise laden thereon, from any port to the places of those who now are or hereafter shall be at enmity with either of the contracting parties. It shall likewise be lawful for the citizens aforesaid to sail with the ships and merchandise before mentioned and to trade with the same liberty and security from the places, ports, and havens of those who are enemies of both or either party, without any opposition or disturbance whatsoever, not only directly from the places of the enemy before mentioned to neutral places, but also from one place belonging to an enemy to another place belonging to an enemy, whether they be under the jurisdiction of one power or under several. And it is hereby stipulated that free ships shall also give freedom to goods, and that every thing which shall be found on board the ships belonging to the citizens of either of the contracting parties, shall be deemed to be free and exempt, although the whole lading or any part thereof should appertain to the enemies of either (contraband goods being always excepted). It is also agreed in like manner, that the same liberty shall be extended to persons who are on board a free ship, with this effect, that although they be enemies to both or either party, they are not to be taken out of that free ship, unless they are officers and soldiers, and in the actual service of the enemies; provided, however, and it is hereby agreed; that the stipulations in this article contained, declaring that the flag shall cover the property, shall be understood as applying to those powers only, who recognize this principle, but if either of the two contracting parties shall be at war with a third, and the other remains neutral, the flag of the neutral shall cover the property of enemies whose Government acknowledge this principle and not of others.

ART. XVI. It is likewise agreed that in the case where the neutral flag of one of the contracting parties shall protect the property of the enemies of the other, by virtue of the above stipulation, it shall always be understood that the neutral property found on board such enemy's vessels shall be held and considered as enemy's property, and as such shall be liable to detention and confiscation, except such property as was put on board such vessel before the declaration of war, or even afterwards, if it were done without the knowledge of it; but the contracting parties agree that two months having elapsed after the declaration of war, their citizens shall not plead ignorance thereof. On the contrary, if the flag of the neutral does not protect the enemy's property, in that case, the goods and merchandise of the neutral embarked on such enemy's ship shall be free.

Art. XVII. This liberty of navigation and commerce shall extend to all kinds of merchandise, excepting those only which are distinguished by the name of contraband; and under this name of contraband, or prohibted goods, shall be comprehended.

First. Cannons, mortars, howitzers, swivels, blunderbusses, muskets, rifles, carbines, pistols, pikes, swords, sabers, lances, spears, halberts; and grenades, bombs, powder, matches, balls, and all other things belonging to the use of these arms.

Second. Bucklers, helmets, breastplates, coats of mail, infantry belts, and clothes made up in the form and for the military use.

Third. Cavalry belts, and horses with their furniture.

Fourth. And generally all kinds of arms and instruments of iron, steel, brass, and copper, or of any other materials manufactured, prepared and formed, expressly to make war by sea or land.

Fifth. Provisions that are imported into a besieged or blockaded place.

Art. XVIII. All other merchandise, and things not comprehended in the articles of contraband, explicitly enumerated and classified as above, shall be held and considered as free, and subjects of free and lawful commerce, so that they may be carried and transported in the freest manner by the citizens of both the contracting parties, even to places belonging to an enemy, excepting those places only which are at that time besieged or blockaded; and to avoid all doubt in this particular it is declared that those places only are besieged or blockaded which are actually attacked by a belligerent force capable of preventing the entry of the neutral.

Art. XIX. The articles of contraband, before enumerated and classified, which may be found in a vessel bound for an enemy's port, shall be subject to detention and confiscation, leaving free the rest of the cargo and the ship, that the owners may dispose of them as they see proper. No vessel of either of the two nations shall be detained on the high seas on account of having on board articles of contraband, whenever the master, captain, or supercargo of said vessels will deliver up the articles of contraband to the captor, unless the quantity of such articles be so great and of so large a bulk that they can not be received on board the capturing ship without great inconvenience; but in this and all other cases of just detention the vessel detained shall be sent to the nearest convenient and safe port for trial and judgment according to law.

Art. XX. And whereas it frequently happens that vessels sail for a port or place belonging to an enemy without knowing that the same is besieged or blockaded or invested, it is agreed that every vessel so circumstanced may be turned away from such port or place, but shall not be detained, nor shall any part of her cargo, if not contraband, be confiscated, unless after warning of such blockade or investment, from the commanding officer of the blockading forces, she shall again attempt to enter; but she shall be permitted to go to any other port or place she shall think proper. Nor shall any vessel that may have entered into such port before the same was actually besieged, blockaded, or invested by the other be restrained from quitting that place with her cargo, nor if found therein, after the reduction and surrender, shall such vessel or her cargo be liable to confiscation, but they shall be restored to the owners thereof.

Art. XXI. In order to prevent all kinds of disorder in the visiting and examination of the ships and cargoes of both the contracting parties on the high seas, they have agreed mutually that whenever a national vessel of war, public or private, shall meet with a neutral of the other contracting party, the first shall remain out of cannon shot, unless in stress of weather, and may send its boat with two or three men only, in order to execute the said examination of the papers concerning the ownership and cargo of the vessel, without causing the least extortion, violence, or ill treatment, for which the commanders of said armed ships shall be responsible with their persons and property; for which purpose the commanders of private armed vessels shall, before receiving their commissions, give sufficient security to answer for all the damages they may commit. And it is expressly agreed that the neutral party shall in no case be required to go on board the examining vessel for the purpose of exhibiting her papers or for any other purpose whatever.

Art. XXII. To avoid all kind of vexation and abuse in the examination of the papers relating to the ownership of the vessels belonging to the citizens of the two contracting parties, they have agreed, and do hereby agree, that in case one of them should be engaged in war, the ships and vessels belonging to the citizens of the other must be furnished with sea letters or passports, expressing the name, property, and bulk of the ship, as also the name and place of habitation of the master and commander of the said vessel, in order that it may thereby appear that the ship really and truly belongs to the citizens of one of the parties; they have likewise agreed that when such ships have a cargo they shall also be provided, besides the said sea letters or passports, with certificates containing the several particulars of the cargo and the place whence the ship sailed, so that it may be known whether any forbidden or contraband goods are on board the same, which certificates shall be made out by the officers of the place whence the ship sailed in the accustomed form, without which requisites said vessel may be detained, to be adjudged by the competent tribunal, and may be declared lawful prize unless the said defect shall be proved to be owing to accident, and shall be satisfied or supplied by testimony entirely equivalent.

ART. XXIII. It is further agreed that the stipulations above expressed relative to the visiting and examination of vessels shall apply only to those which sail without convoy, and when said vessels shall be under convoy the verbal declaration of the commander of the convoy, on his word of honor, that the vessels under his protection belong to the nation whose flag he carries, and, when they may be bound to an enemy's port, that they have no contraband goods on board, shall be sufficient.

ART. XXIV. It is further agreed that in all cases the established courts for prize causes in the country to which the prizes may be conducted shall alone take cognizance of them. And whenever such tribunals of either party shall pronounce judgment against any vessel or goods or property claimed by the citizens of the other party the sentence or decree shall mention the reasons or motives upon which the same shall have been founded, and an authenticated copy of the sentence or decree and of all the proceedings in the case, shall, if demanded, be delivered to the commander or agent of said vessel without any delay, he paying the legal fees for the same.

ART. XXV. For the purpose of lessening the evils of war, the two high contracting parties further agree that in case a war should unfortunately take place between them, hostilities shall only be carried on by persons duly commissioned by the Government, and by those under their orders, except in repelling an attack or invasion, and in the defense of property.

ART. XXVI. Whenever one of the contracting parties shall be engaged in war with another State, no citizen of the other contracting party shall accept a commission or letter of marque for the purpose of assisting or cooperating hostilely with the said enemy against the said parties so at war under the pain of being treated as a pirate.

ART. XXVII. If by any fatality which can not be expected, and God forbid, the two contracting parties should be engaged in a war with each other, they have agreed and do agree now for then, that there shall be allowed the term of six months to the merchants residing on the coasts and in the ports of each other, and the term of one year to those who dwell in the interior, to arrange their business and transport their effects wherever they please, giving to them the safe conduct necessary for it, which may serve as a sufficient protection until they arrive at the designated port. The citizens of all other occupations, who may be established in the territories or dominions of the United States or of New Granada, shall be respected, and maintained in the full enjoyment of their personal liberty and property, unless their particular conduct shall cause them to forfeit this protection which, in consideration of humanity, the contracting parties engage to give them.

ART. XXVIII. Neither the debts due from individuals of the one nation to the individuals of the other, nor shares, nor money which they may have in public funds, nor in public or private banks, shall ever in any event of war or of national difference be sequestered or confiscated.

ART. XXIX. Both the contracting parties, being desirous of avoiding all inequality in relation to their public communications and official intercourse, have agreed and do agree to grant to the envoys, ministers, and other public agents the same favors, immunities, and exemptions which those of the most-favored nations do or shall enjoy, it being understood that whatever favors, immunities, or privileges the United States of America or the Republic of New Granada may find it proper to give to the ministers and public agents of any other power shall, by the same act, be extended to those of each of the contracting parties.

ART. XXX. To make more effectual the protection which the United States and the Republic of New Grenada shall afford in future to the navigation and commerce of the citizens of each other, they agree to receive and admit consuls and vice consuls in all the ports open to foreign commerce, who shall enjoy in them all the rights, prerogatives, and immunities of the consuls and vice consuls of the most favored nation, each contracting party, however, remaining at liberty to except those ports and places in which the admission and residence of such consuls may not seem convenient.

ART. XXXI. In order that the consuls and vice consuls of the two contracting parties may enjoy the rights, prerogatives, and immunities which belong to them by their public character, they shall, before entering on the exercise of their functions, exhibit their commission, or patent, in due form, to the Government to which they are accredited, and having obtained their exequatur, they shall be held and considered as such by all the authorities, magistrates, and inhabitants in the consular district in which they reside.

Art. XXXII. It is likewise agreed that the consuls, their secretaries, officers, and persons attached to the service of consuls, they not being citizens of the country in which the consul resides, shall be exempt from all public service, and also from all kind of taxes, imposts, and contributions, except those which they shall be obliged to pay on account of commerce or their property, to which the citizens and inhabitants, native and foreign, of the country in which they reside are subject, being in everything besides subject to the laws of the respective States. The archives and papers of the consulates shall be respected inviolably, and under no pretext whatever shall any magistrate seize or in any way interfere with them.

Art. XXXIII. The said consuls shall have power to require the assistance of the authorities of the country for the arrest, detention, and custody of deserters from the public and private vessels of their country, and for that purpose they shall address themselves to the courts, judges, and officers competent, and shall demand in writing the said deserters, proving by an exhibition of the registers of the vessel's or ship's roll, or other public documents, that those men were part of the said crews; and on this demand so proved (saving, however, where the contrary is proved by other testimonies) the delivery shall not be refused. Such deserters, when arrested, shall be put at the disposal of the said consuls, and may be put in the public prisons, at the request and expense of those who reclaim them, to be sent to the ships to which they belonged, or to others of the same nation. But if they be not sent back within two months, to be counted from the day of their arrest, they shall be set at liberty, and shall be no more arrested for the same cause.

Art. XXXIV. For the purpose of more effectually protecting their commerce and navigation, the two contracting parties do hereby agree to form as soon hereafter as circumstances will permit a consular convention, which shall declare specially the powers and immunities of the consuls and vice consuls of the respective parties.

Art. XXXV. The United States of America and the Republic of New Grenada, desiring to make as durable as possible the relations which are to be established between the two parties by virtue of this treaty, have declared solemnly and do agree to the following points:

First. For the better understanding of the preceding articles, it is and has been stipulated between the high contracting parties that the citizens, vessels, and merchandise of the United States shall enjoy in the ports of New Granada, including those of the part of the Granadian territory generally denominated Isthmus of Panama, from its southernmost extremity until the boundary of Costa Rica, all the exemptions, privileges, and immunities concerning commerce and navigation which are now, or may hereafter be, enjoyed by Granadian citizens, their vessels and merchandise; and that this equality of favors shall be made to extend to the passengers, correspondence, and merchandise of the United States in their transit across the said territory from one sea to the other. The Government of New Granada guarantees to the Government of the United States that the right of way or transit across the Isthmus of Panama, upon any modes of communication that now exist or that may be hereafter constructed, shall be open and free to the Government and citizens of the United States, and for the transportation of any articles of produce, manufactures, or merchandise of lawful commerce belonging to the citizens of the United States; that no other tolls or charges shall be levied or collected upon the citizens of the United States, or their said merchandise thus passing over any road or canal that may be made by the Government of New Granada, or by the authority of the same, than is under like circumstances levied upon and collected from the Granadian citizens: that any lawful produce, manufactures, or merchandise belonging to citizens of the United States thus passing from one sea to the other, in either direction, for the purpose of exportation to any other foreign country shall not be liable to any import duties whatever, or having paid such duties they shall be entitled to drawback upon their exportation; nor shall the citizens of the United States be liable to any duties, tolls, or charges of any kind to which native citizens are not subjected for thus passing the said Isthmus. And in order to secure to themselves the tranquil and constant enjoyment of these advantages, and as an especial compensation for the said advantages and for the favors they have acquired by the fourth, fifth, and sixth articles of this treaty, the United States guarantee positively and efficaciously to New Granada, by the present stipulation, the perfect neutrality of the beforementioned Isthmus, with the view that the free transit from the one to the other sea may not be interrupted or embarrassed in any future time while this treaty exists; and in consequence the United States also guarantee, in the same manner, the rights of sovereignty and property which New Granada has and possesses over the said territory.

Second. The present treaty shall remain in full force and vigor for the term of 20 years from the day of the exchange of the ratifications; and, from the same day, the treaty that was concluded between the United States and Colombia on the 3d of October, 1824, shall cease to have effect, notwithstanding what was disposed in the first point of its thirty-first article.

Third. Notwithstanding the foregoing, if neither party notifies to the other its intention of reforming any of or all the articles of this treaty 12 months before the expiration of the 20 years stipulated above, the said treaty shall continue binding on both parties, beyond the said 20 years, until 12 months from the time that one of the parties notifies its intention of proceeding to a reform.

Fourth. If any one or more of the citizens of either party shall infringe any of the articles of this trenty, such citizens shall be held personally responsible for the same, and the harmony and good correspondence between the nations shall not be interrupted thereby; each party engaging in no way to protect the offender or sanction such violation.

Fifth. If unfortunately any of the articles contained in this treaty should be violated or infringed in any way whatever, it is expressly stipulated that neither of the two contracting parties shall ordain or authorize any acts of reprisal, nor shall declare war against the other on complaints of injuries or damages, until the said party considering itself offended shall have laid before the other a statement of such injuries or damages, verified by competent proofs, demanding justice and satisfaction, and the same shall have been denied, in violation of the laws and of international right.

Sixth. Any special or remarkable advantage that one or the other power may enjoy, from the foregoing stipulation, are and ought to be always understood in virtue and as in compensation of the obligations they have just contracted and which have been specified in the first number of this article.

Art. XXXVI. The present treaty of peace, amity, commerce, and navigation shall be approved and ratified by the President of the United States, by and with the advice and consent of the Senate thereof, and by the President of the Republic of New Granada, with the consent and approbation of the Congress of the same; and the ratifications shall be exchanged in the city of Washington within 18 months from the date of the signature thereof, or sooner, if possible.

In faith whereof we, the plenipotentiaries of the United States of America and of the Republic of New Granada, have signed and sealed these presents in the city of Bogota on the 12th day of December, in the year of our Lord 1846.

B. A. Bidlack. [seal.]
M. M. Mallarino. [seal.]

Additional article. The Republics of the United States and of New Granada will hold and admit as national ships of one or the other all those that shall be provided by the respective Government with a patent issued according to its laws.

The present additional article shall have the same force and validity as if it were inserted, word for word, in the treaty signed this day. It shall be ratified, and the ratifications shall be exchanged at the same time.

In witness whereof the respective plenipotentiaries have signed the same and have affixed thereto their seals.

Done in the city of Bogota the 12th day of December, in the year of our Lord 1846.

B. A. Bidlack. [seal.]
M. M. Mallarino. [seal.]

Convention Between the United States and the Republic of Panama for the Construction of a Ship Canal to Connect the Waters of the Atlantic and Pacific Oceans.

[Signed at Washington, Nov. 18, 1903. Ratification advised by the Senate, Feb. 23, 1904. Ratified by the President, Feb. 25, 1904. Ratified by Panama, Dec. 2, 1903. Ratifications exchanged at Washington, Feb. 26, 1904. Proclaimed, Feb. 26, 1904.]

A proclamation by the President of the United States of America.

Whereas a convention between the United States of America and the Republic of Panama to insure the construction of a ship canal across the Isthmus of Panama to connect the Atlantic and Pacific Oceans was concluded and signed by their respective plenipotentiaries at Washington, on the 18th day of November, 1903, the original of which convention, being in the English language, is, word for word, as follows:

ISTHMIAN CANAL CONVENTION.

The United States of America and the Republic of Panama, being desirous to insure the construction of a ship canal across the Isthmus of Panama to connect the Atlantic and Pacific Oceans, and the Congress of the United States of America having passed an act, approved June 28, 1902, in furtherance of that object, by which the President of the United States is authorized to acquire within a reasonable time the control of the necessary territory of the Republic of Colombia, and the sovereignty of such territory being actually vested in the Republic of Panama, the high contracting parties have resolved for that purpose to conclude a convention and have accordingly appointed as their plenipotentiaries—

The President of the United States of America, John Hay, Secretary of State, and the Government of the Republic of Panama, Philippe Bunau-Varilla, envoy extraordinary and minister plenipotentiary of the Republic of Panama, thereunto specially empowered by said Government, who after communicating with each other their respective full powers, found to be in good and due form, have agreed upon and concluded the following articles:

ARTICLE I. The United States guarantees and will miantain the independence of the Republic of Panama.

ART. II. The Republic of Panama grants to the United States in perpetuity the use, occupation, and control of a zone of land and land under water for the construction, maintenance, operation, sanitation, and protection of said canal of the width of 10 miles, extending to the distance of 5 miles on each side of the center line of the route of the canal to be constructed; the said zone beginning in the Carribean Sea 3 marine miles from mean low-water mark and extending to and across the Isthmus of Panama into the Pacific Ocean to a distance of 3 marine miles from mean low-water mark; with the proviso that the cities of Panama and Colon and the harbors adjacent to said cities, which are included within the boundaries of the zone above described, shall not be included within this grant. The Republic of Panama further grants to the United States in perpetuity the use, occupation, and control of any other lands and waters outside of the zone above described which may be necessary and convenient for the construction, maintenance, operation, sanitation, and protection of the said canal or of any auxiliary canals or other works necessary and convenient for the construction, maintenance, operation, sanitation, and protection of the said enterprise.

The Republic of Panama further grants, in like manner, to the United States in perpetuity all islands within the limits of the zone above described, and in addition thereto the group of small islands in the Bay of Panama, named Perico, Naos, Culebra, and Flamenco.

ART. III. The Republic of Panama grants to the United States all the rights, power, and authority within the zone mentioned and described in Article II of this agreement and within the limits of all auxiliary lands and waters mentioned and described in said Article II which the United States would possess and exercise if it were the sovereign of the territory within which said lands and waters are located, to the entire exclusion of the exercise by the Republic of Panama of any such sovereign rights, power, or authority.

ART IV. As rights subsidiary to the above grants, the Republic of Panama grants in perpetuity to the United States the right to use the rivers, streams, lakes, and other bodies of water within its limits for navigation, the supply of water or water power or other purposes, so far as the use of said rivers, streams, lakes, and bodies of water and the waters thereof may be necessary and convenient for the construction, maintenance, operation, sanitation, and protection of the said canal.

ART. V. The Republic of Panama grants to the United States in perpetuity a monopoly for the construction, maintenance, and operation of any system of communication by means of canal or railroad across its territory between the Caribbean Sea and the Pacific Ocean.

ART. VI. The grants herein contained shall in no manner invalidate the titles or rights of private landholders or owners of private property in the said zone, or in or to any of the lands or waters granted to the United States by the provisions of any article of this treaty, nor shall they interfere with the rights of way over the public roads passing through the said zone or over any of the said lands or waters, unless said rights of way or private rights shall conflict with rights herein granted to the United States; in which case the rights of the United States shall be superior. All damages caused to the owners of private lands or private property of any kind by reason of the grants contained in this treaty, or by reason of the operations of the United States, its agents, or employees, or by reason of the construction, maintenance, operation, sanitation, and protection of the said canal, or of the works of sanitation and protection herein provided for, shall be appraised and settled by a joint commission appointed by the Governments of the United States and the Republic of Panama, whose decisions as to such damages shall be final, and whose awards as to such damages shall be paid solely by the United States. No part of the work on said canal or the Panama Railroad, or on any auxiliary works relating thereto and authorized by the terms of this treaty, shall be prevented, delayed, or impeded by or pending such proceedings to ascertain such damages. The apprisal of said private lands and private property and the assessment of damages to them shall be based upon their value before the date of this convention.

ART. VII. The Republic of Panama grants to the United States within the limits of the cities of Panama and Colon and their adjacent harbors and within the territory adjacent thereto the right to acquire by purchase, or by the exercise of the right of eminent domain, any lands, buildings, water rights, or other properties necessary and convenient for the construction, maintenance, operation, and protection of the canal and of any works of sanitation, such as the collection and disposition of sewage and the distribution of water in the said cities of Panama and Colon, which, in the discretion of the United States, may be necessary and convenient for the construction, maintenance, operation, sanitation, and protection of the said canal and railroad. All such works of sanitation, collection, and disposition of sewage and distribution of water in the cities of Panama and Colon shall be made at the expense of the United States, and the Government of the United States, its agents, or nominees shall be authorized to impose and collect water rates and sewerage rates which shall be sufficient to provide for the payment of interest and the amortization of the principal of the cost of said works within a period of 50 years; and upon the expiration of said term of 50 years the system of sewers and waterworks shall revert to and become the properties of the cities of Panama and Colon, respectively, and the use of the water shall be free to the inhabitants of Panama and Colon, except to the extent that water rates may be necessary for the operation and maintenance of said system of sewers and water.

The Republic of Panama agrees that the cities of Panama and Colon shall comply in perpetuity with the sanitary ordinances, whether of a preventive or curative character, prescribed by the United States; and in case the Government of Panama is unable or fails in its duty to enforce this compliance by the cities of Panama and Colon with the sanitary ordinances of the United States, the Republic of Panama grants to the United States the right and authority to enforce the same.

The same right and authority are granted to the United States for the maintenance of public order in the cities of Panama and Colon and the territories and harbors adjacent thereto in case the Republic of Panama should not be, in the judgment of the United States, able to maintain such order.

ART. VIII. The Republic of Panama grants to the United States all rights which it now has or hereafter may acquire to the property of the New Panama Canal Co. and the Panama Railroad Co., as a result of the transfer of sovereignty from the Republic of Colombia to the Republic of Panama over the Isthmus of Panama, and authorizes the New Panama Canal Co. to sell and transfer to the United States its rights, privileges, properties, and concessions, as well as the Panama Railroad and all the shares or part of the shares of that company; but the public lands situated outside of the zone described in Article II of this treaty, now included in the concessions to both said enterprises and not required in the construction or operation of the canal, shall revert to the Republic of Panama, except any property now owned by or in the possession of said companies within Panama or Colon or the ports or terminals thereof.

ART. IX. The United States agrees that the ports at either entrance of the canal and the waters thereof, and the Republic of Panama agrees that the towns of Panama and Colon, shall be free for all time, so that there shall not be imposed or collected customhouse tolls, tonnage, anchorage, lighthouse, wharf, pilot, of quarantine dues or any other charges or taxes of any kind upon any vessel using or passing through the canal or belonging to or employed by the United States, directly or indirectly, in connection with the construction, maintenance, operation, sanitation, and protection of the main canal or auxiliary works, or upon the cargo, officers, crew, or passengers of any such vessels, except such tolls and charges as may be imposed by the United States for the use of the canal and other works, and except tolls and charges imposed by the Republic of Panama upon merchandise destined to be introduced for the consumption of the rest of the Republic of Panama, and upon vessels touching at the ports of Colon and Panama and which do not cross the canal.

The Government of the Republic of Panama shall have the right to establish in such ports and in the towns of Panama and Colon such houses and guards as it may deem necessary to collect duties on importations destined to other portions of Panama and to prevent contraband trade. The United States shall have the right to make use of the towns and harbors of Panama and Colon as places of anchorage and for making repairs, for loading, unloading, depositing, or transshipping cargoes either in transit or destined for the service of the canal and for other works pertaining to the canal.

ART. X. The Republic of Panama agrees that there shall not be imposed any taxes, national, municipal, departmental, or of any other class, upon the canal, the railways, and auxiliary works, tugs, and other vessels employed in the service of the canal, storehouses, workshops, offices, quarters for laborers, factories of all kinds, warehouses, wharves, machinery, and other works, property, and effects appertaining to the canal or railroad and auxiliary works, or their officers or employees, situated within the cities of Panama and Colon, and that there shall not be imposed contributions or charges of a personal character of any kind upon officers, employees, laborers, and other individuals in the service of the canal and railroad and auxiliary works.

ART. XI. The United States agrees that the official dispatches of the Government of the Republic of Panama shall be transmitted over any telegraph and telephone lines established fo rcanal purposes, and used for public and private business, at rates not higher than those required from officials in the service of the United States.

ART. XII. The Government of the Republic of Panama shall permit the immigration and free access to the lands and workshops of the canal and its auxiliary works of all employees and workmen of whatever nationality under contract to work upon or seeking employment upon or in anywise connected with the said canal and its auxiliary works, with their respective families, and all such persons shall be free and exempt from the military service of the Republic of Panama.

ART. XIII. The United States may import at any time into the said zone and auxiliary lands, free of customs duties, imposts, taxes, or other charges, and without any restrictions, any and all vessels, dredges, engines, cars, machinery, tools, explosives, materials, supplies, and other articles necessary and convenient in the construction, maintenance, operation, sanitation, and protection of the canal and auxiliary works, and all provisions, medicines clothing, supplies, and other things necessary and convenient for the officers, employees, workmen, and laborers in the service and employ of the United States, and for their families. If any such articles are disposed of for use outside of the zone and auxiliary lands granted to the United States and within the territory of the Republic they shall be subject to the same import or other duties as like articles imported under the laws of the Republic of Panama.

ART. XIV. As the price or compensation for the rights, powers, and privileges granted in this convention by the Republic of Panama to the United States, the Government of the United States agrees to pay to the Republic of Panama the sum of $10,000,000 in gold coin of the United States on the exchange of the ratification of this convention, and also an annual payment during the life of this convention of $250,000 in like gold coin, beginning nine years after the date aforesaid.

The provisions of this article shall be in addition to all other benefits assured to the Republic of Panama under this convention.

But no delay or difference of opinion under this article or any other provisions of this treaty shall affect or interrupt the full operation and effect of this convention in all other respects.

ART. XV. The joint commission referred to in Article VI shall be established as follows:

The President of the United States shall nominate two persons, and the President of the Republic of Panama shall nominate two persons, and they shall proceed to a decision; but in case of disagreement of the commission (by reason of their being equally divided in conclusion) an umpire shall be appointed by the two Governments who shall render the decision. In the event of the death, absence, or incapacity of a commissioner or umpire, or of his omitting, declining, or ceasing to act, his place shall be filled by the appointment of another person in the manner above indicated. All decisions by a majority of the commission or by the umpire shall be final.

ART. XVI. The two Governments shall make adequate provision by future agreement for the pursuit, capture, imprisonment, detention, and delivery within said zone and auxiliary lands to the authorities of the Republic of Panama of persons charged with the commitment of crimes, felonies, or misdemeanors without said zone and for the pursuit, capture, imprisonment, detention, and delivery without said zone to the authorities of the United States of persons charged with the commitment of crimes, felonies, and misdemeanors within said zone and auxiliary lands.

ART. XVII. The Republic of Panama grants to the United States the use of all the ports of the Republic open to commerce as places of refuge for any vessels employed in the canal enterprise, and for all vessels passing or bound to pass through the canal which may be in distress and be driven to seek refuge in said ports. Such vessels shall be exempt from anchorage and tonnage dues on the part of the Republic of Panama.

ART. XVIII. The canal, when constructed, and the entrances thereto shall be neutral in perpetuity, and shall be opened upon the terms provided for by section 1 of Article III of, and in conformity with all the stipulations of, the treaty entered into by the Governments of the United States and Great Britain on November 18, 1901.

ART. XIX. The Government of the Republic of Panama shall have the right to transport over the canal its vessels and its troops and munitions of war in such vessels at all times without paying charges of any kind. The exemption is to be extended to the auxiliary railway for the transportation of persons in the service of the Republic of Panama, or of the police force charged with the preservation of public order outside of said zone, as well as to their baggage, munitions of war, and supplies.

ART. XX. If by virtue of any existing treaty in relation to the territory of the Isthmus of Panama, whereof the obligations shall descend or be assumed by the Republic of Panama, there may be any privilege or concession in favor of the Government or the citizens and subjects of a third power relative to an interoceanic means of communication which in any of its terms may be incompatible with the terms of the present convention, the Republic of Panama agrees to cancel or modify such treaty in due form, for which purpose it shall give to the said third power the requisite notification within the term of four months from the date of the present convention, and in case the existing treaty contains no clause permitting its modifications or annulment, the Republic of Panama agrees to procure its modification or annulment in such form that there shall not exist any conflict with the stipulations of the present convention.

ART. XXI. The rights and privileges granted by the Republic of Panama to the United States in the preceding articles are understood to be free of all anterior debts, liens, trusts, or liabilities, or concessions, or privileges to other Governments, corporations, syndicates, or individuals, and consequently, if there should arise any claims on account of the present concessions and privileges or otherwise, the claimants shall resort to the Government of the Republic of Panama and not to the United States for any indemnity or compromise which may be required.

ART. XXII. The Republic of Panama renounces and grants to the United States the participation to which it might be entitled in the future earnings of the canal under Article XV of the concessionary contract with Lucien N. B. Wyse now owned by the New Panama Canal Co., and any and all other rights or claims of a pecuniary nature arising under or relating to said concession, or arising under or relating to the concessions to the Panama Railroad Co., or any extension or modification thereof; and it likewise renounces, confirms, and grants to the United States, now and hereafter, all the rights and property reserved in the said concessions which otherwise would belong to Panama at or before the expiration of the term of 99 years of the concessions granted to or held by the above-mentioned party and companies, and all right, title, and interest which it now has, or may hereafter have, in and to the lands, canal, works, property, and rights held by the said companies under said concessions or otherwise, and acquired or to be acquired by the United States from or through the New Panama Canal Co., including any property and rights which might or may in the future either by lapse of time, forfeiture, or otherwise, revert to the Republic of Panama under any contracts or concessions, with said Wyse, the Universal Panama Canal Co., the Panama Railroad Co., and the New Panama Canal Co.

The aforesaid rights and property shall be and are free and released from any present or reversionary interest in or claims of Panama, and the title of the United States thereto upon consummation of the contemplated purchase by the United States from the New Panama Canal Co. shall be absolute, so far as concerns the Republic of Panama, excepting always the rights of the Republic specifically secured under this treaty.

ART. XXIII. If it should become necessary at any time to employ armed forces for the safety or protection of the canal, or of the ships that make use of the same, or the railways and auxiliary works, the United States shall have the right, at all times and in its discretion, to use its police and its land and naval forces or to establish fortifications for these purposes.

ART. XXIV. No change either in the Government or in the laws and treaties of the Republic of Panama shall, without the consent of the United States, affect any right of the United States under the present convention or under any treaty stipulation between the two countries that now exists or may hereafter exist touching the subject matter of this convention.

If the Republic of Panama shall hereafter enter as a constituent into any other Government or into any union or confederation of States, so as to merge her sovereignty or independence in such Government, union, or confederation, the rights of the United States under this convention shall not be in any respect lessened or impaired.

ART. XXV. For the better performance of the engagements of this convention and to the end of the efficient protection of the canal and the preservation of its neutrality, the Government of the Republic of Panama will sell or lease to the United States lands adequate and necessary for naval or coaling stations on the Pacific coast and on the western Caribbean coast of the Republic at certain points to be agreed upon with the President of the United States.

ART. XXVI. This convention when signed by the plenipotentiaries of the contracting parties shall be ratified by the respective Governments and the ratifications shall be exchanged at Washington at the earliest date possible.

In faith whereof the respective plenipotentiaries have signed the present convention in duplicate and have hereunto affixed their respective seals.

Done at the city of Washington the 18th day of November in the year of our Lord 1903.

JOHN HAY. [SEAL.]
P. BUNAU VARILLA. [SEAL.]

And whereas the said convention has been duly ratified on both parts, and the ratifications of the two Governments were exchanged in the city of Washington, on the 26th day of February, 1904;

Now, therefore, be it known that I, Theodore Roosevelt, President of the United States of America, have caused the said convention to be made public, to the end that the same and every article and clause thereof may be observed and fulfilled with good faith by the United States and the citizens thereof.

In testimony whereof I have hereunto set my hand and caused the seal of the United States of America to be affixed.

Done at the city of Washington this 26th day of February, in the year of our Lord 1904, and of the independence of the United States the one hundred and twenty-eighth.

[SEAL.] THEODORE ROOSEVELT.

By the President:
JOHN HAY,
Secretary of State.

LEGACIÓN DE LA REPÚBLICA DE
PANAMÁ EN WASHINGTON,
Washington, D. C., February 18, 1904.

His Excellency JOHN HAY,
Secretary of State, etc., Washington, D. C.

SIR: I have the honor of acknowledging the receipt of your communication, No. 23, of January 30, 1904, in which you express to me certain observations about the translation of the treaty of November 18, 1903, contained in the decree ratifying the treaty.

I accept in the name of the Government of the Republic what you propose in said letter, which reads as follows:

"SIR: I have the honor to acknowledge the receipt of your note of the 9th instant transmitting a copy of the decree ratifying the treaty of November 18, 1903, and containing its text in the Spanish language.

"In reply to your request to be notified 'in case the translation is in every respect satisfactory,' I have the honor to invite your attention to a few omissions, as follows:

"1. In Article VIII, line 4, of page 6 of the translation, the words 'á la República de Panamá,' after 'traspaso de soberanía de la República de Colombia,' should be added.

"2. In the same article, last line of the article, the word 'ó' should be inserted between 'puertos' and 'terminales.'

"3. In Article IX, last line but two in the second paragraph of the article on page 7, the words 'cargar, descargar, almacenar y,' omitted from the English text, should come before the words 'trasbordar cargas.'

"In Article XXII, page 11, line 2 of the last paragraph, the words 'present or' in the English text have been omitted, and should be represented by the words 'ó actuales' placed in the Spanish text after the words 'derechos de reversión.'

"In regard to the exact equivalence of words in both languages, I have to indicate the following changes which appear to be necessary:

"1. In Article VII, line 2 of page 5, the word 'puertos' should be used instead of 'bahías' for the English word 'harbors.'

"2. In Article IX, line 4 of the article, page 6 of the copy submitted by you, the words 'customhouse tolls' have been rendered into 'derechos de aduana,' which are understood to mean duties collected on merchandise entered for actual consumption in the country. It is believed that the word 'peajes' would be preferable.

"3. In Article XIII, line 2 of page 8, the English word 'lands' has been translated 'obras,' for which 'terrenos' should obviously be substituted.

"There are a number of other words the accurate meaning of which may give rise to a difference of interpretation, but inasmuch as there could be no other difficulty in connection with the said words, and in view of the fact that the Spanish text has already been formally approved by your Government, the necessity of making further changes therein will be obviated by your official statement that the English text shall prevail in case of such difference of interpretation.

"Accept, Mr. Minister, the renewed assurances of my highest consideration.

"FRANCIS B. LOOMIS,
"*Acting Secretary*."

I am, sir, with great respect, your very obedient servant,

P. BUNAU VARILLA.

THE STORY OF PANAMA.

No. 2.

HEARINGS ON THE RAINEY RESOLUTION BEFORE THE COMMITTEE ON FOREIGN AFFAIRS OF THE HOUSE OF REPRESENTATIVES.

FEBRUARY 9 AND 12, 1912.

THE STORY OF PANAMA.

STATEMENT BY MR. HENRY N. HALL, A STAFF CORRESPONDENT OF THE NEW YORK WORLD.

The CHAIRMAN. The committee will be glad to hear from Mr. Hall.

Mr. HALL. Before I begin the presentation of the facts in their chronological order I wish to show the committee photographs of the two documents of which Mr. Rainey has just spoken.

Photographs of letter written by Dr. Amador to his son, dated October 18, 1903, and note from Dr. Amador to H. G. Prescott, Colon, dated November 7, 1903, are shown to the committee. The following is an exact transcript of these documents, and a translation of the Spanish letter:

. OBRE. 18/903.

QUERIDO HIJITO: Recibo tu telegrama que no vienes por que te habian negado el permiso.

Tambien recibo to carta del 17. La corona si no llega la mandadan del Endicott por el prox. vapor.

El objeto de que vinieras era por que vieras a Bunau-Varilla a quien he hablado de ti. Dice que si todo sale bien, tendras un buen puesto en la Comision Medica que es la primera que iniciara los trabajos, que mi nombre esta en la oficina de Hay y que seguro nada le negaran para ti.

El plan me parece bueno. Se declara independiente una porcion del Istmo al cual no permiten los E. U. llegar fuerzas de Col. a atacarnos. Se convoca una asamblea y esta da facultades a un ministro que nombra el Nuevo Gobierno para que haga un tratado sin necessidad de ulterior aprovacion de esa asamblea.

Aprobado el tratado por ambas partes ya queda la nueva Rep. protegida por los E. U. y se agregaran los demas pueblos del Istmo que no estaban formando parte de esa Rep. y que quedan tambien bajo la protec. de E. U.

El movimiento demorara unos dias, queremos tener aqui el Ministro que va a nombrarse para que hecho el movimiento, se le nombre por cable y se ocupe del tratado. En 30 dias todo quedara concluido.

Tenemos algunos recursos al hacerse el movimiento, y ya esta todo arreglado con un banco.

Apenas este todo arreglado dire a B. V. que se ocupe de ti. Dice que si no quieres ir el buscara un destino aqui en N. Y. Es hombre de gran influencia.

Mil abrazos a Pope y mis recuerdos a Jennie y Mr. Smith.

Tuaffpadre, AMADOR.

Te dejo dos encomienditas donde Annie. No van por que no hay objeto en que to las vuelvas a traer.

A. DIOS.

NEW YORK, *October 18, 1903.*

DEAR LITTLE SON: I received your telegram that you are not coming, as they have refused you permission.

Also received your letter of the 17th. If the wreathe does not come they will send it from the Endicott by the next steamer.

The reason for your coming was for you to meet Bunau-Varilla, to whom I have spoken of you. He says that if all turns out well you will have a good place on the medical commission, which is the first that will begin work; that my name is in Hay's office and that certainly nothing will be refused you.

The plan seems to me good. A portion of the Isthmus declares itself independent and that portion the United States will not allow any Colombian forces to attack. An Assembly is called and this gives authority to a minister to be appointed by the new Government in order to make a treaty without need of ratification by that Assembly. The treaty being approved by both parties, the new Republic remains under the protection of the United States, and to it are added the other districts of the Isthmus which do not already form part of the new Republic, and these also remain under the protection of the United States.

The movement will be delayed a few days; we want to have here the new minister who is going to be named, so that once the movement is made he can be appointed by cable and take up the treaty. In thirty days everything will be concluded.

We have some resources on the movement being made, and already this has been arranged with a bank.

As soon as everything is arranged I will tell B. V. to look out for you. He says if you do not wish to go he will look out for a position for you in New York. He is a man of great influence.

A thousand embraces to Pepe, and my remembrances to Jennie and Mr. Smith.

Your affectionate father, AMADOR.

NOVEMBER 7, 1903.

H. G. PRESCOTT,
Colon.

The chief conspirator congratulate (sic) his first aid-de-camp for the manner that he behaved during the conspiration. (sic)

DR. AMADOR.

Mr. KENDALL. I presume the originals of these documents will be produced?

Mr. HALL. They form a part of the court records in the case of the United States *v.* The Press Publishing Co. (the New York World).

Mr. KENDALL. They are exhibits produced on that trial?

Mr. HALL. Yes, sir; before the rogatory commission sitting in Panama. I will read the evidence bearing on these documents.

[Circuit Court of the United States, Southern District of New York. The United States *v.* The Press Publishing Co. Before Judge Hector Valdes; Gregorio Conte, secretary.]

PANAMA, REPUBLIC OF PANAMA,
June 11, 1909.

There appeared before the second judge of the circuit Mr. H. G. Prescott, summoned as a witness to give testimony according to the examination which is to be made by Mr. Fuller, attorney for the defendant, and Mr. Knapp, attorney for the United States, in accordance with letters rogatory issued to the Republic of Panama under an order of this court on the 25th day of May, 1909. It is stipulated that all objections are reserved to be made at the time of the trial, except as to the form of question, it being understood that no objections to form shall be made at the trial.

H. G. PRESCOTT, a witness on behalf of the defendant, having been duly sworn to tell the truth, the whole truth, and nothing but the truth, testified as follows:

By Mr. FULLER:

Q. Did you ever receive a communication after the revolution from any prominent member thereof?—A. Yes; I received several.

Q. Did you ever receive one from Dr. Amador?—A. Yes.

Q. Is that the communication?—A. Yes; that is his own handwriting.

Q. And signed by him?—A. Yes, sir.

It is hereby stipulated that the following is a true copy of the original:

NOVEMBER 7, 1903.

H. G. PRESCOTT, *Colon:*

The chief conspirator congratulate his chief aid-de-camp for the manner he behaved during the conspiration.

DR. AMADOR.

And further:

Q. You are familiar with the handwriting of Dr. Amador, I believe you told me?—A. I am.

Q. Will you please look at this paper and see if it is in his handwriting and his signature thereto.—A. Yes; that looks like his handwriting. I know his signature. Yes; that is his signature.

Q. And is the letter in his handwriting?—A. Yes; I should say it was.

Mr. FULLER. I should like this marked for identification No. 5.

And again, in the same proceeding, on June 16, 1909:

Dr. RAOUL A. AMADOR, a witness on behalf of the defendant, having been duly sworn to tell the truth, the whole truth, and nothing but the truth, testified as follows:

By Mr. FULLER:

Q. What was your father's name?—A. Manuel Amador Guerrero.

Q. Was he the first president of the Republic of Panama?—A. To my knowledge he was.

Q. Was he the same Dr. Amador who was influential in promoting the revolution?—A. He was.

Q. Where were you during the months of September, October, and November, 1903?—A. I was in the neighborhod of Boston, Massachusetts. I was serving as a surgeon in the United States Army at Fort Revere.

Q. Did you receive any letters from your father while he was in New York?—A. Yes; I received several letters from him.

Q. Did you receive a letter from him on or about the 18th of October, 1903?—A. I did.

Q. Was that letter from New York?—A. From New York.

Q. And received by you at Fort Revere?—A. Fort Revere.

Q. You are familiar with your father's handwriting; you have seen him write?—A. Yes.

Q. Is that the letter that your father wrote you? [Mr. Fuller hands paper to witness.]—A. Yes, sir.

Mr. FULLER. I now offer in evidence the paper handed to witness, which is Exhibit No. 5, for identification, and which was identified by Mr. H. G. Prescott as being written by Dr. Amador.

It is hereby stipulated that the following is a true photograph of the original Spanish and a true copy of its English translation:

(Here follow in the court record the photograph shown the committee, and the English translation which Mr. Rainey read to the committee.)

Further down in his examination of Dr. Amador Mr. Fuller asked:

"Q. Now, do you know what man your father meant by 'Hay'?—A. Yes.

"Q. Who was it?—A. It was Mr. John Hay, the Secretary of State.

"Q. Of the United States?—A. Yes, sir."

Mr. KENDALL. Before you proceed with your statement let me ask if there was a transcript made of the testimony adduced on the trial of that case?

Mr. HALL. Yes, sir.

Mr. KENDALL. And certified by the stenographer?

Mr. HALL. Oh, yes.

Mr. KENDALL. You have that?

Mr. HALL. Oh, yes.

Mr. KENDALL. All right.

Mr. FLOOD. Let me ask, What is this case from which you are about to read a part of the record?

Mr. HALL. The case of the United States *v.* The Press Publishing Co., the corporation which publishes the New York World. I have only read that part of Mr. Prescott's testimony which is relevant to these documents.

Mr. FLOOD. What relation do you bear to this inquiry?

Mr. HALL. I am a staff correspondent of the New York World.

Mr. FLOOD. You are here representing the New York World?

Mr. HALL. Yes, sir; I am here at the request of the chairman of this committee to produce the evidence we have in this matter.

Mr. KENDALL. What are you now proposing to read from?

Mr. HALL. For my own convenience merely I have here a copy that I had made of the court proceedings in the case of the United States *v.* Press Publishing Co.

Mr. KENDALL. You are proposing to read from a digest of the court proceedings in that case?

Mr. HALL. No; it is not a digest but a copy of a certain portion of the proceedings bearing on this particular point, bearing upon these documents.

Mr. KENDALL. It is a collation of the record?

Mr. HALL. You might so term it. For my own convenience in presenting this matter to you with as little waste of time as possible I have had made a copy of this particular evidence.

Mr. SHARP. But, as I understand you, it is an exact copy of the stenographer's transcript of proceedings had in the case of the United States *v.* The Press Publishing Co.?

Mr. HALL. Yes, sir.

Mr. FLOOD. It is an exact copy of the stenographer's transcript so far as that particular evidence is concerned, the copy having been made for the purpose of convenience in presenting the matter to this committee?

Mr. HALL. That is it exactly.

Mr. KENDALL. I think you should make clear in the record of our hearing at what pages of the stenographer's transcript of the proceedings in the case of the United States *v.* The Press Publishing Co. we might find the evidence referred to.

Mr. HALL. I shall be very glad to do so. Here is the stenographer's transcript in the case of the United States *v.* The Press Publishing Co. [holding up a record so that members of committee may see it]. The examination of Mr. H. G. Prescott may be found, beginning on page 204 of the stenographer's transcript, and the examination of Mr. Amador may be found, beginning on page 262 of the same record.

Mr. CLINE. That record is properly certified?

Mr. HALL. I do not know whether it is regularly certified or not, but I understand such a certified record is in the office of counsel for The Press Publishing Co. in this case—Messrs. Nicoll, Annable, Lindsay & Fuller, New York City.

Mr. GOODWIN. As I understand you, Mr. Hall, the complete record in the case of the United States *v.* The Press Publishing Co. is quite voluminous, but you are only proposing now to read to this committee that part of the record pertaining to the letter and telegram?

Mr. HALL. That is all I have done. But I now propose to give the committee a history of the events leading up to what took place on the Isthmus of Panama.

Mr. GARNER. You are simply undertaking to read from a portion of that court record in order to identify and conclusively show that these are true copies of the original papers passing between the parties referred to?

Mr. HALL. Yes, sir.

Mr. GARNER. And later on you may use the record to prove other facts that Mr. Rainey has alleged?

Mr. HALL. Most certainly.

Mr. KENDALL. It seems to me there ought not to be the slightest difficulty about identifying these papers. If they were introduced in court in the case of the United States *v.* The Press Publishing Co., they should show on their face that fact; and the transcript should bear upon its face the certificate of the official court reporter who made it.

Mr. FLOOD. Mr. Hall said he did not have the certificate.

Mr. HALL. I do not know that such certificate appears upon this copy of the record.

Mr. KENDALL. I think that is a very essential thing to have. This is not a statement, but testimony. Of course, if it is to be allowed the dignity of testimony, it ought to be authentic.

Mr. TOWNSEND. I hink there is going to be a great deal of unnecessary delay if we proceed upon the assumption that we are sitting here as a court, which, of course, we are not. We are sitting here as investigators. That question was thrashed out in the first Lorimer case; they were assuming that they were sitting as a court, and consequently had to have another investigation. As we are sitting here as investigators, I think it perfectly fair for us to assume that Mr. Hall is giving us an honest reading from an accurate transcript of the testimony. If such is not the case, it may be easily demonstrated, and, of course, if such were shown to be a fact, Mr. Rainey and Mr. Hall would be discredited. If Brother Kendall will permit me to say so, I think we are unnecessarily consuming time that might be occupied in listening to the presentation of this evidence. Both of these gentlemen may be sent to jail if they are not presenting the matter in the manner they claim to be presenting it.

Mr. KENDALL. It would be an interesting thing to know how they might be sent to jail. We will have a new principle of jurisprudence put in effect here if Mr. Townsend can maintain that position.

The CHAIRMAN. I think the committee will make progress in the matter if we let Mr. Hall present the case in his own way, and then when he finishes, if we want to take up anything, or prove anything, or get more light on anything that we think Mr. Hall has not submitted sufficient proof upon, it may be done.

Mr. TOWNSEND. This interests me enormously, and it seems to me that the hearer may get a better impression of the whole matter if the story is presented without interruption and in the manner in which the gentleman has prepared himself to present it.

Mr. KENDALL. I wish to say that I also am deeply interested, but here is a question that involves John Hay, who is dead, and Senator Hanna, who is dead, and Dr. Amador, whom I have heard here is dead, and I think before we go too far listening to charges against these men we ought to have proof in some authentic way, and especially ought that to be true in a case like this, where there is not the slightest difficulty in producing it.

Mr. HALL. If the committee so desires, I will send a telegram to New York and get a certified copy here to-morrow morning from the Press Publishing Co.'s attorneys. That may be done without the slightest difficulty.

Mr. KENDALL. The official court stenographer who took down that testimony in shorthand and had it transcribed on the typewriter is the man to give a certificate as to the accuracy of the record.

Mr. HALL. Our attorneys in the case of the United States *v.* The Press Publishing Co., Messrs. Nicoll, Annable, Lindsay & Fuller, have a certified copy of the record.

Mr. GOODWIN. I suggest that if there is going to be any question about having a certified copy of the record in the case of the United States *v.* The Press Publishing Co. from which to read before this committee, that the committee now adjourn until to-morrow morning, and in the meantime let Mr. Hall get a certified copy of the proceedings in that case here.

Mr. FOSTER. As I understand this hearing, it is just a preliminary proceeding to see whether there may be produced enough evidence to warrant this committee in going ahead and making an investigation. We do not need to delay on technicalities.

Mr. KENDALL. If it is a technicality, the committee can afterwards override it.

Mr. FOSTER. Well, I did not mean a technicality exactly. But if they can produce a certified copy of the transcript of proceedings in the case of the United States *v.* The Press Publishing Co. when we come to an investigation, if it is the sense of the committee that such an investigation should be made, we can go ahead.

Mr. FLOOD. Mr. Hall, I take it, will be in a position to do that. What is this record which you now have, Mr. Hall?

Mr. HALL. This was given to me by the World's attorneys. It is a carbon copy of the record in their possession which record is certified.

Mr. KENDALL. This is a copy furnished to the attorneys for the New York World by the official court reporter, is it not?

Mr. HALL. Yes, sir; this is a copy made by the official reporter.

Mr. KENDALL. In our country the official reporter always attaches a certificate to the record, but I do not know whether that is customary in New York City or not.

Mr. GARNER. All of the original papers presented in the case of the United States *v.* The Press Publishing Co. are either in court or in the hands of the attorneys?

Mr. HALL. Some of them are here.

Mr. GARNER. Mr. Chairman, Mr. Hall purports to offer a copy. The point made by Mr. Foster and others is that this present hearing being merely a preliminary matter to determine whether or not the committee will recommend an investigation, we might take this copy as being correct for the time being, and if the committee sees fit to recommend an investigation, of course then the committee may formulate some rules for the introduction of testimony for the purpose of getting at the particular facts.

The CHAIRMAN. I think that the easiest way to get along and make progress. Mr. Hall, you may now proceed in your own way.

Mr. HALL. Gentlemen, I have here the evidence gathered by the New York World for its defense in the case of the United States *v.* The Press Publishing Co.

When Mr. Rainey introduced his resolution (H. Res. 32), as he has told you, he asked the World to show him this evidence. We did so. This evidence proves, and proves most conclusively:

First. That Mr. Roosevelt and some members of his administration were cognizant of and gave their support to the preparations being made for the Panama revolution;

Second. That the steps taken by Mr. Roosevelt to prevent Columbia from maintaining her sovereignty over the Isthmus of Panama and to prevent the landing of troops within the State of Panama and the suppression of the fake rebellion were in violation of the treaty of 1846–48; and

Third. That the acts of Mr. Roosevelt in respect to the creation and recognition of the Republic of Panama were in violation, not only of the treaty obligations of the United States, but of fundamental principles of international law, which have been and are recognized by the United States as binding upon nations in their dealings with one another.

In the Compilation of Treaties in Force, prepared in 1904 under the direction of the Senate Committee on Foreign Relations, in compliance with the Senate resolution of February 11, 1904, and which—

before it was finally sent to the Public Printer was submitted by the chairman of the committee to the Secretary of State, and was examined by the State Department with a view to excluding agreements and parts of agreements in whatever form which are regarded as no longer operative, and including all that are so—

You will find, under the heading Colombia, on page 194, the text of the treaty of peace, amity, navigation, and commerce referred to by Mr. Rainey in his address, the treaty of 1846–1848, concluded on December 12, 1846, and finally proclaimed June 12, 1848. At the top of page 205 you will find in Article XXXV, section 1, the stipulation that the United States "guarantee the rights of sovereignty and property which New Granada (now Colombia) has and possesses over the Isthmus of Panama"; and if you turn to page 607 of the same official publication, under the heading Panama, you will find in Article I of the treaty of 1904 that the United States also "guarantees and will maintain the independence of the Republic of Panama" over this same territory.

Here are two public treaties, both of which are in force, whereby the United States is pledged to opposite and entirely irreconcilable things.

Mr. Legare. Will you read that article about the Republic of Panama again?

Mr. Hall. Article I of the treaty of 1904 reads: "The United States guarantees and will maintain the independence of the Republic of Panama."

Mr. Goodwin. In that treaty of 1846–1848 that you referred to, as I recall Article XXVII, what is provided?

Mr. Hall. It provides as follows:

Article XXVII. If by any fatality which can not be expected, and God forbid, the two contracting parties should be engaged in a war with each other, they have agreed and do agree now for then, that there shall be allowed the term of six months to the merchants residing on the coast and in the ports of each other, and the term of one year to those who dwell in the interior, to arrange their business and transport their effects wherever they please, giving to them the safe conduct necessary for it which may as a sufficient protection until they arrive at the designated port. The citizens of all other occupations, who may be established in the territories or dominions of the United States or of New Granada, shall be respected and maintained in the full enjoyment of their personal liberty and property, unless their particular conduct shall cause them to forfeit this protection, which in consideration of humanity the contracting parties engage to give them.

Mr. GOODWIN. That is a pretty solemn compact, is it not?

Mr. HALL. It is very solemn, but perhaps not quite so conclusive as Article XXXV, which I hope to read to you in a few minutes.

With your permission I shall retrace from these papers and documents the events which took place between the negotiations of the treaty with New Granada in 1846, and the ratification of the treaty with Panama in 1904; and in so doing I shall endeavor to avoid all reference to matters which are not germane to the legal question embodied in Mr. Rainey's resolution. Gentlemen, what became of the $40,000,000 paid by the United States for the property and archives of the New Panama Canal Co., or of the $10,000,000 paid to the Republic of Panama; whether there was or was not a syndicate of Americans interested in the sale of the Panama Canal to the United States and who the members of that syndicate were; how the infant Republic of Panama has been protected or exploited by those responsible for its creation—are all matters which I conceive to be foreign to the purely legal and international questions covered by Mr. Rainey's resolution, and I shall, therefore, make no reference to them.

Now, in 1846 there were——

Mr. SHARP. I asked this question of Congressman Rainey when he was here before us, and he made substantially the same reply as was contained in your statement just now. For my own information, I would like to ask why there is any disposition to fight shy of the other phase of this question just mentioned by you. It seems to me that has considerable bearing upon the motives that led to the so-called intrigue.

Mr. GOODWIN. Do you not think that rather fundamental?

Mr. SHARP. I think it would have some bearing upon the motives we are to pass upon in considering this resolution (H. Res. 32).

Mr. HALL. As I read Mr. Rainey's resolution—well, I will just read it:

Whereas a former President of the United States has declared that he "took" Panama from the Republic of Colombia without consulting Congress; and

Whereas the Republic of Colombia has ever since petitioned this country to submit to The Hague Tribunal the legal and equitable question whether such taking was in accordance with or in violation of the treaty then existing between the two countries, and also whether such taking was in accordance with or in violation of the well-established principles of the law of nations; and

Whereas the Government of the United States professes its desire to submit all international controversies to arbitration, and has conducted treaties with many other nations agreeing to submit all legal questions to arbitration, but has steadily refused arbitration to the Republic of Colombia: Therefore be it

Resolved, That the Committee on Foreign Affairs of the House of Representatives be, and the same hereby is, directed to inquire into the same; send for books, papers, and documents; summon witnesses, take testimony, and report the same, with its opinion and conclusions thereon, to this House, with all convenient speed.

Now, I am here in obedience to the request of the committee to give you anything you wish, but had thought I would best serve the committee and save it valuable time if I confine myself purely to the legal and international aspect of this question, so that the committee may be able to decide, without considering any of these extraneous matters, whether or not this is a matter that the House of Representatives should investigate by a special committee or should refer to you for investigation, or that they should endeavor to send to The Hague for arbitration. I wanted to put it on the highest possible plane. As far as I am prepared here at this time, I will say that I have merely brought those documents from among the number which the New York World collected for its defense which seemed to me to bear directly upon Mr. Rainey's resolution. The investigation will be almost interminable if we try to follow out the various ramifications, though a great deal will come out, I have no doubt, and will be bound to come out in the discussion of the actions of Mr. William Nelson Cromwell, general counsel for the Panama Railroad Co. and the New Panama Canal Co. In preparing the presentation of this matter I have endeavored to put it on as high a plane as possible and to leave aside matters which would prompt some people to think that the New York World is appearing here in the rôle of prosecutor and wishes to stir up a scandal. Nothing could possibly be further from the intention of that newspaper, and this is evidenced by the fact that after the case of The United States *v.* The Press Publishing Co. was decided in favor of the defendant the New York World, both by the United States circuit court and the Supreme Court of the United States, it kept all this evidence that had been gathered for its defense and never attempted to make capital out of it, and has never published any of it in its news columns. I am particularly anxious it shall not appear in any way, shape, or form that the New York World is here as a prosecutor. We are here at the request of Mr. Rainey, the author of the resolution, and of Mr. Sulzer, the chairman of the committee, to show you the evidence we collected so far as it bears upon Mr. Rainey's resolution and in order that you may form your opinion as to what is the right solution to give to this delicate matter.

Mr. FLOOD. If the committee later on should want to go into other phases of this subject, we can have you before us again?

Mr. HALL. Certainly; especially if the committee decides that there should be a thorough and searching investigation into all phases of this matter and the House of Representatives votes such an investigation. In that event, I will come and answer any question that may be propounded to me about matters of which I have knowledge.

Mr. DIFENDERFER. You have put yourself in a position to give this committee a prima facie case?

Mr. HALL. Yes; I think so. There is a complete chain of evidence that binds this country, from the negotiations for the treaty of 1846 to the ratification of the treaty of 1904. I want to take this question up link by link with the committee. As we go along this chain of evidence some links will be found dull with the dust of diplomatic documents, others hard as the iron of self-interest, others again shine with the pure gold of patriotism or glitter with rare gems of intellect, some are grotesque, while not a few are covered with the slime of shame; but you can only arrive at the truth by taking up this evidence link by link and going right through to the end. I am anxious to do this so as to save the time of the committee and arrive at a result.

Mr. FLOOD. I suggest that you just proceed as you have prepared yourself.

Mr. GARNER. Mr. Hall, as I understand, it is your preference and request that the committee permit you to resume and continue with your presentation of the issue, and after you have concluded you will answer any questions?

Mr. HALL. I shall be entirely ready to answer any question any member of the committee may ask; and if, as I go along, I should be so unfortunate as not to make myself perfectly clear, I shall be glad to answer any questions propounded to me with a view of eliciting fuller information on the subject.

The CHAIRMAN. With that understanding, Mr. Hall, you may proceed and present the case in your own way.

Mr. HALL. All right, gentlemen. To begin at the beginning: In 1846 there were no transcontinental railroads, and communication between the United States and its possessions on the northwest coast of America was extremely difficult and dangerous. The trip across the continent took 8 or 9 months; 4 or 5 months were required for the sea voyage around the Horn; and the anger of the sea was scarce less to be feared than the scalp-hunting Indians of the plains. The only practical way of reaching the Pacific Ocean was over the Isthmus of Panama—as you will recall, at that time the War with Mexico was in progress and there was great interest in California—and, on the Isthmus of Panama, the Republic of New Granada levied, and had levied for more than 20 years, differential duties which made trans-Isthmian travel all but prohibitive under ordinary circumstances. For more than 20 years the United States had tried to obtain the abolition of these differential dues, but without success.

Benjamin A. Bidlack was then the American chargé d'affaires in Bogota and, although he had no specific instructions from his Government as to the compensation he might offer, he was urging upon New Granada to make a treaty of commerce and navigation which would enable the citizens of the United States to pass freely over the Isthmus. At that time England was casting wistful and longing glances toward the most mercantile spot on earth. From her colony of British Honduras she had extended her influence down the Mosquito coast, farther south even than Cape Gracias a Dios. She claimed the right of extraterritoriality for her flag up the thousands of miles of the mighty rivers of South America—the La Plata, the Amazon, the Orinoco. Colombia feared that if England once sent her ships up the Atrato she would close in upon the Isthmus, and so New Granada turned for protection to the great Republic of the North.

After considerable negotiation the Granadian secretary of state, Señor Mallarino, on December 10, 1846, sent to Mr. Bidlack a confidential note setting out the advantages that would accrue to the United States and the favored position in which it would find itself with regard to England if, in turn for the abolition of the differential dues and a guaranty of free transit across the Isthmus of Panama in perpetuity, it guaranteed the sovereignty and rights of property of New Granada across the Isthmus.

Mr. Bidlack, acting on his own responsibility, signed the treaty with New Granada on December 12, 1846, subject to the approval and ratification of the President of the United States, by and with the advice and consent of the Senate thereof.

I will not take up much of your time with this treaty of 1846 except to read to you from Article XXXV, the preamble of which is a very solemn one. I will read it first:

The United States of North America and the Republic of New Granada in South America, desiring to make lasting and firm the friendship and good understanding which happily exists between both nations, have resolved to fix in a manner clear, distinct, and positive the rules which shall in future be religiously observed between each other by means of a treaty or general convention of peace and friendship, commerce, and navigation.

Article XXXV reads as follows:

The United States of America and the Republic of New Granada, desiring to make as durable as possible the relations which are to be established between the two parties by virtue of this treaty, have declared solemnly and do agree to the following points:

First. For the better understanding of the preceding articles it is and has been stipulated between the high contracting parties that the citizens, vessels, and merchandise of the United States shall enjoy in the ports of New Granada, including those of that part of the Granadian Territory generally denominated Isthmus of Panama, from its southernmost extremity until the boundary of Costa Rica, all the exemptions, privileges, and immunities concerning commerce and navigation which are now or may hereafter be enjoyed by Granadian citizens, their vessels and merchandise; and that this equality of favors shall be made to extend to the passengers, correspondence, and merchandise of the United States in their transit across the said territory from one sea to the other.

I call your attention to the words "Isthmus of Panama" as mentioned in this article, because you will find later on, in the Panama Railroad contract of 1850 and the Panama Ralroad contract of 1867, and the Salger-Wyse contract, which was the basis of the New Panama Canal Co.'s concession of 1878, that the Isthmus of Panama is well defined, as anyone who may look at the map can see it should be defined, and that its southernmost boundary is a line from Cape Tiburon to Point Garachine; on one side of that line is the Isthmus of Panama and on the other side the Continent of South America.

I shall be able to show you that in the year 1903, at a time when the United States was at peace with the Republic of Colombia and when the United States had no treaty with the Republic of Panama, President Roosevelt, without any authority from Congress, sent a large force of American marines and sailors, with artillery, into the Continent of South America. He did not merely occupy the Isthmus of Panama to protect the line of the Panama Railroad, but he invaded the Continent of South America. Article XXXV continues:

The Government of New Granada guarantees to the Government of the United States that the right of way or transit across the Isthmus of Panama upon any modes of communication that now exist or that may be hereafer constructed shall be open and free to the Government and citizens of the United States and for the transportation of any articles of produce manufactured or merchandise of lawful commerce belonging to the citizens of the United States; that no other tolls or charges shall be levied or collected upon the citizens of the United States or their said merchandise thus passing over any road or canal that may be made by the Government of New Granada, or by the authority of the same, than is under like circumstances levied upon and collected from Granadian citizens; that any lawful produce, manufactures, or merchandise belonging to citizens of the United States thus passing from one sea to the other, in either direction, for the purpose of exportation to any foreign country shall not be liable to any import duties whatever, or, having paid such duties, they shall be entitled to drawback upon their exportation; nor shall the citizens of the United States be liable to any duties, tolls, or charges of any kind to which native citizens are not subjected for thus passing the said Isthmus. And in order to secure to themselves the tranquil and constant enjoyment of these advantages, and as a special compensation for the said advantages and for the favors they have acquired by the fourth, fifth, and sixth articles of this treaty, the United States guarantees positively and efficaciously to New Granada by the present stipulation the perfect neutrality of the before-mentioned Isthmus, with the view that the free transit from the one to the other sea may not be interrupted or embarrassed in any future time while this treaty exists; and, in consequence, the United States also guarantees, in the same manner, the rights of sovereignty and property which New Granada has and possesses over the said territory.

In paragraph 4 of this same article (XXXV) a peculiar stipulation was entered into. Mr. Bidlack knew well the unsettled conditions which prevailed in the Provinces of South American countries, where police protection is not perhaps always sufficient to meet and control conditions, and he insisted upon the insertion of this clause:

Fourth. If any one or more of the citizens of either party shall infringe any of the articles of this treaty, such citizens shall be held personally responsible for the same and the harmony and good correspondence between the Nations shall not be interrupted thereby, each party engaging in no way to protect the offender or sanction such violation.

It was under that article of the treaty of 1846 that in the year 1885 President Cleveland sent a force from the United States down to Colon to maintain transit, as he was obliged to do under this treaty, and three Colombians who had violated the provisions of the treaty were hanged.

Section 5 of this article (XXXV) provides—and this is of importance to this committee because, although it does not in terms so stipulate, yet it does provide for arbitration:

Fifth. If, unfortunately, any of the articles contained in this treaty should be violated or infringed in any way whatever, it is expressly stipulated that neither of the two contracting parties shall ordain or authorize any acts of reprisal nor shall declare war against the other on complaints of injuries or damages until the said party considering herself offended shall have laid before the other a statement of such injuries or damages, verified by competent proofs, demanding justice and satisfaction, and the same shall have been denied, in violation of the laws and of international right.

And, lastly, paragraph 6 of Article XXXV provides that this treaty is not one of those entangling foreign alliances against which George Washington warned his countrymen, but was a common contract:

Sixth. Any special or remarkable advantage that one or the other power may enjoy from the foregoing stipulations are and ought to be always understood in virtue and as in compensation of the obligations they have just contracted and which have been specified in the first number of this article.

President Polk, in transmitting this treaty to the Senate for ratification, sent with it a message in which he said:

It will be perceived by the thirty-fifth article of this treaty that New Granada proposes to guarantee to the Government and citizens of the United States the right of passage across the Isthmus of Panama, or by the natural roads, and over any canal or railroad which may be constructed to unite the two seas, on condition that the United States shall make a similar guaranty to New Granada of the neutrality of this portion of her territory and her sovereignty over the same.

The reasons which caused the insertion of this important stipulation in the treaty will be fully made known to the Senate by the accompanying documents. From these it will appear that our chargé d'affaires acted, in this particular, upon his own responsibility and without instruction. Under such circumstances it became my duty to decide whether I would submit the treaty to the Senate; and, after mature consideration, I have determined to adopt this course.

The importance of this concession to the commercial and political interests of the United States can not easily be overrated. The route by the Isthmus of Panama is the shortest between the two oceans; and, from the information herewith communicated, it would seem to be the most practical route for a railroad or canal.

The vast advantages to our commerce which would result from such a communication, not only with the west coast of America, but with Asia and the islands of the Pacific, are too obvious to require any detail. Such a passage would relieve us from a long and dangerous navigation of more than 9,000 miles around Cape Horn, and render our communication with our own possessions on the northwest coast of America comparatively easy and speedy.

* * * * * * *

No person can be more deeply sensible than myself of the danger of entangling alliances with any foreign nation. That we should avoid such alliances has become a maxim of our policy, consecrated by the most venerated names which adorn our history, and sanctioned by the unanimous voice of the American people.

* * * * * * *

The guarantee of the sovereignty of New Granada over the Isthmus is a natural consequence of the guarantee of its neutrality, and there does not seem to be any other practicable mode of securing the neutrality of this territory.

* * * * * * *

This treaty removes the heavy discriminating duties against us in the ports of New Granada which have nearly destroyed our commerce and navigation with that Republic and which we have been in vain endeavoring to abolish for the last 20 years.

You will find all of the documents bearing upon this treaty republished in Senate Document No. 17, Fifty-eighth Congress, second session.

Ratification of this treaty was advised by the Senate of the United States on June 3, 1848. On June 10, 1848, it was ratified by the President, and on the same day the ratifications were exchanged. The treaty was finally proclaimed on June 12, 1848.

Gentlemen, I think I have said enough to show you that this treaty was not an entangling alliance with New Granada, but a common contract under which, in return for valuable consideration received, President Polk, by and with the advice and consent of the Senate, solemnly pledged the honor of the United States that so long as it remained a power among the nations of the earth the flag of Colombia should float over the Isthmus of Panama.

Mr. Sharp. In that connection I would make the observation that at this distant day it would look as though the abundant precaution our people took in those days had returned, in a way at least, to plague us.

Mr. Hall. It would seem that way. Not six months had elapsed from the proclamation of the treaty in 1848—you will recall that gold had been discovered in California while we were still engaged in the Mexican War—when a contract was entered into in Washington (on the 28th of December, 1848) for the construction of the Panama Railroad. This contract of 1848, which was finally ratified by the Colombian Congress in 1850, gave to the Panama Railroad Co. a monopoly of transit across the Isthmus of Panama. It was an American corporation chartered under an act of the Legislature of the State of New York in 1849. New Granada (now Colombia) was doing everything she could to comply with the terms of the treaty, and facilitated, as much as she could, the transit across the Isthmus of Panama of the citizens of the United States.

It is, perhaps, well to mention that Colombia paid a very heavy price for this treaty. During the first 10 years of existence of the Panama Railroad $700,000,000 of specie, to say nothing of household goods and merchandise of every kind, were carried over the Isthmus of Panama, and $300,000,000 of imports for construction in California were carried across the Isthmus, on all of which, had differential dues still been enforced, Colombia would have levied from 10 to 30 per cent, which would have made her, in those days, one of the richest countries in South America—the richest, I would say—and she would have been able to build railroads and develop her own resources in the same way that this country was able to do, and yet not one cent did she ever get for this transisthmian traffic.

Mr. GOODWIN. That was all covered by Article XXXV of the treaty of 1846–1848?

Mr. HALL. Yes, sir.

Mr. HARRISON. When was that Panama Railroad constructed?

Mr. HALL. It was begun in 1850; a train was run to Gatun in 1851, but the railroad was not open for traffic until 1855. The flow of traffic across the Isthmus, however, did not wait for the construction of the Panama Railroad. They had the old Spanish trail from the Chagres River on across the dip at Culebra to the Pacific Ocean near the city of Panama.

This had brought to the front the great strategic importance to the United States of the Island of Cuba, and the Democratic Party, then in power, conceived the plan of acquiring Cuba from Spain by purchase and admitting it to statehood—which, by the way, would have given the Democratic Party two extra Senators. In 1854 Messrs. Buchanan, Mason, and Soulé, the ministers of the United States at London, Paris, and Madrid, met at Ostend and issued a joint declaration advising the purchase of Cuba by the United States from Spain for $120,000,000.

This document, known as the Ostend manifesto, declared:

> If Spain, dead to the voice of her own interest and actuated by stubborn pride and a false sense of honor, should refuse to sell Cuba to the United States, then the question will arise, What ought to be the course of the United States under the circumstances?

They answered their own question by saying:

> After we shall have offered Spain a price for Cuba far beyond its present value and this shall have been refused * * * then by every law, human and divine, we shall be justified in wresting it from Spain, if we have the power.

Mr. COOPER. What is that paper?

Mr. HALL. The Olstend manifesto. This un-American manifesto was repudiated by the people of this country, and especially by the Republican Party——

Mr. COOPER. Was the Mr. Buchanan who signed that manifesto the Buchanan afterwards elected by the Democratic Party to be President of the United States?

Mr. HALL. Yes, sir.

Mr. COOPER. That was not the Republican Party doing that?

Mr. HALL. No, sir. I was about to add that the Republican Party, to its honor, be it said, in its national platform in 1856 asserted the true American doctrine in these words—and they were applicable to Mr. Roosevelt in 1904 just as much as they were applicable to the Democrats in 1854:

The highwayman's plea that "might makes right," embodied in the Ostend circular, was in every respect unworthy of American diplomacy, and would bring shame and dishonor upon any government or people that gave it their sanction.

Mr. CLINE. Did you say that Mr. Roosevelt repudiated that?

Mr. HALL. I said that the Republican platform declaration on that subject in 1856 might be applied to Mr. Roosevelt in 1904.

Mr. KENDALL. That had not been the fixed principle of our Government, because we had substantially violated it, just eight years previous to that time, in the war with Mexico.

Mr. HALL. It is to be hoped that it will become the fixed principle of the Government—that "Thou shalt not steal."

Mr. CLINE. Hasn't that been the fixed principle of this Government for the last 100 years?

Mr. HALL. Certainly.

Mr. KENDALL. Was it in 1846?

Mr. HALL. That "Thou shalt not steal"?

Mr. KENDALL. Yes.

Mr. HALL. I think so. It is a fundamental principle.

Mr. LEVY. You can go back to the Ten Commandments for that principle?

Mr. HALL. Yes, sir.

Mr. GOODWIN. Mr. Hall is simply contrasting the Republican platform of 1856 with the subsequent acts of the Republican Party in 1904 to show how the mighty have fallen.

At 12 o'clock noon the committee takes a recess until Monday morning, February 12, 1912, at 10 o'clock.

COMMITTEE ON FOREIGN AFFAIRS,
HOUSE OF REPRESENTATIVES,
Washington, D. C., February 12, 1912.

The committee met at 10 o'clock a. m.

The CHAIRMAN. Mr. Hall, you may proceed.

STATEMENT OF MR. HENRY N. HALL—Resumed.

Mr. HALL. Mr. Chairman and gentlemen, immediately after the recess on Friday I sent a telegram to Mr. Don C. Seitz, the manager of the Press Publishing Co., the corporation which publishes the New York World, asking him to send me a certified copy of the court record of the rogatory proceedings had in Panama in the case of United States *v.* The Press Publishing Co. I have received from Mr. Thomas S. Fuller, of counsel for the Press Publishing Co., a member of the firm of Nicoll, Annable, Lindsay & Fuller, of New York, the following letter:

NEW YORK, *February 9, 1912.*

HENRY N. HALL, Esq.,
New York World Bureau, Washington, D. C.

DEAR MR. HALL: Mr. Seitz has referred to me your telegram to him of February 9, relative to the testimony taken in Panama. It is impossible to send the original transcript of the testimony which is certified by the judge of the Panaman court before whom the same was taken. This, of course, has never been out of his possession until he returned it sealed to the circuit court (now the district court) for the southern district of New York. It is in the clerk's office as a record of that court, and neither we nor any other person can get it. That was certified to by Judge Hector Valdez, before whom it was taken, and his authority was certified to by the proper authorities in Panama, and so on, as is customary under letters rogatory.

In lieu of this I am sending you a copy of the testimony which I have, and which is a true copy of that taken in Panama. This I have certified to as being a true copy, and you will find my certificate to that effect on the last page in the bound volume. This copy which I send you was made from another copy that I had originally. The copy that I had originally was carbon sheets made at the same time that the original testimony was transcribed, and those were compared personally by me with the originals, and such corrections as were made in the originals were noted on my copy. The bound volume that I send you is a faithful transcription of that copy.

If the committee wants any further assurances from me as to the authenticity, I shall, of course, be delighted to give them such facts as are in my power.

Yours, very truly,

THOS. S. FULLER.

The certificate to which Mr. Fuller refers is:

UNITED STATES OF AMERICA,
Southern District of New York, ss:

I, Thomas S. Fuller, attorney and counselor at law, do hereby certify that the foregoing are true copies of the depositions of the witnesses who were examined at the city of Panama, in the Republic of Panama, before Judge Hector Valdez, June 11 to June 19, 1909, inclusive, pursuant to letters rogatory issued out of and under the seal of the circuit court of the United States for the Southern District of New York, on the 25th day of May, 1909, in a certain criminal action then pending in the said court between the United States of America, plaintiff, and the Press Publishing Co., defendant, and that I am the same Thomas S. Fuller therein mentioned who attended before the said judge upon the taking of the said depositions.

Dated at the city of New York this 9th day of February, 1912.

THOS. S. FULLER.

STATE OF NEW YORK,
County of New York, ss:

On this 9th day of February, 1912, before me personally came Thomas S. Fuller, to me known and known to me to be the person described in and who executed the above certificate and acknowledged to me that he executed the same.

E. MORTIMER BOYLE,
Notary Public, New York County.

[Seal of the notary public.]

The CHAIRMAN. That is a certified copy of the proceedings?

Mr. HALL. Yes, sir.

The CHAIRMAN. That will do.

Mr. HALL. Now, to continue my presentation of the facts in their chronological order. The opening of the Panama Railroad in 1855 gave an even greater impetus to transisthmian traffic, and the stream of men seeking fortune in the West was very great. The fact that virtually none of them could speak or understand the language of the country through which they were traveling and their rough and ready manners caused ill feeling which culminated in a serious riot at Panama in 1856. The Government of Bogota had not realized the nature or extent of the traffic across the Isthmus, and the local authorities had no adequate means for the quelling of the disturbance, as a result of which many Americans were killed and much valuable property destroyed.

This led to the treaty of 1857 between the United States and the Republic of New Granada for the adjustment of claims of American citizens against New Granada arising out of the riot. By Article I of this treaty it was specifically acknowledged that the duty of maintaining order on the Isthmus and assuring free transit from one to the other sea devolved upon New Granada, and that she was responsible for failure to do so. Article I reads:

ARTICLE 1. All claims on the part of corporations, companies, or individuals, citizens of the United States upon the Government of New Granada which have been presented prior to the signature of this convention either to the Department of State at Washington or to the minister of the United States at Bogota, and especially those for damages which were caused by the riot at Panama on the 15th April, 1856, for which the said Government of New Granada acknowledges its liability, arising out of its privilege and obligation to preserve peace and good order along the transit route, shall be referred to a board of commissioners consisting of two members, one of whom shall be appointed by the Government of the United States and one by the Government of New Granada. In case of the death, absence, or incapacity of either commissioner, or in the event of either commissioner omitting or ceasing to act, the Government of the United States or that of New Granada, respectively, or the minister of the latter in the United States acting by its direction, shall forthwith proceed to fill the vacancy thus occasioned.

The commissioners so named shall meet in the city of Washington within 90 days of the exchange of the ratification of this convention, and before proceeding to business shall make and subscribe a solemn oath that they will carefully examine and impartially decide according to justice and equity upon all the claims laid before them under the provisions of this convention by the Government of the United States. And such oath shall be entered on the records of their proceedings.

The commissioners shall then proceed to name an arbiter or umpire to decide upon any case or cases on which they may differ in opinion. And if they can not agree in the selection the umpire shall be appointed by the minister of Prussia to the United States, whom the two contracting parties shall invite to make such appointment and whose selection shall be conclusive on both parties.

The United States took advantage of this new treaty to obtain from New Granada some further concessions. By article 7 it was stipulated that the United States might acquire land upon one of the islands of the Bay of Panama for the purpose of establishing a coaling station. But here again the United States specifically acknowledged the territorial sovereignty of the Republic of New Granada over the Isthmus. Article 7 reads:

ART. VII. Whereas the United States may desire to purchase or lease a piece of ground upon one of the islands in the Bay of Panama for a coal depot, the Government of New Granada, willing to promote in this matter the wishes of a friendly nation, concedes to the United States the privilege of purchasing or leasing such a piece of ground, not exceeding 100 English acres in extent, whereupon the United States may erect wharves, piers, and any buildings which may be necessary for the enjoyment of the same for the above-mentioned purpose, and while the said land is held by the United States no tax of any kind shall be bored thereon, nor upon the wharves, piers, or other buildings erected thereon, nor upon the property of the United States employed or deposited there.

But it is understood and expressly stipulated that the aforesaid concession is in no respect to impair or affect the territorial sovereignty of the Republic of New Granada over the land so purchased or leased.

Mr. FLOOD. Mr. Chairman, I want to interrupt Mr. Hall just a moment to ask you this. I was not here at the hearing at which Mr. Rainey was heard. I would like to know what the purpose of this resolution is.

The CHAIRMAN. The resolution of Mr. Rainey?

Mr. FLOOD. Yes.

The CHAIRMAN. It is to investigate the question of how we took Panama.

(After informal discussion:)

The CHAIRMAN. You may proceed, Mr. Hall.

Mr. HALL. In 1862 the Republic of New Granada changed its name to the United States of Colombia. When Bolivar had wrested the northern half of South America from the Dominion of Spain he had established the great Republic of Colombia, which was divided in 1833 into three independent nations, the Republic of New Granada, the United States of Venezuela, and the Republic of Ecuador. In 1863 the Republic of New Granada changed its name to the United States of Colombia without affecting, however, the territorial limits over which it exercised sovereignty.

In 1865 there was a rising in the State of Panama against the central government at Bogota, and the question arose as to what the obligations of the United States were toward Colombia under Article XXXV of the treaty with New Granada. Mr. Allen A. Burton, United States minister at Bogota, in a dispatch bearing on this matter to Mr. Seward, then Secretary of State of the United States, referring to the argument advanced by the officer in command of the naval forces at Colon, who held that the treaty only obligated the United States to defend the line of traffic on the railroad, wrote:

The point of departure, in the argument advanced by them, is the force given to the words of the thirty-fifth article of the treaty, "with the view that the free transit of the Isthmus may not be interrupted;" and the conclusion reached that the obligation contracted by the United States is coextensive only with the view declared. This, at first sight, has some claim to plausibility, but is plausible only. Had the treaty stopped here, leaving no other clew to the limits of the obligation, the inference drawn would not have been entirely wanting in force. But the treaty itself fixes unmistakably, without leaving anything to interpretation or conjecture, precisely what is to be done or order to fulfill that obligation and to effect the object in view—the securing by the United States to Colombia of the perfect neutrality of the Isthmus and, in like manner, her sovereignty and property in that territory, not partially or of the transit alone, but of the whole Isthmus, and that perfectly.

If transit only was to be thus secured it would have been more natural and logical to have said so and no more by employing words more precise and in harmony with the idea intended to be expressed. To thus limit the duty imposed by the treaty on the United States does violence to that part of it which, in plain and appropriate words, extends the guaranty of perfect neutrality, sovereignty, and property to the whole territory of the Isthmus "from its southernmost extremity until the boundary of Costa Rica," and consequently at the same time renders superfluous, meaningless, and inoperative no inconsiderable part of its language, a supposition not to be attributed to the negotiators of so important an agreement and their Governments who ratified it in the entire absence of ambiguity or unreasonableness.

Besides, a named view, or object of the guaranty, is of subordinate importance and must yield to the explicit and unconditional terms of the guaranty itself. It is a legitimate presumption, not to be repelled or weakened by time or subsequent changes, that the contracting parties had fixed and well-defined ideas of, and specified accordingly, what acts should constitute a compliance with the obligations into which they were entering, and although such acts may now appear disproportionate to the end to be achieved, it is not for one party to disregard or diminish them without the consent of the other.

This inclination to define runs through the entire treaty, is one of its notable features, and a wise one, as it tends to avert misunderstandings and consequently to make more efficacious its stipulations. Many other convenient objects not necessary or polite to have been declared and which neither party was bound to disclose, may have induced one or both to enter into the compact. There are patent and forcible reasons for this supposition as to Colombia. This part of her territory is remote and almost detached from the rest of the Republic. It is of the highest importance to the world, and she might well have apprehended that it was looked to with a covetous eye by stronger powers. It is difficult of defense, and she had not the means of defending it. Its inhabitants were but partially civilized, and its quiet and order impose on her a weighty responsibility. Well might Colombia, then, with her sad internal revolutionary experience and menaces from abroad have feared that the presence of any body of men, from anywhere, operating hostilely to her rights and authority on any part of that peculiar territory, and especially such a body as that which invaded it from Cauca, would be dangerous not to this part alone, but to the Republic itself, and therefore have sought a stipulation from the United States which would be likely to preclude all possibility of consequences so disastrous to her security and welfare.

Furthermore, the treaty presupposes that the "tranquil and constant enjoyment" of the advantages secured by it on the Isthmus to the United States is to rebound chiefly to the interest of the latter. The view, then, of keeping the transit uninterrupted, and which the United States are permitted to do, is, in effect, a permission to them to protect their newly acquired rights on Colombian soil (the free transit to the Isthmus being the principal one), and is in reality one of the privileges conceded to the United States as conducive to the full enjoyment of those rights for their own benefit, and can not in any sense be regarded as a burden to them. But as a compensation for granting the rights and privileges and for other important concessions made to the United States of Colombia in articles 4, 5, and 6 of the treaty the former take upon themselves in turn the burden of guaranteeing to the latter the perfect neutrality, sovereignty, and property of the whole Isthmus, which Colombia, whether with or without cause is immaterial, imagined was or might be in danger. She has paid for this security, and the United States have accepted and enjoy a consideration mutually agreed upon as adequate and just; and the views or objects, many or few, which may then have moved Colombia to purchase the right to or that may now influence her to ask for the lawful enjoyment of the benefits resulting from her agreement can not concern the United States or excuse them for failing to comply with a plain duty to which they have bound themselves.

Another feature of the guaranty is not to be overlooked. It extends to "all the rights of sovereignty and property which New Granada (now Colombia) has and possesses over the said territory." At the date of the treaty the now State of Panama was simply a canton of the Republic, over which the national authority was supreme.

Whether, therefore, an invasion of the Isthmus of Panama, or even an internal movement which puts in jeopardy the rights guaranteed to Colombia in that territory, does or does not endanger the freedom of the transit would seem in no case to be a material or open question. It is concluded by positive stipulation. This appears to be the clearly expressed meaning and spirit of the treaty. The duty assumed by the United States may be inconvenient, embarrassing, and even onerous. It is nevertheless one which, when required to do so, they can not fail to respect without dishonor so long as they retain the corresponding benefits ceded by Colombia.

Mr. Flood. What is that you are reading from, Mr. Hall?

Mr. Hall. This is from a dispatch from Mr. Allan A. Burton, United States minister at Bogota, to Secretary of State Seward. It is in the collected papers of R. R. Hitt, who was for many years chairman of this committee, and whose papers bearing on this controversy passed into the possession of the World.

Mr. Flood. Suppose, Mr. Hall, we should decide that this Government violated that treaty and that the taking of Panama was not in accordance with, but was in violation of, the well-established principles of the law of nations, what would be the measure of relief? What do you think we ought to give Colombia?

Mr. Hall. Far be it from me, sir, to express an opinion on that matter. I understand that is the very matter this committee has to pass upon.

Mr. Goodwin. The nature of the relief sought, Mr. Flood, and the manner of compensation?

Mr. Flood. Yes. Suppose the issue is presented: If we decide that our Government did violate the treaty and did act in violation of international law, Colombia is entitled to some relief. What kind of relief would you suggest?

Mr. Hall. I have absolutely no suggestion to make on that head, sir. I am here at the request of Mr. Rainey and of your chairman, who, at Mr. Rainey's request, wrote to Mr. Don C. Seitz, of the World, and asked him to send down here for the committee the evidence which the Press Publishing Co. gathered for its defense in the criminal action for libel which was started against it by Mr. Roosevelt. That evidence I have brought here, and I was endeavoring to present the facts to you, to present all the facts bearing on this particular controversy, in their chronological order, just as they would have been presented to a jury if this matter had come to trial, as the World was anxious it should come to trial, before the courts of competent jurisdiction.

Mr. Flood. But, you know, if it had been presented to a jury, they would also deal with the question of damages.

Mr. Goodwin. As I understand it, this hearing is to determine, or rather it is for the committee to determine, what action shall be taken with reference to that feature of the matter, and if we go into a hearing of all the facts, why the matter, then, will come before Congress.

Mr. Flood. Do you think that is all it contemplates? This resolution contemplates our going into all the facts and reporting those facts to Congress.

Mr. HALL. I can say, Mr. Flood, that it will be of material advantage, not only to this committee but to Congress, to have a calm, clear, dispassionate statement of all the facts in this case. I will say now that a great many of the essential facts are not known to Congress or to the people of the United States. The truth in this matter has never yet been told, and I am here to present to you—and I desire to do so by your leave—documents and papers which were withheld from Congress——

Mr. FLOOD. I did not mean to interrupt you, but I wanted to see if you had any idea——

Mr. HALL. Before going that far, I was endeavoring to build up on a solid foundation of truth a pedestal which would enable you to have clear comprehension of the monumental array of papers and facts which I shall later adduce.

Mr. FLOOD. Without having that access to all those facts and papers, I have never had any doubt that the conduct of this Government was in violation of that treaty and of international law, and I just simply asked you the question I did, Mr. Hall, to see if you had formed any idea in your own mind as to the relief we should give the injured party, so if it should be solemnly resolved by Congress that that was the case——

Mr. HALL. It would seem that for the settlement of just such controversies this Government at the present moment is trying to get the whole world to enter into treaties of general arbitration. I presume that Colombia is willing to enter into a treaty of general arbitration, because she has signed one within the last 10 days with the Republic of Argentina, and for years has been asking the United States to arbitrate this Panama controversy.

Mr. FLOOD. If we sit here, though, and find the facts against our Government, we would not stand much chance before an arbitration tribunal, do you think?

Mr. GOODWIN. I do not think, Mr. Flood, that Mr. Hall would care to encroach upon the prerogatives of Congress to say how much relief should be granted, or if relief should be granted; but——

Mr. HALL. If the committee in its wisdom——

Mr. FLOOD. We are going into a tremendous question.

Mr. KENDALL. Do you not think it ought to be done by a joint committee of Congress?

The CHAIRMAN. Just a moment. Mr. Hall is here to put into the record the essential proofs in chronological order. When we close that, there are very distinguished international lawyers who will appear before the committee and discuss the question of remedies and equities and what this Government should do in good faith.

Mr. HALL. I will say that I have no doubt that when these documents are all before the committee they will necessitate the presence before the committee of some very high officials of the State Department.

The CHAIRMAN. Proceed, Mr. Hall, in your own way.

Mr. HALL. This dispatch of Mr. Allan A. Burton, which was sent from Bogota on November 5, 1865, curiously enough, crossed with a dispatch from Mr. Seward himself to Mr. Burton, dated November

9, in which Mr. Seward answered in advance the points raised by Mr. Burton. Mr. Seward wrote:

No. 134.] DEPARTMENT OF STATE,
Washington, November 9, 1865.

SIR: The question which has recently arisen under the thirty-fifth article of the treaty with New Granada as to the obligation of this Government to comply with requisition of the President of the United States of Colombia for a force to protect the Isthmus of Panama from invasion by a body of insurgents of that country has been submitted to the consideration of the Attorney General. His opinion, by which the United States engages to preserve the neutrality of the Isthmus of Panama, imposes an obligation on this Government to comply with a requisition like that referred to. The purpose of the stipulation was to guarantee the Isthmus against seizure or invasion by a foreign power only——

Mr. GARNER. Just what did you say?

Mr. HALL (reading):

The purpose of the stipulation was to guarantee the Isthmus against seizure or invasion by a foreign power only.

Mr. KENDALL. Foreign from Colombia?

Mr. HALL. Yes. [Reading:]

It could not have been contemplated that we would ever become a party to any civil war in that country by defending the Isthmus against another party. As it may be presumed, however, that our object in entering into such a stipulation was to secure the freedom of transit across the Isthmus, if that freedom should be endangered or obstructed, the employment of force on our part to prevent this would be a question of grave expediency to be determined by circumstances. The department is not aware that there is yet occasion for a decision upon this point.

Your dispatches to No. —, inclusive, have been received.

I am, sir, etc.,

WILLIAM H. SEWARD.

Mr. KENDALL. I understand that dispatch of Seward as meaning that that treaty devolved no duty upon us to settle any difficulties that might arise between Colombia and Panama. Our only duty was to repel invasion from some foreign power upon the Isthmus.

Mr. HULL. Yes, sir; I think that is a perfectly fair presumption of what Mr. Seward's interpretation was.

Mr. GOODWIN. Notwithstanding the treaty itself stipulates we might have access across the Isthmus, if that was denied it would still be a matter of grave doubt upon Mr. Seward's part whether we should resort to force to enforce the treaty?

Mr. HALL. That would seem so.

Two years later, in 1867, the Panama Railroad contract was modified by the United States of Colombia and the Panama Railroad Co. All of the obligations of the Panama Railroad Co. have since been assumed by the Government of the United States, which owns all of the stock of that corporation.

Mr. KENDALL. May I ask a question? I only ask you because I know you have the information. When was the first Panama Railroad Co. organized?

Mr. HALL. The first Panama Railroad Co. was chartered by the Legislature of the State of New York in 1849, but I think it was first started in December, 1848, when the preliminary contract was signed in Washington.

Mr. GOODWIN. It was completed in 1855.

Mr. HALL. The treaty between the United States and New Granada was ratified in June, 1848, and in December the Panama Railroad contract was signed in Washington. Construction began in 1850. In 1851 a train was run to Gatun, and in 1855 the railroad was opened.

Mr. GOODWIN. Was that corporation chartered by the Colombian Government?

Mr. HALL. Yes, sir; by the law of 1850.

Mr. GOODWIN. The law passed by the Parliament of Colombia?

Mr. HALL. Yes, sir. Now, in 1867, as I was saying, the Panama Railroad contract was modified by the United States of Colombia and the Panama Railroad Co. The preamble to this important contract recites the reasons for this modification in these terms——

Mr. FLOOD. What is the date of this modification?

Mr. HALL. 1867. In the preamble of this contract of 1867 the reasons for the modifications of the original contract were recited in these terms by the Government of Colombia and the Panama Railroad Co.:

> * * * desiring to provide whatever may be needful for the perfection of the work of the said railroad, in order that it may better answer the necessities of the commerce of the world, and at the same time furnish a sure and permanent revenue to the treasury of the Republic, have agreed to modify and reform the said contract in the terms set forth in the following stipulations——

Mr. GOODWIN. What are you quoting from, Mr. Hall?

Mr. HALL. From the report of the Hon. Joseph L. Bristow, now Senator Bristow, to the Secretary of War on June 24, 1905, Senate Document No. 429, of the Fifty-ninth Congress, first session, Exhibit E 2, on page 219.

Articles I, II, and III of this contract of 1867 read:

> ARTICLE I. The Government of the United States of Colombia concedes to the Panama Railroad Co. the use and possession for 99 years of the railroad constructed by it and which actually exists between the cities of Colon and Panama. This concession comprises not only the road but also the buildings, warehouses, wharves, dock yards, telegraph between Colon and Panama, belonging to the road, and in general all the dependencies and other works of which the said company is now in possession, necessary to the service and development of the enterprise, and those which in the future it may establish with the same purpose.
>
> ART. II. The Government of the Republic binds itself, during the time that the exclusive privilege which is conceded to the company for the working of the railroad remains in force, not to construct for itself, nor to concede to any person or company, by any title whatever, the power to establish any other railroad on the Isthmus of Panama, and it also stipulates that, while the said privilege continues in force, the Government shall not have the power of undertaking for itself, nor permitting any person to undertake, without the concurrence and consent of said company, the opening or working of any maritime canal which may unite the two oceans across the said Isthmus of Panama to the west of the line of Cape Tiburon on the Atlantic and Point Garachine on the Pacific. But it remains stipulated that the right which is conceded to the company to give its consent does not extend to its opposing the construction of a canal across the Isthmus of Panama (except on the actual route of the railroad itself), but only to its exacting an equitable price for such a privilege and as indemnification for the damages which the railroad company may suffer by the rivalry or competition of the canal.
>
> If the sum, which may be demanded by the company, shall not appear equitable to the Government of the United States of Colombia, then it shall be fixed by arbiters in New York or Panama, one to be named by the Government and the other by the company, and in case of their not agreeing the two shall name a third, whose decision shall be without appeal.

In pronouncing their decision the arbiters shall take into consideration the grounds upon which the company rests, and the information which the Government shall give upon the matter, and in view thereof they shall decide without appeal as they may deem most just and equitable.

The sum, whatever it may be, which shall be finally designated, shall belong one-half to the railroad company and one-half to the Government of Colombia.

ART. III. In compensation of and as a price for these concessions the railroad company binds itself to pay to the Government of the United States of Colombia $1,000,000 in American gold, or in bills on New York, payable in the same kind, as the Government may elect, on the day on which this contract shall be approved by Congress, and to pay from the present time, and until the expiration of the present privilege, an annual revenue of $250,000 in American gold. The company will make the payments quarterly in New York to the agent designated by the Government of the United States of Colombia, or, if the Government should desire, the company will place the money in London or Panama, the Government giving the necessary notice to the company in New York. These quarterly payments shall commence to count from the date of approval of the contract by the Congress.

From the revenue which the Government acquires by this contract there shall be set apart annually during 20 years $25,000, which the company shall deliver to the Government of the State of Panama.

The other articles gave the Panama Railroad the most complete monopoly of building even carriage roads across the Isthmus. This was provided for by Article V:

ART. V. During the whole term of this privilege the company shall have the exclusive right to establish across the Isthmus of Panama, within the zone indicated in Article II, any class of carriage roads whatever, from one ocean to the other. The Colombian Government binds itself not to undertake for itself, nor to permit any other company or person to undertake within said zone any other carriage road, either macadamized or of plank, or of any other class suitable for the use of wheeled vehicles, between the two oceans across the Isthmus of Panama. It being nevertheless well understood that the privilege of which this article treats can not and must not in any manner prevent the construction of any kind of roads in a direction distinct from that expressed, nor the completing, preserving, and improving of roads already existing, or which are actually being constructed on said Isthmus.

Now, I would especially call your attention to Article XXXVI of this contract, wherein lies one of the main reasons for the rejection of the Hay-Herran treaty by Colombia. It is this article which gave Colombia a reversionary right in the Panama Railroad:

ART. XXXVI. At the expiration of the term of the privilege, and by the sole fact of its expiration, the Government of the Colombian Union shall be substituted in all the rights of the company, and shall enter immediately into the enjoyment of the line of communication, of all its fixtures, of all its dependencies, and of all its products. The company shall be bound to deliver to the Government in good order the roads, the works which compose them and their dependencies, such as landing and discharging places, offices, machines, and, in general, whatever movable, or immovable objects, whether destined for the especial service of transportation or applicable to any other object connected with the enterprise.

Mr. KENDALL. That was executed by the officers of the company.

Mr. HALL. Executed by the officers of the company. Here is a binding civil contract, under the terms of which the United States of Colombia, while retaining its reversionary right, ceded the railroad to the company for a period of 99 years in exchange for $1,000,000 in cash and $250,000 a year payable every year for 99 years.

Mr. KENDALL. By whom and to whom?

Mr. HALL. By the Panama Railroad Co. I have heard it advanced in conversation by men of very high repute as lawyers that if it were possible for the United States of America to be sued in the courts of this country there is no doubt that, this being a civil contract and the United States being the successors in the rights of the Panama Railroad, the recognition of any other Republic in the territory through which that railroad passes would not in any way affect the obligation of continuing the payment of $250,000 a year to the Republic of Colombia and the reversion of the property to that power in 1966.

Mr. KENDALL. That question is involved in the bona fide nature of the revolution and the independence that was achieved?

Mr. HALL. Undoubtedly.

Mr. FLOOD. How long was this $250,000 paid?

Mr. HALL. Up to the date of the revolution in 1903. To resume, in 1868 Secretary of State Seward entered into diplomatic negotiations with the Republic of Colombia for the construction by the United States of an interoceanic canal across the Isthmus of Panama. He sent to the American minister in Bogota instructions covering a draft of the projected treaty, and was so anxious to conclude a satisfactory arrangement that Mr. Caleb Cushing was sent as special agent of the State Department to join Peter J. Sullivan, minister resident of the United States at Bogota, and to endeavor to procure the adoption of the treaty desired by the United States. Mr. Sullivan and Mr. Cushing were entirely successful in their efforts, and on January 14, 1869, a treaty was signed at Bogota for the construction of the Panama Canal by the United States. The terms of this treaty were fully as advantageous and even more liberal than those of the Hay-Herran and Hay-Bunau-Varilla treaties, and it was sent by President Andrew Johnson to the Senate of the United States for ratification on February 15, 1869. I will now read the stipulations of this most important treaty:

CONVENTION BETWEEN THE UNITED STATES OF AMERICA AND THE UNITED STATES OF COLOMBIA RELATING TO THE CONSTRUCTION OF A SHIP CANAL BETWEEN THE ATLANTIC AND PACIFIC OCEANS. CONCLUDED AT BOGOTA THE 14TH JANUARY, 1869.

Whereas the construction of a ship canal between the Atlantic and Pacific Oceans through the continental isthmus which lies within the jurisdiction of the United States of Colombia is essential to the prosperity and welfare of the United States of America and the United States of Colombia, as well as to the interests of commerce and civilization throughout the world, now, therefore, the United States of America and the United States of Colombia have agreed to enter into a convention for the purpose of facilitating and ultimately securing that great object, and with that view have appointed their plenipotentiaries, namely: The President of the United States of America, Peter J. Sullivan, minister resident of the United States to the United States of Colombia; and the President of the United States of Colombia, Miguel Samper, secretary of finance and internal improvement of the Colombia Union, and Tomas Cuenca: and the said plenipotentiaries, having exchanged their full powers in due form, have agreed upon the following articles:

Mr. GOODWIN. You are quoting from the treaty of 1869?

Mr. HALL. 1869; yes, sir [reading]:

ARTICLE I. The United States of Colombia agree and consent that the United States of America shall make and the United States of America agree to make the necessary survey for such ship canal; and if they ascertain the same to be feasible then to locate the same, together with all its necessary appendages and appurtenances of locks, ports, harbors, stations, supply feeders, and sluices, etc., on land and sea upon the domain and within the jurisdiction of the United States of Colombia, and to adopt a plan of construction and to make a thorough and detailed estimate of the expense and cost of construction; and for that purpose the United States of America may employ proper military superintendents, engineers, accountants, and other agents and laborers, ships of war and transports, the military force, however, not to exceed at any time 500 rank and file without express consent of the United States of Colombia first obtained; and all persons engaged in such service, whether civil, naval, or military, shall while so engaged render lawful submission and obedience to the civil authorities of Colombia.

When the survey and location shall be completed the President of the United States of America shall certify the same, with the necessary maps and descriptions, to the President of the United States of Colombia, and the same surveys, locations, and descriptions shall be filed in the archives of the two Governments.

The route and plan thus fixed may afterwards be varied, as occasion shall require, under the authority of the United States of America, due notice being given of such modifications to the United States of Colombia. Said canal shall in no case be constructed on or across the route of the Panama Railroad unless the company's consent has been first obtained.

ART. II. The United States of Colombia agree to concede, set apart, appropriate, and devote to the purpose of such ship canal all the territory, including land, ocean, and tributary waters, which shall be designated for the purpose thereof in such plan and may be found necessary, and besides 10 miles of waste, unsettled, and unimproved lands on each side of the canal throughout its entire length, and all the materials for such construction found within the territory so to be conceded; private owners of property being entitled to have a just and reasonable indemnity to the effect whereof the Government of Colombia shall order the expropriations to be made according to its laws, but the valuation thereof in no case to be enhanced by reason of the proposed or actual construction of the canal.

The 10 miles of land granted on each side of the canal shall be measured and divided into equal lots, the front whereof bordering on the canal or its appendages shall not exceed 3,300 yards. Said lots shall be equally distributed between the two Governments so that neither of them shall have two contiguous or consecutive lots nor the two first at either extremity of the canal, both Governments being able to dispose freely of their corresponding lots, but with the conditions that they shall allow free passage thereby to and from the canal and its appendages. To begin the distribution the Government of the United States of America shall chose its first lot, and at the expiration of the term of this treaty shall give back to the Colombian Government, without exacting any amount for improvements made thereon nor for any other reason whatever, all such lots or portions thereof which may not have been disposed of in favor of private individuals.

ART. III. The United States of Colombia stipulate and agree not to undertake or allow the opening of any other interoceanic canal or of any new railway through or across this territory from the Atlantic to the Pacific Ocean without the express consent of the United States of America being first obtained.

ART. IV. The outlay, cost, and expense of the survey, location, construction, and equipment of the said canal and its ports, stations, depots, and harbors, including damages paid for private property and the indemnity that may correspond to the Panama Railroad Co. should the case arrive, in accordance with the contract celebrated by the Colombian Government and approved by Congress on the 15th of August, 1867, shall be for the account of the United States of America, but exclusively with reference to the purpose of this convention. The objects destined in Article II by the United States of Colombia for the construction of the canal shall remain in charge of the United States of America, but exclusively for the purposes of this convention.

ART. V. The United States of America shall construct said canal, with its appurtenances, suitable for the passage of all kinds of vessels, and may employ the necessary force of skill, art, and labor for that purpose. They may also maintain the necessary naval and military force, which shall at no time exceed 1,000 men, without the express consent of the United States of Colombia being first obtained. As soon as the canal be brought into operation, said force shall be withdrawn by the Government of the United States of America, if it be so requested by the Government of the United States of Colombia. The United States of America engage that the employees, laborers, artificers, as well as the naval and military force so engaged, shall conform themselves to the laws and government of the United States of Colombia.

ART. VI. As fast as the canal and its appendages and appurtenances shall be constructed, the control, possession, direction, and government of the same shall belong to, and be exercised by, the United States of America, the Government of the United States of Colombia at the same time being at liberty, after the exchange of this convention, to maintain a permanent committee of agents, with full right to inspect the operations concerned, measure the tonnage of vessels, examine the books and accounts, and report thereon to the Government of the United States of Colombia; but not to interfere with the survey, control, management, direction, and working of the canal.

ART. VII. The Government of the United States of America shall establish a tariff of tolls and freights for the said canal on a basis of perfect equality for all nations, whether in time of peace or war. The proceeds of the canal shall be preferently applied to the reimbursement of the expenses incurred in the management, service, and government of the same and to the reimbursement of the capital invested in its survey, location, and construction, including in the cost of construction the indemnities to be paid for private property, and that which may correspond to the Panama Railroad Co., should the case arrive according to the contract entered into by the Colombian Government with the said company.

Twelve years after the canal be brought into operation the Government of Colombia shall be entitled to an annual 10 per cent of the net proceeds of the undertaking; and as soon as the Government of the United States of America shall have been reimbursed of the capital invested in the undertaking, up to the time when it be brought into operation, said portion shall be 25 per cent of the said net proceeds, even if the reimbursement takes place within the first 12 years. The payment of the portion corresponding to Colombia, above mentioned, shall be made semiannually in the city of New York.

For the purpose of this article it is stipulated: First, that the annual expenses of the undertaking shall in no case exceed 30 per cent of its annual proceeds, unless the express consent of both contracting parties has been obtained; second, that the net proceeds of the undertaking corresponding to the Government of the United States of America shall be preferably applied, from the first year of its being brought into operation, to the reimbursement to the capital; and third, that in order to liquidate the net proceeds of the undertaking no deduction whatever shall be made for interest on capital invested therein, nor for the amount set apart as a reserved or sinking fund.

Mr. GOODWIN. Now, Mr. Hall, inasmuch as Panama was wrested from Colombia, will Colombia get any of that income which is stipulated in the treaty now?

Mr. HALL. This is not the treaty in force.

Mr. KENDALL. That treaty never became effective.

Mr. HALL. The treaty I am now reading never became effective.

ART. VIII. The United States of Colombia shall retain their political sovereignty and jurisdiction over the canal and territory appertaining thereto; but they shall not only allow but guarantee to the United States of America, according to the constitution and laws of Colombia now in force the peaceable enjoyment, control, direction, and management of the same, as before specified.

ART. IX. The United States of America shall have the right to use the canal for the passage of troops, munitions, and vessels of war, in time of peace. The entrance of the canal shall be rigorously closed to the troops of nations which are at war with another or others, including their vessels and munitions of war.

ART. X. Colombia shall not impose tolls or duties of any kind on vessels, passengers, money, merchandise, and other objects conveyed through the canal from one ocean to the other; but such effects as may be destined to be sold or consumed in the interior of Colombia shall be liable to the duties and taxes that are or may be established.

ART. XI. Should a naval or military force be required for the protection of the canal, and the Government of the United States of America agree to furnish the same, said force shall be for the object expressed, and during the time it may be needed act under the concurrent orders of the two Governments, and be paid from the proceeds of the canal.

ART. XII. The mutual rights and privileges hereinbefore specified shall continue for the term of 100 years, reckoned from the day on which the canal be brought into operation; at the end of which time the Government of Colombia shall enter into the possession, property, and enjoyment of the canal and lands appertaining thereto, wharves, stores, and all other appendages of the undertaking built at the extremities or along the canal, without being thereby obliged to pay indemnity of any kind whatever; the United States of America being entitled to retain whatever sums they may have received during the 100 years herein mentioned.

ART. XIII. The United States of America may, by law, devolve all the rights, franchises, duties, property, and obligations touching survey, construction, and preservation of said canal upon any individual citizen or association of citizens of the United States of America; and in that case such citizen or association shall enjoy all the rights, property, and privileges, and be subject to all the obligations and engagements herein contained on the part of the United States of America. The differences which may arise between such citizen or association and the United States of Colombia as to the interpretation or fulfillment of the several clauses of this treaty shall be decided by a tribunal formed in the following manner: Each party shall appoint a commissioner, and these two commissioners shall appoint an umpire who shall decide those cases in which the two former can not agree. This tribunal shall hold its sessions at Bogota, and neither party shall have recourse against its decisions. In case one of the parties be required to appoint its commissioner and should not do it within the 30 days following, or should appoint a person who can not or will not accept the appointment, then this appointment shall be made by the Government of the United States of America. The expenses of the tribunal shall be taken from the gross proceeds of the canal as soon as it be brought into operation; and before this takes place such expenses shall be to the equal charge of both parties, but to be deducted from the first proceeds of the canal. In case the commissioners do not agree as to the appointment of the umpire, then the two contracting governments shall submit their differences to the arbitrament of some other friendly government in the manner stipulated in Article XVII.

The political obligations herein assumed by the United States of America and the United States of Colombia are permanent and indefeasible.

ART. XIV. Such citizen or association shall hold their property, rights, immunities, and privileges in and about the same ship canal subject in like manner to the reservations herein contained in favor of the United States of Colombia.

ART. XV. In case the Government of the United States of America should devolve the undertaking, as mentioned in Article XIII, the privilege shall be forfeited, and the Government of Colombia enter into possession and gratuitous enjoyment of the canal and its appendages in the following cases: First, if such citizen or association should transfer or underlet the enterprise in favor of any foreign government; second, if such citizen or association should cooperate in any rebellious act against the United States of Colombia tending to the withdrawal from the dominion of said Government of the territory wherein the canal may be constructed; and third, if, after the canal be constructed and brought into operation, the passage through the same be suspended for more than three years, save unforeseen cases or superior force beyond the control of said citizens or association. It is understood that the enumerated cases of forfeiture are comprehended in the matters of which the tribunal provided for in Article XIII has jurisdiction, and shall be judged by it both as to fact and law.

ART. XVI. This treaty shall cease and determine if the United States of America shall not make, or cause to be made, the surveys and locations of the canal herein provided for within three years after the ratification and exchange of this convention, or if they shall fail to begin the construction of the canal, or cause it to be begun, within five years after such ratification, or if they shall fail to cause it to be completed within a period of 15 years after such ratification.

ART. XVII. If, unhappily, any difference should arise between the United States of America and the United States of Colombia, growing out of this treaty, such difference shall be submitted to the arbitrament of some impartial government, whose decision shall be, in every case, duly respected and fulfilled.

ART. XVIII. The United States of America and the United States of Colombia mutually agree to second the efforts of each other in procuring the friendship and guarantee of all other nations in favor of the stipulations of neutrality mentioned in Articles VII and IX, as well as the sovereignty of the United States of Colombia over the territory of the Isthmus of Panama and Darien.

ART. XIX. The present convention shall be approved and ratified by the President of the United States of America, by and with the advice and consent of the Senate thereof, and by the President of the United States of Colombia, with the consent and approbation of the Congress of the same; and the ratification shall be exchanged in the city of Bogota within 20 months from the date of the signature of this convention.

In faith whereof we, the plenipotentiaries of the United States of America and of the United States of Colombia, have signed and sealed these presents, in the city of Bogota, on the 14th day of January, 1869.

[SEAL.] PETER J. SULLIVAN,
Minister Resident and Plenipotentiary of the United States of America.

[SEAL.] MIGUEL SAMPER,
THOMAS NUENCIA,
Plenipotentiaries of the United States of Colombia.

Gentlemen, no terms more favorable than those set forth in this treaty could be obtained or expected. Colombia gave to the United States full authority to construct the canal itself, or to confide the building of it by law to the citizens of the United States. She asked for no money, merely 10 per cent of the future annual profits beginning 12 years after the opening of the canal, or 25 per cent when the United States should have recouped the entire cost of the construction of the canal. I think that had the President of Colombia had to send a message to his Congress concerning that treaty, he could have said—and in this case truly—that—

"the treaty was entered into at the urgent solicitation of the people of the United States, and that in drawing up this treaty every concession was made to this Government and to the people of the United States."

Mr. GARNER. Why was not this treaty ratified?

Mr. HALL. The Senate of the United States refused to agree to this treaty.

Mr. HARRISON. What was the reason?

Mr. HALL. There was no reason given. It is immaterial whether the decision of the Senate was influenced by a desire to favor transcontinental railroad projects, or treaties of the United States with other countries, notably England with whom there was then in force the Clayton-Bulwer Treaty of 1850, but the fact remains that all of Colombia's favorable offers were rejected by the United States, which refused to build the canal. In 1870, however, another treaty was negotiated by the United States through Mr. Hulbert, then the American minister at Bogota, and on January 26, 1870, he signed this other treaty with the United States of Colombia containing substantially the same provisions as the draft of the year before.

Mr. FLOOD. What was the date of that?

Mr. HALL. January 26, 1870. It was submitted to the Senate of the United States for ratification by President Grant, on March 31, 1870. There is nothing to show that it was ever acted upon by the Senate of the United States, although it was approved with certain amendments by the Congress of the United States of Colombia by law July 18, 1870. In the words of former Secretary of the Navy Thompson, addressing this very committee on Foreign Affairs of the House of Representatives, on January 20, 1881——

Mr. GOODWIN. What are you reading from now?

Mr. HALL. I am reading from the "House of Representatives Report 224, Forty-sixth Congress, third session," with the attached "Hearing before the Committee on Foreign Affairs, House of Representatives, January 11 and January 20, 1881."

Mr. GOODWIN. At what page?

Mr. HALL. It is page 24.

There are two treaties to be found in the communication from the Secretary of State, one made in 1869 and the other in 1870, in which there is conceded to the United States the right to build that canal; and in one of them—the first—that right is not only conceded to the United States, but it is absolutely made its duty to build the canal, if it should be found practicable. That treaty is found in the message from the President of the United States—Executive Document No. 112, Forty-sixth Congress, second session, commencing on page 34. That treaty was communicated by Mr. Johnson, as President, to the Senate on the 15th of February, 1869. I will not read the treaty, but will refer to its contents. The United States of Colombia agree and consent that the United States of America shall make, and the United States of America agree to make, the necessary survey for such ship canal, and if they ascertain the same to be feasible, then to locate the same, with all the necessary appendages, appurtenances, etc. In Article III the United States of Colombia stipulated and agreed not to undertake or allow the opening of any other interoceanic canal or of any other new railway through or across their territory. Then, in Article V, the United States of America agreed to construct said canal and to establish a tariff of tolls, the political sovereignty, however, of Colombia being retained by that Government. Article IX provides that the United States of America shall have the right to use the canal for the passage of troops, munitions, and vessels of war in time of peace—a right which is conceded to no other government but ours. Then it is provided in Article XIII that the United States of America may by law devolve all their rights, franchises, duties, property, and obligations, etc., upon any individual citizen or association of citizens of the United States. That treaty was signed by the minister resident and plenipotentiary of the United States of America and by the two plenipotentiaries of the Government of Colombia. It gave to the United States of America all possible control of the Panama Canal except that which pertained to the political sovereignty of Colombia. Yet, notwithstanding that that treaty was communicated to the Senate in 1869, it was not ratified, and has not yet been ratified.

Mr. WILSON. Was it rejected?

Mr. THOMPSON. We have no evidence in regard to it. We do not know. Of course we can not tell what the Senate has done in secret session. It was communicated in secret session to the Senate, and that is the last that was ever heard of it.

In 1870 another treaty was made between the United States of Colombia and the United States of America. You will find it commencing at page 38 of the document to which I have referred. Without undertaking to read it, I will state what the terms were of equivalent import. All the rights and privileges that had been granted under the treaty of 1869 by Colombia were granted by this treaty of 1870. But there was a clause in it somewhat broader than in the other. This is Article X: "As soon as the canal, its appendages, and appurtenances shall be completed the entire possession, inspection, direction, and management of the same shall appertain to the United States of America." So that by this treaty of 1870 everything that the United States could ask was proposed to them by Colombia. The United States of America were not only authorized to build the canal by money out of the Public Treasury, if they thought proper to do so, but they were also authorized to confer the right to build it upon any association of United States citizens. That treaty was ratified by the Government of Colombia, but was never ratified by the Government of the United States, and it remains, just as the treaty of 1869, on the archives of the Senate, so far as we know, entirely untouched.

* * * * * * *

The Republic of Colombia did all in her power to put herself under the guardianship and control of the United States. She did what no other independent nation ever did to any other nation on earth. She gave to the United States the right of entire control and protectorate and management of the canal when built either out of the Treasury or by citizens of the United States. And Colombia surrendered to the United States everything which they could by possibility ask, except her own political sovereignty. The United States of America rejected this offer.

Gentlemen, the United States did more than reject that offer. In 1876 the Congress of the United States abolished the mission of the United States to Colombia, and diplomatic relations were not renewed until the restoration of the mission in the summer of 1878, immediately following the steps taken by Colombia in response to the unanimous sentiment of the commercial world and in the exercise of her own right of self-government to cause an interoceanic canal to be built.

Now, on March 20, 1878, the Republic of Colombia granted a concession for the construction of the interoceanic canal——

Mr. HARRISON. Can you give no reason why those treaties were not ratified?

Mr. HALL. They never went out of executive session, sir, but everything I have been able to find out about them in different references shows that first of all it was thought that the transcontinental railroads, then being built, would be harmed by a competing canal; and secondly, the Clayton-Bulwer treaty of 1850 provided for joint control by England and the United States, and the ratification of the treaty signed by Colombia for the construction of that canal would have necessitated the abrogation of the Clayton-Bulwer treaty.

So, on March 20, 1878, the Republic of Colombia granted a concession for the construction of an interoceanic canal to Lucien Napoleon Bonaparte Wyse, an officer of the French Navy. This concession, known as the Salgar-Wyse contract, has been printed innumerable times in American Government documents. It is in the report of the Interoceanic Canal Commission. It is in the report of Mr. Knox on the title of the Panama Canal Company. It is in House Document No. 112, Forty-sixth Congress, second session. This concession, known as the Salgar-Wyse contract, provided that all preliminary studies for the route of the canal should be finished "at latest in 1881," and that "the grantees shall then have a period of two years to organize an universal stock company" for the construction of the canal, which it was specified (Art. V)—

shall be finished and placed at the public service within the subsequent 12 years after the formation of the company which shall undertake its construction, but the executive power is authorized to grant a further maximum term of six years in cases of encountering superhuman obstacles beyond the power of the company, and, if after one-third of the canal is built, the company should acknowledge the impossibility of concluding the work in the said 12 years.

The Salgar-Wyse contract, which left the choice of the route open to the concessionaries, specified in Article III:

Should the route of the canal from one ocean to the other pass to the west and to the north of the straight imaginary line which connects Cape Tiburon with Garachinee Point, the grantees must make an amicable arrangement with the Panama Railroad Co. or pay an indemnity which shall be determined in accordance with the provisions of law 46, of August 16, 1867—

The act amending the original contract of the Panama Railroad Co. Finally the contract provided (Art. XXI) that—

The grantees, or those who in the future may succeed them in their rights, may transfer those rights to other capitalists or financial companies, but it is absolutely prohibited to cede or mortgage them under any consideration whatever to any nation or foreign government.

This stipulation was specifically referred to in the next article, XXII:

The grantees or their representatives shall forfeit their acquired rights in the following cases * * * if they violate the prescriptions of Article XXI.

The Salgar-Wyse contract was confirmed by the Congress of the United States of Colombia by law 28 of 1878 (of May 18), and in

1879 was purchased for $10,000,000 by the Compagnie Universelle du Canal Interoceanique de Panama—the old Panama Canal Co.—of which Ferdinand de Lesseps was president. The Government of France—and this is an important point, because Mr. Roosevelt is on record as having said that he paid the $40,000,000 direct to the French Government—the Government of France formally disavowed all connection with the Panama Canal Co. and all responsibility for it, and declared, through the French ambassador in Washington to the Secretary of the United States, that France—

had no intention * * * to guarantee or protect, or in any way make itself responsible for or on account of the plans of Mr. de Lesseps in negotiations for or the building of an interoceanic canal.

Mr. FLOOD. What date did Mr. de Lesseps purchase that concession?

Mr. HALL. In 1879, the purchase was. In 1885 there occurred a disturbance upon the Isthmus——

Mr. LEVY. That has nothing to do with the $40,000,000——

Mr. HALL. Absolutely nothing, except that the French Government had nothing to do with the Panama Canal Co. in any way, shape, or form, either in 1879 or at any subsequent date.

Mr. GARNER. Therefore, the $40,000,000 could not have been paid to the French Government?

Mr. HALL. It was not paid to the French Government.

Mr. LEVY. Who was the $40,000,000 paid to?

Mr. HALL. The $40,000,000 was paid in actual cash by the United States to J. P. Morgan & Co., the fiscal agents, who are credited with having placed that sum on the books of the Bank of France to the credit of the liquidator of the new company and the receiver of the old company, by whom it is claimed the $40,000,000 was distributed. How, I can not tell.

Mr. LEVY. The receiver—what we call in this country the receiver—received the money in France?

The CHAIRMAN. That is, all that went there.

Mr. HALL. He is supposed to have distributed it.

The CHAIRMAN. You do not know how much went over, do you?

Mr. HALL. No, sir; I do not, nor do I know to whom it went.

Mr. KENDALL. The receipts are filed, I guess.

Mr. LEVY. It went into the hands of the receiver.

Mr. HALL. Now, then, in 1885 there was a very serious disturbance of the transit of the Isthmus. The revolutionists, or insurgents, burned down the city of Colon, interrupted the traffic on the Isthmus which had been secured to the United States by the treaty of 1846, and a force of American warships was sent down there. I would like to read you the note that Don Ricardo Becerra, who was then the minister of Colombia to the United States, addressed to Mr. Bayard. It appears on page 58 of Senate Document 143, Fifty-eighth Congress, second session, "Correspondence from the Secretary of State relating to the use by the United States of a military force in the international affairs of Colombia:"

LEGATION OF COLOMBIA AT WASHINGTON.
Washington, April 2, 1885.
(Received April 2.)

SIR: The Colombian State of Panama, across whose territory exists a railway which brings the two oceans into communication, and where at the present time there is being excavated a canal which will unite their waters, is ruled by its own local institutions and obeys a government whose magistrates are elected by the vote of its citizens. In conformity with the political constitution of the Colombian Nation, to which that State belongs and of which it is an integral part, its government yields obedience to and supports the action of the National Government, which holds its seat at Bogota, in all matters having regard to foreign relations, to international commerce, to public instruction, to the army, to the collection of the general taxes, and to the security of persons and property.

Until 1880 the autonomous rights of the State of Panama, like those of the other States of the Union, extended to the exclusion of all intervention of the Federal Government in the armed contests of the citizens of a State against its authorities; but in 1881 a law of the Federal Congress, explanatory of the constitution, imposed upon the National Government—that is to say, upon its executive department—the duty of defending the existence and the tranquil operation of the legal government of the States against hostile attacks on the part of domestic factions. It may be affirmed that this fundamental innovation upon the Colombian political system was in a great measure effected for the purpose of rendering more efficient and assured than theretofore the national intervention for the protection of the great commercial interests established on the Isthmus and of the enterprises which, like that of the canal now in process of construction, promise to vastly develop those interests for the benefit of civilized peoples.

And, in fact, in the execution of that important law the central government established at Bogota gave paramount attention to the military service of the Isthmus, raising the number of its several garrisons to a thousand men, all veterans, endowing them with the best armament and equipment, and intrusting their command to officers of known capacity, whose appointment was confirmed by the Senate.

Thanks to this special system of defense and precaution, there was no recurrence in the State of the slight but always prejudicial disturbances which in former years had obstructed its progress; the persons and property of natives and foreigners enjoyed the highest possible degree of security; and even the enormous body of laborers employed in the works of the canal, reaching in number some 15,000 men, many of them of the lowest moral condition, has scarcely made itself felt, watched over as it has been and in many cases repressed in its excesses by the soldiery of the national garrisons. This satisfactory state of things lasted until the beginning of the month of March of this year, when, unfortunately, there began to be felt upon the Isthmus the deplorable consequences of the powerful rebellion which had occurred in the interior of the Republic and in the populous State of Cauca, which adjoins that of Panama; a rebellion which had its origin in questions of constitutional form, and proposes as its object to perturb this reform and to overthrow from power the legal magistrates of the nation. In order to repress and suppress it in time, it became necessary to concentrate all the military forces of the Union, and among them those which were doing garrison service in Panama and Colon, a large part of which were removed, although merely as a provisional measure, to the States of Bolivar, upon the Caribbean Sea, and Cauca, upon the Pacific.

The most important points of the Isthmus being thus left ungarrisoned in a way that was almost reckless, it was difficult, if not impossible, for its local government to immediately organize the militia force, and to this was added the adverse circumstances of being relatively distant from the center of purely national population, such as are the Provinces of Chiriqui and Veraguas, in which it was possible to enlist soldiers or levy a conscription in conformity with the law.

In Panama and Colon, whose most active population is either cosmopolitan—or, as in the case of the workmen upon the canal, exempt from all military service in pursuance of the liberal concessions of the Colombian Government, and where, moreover, the attractions of excessive commercial gain relax to a certain extent the ties of citizenship—such an organization of forces needs time, demands expense, and in no case can be the work of the moment.

Meanwhile in these same cities of Panama and Colon there are unfortunately not wanting those professional politicians who are in all countries the pest of modern democracies, partisans whose noxious agitation, curbed and kept within bounds until then by the presence of the national forces, found in their temporary removal a propitious opportunity to devote themselves to their natural machinations.

It thus becomes clear now that notwithstanding that there was at the head of the Government, through legal election by the assembly of the State, one of its most distinguished sons, and notwithstanding the intrinsic excellence and the patriotism of all his public acts, and in spite of this same citizen professing the dominant political opinions of the State those professional agitators, and in their shadow many criminals of diverse nationalities and origin conspired against the public peace and order and at last succeeded in an evil hour in seizing, without resistance, the city of Colon and making a sanguinary attack upon that of Panama.

Thus also are explained the horrible excesses, unprecedented in the political history of Colombia, to which, according to the news furnished by the press, those soulless agitators have abandoned themselves during these last few days, and among which are certainly not the least deserving of chastisement and deplorable the imprisonment of the American consul and of an officer of the Navy of this country, notwithstanding the sentiments of constant amity and respect which have ever been entertained by the people of Colombia and all those of its citizens who have exercised or may exercise therein any power or authority toward this Republic and toward its officers and agents of whatever rank.

The two other circumstances should be here mentioned, in order that this communication, which is a sort of memorandum, may produce the results which he who has the honor to present it to the consideration and judgment of the honorable Secretary of State hopes for from it and these are:

First. That notwithstanding the straitened and painful military situation in the interior of the country there nevertheless remained in the city of Panama certain national forces which have contended against the disturbers of the public, although without the successful result which was to be desired.

Second. That in well-grounded anticipation (based upon a knowledge of men and things upon the Isthmus) of the deplorable excesses of which the city of Colon has been the theater and the victim, conference writer of this communication had the honor, in a verbal conference sought to that end, to intimate clearly to the honorable Secretary of State how expedient it was, and besides being opportune how necessary that sufficient American forces on board of vessels of war stationed at Panama and Colon should be there within sight of events ready and competent to give to the persons and property of American citizens that effective protection and shelter which, by reason of temporary but none the less effective deficiency or material force, the Colombian authorities could not afford for the time being. The honorable Secretary took a note of those intimations, and his remarks indicated his favorable reception thereof.

It follows from what has been herein set forth that Colombia, after having assured at the cost of no small sacrifices on her part the advantages of the Panama transit for the enjoyment and benefit of the interests of all mankind, after having there suppressed the national customs duties and as a concession toward a more expeditious and free communication done away with even the most elementary formalities of her maritime coasting policy, and after, lastly, having contracted without proportionate compensation and solely in a generous spirit of association in the work of common progress, the responsibility of protecting by means of her forces the general schemes of communication from ocean to ocean and the vast interests thereto related, has done since 1849, and especially since 1880, in so far as the great purpose in view involved modification in the constitutional practices of the Government, all that has been in her power in the direction of fulfilling her pledges. Accidents in her political life, which are not to be wondered at in an incipient nation such as Colombia is, since they occur in others of secular growth, have at times prevented, as, for instance, in the present case, effective as is to be desired, but these exceptions, which, as has been observed likewise occur even under the authority of the better-constituted Governments of the world, afford assuredly no ground for forgetting what that Republic has done in contribution to the universal interests of civilisation, to which, as an absolutely free arena, the Colombian territory of the Isthmus has been thrown open.

The present unfortunate state of things in that region will, on the other hand, not be long continued. The rebellion of the interior of Colombia has been overcome, and the recent submission of the coast of the State of Cauca to the authority of the National Government indicates that there will be dispatches from there at no distant day of armed expeditions on the part of the nation, competent to restore peace upon the Isthmus and to subject to the operations of justice those who have disturbed it by attempt like that of Colon.

Entertaining the most justifiable confidence in the high circumspection and never belied spirit of probity of the Government of the United State of America, the undersigned, envoy extraordinary and minister plenipotentiary of the United States of Colombia, has the honor to submit this note and the details and information which it contains to the judgment of the honorable Secretary of State, in the hope that the decision which he will reach concerning the recent deplorable events upon the Isthmus will be as fitting to the occasion as is to be desired.

The undersigned renews, etc. RICARDO BECERRA.

Now, in response to that note, President Cleveland landed American forces, and in rendering account to Congress of his action, in December, 1885, he said:

Emergencies growing out of civil war in the United States of Colombia demanded of the Government at the beginning of his administration, the employment or armed forces to fulfill its guarantees under the thirty-fifth article of the treaty of 1846 in order to keep the transit open across the Isthmus of Panama. Desirous of exercising only the powers expressly reserved to us by the treaty, and mindful of the rights of Colombia, the forces sent to the Isthmus were instructed to confine their action to "positively and efficaciously" preventing the transit and its accessories from being "interrupted or embarrased." The execution of this delicate and responsible task necessarily involved police control where the local authorities was temporarily powerless, but always in aid of the sovereignty of Columbia.

Under the fourth section of the treaty of 1846–1848, which, as you will recall, makes those who violate the treaty of 1846–1848 personally responsible for their acts and engages the two governments in no way to protect the offenders against proceedings from the other government, two men were hanged in Colon for having interrupted the transit of the Isthmus, and later the ringleader, Señor Prestan, who had escaped from Porto Bello, and for whom the high seas had been searched by American vessels of war, was captured in Cartagena, brought back to Colon, and there hanged by the neck until he was dead.

Mr. LEVY. The United States was the only Government that had authority to land troops——

Mr. HALL. No foreign government whatever had any right——

Mr. LEVY. Except the United States.

Mr. HALL. Now, to return in chronological order to the Panama Canal Co. The old Panama Canal Co. in 1888 purchased the great majority of the stock of the Panama Railroad Co., paying for it somewhere in the neighborhood of $18,600,000, and thus, being in control of the Panama Railroad Co., did not have to pay any compensation for the building of a canal across the Isthmus, as they might have been requested to do if the Panama Railroad Co. had been and remained an independent entity.

In 1889 the old Panama Canal Co., having become bankrupt, was dissolved by the Tribunal Civile dela Seine, and Monsieur Brunet was appointed receiver—

with the broadest powers, especially to grant or contribute to any new company all or a part of the corporate assets, to enter into or ratify wih the contributors all agreements having for their purpose the continuance of the works.

Following the collapse of the Compagnie International de Canal Interoceanique de Panama, on February 4, 1889, the Congress of the United States granted a Federal charter to the Maritime Canal Co. for the construction of the Nicaragua Canal, and on May 15, 1889, work in Panama was finally suspended by the liquidator.

Mr. GOODWIN. That is the first time in your recital that the Nicaragua canal proposition has appeared.

Mr. HALL. That is where it comes in for the first time, immediately after the collapse of the Panama scheme; then the United States Congress went ahead and granted this charter for the construction of the Nicaragua Canal.

Mr. HARRISON. Who were the promoters of that Nicaragua Canal Co.?

Mr. HALL. I can furnish you the names of the promoters. I do not happen to have all of them here.

On February 13, 1890, Achille Monchicourt was appointed co-receiver of the old Panama Canal Co. On March 8 Brunet resigned, leaving Monchicourt as sole receiver. Colombia granted a 10-year extension of the concession.

There was a prolonged litigation in the French courts that led to authority being granted to the receivers to dispose of the assets; and, to facilitate the reorganization of the company, Colombia, on April 4, 1893, granted a second extension of the concession. It provided that the 10-year extension granted in 1890 should begin to run not later than October 31, 1894. In a dispatch sent on December 2, 1892, by Secretary of State John Foster to Mr. Jeremiah Coghlan, United States Minister at Bogota, in which the United States minister was urged to ask Colombia not to prolong the French concession, the Isthmus of Panama is admitted by Secretary of State John Foster to be "one of the most important and valuable stretches of territory there is in the world."

In July, 1893, the French courts appointed Mr. Lemarquis as trustee for the bondholders and Mr. Gautron as coreceiver. In 1894 Mr. Monchicourt died and Mr. Gautron continued to act as sole receiver. I am giving this for the purpose of later getting at who were the responsible people to get the money the United States paid.

There remained but a short time to effect before October 31, 1894, the actual reorganization of the old Panama Canal Co. To this end Mr. Gautron, the receiver, and M. Lemarquis, trustee for the bondholders, secured by a series of compromises from the manager of the old company, from the financial institutions, from the contractors, and from a certain number of persons to whom various securities had been assigned, their cooperation in the work of reorganization. The new company was formed to take over the assets of the old company. It was not chartered by the French Government. The new Panama Canal Co. was never chartered by the French Government, nor was it under government supervision. It was incorporated under article 21 of the French law "concerning companies," which provides that "anonymous associations may be formed without authorization from the government." Under this act the La Compagnie Nouvelle du Canal de Panama—the New Panama Canal Co.—was constituted definitely on October 20, 1894. Its headquarters (siege sociale) was: 63, Rue de la Victoire, Paris.

The capital of the New Panama Canal Co. was fixed at 65,000,000 francs, divided into 650,000 shares of 100 francs each. Of the total capital 5,000,000 francs were set apart for the Republic of Colombia to pay for the extension of the concession, 40,620,700 francs were taken by what were known as the penitentiary shareholders—that is, persons who had unduly profited out of syndicates in connection with the old Panama Canal Co. and who obtained the compromise or abandonment of criminal suits brought against them by agreeing to restitute their unlawful gains in the form of subscriptions to the new company, only 3,484,300 francs was obtained by public subscription, the liquidator of the old company taking the balance, 15,895,000 francs.

The 3,484,300 francs ($680,000) subscribed by the public (about 5 per cent of the capitalization) was held by some 6,000 shareholders, the very great majority of whom subscribed for from one to five shares; the balance was held by the big banks and contractors who had "profited" out of the old company.

Mr. LEVY. Did the old shareholders get anything?

Mr. HALL. This was the subscription of 65,000,000 francs to form the new company. Then the old Panama Canal Co., as I shall presently show you, made a contract with the New Panama Canal Co. that provided for a division of anything they could sell the property for.

In payment for the stock of the New Panama Canal Co. the 6,000 small subscribers really paid hard cash. The "syndicators" turned in various claims, receipts, settlements, and some cash. The receiver turned in the cash he had in hand belonging to the old company, and other liquid assets, especially the Panama Railroad stock. Mr. Lemarquis transferred the assets of the old company to the new company for 60 per cent of the profits. These assets included the Panama Railroad shares—68,534 shares out of 70,000 existing—which had been purchased at a cost of about $18,094,000. These shares were deposited with the Comptoir National d'Escompte, subject to an agreement between the two companies which provided that if the canal was built the Panama Railroad was to belong to the new company. If it was not built the new company was to pay 20,000,000 francs for it, and when it was finally turned over to the United States the Panama Railroad was, according to a printed address of Mr. Shonts, merely two streaks of rust.

Prior to the organization of the New Panama Canal Co.—and here, gentlemen, is where comes into the case Mr. William Nelson Cromwell, the man whose masterful mind, whetted on the grindstone of corporation cunning, conceived and carried out the rape of the Isthmus. He was counsel to the Panama Railroad Co. and a director in it. In testifying before the Committee on Interoceanic Canals, February 26, 1906, he said:

> My firm have been general counsel for the Panama Railroad Co. for over 12 years. * * * We never had any connection with the so-called de Lesseps company.

And he further fixes the date of his beginning his connection with the railroad company as 1893. Now, it is to be noted that the Panama Railroad Co. was still the property of the de Lesseps, or old Panama Canal Co., and was not sold to the New Panama Canal Co. until some time after the date of the organization of the latter, the 20th of October, 1894. The actual agreement between the receiver of the old Panama Canal Co. and the New Panama Canal Co. concerning the shares of the Panama Railroad, was not completed until March 24, 1900. Mr. Cromwell's official connection with the New Panama Canal Co. really began in Janury, 1896.

Now, I must run forward a little. For the sum of $40,000,000 the assets, property, and archives of the New Panama Canal Co. had been sold to the United States. Mr. Cromwell, who had done service of unique and invaluable character, very naturally wanted to be paid for it; and he put in a claim for legal services rendered and disbursements made for $800,000, or 4,000,000 francs, just 2 per cent of the $40,000,000. Now, 4,000,000 francs looked a very big sum to the liquidators of the New Panama Canal Co., and no such fee, I venture to say, had ever been heard of in Paris. So, as they could not very well go to law about this matter for obvious reasons, they decided to submit their differences to arbitration. Mr. Cromwell prepared a brief, which he submitted to the three arbitrators in Paris, Maitre Henri Barboux, Maitre Georges Devin, and Maitre Alexandre Ribot, three of the most noted civil lawyers in France, and agreed to abide by their decision. This brief was submitted to the arbitrators in French. I want to be perfectly fair to Mr. Cromwell. I believe the brief was originally written by him in English. It was then translated into French by a well-known French lawyer who practices in New York. A copy of the brief in French as presented to the arbitrators is in possession of the World. It contains a detailed statement of all services rendered to the New Panama Canal Co. that Mr. Cromwell could publicly subscribe to, and contains in the utmost detail the whole history of how he defeated the Nicaraugua bills and put over the sale of the canal for $40,000,000 here in Washington. This brief I have. With your permission, although it is very voluminous, I should like, when I have finished my statement, to have it printed in the record as an appendix to my remarks. It is a valuable document. This is the translation into English.

Mr. Garner. What is the authority for the translation?

Mr. Hall. I translated it, sir, myself. I may say that I was brought up and partly educated in France. I lived in Paris for a number of years, at least a dozen. I exercised my profession as a journalist there and worked on several French newspapers. I have served on several occasions as official interpreter for the Tribunal Civil de la Seine, which is the civil court in Paris, and La Cour d'Appel, which is the court of appeals. Eighteen years ago I married a French lady, and I never speak anything but French in my home life. I made this translation myself from the French original, and did so with the utmost care. I verified everything. I have tried my best to do justice to Mr. Cromwell and to be fair and impartial in this matter.

Mr. Kendall. Has Mr. Cromwell seen your translation?

Hr. Hall. He has not, sir. I do not think he knows it exists.

Mr. Levy. Have you it in French?

Mr. Hall. Yes, sir.

Mr. Levy. It would be well to file the French one as well.

Mr. Hall. I can produce the original in French.

The Chairman. There being no objection, Mr. Hall will have that privilege.

Mr. Cromwell testified before the Morgan committee that he was first employed in June, 1896, as the result of conferences with Mr.

Whalen, then vice president of the Panama Railroad Co. In his brief Mr. Cromwell says:

The board of directors addressed itself to Mr. William Nelson Cromwell, and later to his law firm, Messrs. Sullivan & Cromwell, and officially intrusted them with the representation and defense of the company's interests, appointing them general counsel of the company in the United States. This was in January, 1896.

In Mr. Cromwell's own words his work was legal, judicial, legislative, political, financial, and general. His firm "constituted a force, an organization, and an instrumentality specially adapted to the needs of the Panama Canal Co." In his brief Mr. Cromwell frankly states:

In the course of a very active and very extended professional career, covering a period of more than 30 years, the firm of Sullivan & Cromwell had found itself placed in intimate relations, susceptible of being used to advantage, with men possessing influence and power in all the circles and almost everywhere in the United States; that not only have the members of this firm established close and intimate professional relations with their most distinguished colleagues throughout the United States, but they have also come to know and be in a position to influence a considerable number of public men in political life, in financial circles, and on the press, and all these influences and relations were of great and sometimes decisive utility, and of valuable assistance in the performance of their professional duties in the Panama matter. This fact was formally acknowledged (reconnu) by the company in its letter confirming the renewal of our professional engagement in January, 1902. It would be impossible to detail and enumerate—nor even, perhaps, would it be proper so to do—the innumerable ways in which this influence and this power were utilized in this matter; but what can be easily understood and appreciated is that such relations and connections, the outcome of many years of successful professional activity, were of great value and that our clients in this matter in particular received the benefit of this influence and power. It is not suggested that the remuneration should be based upon this consideration alone, but it was in part such considerations which added weight and power to our professional activities, which contributed materially to the result obtained, and which enabled us in the critical crises of this great affair to ward off what on several occasions looked like the final deathblow to the Panama enterprise, and to drag out of a desperate case a decisive victory.

When Mr. Cromwell was intrusted with the interests of the New Panama Canal Co. in 1896, he found himself face to face with—but I will give it to you in Mr. Cromwell's own words. In his brief he says:

When we were intrusted with the affair in 1896, we found ourselves face to face with a general and almost unanimous opinion in the United States in favor of the Nicaragua Canal, which was looked upon as the American canal; the Nicaragua Canal had been officially recognized by Congress when that body granted a charter to a company formed for its construction; various committees had been appointed by Congress for the survey of this route and favorable reports had been filed; liberal concessions for the building of the canal had been granted by Nicaragua and Costa Rica, and these Governments openly favored the selection of this route by the United States; a large number of citizens of the United States were pecuniarily interested in it; construction work of some importance had been begun by the Maritime Co. on the Nicaragua route; messages of Presidents to Congress had recognized and recommended the Nicaragua route; the matter of the canal was so important that it had become a plank in the platforms formally of both parties, and these platforms formally favored Nicaragua; and above all the Panama Canal was looked upon as an undertaking which was not only a failure from a financial point of view, but as an engineering proposition was a scandalous affair of which nothing but evil was spoken.

The Perkins and Mahon bills were then pending in Congress. In his brief Mr. Cromwell says:

We had personal interviews with Members of Congress; we employed, as assistants, Washington lawyers instructed to follow, day by day, the evidence then being taken by a House committee on the subject of the Nicaragua Canal, and we were in daily communication with them on this subject, studying reports and giving instructions.

Then Mr. Cromwell explains:

At this time the instructions we had received from the company did not permit us to appear publicly in its name, as the company was not ready—by virtue either of a favorable report from its engineering committees or of adequate financial plans—to take a decisive stand before the world. But confidentially we actively circulated information concerning the Panama project and its plans for the revival of the enterprise and the completion of the work, and we laid special stress upon (brought out specially) the flaws and difficulty of execution in the construction of the Nicaragua Canal.

Between January and June, 1896, Mr. Cromwell and Mr. Curtis made alternate stays in Washington for this purpose (on this subject). They devoted themselves actively to the case during a considerable part of this period, and had personal interviews with a number of Senators and Representatives in order to discuss with them and to attack the pending bills. Mr. Cromwell also had frequent interviews with Col. Ludlow in regard to the investigation by his commission, and urged upon him (presented to him) the superior advantages of Panama. As a result of this exposition the Ludlow Commission in its supplementary (ulterieur) report made very favorable references to the Panama route.

Mr. Harrison. What Curtis is that mentioned there?

Mr. Hall. That is Mr. Curtis, Mr. Cromwell's partner.

Now, Mr. Cromwell further on in his brief says:

On June 1 of this year, 1896, Senator Morgan, of Alabama, introduced a new and more comprehensive bill in the Senate, to overcome certain criticisms of the Perkins and Mahon bills; this bill also provided for the adoption of the Nicaragua route, the guarantee by the Government of the bonds of the Maritime Co., and the acquisition of the capital stock of the Maritime Co. by the United States; and it promptly received the indorsement of the committee and was placed on the calendar of the Senate. We at once critically examined this measure, and opposed it, just as we were opposing the other bills.

The reports of the Senate and House committees on the subject of the Nicaragua Canal bills were favorable to those measures, but the opposition Mr. Cromwell had created was sufficient to prevent the passage of any constructive legislation before Congress adjourned. Mr. Cromwell in his brief says:

In December, 1896, when Congress met, the Nicaragua bills were therefore still pending, their passage was recommended by the respective committees, and their supporters (friends) had only to bring them to a vote. The preliminary steps had already been taken. It was certain that in each House the most determined efforts would be made to this end, and a division (vote) would have insured the passage of the bills and the building of the Nicaragua Canal. The period between June and December, 1896, was taken up with such preparations as we were able to make for the following session, in view of the restriction already mentioned; that is to say, in view of the fact that the company was not ready to make public definite engineering and financial plans; but we worked continually on the case (nous occupames constamment de l'affaires), making friends for Panama and keeping ourselves informed of movements and conditions that might be adverse to us. We made frequent reports to the company during the year.

I shall have something to say later about those reports of Mr. Cromwell to the company.

Mr. Kendall. Mr. Cromwell was trying to establish before that board of arbitration that he had used all his ability as a lawyer and his influence as a politician in order to promote the Panama route?

Mr. HALL. In order to defeat legislation in favor of Nicaragua and sell the Panama Canal Co. for the sum of $40,000,000 to the United States.

Mr. KENDALL. In order to do that he had to defeat the Nicaragua project entirely?

Mr. HALL. He is describing how he did that.

The CHAIRMAN. The committee will now take a recess until 2 o'clock, and will give you from 2 o'clock to 4 o'clock to go on.

Mr. HALL. Thank you.

Thereupon at 12 o'clock m. the committee took a recess until this afternoon at 2 o'clock.

AFTER RECESS.

The committee resumed at 2 o'clock p. m., Hon. William Sulzer (chairman) presiding.

STATEMENT OF MR. HENRY N. HALL—Resumed.

The CHAIRMAN. If you are ready to go on, Mr. Hall, you may proceed.

Mr. HALL. As soon as Congress met in December, 1896, Mr. Cromwell came to Washington, bringing with him his partner, Mr. Curtis, and both remained in the Capital to protect the interests of the Panama Canal Co. In his brief, Mr. Cromwell says:

> The supporters of Nicaragua began, as soon as the House met, to circulate a petition addressed to the Committee on Rules, with a view to getting this committee to decide to place their bill on the calendar. Their plan was to obtain so many signatures to this petition that the committee would recognise their strength and be brought to grant their request. We were then kept constantly busy, during the days and evenings, interviewing Members of the House and opposing this action. Despite the 200 signatures of Members they obtained to their petition, the opposition made by us and the Members who were against the bill was such that the attempt failed, to the great surprise and chagrin of its supporters. They then tried to obtain a vote in the Senate, hoping that favorable action there would have a decisive influence on the Committee on Rules in the House. As the bill in the Senate was in favorable posture, Senator Morgan was able to advance it and cooperate with the movement in the House. Mr. Cromwell and Mr. Curtis remained in Washington for several weeks during this critical period, exercising constant vigilance and activity. With the restriction that then hampered our action, our efforts were chiefly bent on showing the drawbacks of the Nicaragua route and the reasons which militated against the passage of legislative measures, rather than on supporting the cause of the Panama Canal.
>
> In spite of the vigorous and almost successful efforts of the Nicaragua party, their bills had not reached a vote when the closure of Congress came on March 4, and we can say, in all justice, that our constant care, our serious opposition, and our varied efforts had contributed in a somewhat considerable degree to this result.

Mr. Cromwell, convinced that the negative policy must be abandoned and that the sole hope for the salvation of the New Panama Canal Co. lay in the adoption of a plan of action upon bases which Mr. Cromwell suggested "different, open, audacious, aggressive," wrote to the company on February 21, 1897, a letter in which he said:

> During the many years of my connection with the railroad and the canal I have been brought into contact with the Government and the most influential Senators and Representatives. I have also informed myself of the general

state of mind of the American press and upon the platforms of each of the political parties. I have come to the conclusion that as far as the general public is concerned, both it and the Government are clearly favorable to the Nicaragua Canal and its control by the American Government. You will thus see that the problem is quite different to that which you have been facing. It is no longer a bankrupt company which is our competitor, it is the Nation itself. Now to turn the Nation from this design becomes the new and weighty problem. I feel that it will be necessary to take active steps in order to stop the Government in its inclination to settle the canal question itself. I know that it is your desire to build the Panama Canal under the auspices or protection of this Government, in some form or other, but what I have told you will show you the difficulty, to wit, that it is clear that our Government wishes to be the virtual owner of the canal. Permit me therefore, respectfully, to suggest that you seriously consider whether the time for us to address our Government in the interest of the Panama Canal has arrived, and if so the basis and form of a proposal on this subject.

This advice was reiterated on February 9, 10, and 13 in letters and telegrams, and brought Monsieur Hutin, director general of the New Panama Canal Co., to New York, where he remained during the latter part of February and the beginning of March. For more than three weeks Mr. Cromwell had daily conferences with him.

On March 4, 1897, the inauguration of Mr. McKinley as President took place, and he immediately called a special session of Congress for the 15th of that month.

In his brief Mr. Cromwell says:

The Nicaragua bills were at once reintroduced. * * * The new Secretary of State was ex-Senator Sherman, who, only a few days previously had been chairman of the Committee on Foreign Relations in the Senate, in charge of the Nicaragua bills, and he was an avowed and powerful supporter of that route. He entered into negotiations with the Central American States, represented by Senor Rodriguez, their minister, with a view to a treaty under which the Nicaragua Canal would be built by the United States itself directly, instead of being built under the concessions of the Maritime Co. He sent official communications to the Senate to this effect and appeared in person before the Senate committee in support of his plan. All these developments (démarches) not only demanded but received the utmost vigilance and diligence on our part; they also necessitated the almost constant presence in Washington of a member of our law firm.

Then Mr. Cromwell goes on to tell how he conceived the idea of making Colombia serve the ends of the Panama Canal Co., and how his clients approved of his plan He says:

Confronted by the unexpected developments (circumstances) of the special session and the active negotiations between the United States and Nicaragua entered upon by Secretary Sherman, we conceived the plan of inducing Colombia herself to intervene and enforce (faire valoir) according to the terms of the treaty of 1846–48 between New Granada (now Colombia) and the United States, and to protect the rights of the Panama Canal Co. as the owner of the concession which had been granted by Colombia on the basis of that treaty. The plan (idea) thus conceived by us was presented to the company, which approved of it at once; and, in consequence, we immediately spoke of it to the representative of Colombia in the United States (Mr. Renfigo, chargé d'affaires at Washington), and a series of interviews ensued, in the course of which we made a full exposition of the new position of the canal company, discussed the treaty of 1848, and furnished arguments in support of these views.

Mr. Cromwell's plan was mapped out in a letter dated March 20, addressed to the New Panama Canal Co., in which he said:

The moment to act has arrived. The Colombian Government and the Panama Co. ought to officially bring to the knowledge of the Government of the United States the existence of the Panama concession, the considerable amount of work accomplished under the concession, the present business like (serieuses) intentions of the parties, and to remind it of the clauses of the treaty of 1848 between the United States and Colombia. In face of such a presentation it will be far more difficult, if not impossible, for our Government to take action with Nicaragua; and in my opinion it is the only means to prevent its so doing. Certainly this is essential to the canal company, for if this Government adopts Nicaragua it will kill our project; but it is equally important to Colombia, which does not wish to see its rival (Nicaragua) obtain the richest prize a South American nation could ever win. Colombia, as well as the Panama Canal Co., must wake up, must come to a keen realization of her danger, and must show herself equal to the opportunity that offers. She ought, immediately and by cable, to notify her minister to present a note covering the grounds we indicate, and to cooperate with us earnestly and at once. Do not let the Government trust to the mails, which are slow. This matter calls for action by cable as rapidly as possible. To gain time, I am myself going to cable you to this effect.

As we have already seen, the plan thus conceived by Mr. Cromwell to make Colombian diplomacy the catspaw of the New Panama Canal Co. was heartily approved of by his clients, and in consequence he immediately turned his attention to Senor Renfigo, the Colombian chargé d'affaires in Washington. What Mr. Cromwell did had best be told in his own words:

We prepared and presented to the representative of Colombia an official protest, and, after discussion, it was accepted by him and presented to the Government of the United States. The effect of this step (mesure) made itself felt, and the attention of the United States was attracted to the Panama Canal through important diplomatic channels. This arrested the attention of the Government and introduced the Panama Canal, advantageously and with effect, as a factor whose consideration imposed itself in the solution of the pending problems; until then it had been completely neglected.

Mr. Cromwell's correspondence with the company shows how fully he was aware of the necessity of defeating all Nicaragua legislation. Writing on April 6 to his clients he said:

Your duty has colossal importance, and we must lay our plans with Napoleonic strategy to prevent any other transisthmian project from taking shape * * *. It is clear that, unless all the other transisthmian projects are thwarted, the hopes of your security holders will be entirely disappointed, and it is equally clear that if this Government makes an agreement with the Nicaragua Government, or even with the present Nicaragua company, our canal project will be henceforth almost hopeless.

Mr. Hutin, who had gone to Panama at the end of March, returned from the Isthmus on April 20. Mr. Cromwell had daily conferences with him, and he spent a great part of the next 30 days in Washington with Mr. Cromwell and Mr. Curtis; then he left for Paris.

Mr. Lemarquis, trustee for the bondholders of the old company, also visited the United States in May of this year, collaborated with Mr. Cromwell daily in the study of the political situation of the parliamentary developments of the public sentiment in favor of Nicaragua and the desire of the United States to itself own a canal, and of the methods Mr. Cromwell was employing and the plans he was advising. In Mr. Cromwell's words:

Mr. Lemarquis's observations and studies permitted him to arrive at wise conclusions, both for his own guidance and that of other interested parties on his return to Paris.

On June 4, 1897, Congress passed the sundry civil appropriation act containing the appropriation to continue surveys in Nicaragua. The act also empowered the President to appoint a commission to report on the Nicaragua route. Under this act President McKinley appointed the Nicaragua Canal Commission, commonly referred as the first Walker Commission. Its members were Rear Admiral John G. Walker, Col. Peter C. Hains, and Prof. Lewis M. Haupt.

Congress met again in December, 1897, and at the very opening of Congress Representative Barham introduced a new bill for the building of the Nicaragua Canal. During this session various new measures were introduced, all with a view to the construction of the Nicaragua Canal under the auspices of the United States. These bills emanated, one from Senator Hansbrough, January 5, 1898; another from Mr. Davidson, January 11, 1898; Senator Morgan, May 5, 1898; Senator Stewart, May 25, 1898; and yet another from Senator Morgan June 20, 1898. The Walker-Hains-Haupt Nicaragua Canal Commission sailed for Nicaragua in December. Mr. Cromwell again wrote to the Panama Canal Co. under date December 24:

> More than ever I am convinced that we ought to make an energetic demonstration before the return of the commission.

On January 26, 1898, Mr. Cromwell again wrote to the company:

> Everywhere one finds proof of a growing confidence in and desire for the construction of a Nicaragua Canal, and I can not help thinking that we have lost and are losing ground every day in regard to our project, and I find myself obliged to insist that the Panama project be called to the attention of our Government before it is too late to stop the drift in favor of the Nicaragua project, and too late to break pledges given or to win against the private and selfish advantage offered by the other plans.

The grave international complications which arose between the United States and Spain over the disturbances in Cuba, followed by the Spanish-American War, absorbed almost the entire attention of Congress during the session of December, 1897–8. Mr. Cromwell's brief continues:

> The celebrated voyage of the American battleship *Oregon* down the Pacific coast, round the Horn, and up the Atlantic coast to Cuba was followed with intense interest not only by the people of the United States, but by the whole civilized world, and this battleship was hurrying to join Admiral Sampson's fleet, which it reached only just in time to take part in the battle of Santiago. The nation understood the danger to which the necessity of such a voyage would have exposed the country in case of war with a more powerful naval power. The enormous advantage of being able—by means of an interoceanic canal—to avoid going round the South American Continent impressed everybody, and a general clamor for the Nicaragua as a measure of public safety arose. * * * Another result of this state of public opinion was to put an end to all ideas of a canal owned by a private company, as Mr. Cromwell had long since predicted. It was to be built, owned, and operated by the United States; it was to be fortified and garrisoned by the United States. It was no longer to be merely a tool of commerce, but, first and foremost, a part of the national defenses, and, as such, not neutral but American. No passage of this kind could be opened to an enemy, it could exist only if held by the United States.

The irritation against France, created in the United States by the open sympathy of the people and press of France with the cause of Spain, led Mr. Cromwell, in April, 1898, to advise a temporary postponement of a public presentation of Panama's case; but he energetically urged upon the company to make this presentation before the Congress which was to meet in the following December.

In May, 1898, a resolution was passed by the Senate inviting the Maritime Co. to make a proposal for the transfer of its capital stock to the United States, carrying with it the ownership of its concessions and the payment of its debt. In response to this resolution, the Maritime Co. made a proposal to the United States in which it offered to effect the necessary transfers on the payment of $5,500,000. It was on these lines that the Morgan bill of June 20, 1898, was presented to Congress.

In June, 1898, the Panama Co. asked Mr. Cromwell to go to Paris to discuss the plans he had urged upon the company. Mr. Cromwell went and was absent from the United States for about six weeks, conferring with the representatives of the canal company in Paris. The result was the complete and unreserved adoption of the plan he had advised, and he was intrusted with its execution. Mr. Cromwell at once returned to the United States and began active work. He organized a press bureau—

for the preparation and publication of technical and popular articles in the various magazines and periodicals of the country, dealing with every phase of the Panama and Nicaragua problems, and to this end employed experienced writers and engineers. The work of the bureau, which lasted for a year or two, * * * extended all over the United States.

Mr. Cromwell hired Gen. Abbot and Mr. Corthell, a distinguished engineer, to assist in the work of this press bureau.

Messrs. Lemarquis and Lampre came to New York in September, and had daily conferences with Mr. Cromwell for several weeks, and accompanied him to Washington.

As the reassembling of Congress drew near (the first session after the Spanish War) a unanimous feeling in favor of the immediate selection of the Nicaragua Canal as a national undertaking made itself manifest throughout the United States. The President of Costa Rica made a special trip to Washington, and in the name of Costa Rica, as well as of Nicaragua, gave President McKinley official assurances that these Governments would adopt all legislation necessary to facilitate the building of the Nicaragua Canal.

In his brief, Mr. Cromwell says:

Keenly alive to the gravity of the situation we insistently urged upon the company to make an official presentation of the case of Panama to President McKinley in the form of a memorial before the reassembling of Congress. We prepared the first draft of the memorial which was to be presented to the Government of the United States in the name of the company, containing a synopsis of the formation of La Compagnie Nouvelle du Canal de Panama, its concessions, the extent of the construction work already accomplished, the organization of the international committee and its findings, the intentions of the company, etc.

Mr. Cromwell went to Washington and communicated to Secretary of State Hay in advance the plan for the official presentation of the case of the New Panama Canal Co., and arranged with the Secretary for an official audience with President McKinley. This was fixed for December 2, 1898, and Mr. Cromwell, with the director general and the chief engineer of the company, who had come from Paris specially for this purpose, officially presented to President McKinley the memorial of the company, accompanied by the report of the international committee, which had just been completed.

At this time the Panama Canal Co. was asking the Colombian Congress for an extension of its concessions, and two days after the presentation of the memorial and report of the technical committee to President McKinley an official statement was given out by the Department of State to the effect that the Colombian Congress in Bogota had refused to grant an extension of its concessions to La Compagnie Nouvelle du Canal de Panama, which naturally meant that the Panama Co. no longer cut any figure in this matter. Mr. Cromwell sent an official communication to the United States Government in which the accuracy of this report from Bogota was denied, and the Colombian minister, at Mr. Cromwell's request, did the same and sent a copy of his note to the press. The same day (Dec. 4) the president of the Maritime Co. sent to the press a note attacking the Panama Canal, and alluding to the interview of its representatives with President McKinley and Secretary Hay on the 2d instant as an insult to the American people.

The following day (Dec. 5) Congress reassembled and President McKinley sent in his message, in which he recommended the building of the Nicaragua Canal under American control.

Two days later Senator Morgan made a violent speech in the Senate, announcing his determination to force the passage of the Nicaragua Canal bill, and attacking the representatives of the Panama Canal as in league with the transcontinental railroads to prevent the American people obtaining an American canal through Nicaragua. Nobody in America thought the session of Congress could pass without the enactment of law for the building of the Nicaragua Canal. Nothing seemed able to resist the influences combined in its favor. Mr. Cromwell, however, proved himself equal to the task. The Nicaragua plan entailed not a neutral canal, but a canal to be built, owned, and controlled by the United States alone, and to be fortified so as to assure to them its exclusive mastership. Mr. Cromwell in his brief says:

We called the attention of Members of Congress and of the administration to the fact that this was contrary to the Clayton-Bulwer treaty with England, and put forward the objection that difficulties with that power would be precipitated if the Nicaragua project were adopted before a modification of this treaty. This objection was made in the Senate and surprised several Senators whose zeal for Nicaragua was not great enough to blind them to other considerations. It was strengthened by a formal protest against the bill presented a few days later by the British Ambassador, Lord Pauncefote, to the Secretary of State and based upon the same grounds. * * * December 23, 1898, the Walker-Hains-Haupt Commission made its preliminary report in favor of the Nicaragua Canal, estimating the cost of its construction at $135,000,000. This settled for the public the practical side of the question, which the report of the Ludlow Commission had left somewhat in doubt. It was assured that the Nicaragua Canal could be built, and at a known cost. Henceforth only one question remained, that of the authorization of Congress.

Mr. Cromwell's next move was to prepare a complete and descriptive pamphlet, explaining in detail the position of the new Panama Canal Co., the progress of the work, the amount of construction already accomplished, the entirely new management of the reorganized company, the concessions and titles, a summary of the report of the technical committee, the plan of the canal itself, accompanied by photographs illustrating the condition of the work, etc.; one of these photographs showed the

sea end of La Boca Pier. This is the pier which connects with the Panama Canal, now open from the ocean.

Speaking of the pamphlet, Mr. Cromwell in his brief says:

We spent several weeks writing this pamphlet, entitled "The New Panama Canal Co." (dated Dec. 26, 1898), of which we circulated a large number of copies. We sent one to each Member of Congress, to all the higher officials of the Federal Government, to the governors and other high officials of all the States, to all the leading newspapers of the East (the number of which reaches several hundreds), to all the commercial bodies of the large cities, to the libraries, to the heads of educational establishments and other influential institutions, and generally wherever the influence of this pamphlet might have weight.

Mr. Cromwell's brief continues:

An examination of the situation convinced us that the Senate bill would soon reach a vote, and would then certainly be adopted, and we wrote to the company along these lines on January 6. We therefore concentrated our attention on the House and planned a new measure of defense. We decided to ask the committee of the House intrusted with the canal matter for a public hearing, although this committee was openly hostile to Panama and had pledged itself to Nicaragua, although it had on several occasions reported in favor of Nicaragua, and although its chairman, Mr. Hepburn, was the most earnest and most able champion of Nicaragua in the House, he having ability, power, and vigor on a par with the capable leader of this cause in the Senate—Senator Morgan. It was, however, the only channel through which the Panama Canal could be officially presented to the House, and we determined to adopt an audacious and aggressive method of exposition. We demanded an audience under circumstances which rendered a refusal impossible, and public hearings were held on January 17, 18, and 19.

We decided upon and had a presentation of the Panama matter made not only by Mr. Cromwell and Mr. Curtis, but, as to its technical aspects, by the chief engineer of the canal company and by Gen. Abbot, member of the International Technical Committee. In prevision of this hearing, a most profound study of the technical sides of the question was made. It necessitated incessant work, night and day, up to the very hour of the hearing.

As we had foreseen, the Morgan bill reached a vote in the Senate, in spite of all opposition, on January 21, and was speedily passed by a vote of 48 to 6. The bill was at once sent to the House, where, as we have said, we had obtained public hearings, in prevision of its arrival, on the 17th, 18th, and 19th of this month.

An enthusiastic and large majority of the House was openly pledged to Nicaragua. The result of a vote in the House was absolutely certain, if a vote were taken. If it could not be deferred, the fate of Panama was sealed. The public and Congress had no real knowledge of the Panama plan. Commission after commission had indorsed Nicaragua, but, as for Panama, the only information available consists of the statements of the Panama Co.'s counsel and officials. These statements, although truthful and precise, had not and could not have the weight a committee report possesses.

How to prevent a vote thus became a vital question, decisive of the fate of the Panama Canal.

In this desperate position, we conceived the plan of obtaining the appointment of a new canal commission for the examination of the Panama route as well as of all the other routes, which would prevent the United States from deciding in favor of Nicaragua before the presentation to Congress of an official report on Panama, with the certainty that we should be able to prove the superiority of Panama. This idea was met almost everywhere with energetic opposition, but Mr. Cromwell and his partners succeeded, by personal interviews and arguments, in convincing several important Members of the House, in particular its Speaker, Mr. Reed, the chairman of the Committee on Ways and Means, Mr. Cannon, who was also leader of the Republican Party in the House, and the chairman of the Committee on Rivers and Harbors, Mr. Burton, of the wisdom, the justice, and the advantages of this plan.

Mr. Kendall. This will all be printed? I suggest that you give that an exhibit number and have it printed with your remarks.

Mr. Hall. This brief is an exhibit. It was made an exhibit this morning. The first thing we introduced it.

Mr. Kendall. You have been reading from the brief?

Mr. Hall. Yes, sir. I have been quoting, verbatim, from the brief the more important passages, but so as not to waste too much of the time of the committee, and to give it a comprehensive story of the means Mr. Cromwell took to defeat Nicaragua legislation, I am joining the links together with a synopsis of the less-important events.

Mr. GOODWIN. Where do you get the information from?

Mr. HALL. The records of Congress and Mr. Cromwell's brief.

As a result of Mr. Cromwell's efforts the Nicaragua bill failed to reach a vote, and its supporters sought some other means of attaining their end. They determined to amend the rivers and harbors bill, which was then before the Committee on Commerce of the Senate; and Senator Morgan obtained the passage in committee of an amendment to this bill, containing almost word for word the pending Nicaragua bill, with an appropriation of $10,000,000 to begin the building of the Nicaragua Canal.

In his brief, Mr. Cromwell said:

The amendment was passed in the Senate by 50 votes for to 3 against, February 25, 1899, just a few days before the end of the session. All that was then needed to make this bill a law, and thus irrevocably pledge the United States to the building of the Nicaragua Canal, was the concurrence of the House in this amendment. The struggle then focused on the question of assent * * *. Thanks to our constant watchfulness, the amendment was known to us as soon as it was introduced in committee.

Mr. Cromwell's brief goes on to say:

At this critical moment we conceived the plan to have the Panama Canal Co. make a proposal assuring to the United States representation in the company and the opportunity of acquiring such interest as it might wish in the canal property, and to this end to offer to reincorporate the Panama Canal Co. in one of the States of the United States, without, however, obliging the United States to make a pecuniary investment in this undertaking unless it decided so to do, and also to carry this proposal immediately and officially before the Committee on Rivers and Harbors, in whose bill the Nicaragua amendment had just been inserted in the Senate, and to back up this proposal by a public hearing.

Messrs. Cromwell and Curtis at once had an interview with the chairman of the Committee on Rivers and Harbors, Mr. Burton, and submitted this proposal to him in writing, signed by the director general and by ourselves as general counsel, and he granted a hearing, which took place immediately before the Committee on Rivers and Harbors in the last days of the session. At this hearing the proposal was officially submitted and an oral statement made by Mr. Cromwell. A copy of this important proposal (Feb. 27, 1899) was addressed and handed to Mr. Burton, chairman of the Committee on Rivers and Harbors, and copies were at once sent to the President of the United States and the Secretary of State.

This proposal, backed up by the public hearings before the Committee on Rivers and Harbors, officially gave the United States the opportunity of participating in the Panama Canal, if it so desired, after an examination of this route. The United States now had a choice of routes for the canal, and this imposed upon Congress the duty of studying and deciding.

Then Mr. Cromwell goes on to tell how he not only defeated the Senate amendment to the rivers and harbors bill, but obtained the passage of a substituted amendment appointing a new commission to examine the Panama route, thus throwing the whole matter back into the investigating stage and effectually preventing the passage of any Nicaraguan legislation. In his brief Mr. Cromwell says:

When the Rivers and Harbors bill (containing the Nicaragua amendment) was substituted to conference the final fate of Panama was at stake. If the conferees retained the Nicaragua amendment, the two Houses of Congress would certainly adopt their report, the United States would be pledged to Nicaragua, and the Panama Co. ruined. The supporters of Nicaragua were confident and even joyful. They were sure of favorable action by the conferees.

The main difference between the two Houses over the bill was in regard to the canal amendment, the House conferees proposing, at our earnest request, the substitution of a clause for the appointment of a new commission to report on all the canal routes and appropriating funds for this purpose. The Senate conferees insisted for a long time on the Nicaragua amendment. The closure of Congress was imminent, and there were only a few hours left for action. If the House conferees stood pat, the entire bill, including the Nicaragua amendment, would fail of passage at this session unless the Senate conferees yielded. The House conferees, led by Mr. Burton, chairman of the Committee on Rivers and Harbors, remained unshaken in their determination to force the substitution of their amendment for the Nicaragua amendment; the Senate conferees (not daring to wreck the whole rivers and harbors bill, which appropriated many millions of dollars) finally yielded, and in the last hours of Congress the substituted amendment became law, to the consternation and great astonishment of the Nicaragua party, all of whose bills failed of passage before the closure of Congress (Mar. 3, 1899). Thus the imminent disaster was avoided and the investigation of the Panama Canal assured. The consequences of this victory can not be computed, as it was a question of life and death for the Panama Co. We think that we are justified in stating that without our efforts the new commission would not have been created, and that the Nicaragua bill would in that case have been passed.

Mr. Cromwell then goes on to tell how "having informed the company of this success we had the pleasure to receive from it the following cablegram," but in the copy of the brief in the possession of the World, this cable is not printed. As one of the reasons for Mr. Cromwell's dismissal by the New Panama Canal Co. on July 1, 1901, was the large sums he had charged to the New Panama Canal Co. as necessary expenses in connection with this very matter and with the changing of the Republican Party platform in 1900 so as to relieve that party from its pledge to Nicaragua, it is, I think, a fair assumption that the cable referred to services which, in Mr. Cromwell's own words, "it would be impossible to detail * * * nor even perhaps would it be proper so to do."

The passage of the law of March 3, 1899, created a new commission to study all the routes, including Panama, entirely changed the situation, and gave Mr. Cromwell the opportunity he wanted. At once, on March 11, he advised an official communication to the President of the United States confirming the assurances previously given by the company, including the proposal of February 27, 1899, and offering every facility for investigation of the Panama route, etc. He drew up this communication, which the director general approved and signed with him. Mr. Cromwell's first consideration was the composition of the commission itself, which had been left to the President himself by law. He urged on President McKinley that neither Admiral Walker, Col. Hains, nor Prof. Haupt should be appointed, as they had already reported in favor of Nicaragua. He prepared a list of engineers, which, after interviews with Secretary Hay and President McKinley, he furnished to the Government. The commission appointed by the President on June 9 was composed of the following men: Rear Admiral John G. Walker, United States Navy, president; Samuel Pasco, ex-Senator from Florida; George S. Morison, Lieut. Col. Oswald H. Ernst, and Col. Peter C. Hains, Corps of Engineers, United States Army; Prof. Lewis M. Haupt, Prof. William H. Burr, and Alfred Noble, and Prof. Emory R. Johnson, of the University of Pennsylvania.

The commission was organized June 15, 1899, and sailed for Paris on August 9, 1899. Their intention from the first was to begin their investigations on the Isthmus of Panama, but there they would be within the zone of discussion and influence of the Nicaragua idea, so Mr. Cromwell persuaded the commissioners to overturn all their plans and start in on the French Co.'s books and maps in Paris, where he would, "with the object of influencing its decisions" (so Mr. Cromwell says) produce before the commission the distinguished English, French, German, and Russian engineers who had served on the French Co.'s "International Technical Commission"—and who were, of course, committed to the Panama route. Mr. Cromwell advised the company by cable when he had brought the Walker commission to this decision, so the company could be ready to receive the Americans in Paris.

The act of March 3, 1899 (that is to say, articles 3, 4, 5, and 6 of the rivers and harbors bill), besides the authority it conferred on the President to appoint a commission charged with investigation and reporting on the various projects, their execution and probable cost, and their rights, concessions, etc., and the cost of acquiring the same, stated as follows:

And in general the President is authorized to make a full and complete inquiry for the purpose of ascertaining which is best and most practical route for a canal across the Isthmus, as well as the cost of its cons'ruction and establishment under the control, management, and ownership of the United States.

The President, on the opinion of the Attorney General of the United States (head of the Department of Justice and Attorney General) adopted an interpretation of this act to the effect that the recommendations of the commission should show not only the technical aspects of the plan, but the possibility of the United States acquiring the control, management, and ownership of the canal. In accordance with these instructions Admiral Walker, chairman of the commission, said that he acknowledged the matter would call for consideration, but that he had broached the subject officially at this time because of instructions from the President.

Mr. Cromwell remained in Paris several weeks longer, and—

held daily conferences with Mr. Bonnardel, the president, and the executive committee on the general business of the company, including its financial situation, its future, and its general plans; on the subject of the formation of syndicates; on the offer of sale that the United States had invited the company to make; on the possibility of obtaining the capital necessary for the continuation of the work from English, American, or other sources; and on the various eventualities that had to be faced in connection with the report of the Isthmian Canal Commission, whether favorable or unfavorable.

One feature of the campaign he had planned was the Americanization of the canal, an idea of his own, which he had incorporated in the proposal of February 27, 1899.

At this time Mr. Cromwell had no illusions about the situation and did not allow the company to have any. He knew that whereas an unfavorable report of the Isthmian Canal Commission would be fatal to the Panama Canal, even a favorable report might not prevail against the national feeling of sympathy for and the enormous influence of the financial interests directly involved in the Nicaragua Canal. His plan for the Americanization of the canal, unanimously approved by the board on October 19, 1899, provided for the organization of a company under the laws of the State of New Jersey, to which the property of La Compagnie Nouvelle du Canal de Panama would be transferred in exchange for a large majority of the shares of the American company, and to which $5,000,000 cash would be subscribed in America. Immediately on his return, November 1, 1899, Mr. Cromwell applied himself to this task and devoted to it nearly all the remainder of the year. On December 27 the Panama Canal Co. of America was organized. The incorporators, all clerks in Mr. Cromwell's office, were: William P. Chapman, jr., now practicing in the Tribune Building; Harvey W. Clark, now at No. 2 Rector Street; and Francis J. Pollock, still with Sullivan & Cromwell. The capital of the company was $30,000,000; its office address, 76 Montgomery Street, Jersey City. Its New Jersey agent was William Brinkerhoff. This company filed no report in Trenton, and, so far as the records show, did nothing. On the next day, December 28, articles appeared in the World, the Sun, the Times, the Tribune, the Herald, etc., and the following list of names of men behind the enterprise was printed as having been given out at the office of Sullivan & Cromwell: J. Edward Simmons; Kuhn, Loeb & Co.; E. C. Converse; Warner Van Worden; August Belmont; H. W. Seligman; Charles P. Flint; George R. Sheldon; Levi P. Morton; Capt. J. R. De la Mar; and Vernon M. Brown.

In this brief Mr. Cromwell says:

> In this matter our connection with the most powerful financiers in the United States played so important a part that but for this factor such a result could not have been obtained. By constant and continuous labor, lasting several weeks, many important financial groups in this country were sounded by us and brought into association with this undertaking, subject in every case to the ratification of the board and of the shareholders. It suffices to say that we obtained assurances and adhesions which would have assured the carrying out of the plan had it been so ratified, as we informed the company prior to the annual meeting. All the preliminary steps to bring the plan to a successful issue were taken upon the condition that this approval should be given.

Mr. Mancini, agent of the company at Bogota, frequently urged that the company should be Americanized so as to protect it against the exactions of Colombia. Some shareholders, in the exercise of the rights the law gave them, were of opinion that it was not to their interest to authorize the transaction, which, therefore, was not carried out. The board of directors, however, looking upon this transaction as an essential part of their administrative plans, thereupon immediately resigned in a body. After a brief interval an election of directors was held on February 12, 1899, at which a new board was chosen.

Mr. Cromwell from Paris directed preparation in the United States for the reassembling of Congress in December, 1899. Two of his partners traveled continuously between New York and Washington, carrying on the work of "argument, enlightenment, and publicity," conferring with public men, and calling the attention of Members of Congress and other influential people to the advantages of the Panama route.

The Isthmian Canal Commission was also in Washington, and—

> Mr. Cromwell kept in constant and personal communication with various members of this body, adding to their information, furnishing documents called for by them, overcoming their hesitations, answering their questions, etc.

They were getting ready to go to the Isthmus to complete their labors by a personal inspection of the routes—Panama, Nicaragua, Darien, Tehuantepec, and others. During the intervening time they had sent exploration parties on ahead of them, and in January following 1900 the commission itself left to make its personal inspection and investigation of all these routes.

Congress met again in December, 1899. The Nicaragua party affected to ignore the Walker Commission, and began to insist more vigorously than ever on the passage of the Nicaragua bills.

Mr. Morgan immediately introduced the Nicaragua bill to the Senate, Mr. Hepburn introduced it in the House, and the partisans of Nicaragua rallied for aggressive action. Besides, the Governments of Nicaragua and Costa Rica kept up a constant agitation, through diplomatic channels, to bring about the adoption of the Nicaragua route by the United States, and to this end offered (to grant) all the rights and concessions asked for. Mr. Cromwell and Mr. Curtis, as before, spent most of their time in Washington, conferring with many Members of Congress and officials, insisting that no action should be taken either by Congress through legislation or by the Department of State concluding a treaty with Nicaragua or Costa Rica.

Public opinion favored Nicaragua, even if the commission in its report declared the Panama plan feasible and practical, a finding which was generally looked upon as impossible. The Nicaragua Canal had on several occasions been declared feasible and practical, its cost had been estimated, and Nicaragua and Costa Rica offered all the necessary treaties and concessions, and the people of the United States favored Nicaragua.

The Panama Canal Co. had given no assurances whatsoever that, even if this route were desired by the United States, it could be acquired from the Panama company, whereas on the other hand Nicaragua and Costa Rica offered everything that was desired, and that in consequence there was no need to wait for an official report of the commission. Besides, the Members of Congress were pledged by their previous votes in favor of Nicaragua.

In order to help delay all action, Mr. Cromwell determined that every Member of Congress should be officially acquainted with all the different documents and statements which we had sent at various times to the President. So he obtained the introduction in the Senate of a resolution by which the President was asked to transmit these documents to the Senate. The resolution was passed and the documents were transmitted in due form, and, by order of the Senate, printed.

On account of the discussion of the preceding year on the subject of the exclusive control of the canal and of Great Britain's protest, based on the clauses of the Clayton-Bulwer treaty, Secretary Hay had negotiated the first Hay-Pauncefote treaty during the parliamentary recess, and this treaty was forwarded to the Senate by the President in January.

The fortification of the proposed canal was at this time a primordial question; Mr. Cromwell pointed out to some Senators the bearing of this subject upon the existing treaty with Great Britain, and laid stress on the fact that the canal had to be neutral. These questions were debated in the Senate during the discussion of this matter in its bearing upon the Hay-Pauncefote treaty. Mr. Cromwell retained Prof. Woolsey, an eminent authority on international law, professor at Yale University, and obtained from him a signed opinion, which he used in support of the arguments he was putting forward among the Senators. All this helped to delay action on the Nicaragua bill.

About this time the director general and secretary general of the New Panama Canal Co. arrived in New York to follow the events.

In his brief Mr. Cromwell thus describes his activities during this period:

On April 13 Senator Morgan introduced a resolution in the Senate providing for the consideration of his bill despite the absence of a report by the commission, and we immediately had interviews with Senators and opposed this action. Thanks to the pending treaty, this resolution was tabled. Stopped on this side, the Nicaragua party returned to the House, under the leadership of Mr. Hepburn, and on April 16 obtained the signatures of more than 150 members to a petition in favor of the bill, urging the Speaker (then Mr. Henderson) to do everything in his power to facilitate its passage by placing it on the calendar. This move was opposed, with our assistance, and, despite considerable support, Mr. Hepburn again failed in his effort to bring about this vote.

On April 28 Mr. Cromwell gave out a statement to the press protesting against any action by Congress before the receipt of the commission's report. On April 30 he sent the President an official protest on the same lines, asking him to transmit it to Congress. He also filed a protest with the Secretary of State. These communications were transmitted by the President to the Senate committee, and there obtained the publicity Mr. Cromwell desired to secure for them.

Mr. Cromwell's brief continues:

On April 3, 1900, the Isthmian Canal Commission returned from the Isthmus, where it had left a numerous staff charged with carrying on the special study of the two plans. But it was not ready to formulate final conclusions and make its report. * * * However, the Nicaragua bill at last took its turn on the calendar of the House and was passed, May 2, 1900 (as had been recognized to be inevitable if it should reach a vote), almost unanimously; that is to say, by 234 votes for to 36 against. * * * The bill was sent to the Senate, where Senator Morgan at once took hold of it and insisted on obtaining action similar to that of the House.

Senator Morgan, as chairman of the Senate Committee on the Nicaragua Canal, summoned before him Admiral Walker and other members of the commission who had previously reported in favor of Nicaragua, with a view to obtaining from them statements which might be used in the Senate debates as preliminary information about the findings of the commission.

Immediately afterward, May 14, 1900, the Senate committee reported the bill favorably to the Senate. Senator Morgan then made the formal motion for the immediate discussion of the bill. The session was drawing to its close. Every day of delay was invaluable to Mr. Cromwell. If Senator Morgan's motion for immediate discussion was carried, it was certain that the bill would be passed. To use Mr. Cromwell's own words, "once more the fate of the Panama Canal Co. hung in the balance." In his brief he says:

One at least of our partners was busy with this matter night and day for several weeks conferring with Senators and members of the commission, preparing arguments, and giving them publicity, and pleading insistently for the defeat of the bill passed by the House. Without going into details, we merely note the fact that Senator Morgan's motion was put to a vote on May 14, 1900, and defeated by a small majority of 7 votes—28 nays, 21 ayes.

But before Congress adjourned Senator Morgan passed a resolution in the Senate fixing the consideration of the bill for the second Monday in December, 1900. Congress adjourned three days later. During all this time Mr. Cromwell and Mr. Curtis with other of their partners spent nearly all their time in Washington lobbying.

Mr. Cromwell's lobbying was so brazen that it was taken official cognizance of by the Senate Committee on Interoceanic Canals, of which Senator Hanna was a member, and which on May 16, 1900, reported thus:

This manifest purpose of this company (the New Panama Canal Co.) to interfere with legislation, by asking the President to inform Congress of a state of facts, as alleged, of which Congress is "presumably without knowledge," is an insult to the intelligence of Congress. It is an insolent invitation to the President to control the action of Congress so that they shall not act upon bills reported by committees in both Houses. * * *

It is a spectacle that is, happily, without precedent, that this foreign corporation, acting in a foreign country and without any recognition even of the honesty of its dealings, while it has all the time been the subject of distrust by our Government, should ask the President to "advise the Congress of the facts of the case" for the purpose of opposing Congress in declaring and enforcing the public policy of our people and Government.

A bill that the House had agreed to consider on the 1st and 2d days of May, 1900, is severely censured by this speculating corporation, because its passage would destroy the hope of that company of unloading a failing enterprise upon the United States under its proposal of February 28, 1899, which is again renewed in this letter.

Aside from the fact that said proposal contains suggestions that provide for the robbery of the stockholders of the "old company" and the violation of the decrees of the courts of France, it proposes a direct violation of the statutes of Colombia, enacted in granting the concessions to that company, and a breach of our treaty of 1846 with Colombia, which binds us to guarantee the sovereignty of that territory over the State of Panama.

The President has never answered said overture, nor has he responded to the suggestions and requests contained in the letter from Sullivan & Cromwell of April 30, 1900, but the Secretary of State has sent that letter to the chairman of the Committee on Interoceanic Canals.

Nineteen hundred was a presidential election year. The Republican platform of 1896 had formally declared in favor of the Nicaragua Canal, the supporters of which made continual use of this plank as an injunction addressed by the party to the Republican members of the legislative bodies. A similar plank in the Republican platform of 1900 would naturally have greatly strengthened the cause of Nicaragua, especially in view of their plan of obtaining a similar indorsement from the Democratic Party, wherein they were successful. So Mr. Cromwell saw Senator Hanna and other Republican leaders and urged that the Republican Party should not again pledge itself to the cause of Nicaragua, but ought to mention the matter in neutral terms, for instance, the "Isthmian" Canal.

The Republican convention met, and in the first draft of its platform the old formula in favor of the Nicaragua project was used. But Mr. Cromwell persuaded Senator Hanna to permit him to amend the Republican national platform in the interest of the Panama route. The words "an isthmian canal" were substituted for the words "the Nicaragua Canal," but only after Mr. Cromwell had contributed $60,000 to the Republican National Committee, of which Senator Hanna was chairman. These $60,000 Mr. Cromwell later charged up to the New Panama Canal Co. as a "necessary expense."

Mr. Goodwin. Is that in Mr. Cromwell's brief?

Mr. Hall. In his brief Mr. Cromwell says:

So we occupied ourselves with this important matter and had personal interviews with the chairman and vice chairman of the platform committee of the Republican convention, who were personally known to us, as well as with other party leaders. * * * Our conferences, our correspondence, and the steps we took in this matter lasted over a period of six weeks without interruption. The convention met, and in the first draft of its platform the old formula in favor of the Nicaragua project was used. We renewed with insistence our arguments and objections, and the justice of our views was at last recognized, the platform was changed, and the words "an isthmian canal" were substituted for the words "the Nicaragua Canal," which for so many years had been used in the party platforms. * * * This was an important step in our fight, since it freed the Republican Members of Congress from a party pledge and was the first occasion on which it was publicly recognized that a canal other than that of Nicaragua was possible.

The CHAIRMAN. But what is your authority for the statement that Mr. Cromwell contributed $60,000 to the Republican campaign fund and charged it to the Panama Canal Co. as a necessary expense?

Mr. HALL. Mr. Bunau-Varilla, sr., in a statement to Mr. Don C. Seitz, of The World.

The CHAIRMAN. You may proceed.

Mr. HALL. It will be remembered that Admiral Walker had asked the company, at the hearing in Paris on September 7, 1899, to name a price for the sale of its property. By a letter to the company, written on April 10, in the year 1900, Admiral Walker made the same official proposal for acquiring the Panama route. He asked the company to state whether it was ready to sell its property and concessions, and if so, at what price.

The French company hesitated to sell, and on November 26, 1900, replied to Admiral Walker's inquiry of April 10, 1900, renewing the Cromwell proposal to reincorporate in the United States and permit the American Government to acquire representation in the company. Four days later the Walker Commission made its preliminary report (Nov. 30, 1900) favorable to Nicaragua, and setting forth that the French company had made no proposition whereby the United States could obtain ownership and control of Panama.

At the same time, December 1, 1900, the Secretary of State, Mr. Hay, concluded and signed protocols with the ministers of Nicaragua and Costa Rica, by which these Governments undertook to negotiate a treaty as soon as the President of the United States should be authorized by Congress to acquire the Nicaragua route; to enter into negotiations for fixing details of the plans and agreements which might be found necessary for its execution; and to stipulate as to the ownership and control of the proposed Nicaragua Canal.

The Hay-Pauncefote treaty was ratified on December 20, 1900, but with modifications which could hardly be acceptable to Great Britain—which proved to be the case—and the delay for its ratification was finally to expire March 4, 1901.

Mr. Cromwell made every effort to delay action on the Nicaragua bill, urging that the Senate ought to wait for action on the part of England in respect to the Hay-Pauncefote treaty, and that it would be improper to pass the Nicaragua bills, which were diametrically opposed to the Clayton-Bulwer treaty which was still in force.

During January, vigorous efforts were made in the Senate and House to advance the Nicaragua bills, the supporters of which made every effort to show that it was not necessary to await the action of England on the Hay-Pauncefote treaty. But Mr. Cromwell and Senator Hanna were determined that there should be no legislation on the canal matter until after the ratification of the Hay-Pauncefote treaty, and the Republican Party adopted this program January 18, 1901.

The supporters of Nicaragua would not accept this conclusion, and succeeded (Feb. 20–26) in advancing the canal bill to a point where it might receive consideration by the Senate. The Nicaragua party also made a new move, in order to get Congress to adopt Nicaragua, by means of an amendment to the sundry civil appropriation bill, then pending before the Senate, authorizing the President to acquire from the Republics of Nicaragua and Costa Rica the route for the construction of the canal, and appropriating public funds for the carrying out of this plan. This amendment was moved by Senator Morgan on February 11, 1901.

The rivers and harbors bill, which had been passed by the House, was pending before the Senate, and Senator Morgan moved the same amendment to this bill, in order to insure its passage. Mr. Cromwell succeeded in having both amendments rejected.

Congress adjourned on the 4th of March and President McKinley was inaugurated without action having been taken on the Nicaragua bills.

The extra session of the Senate, following the inauguration of the new President, only lasted five days, during which there was no attempt at general legislation. Senator Morgan, however, seized the opportunity to again move, March 5, his resolution for the abrogation of the Clayton-Bulwer treaty, and made a speech which lasted for part of three days; but no action was taken by the Senate. No further legislative action was possible before the following December.

The Walker Commission was still at work upon its final report. Mr. Cromwell then devoted himself to bringing the commission to recant its preliminary report in favor of Nicaragua, and to adopt the Panama plan. To accomplish this result it was necessary that the company make an offer of absolute sale; that the consent of Colombia to a cession in favor of a foreign Government (such cession being prohibited by the concession) be obtained; and that the commission recommend the selection of the Panama route.

How to get Colombia to consent to the cession by the New Panama Canal Co. of its rights and property to a foreign Government; such cession being, as we have seen, specifically prohibited under pain of forfeiture by Articles XXI and XXII of the Salgar Wyse Concession, was Mr. Cromwell's next problem. In his brief he says:

During this period the Colombian Legation in Washington had been closed, and that country was not represented here. The official business of the Government was being conducted through the consul general in New York, who at that time was Senor de Brigard.

One part of our plan consisted in getting Colombia to send to Washington a minister competent to take up the canal matter, and it was on our urgent advice that the company gave instructions to its agent in Bogota to suggest this (idea) to the Colombian Government. We also had a personal interview in December, 1900, with the consul general in New York (at that time the only official representative of Colombia in the United States), and we begged him to urge President Marroquin to at once send a minister empowered to deal with the canal question. It was in consequence of our statement, (which contained an account of the whole situation and set forth the necessity for immediate action), that the consul general acceded to our request and cabled President Marroquin an urgent message to this effect, December 23, 1900. President Marroquin answered him by cable (as we were officially notified by the consul general on Dec. 27) that Mr. Martinez Silva, then minister of foreign affairs, would arrive in Washington about the end of January, 1901, for this purpose.

At our request, and after we had convinced him of the urgency of the matter, the consul general sent Secretary Hay an official note, with which he transmitted a copy of President Marroquin's telegraphic communication notifying him of the appointment of Mr. Silva as minister and envoy extraordinary, charged with negotiating with the United States on the subject of the Panama Canal.

Having succeeded in this respect, we took advantage of this fact to urge on Secretary Hay that the negotiations with Nicaragua and Costa Rica ought not to be concluded before the arrival of Mr. Silva, and until the canal company had had an opportunity of negotiating with him.

Minister Silva arrived in New York in the middle of February, 1901, and his first call was on Mr. Cromwell in our law office; then began a series of conferences between the minister and ourselves which lasted several months and of which we shall state the substance.

Here, gentlemen, we have the genesis of those diplomatic negotiations which Mr. Roosevelt told Congress were entered upon "at the urgent solicitation of the people of Colombia." What Colombia's views really were I will allow Mr. Cromwell to tell in his own words:

We soon learned, thanks to our conferences with Mr. Silva, that Colombia considered that the canal concession would necessarily be forfeited in any event in 1910 by reason of the manifest impossibility of the company finishing the canal by that date, and in consequence Colombia judged that in this matter her interest was paramount and should be considered first; that public opinion in Colombia was opposed to the cession to a foreign government, but that the Government then in power was willing to consider such an eventuality on condition that it was based on terms sufficiently advantageous to Colombia.

In the course of a series of conferences we furnished Mr. Silva, at the request of this minister, with a most thorough and detailed explanation of the situation then existing in the United States, * * * and we strongly urged him to immediately make known to the United States the willingness of Colombia to negotiate on these matters and to facilitate the plans of the United States. * * * Mr. Silva, convinced by our explanation and arguments, accepted them in principle, and in the course of an official visit he paid to Secretary Hay, March 13, 1901, assured the latter of his willingness to facilitate the plans of the United States if the terms agreed upon were of a satisfactory nature to Colombia.

This action on Mr. Cromwell's part injected a new element into the canal situation, to wit: An official appearance by Colombia, and during the three months which followed the negotiations between Minister Silva, the Isthmian Canal Commission, and the New Panama Canal Co. continued, with the participation of Admiral Walker, Minister Silva, the president of the company (who was in Washington during this period), and Mr. Cromwell, assisted by one of his partners, Mr. Hill.

Although Colombia sent a minister to negotiate for a canal treaty at the suggestion and instigation of Mr. Cromwell, it thought that it was entering into the bargaining with the United States with its eyes open.

It is very probable—

Said the Colombian foreign minister in his letter of instructions to Minister Silva, dated January 12, 1901—

that the American Government will make extraordinary demands of you, of which you will naturally give opportune advice to this Government, using the cable, so that in the most delicate cases you may operate with special authorization from the Government.

When Minister Silva called on Mr. Cromwell when he landed in New York, one of Mr. Cromwell's first moves was to try to unload on the Colombian Government part of the expense of his publicity campaign, and to utilize the new minister as an assistant to Roger Farnham, Cromwell's chief press agent. Less than three weeks after Minister Silva arrived he wrote to his Government, under date of March 7, 1901:

At present what must be done * * * is to open an active press campaign for the purpose of changing public opinion, which is so decidedly in favor of Nicaragua, and to work directly on the men who dominate Congress and who manage the executive centers of politics. I am already taking measures for this, being advised by men who understand it; but I notify you that from now on this will need money. If the Government is not disposed to spend it, little or nothing can be accomplished.

Minister Silva's first reports to his Government indicate clearly the definite purpose of Colombia not to yield her sovereignty over the canal strip. He pinned his hopes then upon England's rejecting the American amendments to the Hay-Pauncefote treaty. He says in his letter of February 21, 1901:

If England retracts all her former policies and submits to the United States, we are out of the fight, and the Panama enterprise will be dead.

The Hay-Pauncefote treaty, then pending, introduced the clauses of the Constantinople convention neutralizing the Suez Canal, and the amendments proposed by the United States made reservations providing for American control of the canal in the interests of the national defense. Minister Silva considered his negotiations hopeless if England permitted America to control the canal absolutely, because Colombia would not cede her sovereignty, and the United States would then turn to Nicaraugua on account of her willingness to cede anything demanded. In his next letter Minister Silva, pursuing this discussion, tells his Government:

We will take hold of the skirts of the coat of John Bull and will see where we come out, but we will come out on the other side with splendor and profit.

In the diplomatic correspondence of this time, light is shed on the antecedents of another phase of the Panama affair which has caused endless dispute—the threat of Colombia to repudiate the extension of the canal company's concession to 1910. The Colombian Congress having refused the extension, the late Dr. Nicolas Esguerra, one of the most celebrated international lawyers of South America, was sent to Paris as a special commissioner for Colombia, to negotiate with the canal company. In Esguerra's absence, and without his approval, Carlos Calderon-Reyes, then minister of finance, a nephew of Gen. Rafael Reyes, granted the extension from October 31, 1904, to October 31, 1910.

In a letter to his Government of February 28, 1901, Minister Silva questions the legality of this extension and suggests that the question be studied carefully with a view to refunding the 5,000,000 francs which the canal company paid for the extension, and terminating the concession in 1904.

It would be a terrific outrage—

Says Minister Silva—

if the Republic should have to sacrifice itself by recognizing the validity of that infamous contract, the work which was not based on necessities of war but on secret thievery, and assisted by a cynical lie that Mr. Esguerra had recommended the granting of the extension. I have at hand the original communications which prove the contrary.

When the canal negotiations reached their critical state in the summer of 1903 efforts were made to lead the American public to believe that Colombia, purely as an afterthought and without justification, considered and discussed—although it did not act upon the suggestion of cancelling this extension.

Mr. Cromwell was at this time still trying to induce his client to authorize his long-desired proposal of outright sale to the United States. Minister Silva was able to assist him by writing to President Hutin, of the canal company, April 29, 1901, in part as follows:

> To facilitate this (Isthmian Canal) Commission in obtaining the means of presenting a complete report it would be proper that you, as representing the New Panama Canal Co., should tell me, at least in general terms, what are the bases given the previous consent of the Government of Colombia upon which the company would be disposed to transfer its concession to the Government of the United States.

President Hutin complied in part with this request and at the same time called the attention of the Colombian minister to the restrictions in the canal company's concession under which—

> it could not, without the previous consent of Colombia, answer the questions which were put to it nor the propositions which were made to it. By every means in our power—

Continued M. Hutin in this letter—

> we have sought to bring about the necessary intervention of your Government. Your presence and your action, as authorized representatives of the Colombian Government at Washington, establish the proper situation in which our company should be placed in order to discuss the question presented by the Government to the United States.

Here is the genesis of the canal negotiation, clearly and officially stated: The American Government, through the Walker commission, presented questions to the canal company which the canal company could not answer until it brought about, through Mr. Cromwell, the sending of a Colombian minister to Washington to authorize the negotiations.

President Hutin went on to state officially to Minister Silva that the company would transfer its concession to the United States if Colombia were willing, but he named no price. Nor was the Walker commission able to get any definite price set by the canal company until a few days before it made its report the following November. Admiral Walker and Senator Pasco, for the canal commission, submitted to Minister Silva on May 9, 1901, a memorandum of eighteen points to be considered in the negotiations with Colombia, and on June 3, 1901, Minister Silva replied to the commission that he had submitted the memorandum to his Government and asked for instructions. This effectually tied up the report of the canal commission, which was exactly what Mr. Cromwell was seeking to accomplish.

The position was then briefly as follows: The Colombian minister had conditionally consented to the company's making an offer of sale to the United States, and Colombia had announced to the United States that she was disposed to allow the United States to acquire the rights of the canal company on condition that agreements and treaties, the terms of which would be satisfactory to Colombia, be entered into between Colombia and the United States. In consequence the canal company informed the Colombian minister and the Isthmian Canal Commission that it would consent (on the basis of a like consent on the part of Colombia) to the cession of its concessions to the United States at a price which was not fixed, but which was to be determined by private agreement or by arbitration, and that over and above the purchase price of its properties there would be added an indemnity for the future profits which its concessions would have placed the company in position to realize had it built the canal.

Such was the situation on May 16, 1901, when the president of the canal company returned to Paris, but no definite offer had yet been made to the United States. May 1, 1901, the party of Isthmian Canal Co. engineers had returned to Washington, after having virtually completed its studies of the Nicaragua and Panama plans, and thus supplied the latest detailed information for the writing of the final report of the commission. May 21, 1901, the Nicaraguan minister, who had gone to Nicaragua to report to his Government and obtain fresh instructions for the negotiation of a canal treaty, returned to the United States, and it was publicly stated that he was authorized to grant all the demands of the United States on the subject of the Nicaragua Canal.

On June 25, 1901, Admiral Walker, chairman of the Isthmian Canal Commission, called upon Mr. Cromwell in New York and declared that the work of the commission in connection with the preparation of the final report had made such progress that it expected to submit to the President (according to his request) in the first part of July a semiofficial report or summary of its final findings in advance of the filing of its final report, the innumerable details of which would perforce keep it busy several months. He also alluded to the proposal the company had made to Minister Silva and to the commission with a view to fixing a price by agreement or arbitration, with an indemnity for the loss of eventual profits, instead of a fixed price, and he stated that all the members of the commission were agreed that these proposals were insufficient and inacceptable. He spoke of the long-drawn-out correspondence exchanged between the company, and the commission was not authorized to act upon, nor could it act upon, anything except a definite offer of absolute sale for a stated sum. During this interview Admiral Walker inquired of Mr. Cromwell as to the price the company would probably accept, but Mr. Cromwell would not commit himself, and strongly urged Admiral Walker to defer the sending of his advance report to the President in order to permit Mr. Cromwell to inform the company of the views of the commission and of its new request for the fixation of a definite sum. As a result of this conference Admiral Walker promised to defer the filing of his advance report until July 20.

Within a few hours following the departure of Admiral Walker Mr. Cromwell sent the following cable to the canal company:

NEW YORK, *June 25, 1901.*

PANANOVO (COMPAGNIE NOUVELLE DU CANAL DE PANAMA),
Paris:

Admiral Walker came to see us to-day. Declares that commission will finish advance report to President first part July. Declares Pananovo proposal to arbitrate inacceptable; above all because arbitration would delay decision beyond next Congress and because arbitration would take away from Congress the power to fix the amount and would give this power to individuals not subject to the authority of Congress. Admiral asks Pananovo to at once fix definite sum instead of arbitration, and declares that otherwise the proposal of Pananovo must be considered insufficient and inacceptable. He promises me delay his report until July 20 if you come here before then ready to discuss, estimate, and fix definite sum. Am convinced that if Pananovo fixes sum in keeping with views commission, it will have very favorable influence on the report. Cable if you accede to Admiral's request or if you can come and when you can come. Admiral says he expects see President Saturday. If possible instruct me before that date.

CROMWELL.

The company refused to make a definite offer of sale; and Mr. Cromwell's anxiety to induce the New Panama Canal Co. to sell, his syndicate operations, the methods he had employed, and the large sum of money he had spent, having dissatisfied his French clients, on July 1, 1901, they dismissed him. President Hutin here took up and attempted to carry on without Mr. Cromwell's guidance the negotiations in the United States. He failed entirely also; no progress was made by Minister Silva with the Isthmian Canal Commission.

President McKinley, struck down by the bullet of an assassin, died September 14, 1901; Mr. Roosevelt became President, announced to the public in an official statement the policy he intended to follow, and therein recommended the building of the Nicaragua Canal.

On account of the assassination of the President and the inauguration of his successor, the Walker commission delayed the completion of its final report, which gave the company another chance of making the offer which the commission had asked for two years. After an exchange of correspondence with the company in Paris, the commission cabled to the company declaring that if the company intended to name a price for its property and concessions is was necessary to avoid further delay.

The president of the New Panama Canal Co. arrived in the United States on October 15, 1901, but the company adhered firmly to the attitude it had taken in its letter of May 16, 1901 (except that it abandoned its demand for an indemnity for possible future profits). The commission adhered to its attitude that it was not authorized to deal with a proposal in this form, and could only receive and report upon an offer of absolute sale fixing a definite price. The figures presented by the company showed that according to its estimate its properties were worth 565,000,000 francs.

Negotiations between the company and the commission came to a stop on November 6, 1901, and the commission went to work to complete and file its final report. This report, filed 10 days later, November 16, 1901, was signed by all the members of the Isthmian Canal Commission and unanimously recommended the adoption of the Nicaragua plan.

Congress met December 2, 1901, and the supporters of Nicaragua demanded the immediate passage of the Nicaragua bill. Mr. Hepburn introduced in the House on December 6, 1901, a bill authorizing the appropriation of $180,000,000 for the construction of the Nicaragua Canal, $10,000,000 of which was rendered immediately available for this purpose. The Committee on Interstate and Foreign Commerce, of which Mr. Hepburn was chairman, took up this bill, which was backed by the favorable report of the Isthmian Canal Commission, and immediately reported it favorably to the House.

In the Senate several Nicaragua bills were introduced, one by Senator Perkins, two by Senator Morgan. The Senate committee (the

Committee on the Nicaragua Canal), of which Senator Morgan was chairman, acted as promptly as the House committee and unanimously reported a bill in favor of the construction of the Nicaragua Canal. Thus in both houses the Nicaragua bills were favorably reported by the respective committees and supported by the final report of the Isthmian Canal Commission.

On December 10, 1901, a formal convention was signed in Nicaragua between the minister of foreign affairs of Nicaragua and the United States minister, Mr. Merry, with a view to the construction of the Nicaragua Canal by the United States, and this fact was widely advertised by the supporters of Nicaragua as a proof of the adoption of their project by the United States.

On December 17, 1901, the Senate ratified the new Hay-Pauncefote treaty and this assured the passage during that session of laws for the construction of an interoceanic canal by the United States.

On December 19, 1901, the House of Representatives, by unanimous consent, placed the Hepburn bill on the calendar for immediate consideration on January 7, 1902. This assured a vote on the bill within a short time.

It was then that the New Panama Canal Co. decided to make an offer of sale to the United States for $40,000,000, but this offer was rejected by the House of Representatives, which passed the Nicaragua bill by the overwhelming majority of 309 to 2. Mr. Cromwell, in his brief, thus describes these developments:

At the general meeting of the company, which took place on December 21, 1901, the gravity of the situation was fully explained, and resolutions were submitted to the shareholders and adopted by them, authorizing the tender to the United States, through the Isthmian Canal Commission, of a definite and fixed offer, such as that commission had asked for for more than two years, but subject to ratification by the shareholders at a subsequent meeting.

On January 4, 1902, the company in Paris made an offer by cable to the United States, through the commission, covering all its concessions and properties, of which an estimate had been made by the Isthmian Canal Commission, on page 103 of its report, for the sum of $40,000,000, the amount of this estimate; and by other cables sent direct to the commission on January 9 and January 11, 1902, confirmed this offer and declared that it was ready to accept the amount stated for the totality, without exception, of its properties and rights on the Isthmus, and this offer also included all the plans and archives in Paris.

The Hepburn bill reached its turn on the calendar of the House January 8, and the debates continued all through that day and the next. The offer of the company, made on January 4, had been officially transmitted to the President and to the Secretary of State, was published immediately, and was alluded to and considered in the course of the debates in the House on the Hepburn bill.

The House, however, rejected the company's offer, and the Hepburn bill was passed on January 9, almost unanimously, by 309 votes in favor of the Nicaragua plan and only 2 against.

The canal commission had been pressing Minister Silva for an answer as to the position of Colombia, and on January 8, 1902, Minister Silva wrote to his Government a long letter, which he dispatched to Bogota by special diplomatic courier. In part he said:

I have not told the representatives here of the French company on what conditions the permission to transfer the concession would be granted, but it appears to me strictly just that they (the New Panama Canal Co.) should give a good sum to the Government of Colombia, as, if permission is denied them they will lose everything; besides, as the company took advantage of the straitened circumstances of the Government to obtain an extension of six years, which is really what they are going to sell for $40,000,000. I do not think it would be contrary to what is equitable if we exact from them $2,000,000 more in addition to the $1,000,000 which they paid (for the six years' extension).

But, despite the rejection of the New Panama Canal Co.'s offer by the House, President Roosevelt again called the members of the Isthmian Canal Commission together to the White House, on the afternoon of January 16, and asked them to make a supplementary report in view of the offer in question.

The commission met immediately and, on January 18, 1902, decided on the motion of Mr. Cromwell's friend, George S. Morison, that taking into consideration the changed conditions brought about by the offer of the company, the Panama route was preferable.

There was a decided difference of opinion among the members and Prof. Haupt, Senator Pasco and two others were reluctant to abandon Nicaragua. President Roosevelt had made it quite clear to Admiral Walker that he expected the acceptance of the Panama Canal Co.'s offer. Noble and Pasco had given in, but Prof. Haupt stood out, and it was only when Admiral Walker had called Prof. Haupt out of the committee room and pleaded with him to sign the report, stating that the President demanded a unanimous report, that Haupt consented to put his name to it, and he stipulated his reasons in the minutes of the commission.

Mr. HARRISON. Are you quoting now from the brief?

Mr. HALL. No, sir. I am quoting from a statement made by Prof. Haupt.

Mr. KENDALL. From what?

Mr. HALL. From a statement made by Prof. Haupt.

Mr. KENDALL. Are those minutes with Prof. Haupt's reservation printed in some place.

Mr. HALL. I don't know, sir. But the original minutes of the Walker Commission must be in existence.

Mr. KENDALL. That report has been returned of course?

Mr. HALL. I suppose it is in the State Department.

Mr. KENDALL. What is the page of that, if you please?

Mr. HALL. I do not know at all. I suppose the minutes are in existence in the State Department, but I have not been able to get them. I do not know that they have even been printed as a public document.

Mr. KENDALL. I understand you to say that Prof. Haupt made a statement there that Admiral Walker called him out of the committee room and told him that the President insisted upon a unanimous vote of the committee?

Mr. HALL. Yes, sir; that was my statement.

Mr. KENDALL. Where did you get that? I do not mean that offensively. I want to know where the document is that support your statement.

Mr. HALL. The statement is on the authority of Prof. Haupt himself, who made it direct to a staff correspondent of The World.

A BYSTANDER. Mr. Haupt published that statement in an article in one of the magazines after this whole thing was closed, over his own signature.

Mr. HALL. I think Prof. Haupt is on record as to that. His reasons for signing the supplementary report and which he says are inserted at his request in the minutes of the Walker Commission, are printed, if my memory serves me right, in his article in the North American Review of July, 1902.

Mr. GOODWIN. It is a valuable part of the record.

Mr. KENDALL. I think it ought to be in the record. I think it is advisable to have the record rather than an abstract.

Mr. HALL. Oh, undoubtedly. I will get a copy of the statement and put it in the record.

The supplementary report of the Walker Commission, signed by all the members, was transmitted to Congress by President Roosevelt on January 20, 1901.

Minister Silva having cabled his government the offer of the Panama Co. to sell to the United States for $40,000,000, it was decided at Bogota to send another minister, Dr. Jose Vicente Concha, to complete the negotiations. No reason for this change appears in the Colombian diplomatic correspondence, excepting Minister Silva's complaint that he lacked definite instructions and his statement that if his government did not repose sufficient confidence in him, he was entirely willing to resign. Dr. Silva was accused by his government of having exceeded his powers in authorizing the negotiations between the canal company and the United States. His successor, Dr. Concha, was a much different type of man and diplomat.

In his official instructions, issued on January 22, 1902, Minister Concha was enjoined to obtain—

the final adoption of the Isthmus of Panama for the opening of the interoceanic canal on the best terms for Colombia, without affecting the integrity of its territory or its national sovereignty.

He was also authorized to confer with the Washington diplomatic corps to obtain an international control of the Panama Canal and a guarantee of its neutrality by all the powers. Concha's instructions further read:

If you obtain this international arrangement, you will proceed to denounce the treaty of 1846 with the United States.

Concha's supplemental instructions, issued in Bogota January 27, 1902, required his exacting no less than $20,000,000 from the New Panama Canal Co. for Colombia's permission to transfer its concession for the following reasons:

1. Because Colombia's consent is essential, as without its consent the transfer would be void; and if made without its consent, the French company, in penalty, would lose its rights;

2. Because Colombia, by consenting to the transfer of the concession, would lose its expectation of acquiring the Panama Railroad at the expiration of the concession. This railroad was bought by the canal company for 93.000.000 francs ($18.600,000), and on the opening of the canal that would be lost; and

3. Because in the new contract it is proposed that Colombia should renounce the participation it is now entitled to in the future earnings of the canal, which may amount to $1,000,000 a year.

This was the situation when Mr. Cromwell, through the intervention of Senator Hanna and others, was reinstated as general counsel on January 27, 1902, and resumed his lobbying in Washington. The news of his reinstatement was conveyed to Mr. Cromwell by Phillipe Bunau-Varilla, who was then in Washington with the following telegram:

WASHINGTON, *January 27, 1902—10.20 a. m.*

CROMWELL (care Sullivan & Cromwell),
49 Wall Street, New York City.

Your affair was settled this morning, Paris, according to my recommendation, which I had to renew yesterday with great force. Felicitations.

BUNAU-VARILLA.

To which Mr. Cromwell replied:

NEW YORK, *January 27, 1902.*
(Received 2.15 p. m.)

PHILLIPE BUNAU-VARILLA,
New Willard, Washington, D. C.

Many thanks for your kind message; when will confirmation be received by me? I return from Washington Friday filled with deep concern. Not an hour is to be lost, and I will prepare to act at once. Expect important movement in our favor this morning and will give you details.

WM. NELSON CROMWELL.

Mr. Cromwell's acceptance of the mission thus again intrusted to him and the cables of the company, as well as the acknowledgment of his acceptance, was confirmed by the following letter from the company:

No. S. 3759.] PARIS, *January 31, 1902.*

SIR: We have the honor to confirm the telegrams here below, one of which was sent to you direct, whereas the other, fuller and more explicit, was to be handed to you by Mr. Lampre, secretary general of our company:

"JANUARY 29, 1902.

"You will receive through Lampre, after translation, telegram reinstating you as general counsel of Compagnie Nouvelle and containing instructions."

"JANUARY 27, 1902.

"You to be reinstated in your position as general counsel of Compagnie Nouvelle de Panama, rely on your cooperation to conclude matter sale of property; you better than anyone can show title Compagnie Nouvelle de Panama to property and incontestable right she has to sell them. But we require most expressly that no donations be made now or later, nor promises be made, to anyone whomsoever, which might find the Compagnie Nouvelle de Panama. We are convinced you share our sentiments on this point, but we wish it to be well understood between us. It is also understood that the settlement of former accounts and remuneration your future services will be determined sovereignly by the board of directors of Compagnie Nouvelle de Panama, and that no expenditure whatsoever is to be incurred without consent board directors of Compagnie Nouvelle de Panama. Finally, it must be understood that you are to follow instructions of authorized agents of board of directors whoever they be.

"As we say to you in these telegrams, we again intrust you with the functions of general counsel of the company in the United States. We rely on your hearty cooperation to bring to a successful issue, as promptly as possible, the offer we have made to the Government of the United States, to cede to it, for the price of $40,000,000, the totality of our rights, property, and assets of whatever kind on the Isthmus of Panama, as well as the archives and plans in Paris. This offer, as you know, has recently been favorably reported on by the Isthmian Commission. The Panama route presents, as a matter of fact, in the eyes of every competent and impartial judge, inappreciable advantages over any other route. Therefore its opponents seem to focus their attacks (efforts) particularly on the legal question by trying to cast doubts on the validity and extent of the full and absolute title of ownership to the property which we offer to transfer to the buyer.

"Better than anyone you are in a position to defeat this maneuver. Your perfect knowledge of the position of La Compagnie Nouvelle, since its formation, of the unreserved and unrestricted titles it received from the liquidator of the old company, himself acting by virtue of undeniable authority, will permit you easily to dispel every doubt and ally every fear, if really any serious doubts or fears are possible. If needs be, you will find us read to aid you in this task by sending you any records or documents, or by obtaining, with the least possible delay, from a general meeting of shareholders, any special powers of resolutions which may be deemed necessary.

"Finally, we rely that you will know how to utilize your numerous connections and your legitimate influence to bring about the recognition of the superiority of the Panama Canal by all the prominent men whose intervention may be of use to you and who might still hold out against the proof—so complete and so convincing—set forth in the various reports of the Isthmian Commission.

"But it must be clearly understood, and on this point we shall surely be in accord with you, that this result must be sought only by the most legitimate means; that is to say, that in no case could we recourse to methods as dangerous as they are unlawful which consist principally in gifts or promises, of whatsoever nature they may be, and that the reserve must scrupulously be observed by every person acting for us or in our name.

"We also think that we are meeting your views in expressing the desire that you should leave to the board the settlement of all questions of remuneration, referring either to the past or to the future. The board, you may be sure, will know how to recognize in an equitable manner the services you will have rendered it.

"It appears to us superfluous to mention that in all your moves you must be guided by the instructions we have given to our agents in Washington and, should occasion arise, confer with them.

"We congratulate ourselves, sir, on the new connections which are to be established between you and the company, and in the hope that they may contribute to the success of our efforts, we beg you to accept the expression of our highest regard.

"THE PRESIDENT OF THE BOARD OF DIRECTORS,
"M. BO."

Mr. HARRISON. From whom to, Mr. Cromwell?

Mr. HALL. From Mr. Marius Bo, the president of the board of directors of the New Panama Canal Co.

Mr. HARRISON. What date?

Mr. HALL. January 31, 1902.

There is also a postscript:

P. S.—We beg to acknowledge receipt of your telegram received to-day, which we have translated as follows:

"I acknowledge receipt of your cable of 27th reinstating me as counsel of the company, as well as of your other cable communicating to me by Secretary Lampre. I am happy to renew our former connections immediately, and in accordance with the general terms of your cablegrams I have drawn up a general plan of campaign; seeing that no agreement has yet been reached between Colombia and United States, and in view of the erroneous interpretation of our titles, I have inspired a new bill, adopting our project and leaving to the decision of the President all questions relating to titles and to the new treaty to be concluded with Colombia, with discretionary power to choose the other route, if the President is not successful in obtaining a satisfactory title and treaty for our route. I am working to have this bill passed in both houses. My next step will be to obtain from Colombia definite and satisfactory conditions for the treaty with our Government; in the contrary event the whole matter will be jeopardized, and the Senate would probably follow the House in favoring the other route. This capital question has brought Silva to understand the situation and to have conferences with the most important personages."

Mr. Cromwell had been keeping busy all the time he was officially disconnected with the canal company's affairs. On the very day Mr. Cromwell received notice of his reinstatement, Senator Scott, of West Virginia, introduced a joint resolution to appropriate $15,000 and create a special board to investigate the practicability of the Darien Canal route. Whether it was intended as an aid to Mr. Cromwell or was not, the Scott resolution served to divert attention from Nicaragua, and on the very next day, January 28, 1902, Mr. Spooner, of Wisconsin, submitted an amendment intended to be proposed by him to the Nicaragua bill, which had passed the House, and it was ordered printed. This amendment, substituting the Panama for the Nicaragua route, was the basis of the Spooner law under which the Panama Canal is being built.

Senator Spooner protested in the Senate June 12, 1902, that he not only wrote the amendment that bore his name, but devised it. Nevertheless, in a telegram which reached the French Canal Co. on January 31, 1902, Mr. Cromwell said:

I have formulated a general plan of campaign. * * * I have inspired a new bill which adopts our project and which sends to the President for decision all questions relative to titles and to the new treaty to be concluded with Columbia. * * * I am working to have this bill passed by the two Chambers. My next step will be to obtain from Colombia precise and satisfactory conditions for the treaty with our Government.

In his brief Mr. Cromwell says:

At the time when the company had shown, in the preceding spring, its willingness to sell to the United States under certain conditions, we had planned with this end in view, the introduction of a bill in Congress authorzing the building of the Panama Canal by the United States. This bill had been the subject of conferences between us and several eminent statesmen. So, at this critical moment we reverted this idea and had long conferences with Senator Hanna and Senator Spoonor, whom we urged to act in this direction, and these conferences resulted in Senator Spooner preparing and introducing in the Senate a bill for the adoption of the Panama route project and the acquisition of the properties of the Panama Canal Co. for $40,000,000 on the following conditions: (1) That the President should obtain, within a reasonable time, a satisfactory title to all the properties of the company; and (2) that he should obtain, by treaty from the Republic of Colombia, the enjoyment of the necessary right and authority; and that if he did not succeed he should adopt the Nicaragua Canal and obtain, by treaty with Nicaragua and Costa Rica, the territory and rights necessary to its construction.

Mr. Cromwell now set about to prevent the Nicaragua bills, which had been passed by the House a few days previously, from being immediately and favorably reported to the Senate, as Senator Morgan, who had a majority in his committee, was going to do, to bring about a treaty between the United States and Colombia and to procure that the consent of Colombia to a cession by the company be included in this treaty. To obtain the acceptance by Congress of the company's offer and render this offer binding by the ratification of its shareholders, which was essential.

Senator Morgan had brought before his committee much evidence to show that the commission had been illogical in its reports, and that one of its members (Prof. Haupt) had, so to speak, been compelled to sign the report.

Mr. Cromwell thereupon determined to widen the committee's field of inquiry in order to embrace the subject of Panama. He persuaded Senator Hanna and other members of the commiitee to make no report until they had heard all the members of the commission in support of their last report, the hearing of which evidence would directly bring out the advantages of the Panama project and the reaffirmation of the recommendations they had made in favor of the company's offer. Senator Hanna insisted on this course being followed, and all the members of the commission were summoned before the committee by Senator Hanna and testified at length.

Mr. Cromwell, who had conferred with the members of the commission and informed himself in detail as to their individual opinions, prepared for the use of Senator Hanna and his colleague, Senator Kittredge, a series of questions to bring out facts favorable to Panama during the deposition of each of the members of the commission. This procedure also served to gain time to obtain the necessary proposal of a treaty with Colombia and her consent to a cession by the company.

But Senator Morgan had declared that the New Panama Canal Co. could not, in any case, give a valid title to its property; that the company had not the right to sell, that the bondholders of the old company had a reversional interest in the Panama Canal, etc.

To overcome these objections Mr. Cromwell prepared "An opinion on the title of the New Panama Canal Co. and on its right to transfer its property to the United States."

The Senate Committee on Interoceanic Canals had appointed a subcommittee of six members to study and report upon the legal questions. This subcommittee was composed of Senators Foster, Morgan, Mitchell, Turner, Kittredge, and Pritchard. The majority of this subcommittee wrote a detailed report (32 printed pages) to show that the company's titles were defective, and that the company had no power to transfer. Mr. Cromwell's "opinion" had already been published and was furnished to the members forming the minority of this subcommittee, Messrs. Kittredge and Pritchard, and they made a report in accordance with Mr. Cromwell's view.

The majority and minority reports were both submitted to the Senate on March 19, 1902; Mr. Cromwell had the minority report printed at the expense of the Panama Canal Co. and circulated throughout the country.

Mr. Cromwell then applied himself to obtaining the consent of Colombia to the transfer of the canal concession and railroad rights to the United States. In his brief he says:

During this period we applied ourselves actively to the matter of the necessary treaty between the United States and Colombia, and to obtaining by this means the consent of Colombia to the transfer.

Minister Silva was still in Washington, but he was in disfavor in his own country, and accused by his government with having authorized the negotiations between the company and the United States. His powers as minister had been either canceled or considerably curtailed, and his recall was but a matter of time: it took place shortly afterwards in February, 1902.

The Colombian Government in Bogota was preparing either to force the company to pay from 50,000,000 to 60,000,000 francs, as the price of its consent (over and above the advantages Colombia might obtain from the United States), or to treat as null and void the prorogation until 1910; or if these plans failed, to await the forfeiture of the company's concessions in 1910, and then treat directly with the United States or some other nation or interest, at its pleasure, and thus obtain all the pecuniary advantages to be had from the sale of the canal.

Thus the necessity of frustrating the designs of the Colombian Government, and of bringing it to make a proposal to the United States, became of supreme and vital importance to the acceptance of the company's offer.

To back up the company's offer, to retain the support of the friends of Panama in Congress in the Senate, to bring the minority of the Senate committee to make a report recommending Panama, it was absolutely necessary to obtain the proposal by Colombia to the United States of a treaty which should be definite and reasonable. We knew that it was the intention of the Bogota Government to demand a pecuniary tribute of several millions of dollars from the canal company as the price of its consent to the transfer, and we were desirous of obtaining a treaty proposal which would bind the consent of Colombia by an international agreement, and which would thus not only furnish the necessary basis, as far as the United States was concerned, for the acceptance of the canal offer, but also a protection for the company against the demands which might be made on it by Colombia direct.

Hence this became a fundamental and imperative condition of success and we devoted our attention not only to the matter of the acceptance of the company's offer, but also to assuring to it the full advantage of this offer without the heavy deduction that would be caused by a pecuniary tribute to Colombia as the price of her consent.

There was then no official proposal whatever pending between the two countries. The Colombian Government had no desire to assist the sale; Secretary Hay (who was an open partisan of Nicaragua) refused to open negotiations, no law having placed this duty upon him. Neither of the Governments was willing to act, and yet unless there was some agreement between them the offer of the company could not even receive consideration. Mr. Cromwell, therefore, personally and without cooperation opened negotiations with the minister and urged upon him the necessity of a proposal as a basis of a treaty between Colombia and the United States, which proposal should include the consent of Colombia to the transfer.

Fortunately we had already established intimate and cordial relations of mutual confidence with Minister Silva and Mr. Herran, secretary of the legation, a man of wide experience, who was later in charge of the legation.

At last Minister Silva drew up a preliminary proposal which he asked us to examine. This proposal was made on the basis of a lease by Colombia to the United States renting the Canal Zone for 200 years only, at a yearly rental of $600,000, with the added condition that the United States should buy the railroad at a valuation to be made at the expiration of the concession, and until then should pay a yearly rental of $250,000 for the railroad; the United States were to make a loan capitalizing these annual payments.

Mr. Harrison. Mr. Hall, before you go any further I want to ask whether Mr. Silva's actions as minister of Colombia while the treaty was being negotiated were ratified by the authorities of the United States of Colombia.

Mr. Hall. No, sir.

Mr. Harrison. They were not approving of that at all.

Mr. Hall. On the contrary he was recalled. He had exceeded his instructions; and his Government sent Minister Concha to take his place.

Mr. Harrison. That was the reason of the change?

Mr. Hall. That was the reason of the change. When Minister Concha reached the United States he did not come on to Washington at once, but remained in New York. I shall come to that in a moment. Mr. Cromwell goes on to say in his brief:

The situation in the Senate was getting more and more critical every day. Senator Morgan, chairman of the Senate Committee on Interoceanic Canals, supported by the majority of that committee, was using every means to bring the hearings of his committee to an end and to submit to the Senate the report of the majority in favor of Nicaragua and against Panama, so that the question might be voted upon promptly in the Senate, which, according to the partisans of Nicaragua, would support the cause of Nicaragua; and, under the existing circumstances, it was clear to everybody that that would really have been the result. It thus became essential to inform Congress in some manner that Colombia would give her consent, at least on certain conditions, to the transfer to the United States, and in consequence we strongly urged Minister Silva to present his proposal to Secretary Hay, with the idea that once the negotiations were officially opened modifications might be obtained. Mr. Silva yielded to our arguments and agreed to act, and he wrote out a fuller draft of his proposal, which he submitted to us, and which we criticised and corrected at his request.

However, and just as Minister Silva was about to present this proposal, in accordance with our request, he received official notification of his recall, with orders to cease all negotiations, and it became impossible for him to act officially. He had as successor Minister Concha, who arrived in New York February 26, 1902, with new instructions of a radical nature.

Minister Concha had been a political rival of Minister Silva, and he was sent to uphold the politics and pecuniary demands of the Bogota Government, the nature of which we have already outlined, and with which it was recognized that Minister Silva was not in accord.

The arrival of this new minister, in view of the nature of his instructions and of the attitude of the Colombian Government, presented a gravely perilous situation.

The Senate committee was continuing its hearings as we have already said. Senator Spooner, author of the Spooner bill, was asking us for some proof of Colombia's consent in the form of a proper treaty, as well as for proof of the ratification by the shareholders of the canal company of the offer made by its board of directors, which was, on the other hand, perfectly reasonable.

Senator Hanna, whose intelligence was so vast and who had insisted on a decent consideration of the company's offer and on the hearing of witnesses by the committee, in order to elucidate all the aspects of the matter, confessed to us that he was not disposed to support the acceptance of the company's offer or to recommend such acceptance in a minority report of his committee without sufficient assurance that a satisfactory treaty could be obtained, and that the shareholders of the company would ratify the action of the board (of directors) in making the offer.

We arranged an interview at which Senator Hanna, Minister Silva, and Mr. Cromwell were present, but the Colombian minister could not give the definite assurances required.

Minister Silva clearly saw the dangers of the situation although the Government of his country did not see them, but everything depended now on the attitude of his successor Minister Concha. This personage remained in New York after his arrival and would not go to Washington to present his credentials, nor would he at once take up this question. In explanation, he declared that he was awaiting further instructions from Bogota. Mr. Concha refused to yield to the instances of Minister Silva, who urged him to take charge of the legation. It was clear that he would not assist in the matter even by his presence.

This situation became known in Washington among Members of Congress, and gave support to the assertion that Colombia was hostile to the United States and to the conclusion of any treaty, and that in consequence the offer of the Panama Canal Co. ought to be rejected. This gave much anxiety to the supporters of the Panama Canal.

Meantime the Colombian Government, through its consul general in Paris, served notice on the new Panama Canal Co. that it could not transfer its property without first coming to terms with Colombia. The ratification of offer of sale by the shareholders of the company was a fundamental requirement of the Spooner bill then pending, so the company had called a general meeting, to be held in Paris, February 28, 1902, and the advertisements to this effect had been duly published. The Republic of Colombia was owner of 5,000,000 francs' worth of ~~shares, and was also represented on the board of directors by a Government delegate.~~ The Bogota Government had thus been warned of the company's proposed action.

The Republic of Colombia served formal notice on the company the day before the meeting that it forbade the sale of the canal to the United States before the approval of this sale by the Colombian Government under pain of forfeiture of its concessions and the loss of its properties by virtue of articles 21 and 22 of the contract of 1878.

The board abandoned its intention of asking the ratification by the shareholders of the offer of sale made to the United States, abstained from proposing the resolution by which the ratification was to have been given, and introduced an order of the day postponing all action until after the settlement of the difficulties with Colombia. This order of the day was adopted and the meeting adjourned without any action in the matter of the offer made to the United States. As Mr. Cromwell says in his brief:

This action on the part of Colombia furnished official proof that the necessary consent of Colombia had not yet been given.

It clearly showed the intention of Colombia to demand pecuniary tribute from the company as the price of this consent.

It made public and evident the fact that the offer of the company was, so far, incomplete by reason of its nonratification by the shareholders.

The minority of the Senate committee (Messrs. Hanna, Kittredge, Pritchard, and Millard) then told Mr. Cromwell plainly, as Senator Hanna had already done, that they were not disposed to take the responsibility of making a minority report recommending the adoption of the Panama project and the acceptance of the offer of the company, unless the minority was morally certain that the United States could obtain from Colombia the necessary authority over the territory, and that the approval of the shareholders be given in a way to prevent them from disowning the offer that had been made by the board.

So Mr. Cromwell set about to obtain from the new Colombian minister a written statement that the notification by Colombia did not imply opposition to the transfer.

At Mr. Cromwell's request, Minister Silva continued, by telegram and letter, to urge Minister Concha, then in New York, to hasten his arrival in Washington and the assumption of his post, and to take up the negotiations. All the efforts of Minister Silva to this end, however, did not succeed in eliciting a statement from Minister Concha, or even in getting him to go to Washington.

So Mr. Cromwell sent Dr. Mutis Duran, a prominent lawyer and former governor of Panama, who had done legal work for the Panama Railroad Co., to call on Minister Concha in New York and try to persuade him to come to an agreement with the United States and the canal company. Dr. Duran was received by the minister with indifference.

As all the efforts of Minister Silva and Dr. Mutis Duran to bring Minister Concha to take up the negotiations had failed, Mr. Cromwell, who was then in Washington, himself went to New York, called on Minister Concha, and convinced him that the Nicaragua project would inevitably be adopted if Colombia did not neutralize the harmful effects of her official notification in Paris in opposition to the transfer. In his brief Mr. Cromwell says:

As a result of two such prolonged conferences, which lasted all day, on March 7, Mr. Cromwell succeeded in persuading Minister Concha to make a statement, which he authorized us to write out and make public. This statement was written by us; it was addressed to us in our capacity as general counsel of La Compagnie Nouvelle du Canal de Panama, and declared that the notice served on the company by Colombia on February 28 did not imply opposition to the transfer, if a mutually satisfactory convention was concluded between Colombia and the United States in respect to their respective rights and relations in regard to the canal; that Colombia approved the steps taken by the canal company in its negotiations with the United States and would facilitate the transfer with the reservation already mentioned; that Colombia looked with favor on the construction of the Panama Canal by the United States through her territory; that he would continue the negotiations and would soon make clear to the United States the views and proposals of Colombia in this matter, with the object of encouraging the complete and early purchase by the Government of the United States of the rights, concessions, and property of the canal company, in so far as Colombia's constitution and laws would permit her to make the transfer to a foreign government—that is to say, without renouncing her sovereignty. This official note was communicated by us to the press of the United States, and we forwarded a copy officially to the Secretary of State, Mr. Hay, to Minister Silva, to the members of the minority of the Senate committee, and to other influential persons.

This statement by the new Colombian minister was a surprise to all parties interested. It had a powerful effect in all parts and helped a great deal to neutralize the harm that had been done. It had been obtained, thanks to our efforts alone.

The struggle in the Senate committee had continued all this time; hearings ended March 10, and three days later the committee, by a vote of 7 to 4, laid before the Senate a report favorable to the Nicaragua bill and rejecting the Spooner bill and the offer of the company (Mar. 13).

Thus the Hepburn bill concerning the Nicaragua Canal, which had been passed in the House by a vote of 309 to 2, was presented to the Senate with a favorable report of its committee; and the Spooner bill, which had been referred to the same committee, was returned to the Senate with an unfavorable majority report.

The majority of the committee, led by Senator Morgan, did not at this time present a detailed report in support of its findings, as it rested on its numerous preceding reports favorable to Nicaragua, so that the Senate had before it nothing more than the expression of opinion in favor of Nicaragua. The minority was composed of Senators Hanna, Kittredge, Millard, and Pritchard, and Mr. Cromwell begged them to file a detailed minority report. The minority refused to do so then, because of the uncertain status of affairs with Colombia and of the absence of ratification of the company's offer by the shareholders.

Mr. Cromwell then concentrated his efforts on the matter of the proposal of a treaty, and—

for several weeks devoted himself to this matter daily with Minister Concha, Mr. Herran, the secretary of the legation, and influential Senators, with whose views it was necessary to conform.

To continue quoting from Mr. Cromwell's brief:

The new minister (Concha) approached the subject in a very different spirit to that shown by his predecessor (Silva). He had just arrived from Bogota, and was imbued with the extreme views and intentions of the Bogota Government, which had recalled his predecessor because of his over-liberal leanings toward the United States and the company. * * * As the Secretary of State of the United States made no overtures to Minister Concha (because he was not authorized so to do by Congress, which had first to select a route) Minister Concha maintained the same attitude toward the Secretary of State, and, except for diplomatic declarations of good will on either side, neither of the parties took any steps with a view to the negotiation of a treaty.

In the face of this difficulty and to save the situation we once again personally took the initiative; we overcame the repugnance which Minister Concha felt for any discussion with an American, and above all with a representative of the canal company, and were at last requested by the minister to assist him in the wording of any treaty proposal which he might decide to make.

Mr. Cromwell devoted every day of the ensuing month to discussion with the minister at the latter's residence, gave the minister advice on all the questions at issue, and himself wrote out the text of a proposed treaty (projet de traité). These discussions covered the entire ground of international relations and international law; the special interests of Colombia; the treaty of 1846 in force; the general policy of Colombia, as well as that of the United States, in regard to the canal; the special interests of the cities of Panama and Colon, as well as of the Isthmus of Panama; the questions of harbors and of maritime duties; the most vital question of sovereignty; the question of a lease, in perpetuity or for a fixed period; the questions of law courts and judicial procedure; the question of a fixed remuneration and of an annuity, etc. Even above all these questions, in its importance to the company, was the vital consent of Colombia to the transfer and sale of the properties to the United States, consent which, at our own instance, was to be inserted in the treaty itself; and this was our chief aim, although it was also important to insure the conclusion of a treaty satisfactory to both the United States and Colombia, as otherwise the mere consent to a transfer would be without the slightest value. * * * Little by little, in the course of conferences which succeeded each other for whole weeks at a time, Mr. Cromwell led the minister to pledge himself as to various bases for a proposal, but up to March 24, 1902, the best pecuniary conditions Minister Concha was willing to propose were $7,500,000 cash and $600,000 a year from the expiration of a period of 15 years after the completion of the canal, with exemption of the islands of the Bay of Panama, the limitation of the authority of the United States, etc., and a lease for a fixed period. * * * All through these negotiations we particularly bore in mind to obtain, as a matter of the greatest importance in the negotiation, the assent of Colombia to the transfer to the United States; and we inserted in the draft of the treaty a clause to this effect (Art. L) and obtained the assent thereto of Minister Concha.

This was the forerunner of the treaty entered into, according to Mr. Roosevelt, "at the urgent solicitation of the people of Colombia."

Minister Concha had come with instructions to exact an indemnity of from $10,000,000 to $20,000,000 cash, to be paid either by the United States or by the canal company, or by both, and an annual subsidy of a million dollars.

From the start Minister Concha (like his predecessor, Mr. Silva) positively refused to grant a lease in perpetuity, which was imperatively demanded by the United States. Colombia insisted that the lease should be for a fixed and stated period. This was a fundamental difference, and to overcome it Mr. Cromwell hit upon the plan of conceding the principle of a lease (thus recognizing the sovereignty of Columbia) with a provision for the renewal of the lease, at the option of the United States, in succeeding periods of 100 years and on the basis of a new valuation. Mr. Cromwell succeeded in obtaining the assent of Secretary Hay and of Minister Concha to this proposal as constituting an element of the treaty.

Minister Concha had returned to New York. Mr. Cromwell called upon ex-Minister Silva and Dr. Mutis Duran and persuaded them to go to Minister Concha and urge him to reduce the terms, but their efforts were fruitless.

The terms laid down in Minister Concha's instructions, when officially communicated by Mr. Cromwell to Senator Hanna and certain other members of the Senate committee, were declared by them to be inacceptable. Secretary Hay also declared the terms were excessive and impossible and told Mr. Cromwell that the reports he was receiving from the United States minister in Bogota were to the same effect as Minister Concha's proposals.

Minister Concha had not even seen the Secretary of State nor made any offer. As a matter of fact, he was not disposed to make any and was quite seriously considering the advisability of returning to Bogota.

In order to smooth over the difficulties, Mr. Cromwell proposed that instead of stipulating an annuity the amount of which should be unchangeable, this amount was to be fixed and established, in accordance with certain principles laid down in the treaty, by a high commission, the arbiter of which was to be the president of the International Peace Tribunal at The Hague.

After many conferences and discussions Mr. Cromwell persuaded Minister Concha to accept this solution and obtained his written consent thereto.

By March 29, 1902, Mr. Cromwell had completed the preparation, with Minister Concha, of the draft of a treaty, which the minister stated that he was ready to present and which he authorized Mr. Cromwell to discuss with Secretary Hay, Senator Hanna, and others in order to ascertain their views before communicating it officially to the Government of the United States.

But Mr. Cromwell persuaded Minister Concha to sign the proposal and to hand it at once to the Secretary of State, he (Cromwell) arranged an interview for this purpose and accompanied the minister to make the official presentation of the proposal to Secretary Hay March 31, 1902. In his written communication, Minister Concha declared that a further explanatory note would be presented by Mr. Cromwell. The latter wrote, signed, and handed to the Secretary of State this explanatory note, which was forwarded by the President to both Houses of Congress later, at the time of the transmission of the Hay-Concha treaty.

Colombia's trust of the United States found expression even in this first draft of a treaty. Articles 3 and 4 renewed the guarantees of the United States laid down in the treaty of 1846–1848, as follows:

ART. III. All the stipulations contained in article 35 of the treaty of 1846–1848 between the contracting parties shall continue and apply in full force to the cities of Panama and Colon and to the accessory community lands within said zone, and the territory thereon shall be neutral territory, and the United States shall continue to guarantee the neutrality thereof and the sovereignty of Colombia thereover, in conformity with the above-mentioned article 35 of the said treaty.

ART. IV. The rights and privileges guaranteed to the United States by the terms of this convention shall not affect the sovereignty of the Republic of Colombia over the territory within whose boundaries such rights and privileges are to be exercised.

The United States freely acknowledges and recognizes this sovereignty and disavows any intention to impair it in any way whatever or to increase its territory at the expense of Colombia, or of any of the sister Republics in Central or South America, but, on the contrary, it desires to strengthen the power of the Republics on this continent and to promote, develop, and maintain their prosperity and independence.

Minister Concha's reasons are reflected in the following extracts from his letter to the Colombian foreign minister, written April 1, 1902:

The first thing that comes to one's mind in this respect, and especially on account of the present political situation of the Isthmus, is the imminent danger that there may take place a secession movement in that part of the Republic, either spontaneously or by reason of indirect suggestions of foreign interests, which would be a source of incalculable evils for the Republic.

But should the doors of our national territory be closed in hostility to the United States, it would in retaliation denounce, as the press has already suggested, the treaty of 1846, and once the undertakings of this treaty are removed, it (the United States) will view with complacency the events which will then take place in Panama, in order to occupy at once our territory, at the first interruption of the railroad service, or to embrace whatever tendency there may be toward separation whereby they will bring about a lesion of Colombian sovereignty of far greater consequence than any limitation to which the Republic may subject itself in the use of a given zone of its territory.

In a cable to his government, April 10, 1902, Minister Concha announced the failure of his efforts to bring about European intervention to neutralize the canal, at least so far as France was concerned.

The French ambassador—

Said Concha—

has informed me that his government has prohibited his intervening in the affair of the Panama Canal.

A day later Concha confirmed this cable and added that the Washington representatives of all the powers had taken the same position as the French ambassador.

Mr. Cromwell, meantime, continued the negotiations between the United States and Colombia by numerous conferences with Secretary Hay and Minister Concha individually, always acting as the sole intermediary for communications, and gave his advice with a view to modifying the demands of Colombia so as to render them acceptable to the United States. Three weeks were taken up by this work, by rewriting several times the various clauses, and in individual conferences with the representatives of the two governments, so that toward the middle of April he had secured amendments to the proposal of March 31, which met with the approval of the President and the Secretary of State. Among the important points of the protocol was the vital point of the consent of Colombia to the transfers to the United States (Art. I).

How valuable this strategy was considered by the New Panama Canal Co. is shown by the following excerpt from a letter written by President Bo, on April 16, 1902, thanking and complimenting Mr. Cromwell for his successful diplomacy:

We especially appreciate the first article of the protocol, by which Colombia gives our company the right to sell its property to the United States, which, in fact, abrogates articles 21 and 22 of our contracts of concession, which were opposed to us, and will permit us to resist the pecuniary pretensions of Colombia, to which we are absolutely determined.

Mr. Cromwell, with Minister Concha, then wrote a new draft of a treaty and had it transmitted to the Secretary of State, who, after conferences with Mr. Cromwell for the explanation of the provisions of the amendments, finally gave Mr. Cromwell, on April 23, 1902, his official statement dated April 21, 1902, to be transmitted to Minister Concha, in which he declared himself ready to sign the proposed agreement as soon as Congress should authorize the President to conclude an entente, and as soon as the Department of Justice should complete its examination of the title.

Mr. Harrison. That is what Mr. Cromwell says in his brief, is it?

Mr. Hall. Substantially; yes, sir. I will read you his exact words:

After many conferences and discussions we persuaded Minister Concha to accept this solution, and obtained his written consent, accompanied by a letter he wrote to us under date of March 29, 1902. With this consent, Minister Concha handed us a draft of a treaty which we had prepared together, the minister stating that he was ready to present this proposal and authorizing us to discuss its terms with Secretary Hay, Senator Hanna, and others, in order to ascertain their views before communicating it officially to the Government of the United States.

Thus it remained for us to satisfy Secretary Hay and the Senators forming the minority of the committee. We devoted ourselves immediately to this task, and after numerous conferences and explanations succeeded in assuring their acquiescence in sufficient degree for our immediate purpose.

Having informed Minister Concha of this situation, Mr. Cromwell persuaded him to sign the proposal and to hand it at once to the Secretary of State, arranged an interview for this purpose, and accompanied the minister to make the official presentation of it (the proposal) to Secretary Hay March 31, 1902. In his written communication the minister declared that a further explanatory note woulld be presented by Mr. Cromwell. The latter wrote, signed, and handed to the Secretary of State this important document, which strengthened the Colombian proposal and thus buttressed the position of the canal company.

Our explanatory note was forwarded by the President to both Houses of Congress later, at the time of the transmission of the Hay-Concha treaty.

This proposal marked an important step toward the acceptance of the company's offer. It fulfilled our purpose, which was to bring the consent of Colombia within the bounds of international relations and to furnish the basis indispensable to obtaining the support of the Senate.

Mr. Cromwell goes on to tell how he continued to conduct his diplomatic negotiations, and then declares outright:

As a result of these further negotiations, we wrote a new draft of a treaty (known as the Hay-Concha agreement of April 18, 1902) and had it transmitted officially to the Secretary of State by Minister Concha. The Secretary, after other conferences with Mr. Cromwell, for the explanation of the provisions of the amendments, gave Mr. Cromwell, on April 23, 1902, his official statement, dated April 21, 1902, to be transmitted to Minister Concha, in which he declared himself ready to sign the proposed agreement as soon as Congress should authorize the President to conclude an entente and as soon as the Department of Justice should complete its examination of the title.

In all the negotiations concerning the Hay-Concha agreement the minister of the two Governments communicated solely through the intermediary of Mr. Cromwell.

Mr. Cromwell's diplomatic victory was, however, not complete. The minority of the Senate committee insisted, even after President Roosevelt transmitted the Hay-Concha treaty to the Senate, upon having proof that the stockholders of the Panama Canal Company would ratify the offer of sale for $40,000,000. This had not been obtained at the Paris meeting of February 28, 1902, because Colombia had served notice that the concession could not be transferred without permission. The company feared to call another meeting because Colombia might renew its warning at just the time when the treaty was under discussion in the Senate and thereby cause the deathblow to the Panama project.

To meet this emergency Mr. Cromwell conceived the idea of obtaining from at least a minority of the shareholders of the company the written signatures of formal consent to the sale, with a definite pledge to ratify this sale at any general meeting convoked in the future for this purpose. These consents and pledges were obtained by the company and forwarded to Mr. Cromwell, and he was successful in inducing his friends in the Senate to accept this assurance in lieu of ratification by the shareholders.

This obtaining of the signatures of "at least a majority" of the 8,000 shareholders was accomplished, according to Mr. Cromwell's brief, sometime between April 18, 1902, and the filing of the "Hanna minority report" at the end of May. Mr. Cromwell's partner, Curtis, was in Paris at the end of April.

Having fulfilled the two most important conditions (the treaty proposal and ratification by the shareholders), then urged the minority of the Senate committee to make a report. Mr. Cromwell wrote out a complete draft of the report he wanted and discussed it at great length before the minority of the committee. Mr. Cromwell's draft was corrected, adopted, and signed by the minority and became famous under the name of the "Hanna minority report." It was the text-book on the Panama side during the debates which followed in the Senate. Mr. Cromwell had several hundred copies printed, one of which he had sent to each Member of Congress and of the Cabinet.

Mr. HARRISON. Was that minority report written by Mr. Cromwell?

Mr. HALL. Mr. Cromwell says it was written by him and, after he had discussed it before them, was revised by Mr. Hanna and the minority and sent by them to the Senate as their report. I will read you Mr. Cromwell's own words:

> We then urged the members of the minority of the committee to make a minority report. This was a matter to which these members had given much thought during the preceding weeks. As preliminaries, we wrote a complete and thorough draft of a report and also several other treatises of a legal or technical character bearing upon this draft, and we discussed these documents on many occasions and at great length before the minority of the committee. This work had taken up several weeks, and this document had served as a possible draft of a report in the discussion with the minority of the committee. After full consideration this report was corrected, adopted, and signed by the minority and became famous under the name of the "Hanna minority report;" it was the text-book on the Panama side during the debates which followed in the Senate. We had several hundred copies printed, one of which we had sent to each Member of Congress and of the Cabinet before the debates, and also obtained its circulation in numerous other influential circles. This minority report included a summary and a detailed exposition of the entire Panama Canal matter from every point of view—technical, legal, physical, economic, comparative, etc. It was the textbook of the campaign in the coming struggle, and it had a most powerful influence on the outcome—by a barely sufficient majority—of the struggle between Nicaragua and Panama. We added to it a synopsis written by us of the existing claims, concessions, etc., of the Maritime Canal and Nicaragua Construction companies, showing that these companies would demand about $13,000,000 from the United States if that route were adopted, as well as indemnities for the declaration of forfeiture of its concessions by Nicaragua, alleged to be irregular.
>
> The minority also adopted word for word and annexed to its report our opinion on the company's titles, its concessions, its power to transfer, etc., and thus gave to this opinion the seal of official use and approval.
>
> The writing of this minority report, the communication of data, of technical information and legal opinions, the final adoption and circulation of this report constantly occupied two, at least, of our partners for several weeks.
>
> This minority report marked another great step forward.

The final struggle in the Senate lasted from June 4, 1902, till June 19, 1902, in debates on the Hepburn bill (Nicaragua) and the Spooner bill (Panama). Senators Morgan and Harris led the fight for the Hepburn bill, whilst Senators Hanna and Spooner championed the Spooner bill.

The four most formidable and carefully prepared speeches in favor of Panama were made by Senators Hanna, Kittredge, Gallinger, and Cullom. Mr. Cromwell wrote Senator Hanna's speech, if not in its entirety, at least in greater part. Even to the subheads, which appear in the Congressional Record in approved newspaper fashion, the Hanna speech is a strong testimonial to the efficiency of Mr. Cromwell's bureau of seismography, engineering, editorial advertising, diplomacy, legislation, and law. Mr. Hanna spoke from manuscript.

Mr. HARRISON. Where did you get that from, Mr. Hall; that is, the information that Mr. Cromwell wrote Mr. Hanna's speech?

Mr. HALL. Mr. Cromwell does not say so in as many words, in his own brief, but we have testimony on that point. I will quote the authority for that statement.

Mr. KENDALL. I suppose it is, perhaps, the same authority that says he prepared the minority report.

Mr. HALL. Mr. Cromwell says that in his own words.

Mr. KENDALL. He says that in his own words?

Mr. HALL. Yes; I have just read the passage from his brief. As to the speech, Mr. Hanna spoke from manuscript. It was the famous earthquake speech which Mr. Cooper, the other day, said defeated the Nicaragua Canal. Mr. Hanna had his charts up on the wall, and the earthquake territory marked off. Mr. Cromwell in his brief tells in detail how he prepared this information. The speeches of Kittredge, Gallinger, and Cullom also appear carefully subheaded, while on the Nicaragua side this style of editing appears in the Record only in Senator Mitchell's address. Both Senators Hanna and Kittredge, who were Mr. Cromwell's most valuable allies, emphasized that Colombia had consented, in the Concha draft of a treaty (drafted by Mr. Cromwell), to the transfer of the canal concession to the United States—the consent which Mr. Cromwell, for his own ends, had labored to bring within the realm of diplomatic negotiations and international relations.

Senators Kittredge and Cullom both called attention to and quoted from Cromwell's letter to Secretary Hay, which accompanied Concha's draft of a treaty, March 31, 1902. (Mr. Cullom, by the way, had made a speech in favor of the Nicaragua route in the Senate in 1894.)

The final vote took place on a motion to substitute the Spooner bill (Panama), indorsed by the Hanna minority, for the Hepburn bill (Nicaragua), indorsed by the majority. It was decided by the narrow majority of 42 votes in favor of the Spooner bill. against 34 in favor of the Hepburn bill. A slight difference of five votes would have killed the Panama Canal project and have made the Nicaragua Canal the choice of the American people. The supporters of Nicaragua in an effort to neutralize Mr. Cromwell's victory supported a motion directing that any treaty with Colombia be concluded within six months, but this was defeated by 44 votes against and 33 for. They then introduced a similar motion fixing the delay at 12 months, but this also failed, the vote being 39 against and 35 for.

But the struggle was not yet over, as the House strongly favored the Nicaragua bill, which it had passed five months previously by 309 votes for and 2 against. The Spooner bill was at once sent to the House, which rejected it, adhering to its own, the Hepburn bill. This resulted in both bills being sent to a conference between the two Houses. Delegates were appointed, the Senate being represented by Senators Hanna, Morgan, and Kittredge, and the House by Messrs. Hepburn, Fletcher, and Davey. The conferees sat all through the ensuing week. The House delegates yielded at last, and after some opposition the House approved the action of its delegates and passed the Spooner bill.

The Spooner bill was signed by the President on June 28, 1902. Offer made by the Panama Canal Co. was thus accepted and the Panama route chosen, but on condition (1) that the title of the company be approved and (2) that a satisfactory treaty be concluded with Colombia, with the alternative of the adoption of the Nicaragua route in default of one or the other of these conditions.

Mr. Cromwell then applied himself to the task of fulfilling the two conditions of the Spooner Act—the necessary treaty and approval of the titles.

The Hay-Concha agreement, submitted to the Senate, while presenting a sufficient basis for the passage of the Spooner Act, had been found unsatisfactory by many Senators, who insisted that the United States should have the right to establish additional courts in the Canal Zone, maintain a police force, and have control of the sanitation. They also demanded that the forfeiture clause of the proposed treaty be omitted and that a given cash sum, plus a small annuity, be substituted for the pecuniary assignments of the proposed treaty.

After other conferences with Members of the Senate Mr. Cromwell prepared a revision of the treaty and submitted it to Secretary Hay. Numerous conferences between Secretary Hay and Mr. Cromwell followed, and at last the lawyer of the New Panama Canal Co. reached an understanding with Secretary Hay and President Roosevelt.

But it was also necessary to obtain the consent of Minister Concha, and Mr. Cromwell had a series of conferences with him on the subject of these amendments; and at last, on July 18, 1902, Mr. Cromwell succeeded in bringing the representatives of the two Governments to an understanding. Pursuant to arrangements made by him as intermediaries, Secretary Hay officially transmitted the amendments to Minister Concha who, in turn, transmitted them to his Government. In this way the treaty was given a form satisfactory to President Roosevelt, and the revised version thereof was on its way, addressed to the Bogota Government.

Mr. Cromwell says:

In this negotiation, as in the preceding one, the ministers of the two Governments always communicated with each other through the intermediary of Mr. Cromwell and only met to exchange the final documents after the understanding had been reached.

The Colombian Blue Book of 1904 contains a letter of Minister Concha to his Government, dated July 11, 1902, reporting that on July 9, 1902, he had received through an "unofficial source" (Mr. Cromwell says he was always this source) the American draft of the treaty as Secretary Hay (or rather Cromwell) had amended the original Concha (or rather Cromwell) proposal. Minister Concha added:

The Secretary of State before a formal presentation of his amendments has desired to feel out the opinion of the undersigned concerning the changes referred to, but I have expressed no opinion in this matter, pending instructions from your excellency, which were asked for by cable sent yesterday.

The Colombian Government replied by cable July 17, 1902:

Do not break off negotiations. Refer to Congress.

In a letter explaining to Minister Concha the order to refer the negotiations to Congress, the Colombian foreign minister said that the concessions demanded in the American amendments were of a character that could be passed upon only by the Congress.

Minister Concha's correspondence with his Government, from early in June, 1902, indicates that he was anticipating demands by the United States that would be unacceptable. He considered that in the proposals made in March and April of the year he had offered all that Colombia would be willing to concede, and he was determined, as he notified his Government June 20, 1902, to oppose any amendments looking toward the diminution of Colombian sovereignty or affecting the proposed neutrality of the canal. In this attitude he was supported by his Government in a letter from the minister for foreign affairs, dated July 31, 1902. In this letter the Colombian foreign office also approved Concha's suggestion that they should agree upon a new cable code, Minister Concha having warned his Government that he had reasons for suspecting that the Colombian secret code was in possession of the American State Department.

Mr. Cromwell now transferred the field of his activities from lobbying, legislation, and diplomacy, to law, and on July 24, 1902, went to Paris to assist the Special Assistant Attorney General for the United States in reaching the conclusion that the Panama Canal Co. could deliver a valid title. Meanwhile, Farnham was left in charge of Minister Concha in Washington, and Mr. Hill, one of Mr. Cromwell's partners, made frequent trips thither to assist in handling the diplomatic representation of Colombia. They made frequent reports by cable to Mr. Cromwell in Paris.

Attorney General Knox and myself went over later to Paris, and Mr. Cromwell having satisfied him as to the title, the Attorney General, his assistant, and Mr. Cromwell returned to the United States about October 1; finally, Mr. Knox handed, on October 25, his written opinion to the President, declaring that the company's titles were valid and that it had the power to transfer, and at the same time Mr. Knox delivered a copy to Mr. Cromwell.

On his return Mr. Cromwell again took up his headquarters in Washington. He encountered a complete radical change of attitude on the part of Minister Concha, who manifested distrust of Mr. Cromwell and abstained from calling upon Secretary Hay, or even communicating with him. This change of attitude was due in part to warnings Minister Concha had received from Bogota, and to the differences on the Isthmus between the United States Navy officers and those of the Colombian Government caused by the refusal of the American officers to permit the transportation of Colombian troops in arms over the railroad on the ground that action might lead to fighting with the insurgents and thus cause loss to the railroad and interfere with its traffic.

During the summer of 1902 Mr. Carlos Lievano, representing the revolutionary (Liberal) party of Colombia, conferred several times with Charles Burdett Hart, then American minister to Bogota, with the motive of obtaining American intervention to terminate the disastrous civil war then being waged in Colombia in a manner favorable to the Liberals, who had defeated Jose Manuel Marroquin nearly everywhere except in Panama, and were there on the point of apparent victory with an army of 7,000 against a Government force of less than 3,000. Mr. Lievano held out to the American minister the argument that humanity demanded that the struggle should be ended, Colombia already having lost 80,000 men, and that, furthermore, if the Liberal party, constituting a recognized majority of the people of Cololmbia, came into power it would be in a position to negotiate forthwith the desired canal treaty. Mr. Lievano was elated when Minister Hart finally told him that the proposed intervention could be arranged; that he had received his instructions from Washington and that at last the time had arrived when they (the American minister and the Liberal representative) might combine to find means of disrupting the Marroquin Government to which Mr. Hart was the accredited minister.

Three days later, Mr. Lievano declares, he returned to Mr. Hart and was told, in effect, "It's all off; there's no revolution." Upon asking the minister why, Mr. Lievano was told: "You know we have to build the canal." The Liberal representative protested and demanded to know the reason for this reversal of policy, and was told that Lorenz Marroquin, son of the aged President, and Aristides Fernandez had come to the American minister and sought intervention to end the war in behalf of the conservative forces, and in consideration for the promised intervention had pledged the Marroquin Government to enter into a satisfactory canal treaty with the United States. Lorenzo Marroquin declared under oath in October, 1909, that he and Fernandez did confer with the American minister to bring about the American intervention on the Isthmus, resulting in the signing of the treaty of peace of November 21, 1902, aboard the American battleship *Wisconsin.*

Gen. Lucas Caballero, who signed the treaty of the *Wisconsin* in behalf of the Liberals, declares that the American naval officers openly threatened future intervention by the American Government to assist the Panamanians to win their independence—or the outright annexation of Panama by the United States—if the conflict was not ended, and that this was one of the reasons why the Liberals agreed to the abandonment of a successful war.

The Liberal leaders recognized the serious intent of the Roosevelt administration because of the open advances previously made in Washington. The revolutionary headquarters had been for some time in New York, in charge of Gen. Vargas Santos and Dr. Modesto Garces, a Colombian lawyer, who was the emissary of the revolutionists in several conferences at the State Department, whither he had been sent to try to obtain American intervention for the Liberals. On July 31, or August 1, 1902, Dr. Garces returned from one of these missions to Washington and reported that the American Government evidently desired to bring about the independence of Panama, and that David Jayne Hill, then Acting Secretary of State, had suggested that intervention might be arranged with this in view. Dr. Garces thereupon wrote out in Spanish the rough draft of an interrogatory which he said Acting Secretary Hill had suggested should be sent to the State Department, signed by Gen. Vargas Santos, general in chief of the revolutionary forces, who was then in New York purchasing arms and securing financial assistance. In substance this proposed memorandum asked:

What would be the attitude of the United States in the event that the revolutionary forces should declare the independence of the Cauca and Panama?

This memorandum was submitted to Gen. Gargas Santos, who refused to sign it or to become in any way a party to a proposal to dismember his own country. The original memorandum of Dr. Garces is now in possession of Gen. Celso Rodriguez, of Bogota, one of the chief lieutenants of Gen. Vargas Santos. Dr. Garces is dead.

The American naval officers landed marines on the Isthmus and virtually disarmed the fighting forces by preventing transportation of troops on the line of the Panama Railroad. Thus "neutrality" was enforced in order to maintain free and uninterrupted transit on the railroad, notwithstanding it was notorious that the Panama Railroad had been aiding the revolutionists by moving their munitions and refusing transportation to the established government. Freight tags of the railroad taken from revolutionary ordnance transported in contravention of this " neutrality " were exhibits in a suit which the late Gov. Alban, of Panama, was preparing before his death to institute against the Panama Railroad.

Thus the Roosevelt Administration displayed—

our purpose to deal not merely in a spirit of justice but in a spirit of generosity with the people through whose land we might build it [the canal].

Thus early was foreshadowed the design, which Mr. Roosevelt frankly admitted in his message to Congress January 4, 1904—

to announce * * * that if such terms were not agreed to we would enter into an arrangement with Panama direct or take what other steps were needful in order to begin the enterprise.

Whatever exchanges there were on this subject were not published by the Colombian Government when Gen. Reyes, during his administration as President, printed in a Bluebook what purports to be the complete diplomatic correspondence concerning the canal negotiations.

August 9, 1902, President Marroquin cabled Minister Concha:

In order to render the amendments to memorandum presentable to our Congress, demand ten millions cash and annuity of six hundred thousand after fourteen years.

August 13, 1902, the Colombian foreign minister wrote to Concha that, as the drawbacks to the use of the cable were clearly insuperable, the Colombian Government had decided that the negotiations with the United States should not be broken off, but that everything must be submitted to the decision of the Congress. Minister Concha was notified that in a recent conference in the foreign office the Bogota agent of the Panama Canal Co. had been told that Colombia would demand of the company the full par value of the 50,000 shares of canal stock which the Government owned as one of the conditions of consent to the transfer.

August 14, 1902, the Colombian foreign minister cabled Concha:

Special messenger on the 13th instant carries registered instructions Panama Canal.

No trace of these instructions appear in the Libro Azul issued by Reyes.

The hand of Mr. Cromwell appears in the Colombian " Blue Book " in a letter to Minister Concha from Enrique Cortes, who later became Mr. Cromwell's ally when Colombian minister to Washington several years later. Writing from Cazenovia, N. Y., August 27, 1902, Cortes informs the minister that he assisted Concha's predecessor, Dr. Silva—

in the preparation of the bases of the treaty, in which also took part Dr. Facundo Mutis-Duran, as representative of Panama and Mr. Cromwell.

Cortes refers to the American Nation as—

knowing what it wants, and able—should occasion arise—to obtain by the force of its strong right arm what it desires.

In this letter Cortes used the identical expression employed by Mr. Cromwell a year later when the Panama Canal lobbyist assures

Gen. Pedro Velez, of Colombia, that the United States could never be guilty of designing the dismemberment of Colombia, because the United States is "A gentleman among the nations." This phrase, as well as the general line of argument pursued by Cortes, points strongly to Cromwell as the real author of this letter. Cortes recites the dealings of the United States with Spain, Cuba, China, and the Philippines, and continues:

If Colombia tries to be extortionate we shall expose ourselves to loosening the wrath of the Colossus, and then, alas for us! This wrath of the Colossus, which, once its patience is exhaus.ed, ended in a few short months the power of Spain in America, could sweep away in the twinkling of an eye our sovereignty in the Isthmus. The imminence of this danger, and the impossibility of Colombia's maintaining her integrity, have been made more than apparent, apparent, palpable by the events of the civil war on the Isthmus.

Cortes goes on to say that the negotiations now proceeding will—

crystallize the final say in the American Government, and that Colombia will act wisely in giving its simple and full approval.

In reference to the suggestion in Colombia of forfeiting the canal company's concession in 1904, Mr. Cortes says that, besides delaying the negotiations two years, it might provoke in the United States—

an ou burst of indignation that would culminate in the annexation of the Isthmus of Panama to the American Union.

This, Cortes points out, would be a simple and profitable negotiation for the United States which would then give the French company its $40,000,000, and retain unaltered the friendship of its traditional ally, France; of the amount it would have to pay to Colombia and become the absolute owner of the Isthmus as well as of the canal, Mr. Cortes ends:

Our line of conduct can not be other than to approve without delay—and blindfolded—whatever the American Government has arranged with the Colombian legation. Danger is in delay.

August 25, 1902, the Colombian Government cabled Minister Concha:

Tell the American Government that the Colombian Government accepts in principle the last amendments presented. Await instructions which left beginning of August. Ratification by Congress is necessary. In order to convoke it there only lacks the pacification of Panama.

The pacification of Panama by the "strong hand" that Senator Morgan suggested in June, 1902, was very shortly to be begun. News of the surrender of the Government forces to the revolutionists at Aguadulce, Panama, after a month's siege, reached the United States on September 8, 1902, and was confirmed a few days later. September 12, 1902, the Secretary of the Navy cabled to the commander of the *Ranger*, at Panama, not to permit transportation of troops that would convert the Panama Railroad into a theater of hostilities; September 14, 1902, the *Panther* sailed with 320 United States marines and four rapid-fire guns from League Island Navy Yard; September 18, 1902, the *Cincinnati*, which arrived at Colon on the 16th, landed marines and put them aboard the Panama Railroad trains.

Minister Concha did not work in with the pacification plans of his Government, which, having made a secret deal to save its own life, viewed with complacence the intervention on the Isthmus. In a cable to Concha, on September 20, 1902, the Colombian Government notified him of the sending of an army to the Isthmus, and added:

Now is the time to demand from the Government of the United States of America the execution of the treaty of 1846 to assure the transit from Panama to Colon.

September 22, 1902, Concha was informed by cable by his Government:

We are ignorant of the nature of the intervention of the United States of America. All that we demand is execution of Article 35 of the treaty of 1846, as has already been done in analogous circumstances.

And on the same day Concha cabled to Bogota:

I to-day presented to the Secretary of State a memorandum reestablishing truth of events in Panama, without making any comments, reserving the right of my Government to make such declarations as it judges fit.

September 24, 1902, the governor of Panama cabled to President Marroquin:

Americans have disembarked troops in the city of Panama. Concha tells me that he will protest against appeal to force. Should occasion arise prevent him.

September 25, 1902, the Marroquin Government cabled to Concha:

Abstain from treating of the matter of the American intervention in Panama. Minister of foreign affairs will do so here.

Minister Concha protested vehemently to his Government. On October 3, 1902, he cabled to his Government that the governor of Panama had asked him to protest against the order of the American Admiral prohibiting transportation of war munitions or troops on the Panama Railroad—a service which the railroad was bound by its concession to perform. Concha said he replied that he had been forbidden to intervene, and added:

For the fourth time I resign from this legation. Order secretary to take charge.

Concha's Government replied, October 7, 1902:

Your resignation unpatriotic and inadmissible.

On the day Concha cabled his fourth resignation he wrote to his Government in part:

The recent events culminating in the armed intervention of the United States modify from the ground up the negotiations now in progress. The commander of the American forces has assumed de facto the supreme authority in that part of the Isthmus not occupied by the rebels; our Colombian troops are disarmed by those of the United States, their officers travel in the custody of the Americans, even the governor himself is escorted like a viceroy; the American commander notifies the Government employees and the rebels alike of what he will or will not permit in the region he occupies; and lastly, the minister of the Republic in Washington, when he announces that he has asked for details necessary to formulate such protest as international law and the most elementary national dignity demand, has silence peremptorily imposed upon him by the Chief Executive of Colombia and her minister of foreign affairs. Between a power which thus imposes its strength, and a government which does not know how to, or does not care to defend its national sovereignty, treaties can not be consummated; the law of diplomacy gives way to that of conquest, and all discussion ceases between two nations on a footing of equality, and there remains but one to dictate its laws, which the other must accept and obey. In the presence of this new position, for this and other reasons, the undersigned considers his labors in defense of the rights of the Republic at an end.

On October 9, 1902, the Colombian Government cabled Minister Concha:

Do not demand passports. Matter Admiral is being dealt with direct with Hart.

Hart was then American minister in Bogota. Concha wrote to his Government on October 23, 1902, that his convictions would not permit him to sign the pending treaty with the American Government because it was then violating in Panama the treaty of 1846. He recited the grievances expressed in his letter of October 3, 1902, and again insisted that his resignation be accepted.

And then, on October 25, 1902, Concha cabled to his Government:

It is impossible to advance the negotiations of the Panama Canal while there still exists the order prohibiting my discussion of the interpretation of the treaty of 1846–1848, an essential part of the future treaty. * * * I think that prolongation of occupation of the Isthmus by the forces of the United States is unjustifiable, as all danger has disappeared. Silence of the Government of Colombia will cause loss of the Republic.

Minister Concha in a note to the Government, dated October 30, 1902, says in part that the interpretation given to the treaty of 1846, by the acts which American forces are to-day committing in Panama is new, appears to be indisputable.

When, for the first time, the United States used the right of transit via the Isthmus, which is guaranteed them by the existing treaty, it was with the simple object of sending troops to Oregon and California; that was effected by disembarking them and sending them across the Isthmus without having given any previous notice to the authorities; for that our secretary of foreign affairs presented a protest in Washington through the legation, and in a conference in September, of 1858, between the Granadian minister, Gen. Herran, and the Secretary of State, Gen. Casey, it was agreed that in future, whenever it was necessary to send American forces through the territory of the Isthmus, they would come unarmed and as groups of private individuals "without enjoying the exemptions which are customary when troops pass through foreign territory, but, on the contrary, being subject to the territorial jurisdiction exactly like all other strangers." This agreement was punctually fulfilled during the American war of secession on the occasion when forces of the Government of the United States were sent to the Pacific. To-day, so advanced is the interpretation, that American forces are disembarked in Panama to disarm those of the sovereign of the territory. Whatever more extensive comment might be made on this point would be redundant.

In Foreign Relations of the United States, 1885, pages 239 to 251, there is found the correspondence exchanged between the Legation of Colombia in Washington and the Department of State. Therein will be seen clearly that when in that year the United States sent forces to Panama, in spite of the fact that the established government there had practically disappeared, that the railroad line was without defense, and that when contending bands had reached the extreme of imprisoning the American consul, the United States never pretended to execute acts of authority or jurisdiction; on the contrary, when Capt. Kane, commander of the cruiser *Galena*, arrested two of the incendiaries in Colon and stated in a telegram, which he made public, that he would not deliver them to the authorities in Panama, because they would be allowed to escape, a slight protest on the part of the minister of Colombia, Mr. Cecerra, was sufficient to cause the Secretary of State, Mr. Bayard, in a note of April 6, of the same year, to give satisfactory explanations of the case and decide that the prisoners should be delivered to the authorities of the country.

To-day no one, with the slightest particle of reason, could compare the solitary act of Capt. Kane in a condition of total anarchy—which it was difficult not only for a foreigner, but for the people of the country themselves, to locate the legitimate authorities—with the repeated acts, first, of Capt. McLean, and afterwards of Admiral Casey, in very different circumstances, when the transit has not been interrupted, when the Colombian authorities have means and forces sufficient to fulfill their duties, and when the American officers not only have ignored the prerogatives of the Colombians, but have humiliated them, dictating orders, by their acts preventing fulfillment of Colombia's obligations, and authorizing the railroad to violate a perfect civil contract by which it is bound to transport troops, employees, and munitions of the Government. And this is not all. The American Government has detained the troops of the Colombian Government in their march; it has prevented the opportune arrival at their destination of an abundance of elements of war which arrived from abroad at Colon for the campaign of the Pacific; it has attacked and interfered with the disembarkation of Colombian troops from the cruiser *Cartagena* in the Atlantic, and has exercised the right of visit on board the Colombian war vessel in the Bay of Panama; with all of which the marines of the United States in the name of their Government have outraged and ignored the same sovereignty which by a solemn public treaty not only should they respect themselves, but should compel all others to respect.

The acts briefly enumerated have commanded the public and solemn joint approbation of the State and Navy Departments of the American Government, which assert that these acts are the legitimate development of article 35 of the treaty of 1846.

Suppressing, therefore, all other considerations for the object of this note, it is clear that, if the practical interpretation of the treaty is that series of acts, the interpretation is new, and was not known by the minister of Colombia when he prepared the memorandum of the 21st of April (1902) for the canal negotiations, nor was it known either by the minister of foreign affairs when he dictated definite instructions on the 9th of September last.

The memorandum of April above referred to, basis of the canal negotiations, from its very title demonstrates the intimate connection that exists between it and the treaty of 1846, because it expresses that this is the development of the latter, and in Article III it is stated that: "All dispositions of article 35 of the treaty of 1846–1848 celebrated between the contracting parties will continue in force and will be applied in all their force to the cities of Panama and Colon and the accessory islands situated within the said zone, and the territory comprised within them will be neutral and the Government of the United States will continue to guarantee that neutrality and the sovereignty of Colombia, in accordance with article 35."

October 29, 1902, Concha cabled his Government the substance of the foregoing letter to Secretary Hay, and added:

The State Department replied to-day that there was no new interpretation, and that the United States would adopt the Nicaragua route if the treaty was not signed before the American Congress meets in December.

On the following day, October 30, Secretary Hay cabled Minister Concha's refusal to do anything to the Bogota Government and informed it that the President was about to open negotiations with Nicaragua if Minister Concha did not act promptly. At the same time he wrote to Minister Concha that the President would take action under the Spooner Act if the Government of Colombia did not give a prompt reply. At the same time also Secretary Hay told Mr. Cromwell that he had been informed by the Nicaraguan minister that the latter was ready to consider any treaty satisfactory to the United States.

As a result of Secretary Hay's telegraphic notifications, Minister Concha received instructions to act, and accordingly he sought an audience with Secretary Hay on November 4, 1902, and, pursuant to his instructions, demanded that Article XXIII, as he had drafted it in April, and as Secretary Hay had accepted it, should be reinstated instead of the modified Article XXIII which Secretary Hay had proposed in July. Concha contended that his original draft was the correct interpretation of American rights to intervene on the Isthmus under the treaty of 1846.

Minister Concha was not in sympathy with the attitude adopted by the Colombian administration, and told Mr. Cromwell that he considered that the instructions he had received to continue negotiations were unpatriotic and contrary to the real interests of Colombia; that he intended to resign rather than to continue the negotiation of a treaty on the basis demanded by the United States.

Mr. Cromwell begged the minister, personally and by letter, not to act thus, but to negotiate. Minister Concha finally yielded and promised to take up the treaty, but on the condition that the negotiations should be limited at first to the question of sovereignty.

In consequence, on November 5, Concha submitted the question of sovereignty to Mr. Hay. The latter sent for Mr. Cromwell and detailed conferences followed. Finally, according to Mr. Cromwell, the President authorized Mr. Hay to yield.

So on November 18, 1902, Secretary Hay wrote to Minister Concha this:

The President has considered with much attention whether he may admit the amendment that you consider so important for your country—substitution of the first Article XXIII for the last Article XXIII. Desirous of manifesting in unquestionable manner the good will of this nation toward Colombia, the President authorized me to say that if all the other stipulations are accepted to the satisfaction of the United States, he will consent to the substitution of Article XXIII as it appears in the first instrument for the same article in the draft of July 18, 1902, but that not otherwise will he give his acquiescence.

And yet Mr. Roosevelt said in his message to Congress, January 4, 1904:

It has been stated in public prints that Colombia objected to these stipulations on the ground that they involved a relinquishment of her "sovereignty"; but in the light of what has taken place, this alleged objection must be considered as an afterthought.

An "afterthought," gentlemen, of a year before!

Thereupon Minister Concha wrote and presented, first to Mr. Cromwell and later to Secretary Hay (Nov. 11), seven amendments to the proposed treaty, amendments of a fundamental nature, above all that of Article I, as follows:

This same article shall state clearly that the authority given by Colombia to the canal and railroad companies to transfer their rights to the United States shall be governed by the special agreement previously to be made between Colombia and the said companies, for which agreement they have been notified to appoint an agent (mandataire) in Bogota.

Colombia thus made clear that she was acting in good faith in her negotiations with the United States, but that her consent to the transfer was subject to the condition of a previous agreement with the canal company.

Immediately Mr. Cromwell set about to defeat this amendment. He went to see Secretary Hay and also President Roosevelt, and persuaded them to reject this amendment absolutely. This was done by Secretary Hay in his official reply to Minister Concha.

Then at the request of Secretary Hay, Mr. Cromwell prepared a revision of the proposed treaty, which revision Secretary Hay transmitted to Minister Concha on November 18, 1902.

Mr. KENDALL. That is what Mr. Cromwell says in his report to these employers of his?

Mr. HALL. Yes, sir.

Mr. KENDALL. He was trying to get that $800,000 fee.

Mr. HALL. We must presume he was telling the truth.

Mr. KENDALL. His purpose was to convince them how difficult it had been for him to accomplish the results he did.

Mr. HALL. I suppose so, sir.

As I was saying, Mr. Cromwell asserts that at the request of Secretary Hay he, Cromwell, prepared a revision of the proposed treaty, which revision Secretary Hay transmitted to Minister Concha on November 18, 1902. On the theory that Colombia would ultimately yield, the revision admitted none of the demands Minister Concha had made in his proposed seven amendments, except his original draft of Article XXIII.

What Mr. Roosevelt was willing to concede is best seen by a comparison of the two drafts.

[Hay's draft of July 18, 1902.]

ARTICLE XXIII.

If it shall become necessary at any time, in order to enforce the guaranty of neutrality and of freedom from blockade and from the exercise of rights or acts of war within said zone, or within three marine miles of either end thereof, assumed by the United States in the treaty entered into by it with Great Britain on November 18, 1901, or in order efficiently to discharge the performance of the obligations to Colomb'a embodies herein, or in order promptly and efficiently to insure the safety and protection of the canal and dependencies, or of the ships, cargoes, and persons using the same, or of the railways and other works on the said zone or appertaining thereto, the United States shall have the right to employ such of its armed forces to that end as may be necessary according to the circumstances of the case, withdrawing, however, said forces, in whole or in part, so soon as the necessity for their presence has ceased. Said Government shall give immediate advices to Colombia of the measures adopted for the purposes stated.

[Concha's draft of April 18, 1902, which Roosevelt ordered accepted.]

ARTICLE XXIII.

If it should become necessary at any time to employ armed forces for the safety or protection of the canal, or of the ships that make use of the same, or the railways and other works, the Republic of Colombia agrees to provide the forces necessary for such purpose, according to the circumstances of the case, but if the Government of Colombia can not effectively comply with this obligation, then, with the consent of or at the request of Colombia, or of her minister at Washington, or of the local authorities, civil or military, the United States shall employ such force as may be necessary for that sole purpose; and as soon as the necessity shall have ceased will withdraw the forces so employed. Under exceptional circumstances, however, on account of unforeseen or imminent danger to said canal, railways, and other works, or to the lives and property of the persons employed upon the canal, railways, and other works, the Government of the United States is authorized to act in the interest of their protection, without the necessity of obtaining the consent beforehand of the Government of Colombia; and it shall give immediate advice of the measures adopted for the purpose stated; and as soon as sufficient Colombian forces shall arrive to attend to the indicated purpose, those of the United States shall retire.

Transmitting a memorandum of his conference with Secretary Hay, Minister Concha reported to his Government by letter of November 4, 1902, that Secretary Hay voluntarily brought up the subject of interpretation of the treaty of 1846, and said that he could not give any reply as to what recognition should be given to such interpretation in the canal treaty without conferring with President Roosevelt.

Discussing Article XXIII in a letter to Secretary Hay, November 11, 1902, Minister Concha said, in part:

In article 23, which your excellency expressly accepted with the rest of the memorandum in the note which you sent to the legation on the 21st of last April, it appears that, even if Colombia concedes to the United States a certain extension of authority in the Isthmus, should the canal treaty be perfected, by so doing it does not renounce, nor could it renounce, inherent faculties of exercising sovereignty of the Republic * * * without abdicating the elemental right of transporting her officials, her troops, her elements of war, etc., within her own boundaries without any limitation whatever, as is set forth in article 17 of the same memorandum; nor could Colombia agree to have her authorities at any time deprived of the exercise of their legal functions.

The fact that your excellency accepted in the mentioned official note of April 21, the articles of which we are treating, shows well that the explanation there given to the Government of the United States is the correct understanding of the treaty of 1846, and understanding which my Government deems it necessary to have put in statute form in a solemn manner, maintaining and ratifying it for the future. The article proposed by your excellency, instead of the one above mentioned, might give rise to Colombia's being incapacitated, on some occasion, from exercising her power of maintaining order in her territory, or might give rise to contradictions or discussions which could be usefully avoided.

On November 6, 1902, Concha cabled his Government that the State Department had not yet answered to his demands made on the 4th, and added:

Whatever it (Hay's answer) may be, I will not sign any treaty during the American occupation of the Isthmus.

Concha again tendered his resignation by letter on November 7, 1902, when he reiterated that under no circumstances would he sign a treaty with the United States so long as its troops—

against every principle of right and justice, and in violation of a public word of honor, continue to trample under foot Colombian territory and to exercise thereon a usurped jurisdiction.

President Marroquin cabled to Concha November 14, 1902:

Congress meets 1st of March. Ask all possible advantages in respect to Article XXIII. In any case sign the treaty to save our responsibility. The Congress of Colombia must decide definitely.

On November 15, 1902, Minister Concha wrote to his Government expressing his pleasure with the situation in which he had placed Secretary Hay. In part his letter follows:

Although Mr. Hay is very clever, the dilemma that faces him can not but cause him some little mortification; he must either accept Article XXIII of the memorandum of April as a correct interpretation of the treaty of 1846—and then he implicitly recognizes that the occurrences in Panama are violations of this treaty—or he must assert that Article XXIII is not the correct interpretation of the treaty, thereby throwing to the ground his note of April, in which he accepted the memorandum. Of course this would be but a wisp of hay for one having jaws as powerful as this uncle of ours, and he can settle it all with a single crunch. * * * The desire to make themselves appear as the Nation most respectful of the rights of others forces these gentlemen to toy a little with their prey before devouring it, although, when all is said and done, they will do so in one way or the other. The outbursts of the press, of which you will learn when you receive this, and the more or less hidden threats which appear every day in the papers, emanating from Mr. Hay himself or from Cromwell, who is a rat and is very active in fomenting this and other fusses, have not given them the result they hoped for. * * *

So firmly convinced was Dr. Concha of the uselessness of continuing negotiations while American forces occupied the Isthmus that he said in this letter of November 15, 1902:

I must repeat to you that I believe my presence here is not only useless, it is improper.

The CHAIRMAN. The committee will now suspend and take a recess until 10 o'clock to-morrow morning, and you can then resume, Mr. Hall.

Mr. HALL. Thank you, sir. I shall be able to get into the story of the revolution to-morrow.

Thereupon, at 4.30 o'clock, the committee adjourned to meet to-morrow morning at 10 o'clock.

EXHIBIT A.

MR. CROMWELL'S BRIEF.

ARBITRATION BETWEEN MESSRS. SULLIVAN & CROMWELL AND LA COMPAGNIE NOUVELLE DU CANAL DE PANAMA.

(TRANSLATION.)

TRANSLATED BY HENRY N. HALL. MARCH, 1911.

BEFORE

MAITRE BARBOUX, MAITRE DEVIN, MAITRE RIBOT,

Arbitrators.

CONTENTS TO APPENDIX A.

[Pages I and II of the Table of Contents, in the original French, are missing. The following is compiled from the brief, being a literal translation of heads and subheads up to the point indicated.—H. N. H.]

AGREEMENT

Between the undersigned:

La Compagnie Nouvelle du Canal de Panama, having its headquarters in Paris, No. 7 Rue Louis le Grand, represented by Monsieur Monvoisin, vice president of its board of liquidators, of the one part, and

Messrs. Sullivan & Cromwell, of 49 Wall Street, New York, represented by William Nelson Cromwell, of the other part,

It has been set forth and agreed as follows:

Article I.

Messrs. Sullivan & Cromwell have been retained to defend and represent the interests of La Compagnie Nouvelle du Canal de Panama and have rendered it services of various kinds and have made important disbursements.

In order to arrive at a settlement the parties have agreed to appoint a board of arbitration, composed of three arbitrators, and by these presents they appoint Maitres Henri Barboux, Georges Devin, and Alexandre Ribot.

Article II.

The arbitrators shall fix the amount due to Messrs. Sullivan & Cromwell as compensation for the services rendered and the disbursements made by them; the arbitrators, dispensed from the ordinary forms of procedure, may have recourse to such means of information as appear necessary to them.

Article III.

They will sit as friendly arbitrators of last resort, without appeal or legal recourse. They will also fix the costs of the arbitration.

Article IV.

The arbitrators must render their decision within six months from this date. They are hereby relieved from the necessity of placing their decision on file.

Article V.

In the event that in the course of the arbitration one of the arbitrators shall die or resign on account of ill health, the parties shall chose another arbitrator within fifteen days of the death or resignation, after which delay, in default of an agreement, either one of the parties may petition the president of the Tribunal Civil de la Seine to make provision for the replacement of the missing arbitrator.

Signed in duplicate by the parties the twenty-first day of February, one thousand nine hundred and seven.

Read and approved.

For Sullivan & Cromwell,
William Nelson Cromwell.

Read and approved.
F. Monvoisin.

GENERAL STATEMENT OF THE SERVICES RENDERED BY MESSRS. SULLIVAN & CROMWELL AS GENERAL COUNSEL IN AMERICA OF LA COMPAGNIE NOUVELLE DU CANAL DE PANAMA DURING THE EIGHT YEARS, 1896–1904, IN REPRESENTATION, DEFENSE, PROTECTION, AND ADVANCEMENT OF THE INTERESTS OF THE SAID COMPANY.

GENTLEMEN: Accept the sincere expression of our gratitude for your having been willing to undertake the task of determining the compensation justly and reasonably due to us by La Compagnie Nouvelle du Canal de Panama for the services we have rendered in representing, defending, protecting, and furthering its interests, a mission with which we were intrusted by the company in 1896 and which we brought to a successful conclusion in 1904.

We can not better show our appreciation of your action in acceding to the request made to you by the company and by ourselves with a view of obtaining your cooperation as a board of arbitrators than in making every effort to condense within as narrow limits as possible the enormous mass of material bearing upon this subject and in limiting our recital to the chapters of greatest and most decisive importance; and we rely upon your great experience and intelligent appreciation to form for yourselves some idea of the details and multiplicity of incidents which of necessity had place in the accomplishment of the results we successively obtained.

THE PANAMA CANAL AND THE FORMATION OF LA COMPAGNIE NOUVELLE DU CANAL DE PANAMA IN OCTOBER, 1904.

In 1878 Colombia granted the Wyse concession, which was the basis of the formation of La Compagnie Universelle du Canal Interocéanique de Panama. The company became bankrupt, and a receiver was appointed in 1888–89. There is no need for us to analyze the causes of this catastrophe, but it is necessary to say that the conditions in which this collapse took place were the subject of comment, criticism, and prejudice throughout the world, and led to the general belief that the plan of the Panama Canal was not feasible as an engineering feat and that the cost of its construction would have no reasonable limits. Toward the end of the year 1904 there was formed from the colossal ruin a new company, with an entirely new board of directors and a capital of 65,000,000 francs, La Compagnie Nouvelle du Canal de Panama. The board of directors presided over by M. Bonnardel, had had no dealings with the old company. This board took up its task animated by the highest and most patriotic spirit, but it was manifest that the limited capital of the new company did not furnish the basis for a serious advancement of the work, and that its first aim must be the reexamination of all the technical questions. This was recognized by the first important act of the Bonnardel board, which was the creation of a committee of engineers, later known as the international committee or technical committee, composed of distinguished French, Russian, Italian, English, German, Colombian, and American engineers; but this committee had not yet formulated its final conclusions when, in January, 1896, we were intrusted with the interests of the company. At this time the new company had neither organization nor counsel in the United States in respect to the canal question.

Such, in brief, was the situation of La Compagnie Nouvelle du Canal de Panama when we accepted the task which forms the subject submitted for your consideration.

JANUARY, 1896—CIRCUMSTANCES WHICH LED TO OUR EMPLOYMENT.

While the Compagnie Nouvelle, with praiseworthy determination, was studying anew the technical, practical, and financial problems which were involved, the turn which matters in the United States were taking threatened to render all its plans futile and to reduce to nought the hopes of hundreds of thousands of Frenchmen interested in its efforts and toward whom it had assumed a responsibility of unparalled gravity, difficulty, and importance. This menace was the pronounced tendency of the people of the United States to realize their long-cherished plan, to support the building of a canal in Nicaragua under American control. The plan for a canal in Nicaragua had been studied and reported upon under the auspices of the Government of the United States, and measures were pending before the Congress of that country for the adoption of laws decreeing the selection of this route as a national undertaking (instrumentalité nationale). It was manifest that if the United States adopted the Nicaragua route the Panama Canal, whatever its advantages and its superiority from an engineering point of view, could never be completed, as no company would ever be able to raise the capital necessary to build a canal in competition with a Government whose resources are, so to speak, unlimited and which would exploit it not as a source of profit, but to further its national interests.

The board of directors addressed itself to Mr. William Nelson Cromwell and later to his law firm, Messrs. Sullivan & Cromwell, and officially intrusted them, him and his law firm, with the representation and defense of the company's interests, appointing them general counsel of the company in the United States. This was in January, 1896.

FUNCTIONS, DUTIES, AND SERVICES OF GENERAL COUNSEL IN THE UNITED STATES.

Before describing the labors which occupied us it is well to indicate the great differences between the functions and relations of counsel in America, on the one hand, and in France, as in Europe generally, on the other. In Europe this relation is limited to particular subjects which are presented, and does not entail the management or direction of the business in respect to which counsel is consulted. According to custom, the responsibility, as well as the management, rests with the clients. In the United States, however, the powers and duties of counsel in important matters are entirely different and more varied. Besides consultations on points of law and appearances before the courts, counsel often takes charge of the entire business and its actual management, both as to its policies and as to its direction and execution.

In this country there exists no distinction between lawyers as in France and in England between "avocats" and "avoués" between barristers and solicitors. Lawyers admitted to practice before the highest courts in the United States are free to accept all the business which their capacity and ability permit them to undertake. The functions, duties, and privileges of barristers, solicitors, and notaries can all be assumed in America by a single person. In short, a lawyer in America performs all manner of professional work in the practice of his profession. It has also become the custom in the large cities of the United States to form organizations or firms of lawyers comprising numerous partners and their clerks, assistants, and accountants, etc. These firms are so organized that business of any kind whatever can be managed and successfully performed. In these law firms one finds various departments for the management of various kinds of business, such as real estate transactions, the organization and management of corporations, the preparation, prosecution, and pleadings of lawsuits, and the carrying of appeals to the highest courts; the direction and conduct of commercial negotiations; the supervision and organization of mergers of undertakings and enterprises; the management of estates and collection of revenues; mortgage loans; the investment of funds in other securities, and the general administration of estates in trust. To sum up, all the varieties of professional work which in other countries are performed by different classes of legal advisers—notaries or men of affairs—are frequently performed by a single law firm, the various departments of which carry out the entire business. Law firms are often composed of several partners, of numerous attorneys who act as assistants, with the addition of clerks, stenographers, typewriters, agents, cashiers, and accountants. A well-equipped and carefully organized law firm thus constitutes a powerful business force. Although this system is not recognized in France or in England, it is not only permitted but greatly encouraged in our country.

As far as the business of the great corporations is concerned in the United States, the general counsel is, as a rule, the guiding spirit and has almost control. In the exercise of their functions and the accomplishment of the duties which are incumbent upon them, those who hold such positions are obliged to create great law firms through which the work, whether its nature be legal, judicial, legislative, political, financial, or general, is performed. Albeit the nature of the present proceeding would seem to absolve us from our habitual professional reticence concerning the organization and working force of our law firm, we will not dilate upon its standing and its power; but we do not think that anyone will contradict the statement that the law firm of Sullivan & Cromwell occupies a recognized position among the great legal corporations of the Nation, that in the 30 years of its active existence matters of the most far-reaching importance have been conducted under its direction and confined to its exclusive care, and that, in the organization of its offices in which work some 40 persons learned in all branches of their profession, practicing before every court in their country, and possessing extensive connections in all walks of private and public life, our firm constituted a force, an organization, and an instrumentality specially adapted to the needs of the canal company. 'It is also well to state in this connection that in the course of a very active and very extended professional career, covering a period of more than 30 years, the firm of Sullivan & Cromwell had found itself placed in intimate relations, susceptible of being used to advantage, with men possessing influence and power in all the circles and almost everywhere in the United States; that not only have the members of this firm established close and intimate professional relations with their most distinguished colleagues throughout the United States, but they have also come to know, and be in a position to influence, a considerable number of public men in political life, in financial circles, and on the press, and all these influences and relations were of great and sometimes decisive utility, and of valuable assistance in the performance of their professional duties in the Panama matter.' This fact was formally acknowledged (reconnu) by the company in its letter confirming the renewal of our professional engagement in January, 1902. It would be impossible to detail and enumerate—nor even perhaps would it be proper so to do—the innumerable ways in which this influence and this power were utilized in this matter; but what can be easily understood and appreciated is that such relations and connections, the outcome of many years of successful professional activity, were of great value, and that our clients, in this matter in particular, received the benefit of this influence and power. It is not suggested that the remuneration should be based upon this consideration alone, but it was in part such considerations which added weight and power to our professional activities, which contributed materially to the result obtained, and which enabled us in the critical crises of this great affair to ward off what on several occasions looked like the final death blow to the Panama enterprise, and to drag out of a desperate case a decisive victory.

THE CANAL SITUATION AT THE TIME OF OUR EMPLOYMENT.

As soon as the matter was intrusted to us, we first of all engaged in a critical study of the conditions which confronted us. We made frequent trips to Washington during this year, we examined the archives and records of Congress, we had interviews with eminent persons, and we ascertained that the situation which the company faced was, briefly, as follows:

1. *The Nicaragua route.*

The Nicaragua route had always had an attraction for the people of the United States. It had been the object of numerous concessions and conventions, of many surveys and investigations by Americans, beginning in 1826. In 1850–1852 a survey had been made and a definite plan of construction proposed by Col. O. W. Childs, for the American Atlantic & Pacific Canal Co., which then enjoyed a concession for this route. This plan was submitted to the then President of the United States and was approved by the commission of Army engineers to which he had referred it. In 1873 another survey was made by an expedition sent out by the Government of the United States under Frigate Capt. Lull, of the United States Navy. In 1884 the Frelinghuysen-Zavala treaty was negotiated; by this treaty the United States obained from Nicaragua the right to build this canal, and a fresh survey was made by A. G. Menocal, a civil engineer in the naval service. This treaty, however, was not ratified, having been withdrawn from the consideration of the Senate by President Cleveland in 1885. Thus the attention of the United States had been fixed upon Nicaragua ever since 1827. Lull, although he included Panama in his investigation of 1873, did not recommend this route in his report, and neither the United States nor any of its citizens had ever looked upon the building of a canal at Panama as feasible (representing a possibility). Even the work at Panama under De Lesseps had not prevented the negotiation of the Frelinghuysen-Zavala treaty for a Nicaragua canal, and when the work at Panama ceased in 1889, and the company became bankrupt it seemed demonstrated to the entire public that the plan for a canal at Panama was chimerical, its realization impossible, and that the Nicaragua route was the only route possible.

2. *The Nicaragua company and its concessions.*

Already, in 1887, Mr. Menocal had obtained from Nicaragua a concession in favor of the Nicaragua Canal syndicate, and in 1888 he had obtained a similar concession from Costa Rica. An act of Congress was passed (approved Feb. 20, 1889) whereby a charter was granted to the Maritime Canal Co. for the construction of the Nicaragua Canal under these concessions, and the company was accordingly formed.

Charters are very rarely granted by the United States Congress. Except in the case of national banks and of two transcontinental railroads, in the construction and direction of which the Government took part, and except for a few undertakings of Federal interest, such a thing has never been done. The very power of the Federal Government to grant charters had long been a matter of doubt.

The charter granted to the Maritime Canal Co. for the construction of the Nicaragua Canal placed it immediately in an unique and powerful position, gave to it a dignity and importance it could have acquired in no other way, and was considered as an acceptation of the Nicaragua Canal as the canal of the American people; and this canal was popularly known as (received the popular name of) the "American Canal."

The founders and shareholders of the company were persons of high standing in this country, and men as well as groups of great political influence in the United States interested themselves in it, pecuniarly and otherwise. Wide publicity was given to all these developments, and all the interests in favor of a canal were rallied to its support. These interests were numerous and powerful. The entire Pacific coast, for instance, most earnestly desired its construction for the competition it would be able to offer to the transcontinental railroads; and all the manufacturing and commercial interests of the country became its energetic defenders. An ex-Senator of the United States was president of the company, and as an ex-Senator he enjoyed the privilege of access to the floor of the Senate, of which he constantly availed himself to further the interests of the company among the Senators.

3. *The work in Nicaragua.*

The Maritime Co. began its work with vigor. It built works with a view to deepening the entrance to Greytown, its Atlantic terminus; it erected a number of warehouses, barracks, and other buildings, it laid several miles of railroad, it bought two dredgers, which had previously been used in the construction of the Panama Canal, and with these boats it began the actual excavation of its canal in the lowlands back of Greytown. Great publicity was given to all this work and the transfer of the dredgers from Colon in particular was looked upon as furnishing proof of the total and final abandonment of the attempt to build the impossible Panama Canal. Public interest was worked up to a high pitch and it was everywhere believed that a work so promptly begun would be as energetically pushed, and that American energy in possession of the only practical route for a canal (as was believed) would succeed where the French, having attempted the execution of a plan now believed impossible, had failed. National pride played a part (s'y mela) and the whole country came to support the Nicaragua Canal. Excursions, organized at the expense of the company, brought public men and newspaper men to Nicaragua and strengthened their belief in the value of the project.

4. *The situation in Panama.*

During this time the work at Panama had been almost completely stopped. The efforts of the liquidators were necessarily reduced to the preservation of the property in their hands, to the extension of concessions and to attempts to find some basis on which a reconstruction could be effected and the undertaking saved from total ruin. Meanwhile, the scandals in which the old company had been involved had been exploited throughout the world, prosecutions had been begun and their details spread everywhere, and the very name of Panama had been made odious in all lands—nowhere more so than in France itself. In the United States the entire Panama undertaking was unjustly looked upon as having been a gigantic steal and all persons who had even the most insignificant and most innocent dealings with the enterprise found themselves the object of suspicion and were even shunned. This feeling was so pronounced that public men avoided the open discussion of this subject.

5. *Public opinion on the subject of the Panama Canal.*

No one, so to speak, in the United States doubted that the Panama Canal in itself was an impossibility—a failure—and all that one heard on the subject in 1896 were the stories of travelers who had crossed the Isthmus and whose accounts told of nothing but ravage, ruin, and decay. Although in reality—as we now know—the property on the Isthmus was preserved, nothing of this was understood in the United States. Total abandonment was what was spoken of, and nobody believed that there remained anything but a ruin which could serve only to furnish an example of extravagant and dishonest expenditures, and of the folly of an attempt to build a canal at Panama.

This conviction in the public (mind) was not changed when La Compagnie Nouvelle du Canal de Panama was formed and continued the work at Panama in 1894. These happenings were absolutely unknown, even among people generally well informed. Up to the time we made known here that a responsible company was really at work to complete the Panama Canal, the general public was utterly ignorant of the fact that such a company existed, or that the work was going on; and even then it was with great difficulty and only after prolonged efforts that the public could be in some small measure convinced of the reality and seriousness of the Panama undertaking.

6. *Popularity of the Nicaragua route.*

With Nicaragua it was just the contrary. Articles describing the plans and intentions of the company, as well as the work in progress, were constantly published in newspapers and magazines. Lectures and addresses were delivered before many audiences and gatherings, a large size model of the canal as it was planned was exhibited in all the cities of the land, and it was generally believed that the work was progressing toward completion. Many prominent politicians, naval officers, and other public men had closely allied themselves with and were deeply interested in the company. Many distinguished Americans had subscribed to its capital stock and in Congress, on the one hand, by supporting measures presented in favor of the company, and out of Congress (outside), on the other, by creating public sentiment and arousing popular interest they were powerfully helping to make the Nicaragua Canal a national enterprise.

Public opinion demanded the Nicaragua Canal. The only canal known, the only (canal) wanted, the only (canal) spoken of was the Nicaragua Canal. The Panama Canal was looked upon as a vanished dream. The desire for a canal meant only the desire for the Nicaragua Canal. The constant activity of the Maritime Co. and its friends throughout the country had aroused interest and created a demand for its construction. Boards of trade, State legislatures, party conventions all over the country had passed resolutions in which action in favor of the Nicaragua Canal was demanded. The platform, or declaration of principles, of the Republican Party at the time of the presidential election in 1896 formally indorsed the construction of the Nicaragua Canal. This fact shows the influence the company had acquired in political circles (among politicians). Both political parties were pledged to support it. It was evident that in one form or another the United States was about to adopt the Nicaragua Canal. Most conclusive proof of this is found in the bills which had been introduced in the two Houses of Congress in 1891, 1892, 1893, 1894, and 1895, with a view to adopting the Nicaragua route and aiding in the completion of this canal. The bill of 1891 provided for the guarantee by the Government of the United States of the bonds of the Maritime Co. up to 500,000,000 francs. The bill of 1903 provided for an issue of 500,000,000 francs in United States Treasury notes in aid of the Nicaragua Canal. Another bill authorized the President to acquire the route for the construction of the Nicaragua Canal and appropriated 560,000,000 francs for the cost of the undertaking. Another bill authorized the utilization of the credit of the United States for the construction of the Nicaragua Canal. The bill of 1894 authorized the United States to guarantee the bonds of the company up to 350,000,000 francs.

Thus, when we were intrusted with the affair in 1896, we found ourselves face to face with a general and almost unanimous opinion in the United States in favor of the Nicaragua Canal, which was looked upon as the American Canal; the Nicaragua Canal had been officially recognized by Congress when that body granted a charter to a company formed for its construction; various committees had been appointed by Congress for the survey of this route, and favorable reports had been filed; liberal concessions for the building of the canal had been granted by Nicaragua and Costa Rica, and these governments openly favored the selection of this route by the United States; a large number of citizens of the United States were pecuniarily interested in it; construction work of some importance had been begun by the Maritime Co. on the Nicaragua route; messages of Presidents to Congress had recognized and recommended the Nicaragua route; the matter of the canal was so important that it had become a plank in the paltforms of both parties, and these platforms in terms formally favored Nicaragua; and above all, the Panama Canal was looked upon as an undertaking which was not only a failure from a financial point of view, but as an engineering proposition was a scandalous affair, of which nothing but evil was spoken.

7. Legislation then pending with a view to the building of the Nicaragua Canal under the auspices of the United States.

We ascertained also that, in response to this public opinion, bills were pending before the Senate and the House with a view to the adoption of the Nicaragua route, and the building of this canal under the auspices of the United States, through the Maritime Co., and that Congress had recently authorized the appointment of a special commission (the Ludlow Commission), to again survey and report on the feasibility of this route, and the commission was then engaged in this work.

JANUARY-DECEMBER, 1896—RECAPITULATION OF WORK DONE IN 1896.

We studied each of these bills; we prepared comments and arguments in regard to them; we studied the constitutional, diplomatic, or international questions bearing upon them, in connection with the power of Congress to pass such legislation and to lend credit to an enterprise of this kind; we had personal interviews with Members of Congress; we employed as assistants Washington lawyers instructed to follow, day by day, the evidence then being taken by a House committee on the subject of the Nicaragua Canal, and we were in daily communication with them on this subject, studying reports and giving instructions.

To advance the passage of these bills, the supporters of the Nicaragua project had obtained from the House Committee on Interstate Commerce that this committee hold public hearings, and a number of experts and other witnesses, among them the members of the Ludlow Commission, were examined with a view to supporting and favoring the passage through the Senate and House of the Perkins and Mahon Nicaragua bills. We followed this inquiry, day by day, either in person or through our colleagues. At this time the instructions we had received from the company did not permit us to appear publicly in its name, as the company was not ready—by virtue either of a favorable report from its engineering committees, or of adequate financial plans—to take a decisive stand before the world. But confidentially we actively circulated information concerning the Panama project and its plans for the revival of the enterprise and the completion of the work, and we laid special stress upon (brought out specially) the flaws and difficulty of execution in the construction of the Nicaragua Canal.

Between January and June, 1896, Mr. Cromwell and Mr. Curtis made alternate stays in Washington for this purpose (on this subject). They devoted themselves actively to the case during a considerable part of this period, and had personal interviews with a number of Senators and Representatives in order to discuss with them and to assail the pending bills. Mr. Cromwell also had frequent interviews with Col. Ludlow in regard to the investigation by his commission, and urged upon him (presented to him) the superior advantages of Panama. As a result of this exposition the Ludlow Commission in its supplementary (ulterieur) report made very favorable references to the Panama route.

It is important to explain here what a considerable advantage the Nicaragua Canal project possessed over that of Panama in the committees of both houses of Congress, advantage that was maintained from that time until the ratification of the treaty with the Republic of Panama in 1904.

In the Senate all legislation bearing upon an Isthmian canal had first to be submitted to the Nicaragua Canal Committee of the Senate (later the Committee on Interoceanic Canals) for approval, amendment, or rejection by this committee. The chairman of this committee was Senator Morgan, whose stubbornness in favor of Nicaragua was only equaled by his continued efforts in favor of this project, and the animosity with which he constantly attacked and belittled the cause of Panama and everything and everybody connected with that cause.

In the House of Representatives everything bearing upon the canal was first sent to the Committee on Interstate Commerce. The chairman of this committee was Mr. Hepburn, a man whose entire energy and every attainment was devoted to the success of the Nicaragua bill in Congress.

With Senator Morgan, who had effective control of his committee in the Senate, and Representative Hepburn, absolutely dominating his House committee; with these two chairmen, partisans of Nicaragua and devoting their time to the advancement of its interest, both being supported by the, so to speak, unanimous opinion of these two houses of Congress, one realizing that we had before us an almost impossible task, if we were to obtain favorable consideration for Panama.

On June 1 of this year—1896—Senator Morgan, of Alabama, introduced a new and more comprehensive bill in the Senate to overcome certain criticisms of the Perkins and Mahon bills; this bill, also, provided for the adoption of the Nicaragua route, the guaranty by the Government of the bonds of the Maritime Co. and the acquisition of the capital stock of the Maritime Co. by the United States; and it promptly received the indorsement of the committee and was placed on the calender of the Senate. We at once critically examined this measure and opposed it, just as we were opposing the other bills—and made to it the opposition we were keeping up against the other bills.

RESULT: THERE WAS NO LEGISLATION FOR NICARAGUA THAT YEAR—1896.

The reports of the Senate and House committee on the subject of the Nicaragua Canal bills were favorable to those measures, but the arguments we had disseminated and the opposition we had created were sufficient to form an important minority which refused to join with the other members of the committee, and no Nicaragua bill was passed at this session, which closed (came to an end) in the month of June.

Each Congress lasts two years, the length (duration) of the term of the Representatives, who are elected to the legislature for two years, beginning on the 4th of March following their election, comprising (and) two sessions. The first session, generally called the long session, opens (begins) in December of the year following the election of the Representatives and closes (ends) when Congress deems it convenient, generally in the course of the following summer. The second session, popularly called the short session, opens (begins) in the following December and closes (ends) the 4th of March following, on which date the House legislature ends (se termine). In theory each Congress sits uninterruptedly, all business unfinished at the close of the long session remains at the opening of the short session in the same state in which it was at the adjournment and may continue its progress from there on at the short session. Bills pending at the end of the short session, however, die, as the Congress before which they were pending ceases to exist; and if it is desired to get further action on them (leur donner suite), it is necessary to reintroduce them as new measures in the new Congress, where they again follow their course toward being put to a vote.

The session of 1895–96 was the first or long session of the thirty-fifth Congress.

In December, 1896, when Congress met, the Nicaragua bills were therefore still pending, their passage was recommended by the respective committees, and their supporters (friends) had only to bring them to a vote. The preliminary steps had already been taken. It was certain that in each House the most determined efforts would be made to this end, and a division (vote) would have insured the passage of the bills and the building of the Nicaragua Canal.

The period between June and December, 1896, was taken up with such preparations as we were able to make for the following session, in view of the restriction already mentioned, that is to say in view of the fact that the company was not ready to make public definite engineering and financial plans, but we worked continually on the case (nous nous occupames constamment de l'affaire), making friends for Panama and keeping ourselves informed of movements and conditions that might be adverse to us.

We made frequent reports to the company during the year.

DECEMBER, 1896, TO MARCH 4, 1897—ATTACK AND DEFEAT OF THE NICARAGUA LEGISLATION.

The year 1896 was that of the presidential election; it was therefore a year of great political excitement. Each party in nominating its candidates puts forth a statement of the policies it favors and will pursue if it succeeds, which statement is generally called its platform, and in 1896 the platform of the Republican Party announced that this party favored the building of the Nicaragua Canal. That year the Democratic Party evaded this matter in its platform. The Republicans won a decisive victory by the election of Mr. McKinley, and the Nicaragua Canal was therefore adopted as a principle of the Republican policy.

The skillful (adroit) politicians who were managing the Maritime Co. had obtained the support of the leaders of both parties had aroused public opinion and made of the Nicaragua Canal a party as well as a national issue. When Congress met they were able to call on the members of the victorious party (the Republican Party) to support their bill as a measure formally adopted by their party, and this was an almost decisive argument. The Democrats, without having formally pledged themselves as a party, also generally favored the Nicaragua bills. The only questions remaining to be discussed between the parties were, therefore, matters of detail and method, and as for that the Maritime Co. was ready to concede almost anything (tout ce qu'on voulait) to succeed.

With these bills in so advantageous a position for their passage in both Houses, with the dominant party pledged to Nicaragua and the other party cooperating, the future of Nicaragua seemed absolutely assured. We had only been able to make a small beginning in dissipating the dense clouds of ignorance and error on the subject of the Panama Canal which enshrouded Congress and the general public, and in partially enlightening a few minds. This was a work calling for much time and immense labor, and it could not be done properly without an audacious, vigorous, and open propaganda by the Panama Co., which propaganda we were not yet permitted to undertake. The instructions which we received from the company obliged us to remain always on the defensive, without making any real publicity. The difficulties of the situation, with the legislative deathblow apparently about to fall, were serious. The supporters of Nicaragua were full of confidence in their success, the whole country expected it, and neither the one nor the other gave even a moments thought to the Panama Canal as a factor in the situation.

As soon as Congress met in December, 1896, the presidents of both Nicaragua companies—the canal company and the construction company which had been formed to carry out the work—went to Washington to personally direct the campaign. Mr. Cromwell and Mr. Curtis both remained in Washington for an extended period in order to protect the interests of the Panama Canal. On their side the supporters of Nicaragua had a strong sentiment in their favor in both Houses, a popular feeling in the same direction, the approval of the Government, and the declaration of the Republican Party in its platform adopting the Nicaragua Canal project. This party composed the majority of both Houses. Fortunately it was the short session, in which many bills, owing to lack of time, do not reach a vote. But these supporters knew as well as we did that if their bills could be put to the vote they would be passed. So they concentrated their efforts on the plan of getting a vote in the House on the Mahon bill, the passage of which had been recommended by the House committee in charge of this matter.

In the House of Representatives the Speaker is assisted in regard to the order of business and the discussion of bills by a committee called the Committee on Rules, composed of five members—made up of the Speaker, the leader of the majority in the House or the chairman of the Committee on Ways and Means, and, in addition, one influential Member of the majority and two of the minority. When it comes to getting a vote on a bill, especially during the short session, the Committee on Rules must be brought to set a date for its consideration.

So the supporters of Nicaragua began as soon as the Houses met to circulate a petition addressed to the Committee on Rules, with a view to getting this committee to decide to place their bill on the calendar. Their plan was to obtain so many signatures to this petition that the commitee would recognize their strength and be brought to grant their request. We were then kept constantly busy during the days and evenings interviewing Members of the House and opposing this action. Despite the 200 signatures of Members they obtained to their petition, the opposition made by us and the Members who were against the bill was such that the attempt failed, to the great surprise and chagrin of its supporters.

They then tried to obtain a vote in the Senate, hoping that favorable action there would have a decisive influence on the Committee on Rules in the House. As the bill in the Senate was in favorable posture, Senator Morgan was able to advance it and cooperate with the movement in the House. Mr. Cromwell and Mr. Curtis remained in Washington for several weeks during this critical period, exercising constant vigilance and activity. With the restriction that then hampered our action our efforts were chiefly bent on showing the drawbacks of the Nicaragua route and the reasons which militated against the passage of legislative measures rather than on supporting the cause of the Panama Canal.

During this period the proposed treaty between Great Britain and the United States on the subject of the arbitration of the Venezuelan boundary question was pending before the Senate. This treaty contained a clause with a view to the general arbitration of controversies between the two nations, which clause it was asserted would involve the question of the control of the Nicaragua Canal in international difficulties. We thoroughly studied this treaty, and we prepared comments and arguments on this subject for several Members of Congress. In fact, at this time, as well as later, we seized upon and took advantage of every opportunity, whatever it might be, to defeat or delay the consideration of every bill favorable to Nicaragua.

The great Republic of Central America, composed of the Central American States, one of which was Nicaragua, had been created shortly before this, and although Nicaragua had granted concessions this new confederation took its place in international affairs (relations) and at this juncture (time) its minister, Señor Rodriguez, protested against certain clauses of the bill as at variance with (méconnaissant) the Maritime Co.'s concessions. We hastened to seize this opportunity to lay stress upon and make clear the drawbacks of the plans under consideration for the use of the Nicaragua route. The protest of Rodriguez and the discussion it provoked, while offering a temporary obstacle to the Nicaragua bills under consideration, presented a new danger to the Panama cause by reason of this proposal of a treaty between the Central American States and the United States, by virtue of which the United States could itself build and directly control (diriger directment) the canal on the general lines of the Frelinghuysen-Zavala treaty of 1884.

In spite of the vigorous and almost successful efforts of the Nicaragua party, their bills had not reached a vote when the closure of Congress came on March 4, and we can say in all justice that our constant care, our serious opposition, and our varied efforts had contributed in a somewhat considerable degree to this result.

MARCH, 1897—SPECIAL SESSION OF MARCH, 1897—COOPERATION OF COLOMBIA OBTAINED TO MAKE CERTAIN THAT THE PANAMA CANAL PROJECT BE OFFICIALLY RECOGNIZED BY THE UNITED STATES.

On March 4, 1897, the inauguration of Mr. McKinley as President took place, and he immediately called a special session of Congress for the 15th of that month.

Thus, instead of taking a rest, we were obliged to throw ourselves at once into a new struggle. The Nicaragua bills were immediately reintroduced and their passage accelerated (poussée). The new Secretary of State was ex-Senator Sherman, who, only a few days previously, had been chairman of the Committee on Foreign Relations in the Senate, in charge of the Nicaragua bills, and he was an avowed and powerful supporter of that route. He entered into negotiations with the Central American States, represented by Señor Rodriguez, their minister, with a view to a treaty under which the Nicaragua Canal would be built by the United States itself directly instead of being built under the concessions of the Maritime Co. He sent official communications to the Senate to this effect (en ce sens) and appeared in person before the Senate committee in support of his plan. All these developments (démarches) not only demanded but received the utmost vigilance and diligence on our part; they also necessitated the almost constant presence in Washington of a member of our law firm.

Fortunately, the matters most discussed at the special session were the tariff bills, when the conflict of interests and parties became so serious that it was evident to the supporters of Nicaragua that their bills could not reach a vote. They then concentrated their attention on the more practical plan of obtaining a more complete official indorsement of the Nicaragua canal by Congress and the appropriation (vote formel) of funds for the investigation anew of that project. A law to this effect was passed.

Later the President appointed a commission under the name of the "Nicaragua Canal Commission," composed of Admiral Walker, Col. Hains, and Prof. Haupt.

Confronted by the unexpected developments (circonstances) of the special session, and the active negotiations between the United States and Nicaragua entered upon by Secretary Sherman, we conceived the plan of inducing Colombia herself to intervene and enforce (faire valoir), according to the terms of the treaty of 1846–1848 between New Granada (now Colombia) and the United States, and protect the rights of the Panama Canal Co. as the owner of the concession which had been granted by Colombia on the basis of that treaty. The plan (idea) thus conceived by us was presented to the company, which approved of it at once; and, in consequence, we immediately spoke of it to the representative of Colombia in the United States (Mr. Renfigo, chargé d'affaires at Washington), and a series of interviews ensued, in the course of which we made a full exposition of the new position of the canal company, discussed the treaty of 1848, and furnished arguments in support of these views.

We prepared and presented to the representative of Colombia an official protest, and, after discussion, it was accepted by him and presented to the Government of the United States. The effect of this step (Mésure) made itself felt, and the attention of the United States was attracted to the Panama Canal through important diplomatic channels. This arrested the attention of the Government and introduced the Panama Canal, advantageously and with effect, as a factor whose consideration imposed itself in the solution of the pending problems; until then it had been completely neglected.

OUR REPORTS AND ADVICE TO THE COMPANY IN 1897—WE COUNSEL A VIGOROUS POLICY OF PUBLICITY, ENLIGHTENMENT, AND OPPOSITION.

Throughout this difficult period our study and understanding of the position of the canal company both in the United States and beyond the sea imbued us with the idea, which later became apparent to all, that the passive (négative) policy hitherto followed must be abandoned as entirely inadequate to cope with the dangers which threatened the company on all sides, and that the sole hope for its salvation lay in the adoption of a plan of action upon lines which Mr. Cromwell suggested (indiqua), different, open, audacious, and aggressive, and which is set forth as follows in his letter to the company under date of February 2, 1897.

"Permit me to call your attention to other and more fundamental phases (cotés) of the great problem with which your counsel is intrusted.

"As you are aware, I have had occasion during the many years of my connection with the railroad and the canal to study these questions and to weigh public opinion. In the course of this connection, and also while engaged in other professional duties, I have been brought into contact with the Government and the most influential Senators and Representatives. I have also informed myself of the general state of mind of the American press and upon the platforms of each of the political parties. From all my sources of information I am obliged to say that I have come to the conclusion that as far as the general public is concerned, both it and the Government are clearly favorable to the Nicaragua Canal and its control by the American Government. Successive Presidents, successive Congresses, and their successive committees; the political parties by their platforms (déclarations officielles) and the most prominent statesmen by their speeches have supported and favored it for many years; and one can not read the recent debates in the Senate without finding fresh and convincing proof thereof (sur ce point).

"The Nicaragua plan is full of weaknesses, as we well know—it has powerful and intelligent opponents, and the arguments of its supporters are met by (se heurtent à) irrefutable answers in the discussions; but the supreme consideration which is the base of its support is the desire of the nation to extend its coasts to the south in order to extend (encourager) its commerce and protect itself in case of war by a free communication between the two coasts of the national territory (domaine). So arguments tending to show that the undertaking will not be remunerative are not so controlling, and considerations which influence private investments are not so conclusive, in the case of the Government.

"Besides the canal committees in both, the Senate and House have favorably reported the pending bills to lend the credit of the Government up to $100,000,000, and it is very probable that these measures will be passed by the two houses as soon as the opportunity presents itself.

"I presume that, practically, the building of the Nicaragua Canal with the capital and under the protection of the American Government will prevent the building of the Panama Canal. This conclusion is self-evident. At the time the Nicaragua project was grappling with financial difficulties, when the Panama Canal was making continual progress and demonstrating its feasibility, you could face the conditions I have depicted to you with more composure; but I see myself forced to warn you that new conditions have arisen during the past few months; that these conditions are of enormous importance, and that one can not with impunity neglect to take them into consideration. I refer, above all, to the following facts: The canal committees in both House and Senate have favorably reported the pending bill to which the public gives its support; and the Senate debates, since the Rodriguez protest, are proof that the next Secretary of State and the most influential Senators will openly declare themselves in its favor.

"In the course of the discussion of the arbitration treaty between Great Britain and the United States, public opinion in favor of the Nicaragua Canal and the necessity of protecting it from inclusion in the arbitration have developed.

"The effect of all these matters has been to concentrate the attention of Congress and the public on the Nicaragua Canal and the necessity of controlling it (d'en avor la maitrise) and to create popular support for this canal as a matter of national political importance (interet).

"You have already observed that Señor Rodriguez, in the name of the Nicaragua Government, virtually offers our Government to place the canal on the basis of the Frelinghuysen-Zavala treaty, proposed in 1884, and that Senator Sherman, in his capacity of chairman of the Committee on Foreign Affairs (in a month he will be Secretary of State, intrusted, in fact, with the settlement of this question), has openly declared himself in the debates as favoring the canal and preferring that it be built on the basis of the Frelinghuysen-Zavala treaty.

"No one can doubt that if the pending bill is defeated, for whatsoever reason, the new Secretary of State will be disposed to enter into negotiations with Nicaragua on the basis of the treaty referred to, which step the Government has already been invited to take by Señor Rodriguez. This would mean that our Government would then give an equitable indemnity to protect promoters of the Nicaragua Canal and address itself directly to the Nicaragua Government for the establishment of the undertaking.

"We are aware, of course, that if our Government undertakes the Nicaragua Canal it may still have to deal with Great Britain in view of the Clayton-Bulwer treaty; but that is not a matter that concerns us.

"The treaty to which reference is made (Frelinghuysen-Zavala treaty) is a proposed treaty negotiated in 1883 between the two Governments and submitted to our Congress for its approval. Before definite action (was taken) the treaty was withdrawn by the President from the consideration of the Senate. It will, however, perhaps interest you to know its principal clauses.

"It declared that the canal shall be built by the Government of the United States of America and owned by it and the Republic of Nicaragua.

"That there shall be a perpetual alliance between the United States of America and the Republic of Nicaragua, and the United States undertakes to guarantee the integrity of the latter.

"That the United States receives full liberty to build the canal, and that Nicaragua gives the requisite land, rights of way, etc.

"That no customs duties, tolls, taxes, or other assessments shall be levied by the Government of Nicaragua on the ships, their cargoes, passengers, etc.

"That the canal and its auxiliary works and dependencies of all sorts are exempt from all manner of taxation or tonnage dues, etc.

"That the management of the canal shall be intrusted to a board of management, three members of which shall be appointed by the United States and three by Nicaragua, and that the enforcement of the regulations adopted by the board is guaranteed by Nicaragua.

"That the net revenues derived from the operation of the canal shall be divided between the two Governments in the ratio of one-third to Nicaragua and two-thirds to the United States.

"That the United States disavows all intention of infringing upon the independent sovereignty of Nicaragua, and declares its intention to make firm the power of the free Republics of the continent and to favor and develop their prosperity and independence.

"Nicaragua agrees to terminate—as far as possible—every covenant in every treaty to which it is a party that may be repugnant (contraire) to the present treaty.

"The United States undertakes to begin the work within the two years following the ratification (échange) of the treaty and to complete it within the 10 years next ensuing (qui suivent ce commencement); and it is added that this period may be extended if such extension should appear equitable.

"That in the event of difficulties there shall be arbitration by friendly powers.

"That the United States will aid with all its good offices to bring about the union of the five Republics of Central America.

"That the United States shall lend Nicaragua $4,000,000, and the canal profits accruing to Nicaragua shall be applied to the repayment of this sum.

"That neither party shall cede its rights without the consent of the other

"You will thus see that the problem is quite different to that which you have been facing. It is no longer a bankrupt company which is our competitor; it is the nation itself. Now, to turn the nation from this design becomes the new and weighty problem.

"Imbued with (penetrated by) a keen apprehension of my duty toward you, I see myself forced to urge you to give this matter your earliest and best (exclusive) attention.

"Without venturing into details, I am of opinion that we should officially and at once bring to the knowledge of this Government the state of our canal and the serious manner in which the work is being prosecuted. Such silence has been maintained, in compliance with orders from Paris—albeit very wise ones—that our Government and people are completely ignorant of the real development and progress of the Panama Canal and the devoted and worthy manner in which the development of the great enterprise is being pursued. These facts might well lead our own Government to reflect on the subject of its own undertaking if the actual condition of the Panama Canal is proved to its satisfaction by statements emanating from official sources. The popular impression here is that the Panama Canal is not seriously pushed, and wherever I say the contrary people are astonished and interested.

"The appointment of an international engineering committee of the high standing and distinction you contemplate, and the simultaneous announcement of this appointment, would also have some effect on our Government.

"I feel that it will be necessary to take active steps in order to stop the Government in its inclination to settle the canal question itself (directement). I know that it is your desire to build the Panama Canal under the auspices or protection of this Government, in some form or other; but what I have told you will show you the difficulty, to wit: That it is clear that our Government wishes to be the virtual owner of the canal. Permit me, therefore, respectfully to suggest that you seriously consider whether the time for us to address our Government in the interest of the Panama Canal has arrived, and if so, the basis and form of a proposal on this subject."

This advice was reiterated on February 9, 10, and 13, in letters and telegrams, and the plan and policy were further mapped out (elaboré) in a letter dated March 20, addressed to the company, containing the following:

"Permit me then to insistently urge upon you, above all other things, to occupy yourselves immediately with putting into effect the plan I permitted myself to advise, to wit:

"That the moment to act has arrived. That the Colombian Government and the Panama Co. ought to officially bring to the knowledge of the Government of the United States the existence of the Panama concession, the considerable amount of work accomplished under the concession, the present businesslike (serieuses) intentions of the parties, and to remind it of the clauses of the treaty of 1848 between the United States and Colombia.

"In face of such a presentation it will be far more difficult, if not impossible, for our Government to take action with Nicaragua; and in my opinion it is the only means to prevent its so doing. Certainly this is essential to the canal company, for if this Government adopts Nicaragua it will kill our project; but it is equally important to Colombia, which does not wish to see its rival (Nicaragua) obtain the richest prize a South American nation could ever win. Colombia as well as the Panama Canal Co. must wake up, must come to a keen realization of her danger, and must show herself equal to the opportunity that offers. She ought immediately and by cable to notify her minister to present a note covering the grounds we indicate, and to cooperate with us earnestly and at once.

"Do not let the Government trust to the mails, which are slow. This matter calls for action by cable, as rapidly as possible.

"To gain time, I am myself going to cable you to this effect."

Again in his letter to the company of April 6, 1897, he stated:

"I duly received your favor of March 25. I thank you most sincerely for the flattering and encouraging terms of this letter, as well as for your cable and letter to Mr. Whaley. The appreciation so highly expressed by you and all the directors and officials of the company can not fail to inspire me, and it is a pleasure to assist you in the honorable and successful execution of the great task which is confided to you.

"Your duty is of overwhelming (colossale) importance, and we must make our plans with Napoleonic strategy to—

"Prevent any other transisthmian project from taking shape.

"Present our own project in a conscientious and convincing manner.

"Bring the nations of the world together in this matter.

"Raise the enormous capital that is necessary and use it (en disposer) conscientiously and wisely.

"Above all have the courage to abandon the revival of the project if this be for the best.

"Energetically develop the railroad and steamship company with its splendid opportunities for the future, so as to make it a valuable asset (good equivalent) for the satisfaction of your bondholders and for the commerce of the Isthmus.

"All this, in truth, is worthy of the highest ability, and without it ignominious failure must be expected.

"It is clear that unless all the other isthmian projects are thwarted the hopes of your security holders will be entirely disappointed, and it is equally clear that if this Government makes an agreement with the Nicaragua Government, or even with the present Nicaragua company, our canal project will be henceforth almost hopeless.

"You, better than anyone, can foretell the attitude the shareholders of the canal will assume in the presence of such a result.

"Thus you will see how anxious I have been all through the year and, with the formal restrictions you judged prudent to place upon our efforts in America, I have done my best, and up to the present our canal has not suffered.

"The visit of your able director general has afforded the opportunity and the privilege of developing my plans and opinions; first of all, I advised arousing the activity of Colombia in order to obtain its cooperation with the canal company in addressing to this Government energetic and official remonstrances (declarations) based upon the treaty of 1848; I also advised that the canal company emerge from the cloud in which it has enshrouded itself for the past two years and show its real worth (valeur), its honorable intentions, its present plans, and the possible achievement (of the canal)—all the while carefully abstaining from making any promise which would embarrass you later on.

"I do not need to dwell upon the far-reaching importance (grande portée) and great advantages of such a move.

"Mr. Hutin, Mr. Whaley, and Mr. Boyard were quick to approve of and praise this plan; and, subject to your consent, Mr. Hutin has agreed to put it into execution as soon as he arrives on the Isthmus. I am happy to see by your cable, sent to me on March 24, and by your letter, to which the present is in reply, that you give it your full approval. I now feel that we have at last reached the point of action."

And again in his letter of June 25 he said:

"I am of opinion that the best way to impress and to convince our Government and our people is to show the real condition, the seriousness, and the importance of the Panama Canal project by means of official statements which it will be possible for you to give out. Besides, the official announcement, when given out here, of the appointment of an international committee and of its beginning active work would greatly aid our cause and powerfully (especially) support the protest of the Colombian Government. The preparation and presentation of maps, plans, and of the information outlined above, and the announcement of the creation of the international committee, are the two practical things which I urgently advise you to push forward with the greatest energy and to advertise in the most public manner. They will furnish proof of real work, and only real progress and real work will convince anyone to-day about anything that relates to the plans for a canal.

"There has been so much talk on this matter that to-day mere words are unheeded. Only actual results put forward in a convincing manner will hold the attention and satisfy the mind of the Government and people."

However, the company at once sanctioned the adoption of that part of the program dealing with the intervention of Colombia, but it did not deem expedient to carry out the remainder of the plan until a year later.

The director general of the company stayed in New York during February and March, and for two or three weeks we had daily conferences with him in the course of which we rendered him, as representative of the company, full reports; from here he went to the Isthmus, and returned to New York about April 20. We had almost daily conferences with him, and he spent a great part of the next 30 days in Washington with Mr. Cromwell and Mr. Curtis; then he left for Paris.

Mr. Lemarquis, trustee for the bondholders of the old company, also visited the United States in May of this year, and we spent several weeks conferring with him every day and going over the weighty questions in which he was so deeply interested.

Mr. Lemarquis collaborated with us daily in the study of the political situation, of the parliamentary developments, of the public sentiment in favor of Nicaragua, and the desire of the United States to itself own a canal, and of the methods we were employing and the plans we were advising to avoid these disastrous results. He was tireless in his deep devotion to his task and his observations and studies permitted him to arrive at wise conclusions, both for his own guidance and that of other interested parties on his return to Paris.

DECEMBER, 1897–JUNE, 1898, THE SESSION OF CONGRESS—WAR WITH SPAIN—PUBLIC CLAMOR FOR THE ADOPTION OF NICARAGUA BECOMES EMPHATIC—WE ADVISE A PLAN OF PUBLICITY AND DEFENSE.

Congress met again in December, 1897. Bills introduced during the special session were still pending, according to law, and at the very opening of Congress Representative Barham introduced a new bill for the building of the Nicaragua Canal. During this session various new measures were introduced, all in prevision of (prévoyant) the construction of the Nicaragua Canal under the auspices of the United States. These bills emanated, one from Senator Hansbrough, January 5, 1898; others from Mr. Davidson, January 11, 1898; Senator Morgan, May 5, 1898; Senator Stewart, May 25, 1898; and yet another from Senator Morgan, June 20, 1898.

The Walker-Hains-Haput Nicaragua Canal Commission sailed for Nicaragua in December. Mr. Cromwell again wrote to the company under date December 24:

"More than ever I am convinced that we ought to make an energetic demonstration before the return of the commission."

On January 26, 1898, he again wrote to the company:

"Everywhere one finds proof of a growing confidence in and desire for the construction of a Nicaragua Canal, and I can not help thinking that we have lost, and are losing, ground every day in regard to our project, and I find myself obliged to insist that the Panama project be called to the attention of our Government before it is too late to stop the drift in favor of the Nicaragua project, and too late to break pledges given (défaire des engagements pris) or to win in the face of the private and selfish advantages offered by the other plans."

The grave international complications which arose between the United States and Spain over the disturbances in Cuba followed by the Spanish-American War absorbed almost the entire attention of Congress during the session of December, 1897-98.

But while the Nicaraguan bills in Congress demanded less attention, a new and more serious danger to the cause of Panama arose; this was the general (universal) popular demand for the building of the Nicaragua Canal as an offensive and defensive safeguard of national interests.

The celebrated voyage of the American battleship *Oregon* down the Pacific coast, round the Horn, and up the Atlantic coast to Cuba was followed with intense interest not only by the people of the United States, but by the whole civilized world, as this battleship was hurrying to join Admiral Sampson's fleet, which it reached only just in time to take part in the battle of Santiago. The Nation understood the danger to which the necessity of such a voyage would have exposed the country in case of war with a more powerful naval power. The enormous advantage of being able—by means of an interoceanic canal—to avoid going round the South American Continent impressed everybody and a general (universal) clamor for the Nicaragua Canal as a measure of public safety arose. The newspapers were full of articles pointing out the advantages of the canal in case of war (the name Nicaragua was always coupled with the word canal), and of maps and calculations illustrating these advantages, giving the very miles and days to be saved on the trip; and its (the canal's) effect upon the whole Naval Establishment and the defenses of the country. A wave of emotion, always stronger than popular belief (conviction), swept over the whole people. The friends of Nicaragua made the best use of this object lesson in favor of the building of their canal.

Another result of this state of public opinion was to put an end to all idea of a canal owned by a private company, as Mr. Cromwell had long since predicted. It was to be built, owned, and operated by the United States; it was to be fortified and garrisoned by the United States. It was no longer to be merely a tool of commerce, but, first and foremost, a part of the national defenses, and as such not neutral but American. No passage of this kind could be open to an enemy, it could exist only if held (occupé) by the United States.

Another effect of the Spanish-American War was the regretable irritation against France, created in the United States by the open sympathy of the people and press of France with the cause of Spain. This feeling was deplored by us, but it would have been folly not to recognize its existence, in view of the extent of this state of mind and the falsity of this point of view, which would have prevented at that time a fair consideration of any French undertaking, such as the Panama Canal. It was for this reason that in April, 1898, we advised the temporary postponement of a public presentation of Panama's case; but we energetically urged upon the company to make this presentation before the Congress which was to meet in the following December.

In May Mr. Cromwell wrote to the company:

"I am keeping in close touch with affairs in Washington, and I deem the present period important to our project. The enormous importance of a waterway in Nicaragua across the Isthmus has been proven by the present war, and I can clearly see that the drift of official as well as public opinion favors this undertaking more strongly than ever before in the history of the United States. I know that you are wise enough to recognize that this is a natural and legitimate result of the war with Spain. This makes it more and more necessary that we be fully prepared to positively and definitely announce our intentions within the next few months if governmental conditions are in any way propitious. I am giving instructions that the way may be open to you when the time comes, for I am of opinion that the public announcement of our plans should be the first of the important moves the company will have to make. If this public annoucement be delayed too long, there may be nothing left to annouce in a practical way, as we are agreed (d'accord sur l'idee) that there is no room for two canals."

In order to advance their cause the supporters of Nicaragua inspired a resolution, which was passed by the Senate in May, 1898, whereby the Maritime Co. was invited to make a proposal for the transfer of its capital stock to the United

States, carrying with it the ownership of its concessions and the payment of its debt.

In response to this resolution, the Maritime Co. made a proposal to the United States in which it offered to effect the necessary transfers and readjustments (cancellations) on the payment of $5,500,000. It was on these lines that the Morgan bill of June 20, 1898, was presented to Congress.

All these developments were the subject of constant study and lively concern on our part. We often conferred with public men, we closely watched the drift of things, and drew our conclusions, which we communicated to the company by the advice outlined in the above correspondence.

JUNE, 1898—SOJOURN AND CONFERENCE IN PARIS DURING THE SUMMER OF 1898—THE POLICY OF ACTIVE PUBLICITY, ENLIGHTENMENT, DEFENSE, AND PROTECTION IS ADOPTED.

In June of this year (1898) the Panama Co. asked Mr. Cromwell to come to Paris to confer with it on this matter, and specially to discuss the plans he had urged upon the company.

Mr. Cromwell went there and was absent from the United States about six weeks, occupied exclusively in conferring with the representatives of the canal company in Paris, at whose disposal he had placed himself.

He made a detailed exposition of the situation in America and of all the phases of the canal matter, to the president and directors of the company; almost daily conferences were held between the directors and officials on the one hand and himself on the other, for the elucidation and study of his opinions and the plans he had so insistently urged in his letters of the preceding months, quoted above. The president and directors gave close attention to and showed a keen understanding of the situation in the United States.

The result of these detailed conferences with the executive officers of the canal company, which lasted more than six weeks, was the complete and unreserved adoption of the plan we had advised, and we were instructed to carry it out (chargé de le mettre à execution). Mr. Cromwell at once returned to the United States and began active work in accordance with these decisions.

AUGUST–DECEMBER, 1898—PREPARATORY WORK IN VIEW OF THE SESSION OF CONGRESS OF 1898.

Establishment of the press bureau.

The International Technical Committee, which had been formed in the early part of 1896, had pursued its investigations and studies, but so far had not reached any definite conclusions. As part of our advice and plan we pronounced ourselves in favor of the immediate completion of the task of the committee, the publication of its findings, and, should they be favorable, of their immediate presentation to the Government of the United States and of their explanation and circulation as a means of public enlightenment, which was agreed upon with the directors of the company, who took an active part in getting the work of the committee into shape for a final decision and report. On Mr. Cromwell's return to the United States, in August, we at once busied ourselves with the organization of an office or special bureau for the preparation and publication of technical and popular articles in the various magazines and periodicals of the country, dealing with every phase of the Panama and Nicaragua problem, and to this end we employed experienced writers and engineers. The work of this bureau, which lasted for a year or two, was carried out under the constant direction and inspiration of one or more of the members of our law firm and took up our time. It extended all over the United States. The archives of this bureau contain a mass of articles, correspondence, interviews, studies, researches, arguments, etc., which were prepared under our direction and in many cases by ourselves.

Among other things, a compilation of the documents constituting the diplomatic history of the interoceanic canal question in the United States was prepared under our direction and supervision and was circulated by us through influential channels. This work is in three volumes, containing 1,840 pages; it kept us busy for several months, during which we also made researches in the Department of State in Washington. This compilation, the only one extant on the subject, became the manual used in the course of all international negotiations on the matter.

In order to be able to direct the work of this bureau intelligently, and to prepare ourselves for the discussion of all the questions involved, we devoted months to the study of the technical phases of the question, with the assistance of Gen. Abbot and of Mr. Corthell, a distinguished engineer, specially employed by us for this work.

The daily press and the magazines of the country were almost entirely favorable to the Nicaragua Canal, and it was only by the greatest special personal efforts that it was possible to get them to take the slightest interest whatsoever in the cause of Panama or to obtain any publicity whatever for the facts bearing on the matter.

It would be absolutely impossible to detail the thousand and one efforts whereby and occasions when, thanks to personal connections and special efforts, the press was at last awakened and informed of the drawbacks of Nicaragua and of the advantages of the Panama route.

Messrs. Lemarquis and Lampré visited us in September, they had daily conferences with us for several weeks and accompanied us to Washington. During these conferences all the phases of the question were daily the subject of serious examination and consideration, and they were thus enabled on their return to Paris to inform their clients and colleagues of the conditions actually existing and to express their opinion thereon. It was a satisfaction and advantage to us to be able to lay the serious and complicated situation then existing directly before the representative of the new company and the trustee of the bondholders of the old company, and their intelligent and conscientious study of the condition of affairs was of very great assistance.

As the reassembling of Congress drew near—it was to be the first session after the Spanish War—the feeling in favor of the immediate selection of the Nicaragua Canal as a national undertaking took various and aggressive forms throughout the United States. This was shown not only among those who were directly interested in the Nicaragua Canal, but also by the general and apparently irresistible public opinion which, without party distinctions, spread to every part of the United States. Such unanimity has rarely been shown on any national question. Boards of trade, shipping associations, and other commercial organizations throughout the country passed resolutions calling upon Congress to act with a view to the building of the Nicaragua Canal as a matter of public safety and of national development. Petitions to the same effect, signed by tens of thousands of citizens, were sent to their Representatives in Congress. The principal newspapers in the country daily supported similar measures. The leaders of both parties vied with one another in favoring the Nicaragua plan. Under the same influence the President of Costa Rica, in person, made a special trip to Washington, and, in the name of Costa Rica as well as of Nicaragua, gave President McKinley official assurances that these Governments would adopt all legislation necessary to facilitate the building of the Nicaragua Canal.

WE ADVISE AND BRING ABOUT AN OFFICIAL PRESENTATION TO THE UNITED STATES OF THE CONDITION OF THE CANAL AND OF THE COMPANY.

Keenly alive to the gravity of the situation, we insistently urged upon the company to make an official presentation of the case of Panama to President McKinley, in the form of a memorial, prior to the reassembling of Congress. We prepared the first draft of the memorial, which was to be presented to the Government of the United States in the name of the company, containing a synopsis of the formation of La Compagnie Nouvelle du Canal de Panama, its concessions, the extent of the construction work already accomplished, the organization of the international committee and its findings, the intentions of the company, etc.

We went to Washington beforehand and communicated to Secretary of State Hay in advance the plan for the official presentation of the studies (studes), and situation of the Panama Canal, as well as of the proposed memorial and the report of the technical committee; and we arranged with the Secretary for an official audience with President McKinley, soon after, for the official presentation of the Panama Canal's case. In accordance with this arrangement and with the communication from Secretary Hay, the audience was fixed for December 2, 1898, and it was then that Mr. Cromwell, with the director general and the chief engineer of the company, the said official representatives having come from Paris specially for this purpose, officially presented to President McKinley the memorial of the company, accompanied by the report of the international committee which had just been completed (Dec., 1898).

As proof of the rooted prejudice which reigned in the press in favor of Nicaragua, two or three instances, taken from events which occurred during this period, may be cited.

Although the report of the international technical committee, thus officially presented to the President, and the memorial of the company presenting the position of the Panama Canal were documents of the highest importance and greatest public interest, and that copies of these documents had been furnished simultaneously by us to the press of the country, not a newspaper would print them of its own accord, and we could not get them the publicity so essential at this juncture except as paid advertisements. Another instance: About this time, Gen. Abbot wrote an article on the subject of the Panama Canal, which we offered to one of the leading magazines in the country which politely declined to publish it. Later on we procured its publication, but in a less important magazine. Another instance: At this time the company was asking the Colombian Congress for an extension of its concessions, and two days after the presentation of the memorial and report of the technical committee an official statement was given out by the Department of State to the effect that the Colombian Congress in Bogota had refused to grant an extension of its concessions to La Compagnie Nouvelle du Canal de Panama, which naturally meant that the Panama company no longer cut any figure in this matter (ne jouait plus de rôle dans l'affaire). The press of the country gave the widest publicity to this article, a publicity most detrimental to Panama. Within two days, on information of an absolutely reliable source furnished us by the director general to the effect that the extension had not been refused by the Colombian Congress but only that one chamber of that parliament had not acted upon this matter (as we know to-day this extension was afterwards granted by executive decree), we sent an official communication to our Government in which the accuracy of this report from Bogota was denied, and the Colombian minister, at our request, did the same and sent a copy of his note to the press of the country; but the same state of prejudice existed, and it was with difficulty that the slightest publicity could be obtained for these details.

On the other hand, the same day (Dec. 4) the president of the Maritime Co. also sent to the press a note which was reproduced in its entirety in the newspapers throughout the country attacking the Panama Canal and alluding to the interview of its representatives with President McKinley and Secretary Hay on the 2d instant as an insult to the American people. These are merely instances of the general attitude which was almost unanimous.

DECEMBER, 1898—MARCH 4, 1899—SESSION OF CONGRESS.

The following day (Dec. 5) Congress reassembled and President McKinley sent in his message in which he recommended the building of the Nicaragua Canal under American control.

Two days later Senator Morgan made a violent speech in the Senate announcing his determination to force the passage of the Nicaragua Canal bill and attacking the representatives of the Panama Canal as in league with the transcontinental railroads to prevent the American people obtaining an American canal through Nicaragua.

The most influential men in Congress, as well as in the press, all openly supported Nicaragua, and in consequence were all hostile to Panama, which had just declared itself as Nicaragua's competitor; public opinion, although ill informed on the merits of the question, was in harmony with this attitude, and was also at this time hostile to the Panama Co. as a French company on account of the recent attitude of the French Nation, which was believed to be hostile to the United States; two bills were pending before Congress, one in each House, and they were backed by the official recommendation of the President in his message; and the Maritime Canal Co., with its officials and shareholders nearly all important figures in politics, was ready in its own interests to furnish anything that might be lacking, if anything were lacking, to the zeal of the ever-active partisans of Nicaragua in Congress led by Senator Morgan in the Senate and Representative Hepburn in the House.

Such was the situation we were called upon to face when Congress reassembled in December, 1898.

It can be said in all certainty that, so to speak, nobody in America thought the session of Congress could pass without the enactment of a law for the building of the Nicaragua Canal. Nothing seemed able to resist these influences combined in its favor.

(a) We put forward the Clayton-Bulwer treaty as an obstacle to the Nicaragua project.

The plans for Nicaragua, provided for in the bills then under consideration, entailed not a neutral canal, but a canal to be built, owned, and controlled by the United States alone, and to be fortified so as to assure to them its exclusive control.

We called the attention of Members of Congress and of the administration to the fact that this was contrary to the Clayton-Bulwer treaty with England, and put forward the objection that difficulties with that power would be precipitated (engendrées) if the Nicaragua project were adopted before a modification of this treaty. Later this objection was made in the Senate and impressed several Senators, whose zeal for Nicaragua was not great enough to blind them completely to other considerations. It was strengthened by a formal protest against the bill presented a few days later by the British Ambassador, Lord Pauncefote, to the Secretary of State and based upon the same grounds.

Nevertheless Senator Morgan, with other Senators of extreme leanings in favor of Nicaragua, insisted on pushing the bill, despite the treaty, and after a certain amount of opposition from other Senators he succeeded finally in advancing it so much that its immediate discussion was assured. Many Senators and a majority of the Representatives expressed themselves in favor of this bill.

We continued our work of opposition, conferring frequently with certain Senators, and succeeded in convincing several Senators who, in debating the bill, spoke, not against the Nicaragua Canal, but against the passage of the bill before the modification of the treaty. The number of Senators who adopted the view finally became considerable.

However, the public strongly favored the bill, and during the month of December, 1898, the Nicaragua interests persuaded numbers of boards of trade in different parts of the country to adopt resolutions demanding the passage of the Nicaragua bill and calling upon the Senators and Representatives to vote for it. On the Pacific coast associations to push the Nicaragua plan were formed, and funds were subscribed for the necessary and legitimate expenses of the movement.

In the Senate Senator Morgan openly accused the transcontinental railway companies and the Panama interests of placing obstacles in the way of Nicaragua, and obtained the passage of a resolution, which was not put into effect, for an inquiry into their conduct.

December 23, 1898, the Walker-Hains-Haupt Commission made its preliminary report in favor of the Nicaragua Canal, estimating the cost of its construction at $135,000,000.

This settled for the public the practical side of the question, which the report of the Ludlow Commission had left somewhat in doubt. It was assured that the Nicaragua Canal could be built and at a known cost. Henceforth only one question remained, that of the authorization of Congress.

This report, although foreseen, added considerably to the strength of the Nicaragua party, for it destroyed every objection to the canal, even as to the possibility of the enterprise.

(b) We write an elaborate pamphlet containing a full exposition of the Panama Canal and circulate it in Congress, throughout the press, and among all the influential classes in the United States.

The exigencies of the case necessitated the preparation of a complete and descriptive printed pamphlet, explaining in detail the position of La Compagnie Nouvelle du Canal de Panama, the progress of the work, the amount of construction already accomplished, the entirely new management of the reorganized company, the concessions and titles, a summary of the report of the technical committee, the plan of the canal itself, accompanied by photographs illustrating the condition of the work and the serious intentions of the company to complete the undertaking.

This publication was to be used as an authoritative statement by and argument on behalf of the company in the course of its aggressive campaign now decided upon, and the writing of so important a document could be delegated to no one.

We spent several weeks writing this pamphlet, entitled "The New Panama Canal Co." (dated Dec. 26, 1898), of which we circulated a large number of copies. We sent one to each Member of Congress, to all the higher officials of the Federal Government, to the governors and other high officials of all the States, to all the leading newspapers of the East (the number of which reaches several hundreds), to all the commercial bodies of the large cities, to the libraries, to the heads of educational establishments and other influential institutions, and generally wherever the influence of this pamphlet might have weight.

This was of considerable influence, and was the first authoritative and complete statement published in America on the situation of the Panama Canal and of the canal company.

(c) *We obtain a public hearing before the committee of the House, and make a full exposition.*

An examination of the situation convinced us that the Senate bill would soon reach a vote, and would then certainly be adopted, and we wrote to the company along these lines on January 6. We therefore concentrated our attention on the House, and planned a new measure of defense. We decided to ask the committee of the House intrusted with the canal matter for a public hearing, although this committee was openly hostile to Panama and had pledged itself to Nicaragua, although it had on several occasions reported in favor of Nicaragua, and although its chairman, Mr. Hepburn, was the most earnest and most able champion of Nicaragua in the House, he having ability, power, and vigor on a par with the capable leader of this cause in the Senate, Senator Morgan. It was, however, the only channel through which the Panama Canal could be officially presented to the House, and we determined to adopt an audacious and aggressive method of presentation. We demanded an audience under circumstances which rendered a refusal impossible, and public hearings were held on January 17, 18, and 19.

We decided upon and had a presentation of the Panama matter made not only by Mr. Cromwell and Mr. Curtis, but as to its technical aspects, by the chief engineer of the canal company and by Gen. Abbot, member of the International Technical Committee. In prevision of this hearing, a most profound study of the technical sides of the question was made. It necessitated incessant work, night and day, up to the very hour of the hearing.

(d) *The Nicaragua bill is passed in the Senate almost unanimously.*

As we had foreseen, the Morgan bill reached a vote in the Senate, in spite of all opposition, on January 21, and was speedily passed by a vote of 48 to 6. The bill was at once sent to the House, where, as we have said, we had obtained public hearings in prevision of its arrival, on the 17th, 18th, and 19th of this month.

(e) *The situation in the House favorable to Nicaragua.*

An enthusiastic and large majority of the House was openly pledged to Nicaragua. The result of a vote in the House was absolutely certain, if a vote were taken. If it could not be deferred, the fate of Panama was sealed. The public and Congress had no real knowledge of the Panama plan. Commission after commission had indorsed Nicaragua, but as for Panama the only information available consisted of the statements of the Panama Co.'s counsel and officials. These statements, although truthful and precise, had not and could not have the weight a committee report possesses.

(f) *Our plan to prevent a vote favorable to Nicaragua in the House.*

How to prevent a vote thus became a vital question—decisive of the fate of the Panama Canal.

In this desperate position we conceived the plan of obtaining the appointment of a new canal commission, for the examination of the Panama route as well as of all the other routes, which would prevent the United States from deciding in favor of Nicaragua before the presentation to Congress of an official report on Panama, with the certainty that we should be able to prove the superiority of Panama. This idea was met almost everywhere with energetic opposition; but Mr. Cromwell and his partners succeeded, by personal interviews and arguments, in convincing several important Members of the House—in particular its Speaker, Mr. Reed; the chairman of the Committee on Ways and Means, Mr. Cannon, who was also leader of the Republican Party in the House; and the chairman of the Committee on Rivers and Harbors, Mr. Burton—of the wisdom, the justice, and the advantages of this plan.

Their influence in a matter of this kind was great, not alone on account of the general confidence these Members inspired but because of their position and their great power under the rules of parliamentary procedure of the House.

The Speaker of the House was a man of remarkable strength of character. Fortunately, Mr. Curtis, who came from the same State as the Speaker, enjoyed his confidence, and he gave Mr. Curtis the opportunity to present the matter to him in all its details and its every aspect.

As a result of these interviews, the Speaker of the House acquired the conviction that the proposed plan was in keeping with the best interests of the United States, that it was right to follow it under these circumstances, and he lent his great influence to this end.

Similar personal statemens were also made to Mr. Cannon and Mr. Burton, and both came to the same conclusion after a careful study of the matter. However, it is well to state that none of these prominent men (personages) was asked to come to a final decision as to the respective merits of the routes, this not being the object of our proposition, which simply aimed at Congress putting off any decision until after the examination of the various routes.

(g) A vote on the Nicaragua bill is prevented in the House.

As a result of the support we gave to this plan, the efforts of the Nicaragua party to reach a vote on its bill failed, and this party, seeing itself incapable, despite its efforts to bring its bill to a vote, sought some other means of attaining its end. It discovered a way, which was by amendment of the rivers and harbors bill. This bill had the advantage of having been passed by the House and was then pending before the Senate, and its (final) passage as a necessary Government measure was certain.

(h) Each phase of all these developments was followed by us daily, and we constantly studied and discussed the means of opposing the attempt to incorporate the Nicaragua bill in the rivers and harbors bill—How this attempt at first succeeded; how it was finally defeated.

It is well to state that the rivers and harbors bill is a bill under which funds are appropriated for the improvement of rivers and harbors throughout the United States, and that, in consequence, nearly all parts of the country are interested in its provisions; so all the Members of Congress are highly anxious that this bill shall not fail of passage, as their respective constituencies are directly interested in it.

This bill being then before the Committee on Commerce of the Senate, Senator Morgan obtained the passage in committee of an amendment to this bill, containing almost word for word the pending Nicaragua bill, with an appropriation of $10,000,000 to begin the building of the Nicaragua Canal. The amendment was passed in the Senate by 50 votes for to 3 against February 25, 1899, just a few days before the end of the session. All that was then needed to make this bill a law, and thus irrevocably pledge the Unnited States to the building of the Nicaragua Canal, was the concurrence of the House in this amendment. The struggle then focused on the question of assent.

Needless to say that this clever move of the Nicaragua party, which seemed to assure the triumph of its cause, was a complete surprise, caused us the deepest anxiety, and nerved us to make a supreme effort. An irresistible current was carrying Nicaragua to victory, seemingly without an obstacle in its path, and without a thought of the cause of Panama. Fortunately, and thanks to our constant watchfulness, the amendment was known to us as soon as it was introduced in committee.

(i) We conceive the plan of making a conditional proposal to the United States, we obtain a public hearing on this matter before the Committee on Rivers and Harbors, and we thus prevent action in the Nicaragua matter.

At this critical moment we conceived the plan to have the Panama Canal Co. make a proposal, assuring to the United States representation in the company and the opportunity of acquiring such interest as it might wish in the canal property, and to this end to offer to reincorporate the Panama Canal Co. in one of the States of the United States, without, however, obliging the United States to make a pecuniary investment in this undertaking unless it decided so to do, and also to carry this proposal immediately and officially before the Committee on Rivers and Harbors, in whose bill the Nicaragua amendment had just been inserted in the Senate, and to back up this proposal by a public hearing.

We presented this plan to the director general of the canal company, who had arrived from Paris only a few days previously, and we obtained his consent to it. This took place on the 26th and 27th of February, immediately after the passage in the Senate of the Nicaragua amendment to the rivers and harbors bill.

Messrs. Cromwell and Curtis at once had an interview with the chairman of the Committee on Rivers and Harbors, Mr. Burton, and submitted this proposal to him in writing, signed by the director general and by ourselves as general counsel, and he granted a hearing, which took place immediately before the Committee on Rivers and Harbors in the last days of the session. At this hearing the proposal was officially submitted and an oral statement made by Mr. Cromwell. A copy of this important proposal (Feb. 27, 1899) was addressed and handed to Mr. Burton, chairman of the Committee on Rivers and Harbors, and copies were at once sent to the President of the United States and the Secretary of State.

This proposal, backed up by the public hearing before the Committee on Rivers and Harbors, officially gave the United States the opportunity of participating in the Panama Canal if it so desired after an examination of this route. The United States now had a choice of routes for the canal, and this imposed upon Congress the duty of studying and deciding.

(*j*) *We obtain the passage of a bill appointing a new commission to examine the Panama route and report thereon, as also on the other canal routes (Mar. 3, 1899), and by this means we prevent the final passage of the Nicaragua bills.*

This proposal of February 27 had a considerable effect. It afforded sufficient grounds to enable members of the House to insist on an investigation of the two projects by a new commission, and suggested the possibility of the United States obtaining an interest in the undertaking.

Under the rules of Congress, when a bill has been passed in one House and amended in the other it is customary for each House to at first maintain its original position, and then the bill is sent to a conference committee composed of three members of each House, named in the House by the Speaker (then Mr. Reed) and in the Senate by the President of that body. The report of this committee is almost always adopted by the two Houses.

This is what occurred in the present instance, and a conference committee was named in each House. Thus, when the rivers and harbors bill (containing the Nicaragua amendment) was submitted to this conference, the final fate of Panama was at stake. If the conferees retained the Nicaragua amendment, the two Houses of Congress would certainly adopt their report, the United States would be pledged to Nicaragua, and the Panama Co. ruined. The supporters of Nicaragua were confident and even joyful. They were sure of favorable action by the conferees.

The main difference between the two Houses over the bill was in regard to the canal amendment—the House conferees proposing, at our earnest request, the substitution of a clause for the appointment of a new commission to report on all the canal routes and appropriating funds for this purpose. The Senate conferees insisted for a long time on the Nicaragua amendment. The closure of Congress was imminent, and there were only a few hours left for action. If the House conferees stood pat the entire bill, including the Nicaragua amendment, would fail of passage at this session, unless the Senate conferees yielded. The House conferees, led by Mr. Burton, chairman of the Committee on Rivers and Harbors, remained unshaken in their determination to force the substitution of their amendment for the Nicaragua amendment: the Senate conferees (not daring to wreck the whole rivers and harbors bill, which appropriated many millions of dollars) finally yielded, and in the last hours of Congress the substituted amendment became law, to the consternation and great astonishment of the Nicaragua party, all of whose bills failed of passage before the closure of Congress (Mar. 3, 1899). Thus the imminent disaster was avoided, and the investigation of the Panama Canal assured.

The consequences of this victory can not be computed, as it was a question of life and death for the Panama Co. The success thus obtained in face of the hostility to Panama and of the powerful support of Nicaragua by the President and Secretary of State, the great majority of the two Houses of Congress, the press and the public, as an American canal, enabled us not only to prevent the passage of the Nicaragua bills, but to obtain the appointment of a commission with ample means to make an investigation of the two projects at which the Panama Co. could prove the advantages of its route and of its plan, and in this manner bring these advantages to the notice (knowledge) of the Government and people of the United States in an official manner which could not be disregarded.

We think that we are justified in stating that without our efforts the new commission would not have been created, and that the Nicaragua bill would in that case have been passed.

Having informed the company of this success, we had the pleasure to receive from it the following cablegram.[1]

MARCH 3—AUGUST 5, 1899—APPOINTMENT OF THE COMMISSION—STEPS TAKEN TO MAKE KNOWN THE PANAMA CANAL PLANS.

The passage of the law of March 3, 1899, whereby a new commission to study all the routes, including Panama, was created, entirely changed the situation, and gave us the opportunity for which we had struggled. For the first time examination by the United States of the case for Panama was assured. At once, on March 11, we advised an official communication to the President of the United States confirming the assurances previously given by the company, including the proposal of February 27, 1899, and offering every facility for investigation of the Panama route, etc. We drew up this communication, which the director general approved and signed with us.

Our first consideration was the composition of the commission itself, the appointment of which had been left to the President himself by law. We made an investigation and study of the engineers in the United States whose candidacy was possible, and we prepared a list from which we judged the President might well make a selection in case he should call upon us for suggestions. We went to Washington and had interviews with Secretary Hay and President McKinley, to whom we declared that our only desire was to obtain an impartial commission. We refused to propose the appointment of anyone, but at the President's request we furnished him the list of prominent engineers which we had prepared. Later, when the commission was appointed, it was seen that most of the engineers, members of the commission, were included in the list thus furnished. The commission appointed by the President on June 9 was composed of the following men: Admiral John G. Walker, Mr. Samuel Pasco, Mr. Alfred Noble, Mr. George S. Morison, Col. O. H. Ernst, Prof. Lewis R. Haupt, and Prof. Emory R. Johnson.

The commission and the report it was to make became the next field of contention. We understood that even if the report of this commission favored Panama, it would be (as events proved) a tremendous undertaking to make the findings of the commission prevail against the great strength of the Nicaragua cause in Congress, supported by the favor and prejudice of the public, and backed by the power of those who were actively interested in its success. If, however, the report was favorable to Nicaragua, the struggle would be ended; there would not remain the faintest hope of saving the Panama Co. from ruin. Besides, the commission contained three men, one of them its chairman, who had composed the Nicaragua Commission of 1897, and who had recently made a report indorsing the Nicaragua plan—Admiral Walker, Col. Hains, and Prof. Haupt. The latter, in fact, even before his appointment, had publicly declared that nothing could change his preference for Nicaragua. It was generally known that he had been appointed member of the Nicaragua Commission at the instance of the Maritime Co. It was therefore essential not only to convince the commission of the superiority of Panama, but to convince three of its members in spite of their previous opinions and official reports.

Fully recognizing the great advantages which had been obtained by this (the present) defeat of the Nicaragua forces and the passage of the act of March 3, 1899, creating a commission, Mr. Cromwell laid aside all his other business and during the six months following devoted himself exclusively to the official presentation of the Panama matter to the commission so as to convince it of the superiority of this route and of the advantages of having (there were for) the United States (to) adopt the Panama route, or encourage, in some form,

[1] Cable not printed.—H. N. H.

the building of the canal (construction) under its auspices. We judged it of the highest importance that the commission (although three of its members had previously made a report favorable to the Nicaragua route) should treat the Panama project as the controlling and important subject of its investigation. Our first aim was therefore to bring the commission to examine first of all the affairs of the Panama Canal in Paris, where Panama would be the only subject under discussion, instead of beginning by going to the Isthmus, where Panama and Nicaragua would be discussed together and at the same time.

From the very first it was the intention of the commission to begin its work by making a stay on the Isthmus for the purpose of physical study, and that afterwards some of its members should visit Paris, if that were necessary; and that the maps, plans, archives, and information of the Panama Co. which the commission might deem useful should be brought to Washington to be examined there, or if that were not practical that a committee of the commission should go to Paris to make a supplementary investigation, if such investigation were then considered necessary. However, we urged the commission to go in a body to Paris, there to begin its labors. In order to influence its decision, we promised and undertook to have appear before the commission (as was done later) the principal Russian, German, English, and other members of the International Technical Committee, who could not be asked to come to the United States, but who would appear in Paris together with the eminent French engineers. The commission agreed to this plan, and conveyed to us its decision to this effect. We fully advised the company by cable and by letter on this matter in view of the approaching stay of the commission (in Paris), and Mr. Cromwell sailed for Paris on August 5, ahead of the commission, in order to prepare and direct the presentation to be made.

The wisdom of our plan was immediately recognized and approved by the company, and our pledges to the commission were kept by it.

AUGUST–SEPTEMBER, 1899—STAY IN PARIS WITH THE COMMISSION AND APPEARANCE BEFORE IT.

Mr. Cromwell devoted himself to the preparation of the company's case. This necessitated an assiduous study of the history of the company's plans and of its work on the Isthmus, to enable Mr. Cromwell to assist in the presentation of the facts to the commission.

Mr. Cromwell explained, in all their details, to the directors of the company the principal points in doubt and discussion, as he had noted them in his interviews with the commission and from his knowledge of the criticism uttered and questions raised in the course of parliamentary debate and public discussion in the United States. He suggested the basis and general plan of the presentation to be made by the highly efficient engineers of the company, and everything was got in readiness for the arrival of the commission, which took place about the middle of August. The presentation which followed took up five whole weeks; one and sometimes two meetings a day were held. The hearings were conducted with very formal and elaborate procedure, and in the most impressive manner, as before a court of highest jurisdiction, through an interpreter, as some did not understand the language of the others. All the aspects of the technical and engineering questions of Panama were fully and efficiently explained by the engineers of the company and of the International Technical Committee.

Mr. Cromwell was in attendance every day during this time as counsel for the company. Both before and after the sittings of the commission he had interviews and was in frequent communication with the members of the commission, in order to elucidate questions which suggested themselves to them.

The commission left Paris officially about the middle of September.

In the course of the presentation to the Isthmian Canal Commission, and aside from the technical and engineering aspects of the matter, there arose a subject of which we are now going to make mention, and which was of great importance in the subsequent history of the case.

The act of March 3, 1899 (that is to say, articles 3, 4, 5, and 6 of the rivers and harbors bill), besides the authority it conferred on the President to appoint a commission instructed to investigate and report on the various projects, their execution, and probable cost, and their rights, concessions, etc., and the cost of acquiring the same, stated as follows:

"And in general the President is authorized to make a full and complete inquiry for the purpose of ascertaining which is the best and most practical route for a canal across the Isthmus, as well as the cost of its construction and establishment under the control, management, and ownership of the United States."

The President, on the opinion of the Attorney General of the United States (head of the Department of Justice and Attorney General), adopted an interpretation of this act to the effect that the recommendations of the commission should show not only the technical aspects of the plan but the possibility of the United States acquiring the "control, management, and ownership" of the canal (project).

In accordance with these instructions, Admiral Walker, chairman of the commission, in the course of the presentation officially addressed the following question to the company:

"On what terms (conditions de prix) and by what means could the United States become the purchaser of the Panama Canal?"

The company replied virtually that it was not possible to give a definite answer at that time. The chairman of the commission said that he acknowledged the matter would call for consideration, but that he had broached the subject officially at this time because of instructions from the President.

At the request of the directors, Mr. Cromwell remained in Paris several weeks longer and held absorbing daily conferences with Mr. Bonnardel, the president, and the executive committee on the general business of the company, including its financial situation, its future, and its general plans; on the subject of the formation of syndicates; on the offer of sale that the United States had invited the company to make; on the possibility of obtaining the capital necessary for the continuation of the work from English, German, American, or other sources; and on the various eventualities that had to be faced in connection with the report of the Isthmian Canal Commission, whether favorable or unfavorable.

AUGUST–DECEMBER, 1899—THE PLAN FOR THE AMERICANIZATION OF THE CANAL IS ADOPTED; THE BOARD OF DIRECTORS RESIGNS AS A RESULT OF THE ENSUING SITUATION.

One feature of the campaign we had planned was the Americanization of the canal, an idea of our own, which had been incorporated in the proposal of February 27, 1899, and which so greatly influenced the Committee on Rivers and Harbors, and the passage of the law creating the Isthmian Canal Commission. Besides the moral obligations which this proposal had entailed, the events that followed added further to our conviction that it was of the highest importance to the shareholders of the new company, to the receiver of the old company, and to all those interested that the canal should take on an American character by the formation of an American company, with an important group of American stockholders, all the while maintaining the control by La Compagnie Nouvelle du Canal de Panama. The Maritime Canal Co. derived immense advantages from the fact that it was an American corporation, that men of high standing in the financial and political world in the United States and who were citizens of America had a direct personal interest in its fate and lent it the weight of their influence and activity. On the other hand, La Compagnie Nouvelle du Canal de Panama was without support of this kind except from us. Not a citizen of the United States had the least pecuniary interest in the success of the Panama Co., which, being French, was looked upon almost with hostility as a foreign enemy of an American enterprise. The idea obtained, as a matter of fact, in the United States that the new company was only the old de Lesseps company reorganized under a new name, but in reality directed by the same unworthy interests.

To change this situation, to Americanize the Panama Canal, to have it represented by an American company, and to give American citizens some direct pecuniary interest in its success (even if this interest were comparatively small), would change, according to our advice to the company, the nature of the conflict and might eventually decide the result. Furthermore, as the Panama Canal was being built under concessions granted by Colombia, which, according to our contention, were covered and protected by the treaty of 1846 between the United States and Colombia (article 35), there was a special reason for giving the undertaking an American aspect, even if its control was to be retained in France.

At that time we had no illusions about the situation, and we did not allow the company to have any, at least if full information and serious advice could attain that result. We knew that, whereas an unfavorable report of the Isthmian Canal Commission would be fatal to the Panama Canal, even a favorable report might not prevail against the national feeling of sympathy for and the enormous influence of the financial interests directly involved in the Nicaragua Canal. Our plan for the Americanization of the canal was to make use of these two powerful factors of strength and, while leaving to the French company the control of the Panama Canal, to give an American character to the undertaking and to array on its side men and interests in the United States who would defeat those already interested in the success of the Nicaragua Canal.

The company had made known to us the amount needed to finish the canal and had warned us that it would be necessary to raise capital amounting to at least 750,000,000 francs. The company took up the question of raising this capital with Mr. Cromwell in Paris. The result depended not only on the report of the Isthmian Canal Commission and on the future action of the United States as to the selection of a route, but also on the confidence of the financial world; and there (in that world) the attitude and policy of the United States furnished the most important and controlling factor, even if the United States did not select and build a canal of its own, for this country was the nearest to the Isthmus. The most interested in a canal, materially and politically, it would be the one to contribute most commercially to is revenues, and the United States was the nation on which the canal would have to depend most for protection.

Whereas if, on the other hand, the United States selected and built another canal of its own, not only would these considerations disappear, but the canal would be exploited in the interest and for the defense of the Nation without regard to profit. No private canal could live an hour under such conditions.

During this stay, August–October, 1899, that was the constant subject of consideration by the directors and Mr. Cromwell, and after deep study and continuous discussion of all the phases of the question, the board, on October 19, 1899, unanimously approved of the plan and gave us full power to carry it out. This was, of course, subject to the approval by the board of the final details and to the regular approval by the shareholders of the company. The plan provided for the organization of a company under the laws of the State of New Jersey, to which the property of La Compagnie Nouvelle du Canal de Panama would be transferred in exchange for a large majority of the shares of the American company, and to which $5,000,000 cash would be subscribed in America.

Immediately on his return, November 1, 1899, Mr. Cromwell applied himself to this new task, so important in its influence on the future of the company. It is difficult, even for one who recalls all the events of the years that have elapsed since the company was first formed, to appreciate how stupendous was this task. To interest important capitalists in the United States in such an enterprise was an undertaking so arduous as to seem really impossible. The difficulty was increased by the financial panic which, toward the end of the year 1899, shook the money market in the United States to such an extent that capitalists were opposed to the idea of any new investment. Nevertheless, we took up this matter immediately and devoted to it nearly all the remainder of the year. In this matter our connections with the most powerful financiers in the United States played so important a part that but for this factor such a result could not have been obtained. By constant and continuous labor lasting several weeks many important financial groups in this country were sounded by us and brought into association with this undertaking, subject in every case to the ratification of the board and of the shareholders. It suffices to say that we obtained assurances and adhesions which would have assured the carrying out of the plan had it been so ratified, as we informed the company prior to the annual meeting. All the preliminary steps to bring the plan to a successful issue were taken upon the condition that this approval should be given. Mr. Mancini, agent of the company at Bogota, frequently urged that the company should be Americanized so as to protect it against the exactions of Colombia..

Some shareholders in the exercise of the rights the law gave them, were of opinion that it was not to their interest to authorize the transaction, which, therefore, was not carried out.

The board of directors, however, looking upon this transaction as an essential part of their administrative plans, thereupon immediately resigned in a body. After a brief interval a new election of directors was held, on February 12, 1899, at which the present board was elected.

SESSION OF DECEMBER, 1899, TO JUNE, 1900.

While we were conducting these affairs in Paris, we were also making our preparation in the United States for the reassembling of Congress, in December, 1900 (1899?—H. N. H.), as the parliamentary struggle was to be renewed at this session. Two of our partners were constantly occupied with this work and traveled continuously between New York and Washington, carrying on the work of argument, enlightenment, and publicity, conferring with public men, and calling the attention of Members of Congress and other influential people to the advantages of the Panama route.

The Isthmian Canal Commission was also in Washington, and we were in constant and personal communication with various members of this body, now so important, adding to their information, furnishing documents called for by them, overcoming their hesitations, answering their questions, etc. They were getting ready to go to the Isthmus to complete their labors by a personal inspection of the routes—Panama, Nicaragua, Darien, Tehuantepec, and others. During the intervening time they had sent exploration parties on ahead of them, and in January following (1901) (surely 1900.—H. N. H.) the commission itself left to make its personal inspection and investigation of all these routes. We were almost constantly with one or other of the members up to their departure, and we were busy affording them every facility for their inspection as far as Panama was concerned. Their subsequent report we shall discuss in due course.

(a) *Efforts made by the supporters of Nicaragua to have their bill passed without waiting for the report of the commission, and their defeat.*

Congress met again in December, 1899; this was the first, the "long," session of the Fifty-seventh Congress. Every consideration of decency and public duty naturally forbade any action whatever, or even any plan of action, on the part of Congress before the presentation of the report of the canal commission, whose investigation and report now became fundamental for any legislation.

But, casting aside precedent and conventionality, the Nicaragua party defiantly affected to ignore the commission, or treated its coming report in advance as being undoubtedly favorable to the Nicaragua plan, and began to insist more vigorously than ever on the passage of the Nicaragua bills. Their defeat in the previous legislature, by the creation of a new commission, had embittered them; and they were also beginning to recognize our growing strength and the fact that we were making Panama a powerful rival for public favor.

Mr. Morgan immediately introduced the Nicaragua bill in the Senate, Mr. Hepburn introduced it in the House, and the partisans of Nicaragua rallied for aggressive action, just as in the preceding sessions, this time completely discarding the pending investigation of the Panama route by the Isthmian Canal Commission.

Besides, the Governments of Nicaragua and Costa Rica kept up a constant agitation through diplomatic channels and by the open activity of their ministers in Washington, which had its effect and was entirely legitimate, in order to bring about the adoption of the Nicaragua route by the United States, and to this end offered (to grant) all the rights and all the concessions asked for.

The situation was critical and dangerous to the cause of Panama. Mr. Cromwell and Mr. Curtis, as before, spent most of their time in Washington conferring with many Members of Congress and officials, insisting with the greatest possible force that no action should be taken either by Congress through legislation or by the Department of State concluding a treaty with Nicaragua or Costa Rica. Few Members of Congress, however, could be brought to offer open opposition to the Nicaragua bills.

Public opinion favored Nicaragua, even if the commission in its report declared the Panama plan feasible and practical, a finding which was generally looked upon as impossible. It was pointed out that the Nicaragua Canal had on several occasions been declared feasible and practical; that its cost had been estimated, and that Nicaragua and Costa Rica offered all the necessary treaties and concessions, and that the people of the United States favored Nicaragua, whatever might be the possible advantages of Panama.

It was also pointed out that the Panama Canal Co. had given no assurances whatsoever that even if this route were desired by the United States it could be acquired from the Panama Co., whereas on the other hand Nicaragua and

Costa Rica offered everything that was desired, and that in consequence there was no need to wait for an official report of the commission. Although the Members of Congress had no conviction based upon a thorough knowledge of the two projects, they were nevertheless pledged by their previous votes in favor of Nicaragua.

But the situation had to be faced, and we applied ourselves to the new difficulty with all our power. We employed every argument and every resource to bring about a delay until after the filing of the report of the Isthmian Canal Commission.

In order to help delay all action, we judged it necessary that every Member of Congress should be officially acquainted with all the different documents and statements which we had sent at various times to the President. So we obtained the introduction in the Senate of a resolution by which the President was asked to transmit these documents to the Senate. The resolution was passed, and the documents were transmitted in due form, and by order of the Senate printed. It is needless to say that these documents were read by the Senators and that they had an important effect. On account of the discussion of the preceding year on the subject of the exclusive control of the canal and of Great Britain's protest, based on the clauses of the Clayton-Bulwer treaty, Secretary Hay had negotiated the first Hay-Pauncefote treaty during the parliamentary recess, and this treaty was forwarded to the Senate by the President in January.

The fortification of the proposed canal was at this time a primordial question; we pointed out to some Senators the bearing of this subject upon the existing treaty with Great Britain, and laid stress on the fact that the canal had to be neutral. These questions were debated in the Senate during the discussion of this matter in its bearing upon the Hay-Pauncefote treaty. We had very closely studied the subject of a neutral canal. We obtained and made a critical study of the international correspondence and conventions, thanks to which the Suez Canal had been neutralized, and we also examined and weighed carefully the views of writers on international law bearing upon this subject; we retained and had several consultations with Prof. Woolsey, the eminent author of works on international law, professor at Yale University, and obtained from him a formal professional opinion, of which we made use in support of the arguments we were putting forward among the Senators who recognized in him an eminent authority on this subject. We made the most of these points in order to help delay any action on the Nicaragua bill.

The partisans of Nicaragua began their move in the House, where they had certain parliamentary advantages, and directed all their efforts to obtaining a vote on their bill. There again we used the arguments we have just mentioned, and to this end devoted days, and often evenings, to interviews with Members.

About this time, the director general and secretary general of the company arrived here to follow the events. We made detailed reports to them, and they were kept informed day by day.

On April 13, Senator Morgan introduced a resolution in the Senate providing for the consideration of his bill despite the absence of a report by the commission, and we immediately had interviews with Senators and opposed this action. Thanks to the pending treaty, this resolution was tabled. Stopped on this side, the Nicaragua party returned to the House, under the leadership of Mr. Hepburn, and on April 16 obtained the signatures of more than 150 Members to a petition in favor of the bill urging the Speaker (then Mr. Henderson) to do everything in his power to facilitate its passage by placing it on the calendar. This move was opposed with our assistance, and despite considerable support, Mr. Hepburn again failed in his effort to bring about this vote.

At this time the press was full of false and malicious stories about the Panama Canal, disseminated by the adherents of Nicaragua; and particularly of alleged accounts of a proposed consolidation between Panama and the Nicaragua interests.

This was prejudicial, naturally, and on April 28 we caused the publication of a statement to the public reestablishing the facts and denying (containing rectifications and denials on the subject of) these stories, and protesting against any action on the part of Congress before the receipt of the commission's report. We succeeded in obtaining fairly wide publicity for this statement, but its effect was felt more among the public than in Congress, and the great majority was too much bound up with Nicaragua to have an open mind on this matter. On April 30, we sent the President an official protest to the same effect, requesting him to communicate its text to Congress, and we also filed a formal denial of the false stories with the Secretary of State.

These communications were transmitted by the President to the Senate committee, and there obtained the publicity we desired to secure for them.

On April 3, 1900, the Isthmian Canal Commission returned from the Isthmus, where it had left a numerous staff charged with carrying on the special study of the two plans. But it was not ready to formulate final conclusions and make its report.

(*b*) *May 2, 1900–June 7, 1900, the House passes the Nicaragua bill almost unanimously without waiting for the report of the commission. Fight against this bill in the Senate and its defeat there.*

However, the Nicaragua bill at last took its turn on the calendar of the House and was passed May 2, 1900 (as had been recognized to be inevitable if it should reach a vote), almost unanimously—that is to say, by 234 votes for to 36 against.

Nothing could show more conclusively than this ballot and the passage of the bill the popular strength of the Nicaragua Canal project and the difficulties of our case, especially in view of the conditions then existing. The bill was sent to the Senate, where Senator Morgan at once took hold of it, and insisted on obtaining action similar to that of the House. The struggle was thus transferred to the upper House, and we continued to urge upon the Members all possible arguments, above all the irregularity and injustice of any legislation prior to the receipt of the report of the Isthmian Canal Commission and action on the pending Hay-Pauncefote treaty.

In order to overcome the first of these objections, Senator Morgan, the able and resourceful leader of the Nicaraguan party and chairman of the Senate Committee on the Nicaraguan Canal (the committee whose regular duty it was to pass on the House bill), summoned before him Admiral Walker and other members of the commission who had previously reported in favor of Nicaragua, with a view to obtaining from them statements which might be used in the Senate debates as preliminary information about the findings of the commission. Our representatives were present at these hearings and followed them closely, studying every day the testimony taken, preparing arguments, and taking steps to answer them or to explain the facts more advantageously.

Immediately afterwards the Senate Committee on Nicaragua, through its chairman, Mr. Morgan (May 14, 1900), reported the bill favorably to the Senate. Senator Morgan then made the formal motion for the immediate discussion of this bill. This session of Congress, which closed June 7, 1900, was drawing to an end. Every day of delay was of great help to the cause of Panama. If the Nicaragua bill should not manage to receive immediate consideration, the situation in the Senate was such that it would not be passed. But if, on the other hand, Senator Morgan's motion for immediate discussion was carried, it was certain in advance, in view of the state of mind of Congress, that the bill would be passed and promulgated as law. So this motion became the last question of that session, and once more the fate of the Panama Canal Co. hung in the balance. One at least of our partners was busy with the matter night and day for several weeks conferring with Senators and members of the commission, preparing arguments and giving them publicity, and pleading insistently for the defeat of the bill passed by the House. Without going into details, we merely note the fact that Senator Morgan's motion was put to a vote on May 14, 1900, and defeated by a small majority of 7 votes—28 nays, 21 ayes.

Having so nearly succeeded and understanding that unless the Senate reversed its action and took up the bill, it would not be passed, the supporters of Nicaragua, headed by Senator Morgan, filled the press of the country with their furious protests and complaints against the refusal of the Senate to act upon the bill, and they publicly attributed this attitude to the influence of Panama. They aroused the whole country. Telegrams poured in upon Members of the Senate; commercial bodies throughout the land passed resolutions, which they sent to the Senate, in which the immediate passage of the Nicaragua bill was urgently demanded; and the press of the country in general severely criticized the action of the Senate in refusing to consider the bill, demanded its passage, and attacked the cause of Panama and its supporters for their opposition to the measure.

Supported by this expression of popular feeling, and in order to overcome the objections based on the terms of the Clayton-Bulwer treaty, Senator Morgan introduced in the Senate June 4, 1900, a resolution passed by his committee, declaring the Clayton-Bulwer treaty abrogated. In the hurry of the last hours of the legislature, he was unable to obtain a reconsideration of this matter, and recognizing this (fact) to be inevitable he cleverly led the Senate to decide on prompt action at its next session by introducing in the Senate and having it pass a resolution definitely fixing the consideration of the bill for the second Monday in December, 1900.

The adjournment of Congress took place three days later. Thus ended this memorable session.

During all this time Mr. Cromwell and Mr. Curtis with other partners of our law firm spent nearly all their time in Washington and devoted themselves to this matter. It is probable that it had never been in so critical a position; only the most extreme watchfulness, the most direct attention, a cerain skill, and some resourcefulness were able to prevent the passage of the Nicaragua bill, and we make the assertion that but for our labors and our action it would have been passed as a law.

But a grave peril still hung over the situation. At the coming session which was to begin in December, the Nicaragua bill which had already been passed in the House and was awaiting its turn on the Senate Calendar, with a favorable report from the Committee on the Nicaragua Canal, would occupy one of the first places on the senatorial calendar, and we had to make the most thorough preparations to oppose it.

PRESIDENTIAL ELECTION OF 1900—WE PREVENT THE TRADITIONAL INDORSEMENT OF THE NICARAGUA ROUTE AS A PLANK IN THE PLATFORM OF THE REPUBLICAN PARTY, AND WE PROCURE THE SUBSTITUTION OF THE WORDS "AN ISTHMIAN CANAL."

The year 1900 was that of the presidential election, during which the two great parties were to publish their declarations of principles ("platforms"). The Republican platform of 1896 had formally declared, as we have already mentioned, that this party favored the Nicaragua Canal, which declaration had been of enormous value to the Nicaragua faction in Congress; this faction made continual use of this plank as having the value of an injunction addressed by the party to the Republican Members of the legislative bodies. A similar plank in the Republican platform of 1900 would naturally greatly strengthen the cause of Nicaragua and add weight to the efforts of its supporters, especially in view of their plan to obtain a similar indorsement in the platform of the Democratic Party, wherein they were successful.

So we occupied ourselves with this important matter, and had personal interviews with the chairman and vice chairman of the platform committee of the Republican convention, who were personally known to us, as well as with other party leaders. We pointed out to them that the canal matter was a national measure and ought not to be dealt with as a party measure, and that, in view of the law of March 3, 1899, and the unfinished investigation of the commission, the Republican Party ought not to again pledge itself to the cause of Nicaragua to the exclusion of Panama, but ought to mention the matter in neutral terms—for instance, the "Isthmian" Canal. Our conferences, our correspondence, and the steps we took in this matter lasted over a period of six weeks, almost without interruption.

The convention met, and in the first draft of its platform the old formula in favor of the Nicaragua project was used. We renewed with insistence our arguments and objections, and the justice of our views was at last recognized; the platform was changed and the words "an Isthmian Canal" were substituted for the words "the Nicaragua Canal," which for so many years had been used in the party platforms. It was on the strength of this platform, containing this neutral disposition, that the Republican Party went through the election campaign, and in November following secured the election of President McKinley and Vice President Roosevelt.

This was an important step in our fight, since it freed the Republican Members of Congress from a party pledge and was the first occasion on which it was publicly recognized that a canal other than that of Nicaragua was possible.

We derived great advantage from this circumstance throughout the country and in every direction during the ensuing campaign by giving it the widest publicity in congressional circles. This modification was assailed by the Nicaraguan press of the country as constituting a desertion of that cause by the Republican Party, and as being due to the strategy of the Panama party.

1900—THE SITUATION DURING THE AUTUMN OF 1900—MR. CROMWELL'S STAY IN PARIS IN AUGUST AND SEPTEMBER, 1900.

The canal matter had developed, and at this moment four important matters simultaneously demanded our attention:

(I) The findings and report of the Isthmian Canal Commission.

(II) The bills and legislation in Congress bearing on the canal.

(III) The attitude of the company toward an absolute cession to the United States, in accordance with the request of the commission.

(IV) The attitude of Colombia toward such a cession.

We drew up a general plan of campaign, which was to be carried out during the summer, preparatory to the next session of Congress, and then Mr. Cromwell made a stay in Paris at the request of the company, in order to confer with the representatives of the latter during the months of August and September, 1900. During his absence we continued the Panama campaign by means of numerous interviews with members of Congress and of the administration, the circulation of pamphlets the effect of which would be favorable to Panama, and other useful methods.

During his stay in Paris Mr. Cromwell had almost daily conferences with the directors and managers of the company, studying and conferring with them on all the aspects of the case, not only in the United States and Bogota, but also on the general policy of the company and its affairs in France. He presented and described in detail our activities in America, the situation of the affair, his plans for future activity, etc., and on every point he obtained the unreserved approbation and praise of the company.

It will be remembered that Admiral Walker had asked the company at the hearing in Paris, on September 7, 1899, to name a price for the sale of its property. By a letter to the company, written on April 10, in the year 1900, he renewed this question, and asked the company to state whether it was ready to sell its property and concessions, and if so, at what price. This question, which had become the intense and practical point of such highly important bearing upon the future of the canal, was discussed fully and in every one of its details during this stay by Mr. Cromwell with the board (of directors) and managers of the company and at their request.

Mr. Cromwell declared to the company that in his opinion the United States would own and build a canal in Nicaragua if they could not acquire a title of absolute ownership in Panama, and that the construction of such a canal by the United States would, in his opinion, render impossible the raising of sufficient capital to build a canal at Panama, however great the superiority of that project.

The company, however, was not ready at that time to come to a definite decision to sell its property to the United States, as was suggested to it. After passing all these matters in review, Mr. Cromwell returned to the United States and at once took up the matters in hand.

He was thus engaged with the directors and managers during the months of August and September, 1900.

NOVEMBER–DECEMBER, 1900—NEGOTIATIONS WITH THE COMMISSION IN NOVEMBER AND DECEMBER, 1900.

At the approach of the session of Congress (which met again the first Monday in December, 1900), the supporters of Nicaragua rallied their forces to again make determined efforts in every direction. In brief, the situation was as follows:

1. The Isthmian Canal Commission was waiting for the reply of the canal company to its request, renewed April 10, 1900, for a statement as to the terms of sale.

2. The Isthmian Canal Commission was preparing to make its preliminary report (filed later, Nov. 30, 1900), the findings of which were not yet known.

3. The Government of the United States was negotiating a new form of convention with Nicaragua and Costa Rica in reference to the Nicaragua project.

4. The Nicaragua party was preparing to hasten action on its Nicaragua bills, discussion of which had been fixed for the second Monday in December, at the preceding session of Congress.

The president of the canal company came back to the United States from Paris with Mr. Cromwell in October. We made detailed reports to him upon the situation as it existed, and informed him, as a result of interviews with the chairman and other members of the commission, that a reply to the letter of the commission of April 10, 1900, must be made before its report was completed, and that this reply would have a great influence upon the findings of the commission. During the two weeks of his stay two or more of our partners conferred almost daily with the president, informing him as to the various questions pending, the coming report of the commission, and the entire situation, which he acknowledged to be very grave.

In consequence the president returned to Paris to deliberate. Meanwhile we followed the matter closely, giving uninterrupted attention to its various aspects by visits to Washington, conferences with the chairman of the commission, investigations, etc.

The president of the company came back to the United States about November 18, 1900, and informed us that the company was not inclined to make an offer of absolute sale, but wished to adhere to the principle of the proposal of February 27, 1899. We learned that the commission would make its report a few days later, whereof we informed the president. Long and frequent discussions between him and ourselves followed. We assisted the president to draw up, in accordance with his instructions, the reply to the commission, delivered in Washington on November 26, 1900, by which the company made a proposal on the lines he had indicated, but which did not constitute an offer of absolute sale.

THE COMMISSION MAKES A PRELIMINARY REPORT IN FAVOR OF THE NICARAGUA PROJECT, BASED IN PART ON THE FACT THAT THE COMPANY HAD MADE NO OFFER ASSURING TO THE UNITED STATES THE CONTROL, MANAGEMENT, AND OWNERSHIP OF THE CANAL.

Four days later (Nov. 30, 1900) the commission signed and filed its preliminary report of that date, in which it declares itself in favor of Nicaragua. Its findings were based in part on the fact that the company had not made a definite proposal.

We studied this preliminary report in all its aspects, and frequently discussed its clauses with the president of the company; we analyzed and weighed the bases of the findings announced, wrote out commentaries on this subject, and had interviews with several members of the commission to determine with greater precision the bases of its findings on various points, so as to be able to attack them in due course.

The facts revealed by this preliminary report sustained to a great extent the superiority of the Panama route, but it was settled that a route was necessary which the United States could control, own, and manage, and the report stated that the company had made no definite offer.

THE GOVERNMENT OF THE UNITED STATES SIGNS PROTOCOLS WITH NICARAGUA AND COSTA RICA.

At the same time, December 1, 1900, the Secretary of State, Mr. Hay, concluded and signed protocols with the ministers of Nicaragua and Costa Rica, by which these Governments undertook to negotiate a treaty as soon as the President of the United States should be authorized by Congress to acquire the Nicaragua route; to enter into negotiations for fixing details of the plans and agreements which might be found necessary for its execution; and to stipulate as to the ownership and control of the proposed Nicaragua canal.

Naturally the Nicaragua party was delighted with the advantage these events had given it; that is to say, with the favorable report of the Isthmian Canal Commission, and the protocols between the Nicaragua, Costa Rica, and the United States insuring satisfactory treaty rights.

At this time we were constantly conferring with the members of the commission, of the Government, and with the president of the company.

It was a period full of anxiety and worry. What we had learned from all our sources of information forced upon us the conviction that if the company did not give Congress the assurance that it could acquire the Panama Canal on terms acceptable to it, the Nicaragua Canal would be chosen, and we laid these views before the president of the company. However, that was a matter which depended directly on the company, and over which we had no authority. To the best of our ability we faced the situation as it was, with all its difficulties both from without and from within.

THE SESSION OF DECEMBER, 1900, TO MARCH, 1901.

The situation thus created was in fact critical for the Panama company. The Nicaragua bill had been passed by the House, in the Senate its passage had barely been prevented, and its discussion could be demanded at will. The commission had made its preliminary report in favor of Nicaragua, protocols had been signed with Nicaragua and Costa Rica, and on the eve of the reassembling of Congress the press of the country, inspired by the Nicaragua party, was full of articles insistently demanding the construction of the Nicaragua Canal.

The Hay-Pauncefote treaty was ratified on December 20, 1900, but with modifications which could hardly be acceptable to Great Britain (which proved to be the case) and the delay for its ratification was finally to expire March 4, 1901.

We made every effort to delay action on the Nicaragua bill, urging that the Senate ought to wait for action on the part of England in respect to the Hay-Pauncefote treaty, and maintaining also that it would be improper to pass the Nicaragua bills which were diametrically opposed to the Clayton-Bulwer treaty which was in force. This was an argument we used to many Senators, and one that the Government was somewhat inclined to favor.

(*a*) *Uncertainty as to the titles and rights of the Nicaragua company.*

As part of the plan of campaign (strategy of the fight), we were continually devising new moves and new measures. It seemed advantageous to us at this critical time to create a diversion; to distract attention from the weaknesses of Panama; to take up the time and efforts of Nicaragua by placing it on the defensive instead of allowing it to take the offensive by publicly exposing the weaknesses of the Nicaragua company. We devoted ourselves to the investigation, study, and preparations incidental to making revelations on the subject of Nicaragua, and we wrote and circulated printed statements showing up the confusion which existed as to the title of the Nicaragua company, as far as its concessions were concerned, and the forfeiture which, according to Nicaragua, had taken place; its conflicts with that Government and the protests which the company had addressed to it on the subject of this declaration of forfeiture; its efforts to drag the United States into these controversies by invoking the assistance and intervention of the American Government; the rival concessions granted and the complications and controversies between the Nicaragua company and the new concessionaires, etc. We also studied and set forth the conditions under which the acquisition by Americans of lands along the proposed route of the Nicaragua Canal was going on, which lands the United States would later be forced to acquire, to the great profit of these individuals if this route were adopted.

Thanks to this investigation, we also discovered that Nicaragua had granted an exclusive concession to Sir William Forwood for the steam navigation of the San Juan River from Lake Nicaragua to the Atlantic Ocean, which concession only expires in 1920, and would place an obstacle in the way of the construction and operation of the Nicaraguan Canal by the United States, if it adopted this route.

We gave the widest publicity to these revelations, and had them sent generally to Senators and Congressmen as a further argument against the adoption of the Nicaraguan route. This argument had a very beneficial effect.

(*b*) *Efforts of the Nicaraguan party to obtain the passage of its bill by means of amendments to the sundry civil bill and to the rivers and harbors bill—Its defeat.*

During January vigorous efforts were made in the Senate and House to advance the Nicaraguan bills, the supporters of which made every effort to show that it was not necessary to await the action of England on the Hay-Pauncefote treaty; and a great majority of the newspapers of the whole country echoed this view.

We and our friends encouraged in every way action by the Republican Party in Congress with a view to deciding that there should be no legislation on the canal matter until after the ratification of the Hay-Pauncefote treaty. We had interviews with Senators, discussed the matter at length with them, and the party in question adopted this programme January 18, 1901.

Normally, this result would have sufficed to put off the question until after the final ratification of the Hay-Pauncefote treaty, but the supporters of Nicaragua would not accept this conclusion and succeeded (Feb. 20-26), by parliamentary maneuvers, in advancing the canal bill to a point where it might receive consideration by the Senate. Embarrassed, however, by the parliamentary situation which existed, the Nicaraguan party cleverly made a new move in order to get Congress to adopt Nicaragua. This was an amendment to the sundry civil appropriation bill, then pending before the Senate, authorizing the President to acquire from the Republics of Nicaragua and Costa Rica the route for the construction of the canal, and approprating public funds for the carrying out of this plan. This amendment was moved by Senator Morgan on February 11, 1901.

We pointed out to the members of the legislative committee that this amendment had nothing in common with the object of the bill, and that action on this important canal matter ought not to be taken in this roundabout manner.

The rivers and harbors bill, which had been passed by the House, was pending before the Senate, and Senator Morgan moved the same amendment to this bill, in order to insure its passage. We opposed ourselves in the same way to the rivers and harbors bill amendment, for the same reasons. This amendment was rejected.

The 4th of March arrived, date of the adjournment of Congress under the Constitution and of the inauguration of the new President (Mr. McKinley). Thanks to these various obstacles, to which we had actively contributed, the Nicaragua bills failed. Mr. Cromwell and Mr. Curtis had been constantly on the spot with one or more assistants.

The extra session of the Senate, which usually sits on the inauguration of a new President, only lasted five days, during which there was no attempt at general legislation. Senator Morgan, however, seized the opportunity to again move, March 5, his resolution for the abrogation of the Clayton-Bulwer treaty, and made a speech which lasted for part of three days; but no action was taken by the Senate. This guaranteed us against any legislative action before the following December, but no rest was possible.

1901.—WE INSISTENTLY ADVISE THE COMPANY TO MAKE AN OFFER OF ABSOLUTE SALE SO AS TO GET THE COMMISSION TO RECANT ITS PRELIMINARY REPORT.

Although the Isthmian Canal Commission had made a report in favor of the Nicaragua plan, facts cited in the report permitted us to allege that, taking into cosideration the respective advantages of the two plans, that of Panama had been proved to be the best. The report, as well as personal statements made to us by members of the commission, made it clear also that the decision was brought about by the refusal of the company to make an offer of absolute sale.

The commission was still at work upon its final report.

Our greatest effort was then devoted to bringing the commission to recant its preliminary report in favor of Nicaragua and to finally adopt the Panama plan. To accomplish this result it was necessary (primo) that the company make an offer of absolute sale (secundo) that the consent of Colombia to a cession in favor of a foreign government (such cession being prohibited by the concession) be obtained, and (tertio) that the commission be convinced that the Panama plan was the best and that it recommend its selection.

It appeared quite clear to us that to obtain the selection of the Panama plan and to avoid the final adoption of the Nicaragua route it was necessary to make an offer of absolute sale, and we so advised the company insistenly urging it to do so.

We were so convinced of the soundness of our advice on this matter that we insisted on it to the president of the company. But we were convinced that if the point of view of the American Government and people was not appreciated and thoroughly understood by the company the matter could not be considered and judged in its real light, and this was the gist of the advice we gave them. The events which followed, unfortunately, justified our opinion and our advice.

DECEMBER, 1900–MAY, 1901—WE BRING ABOUT THE INTERVENTION OF COLOMBIA—PRELIMINARY DISCUSSION WITH A VIEW TO OBTAINING THE CONSENT OF COLOMBIA.

During this period the Colombian legation in Washington had been closed, and that country was not represented here. The official business of the Government was being conducted through the consul general in New York, who at that time was Señor de Brigard.

One part of our plan consisted in getting Colombia to send to Washington a minister competent to take up the canal matter, and it was on our urgent advice that the company gave instructions to its agent in Bogota to suggest this (idea) to the Colombian Government. We also had a personal interview in December, 1900, with the consul general in New York (at that time the only official representative of Colombia in the United States) and we begged him to urge President Marroquin to at once send a minister empowered to deal with the canal question. It was in consequence of our statement (which contained an account of the whole situation) and set forth the necessity for immediate action that the consul general acceded to our request and cabled President Marroquin an urgent message to this effect December 23, 1900. President Marroquin answered him by cable (as we were officially notified by the consul general on December 27) that Mr. Martinez-Silva, then minister of foreign affairs, would arrive in Washington about the end of January, 1901, for this purpose.

At our request, and after we had convinced him of the urgency of the matter, the consul general sent Secretary Hay an official note, with which he transmitted a copy of President Marroquin's telegraphic communication notifying him of the appointment of Mr. Silva as minister and envoy extraordinary, charged with negotiating with the United States on the subject of the Panama Canal.

Having succeeded in this respect we took advantage of this fact to urge on Secretary Hay that the negotiations with Nicaragua and Costa Rica ought not to be concluded before the arrival of Mr. Silva and until the canal company had had an opportunity of negotiating with him.

Minister Silva arrived in New York in the middle of February, 1901, and his first call was on Mr. Cromwell in our law office; then began a series of conferences between the minister and ourselves which lasted several months and of which we shall state the substance.

We soon learned, thanks to our conferences with Mr. Silva, that Colombia considered that the canal concession would necessarily be forfeited in any event in 1910 by reason of the manifest impossibility of the company finishing the canal by that date, and in consequence Colombia judged that in this matter her interest was paramount and should be considered first; that public opinion in Colombia was opposed to the cession to a foreign government, but that the Government then in power was willing to consider such an eventuality on condition that it was based on terms sufficiently advantageous to Colombia.

In the course of a series of conferences we furnished Mr. Silva, at the request of this minister, with a most thorough and detailed explanation of the situation then existing in the United States, including the political factors; of the state of the treaty negotiations with Nicaragua and Costa Rica; of the state of the legislation affecting the Nicaragua Canal; and of the preliminary report of the commission which showed that its findings were based in part on the uncertainty as to the acquisition of the Panama route and as to the treaty pledges necessary on the part of Colombia; and we strongly urged him to immediately make known to the United States the willingness of Colombia to negotiate on these matters and to facilitate the plans of the United States, as this Government was at that time actively negotiating wih Nicaragua and Cosa Rica on the same matter. Mr. Silva, convinced by our explanation and arguments, accepted them in principle, and in the course of an official visit he paid to Secretary Hay March 13, 1901, assured the latter of his willingness to facilitate the plans of the United States if the terms agreed upon were of a satisfactory nature to Colombia.

This action on our part injected a new element into the canal situation, to wit, an official appearance (act of presence) by Colombia and a possible opportunity for the acquisition of the Panama Canal; opportunity suggested by the advent of Colombia into the affair.

We gave the widest publicity to this incident; it had the effect of demonstrating more clearly to the public understanding the possibility of the United States acquiring the Panama Canal.

During the three months which followed the negotiations between Minister Silva, the Isthmian Canal Commission, and the company continued, with the participation of Admiral Walker, Minister Silva, the president of the company (who was in Washington during this period), and Mr. Cromwell, assisted by one of his partners, Mr. Hill. The result of the various conferences and communications which took place was in brief as follows:

(1) The Colombian minister consented to the company making an offer of sale to the United States; and Colombia announced to the United States that

she was disposed to allow the United States to acquire the rights of the canal company on condition that agreements and treaties the terms of which would be satisfactory to Colombia be entered into between Colombia and the United States.

(2) In consequence the canal company informed the Colombian minister and the Isthmian Canal Commission that it would consent (on the basis of a like consent on the part of Colombia) to the transfer of its concessions to the United States at a price which was not fixed, but which was to be determined by private agreement or by arbitration; and that over and above the purchase price of its properties there would be added an indemnity for the future profits which its concessions would have placed the company in position to realize had it built the canal.

Such was the situation on May 16, 1901, when the president of the canal company returned to Paris, but no definite offer had yet been made to the United States.

We pushed our campaign of information and education with sustained activity until the 1st of July following, and everywhere we found encouraging proofs of a growing disposition to look justly upon the advantages of the Panama cause, for the truth of our public assurances and statements during the preceding years began to be recognized. The years of hard labor we had devoted to the work of publicity were bearing fruit.

MAY-JULY, 1901.—PREPARATION BY THE ISTHMIAN CANAL COMMISSION OF ITS FINAL FINDINGS AND REPORT.

The final report of the Isthmian Canal Commission, which this commission was preparing, was still, however, the central and critical point of interest, and we kept in constant contact with its members, conferring with them, finding out about their progress, etc.

May 1, 1901, the party of Isthmian Canal Co. engineers returned to Washington after having virtually completed its studies of the Nicaragua and Panama plans, and thus supplied the latest detailed information for the writing of the final report of the commission.

May 21, 1901, the Nicaraguan minister, who had gone to Nicaragua to report to his government and obtain fresh instructions for the negotiation of a canal treaty, returned to the United States, and it was publicly stated that he was authorized to grant all the demands of the United States on the subject of the Nicaragua canal.

Placed on the alert by the active negotiations we have mentioned, the supporters of Nicaragua, recognizing the danger their cause was running, began a new campaign of publicity throughout the country, with the result that a feeling in favor of Nicaragua seized upon the country; the press of the Nation demanded the construction of the Nicaragua canal by the United States, and urged that it should lay aside the Panama undertaking, which was denounced as scandalous and abandoned, and once more commercial bodies and other various organizations passed resolutions in favor of the Nicaragua canal to the exclusion of any other.

Until the following month of July we continued to keep in close touch with the commission and to comply with its requests for documents and information in the course of the studies it was still carrying on.

IMPORTANT CONFERENCE WITH THE PRESIDENT OF THE COMMISSION ON THE SUBJECT OF THE BASIS UPON WHICH THE COMMISSION WOULD DOUBTLESS HAVE RECOMMENDED THE SELECTION OF THE PANAMA CANAL IN ITS FINAL REPORT.

On June 25, 1901, an event of enormous importance to the Panama Canal took place.

On that day Admiral Walker, chairman of the Isthmian Canal Commission, voluntarily called upon Mr. Cromwell in our law office in New York and a conference followed, in the course of which Admiral Walker declared that the work of the commission in connection with the preparation of the final report had made such progress that it expected to submit to the President (according to his request) in the first part of July a semiofficial report or summary of its final findings in advance of the filing of its final report, the innumerable details of which would perforce keep it busy for several months. He also alluded to the proposal the company had made to Minister Silva and to the commission with a view to fixing a price by agreement or arbitration with an indemnity for the loss of eventual profits instead of a fixed price, and he stated that all the members of the commission were agreed upon this point; that these proposals could have no result; that they were insufficient and inacceptable. He spoke of the long drawn out correspondence exchanged between the company and the commission on this subject, and declared that the commission was not authorized to act upon, nor could it act upon, anything except a definite offer of absolute sale for a stated sum.

During this interview Admiral Walker inquired of Mr. Cromwell as to the price the company would probably accept, if it fixed a definite figure; to this Mr. Cromwell answered that he was not authorized to make a definite statement on this matter but that the idea of fixing a sum had his approval; and he, in turn, asked what price the commission would probably be disposed to accept, adding that he would immediately telegraph to the company. From the conference which followed Mr. Cromwell felt justified in making a deduction as to the figure which would meet the views of the commission, and this figure greatly exceeded that of the offer the company made later.

From this conference we emerged with the assurance that if the company consented to fix a definite sum, the report would be favorable to Panama; but we understood, in the presence of Admiral Walker's statement, that the company's proposal to fix the price by arbitration or valuation was entirely inacceptable and inadmissable; and that the advance findings to be sent to the President by the commission, and its final report, would follow the findings of its preliminary report already filed, and hence would be unfavorable to Panama if its findings were not changed by a definite and satisfactory offer made in the meantime; and that even if the amount of an offer of this kind was greatly in excess of the commission's estimate its acceptance would be recommended. Therefore Mr. Cromwell strongly urged Admiral Walker to defer the sending of this advance report to the President in order to permit him to inform the company of the views of the commission and of its new request for the fixation of a definite sum. We pointed out that the delay would have to be sufficient to enable the president of the company to come to the United States in person, should be so desire. As a result of this conference Admiral Walker promised to defer the filing of his advance report until July 20, for the purpose stated.

OUR REPORT BY CABLE TO THE COMPANY ON THE SUBJECT OF THIS CONFERENCE, JUNE 25—THE COMPANY PERSISTS IN ITS REFUSAL TO SET A DEFINITE PRICE—CONSEQUENCES.

Within a few hours, following the departure of Admiral Walker, Mr. Cromwell sent a cable to the canal company, worded thus:

NEW YORK, *June 25, 1901.*

PANANOVO (COMPAGNIE NOUVELLE DU CANAL DE PANAMA),
Paris.

Admiral Walker came to see us to-day. Declares that commission will finish advance report to President first part July. Declares Pananovo proposal to arbitrate inacceptable; above all because arbitration would delay decision beyond next Congress and because arbitration would take away from Congress the power to fix the amount and would give this power to individuals not subject to the authority of Congress. Admiral asks Pananovo to at once fix definite sum instead of arbitration, and declares that otherwise the proposal of Pananovo must be considered insufficient and inacceptable. He promises me delay his report until July 20 if you come here before then ready to discuss estimate and fix definite sum. Am convinced that if Pananovo fixes sum in keeping with views commission it will have very favorable influence on the report. Cable if you accede to admiral's request or if you can come and when you can come. Admiral says he expects see President Saturday. If possible instruct me before that date.

CROMWELL.

The company made no definite offer, then or later, prior to the filing of the final report of the commission, and the disastrous consequence, foretold in our cable of June 25, followed, to wit: A unanimous report was made by the commission on November 16, 1901, in favor of the Nicaragua Canal, based above all on the persistent refusal of the company to make a definite offer and on its unwavering adherence to the form of its proposal that a price—in final resort—be fixed, by whatsoever method of appreciation, by third parties.

We do not make allusion to this in any spirit of criticism, as it was the company's business, and it was for it to weigh its own actions; but we think we have the right to point out that if the plan devised by us had been followed, if the situation thus cleared up by us and the negotiations reported by us on June 25 had been taken advantage of, and if a definite offer of a sum far in excess to that proposed later had been made then by the company, the acceptation of this offer would have been recommended by the commission, the final report would have favored Panama instead of Niacaragua, and the final results would have been better for the company.

JULY 1, 1901–JANUARY 27, 1902—OUR INSTRUCTIONS ARE TO CEASE ALL ACTIVITY.

For the period from July 1, 1901, to January 22, 1902, we have no responsibility, as during that period the company, for reasons it deemed sufficient, ordered the cessation of all activity in the United States and itself took over the management of the affair, relieving us of all responsibility during that period.

STATE OF THE PANAMA CASE AT THE POINT TO WHICH WE HAD BROUGHT IT IN JULY, 1901.

We pause to consider the state of the Panama case at the point to which we had brought it at this date, July 1, 1901. Up to then all the bills and legislative measures for the adoption of the Nicaragua plan had been defeated one after the other. The Panama plan had been forced on public attention by the passage, thanks to our efforts, of the law of March 3, 1899, by which the Isthmian Canal Commission was created, and official investigation and consideration of this plan as being part of the canal question which the United States was concerned was thus obtained. The presentation of and investigation into the Panama project had been accomplished, and it was manifest that the commission was disposed to make its final report in favor of Panama if a definite offer of absolute sale at a price it could recommend was made. Not only public opinion no longer unanimously favored Nicaragua, but a strong current of opinion in favor of Panama had been created. Colombia had permitted the company to make an offer on condition that a treaty be entered into between her and the United States, and had announced that she was ready to negotiate such a treaty.

We had virtual assurance that if the company made an offer the commission could accept the report would be favorable to Panama and that we could enter upon the last phase of the struggle which would open immediately on the filing of the report of the commission, with the immense advantage of the formal indorsement of the commission itself.

The supporters of Nicaragua in Congress and elsewhere had powerfully organized and were more embittered than ever by the progress of the cause of Panama. The Nicaragua bills would certainly be introduced anew at the December session, so there was necessity that as far as the legislative aspect of the matter was concerned activity should be continued. In this respect a favorable report of the commission would be of the greatest importance on account of the powerful effect this report would exert on the action of Congress, even though the supporters of Nicaragua should energetically oppose any favorable report and might even obtain its rejection. It was thus of the greatest importance that energetic preparations be pushed in all directions.

Such was the situation on July 1, 1901, when, as we have stated, the company assumed the exclusive management and responsibility, which it retained for the seven months that followed.

EVENTS FROM JULY 1, 1901, TO JANUARY 27, 1902.

(1) President McKinley is assassinated. The inauguration of President Roosevelt takes place; he declares himself publicly in favor of the building of the Nicaragua Canal.

(2) The President of the company negotiates with the commission.

(3) The company adheres to its former attitude, and refuses to make a definite and binding offer. (Nov., 1901.)

(4) Thereupon the commission signs and files its final report against Panama and in favor of Nicaragua. (Nov. 19, 1901.)

(5) The president of the company then returns to Paris and hands in his resignation, which is accepted. Mr. Bô is elected president.
(6) The general meeting (of shareholders) authorizes the communication to the United States of a definite offer subject to ratification later.
(7) The Nicaragua party introduces and pushes its bills in the Senate and House; these bills are reported favorably by the committees of both houses.
(8) The United States negotiates with Nicaragua for a treaty.
(9) The Senate of the United States ratifies the Hay-Pauncefote treaty, which assures the passage of laws for the construction of a neutral canal by the United States.
(10) In the House the debate on the Nicaragua bill is set for January 7.
(11) The company cables to the commission, January 4 (and confirms on the 9th and 11th), an offer of sale to the United States at a price the amount of which is the same as the estimate of the commission—$40,000,000.
(12) The Nicaragua bill is debated by the House for two days after the receipt of the above-mentioned offer, and the House, rejecting this offer, passes the Nicaragua bill almost unanimously—309 ayes, 2 nays.
(13) The Nicaragua bill passed by the House goes at once to the Senate, where prompt action is taken.
(14) The President again calls the commission together (Jan. 16) to consider the offer of the company; the commission files a supplementary report (Jan. 18) recommending the Panama plan because of this offer, and the President sends the said report to Congress (Jan. 20).

Although we did not take part in the events of these seven months—from July 1, 1901, to January 27, 1902—we rehearse them because they created a new and more serious situation which we were called upon to deal with on the resumption of our activities on January 27, 1902.

President McKinley, struck down by the bullet of an assassin in July (? H. N. H.), 1901, died September 8, 1901. Mr. Roosevelt became President, announced to the public in an official statement the policy he intended to follow, and therein recommended the building of the Nicaragua Canal.

On account of the assassination of the President and the inauguration of his successor, the commission necessarily delayed the completion of its final report, which gave the company another opportunity to make the definite and binding offer which the commission had asked for for two years and with which our cable of June 25 dealt.

After an exchange of correspondence with the company in Paris, the commission cabled to the company declaring that if the company intended to name a price for its property and concessions it was necessary to avoid further delay.

The president of the company arrived in the United States on October 15, 1901, and a few days after his arrival sent to us for a copy of the cable of June 25, cited above, which had been sent to the company immediately after the conference held that day between Admiral Walker and Mr. Cromwell and which had been received by the company in due course, as we learned later at the company's offices. In compliance with this request we sent the copy in question.

A continuation of the official correspondence between the company and the commission had as its sole result that the company adhered firmly to the attitude it had taken in its letter of May 16, 1901 (with the exception that it abandoned its demand for an indemnity for possible future profits), and that the commission adhered to its attitude that it was not authorized to deal with a proposal in this form, and could only receive and report upon an offer of absolute sale fixing a definite price.

The figures presented by the company showed that, according to its estimate, its properties were worth 565,000,000 francs.

The negotiations between the company and the commission were concluded thus on November 6, 1901, and the commission went to work to complete and file its annual report. This report, filed 10 days later—November 16, 1901—was signed by all the members of the Isthmian Canal Commission, and unanimously recommended the adoption of the Nicaragua plan, principally because of the fact that the Panama Co. had made no definite, binding, and satisfactory offer.

This was a crushing blow for the cause of Panama, and throughout the country it was looked upon as definitely deciding the adoption of the Nicaragua project by Congress and the abandonment of Panama.

Congress met December 2, 1901, and the supporters of Nicaragua made the utmost use of the enormous advantage they had obtained, and demanded the immediate passage of the Nicaragua bill. Mr. Hepburn introduced in the

House, on December 6, 1901, a bill authorizing the appropriation of $180,000,000 for the construction of the Nicaragua Canal, $10,000,000 of which was rendered immediately available for this purpose. The Committee on Interstate and Foreign Commerce, of which Mr. Hepburn was chairman, gave its prompt consideration to this bill, which was backed up by the favorable report of the Isthmian Canal Commission, and immediately reported it favorably to the House.

A corresponding activity made itself felt in the Senate, where several Nicaragua bills were introduced, one by Senator Perkins, two by Senator Morgan. The Senate committee (the Committee on the Nicaragua Canal), of which Senator Morgan was chairman, acted as promptly as the House committee, and unanimously reported a bill in favor of the construction of the Nicaragua Canal. Thus in both Houses the Nicaragua bills were favorably reported by the respective committees, and supported by the final report of the Isthmian Canal Commission.

On December 10, 1901, a formal convention was signed in Nicaragua between the minister of foreign affairs of Nicaragua and the United States minister, Mr. Merry, with a view to the construction of the Nicaragua Canal by the United States, and this fact was widely advertised by the supporters of Nicaragua as a proof of the adoption of their project by the United States.

On December 17, 1901, the Senate of the United States ratified the new Hay-Pauncefote treaty, and thus overcame the great diplomatic obstacle of the Clayton-Bulwer treaty, the existence of which we had made use of at preceding sessions. This assured the passage, during this session of Congress, of laws decreeing the building of an interoceanic canal by the United States over one or other of the routes.

On December 19, 1901, the House of Representatives, by unanimous consent of its members, placed the Hepburn bill on the calendar for immediate consideration on January 7, 1902, on which date the debates on this bill were to begin and to continue until a decision had been reached on the bill. This assured a vote on the bill within a short time.

At the general meeting of the company, which took place on December 21, 1901, the gravity of the situation was fully explained, and resolutions were submitted to the shareholders and adopted by them, authorizing the tender to the United States, through the Isthmian Canal Commision, of a definite and fixed offer, such as that commission had asked for for more than two years, but subject to ratification by the shareholders at a subsequent meeting.

On January 4, 1902, the company in Paris made an offer by cable to the United States, through the commission, covering all its concessions and properties, of which an estimate had been made by the Isthmian Canal Commission, on page 103 of its report, for the sum of $40,000,000, the amount of this estimate; and by other cables sent direct to the commission on January 9 and January 11, 1902, confirmed this offer and declared that it was ready to accept the amount stated for the totality, without exception, of its properties and rights on the Isthmus, and his offer also included all the plans and archives in Paris.

The Hepburn bill reached its turn on the calendar of the House January 8, and the debates continued all through that day and the next. The offer of the company, made on January 4, had been officially transmitted to the President and to the Secretary of State, was published immediately, and was alluded to and considered in the course of the debates in the House on the Hepburn bill.

The House, however, rejected the company's offer and the Hepburn bill was passed on January 9, almost unanimously, by 309 votes in favor of the Nicaragua plan, and only 2 against.

The bill was immediately sent to the Senate, which referred it to the committee of which Senator Morgan was chairman, and this committee at once took it under advisement.

In consequence of the offer of the company the President again called the Isthmian Canal Commission together on January 16, 1902, to have it reconsider its report, in view of the offer in question. The commission met immediately, and, on January 18, 1902, decided that, after taking into consideration the changed conditions brought about by the offer of the company, the Panama route was preferable. This report was transmitted by the President to Congress on January 20, 1902.

1902, JANUARY 27—RESUMPTION OF OUR ACTIVITIES.

The above résumé shows only too clearly that the situation of the cause of Panama at this moment was in truth dangerous and desperate. In these circumstances the company cabled to Mr. Cromwell, asking him to resume his former connection and activity as general counsel of the company in charge of the matter.

Mr. Cromwell accepted the mission which was thus again intrusted to him and to his law firm, and the cables of the company, as well as the acknowledgment of his acceptance, were confirmed by the following letter from the company:

PARIS, *January 31, 1902.*

No. S. 3759.]

SIR: We have the honor to confirm the two telegrams here below, one of which was sent to you direct, whereas the other, fuller and more explicit, was to be handed to you by Mr. Lampré, secretary general of our company.

"JANUARY 29, 1902.

"You will receive through Lampré, after translation, telegram reinstating you as general counsel of Compagnie Nouvelle and containing instructions."

"JANUARY 27, 1902.

"You to be reinstated in your position as general counsel of Compagnie Nouvelle de Panama; rely on your cooperation to conclude matter sale of property; you better than anyone can show title Compagnie Nouvelle de Panama to property and incontestable right she has to sell them. But we require most expressly that no donations be made now or later, nor promises be made, to anyone whomsoever, which might bind the Compagnie Nouvelle de Panama. We are convinced you share our sentiments on this point, but we wish it to be well understood between us. It is also understood that settlement of former accounts and remuneration your future services will be determined sovereignly by the board of directors of Compagnie Nouvelle de Panama, and that no expenditure whatsoever is to be incurred without consent board directors of Compagnie Nouvelle de Panama. Finally, it must be understood that you are to follow instructions of authorized agents of board of directors, whoever they be."

As we say to you in these telegrams, we again intrust you with the functions of general counsel of the company in the United States. We rely on your hearty cooperation to bring to a successful issue, as promptly as possible, the offer we have made to the Government of the United States to transfer to it, for the price of $40,000,000, the totality of our rights, property, and assets of whatever kind on the Isthmus of Panama, as well as the archives and plans in Paris. This offer, as you know, has recently been favorably reported on by the Isthmian Commission. The Panama route presents, as a matter of fact, in the eyes of every competent and impartial judge, inappreciable advantages over any other route. Therefore, its opponents seem to focus their attacks (efforts) particularly on the legal question by trying to cast doubts on the validity and extent of the full and absolute title of ownership to the property which we offer to transfer to the buyer.

Better than anyone you are in a position to defeat this maneuver. Your perfect knowledge of the position of La Compagnie Nouvelle since its formation, of the unreserved and unrestricted titles it received from the liquidator of the old company, himself acting by virtue of undeniable authority, will permit you easily to dispel every doubt and allay every fear, if really any serious doubts or fears are possible. If needs be, you will find us ready to aid you in this task by sending you any records or documents, or by obtaining, with the least possible delay, from a general meeting of shareholders any special powers or resolutions which may be deemed necessary.

Finally, we rely that you will know how to utilize your numerous connections and your legitimate influence to bring about the recognition of the superiority of the Panama Canal by all the prominent men whose intervention may be of use to you and who might still hold out against the proof—so complete and so convincing—set forth in the various reports of the Isthmian Commission.

But it must be clearly understood, and on this point we shall surely be in accord with you, that this result must be sought only by the most legitimate means; that is to say, that in no case could we have recourse to methods, as dangerous as they are unlawful, which consist principally in gifts or promises, of whatsoever nature they may be, and that the reserve must scrupulously be observed by every person acting for us or in our name.

We also think that we are meeting your views in expressing the desire that you should leave to the board the settlement of all questions of remuneration referring either to the past or to the future. The board, you may be sure, will know how to recognize in an equitable manner the services you will have rendered it.

It appears to us superfluous to mention that in all your moves you must be guided by the instructions we have given to our agents in Washington, and should occasion arise confer with them.

We congratulate ourselves, sir, on the new connections which are to be established between you and the company, and in the hope that they may contribute to the success of our efforts we beg you to accept the expression of our highest regard.

THE PRESIDENT OF THE BOARD OF DIRECTORS,
M. BÔ.

P. S.—We beg to acknowledge receipt of your telegram received to-day, which we have translated as follows:

"I acknowledge receipt of your cable of 27 reinstating me as counsel of the company as well as of your other cable communicated to me by Secretary Lampré. I am happy to renew our former connections immediately, and, in accordance with the general terms of your cablegrams, I have drawn up a general plan of campaign. Seeing that no agreement has yet been reached between Colombia and the United States, and in view of the erroneous interpretation of our titles, I have inspired a new bill adopting our project and leaving to the decision of the President all questions relating to titles and to the new treaty to be concluded with Colombia, with discretionary power to choose the other route if the President is not successful in obtaining a satisfactory title and treaty for our route. I am working to have this bill passed in both Houses. My next step will be to obtain from Colombia definite and satisfactory conditions for the treaty with our Government in the contrary event the whole matter would be jeopardized and the Senate would probably follow the House in favoring the other route. This capital question has brought Silva to understand the situation and to have conferences with the most important personages."

SITUATION IN JANUARY, 1902, WHEN WE RESUMED CONTROL.

Leaving aside all our other business we acceded to this request. From numerous sources we had quite recently been informed of the gravity of the situation, which was so radically different from what we had left in the previous July. At that time we had forced the official recognition of the cause of Panama, a powerful faction had been enlisted on its side, public opinion in favor of Nicaragua had been somewhat overcome, the advantages of the Panama plan had been publicly acknowledged to an important extent, and everything justified the belief that the Isthmian Canal Commission would make a report favorable to Panama.

But when we were again intrusted with this task changes of enormous importance had taken place.

(1) By not complying with the advice we had given to make a definite and fixed offer, which we had declared to be necessary by our cable of June 25, 1901 (of which a copy had been given to the president of the company on his visit to the United States, October 20, 1901), and by ceasing the help given to the commission and the argumentative influences which previously had been employed, a unanimous report of the commission in favor of the Nicaragua cause had been brought about—a result which would have been different had our advice been followed.

(2) Nicaragua and Costa Rica, backed up by the Maritime and Nicaragua companies, were making the most liberal treaty proposals to the United States and urging their acceptance—proposals which the Government of the United States considered satisfactory and which it indorsed—and a protocol had already been signed with Nicaragua.

(3) The Colombian minister, Mr. Silva, who at most had only given a conditional consent to the transfer (of the property), had seen his action, even with this limitation, disapproved by his Government and himself in danger of being relieved of his post (and he was, in fact, recalled later for this very reason); Colombia treated the action of the company as freeing her from all obligations, even as to this conditional consent. The Colombian Government, by mandatory instructions, had limited and decreased the powers of its ministers in Washington, and was directing the matter entirely from Bogota, the capital.

In the Colombian Government opinion was as strong as it was divided as to the policy to be followed in regard to the Panama Canal. An important faction maintained, in public speeches, in the press, and by other methods calculated to influence public opinion, that a forfeiture of the Panama concession in favor of the Government was certain in 1910, at which date the term of its concession would be reached, without any doubt; that its entire assets would be acquired by the Government, and that the canal company ought to be treated as having already defaulted and as having lost its privileges and concessions.

Another faction maintained that even the prorogation until 1910 was null and void, as it had been granted by legislative decree and not by Congress.

Still another faction maintained that no transfer should be made to a foreign Government, such transfer being contrary to national welfare and virtually giving over the national territory on the Isthmus to the people of the United States.

Again, another faction, the Government party, favored the transfer on condition that the canal company paid a tribute of 50,000,000 to 60,000,000 francs, and that the United States undertook to pay an enormous rental, and that the concession be limited to a stated period of 100 years, for instance.

(4) The cause of Panama was languishing, having been left for seven critical months without support in the press and in other channels of public opinion, and all connections of this kind had been broken off.

(5) The legislative situation and public opinion had been entirely neglected. Nothing had been done and nothing said during this long interval to support this cause; its organization in the United States had been done away with, the Nicaragua party had been left free to finally reestablish itself and its cause in every direction, and it had again strongly entrenched itself.

(6) Official and binding consent had not been given by Colombia, as such consent could only be given by a treaty duly ratified by the Colombian Congress, by a law of the Colombian Congress, or by a legislative decree in times of public disorder. No treaty, law, or decree of this kind had been made, and there were neither negotiations nor preparations being made in order to obtain such a treaty, law, or decree.

(7) No preparation whatever had been made in prevision of the Congress, then sitting. No effort whatever had been made by the company to call the attention of Members of Congress to this matter, nor even to its offer; nor to give them special information, nor help them to understand the advantages of the Panama Canal and of the company's offer; nor to refute the tales or counteract the harmful influences of the supporters of Nicaragua. No effort whatever had been made to properly inform the committees of the two Houses of Congress which were considering the matter, and the cause of Panama was without leadership and had no active supporters in either one or the other of the Houses. The line of conduct followed by the company in the course of the negotiations during the preceding six months had alienated the friends of the cause, and public opinion in favor of Panama which had grown up, thanks to so many years' hard work, had become discouraged and ceased to exist.

(8) So when Congress reconvened the supporters of Nicaragua found no opposition whatever to placing their bill on the calendar for a stated date, by unanimous consent of the House, nor to its prompt passage by the House by a, so to speak, unanimous vote, despite the offer of the company to sell its properties for the amount of the commission's estimate, and in absolute disregard of this offer.

This fact alone unfortunately confirms in the most conclusive manner all we have just said.

(9) This bill, which had been passed in the House by such an unheard-of majority, was already receiving the consideration of the Senate committee (of which Senator Morgan was chairman), which, as was known, contained a majority strongly pledged to its passage, and they, by a majority vote, soon afterwards reported this bill favorably to the Senate.

(10) The Hay-Pauncefote treaty had been passed by the Senate, the ratifications had been exchanged by the two Governments, and by this treaty the United States was released from all international difficulties and its right to build the Isthmian canal without reference to any other nation had been formally conceded.

Such was the hopeless situation which confronted us when we resumed the defense of the company's interests in the very midst of a desperate struggle, the outcome of which was doubtful.

1902, JANUARY-FEBRUARY.—WE ENCOURAGE THE PASSAGE OF A LAW, AUTHORIZING THE PURCHASE OF THE PANAMA CANAL ON CERTAIN CONDITIONS, TO BE SUBSTITUTED FOR THE NICARAGUA BILL PASSED BY THE HOUSE.

We threw ourselves into this affair, with the situation of which we had already familiarized ourselves, and which we had anxiously watched and considered with deep solicitude for the company's interests. We undertook the reestablishment of old connections and the awakening of our friends' interest. But we recognized that immediate and heroic measures must be taken, and at once we planned two moves which had a most far-reaching and happy effect.

At the time when the company had shown in the preceding spring its willingness to sell to the United States under certain conditions we had planned with this end in view the introduction of a bill in Congress authorizing the building of the Panama Canal by the United States. This bill had been the subject of conferences between us and several eminent statesmen. So at this critical moment we reverted to this idea and had long conferences with Senator Hanna and Senator Spooner, whom we urged to act in this direction, and these conferences resulted in Senator Spooner preparing and introducing in the Senate a bill for the adoption of the Panama route project and the acquisition of the properties of the Panama Canal Co. for $40,000,000, on the following conditions: (1) That the President should obtain within a reasonable time a satisfactory title to all the properties of the company, and (2) that he should obtain by treaty from the Republic of Colombia the enjoyment of the necessary right and authority; and that if he did not succeed he should adopt the Nicaragua canal and obtain by treaty with Nicaragua and Costa Rica the territory and rights necessary to its construction.

This last clause of Senator Spooner's bill was calculated to gain the support of Senators who wished to assure the building of a canal in any event, by one route or the other, without the delays and uncertainties of new laws.

This bill was at once sent to the committee which had charge of the Nicaragua bill, and by this very fact became its open rival.

This move had a favorable effect. It was the very first time in the history of Congress that a bill for the adoption of the Panama project had been introduced, and, furthermore, this bill in terms authorized the acceptance of the company's offer on the sole condition that the titles be approved and that sufficient control over the Canal Zone be obtained from Colombia by treaty.

At this moment three vital problems, calling for immediate action, faced us—

(1) To prevent the Nicaragua bills, which had been passed by the House a few days previously, from being immediately and favorably reported to the Senate, as Senator Morgan, with a majority of his committee to support him, was going to do.

(2) To bring about a treaty between the United States and Colombia and to procure that the consent of Colombia to a transfer by the company be included in this treaty.

(3) To obtain the acceptance by Congress of the company's offer and render this offer binding by the ratification of its shareholders, which was essential.

STEPS WE TOOK TO OVERCOME ADVERSE OPINION AS TO THE TITLE OF THE COMPANY, ITS RIGHT TO SELL, ETC.

As to the first matter, Senator Morgan had brought before his committee much evidence (prolonged depositions) with a view to undoing the findings of the last report of the commission in favor of Panama by seeking to show that the commission had been guilty (given proof) of inconstancy and vacillation in the writing of its reports, and also that one of its members (Prof. Haupt) had, so to speak, been compelled to sign the report. He laid stress upon the fact that the commission had already reported in favor of Nicaragua in its two preceding reports; that numerous engineers of the country favored Nicaragua, and that all the reports of commissions created by Congress had declared that plan practical, even those of the commission in question.

We considered it essential to the cause of Panama to widen the committee's field of inquiry in order to embrace the subject of Panama, which was not then the intention. We presented these views to Senator Hanna and other members of the committee and urged that the committee make no report until it had heard all the members of the commission in support of their last report, the hearing of which evidence would directly bring out the advantages of the Panama project and the reaffirmation of the recommendations they had made in favor of the company's offer. This line of conduct met with Senator Hanna's approval, and as a member of the committee he insisted on its adoption, and won his point. In consequence, all the members of the commission were summoned before the committee at the instance of Senator Hanna, and testified at length. We followed the hearings day by day; obtained and studied the depositions as fast as they were given, wrote commentaries thereon and made suggestions, and assisted the Senators in sifting (working out) this evidence. Our services and conferences kept us continually occupied, and the matter monopolized our attention, almost night and day, for several weeks.

We had conferred with the members of the commission, we had informed ourselves in detail as to their individual opinions, which they later expressed in the course of their evidence, and we prepared, for the use of Senator Hanna and his colleague, Senator Kittredge, a series of questions which were necessary to bring out the facts during the deposition of each of the members of the commission.

These depositions answered their purpose (succeeded) admirably, not only in enlightening the commission and the Senate as to the facts, but also in gaining time to obtain, if possible, the necessary proposal of a treaty with Colombia and her consent to a transfer by the company.

1902, FEBRUARY–MARCH—WRITING AND CIRCULATION OF OUR OPINION, CONTAINED IN THE PRINTED VOLUME WITH THE TITLE: "OPINION OF SULLIVAN & CROMWELL ON THE TITLE OF OWNERSHIP OF THE NEW PANAMA CANAL CO. AND ITS POWER TO TRANSFER ITS PROPERTY TO THE UNITED STATES."

For many months Senator Morgan and his allies had declared in speeches in the Senate and through the press that the Panama Canal Co. could not, in any case, give a valid title to its property; that the company had not the right to sell; that the affairs of the new company were interwoven with those of the old; that the bondholders of the old company had a reversionary interest in the Panama Canal, and that their consent to the sale was necessary to legalize the title, adding numerous other objections of a legal nature; and all these objections had given rise to doubts in the minds of the Senators and created opposition to Panama in Congress.

To overcome these technical objections, to offset the harmful influence of the publicity given to them by the supporters of Nicaragua, it was necessary to show that the property title of the company was valid, and that its right to sell was legally perfect.

In view not only of these arguments and perversions of the truth, but also of the fact that the Spooner bill was based upon the approval of the title by the President, which rendered it necessary for us to establish the validity of this title, we had undertaken the preparation of an exhaustive opinion on the subject, and we then completed this work and gave it the form of "An opinion on the title of ownership of the New Panama Canal Co. and on its power to transfer its property to the United States." This important document, which played so momentous a part in facilitating the acceptance of the company's offer and the adoption of the Panama Canal route, had necessitated the critical examination (by Mr. Cromwell, Mr. Hill, and other partners of our law firm) of the entire series of concessions and prorogations granted by Colombia to the old and new companies; of the constitution and laws of Colombia; of the formation and organization of the old company; of the liquidation of the old company, and of the records as well as the procedure of that liquidation; of the lottery bonds law of 1888 (bons à lots); of the special French law of 1893 for the Panama liquidation; of the records of the various suits and injunctions by third parties, brought in the course of the liquidation, and bearing upon the conveyance of the assets by the liquidator of the old company to the new company; of the formation and organization of the new company; of the contracts passed between the new company and the liquidator of the old company in regard to the formation of the new company and the sale of the assets of the old company; of the series of agreements bearing upon the general meeting which was to be held under article 75 of the statutes of the new company; of the report of the technical commission appointed under this article; of the agreements between the new company and the liquidator of the old company in the matter of the shares of the Panama Railroad Co.; of the arrangement between the new company and the liquidator of the old company concerning the offer of sale made to the United States and the arbitration clause bearing on the division of the sale price to be realized; of the minutes of the meetings of the arbitration board and its decision; of the provisions of French law and of the statutes of the company bearing upon the voluntary liquidation of the new company in case of sale and the powers to transfer conferred thereby on the liquidators; of the right of the new company, under these laws, to dispose of all its property and effect a valid transfer; and of the answers to the various objections raised in the reports which, from time to time, had emanated from the Morgan committee and which attacked the legal position of the company.

In this opinion we asserted positively and proved that the title of ownership of the company was perfect, and that its right to transfer its properties was full and absolute.

This opinion was completed and signed by us on March 10, 1902; we had it printed and bound, and it received considerable publicity and circulation.

This opinion had a useful effect in maintaining the integrity of the company's legal position, and in overcoming the numerous objections on this ground, which had been and were continually being made, to the acceptance of the company's offer, and which had had an adverse influence on the action of some Senators in this matter. These conclusions were later adopted by some Senators and formed the basis of the minority report of the committee to which we shall refer later, and furnished the supporters of Panama with weapons of inestimable value for the debates. This opinion is submitted herewith.

MARCH, 1902—THE MAJORITY OF THE SPECIAL SENATE COMMITTEE SUBMITS AN UNFAVORABLE REPORT ON THE LEGAL POSITION OF THE PANAMA COMPANY—THE MINORITY ADOPTS OUR ARGUMENTS AND SUBMITS A FAVORABLE REPORT ON THE LEGAL POSITION OF THE COMPANY.

The Senate Committee on Interoceanic Canals had appointed a subcommittee of six members specially instructed to study and report upon the legal questions. This subcommittee was composed of Senators Foster, Morgan, Mitchell, Turner, Kittredge, and Pritchard. The majority of this subcommittee wrote a detailed report (32 printed pages) designed to show that the company's titles were defective, and that the company had no power to transfer. The opinion of Sullivan & Cromwell had already been published and was furnishesd to the members forming the minority of this subcommittee, Messrs. Kittredge and Pritchard, with whom we studied all the questions involved, discussing their bearing, their meaning and interpretation, elucidating all doubtful questions, and producing and explaining all the documents which constituted the title; also we refuted all the objections put forward by the majority of the committee and answered all the conclusions at which it had arrived. This minority of the subcommittee made a report in accordance with the legal views we had discussed before it and which we had embodied in our opinion, and thus gave official sanction to these conclusions.

The majority and minority reports were both submitted to the Senate on March 19, 1902; we had the minority report printed and circulated it among the Senators and wherever it might have influence. It had a great effect.

This was the first time that a member of the Senate or of the House had taken the responsibility of upholding the title of the company and its power to transfer, and this legal argument had been made, thanks to our labors and in accordance with our views.

FEBRUARY–MARCH, 1902—WE NEGOTIATE WITH THE COLOMBIAN MINISTER TO OBTAIN THE CONSENT OF THAT COUNTRY TO A TRANSFER TO THE UNITED STATES.

During this same period we applied ourselves actively to the matter of the necessary treaty between the United States and Colombia and to obtaining by this means the consent of Colombia to the transfer.

Minister Silva was still in Washington, but he was in disfavor in his own country and accused by his Government of having authorized the negotiations between the company and the United States. His powers as minister had been either cancelled or considerably curtailed, and his recall was but a matter of time—it took place shortly afterward, in February, 1902.

The Colombian Government in Bogota was preparing either to force the company to pay from 50,000,000 to 60,000,000 francs as the price of its consent (over and above the advantages Colombia might obtain from the United States) or to treat as null and void the prorogation until 1910; or, if these plans failed, to await the forfeiture of the company's concessions in 1910 and then treat directly with the United States or some other nation or interest, at its pleasure, and thus obtain all the pecuniary advantages to be had from the sale of the canal.

Thus the necessity of frustrating the designs of the Colombian Government and of bringing it to make a proposal to the United States became of supreme and vital importance to the acceptance of the company's offer.

To back up the company's offer, to retain the support of the friends of Panama in the Senate, to bring the minority of the Senate committee to make a report recommending Panama it was absolutely necessary to obtain the proposal by Colombia to the United States of a treaty which should be definite and reasonable. We knew that it was the intention of the Bogota Government to demand a pecuniary tribute of several millions of dollars from the canal company as the price of its consent to the transfer, and we were desirous of obtaining a treaty proposal which would bind the consent of Colombia by an international agreement and which would thus not only furnish the necessary basis, as far as the United States was concerned, for the acceptance of the canal offer, but also a protection for the company against the demands which might be made on it by Colombia direct.

Hence this became a fundamental and imperative condition of success and we devoted our attention not only to the matter of the acceptance of the company's offer, but also to assuring to it the full advantage of this offer without the heavy deduction that would be caused by a pecuniary tribute to Colombia as the price of her consent.

There was then no official proposal whatever pending between the two countries. The Colombian Government had no desire to assist the sale; Secretary Hay (who was an open partisan of Nicaragua) refused to open negotiations, no law having imposed this duty upon him. Neither of the Governments was willing to act, and yet unless there was some agreement between them the offer of the company could not even receive consideration. Mr. Cromwell, therefore, personally and without cooperation, opened negotiations with the minister and urged upon him the necessity of a proposal as a basis of a treaty between Colombia and the United States, which proposal should include the consent of Colombia to the transfer.

Fortunately we had already established intimate and cordial relations of mutual confidence with Minister Silva and Mr. Herran, secretary of the legation, a man of wide experience, who was later in charge of the legation.

At last Minister Silva drew up a preliminary proposal, which he asked us to examine. This proposal was made on the basis of a lease by Colombia to the United States renting the Canal Zone for 200 years only, at a yearly rental of $600,000, with the added condition that the United States should buy the railroad, at a valuation to be made at the expiration of the concession, and until then should pay a yearly rental of $250,000 for the railroad; the United States were to make a loan capitalizing these annual payments.

We protested energeticlly, pointing out that these conditions would be utterly inacceptable to the United States and would only furnish the supporters of Nicaragua arguments for the rejection of Panama and in consequence for the defeat of the Panama bill; but the minister declared formally that these conditions represented the minimum he could propose and that they were much more liberal than the attitude of his Government justified.

The situation in the Senate was getting more and more critical every day. Senator Morgan, chairman of the Senate Committee on Interoceanic Canals, supported by the majority of that committee, was using every means to bring the hearings of his committee, to an end and to submit to the Senate the report of the majority in favor of Nicaragua and against Panama, so that the question might be voted upon promptly in the Senate, which, according to the partisans of Nicaragua, would support the cause of Nicaragua; and, under the existing circumstances, it was clear to everybody that that would really have been the result. It thus became essential to inform Congress in some manner that Colombia would give her consent, at least on certain conditions, to the transfer to the United States, and in consequence we strongly urged Minister Silva to present his proposal to Secretary Hay with the idea that once the negotiations were officially opened modifications might be obtained. Mr. Silva yielded to our arguments and agreed to act, and he wrote out a fuller draft of his proposal, which he submitted to us and which we criticised and corrected at his request.

However, and just as Minister Silva was about to present this proposal in accordance with our request, he received official notification of his recall, with orders to cease all negotiations, and it became impossible for him to act officially. He had as successor Minister Concha, who arrived in New York February 26, 1902, with new instructions of a radical nature.

Minister Concha had been a political rival of Minister Silva, and he was sent to uphold the politics and pecuniary demands of the Bogota Government, the nature of which we have already outlined, and with which it was recognized that Minister Silva was not in accord.

The arrival of this new minister, in view of the nature of his instructions and of the attitude of the Colombian Government, presented a gravely perilous situation.

The Senate committee was continuing its hearings, as we have already said. Senator Spooner, author of the Spooner bill, was asking us for some proof of Colombia's consent in the form of a proper treaty, as well as for proof of the ratification by the shareholders of the canal company of the offer made by its board of directors, which was, on the other hand, perfectly reasonable.

Senator Hanna, whose intelligence was so vast, and who had insisted on a decent consideration of the company's offer and on the hearing of witnesses by the committee, in order to elucidate all the aspects of the matter, confessed to us that he was not disposed to support the acceptance of the company's offer or to recommend such acceptance in a minority report of his committee without sufficient assurance that a satisfactory treaty could be obtained, and that the shareholders of the company would ratify the action of the board (of directors) in making the offer.

We arranged an interview at which Senator Hanna, Minister Silva, and Mr. Cromwell were present, but the Colombian minister could not give the definite assurances required.

Minister Silva clearly saw the dangers of the situation, although the Government of his country did not see them, but everything depended now on the attitude of his successor, Minister Concha. This personage remained in New York after his arrival and would not go to Washington to present his credentials, nor would he at once take up this question. In explanation, he declared that he was awaiting further instructions from Bogota. Mr. Concha refused to yield to the instances of Minister Silva, who urged him to take charge of the legation. It was clear that he would not assist in the matter, even by his presence.

This situation became known in Washington among Members of Congress and gave support to the assertion that Colombia was hostile to the United States and to the conclusion of any treaty, and that in consequence the offer of the Panama Canal Co. ought to be rejected. This gave much anxiety to the supporters of the Panama Canal.

FEBRUARY 28, 1902—COLOMBIA SERVES THE COMPANY WITH FORMAL NOTICE NOT TO SELL ITS ASSETS TO THE UNITED STATES BEFORE COLOMBIA HAS GIVEN HER CONSENT—EFFECT OF THIS NOTIFICATION.

A new event, the effect and danger of which were considerable, took place. It has been seen that the ratification of this offer by the shareholders of the company was a fundamental condition to the acceptance of the company's offer. On January 28, and again on January 31, we told the company that it must fulfill this requirement in order to give support to the Spooner bill then pending and to complete the company's offer. In consequence the company had called a general meeting, which was to be held in Paris on February 28, 1902, and the advertisements to this effect had all been duly published. The Republic of Colombia was carried on the books of the company as owner of 5,000,000 francs' worth of shares, and was also represented on the company's board of directors by a Government delegate, in accordance with the terms of the company's concessions. The Bogota Government had thus been warned of the company's proposed action.

The Republic of Colombia, through its consul general in Paris, served formal notice on the company the day before the meeting that it forbade the sale of the canal to the United States before the approval of this sale by the Colombian Government, under pain of forfeiture of its concessions and the loss of its properties, by virtue of articles 21 and 22 of the contract of 1878.

Naturally the company was much worried by this unexpected action; and, on account of this protest by Colombia, the board abandoned its intention of asking the ratification by the shareholders of the offer of sale made to the United States, abstained from proposing the resolution by which the ratification was to have been given, and introduced an order of the day postponing all action till after the settlement of the difficulties with Colombia. This order of the day was adopted and the meeting adjourned without any action in the matter of the offer made to the United States.

The press of the United States gave great publicity to this event.

This action on the part of Colombia was a grave blow to the cause of Panama.

It furnished official proof that the necessary consent of Colombia had not yet been given.

It clearly showed the intention of Colombia to demand pecuniary tribute from the company as the price of this consent.

It made public and evident the fact that the offer of the company was, so far, incomplete by reason of its nonratification by the shareholders.

Senators in favor of the Spooner bill were not disposed to continue to support it under these circumstances.

And the supporters of Nicaragua gained another powerful and useful argument in their opposition to the passage of the Spooner bill and to the acceptance of the company's offer.

The minority of the Senate committee (Messrs. Hanna, Kittredge, Pritchard, and Millard) then told us plainly, as Senator Hanna had already done, that they were not disposed to take the responsibility of making a minority report recommending the adoption of the Panama project (which these members believed to be the best) and the acceptance of the offer of the company, unless (1) this minority was morally certain that the United States could obtain from Colombia the necessary authority over the territory, and that (2) the approval of the shareholders be given in a way to prevent them from disowning the offer that had been made by the board.

This event called for constant attention on our part, interviews with Senators who were perturbed by these facts, the sending and receipt of cables between the company and ourselves, and the drafting of plans calculated to overcome the harmful effects of the protest of Colombia and of the nonratification by the shareholders.

MARCH 1, 1902—WE OBTAIN FROM THE NEW COLOMBIAN MINISTER A WRITTEN STATEMENT THAT THE NOTIFICATION BY COLOMBIA DID NOT IMPLY OPPOSITION TO THE TRANSFER—GIST OF THIS STATEMENT—USE MADE OF IT AND EFFECT IT HAD.

At our request, Minister Silva continued, by telegram and letter, to urge Minister Concha, then in New York, to hasten his arrival in Washington and the assumption of his post, and to take up the negotiations. All the efforts of Minister Silva to this end, howeevr, did not succeed in eliciting a statement from Minister Concha, or even in getting him to go to Washington.

At the same time and at our request, Dr. Mutis Duran, a prominent citizen and former governor of Panama, called on Minister Concha in New York, and in the course of an interview specially laid before him the views and fears of the population of the Isthmus of Panama, the vital interest which that population had in this matter, and the desire on the part of that population that Colombia should come to an agreement with the United States and the canal company. Dr. Duran informed us that he had been received by the minister with indifference, that the minister had come to the United States with hostile intentions against the transfer of the canal to the United States, and that he (Dr. Duran) could do nothing with him.

Seeing that all the efforts of Minister Silva and Mutis Duran to bring Minister Concha to take up the negotiations had failed, and feeling the pressure of the events already referred to, Mr. Cromwell, who was then in Washington, decided to deal with the situation personally, himself went to New York, called on Minister Concha, forcefully exposed the situation in detail, and convinced him that the Nicaragua project would inevitably be adopted if Colombia did not change her attitude and show a willingness to cooperate with us and to at once help us to neutralize the harmful effects of her official notification in Paris in opposition to the transfer.

As a result of two such prolonged conferences, which lasted all day, on March 7 Mr. Cromwell succeeded in persuading Minister Concha to make a statement, which he authorized us to write out and make public. This statement was written by us; it was addressed to us in our capacity as general counsel of La Compagnie Nouvelle du Canal de Panama, and declared that the notice served on the company by Colombia on February 28 did not imply opposition to the transfer if a mutually satisfactory convention was concluded between Colombia and the United States in respect to their respective rights and relations in regard to the canal; that Colombia approved the steps taken by the canal company in its negotiations with the United States and would facilitate the transfer with the reservation already mentioned; that Colombia looked with favor on the construction of the Panama Canal by the United States through her territory; that he would continue the negotiations and would soon make clear to the United States the views and proposals of Colombia in this matter, with the object of encouraging the complete and early purchase by the Government of the United States of the rights, concessions, and property of the canal company, in so far as Colombia's constitution and laws would permit her to make the transfer to a foreign government—that is to say, without renouncing her sovereignty. This official note was communicated by us to the press of the United States, and we forwarded copies officially to the Secretary of State, Mr. Hay, to Minister Silva, to the members of the minority of the Senate committee, and to other influential persons.

This statement by the new Colombian minister was a surprise to all parties interested. It had a powerful effect in all parts and helped a great deal to neutralize the harm that had been done. It had been obtained, thanks to our efforts alone.

THE MAJORITY REPORT OF THE SENATE COMMITTEE IS UNFAVORABLE TO PANAMA; OUR REVELATIONS AS TO THE CLAIMS THE NICARAGUA COMPANY WOULD MAKE; THE MINORITY OF THE COMMITTEE REFUSES TO REPORT THE PANAMA PROJECT FAVORABLY UNLESS A TREATY BE ENTERED INTO WITH COLOMBIA AND THE SHAREHOLDERS RATIFY THE OFFER.

During this time the struggle in the Senate committee continued and called for our daily and anxious attention. Senator Morgan and his allies, forming the majority of the committee, kept on trying to bring the hearings to a close to make a report favorable to Nicaragua. The officials of the Panama Railroad Co. were called before the committee, at Senator Morgan's request, to show in substance that if the United States acquired the stock of the Panama Railroad Co. it would find itself embarrassed by numerous transportation contracts and by burdensome entanglements with the Government of Colombia and the State of New York; also that the operation of the railroad would not be profitable and that its property was not worth the amount of the appraisal made by the commission. The testimony taken filled 75 printed pages. We had interviews with each one of the officials of the railroad company; we studied and fully discussed before the hearings all the points under consideration, and we expressed ourselves on each point; we obtained minutes of the depositions (which reproduced them verbatim) in the order they were given day by day, studied and analyzed them, and made suggestions in regard thereto. We also had conferences with Senator Hanna and Senator Kittredge, at their request, and furnished them with data and information with a view to bringing out in an examination conducted by them the advantages of the Panama Railroad and proving that the estimate of the commission was justified. The result was that the confidence of the members of the minority in the value of the property to be acquired by the United States, if the Panama offer were accepted, was strengthened.

These labors were most absorbing and occupied several partners of our law firm in New York and Washington, in many conferences, studies, frequent discussions with witnesses, and the consideration of all the economic and transportation questions, as well as the condition of the finances and business of the railroad in all its aspects.

In the course of these hearings we reached the determination to take up the fight against Nicaragua in a more aggressive manner and to show Congress the falsity of its position. Personally and in various ways we made an investigation and acquired information justifying the following premises:

(1) That if the Nicaragua route were adopted the Nicaragua Co. would demand of the United States the reimbursement of the amount it claimed to have spent for concessions, construction, material, etc., which, with interest added, was stated to amount to $13,000,000.

(2) That the Nicaragua Co., or those who were interested in it, had already acquired an important part of the route for the Nicaragua project which it would be necessary for the United States to acquire from them in order to build the canal, at enormous cost to the United States and a corresponding profit to those interested in the Nicaragua Co.

(3) That the Nicaragua Co. would also present to the United States a heavy claim on the ground of the alleged irregular declaration by Nicaragua of the forfeiture of its concession.

We pointed out to Senator Hanna the importance of revealing these facts so as to sufficiently enlighten Congress.

He was of the same opinion, and at his request witnesses were examined later who showed the reliability of these facts as a whole. This created a distinctly unfavorable impression toward Nicaragua, and lay bare to the Senate the complications and dangers which the selection of this project would entail.

Hearings before the committee ended March 10, and three days later the committee, by a vote of seven to four, laid before the Senate a report favorable to the Nicaragua bill and rejecting the Spooner bill and the offer of the company (Mar. 13).

Thus the Hepburn bill concerning the Nicaragua Canal, which had been passed in the House by a vote of 309 to 2, was presented to the Senate with a favorable report of its committee; and the Spooner bill, which had been referred to the same committee, was returned to the Senate with an unfavorable majority report.

The majority of the committee, led by Senator Morgan, did not at this time present a detailed report in support of its findings, as it rested on its numerous preceding reports favorable to Nicaragua. It was clear that the majority had also adopted the strategy of preventing the minority of the committee from making any report whatever, so that the Senate would have before it nothing more than the expression of opinion in favor of Nicaragua. The minority was composed of Senators Hanna, Kittredge, Millard, and Pritchard, and we strongly urged them to file a detailed minority report, setting forth the facts and arguments in support of the passage of the Spooner bill and the acceptance of the company's offer, so that this bill would be presented to the Senate with the support of these distinguished Senators and a clear presentation of the facts and arguments. The minority refused to do so then, because of the uncertain status of affairs with Colombia and of the absence of ratification of the company's offer by the shareholders, to which we have already referred. As to this last matter, we pointed out to the minority of the committee that the company, after the incidents of February 28 (protest of Colombia which prevented carrying out the object for which the meeting of shareholders had been called on that date), could not in prudence call a general meeting of the shareholders before the conclusion of a treaty by Colombia giving her consent to the transfer; and, for the time being, this view was accepted by the abovementioned Senators.

We then concentrated our efforts on the matter of the proposal of a treaty, and for several weeks Mr. Cromwell devoted himself to this matter daily with Minister Concha, Mr. Herran, the secretary of the legation, and influential Senators, with whose views it was necessary to conform.

NEGOTIATIONS WITH MINISTER CONCHA OF COLOMBIA WITH A VIEW TO SECURING THE PROPOSAL TO THE UNITED STATES OF A TREATY MAKING POSSIBLE THE SALE OF THE PANAMA CANAL AND GRANTING THE UNITED STATES THE NECESSARY TREATY RIGHTS; NEGOTIATIONS WITH SECRETARY HAY WITH A VIEW TO OBTAINING ITS ACCEPTANCE; WE BRING ABOUT THE AGREEMENT, THE FIRST RESULT OF WHICH WAS THE CONCHA PROPOSAL OF MARCH 31, WHICH LED TO THE HAY-CONCHA AGREEMENT OF APRIL 18, 1902.

(a) We initiate and conduct the negotiations.

The new minister (Concha) approached the subject in a very different spirit to that shown by his predecessor (Silva). He had just arrived from Bogota and was imbued with the extreme views and intentions of the Bogota Government, which had recalled his predecessor because of his overliberal leanings toward the United States and the company. Although brilliant and very intellectual and a former cabinet minister, he was not only without knowledge of the English language, but entirely without experience of the world outside of Colombia, as he had never before left his own country, or seen the Isthmus of Panama. He took no part in the official life of Washington, and held himself aloof from all those who had had any dealings with the canal matter, all of whom he looked upon with distrust. His predecessor, Minister Silva, had remained in Washington at our request to explain the provisions of the preliminary draft of the treaty, but the new minister only listened to his statements once and (according to what his successor told us) did not ask a single question toward aiding or elucidating these explanations. After waiting many days for an invitation to explain himself at greater length, which did not come, Mr. Silva left Washington for New York, where he remained several weeks more, but Minister Concha did not call upon him. Shortly afterward he returned to Colombia and was obliged to quit public life.

As the Secretary of State of the United States made no overtures to Minister Concha (because he was not authorized so to do by Congress, which had first to select a route), Minister Concha maintained the same attitude toward the Secretary of State and, except for diplomatic declarations of good will on either side, neither of the parties took any steps with a view to the negotiation of a treaty.

In the face of this difficulty, and to save the situation, we once again personally took the initiative; we overcame the repugnance which Minister Concha felt for any discussion with an American, and above all with a representative of the canal company, and were at last requested by the minister to assist him in the wording of any treaty proposal which he might decide to make.

Mr. Cromwell devoted every day of the ensuing month to discussion with the minister at the latter's residence, gave the minister advice on all the questions at issue, and himself wrote out the text of a proposed treaty (projet de traite). These discussions covered the entire ground of international relations and international law; the special interests of Colombia; the treaty of 1846 in force; the general policy of Colombia as well as that of the United States in regard to the canal; the special interests of the cities of Panama and Colon as well as of the Isthmus of Panama; the questions of harbors and of maritime duties; the most vital question of sovereignty; the question of a lease, in perpetuity or for a fixed period; the questions of law courts and judicial procedure; the question of a fixed remuneration and of an annuity, etc. Even above all these questions, in its importance to the company, was the vital consent of Colombia to the transfer and sale of the properties to the United States, consent which, at our own instance, was to be inserted in the treaty itself; and this was our chief aim, although it was also important to insure the conclusion of a treaty satisfactory to both the United States and Colombia, as otherwise the mere consent to a transfer would be without the slightest value.

Minister Concha had come with instructions to exact an indemnity of from $10,000,000 to $20,000,000 cash, to be paid either by the United States or by the canal company or by both, and an annual subsidy of a million dollars. According to his explanations his Government considered that even if the United States adopted the Nicaragua plan, Colombia would derive a greater advantage by acquiring the canal and the Panama Railroad through the forfeiture of their concessions, and moreover the Bogota Government believed that the Panama Canal would be built under the auspices of an European Government if it was not acquired by the United States, from which Colombia would reap great profit.

We recognized that even if a proposal based on these conditions were made it would be entirely inacceptable to the United States, that the Panama Canal would thus be at once eliminated as a factor in the consideration of the problem, and we zealously and warmly discussed these matters in order to obtain less onerous terms.

Little by little, in the course of conferences which succeeded each other for whole weeks at a time, Mr. Cromwell led the minister to pledge himself as to various bases for a proposal, but up to March 24, 1902, the best pecuniary conditions Minister Concha was willing to propose were $7,500,000 cash and $600,000 a year from the expiration of a period of 15 years after the completion of the canal, with exemption of the islands of the bay of Panama, the limitation of the authority of the United States, etc., and a lease for a fixed period.

(b) We devise and carry out a plan whereby the dissensions between the United States and Colombia as to the perpetuity clause are overcome.

From the start Minister Concha (like his predecessor, Mr. Silva) positively refused to grant a lease in perpetuity, which was imperatively demanded by the United States. Colombia insisted that the lease should be for a fixed and stated period. This was a fundamental element of controversy, and if it were not overcome no treaty could be concluded. Mr. Cromwell had numerous and lengthy conferences to overcome this difficulty, and at last hit upon a plan which solved the problem, to wit: While conceding the principle of a lease (thus recongnizing the sovereignty of Colombia) he suggested a provision for the renewal of the lease, at the option of the United States, in succeeding periods of 100 years, and on the basis of a new valuation. Mr. Cromwell succeeded in obtaining the assent of Secretary Hay and of Minister Concha to this proposal as constituting an element of the treaty. All through these negotiations we particularly bore in mind to obtain, as a matter of the greatest importance in the negotiation, the assent of Colombia to the transfer to the United States; and we inserted in the draft of the treaty a clause to this effect (Art. I) and obtained the assent thereto of Minister Concha.

Although this was a long step toward a definite proposal, so essential to the interests of the company, the heavy pecuniary demands, if maintained, would perforce be fatal.

Minister Concha was then in New York. We called upon ex-Minister Concha and Dr. Mutis Duran, we explained the difficulty to them, and persuaded them to go to Minister Concha and urge him to reduce the terms and to bring them to a level where their acceptance would be possible. These gentlemen did as requested, but their efforts were fruitless

The company, which we kept constantly informed as to the progress of these negotiations, expressed its satisfaction by the following cable of March 24, 1902.

"We approve and are satisfied with your manner of conducting the genotiations with Concha. Hope that, thanks to your efforts, you will succeed in getting indispensable protocol filed with least possible delay."

The terms laid down in Minister Concha's instructions, when officiously communicated by us to Senator Hanna and certain other members of the Senate committee, were declared by them to be exorbitant and inacceptible, and they stated that they were not prepared to recommend the adoption of the Panama plan and the acceptance of the company's offer on such terms. Secretary Hay, also, declared that these terms were excessive and impossible, and told us that the reports he was receiving from the United States minister in Bogota were to the same effect as Minister Concha's proposals, and that he foresaw that Colombia's demands would go beyond all reason.

It was clear that if Colombia did not propose a treaty there would be no basis for a minority report, nor for any real opposition to the Nicaragua bill; that the refusal of Colombia to make a proposal of the kind under existing circumstances would be interpreted as a hostile attitude and would discourage those who were well disposed toward the Panama plan to such an extent that they would in all probability abstain from making any active opposition to Nicaragua; whereas, on the other hand, if an unreasonable offer were made, there would be no opportunity to reduce it, it would be sent to the Senate just as it was, and would have the same fatal effect against the passage of bills favorable to Panama.

The situation was exceedingly perilous and disquieting. Minister Concha was keenly alive to the dangers, but he was bound by the imperative instructions of his Government. The matter had reached an impasse. Minister Concha had not even seen the Secretary of State, and had not given him the faintest assurance of any offer; as a matter of fact he was not disposed to make any offer at this time, and quite seriously informed us that he intended to leave his post and return to Bogota without making any offer. In this matter his door was closed to all except ourselves.

The Senators favorable to Nicaragua often asked at the State Department if Colombia had already made a proposal, and her inaction in this matter, which was also commented upon by the press, had a serious and harmful effect on Panama, whose enemies spread the news that no proposal in any way acceptable to the United States or offering a reasonable basis for the acceptance of the company's offer would be made.

(c) We devise and carry out a plan to overcome the fundamental differences between the Governments in the matter of the prohibitive figure of the annuity insisted upon by Colombia.

At this critical moment we devised a plan which solved the difficulty and which led to a supplementary proposal on the part of Colombia, included in article 25 of the proposed treaty of March 31, 1902, to wit: Instead of making provision for an annuity the amount of which should be unchangeable (and prohibitive) this amount was to be fixed and established, in accordance with certain principles laid down in the treaty, by a high commission, the arbiter of which was to be the president of the International Peace Tribunal at The Hague. This solution obviated the immediate mention of a sum, which if fixed at this time would either have been so high as to render the treaty impossible, and thus have caused the rejection of the offer of Panama to the United States, or so low as to be inacceptable to the government at Bogota, and thus have insured the rejection of the treaty in that quarter; this solution removed the base on which the opposition had relied, and placed the two countries in the reasonable attitude of the one being ready to accept and the other ready to give the amount that would be determined by arbitration on an equiable basis.

After many conferences and discussions we persuaded Minister Concha to accept this solution, and obtained his written consent, accompanied by a letter he wrote to us under date of March 29, 1902. With this consent Minister Concha handed us a draft of a treaty which we had prepared together, the minister stating that he was ready to present this proposal and authorizing us to discuss its terms with Secretary Hay, Senator Hanna, and others, in order to ascertain their views before communicating it officially to the Government of the United States.

Thus it remained for us to satisfy Secretary Hay and the Senators forming the minority of the committee. We devoted ourselves immediately to this task, and after numerous conferences and explanations suceeded in assuring their acquiescence in sufficient degree for our immediate purpose.

(*d*) *We obtain from Colombia an official proposal of a treaty and its presentation to Secretary Hay, and we also write the explanatory letter which accompanies it.*

Having informed Minister Concha of this situation, Mr. Cromwell persuaded him to sign the proposal and to hand it at once to the Secretary of State, arranged an interview for this purpose, and accompanied the minister to make the official presentation of it (the proposal) to Secretary Hay, March 31, 1902. In his written communication the minister declared that a further explanatory note would be presented by Mr. Cromwell. The latter wrote, signed, and handed to the Secretary of State this important document, which strengthened the Colombian proposal and thus buttressed the position of the canal company.

Our explanatory note was forwarded by the President to both Houses of Congress later, at the time of the transmission of the Hay-Concha treaty.

This proposal marked an important step toward the acceptance of the company's offer. It fulfilled our purpose, which was to bring the consent of Colombia within the bounds of international relations and to furnish the basis indispensable to obtaining the support of the Senate.

(*e*) *We continue the negotiations in order to obtain modifications of the Colombian proposal deemed necessary to secure the approval of Congress.*

Although this preliminary essential condition of a treaty proposal by Colombia had been fulfilled and the consent of that country to the transfer also shown thereby, we had foreseen from the start that certain of the terms would have to be modified, otherwise it would be rejected by the Senate. We therefore followed up the negotiations between the United States and Colombia by numerous conferences with Secretary Hay and Minister Concha individually, and we studied the amendments and suggestions of each, always acting as the sole intermediary for communications, and we gave our advice with a view to modifying the demands of Colombia so as to render them reasonably acceptable to the United States. The three weeks that followed were taken up by this work, by rewriting several times the various clauses, discussing the laws applicable and the questions at issue, and individual conferences with the representatives of the two Governments, so that toward the middle of April we had secured amendments to the proposal of March 31 which met with the approval of the President and Secretary of State. Among the important points of the protocol was the vital point of the consent of Colombia to the transfers to the United States (Art. I).

(*f*) *Thanks and congratulations from the company.*

Paris having been immediately notified of this important success, we had the satisfaction of receiving from there, on April 15, the following cable of thanks and appreciation:

"The board has studied your second report, appreciates your efforts and the results obtained, especially wording of Article I of the protocol, and expresses to you its heartiest thanks."

This was followed the next day by the following letter:

PARIS, *April 16, 1902.*

DEAR SIR: We have the honor of confirming our telegrams of the 15th instant to this effect:

"Your second bitterish bassisten to enotabamur, who appreciate your efforts and results obtained, specially wording article first protocol, and expresses to you heartiest thanks."

Which must be translated:

"The board has studied your second report, appreciates your efforts and the results obtained, especially wording of Article I of the protocol, and expresses to you its heartiest thanks."

We have specially appreciated Article I of the protocol, whereby Colombia gives our company the right to sell its property to the United States, which, in fact, abrogates articles 21 and 22 of our contracts of concession, which were opposed to us, and will permit us to resist the pecuniary pretensions of Colombia, as we are absolutely determined to do.

Again be pleased, dear sir, to receive our thanks and the assurances of our most distinguished sentiments.

THE PRESIDENT OF THE BOARD OF DIRECTORS,
M. BÔ.

To Mr. CROMWELL.

As a result of these further negotiations, we wrote a new draft of a treaty (known as the Hay-Concha agreement of April 18, 1902) and had it transmitted officially to the Secretary of State by Minister Concha. The Secretary, after other conferences with Mr. Cromwell for the explanation of the provisions of the amendments, gave Mr. Cromwell, on April 23, 1902, his official statement, dated April 21, 1902, to be transmitted to Minister Concha, in which he declared himself ready to sign the proposed agreement as soon as Congress should authorize the President to conclude an entente and as soon as the Department of Justice should complete its examination of the title.

In all the negotiations concerning the Hay-Concha agreement the minister of the two Governments communicated solely through the intermediary of Mr. Cromwell.

On April 24, 1902, the company, which had been notified of this important event, again expressed its thanks by the following cable:

"Sincere thanks for every important success achieved by you. Consider very carefully question of calling general meeting and necessity of avoiding any incident on Colombia's part analagous to that of February."

These thanks were repeated in the course of the following letter of April 25, 1902:

PARIS, *April 25, 1902.*

DEAR SIR: I hand you inclosed various letters from Mr. Mancini which will inform you on the feelings that Colombia cherishes toward us.

I beg you, after reading them, to consider very carefully whether it would not be well to postpone, at least for the present, the calling of a general meeting which would have to ratify our offers to the Government of the United States.

It seems to me that the calling of a meeting would be very dangerous for the following reasons:

You are not ignorant of the fact that we are obliged, every time we call a general meeting of our shareholders, to ask Colombia to designate a representative for the meeting. Now, would not this very fact reawaken her pretension of demanding from us a given sum for the abrogation of articles 21 and 22 of our contract of concession, which articles we consider as being virtually abrogated by Article I of the protocol handed by Concha to Secretary of State Hay.

Supposing she (Colombia) could not prevent us from calling this meeting before we had obtained from her what she intends to force upon us (? H. N. H.) we should be for 21 days under the menace of any incident which she might even provoke on the eve of the meeting, as she did on February 27 last. Such an incident, which might happen at the very moment the canal bill is being debated in the Senate, would have a disastrous effect.

I believe, and I call your attention to this point, that it would be better in every way to call this meeting only after the vote in the Senate, when the decision to be taken will be subject only to the will of the President of the

United States; that would prevent, or at least render ineffective, any incident provoked by Colombia.

I confirm the telegram which I sent to you yesterday and beg to reiterate, in my name and in the name of the board, our sincere thanks for the important and almost decisive success you achieved in the communication to Secretary of State Hay of Mr. Concha's final protocol.

Please accept, dear sir, the assurance of my most distinguished sentiments.

THE PRESIDENT OF THE BOARD OF DIRECTORS.
M. BÔ.

PRESIDENT ROOSEVELT SUBMITS THE HAY-CONCHA AGREEMENT FOR THE CONSIDERATION OF CONGRESS.

This agreement, thus approved by the representatives of Colombia and of the United States, was transmitted by the President of the United States, with Mr. Cromwell's explanatory letter, to the committees of both Houses of Congress on May 15, 1902.

This marked another decisive step toward the acceptance of the company's offer by the official presentation of the negotiations to Congress and furnished the necessary basis for supporting the Panama project.

This step forward enabled us to make sure of the continued support of the friends of Panama and to delay action by the Senate on the Nicaragua bills, the discussion of which was being pressed.

It was of enormous value in the struggle which was about to take place.

CERTAIN SENATORS DEMAND PROOF OF THE RATIFICATION BY THE SHAREHOLDERS OF THE COMPANY'S OFFER TO THE UNITED STATES—DIFFICULTIES AND DANGERS IN THE WAY OF OBTAINING RATIFICATION AT A GENERAL MEETING—WE DEVISE AND CARRY OUT A PLAN WHICH OVERCOMES THE DIFFICULTY.

The debate on the Nicaragua bill was approaching. Up to then the minority of the Senate committee had not decided to file a report in support of Panama. The two things required by this minority and by other Senators were: (1) A satisfactory treaty proposal from Colombia, and (2) the ratification by the shareholders of the canal company. We had fulfilled the first of these two conditions, but the obstacle of the second remained.

In our various reports to the company we had drawn its attention to the necessity of obtaining the ratification of its offer by the shareholders, but the board of directors and we ourselves recognized the danger there would be in again bringing this matter before a general meeting at which Colombia could again intervene, as she had done on February 28 of the same year, or in encouraging Colombia to put in definite shape the great pecuniary demands which were the price of her consent. The intention to make these demands had been learned through the intermediary of the company's agents in Bogota, as well as by information which Secretary Hay gave us and further details which we obtained from other private sources accessible to ourselves and to the company.

Toward the end of April we again specially called the attention of the board to this matter—at this time Mr. Curtis was in Paris conferring with the board—but the company expressed its grave apprehension of an intervention by Colombia similar to that of February 28, if a general meeting were called.

At the same time the company suggested to us the calling of a general meeting to consider the matter of the Hay-Concha treaty of April 18, and to authorize the board of directors after ratification of this treaty by the two countries, to give a release to Colombia of all concessions granted by it to the canal company, and to thus limit the properties offered the United States to the physical properties of the canal company, with the shares of the Panama Railroad Co.; this suggestion was based on the fact that the reports of the Isthmian Canal Commission had treated the canal concessions as having no pecuniary value.

We studied this plan and gave a contrary opinion in regard to it based on the fact that this plan would change and consequently revoke the company's offer to the United States; that it would force the amendment of the Hay-Concha treaty; that if anything arose to prevent the conclusion of the sale after the ratification of the treaty, the company would be in the position of having no concessions; that the election of this plan would look like the abandonment of its concessions; and, lastly, that it would entail a tacit admission that concessions were without value and would prompt a demand in Congress for a reduction in price.

We gave our assent to the conclusion that it would be dangerous for the company at this juncture to risk a conflict with Colombia in the course of a general meeting. It was imperatively necessary, however, to show to the satisfaction of the Senators, and above all to the members of the minority of the committee, that they could rely upon this ratification. In the face of this difficulty we devised a plan which we explained to the Senators in the course of numerous conferences and which we induced them to accept, to wit: That the company should at once obtain from at least a majority of the shareholders of the company the signatures of formal written consents to the sale, with the undertaking to ratify this sale at any future general meeting called for this purpose. This plan after correspondence and examination was adopted by the company, and these consents and undertakings were obtained by it; they were forwarded to us and finally submitted by us to the Senators in accordance with our promise to produce them.

EFFORTS TO OBTAIN A MINORITY REPORT OF THE SENATE COMMITTEE IN FAVOR OF THE PANAMA PROJECT; SUCCESS OF THESE EFFORTS (MAY, 1902).

Thus, for the time being, the two conditions of primordial importance (treaty and ratification by the shareholders) had been fulfilled, and we then urged the members of the minority of the committee to make a minority report. This was a matter to which these members had given much thought during the preceding weeks. As preliminaries, we wrote a complete and thorough draft of a report and also several other treatises of a legal or technical character bearing upon this draft, and we discussed these documents on many occasions and at great length before the minority of the committee. This work had taken up several weeks, and this document had served as a possible draft of a report in the discussion with the minority of the committee. After full consideration, this report was corrected, adopted, and signed by the minority, and became famous under the name of the "Hanna minority report"; it was the textbook on the Panama side during the debates which followed in the Senate. We had several hundred copies printed, one of which we had sent to each Member of Congress and of the Cabinet, before the debates, and also obtained its circulation in numerous other influential circles. This minority report included a summary and a detailed exposition of the entire Panama Canal matter, from every point of view, technical, legal, physical, economic, comparative, etc. It was the textbook of the campaign in the coming struggle, and it had a most powerful influence on the outcome—by a barely sufficient majority—of the struggle between Nicaragua and Panama. We added to it a synopsis written by us of the existing claims, concessions, etc., of the Maritime Canal and Nicaragua Construction Cos., showing that these companies would demand about $13.000 000 from the United States if that route were adopted, as well as indemnities for the declaration of forfeiture of its concessions by Nicaragua, alleged to be irregular.

The minority also adopted word for word and annexed to its report our opinion on the company's titles, its concessions, its power to transfer, etc., and thus gave to this opinion the seal of official use and approval.

The writing of this minority report, the communication of data, of technical information and legal opinions, the final adoption and circulation of this report constantly occupied two, at least, of our partners for several weeks.

This minority report marked another great step forward.

GREAT STRUGGLE IN THE SENATE ON THE OCCASION OF THE VOTE WHICH WAS TO DECIDE THE SELECTION OF NICARAGUA OR OF PANAMA; OUR PREPARATIONS TO ASSURE THE ADOPTION OF THE MINORITY REPORT FAVORABLE TO PANAMA; AND OUR SUCCESS.

(a) Preparations for the struggle and debates that followed.

The decisive battle on which depended the choice between the projects (Nicaragua or Panama) represented, respectively, by the Morgan-Hepburn bill for Nicaragua and the Spooner bill for Panama, and the acceptance or rejection of the company's offer to the United States, was drawing near.

Whilst the incidents we have already recited were taking place, we were occupied daily with conferences with Senators; with the elaborations of arguments in favor of Panama; with the writing of answers to objections; with the writing and circulation of a note on the disadvantages and objections presented by the Nicaragua project and on the situation of the Nicaragua companies; with the exposition and dissemination of legal arguments; with replies to the numerous misleading and malevolent statements of the Nicaragua supporters; and, in general, with supporting the Spooner bill and urging the acceptance of the offer of the company.

During these decisive weeks of May and June several partners of our law firm were constantly in Washington, personally conducting the matter, giving it their exclusive attention, with the support of every instrumentality of our organization. It was understood that the fate of Panama depended on the outcome. Repeated polls of the Senate had led the supporters of Nicaragua to boast of a large majority, and such was the popular expectation. The Nicaragua group was hurrying on the vote. The debate had been set for June 4, and Mr. Cromwell had taken personal command of the Panama interests.

We had made every possible preparation for the struggle:

(*a*) We had negotiated, written, and assured the exchange of a protocol between Colombia and the United States, granting to the latter the necessary territorial rights and concessions.

(*b*) We had obtained the insertion in the proposed treaty of the official consent of Colombia to the transfer by the company, thus overcoming the obstacles presented by the prohibition of articles 21 and 22 of the concession.

(*c*) We had satisfied for the time being, through a plan devised by us, the senatorial demands for proof that the company's offer would be ratified by its shareholders.

(*d*) We had written and circulated an exhaustive and convincing opinion on the subject of the company's titles and its power to transfer, with an appendix which answered the criticism and legal arguments of the Nicaragua group, and this opinion had been adopted by the minority and submitted to the Senate.

(*e*) We had persuaded the members of the minority of the Senate committee that it was right to make a minority report in favor of Panama; that this report would be justified by the facts; and we had thus laid the fundamental basis for a discussion. This report was filed. We had written the best part of it.

(*f*) We had had personal interviews with the political leaders of the Senate, as well as with many influential members of the Government and of the Republican Party, and, by our arguments, had convinced them of the justice of our views.

(*g*) At the same time, general work of a useful character was being carried on by us in all directions. Two matters are deserving of special mention: (1) the matter of comparative volcanic conditions of the Nicaragua and Panama routes, and the dangers of the Nicaragua route from this cause, and (2) the evidence of men who would themselves use the canal—shipowners, captains of vessels, and others.

These results formed a splendid basis of operations, basis without which the best friends of Panama would not have been ready to support further the cause of Panama, which would have led to a victory for Nicaragua.

(1) The volcanic character of the region through which the Nicaragua route passed was constantly utilized by us as an argument against the selection of this route. Prior to this we had secured the advice and assistance of a distinguished scientist, whose name is known throughout America as an acknowledged expert on these matters, who visited the region of Nicaragua and Panama, and who later wrote articles on this aspect of the question, showing the dangers to which the Nicaragua route was exposed on this account. At this juncture, May 8, the great catastrophe of Mount Pelée occurred, and riveted the attention of humanity on this unforeseen and destructive power.

In order to present, in a graphic manner, to the Senate the probabilities of the destruction of the Nicaragua Canal by this force, because of the volcanic nature of the region, we obtained the official records and data of volcanic eruptions in this region and had them illustrated in a graphic manner on maps that we had printed and distributed to all the Senators. These maps brought out the fact that volcanic eruptions were characteristic of Central America, including Nicaragua and Costa Rica, and that no volcanoes existed within 200 miles of the Panama route.

At the beginning of the controversy, on March 7, an eruption took place at Mount Monotombo, on Lake Nicaragua, a few miles north of the line of the Nicaragua Canal, and we also took this fact as a further proof of our state ments, and the fact having been disputed by the Nicaragua minister we confirmed the truth of it by direct cables from Central America to which we gave wide publicity.

The arguments based on volcanic conditions were effectively used by Senator Hanna in the senatorial debates which followed.

(2) Among the objections to the Panama route which had considerable influence upon the Senate was that the calms that obtain in the Gulf of Panama would render that route, so to speak, impracticable to sailing vessels, and that the greater distance separating the United States from the Panama Canal would lessen its value to our shipping.

We deemed that to reply to these objections the most forceful arguments would be those furnished by the testimony of experienced shipowners and captains of vessels who were themselves to use the route of the canal, and at our suggestion Senator Hanna authorized us to obtain this evidence. With his permission we wrote a series of questions covering the entire field of the relative advantages of the two canals for practical navigation, and had them sent to more than 80 shipowners, captains of vessels, and other officers of steamships and sailing vessels of the high seas. The replies to this series of questions, to the number of more than 80, fully confirmed our arguments and justified our attitude; they were given to Senator Hanna who presented them in extenso to the Senate in the course of the debate that followed; they figure in the official report of the Senate debates. The documents in this matter, as on all other matters, will be presented at the hearing of the present case.

Everything was then ready for the final struggle in the Senate, which began on June 4, 1902, and continued till June 19, 1902, in debates on the question of the passage of the Hepburn bill (Nicaragua) or of the Spooner bill (Panama). Senators Morgan and Harris led the supporters of the Hepburn bill, while Senators Hanna and Spooner led those of the Spooner bill. All the prominent Members of the Senate took part in the debates, and many of them made prepared and lengthy speeches.

During every hour of this struggle two at least of the partners of our law firm, with other assistants, kept in constant consultation with the Senators and assisted them in answering the arguments advanced against Panama in the course of the debates, giving information in support of this project, as well as furnishing arguments and information in reply to the arguments advanced in favor of Nicaragua, going to Senators' homes and presenting arguments to them, frustrating the hostile maneuvers and false statements about the Chagres River, the harbors, duration of transit through the canal and other practical questions, and in every way increasing and strengthening the support of Panama. Step by step, as the discussions progressed, we passed in review every detail of the debates and every move in the matter, which were the subjects of advice and suggestions on our part.

Every effort was made by each of the sides to secure the presence of absent Senators or to bring about the pairing of contrary votes, with such success that only about six Members of the Senate were absent at the final vote, and as to those an equal number had agreed to abstain from voting.

The debates attracted great attention; the Senate Chamber was almost always thronged by an attentive audience; the press followed the debate very closely and reported its successive phases; an exceptional number of Senators were present; the struggle was followed with intense interest by the whole country.

(b) Victory for Panama after a fierce struggle in the Senate by 42 votes for and 34 against—the loss of 5 votes to the advantage of Nicaragua would have killed Panama forever.

The final vote took place on a motion to substitute the Spooner bill (Panama), indorsed by the minority report, for the Hepburn bill (Nicaragua), indorced by the majority report. When a vote on this motion was reached it was decided by the narrow majority of 42 votes in favor of the substitution of the Spooner bill against 34 in favor of the Hepburn bill. A slight difference of 5 votes would have killed the Panama Canal project and have made the Nicaragua Canal the choice of the American people. The supporters of Nicaragua in their desperate efforts to neutralize the victory vigorously supported a motion directing that any treaty with Colombia be concluded within six months (which in last analysis would have resulted in the defeat of the Panama project, as the treaty could not be obtained within that time), and this motion was defeated by 44 votes against and 33 for. They then introduced a similar motion fixing the delay at 12 months, and this motion was nearly passed, the vote being 39 against and 35 for. Various other motions were introduced for the same purpose, which was to make the selection of the Panama project impossible, even in spite of the law, if it were voted, but all were rejected with the same slight difference in the number of the votes. But the final ballot having favored Panama, the passage of the bill (according to custom) took place in the Senate, so to speak, without opposition.

Thus our long fight in the Senate had been won for Panama.

(c) *Thanks and congratulations of the company.*

Once again, on receipt of the news of the victory, we had the pleasure of receiving the thanks of the board by the following cable of June 20, 1902:

"In my name and in the name of the board, send you our most sincere congratulations on success obtained, appreciating your action."

These thanks were confirmed by the company in the following letter:

"PARIS, *June 27, 1902.*

"We confirm the congratulations which we sent you by cable on the 20th instant on the result obtained in the Senate by the vote of the Spooner bill. We hope with you that the House will ratify this vote, and that the choice of the Panama route will then be subject only to the assent of Colombia."

JUNE 20–26, 1902.—CONFLICT BETWEEN THE SENATE AND THE HOUSE AS TO THE CHOICE OF ROUTES FOR THE CANAL—THE HOUSE REJECTS PANAMA, ADHERES TO THE NICARAGUA BILL—CONFERENCES BETWEEN THE HOUSES—THE SENATE REFUSES TO RECEDE—THE HOUSE FINALLY SUBMITS AND GIVES ITS ASSENT TO THE SPOONER BILL.

But the struggle was not yet over, as in the House it was still necessary to fight on to the end; and it was this same House which had passed the Nicaragua bill five months previously by 309 votes for and 2 against. The Spooner bill was at once sent to the House, which rejected it, adhering to its own, the Hepburn bill. This action resulted in the two bills being sent to a conference between the two Houses. Delegates were appointed by both Houses; the Senate was represented by Senators Hanna, Morgan, and Kittredge, and the House by Messrs. Hepburn, Fletcher, and Davey. The conferees sat all through the ensuing week and tried to win each other over. The Senate delegates persisted to the end in refusing to yield to the House. The House delegates yielded at last, and the House, after some opposition and discussion, approved the action of its delegates and passed the Spooner bill.

At every step of this critical conflict we were consulted by Senators Hanna and Kittredge, who were delegates and had signed the minority report, and we exchanged views with them on every question; and we had conferences almost day and night with Members of the House, among whom we made efforts to assure the passage of the Spooner bill.

Thus the action of the House in rejecting the offer of the company and in selecting Nicaragua underwent an entire change and Panama was saved from imminent disaster.

We are more than justified in saying that without our efforts this result would not have been obtained, the offer of the company would have been rejected, and the Nicaragua route would have been chosen.

JUNE 28, 1902.—THE SPOONER ACT IS PROMULGATED AS LAW, PANAMA IS ADOPTED SUBJECT TO CERTAIN CONDITIONS IN DEFAULT OF WHICH THE ADOPTION OF THE NICARAGUA ROUTE IS ORDERED.

The bill was signed by the President on June 28, 1902, the offer made by the Panama Canal Co. was thus accepted, and the Panama route chosen, but on condition (1) that the title of the company be approved, and (2) that a satisfactory treaty be concluded with Colombia; with the alernative of the adoption of the Nicaragua route in default of one or the other of these conditions.

Again, on this occasion we had the satisfaction of receiving the thanks of the company by the following cable of July 4, 1902:

"Your wire received. Congratulations on its contents. We call your attention to this fact, that from August 1 to October 15 prominent lawyers will be absent from Paris. Advise you also to ask before August 1 for any legal documents, information, or opinions you may judge useful and necessary."

The secretary general of the company had come to the United States in January in connection with the company's offer, and after this matter had been entrusted to us anew the increasing perils, struggles, and anxieties made it advisable for him to remain here several months. It was extremely gratifying to us to have at our side this intelligent and zealous official of the company, and thus to be able to keep him informed of every phase of the movement which, like a tide, had its ebb and flow, and of the progress we were making.

We then applied ourselves to the task of fulfilling the two conditions of the Spooner Act—the necessary treaty and approval of the titles.

JUNE 28–JULY 24, 1902.—FURTHER NEGOTIATIONS WITH A VIEW TO GIVING THE TREATY WITH COLOMBIA A FORM SATISFACTORY TO THE UNITED STATES, IN ORDER TO OVERCOME THE OBJECTIONS RAISED IN THE SENATE.

As to the treaty: The Hay-Concha agreement, which had been submitted to the Senate, while presenting a sufficient basis for the passage of the Spooner Act, had been found unsatisfactory on several points by many Senators, who insisted that the United States should have the right to establish additional courts in the Canal Zone, to maintain there a police force, and to have control of the sanitation. They also demanded that the forfeiture clause of the proposed treaty be omitted and that a given cash sum, plus a small annuity, be substituted for the enormous and so uncertain pecuniary assignments of the proposed treaty.

According to the Constitution of the United States it is indispensable that a treaty be passed by a majority of two-thirds, and as it had only been possible to obtain a slight majority for the passage of the Spooner Act it was clear that the necessary ratification of a treaty could not be obtained unless all reasonable objections were met in a manner to win a sufficient number of additional votes to make up the two-thirds necessary, and that it mattered a little whether the objections were justified or made in bad faith.

We applied ourselves to this task, and after other conferences with many Senators to learn their views or their objections and after careful study we prepared a revision of the treaty and submitted it to Secretary Hay, at his request. These amendments called for most minute study and examination of all the special factors in the matter and a great deal of original work. Numerous conferences between Secretary Hay and ourselves followed, and at last we reached an understanding with Secretary Hay and the President on the subject of what would appear to be acceptable to the Senate.

It then became also necessary to obtain the consent of Minister Concha, and we had a series of conferences with him on the subject of these amendments which were discussed, studied, and reviewed with him every day, up to July 18, 1902, date on which we succeeded in bringing the representatives of the two Governments to an understanding. Pursuant to arrangements made by us, as intermediaries, Secretary Hay officially transmitted these amendments to Minister Concha who, in turn, transmitted them to his Government. In this way the treaty was given a form satisfactory to the President and also, it was believed, to the Senate, and this revision was on its way addressed to the Bogota Government.

In this negotiation, as in the preceding one, the ministers of the two Governments always communicated with each other through the intermediary of Mr. Cromwell, and only met to exchange the final documents after the understanding had been reached (apres l'entente).

We had thus made another important step.

EXAMINATION OF THE TITLE BY THE ATTORNEY GENERAL—PREPARATION OF DOCUMENTS PROVING THE VALIDITY OF THE TITLE OF LA CAMPAGNIE NOUVELLE DU CANAL DE PANAMA, AND ITS LEGAL RIGHT TO TRANSFER—STAY IN PARIS WITH THE ATTORNEYS GENERAL OF THE UNITED STATES GOVERNMENT—SOLUTION OF ALL LEGAL QUESTIONS TO THEIR SATISFACTION.

The treaty being then underway, we turned our attention to the other fundamental condition of the Spooner Act—that is to say the company's title of ownership and its power to transfer. We had already studied this question, and our printed opinion had been presented to the Senate and adopted as part of the minority report of the Senate committee, as we have already pointed out. But the Spooner Act provided for a critical examination by the United States of all the title deeds and of all legal questions from the point of view of a buyer, in order to assure to the United States an absolute title, free from all liens or complications, and in addition the necessary approval of the stockholders.

On behalf of the United States, the Department of Justice, at the head of which is the Attorney General, was naturally intrusted with this matter. This official appointed a special assistant to help him with the preliminary work. Before the beginning of the investigation we furnished the Attorney General with printed copies of our opinion, with the principal title deeds of the property translated from the French and printed. We arranged with him for the regular examination of these questions in Paris, and Mr. Cromwell left for that city on July 24, 1902, for this purpose.

During the two following months, in Paris, Mr. Cromwell devoted himself exclusively to preparing the presentation, and then to the presentation and explanation, in its smallest details, to the Special Assistant Attorney General and to the Attorney General himself of the company's title and its power to transfer.

For this purpose Mr. Cromwell prepared in advance a general explanation or diagram of the title, which embraced some 60 different subjects, for each of which he had a special file prepared. These files contained the various concessions for the canal and railroad and all their prorogations; numerous court decisions, with the legal proceedings which had led up to them; the statutes of and other documents bearing upon the organization of the old company; the liquidation of the latter; the statutes of and other documents bearing upon the organization of the new company; the agreements between the liquidator and the new company; the transfers from the old company to the new; the charter; the organization and legal history of the Panama Railroad; the special agreements between the liquidator and the new company in regard to the Panama Railroad shares; the financial condition of the canal company; the financial condition of the railroad company; the lists of shareholders of the canal company and of shareholders of the railroad company; the various bond issues and share issues of the Compagnie Universelle; the organization and condition of the holding companies of the lottery bonds; the title deeds of real estate on the Isthmus; the status of the various judgments against the old company in Paris and on the Isthmus; the special French law relating to the liquidation of the old company; certificates proving the payments made to Colombia in accordance with the concession; the history and legal status of the Dounadieu, Joreau, and other injunctions; the proceedings before the civil courts authorizing the liquidator to cooperate in the sale to the United States; the arbitration and agreement between the liquidator and the new company in the matter of the division of the $40,000,000; the various proceedings of the board of directors and the shareholders in the matter of the proposed sale and, in general, everything bearing on the legal history of the canal and railroad companies.

These files, which are presented, were all the object of critical examination on our part, and we also explained them to the Special Assistant Attorney General. We pay high tribute to the skillful assistance rendered by Messrs. Lampré and Marie in the course of the compilation, translation, and classification of the numerous documents and notes.

This also entailed numerous conferences between Mr. Cromwell and the Assistant Attorney General, every day, for the discussion and explanation of doubtful questions and the communication of further documents called for by him.

Although we had given the Attorney General of the United States our opinion, which had been officially accepted by the Senate minority report, approved by the passage of the Spooner Act, we advised that this opinion be indorsed by eminent French jurists. This line of conduct was adopted, and we had our opinion translated, printed in French, and submitted to Maitres Waldeck Rousseau, Léon Devin, H. Du Buit, H. Limbourg, Henri Thiebelin, and Paul Gontard. We also presented our own views to these eminent jurists in support of our opinion, and they, after full deliberation, did us the great honor of adding to it their absolute indorsement, without making any changes.

In the course of his researches the Assistant Attorney General submitted to us a series of objections of a legal nature which had been raised in Congress by partisans of the Nicaragua Canal, the sense of which was that the Panama Canal Co. had neither valid property title nor the power to transfer; that the liquidator of the old company still retained the legal title, at least in part, and that the consent of the bondholders and shareholders of the old company was necessary to a valid transfer; that the concessions and assets of the new company were subject to a trust lien in favor of the creditors and shareholders of the old company; that the French Government also had certain rights and that the transfer could not take place without the consent of that Government; that, under the law of 1888 on the lottery bonds, the materials used in the construction of the canal must be of French manufacture; that the French courts had no jurisdiction to authorize the liquidator to consent to the sale, etc.

Besides our own opinion, which maintained that these objections were ill-founded in law, we advised the company to obtain the opinions of French jurists on these matters, and these questions were submitted to the same eminent jurists. They were discussed by them with us in lengthy conferences and were the object of exhaustive deliberation on their part, that led to opinions which we gave to the Attorney General. These gentlemen indorsed our opinion and, by conclusive arguments, declared that the objections we have mentioned were erroneous and without legal basis according to French law.

The Attorney General of the United States came himself to Paris, before the close of this examination, and Mr. Cromwell had conferences with him on legal matters.

The regular examination of the company's titles and power to transfer was thus brought to an end, but the Attorney General reserved his own examination, the study of the documents and legal questions, and his final decision in the matter till after his return to the United States.

The Attorney General, his assistant, and Mr. Cromwell returned to the United States about October 1 after an absence of two months, during which the latter had devoted his whole time to this matter.

In due course we had various conferences with the Attorney General and his assistant on the legal questions under examination and we made a last oral argument to them on the matter on October 22. After further consideration this distinguished official handed, on October 25, his full and final opinion to the President, declaring that the company's titles were valid and that it had the power to transfer, and at the same time delivered a copy to us.

The company having been informed by us of this result, sent us on October 27, 1902, the following cable:

"Board of directors sends you all its thanks and all its congratulations."

Thus was obtained the confirmation of our opinion on all the points of law originally submitted to Congress and to the Attorney General, and one of the fundamental conditions of the Spooner Act fulfilled.

OCTOBER 25–NOVEMBER 22, 1902—WE RESUME NEGOTIATIONS WITH COLOMBIA FOR THE NECESSARY TREATY—COLOMBIA DEFERS OR REFUSES TO CONTINUE NEGOTIATIONS WITH THE UNITED STATES—WE INDUCE COLOMBIA TO RESUME THE NEGOTIATIONS, BUT COLOMBIA RESUMES NEGOTIATIONS WITH THE DEMAND THAT THE COMPANY FIRST MAKE A PECUNIARY ARRANGEMENT IN EXCHANGE FOR THE CONSENT OF COLOMBIA AND THAT THE UNITED STATES INCREASE THE PAYMENTS, ETC.—THE UNITED STATES REJECTS THE SAID DEMANDS—CONCHA BREAKS OFF NEGOTIATIONS AND LEAVES FOR BOGOTA WITHOUT NOTIFYING THE UNITED STATES.

We then turned our attention anew to the matter of the treaty, as the last condition of the Spooner Act. During this same period of two months (from July 24 to Sept. 30, 1902) Mr. Farnham remained almost constantly in Washington and Mr. Hill frequently joined him there for conferences with Minister Concha, Secretary Herran, and officials of the State Department, keeping themselves informed and watching the various interests of the company in Washington, and making frequent reports by cable to our partner in Paris.

On his return Mr. Cromwell again took up his headquarters in Washington to accelerate the treaty matter. He encountered fresh complications and a complete radical change of attitude on the part of Minister Concha. This official openly showed his hostility to the Government of the United States, and abstained from calling upon Secretary Hay or even communicating with him. This change of attitude was due in part to the determination, every day stronger, in Bogota, to force the canal company to pay a money tribute in exchange for the consent of Colombia, and to the differences on the Isthmus between the United States Navy officers and those of the Colombian Government caused by the refusal of the American officers to permit the transportation of Colombian troops in arms over the railroad on the ground that such action might lead to fighting with the insurgents and thus cause loss to the railroad and interfere with its traffic.

The Bogota Government had not yet given instructions to its minister to conclude the treaty.

Our partner devoted himself for several weeks in Washington to tranquillizing the minister, and trying to reestablish the negotiations on the cordial basis which had existed prior to his departure for Paris, in the preceding July.

Meanwhile the change in Colombia's attitude had been learned in diplomatic circles, the hopes of the supporters of the Nicaragua Canal were reawakened and their activity returned. Secretary Hay informed us that the attitude of Colombia in not continuing and not concluding the negotiations on the basis of the Hay-Concha agreement, was so unreasonable that he could no longer permit himself to defer treating with Nicaragua and Costa Rica and that Senator Morgan was pressing the State Department to open negotiations with these nations, which, he added, were now ready to sign a treaty, in whatever form was demanded by the State Department.

The opening of Congress was at hand, and it became clear that the supporters of the Nicaragua Canal would make fresh efforts to end the negotiations with Colombia by alleging that a reasonable time for obtaining this treaty had elapsed.

Up to October 30 Minister Concha refused to act. On that day Secretary Hay cabled Minister Concha's refusal to do anything to the Bogota Government, and informed it that the President was about to open negotiations with Nicaragua if Minister Concha did not act promptly. At the same time he wrote to Minister Concha that the President would take action under the Spooner Act if the Government of Colombia did not give a prompt reply. At the same time, also, Secretary Hay warned us that he had been informed by the Nicaraguan minister that the latter was ready to consider any treaty satisfactory to the United States.

As a result of Secretary Hay's telegraphic notifications, Minister Concha received instructions to act and to discuss, but this official informed us that he would not obey his instructions; that he considered them unpatriotic and contrary to the real interests of Colombia; that he intended to resign rather than to continue the negotiation of a treaty on the basis demanded by the United States.

Knowing that his resignation would cause confusion, delay, and dangers, we begged the minister, personally and by letter, not to act thus, but to negotiate. Minister Concha wrote to us expressing his high esteem, and finally he yielded and promised to take up the treaty, but on the condition that the negotiations should be limited at first to the question of sovereignty.

In consequence, on November 5, Concha submitted the question of sovereignty to Mr. Hay. The latter sent for Mr. Cromwell and detailed conferences followed. Finally the President authorized Mr. Hay to yield. It was an important point, because, unless sovereignty were granted, the negotiations could have no result.

Minister Concha, now forced to reveal his intentions fully, wrote and presented, first to us and later to Secretary Hay (Nov. 11), seven amendments to the proposed treaty, amendments of a fundamental nature, above all that of Article I, as follows:

"This same article shall state clearly that the authority given by Colombia to the canal and railroad companies to transfer their rights to the United States shall be governed by the special agreement previously to be made between Colombia and the said companies, for which agreement they have been notified to appoint an agent (mandataire) in Bogota."

The purpose of this amendment was astutious, as, while the consent of Colombia was maintained and she thus appeared to be acting in good faith in her negotiations with the United States, this consent was subject to the condition of a previous agreement between the canal company and Colombia and would thus oblige the company to pay an enormous pecuniary tribute or to see the treaty fall through if the company did not yield to the exactions of Colombia.

It was a vital and fundamental point for the company, and Mr. Cromwell deployed all his energy in resisting the acceptance of this amendment. He conferred frequently on this matter with Secretary Hay, and at his request explained to him the full scope of the amendment as well as the relations between the parties. He showed him that it would be disadvantageous to consent to this amendment. The result of these arguments and conferences was that

Secretary Hay declared himself in accord with our views, and in his official reply to Minister Concha he rejected the amendment.

The company expressed its appreciation of this new service by the following cable:

"DECEMBER 1, 1902.

"LADYCOURT, *New York:*

"Cables received. Congratulations and thanks. Hope for favorable conclusion soon. Have decided to call only ordinary meeting."

At the request of Mr. Hay we prepared a revision of the treaty in accordance with the existing status of the negotiations.

On November 24 Minister Concha sent to Secretary Hay, in reply, a long memorial, in which he justified his position and maintained it.

At this juncture Mr. Hay notified us that he had learned from Bogota that the present plan of Colombia was to declare the prorogation till 1910 invalid, forfeit the concessions, and then propose a direct sale to the United States. We expressed the indignation with which such a design filled us. The United States did not accept (fall in with) the suggestion of Colombia.

One of Minister Concha's amendments covered the question of the amount of the annuity to be paid by the United States under the treaty. The sum demanded by Colombia was $600,000 a year; it was based in part on the alleged loss of revenues in tonnage and lighthouse dues at Panama and Colon, a loss which it was pretended would ensue in case these were made free ports under the treaty. In order to acquaint ourselves with the facts and to influence the parties, we began and pushed to a successful conclusion an inquiry on the Isthmus, resulting in the discovery of the fact that the statement that Colombia had made on the subject of the revenues derived from this source was grossly exaggerated, and we obtained and communicated to both parties the exact figures, proving the truth of our assertions, which later brought Colombia to reduce her pretensions.

At last Minister Concha became so violent in his opposition to the terms of the proposed treaty that on November 29, 1902, on the eve of the meeting of Congress, he broke off all negotiations and left the legation to go to New York, without even taking leave of the State Department, or giving it any explanation, and he left shortly afterwards for Bogota. This departure left the Colombian Legation in a state of demoralization, and Mr. Herran, the secretary of the legation, remained in charge, without authority or instructions.

We were deeply perturbed by this fresh complication, and we had to cope with it alone.

NOVEMBER, 1902–JANUARY, 1903—BY OUR EFFORTS WE AVOID THE DANGER OF THE ABANDONMENT BY THE PRESIDENT OF THE EFFORTS TO OBTAIN A SATISFACTORY TREATY WITH COLOMBIA AND THE CHOICE BY HIM OF THE ALTERNATIVE ROUTE.

As soon as the Colombian minister had gone, the partisans of Nicaragua began a campaign in the press and by personal communications to urge the President to open negotitions with Nicaragua and Costa Rica for the conclusion of a treaty, declaring that Colombia had abandoned the negotiations and there was no chance of dealing with that country, and that a reasonable time had already elapsed.

At the same time the ministers of Nicaragua and Costa Rica announced in the newspapers that their Governments were ready to make any treaty with the United States that could be considered fair, and we were again face to face with the necessity of fighting the supporters of the Nicaragua Canal in Congress and in the field of diplomacy.

Secretary Hay, in view of the uncertainties of the situation in the Panama matter, considered it his duty to continue negotiations with Nicaragua and Costa Rica, and it was announced in the press in December, 1902, that he had drawn up the new treaties and that the ministers of these two countries had received instructions to sign them.

At the same time Senator Hanna and other party leaders in the Senate insistently demanded action on the part of Colombia.

The December session of Congress was at hand. The President was strongly urged by the partisans of the Nicaragua Canal to insert in his coming message to Congress a full explanation of the involved condition of the negotiations with Colombia, and to declare that a reasonable delay for the acquisition of the Panama Canal having elapsed and the negotiations having been fruitless it was necessary to adopt the Nicaragua route.

The attitude of Colombia was so extraordinary and so indifferent, her demands were so exaggerated that the President gave serious consideration to the situation to determine whether the Spooner Act did not impose this action upon him as a duty, of which Mr. Hay and Senator Hanna informed us. The situation was full of danger, and Mr. Curtis and Mr. Cromwell remained in Washington for two weeks, endeavoring by continual conferences and efforts to avert this misfortune, insisting that a further delay in which to obtain the necessary treaty should be granted. The President took the responsibility of granting a new and slight delay and abstained from commenting upon the matter in his message.

Congress met and Senator Morgan, on December 20, introduced a motion by the terms of which the President was requested to conclude at once the negotiations for the Nicaragua Canal, as no treaty had been arrived at with Colombia. We organized opposition to this motion, which was defeated. But the situation was nevertheless extremely perilous, as the negotiations with Colombia had arrived at an impasse and neither of the nations was taking any action. But inaction, from whatever cause, was fatal to Panama.

AFTER THE ABANDONMENT OF HIS POST BY MINISTER CONCHA WE CONTINUE NEGOTIATIONS WITH CHARGÉ D'AFFAIRES HERRAN—WE DISCOVER AND CARRY OUT A PLAN TO SOLVE THE EXISTING DIFFICULTIES AND WE BRING ABOUT THE CONCLUSION OF THE HAY-HERRAN TREATY.

The abandonment of his post by Minister Concha and his refusal to continue the negotiations, contrary to the orders of his Government, left the legation in a quandary and the negotiations in a critical position.

Fortunately Chargé d'Affaires Herran continued to have the same confidence in us that had been shown by his predecessors, Ministers Silva and Concha, and he, as they, maintained intimate and confidential relations with us. Through these relations we learned that the Bogota Government had given Minister Herran instructions to continue the negotiations on the basis of the acceptance by the United States of all the Concha amendments (which included a previous agreement between the canal company and the Government) and also the payment by the United States of $10,000,000 cash and a perpetual annuity of $600,000.

The United States continued to firmly resist the Concha amendments and the increase of the payments.

We understood that unless the parties were brought to an agreemeent, the negotiations would fall through and the consequences be disastrous. Two, at least, of our partners were entirely taken up by this matter in conferences with Chargé d'Affaires Herran and Secretary Hay and others. Mr. Cromwell was urging Secretary Hay to increase the annuity, and on December 12, after a long conference with him, the latter (after a conference with the President) authorized us to promise Minister Herran an increase in the annuity payable by the United States from $10,000 to $100,000 a year. Although this offer marked a great advance in the negotiations, there still remained a considerable difference of $500,000 a year, and Minister Herran's instructions prohibited him from accepting the sum offered.

The Secretary of State, whose patience, quite naturally, was well nigh exhausted, prepared to close the negotiations, and he thus informed us. It was clear that such action, although entirely justified, would have a disastrous effect, and as a consequence entail the adoption of Nicaragua; so we had a personal interview with Secretary Hay on January 2, and also wrote him begging him not to send his ultimatum. The next day (Jan. 3) we again had long conferences with Secretary Hay, continuing our insistent urgings against the sending of an ultimatum, giving him details of our last interviews with Minister Herran and assuring him of our conviction that if the United States would grant another delay we would succeed in bringing about an understanding. As a result of these assertions and solicitations Secretary Hay consented to defer for a little longer his ultimatum.

We at once devoted a whole day to a conference with Minister Herran and collaborated in the writing of a cable to Bogota, insistently asking for wider powers in the negotiations, but these instructions did not arrive.

Meanwhile (Jan. 3) the United States minister in Bogota, Mr. Hart, informed Secretary Hay by cable that the Government of Colombia intended to demand an indemnity from the company before ratifying any treaty. We at once had conferences with Secretary Hay and the President to combat Colombia's attitude.

In the course of one of these conferences, Secretary Hay told us that President Roosevelt had informed him that he would approve the Nicaragua and Costa Rica treaties and that he would send them to the Senate for ratification if Colombia did not act promptly; and Secretary Hay authorized us to repeat these words to Chargé d'Affaires Herran, which we did at once.

On January 16, Secretary Hay informed us that he had received a cable from Minister Hart, stating that Colombia was unwilling to accept the offer made by the United States and that she had given instructions to Minister Herran to insist upon the terms previously laid down, and upon all of the Concha amendments; the cable also stated that the Panama Canal Co. was requested to appoint an agent in Bogota. The same day Minister Herran showed us a cable from his Government on the same matter and to the same effect. Secretary Hay then gave instructions, by cable, to the American minister in Bogota, ordering him to announce officially to the Colombian Government that "if the present attitude of Colombia does not change, it will render impossible the continuation of the negotiations and the pourparlers will be closed."

Senator Morgan and others were daily renewing their pleas to the President and to Secretary Hay for the closure of the negotiations with Colombia, and the adoption of the Nicaragua route.

The Bogota Government maintained its obstinate, indifferent, and exacting attitude both toward the United States and toward the canal company. Even the warmest supporters of Panama were utterly discouraged by this deadlock, for it was clear to all that unless the negotiations were at once brought to a successful conclusion, the President would not only be within his rights in abandoning them on account of Colombia's attitude, but would be forced to do so under the very terms of the Spooner Act which provided an alternative and only gave him a reasonable time within which to conclude this treaty.

It is no exaggeration to say that we were almost in despair, for if neither of the Governments could satisfy the other (and they were, so to speak, no longer in communication), a solution seemed impossible. Under these critical conditions we were busy for several successive days placing our arguments before the Colombian chargé d'affaires, examining with him the instructions that had been given, and discussing various plans to bring about an agreement. The chargé d'affaires was well disposed, but almost powerless.

At the request of Secretary Hay, we kept him informed almost hour by hour of the state of the negotiations which still seemed to hold out no hope and which were looked upon by the officials of the United States Government as virtually closed and about to be officially ended by the delivery of this Government's ultimatum and the public announcement of this step. We were in continuous session with Mr. Herran, and at last persuaded him to take the responsibility and abandon all the Concha amendments (including the vital amendment which reserved the consent of Colombia to the transfer provided for in Article 1), except that dealing with the indemnities from the United States.

This was another important step toward success, but as to the pecuniary arrangements we were not out of the deadlock.

We continued our efforts to persuade him through conferences, and again Mr. Cromwell found a solution by devising the following plan to replace Article XXV-B (in the matter of the pecuniary indemnity, to wit, the exact amount of the indemnity was left to a commission of three persons named in the treaty (with the President of The Hague tribunal as arbitrator, but within the maximum and minimum limits proposed by each Government. After prolonged efforts, Mr. Cromwell persuaded Minister Herran to accept this substitution, and to authorize him to propose it to the United States. This is what the minister did in the following communication:

LEGATION OF COLOMBIA,
Washington, D. C., January 16, 1903.

Mr. WILLIAM NELSON CROMWELL.

DEAR SIR: I repeat what I told you this morning; that is, I will sign in the name of my Government the treaty proposed by the United States if Article XXV-B is modified by the substitution of the attached clause which you suggest, and which I have approved with my initials.

Truly, yours, TOMAS HERRAN.

We immediately presented this note to Secretary Hay and to the President urging them to approve it. As a result of long conferences we were authorized to announce to Mr. Herran that his proposal would be accepted unless a given sum were fixed by agreement, which was preferred.

This was an enormous advance, as it delayed the ultimatum and reopened the door to negotiation. Having succeeded so far, we suggested a compromise on the basis of 250,000 a year. This was the amount of the annuity which had been served for so many years under the Panama Railroad Co.'s concessions, and we maintained it was a precedent that furnished an equitable basis for a settlement. The United States, however, had not yet shown the slightest disposition to exceed the figure of $100,000. At last Mr. Herran yielded to our arguments and authorized us to offer Mr. Hay a compromise on the basis of $250,000. Great as was this success it was still necessary to bring the United States to increase the indemnity to this figure. On the 21st of the month, far into the night and the whole of the following day, Mr. Cromwell devoted himself to this task, discussing with Secretary Hay, explaining the dangers of the situation to him, and the necessity for immediate action (because the Bogota Government could at any moment reduce Mr. Herran's powers, which was already a matter of apprehension), and urging insistently the increase of the indemnity offered by the United States to the amount of this figure. As a result of these arguments and of his own conviction the Secretary authorized a compromise at this figure if we could obtain the approval by the chargé d'affaires of all the other clauses of the treaty. We went to that official's house, we made a supreme effort to decide him, and brought him to an agreement on all the questions yet unsettled. Then we rapidly corrected the draft of the treaty to make it conform to this arrangement, and, accompanying Chargé d'Affaires Herran to the Secretary's residence in the evening of January 22, 1903, we announced to the latter that an understanding had been reached and that Mr. Herran was ready to sign the treaty then and there. Mr. Herran confirmed this statement, after the assurance had been given him by Secretary Hay that the said treaty represented the best terms that the United States could grant.

The treaty was then immediately signed by the two ministers; there were present only Secretary Hay, Chargé d'Affaires Herran, and Mr. Cromwell.

(The pen with which the Secretary and the chargé d'affaires signed this treaty is one of the precious souvenirs of this incident; the secretary presented it to Mr. Cromwell as a mark of appreciation of the part he took in the so long and apparently so hopeless negotiations.)

This treaty was at once sent by the President to the Senate of the United States (Jan. 23, 1903) where a great s ruggle was afterwards to take place over its ratification.

Thus was concluded the Hay-Herran treaty which fulfilled the last conditions of the Spooner Act, and saved the fate of the Panama Canal. It became the subject of controversies not only in the United States Senate where it was ratified, but also in Colombia where it failed of ratification, which was what justified the subsequent separation and independence of the Republic of Panama, and the immediate conclusion with the new Republic of a similar treaty wherein were repeated the fundamental clauses of the Hay-Herran treaty which granted the consent to the transfer by the Panama Canal Co. to the United States by authorizing the acceptance of the company's offer to the United States.

It is not through vanity but simply because it is absolutely necessary to sta e the fact, in order to point out the true significance of this service, that it must be noted here that the entire negotiation of the treaty with Colombia was conducted by Mr. Cromwell, with Ministers Concha and Herran and Secretary Hay, who held nearly all their official communications through his intermediary exclusively, without meeting each other, except on one or two official occasions, up to the hour when Mr. Cromwell brought about a meeting of the representatives of the two Governments for the signature of the treaty on January 22, 1903, the matter being then settled.

As an historical detail showing by how narrow a margin we succeeded, we note that a few hours after the signing of the treaty, Mr. Herran received a peremptory cable from his Government to suspend all negotiations till the receipt of fresh instructions. This dispatch which if it had arrived a few hours earlier would have paralyzed all action, and have prevented any result, was on its way from Bogota when, thanks to the strongest pressure, we succeeded in having the treaty concluded in order to avoid this very possibility which we had feared.

On January 21 (? H. N. H.), we wrote to the company to announce the happy conclusion of the treaty, and we had the pleasure of receiving, in reply, the following letter:

PARIS, *January 31, 1903.*

GENTLEMEN: We have duly received your letter of January 21 and have read with very keen interest all the details you give us on the final phases of the negotiations which preceded the signature of the treaty. It gives us pleasure to repeat to you on this occasion that we have known how to appreciate at their true worth all the efforts made by you to bring the two parties to the compromise agreement which made the conclusion of the treaty possible, and it is with great satisfaction that we convey to you once more all our congratulations and our best thanks.

Kindly accept, gentlemen, the assurance of our distinguished sentiments.

THE PRESIDENT OF THE BOARD OF DIRECTORS,
M. BÔ.

Later they wrote us again:

"We have been pleased to hear that Mr. Hay took pains to show, by the gift of the pen which was used to sign the treaty of January 22, how much he appreciated your efforts and the assistance you lent him; and to it we add our most sincere congratulations.

M. BÔ."

LONG AND FIERCE STRUGGLE IN THE UNITED STATES SENATE OVER THE RATIFICATION OF THE TREATY—FINAL SUCCESS.

This deliverance from a situation so involved that it was generally believed that no treaty could be concluded with Colombia and that consequently the President would have to adopt the Nicaragua route, caused interest and surprise everywhere, and defeated the efforts the supporters of Nicaragua were making to bring the President to abandon the negotiations with Colombia and to send to the Senate the treaties which Nicaragua and Costa Rica were offering to the United States.

Senator Morgan made every effort in the Senate to have the treaty referred to the Canal Committee of which he was chairman, but he failed. The treaty was referred to the Committee on Foreign Rela ions, of which Senator Morgan was also a member.

The supporters of Nicaragua, fighting the ground foot by foot, had actively organized to prevent the vote by the necessary two-thirds (majority) and had recourse to every possible parliamentary maneuver to prevent the ratification of the treaty. Senator Morgan introduced resolutions calling for proof that Chargé d'Affaires Herran was authorized to sign the treaty, and also casting doubt upon the constitutional powers of Vice President Marroquin to conclude any treaty. The records of the Senate contain numerous other resolutions in the months of January, February, and March. All these maneuvers which were met by us, called for and received constant attention on our part.

Part of the tactics of the Nicaragua party consisted in riddling the treaty with amendments so as to render it inacceptable to Colombia, to make it fall through and by this means to force the alternative of the Nicaragua route. With this object, Sena'or Morgan submitted to the Committee on Foreign Relations of which he was a member, more than 60 separate amendments to the treaty. These amendments were at once submitted to us by various Senators and we were asked to prepare and furnish information and suggestions to justify their rejection, by reason of our special and almost exclusive knowledge of the history of the negotiations which had culminated in this treaty. We made a critical study of these various amendments and furnished the Senators with arguments in rebuttal which were afterwards used in the debates.

Personally, we had conferences with a number of influential Senators, we made statements to them concerning the treaty negotiations which had lasted more than a year and a half; we expressed to them our conviction that it was the most advantageous treaty that could then be obtained from Colombia; we told them it was the result of hundreds of conferences and of many consecutive months of work; that each clause was the result of careful study, negotiation, and compromise; that its signature had only been obtained at the last moment when all hope had been abandoned and that the day after its signature Chargé d'Affaires Herran had received instructions by cable to suspend negotiations; so that the slightest amendment to the present treaty would undo all the work that had been done and would leave the entire matter in a chaotic state. These statements as well as our personal efforts convinced some prominent Senators that it was necessary to adhere to the treaty as it had been signed and to reject all the amendments.

The report of the Committee on Foreign Relations was in favor of the treaty, but its discussion had to take place in the Senate itself. On this matter the supporters of the Panama Canal and the partisans of Nicaragua were again lined up against each other for a fierce struggle.

The Nicaragua party recognized that it was drawing nearer and nearer to the end of its hopes, which made it fight all the more desperately. Every Senator was solicited by us or by our friends or by Senator Morgan and his supporters; we and our friends trying, on one hand, to obtain a majority of two-thirds in favor of the treaty as it stood and to defeat all the amendments, and Senator Morgan and his allies, on the other hand, trying to prevent this majority and in any case to force the passage of the amendments which would lead to the rejection (of the treaty) by Colombia later on.

The debate lasted several days in the month of February, and we followed its every phase with the greatest attention, entirely taken up by the service we were rendering and giving the Senators every possible assistance in the course of the debates. The opposition was so vigorous and the debates so prolonged that the session of Congress came to an end without action being taken on the treaty.

We had constant conferences with Senator Hanna and other party leaders during this critical period, and persistently urged an extra session to assure action upon the treaty.

At this time the option of the canal company was nearing its expiration (Mar. 4, 1903), and on this subject also we were negotiating with the Government, as will be seen in the next chapter, but we abstained from definite action in the matter of this option until we had received assurances that the extra session would take place, with the object of arriving at a decision on the treaty, as otherwise delays of indeterminate length might lead to complications. On March 2, 1903, the President summoned the extra session of Congress, which gave all reasonable assurance that the treaty would be the subject of early action, either affirmative or negative; and it was then that we took the necessary steps to assure the taking up of the option, as will be seen in the next chapter.

The Nicaragua party, thus checked again, manifested its opposition with even more vigor and raised fresh objections to the treaty, one of which met with the support of the partisans of Panama as well as those of Nicaragua, to wit, that the treaty should be amended so as to give the United States the complete control of the Canal Zone, with the right of fortifying and defending it. This objection was of a nature to be well received, as it touched national interests in a sensitive spot. However, we assured the Senators that the slightest amendment to the treaty would cause its rejection, because Colombia would not be willing to sign another. We put the matter up to Minister Herran; we obtained from him an important letter, addressed to ourselves, stating that any amendment passed by the Senate would cause rejection by Colombia. This letter was shown to prominent Senators and led them to withdraw their support from the proposed amendments.

In the course of the debates some Senators maintained that the clause in the treaty under which the United States was to return to Colombia the valuable concessions of public lands about to be acquired from the canal company would be a violation of the Spooner Act and that, therefore, the treaty had no legal basis. We discussed this objection before the Attorney General and opposed it in other quarters. It was finally abandoned.

In this way the struggle went on and Senator Morgan made 10 separate speeches, which he had printed, against the treaty on the various fundamental aspects of the matter.

On March 16 the Democratic Members held a caucus to agree upon the opposition to be made to the treaty and the support to be given the Morgan amendments.

The next day, March 17, the final vote took place, and ended in the defeat of every one of the Morgan amendments and in the ratification of the treaty without the change of a single line; the text as signed remained intact.

Thus the months of January and February and the first fortnight of March, 1903, were given up almost exclusively by Messrs. Cromwell, Hill, Curtis, and Farnham, together or alternately, in Washington, to conferences with Senators, preparation of arguments, throwing light on controversial points, opposition to the Morgan amendments, and collaborating in the ratification.

The Hay-Herran treaty, ratified by the Senate of the United States, marked another important victory for the cause of Panama and another step toward ultimate success.

We kept the company fully informed of the progress of the struggle as well as of our various movements and successes, and we received from it the following cable expressing its satisfaction:

"Your cables received. Thank you. Are satisfied with the news and, as you, hope for good result. As far as Colombia is concerned, are entirely in accord with you on all points and upon the course to pursue we approve your idea to inform the Government of the United States and to act according to its indications."

It cabled us further when we informed it of our final success:

"MARCH 18, 1902.

"Very pleased with result. Our congratulations and thanks."

1903, FEBRUARY–MARCH—THE OPTION OF THE CANAL COMPANY EXPIRES ON MARCH 4—THE UNITED STATES DEMANDS AN EXTENSION WITHOUT PLEDGING ITSELF—ON OUR SIDE WE PROPOSE A PLAN FOR THE IMMEDIATE ACCEPTANCE BY THE UNITED STATES, SUBJECT ONLY TO THE RATIFICATION OF THE TREATY, AND SECURE THE ADOPTION OF THIS PLAN BY THE UNITED STATES, WHICH THUS ENTERED INTO A CONDITIONAL UNDERTAKING INSTEAD OF CONTINUING TO ENJOY AN OPTION.

The option granted by the canal company on January 4, 9, 11, 1902, was to expire on March 4, 1903, under its own terms. The vicissitudes of the struggle to assure its acceptance had led us to its end without action by the United States on this option, and now the President could not unconditionally accept, even if he had wished to (because of the restriction of the Spooner Act), the offer which had been made, and, on the other hand, the company could not grant an absolute extension of it without running the risk of serious complications.

On February 4 and 7 Secretary Hay asked us to take the necessary steps to obtain the desired extension, which was to be granted without any pledge on the part of the United States, and to confer on this matter with the Attorney General. In consequence we addressed ourselves to this official, and a series of conferences ensued. The struggle in the Senate over the treaty was still going on.

It appeared to us that if the existing offer by the company to the United States was changed in any way whatsoever, even as to its duration, such change might bring about the reopening of the entire matter before the French courts and by the company's shareholders and place the transaction in danger. The offer (limited to Mar. 4, 1903) had been approved by the Tribunal Civile de la Seine, and the liquidator had been authorized to lend it his assistance; controversies had arisen as to this consent and its adversaries had been defeated; some of the shareholders had given it their limited approval; it was very important that this offer be accepted before Colombia should begin a lawsuit to enjoin it (which she did the following year), and also that a further defense against Colombia's pecuniary demands be created.

So we suggested a different plan to the Government, to wit, the immediate acceptance by the United States, subject only to the ratification of the Colombian treaty and of the legal formalities (so as to give to this matter the character of a conditional undertaking), instead of extending the option without obtaining any pledge.

The company had authorized us to take up this matter, and we devoted ourselves to it during the next two weeks, in Washington, by conferences with the President, the Attorney General, the Secretary of State, and the Senators who were conducting the fight in the Senate over the treaty; and we presented arguments in support of the adoption of this plan for the reasons above stated. At first this plan was not well received. It was, however, finally adopted by the United States, and the Attorney General and Mr. Cromwell, in the course of several conferences, agreed upon the form of the acceptance, which was cabled by him (the Attorney General) in our presence to the company on February 17 and of which an official copy was given to us as representatives of the company. The acceptance was worded thus:

WASHINGTON, D. C., *February 17, 1903.*

M. Bô, *President of the Board of Directors of la Compagnie Nouvelle du Canal de Panama, No. 7 Rue Louis le Grand, Paris, France:*

At the direction of the President of the United States I have the honor to announce that the offer of La Compagnie Nouvelle du Canal de Panama, contained in your telegrams of January 9 and 11, 1902, through the intermediary of Admiral Walker, to sell the properties and rights of the company on the Isthmus of Panama and in Paris, offer to which Mr. Gautron, liquidator of La Compagnie Universelle du Canal Interoceanique de Panama, has given his consent, with the approval of the Tribunal Civile de la Seine, is hereby accepted, subject to the modification of articles 21 and 22 of the concession contract by the ratification by both countries and the going into effect of the treaty pending between the United States and Colombia in regard to the Panama Canal, which treaty is already signed and its ratification expected. The President desires that the necessary steps for the transfer of the title and the possession of the property be expedited as much as possible, so that as soon as the pending treaty is ratified and put in effect there will remain nothing more to do but complete the transaction by taking possession and paying the price.

P. C. KNOX, *Attorney General.*

To which we at once replied as follows:

WASHINGTON, D. C., *February 19, 1903.*

To the honorable P. C. KNOX, *Attorney General.*

DEAR SIR: A meeting of directors has been called to consider your cable of the 17th instant. Meanwhile I am requested by Mr. Bô, the president, in order to dispel all doubt on the following questions, to ask you to confirm:

First. That the sentence in your cable, "properities, etc., in Paris," contemplates only the plans and archives in Paris, as stated in the company's cable of January 11, 1902.

Second. That the company gives no undertaking to obtain a modification of Articles XXI and XXII of the concession contract.

Awaiting the favor of a reply in order to cable to Paris, I am,

Yours, very truly,

WILLIAM NELSON CROMWELL,
General Counsel.

And the Attorney General replied as follows:

DEPARTMENT OF JUSTICE,
Washington, D. C., February 19, 1903.

Mr. WILLIAM NELSON CROMWELL,
General Counsel, New Willard Hotel, Washington.

DEAR SIR: In reply to your letter of to-day I must state that as the acceptance by the President of the offer of La Compagnie Nouvelle du Canal de Panama was not made with the intention of including what the negotiations do not show to have been agreed upon by the parties to include in the offer of this company I do not consider it advisable at this time to enter into detailed interpretations of the offer or of the acceptance.

Yours, very sincerely,

P. C. KNOX,
Attorney General.

To which we replied as follows, thus completing the understanding:

WASHINGTON, D. C., *March 3, 1903.*

To the honorable P. C. KNOX,
Attorney General of the United States, Washington.

DEAR SIR: I beg to acknowledge receipt of your favor of the 19th ultimo in reply to my letter of even date, in which I expressed the viewpoint of the company in regard to the subjects therein mentioned and asked you to give your assurance on these matters.

I notice with keen satisfaction the general assurance you express as to the President's intentions and I agree with you that it is not advisable at this moment to enter into detailed interpretations of this great transaction, so unique of its kind.

Above all other considerations the situation demands that the company's offer, as contained in its cables of January 9 and 11, 1902, which has received the consent of the liquidator, with the special approval of the courts, as well as the assent of other important interests, and as accepted by your cable of the 17th ultimo, shall undergo no change or modification, which, moreover, I have neither the wish nor the power to make.

We only put our questions in order to exclude the slightest possibility of a doubt as to the secondary points mentioned; I am now perfectly convinced that no differences whatever on these points can arise between the parties.

It is therefore with pleasure that I hand you herewith the official acknowledgment of your cable of the 17th ultimo.

I have the honor to be, most sincerely, yours,

WILLIAM NELSON CROMWELL,
General Counsel of La Compagnie Nouvelle du Canal de Panama.

WASHINGTON, D. C., *March 3, 1903.*

To the honorable P. C. KNOX,
Attorney General of the United States.

SIR: In accordance with the powers conferred upon me by the President of La Compagnie Nouvelle du Canal de Panama I proceed to notify you that the acceptance by the President of the United States, through your cable of the 17th ult., of the company's offer, as it is contained in its cables of January 9 and 11, 1902, addressed to the chairman of the Isthmian Canal Commission, is acknowledged by these presents as being in accordance with the said offer.

Very respectfully,

WILLIAM NELSON CROMWELL,
General Counsel of La Compagnie Nouvelle du Canal de Panama.

It is to be observed that we refrained until March 3 from sending the letter containing the final agreement. We had decided that it was not to the interest of the company to accept the condition that the agreement was made subject to the going into effect of the treaty unless the President summoned Congress in special session to continue and conclude the discussion of the treaty. The special session was summoned on the 2d, partly on account of the pending treaty, and then we handed in the acknowledgment (agreement).

The aceptance by the United States, with our consent, we being willing, constituted another great step in advance, as it represented the first undertaking on the part of the United States, put an end to all other objections, and constituted a binding contract, subject only to the conditions mentioned.

It also gave the company a great advantage in its resistance to the exactions of Colombia.

Before being suggested by us this measure had not been proposed by the Government.

OCTOBER 29, 1902–AUGUST 12, 1903—COLOMBIA DEMANDS A HEAVY CASH TRIBUTE FROM THE COMPANY AS THE PRICE OF HER CONSENT TO THE TRANSFER—PLANS OF COLOMBIA TO DECLARE THE EXTENSION (OF THE CONCESSION) TO 1910 NULL AND VOID, AND THEN TO PROCLAIM THE FORFEITURE OF THE CONCESSIONS—ALL THESE PLANS FAIL, THANKS TO MEASURES HEREINAFTER DESCRIBED, AND IN CONSEQUENCE THE COMPANY IS SAVED CONSIDERABLE EXPENSE.

By the Hay-Herran treaty we had obtained (subject to ratification) the consent of Colombia (Art. I), but even previously there had been indications, and shortly after there was clear proof, that it was the intention of Colombia to force the company to pay a considerable sum (which according to subsequent indications was to amount to 50,000,000 francs) as the price of the abrogation by Colombia of Articles XXI and XXII of the concessions, which prohibited the transfer to a foreign government.

We have alluded to the official document which had been transmitted to us by Minister Concha calling upon the company to appoint an agent in Bogota to negotiate for the consent of that country as well as the amendment of Article I of the treaty proposed by Minister Concha to Secretary Hay with a view to making the consent of Colombia subject to the reservation that the company must reach a previous agreement with Colombia; we have also dealt with the refusal of the United States to accede to this amendment, thanks to our repeated arguments and objections. We have also made mention of the official protest served on the company in Paris, on February 28, 1901, by Colombia against the transfer to the United States, and which had necessitated the postponement of the proposed ratification.

On October 29, 1902, the minister sent us an official communication in which he announced that the minister of foreign affairs in Bogota demanded that the Panama Canal Co. and the Panama Rilroad Co. appoint agents in Bogota to treat with the Government, should occasion arise, as to the terms of the conditional cancellation of their respective concessions in order to enable these companies to transfer their rights to the American Government in case the pending negotiations with a view to a treaty with this Government should succeed.

As has been mentioned above, Minister Concha later presented (Nov. 11) to Secretary Hay an amendment to Article I, quoted above, in which it was stipulated as a condition of Colombia's consent to the transfer that "a special agreement to be previously made between Colombia and the companies which had been notified to appoint an agent in Bogota for that purpose;" and it will be recalled that, thanks to our opposition, the Secretary rejected this amendment, and shortly afterwards Minister Concha left his post.

January 3, 1903, the United States minister cabled to Secretary Hay that Colombia intended to exact an indemnity from the canal company.

On January 9 the Secretary informed us that he knew positively that the delay which had occurred in the negotiations and the attitude of Colombia were due to the refusal of the Panama Canal Co. to negotiate for the consent of Colombia and to pay the tribute which Colombia was determined to exact before concluding any treaty; and on January 16 the United States minister cabled to the Secretary: "Colombia will not accept the offer of the United States, and has given Herran instructions to insist on the terms stated and upon all the Concha amendments, and, further, an agent of the Panama Canal Co. in Bogota must be appointed."

The same day (Jan. 16) Minister Herran showed us a cable to the same effect which he had received from his Government.

In February Colombia sent to the canal company and to the railroad company official written requests (signed by the minister of foreign affairs, under date Dec. 24, 1902), calling upon these companies to appoint an agent in Bogota empowered to negotiate; and declaring that, as to any permission to transfer the concessions, "she would demand and exact from the concessionary company in return a sum of money previously agreed upon, and a release by the company from all undertaking or obligation on the part of Colombia under the concession for the opening of Isthmus of Panama until such date as this concession should be transferred to another party."

Mr. Mancini, the company's agent in Bogota, wrote frequently to the company and to ourselves, declaring that Colombia would neither make nor ratify any treaty unless the company came to a previous arrangement with her for a cash payment; and on May 7, 1903, he cabled that this demand amounted to 50,000,000 francs and that he had been requested to state the company's intentions. Other news received through the State Department and its minister in Bogota, which Secretary Hay communicated to us as soon as received, was equally significant and plain.

On May 30 the United States minister in Bogota arrived in New York. He called upon us and fully informed us, more than confirming the unswerving determination of Colombia to reserve her consent until after the payment of many millions of francs by the company; this was again confirmed several days later (June 2) by a cable which Mr. Hay received from the chargé d'affaires in Bogota, who stated that "Colombia intends to force the company to make a heavy payment; without which no ratification."

On July 9 the United States minister cabled Mr. Hay an official note from the minister of foreign affairs, in reply to Secretary Hay, stating that the Congress would have to take into consideration the notifications served upon the companies by Colombia, notifications to which they had not conformed, and the effect of which could not be removed by the treaty.

On August 9 Mr. Mancini cabled that the committee of the Colombian Congress demanded that Article I of the treaty be amended in accordance with Minister Concha's proposal, of which Secretary Hay was at once informed.

On August 12 the American minister cabled to the Secretary that the treaty would not be ratified without "the amendment whereby a previous agreement between the company and Colombia is to be provided for."

The debates in the Colombian Congress when the treaty was pending in Bogota, the articles in the Colombian press, and the official reports addressed to the Secretary of State by the American minister also showed that there was in Colombia and in the Colombian Congress a powerful faction which was trying to officially repudiate the last extension of the company's concession until 1910, and then to proclaim the forfeiture of the concession at its expiration, which would then take place in 1906, and afterwards to negotiate a direct sale either to the United States or some other government and to obtain thus the totality of the purchase price and advantages of the canal.

The extension in question had been granted by a legislative decree of the President and not by Congress, which furnished the pretext for this maneuver.

It was clear, both to the company and to ourselves, that if the company entered into the negotiations demanded by Colombia the inevitable result would be the payment of many millions of francs. In order to save the company from this expense, we made active and successful efforts. It was the desire of the company not to comply with Colombia's demands, and it was the advice which we strongly and continually gave and which was also given to it by its eminent counsellors in France; but while that was a most natural desire on the part of the company, the company itself was powerless to carry out its desire, except through our efforts.

During this period (October, 1902–August, 1903) this matter caused us deep anxiety and demanded constant attention and services. It appeared to us that the only way to escape these exactions, to defeat these maneuvers, and to save the company from paying a tribute of many millions of francs, was to convince the American Government that it should refuse to consent to any amendment of Article I or to permit that the treaty should depend in any way on a previous agreement with the canal company, as Colombia was demanding. To this end we had numerous interviews with Secretary Hay, Senators Hanna, Spooner, and Kittredge, Congressman Burton, and other party leaders in Congress, and on certain occasions with the President. We pointed out that Colombia had already pledged herself morally to consent, and that her consent should be imposed upon her as being demanded by international good faith, and we thus created a feeling favorable to the support and protection of the company against these demands. As a result of these conferences and efforts, the American Government adopted this view, and on several occasions the Secretary sent to the American minister, for transmission to the Colombian Government, firm and positive refusals to consent to the amendment or transaction proposed. It was in recognition of our success in this direction that the company sent us on April 10, 1903, the following cable:

"Your cables received. We are very pleased and send you our congratulations and thanks."

Secretary Hay honored us with his confidence by permitting us to collaborate with him in the writing of these instructions, which conveyed the determinations arrived at. Almost on every occasion he had previously sent for us and had conferred with us as representatives of the canal company, in order to obtain our views.

We also wrote, at the request of the Secretary, a detailed note covering the whole history of the negotiations and arguments in support of the attitude thus taken by the United States, which note the Secretary used as a basis for his official instructions to the American minister and to which the United States adhered to the end. We sent a copy of these instructions to the company, which expressed its approval by the following cable:

"We have received Mr. Hay's letter of instructions to the minister of the United States in Bogota, which satisfies us and for which we thank you."

These instructions (communications) were officially communicated to the Colombian Government, and they were bitterly attacked as contrary to the attitude that Colombia had taken. The President and Secretary Hay, however, giving the highest proof of their honor, stoutly maintained the attitude which had been thus assumed by common consent.

It is not exaggerated to say that it was due, in great part, to our services in this matter during these 10 months and to subsequent efforts of ours that the company effected a saving of many millions of francs, which it would have been otherwise necessary to pay in order to obtain the consent requisite to the acceptance of its offer and to the carrying out of the sale which it had found it essential to make.

MARCH–AUGUST, 1903—STRUGGLE IN THE COLOMBIAN CONGRESS OVER THE RATIFICATION OF THE HAY-HERRAN TREATY—ADJOURNMENT OF THE CONGRESS WITHOUT ACTION ON AUGUST 12—THE TREATY IS NOT RATIFIED—COLOMBIA RESUMES NEGOTIATIONS.

This was a period full of anxiety and effort, and two or more of our partners devoted themselves almost constantly to this matter in Washington and New York. It was clear that, whatever the cause, and no matter whose duty it was, if the necessary consent and treaty rights were not obtained from Colombia by the United States, the result would be disastrous to the company, for then the United States would adopt the alternative route. The fact that the United States had this alternative rendered it independent of the company.

For the company it was a matter of life and death. For the United States it was only a question of adopting Panama or having easy recourse to the alternative route, which was offered it on its own terms and which, besides, was the popular route. It was therefore of the greatest importance to the company to further the treaty, to defeat the demands and designs of Colombia, and to maintain the confidence and support of the friends of Panama in view of new plans, in case the treaty should fail.

During these months two or more of our partners were constantly traveling between New York and Washington; they were often occupied for days and sometimes weeks at a time conferring with the Secretary of State and party leaders in Congress, sometimes with the President himself; communicating with Senator Hanna or keeping him informed of every phase by letter; on two occasions Mr. Farnham also went for this purpose to the Senator's residence in Ohio; we were conferring with Mr. Hart, United States minister (temporarily back from Bogota) upon the critical points of the situation in Colombia, and Mr. Farnham went to see him in Virginia on this subject; we were keeping up constant correspondence with Mr. Mancini, by mail and cable; we were examining, studying, and forming plans of action, relying upon the newspapers and prints published in Colombia, which were discussing the pending treaty; we were conferring with prominent Colombians and Panamans who came to see us, and urging upon them arguments in support of the treaty; we were deciding upon maneuvers for the campaign, etc.

A constant exchange of reports and information was maintained between the State Department and ourselves. We were in constant and daily communication; the Secretary consulted with us on every important development, and we conferred with him on all the important instructions given by the Government to its minister in Bogota and on the reports of the latter.

The Colombian Government put off the calling of Congress from one date to another until June 20. Meantime it maintained its demand on the canal company for negotiations as to the pecuniary tribute of which we have spoken and on which its consent was to depend; and, from information derived from various sources, it was clear that Colombia was contemplating amendments to the treaty, including the amendment of Article I, mention of which has already been made.

The hostile dispositions of the Colombian press and Government were so manifest that we suggested to Secretary Hay (on June 9) to have the American Government announce to the Colombian Government in advance of the meeting of its Congress and with absolute frankness and firmness, that the United States had been led to adopt the Panama route and to enter into an undertaking with the canal company relying upon Colombia's treaty proposals and on the consent to the transfer included in these proposals.

The Secretary accepted these views and submitted them to the President, who, a few days later, sent for Mr. Cromwell, and after due consideration directed that instructions be sent to Colombia, which was done by Secretary Hay in a communication wherein it was stated:

"In virtue of this agreement (referred to above) our Congress reversed its previous judgment and decided upon the Panama route. If Colombia should now reject the treaty or unduly delay its ratification the friendly understanding between the two Governments would be so seriously compromised that action might be taken by the Congress next winter which every friend of Colombia would regret."

We on our side made the same observations to Minister Herran, and we expressed to him our personal conviction of what would be the consequences to the Isthmus of a violation by Colombia of her solemn undertakings. He fully recognized the gravity of the situation and sent his Government a cable message in support of that of Secretary Hay which we had communicated to him with the approval of the latter. It is significant that at that time (June, 1903) he inserted in his cable the declaration to his Government that he was convinced that if the treaty were not soon ratified Panama would secede and conclude the treaty itself.

It was this attitude, taken by the American Government under the circumstances we have just set forth, that furnished the basis of and justification for the subsequent events, the consequences of which were so transcendent.

The company, fully informed by us by cable, cabled to us in these generous terms:

"Paris, *June 13, 1903.*

"Your cables and letters received. Are completely in accord with you on the program and are happy commencement execution. We hope for favorable results; we thank you for all your efforts."

And again:

"PARIS, *June 19, 1903.*

"We have received your dispatch of 15th. We hope step taken will produce decisive result. Thank you."

During this period we were also in constant communication with Minister Herran, exchanging information and consulting together upon the developments.

It should be noted here that all the cables and other messages between Secretary Hay, Minister Herran, and ourselves were necessarily communicated by each of us to the others, with a view to thorough cooperation.

The exactions of Colombia toward the canal company were also, about this time, the subject of consideration and action, as we have shown in the preceding chapter.

The relations of the Isthmus of Panama to the treaty furnished one of the most important aspects of the matter, as the choice of the Nicaragua route as an alternative entailed the commercial and material death of this region, which for a generation had patiently endured many national evils solely in the hope that the canal would be built. As we were general counsel of the Panama Railroad as well as of the canal, we had maintained for 10 years close professional and personal relations with influential people on the Isthmus. We utilized their interest and their zeal to create active support for the treaty, which they were giving by petitions to Bogota and by every means in their power. We kept them constantly informed as to the state of affairs; they, on their side, kept us perfectly informed as to the state of affairs on the Isthmus; we maintained the closest intimacy with them and they relied much upon our advice.

The debates in the Colombian Congress were transmitted to us by cable as they took place and called for our consideration and the taking of measures (decisions) on our part. This body, in the course of its sessions, had appointed committees intrusted with the matter, and we studied and passed upon the reports of these committees.

At last it became evident that the Colombian Congress would insist upon the amendment of Article I and other clauses of the treaty; and on August 12, basing itself upon this reason, Congress voted to adjourn without ratifying.

AUGUST-NOVEMBER, 1903—BECAUSE OF COLOMBIA'S INACTION, THE NICARAGUA PARTY DEMANDS THE ABANDONMENT OF THE PANAMA PLAN AND THE ADOPTION OF THE ALTERNATIVE ROUTE, WITH THE APPROVAL OF THE PUBLIC AS A RESULT OF COLOMBIA'S CONDUCT TOWARD THE UNITED STATES.

The selection of Nicaragua is demanded.

The natural consequence of Colombia's attitude and inaction was to create a strong national tendency in favor of the selection of the Nicaragua route. The supporters of that route, led by Senator Morgan and Congressman Hepburn, urged the President to declare the negotiations with Colombia abandoned and to adopt the alternative. They inflamed and aroused the press of the country, which gave active support to these views.

Colombia renews overtures after the adjournment.

The Colombian Government made overtures of an indefinite nature and the State Department consulted us on the subject.

On August 25 the company wrote to us:

"It is still a little difficult to see by what road we shall attain our end, but by no reasoning is it admissible that we can ever lose the fruits of your long and successful efforts * * *

"Among the motives assigned to the unanimous decision of the Colombian Senate, we have noted the refusal of our company to enter into direct negotiations with the Bogota Government. You know better than we ourselves the reasons for our attitude. We shall persist in it until the Government of the United States shall agree with you that we ought to adopt some other."

Message of the President to Congress is imminent.

The President had called Congress in extra session for November, and he was preparing to present a full report of the negotiations with Columbia in his message, with recommendations regarding action by Congress.

Even the friends of the Panama project were indignant at Colombia's action. We were in great anxiety.

Another crisis was upon us. What was to be done? As before, the company itself could give us no direct assistance. It encouraged us, however, by cabling us as follows:

"PARIS, *August 17, 1903.*

"We have received your three cables. Trust that the existing difficulties will be overcome, thanks to your efforts."

We make a proposal which insures delay and prevents any action by Congress.

At this juncture we proposed to the President and Secretary of State to extend the conditional agreement while awaiting fresh negotiations with Colombia or until it should be possible to successfully cope (resoudre) with the new situation in some other satisfactory manner, and that in the meantime the company should continue the construction work on the Isthmus.

We urged the President to adopt this plan and to defer any action on his part. He accepted it on our promise to promptly obtain the official confirmation of this proposal by the company.

Trip to Paris—We obtain the approval by the company of our proposal and cable the understanding to the President October 31, 1903.

Events in Washington, Bogota, and Panama rendered it necessary for Mr. Cromwell to confer in person with the directors, and he sailed on October 15 for Paris to confer rapidly and return. Meanwhile Mr. Curtis at once took up the management of the company's interests, of which we notified the President and Secretary of State by letter. Arriving in Paris on October 23, Mr. Cromwell devoted his whole time during the three following weeks to conferences with the directors, managers, and the liquidator. He explained to them and discussed the situation in Bogota, in Washington, and in Panama, as well as the proposal he had made to the President. After a thorough examination, the board of directors unanimously approved his proposal to the President, and because of that approval Mr. Cromwell cabled to the President of the United States on October 31, 1903, before the independence, as follows:

"PARIS, *October 31, 1903.*

"To the PRESIDENT OF THE UNITED STATES,
"*Washington, D. C.:*

"Referring you respectfully to my letter of October 13, I am authorized, in the name of the president of the canal company, with the unanimous approval of the board of directors at its meeting to-day, and with that of the liquidator of the old company, to give you personally and to the Government of the United States the assurance of their loyal support, which they firmly maintain, and to express to you their entire confidence in the success of your masterful policy.

"I have received full powers to complete all details on my coming return.

"WILLIAM NELSON CROMWELL,
"*General Counsel of La Compagnie Nouville du Canal de Panama.*"

Mr. Curtis immediately waited upon the President, and the Chief Executive expressed to him his satisfaction at this cable, which fully confirmed the assurance he had received.

AUGUST 12–NOVEMBER 3, 1903—THE COLOMBIAN CONGRESS REASSEMBLES—VOTES ITS CLOSURE WITHOUT ACTION, LEAVING FURTHER NEGOTIATIONS IN THE HANDS OF THE GOVERNMENT—SECESSION OF THE DEPARTMENT OF PANAMA—ESTABLISHMENT OF THE REPUBLIC OF PANAMA—PROTECTION AND MAINTENANCE OF THE CONCESSIONS AND PROPERTY OF THE COMPANY AGAINST DIFFICULTIES WITH COLOMBIA.

The Isthmus.

But Colombia having omitted to ratify the treaty in August, other events of great importance followed.

While the treaty was under discussion, the possibility of secession by Panama if there was any further delay in the conclusion of the treaty, was generally recognized. In fact, as we have pointed out, Minister Herran himself had cabled in June to his Government that that would be the probable result. We, ourselves, had not then and did not have later any doubt of this result, and this made us even more watchful that the vast interests entrusted to us should not be placed in danger or compromised.

The Colombian Congress met again in October, the treaty was discussed anew, and it was still hoped on the Isthmus (although with some misgivings) that Congress would ratify it during this session.

We were in constant communication with the Isthmus during this period, and we had interviews in New York with representatives of the Isthmus.

Protection of the concessions and property against Colombia.

We did not deem it necessary to enter into the details of the events of this period, but it is proper to mention that the protection of the concession and property of the company against confiscation by, or difficulties with, Colombia presented a problem which called for and obtained our vigilance, care, and energetic services.

The Colombian Congress was in session and was hostile to the company. As has already been stated, its committees recommended the repudiation of the extension till 1910 and the forfeiture that would ensue.

The canal and railroad companies, the dominant powers and commercial organizations on the Isthmus, were publicly accused of encouraging and assisting the revolutionary movements, and it was only too plain that Colombia would seize the slightest indication of such a thing to confiscate the concessions and take possession of the properties, or subject them to serious complications. We exercised incessant care, and in September, seeing that a storm was approaching, we cabled to all the officials on the Isthmus explicit instructions to carefully avoid giving any cause for confiscation or seizure, which was supplemented by personal interviews we had with the general superintendent of the railroad, who came to New York partly to confer with us about the situation on the Isthmus.

The Colombian Congress voted its closure on November 2, once again without action, and left the matter in the hands of the executive power as to future negotiations. The President at once began negotiations on a modified basis.

The following day, November 3, 1903, the Department of Panama declared and maintained its independence as the sovereign Republic of Panama, and it became useless to continue negotiations with Colombia.

It is not necessary to set forth here in detail the incidents of this so important event. Suffice to say that in our capacity as general counsel of the railroad company (an American company) we called upon the American Government to protect the property of the canal and railroad and to apply the clauses of the treaty of 1848, which guaranteed the free and uninterrupted transit across the Isthmus; that three of our partners were in frequent conference and communication with the United States Government, the directors of the railroad, and its officials on the Isthmus; and that we assured the complete protection and conservation, without damage or inconvenience, of the property of the two companies.

We confirm by cable to the President the application of the understanding to the new situation.

On November 7, Mr. Curtis had an audience with the President, who asked that the company formally declare that it agreed to the application of the existing understanding to the new situation as it had been generally set forth by cable on October 31. Mr. Cromwell, having been notified by cable, immediately wrote and, in accordance with instructions from the board of directors and the liquidator, sent, on November 9, the following cable:

PARIS, *November 9, 1903.*

To the PRESIDENT OF THE UNITED STATES,
Washington, D. C.

I am authorized to confirm the cable that I had the honor to address you on October 31, in the Name of President Bô, with the unanimous approval of the board of directors, as well as of the liquidator of the old company, and to add in their name, that they fully confirm the understanding that the agreement entered into on March 3 last between your excellency and the Compagnie Nouvelle, covers and equally applies to the new situation with which you are dealing. You can have the utmost confidence in the good faith of the company, whose attitude remains the same. I am sailing on Wednesday with powers to settle any details that may have to be arranged.

WILLIAM NELSON CROMWELL,
General Counsel of La Compagnie Nouvelle du Canal de Panama.

During his stay in Paris Mr. Cromwell was in constant communication with the United States, giving advice and instructions, and having accomplished the object of his brief stay, he sailed on November 11 for the United States, to be present at the conference previously arranged with the special delegates of the new Republic of Panama on their arrival in New York.

NOVEMBER, 1903—WE OBTAIN SUPPORT AND PROTECTION FOR THE INTERESTS OF THE PANAMA CANAL ON THE ISTHMUS FROM THE PROVISIONAL GOVERNMENT OF PANAMA (JUNTA).

The provisional government of Panama was composed of a junta of three citizens invested with all the powers of government until a constitution should be adopted.

There was no doubt that the new republic would immediately ratify the pending Hay-Herran treaty or another treaty that would be satisfactory, and to this end it at once sent special delegates to the United States to assist its distinguished and capable minister in Washington with the treaty and matters connected with it. The special delegates were Dr. Amador (later President of the Republic) and Mr. Boyd, with Dr. Pablo Arosemena (later Vice President), as counsellor. Before leaving Panama these personages had arranged by cable to meet Mr. Cromwell in New York for a conference, Mr. Cromwell being on his way at the same time from Paris to New York. They arrived before him, but awaited his arrival in New York some hours later on November 18. An important conference which lasted a whole day followed, in the course of which we obtained the assurrance that the concessions and property of the Panama Canal Co. on the Isthmus would be fully recognized and protected. At their request we met these personages in Washington to assist them in taking up pending questions.

The treaty had been signed a few hours before their arrival in Washington. In order to assure its ratification, we arranged interviews between the special delegates and Senators Hanna, Fairbanks, Kittredge, Platt, and other Members of Congress, so as to inform the latter on the situation and permit them to acquaint themselves with the new situation by personal inquiry, with a view to the coming debates in Congress. The advantages of this procedure became clearly evident during the debates in the Senate.

During their stay in Washington and New York, which lasted a long time, the special delegates conferred daily with one or several of our partners, asked and followed our advice on all phases of the unique situation which had been recently created. It may be mentioned that this connection has been maintained to this day.

The supreme interest of the canal company as to the treaty between the United States and Panama related to the terms contained in articles 1 and 22 of the Hay-Herran treaty. Mr. Curtis conferred about them with Secretary Hay after the independence and before the signature of the treaty. He received assurances from Mr. Hay that these two clauses would be preserved. The terms of these articles were reincorporated, so to speak, verbatim in the treaty between the United States and Panama.

NOVEMBER 20–27, 1903—WE OBTAIN FROM THE NEW REPUBLIC THE OFFICIAL GUARANTEE OF THE CANAL CONCESSIONS AND A NOTIFICATION OF THE DEVOLUTION OF SOVEREIGNTY, AS WELL AS A CLAIM FOR ALL THE RIGHTS PASSED FROM COLOMBIA TO PANAMA, INCLUDING THE CANAL SHARES.

After the independence the company cables us to obtain, if possible, formal statements defining the official attitude of the new republic as to the concessions, the canal stock, and the question of sovereignty. We immediately took this matter up, had conferences with the special delegates for three successive days, and obtained an official formal declaration signed by them (Nov. 27), which was addressed to us as general counsel of the company, as well as similar declarations for the railroad company.

By these official statements the Republic, as the new sovereign, confirmed all the concessions of the canal and railroad companies and acknowledged and approved the disputed extension to 1910; it claimed for Panama the absolute succession to the sovereignty of Colombia; it demanded the appointment of a delegate to the board of directors and the appointment of agents in Panama in accordance with the concessions; and it also claimed all the assets and rights belonging to the Government which had granted the concession, including the Panama Canal shares.

These important documents not only officially established and confirmed the title and protected the property of the canal and railroad companies under the new republic, but they also supplied a full answer to the later demands that Colombia made on the company in Paris in suits which were afterwards begun by Colombia.

Soon after, the Colombian Government made a formal claim on the company in Paris for the said shares and contested the devolution of sovereignty to Panama. The company, sustained by the governmental declarations mentioned above, resisted these claims. It will be seen below that Colombia began an action in Paris, in 1904, to enjoin the transfer to the United States, to establish its right to continue to vote as owner of the canal shares, and to retain its representation on the board of the canal company. In its decision on this matter the court cited these documents as decisive factors in support of the attitude of the company in its refusal to recognize that the sovereignty of Colombia still existed.

Following this important step, we had the Republic of Panama appoint as its agent on the board of the canal company, Mr. Poylo, of Paris, in order to show its sovereignty, and we also had it recognize Mr. Renaudin and M. Shaler as agents on the Isthmus of the canal and railroad companies respectively, under the concessions. All the documents and notices on this subject were written and filed under our supervision.

The company was thus fully protected and strengthened in its concessions and property under the new régime.

STRUGGLE FOR THE RATIFICATION BY THE UNITED STATES SENATE OF THE TREATY BETWEEN THE UNITED STATES AND PANAMA, AND FURTHER PROPOSALS BY COLOMBIA (REYES MISSION).

The treaty had been signed on November 18, 1903, ratified by Panama on December 2, 1903, and submitted to the Senate of the United States by the President on December 7, 1903.

Although its terms were entirely satisfactory to the American Government, and it contained the special clauses of the Hay-Herran treaty of interest to the canal company, the conditions which had surrounded the independence created a serious division of opinion in the United States. As to the terms of the treaty itself there was little opposition, but as to the circumstances under which it had been concluded there was grave diversion of opinion.

The opposition was composed of four groups: The Democratic element which wanted to defeat thé Government on so important a matter of government policy; the critical element which took the point of view that the United States had infringed the rights of Colombia; an important faction of insurgents in the government party itself; and the Nicaragua party which eagerly seized the opportunity to throw this matter into such difficulties that the adoption of their alternative route might result.

Senator Hanna and other party leaders asked us for information. To overcome adverse opinion we arranged and conducted conferences between the special delegates of Panama and the party leaders of the Senate, as we have already related; and we prepared an exhaustive statement of the unjust wrongs that Panama had suffered for a period of 50 years, which statement we communicated to the Government officials and Members of Congress to justify the independence and we created a current of opinion favorable to the new republic and to a treaty with it. We also advanced arguments in support of the Government's action, which was fully justified and correct. But adverse influences and public comment created such bitter opposition to the Government that the ratification of the treaty was, for some time, believed to be very doubtful.

We were relied upon to devote ourselves to the ratification of the treaty between the United States and Panama as we had already done for the Hay-Herran treaty, and we devoted ourselves to this task during the six following weeks with every resource at our command. Two or three of the partners of our law firm made constant stays in Washington, conferring with the party leaders, obtaining and disseminating information and arguments, overcoming the opposition to and gaining support for the treaty.

A disquieting and serious complication arose: Colombia was making tardy proposals with a view to a treaty and was asking the United States to reconsider its recognition of Panama. Gen. Reyes was sent with full powers for this purpose from Bogota to Washington, where he arrived on November 20, 1903. A series of communications followed between Gen. Reyes and Secretary

Hay, in the course of which Colombia protested against the secession of Panama, accused the United States of having aided it in violation of relations established by existing treaties, offered a treaty in almost any form demanded by the United States and, in brief, asked the United States to reconsider its recognition of Panama and to lay aside the treaty in question. Acting on the facts of the case and on honor, the United States maintained its position, refused to discuss the proposal, and the entire correspondence was published.

We ourselves had taken no direct part in this negotiation or in this correspondence, although necessarily we had been informed of its progress; but its effect was to powerfully stimulate the opposition to the treaty and to furnish support to the opposition factors we have already mentioned. In fact, the members of some of these factions were discussing directly with the Colombian envoy, and supported resolutions in the Senate having for their object an investigation of the participation of the United States in the independence movement, the payment of $10,000,000 indemnity demanded by Colombia, and other similar measures.

On December 17 Senator Morgan introduced (in the Senate) a resolution forbidding the conclusion of the purchase from the canal company until after fresh action by both Houses of Congress, as well as a resolution calling upon the Attorney General to report to Congress on the status of the negotiations between Panama and the United States in the matter of the title. On January 4 a Senator introduced a resolution in respect to a treaty with Colombia to settle the differences arising out of the action of the United States in Panama. On January 13 another Senator introduced a resolution for an investigation into the events of the revolution. On January 18 Senator Morgan introduced a resolution rejecting Article XXII, by which the transfer by the canal company was authorized. On January 26 the situation was considered so grave that the group of Democratic Senators met, discussed the whole matter, and adopted resolutions in favor of an investigation and report to the Senate on the revolution by the Senate Committee on Foreign Relations. A resolution declaring that the action of the United States constituted an act of war and that the President had no power to declare war without the consent of Congress, was also pending, as well as another resolution declaring that the action of the Government was contrary to the Spooner Act, which did not apply to the new conditions.

As fast as these resolutions were introduced we conferred with prominent Senators and presented to them arguments against these resolutions. The resolutions thus introduced had been submitted to the Colombian envoy and corrected and approved by him. They were very fully discussed, but nevertheless they were all ultimately rejected.

Having failed in his mission, Gen. Reyes left Washington and came to New York, where, through mutual friends, Mr. Cromwell and he met for a series of conferences, which later were of great importance and in the course of which a warm friendship sprang up, a friendship which still endures.

It was during this period (Feb., 1904) that Mr. Cromwell proposed the following transaction to Gen. Reyes:

(1) The treaty between the United States and Panama was to be ratified without further complaint from Colombia, and the independence of Panama, which was an accomplished fact, was to be recognized by Colombia; (2) the United States should then be asked to act as arbitrator between the two nations; (3) new treaties should be concluded between the three nations, respectively, and Colombia was thus to obtain, in a great measure, the advantages accruing from the construction of the canal which had been lost by her delay in the ratification of the Hay-Herran treaty, and Panama and Colombia were to send special delegates to conduct negotiations to this end.

We do not consider ourselves at liberty to set forth here the details of these conferences, but we can mention that Gen. Reyes gave them such great consideration and encouragement that we at once sent Capt. Beers, of the Panama Railroad, to the Isthmus of Panama to explain the plan in detail to the Government of Panama, which promptly authorized its study.

We notified the company of this plan on February 3, 1904, and received its reply by cable on February 5, as follows:

"Your cable received. We thank you for information and congratulate you on your plan."

(We take the liberty of setting forth here as interesting historical facts—which have all been published—that Gen. Reyes was later elected President of Colombia, that quite recently the identical plan outlined above has ripened, and that on August 17, 1907, protocols were signed between Colombia, Panama, and the United States through the media ion of the latter and by ministers specially authorized to that effect by each of the Governments, with our collaboration as counsel of the Republic of Panama.)

The Commi tee on Foreign Relations, however, insisted on amendments which would give the United States greater authority and more complete sanitary control over the terminal ports on the Atlantic and Pacific, and reported the treaty to the Senate on January 18 with these amendmen s. We were at once consulted by Senators on the subject of these amendments, and we strongly advised their rejection, as they would indefini ely delay the treaty, as Panama itself desired to insert, if any changes were to be made, the clauses which had been omitted at the time of its signature and the discussion of which had been prevented by the rapid march of events. Later, on January 29, the committee yielded to these considerations, reconsidered its action, and withdrew the amendments.

The treaty was put to a vote on February 23, 1904, and after debate was passed by the necessary two-thirds majority, but with 17 adverse votes which were maintained to the end. The ratifications were duly exchanged on February 26, 1904.

That was another important step toward the goal.

DECEMBER, 1903–FEBRUARY, 1904—COLOMBIA BRINGS SUIT IN THE TRIBUNAL CIVILE DE LA SEINE IN PARIS TO ENJOIN AND PROHIBIT THE TRANSFER TO THE UNITED STATES, TO OBTAIN AN ORDER FOR THE ADMISSION OF ITS DELEGATE TO THE BOARD OF DIRECTORS, TO OBTAIN RECOGNITION OF ITS RIGHT TO VOTE AS THE OWNER OF THE SHARES ENTERED IN ITS NAME, ETC.—WYSE JOINS WITH COLOMBIA IN THE INJUNCTION SUIT.

The defense of these suits was conducted entirely by the able lawyers of the company in Paris. It was necessary for us, however, to study and explain to the American Government, to the Senators, and to the press the true meaning of these suits, the principles at stake, our own views on the result of the suits in case they were won or lost. We received and studied all the papers in the case and closely followed every step taken.

Quite naturally, the American Government was deeply perturbed by suits brought by such powerful interests. Gen. Reyes had gone to Paris to assist in their prosecution. It was necessary to reassure the Attorney General himself on all the points, as his action was not going to be governed by any argument or decision in France, but by his own opinion and upon his own responsibility; and if a serious doubt arose in his mind it was probable that the President would refer the whole matter back to Congress.

Consequently we had frequent discussions with the Attorneys General about the points involved, and in this connection we made a critical study with them of all the points in the various cases, studied and discussed the French code, decisions of French courts, and questions of international law raised by the change of sovereignty on the Isthmus.

The press was also continually publishing articles giving reports of various phases of the cases, announcing that the Panama title was invalidated, that legal contests had been started by Colombia, the grantor of the Panama concessions, etc. We were constantly obliged to deny these harmful statements and to offset their effect.

The supporters of Nicaragua also utilized these lawsuits to arouse opposition to the Government and to the ratification of the treaty in a vain effort to obtain the adoption of the Nicaragua alternative. It was necessary for us to defeat these adverse influences, and we had numerous conferences with Members of Congress on the subject, to whom we made a complete explanation and to whom we gave our personal opinions and conclusions.

JANUARY, 1904, TO MARCH 3, 1904—WE PROPOSE AND OBTAIN FROM THE UNITED STATES AN AGREEMENT BY WHICH IT UNDERTAKES TO COMPLETE THE PURCHASE WITHOUT REGARD TO THE COLOMBIAN LAWSUITS AND TO THE COMPLICATIONS ON THE ISTHMUS—AND WE THUS OBTAIN A DEFINITE AND BINDING UNDERTAKING FROM THE UNITED STATES IN FAVOR OF THE COMPANY.

During the same period other matters called for action.

It will be recalled that in the early part of October it had been agreed between the President and ourselves that we would obtain from the canal company a further agreement stating that the existing contract of March 3, 1903, would be maintained whilst awaiting fresh negotiations with Colombia or other events; that Mr. Cromwell went in haste to Paris, accomplished this result as well as others, and cabled the fact to the President with the unanimous approval of the directors and of the liquidator, which took place on October 31 and was further confirmed on November 9.

Immediately on his return Mr. Cromwell made a detailed report to the President (Nov. 23), who expressed to him his satisfaction at the cables of October 31 and November 9.

It seemed highly important to us, in view of public complications, to obtain for the company an official declaration by the United States expressing its determination to close the matter on the basis of the original contract, and we asked the Government to furnish us such a statement.

The lawsuits of the Colombian Government against the company to enjoin and prohibit the proposed transfer in favor of the United States were pending in Paris, and there was a public controversy, within Congress and without, on the subject of the questions raised by the secession of Panama. The situation was complicated from a political, legal, and international point of view, and there existed good reasons of state of a nature to cause the Attorney General to reflect very seriously before entering into any new undertaking at this juncture.

The Attorney General continued to insist for the closure of the sale on a method to which the company was opposed as not being in accord with French law. We were kept busy for many days communicating with the company and discussing with the Attorney General.

The prosecutions in Paris would inevitably entail a delay of a year before the final decisions of the French courts. That was an important difficulty. We urged the Government to close the matter immediately. After consideration the special assistant to the Attorney General proposed to use the choice of two plans

(1) The company was to sign all the deeds of transfer, which would be deposited, together with the $40,000,000, with bankers acting as trustees until the end of the lawsuits, or (2) the matter was to be settled as far as the transfer of the Panama Railroad shares and other chattels not affected by the concessions were concerned, and $10,000,000 was to be paid on account, the disposition of the remainder of the property and of the balance of the purchase price to await the end of the Colombian lawsuits.

We expressed our disapproval of these proposals, but at the request of this official we cabled them to the company, which approved of our attitude.

It was expected that the injunction suit brought by Colombia would be decided about March 31, but the appeals would lead to long delays. The numerous dangers of the affair appeared to us to call for audacious and decisive action, and we suggested to the American Government, as well as to the company, that each side assume the ricks inherent to the Colombian lawsuits (as the company was not under the ban of a court injunction) and that the matter be immediately concluded. This proposal was presented by us personally to the President, to Secretary Hay, and to the Attorney General and energetically pressed by us. We pointed out the dangers of delay, of fresh prosecutions, and renewed complications if the conclusion of the purchase were long delayed. We transmitted this proposal by cable to the company, which promptly acceded to it and cabled us:

"PARIS, *March 1, 1904*.

"We confirm our last cable of yesterday. We rely entirely upon your skill and efforts to overcome hesitations of the Government of the United States and its high officials."

As a result of these arguments and discussions the Government entered into an agreement with us and handed to us a definite and decisive undertaking, which provided for the immediate conclusion of the transaction, in the following form:

WASHINGTON, D. C., *March 2, 1904*.

Mr. WILLIAM NELSON CROMWELL,
General Counsel of La Compagnie Nouvelle du Canal de Panama.

SIR: At the direction of the President, I beg to inform you that the Government of the United States is now ready to carry out its contract of purchase with La Compagnie Nouvelle du Canal de Panama by receiving the property of the company and the deed or deeds of transfer of these properties and by paying the price agreed upon.

P. C. KNOX,
Attorney General.

The company was at once notified by us of this result, and on March 4, 1904, we had the pleasure of receiving from it the following cable:

"PARIS, *March 4, 1904*.

"Very pleased with your telegrams. We send you our sincerest congratulations."

Thus we had at last arrived at a binding and complete contract of purchase.

MARCH 3–APRIL 2, 1904—WE GO TO PARIS BEFORE THE ARRIVAL OF THE REPRESENTATIVES OF THE GOVERNMENT AND PREPARE A PROGRAM FOR THE CONCLUSION OF THE TRANSACTION—WE DRAW UP THE DEEDS OF TRANSFER AND OTHER PAPERS READY FOR SUBMISSION TO THE ASSISTANTS TO THE ATTORNEY GENERAL ON THEIR ARRIVAL—WE NOTIFY THE PRESIDENT (OF THE UNITED STATES) OF FAVORABLE DECISIONS RENDERED BY THE FRENCH COURTS, OF THE CALLING OF A GENERAL MEETING OF SHAREHOLDERS, ETC.

Happily we now reach the time of the conclusion of the transaction. It had been mutually agreed that the payment and the delivery of the documents should take place in Washington, but that the details should be supervised in Paris by special assistants to the Attorney General and all the preparations made for the conclusion of the transaction in the United States; and that, for this purpose, Mr. Cromwell, for the company, and Mr. Day, Assistant Attorney General, and Mr. Russell, special assistant to the Attorney General, for the United States, should go to Paris. In consequence, Mr. Cromwell sailed on March 23.

Before his departure Mr. Cromwell sent to the President, to Secretary Hay, to Mr. Knox, the Attorney General, to Mr. Payne, Postmaster General, and to Secretary Shaw letters explaining his departure and assuring them that the Colombian lawsuits would be overcome, that the ratification of the shareholders would be obtained, and that the transaction would be concluded.

He arrived in Paris on March 21, at once met the directors and managers of the company and the liquidator of the old company, and made a detailed report to them, with which they expressed themselves as extremely satisfied. He prepared a general program for the conclusion of the transaction as far as the company was concerned, which program was ultimately carried out. During the 12 days following he devoted himself exclusively to the work of the final wording of the papers, resolutions, and other details, so as to be ready to communicate them to the assistants to the Attorney General on their arrival (Apr. 2).

The Procureur de la Republique (French public prosecutor) having intervened in the Colombian and Wyse suits, a fact which had been published in such a manner as to indicate hostility to the attitude by the company, Mr. Cromwell, at the request of the company, on March 27, sent a long explanatory cable to the President.

On March 31 the Tribunal Civile de la Seine rendered its decision in favor of the company in the Colombian and Wyse suits to enjoin the transfer to the United States; and the same day Mr. Cromwell sent to the President and to Mr. Knox, the Attorney General in Washington, detailed information by cable on this decision, which fully confirmed the assurance he had given them before his departure.

The same day the board of directors called a general meeting for April 23, of which we informed the President and the Attorney General the same day by cable.

At this time (Mar. 30) a suit was begun in Washington by a man named Wilson, in his capacity as a citizen of the United States, to prevent the payment of the $40,000,000 by the Secretary of the Treasury. Publicity having been given to this suit, we examined with the company the effect it might have upon the business in hand and promptly concluded that this matter should not hold us back. Consequently in our cables of March 31 to President Roosevelt and to the Attorney General we inserted a statement as to the company's attitude in this respect and asked the United States to conclude the transaction without paying heed to this suit.

We also arranged with the company to have inventories made of the very voluminous plans and archives in Paris and of the properties on the Isthmus.

We also studied the legal status of the Panama Railroad Co.'s shares, which were held under special agreements, according to which the consent of the liquidator was to be obtained for their transfer to the United States. We therefore made all the preparations for the presentation to the assistants to the Attorney General, immediately on their arrival, of the documents establishing the title of the company. These distinguished officials arrived in Paris on April 2, and the same day Mr. Cromwell sent them a message informing them (1) of the favorable decision of the French courts, and (2) of the calling of the general meeting for the 23d of the same month, the summons for which was issued while they were on their way; we also handed to them drafts (3) of a general deed of transfer by the company, (4) of a deed of consent thereto by the liquidator; (5) of resolutions which were to be passed at the general meeting; (6) of the formula of acceptance by the President of the function of arbitrator in the matter of the work performed, formula which had been drawn up by Mr. Cromwell for their consideration; and we also informed them that (7) the inventories of the properties on the Isthmus and in Paris had been prepared and were at their disposal for examination; that (8) the Panama railroad shares were ready and that (9) ample security was offered for the existing judgments on the Isthmus.

Thus, the preparations for the conclusion of the transaction were far advanced at this date.

APRIL 4, 1904—FINAL SETTLEMENT OF ACCOUNTS BETWEEN THE CANAL AND RAILROAD COMPANIES.

As the canal company, as proprietor of nearly all the capital stock of the railroad company, had held for many years a controlling interest in this company, and had also built for the railroad company its La Boca Wharf (which cost about 10,000,000 francs), and as various accounts had not been settled, it was considered by the canal company that it would be well to draw up and settle all questions of accounts between the two companies, and the company asked us to bring about this result. In accordance with our advice each of the companies appointed committees with full powers; these committees fulfilled their duties, reached an agreement, and advised the exchange of mutual receipts in full and releases.

The consideration of this matter dragged on for a year, and led, on April 2, 1904, to an official exchange of the papers called for by such a case, in accordance with the action of the respective boards, which documents were drawn up by us; and the companies exchanged reciprocal releases.

APRIL 2–16, 1904—WE REACH AN UNDERSTANDING WITH THE ASSISTANTS TO THE ATTORNEY GENERAL ON ALL QUESTIONS AND DOCUMENTS—SIGNATURE AND OFFICIAL DELIVERY OF THE DEEDS OF TRANSFER AT THE AMERICAN EMBASSY, APRIL 16, 1904.

During the two weeks which followed the arrival of the assistants to the Attorney General the latter had daily conferences with Mr. Cromwell and were in consultation for the examination and revision of the documents, the study of points of law, decisions to be taken, etc. Among these numerous matters it is necessary to mention a few:

(1) *The general deed of transfer from the company, and the assent of the liquidator, deliberations of the directors, shareholders, and documents of the same kind.*

Many questions of law and politics were involved; all these documents were discussed on numerous occasions, corrected according to the conclusions arrived at, and finally mutually agreed upon.

(2) *The lawsuit of the company with Wyse.*

The decision and the question of appeal were studied and discussed and a plan of action mutually decided on.

(3) *The suit of Wilson against the Secretary of the Treasury and La Compagnie Nouvelle du Canal de Panama.*

This suit, as we have stated, had been begun in Washington on March 30, 1904, against the Secretary of the Treasury and La Compagnie Nouvelle du Canal de Panama for the avowed purpose of obtaining the injunction to prevent the payment by the Government, or the receipt by the company, of the $40,000,000 for the following reasons: That the Spooner Act applied only to a treaty with Colombia and not to the new situation; that the contract between the United States and the company was illegal; that the Constitution of the United

States did not permit the use of public funds for such a purpose; and that the payment should not be made by the Government or received by the company.

We retained a lawyer in Chicago (where the plaintiff resided) to make an inquiry into the purpose of the lawsuit, studied the papers in the case in Washington, and had conferences with Government officials. We also examined the court decisions and questions of law, and we prepared, in case of necessity, to show that the demand was ill founded.

Our partner in Paris was kept informed of all this by cable so that he could take the matter up on the spot.

After discussion it was agreed with the assistants to the Attorney General to conclude the transaction without regard to this suit.

(4) *Transfer and registration fees.*

This question involved a possible claim by the registrar of 5,000,000 francs. The assistants to the Attorney General after a careful examination of the matter informed Mr. Cromwell that they would not reject the title for this cause; but he was of opinion that it was necessary for the United States to promise to indemnify the company for these fees, and he wrote and made the assistants to the Attorney General sign a formal agreement to this effect.

(5) *Ratification by the shareholders.*

This matter was of extreme importance, and the assistants to the Attorney General and ourselves gave it special care and attention. It was the subject of many discussions.

All the technical procedure that was to precede the calling of the meeting and the meeting itself was studied and discussed.

The report of the company's board containing the account of the negotiations with the United States was communicated and explained by us to the assistants to the Attorney General before the meeting and was approved by them.

(6) *Inventories of the plan and archives in Paris.*

These documents were examined by the assistants to the Attorney General and the inventories verified under our supervision.

(7) *Inventories of the lands on the Isthmus and property title.*

These documents were all examined by the assistants to the Attorney General under our supervision.

(8) *Panama Railroad shares.*

These shares were not transferable, but were held under special agreements with the liquidator. These documents were examined and discussed by Mr. Cromwell with the assistants to the Attorney General, and an understanding was reached as to their legal effect and the delivery of the necessary releases by the liquidator.

(9) *Judgments against the liquidator on the Isthmus.*

At the time of the bankruptcy of the old company in 1889 various judgments had been registered against the liquidator on the Isthmus of Panama, and some of the buildings and property of the canal had been seized under these judgments. The liquidator disputed the mortgage effect of these judgments, but certain decisions had been against him.

In the early part of March, 1904, the special assistant to the Attorney General asked us to obtain the cancellation of these judgments. In consequence we directed Mr. Farnham to ascertain the exact position of these judgments and the basis on which they could be compromised; so he went down to the Isthmus (Mar. 29) for this purpose and other matters connected with the company. Mr. Farnham examined the records, discussed the matter personally with the creditors, conferred with counsel in these cases, learned that the creditors were going to appeal to the courts to force the public sale of the properties, and that they insisted on payment in full with interest, of which he informed our partner in Paris, by cable from the Isthmus. Mr. Farnham persuaded the creditors to defer their action pending a conference with Mr. Cromwell whom they knew personally.

This was, however, a question which it was necessary to settle before the transfer of the title; but the liquidator of the company, quite naturally, wished to reduce the amount if possible, which entailed delay. Consequently, we proposed to the assistants to the Attorney General that they should not insist on the cancellation of these judgments (which could only be brought about by a payment in full), but to accept a deposit for the amount and give time for negotiation. This was agreed upon, and we took the necessary measures for the deposit of 350,000 francs by the company and drew up and had signed the appropriate agreements to this effect.

(10) *Basis of the title—Power to transfer.*

It had been mutually agreed that the transfer proper should be effected by the dissolution of the existing company and the appointment of liquidators with full powers, in accordance with the law bearing on such cases and in confirmation of deeds to be signed by the company itself prior to liquidation.

This matter was again studied by the assistants to the Attorney General and Mr. Cromwell in view of the particular arrangements then in progress and of the resolutions of the shareholders to effect the dissolution of the company, the transformation of the existing board of directors into a board of liquidators, the authorization of a transfer through them, etc., and the deeds of transfer themselves were drawn up and critically examined with a view to this fundamental program.

An agreement had been reached on all these points on April 16. On account of the pending and threatened litigation, it was mutually agreed in writing that all the documents should be signed at once and prior to the general meeting, subject to ratification by the meeting.

It was also mutually agreed upon that the signature and delivery of the documents should be effected under the protection and auspices of the United States at its embassy in Paris. Mr. Cromwell, as well as the assistants to the Attorney General, explained the situation to the American ambassador, and this distinguished official graciously facilitated this plan and was present in person at the signature of the documents.

This event was considered by all as being of historic importance. It marked the acquisition of the Panama Canal by the United States and thus assured to mankind that the efforts made for 400 years to join the waters of the Atlantic and Pacific Oceans, to guarantee the transit of the world's commerce on conditions of equality, the necessary protection of the American shores, and the advancement of civilization, thanks to a neutral canal, would succeed. We therefore record here that the ceremony of the signature of the deeds of transfer of the Panama Railroad and Canal by La Compagnie Nouvelle du Canal de Panama and their delivery to the United States of America took place at the American Embassy in Paris on April 16, 1904, in presence of the following persons:

Gen. Porter, ambassador of the United States in Paris.

For the company: Mr. Bô, president of La Compagnie Nouvelle du Canal de Panama; Mr. Rischmann, director of the company; Mr. Cromwell, general counsel of the company in America; Mr. Lampré, secretary general of the company.

For the liquidation: Mr. Gautron, liquidator of La Compagnie Universelle du Canal Interoceanique de Panama.

For the United States: Mr. Day, Assistant Attorney General of the United States; Mr. Russell, special assistant to the Attorney General; Mr. Gowdy, consul general of the United States in Paris, and his assistant, by whom the documents were legalized.

APRIL 23—GENERAL MEETING FOR THE RATIFICATION OF THE SALE, THE DISSOLUTION OF THE COMPANY, AND AUTHORIZATION TO COMPLETE THE TRANSACTION AND LIQUIDATE.

The momentous day for which so many preparations had been made arrived. The general meeting was held regularly, with a large attendance. The proposed deeds of transfer were submitted to the meeting with the reports and recommendations of the board. A discussion followed. Resolutions were duly passed, ratifying the agreement with the United States and the deeds of transfer in their favor, declaring the company dissolved, and transforming the existing board of directors into a board of liquidation with full powers to complete the transaction and liquidate all the affairs of the company.

APRIL 23—CONFIRMATORY DEEDS OF TRANSFER AND GENERAL POWER OF ATTORNEY TO PASS AND SIGN ALL CONFIRMATORY DEEDS AFTER THE GENERAL MEETING.

It had been previously agreed between the assistants to the Attorney General and Mr. Cromwell that, immediately after the ratification of the shareholders, confirmatory deeds of transfer rehearsing the original deeds of transfer should be signed, together with a general power of attorney. These deeds had already been drawn up and were in due course signed the same day by the same officials under our supervision. They were also regularly legalized in presence of the consul general of Panama as well as of the United States. We had all these deeds of transfer signed in English and in French, with the stipulation that for their interpretation the English text should prevail, and had certified as true copies and delivered to the assistants to the Attorney General duplicates of the minutes of the meetings of the board of directors and shareholders in the course of which the series of documents drawn up had been authorized.

Once again we enjoyed the intelligent cooperation of Messrs. Lampré and Marie in connection with the company's records and archives.

APRIL 15-28—WE PROPOSE AND ARRANGE THE CONCLUSION OF THE TRANSACTION IN PARIS INSTEAD OF IN WASHINGTON AND OBTAIN THE APPOINTMENT OF MESSRS. J. P. MORGAN & CO. AS FISCAL AGENTS ACCORDING TO CONTRACTS MADE WITH THE COMPANY, IN ORDER TO PROTECT THE 206,000,000 FRANCS AGAINST INJUNCTIONS, SEIZURE, OR COMPLICATIONS.

As has already been described, the transaction under the agreement and understanding between the parties was to be completed in Washington, where the contract had been made, and the delivery of the documents as well as the payment of the $40,000,000 were to be effected in that place. All the plans and arrangements up to then had been made in this expectation and in accordance with this understanding.

In fact, before leaving for Paris we had, at the request of the company, proposed to the Secretary of the Treasury that the company would accept in payment (1) United States bonds at 2 per cent or (2) payment by installments in cash in Washington in such amounts as the Secretary of the Treasury might find convenient, on condition that deferred payments should bear 2 per cent interest. The Secretary was deeply interested in this proposal, conferred with other members of the Cabinet, and in the course of a later conference with Mr. Cromwell replied that the Government was of opinion that the Spooner Act did not furnish authority for any change in the mode of payment, and that he would therefore be ready to pay the entire sum in cash in Washington, or at the subtreasury of the United States in New York. He made arrangements for this purpose. On account of the pending suits of Colombia, Wyse, and Wilson, and other suits that might be started by these parties or others, and of threats of injunction and seizure by these and other enemies of the company in the United States and in France, we deemed it dangerous to the interest of the company that the payment should be made in the United States or in any part of France except the Bank of France, which, under the laws of the country, receives deposits exempt from the effects of legal process.

The company also expressed the gravest apprehension of difficulties and urged Mr. Cromwell to make arrangements which would obviate the complications and dangers which it considered possible.

On account of this situation Mr. Cromwell conceived and proposed a radical modification of the plan of action, to wit: That the payment should be made at the Bank of France instead of in Washington, and that, if possible, Messrs. J. P. Morgan & Co., the bankers, should be appointed to effect the remittance to the Bank of France, on behalf of the Government of the United States, if this Government would consent to change the place of payment, if it appointed the said bankers as its agents for this purpose, at the expense of the company, and if the said bankers were willing; so that the legal title to the funds would remain with the United States until their actual payment by its financial agents into the Bank of France under the said arrangement; and thus the funds would be free from all injunctions, seizure, and complications. The directors approved of this plan and authorized us to propose it and carry it out if possible. Learning by inquiry at the offices of Messrs. J. P. Morgan & Co. in Paris that Mr. Morgan was then in London, Mr. Cromwell telegraphed him, asking for a personal interview, and Mr. Morgan came over to Paris two days later for this purpose. Mr. Cromwell, in the name of the company, made and explained to Mr. Morgan the above-mentioned proposal in the course of several personal conferences. The latter accepted the proposal in principle, of which we immediately informed Mr. Bô, the president.

Meanwhile we had submitted this proposal to the assistants to the Attorney General and had insisted on its adoption for the reasons stated above. These officials declared that they shared our opinion as to the prudence and advantages of this plan, but they were not authorized to make the proposed change without the direct sanction of the Attorney General. They cabled to this office and a few days later (Apr. 27) announced to Mr. Cromwell that they had received from the Attorney General a reply by cable authorizing them to agree to this plan, that the Government would appoint the said bankers as its agents for the purpose stated, in prevision of arrangements to be made with them by the company at its own expense, and that the assistants to the Attorney General would conclude the transaction in this manner.

Awaiting the reply of the Attorney General we had negotiated with Mr. Morgan, in the name of the company, the various agreements, details, and conditions, on the basis of which the transaction should be concluded in case the United States accepted the plan. With the exception of one or two formal interviews the entire negotiation involving the details of the plan and the legal and financial conditions between the company and the bankers was conducted by Mr. Cromwell, who brought about a complete agreement between the parties. He then wrote a series of contracts between (1) the company and the United States, (2) the company and J. P. Morgan & Co., and (3) J. P. Morgan & Co. and the United States, in accordance with which the transaction was completed, and the last-mentioned contract was corrected and agreed to by the assistants to the Attorney General.

These contracts were signed on April 28 and their terms satisfactorily provided for the receipt of the funds in New York by the bankers, their transmission and deposit in the Bank of France, in accordance with the instructions of the company, the calculation of the exchange in French francs at a given rate (that 206,000,000 francs should be the equivalent of the $40,000,000), that the legal title to the funds should be retained by the United States up to their actual arrival in the Bank of France, and that the total payment should be effected within a short and stipulated time.

On account of the possible controversies against which we were taking precautions we inserted a clause stating that "in the meantime the United States shall be responsible to the company for the said purchase price up to the time of the total payment of the price to the company or for its account, in the manner above mentioned, and the United States agrees that this payment shall be effected without regard to any such injunction, seizure, or claim of any nature whatsoever."

By the carrying out of this plan the enemies of the affair in the United States and in France were thwarted, the funds were paid to the company without complications or reductions, and the company was assured against the risks of payment in Washington without any real increase in expense to itself, as the banking charges were less under this method than would have been the expenses of transmission if the funds had been paid in Washington, as had been agreed.

It is due to the bankers to state that they acted at the personal request of Mr. Cromwell and that they lent to the transaction the protection of their great name, of their great credit, and of their important system without hope of profit, and that their compensation (according to subsequent official information to Congress) amounted to the comparatively insignificant sum of 175,500 francs, which included what was due for exchange, the transportation of gold, and the moral responsibility imposed by the receipt and transmission of 206,000,000 francs.

MAY 7, 1904—FINAL SETTLEMENT BY THE DELIVERY OF THE PROPERTY AND ARRANGEMENTS FOR PAYMENT BY MESSRS. J. P. MORGAN & CO., THE BANKERS.

The last days were devoted entirely to arrangements for the final details of the delivery.

On May 4 the delivery of the Panama Canal and other property on the Isthmus was effected to the representative of the United States on the Isthmus according to instructions by cable. On May 6 all the plans and archives of the company in Paris were delivered to the assistants to the Attorney General, who were in Paris.

On May 7, at the head offices of the company in Paris, in the presence of Mr. Bô, president; of Mr. Lampré, secretary general; of the assistants to the Attorney General, Day and Russell; of Mr. Gautron, the liquidator; and of Mr. Cromwell, the shares of the Panama Railroad Co., comprising almost the whole of its capital stock, were delivered, this being the final operation.

Having thus concluded the transaction, we demanded of the representatives of the American Government an official acknowledgment of the complete delivery of the properties in accordance with the undertakings of the company.

This document was duly signed and delivered on the 7th of the same month by the assistants to the Attorney General in the following form:

"PARIS, *May 7, 1904*.

"The United States of America acknowledges and declares by these presents that delivery has been made to it or its representatives of the totality of the properties and rights of La Compagnie Nouvelle du Canal de Panama (and of the said company in liquidation) on the Isthmus of Panama and of its plans and archives in Paris, as well as the certificates representing 68,887 shares of the capital stock of the Panama Railroad Co., in accordance with the general deeds of transfer of the 16th–23d of April, 1904, and the agreement of April 28, 1904, made and entered into between the said parties and the United States, and that payment of the purchase price, as it has already been agreed upon, is now due by the United States."

(Signed on behalf of the United States by the assistants to the Attorney General.)

Thus we had attained the object of our hopes and brought to a successful conclusion our incessant and intense struggle of eight years for the preservation and realization of the great investment of the company in the Panama Canal and its property on the Isthmus.

SUBSEQUENT DETAILS.

MAY 7, 1904–NOVEMBER, 1904—JUDGMENTS ON THE ISTHMUS.

Mr. Cromwell left Paris on May 11 with Mr. Russell, assistant to the Attorney General. Before leaving he had been authorized and instructed by the company and the liquidator to negotiate with a view to a compromise of the judgments on the Isthmus, in regard to which the company had deposited with the Government security for 350,000 francs, and to carry out the company's agreement of April 16.

On his return Mr. Cromwell opened negotiations with the various legal creditors. He had numerous conferences in New York with their lawyer, Señor Morales, corresponded with the principals on the Isthmus, and succeeded in compromising and settling all the judgments one after the other. In order to carry out the various compromises he employed and gave instructions to Señor Arango and Dr. Arosemena, as agents and counsel on the spot, to obtain receipts, certificates of release, etc.

As it was not practical to withdraw any part of the funds deposited until the discharge of all the judgments, we personally advanced for the time being the funds for the account of the company.

On November 14 we addressed a complete report to the Attorney General, to which were attached the official certificates proving the discharge and cancellation of all the judgments which completed the company's execution of its undertaking of April 16, 1904.

The report and the certificates were found complete and satisfactory by the Attorney General, who then returned to us the amount on deposit.

The entire balance over and above the settlement was forwarded by us to the company without any deduction by us for fees.

Besides carrying out the company's undertaking, this service resulted in a saving of more than 40,000 francs.

NOVEMBER, 1904–FEBRUARY, 1905—CONFIRMATORY DEEDS OF TRANSFER OF CANAL PROPERTY OUTSIDE OF THE CANAL ZONE.

By the transfer deeds signed in Paris the company had agreed to sign all other deeds which might be required from time to time to give effect to the transfer. To this end the company had then signed a power of attorney appointing as its proxy Mr. Renaudin its agent on the Isthmus. This gentleman having withdrawn from the Isthmus, the Attorney General requested the company to sign a similar power of attorney appointing some other proxy. In consequence we wrote a similar power of attorney, in collaboration with the special assistant to the Attorney General, which we forwarded to the company for signature. The suggestion having been made that Mr. Cromwell act in this capacity, be accepted.

In order to overcome certain difficulties as to the registration of the company's deeds of transfer covering properties outside of the Canal Zone, the Attorney General requested Mr. Cromwell in writing, on February 17, 1905, to sign and deliver a confirmatory act of transfer of the buildings within the city of Panama, as well as of the company's rights in the island of Taboga.

We had previously studied and verified the situation in regard to this matter, and we had conferences with the officials of the Panama Government; with Gen. Davis, governor of the Canal Zone; with the Secretary of War; and with the special assistant to the Attorney General. We then signed as representatives of the company, together with the Secreary of War, the necessary confirmatory act of transfer, of which we notified the company in due course.

MAY 7–JULY, 1904—ARRANGEMENTS TO PREVENT THE SEIZURE OF FUNDS, AND FINAL RECEIPTS BETWEEN THE BANKERS AND THE GOVERNMENT, IN ACCORDANCE WITH THE AGREEMENT WITH THE COMPANY OF APRIL 16.

When in Paris we had discussed and settled with Mr. Morgan the various details which were to be followed in the United States to assure the protection of the funds against legal attack, and we had also arranged with him, at the request of the company, to hasten the payment of the 20,000,000 francs applicable to the railroad shares.

With a view to immediate action in New York we cabled to the bankers in New York, as well as to Mr. Curtis, the complete text of the contracts with the bankers, and an announcement of the conditions and of the methods which were to be carefully followed so as to prevent seizures, injunctions, or other legal actions whatever in New York or on the way. Mr. Curtis in New York had conferences at the same time with the bankers, gave his advice as to the steps to be taken for this purpose, and took every possible precaution against legal complications, pronouncing himself with the utmost care on the technical requirements of the case. To this end one of our partners also went to Washington with the bankers to give his advice and assistance.

Later on, in New York, the payments having been completed and the Government having called for certificates (of deposit) and receipts in due form to this effect from the bankers, in accordance with the contracts signed in Paris, the latter communicated to us for our approval the final documents, we examined and corrected them, and then gave our approval.

The agreements with the bankers which we had proposed and negotiated in Paris in April were fully and successfully carried out and the payment completed to the entire satisfaction of the company, of the United States, and of the bankers; and the new method of procedure (to which we had at that time given publicity so as to discourage attacks) was shown to be efficacious and successful—from every point of view.

General Remarks.

If we have permitted this brief to run to some length it is because our labors forced us to deal with situations and conditions as well as with facts; and also because the study of this matter will be facilitated by the incorporation of certain documents in the text. But the foregoing is at most only a sketch, for no summary could describe in their true proportion the variety, the scope, the gravity, the responsibility, the difficulty, and the absorbing nature of the labors imposed by the exigencies of this case.

At the outset of our employment the case took up less of our time, because of the policy then adopted by the company, the formation of which was recent and which had no definite engineering or financial plans, of not appearing openly in any public movement in the United States; but even then one at least of our partners gave the matter continuous attention, and for us it was from the first (sa genese) a weighty and absorbing professional task. It dealt not only with the Panama Canal, but also with the study and observation of its great rival and of the railroad interests which were hostile to it. In fact, it will be seen that it was our careful study of these conditions which led us to give early warning to the company of the approaching dangers and to strongly advise an open, audacious, and vigorous campaign for the preservation and protection of its vast interests, advice which led the company two years later to adopt this plan.

From then on the opportunities for the employment of our time and efforts multiplied from day to day. The work developed, spread out, and became more and more arduous and absorbing.

During the first part of this time one at least of our partners, with the assistance of clerks, devoted a considerable part of his time and efforts to the matter, and was often obliged to pass weeks and sometimes months at a time in Washington and to abandon in consequence other professional work of the law office.

During the years from 1899 to 1904, with the exception of the seven months from July, 1901, to January 27, 1902, several of our partners devoted their time, their attention, and their efforts almost exclusively to this matter for the direct and personal conduct of the campaign in its various details in Washington, New York, and other places, whilst the senior member of our firm was called upon to absent himself for months at a time to make stays in Paris devoted to reports and conferences.

Besides the devotion which Mr. Cromwell has displayed in this matter, to the extent of allowing himself to be almost entirely absorbed by it, in the general direction of the case in all its phases during the eight years (except always the period mentioned) the unforeseen developments were so considerable and so critical and the exigencies (of the case) so varied and so grave that several other partners of our law firm—Mr. Curtis, Mr. Hill, Mr. Jaretzki, and others again—were obliged to devote themselves to equal activity. At the critical periods—which were only too frequent—the greater part of the entire staff of the office was enlisted to cope with the crisis while it lasted. To say that at least half of the potentiality which gives our law firm its usefulness and its income was actually withdrawn from all other professional activity, and necessarily devoted to this particular matter for a consecutive period of three or four years, is to make a very conservative estimate. The incessant calls upon us, the prolonged absence, and the absorbing nature of the work prevented the accustomed, continuous, and remunerative exercise of our functions in other directions. In fact, our attention to this matter absorbed us to such an extent that the clients of our law firm and the public came to understand and to recognize that we were not available as formerly for other professional work, and in consequence we were obliged to give up these cases and the fees they offered. The matter was in a perpetual condition of controversy and danger, and it was only by incessant vigilance and activity that the final result could be attained.

As to the extensive correspondence (letters, cables, and telegrams are there by the thousand), the innumerable conferences; the journeys in the United States, to be counted by hundreds, and the many trips to Europe; the arguments and papers written for circulation among the public and for use in Congress; the instruction and direction of agents and assistants; the incessant efforts to bring about an appreciation of the Panama route, efforts which came to be part of our daily activity; the constant watching of public events and political maneuvers in Congress, and the movements of attack and defense which we conceived and carried out at every stage of the long struggle; the many problems solved and difficulties overcome; the disaster of January, 1902, and the successive victories afterwards won; the difficulties within the company itself, which became an important factor in the case; the unceasing resourcefulness and opposition, which lasted throughout the period, of the leaders of the Nicaragua party, whose bitterness and hostility increased as their plans were defeated or thwarted; the vicissitudes of the treaty negotiations in regard to which one of the Governments was indifferent and the other powerless to enter before the previous adoption by Congress of a route for the canal, but which it was essential for the company to bring to a successful issue from one side or the other; the exactions and machinations whereby Colombia was doing her best to force money from the company, and the measures taken to prevent their being successful; the situation on the Isthmus which culminated in the independence, all the anxiety and the precautions taken for the protection of the company's interests while these grave events were taking place; the campaign of belittlement and deception incessantly carried on by the hostile interests of Nicaragua and the railroads against the cause of Panama and those who were supporting it—as to all this, it would be altogether impossible to give details in this brief, even if it were proper to do so. If it is desired, these matters will be dealt with at the hearing.

The work included almost every branch of professional activity—engineering, law, legislation, finance, diplomacy, administration, and direction.

Whether one considers the labors entailed, the responsibility which weighed upon us, the nature of the work, the importance of the results attained, or the sacrifices imposed, we respectfully assert that these services deserve to be recognized in a just and adequate manner.

September 5, 1907.

SULLIVAN & CROMWELL.

EXHIBIT B.

THE PANAMA LIBEL SUIT.

HISTORY OF THE CASE OF THE UNITED STATES v. THE PRESS PUBLISHING COMPANY DECIDED IN FAVOR OF "THE WORLD" BY THE UNITED STATES CIRCUIT COURT AND BY THE SUPREME COURT OF THE UNITED STATES, TOGETHER WITH A STATEMENT OF HOW "THE WORLD" CAME TO PRINT THE NEWS ARTICLE OF OCTOBER 3, 1908; MR. CROMWELL'S PART IN ITS PUBLICATION, ETC.

THE PANAMA LIBEL SUIT.

Mr. Roosevelt's Panama libel suit against the World had its genesis during the last presidential campaign in a complaint made by William Nelson Cromwell through his lawyer, W. J. Curtis, to District Attorney Jerome on October 1, 1908, that certain persons were trying to blackmail him by reason of his connection with the sale of the Panama Canal to the United States.

On October 2 the World received information of Mr. Cromwell's complaint, and a reporter was sent out to cover the story. He was unable to get any conformation from the district attorney's office, and so reported to the city editor. Nothing was written and the matter was dropped.

Late the same evening Jonas Whitley, a former newspaper man employed by Mr. Cromwell as a press agent, came to the World office and told the managing editor that the World was about to print a Panama news article that was entirely false. The managing editor knew nothing about it, so he inquired at the city editor's desk. He was told that the World had no Panama article of any kind or description, but that it had been trying to verify a report of a complaint made by Mr. Cromwell to the district attorney and had been unable to do so.

MR. WHITLEY STATED SUBSTANCE OF THE COMPLAINT.

Mr. Whitley had voluntarily related the substance of the complaint. He said that the persons who were alleged to be trying to blackmail Mr. Cromwell pretended that Charles P. Taft and Douglas Robinson were members of a syndicate interested in the sale of the Panama Canal, and these persons threatened to exploit the story for political purposes unless Mr. Cromwell bought them off.

A synopsis of Mr. Whitley's account of the Cromwell complaint was then dictated to a stenographer, and the typewritten copy was turned over to Mr. Whitley to revise. This manuscript is still in possession of the World. It shows that Mr. Whitley scratched out the name of Charles P. Taft and substituted the name of Henry W. Taft. Then he erased the name of Henry W. Taft and restored the name of Charles P. Taft.

The news article, as revised by Mr. Whitley, was printed in the World the following morning—October 3, 1908. It contained the following:

"In brief Mr. Curtis told Mr. Jerome it had been represented to Mr. Cromwell that the Democratic national committee was considering the advisability of making public a statement that William Nelson Cromwell, in connection with Mr. Bunau-Varilla, a French speculator, had formed a syndicate at the time when it was quite evident that the United States would take over the rights of the French bondholders in the De Lesseps Canal, and that this syndicate included among others Charles P. Taft, brother of William H. Taft, and Douglas Robinson, brother-in-law of President Roosevelt. Other men more prominent in the New York world of finance were also mentioned. According to the story unfolded by Mr. Curtis it was said that * * * these financiers invested their money because of a full knowledge of the intention of the Government to acquire the French property at a price of about $40,000,000, and thus—because of the alleged information from high Government sources—were enabled to reap a rich profit."

After Mr. Whitley had finished revising this article he telephoned to Mr. Cromwell and then told the managing editor of the World that Mr. Cromwell would like to make a statement.

Very late that night Mr. Cromwell telephoned to the World office and dictated a statement to one of the World's stenographers. The stenographer's notes were read over to him to make sure that there was no error; he approved them, and this statement was printed exactly as dictated by Mr. Cromwell.

It said in part:

"Neither I nor any one allied with me, either directly or indirectly, at any time or in any place in America or abroad, ever bought, sold, dealt in, or ever made a penny of profit out of any stocks, bonds, or other securities of either the old Panama Canal Co. or the New Panama Canal Co., or ever received for the same a single dollar of the 40 millions paid by the United States. I make this the most sweeping statement that language can convey. As everybody connected with the affair knows, I abstained from receiving the 40 millions in my own hands at Washington or New York as the general counsel of the company, and myself arranged for the payment of the entire 40 millions direct from the Treasury of the United States through the bankers of the Government into the Bank of France at Paris to the credit of the liquidators of the two companies. There it remained subject to the order of the liquidators until distributed by them to the hundreds of thousands of beneficiaries, and not one dollar of it ever came to me or anyone in anywise connected with me. Of course, I do not refer to our regular compensation as counsel. I suppose it will be years before the beneficiaries will all be identified and the distribution completely made."

The Cromwell complaint was never submitted to a grand jury; there was no grand jury inquiry as to this alleged attempt at blackmail, and the legal proceedings on Mr. Cromwell's part against the alleged blackmailers ended with the filing of the Cromwell complaint.

It was Mr. Cromwell's complaint and that alone which brought the name of Charles P. Taft into the Panama matter. It was Mr. Cromwell's press agent who brought the names of Charles P. Taft and Douglas Robinson into the World office. But for Mr. Cromwell it is probable that no Panama story would have been printed during the campaign, and it is certain that the names of Charles P. Taft and Douglas Robinson would never have been published in connection with the affair.

INDEBTED TO MR. CROMWELL FOR NOTORIETY.

When Mr. Cromwell's complaint was made public Mr. Charles P. Taft emphatically denied that he had any connection whatever with a Panama syndicate or with the sale of the canal. Mr. Robinson refused to discuss the matter for publication. It is fair to say that the information in the possession of the World completely substantiates Mr. Charles P. Taft's denial that he had any interest, direct or indirect, in the sale of the Panama Canal. Why his name should have appeared in Mr. Cromwell's complaint to Mr. Jerome the World has no means of knowing. As to Mr. Douglas Robinson there is nothing to show that he was an associate of Mr. Cromwell's in the sale of the canal. He also is indebted solely to Mr. Cromwell for the notoriety.

Great interest was aroused in political circles by Mr. Cromwell's complaint, and the World, as well as other newspapers, tried to ascertain if any facts could be discovered in addition to those which had been dragged to light by Senator Morgan in 1906 in the course of the investigation of the Panama Canal matter by a committee of the United States Senate, which investigation had been thwarted by Mr. Cromwell's refusal to answer the most pertinent questions put to him on the ground that as counsel for the New Panama Canal Co. his relations with the canal vendors were privileged and confidential.

Unsuccessful attempts were made to get at the records in Paris and Washington. The World at great expense retained an eminent English lawyer, a member of Parliament, who went to Paris and made an investigation on behalf of this paper. Very little additional information could be obtained, and he reported in part as follows:

"I have never known in my lengthy experience of company matters any public corporation, much less one of such vast importance, having so completely disappeared and removed all traces of its existence as the New Panama Canal Co. This company having purchased the assets of La Compagnie Universelle du Canal Interoceanique de Panama (the old or De Lesseps Panama Canal Co.), brought off the deal with the American Government. So thorough has been its obliteration that only the United States Government can now give information respecting the new company's transactions and the identity of the individuals who created it to effectuate this deal, and who for reasons best known to themselves wiped it off the face of the earth when the deal was carried through. * * * I consulted leading French lawyers, and they declared that there was no machinery, legal or otherwise, by which its records could be brought to light. * * * The stock of the new company was originally registered, so transactions in it could be traced, but power was subsequently obtained to transform it into "bearer" stock, which passed from hand to hand without any record being preserved. * * * There is nothing to show the names of the owners of the stock at the time of the liquidation of the company and who actually received their proportions of the purchase money paid by the United States. * * * No record exists here of a single person who received the money or of the proportions in which it was paid. The liquidation of the new company was finally closed on June 30 last, and the offices of the liquidators were shut. No one is there to give the slightest information concerning it, although questions are still arising necessitating information. The American ambassador in Paris was entitled to the archives of the company for his Government, and those archives should include a list of the persons who received the purchase money paid by the United States."

CHARGES WERE UNCHALLENGED DURING CAMPAIGN.

In all, The World printed six articles on the Panama Canal purchase and on the Panama revolution of 1903, giving currency to the charges that there was a syndicate of Americans who were interested in and received some of the $40,000,000 which the United States paid to the French canal company for the canal property, and that the Administration at Washington and some of the individuals who then composed it were cognizant of and had supported the plans for the revolution in Panama, as a result of which the present Republic of Panama seceded from the Republic of Colombia and gave to the United States those sovereign rights over the Canal Zone which, under its constitution, Colombia was unable to grant.

These articles were reproduced in many papers throughout the country, and Mr. Rainey, of Illinois, expressed his intention of forcing a full congressional investigation, if possible, when Congress convened in December.

At this time Mr. Roosevelt, oblivious of the traditions of his high office, was personally managing Mr. Taft's candidacy. Regardless of his obligations as President of the United States, he had taken charge of the Republican campaign and was the actual boss of the Republican Party. He allowed the Panama charges to pass unchallenged, paid no attention to the Panama articles, and refused to regard Panama as an issue. Much less did he look upon these articles as a libel upon the United States Government, upon himself, or upon any of his associates.

On the day before election, however, the Indianapolis News, the leading paper in Indiana, which had refused to support the Republican national and State tickets in the campaign, printed an editorial on the Panama scandal and asking who got the $40,000,000 the United States had paid for the canal. Morally the election in Indiana was a decisive Republican defeat, as, although Mr. Taft carried the State by a narrow plurality of 10,731, a Democratic governor and a Democratic legislature were elected, a Democrat was sent to the United States Senate in place of Mr. Hemenway, and only three Republican Representatives were elected out of a delegation of 13. Mr. Roosevelt and Mr. Roosevelt's friends were greatly mortified and attributed the result largely to the Indianapolis News.

PRESIDENT ROOSEVELT BREAKS OUT IN DENUNCIATION.

Accordingly, on November 29, 1908, William Dudley Foulke (the convenient gentleman to whom Mr. Roosevelt wrote the famous letter denying that he had used the Federal patronage to bring about Mr. Taft's nomination) sent to the President the Panama editorial printed in the Indianapolis News on November 2, and informed Mr. Roosevelt that "if the statements of the News are true our people ought to know it; if not true, they ought to have some just means of estimating what credit should be given in other matters to a journal which disseminates falsehoods."

Mr. Roosevelt in reply on December 1, 1908, denounced the conduct of Mr. Delavan Smith, editor of the Indianapolis News, as "not merely scandalous but infamous." He called him "a conspicuous offender against the laws of honesty and truthfulness," occupying "the same evil eminence with such men as Mr. Laffan of the New York Sun." He said that such newspapers as the Indianapolis News and the New York Sun "habitually and continually and as a matter of business practice every form of mendacity known to man"; that "the most corrupt financiers, the most corrupt politicians, are no greater menace to the country than the newspaper men of the type I have described."

Dealing with the purchase of the Panama Canal, Mr. Roosevelt asserted that the United States "paid $40,000,000 direct to the French Government, getting the receipt of the liquidator appointed by the French Government to receive the same"; that "the United States Government has not the slightest knowledge as to the particular individuals among whom the French Government distributed the sum"; that "this was the business of the French Government"; that "so far as I know there was no syndicate"; that "there certainly was no syndicate in the United States that to my knowledge had any dealings with the Government, directly or indirectly"; that "the people have had the most minute official knowledge" of the Panama affair; that "every important step and every important document have been made public"; and that the "abominable falsehood" that any American citizen had profited from the sale of the Panama Canal "is a slander, not against the American Government, but against the French Government."

THE WORLD'S EDITORIAL REPLY TO PRESIDENT ROOSEVELT.

Up to this time the World had not discussed the Panama matter editorially, but when Mr. Roosevelt went so far as to tell the American people that the United States Government "paid the $40,000,000 direct to the French Government" it seemed to the World that the time had arrived when the country was entitled to the truth, the whole truth, and nothing but the truth. In an editorial flatly challenging some of Mr. Roosevelt's statements, and proving its case by the official records, the World demanded a congressional investigation into the Panama scandal. It said:

"In view of President Roosevelt's deliberate misstatements of facts in his scandalous personal attack upon Mr. Delavan Smith, of the Indianapolis News, the World calls on the Congress of the United States to make immediately a full and impartial investigation of the entire Panama Canal scandal. * * *

"The natural query of the Indianapolis News as to 'Who got the money?' was based on the World's historical summary of Mr. Cromwell's connection with the Panama Canal. The inquiry was originally the World's and the World accepts Mr. Roosevelt's challenge. If Congress can have all the documents in the case, as Mr. Roosevelt says, let Congress make a full and complete investigation of the Panama Canal affair, and in particular of William Nelson Cromwell's relations with the French company, with Panama, and with the Government of the United States. Let Congress officially answer the question, 'Who got the money?' * * *

"Mr. Roosevelt says 'the Government paid this $40,000,000 direct to the French Government'; Mr. Cromwell testifies that the United States paid the money to J. P. Morgan & Co. Mr. Roosevelt says 'the French Government distributed the sum'; Mr. Cromwell testified as to how he distributed it. Mr. Roosevelt talks of 'getting the receipt of the liquidator appointed by the French Government to receive the same;' Mr. Cromwell testified: 'Of the $40,000,000 thus paid by the United States Government $25,000,000 was paid to the liquidator of the old Panama Canal Co. under and in pursuance of an agreement entered into between the liquidator and the new company. Of the balance of $15,000,000 paid to the New Panama Canal Co. $12,000,000 have already been distributed among its stockholders and the remainder is now being held awaiting final distribution and payment.' * * *

"Whether Douglas Robinson, who is Mr. Roosevelt's brother-in-law, or any of Mr. Taft's brothers associated himself with Mr. Cromwell in Panama exploitation, or shared in these profits, is incidental to the main issue of letting in the light. Whether they did or not, whether all the profits went into William Nelson Cromwell's hands or whatever became of them, the fact that Theodore Roosevelt, as President of the United States, issued a public statement about such an important matter full of flagrant untruths, reeking with misstatements, challenging line by line the testimony of his associate, Cromwell, and the official record, makes it imperative that full publicity come at once through the authority and by the action of Congress."

President Roosevelt then took steps to find out if among the records and archives received by the Isthmian Canal Commission from the New Panama Canal Co. there were any compromising documents. In obedience to his orders the documents were examined by Judge Paul Charlton, of the War Department, and Mr. Rogers, general counsel of the Isthmian Canal Commission. Their report was transmitted by Gen. Luke Wright, then Secretary of War, to President Roosevelt on December 14, 1908. It was to the effect that the records and archives received from Paris contained solely engineering data.

PRESIDENT ROOSEVELT'S AMAZING SPECIAL MESSAGE.

On the following day President Roosevelt sent a special message to the Congress of the United States which is unique in American history. In it he said:

"In view of the constant reiteration of the assertion that there was some corrupt action by or on behalf of the United States Government in connection with the acquisition of the title of the French company to the Panama Canal, and of the repetition of the story that a syndicate of American citizens owned either one or both of the Panama companies, I deem it wise to submit to the Congress all the information I have on the subject. These stories were first brought to my attention as published in a paper in Indianapolis called the News, edited by Mr. Delavan Smith. These stories were scurrilous and libelous in character and false in every essential particular. Mr. Smith shelters himself behind the excuse that he merely accepted the statement which had appeared in a paper published in New York, the World, owned by Mr. Joseph Pulitzer. It is idle to say that the known character of Mr. Pulitzer and his newspaper are such that the statements in that paper will be believed by nobody. Unfortunately thousands of persons are ill-informed in this respect and believe the statements they see in print, even though they appear in a newspaper published by Mr. Pulitzer. * * *

"These stories * * * need no investigation whatever; * * * they are in fact wholly and in form partly a libel upon the United States Government. * * * The real offender is Mr. Joseph Pulitzer, editor and proprietor of the World. While the criminal offense of which Mr. Pulitzer has been guilty is in form a libel upon individuals, the great injury done is in blackening the good name of the American people. It should not be left to a private citizen to sue Mr. Pulitzer for libel. He should be prosecuted for libel by the governmental authorities.

"In point of encouragement of iniquity, in point of infamy, of wrongdoing, there is nothing to choose between a public servant who betrays his trust, a public servant who is guilty of blackmail or theft or public dishonesty of any kind and a man guilty as Mr. Pulitzer has been guilty in this instance. It is therefore a high national duty to bring to justice this villifier of the American people, this man who wantonly and wickedly and without one shadow of justification seeks to blacken the character of reputable private citizens and to convict the Government of his own country in the eyes of the civilized world of wrongdoing of the basest and foulest kind, when he has not one shadow of justification of any sort or description for the charges he has made. The Attorney General has under consideration the form in which the proceedings against Mr. Pulitzer shall be brought."

ATTORNEY GENERAL BONAPARTE STARTED CRIMINAL PROCEEDINGS.

Under orders from Mr. Roosevelt, Attorney General Bonaparte instituted criminal proceedings in the courts of the District of Columbia against both the World and the Indianapolis News, and on February 17, 1909, the grand jury of the District of Columbia returned an indictment against the Press Publishing Co., proprietor and publisher of the World; Joseph Pulitzer, the president of the company; and Caleb M. Van Hamm and Robert H. Lyman, two of the news editors of the World, based on the circulation within the District of Columbia of copies of the World containing the news articles and the editorial above referred to, and a further indictment against Delavan Smith and Charles R. Williams, the owners and proprietors of the Indianapolis News, based on the circulation in the District of Columbia of copies of the News which reflected, as charged, upon ex-President Roosevelt, President Taft, Charles P. Taft, Douglas Robinson, ex-Secretary of State Elihu Root, William Nelson Cromwell, and J. P. Morgan, alleged to have been libeled by the World.

GOVERNMENT COMPLETELY DEFEATED IN INDIANAPOLIS.

The Government was completely defeated in the Indianapolis News case. United States Attorney Kealing, of Indianapolis, a Roosevelt appointee, resigned his position rather than assist in the attempt to remove the defendants from their homes to the District of Columbia for trial. In his letter of resignation to the Attorney General of the United States he said:

"For almost eight years I have had the honor of representing the Government as United States attorney. During that time I have prosecuted all alike, without fear or favor, where I had honest belief in their guilt. I have been compelled on several occasions to prosecute personal friends, but in each case I only did so after a thorough investigation had convinced me of their guilt. In this case I have made a careful investigation of the law applicable thereto. As to the guilt or innocence of the defendants on the question of libel I do not pretend to say. If guilty they should be prosecuted, but properly indicted and prosecuted in the right place, viz, in their homes. It is only with the question of removal that I have to do.

"I am not in accord with the Government in its attempt to put a strained construction on the law; to drag these defendants from their homes to the seat of the Government, to be tried and punished, while there is good and sufficient law in this jurisdiction in the State court. I believe the principle involved is dangerous, striking at the very foundation of our form of Government. I can not therefore honestly and conscientiously insist to the court that such is the law, or that such construction should be put on it. Not being able to do this, I do not feel that I can, in justice to my office, continue to hold it, and decline to assist."

JUDGE ANDERSON'S ILLUMINATING OPINION.

United States District Judge Anderson decided against the contention of the Government, and in discharging Messrs. Smith and Williams from custody said:

"It was well stated by a former President of the United States that it is the duty of a newspaper to print the news and tell the truth about it. It is the duty of a public newspaper, such as is owned and conducted by these defendants, to tell the people, its subscribers, its readers, the facts that it may find out about public questions, or matters of public interest; it is its duty and its right to draw inferences from the facts known—draw them for the people. * * *

"Here was a great public question. There are many very peculiar circumstances about the history of this Panama Canal or Panama Canal business. I do not wish to be understood as reflecting upon anybody, in office or out, in connection with this matter, except such persons as I may name in that way. The circumstances surrounding the revolution in Panama were unusual and peculiar. The people were interested in the construction of a canal; it was a matter of great public concern, it was much discussed. A large portion of the people favored the Nicaragua route. Another portion of those who were interested in it, officially or personally, preferred the Panama route. A committee was appointed to investigate the relative merits of the two routes. They investigated and reported in favor of the Nicaragua route. Shortly afterwards—I do not recall just how soon afterwards—they changed to the Panama route. Up to the time of that change, as I gathered from the evidence, the lowest sum that had been suggested at which the property of the Panama Canal Co. could be procured was something over $100,000,000. Then, rather suddenly, it became known that it could be procured for $40,000,000. There were a number of people who thought there was something not just exactly right about that transaction, and I will say for myself that I have a curiosity to know what the real truth was.

"Thereupon a committee of the United States Senate was appointed to investigate these matters—about the only way the matter could be investigated. The committee met. As stated in these articles, the man who knew all about it—I think that is the proper way to speak of Mr. Cromwell—who knew all about it, was called before the committee. Mr. Cromwell, upon certain questions being put to him, more or less pertinent, stood upon his privilege as an attorney and refused to answer. * * * Mr. Cromwell stood upon his privilege whenever questions were asked, the answers to which would or might reflect upon him and his associates. But whenever a question was asked which gave him an opportunity to say something in their behalf, he ostentatiously thanked the examiner for the question and proceeded to answer. To my mind that gave just ground for suspicion. I am suspicious about it now. * * * Now * * * the question is: Did these defendants, under the circumstances, act honestly in the discharge of this duty, of which I have spoken and which the law recognizes, or were they prompted by a desire to injure the person who is affected by their acts? If it were necessary to decide this case upon the question of privilege, the lack of malice, I would hesitate quite a while before I would conclude that it was my duty to send these people to Washington for trial.

"But that is not all. This indictment charges these defendants with the commission of a crime in the District of Columbia. The sixth amendment to the Constitution of the United States provides: In all criminal prosecutions the accused shall enjoy the right to a speedy and public trial by an impartial jury of the State or district wherein the crime shall have been committed, which district shall have been previously ascertained by law. * * *

"To my mind that man has read the history of our institutions to little purpose who does not look with grave apprehension upon the possibility of the success of a proceeding such as this. If the history of liberty means anything—if constitutional guarantees are worth anything—this proceeding must fail. If the prosecuting authorities have the authority to select the tribunal; if there be more than one tribunal to select from; if the Government has the power and can drag citizens from distant States to the capital of the Nation, there to be tried, then, as Judge Cooley says, this is a strange result of a revolution where one of the grievances complained of was the assertion of the right to send parties abroad for trial."

ANOTHER ATTEMPT MADE TO STRETCH THE LAW.

In the face of this decision there was no attempt by the Government to remove Mr. Pulitzer, Mr. Van Hamm, and Mr. Lyman from the New York jurisdiction to the District of Columbia on the indictment pending against them in that district; but, to please Mr. Roosevelt, another attempt had been made to stretch the law so as to permit the prosecution of the World before the Federal courts without again raising the question of removal.

Under instructions from President Roosevelt, United States Attorney Henry L. Stimson, who was Mr. Roosevelt's candidate for governor of the State of New York at the recent State election, had also obtained further separate indictments for criminal libel from the Federal grand jury in the southern district of New York against the Press Publishing Co. (the corporation which publishes the World) and against Mr. Van Hamm, charging the circulation of 29 copies of each of the issues complained of at and within "the fort and military post and reservation of West Point" and at and within "the tract of land in the borough of Manhattan, in the city of New York," whereon stands "a needful building used by the United States as a post office," both being "places which had been ceded by the State of New York to the United States."

This indictment, couched in the very language of the notorious alien and sedition acts, expressly charged that it was the purpose of the World to "stir up disorder among the people" (the language of the sedition act was "to stir up sedition among the people"). In substance and in fact it was an indictment for the publication of what in 1798 would have been alleged in terms to constitute a seditious libel, tending to stir up discontent and disaffections and to bring the Government into contempt.

The act on which the Government relied as authority for this unprecedented prosecution was that of July 7, 1898, entitled "An act to protect the harbor defenses and fortifications constructed or used by the United States from malicious injury, and for other purposes." It was founded on the act of March 3, 1825, which was the first Federal enactment of this character. Eighty-five years had passed since Judge Story conceived this statute and since Congress made it a part of the laws of the United States. It had never before been invoked by the Federal authorities as giving them the right to punish libel.

It was further asserted by United States Attorney Stimson in a letter to Mr. Jerome that:

"These publications * * * appear to have been circulated by the newspaper in question in a number of distinct and independent jurisdictions and to contain charges reflecting on the personal character of a number of men, of whom some are in public life and some are private citizens. In each of these jurisdictions, under well-known principles of law, each of these publications would constitute a separate offense, and, as it happens in this case, each one is characterized by distinct and peculiar features."

SWEEPING SCOPE OF GOVERNMENT CLAIM.

As there are no fewer than 2,809 Government reservations corresponding to West Point and the post-office building, a newspaper of large circulation under this Rooseveltian theory of law might be prosecuted from one end of the country to the other by the Federal authorities for an article that was neither written nor printed on any of these reservations, but happened to reach them in the ordinary course of circulation.

At the suggestion of counsel for the World court orders for the issuance of letters rogatory for the examination of witnesses were addressed through the usual diplomatic channels to the proper judicial authorities of the French and Panaman Governments.

In order to obtain the Government's consent to this procedure it was necessary for the World to pay the expenses of United States Attorney Wise and Deputy Attorney General Stuart McNamara to Paris, and of Mr. Knapp, of the United States attorney's office, to Panama, as the Government refused to assume any part of the cost of procuring the evidence needed.

The letters rogatory having been issued, the State Department in Washington notified De Lancey Nicoll, the World's counsel in New York, that the American ambassador to France had been instructed to assist Coudert Bros., the World's counsel in Paris, in obtaining the authorization of the minister of justice in order that the examination of witnesses could begin about July 12, 1909. On July 18 Mr. Wise wrote to Mr. De Lancey Nicoll that he had received a letter from the Attorney General "in which he informs me that he has made request for instructions to the American ambassador at Paris to facilitate you in all ways to a full and thorough access to the papers of the old and new Panama canal companies."

Mr. Wise also informed John D. Lindsay, Mr. Nicoll's law partner, that if a personal note from Mr. Taft to the President of the French Republic was necessary to secure evidence in the matter contemplated he would obtain such a letter.

EFFORTS TO GET AT FACTS IMPEDED.

This looked very promising, and it seemed certain that the American people would finally know "Who got the money." But on June 21 Mr. Nicoll received the following cable from Coudert Bros.: "Government interfering. Wants know nature of case, names, witnesses, list of questions." Mr. Nicoll at once took the matter up with the Attorney General and with the State Department, but the French authorities insisted that the rogatory letters could not be issued, and in a letter written to Mr. Lindsay July 13 Mr. Wise said the American ambassador had been informed by the French foreign office "that no such examination as was contemplated by us can be had." Mr. Wise added:

"As you know, I have been in Paris for the past week, during which time I have known of the before-mentioned difficulties, and being desirous of affording your client every opportunity to have a full and fair opportunity to conduct its examination, I have arranged with the American ambassador to permit the use of the rooms at the embassy for the examination of such witnesses as you may desire to call; he has also agreed that if you and I join in a written request to him to invite such witnesses to come to the embassy to be examined he will immediately communicate with the Secretary of State of the United States for his approval of such course, and upon receiving such approval, if the French Government does not object, he will invite them. I am reliably informed that the French Government will make no objection, and I am sure the Secretary of State will give his approval."

This simply meant that such witnesses as might choose to come would give such testimony as they saw fit, and that there could be no thorough examination, such as the case demanded. However, there was nothing to do but to make the best of the situation. So on July 15 Mr. Lindsay wrote to Mr. Wise asking him to make arrangements "so that I can see to-morrow, if possible, at any time suitable to your convenience, the records of the two companies."

In his reply, Mr. Wise said:

"* * * You seem to assume that I have a power of control over the affairs of these two companies and that it is only necessary for me to signify my desire that the records of these companies should be examined and the wish would be gratified. * * * You are greatly in error. * * * First * * * the New Panama Canal Co. was a going corporation at the time when it sold its properties to the United States, and under the French law, which is quite similar to that of the State of New York, the corporation having no further function to perform, went out of existence by its board of directors assuming the functions of a board of trustees for the distribution of its assets; and this having been fully performed, * * * the board of trustees * * * deposited all of the books of the company with a depository, which in this case happened to be the Crédit Lyonnais, where under the laws of France such books must remain for a period of 20 years. This having been done, the board of directors or the board of trustees have no further control over these books and can not have access thereto. I know of no way by which it will be possible for me to arrange for you to see the records of these companies. I do not believe you would be able to examine these records through any court proceeding. I have consulted with eminent French counsel on this subject and am informed that no court in France could make any order compelling the Crédit Lyonnais or its officers to submit the papers to our examination."

THE WORLD PREPARED TO CLAIM JUSTIFICATION.

Although thwarted in its attempt to get access to the records of the canal companies, which under the terms of the agreement of sale belong by right to the United States Government and ought to be in Washington, the World pursued its investigations and collected much valuable evidence in Paris and in Panama. A staff correspondent was sent to Bogota and by the courtesy of the Colombian Government was given certified copies of original records bearing upon the case and other documentary evidence of great value.

When the case came up for trial in the United States district court in New York City on January 25, 1910, before Judge Charles M. Hough, the World was fully prepared to submit to the jury evidence to sustain the defense of justification which would have been entered had the case gone to trial on its merits. But the form in which the prosecution was brought forced upon the World responsibilities which could not be disregarded.

After stating to the court that, quite apart from the legal questions involved, he proposed to interpose the defense of justification, De Lancey Nicoll, counsel for the World, moved that the court quash the indictment, dismiss the proceedings, or instruct the jury to acquit the defendant upon the following grounds:

1. The court has no jurisdiction in this case. There is no statute of the United States authorizing this prosecution.
2. The act of 1898 does not apply to the case, as disclosed by the evidence.
3. If the act of 1898 is so construed as to cover the acts shown by the evidence it is unconstitutional.
4. The offense, if any, was committed wholly within the jurisdiction of the State of New York, and was punishable there.
5. The defendant, being a corporation, is incapable of committing the offense charged in the indictment.

But for the menace to the freedom of the press presented by Mr. Roosevelt's unprecedented prosecution, and but for the question of constitutional liberty in its relation to freedom of speech and of the press involved, the World would very much have preferred to let the case go to trial on its merits and present the evidence in its possession to a jury.

This could not be done, however, without conceding the existence of a Federal libel law, thereby placing the press of the entire country at the mercy of the President of the United States or of the party in power. While in some future case that might arise, the great constitutional issue raised by the World would undoubtedly have been settled by the courts, yet smaller and weaker newspapers, unable to match their resources against the limitless power of the United States Government, might have been bankrupted and ruined in defending their rights.

THE WORLD'S FIGHT WAS FOR THE PRESS OF WHOLE COUNTRY.

The World, therefore, not merely in its own interest, but in the interest of the freedom of the press and in order to safeguard the public's right to a full, free, and untrammeled discussion of all national and political questions, felt obliged to resist to the utmost every pretense on the part of the Federal authorities that there was a Federal libel law; that Federal authorities had a coordinate jurisdiction with the State authorities in prosecuting alleged libel if it could be shown that the paper or periodical which had offended the Government happened in the ordinary course of its circulation to reach any one of the 2,809 Government reservations.

So Mr. Nicoll contended that the libels with which the World was charged—even if they were libels—were cognizable in the State courts and could have been punished there, but that there was no Federal libel law, and whatever the language of the act to protect harbor defenses and fortifications, the whole history of the law of libel in the United States, the history of the statute and the history of the passage of the act of 1825 through Congress all plainly showed that Congress did not intend and the law did not authorize any such purpose as claimed by the Government.

On behalf of the Government, United States Attorney Wise argued that the act under which the indictment was being pressed could be construed as a Federal libel law. He contended that newspapers were subject to prosecution for libel in the Federal courts as well as in the State courts, with the result that the President of the United States could instigate criminal proceedings against a newspaper in any or all of the 2,809 Federal jurisdictions in which it might happen to circulate, and that a conviction in any one of these jurisdictions would not be a bar to further convictions in others and to further convictions—should such be obtainable—in each and every State of the Union.

JUDGE HOUGH QUASHED THE INDICTMENT.

Judge Hough refused to accept this view. In his judgment quashing the indictment he said:

"The court is relieved of much embarrassment by the form of one of the motions made. The jurisdiction of this court is peremptorily challenged by the motion to quash. Other motions have been made which will not be considered. But inasmuch as a decision under a motion to quash is now speedily reviewable by the highest court, I shall dispose of the case under that motion. * * * It seems to me that there is a plain distinction between that jurisdiction which grows out of the necessary exercise of national powers and that which is based on the physical ownership of areas of land. The first basis or foundation of jurisdiction is governmental and fundamentally governmental. The existence and exercise of that species of jurisdiction is vital to the National Government, but territorial jurisdiction is merely a convenience. It is frequently a very great convenience, but it is no more than that.

"The criminal statutes passed in the exercise of congressional authority have always, as far as they have come under my observation, seemed to me to view offenses and offenders from one or two standpoints. The proscribed act is made an offense or crime because it either lessens the authority or attacks the sovereignty, or interferes with the operation of or injures the property of the United States, or else it is an offense against general municipal law which happens to be committed upon a place within the exclusive jurisdiction of the nation. Now, it may be, it has in the past been thought, that under some circumstances the crime of libel might be considered to impair the authority and interfere with the efficiency of the Government of the United States, but so far as I know or am informed by counsel, this thought has not found expression in any national statute now in force. Therefore in this court the crime charged in this indictment is to be regarded only as an offense against the United States, if it is an offense against the law of New York, which happened to be committed upon national land physically within the southern district of New York. * * * The question is this: The libelous matter here complained of was printed and published in the county of New York. Therefore the State court sitting in that county has jurisdiction. It was also published in the county of Orange; therefore the State court sitting in that county has jurisdiction. But it was also published in the West Point reservation, which is both in the county of Orange and in the southern district of New York, and therefore this court has jurisdiction. To the proposition that this can be true I am unwilling to yield assent until instructed by higher authority. * * *

"I am of the opinion that the construction of this act claimed by the prosecution is opposed to the spirit and tenor of legislation for many years on the subject of national territorial jurisdiction. It is a novelty, and the burden of upholding a novelty is upon him who alleges it. * * * It is therefore ordered that a judgment of this court be entered quashing the indictment herein, because upon the construction of the statute, hereinbefore stated, the indictment is not authorized by the statute on which it rests."

On the day following Judge Hough's decision the World printed an editorial in which it said:

"If there exists in Washington the shadow of a suspicion that a Federal libel law can be created by construction or interpretation—if there still remains the likelihood that some day another Roosevelt will prostitute his powers by invoking the act to protect harbor defenses in order to prosecute newspapers that have offended him—if there be the ghost of a belief that the Federal Government has coordinate power with State governments in the prosecution of alleged libel, and that every American newspaper is at the mercy of the President—then the sooner there is a final decision of the Supreme Court of the United States the better."

NEWSPAPERS EVERYWHERE CONGRATULATED THE WORLD.

Newspapers of every shade of political opinion in every State of the Union congratulated the World upon its signal victory and joined with this paper in urging President Taft to appeal the case to the Supreme Court. Said the World on January 31, 1910:

"As the Panama case now stands there is nothing to prevent a future Roosevelt from making another assault upon the freedom of the press in order to gratify his own personal malice. He can pretend that the United States Government or some official of the United States Government has been libeled. He can select the alleged offender, declare that 'he should be prosecuted for libel by the governmental authorities,' and order a subservient Attorney General to institute criminal proceedings in the name of the people of the United States. * * *

"Freedom of speech and of the press is not a favor to be exercised at the pleasure of a President. The immunity of newspapers from wholesale Federal prosecution, with the attendant possibility of bankruptcy and ruin, is either a matter of law or it is nothing. The press is not free if it is to be free only on condition that a President refrains from abusing his power and prostituting his authority.

"The Federal Government, through its officers having claimed the right to prosecute newspapers for criminal libel under the provisions of the act to protect harbor defenses, is morally obligated to either make that claim good in the court of last resort or to establish beyond quibble or cavil the constitutional irregularity of the whole proceeding. It has no right to leave the issue in doubt. It has no right to leave 22,000 newspapers and periodicals uncertain as to their responsibility under the law. Mr. Taft and Mr. Wickersham may both agree with Judge Hough's decision. The World assumes that they do. But Mr. Taft will not always be President of the United States and Mr. Wickersham will not always be Attorney General of the United States. Their opinions bind none of their successors.

"The power to determine great constitutional questions rests with the Supreme Court of the United States. In this department of Government it alone can speak with full authority; and in dealing with a revolutionary issue that involves public freedom and public liberty, nothing is to be taken for granted, nothing is to be left to chance, nothing is to be left to the whim or pleasure of a President or of a political party in power."

On February 26, 1910, the Government filed a writ of error and the appeal came before the Supreme Court of the United States on Monday, October 24, 1910. It was heard by Mr. Justice Harlan, Mr. Justice White (now Chief Justice of the United States), Mr. Justice Day, Mr. Justice Holmes, Mr. Justice McKenna, Mr. Justice Lurton, and Mr. Justice Hughes. The unanimous decision of the courts in favor of the World was handed down on January 3, 1911, by Mr. Chief Justice White.

DISMISSAL OF THE WASHINGTON INDICTMENTS.

There still remained in force the indictments handed up February 17, 1909, in the Supreme Court of the District of Columbia under the direction of Attorney General Bonaparte, acting on the direct orders of President Roosevelt. No attempt had ever been made to serve warrants on Mr. Pulitzer or the two news editors of the World, although word had been formally sent to the United States attorney for the southern district of New York that each held himself subject to the latter's call whenever he wished to push the matter. The effort made before Federal Judge Anderson in Indianapolis in October, 1909, to drag Delevan Smith and Charles R. Williams to Washington for trial had failed utterly.

In due course, after a careful consideration of all the papers in the case in the Department of Justice, United States Attorney Clarence R. Wilson, acting under instructions from Attorney General Wickersham, made a formal motion on March 31, 1911, before Justice Daniel Thew Wright in the Supreme Court of the District of Columbia for the dismissal of these indictments.

"It is so ordered," said the justice.

"The indictments were dismissed," said the district attorney later, "because the Attorney General, after considering the decision of the United States Supreme Court in this same matter, came to the conclusion that there was nothing more to be done in those cases."

The effort to revive the spirit of the alien and sedition laws, to establish the doctrine of lese majesty, had come to an inglorious end.

The decision of the Supreme Court of the United States, while safeguarding the liberty of the press for all time against the encroachments of Federal authority, and more than justifying the great effort of the World in a cause it knew to be just, yet leaves unanswered the question: "Who got the money?"

THE STORY OF PANAMA.

No. 3.

HEARINGS ON THE RAINEY RESOLUTION BEFORE THE COMMITTEE ON FOREIGN AFFAIRS OF THE HOUSE OF REPRESENTATIVES.

FEBRUARY 13 AND 14, 1912.

THE STORY OF PANAMA.

COMMITTEE ON FOREIGN AFFAIRS,
HOUSE OF REPRESENTATIVES,
Washington, D. C., February 13, 1912.

The committee met at 10 o'clock a. m., Hon. William Sulzer (chairman) presiding.

The CHAIRMAN. The committee will come to order. Mr. Hall, you may resume your statement.

STATEMENT OF MR. HENRY N. HALL—Resumed.

Mr. HALL. On November 18, 1902, Secretary Hay submitted to Minister Concha the Cromwell revision of the treaty, with the compromise on Article XXIII, as heretofore related. It was proposed to settle the question of Colombia's indemnity from the United States by payment of $7,000,000 and an annuity of $100,000, or $10,000,000 and an annuity of $10,000. Secretary Hay suggested in his note that Dr. Concha's Government should no longer delay indicating which alternative it would choose.

Concha cabled the Bogota foreign office on the following day, November 19, 1902:

> The Department of State in Washington answered me regarding the matter of the Panama Canal in the form of an ultimatum * * *. Refuses increase of the amount of indemnity; sustains change in the counter memorandum of July 18; * * * does not permit the canal company to enter into a previous arrangement with the Government of Colombia, but pretends that the treaty constitutes permission for cession of the rights to the Government of the United States without other conditions; denies the return to Colombia of Government lands; does not accept indicated termination of period (of lease) * * *. I do not believe the treaty is admissible in this form * * *. Communication of the State Department does not admit of new objections.

In another cable on November 19, 1902, Concha notified his Government:

> I can not conscientiously agree to treaty last proposed by State Department in Washington, as it sacrifices Colombia without even the excuse of a pecuniary advantage, because she will receive less than she now gets from the Panama Railroad alone. [$250,000 a year.]

He added that his determination to leave his post was irrevocable.

November 22, 1902, Minister Concha replied to Secretary Hay at great length, setting forth Colombia's objections to the treaty as Mr. Hay had submitted it. Respecting the refusal of the United States to admit Colombia's right to exact conditions from the canal and railroad companies before transferring their concessions. Dr. Concha said, in part:

> Limited as is the time during which the companies will enjoy the usufruct from these properties, it is clear that if these have a great price it pertains to Colombia,

and there is no reason or motive for its being paid to the companies or that its owner shall cede it gratuitously. Already Colombia has exercised an act of exceptional liberality in extending to the canal company the period of construction of the works, the only effect of which has been that the latter is now in a position possibly to recover a part of its capital which, without this circumstance, would have passed to Colombia within a few months.

The undersigned does not demand nor suggest that the United States shall intervene in the questions that are to be discussed between the Government of Colombia and the said companies, but he does present these questions so that there may be clearly seen the equity with which Colombia proceeds in her petitions. At present, if there is lacking any example of her liberality in concessions of land, it will be sufficient to demonstrate the increase of the Canal Zone from the 200 meters conceded to the company to the 5,000 meters offered to the United States.

The preceding reasons serve in part also to demonstrate the necessity that exists that the Government of Colombia shall celebrate a special contract with the companies which are to cede their rights; but to them we add that the treaty between Colombia and the United States can not have the judicial faculties of adjusting or canceling the bonds which exist between the Republic of Colombia and those companies, bonds arising from perfect contracts which can not be undone, in conformity with the principles of universal jurisprudence, because one of the parties celebrates a pact concerning the same material with a third party, which in this case would be the United States. No matter how sincere and earnest may be the desire of the Colombian Government to remove the difficulties from the negotiations, it could not, without causing irreparable damage to interests of the Colombian people, withdraw the conditions which have been expressed regarding article.

Dr. Concha cabled to Bogota on November 28, 1902, that Dr. Tomas Herran, secretary, would take his place as chargé d'affaires, and the same day, without waiting for his letters of recall, Dr. Concha left Washington. He did not even take leave of the State Department. His last official act before leaving was to transmit to Bogota the Cromwell-Hay draft of the treaty of November 18, 1902, which he refused to sign.

Dr. Herran entered upon his work with the following instructions cabled December 11, 1902, from Bogota:

Do all you can to get $10,000,000 cash and $600,000 yearly payment, and all possible advantages as per former instructions. Demand a written declaration from the United States Government that it will not make any better terms, if such be the case, and sign the treaty with the indispensable stipulation that it be subjected to whatever the Colombian Congress decides.

At this time, however, Secretary Hay considered that his duty was to continue the negotiations with Nicaragua and Costa Rica, but President Roosevelt took the responsibility of granting Mr. Cromwell a new and brief delay and abstained from making remarks upon the matter in his message.

Dr. Herran gave his Government an account of the juggling of Roosevelt's message in a letter dated December 19, 1902, in which he said that he had been told confidentially that the President in the first draft of his message had discussed the inactivity of Colombia and had proposed demanding an answer by January 5, 1903. Herran added that his confidential informant (presumably Cromwell) told him that "at the instance of various members of the Cabinet and several Senators, this part of the message was suppressed and was replaced by the colorless paragraph on Colombia." The "colorless paragraph," or rather paragraphs, on the canal in Mr. Roosevelt's message of December 2, 1902, follows:

The Congress has wisely provided that we shall build at once an isthmian canal, if possible at Panama. The Attorney General reports that we can undoubtedly acquire good title from the French Panama Canal Co. Negotiations are now pending with Colombia to secure her assent to our building the canal. This canal will be one of the greatest engineering feats of the twentieth century; a greater engineering feat than has yet been accomplished during the history of mankind. The work should be carried out as a continuing policy without regard to change of administration; and it should be begun under circumstances which will make it a matter of pride for all administrations to continue the policy.

The canal will be of great benefit to America and of importance to all the world. It will be of advantage to us industrially and also as improving our military position. It will be advantageous to the countries of tropical America. It is earnestly to be hoped that all of these countries will do as some of them have already done with signal success, and will invite to their shores commerce and improve their material conditions by recognizing that stability and order are the prerequisites of successful development. No independent nation in America need have the slightest fear of aggression from the United States. It behooves each one to maintain order within its own borders and to discharge its just obligations to foreigners. When this is done, they can rest assured that, be they strong or weak, they will have nothing to dread from outside interference. More and more the increasing interdependence and complexity of international, political, and economic relations render it incumbent on all civilized and orderly powers to insist on the proper policing of the world.

Mr. Cromwell maintained intimate and confidential relations with Dr. Herran. He knew what Herran's instructions were. At first the United States continued firmly to oppose the Concha amendments and the increase of indemnities, but Mr. Cromwell urged Mr. Hay to increase the annuity, and on December 12, after a long conference with the Secretary of State, the latter, after a conference with the President, authorized Mr. Cromwell to promise Minister Herran an increase of annuity payable by the United States from $10,000 to $100,000 a year.

On December 13, 1902, Dr. Herran cabled to his Government:

Government of the United States after various discussions offers maximum $10,000,000 cash and afterwards an annuity of $100,000. I think this is unacceptable, but await orders of the Colombian Government.

In his letter of December 19, 1902, in addition to reporting to his Government the change in Roosevelt's message, whereby further delay was granted, Dr. Herran said:

Besides this deferred ultimatum, another danger threatens us. Mr. Shelby M. Cullom, Senator from Illinois and chairman of the Committee on Foreign Relations, maintains that in case Colombia does not lend itself to a satisfactory agreement, the Government of the United States can come to an understanding with the canal company direct, passing over the head of Colombia and expropriating part of our territory, justifying this on the ground of universal public utility, and leaving the compensation due to Colombia to be decided upon later. * * * President Roosevelt is a determined partisan of the Panama route, and in view of his impetuous and violent disposition it is to be feared that the scheme of Senator Cullom is not distasteful to him.

You will, of course, recall that Mr. Roosevelt admitted in his message to Congress on January 4, 1904, that he had entertained this very purpose. He said:

My intention was to consult the Congress as to whether under such circumstances it would not be proper to announce that the canal was to be dug forthwith; that we would give the terms that we had offered and no others; and that if such terms were not agreed to we would enter into an arrangement with Panama direct, or take what other steps were needful in order to begin the enterprise.

Senator Morgan, on December 20, introduced a motion by the terms of which the President was requested to conclude, at once, the negotiations for the Nicaragua Canal, as no treaty had been arrived at with Colombia. Mr. Cromwell organized opposition to this motion, which was defeated, but fearing the results of inaction he went to Dr. Herran and persuaded him that action on the part of

Colombia was imperative, as the State Department would present an ultimatum on January 5.

His fears more fully confirmed, Dr. Herran cabled to his Government December 25, 1902:

Probable that State Department will present ultimatum January 5.

December 31, 1902, the Colombian Government cabled Herran:

We await with impatience ultimatum announced, so as to decide whether you shall sign.

Instead of the ultimatum, which Dr. Herran was expecting, he received the following letter:

DEPARTMENT OF STATE,
Washington, December 30, 1902.

ESTEEMED MR. MINISTER: I regret appearing to importune you, but to-day it is absolutely necessary that I report to the President regarding the condition of our negotiations. Will you have the kindness to let me know as briefly as possible what I should say?

JOHN HAY.

December 31, 1902, Dr. Herran replied to Secretary Hay:

MY DEAR SIR: In answer to your letter of yesterday I hasten to inform you that although I immediately telegraphed Bogota synopsis of our last conference, I have not yet received instructions that enable me to resolve in a satisfactory manner the difficulty that exists regarding the annuity to be authorized to Colombia.

The instructions according to which I am proceeding fix that annuity in $600,000, considering that this sum is a just equivalent of the rent which Colombia should receive in view of the stipulation of the projected treaty.

The discrepancy between the sum offered and the sum demanded is so great that it does not appear as if we can arrive at an advantageous agreement; but, as before the annuity shall begin several years must elapse, possibly the present difficulty can be overcome by deferring determination of the annuity for a future contract between the two Governments.

Secretary Hay prepared to close the negotiations, and so informed Mr. Cromwell, who at once called at the State Department and conferred personally with Secretary Hay on January 2, 1903, and also wrote him beseeching him not to send his ultimatum. As a result of this beseeching and more urgent pleadings in another long conference on January 3, 1903, Secretary Hay consented to put off his ultimatum for a brief time.

Mr. Cromwell immediately devoted one whole day to a conference with Minister Herran and collaborated in preparing a cablegram to Bogota urgently demanding wider powers in the negotiations, but these instructions did not arrive.

This cablegram does not appear in the Colombian Blue Book.

On January 3, 1903, Dr. Herran cabled to the Colombian Government:

Final proposition of American Government ten millions cash and $100,000 annually after nine years. They add stipulation that once Panama Canal is open the two Governments can negotiate an equitable increase of the annuity. This cablegram is urgent, because the Congress will make a definite decision soon.

In a dispatch to his Government, Dr. Herran confirmed this cable and supplied a copy of Secretary Hay's proposal, as follows:

[Translation.]

Stipulation proposed by Secretary Hay January 3, 1903:

"It is agreed that, when the canal shall have been finished, if the circumstances appear to justify an increase in the annuity above stipulated ($100,000) the two Governments, by mutual initiative, may discuss the point by diplomatic negotiations."

Meanwhile (January 3) the United States minister in Bogota, Mr. Hart, informed Secretary Hay by cable that the Government of Colombia intended to demand an indemnity from the company before ratifying any treaty. Mr. Cromwell at once had conferences with Secretary Hay and the President to combat Colombia's attitude.

In the course of one of these conferences Secretary Hay told Mr. Cromwell that President Roosevelt had informed him that he would approve the Nicaragua and Costa Rica treaties and that he would send them to the Senate for ratification if Colombia did not act promptly, and Secretary Hay authorized Mr. Cromwell to repeat these words to Chargé d'Affaires Herran, which he lost no time in doing.

Advising his Government by mail of January 8, 1903, Dr. Herran wrote in part:

The President shows that he is determined to terminate negotiations for the construction of the interoceanic canal, whether it be by Panama or Nicaragua, before the 4th of March, the date on which the present Congress will close its meetings. He is a decided partisan of the Panama route, but he does not reject that of Nicaragua, and probably will adopt the latter in case he does not arrive at a satisfactory arrangement with Colombia.

Another alternative presented to us is the adoption of the treacherous project of Senator Cullom—expropriation of the coveted zone in Panama—invoking therefor "universal public utility" and offering to pay Colombia the value of the territory so usurped in accordance with appraisal by experts. This contingency appears very improbable, but I do not venture to qualify it as being absolutely impossible.

Dr. Herran's confidence in Mr. Cromwell had disappeared by this time, if we may judge from Dr. Herran's letter to his Government on January 9, 1903, in which he said:

In the initial period of our work here, when it was necessary to gain adherents to the Panama route in competition with that of Nicaragua, the agents of the Panama Canal Co. were very useful allies, especially Mr. William Nelson Cromwell, the clever lawyer of the company, a man of indefatigable activity and great influence. So long as the interests of Colombia and the canal company were identical, this powerful cooperation was most useful, but now these interests are no longer common, and I am working independently of our former allies. Now that the Panama route has been preferred, the agents of the company, in order to clinch the negotiations they have begun with the United States, are doing all they can to have the treaty signed, no matter what the cost to Colombia. Mr. Philippe Bunau-Varilla is trying to intervene officiously in this affair, and I know that he has been sending cables to the Colombian Government. This gentleman is an important shareholder of the canal company, but he holds no official position in it; his activity is entirely on his own account, and he represents solely his own interests.

January 10, 1903, President Marroquin and Foreign Minister Paul stated by cable that they supposed the Chonca amendments had been accepted by the United States. They instructed Dr. Herran to try to get better pecuniary terms and some reduction in the delay to elapse before the annuity payments begin. "If this is not possible and you see that by the delay everything may be lost, sign the treaty," is the final instruction. Herran did not receive this cable until January 16, when he immediately showed it to Cromwell.

On the same day, January 16, Secretary Hay informed Cromwell that he had received a cable from Minister Hart stating that Colombia was unwilling to accept the offer made by the United States, and that she had given instructions to Minister Herran to insist upon the terms previously laid down and upon all of the Concha amendments; the cable also stated that the Panama Canal Co. was requested to appoint an agent in Bogota.

Secretary Hay then gave instructions, by cable, to the American minister in Bogota ordering him to announce officially to the Colombian Government that "if the present attitude of Colombia does not change, it will render impossible the continuation of the negotiations and the pourparlers will be closed."

This ultimatum was also communicated to Dr. Herran in the following letter, dated January 16:

DEAR MR. HERRAN: I must inform you that by telegram to-day I have told our minister in Bogota that if the Government persists in its present attitude it will make impossible further negotiations.

Dr. Herran acknowledged with thanks the receipt of this note from Secretary Hay, but added no comment.

Mr. Cromwell was almost in despair, for neither of the Governments could satisfy the other; they were, so to speak, no longer in communication.

Mr. HARRISON. How do you know that, Mr. Hall?

Mr. HALL. I will read this from Mr. Cromwell's own brief, because it is very important. Mr. Cromwell says:

It is no exaggeration to say that we were almost in despair, for if neither of the Governments could satisfy the other (and they were, so to speak, no longer in communication) a solution seemed impossible. Under these critical conditions we were busy for several successive days placing our arguments before the Colombian chargé d'affaires, examining with him the instructions that had been given and discussing various plans to bring about an agreement. The chargé d'affaires was well disposed, but almost powerless.

At the request of Secretary Hay we kept him informed almost hour by hour of the state of the negotiations, which still seemed to hold out no hope, and which were looked upon by the officials of the United States Government as virtually closed, and about to be officially ended by the delivery of this Government's ultimatum and the public announcement of this step. We were in continuous session with Mr. Herran, and at last persuaded him to take the responsibility and abandon all the Concha amendments (including the vital amendment which reserved the consent of Colombia to the transfer provided for in Article I) except that dealing with the indemnities from the United States.

This was another important step toward success, but as to the pecuniary arrangements we were not out of the deadlock.

We continued our efforts to persuade him through conferences, and again Mr. Cromwell found a solution by devising the following plan to replace Article XXV-B (in the matter of the pecuniary indemnity), to wit, the exact amount of the indemnity was left to a commission of three persons named in the treaty (with the president of The Hague tribunal as arbitrator), but within the maximum and minimum limits proposed by each Government. After prolonged efforts, Mr. Cromwell persuaded Minister Herran to accept this substitution and to authorize him to propose it to the United States. This is what the minister did, in the following communication:

LEGATION OF COLOMBIA,
Washington, D. C., January 16, 1903.

Mr. WILLIAM NELSON CROMWELL.

DEAR SIR: I repeat what I told you this morning; that is, I will sign in the name of my Government the treaty proposed by the United States if Article XXV-B is modified by the substitution of the attached clause, which you suggest and which I have approved with my initials.

Truly, yours, TOMAS HERRAN.

We immediately presented this note to Secretary Hay and to the President, urging them to approve it. As a result of long conferences we were authorized to announce to Mr. Herran that his proposal would be accepted, unless a given sum were fixed by agreement, which was preferred.

This was an enormous advance, as it delayed the ultimatum and reopened the door to negotiation. Having succeeded so far, we suggested a compromise on the basis of $250,000 a year. This was the amount of the annuity which had been served for so many years under the Panama Railroad Co's concessions, and we maintained it was a precedent that furnished an equitable basis for a settlement. The United States, however, had not yet shown the slightest disposition to exceed the figure of $100,000. At last Mr. Herran yielded to our arguments, and authorized us to offer Mr. Hay a compromise on the basis of $250,000. Great as was this success, it was still necessary to bring the United States to increase the indemnity to this figure. On the 21st of the month, far into the night, and the whole of the following day, Mr. Cromwell devoted himself to this task, discussing with Secretary Hay, explaining the dangers of the situation to him, and the necessity for immediate action, because the Bogota Government could at any moment reduce Mr. Herran's powers, which were already a matter of apprehension, and urging insistently the increase of the indemnity offered by the United States to the amount of this figure. As a result of these arguments and of his own conviction, the Secretary authorized a compromise at this figure if we could obtain the approval by the chargé d'affaires of all the other clauses of the treaty. We went to that official's house, we made a supreme effort to decide him, and brought him to an agreement on all the questions yet unsettled. Then we rapidly corrected the draft of the treaty to make it conform to this arrangement, and, accompanying Chargé d'Affaires Herran to the Secretary's residence, in the evening of January 22, 1903, we announced to the latter that an understanding had been reached and that Mr. Herran was ready to sign the treaty then and there. Mr. Herran confirmed this statement after the assurance had been given him by Secretary Hay that the said treaty represented the best terms that the United States could grant.

(The pen with which the Secretary and the chargé d'affaires signed this treaty is one of the precious souvenirs of this incident. The Secretary presented it to Mr. Cromwell as a mark of appreciation of the part he took in the so long and apparently so hopeless negotiations.)

This treaty was at once sent by the President to the Senate of the United States (January 23, 1903), where a great struggle was afterwards to take place over its ratification.

Thus was concluded the Hay-Herran treaty, which fulfilled the last conditions of the Spooner Act and saved the fate of the Panama Canal. It became the subject of controversies not only in the Unites Stated Senate, where it was ratified, but also in Colombia, where it failed of ratification, and was what justified the subsequent separation and independence of the Republic of Panama and the immediate conclusion with the new Republic of a similar treaty wherein were repeated the fundamental clauses of the Hay-Herran treaty, which granted the consent to the transfer by the Panama Canal Co. to the United States by authorizing the acceptance of the company's offer to the United States.

It is not through vanity, but simply because it is absolutely necessary to state the fact in order to point out the true significance of this service, that it must be noted here that the entire negotiation of the treaty with Colombia was conducted by Mr. Cromwell, with Ministers Concha and Herran and Secretary Hay, who held nearly all their official communications through his intermediary exclusively, without meeting each other, except on one or two official occasions, up to the hour when Mr. Cromwell brought about a meeting of the representatives of the two Governments for the signature of the treaty, on January 22, 1903, the matter being then settled.

As an historical detail showing by how narrow a margin we succeeded, we note that a few hours after the signing of the treaty Mr. Herran received a peremptory cable from his Government to suspend all negotiations till the receipt of fresh instructions. This dispatch which if it had arrived a few hours earlier would have paralyzed all action and have prevented any result, was on its way from Bogota when, thanks to the strongest pressure, we succeeded in having the treaty concluded in order to avoid this very possibility which we had feared.

The CHAIRMAN. Mr. Hall, Mr. Herran, I understand, is dead?

Mr. HALL. Mr. Herran is dead; yes, sir.

The CHAIRMAN. When did he die?

Mr. HALL. He died in 1904, if I am not mistaken, sir. I can supply the exact date.

The CHAIRMAN. In this country or Colombia?

Mr. HALL. I do not know, sir. My own impression is that he died in this country. I think he never really got back to Colombia.

The CHAIRMAN. You may proceed.

Mr. HARRISON. Was he still in the service of the United States of Colombia when he died?

Mr. HALL. My understanding of it is that he was no longer in the Diplomatic Service. He had retired to private life.

Now, to Mr. Cromwell's account I may add a letter written by John Hay, on January 22, which no doubt very greatly influenced Mr. Herran's decision to sign that treaty.

DEPARTMENT OF STATE,
Washington, January 22, 1903.

DEAR MR. HERRAN: I am commanded by the President to say to you that the reasonable time that the statute accords for the conclusion of negotiations with Colombia for the excavation of a canal of the Isthmus has expired, and he has authorized me to sign with you the treaty of which I had the honor to give you a draft, with the modification that the sum of $100,000, fixed therein as the annual payment, be increased $250,000. I am not authorized to consider or discuss any other change.

With sentiments of high consideration, etc.,

JOHN HAY.

The dispatch ordering Dr. Herran not to sign the treaty, a treaty which Mr. Roosevelt afterwards told Congress had been "entered into at the urgent solicitation of the people of Colombia," was as follows:

BOGOTA, *January 24, 1903.*
(Received Washington, Jan. 25, 11 p. m.)

COLOMBIAN MINISTER,
Washington:

Do not sign canal treaty. You will receive instructions in letter of to-day.

MARROQUIN.

The letter of instructions referred to in the above cable was not printed in the Colombian Blue Book published by Gen. Reyes.

It is interesting to note that on January 21, the day before Secretary Hay delivered the ultimatum by order of President Roosevelt, and the day before Mr. Cromwell led Chargé d'Affaires Herran to Secretary Hay's house to sign the treaty, Mr. Cromwell wrote to the New Panama Canal Co. announcing to it the happy conclusion of the treaty. In reply he received the following letter:

PARIS, *January 31, 1903.*

GENTLEMEN: We have duly received your letter of January 21 and have read with very keen interest all the details you give us on the final phases of the negotiations which preceded the signature of the treaty. It gives us pleasure to repeat to you on this occasion that we have known how to appreciate at their true worth all the efforts made by you to bring the two parties to the compromise agreement which made the conclusion of the treaty possible, and it is with great satisfaction that we convey to you once more all our congratulations and our best thanks.

Kindly accept, gentlemen, the assurance of our distinguished sentiments.

M. BO,
President of the Board of Directors.

Dr. Herran reported to his Government on the signing of the treaty, and his reasons for so doing, by cable as follows:

WASHINGTON, *January 22, 1903.*

FOREIGN AFFAIRS, *Bogota:*

Treaty signed to-day accepting ultimatum ten millions and two hundred and fifty thousand dollars annuity.

HERRAN.

The Colombian chargé d'affaires also sent the following dispatch to the Colombian foreign office by the next outgoing mail.

WASHINGTON, *January 29, 1903.*

Dr. FELIPE F. PAUL,
Minister of Foreign Affairs, Bogota:

On the evening of the 22d of this month, after having dispatched the letter which I directed to your excellency on that date, I received the ultimatum, a copy of which I inclose.

The same evening I had an interview with the Secretary of State in his house, and there signed the treaty accepting the ultimate conditions of his final proposal. This matter did not admit of any further postponement, and I was obliged to take one of the two courses that presented themselves—either to accept a treaty which does not satisfy us or abandon all hope that the interoceanic canal will be opened through Colombian territory. Being guided by the categorical orders which your excellency has communicated to me and reiterated respecting the acceptance of an ultimatum in such a case as actually has presented itself, I decided upon the first alternative. It is now incumbent on the Colombian Congress finally to resolve this important matter, as without its acceptance the treaty signed has no value, and the Congress is entirely at liberty to approve or reject it.

To the many difficulties that have surrounded me in the course of these arduous negotiations have been added additional embarrassments caused by recent cables from the American minister in Bogota and the agent of the canal company. Both asserted and reiterated that the Colombian Government had ordered me to accept the ultimatum that would be persented to me, even if the annuity of $100,000 were not increased. This was communicated to me by the Secretary of State. I answered that the information furnished him was not trustworthy, and added that I should persist in my resolution to reject so small an annuity. This reply resulted in the ultimatum which is inclosed, in which the annuity is increased to $250,000. For the reasons that I already have pointed out I accepted this final proposition, although I did not give it my approval.

THOMAS HERRAN.

On January 23, 1903, the day after it was signed, President Roosevelt sent the Hay-Herran treaty to the Senate, and it was at once referred to the Committee on Foreign Relations, despite the efforts of Senator Morgan, who did everything he could to have it referred to the Canal Committee, of which he was chairman. Senator Morgan was a member of the Committee on Foreign Relations and introduced resolutions calling for proof that Chargé d'Affaires Herran was authorized to sign the treaty and also casting doubt upon the constitutional powers of Vice President Marroquin to conclude any treaty. Mr. Cromwell was able to compass the defeat of these motions as well as the rejection of other resolutions in the months of January, February, and March.

Senator Morgan submitted to the Committee on Foreign Relations more than 60 separate amendments to the treaty. Mr. Cromwell says these amendments were at once submitted to him by friendly Senators, and that he furnished the Senators with arguments in rebuttal which were afterwards used in the debates.

Mr. HARRISON. Do you get that from Mr. Cromwell's brief also?

Mr. HALL. Yes, sir.

The report of the Committee on Foreign Relations was in favor of the treaty, but in the Senate itself the supporters of the Panama Canal and the partisans of Nicaragua were lined up against each other.

Mr. Cromwell says that every Senator was solicited by him and his friends in an endeavor to obtain a two-thirds majority in favor of the treaty as it stood, and to defeat all amendments. Certain it is that he remained in Washington, and made every effort to lobby the treaty through to ratification, but the opposition was so vigorous that the session of Congress came to an end without action being taken by the Senate.

But Mr. Cromwell would brook no delay; he had constant conferences with Senator Hanna and other party leaders, and persistently urged an extra session to assure action upon the treaty. Now, we arrive at a particularly Cromwellian piece of diplomacy.

At this time the option granted by the canal company on January 4, 9, 11, 1902, was nearing its expiration (March 4, 1903). The delay over the Hay-Herran treaty had brought the option almost to its term without action by the United States, and President Roosevelt, although willing, could not, because of the restrictions of the Spooner act, definitely accept the offer made. On February 4 and 7 Secretary Hay asked Mr. Cromwell to take the necessary steps to obtain an extension of the option and to confer on this matter with the Attorney General. Mr. Cromwell and Mr. Knox conferred on the matter. The struggle in the Senate over the treaty was still going on.

The offer of the New Panama Canal Co. (limited to March 4, 1903) had been approved by the Tribunal Civile de la Seine and the liquidator had been authorized to lend it his assistance; controversies had arisen as to this consent. It was very important that this offer be accepted by the United States before Colombia could begin a lawsuit to enjoin it (which she did the following year), and also that a further means of escape from Colombia's pecuniary demands be created for Mr. Cromwell's clients.

So Mr. Cromwell boldly suggested to Mr. Knox the immediate acceptance by the United States subject only to the ratification of the Colombian treaty and of the legal formalities (so as to give this matter the character of a conditional contract) instead of extending the option without obtaining any pledge. At first this plan was not well received. It was, however, finally adopted by the United States, and the Attorney General and Mr. Cromwell in the course of several conferences agreed upon the form of the acceptance, which was cabled by Mr. Knox, in Mr. Cromwell's presence, to the company on February 17. The acceptance of the United States was worded thus:

WASHINGTON, D. C., *February 17, 1903.*

M. Bo,
President of the Board of Directors of La Compagnie Nouvelle du Canal de Panama, No. 7 Rue Louis le Grand, Paris, France.

At the direction of the President of the United States I have the honor to announce that the offer of La Compagnie Nouvelle du Canal de Panama, contained in your telegrams of January 9 and 11, 1902, through the intermediary of Admiral Walker, to sell the properties and rights of the company on the Isthmus of Panama and in Paris, offer to which Mr. Gautron, liquidator of La Compagnie Universelle du Canal Interoceanique de Panama, has given his consent, with the approval of the Tribunal Civile de la Seine, is hereby accepted, subject to the modification of articles 21 and 22 of the concession contract by the ratification by both countries and the going into effect of the treaty pending between the United States and Colombia in regard to the Panama Canal, which treaty is already signed and its ratification expected. The President desires that the necessary steps for the transfer of the title and the possession of the property be expedited as much as possible, so that as soon as the pending treaty is ratified and put in effect there will remain nothing more to do but complete the transaction by taking possession and paying the price.

P. C. KNOX, *Attorney General.*

To which Mr. Cromwell at once replied as follows:

WASHINGTON, D. C., *February 19, 1903.*

Hon. P. C. KNOX, *Attorney General.*

DEAR SIR: A meeting of directors has been called to consider your cable of the 17th instant. Meanwhile, I am requested by Mr. Bo, the president, in order to dispel all doubt on the following questions, to ask you to confirm—

First. That the sentence in your cable, "properties, etc., in Paris," contemplates only the plans and archives in Paris as stated in the company's cable of January 11, 1902.

Second. That the company gives no undertaking to obtain a modification of Articles XXI and XXII of the concession contract.

Awaiting the favor of a reply in order to cable to Paris, I am,

Yours, very truly,

WILLIAM NELSON CROMWELL,
General Counsel.

And the Attorney General replied as follows:

DEPARTMENT OF JUSTICE,
Washington, D. C., February 19, 1903.

Mr. WILLIAM NELSON CROMWELL,
General Counsel, New Willard Hotel, Washington.

DEAR SIR: In reply to your letter of to-day, I must state that, as the acceptance by the President of the offer of La Compagnie Nouvelle du Canal de Panama was not made with the intention of including what the negotiations do not show to have been agreed upon by the parties to include in the offer of this company, I do not consider it advisable at this time to enter into detailed interpretations of the offer or of the acceptance.

Yours, very sincerely,

P. C. KNOX,
Attorney General.

To which Mr. Cromwell replied as follows, completing the understanding:

WASHINGTON, D. C., *March 3, 1903.*

Hon. P. C. KNOX,
Attorney General of the United States, Washington.

DEAR SIR: I beg to acknowledge receipt of your favor of the 19th ultimo, in reply to my letter of even date, in which I expressed the viewpoint of the company in regard to the subjects therein mentioned and asked you to give your assurance on these matters.

I notice with keen satisfaction the general assurance you express as to the President's intentions, and I agree with you that it is not advisable at this moment to enter into detailed interpretations of this great transaction, so unique of its kind.

Above all other considerations the situation demands that the company's offer, as contained in its cables of January 9 and 11, 1902, which has received the consent of the liquidator with the special approval of the courts, as well as the assent of other important interests, and as accepted by your cable of the 17th ultimo, shall undergo no change or modification, which moreover I have neither the wish nor the power to make.

We only put our questions in order to exclude the slightest possibility of a doubt as to the secondary points mentioned; I am now perfectly convinced that no differences whatever on these points can arise between the parties.

It is therefore with pleasure that I hand you herewith the official acknowledgment of your cable of the 17th ultimo.

I have the honor to be, most sincerely, yours,

WILLIAM NELSON CROMWELL,
General Counsel of La Compagnie Nouvelle du Canal de Panama.

WASHINGTON, D. C., *March 3, 1903.*

Hon. P. C. KNOX,
Attorney General of the United States.

SIR: In accordance with the powers conferred upon me by the president of La Compagnie Nouvelle du Canal de Panama, I proceed to notify you that the acceptance by the President of the United States through your cable of the 17th ultimo of the company's offer as it is contained in its cables of January 9 and 11, 1902, addressed to the chairman of the Isthmian Canal Commission, is acknowledged by these presents as being in accordance with the said offer.

Very respectfully,

WILLIAM NELSON CROMWELL,
General Counsel of La Compagnie Nouvelle du Canal de Panama.

Now, in connection with the offer of sale for $40,000,000 of the property and archives of the New Panama Canal Co. and its acceptance by the Government of the United States and the contract afterwards entered into between the United States and the New Panama Canal Co. by which the property and the archives were purchased, there can be no possible doubt whatever that what the United States purchased was not only the property on the Isthmus, but also all the technical plans and commercial archives in Paris. Now, the United States received the property on the Isthmus and all the technical plans, but it has never received the archives, which archives contain all of Mr. Cromwell's confidential reports as to the manner in which he advanced the changing of the views of many public men from the Nicaragua to the Panama route and also contain all of Mr. Cromwell's accounts, and more important than anything else contain the actual list of shareholders to whom the $40,000,000 was paid.

Mr. KENDALL. Mr. Hall, I was going to ask you yesterday, and this seems to be an opportune time at which to do it, who appointed what we call the court of liquidation in Paris? How was it constituted?

Mr. HALL. It was constituted under the French law that when any "societe anonyme"—what we would call a limited liability company in this country—goes into liquidation, they go to the court and the court almost invariably, unless some very special reason exists for doing otherwise, appoints the board of directors of the company, the men who had active charge of its affairs, to be the board of liquidation.

Mr. KENDALL. I suppose it corresponds somewhat to our procedure in bankruptcy in this country.

Mr. HALL. They were not bankrupt. It was a voluntary winding up of the affairs of the company. They went to the court and the court decided that the board of directors should be the board of liquidators, and made the necessary order so appointing them.

Mr. KENDALL. Are they required to submit reports to the court?

Mr. HALL I believe they are, sir.

Mr. KENDALL. And those reports are published, of course?

Mr. HALL. I do not know, sir; but I do not think so, as I understand the procedure under the French law. I will read from a statement which I have prepared of the history of the case of The United States *v.* The Press Publishing Co, already printed as an appendix to the record:

At the suggestion of counsel for the World, court orders for the issuance of letters rogatory for the examination of witnesses were addressed through the usual diplomatic channels to the proper judicial authorities of the French and Panaman Governments.

In order to obtain the Government's consent to this procedure, it was necessary for the World to pay the expenses of United States Attorney Wise and Deputy Attorney General Stuart McNamara to Paris and of Mr. Knapp, of the United States attorney's office, to Panama, as the Government refused to assume any part of the cost of procuring the evidence needed.

The letters rogatory having been issued, the State Department, in Washington, notified De Lancey Nicoll, the World's counsel in New York, that the American ambassador to France had been instructed to assist Coudert Bros., the World's counsel in Paris, in obtaining the authorization of the minister of justice in order that the examination of witnesses could begin about July 12, 1909. On July 18 Mr. Wise wrote to Mr. De Lancey Nicoll that he had received a letter from the Attorney General "in which he informs me that he has made request for instructions to the American ambassador at Paris to facilitate you in all ways to a full and thorough access to the papers of the old and new Panama Canal companies."

Mr. Wise also informed John D. Lindsay, Mr. Nicoll's law partner, that if a personal note from Mr. Taft to the President of the French Republic was necessary to secure evidence in the matter contemplated he would obtain such a letter.

This looked very promising, and it seemed certain that the American people would finally know "who got the money." But on June 21 Mr. Nicoll received the following cable from Coudert Bros.: "Government interfering. Wants know nature of case, names, witnesses, list of questions." Mr. Nicoll at once took the matter up with the Attorney General and with the State Department, but the French authorities insisted that the rogatory letters could not be issued, and in a letter written to Mr. Lindsay July 13 Mr. Wise said the American ambassador had been informed by the French foreign office "that no such examination as was contemplated by us can be had." Mr. Wise added:

"As you know, I have been in Paris for the past week, during which time I have known of the before-mentioned difficulties, and being desirous of affording your client every opportunity to have a full and fair opportunity to conduct its examination, I have arranged with the American ambassador to permit the use of the rooms at the embassy for the examination of such witnesses as you may desire to call; he has also agreed that if you and I join in a written request to him to invite such witnesses to come to the embassy to be examined he will immediately communicate with the Secretary of State of the United States for his approval of such course, and upon receiving such approval, if the French Government does not object, he will invite them. I am reliably informed that the French Government will make no objection, and I am sure the Secretary of State will give his approval."

This simply meant that such witnesses as might choose to come would give such testimony as they saw fit, and that there could be no thorough examination, such as the case demanded. However, there was nothing to do but to make the best of the situation. So, on July 15, Mr. Lindsay wrote to Mr. Wise asking him to make arrangements "so that I can see to-morrow, if possible, at any time suitable to your convenience, the records of the two companies."

In his reply Mr. Wise said:

"* * * You seem to assume that I have a power of control over the affairs of these two companies, and that it is only necessary for me to signify my desire that the records of these companies should be examined and the wish would be gratified. * * * You are greatly in error. * * * First * * * the New Panama Canal Co. was a going corporation at the time when it sold its properties to the United States, and under the French law, which is quite similar to that of the State of New York, the corporation, having no further function to perform, went out of existence by its board of directors assuming the functions of a board of trustees for the distribution of its assets, and this having been fully performed, * * * the board of trustees * * * deposited all the books of the company with a depository, which in this case happened to be the Credit Lyonnais, where under the laws of France such books must remain for a period of 20 years. This having been done, the board of directors or the board of trustees have no further control over these books and can not have access thereto. I know of no way by which it will be possible for me to arrange for you to see the records of these companies. I do not believe you would be able to examine these records through any court proceeding. I have consulted with eminent French counsel on this subject and am informed that no court in France could make any order compelling the Credit Lyonnaise or its officers to submit the papers to our examination."

Mr. KENDALL. That means, under the French law, they were retired for 20 years?

Mr. HALL. Yes, sir. That does not get over the fact that those archives belong to the Government of the United States and were purchased by the United States, and specifically declared to be part of the property for which a consideration of $40,000,000 was paid.

Mr. KENDALL. If that is the correct interpretation of the French law, it seems to me to afford a splendid opportunity for this company to let its transactions remain sealed for 20 years.

Mr. HALL. That is just the point. The World, at great expense, retained an eminent English lawyer, a member of Parliament, who went to Paris and made an investigation on our behalf. Very little additional information could be obtained, and he reported in part as follows:

I have never known, in my lengthy experience of company matters, any public corporation, much less one of such vast importance, having so completely disappeared and removed all traces of its existence as the New Panama Canal Co. This company having purchased the assets of La Compagne Universelle du Canal Interoceanique de Panama (the old or De Lesseps Panama Canal Co.), brought off the deal with the American Government. So thorough has been its obliteration that only the United States Government can now give information respecting the new company's transactions and the identity of the individuals who created it to effectuate this deal, and who for reasons best known to themselves wiped it off the face of the earth when the deal was carried through. * * * I consulted leading French lawyers, and they declared that there was no machinery, legal or otherwise, by which its records could be brought to light. * * * The stock of the new company was originally registered, so transactions in it could be traced, but power was subsequently obtained to transform it into "bearer" stock, which passed from hand to hand without any record being preserved. * * * There is nothing to show the names of the owners of the stock at the time of the liquidation of the company and who actully received their proportions of the purchase money paid by the United States. * * * No record exists here of a single person who received the money or of the proportions in which it was paid. The liquidation of the new company was finally closed on June 30 last, and the offices of the liquidators were shut. No one is there to give the slighest information concerning it, although questions are still arising necessitating information. The American ambassador in Paris was entitled to the archives of the company for his Government, and those archives should include a list of the persons who received the purchase money paid by the United States.

Mr. KENDALL. Was Delancey Nicoll your counsel?

Mr. HALL. Yes, sir.

Mr. KENDALL. Did he examine this law?

Mr. HALL. I presume so. His partner, John D. Lindsay, was in Paris and most certainly did.

Mr. KENDALL. Did he join Mr. Wise in the construction you read?

Mr. HALL. I believe so, sir.

The CHAIRMAN. Mr. Wise is the United States district attorney for the southern district of New York, is he not?

Mr. HALL. Yes, sir.

Mr. LEVY. Mr. Hall, the old company had 60 per cent of the profits; that was the contract with the new French company. How many stockholders or how much capital represented that 60 per cent of the old company, do you know the number?

Mr. HALL. I do not remember offhand, sir. That is the financial end of this thing, and once we get going into that, it will be endless.

Mr. Cromwell very cleverly refrained, until March 3, from sending the letter containing the final agreement. He would not accept the condition that the agreement was made subject to the going into effect of the treaty until the President had summoned Congress in special session to continue and conclude the discussion of the treaty. The special session was summoned on the 2d of March, and on the following day Mr. Cromwell handed in the agreement.

As soon as Congress met in extra session, the Nicaragua party raised fresh objections to the treaty, one of which met with the support of a large majority of the Senate, to wit, that the treaty should be amended so as to give the United States the complete control of the Canal Zone, with the right of fortifying and defending it.

But Mr. Cromwell would take no chances. He assured the Senators that the slightest amendment to the treaty would cause its rejection, because Colombia would not be willing to sign another. He put the matter up to Chargé d'Affaires Herran, obtained from him an important letter, dictated by Mr. Cromwell and addressed to him, stating that any amendment passed by the Senate would cause rejection by Colombia. This letter was shown to prominent Senators.

On March 16 the Democratic Members held a caucus to agree upon the support to be given the Morgan amendments.

The next day, March 17, the final vote took place and ended in the defeat of every one of the amendments and in the ratification of the treaty without the change of a single line; the text as signed remained intact.

Mr. Cromwell made a number of reports to the company and kept it fully informed of the progress of the struggle in Washington. About this time he received the following cable:

Your cables received. Thank you. Are satisfied with the news and, as you, hope for good result. As far as Colombia is concerned, are entirely in accord with you on all points, and upon the course to pursue we approve your idea to inform the Government of the United States and to act according to its indications.

That is the first intimation of an understanding between Mr. Cromwell and the Government of the United States that he eventually put some plan, which he has not yet told us of, up to the directors of the New Panama Canal Co., and they in their telegram told him that they approved the course he was going to pursue and asked him to inform the Government of the United States and to act according to its instructions—the instructions of the Government of the United States to the Panama Canal Co. as to the course it was to pursue.

By the Hay-Herran treaty Mr. Cromwell had obtained (subject to ratification) the consent of Colombia (Art. I), but he knew perfectly well that it was the intention of Colombia to force the company to pay a considerable sum before consenting to the transfer. He was in possession of the official protest served on the company in Paris, on February 28, 1901, by Colombia against the transfer to the United States, and which had necessitated the postponement of the proposed ratification. In his brief Mr. Cromwell further says:

On October 29, 1902, the minister sent us an official communication in which he announced that the minister of foreign affairs in Bogota demanded that the Panama Canal Co. and the Panama Railroad Co. appoint agents in Bogota to treat with the Government, should occasion arise, as to the terms of the conditional cancellation of their respective concessions in order to enable these companies to transfer their rights to the American Government in case the pending negotiations with a view to a treaty with this Government should succeed.

As has been mentioned above, Minister Concha later presented (November 11) to Secretary Hay an amendment to Article I, quoted above, in which it was stipulated as a condition of Colombia's consent to the transfer that "a special agreement to be previously made between Colombia and the companies, which had been notified to appoint an agent in Bogota for that purpose;" and it will be recalled that thanks to our opposition the Secretary rejected this amendment, and shortly afterwards Minister Concha left his post.

January 3, 1903, the United States minister cabled to Secretary Hay that Colombia intended to exact an indemnity from the canal company.

On January 9 the Secretary informed us that he knew positively that the delay which had occurred in the negotiations and the attitude of Colombia were due to the refusal of the Panama Canal Co. to negotiate for the consent of Colombia and to pay the tribute which Colombia was determined to exact before concluding any treaty; and on January 16 the United States minister cabled to the Secretary: "Colombia will not accept the offer of the United States, and has given Herran instructions to insist on the terms stated and upon all the Concha amendments; and, further, an agent of the Panama Canal Co. in Bogota must be appointed."

The same day (January 16) Minister Herran showed us a cable to the same effect which he had received from his Government.

In February Colombia sent to the canal company and to the railroad company official written requests (signed by the minister of foreign affairs, under date December 24, 1902) calling upon these companies to appoint an agent in Bogota empowered to negotiate, and declaring that, as to any permission to transfer the concessions, "she would demand and exact from the concessionary company in return a sum of money previously agreed upon, and a release by the company from all undertaking or obligation on the part of Colombia under the concession for the opening of the Isthmus of Panama until such date as this concession should be transferred to another party."

Mr. Mancini, the company's agent in Bogota, wrote frequently to the company and to ourselves, declaring that Colombia would neither make nor ratify any treaty unless the company came to a previous arrangement with her for a cash payment; and on May 7, 1903, he cabled that this demand amounted to 50,000,000 francs and that he had been requested to state the company's intentions. Other news received through the State Department and its minister in Bogota, which Secretary Hay communicated to us as soon as received, was equally significant and plain.

But Mr. Cromwell and the Panama Canal Co. set about to defeat the demand of Colombia. They succeeded in virtually freezing out Colombia as a shareholder in the canal company and then in setting in motion the machinery of the State Department to protect themselves against her first demands.

Jose Pablo Uribe, then Colombian minister to France, wrote on February 7, 1903, from Paris, to the Colombian minister for foreign affairs, Bogota, in part as follows:

In the journal of quotations of the Paris Bourse there has been published a notice of the syndicate of bankers (corresponding to the board of governors of the stock exchange), announcing that they will admit to purchase and sale only the shares of the New Panama Canal Co. marked with the numbers from 1 to 600,000. This action excludes the shares of the Government of Colombia, which are those numbered from 600,001 to 650,000, and can not be negotiated as are the others; naturally, this measure serves as a pretext for depreciating their value, which should be the same as the others.

We clearly see the intention to impede the sale of the shares that belong to Colombia or the idea of buying them cheap.

Possibly they figure that in this way Colombia will accelerate the signing and ratification of the treaties referring to the canal, so that they may, with greater facility, have this security for negotiation. In this there is an error, because it is not the way to compel us to do what is desired by the speculators, nor do I think that this measure conforms to the law and practice in such matters.

The first move of the State Department to protect Mr. Cromwell's clients, so far as the published correspondence shows, was the following cable from Secretary of State Hay to the American minister at Bogota on April 7, 1903:

Referring to the requests of Colombia to the canal and railroad companies for appointment of agents to negotiate cancellation of present concessions, etc., if the subject arises, inform the Colombian Government that the treaty covers entire matter, and any change would be in violation of the Spooner law and not permissible.

Just imagine, gentlemen, what the American Government would have done when the Hay-Pauncefote treaty was submitted to the Senate of the United States for ratification if England had declared that any amendment would be in violation of the navigation act and not permissible. The treaty would have been thrown out neck and crop. That is just what happened to the Hay-Herran treaty in Bogota, and although there were other and graver reasons, it can not be doubted that Mr. Roosevelt's extraordinary pretension that Colombia could not amend the treaty had a direct bearing on its final unanimous rejection by the Colombian Senate.

The diplomatic correspondence sent to the United States Senate shows that from this time on all the power of the American Government was incessantly exerted in support of the ridiculous proposition that the payment of an indemnity by the canal company to

Colombia in compensation for the abandonment of Colombia's reversionary right in the Panama Railroad and the $250,000 annuity would be in violation of the Spooner law.

Mr. Beaupré was keeping the State Department well advised, and Secretary Hay communicated to Mr. Cromwell as fast as they were received all views of this danger threatening the canal company in Bogota.

On April 24, 1903, Mr. Beaupré deemed it best, although the subject had not arisen, to sound the Colombian minister of foreign affairs upon the intention of the Colombian Government to exact payment from the canal company prior to the transfer of the concession, and he notified Secretary Hay by letter of the same date.

Further, Mr. Cromwell in his brief says:

On May 30 the United States minister in Bogota arrived in New York. He called upon Mr. Cromwell and fully informed him of the situation in Bogota, more than confirming the unswerving determination of Colombia to reserve her consent until after the payment of many millions of francs by the company; this was again confirmed several days later (June 2) by a cable which Mr. Hay received from the chargé d'affaires in Bogota, who stated that "Colombia intends to force the company to make a heavy payment, without which no ratification."

This cable was suppressed by President Roosevelt when the diplomatic correspondence was called for by the Senate.

Now, gentlemen, here is a cable from the chargé d'affaires of the United States, which Mr. Cromwell quotes in his brief: "Colombia intends to force the company to make a heavy payment without which no ratification." I have searched in vain through all the diplomatic correspondence published by Mr. Roosevelt at the request of the Senate of the United States bearing upon this matter for any trace of that cable. The correspondence was published in Senate Document No. 51, Fifty-eighth Congress, second session, and I will now present to this committee all of the correspondence of the Government of the United States with its minister in Bogota in the original cipher of the State Department.

Mr. HARRISON. Is that the only instance where that correspondence is not embodied in the public document?

Mr. HALL. No, sir.

For obvious reasons, as these dispatches have all been published and as this cipher is a numeral cipher, and it would only be necessary to collate one with the other, I will not ask that the secret cipher of the State Department be embodied in the record, but I will as I go along read into the record those dispatches which were suppressed, and I will read them in the cipher of the State Department, so that if the committee deems it necessary it can ask the State Department to translate them, it can do so.

Mr. LEVY. But they are all in the correspondence sent to the Senate.

Mr. HALL. No, sir; I will read into the record the dispatches that were suppressed, and I will read them in the cipher of the State Department. Of course, it is up to the committee to decide if it wants to print the whole correspondence.

The CHAIRMAN. Yes; we will put it all in the appendix to the record.

Mr. HARRISON. Are those the suppressed telegrams?

Mr. HALL. No; this is the entire correspondence of the United States Government——

The CHAIRMAN. You have made the translation?

Mr. HALL. I have not got the secret cipher.

The CHAIRMAN. Let me ask you a question for the purpose of information. Where did you get those cipher telegrams? If you do not want to answer, you do not need to answer.

Mr. HALL. In order to avoid the possibility of anybody suggesting that any of the evidence obtained by the Press Publishing Co. for its defense in the criminal action brought against it by the Government was improperly obtained, I will tell the committee how these were obtained, although in so doing I am overstepping the bounds of professional etiquette. A staff correspondent of the New York World was sent to Bogota, and he obtained these transcripts, made from the original telegrams delivered to the American Legation in Bogota, from the head of the national telegraph system of the Republic of Colombia. These are all on the official paper. The heading reads "Republica de Colombia—Direccion General de Correos y Telegrafos—Seccion de Telegrafos." The manager of the national telegraph system of Colombia, when he gave these copies of this official correspondence to the correspondent of the World, was actuated solely by motives of the highest patriotism, and acted without either the consent or the authority of his superiors.

Mr. HARRISON. Do I understand these are copies of originals?

Mr. HALL. Those are copies; the originals are on file in the telegraph department, the national telegraph department of Colombia; the Government owns the telegraphs.

Mr. HARRISON. Are those the originals that were used in the trial of the libel case?

Mr. HALL. No, sir; they were never introduced in evidence. We never got so far as that.

The CHAIRMAN. The case was dismissed by the United States courts for lack of jurisdiction.

Mr. KENDALL. You say these are the telegrams that were suppressed?

Mr. HALL. Only certain of the cables were suppressed, and those I proposed to read into the record in their chronological order.

Mr. KENDALL. Suppressed by whom?

Mr. HALL. Suppressed by Mr. Roosevelt from the diplomatic correspondence transmitted to the Senate by the State Department.

Mr. KENDALL. Mr. Roosevelt was President then?

Mr. HALL. Yes, sir.

The CHAIRMAN. These telegrams to which you refer now are the telegrams which the President did not send to the Senate in response to the Senate's resolution?

Mr. HALL. Yes, sir.

The CHAIRMAN. How about the dispatches?

Mr. HALL. I do not know; I presume that if some of the cables were suppressed some of the dispatches were also. Of course the great majority of the correspondence was sent to the Senate.

The CHAIRMAN. And that which you hold in your hand is the correspondence that the President sent to the Senate?

Mr. HALL. This printed document is Senate Document No. 51, Fifty-eighth Congress, second session.

The CHAIRMAN. And the other telegrams to which you refer now are those which were not sent in?

Mr. HALL. Yes; and I think it is a fair presumption that if some of the cables were suppressed some of the dispatches were suppressed also.

Mr. KENDALL. How did you acquire those, Mr. Hall—the copies that you have of the suppressed telegrams?

Mr. HALL. Why, it was only necessary to compare the dates of cables in cipher and the dates of cables published.

Mr. KENDALL. The dates in the cables that were delivered for transmission at Bogota?

Mr. HALL. No; these cables were delivered to the legation in Bogota. These are cables from the State Department to the American minister in Bogota.

Mr. KENDALL. The original of these cables would be where?

Mr. HALL. The original of the cables must be in the State Department here in Washington.

Mr. KENDALL. And the transmitted cables are in the legation at Bogota?

Mr. HALL. In the legation at Bogota. And the record of transmission kept by the telegraph and cable companies is in the possession of the telegraph and cable companies.

Mr. KENDALL. Then the telegraph company at Bogota would have the cable transmitted by the State Department here to the legation at Bogota, and also the answer of the legation at Bogota to the State Department here?

Mr. HALL. Yes, sir.

Mr. KENDALL. And that is the record you have here complete?

Mr. HALL. Yes, sir; and it does not agree entirely with the correspondence sent to the Senate. Some of the messages were suppressed.

Mr. HARRISON. Have you a copy of the resolution that passed the Senate calling for this correspondence?

Mr. HALL. It is a public document.

Mr. LEVY. The question is whether we can publish the dispatches but withhold the cipher.

The CHAIRMAN. There is no particular secrecy.

Mr. LEVY. That is not the question. It is a question that the cipher might be found out by foreign powers.

Mr. HALL. That is the very point I made. Here are the cipher dispatches; here is the entire correspondence of the United States Government with its minister in Bogota referring to this matter. It is in the original cipher of the State Department. On comparison with the dispatches published in Senate Document No. 51, of the Fifty-eighth Congress, second session, it is clear that part of that cable correspondence was suppressed by Mr. Roosevelt. Now, if you print in the record the whole of this cipher, which is a numeral cipher, anybody—I have done it myself—can take the corresponding telegram printed here, superpose the words, and they will fit in. I am able to tell you that the suppressed telegrams here refer to this matter. They contain such words as "revolution," "Panama," "Colombia," and so forth. Now, if you print the whole of this in the record, anybody will be able to find out what was the cipher of the United States with its legation in Bogota in 1903. Whether that cipher has since been changed, whether the United States uses a different cipher for every legation, I do not know. I was intending merely to read into the record at the appropriate place such telegrams as I say were suppressed.

The CHAIRMAN. Well, you can print the suppressed ones here in the record.

The following cables are among those not included in Senate Document No. 51, Fifty-eighth Congress, second session, December 19, 1903; in all, some 50 cables were withheld:

WASHINGTON, *September 29, 1903.*

BEAUPRE, *Minister, Bogota:*

ABJMM 44390 18918 21129 52421 38908 52579 55397 27480 41621 50838 53149 18405 12674 11049 41621 25825 17788 33437 21129 12926 31700 206002 53006 41680 52608 21129 32735 35885 52608 19257 41598 36606 18918 49684 53149 24712 10788 54653 19100 47151 44869 56833 45175 52608 25369 10138 41598 44963 12792 24771 10788 18529 41662 56755 24225 33189 57371 18926 25126 41788 38825.

ADEE, *Acting.*

WASHINGTON, *September 29, 1903.*

BEAUPRE, *Minister, Bogota:*

JBJBP 47375 41598 44365 of 19597 12792 50462 52392 21129 43518 14803 LUIS CUERVO MARQUEZ 53149 49805 57349 19661 23028 41598 CONCHA 11927 12792 10436 38452 MARQUEZ 34527 37757 36899 52868 30073 12293 MARQUEZ 39429 158454 22428 34549 39173 41598 36899 49497 50941 31694 32005 21475 30333 42402 20466.

ADEE, *Acting.*

WASHINGTON, *October 1, 1903.*
(Received Buenaventura Oct. 3.)

BEAUPRE, *Minister, Bogota:*

KOCDP 57371 52891 53834 52868 12792 30073 46174 18918 21129 54198 52561 of 52867 38927 20328 31785 21129 28741 21455 for 41798 39923 51318 18926 41783 42402 20466 for 53825 57322 31694 17907 36607 31008 54917 39220 41598 telegraphing 42097 51318 18926 11668 52969 57322 17360 15428 53062 43000 21129 11942 to 31734 45044 45292 28747 21475 30333 18927 28362 for 52838 57322 35449 53825 on 16382 41598 14480 52969 CONCHA 11927 39738 10251 56942 34191 21129 16672 30910 53938 36606 18926 56963 37805 31018 20624 50916 56211 42086 39222 41598 telegraphing 16672 28426 18742 43037 of 31691 527744 21208 56902 21129 43000 12057 20''78 for 54015 44594 45929 41625 22647 53155 19118 bj 18209 31694 12792 21129 43000 21826 45950 21475 10546 52608 52504 52891 11927 43000 21129 28449 47010 12792 47042 53149 18926 17788 42467 12792 18529 56755 23225 41798 33789 and 29962 52955 26793 16366 CONCHA 11927 41598 40870 44789 53846 20624 52392 53309 36977 21129 34527 34893 50253 37352 29029 30391 18926 12792 47010 31055 56902 48070 41598 21209 11668 52969 57322 54459 21475 30461 38115 52491 52542 53825 57322 52776 21129 45088 52868 57322.

LOOMIS, *Acting.*

WASHINGTON, *October 14, 1903.*

BEAUPRE, *Minister, Bogota:*

KADDP 18918 21129 10474 52504 39118 in 52390 41581 27505 21129 22557 57349 30457 51680.

LOOMIS, *Acting.*

WASHINGTON, *October 17, 1903.*

BEAUPRE, *Minister, Bogota:*

49497 18918 21129 14596 10685 52394 46154 25131 52356 41598 30825 35636 56382 21129 10446 20624 31734 52504 12293 52408 25103 56213 20626 45943 22647 56902 21129.

HAY.

Mr. KENDALL. What is to become of this other mass of telegrams?

Mr. HALL. I understand they are to be printed in the appendix.

Mr. KENDALL. It is not our purpose to incorporate that?

The CHAIRMAN. I think all should go into the record.

After informal discussion—

The CHAIRMAN. You understand that it is a numerical cipher; just so many numbers?

Mr. HALL. Yes.

The CHAIRMAN. And some of these dispatches have been sent to the Senate of the United States?

Mr. HALL. Yes.

The CHAIRMAN. And some have not?

Mr. HALL. Yes.

The CHAIRMAN. And they are all matters of record in the State Department; hence there is no secrecy about them.

Mr. LEVY. There is the secrecy of that cipher; you are giving the United States cipher away.

The CHAIRMAN. That was a cipher used between the United States and its Colombian legation in 1903?

Mr. HARRISON. If you embody some of these quotations you give it away.

Mr. LEVY. They give the translation in the Senate document without the cipher. Now, we could say to the State Department, "We would like you to decipher these for us," but do not put our cipher in the record.

Mr. RAINEY. May I make a suggestion, Mr. Chairman? This is not intended to be a secret code in the sense used by Mr. Levy. It is a method of economical communication by cable.

The CHAIRMAN. So I understand.

Mr. RAINEY. It is a number cipher and each number means a certain number of words.

Mr. HALL. No, sir; I think you are mistaken. Very nearly each number means one word. It costs just as much as to transmit them in plain English.

Mr. RAINEY. Oh; I was mistaken about that. I remember President Roosevelt sent a message to the House saying in effect that all documents in the State Department or in any other departments bearing upon this subject could be seen by any Member of Congress or any reputable person—I think that was the language used.

Mr. LEVY. If we give this cipher away, anyone who gets the dispatches can use the United States cipher. They would have to change the cipher they are using at the present time. I would like to suggest that the chairman ask the Secretary of State to give him a copy of those ciphers, but do not put the cipher dispatches in the record.

Mr. RAINEY. Just so as we get them in the record in some way.

Mr. HARRISON. Are these same ciphers used to-day?

The CHAIRMAN. I will call up the State Department and ask them.

Mr. LEVY. I will call them up.

After an interval.

Mr. LEVY. Mr. Chairman, the State Department says it makes no difference now; but they are very much obliged we have taken that into consideration.

The CHAIRMAN. I think it was wise for you to be safe.

Mr. HALL. Mr. Cromwell not only received a detailed report from Charles Burdett Hart upon his return from Bogota, May 30, 1903, but he sent Mr. Farnham to see Hart in Virginia later in the summer

This is Roger L. Farnham, who was for some years a reporter on the World staff, and who for a long time has been one of Mr. Cromwell's henchmen and his confidential agent. Mr. Hart came from Bogota at this time, having been permitted to return to Colombia to remove his belongings and resign after answering charges filed against him. Hart's son was engaged in business in Bogota with the son of J. Gabriel Duque, owner of the Panama lottery and the Panama Star and Herald. While ex-Minister Hart was advising Cromwell, the younger Duque was lobbying at Bogota for the ratification of the treaty.

The debates in the Colombian Congress when the treaty was pending in Bogota, the articles in Colombian press, and the official reports addressed to the Secretary of State by the American minister, also showed that there was in Colombia and in the Colombian Congress a powerful faction in favor of testing the legalists of the last extension of the company's concession until 1910, and, if illegal, of insisting on the forfeiture of the concession at its expiration, which would then take place in 1906.

The extension of the concession had been granted by legislative decree of the President and not by Congress; it had never been confirmed by Congress and was of very doubtful legality.

Mr. Cromwell saw clearly that the only way to escape satisfying the just demands of Colombia was to keep on using the American Government, and make it maintain its refusal to consent to any amendment of Article I or to permit that the treaty should depend in any way on a previous agreement with the canal company, as Colombia was demanding. Mr. Cromwell had numerous interviews with Secretary Hay, Senators Hanna, Spooner, and Kittredge, Congressman Burton, and other party leaders in Congress, and on certain occasions with President Roosevelt. He urged that Colombia had already pledged herself morally to consent and that her consent should be imposed upon her as being demanded by international good faith, and thus succeeded in getting the American Government to use all its influence in favor of the French company, and on several occasions Secretary Hay sent to the American minister, for transmission to the Colombian Government, firm and positive refusals to consent to the amendment or transaction proposed.

Secretary Hay even permitted Mr. Cromwell to collaborate with him in the writing of these instructions. In his brief Mr. Cromwell says:

It was clear, both to the company and to ourselves, that if the company entered into the negotiations demanded by Colombia the inevitable result would be the payment of many millions of francs. In order to save the company from this expense, we made active and successful efforts. It was the desire of the company not to comply with Colombia's demands, and it was the advice which we strongly and continually gave and which was also given to it by its eminent counsellors in France; but while that was a most natural desire on the part of the company, the company itself was powerless to carry out its desire except through our efforts.

During this period (October, 1902–August, 1903) this matter caused us deep anxiety and demanded constant attention and services. It appeared to us that the only way to escape these exactions, to defeat these maneuvers, and to save the company from paying a tribute of many millions of francs was to convince the American Government that it should refuse to consent to any amendment of Article I or to permit that the treaty should depend in any way on a previous agreement with the canal company, as Colombia was demanding. To this end we had numerous interviews with Secretary Hay, Senators Hanna, Spooner, and Kittredge, Congressman Burton, and other party leaders in Congress, and on certain occasions with the President. We pointed out that Colombia had already pledged herself morally to consent and that her consent should be imposed upon her as being demanded by international good faith, and we thus created a feeling favorable to the support and protection of the company against these demands. As a result of these conferences and efforts the American Government adopted this view and on several occasions the Secretary sent to the American minister for transmission to the Colombian Government firm and positive refusals to consent to the amendment or transaction proposed. It was in recognition of our success in this direction that the company sent us on April 10, 1903, the following cable:

"Your cables received. We are very pleased and send you our congratulations and thanks."

Secretary Hay honored us with his confidence by permitting us to collaborate with him in the writing of these instructions, which conveyed the determinations arrived at. Almost on every occasion he had previously sent for us and had conferred with us as representatives of the canal company, in order to obtain our views.

We also wrote, at the request of the Secretary, a detailed note covering the whole history of the negotiations and arguments in support of the attitude thus taken by the United States, which note the Secretary used as a basis for his official instructions to the American minister and to which the United States adhered to the end. We sent a copy of these instructions to the company, which expressed its approval by the following cable:

"We have received Mr. Hay's letter of instructions to the minister of the United States in Bogota, which satisfies us and for which we thank you."

There, gentlemen, you have this semibankrupt French company thanking Mr. Cromwell for a copy of and expressing its satisfaction with the instructions issued by the State Department of the United States to the American minister in Bogota.

Mr. Goodwin. That is what Mr. Cromwell says.

Mr. Hall. It is not likely he would quote to the company itself a letter from them if they had not written it.

Now, these Hay-Cromwell instructions were officially communicated to the Colombian Government, and they were bitterly attacked as being predicated on an incorrect statement of the facts and as contrary to the attitude that Colombia had taken. But President Roosevelt and Secretary Hay stood by Mr. Cromwell and his clients, and, as Mr. Cromwell says, "stoutly maintained the attitude which had been thus assumed by common consent."

Secretary Hay's letter to Mr. Beaupre plainly bears the imprint of Mr. Cromwell's argument and style. The instructions read as though Mr. Cromwell had written them himself. In part, this letter to the American minister says:

Such action on the part of Colombia or on that of the companies would be inconsistent with the agreements already made between this Government and the canal company, with the act of June 28, 1902, under the authority of which the treaty was made and with the express terms of the treaty itself.

By the act of June 28, 1902, the President was authorized to acquire, at a cost not exceeding $40,000,000, the "rights, privileges, franchises, and concessions" and other property of the New Panama Canal Co., and an agreement to that end was made by him with the company and to the Government of Colombia that by articles 21 and 22 of the Salgar-Wyse concession of 1878 the company could not transfer to the United States its "rights, privileges, franchises, and concessions" without the consent of Colombia. Therefore, and before entering upon any dealings with the New Panama Canal Co., the present treaty with Colombia was negotiated and signed.

This statement by Secretary Hay was an absolute misstatement, as long before the canal treaty was negotiated or signed the United States, through the Isthmian Canal Commission, had "entered upon dealings with the New Panama Canal Co." formally asking that company to name a price at which it would transfer these "rights, privileges, franchises, and concessions," and the Spooner law had been passed, because the United States held that company's option to sell for $40,000,000.

The Hay-Cromwell instructions to the American minister continue:

The first article of that treaty provides as follows:

"The Government of Colombia authorizes the New Panama Canal Co. to sell and transfer to the United States its rights, privileges, properties, and concessions, as well as the Panama Railroad, and all the shares or parts of shares of said company."

The authorization thus given, it will be observed, covers expressly the "rights, privileges, * * * and concessions" of the company, as well as its other property.

Colombia now, by these notices, indicates a purpose not only of disregarding the authorization thus explicitly given, * * * but to destroy a great part of the subject matter to which it refers. She states an intention of requiring the company to cancel all obligations of Colombia to it, and thus to deprive the United States of the rights, privileges, and concessions which she has expressly authorized the company to transfer to them and which the canal company has contracted to sell and convey to the United States.

This Government can not approve such a transaction either by Colombia or by the company. * * * The Government of Colombia initiated the negotiations, and it can not be conceived that it should now disclaim its own propositions, nor can this Government acquiesce in such a course. * * * It is not necessary here to consider the question of good faith toward the canal company which would be raised by new exactions of that company at this time.

You have seen, gentlemen, from what I have already said that there is no possible chance for anybody sustaining the attitude taken in this by Secretary Hay, and later so often repeated by Mr. Roosevelt, that the treaty was entered into at the earnest solicitation of the people of Colombia, and that the Government of Colombia initiated the negotiations. We have seen that the negotiations were initiated by Mr. Cromwell himself, and that they were all dependent upon the request made by Admiral Walker to the New Panama Canal Co. to state a price at which it would sell its properties to the United States. Mr. Hay's instructions continue:

The foregoing instuctions, however, though sufficient in themselves to justify this Government in declining to recognize any right of the Republic of Colombia to limit the consent given by Article I of the treaty by any terms or conditions of any kind, are less important than others arising from the actual negotiations attending the making of the treaty. These other considerations render it impossible that any such new limitations should even be considered, and give any attempt by Colombia in that direction the character of a serious departure from the agreement reached between the executive Governments of the two nations.

Mr. Hay then sets forth as "these other considerations" the supposed Colombian origin of the treaty (negotiated and drafted by Mr. Cromwell himself), and cites Colombia's consent in the treaty to the transfer of the canal concession—which Mr. Cromwell cajoled or bullied Minister Concah into including the first draft of March 31, 1902. Mr. Hay declares that Concha assented to this proposal until November 11, 1902, when he proposed amendment of Article I, which the United States rejected as "wholly inadmissible." And here is what Mr. Cromwell had been playing for in getting the question of consent brought "within the domain of international relations." The Hay-Cromwell instructions continue:

The consent of Colombia to the sale of the canal company's property and concessions to the United States is a matter of agreement between the two nations. It has not been granted by Colombia to the company alone, but also to the United States. To that agreement neither the canal nor the railroad company is or can be a party; nor can the United States permit its international compacts to be dependent in any degree upon the action of any private corporation. Such a course would be consistent neither with the dignity of either nation nor with their interests. To make the effectiveness of the agreement between Colombia and the United States depend upon the willingness of the canal company to enter into arrangements with Colombia, of a character satisfactory to that country, would not only give that company an influence which it can never be permitted to exercise in the diplomatic affairs and international relations of this country, but would enable it to control the acquisition by the United States of the rights granted by Colombia, and the enjoyment by Colombia of the equivalent advantages secured to her by the United States.

Mr. Hay's saying there that the New Panama Canal Co. should never be allowed to acquire "an influence which it can never be permitted to exercise in the diplomatic affairs and relations of this country" is strange indeed, when we have Mr. Cromwell's assertion that these very instructions that I have been reading from were drafted by him as counsel for the company.

Mr. GARNER. In behalf of Mr. Hay, who is deceased, would it not be assumed that Mr. Cromwell was making statements that could not be sustained by facts in order to secure a fee from the French company? In other words, to use a harsh term, is it not possible that Mr. Cromwell is lying about the matter of what Mr. Hay did?

Mr. HALL. Quite possible.

The CHAIRMAN. He certainly was trying to get a big fee.

Mr. HALL. Yes, sir; there is no doubt about that. But it is hard to get over the company's cable acknowledging receipt of a copy of these very instructions and expressing its approval of them. Mr. Cromwell asserts that a constant exchange of reports and information was maintained between the State Department and Mr. Cromwell. They were in constant and daily communication; Secretary Hay consulted with Mr. Cromwell on every important development, and Mr. Cromwell conferred with him on all the important instructions given by the United States Government to its minister in Bogota and on the reports of the latter.

From the very first the Hay-Herran treaty was opposed by public sentiment in Colombia; on March 30, 1903, Mr. Beaupre, who had succeeded Hart as minister, reported by letter to Secretary Hay that "without question public opinion is strongly against its ratification," and that "it is apparent lately that the French canal company is to take a decided interest in securing the ratification of the convention, and that its influence to that end will be of much importance."

On April 15, 1903, Mr. Beaupre advised Secretary Hay that "from approbation to suspicion and from suspicion to decided opposition have been the phases of change in public sentiment during the last month," and that "this fact is clear, that if the proposed convention were to be submitted to the free opinion of the people it would not pass."

On May 4, 1903, a letter of Mr. Beaupre to Secretary Hay represents Alexander Mancini, agent of the French canal company at Bogota, as being emphatically of the opinion "that the Congress will refuse to ratify the convention and that he (Mancini) has written to his company to that effect." Thus early was Mr. Cromwell given reason for his abiding faith that the canal treaty would be rejected and that it would be necessary to make a revolution in Panama.

Mr. Beaupre notified the State Department on May 7, 1903, by cable that the Colombian Congress had been called to meet June 20, 1903. On the same day by letter he makes the first reference which appears in the published diplomatic correspondence of the United States to the secession of Panama. Says Mr. Beaupre:

The probabilities are that when the measure is presented to Congress there will be a lengthy debate and an adverse report. Then the representatives of the coast departments of the Cauca, Panama, and Bolivar will ask for a reconsideration and urge a ratification of the convention as the only means of preventing a secession of those departments and the attempt to constitute of their territories an independent republic. The debate will be resumed, and in the end the friends of the Government and of confirmation will prevail.

On May 12, 1903, Mr. Beaupre transmitted to the State Department translation of an extract from an article written by Dr. Juan B. Perzy Sota, who had been elected a Senator from the Department of Panama, as indicative of the popular feeling against the Hay-Herran convention. In this article the Panama Senator said:

The Herran treaty will be rejected, and rejected by a unanimous vote, in both Chambers. * * * The insult, however, which Herran has cast upon Colombian name will never be wiped out. The gallows would be a small punishment for a criminal of this class.

That, gentlemen, is what the Colombians thought of the minister who signed the treaty. Now on July 9, the United States minister—well, this is very important and I will read from Mr. Cromwell again because of what Mr. Garner said with reference to Mr. Hay, who is dead; so in speaking of Mr. Hay in this matter I will use Mr. Cromwell's own words or quote whatever other authority I have.

Mr. GARNER. In other words, you make no direct charges yourself except what the record bears out?

Mr. HALL. Yes, sir; it is to be presumed Mr. Cromwell would, of course, certify under oath that he was telling the truth in his brief. He presented it as a member of the bar seeking just remuneration for his services to men who stood at the very head of the legal profession in France, and were acting as arbiters in a matter of professional delicacy.

Mr. HARRISON. Were these statements made by Mr. Cromwell before Mr. Hay died?

Mr. HALL. Mr. Hay was dead when this brief was presented. This testimony of Mr. Cromwell's in this matter was presented at an arbitration, the terms of which were fixed by an instrument which I hold in my hand, signed in duplicate on the 21st day of January, 1907. At that time Mr. Hay was dead and could not have contradicted Mr. Cromwell.

Mr. DIFENDERFER. Mr. Cromwell made these statements under oath?

Mr. HALL. I will read you the exact text of the instrument to which I have referred:

Agreement between the undersigned La Compagnie Nouvelle du Canal de Panama, having its headquarters in Paris, No. 7 Rue Louis le Grand, represented by Monsieur Monvoisin, vice president of its board of liquidators, of the one part, and Messrs. Sullivan & Cromwell, of 49 Wall Street, New York, represented by William Nelson Cromwell of the other part.

It has been set forth and agreed as follows:

ARTICLE I. Messrs. Sullivan & Cromwell have been retained to defend and represent the interests of La Compagnie Nouvelle du Canal de Panama and have rendered it services of various kinds and have made important disbursements.

In order to arrive at a settlement the parties have agreed to appoint a board of arbitration, composed of three arbitrators and by these presents they appoint Maitres Henri Barboux, Georges Devin, and Alexandre Ribot.

ART. II. The arbitrators shall fix the amount due to Messrs. Sullivan & Cromwell as compensation for the services rendered and the disbursements made by them; the arbitrators dispensed from the ordinary forms of procedure may have recourse to such means of information as appear necessary to them.

ART. III. They will sit as friendly arbitrators of last resort, without appeal or legal recourse. They will also fix the costs of the arbitration.

ART. IV. The arbitrators must render their decision within six months from this date. They are hereby relieved from the necessity of placing their decision on file.

ART. V. In the event that in the course of the arbitration, one of the arbitrators shall die or resign on account of ill health, the parties shall choose another arbitrator within 15 days of the death or resignation, after which delay, in default of an agreement either one of the parties may petition the president of the tribunal civil de la Seine to make provision for the replacement of the missing arbitrator.

Signed in duplicate by the parties, the 21st day of February, 1907.

Read and approved for Sullivan & Cromwell.

WILLIAM NELSON CROMWELL.

Read and approved:

F. MONVOISIN.

Mr. KENDALL. These statements of Mr. Cromwell, involving Mr. Hay, as Judge Difenderfer inquires, were not under oath; they were simply incorporated in his brief filed with that board?

Mr. HALL. This is his brief. The point I was making was not in any way, shape, or form a reflection upon the late Secretary of State, but in justice to Mr. Cromwell it is inconceivable that a man of Mr. Cromwell's standing at the New York bar should in a brief presented to arbitrators in a matter of this kind make statements which he would not be ready to substantiate under oath.

Mr. KENDALL. The concrete question is this: Has he sworn to what you have read?

Mr. HALL. Not that I am aware of.

Mr. KENDALL. I have not any particular solicitude about Mr. Cromwell, but I do have——

Mr. HALL. Some solicitude about Mr. Hay?

Mr. KENDALL. Yes; he being dead.

Mr. HALL. Certainly; and everybody has that solicitude.

Mr. HARRISON. Mr. Cromwell has made allegations in that brief in respect to Senator Spooner, Mr. Burton, Mr. Roosevelt, and others. Have any of these men denied the statements he has made?

Mr. HALL. I do not believe any of Mr. Cromwell's statements have been made public before.

Mr. KENDALL. Your opinion is that these men have not been aware of these statements?

Mr. HALL. They have not been aware of these statements, but my contention is that the matter is one that is susceptible of very clean proof, because if you once got Mr. Cromwell's reports to the New Panama Canal Co., now in the vaults of the Credit Lyonnais, and his accounts, you will get documentary evidence bearing upon these points. There is no doubt that the average intelligent man, reading this brief, will assume that Mr. Cromwell made a very liberal and supposedly improper use of money. If he did so it will show, undoubtedly, in his accounts and on the books of the New Panama Canal Co. His reports made to his employers, from week to week and month to month, for a period of six years, ought to bear out in detail his statements there. And it is to be supposed that the company, having Mr. Cromwell's report in its possession at the time of this arbitration, would be able to check up and see whether those reports in some way or very closely carried out the contentions he made in his brief.

Mr. GARNER. In other words, it is supposed Mr. Cromwell would not have made this contention when the company could have shown it to be false by the vouchers on file in their office.

Mr. LEVY. He does not make any innuendoes or charges against Senator Spooner?

Mr. HALL. Yes, sir; he flat-footedly tells the committee that he inspired the Spooner amendment to the Nicaragua bill, and Mr. Spooner flat-footedly denied it on the floor of the Senate when Mr. Morgan of Alabama charged him with it. Now, to read from Mr. Cromwell's brief.

Mr. Cromwell says:

The hostile dispositions of the Colombian press and Government was so manifest that we suggested to Mr. Hay on June 9——

Mr. GARNER. June 9 of what year?

Mr. HALL. June 9, 1903—

The hostile dispositions of the Colombian press and Government were so manifest that we suggested to Secretary Hay, on June 9, to have the American Government announce to the Colombian Government, in advance of the meeting of its congress and with absolute frankness and firmness, that the United States had been led to adopt the Panama route and to enter into an undertaking with the canal company relying upon Colombia's treaty proposals and on the consent to the transfer included in these proposals.

The Secretary accepted these views and submitted them to the President who, a few days later, sent for Mr. Cromwell and, after due consideration, directed that instructions be sent to Colombia, which was done by Secretary Hay in a communication wherein it was stated:

"In virtue of this agreement (referred to above) our Congress reversed its previous judgment and decided upon the Panama route. If Colombia should now reject the treaty or unduly delay its ratification, the friendly understanding between the two Governments would be so seriously compromised that action might be taken by the Congress next winter which every friend of Colombia would regret."

Now, this is what Mr. Cromwell says he inspired. The actual text of the ultimatum sent by the United States—as published in Senate Document No. 51—differs only very slightly, and reads:

The Colombian Government apparently does not appreciate the gravity of the situation. The canal negotiations were initiated by Colombia, and were energetically pressed upon this Government for several years. The propositions presented by Colombia, with slight modifications, were finally accepted by us. In virtue of this agreement our Congress reversed its previous judgment and decided upon the Panama route.

If Colombia should now reject the treaty or unduly delay its ratification, the friendly understanding between the two countries would be so seriously compromised that action might be taken by the Congress next winter which every friend of Colombia would regret. Confidential. Communicate substance of this verbally to the minister of foreign affairs. If he desires it, give him a copy in form of memorandum.

Mr. KENDALL. The terms of that ultimatum were available to Mr. Cromwell when he made this statement before the board?

Mr. HALL. Undoubtedly.

Mr. GARNER. They must have been available.

Mr. KENDALL. They had been published?

Mr. HALL. They had been published.

Mr. GARNER. If what Mr. Cromwell says in his brief is true, I think he earned his fee. I should like very much to know what the award was.

Mr. HALL. I think it was $200,000—1,000,000 francs—and I must say if what he says in his brief is true, it was remarkably small remuneration for a man of his intelligence and activity.

June 18, 1903, Dr. Rice answered the ultimatum. He cited the long delay and the narrow margin by which the treaty had been ratified by the United States Senate, "And if it had been rejected," the Colombian foreign minister wrote, "it would have been without any diminution of the right of Colombia, just as its rejection here will be without any diminution of any right of the United States." Answering the argument that Colombia was bound to complete the negotiations because she had initiated them—a statement which is untrue—Dr. Rice said:

Having proposed a negotiation does not necessarily imply that it is to be approved, either in whole or in part, by the legislative body of the country that began it. As a notable example Dr. Rice cited the United States' rejection of the convention abrogating the Clayton-Bulwer treaty after the project had been proposed by the United States, because it would not accept the British amendments. The foreign minister indicated that Colombia did not consider as within the bounds of possibility the seizure of Panama, which Mr. Roosevelt has confessed he did contemplate. On this point the answer to the ultimatum says: "The Colombian Government has derived the correct conclusion that the only results that can affect adversely the interests of this nation, if their Congress should reject the project of the treaty, is that the Government of the United States will cease negotiations and adopt the Nicaragua route."

"When is there such an undue delay in the ratification of a treaty which will tend to cause a serious compromise in the friendly relations with the contracting party?" asks the Colombian foreign minister. "In this country there would be an undue delay if, the ratification having been ordered by the law, the executive power should show a disposition to disregard it with the evident purpose of causing injury to his own country or the other nation interested in the pact."

After citing interference in Cuba and in Venezuela as proof of America's "determination to procure and preserve the independence, sovereignty, and integrity of the American nations," the foreign minister concludes his reply to the ultimatum in the following paragraph:

If the Congress, using its inherent prerogative of national sovereignty, rejects the pact in question because in their judgment it is not for the benefit of the Republic it will be, I am sure, with much regret that it can not comply with the desires of the Government and the Congress of the United States; but feeling confident for the reasons of justice that by this act it will not have altered in any particular the friendly relations which fortunately exist between the two Republics and to the preservation of which Colombia attaches the highest importance.

Mr. Cromwell on his side reported Secretary Hay's warning to Dr. Herran, and expressed to him his personal conviction that Colombia would lose Panama if she did not ratify the treaty without amendment. Dr. Herran sent his Government a cable message in support of that of Secretary Hay, which we had communicated to him with the approval of the latter. It is significant that at that time—June, 1903—he inserted in his cable the declaration to his Government that he was convinced that if the treaty were not soon ratified Panama would secede and conclude the treaty itself.

This cable was approved by Gen. Reges when the Colombian diplomatic correspondence was published in the Libro Azul.

The CHAIRMAN. The committee will take a recess until 2 o'clock.

Thereupon, at 12 o'clock m., the committee took a recess until this afternoon at 2 o'clock.

AFTERNOON SESSION.

CONTINUATION OF STATEMENT OF MR. HALL.

Mr. HALL. Referring to the ultimatum of June 9, Mr. Cromwell says in his brief:

We on our side made the same observations to Minister Herran, and we expressed to him our personal conviction of what would be the consequences to the Isthmus of a violation by Colombia of her solemn undertakings. He fully recognized the gravity of the situation, and sent his Government a cable message in support of that of Secretary Hay, which we had communicated to him with the approval of the latter. It is significant that at that time (June, 1903) he inserted in his cable the declaration to his Government that he was convinced that if the treaty were not soon ratified Panama would secede and conclude the treaty itself.

It was this attitude, taken by the American Government under the circumstances we have just set forth, that furnished the basis of and justification for the subsequent events, the consequences of which were so transcendent.

The company, fully informed by us by cable, cabled to us in these generous terms:

"PARIS, *June 13, 1903.*

"Your cables and letters received. Are completely in accord with you on the program and are happy commencement execution. We hope for favorable results. We thank you for all your efforts."

Mr. KENDALL. Who sent that, Mr. Hall.

Mr. HALL. There is no signature to this cablegram. It is given out by Mr. Cromwell. This is in his own brief, and it is to be presumed that he would not have quoted their own telegram to the New Panama Canal Co. unless it was correctly transcribed.

In Mr. Cromwell's brief this is followed by another cable:

"JUNE 19, 1903.

"We have received your dispatch of the 15th. We hope step taken will produce decisive results."

Now, gentlemen, what was the step taken between the 13th and 15th of June which was to produce decisive results? On June 13 Mr. Cromwell had a long conference at the White House with President Roosevelt, and on leaving the White House the attorney for the New Panama Canal Co. sent his press agent, Mr. Richard L. Farnham, formerly in the employ of the World, over to the Washington bureau of the World. Mr. Cromwell lived at the New Willard, and the Washington bureau of the World is at the corner of Fourteenth and F. Mr. Farnham made to one of the members of the World's staff a suggestion for an article on the Panama Canal matter. Mr. Farnham stipulated that his name should not be used and that he was not to be quoted in the article; but he assured the World correspondent that there would be an uprising on the Isthmus; that it would probably take place on election day, November 3; and that five or six citizens of Panama would soon arrive in Washington to consult with Secretary Hay and other State Department officials concerning the proposed uprising.

Mr. KENDALL. That is a very interesting development. Mr. Farnham is now living?

Mr. HALL. Yes, sir.

Mr. KENDALL. How did you ascertain that this conference was held in the White House?

Mr. HALL. It is on record in the daily papers.

Mr. KENDALL. About Mr. Cromwell calling at the White House?

Mr. HALL. Yes, sir; also, I think that the records of the White House will show who called on the President on that day.

Now, from the information thus obtained the World correspondent, who is also living, wrote an article which appeared in the World on June 14, in which every detail of the Panama revolution of November 3 was accurately forecasted. Everything was eventually carried out exactly as it was printed in this article more than four and a half months before. This article read—with your permission, I will read the whole article:

WASHINGTON, *June 13, 1903.*

President Roosevelt is determined to have the Panama Canal route. He has no ntention of beginning negotiations for the Nicaragua route.

The view of the President is known to be that as the United States has spent millions of dollars in ascertaining which route is most feasible, as three different ministers from Colombia have declared their Government willing to grant every concession for the construction of a canal, and as two treaties have been signed granting rights of way across the Isthmus of Panama, it would be unfair to the United States if the best route be not obtained.

Advices received here daily indicate great opposition to the canal treaty at Bogota. Its defeat seems probable for two reasons:

(1) The greed of the Colombian Government, which insists on a largely increased payment for the property and concession.

(2) The fact that certain factions have worked themselves into a frenzy over the alleged relinquishment of sovereignty to lands necessary for building the canal.

Information also has reached this city that the State of Panama, which embraces all the proposed Canal Zone, stands ready to secede from Colombia and enter into a canal treaty with the United States.

The State of Panama, in the view of its citizens of this State, prepared a form of government and were ready to establish the Republic of Panama. The making of this plan operative at that time was considered inexpedient, but it is now ready for prompt execution. It is known that the following suggestion has been communicated to representatives of the administration:

The State of Panama will secede if the Colombian Congress fails to ratify the canal treaty. A republican form of government will be organized. This plan is said to be easy of execution, as not more than 100 Colombian soldiers are stationed in the State of Panama.

The citizens of Panama propose, after seceding, to make a treaty with the United States, giving this Government the equivalent of absolute sovereignty over the Canal Zone. The city of Panama alone will be excepted from this zone, and the United States will be given police and sanitary control there. The jurisdiction of this Government over the zone will be regarded as supreme. There will be no increase in price or yearly rental.

In return the President of the United States would promptly recognize the new Government, when established, and would at once appoint a minister to negotiate and sign a canal treaty. This can be done expeditiously, as all the data has already been supplied.

President Roosevelt is said to strongly favor this plan if the treaty is rejected. The treaty of 1846, by which the United States guarantees the sovereignty of Colombia over the Isthmus of Panama, is now construed as applicable only to foreign interference and not to the uprisings of her own people. The formal abrogation of the treaty of 1846 is, however, under consideration.

It is known that the Cabinet favors the President's idea of recognizing the Republic of Panama if necessary to secure the canal territory. The President has been in consultation both personally and by wire with leading Senators and has received unanimous encouragement.

The President, Secretary Hay, and other high officials say that no foreign government must be permitted to construct a canal along the Panama route. They realize that if the United States utilizes this route there is no danger of a competing canal being built over the Nicaragua route because of the enormous cost and because it would then be within the zone of this country. On the contrary, if the United States builds on the Nicaragua route the Panama could be taken by a foreign government and still be beyond the zone of this country.

It is intended to wait a reasonable time for action by the Colombian Congress which convenes June 20, and then if nothing is done, to make the above plan operative.

William Nelson Cromwell, general counsel of the Panama Canal Co., had a long conference with the President to-day. Mr. Cromwell's advices are that much opposition to the treaty has developed, but he still expects ratification.

According to information received here a bitter fight is being made on the treaty by representatives of foreign governments at Bogota and by the transcontinental railroad interests opposed to the canal. Lobbyists from the United States have gone to Colombia and are prepared to spend unlimited money to defeat the treaty.

Mr. DIFENDERFER. Who wrote that article, Mr. Hall?

Mr. HALL. Of course if the committee insists that I give the name of the special correspondent who wrote that article I have no doubt that I shall be authorized by the World to do so, but it would be a breach of professional etiquette for me to divulge the name of the author of any article appearing in the paper. However, I will say this, that the man who wrote that article is a newspaper man of the very highest standing, he is personally known to every Senator of the United States, he has been in the employ of the World here in Washington from 16 to 18 years, and he has made an affidavit, which if necessary can be produced, swearing to the exactitude of the sources of his information. He is still living.

Mr. KENDALL. Your theory, Mr. Hall, is that on this date in June Mr. Cromwell had a protracted conference with President Roosevelt, and that immediately following that conference Mr. Farnham, his personal representative, conferred with the correspondent of the World in Washington, inspiring the publication of this article which you have just read?

Mr. HALL. I have no theory, sir, in this matter. I am trying my best to avoid theories. I am merely stating a fact, that Mr. Roosevelt did have a conference that day with Mr. Cromwell, that Mr. Cromwell did go immediately to the Hotel Willard on leaving that conference, and that Mr. Cromwell did send his personal representative, Mr. Roger L. Farnham, to the New York World with this story, and obtained its publication in our paper.

Mr. KENDALL. I think that is only a more elaborate way of saying what I said.

Mr. HALL. I am anxious to avoid the word "theory," because what I have put forward is a statement of fact.

Now, on July 5, 1903, Mr. Beaupre cabled to Secretary Hay that a part of the ultimatum, which we have seen—Mr. Cromwell claims he inspired—had been read in a secret session of the Colombian Senate, that it had created a sensation, and was "construed by many as a threat of direct retaliation against Colombia in case the treaty is not ratified. This and the statement of just-arrived Members of Congress from Panama that this department would revolt if the treaty is not ratified caused alarm, and the effect is favorable."

On July 7, after the attitude of the American Government had been made plain to the Colombian Senate, Dr. Concha, for minister of Colombia in Washington, wrote to President Maroquin:

It would be well, in the course of debates, to rectify the error that Colombia proposed the negotiation to the American Government, when, on the contrary, it was the Isthmian Canal Commission, presided over by Admiral Walker, which began the discussion of the matter with Dr. Silva.

On July 11, 1903, Mr. Beaupre cabled to Secretary Hay:

I think strong intimation from you, through Colombian minister or this legation, that unnecessary delay should be avoided would be effective.

On July 13, 1903, Secretary Hay replied by cable:

Any amendment whatever or unnecessary delay in the ratification of the treaty would greatly imperil its consummation.

Mr. Cromwell during this period was busy fomenting the Panama revolution. He had his agents on the Isthmus. As general counsel of the Panama Railroad, as well as the canal, he had maintained for 10 years close professional and personal relations with influential people on the Isthmus. He kept them constantly informed as to the state of affairs; they, on their side, kept him perfectly informed as to the state of affairs on the Isthmus; he maintained the closest intimacy with them, and they relied much upon his advice.

Although Mr. Cromwell was receiving cable reports from his agent in Bogota, as well as through the American minister, on the progress of the treaty in the Colombian Congress, he was satisfied, even before Congress met, that the treaty would be rejected and was making his plans for the revolution which would bring about the separation of Panama. In his brief he says:

In fact, as we have explained, Minister Herran himself had cabled in June to his Government that this (separation of Panama) would be the probable result. We ourselves had not then and did not have later any doubt of the result, and this rendered us more attentive in order that the vast interests which were confided to us might not be imperiled or complicated.

How generally it was recognized in Washington that the Roosevelt administration was ready to violate the treaty of 1846 and seize the territory of Colombia is indicated by a letter written from Washington July 6, 1903, by Gen. Pedro Velez R., of Barranquilla, Colombia, to his brother, Luis Velez R., then governor of the Department of Bolivar. So impressed was Gov. Velez that he sent the following telegram to President Marroquin, to the minister of foreign affairs and war, and to the president of the Colombian Senate:

Pedro Velez R., now in the United States, writes in effect as follows under date of July 6: The position of our country is looked upon here with many misgivings. Some people believe that if the treaty is not ratified the American Government will take possession of the canal works by force; others believe that a revolution will be fomented in Panama, the independence of which will be recognized. It is asserted by newspaper men that a deputation has come from Panama to arrive at an understanding with the Washington Government and to find out if the latter will support the independence; that this Government has made inquiries in Europe as to whether the Governments there would object in case it recognized the independence and negotiated for the construction of the canal immediately afterwards, and that the answers were favorable. He (Pedro Velez) considers it urgent to send and maintain sufficient forces in the principal centers of population in Panama to repress any uprising and also to hold in readiness considerable reenforcements in Bolivar so as not to attract too much attention.

The American Government is absolutely considering the Nicaragua route. Consider it my duty inform Government.

LUIS VELEZ R., *Governor.*

Before leaving the United States Gen. Pedro Velez R. went to talk over the situation with Mr. Cromwell, and was assured by him, in Mr. Cromwell's office, on July 20, 1903, "that the United States never followed a crooked policy; that perhaps from a lack of refinement, only acquired by nations of very ancient civilization, it had not displayed and did not then display that deep and wily diplomacy, but little sincere at times, of which some European nations can boast," but that the American Government was "open and honest, respectful of its obligations," as witness Cuba; and that "the American Government wished to be a gentleman among the nations." Mr. Cromwell also assured Gen. Velez that "if ever the day came when an administration in the United States should depart from this line of conduct, the American people would rise as one man to bring back to the paths of honesty and righteousness the disloyal men who had been misled to break with the antecedents and the irrevocable desires of the Nation."

I call your attention, gentlemen, to that phrase: The American people "would rise as one man." It will recur at intervals. We will find it being used by the Panaman conspirators in the correspondence with Mr. Cromwell, and by Mr. Roosevelt in his message to the Congress of the United States.

But all the while Mr. Cromwell was rushing preparations to resolve the situation "in some other satisfactory manner." To this end it had been arranged that Jose Agustin Arango, attorney and lobbyist of the Panama Railroad Co., and a senator from the Department of Panama, should meet Mr. Cromwell or his representatives in Kingston, Jamaica, before proceeding in Bogota to the opening of Congress on June 20, 1903. At the last moment, according to the present recollection of his family, Senator Arango received a cable canceling this appointment.

In his "Data for a history" Senator Arango says he refused to assist in the work of the Colombian Congress, "because I had complete conviction that the Herran-Hay treaty * * * would be rejected; consequently I saw only one means of saving the Isthmus from the ruin toward which it was trending * * * our separation from Colombia."

The same month Capt. Chauncey B. Humphrey, Twenty-second Infantry, instructor in drawing at West Point, and Second Lieut. Grayson Mallet-Prevost Murphy, graduated from West Point June 11, 1903, and assigned to the Seventeenth Infantry, United States Army, were sent as military intelligences on a four months' tour through the northern portions of Venezuela and Colombia.

The movements of Arango in the early part of the summer of 1903 are difficult to trace. Various persons in Panama are positive that he was absent for some time, and they were given to understand that he left for the Congress at Bogota, but were told afterwards that he went to Kingston to keep the appointment with Cromwell. He certainly did not take his seat in the Colombia Senate, but there is, however, no record discoverable of his having been in Kingston.

In his own account of the revolutionary movement Arango wrote that he commissioned Capt. James R. Beers, freight agent and port captain for the Panama Railroad at its western terminus, "a man of sane and clear views, of absolute probity and honor," and possessed of the confidence of William Nelson Cromwell, to go to New York. Beers left early in June, while Arango remained in Panama to foment discontent and nurse hopes.

That the object of Capt. Beers's visit to the United States was to confer with William Nelson Cromwell on a revolution in order to declare the independence of the Department of Panama was well known to his most intimate associates on the Isthmus before his departure. It was also known, especially to Herbert G. Prescott, assistant superintendent of the Panama Railroad, that Capt. Beers went as the authorized spokesman of Arango and a very few of Arango's relatives and friends.

In an effort to protect Mr. Cromwell and give to the world the impression that the secession was a "spontaneous" movement, Arango suppressed Cromwell's name altogether in his "Date for a History of the Independence," published in El Heraldo del Istmo, December 15, 1905, and referred to him only as "the responsible person who, through Capt. Beers, had opened the road to our hopes and thus stimulated the sending of a representative of the committee."

Now, I have no letter or written document to prove that it was Mr. Cromwell who sent for Capt. Beers, but everyone of at least five or six men who took a prominent part in that revolution, to whom I have spoken personally, have assured me that Mr. Cromwell did send for Capt. Beers, and that Capt. Beers was not the type of man to go off and leave his job on the Panama Railroad and journey to New York to stir up a revolution unless he had been sent for by a man who was his superior in the Panama Railroad Co. There is no doubt whatever that Capt. Beers acted as Cromwell's agent in the matter. It was through him that the revolution was fomented, and it was Capt. Beers who first suggested the revolution to Arango and told Arango that the Panamans could count on Cromwell's support.

While Capt. Beers was in the States getting Mr. Cromwell's orders, Senator Arango was cautiously sounding influential Panamanians. On a Sunday late in July, just before Capt. Beer's return from New York, 26 or 28 prominent Americans and Panamanians were gathered at a luncheon as guests of Ramon and Pedro Arias at their house in the Savannahs.

The plans for the revolution were freely discussed, and numerous speeches made in favor of setting up an independent republic on the Isthmus under the protection of the United States, which would build the canal.

Hezekiah A. Gudger, then American consul general in Panama, now chief justice of the supreme court of the Canal Zone, was among the speakers. Judge Gudger doesn't remember what he said; J. Gabriel Duque, proprietor of the Panama Star and Herald, was present, as were Herbert G. Prescott, assistant superintendent of the Panama Railroad in charge of transportation; Maj. (now Col.) William Murray Black, United States Army, Engineer Corps, in charge of inspection of canal excavation by the French Canal Co. in behalf of the Isthmian Canal Commission; Lieut. Mark Brooke, United States Army, Engineer Corps, assistant to Maj. Black; Austin C. Harper, of Phillipsburg, Pa., and American civilian engineer under Maj. Black; Carlos Constantino Arosemena, later secretary of the revolutionary commmittee, and recently minister of Panama in Washington; Gen. Ruben Varon, Colombian "admiral," who was bought by the Panama rebels with a bribe of $35,000 silver; Mr. Arango, and others.

The date of this luncheon at the Arias House is very strangely fixed in Col. Black's diary as July 28, 1903, which was a Tuesday. The host and several guests fix the day positively as Sunday. This and other entries in the book lead one to suspect that Col. Black "wrote up" his diary when his memory was none too fresh, possibly after the revolution or after he was criticized publicly by the late Senator Carmack, of Tennessee, for having, in United States Army uniform, raised the Panaman flag of independence in Colon on November 6.

Before Capt. Beers left New York Mr. Cromwell furnished him a cable code book, with additions and special instructions for its use written in the blank pages in the back of the book. And when Beers exhibited the code upon his return to the Isthmus, August 4, 1903, he told his friends that Mr. Cromwell could be depended upon to "go the limit" with them in their revolutionary project.

On the Sunday following his emissary's return, Arango gave a luncheon at his country house in honor of Capt. Beers. Only a half dozen or so of Arango's most intimate friends were invited, with only two Americans, Prescott and Beers. Before the luncheon Beers had made his report to each conspirator, and at the table he did not go into these details again, except to say that the plan for the revolution could be carried out successfully, and that they could depend on Cromwell not only to assist them himself, but to obtain other assistance which he had promised to secure for the movement.

From this Sunday the propaganda was pushed in earnest, and frequent conferences were held in the office of Arango, attorney and land agent of the Panama Railroad, or in the adjoining office of Dr. Manuel Amador Guerrero, intimate friend of Arango and physician to the Panama Railroad. Amador had been taken into the plot by Arango during Beers's absence in the States, and had been told of Beers's mission, and had entered into the conspiracy with enthusiasm.

At the outset Amador promised that Arango should be the first President of the projected Republic, and Arango in turn put Amador forward for the honor.

Returning to the diplomatic negotiations. On July 21, 1903, the Colombian minister for foreign affairs interrogated Minister Beaupre as to the meaning of his note of April 24, 1903, when Mr. Beaupre transmitted in a letter the cabled instructions of April 7, 1903, when Secretary Hay told him to inform the Colombian Government, if the subject arose, that any change in the Hay-Herran treaty affecting the clause granting permission to transfer the concessions "would be in violation of the Spooner law and therefore not permissible." The foreign minister now wished to know whether any other amendments to the treaty would be regarded by the American Government as violations of the Spooner law. To this Mr. Beaupre responded on July 22, 1903, with the following argument:

I have the honor to say to your excellency that with the approval by the United States Senate of the treaty between Colombia and the United States, signed on the 22d of January, 1903, the Spooner law, which authorized the making of that treaty, was fully complied with, in the opinion of the Senate, so far as the Panama route was concerned. * * * Hence, the said law went out of active existence with reference to Panama, and can only again become a subject of discussion, and then in reference to the Nicaragua route, in the event of the rejection of the treaty by Colombia. * * * I consider it my duty to inform your excellency that I have no reason to believe that my Government will consider or discuss any modifications whatever to the treaty as it stands. * * * It would seem that the treaty itself, as the official interpretation of the law, can not be modified at all without violating that law.

The cables between Bogota and Washington were badly delayed, and on July 29, 1903, Acting Secretary of State Loomis cabled Mr. Beaupre:

Would like information as to present situation.

Receiving no reply, Secretary Hay sent another cable reiterating the views which Mr. Cromwell in the interest of his client had forced upon the administration. Mr. Hay's cable in full follows:

Instructions heretofore sent to you show the great danger of amending the treaty. This Government has no right or competence to covenant with Colombia to impose new financial obligations upon canal company and the President would not submit to our Senate any amendment in that sense, but would treat it as voiding the negotiations and bringing about a failure to conclude a satisfactory treaty with Colombia. No additional payment by the United States can hope for approval by United States Senate, while any amendment whatever requiring consideration by that body would most certainly imperil its consummation. You are at liberty to make discreet unofficial use of your instructions in the proper quarters. The Colombian Government and

Congress should realize the grave risk of ruining the negotiation by improvident amendment.

August 5, 1903, Mr. Beaupre cabled:

From conversations with prominent Senators I believe the Government does not consider my opinions as final or authoritative. I beg for an emphatic statement from you or instructions under my telegram of July 15. There is much danger that the treaty will be amended.

August 5, 1903, was a day of anxiety for Minister Beaupre. His cables, which Mr. Cumneh says were placed by Secretary Hay at his disposition as general counsel of the Panama Canal Co., for this one day alone cost the United States $992.20 at regular tariff rates now in force. In one $600 message, which did not reach Washington until August 12, 1903, Mr. Beaupre transmitted a summary of the report of the Senate committee recommending nine amendments to the treaty. Another cable of this date transmits the substance of Mr. Beaupre's note which he addressed to the Colombian minister of foreign affairs. In this note, dated August 5, 1903, Mr. Beaupre said to the Colombian Government:

It is clear that the committee's proposed modification of Article I (so as to provide that the canal company should pay Colombia for the privilege of transferring its concession to the United States) is alone tantamount of an absolute rejection of the treaty. I feel it my duty to reiterate the opinion I have before expressed to your excellency that my Government will not consider or discuss such an amendment at all.

Mr. Beaupre cited as the next serious objection a proposed amendment of the form of the tribunals for the Canal Zone, and said that "the other modifications, though not equally serious in principle," were so inconsequential to Colombia that she should not place them in the way of approval of the treaty. By Mr. Beaupre's letter it is seen that he interpreted his instructions as giving first importance to the protection of the French Panama Canal Co.'s $40,000,000 from the demands of Colombia.

I take this opportunity to respectfully reiterate what I have before expressed to your excellency, that if Colombia really desires to maintain the present friendly relations existing between the two countries * * * the pending treaty should be ratified exactly in its present form, without any modifications whatever. I say this from a deep conviction that my Government will not in any case accept amendments.

Later in the same day Secretary Hay's cabled instructions of July 31, 1903, reached the Bogota Legation and Mr. Beaupre wrote another note to the Colombian foreign minister, in which he said that he had received such definite instructions from his Government as to enable him not only fully to confirm, but to amplify materially all his previous notes. Mr. Beaupre said in part:

I may say that the antecedent circumstances of the whole negotiation of the canal treaty, from official information in the hands of my Government, are of such nature as to fully warrant the United States in considering any modification of the terms of the treaty as practically a breach of faith on the part of the Government of Colombia, such as may involve the very greatest complications in the friendly relations which have hitherto existed between the two countries.

Mr. Beaupre concludes this amazing diplomatic threat with the following assurance concerning the treaty of 1846–1848:

It is to be regretted that the reference to the necessity for the practical reenactment of the treaty of 1846–1848 in the (Colombian) Senate committee's report should constitute almost a doubt as to the good faith of the intention of the United States in its compliance therewith. I must assure your excellency that unless that treaty be denounced in accordance with its own provisions my Government is not capable of violating it, either in letter or spirit, nor should there be any fear on the part of Colombia that if ratified the clauses guaranteeing her sovereignty in the pending treaty, couched as they are in still more precise and solemn terms than those of 1846, will ever be disregarded in the slightest degree by the Government of the United States.

Both of Mr. Breaupre's notes of August 5, 1903, were read in secret sessions of the Colombian Senate and served to intensify the resentment which had been rising ever since the reading of his celebrated ultimatum of June 13, 1903.

August 6, 1903, Mr. Beaupre cabled to Secretary Hay:

Confidential. Note reference to treaty 1846 in the committee report. Colombia dreads above all things newspaper reported intention of the United States to denounce the treaty in the event of rejecting canal treaty. I have additional confirmation the statement of my dispatch No. 49, June 15.

Mr. Beaupre's dispatch, No. 49, of June 15, 1903, is one which Mr. Roosevelt failed to transmit to the Senate of the United States.

August 11, 1903, the day before the rejection of the treaty, Foreign Minister Rice in a long letter replied to Mr. Beaupre's various threats and warnings. In part, he said:

In the opinion of the Colombian Government the view expressed by your excellency's Government that the circumstances attending the whole negotiation of the canal treaty are of such a nature as would fully authorize the United States in considering a violation of the pact any modification whatever of the conditions of the treaty is not compatible with diplomatic usages nor with the express stipulations of article 28 of the same convention. (Article 28 provides for exchange of ratifications by the Congresses of the countries.)

In fact, plenipotentiaries in concluding public treaties propose and accept conditions with the purpose of facilitating the negotiation, which is not final except by means of ratification, which in republics is vested in the executive power, with the concurrence, direct or indirect, of some other high power of state.

I suppose that your excellency's Government has never denied to the Senate the right to introduce modifications in the international pacts, and that this right has the same legal force as that of approving or disapproving public treaties, and I understand that the Senate has exercised its right to propose modifications not only in this case but also in others, as I pointed out to your excellency in my contra memorandum of June 18, in connection with the project of convention date November 28, 1902, between the United States and Great Britain for the abrogation of the Clayton-Bulwer treaty of 1850.

Dr. Rice in this letter reiterates Colombia's confidence "that justice and equity govern the course of the United States in its relations with all powers," and his own belief that the United States must recognize the right of the Colombian Congress not only to propose modifications in the treaty but even to reject it, and that exercise of that right "can not in any manner entail complications great or small in the relations of the two countries, which it is to be hoped will continue on the same equal footing and in the same good understanding which has happily existed until now."

Now, on August 12, 1903, came the rejection of the treaty by unanimous vote of the Colombian Senate. Senator (later governor) Obaldia, of Panama, refrained from voting. Minister Beaupre had made it so plain by his threats and warnings, all of which were read to the Senate, that the United States would accept no amendment of the treaty that it was decided to reject it entirely.

The principal argument was made by Gen. Pedro Nel Ospina, now minister of Colombia to the United States, who contended that the treaty could be passed as demanded by the United States.

News of the rejection was cabled on August 12, by Minister Beaupre to the State Department, but was not received in Washington until August 15. But the State Department did receive on the 12th Mr. Beaupre's cable of August 5, 1903, announcing the report of the committee recommending nine amendments to the treaty. These proposed amendments were to compel Mr. Cromwell's client to pay part of its $40,000,000 to the Colombian Government for permission to transfer its concession, and altering the form of tribunals proposed for the Canal Zone. Nothing in these nine amendments suggested any change in the amount of indemnity the United States itself should pay to the canal company or to Colombia. Receipt of this cable was not announced at the State Department until the following day, when press dispatches brought news of the committee's action.

Fifty-four days elapsed between submission of the treaty by President Roosevelt and its ratification by the American Senate, and 54 days between the convening of the special session of the Colombian Congress and the treaty's rejection by its Senate.

Dr. Herran's fears, expressed in his letter of December 19, 1902, that President Roosevelt's "impetuous and violent disposition" might lead him to adopt the scheme of Senator Cullom to seize Panama "on the ground of universal public utility," received justification at this time. After getting news of the action of the Colombian Senate's committee in favor of amending the treaty, and without knowing that the treaty had been rejected, Mr. Roosevelt sent for Senator Cullom, chairman of the Senate Committee on Foreign Relations. Mr. Cullom went to Oyster Bay on Friday, August 14, 1903, accompanied by his son-in-law, William Barrett Ridgely, then Comptroller of the Currency. Secretary Hitchcock and T. E. Burns, of Minneapolis, were also of the luncheon party this day at Sagamore Hill. Aside, the President discussed with Senator Cullom the canal situation. The conference was reported the next morning in the New York Herald, in part, as follows:

> One might expect from a statement previously made by the President to the effect that he considered either canal route practicable, and from the two reports of the Isthmian Canal Commission, one of which favored Nicaragua and the other Panama, that the administration, as soon as the Colombian Congress killed the treaty by amending it, would be willing to follow out the act of Congress under which the canal is to be built and turn to Nicaragua.
>
> No such intention can yet be discovered. The administration is still wedded to the Panama route. It does not yet seem willing to go so far as to invade Panama, as soon as Colombia acts adversly and with an armed force to protect the workmen, proceed to dig the canal, but there has been significant talk in administration circles of getting around the matter in some other way.
>
> This intention, which is not clearly defined, was voiced this evening by Senator Cullom in an interview soon after he left Sagamore Hill.

The Herald, in the interview, quoted Senator Cullom as saying:

> We might make another treaty, not with Colombia, but with Panama.

On the same day the State Department gave out information concerning the proposed amendment of the treaty in Bogota, the New York Herald's Washington correspondent, after a visit to the State Department, telegraphed his paper, August 13, 1903:

> Mr. Beaupre, the American minister at Bogota, has cabled the State Department discouraging news about the canal treaty. The cablegram says that amendments to the treaty have been recommended and the minister believes one of the principal amendments, which provides for an increase in the purchase price for the canal concession, will probably be adopted.

Other newspapers were led into making the same misstatement. Mr. Beaupre's $600 cable of August 5, 1903, which reached the State Department the day before this false information was handed to the Washington correspondents, contained absolutely no basis for such a statement or surmise. Mr. Beaupre's cable set out the proposed amendments seriatim.

Yet the State Department permitted the information to go abroad through the press without contradiction, that Colombia was attempting to hold up the United States for more money, and President Roosevelt has persistently stood by this falsehood ever since.

On August 14, 1903, the day Senator Cullom dropped the suggestion that "We might make another treaty, not with Colombia, but with Panama," Mr. Cromwell became very active at the State Department. The New York Herald's dispatch of August 14, 1903, says:

> Alarmed at the gravity of the situation at Bogota, William Nelson Cromwell, counsel for the Panama Canal Co., made two calls at the State Department to-day to see Acting Secretary Loomis and Mr. Adee, the Third Assistant Secretary. In a last effort to save the treaty from annihilation by amendment, Mr. Cromwell and Dr. Herran are sending detailed cables to Bogota reiterating that the United States insists upon the treaty's ratification without amendment.

On August 25, the New Panama Canal Co. wrote to Mr. Cromwell, "It is still a little difficult to see by what road we shall attain our end."

Mr. Cromwell knew that no revolution in Panama could be successful if the governor remained loyal to the national administration. The first necessary step was to bring about the removal of the governor of the department, and to install in his place one who would close his eyes to secessionist preparations and join in the movement when it was made. Such a man was Jose Domingo de Obaldia, one of the Panaman senators, and an advocate of the treaty, although he, as one of the committee, signed the report amending the treaty, thereby killing it. In spite of private and public warnings and pleadings President Marroquin, at the instance of his son, Lorenzo, an intimate friend of young Dughe agreed late in August to name Obaldia governor, and offered Mutis-Duran the governor of Panama, a place in the cabinet of Bogota.

Since 1903, the charge has repeatedly been made in Colombia and in Panama that a corruption fund was sent to Bogota to buy this appointment and that $40,000 was paid to young Marroquin. I have no documentary proof of that, but I understand that documentary proof has been obtained by a special committee of the Colombian Congress which has been investigating these matters.

President Marroquin's excuse for appointing Obaldia as governor of Panama was that Obaldia had agreed to cooperate to elect Gen. Rafeal Reyes as Marroquin's successor and assure a congress that would pass the canal treaty at the next session. At the time, Gov. Velez, of the department of Bolivar, who had warned his Government in July, 1903, that the United States might seize Panama and that troops should be held ready to suppress any uprising, was rewarded for his loyalty, and that of his brother who was visiting the United States, by being removed. The governor of the adjoining department of Magdalena also was replaced.

Minister Beaupre announced by cable of August 30, 1903, to the State Department, two days before the appointment was officially made, that Gov. Obaldia had been named; and on the following day cabled:

I had an interview with Senator Obaldia to-day. He informed me that he is willing to remain so long as there is hope for the treaty, but he is convinced that there is none, and will leave, therefore, on the 6th proximo. Confirms Gen. Reye's statement concerning presidential candidate, and says that the next Senate was made certain for the treaty; * * * that in accepting the governorship of Panama he told the President that in case that the department found it necessary to revolt to secure canal, he would stand by Panama; but he added that if the Government of the United States will wait for the next session of Congress canal can be secured without a revolution. * * * Confidential. My opinion is that nothing satisfactory can be expected from this Congress.

Meantime, Mr. Roosevelt had been discussing the uglier and shorter means to his end—openly seizing the canal strip and fighting Colombia, if she dared to protest, with arms. The New York Herald's correspondent at the summer capital telegraphed from Oyster Bay under date of August 28, 1903:

Public sentiment may yet be called on to determine whether the United States shall take action which would lead to war with a sister republic over the right to complete the Panama Canal.

A step which might lead to war with the United States of Colombia is one of the contingencies discussed by representatives of the administration in seeking to find some way out of the difficulty arising through the failure of the Colombian Congress to ratify the Panama Canal treaty without amendments.

The canal question was the chief reason why Secretary of State Hay came here to see the President to-day * * * President Roosevelt and Secretary Hay regard the treaty as probably dead. They take little interest in the dispatches from Minister Beaupre at Bogota, which purport to detail efforts being made by the Colombians to "save the treaty" by amending it.

The United States long ago informed the little Republic that if any amendments were made to the treaty they would not be acceptable to this Government. It is impossible for this Government to recede from this statement, soberly made, and to consider talk of negotiating a new treaty which would give Colombia greater advantages and an annuity of $500,000, instead of $250,000, which some of the Colombians demand. This demand is termed "blackmail" in the United States by demanding more money for the canal; the State Department knew that there was absolutely no formation for or truth in the statements being circulated from Oyster Bay.

Furthermore, the administration had been informed before this conference of Roosevelt and Hay, by Dr. Herran, of the receipt from his Government of the following cable, which had also been published in Panama:

BOGOTA, *August 13, 1903.*

COLOMBIAN MINISTER,
Washington:

Senate unanimously disapproved canal treaty; among other reasons advanced in the debate being the diminished sovereignty and the companies not having previously arranged for transfer of their concessions. All the notes of the American minister against the introduction of amendments and his memorandum (the Beaupre-Cromwell ultimatum of June 13) on the possible rejection of the treaty or delay in its exchange contributed to its rejection. It is considered probable that Congress will fix the bases for renewing the negotiations.

ROCO,
Foreign Minister.

And also, the administration, before this conference of Mr. Roosevelt and Mr. Hay at Oyster Bay, had received in the dispatches from Mr. Beaupre repeated assurances that the rejection of the treaty was not, in all probability, final. On August 23, 1903, Mr. Beaupre's cable of the 17th had arrived, stating:

The President (of Colombia) informs me that Congress will pass law authorizing him to continue and finish negotiations for canal, but what conditions will be specified he can not state at present moment.

Prior to this Dr. Herran had received from his Government on August 21, 1903, and by its order had communicated to Secretary Hay the following cable, dated in Bogota, August 16, 1903:

The Senate, considering that the people of Colombia desire to maintain the most cordial relations with the United States, and that completion of the canal is of the greatest importance for universal American commerce, have named a commission of three Senators to study the manner of satisfying the desire of digging the canal, harmonizing legal and national interests.

And prior to this also Secretary Hay had cabled to Minister Beaupre, on August 24, 1903:

The President (Roosevelt) will make no engagement as to his actions on the canal matter, but I regard it as improbable that any definite action will be taken within two weeks.

On the day of the Roosevelt-Hay conference the following cable from Mr. Beaupre, dated August 24, 1903, reached the State Department:

Nothing has been done, and very little satisfactory action, this depending upon the attitude of the Government of the United States, which is waited for in great anxiety. The report of the committee prepared.

Reverting to the Herald's report of the Roosevelt-Hay council of August 28, 1903—

The conference of the President and Secretary Hay was to map out a plan to be pursued in view of the admitted failure of the treaty. There are three alternatives for the administration, and none will be taken until after full consultation with leaders in Congress.

The first is to ignore Colombia, proceed to construct the canal under the treaty with New Granada of 1846, fight Colombia if she objects, and create the independent Government of Panama out of the present State of Panama. This would give the United States what would be expected to be a short and inexpensive war, but would insure a permanent settlement of the question of the sovereignty of a canal zone across the Isthmus of Panama.

The second alternative is that the President shall act in accordance with the provisions of the Spooner law, and, having failed to make a treaty of a satisfactory kind with Colombia, turn to the Nicaragua route.

The third course is to delay this great work until something transpires to make Colombia see light, and then negotiate for another treaty * * *.

It will, doubtless, be a surprise to the public that a course which is sure to involve the country with war with a South American Republic is one of the methods of procedure being soberly contemplated by the United States * * *.

The position taken by those who are now advising extreme action by the United States is that the State Department has met Colombia more than half way, and that her statesmen are trifling with this Government and seeking to blackmail it in a matter of great importance to the security of the United States.

Persons interested in getting the $40,000,000 for the Panama Canal Co. are, of course, eager that this Government shall go ahead and seize the property, even though it leads to war.

August 29, 1903, the day after the Roosevelt-Hay conference, Secretary Hay cabled to Minister Beaupre as follows:

The President is bound by the Isthmian Canal statute, commonly called the Spooner law. By its provision he is given a reasonable time to arrange a satisfactory treaty with Colombia. When, in his judgment, the reasonable time has expired and he has not been able to make a satisfactory arrangement as to the Panama route, he will then proceed to carry into effect the alternative of the statute. Meantime the President will enter into no engagement restraining his freedom of action under the statute.

We are now at the end of August, 1903. Mr. Cromwell has managed to keep public attention fixed on the diplomatic exchanges. His revolutionary plans had been worked up silently without attracting attention.

Jose Augustin Arango, the land agent, lobbyist, and local lawyer for the Panama Railroad; Capt. James R. Beers, an American freight agent and port captain; and Dr. Manual Amador Guerrero, the company's physician, all of them directly dependent upon Mr. Cromwell's favor, formed the nucleus of the revolutionary conspiracy in Panama. Beers, who had returned on August 4, 1903, with Mr. Cromwell's code book and instructions, was keeping his principal fully informed by cable and by letter, and the time was ripe to put to the front a native Panaman.

Herbert G. Prescott, the most popular American on the Isthmus, married there, and, on account of his family ties and his position as assistant superintendent of the Panama Railroad, was intrusted with all that the conspirators were doing. For appearance's sake, Prescott, as well as Beers, kept in the background.

Before Capt. Beers had been sent to New York, Arango had only confided in his sons and sons-in-law, and after the plot was well outlined he did not, for diplomatic reasons, admit any of his family to the revolutionary committee, but depended upon them as a family counsel for his own guidance and support. The revolutionary committee was composed at first of Arango, Amador, and Carlos Constantine Arosemena, later minister to Washington. To this committee were added by the end of August, Nicanor A. de Obarrie, Ricardo Arias, Federico Boyd, Tomas Arias, and Manuel Espinosa B.

Dr. Amador expressed a desire to be one of the commissioners to be sent to the United States for the work that was necessary there. To allay suspicion, Dr. Amador wrote to his son, Dr. Raoul A. Amador, then acting assistant surgeon in the United States Army, stationed at Fort Revere, Mass., instructing him to send a cable, "I am sick; come." This the younger Amador did before his father embarked from Colon on the Panama Railroad Steamship Co.'s steamer *Seguranca*, August 26, 1903, for New York. Ricardo Arias, who was designated as another commissioner to accompany Dr. Amador, was obliged at the last moment to remain in Panama, and Amador was intrusted alone with the mission.

The purpose of Dr. Amador's mission was (1) to confirm to the satisfaction of the native Panamans the promises of assistance brought back from Mr. Cromwell by Capt. Beers and obtain the aid of the other forces which Cromwell told Beers he could enlist for the movement; (2) to secure assurance, if possible, directly from the American Secretary of State or the President, that the revolution would be supported by the armed forces of the United States, and that the infant Republic, once born, would be promptly recognized and treated with by the United States and made financially secure and protected by American warships and soldiers from retaliation by Colombia; and (3) to secure the resources, in money and arms, necessary for the movement.

Before Amador's departure the conspirators drafted a cable code which reveals clearly what were their plans and purposes. It was in two sections, headed "From there to here," and "From here to there." Not a single name was mentioned, but in the code "X" stood for John Hay, Secretary of State; "W" was William Nelson Cromwell, and "Ministro" referred to the Colombian chargé d'affaires, Dr. Thomas Herran. "B," Beers or Beaupre, appears also once in the code. In the code to be used by Amador in cabling from New

York there were 30 expressions, providing for all manner of contingencies, even for Cromwell's turning out to be only a boastful liar. Sixteen code messages were provided for the revolutionists to cable to Amador. The code word in each case was to be a numeral.

Here is a copy of this code [showing code to committee], the code Amador left in Panama when he went to New York on August 26, 1903. I have it here in the original Spanish, and I have an English translation of it. I also have the identification of a reputable member of the Panaman bar, who was counsel for the Press Publishing Co., and who himself copied it out of the letterpress book of one of the Arias, who was a member of this conspiracy. I will read the code, because this code was used by Madero and cabled from New York. There are 30 expressions, providing for all manner of contingencies. The code is:

FROM HERE TO THERE.

(For Amador's advices from New York to Panama.)

I. Have not been satisfied with Hay in my first conference.

II. Have had my first conference with Hay, and I found him determined to support the movement effectively.

III. Have not been able to talk to Hay personally, only through a third person; I believe that everything will turn out in line with our desires.

IV. Hay is determined to aid us in every way, and has asked me for exact details of what we need to insure success.

V. My agent is going with me, fully authorized to settle everything there.

VI. Cromwell has behaved very well, and has facilitated my interviews with important men who are disposed to cooperate.

VII. You can hurry up matters, as everything here goes well.

VIII. I am satisfied with the result and can assure success.

IX. Minister Herran has suspected something and is watching.

X. Have not been able to obtain assurances of support in the form in which I demanded it.

XI. Delay of Cromwell in introducing me to Hay makes me suspect that all he has said has been imagination and that he knows nothing.

XII. It appears that Hay will not decide anything definitely until he has received advices from the commissioner who is there (in Panama).

XIII. I understand that Hay does not wish to pledge himself to anything until he sees the result of the operation there (in Panama).

XIV. The people from whom I expected support have attached little importance to my mission.

XV. Those who are decided can do nothing practical for lack of necessary means.

XVI. I have convinced myself that Hay is in favor of the rival route, and for that reason will do nothing in support of our plan.

XVII. News that has arrived from there (Panama) on facilitating the construction of the canal has caused opinion here to shift in regard to our plan.

XVIII. The pretensions manifested in the new draft of an agreement (treaty) render all negotiations between the two Governments impossible, and for this reason I have again resumed conferences.

XIX. The new commissioner is expected here to negotiate. On this depends my future movements.

XX. I consider that I can do nothing practical here now, and for this reason I have decided to take passage for home.

XXI. Await my letter, which I write to-day.

XXII. Here it is thought best to adopt a different plan in order to obtain a favorable result for the construction of the work.

XXIII. Cromwell is determined to go the limit, but the means at his disposal are not sufficient to insure success.

XXIV. Hay, Cromwell, and myself are studying a general plan of procedure.

XXV. The commissioner there (in Panama) is an agent of Cromwell's, of which fact Hay is ignorant.

XXVI. I wish to know if anything has been advanced there (in Panama) and can I fix date here to proceed.

XXVII. Delay in getting a satisfactory reply obliges me to maintain silence.

XXVIII. B. communicates here (New York) that the contract can be satisfactorily arranged.

XXIX. I have considered it prudent to leave the capital (Washington) and continue negotiations from here (New York) by correspondence.

XXX. I await letters from there (Panama) in reply to mine, in order to bring matters to a close.

FROM THERE TO HERE.

(For the conspirators' advices from Panama to Amador in New York.)

Forty. The situation here is the same as when you left in every respect.

Fifty. The object of your trip is suspected here, and in consequence you must be circumspect.

Sixty. New military commander expected here shortly.

Seventy. Letters received. All is well. You can proceed.

Eighty. We write at length on variation of plan, as the one outlined has certain drawbacks.

Ninety. We accept indications contained in cable.

One hundred. Cable received. Go ahead.

Two hundred. Forces coming from Bolivar will arrive shortly.

Three hundred. Forces coming from Cauca will arrive here soon.

Four hundred. From Bogota they ask what has been done in the matter.

Five hundred. The matter is being much talked about. In consequence much precaution is necessary in acting.

Six hundred. Newspapers of there (Panama) give account of object of your journey.

Seven hundred. Strong opinion shown in favor of the plan, but this may hamper its realization.

Eight hundred. Here nothing has been done, awaiting what you have to communicate.

Nine hundred. Without our being able to tell how, the Government has discovered the secret and is on the watch.

One thousand. We must have the resources asked for to proceed with probabilities of success.

Thus provided with means of secret communication—a copy of the code being left with Arango, Boyd, and Arias—Dr. Amador embarked for New York. An indication of the financial condition of the "patriots' committee"—if not of its own poverty, at any rate of its determination that the Americans should pay the costs of the movement—is the fact that Amador was not supplied with even enough money to pay the expenses of his trip. This he had to borrow later in New York on his personal credit from Joshua Lindo, a Panaman banker. Dr. Amador was a good poker player, and on the voyage won from his fellow passengers enough to tide him over several days. On the *Seguranca*, with Dr. Amador, were J. Gabriel Duque, proprietor of the Panama Lottery and the Panama Star and Herald, and Tracy Robinson, both American citizens, old and influential residents of the Isthmus.

From the steamer Dr. Amador went to the Hotel Endicott, Columbus Avenue and Eighty-first Street, where he registered on September 1, 1903. He retained room No. 152-C from his arrival till departure for Panama on October 20, 1903.

Mr. Duque had come to New York on one of his customary business trips, but upon arriving at the exporting office of Andreas & Co., Mr. Duque met Roger L. Farnham, man Friday of the general corps for the Panama Canal Co., who told Mr. Duque that Mr. Cromwell wished to see him, and together Farnham and Duque went to No. 49 Wall Street. Mr. Duque had met Mr. Cromwell two or three years before this time, but had no intimate acquaintance.

Mr. Cromwell told Mr. Duque that there was no prospect of favorable action on the pending treaty by the Colombian Congress, and that the Department of Panama should make a revolution and declare its independence. He asked Mr. Duque whether the leading men of Panama would or could furnish the necessary funds for a revolution, and Mr. Duque replied that he did not think so. Cromwell said that if Mr. Duque would advance the necessary $100,000, he (Cromwell) would furnish the security for such a loan, to be repaid after independence, and that if Mr. Duque would make the Republic of Panama, he (Cromwell) would make Duque its first president.

Mr. Cromwell, after thoroughly discussing the situation in Panama and Bogota, said that Secretary of State Hay wished to confer with Mr. Duque in Washington. He called up the Secretary of State on the long-distance telephone, made an appointment, and gave Mr. Duque a note of introduction to Mr. Hay.

Farnham cautioned Mr. Duque not to remain over night in Washington, and suggested that, in order to avoid registering at a hotel and leaving a record of his visit, he take the night train from New York, arriving in Washington at 7 o'clock in the morning, see Mr. Hay, and come promptly away. This suggestion Mr. Duque followed.

Before leaving New York, however, he met Charles Burdett Hart, former American minister to Bogota, in the office of Andreas & Co., and Hart said he would introduce Mr. Duque to Secretary Hay. They therefore journeyed to Washington together, on the night of September 2, 1903, and after breakfasting at Harvey's, went to the Department of State at half past 9 o'clock and waited until the arrival of Secretary Hay about 10 a. m. Hart then presented Mr. Duque and shortly afterwards left them in a conference which lasted until between 12 and 1 o'clock.

In this conference the Secretary of State made no promise of direct assistance to the revolutionists of Panama, saying that he "would not cross that bridge until he got to it," but he did say distinctly that "the United States would build the Panama Canal and that it did not purpose to permit Colombia's standing in the way."

Secretary Hay also said that should the revolutionists take possession of the cities of Colon and Panama they could depend upon the United States to prohibit Colombia's landing troops to attack them and disturb the "free and uninterrupted transit" which the American Government was bound by treaty with Colombia to maintain.

Further, the Secretary of State asked Mr. Duque (representative of a plot against the Colombian Government) to remain in Washington or return to confer with the President when Mr. Roosevelt should come back from Oyster Bay the day after Labor Day. This was Mr. Hay's proposal, but it was impossible of acceptance because Mr. Duque had arranged to sail on September 7, 1903.

Having conferred two hours and more, during which he says Mr. Hay tried his best to pump him of all the information he possessed relative to the situation in Panama and Bogota, Mr. Duque left the State Department to call on his friend Mr. Herran, the Colombian chargé d'affaires.

Mr. Duque, a Cuban by birth and an American citizen by adoption, had many friends in Colombia; his son had prospered in business in Bogota and married into one of the foremost families of that capital. He went to Dr. Herran, thinking that a friendly warning might be communicated to Bogota in time to be effective. He told Dr. Herran that if the treaty was not ratified Panama would revolt and Colombia would lose everything.

The day after Duque's visit Dr. Herran sent his Government the following cable:

Revolutionary agents of Panama here. Yesterday the editor of the Estrella de Panama had a long conference with the Secretary of State. If treaty is not approved by September 22 (date Hay-Herran treaty expired by limitation), it is probable that there will be a revolution with American support.

On the same day that he sent this cable to Bogota, September 4, 1903, Dr. Herran wrote to the Colombian consul general in New York, Arturo de Brigard:

Yesterday Mr. J. G. Duque, editor and proprietor of the Star and Herald, had a long interview with the Secretary of State, and I understand that the plan for a revolution which he brought with him has been well received by the Government here, and it is most probable that in the event that the canal treaty is not approved before the 22d of this month there will be a revolutionary separatist movement on the Isthmus with the powerful support of this country.

Besides Duque there have come from Panama the following persons, and some of them, if not all, are compromised on this projected revolution; Tracy Robinson, G. Lewis, Amador, Arosemena. It appears that the headquarters of the revolution in New York is in the offices of Andreas & Co., whose address you know.

The canal and Panama Railroad companies are deeply implicated in this matter.

Duque will return to Panama on Tuesday next.

I have already informed our Government of this matter by cable, but you may perhaps be able to discover something more with the information I give you.

The situation is exceedingly critical, and I fear we shall not be able to ward off the blow which threatens us if the treaty is not approved in time and without substantial modifications.

Dr. Herran immediately put detectives on the track of Amador and wrote to Mr. Cromwell and to the canal company in Paris, warning them that Colombia would hold them responsible for any secessionist plot on the Isthmus.

On August 29, 1903, Dr. Herran received the following cable from the Colombian minister of foreign affairs:

Please inform me by cable and in code what effect the rejection of the treaty has produced on the Government of the United States.

RICO.

He replied, on September 5:

Disapproval of treaty has produced a bad impression, but the Government of the United States awaits a favorable reaction before September 22. Otherwise, it is probable that the President of the United States will assume a hostile attitude.

HERRAN.

Then the foreign minister asked him by cable, September 10:

Tell me in what hostile attitude will consist.

RICO.

And he replied September 15:

Hostile attitude will consist in favoring indirectly a revolution in Panama.

HERRAN.

Dr. Herran explained his statement respecting the probable hostile attitude of President Roosevelt in the following paragraph of a letter to the Colombian foreign minister, written in Washington September 11, 1903:

The warning that I gave relative to the probable future attitude of the President is founded on threatening statements which he has uttered in private conversations, and which by indirect means have come to my knowledge. Special reference is made to the promptness with which the independence of our department of Panama will be recognized. President Roosevelt is a decided partisan of the Panama route, and hopes to begin excavation of the canal during his administration. Your excellency already knows the vehement character of the President, and you are aware of the persistence and decision with which he pursues anything to which he may be committed. These considerations have led me to give credit and importance to the threatening expressions attributed to him.

To return to the conspirators. As an employee of the Panama Railroad, Dr. Amador reported, after his arrival on September 1, 1903, to the company's offices in New York, and with the vice president, E. A. Drake, went to call on Mr. Cromwell. He presented a letter to Mr. Cromwell from Jose Augustin Arango. Dr. Amador was received most cordially. Mr. Cromwell made him a thousand offers in the direction of assisting the revolution.

He told Dr. Amador to go back to see him, which Amador did. Cromwell promised Amador that he would finance the revolution. Immediately afterwards he found out that Duque had been to call on Herran, and the following day received a letter from Dr. Herran, warning him that the concession of both the Panama Railroad and Panama Canal Co. would be canceled if they took any part in the revolutionary movement.

Mr. Cromwell determined to protect himself and safeguard to the best of his ability the interests of his clients, all the while pushing the revolution in secret.

His first overt act was to openly sever connections with Dr. Amador. He did not keep another appointment he had made with the Panaman conspirator; sent word that he was out when Dr. Amador called at his office. Finally, on Dr. Amador insisting that he be received by Mr. Cromwell, the latter came out into the lobby of his office, and told Dr. Amador he did not wish to have anything to do with him and not to come back. Dr. Amador was, finally, almost thrown out of Mr. Cromwell's office.

To further protect himself Mr. Cromwell, who knew all the higher officials of the Panama Railroad were in the company, sent the following cable to Col. James R. Shaler, superintendent of the Panama Railroad, on the 10th instant:

While there may be no real foundation for newspaper statements of possible revolution at Panama, I advise and request that you take extra and every precaution to strictly perform our obligations to Colombia under concession, and instruct officials and employees to be careful as heretofore not to participate in any movements or hostilities whatever, and that you make at once your attitude known to Government officials there, and make careful record of your acts in this regard in order to prevent even a pretext for complaint or claims by Bogota or Panama Governments; also take every precaution to protect the property in your care from possible damage or interruption of service.

CROMWELL, *General Counsel.*

Both Col. Shaler and Capt. Beers had been to New York and received instructions direct from Mr. Cromwell. They considered that the sincerity of Mr. Cromwell's cabled instructions of September 10, 1903, was in keeping with that of his statement therein, that "there may be no real foundation for newspaper statements of possible revolution"—the same revolution which Mr. Cromwell had been promoting and discussing with them himself. They knew that Cromwell had sent the cable solely for the purpose of protecting the company in the event that the revolution should fail. They well knew that he didn't want it to fail, and consequently they acted as they did. And they were neither reprimanded nor discharged therefor. In his brief Mr. Cromwell says:

The protection of the concessions and the property of the company against confiscation or difficulties on the part of Colombia presented a subject which exacted and obtained from us vigilance, care, and energetic services.

Mr. Prescott came up to New York, on his regular leave of absence, September 18, 19. On the same boat came Hezekiah A. Gudger, the American consul general in Panama, who made a speech at the first luncheon where independence of Panama was publicly discussed, in July, 1903. Immediately after they landed they took luncheon at Miller's Hotel, and from there went to the offices of the Panama Railroad, where, with Judge Gudger, he met Cromwell, and while Gudger had a long conference in an inner office with him, Prescott remained outside with Vice President Drake.

Judge Gudger declares that neither he nor Mr. Cromwell discussed the revolutionary situation. Prescott was talking nothing but revolution to Vice President Drake. He knew that Capt. Beers's cables to Cromwell were transmitted through Drake, so he freely discussed the plans. Drake was strongly in favor of revolution, which he believed was the only solution. Gudger was engaged so long in his conference that when he left Cromwell asked Prescott to come to his law office the following morning at 10 o'clock, there being no more time for conferences that evening.

Arriving at Cromwell's office, as per appointment, Prescott was met by Roger L. Farnham, who said Mr. Cromwell was busy. In a few minutes Edward B. Hill, one of Cromwell's firm, came out and invited Prescott into his office after Farnham had introduced them. Hill talked very frankly. He said that the Panamans must be fools if they expected the United States to give them any guaranty before the revolution took place; that they must make the movement themselves, but that they surely could understand that once they had established their independence the United States would never permit Colombian troops to land to attack them, as there was precedent for such a course. Hill also called Prescott's attention to the order to the employees on the Isthmus, and said that of course the railroad could not afford to take any chances of forfeiting its concession in the event of the movement failing. Hill asked Prescott's opinion as to whether the Panamans had enough "sand" to carry the movement out successfully, and Prescott replied that he did not believe they would take such risks unless they felt sure of protection from the United States, as otherwise the Colombian troops would overrun them.

During this conversation, which lasted from 10 o'clock until nearly noon, Farnham came in and out of Hill's office several times, joined freely in the discussion, asked many questions, and expressed his desire to go to the Isthmus and help pull off the revolution himself. No reason was offered for Cromwell's failure to keep the appointment, and supposing that Cromwell was occupied, and having no reason of his own to confer with him, Prescott left when Hill was through.

Cromwell's attention was called several times to Prescott's being in Hill's office, but he excused himself from seeing him. Prescott had committed himself to the cause of the revolution in his conversation with Drake, and Drake had communicated this fact to Cromwell overnight.

On September 4, 1903, two very important letters were written by Arango. One of them was to Mr. Prescott and one of them was to Dr. Amador.

The letter to Mr. Prescott is as follows:

Confidential.] PANAMA, *September 14, 1903.*

H. G. PRESCOTT, Esq., *New York.*

DEAR MR. PRESCOTT: I have read with pleasure your lines, as also the cuttings of the New York Herald you kindly sent me.

We are anxious to do something in the direction, you know, as opportunity is excellent now and we are prepared and ready, only depending on your Government to decide. Delay is dangerous.

Try to see our friend Dr. Amador, who is there, and give him a help if possible for you to do so.

Yours, very truly, J. A. ARANGO.

The letter to Dr. Amador reads as follows: I will put in an exact transcript of the original Spanish.

PANAMA, *Sept. 14, 1903.*

Mi querido amigo:

Como manana Martes debe llegar a Colon el "Seguranca," espero que durante el dia recibiremos la esperada carta de Ud. que nos de la explicacion de su desalentador cablegrama: "disappointed" "esperen cartas"—Despues hemos recibido el que dice "Hope" y......mas nada; de manera que estamos en una situacion de temerosa expectativa, puesto que setamos ignorantes de lo que alla este occurriendo a UD. y del motivo del profundo silencio que guarda Mr. Cromwell.

Cansados de tanta incertidumbre resolvimos dirigir a ese Senor los siguientes cables, aun no contestados; pero que esperemos atendera y correspondera dentro de dos o tres dias:

El 10 de Sept—en clave.

(Confidential.) Regret Captain Berr's letters and cables are not replied. Opportunity now excellent to secure success provided United States promptly recognizes our independence under conditions with our agent there who is fully authorized to contract for us. Should Congress concede contract although improbable will be through fear of our attitude. Congress controlled by enemies of contract. Answer by wire in cipher through Beers. Tell our agent that to use all caution possible must send his cables through Beers not to use Brandon again. Arango.

El 12 de Septe, tambien en clave:

"Our position being critical we must have immediate answer to act promptly or abandon business."

La recomendacion que se hace a Ud. en el primer cable que dejo copiado, de no valerse de Brandon, es porque se hizo casi-publico el de Ud. "disappointed" y sospecho que tambien el otro ha sido conocido de algunos, lo que proviene sin duda de que el cable haya sido conocido del joven Brandon y este lo haya comunicado a Gustavo Leeman, quien debio divulgarlo; pero sea de ello lo que quiera, es preferible que Ud. se comunique por conducta del Capitan Beers, aun usandon el clave de Arias o Boyd.

Ya Ud. sabrá el cambio de gobernador; y esta tarde llego a Colon el General Baron, trayendo noticia de hallarse en Baranquilla ya Obaldia y Sarria con quince oficiales o jefes y oficiales, lo cual se explica, porque como Sarria esta en malos terminos con Huertas, habrá pedido traer oficialidad nueva, lo qual es una contratiempo para nosotros, aun quando todo pueda ser allanable. En fin, veremos "si se nos quema el pan en la puerta del horno."

La occasion que está perdiendose es brilliante—aqui todo el pai se levatara como un solo hombre. Desde que Ud. fue ha aumentado considerablamente el deseo de independencia con protectorado. Todos de afuera y adentro le piden sin misterios. Lastima seria perder esta brillante ocasion.

Supongo que noticias generales le daria Maria y su hijo Manuel etc. por lo cual solo me ocupo de lo urgente y que nos incombe.

Contra mi costumbre le escribo en lenguage llano sin reservas, confiando en que Ud. rompera esta tan pronto la lea y tome nota de lo que convenga.

No recuerdo mas que decir y me despide, deseando que nuestros esfuerzos no sean esteriles;

Su invariable amigo, J. A. ARANGO.

Now, translated, that letter reads:

PANAMA, *September 14, 1903.*

MY DEAR FRIEND: As to-morrow, Tuesday, the *Seguranca* should arrive at Colon, I trust that during the day we shall receive your expected letter, which will give us the explanation of your discouraging cablegram, "Disappointed; await letters." Since then we have received the cable saying, "Hope," and nothing more, so that we are in a position of fearful expectancy, as we are ignorant of what has happened to you over there and of the reasons for the profound silence which Mr. Cromwell maintains.

Tired of so much incertitude, we decided to send the following cables to that gentleman. They are as yet unanswered, but which we trust he will give attention and reply to within two or three days:

On September 10, in cipher:

"Confidential. Regret Capt. Beers's letters and cables are not replied. Opportunity now excellent to secure success provided United States promptly recognizes our independence under conditions with our agent there, who is fully authorized to contract for us. Should Congress concede contract, although improbable, will be through fear of our attitude. Congress controlled by enemies of contract. Answer by wire in cipher through Beers. Tell our agent that to use all caution possible must send his cables through Beers; not to use Brandon again.

"ARANGO."

On the 12th of September, also in cipher:

"Our position being critical, we must have immediate answer to act promptly or abandon business."

The recommendation made to you in the first cable set out above, not to use Brandon, is because your cable, "Disappointed," was made quasi public, and I suspect that the other one also has been known to several persons, which doubtless comes from the cable having been known to young Brandon and by him communicated to Gustave Leeman, who must have divulged it; but, be that as it may, it is better for you to communicate through Capt. Beers, even when using Arias's or Boyd's cipher.

You already know of the change of governor; and this afternoon there arrived in Colon Gen. Baron (Varon), bringing news that Obaldia and Sarria are already in Barranquilla with 15 officers and officials, which is explained by the fact that as Sarria is on bad terms with Huertas he has asked to be allowed to bring fresh officials, which is a contretemps for us, even if everything can be arranged. Anyhow, we shall see if there will be "a slip betwixt the cup and the lip."

The opportunity which is being lost is a brilliant one. Here the whole country will rise as one man. Since you left the desire for independence with a protectorate has greatly increased. Everyone in town and country ask for it openly. It would be a pity to lose this brilliant opportunity.

I suppose that Maria and your son Manuel will give you general news; therefore I have only referred to urgent matters which are incumbent upon me.

Against my custom, I am writing this in plain language and without reserve, confident that you will tear up this letter as soon as you have read it and taken note of its contents.

I can think of nothing more to say and take leave, wishing that our efforts may not be fruitless.

Your unswerving friend, J. A. ARANGO.

Dr. Amador's cables "Disappointed" and "Hope" were written the first after Mr. Cromwell had told him he would have nothing to do with the revolution; the second after information had been conferred to him that if he would remain quiet in New York he would receive help from another quarter. Help did come from another quarter. Summoned in haste from Paris, Philippe Bunau-Varilla, one of the New Panama Canal Co., who had been instrumental in getting Mr. Cromwell reappointed as counsel, arrived in New York on September 23, 1903, some two weeks after Dr. Amador had sent his cable "Disappointed" to the Isthmus, or just in time for Mr. Cromwell, who was anxious to get under cover after Dr. Herran's warning, to cable to Paris and have Bunau-Varilla take the first steamer across.

Unfortunately I do not have the cable that I believe Mr. Cromwell sent to the New Panama Canal Co. to have Bunau-Varilla sent over here; but that cable is also among the archives of the New Panama

Canal Co., which are the property of the United States and which are still in France, kept in the vaults there.

Dr. Amador sought Bunau-Varilla at the Waldorf-Astoria on the very night of the latter's arrival. He discussed the revolutionary plans with him. Bunau-Varilla promised all the financial support needed, and undertook to make the arrangements with the United States Government for the presence of warships to protect the Panamans against any effort by Colombia to suppress the revolution.

On October 7, 1903, Amador went down to the pier to see Prescott off for Panama. He told him that Bunau-Varilla would take him to Washington on the following day and obtain the hoped-for promises of American assistance. Amador told Prescott to communicate to the friends on the Isthmus this news; to tell them that Bunau-Varilla would arrange everything satisfactorily, including the finances; that they might expect Amador down on the next steamer; and that they should be prepared to make the movement shortly after he arrived in Panama.

On October 7 the New York Herald's Washington correspondent telegraphed his paper:

> William Nelson Cromwell * * * called on President Roosevelt to-day. Mr. Cromwell declared this afternoon: "The Panama Canal will be built, and by the United States Government." He would not say what new development had made this possible.

On October 10 President Roosevelt wrote to Dr. Albert Shaw, editor of the American Review of Reviews, who had been forecasting with the accuracy of an inspired prophet the events soon to take place in Panama:

> I cast aside the proposition made at this time to foment the secession of Panama * * *. Privately I feel free to say to you that I should be delighted if Panama were an independent State or if it made itself so at this moment; but for me to say so publicly would amount to an instigation of a revolt, and therefore I can not say it.

On October 10 Mr. Beaupre wrote to Secretary Hay:

> Monsieur Mancini (the Panama Canal Co.'s agent in Bogota) informs me, moreover, that some time before the rejection of the Hay-Herran treaty he wrote to Mr. Cromwell informing him that in all probability an attempt would be made to override the rights of the French company and to call in question the validity of the extension of time (of the canal concession) granted to it. To this he received no reply beyond the mere acknowledgment of his message, and his only instructions have been not to move in the matter at all. He therefore concludes, so he told me, that the United States Government and the French company have arrived at some satisfactory understanding.

On October 13 William Nelson Cromwell wrote a letter to President Roosevelt, to which Cromwell refers in a cable to Roosevelt from Paris, October 31, 1903. This letter, as well as the conference at the White House on October 7, 1903, appears to have been in relation to Mr. Cromwell's inducing Mr. Roosevelt "to extend the conditional agreement while awaiting new negotiations with Colombia or until such time as it should be possible to resolve the new situations in some other satisfactory manner."

On October 13 Dr. Amador saw Bunau-Varilla at night at the Waldorf-Astoria and discussed Bunau-Varilla's proposal, then outlined for the first time, to confine the revolution to the Canal Zone. Amador called the next morning and agreed to the plan.

On October 14 the State Department received Mr. Beaupre's cables of October 9 and 10, forecasting an unfavorable report of the Senate committee in Bogota.

Mr. Cromwell along and Mr. Bunau-Varilla and Dr. Amador in company had all made trips to Washington, and on October 15 Mr. Cromwell, all arrangements having been made, left for Paris to "confer with the directors of the Panama Canal Co."

On October 15 the Navy Department ordered Admiral Glass, in command of the Pacific Squadron, to proceed "about 22d instant on exercise cruise to Acapulco."

Mr. DIFENDERFER. Have you a copy of that order?

Mr. HALL. Yes, sir. Now, from here on I shall have to refer to and go over the confidential files of the Navy Department. This is the information which Mr. Roosevelt refused to transmit to Congress, but I obtained from the Secretary of the Navy permission to inspect and make copies of those files. I will put in here the letter from the Secretary of the Navy, so as to make it quite clear that this information which was refused to Congress was not improperly obtained by the World:

NAVY DEPARTMENT,
Washington, June 11, 1910.

SIR: In compliance with your request of the 6th instant the department grants you permission to inspect its records and documents bearing upon the Panama revolution of 1903 and make such extracts from and copies of said papers as you may desire, extracts and copies to be made in duplicate and one of the duplicates initialed by you and placed on file in accordance with your suggestion.

If you will advise the department as to when you wish to begin an examination of these records, suitable arrangements will be made therefor and a representative of the department designated to assist you in the matter.

Very respectfully,
GEO. L. VON MEYER,
Secretary of the Navy.

MR. HENRY N. HALL,
The New York World,
Washington Bureau, Washington, D. C.

On October 16, Mr. Roosevelt received in person the reports of Capt. Humphrey and Lieut. Murphy, who, as an "unpremeditated incident of their return journey," had reported every detail that might be useful in a campaign on the Isthmus, even to the best positions for artillery to command Panama and Colon and the number of mules that might be procured in far interior villages.

On October 16, a New York Herald dispatch from Bogota stated that—

As a consequence of Gov. Obaldia's quieting dispatches the fear formerly felt in Bogota regarding a secession of the Isthmus has been entirely dissipated, and public opinion is now assured that no further danger is threatened.

The bank account of the American minister in Bogota for this period shows that the Herald correspondent from time to time received checks for various small amounts.

Capt. Humphrey and Lieut. Murphy having reported in person to President Roosevelt on the 16th, it was found advisable on October 17, the next day, to detail military attachés to the American Legation in Bogota. Capt. Sidney A. Cloman, whose detail to the Military Information Division had been announced on September 16, 1903, and Capt. William G. Haan were assigned, though only Cloman's detail appeared in the press dispatches from Washington. The reason for Cloman's assignment to Bogota announced at the State Department was that the United States was going to pursue a new policy and send Army men to all of the American legations in South America to forearm this country with military information on account of the activity of Germany there and its evident purpose to oppose us in enforcing the Monroe doctrine. Notice of the return of Capt. Humphrey and Lieut. Murphy inconveniently found its way into the papers, and a Washington dispatch explained that they had been exploring northern Venezuela to this purpose, estimating carefully the sized army that country could put in the field to back up the United States in a crisis, and that these officers "also went to Panama and studied it from a soldier's point of view."

On the same day, October 17, Bunau-Varilla gave full and final instructions to Amador and told him to sail on the first boat, October 20, for Panama, and pull off the revolution on November 3.

The CHAIRMAN. November 3 was election day?

Mr. HALL. Yes, sir. It is a date well remembered in every newspaper office in this country, because although the telegram telling of the revolution should have left Panama at 6 o'clock in the evening, it only got to the newspaper offices in this country late at night. The Associated Press man, for certain reasons, was not on his job, and the cables were sent a little later than they should have been. Every newspaper was full of election news, and the night editors had the time of their existence tearing down and making up the papers that morning.

Mr. CLINE. Suppose that the revolution had occurred on the 3d, and the papers on account of the election were full of election news and consequently the people wouldn't see it, how would that effect the situation, even if the facts didn't get out until the next day?

Mr. HALL. It would make no difference. It was simply a piece of shrewd political strategy, an idea that they would give as little prominence to the revolution as possible.

Mr. DIFENDERFER. It was done under cover.

Mr. HALL. It was a shrewd political move, such as would only suggest itself to a particularly slick politician.

Mr. KENDALL. It is the supposition that these gentlemen designed back there in June to defer the revolution until the 3d of November, because there were certain subordinate elections being held on that day.

Mr. HALL. Were they subordinate?

Mr. KENDALL. There was no President elected in 1903.

Mr. HALL. For myself, I will say in all frankness that I do not consider the evidence that the date was fixed upon way back in June as absolutely conclusive in that matter. We have seen that Dr. Herran, after Mr. Duque had seen Secretary Hay, cabled to his Government, setting the last date at which Mr. Roosevelt would wait before "assuming a hostile attitude" as September 22. Afterwards it may have been changed to November 3. Now, in such matters there is always a sprinkling of legend and tradition that finds its way, creeps into the public mind; and down in the Isthmus of Panama no one has any doubt whatever that the suggestion was made at the time this thing was really decided upon in June. But I am willing to waive that. It is not an essential point, anyway.

Mr. CLINE. The only question I was raising was that there seems to be undue prominence given to that date. It is immaterial whether they got the news that day or the next day.

Mr. HALL. Certainly, sir.

Now, to go back to my story. Bunau Varilla promised to advance $100,000 for the expenses of the revolution out of his own pocket, and asked Amador to promise that he (Bunau Varilla) should be appointed first minister of the new republic in Washington. Dr. Amador was not willing to give this undertaking until he had conferred with his friends on the Isthmus, and later it was only through the insistence of Arango, as one of the provisional government established after the revolution, that Bunau Varilla received his appointment.

On October 19 President Roosevelt ordered the Navy Department to hold warships within striking distance of the Isthmus of Panama on both the Atlantic and Pacific sides. Pursuant to this order instructions were issued the same day as follows:

GLASS, *Marblehead, San Francisco, Cal.:*

Send *Boston* or other vessel ahead of squadron to Acapulco. (In cipher.) Send the *Boston* with all possible dispatch to San Juan del Sur, Nicaragua. She must arrive by November 1, with coal sufficient for returning to Acapulco. Secret and confidential. Her ostensible destination Acapulco only.

MOODY.

NAVY YARD, *Brooklyn, N. Y.:*

Desire *Dixie* sail for League Island in time embark battalion and be ready for sea 23d.

MOODY.

BARKER, *Kearsarge, Navy Yard, Brooklyn, N. Y.:*

Dixie must be ready to sail from League Island with battalion about 23d.

MOODY.

Orders were given to place a contingent of 400 marines on board the *Dixie*, and the U. S. S. *Atlanta* was ordered to proceed to Guantanamo.

President Roosevelt, as Commander in Chief of the Army, also gave instructions to the General Staff to prepare for the eventuality of a campaign on the Isthmus. The second division of the General Staff, which is known as the Military Information Bureau, compiled in great haste confidential notes on Panama "for the sole use of the officer to whom issued," bearing the imprint of the Government Printing Office and the date November, 1903 (copy in possession of the World). The scope of the operations contemplated may be gathered from the following excerpts:

An advance across the Isthmus from Colon toward Panama would be, of course, easiest by the railroad line, as the trails are all generally very difficult and overgrown with brush. There is a telegraph and telephone line which runs across the Isthmus along the railroad. The railroad is ballasted with rock nearly the whole distance from Colon to Panama. Light artillery could be taken along the railroad on trains or could be taken along the railroad tracks, when the necessary amount of boards and planks would have to be carried to lay over the bridges. * * * Three equipped men could march abreast on foot along the railroad line. * * * There is water communication from the mouth of the Chagres to Gatun. * * * There are several hills which could be occupied to prevent an advance along the line. The railroad is quite well equipped with rolling stock. There are about 65 bridges, principally steel, the most important and longest crossing the Chagres River above Gatun. * * * About 150 small cart mules and horses could be obtained at Panama, about 70 pack mules at Chorrera, while not more than 60 or 70 animals could be obtained at Colon. * * * Guns could be mounted upon a point near the lighthouse in the city of Colon. * * * Fresh water is obtainable at Colon for vessels, but is of poor quality. * * * About one-half mile from the city of Panama is a large hill, about 600 feet in height (Ancon). * * * Modern artillery could be placed upon this hill and command the city of Panama and harbors; also the anchorage at Culebra Island. The only points where troop could be landed near Colon, on the Atlantic side, are

Portobello Harbor, Manzanilla or Limon Bay, and Bocas del Toro, or, in favorable weather, at the mouth of the Chagres. The only place where troops could be landed on the south side of the Isthmus is at the harbors of Panama or La Boca or at the mouth of the Camite River, near Chorrera.

Notes on Panama describes all the roads and trails of the Intercontinental Railway Commission. Capt. Humphrey's report is called upon for the following detail:

The country between Panama and Panama Viejo (old Panama) is very rolling and grown with grass, affording fine pasturage for cattle. Along this road the country would also afford excellent camping facilities for large bodies of troops. The water supply of Panama at the present time is very poor, the only good water being stored in cisterns in the city. Water is also drawn from wells along the railroad near the city, but this is exceedingly impure.

The next contribution in the Notes on Panama by Capt. Humphrey is a reproduction of his map of La Boca, the mouth of the canal, and Ancon Hill, which Admiral Glass, on November 2, 1903, was ordered by cable to "occupy strongly with artillery," if necessary to prevent the landing of Colombian forces.

Among the data accumulated by these two young Army officers on their "unpremeditated" and incidental sojourn on the Isthmus was an estimate of the number of mules that "may be obtained in numbers and in localities and in one week's notice, as follows: Pedregal, 100; Puerto Mutis, 30; Mensable, 50; Aguadulce, 50; Chepo, 10; Chorrera, 10; Panama, 50."

All of the aforementioned settlements outside of Panama are far in the interior without means of communication and no reliable information could have been obtained therefrom without going there.

One feature of Capt. Humphrey's "unpremeditated" investigations in Panama must have consumed a week's time. The resulting detailed information set forth in Notes on Panama, pages 186–189. It is a report on each of the 25 stations between Panama and Colon on the railroad. Distance from Panama, population, topographical features, and capacity of sidetrack at each station are given. Topographical sketches of several of the principal stations are reproduced in the War Department handbook for the campaign on the Isthmus. Concluding this section of his report Capt. Humphrey says:

About 2 miles south of Colon along the railroad is a small station of five or six frame houses, near the foot of a small hill about 150 feet in height, known as "Monkey Hill." Artillery placed here would command all approaches to Colon from the south. It would also command the city of Colon, and were the artillery of sufficient power would command both the harbors of Manzanilla and Limon Bay.

The north entrance to the canal is located about one-half mile west of "Monkey Hill," and can be plainly seen from the top of the hill. All along the railroad and canal line between Colon and Panama the country is overgrown with a dense underbrush, rendering communication along the trails very difficult. There is no wagon road or cart road across the Isthmus, only a narrow trail 2 feet wide, with low-hanging vines and underbrush overhead, quite impracticable during the rainy season for travel. There is absolutely no land communication either from Colon or Panama along the neck of the Isthmus with the interior of Colombia. From the State of Panama communication is by steamship from Buenaventura Harbor on the west coast of Colombia to Panama, while the only communication on the Atlantic side is by a steamship from either Cartagena or Savanilla.

There is at present communication from Porto Bello Harbor across the Isthmus with Panama by means of the old Spanish mule trail. The trail was at one time in very good condition, having been paved with cobblestones by the Spanish, but it is now in very bad repair, and during the rainy season almost impossible for mules and horses.

November—when the Roosevelt-Cromwell revolution was to be pulled off—is in the rainy season.

On October 20, 1903, Dr. Amador left New York for Panama on the Panama Railroad Steamer *Yucatan*. Before sailing, Dr. Amador wrote the following letter to his son, Raone A. Amador, who was then serving as a surgeon in the United States Army at Fort Revere, near Boston, Mass.

OCTOBER 18, 1903.

DEAR LITTLE SON: I received your telegram that you are not coming, as they have refused you permission.

Also received your letter of the 17th. If the wreath does not come, they will send it from the Endicott by the next steamer.

The reason for your coming was for you to meet Bunau-Varilla, to whom I have spoken of you. He said that if all turns out well, you shall have a good place on the medical commission, which is the first that will begin work; that my name is in Hay's office and that certainly nothing will be refused you.

The plan seems to me good. A portion of the Isthmus declares itself independent and that portion the United States will not allow any Colombian forces to attack. An assembly is called and this given authority to a minister to be appointed by the new Government in order to make a treaty without need of ratification by that assembly. The treaty being approved by both parties, the new Republic remains under the protection of the United States and to it are added the other districts of the Isthmus which do not already form part of the new Republic and these also remain under the protection of the United States.

The movement will be delayed a few days. We want to have here the minister who is going to be named, so that once the movement is made he can be appointed by cable and take up the treaty. In 30 days everything will be concluded.

We have some resources on the movement being made, and already this has been arranged with a bank.

As soon as everything is arranged I will tell B. V. to look out for you.

He says if you do not wish to go he will look out for a position for you in New York. He is a man of great influence.

A thousand embraces to Pepe and my remembrances to Jennie and Mr. Smith.

Your affectionate father,

AMADOR.

P. S.—I leave two parcels at Annies's. I did not send them, as it will be no use to have you bring them back with you. Adios.

Mr. DIFENDERFER. It is very evident then that in connection with such promises of official positions there was also some money paid to these insurrectionists, was there not?

Mr. HALL. No, sir; I am convinced that at that time, October, 1903, no money had been paid to these conspirators or insurrectionists. But I have no doubt whatever that when the United States transferred to Messrs. J. P. Morgan & Co. the first million dollars of the ten million which was paid to the Republic of Panama under the Hay-Bunau-Varilla treaty a considerable sum was paid to some of those who took part in the movement, and as I go along I shall be able to show you the numerous small sums paid on the Isthmus.

Mr. DIFENDERFER. Do you believe that a large amount of money had been promised these men in connection with the revolution or that they had received the promise of appointment to official positions?

Mr. HALL. I believe that Dr. Amador had been told that if he followed out Mr. Cromwell's instructions implicitly he would get something, but I don't think that the Panamans, the men who formed the junta, or revolutionary committee, were paid. The people who were paid were the Colombian soldiers. Bribery was resorted to on the Isthmus of Panama, and I shall be able to show you just how much money was paid and give you every detail of that. But I don't think that these gentlemen, many of whom I know personally, and who, as Panamans, I can well understand wanted to establish their own State as a little independent republic, were paid any money. They would be not only pleased, but greatly flattered to be mixed up in an international thing of this kind. I believe that Dr. Amador and perhaps one or two others got something after the revolution, but I don't think they were paid in advance. I don't think that at all.

Mr. Cline. Don't you think that Mr. Cromwell advanced some money to these parties prior to the revolution?

Mr. Hall. $100,000 was telegraphed over by the Credit Lyonnaise, for account of the New Panama Canal Co., to Heidlebach, Ikleheimer & Co., and credited to Bunau-Varilla, and then there was also a loan of $100,000 from the Bowling Green Trust Co., secured, as I shall show you later, by securities deposited by Mr. Cromwell; but the money that was forthcoming to meet the expenses of the revolution on the Isthmus, the several thousands of dollars used to bribe the soldiers and initial expenses of that kind, were advanced by the Panama Railroad Co., the bank of Ehrman, of which the senior partner, Felix Ehrman, was vice consul general of the United States in Panama, Isaac Brandon & Bros., Pisa Nephews, and other bankers in Panama who knew the deal was going through.

Mr. Difenderfer. The Bowling Green Trust Co. is a Standard Oil institution, is it not?

Mr. Hall. I do not know, sir.

Now in this letter of Amador to his son there are two things. One of them is that the first plan, the real plan of which Mr. Roosevelt and some members of his administration were cognizant and to which they gave their support, only provided for the "taking" of the Canal Zone. They didn't want to be burdened with the whole expense of Panama, and their intention was to seize and make independent a small republic at the Canal Zone, including the two cities of Panama and Colon and that portion of the Isthmus between those places and for 50 miles on either side of Panama and Colon. That was all that was necessary for their purposes, and if that had been followed out—and I shall show you the reasons why it was not followed out—it would have obviated a great deal of trouble.

Mr. Difenderfer. The zone was afterwards reduced to 10 miles.

Mr. Hall. It is 10 miles now.

Meet minister on the wharf	Abrupt.
Pablo Arosemena	Accuse.
J. A. Arango	Absurd.
Tomas Arias	Accent.
Federico Boyd	Account.
They do not accept the plan	Accord.
I have received of B. V. the 4,000	Adult.
I have received from B. V. the balance up to 100,000	Advent.
The minister will negotiate loan	Adept.
This work in your cable to Maduro means that it is for me	Obscure.
Cables with this work are for B. V. transmit them (to him)	Fate.
Minister sailed from Colon the 3	Three.
Minister sailed from Colon the 10	Ten.
Minister sailed from Colon the 17	Seventeen.
Minister sailed from Colon the 24	Twenty-four.
Minister sailed from Colon the 1st of December	First.

Code of Liebert (Lieber).

To go back to Dr. Amador. As soon as he got on board the steamship *Yucatan* he went to the purser of the ship, George Beers—a son of Capt. Beers, Mr. William Nelson Cromwell's agent on the Isthmus—and handed the young man a package, telling him to place it in the safe and guard it carefully, as it was vital to Panama. Mrs. Federico Boyd and her son, F. Boyd, jr., were passengers on the same boat.

Dr. Amador had arranged cable codes with Joshua Lindo and Bunau-Varilla before sailing. They are in Spanish, in Dr. Amador's handwriting. Translated, they read:

In Dr. Amador's handwriting:

CODE WITH LINDO.

The plan is accepted; minister will start....................Abete.
Ask Bunau-Varilla for the $4,000..............................Abbot.
Ask Bunau-Varilla for the balance up to $100,000..............Ably.
Send the 50 revolvers, not very large ones, with 1,500 cartridges; must be handy, but not small Smith & Wessons..............Abode.
Read the sixth work, counting that of the cable as the first.

In Dr. Amador's handwriting, on the back of a sheet of letter-head of the Hotel Endicott:

ADDITION TO CODE WITH LINDO.

Send 500 Remington rifles and 500,000 cartridges..............Sorry.
Movement delayed for lack of arms.............................Truble.
Movement delayed for six days.................................Sintruble.
B. V. agrees to the delay.....................................O. K.

The following was written and crossed out by Amador:

For the $100,000 loan they charge 5-10 per cent................5-10 per cent.

Heading written in ink in the handwriting of Jose Agustin Arango:

CODE WITH (JONES) BUNAU-VARILLA.

Typewritten by some one who did not know Spanish, and evidently copied from Amador's manuscript:

Tomorrow at daybreak the movement will take place..........Galveston.
We have great hopes of good result..........................Mobile.
The movement is effected with good success without casualties.Safe.
The movement is effected with losses of life of small importance.Serious.
The movement is effected with losses of life of grave importance.Grave.
From 1 to 10 killed or wounded..............................Belgium.
From 10 to 20 killed or wounded.............................France.
From 40 to 80 killed or wounded.............................Turkey.
More than 80 killed or wounded..............................Russia.
We have taken several Colombian warships....................Take.
Warship Bogota..Wood.
Warship Padilla...Crowd.
Warship Boyaca..Female.
Warship Chucuito..Small.
They have left for the Cauca................................South.
Rendered useless..Spoiled.
They are in Buenaventura, or absent from Panama.............Laugh.
We have news of the arrival of Colombian forces.............News.
The Pacific...Good.
The Atlantic..Bad.
One day...Word.

Two days	Ton.
Four days	Heavy.
Five days	Powerful.
All the friends approve plan and we are proceeding to carry it out	Sad.
Enthusiasm	Faithful.
Discouragement	Great.
Met troops disembarking or disembarked	Tradition.
One hundred	Rabbit.
One hundred and fifty	Cat.
Two hundred	Lion.
More than two hundred	Tiger.
The great number of troops prevents us making the movement.	Elephant.
This cable is for Jones New York	Fate.
This cable is for Smith Panama	Obscure.
Tell me if anything had happened which obliges them not to, follow plans agreed upon	Content.
Nothing has occurred which necessitates modification	Boy.
Something has happened which compels abandonment of all idea of movement	Heaven.
We have issued the declaration of independence with the six declarations without changing a word	London.
Repeat your cable where occurs the word X, in order to be perfectly certain	Plus X.
I repeat the word X, which is perfectly correct	X plus.
I think it is extremely dangerous to refuse that which the United States desires	India.
I think that to arrive at our ends it is necessary to show some resistance	Japan.
It is impossible to resist longer; you accept	China.
Here is that which they desire to change	Mongolia.
I think these changes extremely advantageous and that they should be accepted	Indochina.
I think these changes acceptable	Manchuria.
I think it can not be accepted	Liberia.
Accept everything that you think just	Arabia.
Do not be worried by the delay, all is well	Canada.

Added in Amador's handwriting:

The movement will take place within	United.
Days	River.
One	Kentucky.
Two	Ohio.
Three	Mississippi.
Four	Hudson.
Five	Missouri.

The CHAIRMAN. We will take a recess at this point and go on with the hearing on Thursday morning at 10 o'clock.

COMMITTEE ON FOREIGN AFFAIRS,
Thursday, February 15, 1912.

The committee met at 10 o'clock a. m., Hon. William Sulzer (chairman) presiding.

STATEMENT OF MR. HENRY N. HALL—Resumed.

The CHAIRMAN. Mr. Hall, you may proceed.

Mr. HALL. On October 20, the same day that Dr. Amador left New York and five days after Mr. Roosevelt had ordered warships to proceed within striking distance of Panama and Colon, the American minister to Colombia wrote the following letter to the Secretary of State:

No. 185.] LEGATION OF THE UNITED STATES,
Bogota, October 20, 1903.

SIR: I have the honor to inform you that it would be of great utility and satisfaction to me to be kept posted as to the course of events on the Isthmus, and, if not inconsistent with the rules, I would be glad to have it arranged so that our consular offices at Panama and Colon could send me copies of their dispatches to the department on the political situation and that the consul general at Panama could telegraph me whenever anything of unusual importance occurs.

I am, sir, your obedient servant, A. M. BEAUPRE.

Mr. Beaupre, on the next day, October 21, wrote to Secretary Hay as follows:

I have the honor to inform you that there is no disguising the alarm existing as to the possible action of the Government of the United States should the feeling of dissatisfaction undoubtedly existing in the Department of Panama find expression in overt acts. The alarm took the form of a heated debate in the Senate yesterday, when the Government was again attacked for the appointment of Señor Obaldia as governor of Panama. The reply elicited from the minister for foreign affairs was rather significant. He read an extract from the treaty of 1846, in which the United States guaranteed Colombian sovereignty on the Isthmus, and assured the Senate that in case of an insurrection in the Department of Panama the United States would be bound to support the Government.

The next day, October 22, Secretary Hay cabled to Minister Beaupre:

Referring to your telegram 17th, if you find disposition on the part of Colombia to ask terms more favorable to Colombia than those heretofore negotiated, you may intimate orally, but not in writing, that it will be useless to send a special envoy.

On October 23 Mr. Cromwell arrived in Paris. According to his own brief, he discussed and explained to the adminstrators, the director and the liquidator of the old and new canal companies, "the situation in Bogota, that in Washington, and that in Panama, as well as the proposition he had made to the President."

On October 24 the State Department received Minister Beaupre's cable of October 22, stating that the minister for foreign affairs had informed him that at its next meeting the cabinet would consider a proposal to send a new minister and a special commission of three prominent men to renew canal negotiations.

All this was taking place while Dr. Amador was on board the steamship *Yucatan* on his way from New York down to Colon, and the American warships were being rushed to within striking distance of the Isthmus.

At the same moment President Roosevelt, standing within the shadow of the Peace Cross on Mount St. Albans, addressed a missionary meeting on October 25. Pleading aggressive Christianity, the man who "took" the Isthmus said:

In our civil life, although we need that the average public servant shall have far more than honesty, yet all other qualities go for nothing, or for worse than nothing, unless honesty underlies them, not only the honesty that keeps its skirts technically clean, but the honesty that is such according to the spirit as well as the letter of the law.

I wonder what Mr. Roosevelt would have said if one of those missionaries had asked him what he thought of a man who coveted his neighbor's watch, and not being able to acquire it on his own terms, sent a little boy to steal it, and then bought it from the little boy.

On October 26, three days after Mr. Cromwell's arrival in Paris, the Credit Lyonnais, by cable to Heidelbach, Ickelheimer & Co., of

New York, opened in favor of Bunau-Varilla a credit of $100,000. The president of Credit Lyonnais was Marius Bo, also president of the New Panama Canal Co., and Cromwell's chief instrument in France in its manipulation. Mr. Bo's election as president of the canal company, December 24, 1901, was followed almost immediately by Mr. Cromwell's reinstatement as general counsel for the New Panama Canal Co., and Mr. Cromwell is of record as counsel for the Credit Lyonnais in the United States.

The *Yucatan*, on which Dr. Amador was, arrived in the harbor of Colon on October 27, a few minutes after 11 a. m. None of the revolutionary committee went over to meet Amador in compliance with a request he made in his last letter, in which he wrote:

> I am entirely satisfied with the situation. I wish you all to drink a glass of champagne in my name, but no one must go to the station on my return.

The committee, however, sent over Mr. Prescott, of the Panama Railroad, who went on board with the port captain, and taking Amador aside, asked him if he had any papers or documents that he, Prescott, could take for greater safety. Amador thanked Prescott, and said that he had nothing with him but the flag of the new Republic, which was wound around his body.

This flag, I might here mention, had been made in the Waldorf-Astoria by Mrs. Bunau-Varilla, and was a silk flag of the United States, out of which she had cut the jack containing the stars and substituted a piece of blue silk, on which two white stars were joined together by a line symbolical of the canal.

Mr. HARRISON. The flag, then, looks a great deal like the flag of the United States?

Mr. HALL. A great deal the same, only the jack being taken out and this other substituted.

Amador, accompanied by Prescott, immediately went over to Panama. On the way over Amador told Prescott that everything was settled and that all the arrangements had been completed through Bunau-Varilla, who had promised to have American warships on hand to protect the revolutionists after they had declared their independence. Amador expressed to Prescott his most implicit confidence in the fulfillment of Bunau-Varilla's promise and did not seem to apprehend any doubts or hesitation on the part of his fellow conspirators. It had been decided that on Amador's arrival in Panama the revolutionary committee should meet the same evening at Federico Boyd's house on the Cathedral Plaza and receive Amador's report.

As a rule, the revolutionary committee used to meet late at night, either at Dr. Amador's house or at the electric-light company's office in Panama. On this occasion they met at the house of Mr. Federico Boyd.

Mr. CLINE. Let me ask you this question: How long before the revolution actually occurred had Dr. Amador taken up his residence in Panama?

Mr. HALL. Dr. Amador returned to Panama on the 27th of October, and the revolution occurred on the 3d of November.

Mr. CLINE. Had he been there any length of time prior to that?

Mr. HALL. He had lived there for many years, as physician of the Panama Railroad, and was known, of course, to everybody on the Isthmus.

Mr. CLINE. I take it from the statement that you have given here that he was a member of——

Mr. HALL (interposing). The revolutionary committee.

Mr. CLINE. At the same time was he a member of the Colombian Cabinet or Legislature?

Mr. HALL. No, sir; it was Mr. Arango who was senator of the State of Panama in the Colombian Senate, but, as we have seen, did not go to Bogota to take his seat at the session at which the Hay-Herran treaty was discussed, he having declared that his going was of no use because he knew the treaty would fail, and the recollection of his family is he had an appointment to meet Mr. Cromwell or his agent in Jamaica, but they are not sure whether he went, and it is impossible to prove his presence there because the records of the hotels in Jamaica were destroyed in the Kingston earthquake.

The meeting of the conspirators was held at Federico Boyd's house at 7 o'clock on the evening of the 27th. At it there were present all the members of the revolutionary committee, with the exception of Espinosa and Obarrio. Mr. Prescott was the only American present. Dr. Amador had outlined to his fellow conspirators the plan agreed upon between Bunau-Varilla and the authorities in Washington, which was to declare independent only the Canal Zone and the cities of Panama and Colon, and the United States warships and marines would be both at Colon and Panama to prevent the Colombian forces from attacking the Panamans, and that as soon as the government could be formed the United States would recognize the independence of Panama, which was to take its place among the nations of the world as the "Republic of the Isthmus."

It was not the original plan to call it the Republic of Panama. I will show you how that change was brought about.

Finally Amador showed a draft of the declaration of independence, which had been prepared in New York, and cable codes to enable the conspirators to communicate with Bunau-Varilla through Joshua Lindo, of Piza Nephews & Co., 18 Broadway, New York. Amador then showed his fellow conspirators the flag of the new Republic. It was merely a silk American flag, as I have told you, with the jack cut out, and in its place, on a blue silk ground, two white stars joined by a narrow strip of white ribbon, symbolical of the canal. It had been designed by Madam Bunau-Varilla.

When Amador pulled out this flag the impatience and disappointment of his hearers, which had been growing steadily throughout the narration, found vent in disapproval of the proposed emblem, which was declared to be too much like the American flag.

These Panamans really thought that Dr. Amador was coming back to them with some secret treaty signed by Mr. Hay or President Roosevelt, and the discussion of the merits of the emblem was interrupted by Ricardo Arias, who is one of the most wealthy men in the Republic of Panama and one of the conspirators, and who has great cattle interests in the interior outside of the proposed zone to be placed under the protection of the United States. He made a strong speech in which he ridiculed and denounced the plan to declare independent only the narrow strip of land in the vicinity of the canal. He pointed out that he, in common with all the other substantial men of Panama, had large estates and cattle interests throughout the entire department, and that they would all be ruined if their property was not protected from the Colombians. His remarks met with unanimous approval, and it was then and there agreed that if the movement were to take place at all it must extend to the whole State of Panama.

Now, the State of Panama is not limited by the geographical limitations of the Isthmus. The Isthmus of Panama, we have seen, as laid down in the treaties and recognized by all the authorities, is bounded on the south by an imaginary line running from Cape Tiburon to Point Garachine.

Mr. CLINE. It would seem from your statement that the whole body of conspirators, as to the real purpose of the resolution, had not been taken into the confidence of——

Mr. HALL (interposing). Of Mr. Cromwell; no, sir.

It was then decided by the conspirators to send men into the interior to initiate the revolutionary propaganda which until then had been confined solely to these few people in the city of Panama, and was not even known to the men who later led the movement in Colon, and to let the other towns know that a movement was in progress. Amador said that the proposal that he had laid before them was only what had been urged by Bunau-Varilla. He did not want to tell his fellow conspirators he had agreed to sacrificing their interests. Mr. Bunau-Varilla says that Amador had agreed they should only declare independent the 50-mile strip, but Dr. Amador told his fellow conspirators—and they are all agreed on this point—that pledges given by the American Government in Washington to Mr. Bunau-Varilla were such that no Colombian troops would be allowed to attack the Panamans anywhere after they had once declared their independence, and that the agreement with the American authorities was such as to cover whatever action they might take, if they declared a larger or smaller portion of the Isthmus independent. Thomas Arias and Federico Boyd, two of the junta, however, voiced the uneasiness of the conspirators, who, with the exception of Prescott, had expected that Amador would bring back with him some secret treaty signed by the United States. They were, on the whole, much disappointed, and said so in unmistakable terms, because Amador had absolutely nothing to show them in writing from either Mr. Roosevelt or Mr. Hay. The meeting broke up at about midnight, and Amador returned to his house, where he told his wife of the lack of enthusiasm that had been shown by his fellow conspirators.

The fact that it was only at this meeting on the night of October 27 that it was decided to extend the revolutionary movement to the whole Isthmus, shows that Mr. Roosevelt misstated the facts to the Congress of the United States when, in his message of January 4, 1904, quoting from the report of his military investigators whom he had interviewed in person on October 16, he said "that there were representatives of the revolutionary organization at all important points on the Isthmus"; and also that Mr. Roosevelt misstated the facts when in his notification to Colombia of the recognition of the independence of Panama on November 6 he said "that the people of Panama had 'by an apparently unanimous movement dissolved their political connection with the Republic of Colombia.'" Up to November 1, no one on the Isthmus, with the exception of these seven conspirators and the high officials of the Panama Railroad and the officers of the United States Army, who had been detailed to make a report on the French work for the Isthmian Canal Commission, were aware it was intended to pull off a revolution.

Mr. CLINE. Do you not think, Mr. Hall, that the history of this conspiracy among the seven conspirators, as you have detailed it here, five of whom apparently had no knowledge of what the real purpose was, is at total variance with the histories of conspiracies of this kind; that is to say, is it not the rule that in the formation of a conspiracy by such a small number of men everybody is taken in on the ground floor, so to speak?

Mr. HALL. Yes, sir.

Mr. CLINE. But in this case it was entirely different.

Mr. HALL. Dr. Amador is dead, and although I have not got the draft he cashed for the money paid to him out of the first million dollars, yet I am quite sure he received in the neighborhood of $100,000, and that he was virtually the only one of the conspirators who was paid any large sum; and he was paid this in order that he might assist in covering up Mr. Cromwell's tracks.

Mr. CLINE. Knowing your familiarity with the whole history of these conspiracies, I was simply asking for my own information whether it did not occur to you that this was out of the ordinary?

Mr. HALL. Undoubtedly.

On the following day, October 28, Tomas Arias went to Amador and told him that he did not want to go on with the plan——

Mr. HARRISON. What is your authority for that, Mr. Hall?

Mr. HALL. Tomas Arias's own sworn statement. Of course, in the narration I am now making every fact advanced by me is based upon sworn statements or can be satisfactorily proved.

On the following day, October 28, Tomas Arias went to Amador and told him that he did not want to go on with the plan, as he was afraid that things would not turn out well, and he said that he would suffer more than anyone else. As I have said, Tomas Arias was a man of large wealth. Amador tried to reassure him, appealing to his patriotism and saying that both he and Arango were willing to give their lives that the Isthmus might be free; but Tomas Arias said: "You are an old man, Arango is an old man, and you don't care if you are hung. I do not like to be hung." Tomas Arias's intention to withdraw, and the knowledge that his defection would undoubtedly start a panic among the conspirators and upset the entire plan, caused Amador great uneasiness, which was further intensified by Gov. Obaldia, who confidentially conveyed to him the news that a strong force of picked Colombian troops was on its way to the Isthmus under Gen. Juan B. Tovar and Ramon G. Amaya.

Obaldia, who was a Panaman and whose appointment as governor of Panama, it is charged by the committee of the Colombian Congress which investigated these matters, was obtained by an improper payment to the son of the then President of Colombia, and who actually lived in Amador's house, secretly favored the secessionists' plan, but he was afraid to take any risk himself. I do not think there is any doubt about that. He was afterwards the President of the Republic of Panama, and I have had numerous personal conversations with him, and while I do not want to quote a dead man in terms, I will say he certainly did favor the secessionists' plan and did everything he could to promote it.

In order to secretly favor the plan of the revolutionists, which had to some extent been disclosed to him by Arango, Obaldia, after news of Amador's departure from the States had been received, and he had been assured by Arango that all was well, and that they could count on American support, had, on October 25, sent away to Penonome, a town in the interior, on the pretext of an invasion from Nicaragua, that never occurred and was purely a pretext, a detachment of Colomiban troops which the conspirators believed would remain loyal and whose officers it had not been possible to bribe.

Now, here is where Mr. Obaldia overstepped the mark a little. On the same day an account of this fake invasion was cabled to the New York Herald by its Panama correspondent, Mr. Samuel Boyd, the brother of Federico Boyd, who thus hoped to afford a feasible pretext for the sending of the warships they knew were to come. But this report spread by Obaldia to justify his depleting the garrison of Panama precipitated action on the part of the Colombian Government, and on receipt of Obaldia's cable a telegram was sent by the governor of Bogota to Tovar to proceed to the Isthmus to suppress the reported invasion.

Obaldia was notified by the Colombian Government that Tovar was on his way, and was told to at once send the gunboat *Padilla* to Buenaventura to fetch other troops that were available there. When he received this cable he at once communicated it to Amador, who, knowing the misgivings that already existed among his fellow conspirators, decided not to tell them of the Colombian troops.

Now, Amador was in the conspiracy up to his neck. He was a brave man and an impulsive man. He put on a bold front and took Prescott into his confidence, and he and Prescott, who was and is very energetic and a typical railroad man, one who does not do things half way, decided to bluff it out, and they told the other members of the revolutionary committee they were going to send a cable to Bunau-Varilla in the United States to obtain definite assurances as to the presence of the warships, and Amador asked Arias to withhold his decision to withdraw until a satisfactory answer could be received from the United States. Arias said that if Amador got an answer that satisfied him, and he saw something really substantial in the way of a cable, he would have more confidence and would go on.

They sent to the United States this cable:

[No. 3 transmitting form.]

WEST INDIA & PANAMA TELEGRAPH CO. (LTD.),
Panama Station, October 29, 1903.

Sent at 8.49 a. m. to P. R. R. by H., from Smith.

To TOWER, *New York:*

Fate news bad powerful tiger urge vapor Colon.

Translated by the Amador-Lindo-Bunau-Varilla code, this reads:

From Amador, Panama, to Lindo, New York.

This cable is for Bunau-Varilla. We have news of the arrival of the Colombian forces on the Atlantic side within five days. They are more than 200 strong. Urge warships Colon.

Smith was the name used by Amador for all his communications with his fellow conspirators in New York, because it is the maiden name of his son's wife. Tower was the cable address of Joshua Lindo, of Piza, Nephews & Co., in whose office Amador had arranged to address all the messages intended for Bunau-Varilla.

Immediately on receipt of this cable Mr. Lindo took it in person to Bunau-Varilla at the Waldorf-Astoria Hotel, and Bunau-Varilla came on to Washington at once. Mr. Bunau-Varilla says that he saw Secretary Hay, and he is not sure whether he saw President Roosevelt or not; but he says he went to the State Department and urged that the ships should be sent at once. As a result of his efforts an urgent cable was sent to Commander Hubbard, of the U. S. S. *Nashville*, to proceed at once to Colon with all possible speed. This cable was not communicated to Congress. It is in the confidential files of the Navy Department, and reads as follows:

OCTOBER 30, 1903.

NASHVILLE, *Kingston, Jamaica:*

Hold vessel in readiness to return to Guantanamo.

That is in plain English, but the following is in cipher:

Secret and confidential. Proceed at once to Colon. Telegraph in cipher the situation after consulting with the United States consul. Your destination is a secret. Telegraph in cipher your departure from Kingston.

DARLING, *Acting.*

Satisfied with the assurance he had received from Secretary Hay, Bunau-Varilla went back to New York on the Congressional Limited, and on his way he telegraphed to the conspirators in Panama. He had the cable sent from Baltimore, and it read:

SMITH, *Panama:*

Thirty-six hours Atlantic, forty-eight Pacific.

This cable was received in Panama on November 1, and had the effect of putting fresh life into the conspirators. The news of the coming of the Colombian troops was generally rumored about town and had been cabled up to the New York Herald by Sam Boyd on the evening of the previous day.

The conspirators had been further encouraged by the active support given to their cause by the Panama Railroad Co., which had refused to supply any coal to the Colombian gunboats *Padilla* and *Bogota*, although the supply had been requisitioned for both by the Colombian military authorities and Gov. Obaldia, in compliance with instructions received from Bogota.

When the request for coal had been made to Col. Shaler, superintendent of the Panama Railroad Co., he had consulted with Prescott, and they had decided to leave the matter in the hands of Capt. Beers, Mr. William Nelson Cromwell's agent on the Isthmus; but Beers was sick, so the matter was turned over to Arango, who went through the farce of informing Obaldia that all the coal was in Colon—as a matter of fact, there were large quantities in Panama—and later that all the available coal had been contracted for by the steamship companies; he expressed the regrets of the Panama Railroad Co. at its inability to supply the Government and advised Obaldia to try to get coal from the Pacific Mail, knowing full well that the latter corporation would do nothing contrary to Mr. Cromwell's wishes.

Whereupon Gov. Obaldia sent the following cable to Bogota and to the governors of Cauca and Pompayan:

[Certified copy of cable.]

OCTOBER 31.

Have cabled to San Francisco to get coal from the Pacific Mail. Expect reply to-day. Railroad refuses to give it. *Padilla* ready. Will advise of her leaving. There is no invasion. Both parties on the Isthmus condemn it.

The reference to the *Padilla* being ready was based on the fact that a small supply of coal had been placed on board this boat after Amador and Arango had obtained positive assurances from her commander, Gen. Ruben Varon, that he would support the revolutionary movement and turn his vessel over to them the moment they declared Panama independent. He agreed to do this for $35,000 silver as soon as Amador and Arango had satisfied him that they had the promise of the American Government that American warships would be on hand to protect them from any attack by the Colombian troops.

Arrangements had been made for the movement to take place in Colon at the same time as in Panama. Sr. Don Porfirio Melendez had been sent for by Arango and had had a long conference with Amador, Boyd, and Arango in room 11 in the Hotel Central in Panama on November 1. He agreed to take the active leadership of the secessionist movement on the Atlantic side, and made arrangements to get 300 men who were engaged along the line of the Panama Railroad. They were told to muster at Colon for work on the United Fruit Co.'s plantation at Bocas del Toro at higher wages than the railroad was offering. The leaders, however, were taken into Melendez's confidence and told that the men might be needed to overcome the police force in Colon, about 150 strong, in case the latter should refuse to join the movement.

Not even the people of Colon, which is quite near Panama, just on the other side of the Isthmus, knew of this movement.

Bunau-Varilla had insisted on November 3 as the date for the revolution, but the conspirators wanted to make assurance doubly sure, and they decided to delay the movement for one day more, so as to give the American warships, which were to protect them from attack, ample time in which to arrive. They, of course, did not know the object of having it on November 3. Another reason was they wanted to delay acting at all until after the departure of the French steamer for Cartagena, in order that news of the uprising might not be carried by her.

So it was settled that the movement should take place on November 4, and Amador so notified all his friends, and told Mr. J. Gabriel Duque, editor and proprietor of the Panama Star and Herald, who we have seen had had that conference with Mr. Hay, and Duque, who was at the head of the fire brigade, which he supported to some extent out of his private purse, said that he had 287 young men who could be counted upon to support the movement.

As a result of Bunau-Varilla's visit to Washington, President Roosevelt, in orders to the Navy Department on the morning of November 2, sent the following instructions by cable to the various warships "within striking distance of the Isthmus." These are published in Senate Document 51, Fifty-eighth Congress, second session:

NAVY DEPARTMENT,
Washington, D. C., November 2, 1903.

DIXIE, *Kingston, Jamaica:*

Secret and confidential. Proceed with all possible dispatch to Colon. Maintain free and uninterrupted transit. If interruption threatened by armed force, occupy the line of railroad. Prevent landing of any armed force with hostile intent, either government or insurgent, either at Colon, Porto Bello, or other port. Send copy of instructions to the senior officer present at Panama upon arrival of *Boston*. Government force reported approaching the Isthmus in vessels. Prevent their landing if in your judgment this would precipitate a conflict. Acknowledgement is required.

DARLING, *Acting.*

[Translation.]

NAVY DEPARTMENT,
Washington, D. C., November 2, 1903.

NASHVILLE, *care American Consul, Colon:*

Secret and confidential. Maintain free and uninterrupted transit. If interruption threatened by armed force with hostile intent, either government or insurgent, either at Colon, Porto Bello, or other point. Send copy of instructions to the senior officer present at Panama upon arrival of *Boston*. Have sent copy of instructions and have telegraphed *Dixie* to proceed with all possible dispatch from Kingston to Colon. Government force reported approaching Colon in vessels. Prevent their landing if in your judgment this would precipitate a conflict. Acknowledgment is required.

DARLING, *Acting.*

NAVY DEPARTMENT,
Washington, D. C., November 2, 1903.

GLASS, *Marblehead, Acapulco:*

Proceed with all possible dispatch to Panama. Your destination is secret. Telegraph in cipher your departure. Secret and confidential. Maintain free and uninterrupted transit. If interruption is threatened by armed force, occupy the line of railroad. Prevent landing of any armed force, either Government or insurgent, with hostile intent, at any point within 50 miles of Panama. If doubtful of the intention of any armed force, occupy Ancon Hill strongly with artillery. If the *Wyoming* would delay *Concord* and *Marblehead*, her disposition must be left to your discretion. Government forces reported approaching the Isthmus in vessels. Prevent their landing if in your judgment landing would precipitate a conflict.

DARLING, *Acting.*

WASHINGTON, D. C., *November 2, 1903.*

BOSTON, *San Juan del Sur, Nicaragua:*

Proceed with all possible dispatch to Panama. Your destination is secret. Telegraph in cipher your departure. Secret and confidential. Maintain free and uninterrupted transit. If interruption is threatened by armed force, occupy the line of railroad. Prevent landing of any armed force, either Government or insurgent, with hostile intent, at any point within 50 miles of Panama. If doubtful of the intention of any armed force, occupy Ancon Hill strongly with artillery. Government forces reported approaching the Isthmus in vessels. Prevent their landing if in your judgment landing would precipitate a conflict.

DARLING, *Acting.*

The special instructions given to the U. S. S. *Nashville*, copies of which were sent to the commander of the *Dixie* and which Commander Hubbard was ordered to communicate to the senior officer present at Panama on the arrival of the *Boston*, have never been published, and were not communicated to Congress by President Roosevelt. It is also worthy of remark that the feasibility of placing artillery on Ancon Hill, mentioned in the War Department's notes on Panama, did not escape President Roosevelt and that the following passage is found in orders sent both to the *Marblehead* and the *Boston:*

If doubtful of the intention of any armed force, occupy Ancon Hill strongly with artillery.

In the confidential instructions printed for the sole use of the officer to whom issued by the War Department, the following passage is found:

If doubtful of the intention of any armed force, occupy Ancon Hill strongly with artillery.

Mr. DIFENDERFER. That was a good strategic position, overlooking the city of Panama?

Mr. HALL. Yes, sir; and commanding the harbor and commanding the Panama Railroad depot.

And yet, on October 29, Dr. Herran, this poor chargé d'affaires of Colombia in Washington, was given assurances by the State Department in Washington that the Government of the United States would only intervene on the Isthmus to maintain traffic. Answering a cable inquiry from his Government respecting the report of the fake invasion of the Isthmus which Gov. Obaldia had sent to Bogota, Dr. Herran cabled:

The Government of the United States is unaware of the character of the invasion of the Isthmus. The Secretary of State declared to me to-day that the Government of the United States would only intervene to maintain traffic.

Secretary Hay, on October 30, cabled to Minister Beaupre:

You may avail yourself of leave of absence under authorization cabled to you July 9.

On October 31 William Nelson Cromwell cabled from Paris to President Roosevelt that he was authorized in the name of the president of the canal company (Marius Bô), also president of Credit Lyonnais—(which had cabled $100,000 to finance the independence of Panama)—and in the name of other canal officials "to give you and the Government of the United States the assurance of loyal adherence, which they firmly maintain, and to express to you their entire confidence in the outcome of your masterly policy. I have received plenary power to complete all details on my coming return."

Here is the text of the cable, which is on file in the Department of Justice here in Washington:

PARIS, *October 31, 1903.*

To the PRESIDENT OF THE UNITED STATES,
Washington, D. C.:

Referring you respectfully to my letter of October 13. I am authorized in the name of the president of the canal company, with the unanimous approval of the board of directors at its meeting to-day, and with that of the liquidator of the old company, to give you, personally, and to the Government of the United States, the assurance of their loyal support, which they firmly maintain, and to express to you their confidence in the success of your masterful policy.

I have received full power to complete all details on my coming return.

WILLIAM NELSON CROMWELL,
General Counsel of La Compagnie Nouvelle du Canal de Panama.

Mr. Curtis, Mr. Cromwell's partner, immediately left for Washington, waited upon the President, and Mr. Roosevelt expressed to him his satisfaction at this cable, which fully confirmed the assurance he had received from Mr. Cromwell. That is from Mr. Cromwell's brief. Mr. Curtis also went through the formality of officially, as representing the Panama Railroad Co., asking the Government of the United States to protect the American property of the Panama Railroad Co. on the Isthmus.

While the Washington authorities were carrying out their part of the agreement to provide sufficient force at Colon and Panama to prevent Colombia exercising her sovereign right of suppressing the intended revolutionary movement, the conspirators in Panama were not idle. A new national flag had been designed by Manuel Amador, a son of Dr. Amador, and the first of the new emblems had been sewn together by Senorita Maria Amelia de la Ossa, who was engaged to marry Mr. "Dick" Prescott, the brother of Herbert G. Prescott, of the Panama Railroad. Mrs. Amador and her daughter Elmira, the latter married to Mr. William Ehrman, nephew of Felix Ehrman, United States consul general in Panama, Mrs. Lefevre, Mrs. Espinosa, the Arango and Arosemena families, all engaged in making flags, but nowhere was the activity shown in this work greater than at the house of Dr. Amador, in which Gov. Obaldia, the ranking Colombian official on the Isthmus, was then living.

The final plans for the separatist movement were perfected. It was arranged, this suggestion having been made to Capt. Beers by Mr. Cromwell, that at 5 o'clock on the morning of the 4th Gov. Obaldia and the highest Colombian officials, together with any prominent persons who were known not to favor Panaman independence, should be seized in their beds by Panaman police and members of the fire department, supported by troops from the Colombian regiments which were stationed in Panama under the command of Huertas. From the first the conspirators had seen the necessity of securing the cooperation of these Colombian troops, and money with which to bribe them was one of the things which Amador had been sent to New York to obtain.

And in the cable codes you will find a provision for the sending of 50 revolvers of small caliber which the members of the fire department were to use in their early morning arrests of any citizens loyal to Colombia.

This had been agreed to by Gen. Huertas after Amador had satisfied him that he had the support of the United States Government, and that not only Huertas, but all his officers and men, would receive liberal pecuniary reward for their assistance. Huertas in turn had won over his officers with the exception of Tascon, who had been sent by Obaldia to Penonome with about 100 men to meet this fake invasion which never existed at all. It was further planned in accordance with Mr Cromwell's suggestion that as soon as these arrests had been made the volunteer fire brigade, which was composed almost exclusively of the younger relatives of leading families favoring independence and had been recruited by Duque with a view to its participation in any separatist movement that might be projected, should be called out by a preconcerted signal, the sending up of a skyrocket, and that the 287 men composing it should rejoin their company stations, collecting the people on their way, and after indulging in whatever cart-tail oratory they could, they should then be gathered down at the Cathedral Plaza where they should hear the declaration of independence read and see the new flag of the Republic raised.

Prescott, after Amador had sent his cable to Bunau-Varilla asking for the warships, had gone over to Colon, and in order to be prepared for all eventualities, had shifted all the available rolling stock of the company from the Colon to the Panama end of the line, and by November 1 there were no cars in which any troops could have been moved from Colon to Panama. If questioned concerning this, it was his intention to state that "as assistant superintendent he was guarding the property of the company from liability of seizure by a hostile force for purposes that might have disturbed the free and uninterrupted transit which the United States was pledged to maintain."

That sounds more like Mr. Cromwell, the corporation lawyer, than it sounds like Herbert Prescott, the practical railroad man.

On November 1 Prescott was told by Col. Shaler, superintendent of the Panama Railroad, to "go over to Panama and wait until something turns up." He was in perfect accord with his chief, and both were determined to assist in every possible manner the revolutionary movement.

On the morning of November 2, at about 10 o'clock, Gov. Obaldia sent for Gen. Huertas, the commander of the Colombian forces on the Isthmus, which consisted of the Colombia regiment. When Huertas arrived he was at once conducted to the private office of the governor, who was already closeted with Amador, and the three remained together for more than an hour. On leaving this conference, Gen. Huertas told Col. Guillermo Calderon that Gen. Juan B. Tovar and the Tiradores regiment under Col. Eliseo Torres were coming in to relieve him, but that they would arrive too late, as the American warships which were to aid Panama to defy the Colombian Government were already on their way to Panama and Colon, and that if the Tiradores were disembarked the American forces would seek some pretext to take part in the fight if there was one. Huertas said that the salvation of Panama was in the treaty with the United States.

On the evening of November 2 the U. S. S. *Nashville* was sighted from Colon. The Colombian officials were much surprised at her arrival, as it had not been announced to them, and only a couple of weeks before the same vessel had left Colon after a short stay from October 11 to October 19, in the course of which her commander had called on Gen. Pedro A. Guandros, the prefect, and assured him that he was only visiting the Atlantic coasts of the Americas on an official tour. It has, however, been noticed that on her arrival the *Nashville's* launch had brought a big bundle of correspondence on shore, part of which had been delivered to the American consulate and part to the Panama Railroad Co.

With your permission, I will print in the appendix the log of the *Nashville* and the log of the *Dixie*.

Mr. Difenderfer. Was McCalla captain of the *Nashville*?

Mr. Hall. Commander Hubbard was in command of the *Nashville* at that time. These logs were copied by me in the Navy Department, and Mr. Charles W. Stewart, the keeper of the war records of the Navy Department, will, I have no doubt, be willing to certify to their correctness.

As soon as Shaler learned that the *Nashville* had been sighted he wired that fact to Prescott, who was in charge of the Panama Railroad Co.'s interests in Panama, and he also wrote him the following letters:

Monday, November 2, 1903.

Dear Mr. Prescott: Have just wired you that the *Nashville* has been sighted. This, I presume, settles the question. I have to suggest that the new Government should address a communication to the general superintendent stating the facts that may have transpired up to that time when they may want to make any requests of us. They should state the facts as to their assumption of authority of government. They should give assurance that they will render absolute protection to the railroad in its properties and its rights, the same as secured to the railroad by contracts 1850 and 1867, article 30 and elsewhere, with the Bogota Government. In consideration of this action on the part of the Government, they will expect the railroad company to comply with provisions of article 19 and furnish promptly all cars necessary for complying with the provisions of said article 19 to the new Government. They must notify the railroad company that the new Government "by whatever its name may be," has the military force necessary to enforce their requests, and it will be used for that purpose, and that such military force will be kept in readiness for service at all times. Government should notify railroad company that they should expect railroad company to operate their trains regularly, and the Government will see to it that such movement of trains shall not be interfered with by other parties or forces.

This is in a general way. See my letter even date accompanying this.

J. R. Shaler.

The letter of even date is a little confidential note which I will also show and read to you:

NOVEMBER 2, 1903.

DEAR PRESCOTT: I send you herewith memo. of points that should be covered in any communication addressed to us. Of course, there are many others, and you had better see Dr. Pablo Arosemena as soon as you can do so consistently and let him advise you fully.

The object is to have the new Government send us such communication as will free us from liability in case there is a failure.

Don't fail to get full advice and be governed by it.

I send this by No. 5 to-morrow, that you may have it early.

Yours, truly,

J. R. SHALER, *General Superintendent.*

Of course you understand that we will not accept any requests from the proposed new Government unless they are backed up by military force. But I advise you thus fully in case there may be interruption of communication between Panama and Colon.

Immediately on receipt of these letters, Prescott showed them to Arrango and Amador and allowed the former to make a copy of what Col. Shaler wanted written to him. The letter notifying the railroad company of the establishment of the new Government was drawn up on the morning of the 3d, all ready for the signatures of the members of the new Government to be attached, and Prescott was so informed when he went around and reminded them of it.

The United States ship *Nashville* cast anchor in Limon Bay, just inside the harbor of Colon, at 6.30 p. m. on November 2, 1903. Commander Hubbard went on shore and found, to use his own words, "that everything on the Isthmus was quiet." At about midnight another vessel was reported. This proved to be the Colombian gunboat *Cartagena*, carrying Gens. Tovar and Amaya and nearly 500 picked Colombian troops. Commander Hubbard of the United States ship *Nashville* had her boarded at daybreak—that is in Commander Hubbard's report—and ascertained that these troops were for the garrison at Panama. Commander Hubbard, who had knowledge of the conspirators' plans, says in his report:

Inasmuch as the independent party had not acted and the Government of Colombia was at that time in undisputed control of the Provice of Panama, I did not feel, in the absence of any instructions, that I was justified in preventing the landing of these troops, and at 8.30 they were disembarked.

The news of the arrival of the *Cartagena* was telephoned over to Mr. Prescott and the conspirators, who had been kept in the dark all this time by Amador and doubted the current rumors, and they almost completely lost heart at the unexpected arrival of such a large number of Colombian troops. They were encouraged, however, by Dr. Amador's wife, Señora Dona Maria de la Ossa de Amador, who declared that it was now too late to go back on what had been agreed, and that soldiers or no soldiers, they must put up a fight. It was agreed to have Col. Shaler bring over the Colombian generals and leave the troops in Colon; and it was decided that if the troops obtained rolling stock by force to come over, Prescott should go to Miraflores with a powder gang and dynamite the train, when the soldiers could be either shot or taken prisoners by Huertas and his men.

I think credit should be given to Mrs. Amador, with her woman's wit, for the plan to send the generals over and leave the soldiers in Colon. We shall see how afterwards the generals were arrested in

Panama and put out of the way, and the soldiers in Colon were bribed to return to their own country.

There was no need, however, for resorting to extreme measures. At 8 a. m. on November 3, the Colombian gunboat, passing quite close to the *Nashville*, came along the old Panama Railroad wharf and Gens. Juan B. Tovar and Ramon G. Amaya with their aides disembarked. They were met by Gen. Pedro A. Cuadros, prefect of Colon, Dr. Benjamin Aguillera, his secretary, Señor Alejandro Ortiz, chief of the harbor police, Gen. Emiliano Chamorro, and a number of others, among whom was Jose Segundo Ruiz, port captain of Bocas del Toro, who had left his post and come to Colon to warn the Colombian generals of the threatened revolution.

In an affidavit Ruiz thus describes his reasons for coming:

Some time in October, either on the 10th or the 11th, the Norwegian vessel *Breeton* anchored in Admiralty Bay and the captain told me that "he knew for certainty" that a separatist movement was planned in Panama and that it was openly favored by the American Government. That the reason for the separation was the rejection by the Colombian Senate of the Hay-Herran treaty for the opening of an interoceanic canal.

After the generals had exchanged greetings with the Colombian officials, Gen. Tovar called the prefect aside and the two remained talking together for about 10 minutes. They were interrupted by the arrival of Col. Shaler, general superintendent of the Panama Railroad Co., who, as we have seen, was in hearty sympathy with the plans of the revolution and who had that morning already had a conference with Porfilio Melendez and had decided to retain the soldiers in Colon and send the generals over to Panama. Shaler at once addressed himself to Gen. Tovar.

Now what then ensued and the facts which bear upon the actions of Gen. Tovar, I am able to quote from the contemporaneous documents and reports sent by the Colombian general to the minister of war of the Republic of Colombia, which are on file in the war department in Bogota. Gen. Tovar's own words are:

Mr. Shaler invited me at once to take a seat in a special car which by order of Gen. Obaldia he had in readiness for me, and he even insisted that I should do so, telling me that the hour fixed for the departure of the train had already passed, and that it had been held for my arrival.

I pointed out to him that it was not possible for me to accept his invitation, as it was necessary for me to take the proper measures for the disembarkation of the troops I had brought with me, and because I wished to take them with me to Panama; further, as he insisted in his efforts, and I was able to satisfy myself, even by the assurance of the prefect himself, that the troops could and would go over in a special train to be dispatched at 1 p. m., I found no justifiable reason to persist in my refusal, all the more so as I had been sent to Panama to assist the Government against a reported invasion from Nicaragua, and that I had not the slightest idea that a barrack uprising was planned.

When the generals were seated in the special car Gen. Amaya turned to Tovar and said: "Let me remain here with my soldiers. I can not go." "No. You mustn't leave me here all alone," was the commander in chief's rejoinder.

That is the sworn testimony of Ruiz, who was standing by with the general.

But Col. Shaler put an end to all hesitation by blowing his whistle as a signal for the train to start. The general superintendent of the Panama Railroad was acting as train dispatcher that morning. When it had pulled out he went to his office and called up Mr. Prescott on the telephone. He told him that the Colombian generals would arrive at about 11 o'clock; and that he would try to keep the troops in Colon, but he warned Prescott of the danger of the troops taking a train by force.

Immediately after the generals had gone Ruiz went back to Torres and told him that he had come all the way from Bocas del Toro on purpose to warn Gen. Tovar of the plan for a revolution, and pointing to the *Nashville* he said: "That warship is here for no other purpose than to support the separatist movement which is about to break out."

Shortly afterwards Commander Hubbard, who had just received the Navy Department's message of November 2, telling him to prevent the landing of the Government troops, it having been delivered to one of the ship's boats while he was at the consulate and not to the consul, as directed; went to Shaler, who told him that he had already decided not to transport the Colombian troops.

Hubbard remained in Shaler's office "until it was sure that no action on his part would be needed to prevent the transportation of the troops," and he then sent off the following cable:

COLON, *November 3, 1903.*

SECNAY, *Washington:*

Receipt of your telegram of November 2 is acknowledged. Prior to receipt this morning about 400 men were landed here by Government of Colombia from Cartagena. No revolution has been declared on the Isthmus—

Who had been telling him about a revolution?

and no disturbances. Railway company has declined to transport these troops except by request of governor of Panama. Request has not been made. It is possible that movement may be made to-night at Panama to declare independence, in which case I will * * *.

Here the dispatch is said to be mutilated. It ends:

Situation is most critical if revolutionary leaders act.

(Signed) HUBBARD.

Commander Hubbard knew perfectly well that the revolutionary leaders were going to act. He was kept fully informed of what was passing by Col. Shaler, who, immediately after the generals had left, had had a conference with Melendez, with the result that Melendez's daughter, Señorita Aminta Melendez, was sent over to Panama on a fast freight train, with two letters, Amador proposing a plan of action agreed on between Shaler and Melendez. The substance of the letter was that if the Colombian soldiers seized a train to go over to Panama, all their arms and ammunition would be placed in the rear coach, and that when the train got to L'Ion Hill one of Melendez's men would pull the coupling pins and leave the arms stalled in the jungle. (Evidently they had not heard of Prescott's idea that he would go to Miraflores and dynamite the train.) The engineer was then to run his train straight on to Culebra, where he was to abandon the train and leave the army helpless halfway across the Isthmus. It was also proposed to capture the Colombian gunboat *Cartagena*, which had brought the Tiradores regiment to Colon. Knowing that this vessel would need coal and water, Shaler proposed that when she was taking on supplies her commander and officers should be enticed away by Melendez, and that the gunboat should then be boarded and seized by about 30 men under the orders of Capt. Achurra, one of Melendez's lieutenants.

When Prescott, in Panama, received Shaler's message that the Colombian generals were on their way, he went to Amador's house and told him that now or never was the day to act. Amador at once ordered his carriage and drove straight to the Chiriqui Barracks, where he called for Huertas. When the latter came out Amador made a strong appeal to him to remain firm and stick to the agreement made in the governor's office on the preceding day.

Curiously enough, we have a note made by one of Huertas's men, who was standing by and who overheard the conversation. He said: "Huertas, what you are to-day you owe to Panama. From Bogota you can hope for nothing. I am old and tired of life; it is of no importance to me to die. If you will aid us, we shall reach to immortality in the history of the new Republic. Here you will have four American war ships. There will be the same number in Colon. (That turned out to be absolutely true.) You and your battalion can accomplish nothing against the superior force of the cruisers, which have their orders. Choose here, glory and riches; in Bogota, misery and ingratitude."

Huertas remained impassive for a moment, then looked up to Amador and holding out his hand, said: "I accept. Castro does not bother me." Amador shook Huertas warmly by the hand and at once reentered his carriage.

At 10.30 Huertas, at the head of the Colombia regiment, marched down to the Panama Railroad station to receive the generals. On passing the Hotel Italia, on what is now the Avenida Central, Huertas smiled and nodded to Amador, who was standing there.

General Juan B. Tovar arrived in Panama at 11.30 a. m., and if any doubt had ever entered his mind it would quickly have been dispelled by the enthusiastic reception accorded to him on arrival of the train at the Panama Railroad depot.

Gov. Obaldio was there, accompanied by all his official family, including Señor Julio Fabrega Manuel Amador, the son of Dr. Amador; and Nicholas Victoria B. Eduardo, de la Guardia; Dr. Efraim de J. Navia, and Gen. Francisco de P. Castro, military commander of Panama, with his aids, and a large representative gathering of prominent citizens.

On the wide unpaved street leading from the railroad depot to the Plaze, just opposite the depot, the Colombian regiment was drawn up in review order under its commander, Gen. Estaban Huertas, to render the generals military honors, and there was also a strong detachment of the departmental police. The generals entered Gov. Obaldia's carriage and, preceded by the Colombian regiment under Huertas and followed by a long train of carriages with officials, among whom was Felix Ehrman, the United States consul general, he was driven to the Government House. In Tovar's own words, "There was nothing that did not show the greatest cordiality and give me the most complete assurance that peace reigned throughout the department."

On arrival at the governor's house, Obaldia showed Tovar a number of telegrams saying that the reported invasion from Nicaragua had no foundation in fact, and that everything in the interior was perfectly quiet. At about 1 p. m. Obaldia ordered his carriage and accompanied Tovar to the comandancia general above the present post office, where lodgings had been prepared for him.

In the meantime the revolutionary committee was busy. Urged on by his wife, Dr. Amador had notified all the members, most of whom had almost entirely lost heart, that the blow would be struck that very evening, and the young men who were in the fire brigade got their instructions. There was a general rumor all through the town that there was going to be a mass meeting the same evening, but no one outside of the conspirators and the immediate families and friends knew exactly what was going to happen five hours before the fake revolution actually took place. News of this general public rumor first reached Gen. Tovar at 1.30, when Gen. Jose M. Nunez Roca called on him and informed him that his arrival had created great excitement and alarm throughout the city. Gen. Tovar was still talking with Gen. Roca when he received a card from Dr. Jose Angel Porras warning him to be careful, and telling him to place no confidence in anybody. Alarmed by these reports, Gen. Tovar immediately went to the military headquarters, where he assumed command. He was accompanied by Gen. Amaya and, on his order, the latter sent two aids-de-camp to the governor to inform him of the disquieting rumors and to request him to order the immediate dispatch of the train which was to bring the troops from Colon, as word had just been brought that the railroad company would accept such orders only from the governor. In less than half an hour the aides returned, saying that Gov. Obaldia said that all the necessary orders had been given and that it was certain the troops would arrive in the afternoon.

From military headquarters the Colombian generals went to the barracks of the Colombian battalion to take command there and inspect the armory. They were received there by Gen. Huertas and his officers, and inspected the men's quarters and arms.

This having been done, Gen. Tovar went to the sea wall, and just as he was giving instructions to Huertas as how best to defend the position in case of an attack, Senor Julio Fabrega, Gov. Obaldia's secretary, arrived, and told him that the superintendent of the railroad was placing difficulties in the way of dispatching the troops from Colon, according to a telegram that was shown to him, alleging as his reason that certain sums of money were owing to the company.

Gen. Tovar told Senor Fabrega to go straight back to Gen. Obaldia and say that he was ready to pay cash and even to meet all outstanding debt and be personally responsible for all moneys owing, but that the troops must be sent over.

Gen. Tovar was well supplied with money, as the Bogota Government, having informed him that there was little or no cash in the national treasury at Panama, had instructed him that he must take sufficient funds to meet the pay rolls and expenses of his troops, and he had obtained from the collectors of customs in Barranquilla and Cartagena $65,272, American money, which he had brought with him in specie and drafts.

Immediately after Senor Fabrega had left, Gen. Tovar sent two officers to Gov. Obaldia to urge him to obtain the immediate dispatch of his forces from Colon. Gen. Tovar, taking Gens. Amaya and Castro with him, then went to the barracks known as Las Monjas, and from there returned to headquarters to get the report of the aides he had sent to the governor, and they came back, saying that Senor Obaldia had expressed great surprise at the procedure of Col. Shaler, as he (the governor) was sure that nothing was owing to the railroad company, but that in any case the governor was certain that the troops would be dispatched. Still not satisfied, Gen. Tovar sent his colleague, Gen. Amaya, to the Government House to impress upon Gov. Obaldia the necessity for at once transporting the troops. Gen. Amaya, in his report to the minister of war of the Republic of Colombia, on November 14, 1903, thus describes his visit:

When I presented myself I could see that the governor's mind was not at ease, and I made clear to him the necessity of bringing over the troops, offering him in the name of my superior officer the money necessary to pay for the trains. Gov. Obaldia protested to me that there was no need of that, that the orders had been given, and that it was certain that the battalion would be over at 5 p. m.

Gen. Amaya returned to military headquarters, where Gen. Tovar was waiting for him. He found his chief with Dr. Nicolas Victoria J., secretary of public instructions, who said that he did not believe that Gov. Obaldia could control the movement, which was about to break out. Just after Dr. Victoria left, Senor Don Eduardo de la Guardia, departmental head of the national treasury, arrived and told the generals that he was certain the disorder would begin before long, and assume alarming proportions. Pressed by Gen. Tovar for further information, Senor de la Guardia said that he did not believe the governor had given any orders to bring the battalion Tiradores over from Colon, and that he did not believe the governor would give any orders to suppress the threatened uprising, in which he asserted that both the battalion Colombia and the departmental police were involved.

Gen. Tovar immediately sent two of his aids, Gen. Angel M. and Luis Alberto Tovar, to the Panama Railroad telegraph office to see if the telegrams Gov. Obaldia said had been sent had really been taken to the office and dispatched.

He told them on their way back from the telegraph office to call on the governor again, and tell him that as the police had not yet appeared on the streets to maintain order, that he, Gen. Tovar, would go personally at the head of the Colombia battalion and disperse any gathering, so as to restore to the inhabitants the calm they seemed to be rapidly losing.

Telling two other aids, Cols. Jose M. Tovar and Alfredo Campusano, to close up the offices at headquarters and rejoin him at the barracks, Gen. Tovar, accompanied by Gen. Amaya and Gen. Castro, started for the barracks, where Huertas was with his troops.

It was then half-past 4, and the news had spread rapidly all over the town that something was going to happen. Urged on by his wife and encouraged by Prescott, Amador had completed his arrangements. Arango had been sent to tell Dr. Carlos A. Mendoza, the leader of the liberal party, that the movement would take place the same day and ask him to get ready the manifesto and declaration of independence which he had been asked to draft with Dr. Eusebic A. Morales and Señor Juan A. Henrique. Amador had told Duque that the uprising would start at 5 p. m., and it had been decided to vary the original plan to the extent that the members of the fire brigade in answer to the skyrocket signal would go to the armory near the barracks, and that they would break in and distribute arms to the people and make their way to the Plaza de la Catedral and from hence to the barracks to take the Colombian officers prisoners.

Ever since noon messengers had been busy carrying word to friends and relatives of the conspirators that they should arm and meet in the Santa Ana Plaza at 5 p. m. The public generally had been informed that there would be a great mass meeting at that time and place.

These plans narrowly missing going awry, however, as at a little after 2 o'clock Arango, seeing that Arias and Espinosa had shut themselves up in their houses, and feeling disheartened by the evident indecision of the majority of the revolutionary committee, had sent his son Belissario to tell Amador that he had reason to believe that some of the conspirators were going to abandon the cause, but that he and his sons would stand by him and share whatever fate might be his. (Arango's notes.)

Young Arango did not find Amador at his house, but learned that he was at Carlos R. Zachrisson's near the barracks, where he found the chief conspirator and delivered his father's message, further informing him that they would all be in the Santa Ana Plaza at 5 o'clock.

Just as Amador was nearing the house with young Arango on the way to Prescott's, they met Gen. Huertas with one of his adjutants. Huertas then made a proposition to change the plan, and he proposed that the arrest of the Colombian generals should be postponed, and urged that the generals should be arrested at 8 o'clock in the evening, when there was to be a band concert and parade in honor of the officers, and that they would in all probability find themselves separated from one another, and it would be easy to take them prisoner separately.

Belissario Arango at once went back to tell his father, and word was sent to Felix Ehrman, United States vice consul general, who, just as the Colombian generals were on their way to the barracks, received the following cable from the State Department:

WASHINGTON, *November 3, 1903.*

EHRMAN, *Panama:*

Uprising on Isthmus reported. Keep department promptly and fully informed.

LOOMIS, *Acting.*

This cable was brought to Mr. Felix Ehrman at his desk in the Ehrman Bank on the Cathedral Plaza. Young Herman Gudger, the son of the United States Consul General Gudger, who as we have seen was present at the first luncheon at which the independence was considered, was keeping in close touch with the revolutionists during his father's absence. He sat down and at Mr. Ehrman's dictation, wrote and sent off the following reply:

PANAMA, *November 3, 1903.*

SECRETARY OF STATE, *Washington:*

No uprising yet. Reported will be in the night. Situation is critical.

EHRMAN.

Meanwhile the Colombian generals had reached the barracks, where they had found Huertas surrounded by his officers sitting about on benches near the gate to the sea wall. Gen. Tovar at once took Huertas aside and told him that the situation was critical and that he feared the people en masse although unarmed were coming to make a demonstration in front of the barracks. He told Huertas to prepare to defend the barracks, and showed him where he wanted the best marksmen he had placed along the sea wall and at certain points in the barracks inclosure; and he ordered a detachment to form and go out to patrol the streets and maintain order.

At the same time Gen. Tovar said that with his comrades and their aides he would spend the night in the barracks. The Colombian generals then discussed plans and were waiting the return of the aides when Capt. Romero called Gen. Castro aside and told him that groups of rioters were already arriving opposite the barracks. Gen. Amaya went out and returned with Gen. Caycedo Alban and confirmed the news. Gen. Huertas then approached the group and asked Gen. Tovar's permission to order out the first patrol. Gen. Tovar assented, and Huertas, excusing himself to change his coat, went upstairs in the guardhouse, followed a few moments later by Gen. Castro.

A company of soldiers, fully armed for patrol duty, marched out under the command of Capt. Marco A. Salazar, and turning to the right of the sea-wall gate, as if to pass in front of the Colombian officers, opened into two files, one of which passed on either side of the generals. At a word of command the soldiers lowered their bayonets and hemmed the generals in, rendering them completely helpless.

"Generals, you are prisoners," said Salazar.

"I am—the commander in chief," was all Gen. Tovar could say.

"You and your aides," answered Salazar, laughing.

"By whose orders?"

"Gen. Huertas."

In a desperate effort to break through, Gen. Tovar threw himself on the man next to him, but a dozen bayonets were shoved toward him. He ceased to struggle and called to the commander of the patrol, Capt. Salazar, begging him not to be a traitor, but his appeal was only met with jeers. Then he called on the sentinels and soldiers to come to the defense of their country, and denounced the treachery of which he was the victim. All his appeals were useless, and the group of officers was kept standing as prisoners for some minutes. Gen. Tovar called for Huertas, who was not to be seen, and his cries for Gen. Castro failed to elicit any response from that officer.

Gen. Huertas had been taken by surprise at the appearance of the mob in front of the barracks, as he was convinced that his suggestions that the Colombian generals be made prisoners in the evening had been accepted. Young Arango had gone to tell Gen. Domingo Diaz and Mr. Duque that the hour had been changed, but when he got to the Plaza Santa Ana he found Gen. Diaz already surrounded by a crowd. Diaz would not hear of any delay, as it was then nearly 5 o'clock, and he said that he and his brother, Pedro A. Diaz, would themselves lead the populace to the barracks. When they arrived at the Plaza de la Cathedral, the fire brigade was already giving out arms to the people, and they moved on to the barracks. As soon as Huertas saw them he made up his mind to act at once and gave the necessary orders to Capt. Marcos A. Salazar.

The crowd in front of the barracks led by the Diazes, Francisco de la Ossa, young Arango, and a number of younger revolutionists and members of the fire brigade, had grown to several thousand, most of them armed, and surrounded by this throng the generals were marched out of the barracks through the gate to the sea wall across Cathedral Plaza and up what is now Central Avenue to police headquarters, where they were given rooms on the first floor.

All the way the crowd was shouting itself hoarse with cries of "Viva el Istmo libre!" "Viva Huertas!" "Viva el Presidents Amador!" etc., and everyone who had a firearm of any description was discharging it in the air to the no small danger of the many women and children thronging the balconies on the streets.

On the way to the prison the generals were met by their aides, Angel M. and Luis Alberto Tovar, whom they had sent to the telegraph office, who had searched the telegraph office in vain for any sign of the message Gov. Obaldia said he had sent. These two officers, with Col. Carlos Morales, made an attempt to rescue their chiefs, but they were themselves taken into custody and led to prison in the police headquarters.

Amador was in conference with Mr. Prescott at the latter's house when news that the Colombian generals had been arrested was brought to him. Prescott at once called up Colon on the Panama Railroad telephone and got in communication with Señor Porfilio Melendez, the agent of the revolutionists there, and according to a prearranged agreement said: "The sancocho is about to begin." It was then 5.49 p. m.

On the anniversary of that day a year afterwards, Porfilio Melendez sent to Mr. Prescott this card [shows card]:

DEAR PRESCOTT:

I received your card and am very sorry you will not accompany us to-day. Do not forget at 5.49 p. m. to take a drink at this same hour. I shall take it here in commemoration of your words of the 3d of November last year, "the sanchcho is about to begin."

Yours, very truly,

PORFILIO A. MELENDEZ.

Amador at once sent Commander Antonio A. Valdez to arrest Gov. Obaldia, and then went straight to Mr. Felix Ehrman, acting United States consul general, and apprised him of the fact that Panama had severed her bonds with Colombia and that a provisional government of three consuls would at once be formed. Mr. Ehrman immediately dispatched the following cable to the State Department in Washington:

PANAMA, *November 3, 1903.*

Uprising occurred to-night, 6; no bloodshed. Army and Navy officials taken prisoners. Government will be organized to-night, consisting three consuls, also cabinet. Soldiers changed. Supposed same movement will be effected in Colon. Order prevails so far. Situation serious. Four hundred soldiers landed to-day, Paranquilla.

When Arango heard of the general's arrest, he at once went to the Government House, arriving just after Commander Valdez, who found Gov. Obaldia sitting in the drawing room with the keys of the treasury in his hand. Obaldia at once handed the keys to Arango, and, accompanied by Commander Valdez and Col. Augustin Arango, they went to Amador's house, where the governor was informed that he would be left as a prisoner under the guard of the two officers.

I have here a picture of Gov. Obaldia in Amador's house under arrest. He looks a very resigned prisoner! [Shows photograph.]

Coming out of Amador's house, Arango met Amador, Boyd, and Arias in front of the archbishop's palace at the corner of the Cathedral Plaza, and as it had previously been decided that Arango, Boyd, and Arias should form the provisional government, they at once went and signed the letter which had been prepared in the morning in accordance with what Col. Shaler had written to Prescott that the new Government should address to the railroad.

They then went to the Cathedral Plaza, where they were cheered by the crowd. Prescott was standing just in front of Central Hotel, and Arango handed him the letter they had prepared in accordance with Shaler's instructions. It was an almost literal translation of the corresponding part of Shaler's letter to Prescott, and read as follows:

TO THE GENERAL SUPERINTENDENT OF THE PANAMA RAILROAD CO.,
Colon:

We inform you that to-day at 6 p. m. a popular movement took place in this city whereby the independence of this department was declared. It will in future be known as the Republic of the Isthmus.

There has been appointed a provisional junta of government, composed of Senores Jose Augustin Arango, Federico Boyd, and Tomas Ariaz, who, in their official capacity, inform you that, as the government de facto, they are willing to comply with all the obligations of the contract entered into between the Republic of Colombia and the railroad which you represent on the Isthmus in 1850 and 1867, and that in consequence it hopes that you will in turn comply with the provisions of article 19 and other similar depositions of the same contract.

We also inform you that the new government, besides the prestige unanimously conferred on it by all the citizens, has sufficient military force to give complete protection to the interests and property of the railroad whenever you may so request, for which reason it hopes that the transit between this city and Colon will be maintained without interruption as in normal times, and that the government which we represent will not permit under any circumstances foreign elements to interrupt or in any manner interfere with the regular movement of trains.

We are, General Superintendent, your faithful and obedient servants,

JOSE AUGUSTIN ARANGO.
FEDERICO BOYD.
TOMAS ARIAS.

At the same time, Mr. Arango handed a telegram for Col. Shaler to Mr. Prescott with a request that it be at once sent. This telegram read:

HONORABLE SUPERINTENDENT OF THE RAILROAD, *Colon:*

This junta of government has knowledge that the military forces brought to Colon by the steamship *Cartagena* have asked you to transport them to this side, and as this act would be of grave consequences for the company you represent, we urge you not to accede to such request, because the junta of government would see itself obliged to use its armed forces to attack the trains bringing over soldiers at whatever point on the railroad line. We hope that you will inform us of your decision on this most important matter.

J. A. ARANGO.
FEDERICO BOYD.
THOMAS ARIAS.

Mr. Prescott at once borrowed a chestnut horse from Don Francisco de la Ossa, the alcalde of Panama, and rode down to the railroad station where he found his brother Dick. He went to the telegraph office and told Col. Shaler over the wire that the plan had been carried out as agreed, and he gave the two preceding messages to his brother Dick to transmit.

There was quite a crowd of railroad men and other people at the depot, and some little delay ensued in sending the messages.

Just after Dick Prescott had finished, a shell tore through the air overhead and a moment later a report followed. The bombardment of Panama by the Colombian gunboat *Bogota* had begun.

This was in execution of a threat made nearly two hours previously by Col. Martinez, the paymaster of the *Bogota*, who was in charge of the vessel, and who, on hearing that the generals had been arrested and with them Gen. Luis Alberto Tovar, the commander of the *Bogota*, had sent a message that if they were not released within two hours he would bombard the city. For nearly half an hour the firing continued, some five or six shells being thrown in all, to which the battery on the Bovedas sea wall replied; and the *Bogota* "finally withdrew after killing a Chinaman in Salsipuedes Street and mortally wounding an ass in the slaughterhouse. The shell that killed the Chinaman is now in the possession of Prescott, to whom it was presented by Nicanor de Obarrio, one of the members of the revolutionary committee, who afterwards became minister of war.

While the bombardment was still going on the municipal council met under the presidency of Demetrio Brid, editor of the English section of Mr. Suques's Panama Star and Herald, and in the presen e of all of the most prominent conspirators recognized as a de facto government a junta composed of Jose Augustin Arango, Federico Boyd, and Tomas Arias. It also read over the manifesto and declaration of independence and fixed 2 p. m. on the following day for a solemn meeting of the council to be followed by the public reading of the declaration of independence and the formal proclamation of the Republic of Panama. It was there that the almost unanimous sentiment of the people was manifested, and when they were told "We are going to have a republic of our own and it is going to be called the Republic of the Isthmus," they protested and demanded that it be called the Republic of Panama. The manifesto was signed by the three members of the provisional junta, and recited the reasons for the separation in the following terms.

I am not able to prove to you that this is the declaration of independence mentioned in the cable codes as having been prepared in New York, but it reads somewhat as if it might have been:

> The far-reaching act which the inhabitants of the Isthmus of Panama have just executed by a spontaneous movement is the inevitable consequence of a situation which had daily become graver.
>
> Long indeed is the recital of the grievance that the inhabitants of the Isthmus have suffered at the hands of their Colombian brothers, but these grievances would have been borne with resignation for the sake of harmony and national union if it had been possible and if we could have entertained well-founded hopes of improvement and effective progress under the system to which we were subjected by that Republic. We most solemnly declare that we have the sincere and profound conviction that all hopes were futile and all sacrifices on our part vain. The Isthmus of Panama has been governed by the Republic of Colombia with the narrowmindedness which was once shown to their colonies by European nations; the Isthmian people and their territory were a source of fiscal resources and nothing more.

That reference to the narrowmindedness once shown by other European nations never suggested itself to a Latin American mind. Why should a Panaman make direct reference to England's government of her colonies? The manifesto continues:

> The contracts and negotiations regarding the railroad and the Panama Canal and the national taxes collected on the Isthmus have netted to Colombia tremendous sums, which we will not detail here, not wishing to appear in this recital as being animated by a mercenary spirit, which never has been nor is now our purpose.

That is the very last thing those people would have mentioned. Then it goes on to say:

> Of these large sums the Isthmus has not received the benefit of a single road between its towns, nor a public building, nor a single college; neither has it seen any interest displayed in advancing its industries, nor has the most infinitesimal part of those sums ever been applied toward its prosperity.

A very recent example of what we have here set out has occurred with the Panama Canal negotiations, which, when taken under consideration by Congress, were summarily rejected. There were a few public men who expressed their adverse opinion on the ground that the Isthmus of Panama alone was to be favored by the opening of a canal under a treaty with the United States, and that the rest of Colombia would not receive direct benefits of any sort by the work, as if this method of reasoning, even if correct, could justify the irreparable and perpetual damages which would be caused to the Isthmus by the rejection of the treaty in the manner in which it was done, which amounted to closing the door to all future negotiations.

In the presence of such notorious reasons the population of the Isthmus has decided to recover its sovereignty, and to begin to form part of the society of free and independent nations, in order to work out its own destiny, to insure its future in a stable manner, and to discharge the duties incumbent upon it by the situation of its territory and its immense wealth.

To that we, the initiators of the movement, aspire, and we have obtained unanimous approval. We aspire to the formation of a true republic, where tolerance shall prevail, where the law shall be the invariable guide of those who govern, where effective peace shall be established, to consist in the free and harmonious play of all interests and activities, and where, finally, civilization and progress shall find perpetual stability.

At the commencement of the life of an independent nation we fully appreciate the responsibilities of statehood, but we have deep faith in the good sense and patriotism of the isthmian people, and we possess sufficient energy to blaze our way by means of labor to a happy future devoid of troubles or dangers.

In separating from our brothers of Colombia we do so without hatred and without joy. Just as a son withdraws from under the paternal roof, the isthmian people in adopting the course they have chosen have done so in sorrow, but in obedience to the supreme and inevitable duty they owe to themselves and to their own welfare.

We therefore begin to form a nation, one of the free nations of the world, considering Colombia as a sister nation by which we shall stand whenever circumstances so require and for whose prosperity we make the most fervent and sincere wishes.

JOSE AUGUSTIN ARANGO.
FEDERICO BOYD.
TOMAS ARIAS.
PANAMA, *November 3, 1905.*

This manifesto was nominally the work of Dr. Eusebio A. Morales, but is commonly reported in Panama to have been based upon the draft brought back from New York by Amador, referred to in the Amador-Lindo-Bunau-Varilla cable code.

Before the meeting of the municipal council broke up the following cable was sent to President Roosevelt:

A SU EXCELENCIA EL PRESIDENTE DE LOS ESTADOS UNIDOS,
Washington:

The municipality of Panama is now (10 p. m.) holding a solemn session and joins in the movement of separation of the Isthmus of Panama from the rest of Colombia. It hopes for recognition of our cause by your Government.

DEMETRIC H. BRID.

After the meeting of the municipal council and fearing that the *Bogota*, which had steamed out of the bay, might make her way up the coast and, after taking on board the soldiers of the Colombian regiment sent to Penonome under Leoncio Tascon, return to attack the town, Huertas sent the following letter to Tascon to apprise him of what had happened:

No. —.

BATTALION COLOMBIA,
OFFICE OF THE COMMANDING OFFICER,
Panama, November 3, 1903.

TO COMMANDANTE LEONCIO TASCON,
Penonome:

There having broken out to-day a movement for the independence of the Isthmus, which has been carried into effect without the shedding of a single drop of blood, the Government which now holds sway here has been recognized. By necessity, in order to avoid their taking me a prisoner I was obliged to commit to prison some of my superior officers. You must prepare with the men you have with you to come here as soon as you receive this, my order.

The *Bogota* is the only vessel which was hostile, but it is now steaming out of the bay. The *Cartagena* and the *Padilla* are for us.

You are hereby appointed chief of the battalion. I repeat that you are to accept no orders except from me or those sent to you by Dr. Manuel Amador Guerrero.

In Colon there are two American warships which have disembarked forces, and to-morrow morning two more are to arrive here. Thus this movement is supported to overflowing by the Americans. Any effort would have been a useless sacrifice. Therefore we have decided, after careful consideration, to recognize the Government of the Isthmus, as any hostility on our part would have lost us.

In you I have placed my entire confidence.

Your obedient servant and friend, E. HUERTAS.

The letter was taken to Tascon by Don Antonio Burges, who made the trip during the night in a little gasoline launch, the *Campo-Serrano*, at the risk of being taken prisoner by the *Bogota*, which had only taken shelter behind the island in the bay.

Some time after midnight Mr. Felix Ehrman, the acting United States consul general, was roused out of bed by a cable from the State Department, sent from Washington at 11.18. (S. Doc. No. 51, 58th Cong.) It read:

EHRMAN, *Panama:*

Message sent to *Nashville* to Colon may not have been delivered. Accordingly, see that the following message is sent to *Nashville* immediately:

"NASHVILLE, *Colon:*

"In the interests of peace make every effort to prevent Government troops at Colon from proceeding to Panama. The transit of the Isthmus must be kept open and order maintained. Acknowledge.

"DARLING, *Acting.*"

Secure special train if necessary. Act promptly.

LOOMIS, *Acting.*

Mr. Ehrman at once called up Col. Shaler in Colon, and the latter promised to immediately send the message to Commander Hubbard. He also told Mr. Ehrman that under no circumstances would he move the troops. This was the last telephone communication between the city of Panama and Colon, as at daybreak the next morning all the wires had been cut by Dick Prescott and Ernesto Lefevre, acting under instructions from Prescott. Prescott, however, had intended to leave one wire running to his own house, and had given his brother a diagram showing which wire not to cut, but in the excitement Prescott's wire was cut with the rest, and the only place from which communication could be had with Colon was the Panama railroad station.

The CHAIRMAN. Mr. Hale, if this is a convenient place, we will take a recess.

The committee thereupon took a recess until 2 o'clock p. m.

BOGOTA, *January 29, 1902.*

SECSTATE, *Washington:*

48457 38443 53236 56324 55266 39549.

HART.

BOGOTA, *January 29, 1902.*

SECSTATE, *Washington:*

ABTCP 21474 32484 35008 20823 21271 46255 20844 56527 50526 14013 50526 37779 46256 31700.

HART.

BOGOTA, *January 27, 1901.*

SECSTATE, *Washington:*

OABGM 21470 42862 53811 53797 39940 31891 36808 54019 37371 13634 54688 53797 54019 28162 16290 21308 11717 31361 46686 31260 36808 57154 48800 50673 32681 11646.

HART.

BOGOTA, *February 1, 1902.*

SECSTATE, *Washington:*

OBACP 47366 53236 37553 54669 39673 20217 21966 47045 44360 36523 15551 13547 35801 20645 22454 34186 41395 30913 13634 56251 40292 33577 38862 28299 29727.

HART.

BOGOTA, *February 20, 1902.*

SECSTATE, *Washington:*

Bajla 47358 53217 30798 36478 39673 43309 19955 36155 45464 53403 39883 42440 21770 31665 42463 30946 53846 29645 16716 35406 45096 53403 42654 22772 22045 19846 22766 47462 26683 13707 20965 53579 52049 27281 38971 55558 37374 15393 35993 24882 43750 56527 19955 21971 42503 32571 54688 40170 27635.

HART.

BOGOTA, *22 de Feb. de 1902.*

SECSTATE, *Washington:*

BBAKP 22584 12640 42463 43309 19955 21971 34186 19768 34279 21971 54011 53846 31779 31150 46619 42712 34875 21971 11722 37449 26802 53468 21470 15731 16696 50051 37448 22317 53991 32567 53720 27699 57744 40950 46177 58727 48214 17644 32629 42654 57744 56133 42652 22454 53450 42654 28164 13634 35006 56706 53992 30539 51181 17644 53991 50051 45860 13634 22318 53991 13501 21971 57288 42638 13634 28157 15130 57744 32567 57746 21470 42929 51186 17644 24882 27553 57728 36401 40741 28714 46619 12640 27601 37996 53403 33700 23887 34279 53198.

HART.

BOGOTA, *February 24, 1902.*

SECSTATE, *Washington:*

BBDCP 32536 21664 58170 38944 29784 32225 40916 12588 48810 57492 32196 31361 41339 18944 30818 23476 53999 50735 39036 34103 58170 13244 21989 51030 31361 28827 32536 30024 49468 58172 48548.

HART.

BOGOTA, *February 26, 1902.*

SECSTATE, *Washington:*

BBGCP 47358 53215 54671 36478 15096 53464 41791 30946 53797 53464 18555 54524 24314 15269 47320 32563 30818 23476 19461 41732 47658 26409 47028 32563 44302 37330 24727 42473 44747 28781 29224.

HART.

BOGOTA, *February 27, 1902.*

SECSTATE, *Washington:*

BBGAP 47358 53217 58170 32565 12274 37446 31361 58170 42391 41238 43579 10861 24999 10863 33445 28158 42440 18944 67250 39388 35228 29224 48810 54130 56036 18393 30818 23476 53999.

HART.

BOGOTA, *March 3, 1902.*

SECSTATE, *Washington:*

COCCP 32536 31361 12091 51792 43633 56822 42407 35187 34708 41339 18944 55898 19584 48810 57473 11396 32536 12239 14859 26334 50917 13634 49968 29224.

HART.

BOGOTA, *March 6, 1902.*

SECSTATE, *Washington:*

OCTTP 53999 36472 41630 40216 36919 34242 39673 19955 55025 21204 33700 36550 41786 36148 31850 32555 52136 49258 36929 57923 36142 19493 53787 56840 31226 53991 37980 17224 55601 21470 26236 44240 19955 41485 40263 33475 39750 22587 39926 52238 31150 22432 44927 53995 41494 55266 12774 57744 19955 21971 12539 12774 57744 55266 33927 41381 22454 32830 51314 57510 37371 32830 41594 19955 57250 17514 42680 13327

43703 13707 56527 31175 41258 23489 31175 41724 58164 12553 19955 13641 14717 17805 45860 21458 20511 58314 53811 40160 50721 19955 21466 44506 43263 19584 55266 43700 19584 55266 45456 53037 22317 21301 51764 43309 17272 37345 27943 38754 42463 23489 35685 21466 45874 32793 28137 19955 38159 32624 47709 15467 45164 23489 24067 22317 53991 55266 26507 56236 13540 46858 53460 21971 30850 14218 23489 57744 55266 41039 52177 22737 26644 24561 14226 44493 41786 28993 27070 40263 49264 41633 21450 37317 31972 12274 53626 56251 33927 38494 18944 18126 39679 17878 53766 52072.

HART.

BOGOTA, *March 20, 1902.*

SECSTATE, *Washington:*

President Sanclemente died nineteenth instant.

BEAUPRE.

BOGOTA, *March 22, 1902.*

SECSTATE, *Washington:*

21470 33577 32629 Asphaltum 22317 53991 Bidlake 13501.

BEAUPRE.

BOGOTA, *March 22, 1902.*

SECSTATE, *Washington:*

CBBKA 32563 13960 35187 56227 41351 18944 15100 32225 55913 43036 53450 55263 48803 31333 57301 39945 20081 38208 40699.

BEAUPRE.

BOGOTA, *May 15, 1902.*

SECSTATE, *Washington:*

EAEJA 35692 54195 35369 18954 13634 52681 24303 47625 52025 40161 49047 18394 56537 41364 28756 54524 38469 21308.

BEAUPRE.

BOGOTA, *May 15, 1902.*

SECSTATE, *Washington:*

EAEEP 47358 53248 37553 54669 22305 20217 Fluvial 21971 47036 47974 30915 21470 56278 48865 22221 55677 39230 56171 15393 18260 37797 27938 27463 42440 46195 42842 19584 55635 41414 44927 36843 13634 54403 46623 15322 28344 49761 40216 23329 21971 33634 18475 50015 17767 47014 34273 13634 35790 57220 42942 18102 31354 17282 34821 53703 30353 53346 42440 50327 19051 15551 48700 56171 34273 13634 35790 17922 42500 21971 48099 19584 32580 Bolivar 30336 43126 44074 42440 Ford 57909 22249 54688 44489 36410 32539 56352 53403 32563 57937 12573 53016 56171 53403 32563 57937 36792 56171 20213 31764 31175 32563 31668 36539 57622 54292 32577 48701 56171 53991 21971 50317 46548 42440 34273 13634 35790 13792 12076 40656 41377 31175 47884 15551 46675 21971 32577 36532 48027 15551 22098 56508 46020 47247 28592 36804 35369 54171 40216 22084 56508 44960 35369 51733 32782 15551 53336 21971 40216 39388 49367 22086 56278 48865 21470 38643 27898 35369 32501 19461 25883 21971 17922 50886 42986 31175 33573 54381 32232 40216 21715 55156 42625 27280 Ford 30915 14750 30977 46675 46761 35369 24680 55407 24314 45070 21739 20217 49761 14278 53991 26763 47230 54472 24316 53703 49024 13634 44074 35369 25078 57744 32545 53379 39285.

BEAUPRE.

BOGOTA, *May 28, 1902.*

SECSTATE, *Washington:*

EBHDP 12862 Dobson 21037 42440 Morgan 41793 27867 39704 54673.

BEAUPRE.

BOGOTA, *June 12, 1902.*

SECSTATE, *Washington:*

FABKA 25410 46202 41726 36478 35693 35179 42604 31398 39971 30804 43787 31850 37741 30915.

BEAUPRE.

BOGOTA, *June 12, 1902.*

SECSTATE, *Washington:*

FABJA 47366 53238 39704 50927 22305 25409 42440 32577 16237 Bocas 40216 47390 32580 43309 53991 42842 35006 11113 53464 25409 15393 14393 38276 42440 31927 21971.

BEAUPRE.

BOGOTA, *June 27, 1902.*

SECSTATE, *Washington:*

FBGCP 47366 53238 37755 28346 21470 47425 43888 29074 20099 Robinson 57744 32964 13634 13527.

BEAUPRE.

BOGOTA, *July 23, 1902.*

SECSTATE, *Washington:*

15269 50919 41803 35328.

HART.

BOGOTA, *July 25, 1902.*

SECSTATE, *Washington:*

GBECP 32536 13960 52677 Caicedo 35187 32915 20805 13702 17084 25959 Tolima 57168 17908 27622 32681 24854 53720 28686 32536 29774 28116 43245 25961.

HART.

BOGOTA, *August 6, 1902.*

SECSTATE, *Washington:*

OHFDP 47366 53238 49765 36478 39673 43632 31175 Granger and Kennedy 40216 33577 50172 32225 42869 19584 39283 57598 53242 32626 43632 20246 22008 53471 56195 42842 53580 41630 32577 13768 40216 16189 53417 17318 38567.

HART.

BOGOTA, *August* 7.

SECSTATE, *Washington:*

44371 Amsink 41631 31147 19760 37892 42092 43242 43242 31722 42625 39299 47706 47781 28092 39192 10842 37892.

HART.

BOGOTA, *August 8, 1902.*

SECSTATE, *Washington:*

OHHAP 47366 53811 41723 54661 37757 13831 53811 30807 14719 53707 58153 46994 38252 58050 35007 Ellerby Bucaramanga 15769 45837 21073 47967 37985 57154 30870 21109.

HART.

BOGOTA, *August 8, 1902.*

SECSTATE, *Washington:*

OHHAP 52419 53403 53243 18260 41945 32505 13634 39283 56149 14243 35187 17282 53238.

HART.

BOGOTA, *August 12, 1902.*

SECSTATE, *Washington:*

OHMLA 53224 28347 36478 47036 Ellerbys 45836 53416 21037.

HART.

BOGOTA, *August 11, 1902.*

SECSTATE, *Washington:*

OHKAP 47366 53238 30799 37757 22305 46026 24629 21054 13634 36779 19584 55268 23169 21470 41913 39750 53999 53423 32636 48214 36526 32582 11402 53254 23169.

HART.

BOGOTA, *August 13, 1902.*

SECSTATE, *Washington:*

HACEP 14563 22305 22438 42625 37371 35194 34186 13634 35229 32352 41651 31850 43309 32563 37289 34657 54524 53468 21308 13634 35276 40741 22584 17927 43902 49932 24016 21474 13634 19265 57260 21470 15984 52054 48866 53016 31175 40161 55677 14218 31398 56167 31617 35369 21466 44657 13634 25384 53991 12708 47396 29681 48864 47459 19281.

HART.

BOGOTA, *August 21, 1902.*

SECSTATE, *Washington:*

HBABP 47366 31665 34631 31665 54672 37757 47045 53579 41732 56706 49501 41102 34186 42440 Amsincks 21073.

HART.

BOGOTA, *August 21, 1902.*

SECSTATE, *Washington:*

HBABP 47366 31665 34631 50337 54675 37757 13368 55031 53403 27891 22030 39239 53911 50016 45860 34866 13489 21054 41030 23411 52363 57803 44868 47751.

HART.

BOGOTA, *August 27, 1902.*

SECSTATE, *Washington:*

HBGDP 47358 53217 58170 53450 43984 15216 50185 40795 53992 47800 54136 53465 32681 44284 54019 28158 19632 52558 53441 17101 56196 56036 51194 31829 32563 47492 53626 15223 15393 31742 24889 54019 32536.

HART.

BOGOTA, *August 26, 1902.*

SECSTATE, *Washington:*

HBTTP 41705 32563 46341 45440 53450 35006 44981 42463 45164 21473 56675 57473 15258 34186 11058 54688 40704 13634 57507 13536 31408 44273 35369 44828 53450 45164 45207 13135 50356 42941 45779 35406 44534 13634 21736 57858 51885 42941 18263 49722 31175 53450 42481 23020 35369 50798 10842 39930 11751 45211 46068 12609 52464 50560 42440 48810 57493 20121 42815 52683 34405 47062 13529 13536 50784 41832 15216 37323 32225 57507 35369 21618 18944 57055 32563 35007 44934 53450 45164 56577 43103 13634 57803 57521 44306 49741 45164 35718 33680 52274 53720 32225 33577 53999 50172 45211 13634 40224 52049 41859 46068 12609 15223 39204 41705 49541 34004 27601 57731 53997 54374 26675 31870 30708 50784 13634 44488 53450 36225 42440 45211 54124 53768 57473 39204 34242 53626 15223 33634 51669 53450 21954 13656 26874 19585 18194 28419 57400 52583 32571 53450 15216 17922 52049 43970 15564 44534 31829 45211 49262 53626 43984 56869 23059 43101 32571 57318 17454 49254 22587 37289 42747 52054 19584 39525 36122 31502 52590 13634 33577 38862 29499 15068 52737 37374 57797 37448 43135 43567 15223 33634 20314 55154 35277 13656 47461 15393 11951 56782 32539 50919 37289 17008 13634 45790 47869.

HART.

BOGOTA, *August 29, 1902.*

SECSTATE, *Washington:*

HBJMM 22584 47358 53217 54673 36478 32580 53720 25944 48372 35369 46041 40216 53263 39750 35369 52020 22565 53403 34245 13768 40219 12274 45211 53491 11379 39930 45184 13634 36945 48376 45208 18185 53500 51782 16807 24545 49538 53417 48628 51213 53450 24198 50042 52316 40216 47471 50920 32563 15393 36983 40224 37289 32535 45211 27357 34279 24340 13634 30607 27175 34242.

HART.

BOGOTA, *May 1°, 1902.*

SECSTATE, *Washington:*

OEALA 21470 36544 32580 43309 25311 31751 20422 12899 53233 18630 23183 13634 18630 38512 13634 23183 55242 18630 40213 42785 23183 13634 21642 56169 42440 55266.

BEAUPRE.

BOGOTA, *March 31, 1902.*

SECSTATE, *Washington:*

CCAJA 30793 30818 23478 54019 41791 41339 Guatavita 31566 40160 31868 30797 53797 39940 28829 11396 32536 12324 15100 Uribe Uribe 48809 25497 54677 13711 48671 32536 31361 23478 12086.

BEAUPRE.

BOGOTA, *April 9, 1902.*

SECSTATE, *Washington:*

ODJDP 38201 36630 32536 51298 15100 48810 21629 Uribe Uribe 25497 26885 41339 Medina 13634 34013 31109 54130 56036 14292 56537 38207.

BEAUPRE.

BOGOTA, *April 15, 1902.*

SECSTATE, *Washington:*

DAEKA 32225 55913 15112 53811 53797 52049 32550 38463 37372 43309.

BEAUPRE.

BOGOTA, *October 9, 1903.*

SECSTATE, *Washington:*

OKJLA 47183 20916 46513 52371 49381 52867 56780 44335 11724 43000 35329 44567 46322 16772 53149 13152 14336 38396 19113 21129 34527 40870 33789 29206 36606 21475 43000 18793 10788 20628 28573 33600 47008 40653 46506 21129 12792 38937 20622 16802 27792 10320 52608 39812 21188 42100 10640 52626 21129 11430 31177 50371 33900 49093 47151.

BEAUPRE.

BOGOTA, *October 10, 1903.*

SECSTATE, *Washington:*

OKKAP 44333 20983 47151 43956 54653 53819 52375 49381 52867 50899 30077 53846 20326 47168 52608 52861 37360 44351 44913 37444 13859 29208 53082 31787 19113 21129 43000 13433 52895 45074 56902 28940 52561 49228 56755 40615 44917 and 13152 29208 53026 10533 41290 50872 52371 40884 33743 52845 19385 30000 55545 29208 53082 53177 21129 16787 13153 44658 21908 56961 52236 21524 10788 41788 47151.

BEAUPRE.

BOGOTA, *October 8, 1903.*

SECSTATE, *Washington:*

KOHJA 21742 20629 51429 tgxxuj 49344 53149 55832 11668 21899 33344.

BEAUPRE.

BOGOTA, *October 17, 1903.*

SECSTATE, *Washington:*

KAGAP 35313 21745 52561 18914 57328 26215 45706 41598 47012 19113 40652 54424 12925 11014 16772 30300 18742 39625 50566 28265 53149 55832 45454 39178 26550 21930 24942 17325 52867 35636.

BEAUPRE.

BOGOTA, *October 23, 1903.*

SECSTATE, *Washington:*

KDCLA 47183 20960 40990 26216 13469 53166 21930 36447 43500 10000 55621 31325 28563 41294 14784 15645 44391 34549 39173 53177 21912 12892 52561 18091 48420 21911 54653 30825 45333 18909 30656 39374 31575 38908 35321 52561 15395 39046 18912 11744 26214 19113 45692 36532 17418 45074 49294 12742 28268 12803 20917 41598 52969 44937 39098 53149 55832 47008 40643.

BEAUPRE.

BOGOTA, *October 27, 1903.*

SECSTATE, *Washington:*

·KBGGP 47176 20960 26219 24188 49224 41812 30823 49235 50693 Caro 41905 45086 37444 41598 15875 14551 54089 31956 52561 13376 31201 10788 56408 31721 39285 52174 12792 30913 52189 55735 51291 13809 31201 21895 12925 52878 21895 48015 17901 10797 41598 40814 41598 33162 51212 25082 53574 36607 12926 49206 40019 41598 54424 34527 25413 51505 53541 49234 Groot 41804 15836 41168 50693 34527 48531 53208 49234 Ospina 24695 45086 37455 15875 30008 49234 Arango 11668 43646 52608 31200 41598 45086 37444 56525 41812 53574 56902 39763 56408 31725 24478 53977 45074 26233 of 56672 38825 16440 43956 34941 14696 55735 53086 30333 49228 26215 36532 52608 49235 13452 53149 11866 45053 52613 44402 41668 20430 24277 56961 55545 52209 10788 16612 52195 53169 49943 14629 12293 44663 38837 16612 12182 to 27018 28203 21908 41783 52869 35636.

BEAUPRE.

BOGOTA, *Julio 8 de 1902.*

GUSTATORIS, *New York:*

Arrived June thirty mahlon.

BEAUPRE.

BOGOTA, *July 24, 1902.*

SENATOR SCOTT, *Washington:*

You, Elkins, Hopkins, arrange for Beaupre. Cable result.

HART.

BOGOTA, *July 25, 1902.*

HOPKINS, *Aurora, Illinois:*

Hart cabled Scott see you and arrange for me.

BEAUPRE.

BOGOTA, *July 30, 1902.*

BEAUPRE, *Aurora, Illinois:*

Conflexure Comique Hopkins Hart Cabled Scott controller appeach for Beaupre deganeur technical.

BEAUPRE.

BOGOTA, *August 7, 1902.*

GUDGER, *Consul Americano, Panama:*

46216 11460.

HART.

BOGOTA, *August 5, 1902.*

CONSUL AMERICANO, *Panama:*

43518 52392 38908 20113 50077 52623 36529.

HART.

BOGOTA, *August 11, 1902.*

GUDGER, *Consul Americano, Panama:*

At the request of the President of Cuba, expressed through the Department of State and this legation, the Colombian Government permits United States consular officers within its jurisdiction to use their good offices in representation of the interests of Cuba and of its citizens until Cuban consuls shall have been appointed, and will so notify governors. Notify your dependencies, also Cartagena and Barranquilla.

HART.

BOGOTA, *August 23, 1902.*

GUDGER, *Consul Americano, Panama:*

56167 50077 41783 36529 11460 54917 40366 41851 44506 24948 41598 52391 31721 45375 11482 53354 36709 41598 24646 41598 47958 41783 36529 41034 17066 31566 41693.

HART, *Minister.*

WASHINGTON 6, BUENAVA 6, HONDA 16 *Mayo, 1902.*

BEAUPRE, *Charge, Bogota:*

EOFDP 48073 3991 21410 that 32577 16237 Bocas 19584 25409 47433 43890 for 38276 38445 35006 34533 57803 42640 53797 27635 49902 28099 53404 34828 36598 20119 38274 40654 31436 13634 53985 38274 56179 ipso facto 35569 32536 43842 47793 12588 42842 as 55405 13634 42777 54019 38276 65734 38894 31927 32571 24143 11549 in 31439 42430 40654 13634 39034 of 53985 53991 43139 53830 36303.

HILL, *Acting.*

WASHINGTON 18, BUENAVA 18, *de Junio, 1902.*

BEAUPRE, *Charge, Bogata:*

Ask Government telegraph customs Barranquilla to permit entry Captain Robinson, United States Army, and brother, with outfit for collecting zoological specimens, including specimens, guns, and limited amount ammunition. Mission entirely scientific. Sailed June fourteenth.

HAY.

WASHINGTON 2, BUENAVA 2, *de Agosto, 1902.*

HART, *Minister, Bogata:*

Ask Government instruct governor of Bolivar to issue passports to Granger and Kennedy at Barranquilla allowing them to carry food supplies to mining dredger on Atrato River. Operatives, including sick woman, are in actual need.

ADEE, *Acting.*

WASHINGTON 28, BUENAVENTURA 28, *Augusto, 1902.*

HART, *Minister, Bogota:*

HBHKA 15322 28344 54383 31567 51915 29156 and 52386 55790 43842 53383 27604 51911 57055 22030 17514 39204 but 11396 45419 36843 45456 is 52183 50015 42654 56707 40161 41414 and 53301 22030 39213 53911 50015 40161 21633 41030 20303 47003 53997 32408 57372 50256 43138 42300 35790 32847 19584 54383.

ADEE, *Acting.*

WASHINGTON, 4, BUENAVA 4 *setiembre, 1902.*

HART, *Minister, Bogota:*

Replying to cable August 25, Amsinck has presented evidence of citizenship.

ADEE, *Acting.*

WASHINGTON 16, BUENAVA 16, *Septiembre, 1902.*

HART, *Minister, Bogota:*

14090 58213 53198 28429 22403 28313 53991 19247 43703 95211 33577 16723 21635 20951 53991 55693 42522 27034 11386 44927 54019 26233 28706 43842 23140 21478 57597 23834 26688 42440 21925 18944 39388 26770 21923 58191 impractical 45165.

ADEE, *Acting.*

WASHINGTON 28, BUENAVA 29, *Septiembre, 1902.*

HART, *Minister, Bogota:*

JDJOP 47987 58227 19760 42440 54669 19246 20222 to 16463 21470 13634 25804 3500 and 49726 37149 56241 46249 of 24646 42536 48334 48865 32571 45173 21096 For 35799 18229 36286 43567 36523 43070 31515 and 45164 21102 53720 25945 35369 55760 39492.

ADEE, *Acting.*

WASHINGTON 7, BUENVA 7, *Octe., 1902.*

HART, *Bogota:*

33634 23211 49808 43842 35810 42463 35227 of 27277 42441 56166 57803 22876 22737 the 29715 42463 50276 1494 53403 41732 56160 17392 51380 30005 47492 16237 18331 10990 to 22158 21466 48214.

HAY.

WASHINGTON 7, BUENAVA 7, *Octubre, 1902.*

HART, *Bogota:*

33634 23211 49808 43842 35810 42463 35227 of 27277 42441 56166 57803 22876 22737 the 29715 42463 50276 1494 53403 41732 56160 17392 51380 30005 47492 16237 18331 10991 to 22158 21466 48214.

HAY.

WASHINGTON 16, BUENAVA 16, *Octe., 1902.*

HART, *Minister, Bogota:*

KAFVP 32571 47501 40514 57300 14275 15022 in 43309 41732 36688 to 36195 51314 42785 57963 26715 of 21444 13489 21632 56577 36527 35404 50158 42423 53326.

HAY.

WASHINGTON 27, BUENAVA 27, *Octe., 1902.*

HART, *Minister, Bogota:*

KBGDP 32225 qszmlv 47023 34279 36539 19461 25384 21885 53500 54008 32798 53416 27339 53471 11630 42457 42517 42625 37371 54581 39391 21470 55017 53419 53627 25349 39381 54384 57774 45211 is 19072 19637 urssrua 38286 53991 19374 10842 19955 56196 41658 53404 32021 25676 17614 45074.

HAY.

WASHINGTON 29, BUENAVA 29, *Octubre, 1902.*

HART, *Minister, Bogota:*

KBJLA 55268 56051 17908 53253 42300 22876 the 56064 53031 54952 34279 20669 the 53279 46026 21466 49192.

HAY.

WASHINGTON 22, BUENAVA 23, *Novbre., 1902.*

HART, *American Minister, Bogota:*

LBBLA 42640 22717 21470 on 511 21079 56527 in 21444 13768 18203 42440 56980 34419 17614 43843 of 43703 13634 46002 43843 54688 56752 39204 12899 44748 22318 to 21444 35369 19955 39267 33634 20390 15322 54670 13135 46534 of 143924 13634 50306 40314 22318 19540 32472 30454 37384 35718 on 21444 41945 49537 45810 57247 56495 the 1995 5 42800 41658 42503 43821 49475 54383.

HAY.

WASHINGTON 21, BUENAVA 21, *Novbre., 1902.*

HART, *Ministro, Bogota:*

Protectu cffee of meckc at predonia Medellín and Caracolí on proof american oflnershes.

HAY.

WASHINGTON 25, BUENAVA 25, *Novbre, 1902.*

HART, *Bogota:*

Assomoning.

GUILFORD.

WASHINGTON 25, BUENAVA 25, *Novbre, 1902.*

HART, *Ministro, Bogota:*

LBEAP 17032 31850 40213 JGUQEC 10842 39926 47434 11264 42979 45940 41923 12899 42979 22318 43842 55301 21470 36523 34242 50758 45211 22022 22933 50251 57009 41655 53997 27669.

HAY.

WASHINGTON 1°, BUENAVA 1°, *Dicbre, 1902.*

HART, *Minister, Bogota:*

Dobson sec consular convention article 3 section ten lait sentence do not incur indefinite exprense unless estate will certainly de fray.

HILL, *Acting.*

WASHINGTON 3, BUENAVA 3, *Dicbre, 1902.*

HART, *Ministro, Bogota:*

MPCDP 42290 27409 16156 53403 34179 46706 37289 16723 72347 19955 41478.

HAY.

WASHINGTON 9, BUENAVA 9, *Dicbre, 1902.*

HART, *Minister, Bogota:*

Duque brought suit shivering doctor settlement.

MORGAN.

WASHINGTON 10, BUENAVA 11, *Dicbre, 1902.*

HART, *Minister, Bogota:*

MOKLA 44360 38593 57231 42800 34179 46706 37330 47005 34279 44849 53945 24553.

HAY.

WASHINGTON 17, BUENAVA 17, *Dicbre, 1902.*

GUIFORD, *American Legation, Bogota:*

Bimanous afueeken.

WASHINGTON 30, BUENAVA 30, *Dicbre., 1902.*

MCODP 50556 56824 12692 42500 34179 46706 53298 40171 27781 13634 42640 34631 53797 43786 47864 al 32343 34243 28359 11278 or 47414 55632 32536 50136 29959 36539 13634 34872 50078 23892 53500 54008 40916 35105 22761 12015 41658 49002.

HAY.

WASHINGTON 3, BUENAVA 3, *Enero, 1903.*

HART, *Minister, Bogota:*

AOCLA 21271 41478 33700 42500 34179 46706 53720 46146 46621 37384 12751 that 12540 22118 42463 19965 34828 21000 50594 49970 37817 an 35685 42465 71087 13993 54691 32576 55590 36274 of 28369 39704 22921 52134 of 52341 35685 53830 26755 41478 28706 46621 13585 35006 14019 37289 55636 26233.

HAY.

WASHINGTON 16, BUENAVA 16, *Enero, 1903.*

HART, *Minister, Bogota:*

AAFKA 58233 37553 30946 47016 53707 38428 21470 43960 in 45164 16481 37374 47847 32019 41485 35228.

HAY.

WASHINGTON 28, BUENAVA 28, *Enero, 1903.*

HART, *Bogota:*

Bring october.

——— ———.

WASHINGTON 4, BUENAVA 4, *Febr°., 1903.*

HART, *Bogota:*

Minister Yes.

SCOTT.

WASHINGTON 18, BUENAVA 18, *Mayo, 1903.*

BEAUPRÉ, *American Legation, Bogota:*

Inform Colombian Government Senate yesterday approved canal convention without amendment.

LOOMIS, *Acting.*

WASHINGTON 6, BUENAVA 6, *Abril, 1903.*

BEAUPRÉ, *Minister, Bogota:*

Pan American Investment Company understands that supreme court on application attorney general has canceled concessions without due process of law. Investigate and report final proceedings and judgment of supreme court.

LOOMIS.

WASHINGTON 7, BUENAVA 7, *Abril, 1903.*

BEAUPRÉ, *Minister, Bogota:*

47358 48249 42440 21444 to 19955 13634 46672 21966 31175 14471 of 12642 41469 Cancellation 42463 45164 22318 29298 34875 52124 15016 36134 21470 53439 54383 24418 29044 39667 13653 20583 17644 56293 ipronor 38286 13731 43878.

HAY.

WASHINGTON 12, BUENAVA 12, *May, 1903.*

BEAUPRÉ, *Minister, Bogota:*

33577 45232 21444 48370.

LOOMIS, *Acting.*

BOGOTA, *September 6, 1902.*

SECSTATE, *Washington:*

OJTDP 40216 26253 36140 53403 34279 32536 57905 14523 58213 42522 53991 19247 43703 24314 29236 42625 37371 57200 48800 37289 52051 32571 33584 41630 53346 42498 19461 53697 58213 42522 39704 16750 35926 48810 11264 53346 34197 42500 13790 45336 42942 35981 34106 39034 42440 38754 40216 11688 41822 37289 46548 42440 34605 37203 19461 38953 56537 38231 22752 17282 23650 13774 23408 56537 25692 52163 53464 19955 39667 54019 22737 40216 28576 53720 38200 44472 15393 18260 56840 45L73 22958.

HART.

BOGOTA, *September 10, 1902.*

SECSTATE, *Washington:*

OJKMM 32563 13960 35187 52676 42440 32225 Carriago 56491 42700 57744 52049 48803 31333 42625 32681 44284 28158 42440 18944 53721 47462 43245 42463 57510 28162 47477 32563 13960 13150 48201 42441 48803 16337 42603 32536 56166 42625 39258 48929 42625 53703 36478.

HART.

BOGOTA, *September 15, 1902.*

SECSTATE, *Washington:*

JAEDP General Perdomo 14448 40213 42440 32536 57744 45238 44847 13694 33577 38494 31175 43309 34013 52049 39438 13711 50038 31282 40463 34406 53417 24614 48802 42625 37371 30593 34279 37686 17454 36802 50251 19637 45162 42441 38194 31333 48810 57744 15382 42625 39258 48929 32563 33577 26326 54688 53797 39940 54584 27235 53627 48810 40213 42440 54367 32484 15393 23150 33937 54584 22106 30856 15180 47670 45254 41452.

HART.

BOGOTA, *September 20, 1902.*

SECSTATE, *Washington:*

JBOCP Marin 40843 20056 13634 54534 42463 32915 20813 33577 52679 53471 30771 31144 47713 54005 45517 17282 50593 15504 20813 17922 38237 53579 38961 14218 35187 48803 18933 35406 36808.

HART.

BOGOTA, *September 22, 1902.*

SECSTATE, *Washington:*

JBBCP 21037 56180 42457 21079 56527 48317 36577 52056 54688 39940 57760 51864 15221 13816 18260 53037 45441 17690 53471 31002 42441 52875 19591 42510 54984 42869 51148 17689 34242 53471 19578 42465 48848 43842 45440 56580 17690 12573 35406 19186 13634 30255 13634 11396 51738 44131 57473 56326 34242 30946 25035 38242 56577 36286 50251 12510 41710 25035 35370 31615 45440 56580 47639 13586 28888 32423 30946 34631 27637 19009 37909 43703 43842 18405 38754 53997 24874 33581 21272 34279 19455 13634 21570 53991 18944 34010 33634 14218 51268 42440 34077 55495 56580 47639 53513 34279 51730 53063 19637 12853 12343 42410 11058 53298 25035 27402 31475 18944 13634 52628 12911 29254 30300 17614 25875 16687 53536 45369 37780 54019 43019 39438 13707 36786 42934 13506 35413 53950 42440 25856 34742 15645 36539 25813 35006 35799 53997 30958 19637 25951 35395 37727 35799 17544 38410 53298 53797 27636.

HART.

BOGOTA, *September 26, 1902.*

SECSTATE, *Washington:*

JBTMM 47358 53217 58170 39673 56268 54524 43309 56582 37181 54019 43278 40795 57170 47051 19584 45211 40216 13634 40224 57508 40940 27469 19585 53227 32580 43309 12325 38164 56268 54524 57252 11590 25341 30882 37795 35406 50917 43842 56246 23775 53213 58170 56869 47558 28580 19461 44531 13705 56577 55633 53250 35007 25967 53403 32571 48249 57783 42463 56268 54524 13767 53627 17325 38163 12573 55301 32580 43309 51095 48214 43842 52011 38126 42625 24873 21435 42625 37371 13734 34494 46195 25853 28453 24314 43842 32571 16856 14216 58213 56244.

HART.

BOGOTA, *September 24, 1902.*

SECSTATE, *Washington:*

JBDEP 21470 36154 53403 42979 21633 16237 21478 27604 43883 43588 43036 46672 53991 43309 42440 15049 32536 54524 43842 40216 48249 39750 12271 58191 53442 37289 47461 19637 21466 43773 15410 55343 34622 39705 46162 34866 42625 37371 53512 34186 35406 36808 44579 25853 48574 57964 41249 45383 57250 25853 21470 57905 47492 57906 45515 17282 54810 45345 43842 56235 53720 13734 32019 30277 53419 15049 32536 31361 19983 45548 43309 21470 17614 44869 44846 25075 53471 48800 42625 37371 13768 56527 39704 53618 23402 35783 43842 56235 31393 40216 15789 42979 21633 42625 37371 17282 36531 12992 15049 32536 31361 43579 31763 31850 44240 44252 15393 42344 39704 48253 43842 40216 57597 53388 58191 31185 48475 53830 53720 38512 23655.

HART.

BOGOTA, *September 25, 1902.*

SECSTATE, *Washington:*

JBEDP 40216 50149 39750 41838 35568 23887 53228 31891 32577 43309 24974 54670 50223 49538 21633 20951 16173 34242 37604 38159 54524 43309 46016 13489 38754 13634 45860 43842 32577 49540 21470 33577 13562 31333 53536 46298 13634 24879 53991 31406 48810 33927 48637 42640 34631 40160 43842 21718 42625 31393 40216 49540 46621 15534 38164 42440 55268 54524 18540 18260 55343 45168 11399 11085 53198 57905 35685 41974 42440 54524 15237 43309 13827 43836 42344 21437 57379 18595 45345 41945 50403 53383 58213 29493 49537 54019 25951 53439 38164 42440 54524 53464 55268 42785 42933 39810 31175 39389 28299 31758 13634 49902 42463 54171 17325 28281 29499 48217 42463 32577 42817 34279 22863 28714 46621.

HART.

BOGOTA, *September 26, 1902.*

SECSTATE, *Washington:*

JBTDP 12077 35369 29980 27958 12899 43696 35369 21466 32501 37289 25420 Coffee 21175 50344 20449 Coffee 53462 34601 30804 20449 34232 42640 27634 vegetable ivory 54667 20449 12899 43785 quintal 19394 42640 20449 42640 53797 30686 23116 57837 54688 27635 31561 20449 42640 53797 Cocoanuts 42640 27634 31767 53465 55610 39258 48929 30804 20449 53465 39050 39258 31561 20449 quintal 45662 13634 25077 49536 29980 42440 Coffee 31896 43469 24319 57622 35228 54978 22454 13489 34326 38194.

HART.

BOGOTA, *October 1, 1902.*

SECSTATE, *Washington:*

OKACP 32571 55637 39750 48220 53449 50051 37374 54688 51030 56173 43842 57772 49544 24188 19247 43703 46584 15878 22772 13634 21264 19955 39667 57744 25687.

HART.

BOGOTA, *September 29, 1902.*

SECSTATE, *Washington:*

JBJCP 32571 12294 19637 21456 16237 56674 53439 18944 46256 35369 49387 13634 30942 15397 56166 13027 25942 32571 15789 56165 17282 13024 25942 57803 25685 34179 34179 45162 43309 11155 41377 42942 38322 32539 43351 53403 25945 57622 54964 58213 14022 53830 53720 38512 37289 38983 14216.

HART.

BOGOTA, *October 6, 1902.*

SECSTATE, *Washington:*

OKFDP 45211 37181 39750 53992 22518 12566 50659 39750 53201 35420 32580 43309 22083 53439 13489 11928 31330 43588 42440 21466 54524 13634 41003 43036 46672 45211 26253 35266 55604 53403 55301 46672 21971 17282 13024 22159 57744 15322 41712 42440 23489 57744 21470 17624 35228 25075 52306 53471 48800 53462 25949 43309 15779 53449 36523 13489 21633 43888 46672 21971 22159 57744 23489.

HART.

BOGOTA, *October 13, 1902.*

SECSTATE, *Washington:*

KACAP 21470 13962 37382 27853 48810 31891 39258 48929 13767 32225 13634 40213 47355 53213 30798 50225 15270 57760 31361 16237 21308 28962 43309 21470 47984 54014 53198 51927 36478.

HART.

BOGOTA, *October 24, 1902.*

SECSTATE, *Washington:*

KBDAP 56236 30277 21444 33584 38512 56047 13759 21444 36172 39525 21466 21054 14799 35267 36976 50280 19637 56045 13634 42942 39433 21470 48251 12992 21466 21054 53997 53037 46031 38518 20127 43842 58213 14022 48235.

HART.

BOGOTA, *November 30, 1902.*

SECSTATE, *Washington:*

LCOCP 47358 41975 50922 34531 13134 27928 30798 39713 32571 42869 53403 12911 39258 48929 18919 29499 53811 57281 41214 17282 48709 54020 43139 15465 55017 18917 20217 21971 47056 55495 35801 30969.

HART.

BOGOTA, *November 3, 1902.*

SECSTATE, *Washington:*

OLCBP 47366 53238 54674 42425 32571 49983 14523 31972 50919 43842 53214 50779 45211 13634 40216 21471 36532 23435 19955 41478 13792 27174 31870 40181 16489 42463 13489 11928 42625 37371 43842 QSZMLV 33927 17817 40940 29679 11063 36863 42440 15322 53715 54420 31567 36532 31213 23026 53442 37289 42738 39381 21186 53450 36863 42462 15322 22584 40216 47767 39750 53403 QSZMLV 37289 52133 32681 41529 29568 19546 53751 43902 25488 54416 43842 40216 11688 53419 QSZMLV 57643 45549 41495 34004 46962.

HART.

BOGOTA, *November 7, 1902.*

SECSTATE, *Washington:*

OLGAP 21470 49968 53991 34678 42785 50051 53478 50460 35406 19955.

HART.

BOGOTA, *November 7, 1902.*

SECSTATE, *Washington:*

OLGAP 21470 12784 53991 43695 50930 53797 38343 31260 20844 51805 50008 19600 13634 26386 17275 43309 37555.

HART.

BOGOTA, *November 14, 1902.*

SECSTATE, *Washington:*

LADBP QSZMLV 33927 12573 53253 32571 53430 11405 13489 16481 42625 37371 34022 45549 19955 54383 32571 53254 34242 12573 53403 44015 45537 40216 36189 39750 13149 45515 22737 23649 39551 32563 18264 45113 31260 28404.

HART.

BOGOTA, *November 24, 1902.*

SECSTATE, *Washington:*

LBDKA 47358 41975 50922 34631 13634 50925 54675 39713 39673 Dobson 34849 16724 35725 29865 53997 43263 19637 29273 34186 19937 49515 22935 40890 45860 57250 42942 24878 42440 39033 45860 47801 31850 18944 13705 32382 37374 43970 16445 44750 36560 53236.

HART.

NOVEMBER 25, 1902.

SECSTATE, *Washington:*

LBEGP 36560 53236 54669 36478 47044 23123 35006 36084 57473 33073 37181 39750 36138 42440 53398 41713 36478 31850 21473 56674 49538 34979 22949 57643 43883 34242 48758 54384 32423 51108 31175 51095 38862 40216 57738 58191 36170 53403 21444 56526 19953 13767 53236 16487 21471 49798 17908 53253 31150 30875 34828 40213 47433 50758 54384 49798 53024 20669 38520 13634 50758 49761 38520 37330 48253 38031 58213 54798 25389 39370 32019 22318 53891 21444 53703 38520 15731 35685 35406 52458 53997 43263 21444 41837 53720 42853 49500 56246 22737 29805 29013 13634 50651 28320 39245 31668 41036 55045 53439 57510 54383 52173 22758 22737 41837 53720 17741 37472 41652 46197 50182 21471 40216 49540 32536 34442 23648 22737 14722 13767 46777 54384 17644 40741 45505 34828 45378 35692 19461 41923 32551 29685 37449 49857 46771 40216 34442 12911 31393 34141 52024 22580 53399 58191 31175 43703 22727.

HART.

BOGOTA, *November 27, 1902.*

SECSTATE, *Washington:*

LBGLA 25409 56202 19846 22781 28403 40118 39551 14013 25409 43414 12899 44534 45449 13634 43880 48700 29720.

HART.

BOGOTA, *December 2, 1902.*

SECSTATE, *Washington:*

MOBEP 21530 25411 47302 15302 30804 53797 39940 22584 51095 48194 51655 15075 20321 52670 13634 26962.

HART.

BOGOTA, *December 8, 1902.*

SECSTATE, *Washington:*

OMHZA 47358 53232 53703 36478 40216 32417 27409 16156 53403 14179 46706 37289 31972 16723 53338 19955 41478 49542 34828 53751 52386 58035 16717 57597 32472 19605 45036 16853 53403 40216 12573 15778 39750 49537 53403 53607 40956 45493 46771 54383 44828 43700 35692 53991 53298 40171 13545 42633 42718 30969 22584 40216 26250 39381 34179 56706 29110 13822 16265 45245 39679 42600 45211 57527 48691 53991 18944 29804 53999.

HART.

BOGOTA, *December 12. 1902.*

SECSTATE, *Washington:*

MABDP 47358 53232 53326 36478 47044 40216 50673 39750 23892 53198 34004 50172 58170 53991 34179 46706 47907 16162 53416 37131 57744 44849 53991 54409 13634 12325 34242 53403 34279 44849 31484 32472 39285 40216 16189 39750 53439 44849 47014 50772 45211 53924 53991 32472 19637 39283 38466 54011.

HART.

BOGOTA, *December 12, 1902.*

SECSTATE, *Washington:*

MABDP 39673 29980 27958 32571 25422 45730 47303 42440 53298 43787 40697 18202 30919 37556.

HART.

BOGOTA, *December 12, 1902.*

SECSTATE, *Washington:*

MABTP 47357 32019 53232 53326 36478 13634 40196 53999 40216 33577 37779 32003 39750 23890 44849 16732 34179 46706 20684 27057 41468 13634 50751 41206 21444 53471 32542 55268 54384 47603 23116 42463 43309 19955 11388 34279 36539 13634 52134 14652 21466 22737.

HART.

BOGOTA, *December 31, 1902.*

SECSTATE, *Washington:*

MCAFP 22584 48100 42463 19955 21971 53263 39750 32571 41913 21971 53423 41030 48214 43879 53991 54225 41032 43695 31175 43879 49349 41888 53991 43309 46672 21971.

HART.

BOGOTA, *January 5, 1903.*

SECSTATE, *Washington:*

AOEBP 47358 53232 53709 54801 47045 40216 49540 34179 46706 36532 36402 44493 39225 21466 41837 54029 41939 54669 43842 34015 47993 48548 13634 56450 36542 50800 54416 29236 34013 36402 53298 40171 27781 13634 50922 34631 53797 13989 18196 35007 13634 34013 36170 53403 22737 19988 23650 55495 12510 39547 40216 49540 36539 53991 20684 54073 32002 23885 13767 31393 14799 44492 40218 49540 34279 32536 37289 42714 53403 18126 21444 19893 22345 39679 57744 55266 41386 53403 19955 13634 46672 21966 50078 34186 48101 16723 53991 19959 29733 23500.

HART.

BOGOTA, *January 10, 1903.*

SECSTATE, *Washington:*

AOKEP 12284 40216 36557 57622 53255 53991 34179 56706 50758 54416 34841 19893 49839 46621 50996 40578 57318 57289 53787 11311 32539 42440 55266 28714 46621.

HART.

BOGOTA, *January 9, 1903.*

SECSTATE, *Washington:*

AOJEP 47358 53232 53703 36478 47044 34179 46706 50149 49373 29500 34279 56129 46841 42688 36491 22118 42463 19955 13634 40216 45058 42688 45211 29805 48698 18944 19584 40647 57126 39667 17614 22968 43842 44755 45211 57473 12294 39704 16718 28113 19745 11630 35369 11126.

HART.

BOGOTA, *February 2, 1903.*

SECSTATE, *Washington:*

OBBCP 32571 25411 11034 12899 29980 27958 29499 42600 44939 40040 28287 51213 41888 53621 46822 24724 34536.

HART.

FEBRUARY 12, 1903.

SECSTATE, *Washington:*

BABJA 41043 16848 46943 42785 39720 38444 40695 37951 14022.

HART.

BOGOTA, *February 12, 1903.*

SECSTATE, *Washington:*

BABBP 22896 49574 21470 25411 29664 31850 35179 lard butter sugar flour 13641 vegetable 45674 35411 41272 51678 57805 37943 42440 45106.

HART.

BOGOTA, *February 17, 1903.*

SECSTATE, *Washington:*

BAGAP 21470 25411 48775 12899 35179 29499 53768 11026 11396 53217 54661 36478 17233 45164 29527 41630 27958 14881 24106 32519 31850 50930 53991 42640 34631 43787 12074 hardware 31850 30804 53991 42640 34631 43787 57701 13634 51510 31850 42640 34631 53991 54688 34631 30804 43787 35208 32232 14799 24277 53236 42869 44263 29310 13634 55266.

HART.

BOGOTA, *April 24, 1903.*

SECSTATE, *Washington:*

DBDJA 47366 53238 50927 36478 45566 35369 52624 24349 43745 13684 30842 37727 57643 32411 53919 41895 21971 19584 55268 39592 56675 50225.

BEAUPRE.

BOGOTA, *May 7, 1903.*

SECSTATE, *Washington:*

EOGDP 51402 50303 17908 19832 37755 54665.

BEAUPRE.

BOGOTA, *May 16, 1903.*

SECSTATE, *Washington:*

EAFBP 53232 54661 36478 47044 45232 21444 48371.

BEAUPRE.

BOGOTA, *May 19, 1903.*

SECSTATE, *Washington:*

EAJCP 40273 WGXZUJNEM 40213 42440 32536 12336 48790 42440 25409 19846 22754 13634 25578 25284 43703 29298 25501 40289 13634 48639 32225 IVZLK 38232 32580 QKAMU 52273 34242 22438 43707.

BEAUPRE.

BOGOTA, *May 28, 1903.*

SECSTATE, *Washington:*

EBHJA 36171 45211 53204 47603 38194 41974 55268 28592 38237 15258 16237 37371 34828 29934 15764 14052 39380 54543 57606 36680 42768 46777 23675.

BEAUPRE.

BOGOTA, *June 1, 1903.*

SECSTATE, *Washington:*

TOAEP 24568 36525 53157 24490 45353 42000 47669 53009 52608 40406.

BEAUPRE.

BOGOTA, *June 5, 1903.*

SECSTATE, *Washington:*

TOCBP 46524 30823 29964 49497 29787 20628 46583 43046 36060 20283 19375 21124 12302 12069 20275 14184 37379 47958 28657 19406 25031 41598 36938 53426 53446.

BEAUPRE.

BOGOTA, *June 17, 1903.*

SECSTATE, *Washington:*

TAGDP 39070 14453 41926 45935 19113 22833 55298 51207 41876 36480 22878 16787 45940.

BEAUPRE.

BOGOTA, *June 17, 1903.*

SECSTATE, *Washington:*

TAGDP 19195 41448 31049 20628 56941 41621 45631 15395 42467 41943 39733 41598 42027 38837 37652 53149 31738 42467 56902 26203.

BEAUPRE.

BOGOTA, *June 18, 1903.*

SECSTATE, *Washington:*

TAHDP 33986 40890 43435 15395 18986 45638 42467 56780 56943 39374 52366 35306 41758 43641.

BEAUPRE.

BOGOTA, *June 23, 1903.*

SECSTATE, *Washington:*

TBCCP 21742 30987 31721 22767 21919 43000 17543 13376 37692 49409 25392 31721 42740.

BEAUPRE.

BOGOTA, *June 25, 1903.*

SECSTATE, *Washington:*

TBELA 41919 19699 41845 19113 26227 57328 24978 26746 46761 53474 31721 41296 16883 55788 46000 44331 53574 31721 51901 55545 52876 53149 30104.

BEAUPRE.

BOGOTA, *June 26, 1903.*

SECSTATE, *Washington:*

TBTLA 21742 35329 53574 16787 44335 54653 21741 36560 21789 19699 29706 18619 54349 35278 38546 38525 49224 54051 10309 49335 30333 12792 31721 54917 35253 49235 33344 26708 25393 52408 33322.

BEAUPRE.

BOGOTA, *July 2, 1903.*

SECSTATE, *Washington:*

GOBJA 21742 35313 44622 52561 44369 32272 39038 49235 15432 42436 57328 54796 40585 53571 33250 26227 28131 38525 24502 41923 53574 44323 38525 49224 49128 11746 45929.

BEAUPRE.

BOGOTA, *July 5, 1903.*

SECSTATE, *Washington:*

GOEGP 33927 31130 10701 20628 56902 35718 41598 13877 53833 47138 39450 53455 36899 30073 51623 47103 30308 41001 56780 46513 21895 52581 38862 37138 22280 31566 14480 41798 18742 31725 25630 38928 14480 41798 21907 22112 12057 40643 44594 49956 53574 34763 41063 39371 Hacienda 53149 21124 56408 13284 53574 14034 29115 52779 35825 13330 30577 28514 34527 40653 49090 42506 16150 48991 10000 39088 20630 25126 53827 41099 53574 12265 19141 19117 41317 17788 20602 12792 21124 55999 54424 40188 38528 22647 10715 48033 21124 56445 16440 34747 34527 53574 56101 50253 20602 56547 46846 33337 48032 57116 16440 18230 18742 41327 53149 21124 41752 22647 20602 33055 31996 52617 42858 41598 33337 49618 34527 19113 21129 28394 14625 14480 41798 41621 39086 13877 41324 41625 37101 36447 55634 18742 54424 40579 22021 41598 20602 53149 48440 41598 49618 42467 45833 46291 34527 14480 41798 53574 39421 11602 44905 29207 53149 45413 41598 41798 41957 49618 14551 38937 22755 16550 49017 12792 44905 27620.

BEAUPRE.

BOGOTA, *July 5, 1903.*

SECSTATE, *Washington:*

GOEGP 21742 35313 44622 52565 42554 41598 52390 36913 40868 55735 45990 49224 48931 49454 23613 49313 22291 18742 38683 14555 52962 41598 25928 47773 11746 20602 19384 53574 45945 43000 52878 12792 50996 14439 39070 31008 42467 52600 25103 57063 47953 33986 53574 45945 19472 11997 12792 27436 29706 43000 54669 33549 29205 37675 36900.

BEAUPRE.

BOGOTA, *July 9, 1903.*

SECSTATE, *Washington:*

GOJJA 21742 31383 JGGYGG 47390 38908 48695 57362 33170 52843 53574 16520 45940 56961 53846 12625 43000 53149 14480 41798 51076 42858 52456 39329 18795 19113 21129 30333 48024 53383 53149 14480 53830 34852 42858 53149 29955 39329 48700 53574 16520 45940 41796 56930 12625 33162 14957 55402 21745.

BEAUPRE.

BOGOTA, *July 11, 1903.*

SECSTATE, *Washington:*

GAAAP 21742 38525 49224 41907 53574 43000 13433 31723 40961 24702 53574 12425 38862 35819 37400 36606 29735 41876 12926 23726 41598 37836 55309 24034 36447 24834 56408 41919 29977 30333 43000 52845 51207 36110 31062 53004 20629 41943 52878 37670 52561 24858 15992 57081 27457 42100 24277 22583 54653 49381 40570 35697 52396 30333 28688.

BEAUPRE.

BOGOTA, *July 15, 1903.*

SECSTATE, *Washington:*

GAEAP 21742 50077 39900 29703 53574 43000 17552 16782 45940 18725 12625 43000 43913 16530 42759 12625 18630 17564 44482 52561 10875 21476 16520 49017 34348 52561 31729 16440 35328 53004 20629 41943 38908 41598 43865 38828 28510 33900 57063 13681 35712 32088 27700 57328 53574 51328 20995 41598 40868 49224 30823 12792 39926 41629 14000 45929.

BEAUPRE.

[Cablegrama.]

SAN JOSE, C. R., *26 Sbre, 1909. Buenaver 26.*

AMLEGATION, *Bogota:*

Esta-bueno Salgo. Sandy. Antt°. Guarnizo. Es copie.

VÁSQUEZ.

AMERICAN LEGATION, *Bogota, September, 1909.*

CONSUL, *San Jose (Costarrica):*

11412 12020 SAINTECROIX 30308 45779 FRAZT GUYOL 32735 18022 49228 36307 51102 36887 47435 15225 35290 44565 50075 56138 32663 57362 27872 45779.

HIBBEN.

BOGOTA, *August 5, 1903.*

SECSTATE, *Washington:*

HOEKL 32858 10907 40996 39374 21463 47174 20994 53574 27450 45086 39732 14480 41798 36447 52293 46729 53574 41870 31713 57063 22090 41943 26214 12624 52597 20960 17066 35734 10702 40244 41017 13877 53829 36913 52456 41943 29490 31559 34338 52785 24962 14551 24771 29187 12792 35854 31735 12624 14480 52864 51778 53630 10470 28510 42089 39736 40983 49400 34527 44572 14090 55094 53149 20602 51325 26232 52622 49231 16562 11045 15327 41943 50562 37692 56284 20916 53564 13606 20433 56902 51207 46926 41621 24040 22066 41598 31177 24858 54796 52577 20602 46019 25408 44356 46766 48999 11320 19113 16153 18789 20422 12129 41598 40407 35937 53574 16702 45940 39732.

BEAUPRE.

BOGOTA, *August 5, 1903.*

SECSTATE, *Washington:*

HOEKA 36542 41103 13427 52561 53574 16787 45940 56961 12613 16918 43867 35243 31717 28946 52734 18619 27502 49235 41621 53829 34548 41610 18670 52542 53846 52863 29682 47183 20960 56472 30308 30073 34564 44067 52608 46499 53177 Spooner 37444 49571 51776 48919 34527 14480 41798 21607 16672 36181 52597 42467 45830 12792 19113 21124 41348 17328 38539 14343 20628 34578 52608 21612 49571 28426 54140 31720 31785 22021 40535 27786 52784 21124 53149 53383 52636 48032 53149 54424 16682 29171 52561 20602 49558 46389 42298 41600 37317 31794 56438 44323 53890 21124 28663 13384 51499 37325 53149 27879 52597 20191 42467 12792 20636 38862 46867 27458 12792 21272 28739 57472 56475 51289 21475 52861 52504 41598 14502 53846 12792 52969 16672 39738 38656 14551 29161 20362 52561 20602 31794 54424 41812 48023 54835 41621 57472 12792 42724 10980 52515 16712 29171 56902 44118 52597 48032 31787 54424 14017 40458 tenancy 28743 33952 42298 12792 28428 34528 42967 38650 52608 43082 41621 21475 52608 18238 57472 49571 34991 52629 31883 44118 52610 40535 45017 53185 21475 29207 49571 20362 25633 28743 31049 21475 34537 54283 38650 20191 42467 12792 20636 17698 56408 16682 50872 52597 31988 41598 53578 30725 30727 16687 39738 34527 13387 56210 12913 22569 34527 36606 13530 52626 56668 25107 42467 34766 41621 57472 30826 34527 14480 49495 21475 41621 48021 31827 54835 52622 55852 41598 37293 lagoons 48088 42089 51156 56389 40430 41943 14538 56479 16440 25756 52626 51733 52622 19113 41943 15905 19801 41943 56479 16440 38362 54835 41598 27095 36606 22274 38503 41943 41859 16672 20362 37962 42010 16624 25714 52647 23498 27582 41943 37742 52647 37793 22910 36123 37293 56728 41943 40397 33986 40535 30413 45470 16682 28426 52600 48011 36447 28747 41812 34527 50265 14630 46525 54843 41598 51499 55852 30418 51733 12792 38503 41621 19113 41959 15905 19801 56961 12192 52561 21475 44503 54941 41598 51499 55852 18778 34527 55462 52649 37700 48032 45452 56474 41804 40481 12986 26619 38528 25837 41943 44222 27754 52597 54426 25382 31556 51499 55852 30418 10245 45470 52608 54835 41598 55852 41943 48088 42184 57472 52622 19113 30418 53472 38819 28456 16687 12743 28747 48021 54424 52613 48011 49558 31568 52664 54843 52608 55852 56961 52329 41943 19827 41602 37101 34527 50253 29590 14690 54835 46759 38503 12792 41859 41621 21475 52608 40430 44823 45018 41621 47336 56408 54424 38884 52617 57012 16672 25633 52629 31883 44118 43906 limiting 52878 21475 52626 25107 42467 12792 25669 52597 21195 56408 32887

52189 43398 54132 14480 49495 34527 12057 52842 16672 51291 56167 45281 34527 14480 30824 29957 34527 14480 27502 54058 41621 20323 16672 23140 54140 40890 27116 41602 37101 16672 20566 34564 20191 42467 12792 20636 28675 39129 25532 53155 36181 52617 22420 41621 47654 41621 47336 50085 34527 14480 52864 12057 46761 28429 41598 53630 41621 54426 12950 13530 41621 37472 54426 34527 20624 52515 16672 51776 14630 22696 14480 52456 22255 12792 16682 28426 52561 46685 43664 12792 48590 56531 30501 41621 57472 16672 51282 53152 11927 17803 31734 49498 34956 56514 21475 39118 34527 14480 30824 24361 54716 52617 49177 56479 32792 38402 19407 56438 38118 34564 48507 14480 16672 25633 12792 42421 18742 54424 10546 52636 55084 52612 53062 27505 34527 14480 53829 20325 41598 30597 16672 36181 30135 52491 56470 28641 12864 57012 17173 28791 12069 21476 19527 28883 12799 45017 12792 48033 54221 49558 47914 20602 37379 42506 14480 53830 17360 18619 24852 16672 51776 40884 34537 10875 20323 52608 53628 56482 24354 54748 25825 56479 14174 17802 22650 14710 31120 41621 53541 16672 34991.

BEAUPRE.

BOGOTA, *August 5, 1903.*

SECSTATE, *Washington:*

HOEJA 46517 13877 53829 22429 52390 13877 49495 46194 40996 31008 39374 14928 45779 39733 34527 53574 36607 16802 22126 55451 Spooner 37444 48531 14551 51582 30333 19119 21476 41598 21124 22133 18742 31725 27872 45779 47099 36899 53827 51391 30308 52629 13809 53574 18742 49231 52608 Spooner 37444 56408 15881 36606 38547 55735 31130 21305 50265 14692 42467 48160 21457 33330 48412 37444 56021 42144 41598 10802 28885 46505 42467 12829 41812 16946 51288 26227 12927 46505 40816 28511 46730 41598 53574 18742 20602 52895 40244 43128 41864 56469 12525 53973 21773 18919 46499 53149 31713 18656 17539 27145 35298 33927 46047 17544 31713 11744 22079 41943 26214 39733 56210 53177 53541 14630 50815 34451 33900 31346 31015 19317 45997 12792 51234 41621 41017 12292 43892 30374 34542 21476 41621 21124 31713 57063 22079 52636 39732 55451 Spooner 37444 52670 46055 36562 49128 53574 36607 14692 41681 36021 41598 19146 39738 15460 56961 55449 52561 37444 43000 31008 22901 56902 44937 49235 17543 31721 22086 41869 30001 41943 15837 17338 30346 27736 50888 57357 41943 35697 54110 52375 36899 29956 24036 52561 53574 16772 12610.

BEAUPRE.

BOGOTA, *August 6, 1903.*

SECSTATE, *Washington:*

HOTKA 21742 40995 46499 53149 53541 27503 30725 20982 47151 20602 26991 10240 52842 40810 47187 35854 54426 25081 53574 28511 46729 19113 53541 43000 32858 10875 21775 50896 25468 30728 36913 29955.

BEAUPRE.

BOGOTA, *August 6, 1903.*

SECSTATE, *Washington:*

HOFBP 20628 47407 38908 48695 52597 20433 41598 36609 41662 11746 20602 17284 29061 22647 18919 21129 36447 54441 12792 14957 41680 49015 22566 49434.

BEAUPRE.

BOGOTA, *August 10, 1903.*

SECSTATE, *Washington:*

HOKJA 35288 31697 52561 42000 17418 47669 34527 42467 55328 47385 18795 22305 36447 54501.

BEAUPRE.

BOGOTA, *August 12, 1903.*

SECSTATE, *Washington:*

HABGP 53574 46727 49228 53157 28205 21742 10416 52878 30001 52694 51046 50352 33550 55614 31177 11482.

BEAUPRE.

BOGOTA, *August 12, 1903.*

SECSTATE, *Washington:*

HABKP 21742 31383 JGYGG 18987 35296 52561 24220 21897 10548 43474 37395 42976 31697 12792 35280 49235 and 20212 17533 53574 23301 41103 16440 42750 56961 12625 18704 56955 49727 51505 45986 45353 49358 16520 23613 14551 27789 44369 44331 53574 11731 49232 48998 36606 42744 56955 12625 17085 16042 40081 30333 24216 33330 52374 11483 52561 52757 33572 52608 31383 14936 57358 31561 53846 55982 39899 30418 22419 41625 43460 17284 52236 42086 10788 and 47407 34164 47103 33162 26932 56389 22256 16520 12610 53082 12792 52855 40545.

BEAUPRE.

BOGOTA, *August 12, 1903.*

SECSTATE, *Washington:*

HABJP 46516 52375 HABGP 33900 17540 52561 46730 41598 53545 30003 30333 30305 46068 57330 24267 12792 55545 55735 54264 44530 14305 52878 17543 18209 31008 53209 24277 31010 35306 56469 32211 12292 46174 52988 43142 Of 33391 35243 24270 30104 33673 12057 21099 17788 40260 12926 20628 45990 29446 31725 10415 39736 41943 24834 38003 20344 49232 40001 34345 50615 38362 55804 41598 31383 Ospina 55745 27450 56547 25413 19113 23343 31547 55545 30333 53571 16918 52504 56027 22693 the 45314 22255 33162 34320 52561 to 18404 40643 53150 21518 22256 49752 16440 39738 50264 12164 40642 53155 18478 53150 51459 21518 44229 to 33539 23477 50877 52561 27448 52878 24852 40550 14551 53846 24281 51568 45454 36104 21930 16702 34165 26336 18742 44369 12927 56961 24834 re 22968 18742 24568 45455 39747 22256 43000 54747 37445 42764 15890 28807 56961 31177 46386 21895 21505 10000 19113 53541 56902 54424 49787 45251 53700 52539 44322 53541 16550 10446 33383 43000 38937 21895 10168 21505 40642 56961 35056 49235 45357 50558 29686 36532.

BEAUPRE.

BOGOTA, *August 15, 1903.*

SECSTATE, *Washington:*

HAEAP 44937 49234 49698 52597 55545 55977 54765 39479 47176 20960 33332 17546 46364 36447 43906 41758 37971 38521 47151 53020 49221 13596 40788 20960 41598 52969 31383 Ospina 19685 23007 56902 49972 20960 13596 30963 18742 19699 47185 as 36823 20960 18217 33694 13450 26439 30018 38944 45951 53574 20992 49134 41807 56755 57012 53176 27864.

BEAUPRE.

BOGOTA, *August 17, 1903.*

SECSTATE, *Washington:*

HAGDP 44369 35347 38908 52561 21895 42740 37445 15890 33400 22593 12792 30056 40647 19113 56141 21612 56780 50586 19194 50836 44324.

BEAUPRE.

BOGOTA, *August 17, 1903.*

SECSTATE, *Washington:*

HAGTP 33927 38374 14321 21463 20283 19375 21124 48641 39662 wsxh 12792 31729 43000 42858 29962 52955 26794 19409 29962 52955 34527 52969 39856 18209 10574 17871 30333 49448 41598 45830 43000 20375 for 24013 12792 49173 18077 22128 12889 21371 18801 42858.

BEAUPRE.

BOGOTA, *August 24, 1903.*

SECSTATE, *Washington:*

HBDLA 41019 26845 12792 38032 48633 10788 52878 25185 54748 15645 31725 56472 55620 13351 47183 20960 44277 52365 41598 52865 40938 37400.

BEAUPRE.

BOGOTA, *August 26, 1903.*

SECSTATE, *Washington:*

HBTJA 52365 40871 46188 25131 39179 41598 36899 53829 53834 12792 15761 29955 56472 39989 54339 30418 50075 36447 31832 40099 25186 54763 15639 45215.

BEAUPRE.

BOGOTA, *August 31, 1903.*

SECSTATE, *Washington:*

HCABP 36078 49234 VFKTRPH 24188 35332 52574 56843 46867 38111 52737 33550 52617 53541 18651 22959 52598 36447 40938 37577 52776 52623 50085 45333 33162 21815 31383 TGYGG 50888 21461 44396 19123 48700 40814 49221 38406 19620 30333 53574 52561 33162 16846 35697 53149 31740 MZBVBJHAEP 12792 JKXXAQJ 21463 27562 56408 33305 24341 52579 10471 31741 OF 42467 33162 53196 44369 THAT 19384 52561 25103 30775 it 40535 47954 49015 19113 57066 50810 18742 42467 18651 10846 33986 31725 55617 30418 21923 THE 19113 16520 49017 56961 47959 49234 Campo 52618 Cauca 36454 37603 52854 33650 for 53574 31662 21742 41870 41019 48633 16520 28942 31054 21895 Caros 42725 17066 76820 18742 Valez 12792 Soto 52638 30302 22247 24428 38521 11746 53574 31383 TGYGG 49141 51042 28171 33600.

BEAUPRE.

79669—13——27

BOGOTA, *August 29, 1903.*

SECSTATE, *Washington:*

HBJMM 46189 13376 39179 25112 21463 46730 41621 53541 40944 52926 39118 52371 53831 20992 32735 47203 12926 45148 48633 47151 14034 31663.

BEAUPRE.

BOGOTA, *August 30, 1903.*

SECSTATE, *Washington:*

HCOHP 21742 12531 15839 52561 15330 52608 27561 41598 TGYGG NKXXK YCT 32735 12292 19778 the 31740 41598 Bolivar 38416 a 12792 42467 40931 47619 MZBVB JHAEP JKXXA QJ and 49234 VFKTR PH 12057 43553 to 53574 12950 TGYGG.

BEAUPRE.

BOGOTA, *August 30, 1903.*

SECSTATE, *Washington:*

HCOGP 21742 31383 JGYGG 47407 38908 35298 52597 44396 19122 ature 17066 41658 33402 18742 NKXXK YCJP 12926 31740 12082 25131 32739 44622 13215 52575 10408 56961 19620 37166 52597 53541 13850 18801 21895 41943 40814 30333 56961 53571 12926 15333 30989 41598 54424 33162 25377 16962 44365 He 37163 56389 51544 53062 57081 31787 18742 31725 12164 21930 of 36899 53825 57312 56464 19634 33162 22781 46363 53574 19384 43915 30503 it 53004 44322 21895 40540 52600 21895 10794 33162 37163 34052 10408 39733 56210 12792 38105 56833 55613 53571.

BEAUPRE.

BOGOTA, *September 2, 1903.*

SECSTATE, *Washington*·

OJBLA 46191 52356 53829.

BEAUPRE.

BOGOTA, *September 5, 1903.*

SECSTATE, *Washington:*

52365 53834 20992 47193 a 37444 56408 13858 46129 Of 53574 15889 44369 53149 21503 53533 30333 42467 19113 41943 22647 30333 48507 56903 44610 42700 51291 48032 of 21124 45830 21129 43060 53383 45415 15301 all 41327 34759 13147 42859 41598 53846 33789 29962 52955 26793 12792 53383 41598 45018 to 20602 34527 40870 50095 19113 21129 43060 53383 41758 42858 53149 20602 41598 52456 39328 26793 44369 15881 38539 30303 21476 37564 Of 57472 30333 41798 33789 57322 40961 34759 42467 41943 20636 13147 47022 41798 33789 29962 52955 26793 54653 40870 50095 37564 47012 28522 33789 57322 41758 42858 41598 53830 42945 34843 40746 19113 12792 46280 20624 50472 42194 56672 52515 and 35391 39692 53630 41812 43664 12792 48590 20948 20624 41812 11083 16430 28739 57472 53062 37951 30333 21276 Of 57012 20602 46170 31008 22649 31694 53825 39328 26793 41758 53571 30135 46681 21461 45413 18742 44610 21129 44668 28499 52878 10459 18742 49228 28510 41034 48633 28966 31054 21895 24283 17355 39805.

BEAUPRE.

BOGOTA, *September 10, 1903.*

SECSTATE, *Washington:*

JAOEP 50022 47176 19113 20960 45706 17073 41795 26218 49228 30073 22102 47151 43956 54653 30825 35636 29951 15495 53157 49224 54716 13647 VFKTRPH 14551 31738 42467 13645 46620 17474 30568 41598 49377 43000 49518 49235 56631 50693 41826 50365 52622 44365 24695 10797 52622 31694 47550 42757 12243 53995 55545 56472 28319 55545 of 19584 11731 31721 50077 32742 34486 45139 48633 10788.

BEAUPRE.

BOGOTA, *September 14, 1903.*

SECSTATE, *Washington:*

JADDP 19113 20960 47151 54003 30073 45997 24188 Perez Soto 41049 12613 10313 47694 28807 53149 52504 of 45074 37444 50077 32742 19778 41020 17768 52878 37444 28966.

BEAUPRE.

BOGOTA, *September 17, 1903*

SECSTATE, *Washington:*

JAGLA 40890 26231 19113 45692 40891 34527 50077 44658 21911 17284 53823 45333.

BEAUPRE.

BOGOTA, *September 22, 1903.*

SECSTATE, *Washington:*

JBBTP 45086 37444 21463 19113 53541 17073 26216 50022 30073 45997 40890 40788 25708.

BEAUPRE.

BOGOTA, *September 22, 1903.*

SECSTATE, *Washington:*

JBBKA 44369 35331 38908 52597 18918 21129 52967 51872 49434 30077 39854 54459 40789 22647 49934.

BEAUPRE.

BOGOTA, *September 22, 1903.*

SECSTATE, *Washington:*

JBBJA 23254 46203 39623 36488 11040 18237 12079 20362 25642 13933 49574 10794 41598 40456.

BEAUPRE.

BOGOTA, *September 27, 1903.*

SECSTATE, *Washington:*

JBGTP 44369 36475 20234 53744 14301 25825 17802 31694 12792 18918 21129 53169 56902 39374 26917 34007 51426 57063 51576 11409 21129 24736 10788 24194 31557 53102 40636 52737 52401 56902 Barranquilla 34527 16176 21590 37815 36041 53067 18660 36447 41828 42086 15920 21075 31047 43758 52391 49340 50975 53149 20636.

BEAUPRE.

BOGOTA, *September 27, 1903.*

SECSTATE, *Washington:*

JBGHP 19759 19113 38825 48919 24267 41598 44919 37444 44678 16440 24428 52889 56755 41566 56957 24193 10875 12625 44027 19620.

BEAUPRE.

BOGOTA, *September 29, 1903.*

SECSTATE, *Washington:*

JBJDP 31721 41661 29204 22647 18918 21129 53847 57322 31008 15763 56902 28747 44629 53155 47011 30333 53089 33986 17777 52065 36447 34527 44026 41859 11648 11932 16535 45979 10256 36475 53957.

BEAUPRE.

BOGOTA, *September 30, 1903.*

SECSTATE, *Washington:*

JCOMM 49228 20916 13596 15432 30073 24267 41758 19113 20998 47174 49381 53819 44271 38837 30333 48919 24267 32792 44272 52636 47151 12870 16772 44335 24211 36432 13858 46730 41598 53574 15761 53819 18619 36033 45086 37444 15890 28807 40627 22278 41599 19113 54124 21612 43000 41291 37603 31721 37884 40627 40789 53541 47698 45138 52561 11190.

BEAUPRE.

WASHINGTON 29, BUENAVA 29, *Septiembre, 1903.*

BEAUPRE, *Minister, Bogota:*

ABJMM 44390 18918 21129 52421 38908 52579 55397 27480 41621 50838 53149 18405 12674 11049 41621 25825 17788 33437 21129 12926 31700 206002 53006 41680 52608 21129 32735 35885 52608 19257 41598 36606 18918 49684 53149 24712 10788 54653 19100 47151 44869 56833 45175 52608 25369 10138 41598 44963 12792 24771 10788 18529 41662 56755 24225 33189 57371 18926 25126 41788 38825.

ADEE, *Acting.*

WASHINGTON 29, BUENAVA 29, *Stbre, 1903.*

BEAUPRE, *Minister, Bogota:*

JBJBP 47375 41598 44365 of 19597 12792 50462 52392 21129 43518 14803 Luis Cuervo Marquez 53149 49805 57349 19661 23028 41598 Concha 11927 12792 10436 38452 Marquez 34527 37757 36899 52868 30073 12293 Marquez 39429 158454 22428 34549 39175 41598 36899 49497 50914 31694 32005 21475 30333 42402 20466.

ADEE, *Acting.*

WASHINGTON 1°, BUENAVA 3, *Octbre, 1903.*

BEAUPRE, *Minister, Bogota:*

KOCDP 57371 52391 53834 52868 12792 30073 46174 18918 21129 54198 52561 of 52867 38927 20328 31785 21129 28741 21455 for 41798 39923 51318 18926 41783 42402 20466 for 53825 57322 31694 17907 36607 31008 54917 39220 41598 telegraphing 42097 51318 18926 11668 52969 57322 17360 15428 53062 43000 21129 11942 to 31734 45044 45292 28747 21475 30333 18927 28362 for 52838 57322 35449 53825 on 16382 41598 14480 52969 Concha 11927 39738 10251 56942 34191 21129 16672 30910 53938 36606 18926 56963 37805 31018 20624 50916 56211 42086 39222 41598 telegraphing 16672 28426 18742 43037 of 31694 527744 21208 56902 21129 43000 12057 20″78 for 24015 44594 45929 41625 22647 53155 19118 bj 18209 31694 12792 21129 43000 20826 45950 21475 10546 52608 52504 52891 11927 43000 21129 28449 47010 12792 47042 53149 18926 17788 42467 12792 18529 56755 23225 41798 33789 and 29962 52955 26793 16366 Concha 11927 41598 40870 44789 53846 20624 52392 53309 36977 21129 34527 34893 50253 37352 29029 30391 18926 12792 47010 31055 56902 48070 41598 21209 11668 52969 57322 54459 21475 30461 38115 52491 52542 53825 57322 52776 21129 45088 52868 57322.

LOOMIS, *Acting.*

WASHINGTON 14, BUENAVA 14, *Octbre, 1903.*

BEAUPRE, *Minister, Bogota:*

KADDP 18918 21129 10474 52504 39118 in 52390 41581 27505 21129 52557 57349 30457 41680.

LOOMIS, *Acting.*

WASHINGTON 17, BUENAVA 17, *Octbre, 1903.*

BEAUPRE, *Minister, Bogota:*

49497 18918 21129 14956 10685 52394 46154 25131 52356 41598 30825 35636 56382 21129 10446 20624 31734 52504 12293 52408 25103 56213 20626 45943 22647 56902 21129.

HAY.

WASHINGTON 20, BUENAVA 20, *Octbre, 1903.*

BEAUPRE, *American Minister, Bogota:*

Have been designated military attaché Colombia; please obtain customs courtesies baggage Capitain Sidney a cloman general staff Capitain William G. Haan General Staff sail New York twenty-fourth.

S. A. CLOMAN, *Military Attaché.*

WASHINGTON 22, BUENAVA. 22, *Octbre. 1903.*

BEAUPRE; *Minister, Bogota:*

53827 46516 52390 49497 34049 30018 26436 42624 20602 14889 52504 39899 29704 20602 52542 52926 33355 40629 36102 41985 18680 57189 52561 16782 54908 49294 a 50560 28265.

HAY.

WASHINGTON 30, BUENAVA. 30, *Octe. 1903.*

BEAUPRE, *Minister, Bogota:*

52867 38898 15909 10288 54110 15875 18925 57362 36899 40884.

HAY.

WASHINGTON 6, BUENAVA. 8, *Novbre 1903.*

BEAUPRE, *Minister, Bogota:*

LOFAP 42938 41598 42467 33085 18749 13433 53995 40074 26548 52636 43692 21978 47336 of 20602 12792 47738 52636 34963 and 11186 31695 41623 42293 47338 30643 56934 31725 of 12641 32735 28155 46763 44391 10546 52608 53048 of 30989 56460 50253 38102 12792 so 32671 28884 17802 47618 40415 39989 27292 20861 53177 31734 of 20602 12892 42667 52608 42865 and 28314 49487 12057 4575 36517 17805 33162 33485 52574 18230 39150 18742 53541 41327 18636 35945 20244 49111 52597 42863 53329 57019 10747 36530 42467 49580 38115 16440 26617 18743 22221 51467 54501 12792 55837 20237 55685 48350.

HAY.

WASHINGTON 11, BUENAVA, *13 Novbre, 1903.*

BEAUPRE, *Bogota:*

27292 25413 12743 12674 50339 41598 38842 36517 17788 20602 12792 42467 55910 35685 42137 22303 42467 54843 41680 49015 30333 31383 tgygg 10000 23536 46231 12792 22096

33235 36545 52945 25362 43041 37322 41598 20624 53682 41758 36529 14551 51505 23498 57063 44099 20237 55685 12792 26619 30346 34940 43000 52608 30905 53406 56527 13957 43553 45175 33900 52411 57349 41758 31079 50085 52603 32211 28155 46763 52629 45310 31694.

HAY.

WASHINGTON 15, BUENAVA, *16 Novbre, 1903.*

BEAUPRE, *Bogota:*

LASCP 33986 20628 51585 47801 37602 Snyder 38862 10507 57349 52847 17713 penod 37574 37670 54110 45184 56210 39371 57349 24607 39989 13775 54110 38068 21612.

HAY.

WASHINGTON 14, BUENAVA, *16 Novbre, 1903.*

BEAUPRE, *Minister, Bogota:*

LACBP 14117 10313 30910 11290 10288 15442 43128 12792 41680 22810.

HAY.

WASHINGTON 14, BUENAVA, *16 Novbre, 1903.*

BEAUPRE, *Minister, Bogota:*

LADDP 32735 18918 21129 22647 16975 30656 28791 24114.

LOOMIS, *Acting.*

WASHINGTON 14, BUENAVA, *16 Novbre, 1903.*

BEAUPRE, *Minister, Bogota:*

The President yesterday fully recognized the Republic of Panama and formally received its minister plenipotentiary; you will promptly communicate this to the Government to which you are accredited.

HAY.

WASHINGTON 18, BUENAVA, *19 Novbre, 1903.*

BEAUPRE, *Bogota:*

56833 41797 35281 20628 52603 32792 46291 47337 42467 52561 42137 10781 52201 34564 35898 41598 42861 12792 42000 41783 36529 52603 27292 25369 12743 12674 49487 45692 36517 17788 20602 12792 42467 and 57063 31596 46999 56138 49448 14017 41137 43986 53176 27864 43000 33900 47057 52607 12926 48956 15883 52174 57371 10288 56311 57349 52843 17713 47402 41804 57371 20573 52189 19827 41598 your 37670 33986 12215 57349 20728 16050.

HAY.

WASHINGTON 21, BUENAVA, *21 Novbre, 1903.*

BEAUPRE, *Minister, Bogota:*

Are caudors grahams and toueans safe 52416 52658 44311 18060 31579 31121 26197 14551 11433 57349.

HAY.

WASHINGTON 24, BUENAVA, *24 Novbre, 1903.*

BEAUPRE, *Minister, Bogota:*

LBDBP 43518 48690 93149 38735 57450 44021 32792 24087 28800 18918 22647 38362 44594 41097 48919.

HAY.

WASHINGTON 23, BUENAVA, *23 May, 1903.*

BEAUPRE, *Minister, Bogota:*

55301 58191 37980 52386 46880 54019 23534 26967 55759 28344 31563 29045.

HAY.

WASHINGTON 8, BUENAVA, *8 Junio, 1903.*

BEAUPRE, *Minister, Bogota:*

FOHDP 22314 42467 18926 45779 49698 31049 50461 45639 27675 38268 20628 46828 50077 49698 56839 disinfect 1849 56841 30925 42766 12187 37319 10646 30925 31008 54424 43763 12664 18061 54220 27485 39742 42027 56961 27436 27872 45779 54835 41680 35084 20628 39744 42027.

LOOMIS, *Acting.*

WASHINGTON 1°, BUENAVA, *1° Julio 1903.*

BEAUPRE, *Minister, Bogota:*

32857 31130 10701 20628 56902 25103 35696 41598 13877 53833 37057 25103 35328 14709 50075.

LOOMIS, *Acting.*

WASHINGTON 9, BUENAVA, *9 Julio 1903.*

BEAUPRE, *Bogota:*

57595 51291 21775 17284 37624 43923.

HAY.

WASHINGTON 13, BUENAVA, *13 Julio 1903.*

BEAUPRE, *Minister, Bogota:*

40671 45086 12625 39118 34580 52386 53157 57063 50810 13376 19719 41598 10436 18742 49231 56557 12613 56210 or 24858 52620 54929 41621 53541 57063 31884 34283 36606 22419.

HAY.

WASHINGTON 10, BUENAVA, *10 Agosto 1903.*

BEAUPRE, *Minister, Bogota:*

HOKMM 37057 25123 11432 27681 24082 34527 39179.

LOOMIS, *Acting.*

WASHINGTON 13, BUENAVA, *13 Agosto 1903.*

BEAUPRE, *Minister, Bogota:*

52865 32857 46174 25103 18918 41598 36899 52879 12625 51579 34580 18918 41621 29937 57061 29643 53149 53574.

LOOMIS, *Acting.*

WASHINGTON 19, BUENAVA, *19 Agosto, 1903.*

BEAUPRE, *Minister, Bogota:*

40871 52357 31008 22298 20636 21071 52357 34527 50512 24118 15761 29957 48696 40890 18918 46174 50003 36899 52864 25109 52411 57349 on 36899 52864 53829 53834 52869 15761 52456 52864 12792 29955 and 46131 52391 31062 24118 36899 29955 30104 24118 15761 29957 41798 15761 50085 52484 12792 54819 42857 46174 25131 19179 34024 45199 11746 39962 56938 41681 21099 56438 28210 44625.

ADEE, *Acting.*

WASHINGTON 24, BUENAVA, *24 Agosto, 1903.*

BEAUPRE, *Minister, Bogota:*

53829 44369 38540 40890 28006 14709 33437 10788 41783 19113 38825 18656 46607 36532 34472 52561 13376 24771 10788 56780 52195 56955 53846 55982.

HAY.

WASHINGTON 31, BUENAVA, *31 Agosto, 1903.*

BEAUPRE, *Minister, Bogota:*

53834 244369 is 18230 18795 36528 12113 50928 21023 18927 52608 Spooner 37444 18759 43314 33171 31566 46056 53062 14301 a 48633 53600 20602 43000 56213 34549 36885 52608 46056 53062 has 29063 12792 17077 10149 38539 a 48633 14321 14710 42467 48160 33177 52670 44706 19367 36123 27436 12392 45098 41621 50928 38954 44369 56755 28149 40890 28006 47687 33437 30918 10788 54132.

HAY.

WASHINGTON 14, BUENAVA, *15 Dicbre, 1903.*

BEAUPRE, *Minister, Bogota:*

55324 56755 39036 57349 15395 19375 47389.

LOOMIS, *Acting.*

WASHINGTON 16, BUENAVA, *17 Dicbre, 1903.*

BEAUPRE, *Minister, Bogota:*

55322 56755 39036 57349 at 18375 53832 11086 56755 31630 43130 44021 34496 41888 to 42853 35998 23540 15395 19375.

ADEE.

BOGOTA, *September 20, 1902.*

CONSUL AMERICANO, *Panama:*

56169 50075 52623 36529 41172 12792 30952 13957 42861 40643 44879 12874 50253 45140.

HART.

BOGOTA, *October 17, 1902.*

CONSUL AMERICANO, *Panama:*

13957 14207 20624 53682 42768 42194 45830 56169 50075 41783 36529.

HART.

BOGOTA, *November 10, 1902.*

AMERICAN CONSUL, *Panama:*

48226 31721 36447 15497 41783 36529 12307 36542 40631 42861 36447 27517 48214 53700 12864 50253 56138 44869 38549 52404 50077.

HART.

BOGOTA, *November 21, 1902.*

MILLARD, *Bolivian Legation, Washington:*

Shivering Guilford ricolorate Banco Colombia.

AMERICAN MINISTER.

BOGOTA, *November 24, 1902.*

CONSUL AMERICANO, *Panama:*

31694 45375 52565 53559 49934 41783 36529 26761 11886 42853 30333 14226 12792 18077 51837 12950 49236 47968 33495 56169 28448 23225 34527 31659.

HART.

BOGOTA, *November de 1902.*

RICARDO DEEB, *93 Washington Street, New York:*

Frutos Honda bajaron primer buque. Sombreros embarcaranse pronto. Casa Victorino vendida seis mil oro. Urge poder Teofilo.

MINISTRO AMERICANO.

BOGOTA, *Diciembre 3 de 1902.*

CONSUL AMERICANO, *Panama:*

32735 47961 20792 24931 14296 12792 18076 53149 31721 34006 56705 21074 52394 15973 54919 40382 52390 41097 53830 46202.

HART.

BOGOTA, *October 2, 1903.*

SECSTATE, *Washington:*

KOBCP 37444 42764 34202 37846 TKHOKWN 33171 25540 30985 49752 15217 33400.

BEAUPRE.

BOGOTA, *October 9, 1903.*

SECSTATE, *Washington:*

OKJLA 47183 20916 46513 52371 49381 52867 56780 44335 11724 43000 35329 44567 46322 16772 53149 13152 14336 38396 19113 21129 34527 40870 33789 29206 36606 21475 43000 18793 10788 20628 28563 33600 47008 40653 46605 21129 12792 38937 20622 16802 27792 10320 52608 39812 21188 42100 10640 52626 21129 11430 31177 50371 33900 49093 47151.

BEAUPRE.

BOGOTA, *October 10, 1903.*

SECSTATE, *Washington:*

OKKAP 44333 20983 47151 43956 54653 53819 52375 49381 52867 50899 30077 53846 20326 47168 52608 52861 37360 44351 44913 37444 13859 29208 53082 31787 19113 21129 43000 13433 52895 45074 56902 28940 52561 49228 56755 40615 44917 and 13152 29208 53026 10533 41290 50872 52371 40884 33743 52845 19385 30000 55545 29208 53082 53177 21129 16787 13153 44658 21908 56961 52236 21524 10788 41788 47151.

BEAUPRE.

BOGOTA, *October 8, 1903.*

SECSTATE, *Washington:*

KOHJA 21742 20629 51429 TGXXUJ 49344 53149 55832 11668 21899 33344.

BEAUPRE.

BOGOTA, *October 17, 1903.*

SECSTATE, *Washington:*

KAGAP 35313 21745 52561 18914 57328 26215 45706 41598 47012 19113 40652 54424 12925 11014 16772 30300 18742 39625 50566 28265 53149 55832 45454 39178 26550 21930 24942 17325 52867 35636.

BEAUPRE.

BOGOTA, *October 15, 1903.*

SECSTATE, *Washington:*

KAEGP 47183 20960 46513 52371 52484 17066 45990 49224 42023 44586 44675 26217 40813 55980 43000 53704 52597 20960 45088 44913 37444 45951 53095 29208 31787 19113 21129 18619 53209 47151 20362 31575 54189 52561 20602 57063 31884 17623 18795 19119 41620 29208 12792 50899 52561 19389 20602 57063 57312 43893 41600 48035 12792 45017 41621 19113 21129 52774 16440 30910 20731 52504 56902 31725 54110 11305 20158 20992 45291 30418 19380 41621 13161 41598 53095 29208 18742 46339 13801 41621 40535 51616 52617 47050 56902 35898 52622 30104 39328 30874 42421 18795 30926 21129 43000 55393 25706 49358 41869 41598 30000 47706 37732 24362 52542 50872 52371 52484.

BEAUPRE.

BOGOTA, *October 23, 1903.*

SECSTATE, *Washington:*

KBCLA 47183 20960 40990 26216 13469 53166 21930 36447 43500 10000 55621 31325 28563 41294 14784 15645 44391 34549 39173 53177 21912 12892 52561 18091 48420 21911 54653 30825 45333 18909 30656 39374 31575 38908 35321 52561 15395 39046 18912 11744 26214 19113 45692 36532 17418 45074 49294 12742 28268 12803 20917 41598 52969 44937 39098 53149 55832 47008 40643.

BEAUPRE.

BOGOTA, *October 27, 1903.*

SECSTATE, *Washington:*

KBGGP 47176 20960 26219 24188 49224 41812 30823 49235 50693 Caro 41905 45086 37444 41598 15875 14551 54089 31956 52561 13376 31201 10788 56408 31721 39285 52174 12792 30913 52189 55735 51291 13809 31201 21895 12925 52878 21895 48015 17901 10797 41598 40814 41598 33162 51212 25082 53574 36607 12926 49206 40019 41598 54424 34527 25413 51505 53541 49234 Groot 41804 15836 47168 50693 34527 48531 53208 49234 Ospina 24695 45086 37455 15875 30008 49234 Arango 11668 43646 52608 31200 41598 45086 37444 56525 41812 53574 56902 39736 56408 31725 24478 53977 45074 26233 Of 56672 38825 16440 43956 34941 14696 55735 53086 30333 49228 26215 36532 52608 49235 13452 53149 11866 45053 52613 44402 41668 20430 24277 56961 55545 52209 10788 16612 52195 53169 41943 14629 12293 44663 38837 16612 12182 To 27018 28203 21908 41783 52869 35636.

BEAUPRE.

BOGOTA, *November 4, 1903.*

SECSTATE, *Washington:*

OLDEP 21742 17085 49821 52385 46816 50452 34527 42467 27450 36529 36447 44284 48911 12925 44746 34963 28966 50369 42699 19318 32023 46816 35306 32695 41458 31729 28572 11998 12792 53682 49331 36529 47057 52391 Of 34338 31008 22316 33437 52391 38915 16612 35960.

BEAUPRE.

BOGOTA, *November 1, 1903.*

SECSTATE, *Washington:*

LOAJA 43039 25123 15912 10288 38709.

BEAUPRE.

BOGOTA, *November 1, 1903.*

SECSTATE, *Washington:*

LOAKA 31721 36525 38636 53177 40406 53157 49524 23724 10809 12792 26223 45717 56461 44335 12792 54584 24239 56902 43000 46617 19113 50901 20624 19842 17066 35685 35295 31725 52597 20628 57063 22079 40788 40643 56408 17551 10469 18795 21923 52776 33986 31725 51042 25408 41843 19113 56408 44423 26770 14551 40666 18742 10748 40944 57002 32735 49826 42090 35846 33587 31849 57012 19361 27873 52921 20624 52515 42506 33900 43240 41896 41598 35300 55489 53149 44369 57328 35295 33400 41598 51388 52390 41581 53827.

BEAUPRE.

BOGOTA, *October 31, 1903.*

SECSTATE, *Washington:*

52869 21904 53157 40890 10788 52201 54716 37379 47151 21463 19113 52776 39922 52542 52608 55545 13761 53819 46729 53574 26845 42939 13351 42194 47213 41598 48911 40084 34564 QKAMU 12792 42467.

BEAUPRE.

BOGOTA, *October 29, 1903.*

SECSTATE, *Washington:*

KBJAP 43518 35702 22306 42467 11460 18919 38848 43000 19113 50075 54061.

BEAUPRE.

BOGOTA, *November 6, 1903.*

SECSTATE, *Washington:*

OLFFP 37164 52597 47958 20831 34527 42467 31383 TGYGG 48698 52577 31725 37320 53682 44356 20624 50472 12926 53406 47392 18742 20624 19842 31729 24471 38760 12828 55462 41598 55334 22261 15854 56213 45353 42000 36447 (26627) 56755 13816 18742 24567 19113 53541 14551 49932 41955 31725 44216 56755 18967 21912 56902 40788 12792 30976 39062 38891 13823 53574 31383 7GYGG 32735 52608 42968 21723 52622 55362 33162 48698 12864 16971 40535 56755 31630 52626 36529 41943 49236 47257 52694 11042 38842 12279 10238 37975 53177 48626 41598 42938 52694 33999 31642 57066 37928 10767 34527 32724 56902 20793 54426 30519 52900 43128 41864 41598 7GYGG 12792 33162 11430 31729 10767 10560 52738 31839 44986 41598 45353 41864 29686 53574 12792 22140 19620 52597 53541 55788 37688 46723 21903 53169 38760 56780 24473 41798 52955 53682 56780 49330 31049 42402 49873 10221 48507 41132 31049 15448 49873 43518 13180.

BEAUPRE.

BOGOTA, *November 7, 1903.*

SECSTATE, *Washington:*

OLGBP 31383 TGYGG 37617 39805 30333 42467 36289 56902 44007 52739 52411 19971 52622 35760 52561 39623 36488 35945 36529 33162 56899 13177 31062 17284 37624 52626 35494 52371 57328 12792 37163 34033 12647 20791 42024 22993 56917 56904 40788 42467 31694 14301 42861 12926 13809 19113 53541 56531 10446 21604 52597 35768 41598 20602 16440 44357 52739 52411 39263 14889 31725 12792 23449 47268 15432 Pan 12647 21676 11957 20602 44356 33337 35768 45706 41621 13809 53574 39118 52371 57328 16772 14305 34527 42467 33162 14947 17284 52236 24771 10788 56833 16006 33437 14382 52694 52562 31725 34564 38954 44355 40751 12792 53406 41621 36529 12792 26700 46285 40791 31694 31839 28726 33344 38760 17066 24473 34564 Cauca 12792 42467 13177.

BEAUPRE.

BOGOTA, *November 7, 1903.*

SECSTATE, *Washington:*

OLGFP 14551 31725 32735 55331 15395 42467 12792 20636 39374 47390 38908 14889 12165 20628 37319 53682 52929 43815 29973 52694 12894 37971 45830 43000 12293 33986 31725 56755 10798 38467 20624 48032 12792 50472 41783 36529 10546 14480 52873 53578 30725 19386 20628 36447 28203 53974 51774 52608 48911 40074 52694 42506 21742 12529 28203 53974 27588 31008 39374 21775 41621 44948 38375 31383 TGYGG 51042 37415 36453 43980 23472 44323 14629 45258 18742 39623 53149 42467.

BEAUPRE.

BOGOTA, *November 9, 1903.*

SECSTATE, *Washington:*

OLJJA 35288 18742 31383 JGYGG 52561 31383 JGHXK JES XPWCMR 12792 OAMKG DHGEIJLNH 44937 42725 37504 10507 33400 41758 39623 43000 31851 28726 33344 37352 23741 42498 51158 57328 23778 26939 56902 NKXXKYCJP 38781 39037 25082 33400 18990 19742 41598 31694 33790 31352 15432 42436 52638 41990 A 44937 40407 31383 10907 44369 19005 33437 47521 53682 26394 31354 57123 49514 38760 24483 33344 12926 20232 17488 32023 18742 50306 37675 54110 51207 32016 18619 13433 34998 33652 25010 42506 47506 OSXGWEX NK KYCJP 15496 56902 51095 46521 45715 44338 39374 52371 49498 32858 44357 49959 18619 39340 42416 30104 33789 49510 30563 42611 52969 27503 50094 12792 35697 41798 33789 52872 53149 20615 27503 50093.

BEAUPRE.

BOGOTA, *November 10, 1903.*

SECSTATE, *Washington:*

OLKKA 26708 25372 20741 53149 55832 41796 26700 54178 38928 52390 52867.

BEAUPRE.

BOGOTA, *November 11, 1903.*

SECSTATE, *Washington:*

OLLKA 50077 33344 22777 18619 38105 52878 22597 54053 14693 36447 35835 29818 11746 31721 43000 52737 12293 29819 11746 54424 16899 17534 52561 31725 27836 52608 48911 40074 12892 50896 52391 46174 31697 27450 54424 30519 35960 20624 53682 54110 31383 ZSFKH 15395 20636 40570 52636 51834 43000 12743 14233 52456 52955 51207 17418 45842 33344 12895 41598 30104 52955 34564 QKAMU 41855 11746 42467 20787 31383 Reyes 45281 54424 56755 12150 20602 37319 53682 42506 39040 54132 37505 41598 49234 QKXS 12792 47550 42761 47402 31721 53149 18977 22834 45455 12611 22256 42011 46999 43906 34164 53571 52895 41905 31697 12792 31383 REYES 14551 17418 35476.

BEAUPRE.

BOGOTA, *November 12, 1903.*

SECSTATE, *Washington:*

OLMFP 35313 44622 52561 31723 22145 51580 11409 37675 17418 52436 47795 15982 31201 21298 10574 24031 15495 18742 43736 56213 37188 52561 54424 12155 53682 37319 34019 51579 33700 49574 10748

BEAUPRE.

BOGOTA, *November 12, 1903.*

SECSTATE, *Washington:*

OLMKA 55740 36339 53177 42436 40863 21671 56902 44369 12860 18903 21049 51388 41598 52390 41621 50085 30644 40996 53177 39374 55740 14904 38900 57073 41693 22289 37379 20323 38927 54424 57095 43041 52608 37322 41598 20624 53682 47099 41870 52608 37330 54872 40610 40890 36021 18704 32281 31111 40244 27148 34527 24946 41005 12849 20866 38539 44369 52670 28065 48930 54756 44322 54653 25928 13177 46177 53177 53846 45715 41621 39374 22428 52371 49498 42506 52737 22228 34527 31694 20119 12792 29740 49400 53688 56284 45353 36447 35328 52622 46010 50075 17543 24036 40980 53149 31721 18715 12664 34564 35966 28394 34527 18102.

BEAUPRE.

BOGOTA, *November 14, 1903.*

SECSTATE, *Washington:*

LADLA 34527 41682 40995 24118 30825 39374 57185 30308 52608 34164 46278 52622 50263 31700 42467 18742 31725 28161 46763 56919 36453 20155 11814 18742 29443 52596 46278 36453 55450 41598 53578 27504 30725 56408 21182 31724 20602 45212 14629 26759 34551 50310 12792 27736 38650 12950 22079 52597 30989 52891 31694 56902 31725 32735 45979 51505 31832 43630 52582 43916 22593 46765 54459 31725 50901 36545 36606 35846 53149 35950 20602 34527 41473 51321 52622 36529 40944 46288 52608 46095 17573 33562 51324 52784 43647 53188 31694 34124 52784 43647 53188 31694 34165 14248 36456 38713 53149 36530 42467 41005 36447 38114 27450 52878 46278 22696 12057 44088 12792 55451 53578 27504 30725 41659 51325 37415 43638 32595 56902 54195 52579 52608 38954 52754 40890 35962 52629 39319 41860 40535 53149 46484 35768 41598 20602 42506 23372 50568 27559 11429 28807 27701 24379 18742 52456 55550 53149 41798 32630 38908 42786 31721 54198 52596 10788 16902 52293 53150 24444 12792 11451 38908 50995 16787 52195 35713 32088 19385 49522 46765

BEAUPRE.

BOGOTA, *November 17, 1903.*

SECSTATE, *Washington:*

LAGDP 39374 49307 13171 40995 47403 53436 18919 10346 30308 14551 31725 26762 24783 50862 36532 41904 37322 41598 20624 53682 56760 48997 33235 30333 31383 Reyes 51765 36606 45447 36488 18405 20602 12792 42467 53149 27879 52561 37415 49558 47014 34963 12948 15973 14207 10788 42100 35139 33986 52895 35854 54426 20602 10426 45281 52513 48032 41598 20602 41783 36529 14034 44230 38503 41598 42000 29535 53177 43986 33484 50472 56408 54424 32735 33355 46221 10560 36532 12755 34603 52693 52561 54424 49752 41103 43041 41943 11954 26330 of 20602 39143 44503 52437 26621 41621 53406 20602 32735 30333 29962 57322 38472 30905 53406 18619 49632 16535 14907 19367 52878 29225 11926 52626 38192 of 44097 52515 49988 31008 29733 50352 36043 of 53406 38862 41566 50472 of 40415 16627 25544 45455 15995 35410 44222 to 20881 14161 14709 27447 28895 53541 12925 20244 51523 39899 18795 55450 10043 45353 53541 52542 10000 52437 36043 41598 53329 40001 27469 38933 54424 23268 27747 44503 36043 of 53406 57081 41073 46095 10336 41441 20628 in 46487 42000 and 22261 48205 36494 24976 41598 54424 by 53541 33986 54424 53682 17080 54892 26035 20624 14233 36542 in 51419 of 40407 50472 and 22693 53574.

BEAUPRE.

BOGOTA, *November 17, 1903.*

SECSTATE, *Washington:*

LAGLA 46045 52940 45003 43867 52561 31433 35278 13978 57012 29686 20628 11746 54424 34527 52467 38825 31438 36453 57369 38596 13433 27315 35264.

BEAUPRE.

BOGOTA, *November 15, 1903.*

SECSTATE, *Washington:*

LAEGP 31723 34527 21261 22759 50075 12792 28726 10092 43000 50519 18925 53149 38413 45207 20628 53155 44586 12792 49330 52626 40415 43000 18428 17066 14898 53439 53004 27662 55832 21076 53149 44390 49231 31049 20634 13436 49232 53149 41897 10797 41598 44391 21461 42477 12567 47398 18795 18428 32630 52878 57361 12402 39374 30075 25391 52607 49778 49090 36532 18428 53444 16854 20628 29733 42467 15842 42739 39174 30333 20628.

BEAUPRE.

BOGOTA, *November 20, 1903.*

SECSTATE, *Washington:*

LBOAP 44405 45362 55467 12792 10377 15498 54716 44369 12792 31725 41805 57045 49937 15652 56605 49937 44369 13957 42178 55394 29458 51499 31951 10369 12792 54663 14027 28638 39319 44268 38363 25611 53149 15495 42467 13088.

BEAUPRE.

BOGOTA, *November 21, 1903.*

SECSTATE, *Washington:*

LBAAP 39374 34527 40996 25411 35298 36545 52608 35854 20628 33406 53329 41758 37971 53406 17788 41580 43464 of 19046 36447 36240 52608 29210 45298 of 25124 42467 39998 56438 50074 29590 26564 31008 20636 12792 42467 12946 56408 40890 35866 41579 53329 42767 12940 41860 56801 33406 30905 53329 56514 20628 32007 38467 39374 56897 31725 53149 37138 10256 to 27879 52561 52784 41860 16627 35960.

BEAUPRE.

BOGOTA, *November 23, 1903.*

SECSTATE, *Washington:*

LBCAP 44311 39628 48390 54871 26197 31566 31721 51045 21261 22755 18628 54146 of 35835 29818 12792 32780 38546 31213 54051.

BEAUPRE.

BOGOTA, *November 25, 1903.*

SECSTATE, *Washington:*

LBEMM 51207 42725 34564 31694 33193 39382 16153 18742 41876 29682 31581 38908 42786 12792 20846 55685 42086 42725 33193 39374 29682 28857 25913 38968 30073 51119 39048 41621 18903 57328 14551 31383 Reyes 36447 41768 55864 53149 55832 44669 40890 24771 10788 52228 31721 54653 47717 39623 37179 36542 13084 39623 36488 35425 12743 10802 19046 12688 41919 49235 11767 10808 44391 17552 42467 19146 46391 12926 29818 11746 54424 12792 30846 35837 12003 47215 48911 40074 34564 QKAMU 14435 37188 52360 17663 52561 31465 56755 46285 42467 11668 28029 10775.

BEAUPRE.

BOGOTA, *November 27, 1903.*

SECSTATE, *Washington:*

LBGMM 39382 18987 38908 21682 24188 33682 10043 30969 35332 52579 21617 56902 44369 57328 36558 21508 52597 39374 32211 49409 18046 31008 30073 37380 34549 38610 41621 19113 40643 33162 14905 27896 49015 57371 41680 11042 38837 56902 42467 42010 52561 25103 57063 47849 53149 20602 12792 48422 16385 30440 20628 57063 33986 52878 16802 10429 34165 18967 47257 22833 56537 13816 53542 56902 54424 52620 44107 52504 12792 21612 41621 53541 19553 18742 54424 56902 47337 42467 52600 16550 26827 39846 43000 33986 51499 14322 16550 38362 48641 57349 12792 42467 39382 15347 38908 16812 41796 19345 42144 33344 43000 52878 21744 12792 44369 56899 32831 57371 55402 17284 35697 49336 31383 Reyes 39382 48422 46765 16817 18460 56931 37670 12925 12451 43142 17080 43593 to 15495 37678 31721 52194 38974 44503 51499 41575.

BEAUPRE.

BOGOTA, *December 8, 1903.*

SECSTATE, *Washington:*

OMHGP 22954 40586 46871 33344 12892 52608 31200 41612 31177 40650 40244 42611 27448 12674 49487 45719 42467 52776 37605 30333 54424 56902 56740 10216 24338 53825 37624 48956 37673 31738 Bolivar 24569 20433 43815 19375 and Barranquilla 53149 55325 to 31010 20636 19090 19461 55320 to 39036 54832 at 19375 17788 24338 53832 and 52868 52189 54832 to 20636 41072 29569.

BEAUPRE.

BOGOTA, *December 26, 1903.*

SECSTATE, *Washington:*

MBFCP QEKRAEGXS 37967 18102 20232 45833 21129 12647 23121 40799 20232 30531 49169 15842 25119 QAZHAEKUKHQK 20083 42484 30291 38443 16008 35697.

SNYDER.

BOGOTA, *December 26, 1903.*

SECSTATE, *Washington:*

MBFLA 22954 53682 49331 52608 20466 52613 35864 41621 31694 54052 33900 35329 29003 41598 53846 52955 39098 37652 53756 12925 49514 42099 32792 37652 41294 31645 42230 53149 42467 53149 55605 32074 31832 13718 14710 15645 QKAMU 12792 AZLVK DAVK 12792 36549 44663 53682 49331 30583 13376 48911 40074 34571 25131 10649 35306 32695 41458 45743 44482.

SNYDER.

EXHIBIT D.

EXTRACTS FROM LOGS OF U. S. S. "NASHVILLE" AND U. S. S. "DIXIE."

EXCERPTS FROM THE LOG BOOK OF THE U. S. S. "NASHVILLE" UNDER THE COMMAND OF COMMANDER J. HUBBARD, UNITED STATES NAVY.

Sunday, September 27, 1903. At anchor off Pensacola Island, Fla. The commanding officer inspected crew and ship. Had on board 338 tons 1,661 pounds of coal.

Monday, September 28, 1903. At anchor off Pensacola Island, Fla., and making passage to ——. 9.15 a. m., mustered to quarters, fighting-efficiency drills. Making preparations for getting under way. At 10 a. m. lighted fires under boilers. At 1.25 p. m. got under way and stood out of Pensacola Bay. Magazines inspected and found in satisfactory condition.

Tuesday, September 29, 1903. At sea, and making passage to ——. Mustered to quarters, exercised at fighting-efficiency drills. Target practice. (172 miles.)

Wednesday, September 30, 1903. At sea and making passage to ——. (200 miles.)

Thursday, October 1, 1903. At sea making progress to ——. Fighting-efficiency drills. (156 miles.)

Friday, October 2, 1903. At sea, making passage to ——. Mustered at quarters. Division and fighting-efficiency drills, sounded drill calls, and overhauled batteries. (169 miles.)

Saturday, October 3, 1903. At sea, making passage to ——. General cleaning day. (188 miles.)

Sunday, October 4, 1903. At sea, making passage to ——. Mustered crew at 9.15; assembled on quarter deck and held general muster. At 10.45 sighted Old Providence Rock. At 7 p. m. stopped engines; 8 p. m., lying dead in the water, with engines stopped. At 11.50 p. m. went ahead slow on both engines for five minutes. (174.7 miles.)

Monday, October 5, 1903. At sea, and stood into harbor and anchored off St. Andrews Island. Lying dead in the water. Went ahead full steam on both engines at 3.47 a. m., for five minutes, bringing the ship to her course back south. Stopped engines at 3.52. Went ahead, both engines, at 5.40. Land sighted at dawn. At 5.30 slowed down to three-fourths speed. Sail sighted near St. Andrews Island at 6.37. Made sail out to be a schooner, bearing north. Turned with starboard helm and gave chase at full speed. Overhauled schooner and made her out to be the *Kearsarge* (sic) with passengers aboard. At 7.14 p. m. turned with port helm heading for St. Andrews Island. At 9.30 pilot came aboard then stood in for an anchorage; 9.40 hoisted ensign and sounded to quarters. On advice of pilot stood to the westward. At a little before 10.15, after a reported sounding of 15 feet, the ship grounded. Floated at 12.50 and at 12.53 let go the port anchor in 3½ fathoms. Got under way at 3.10 and stood in slowly toward the village. At 3.30 p. m. anchored in 6½ fathoms.

Tuesday, October 6, 1903. At anchor off St. Andrews Island. The commanding officer visited the prefect officially. At 3.40 got underway and shifted our anchorage about 90 yards to the northeast in a better anchorage. Swimming parties sent ashore.

Wednesday, October 7, 1903. At anchor off St. Andrews Island. The prefect of the Province made an official call on the commanding officer and was received with appropriate honors. Liberty party sent ashore.

Thursday, October 8, 1903. At anchor off St. Andrews Island. Surveying party left the ship at 8.30; returned at 12.15, and left again at 1.15 and returned at 6.15. Swimming and liberty parties sent ashore.

Friday, October 9, 1903. At anchor off St. Andrews Island. Surveying party left ship at 7 a. m., under Lieut. Commander H. M. Witzel and Ensign W. S. Chase.

Saturday, October 10, 1903. At St. Andrews Island, and stood out en route to Colon. Surveying party left ship 8 a. m. Commanding officer left with a pilot to plant some buoys on shoals. Surveying party returned at 10.30 and commanding officer at 10.45. Fires started at 9.30. Received on board for transportation one bag of mail for the prefect. Got under way at 12.25.

Sunday, October 11, 1903. At sea and stood into Colon, Colombia, where anchored. At 9.15 mustered to quarters, followed by inspection of crew and ship by the commanding officer. Sighted land on starboard bow at 9.30 a. m., at 12.39 made out Colon, at 2.22 let go anchor. Ensign Chase called at consulates ashore and presented the commanding officer's compliments. 7 p. m. engines secured.

Monday, October 12, 1903. At anchor off Colon, Colombia. At 9.15 sounded general quarters. 10.10 United States consul made an official call on the commanding officer. On the departure of the United States consul at 10.50 a salute of 7 guns with the national ensign at the fore in his honor. The commanding officer returned the call of the United States consul.

Tuesday, October 13, 1903. At anchor, and stood in and moored to dock at Colon, Colombia. 5.49 a. m. got under way and went alongside the Panama Railroad Wharf No. 1 for coal. Moored to dock at 7. Started coaling with natives. Panama Railroad steamer *Seguranca* came in from New York. The commanding officer left the ship to pay an official call on the prefect. Took in altogether 121½ tons of coal. At 5.24 p. m. warped the ship astern and anchored in 5½ fathoms.

Wednesday, October 14, 1903. At anchor off Colon, Colombia. The U. S. S. *Louisiana* left the harbor. British steamer *Tagus* entered the harbor. Received in Supplies and Accounts department $4,000 in gold, United States currency. Mustered crew at 5.30 p. m.

Thursday, October 15, 1903. At anchor off Colon, Colombia. Norwegian steamer *Beacon* came in. At 3 p. m. the prefect and alcalde of Colon made an official call on the commanding officer. Upon the departure of prefect a salute of 7 guns and the Colombian ensign at the fore in his honor.

Friday, October 16, 1903. At anchor off Colon, Colombia. French vice consul paid an official visit on the commanding officer. Five guns and the French ensign at the fore in his honor. The commanding officer returned the official visit of the French vice consul. Royal Mail Steam Packet *Tagus* left.

Saturday, October 17, 1903. At anchor off Colon, Colombia, and at sea. Received aboard ship gratis an unlimited supply of bananas from the United Fruit Co. At 5.32 ship under way, stood out to sea.

Sunday, October 18, 1903. At sea making passage to Guantanamo, Cuba. Mustered crew at 9.15. Inspection of crew and ship by commanding officer, followed by the reading of "Articles of War."

Monday, October 19, 1903. At sea making passage to Guantanamo, Cuba. Drills (fighting efficiency, etc.).

Tuesday, October 20, 1903. At sea making passage to Guantanamo, Cuba. Drills (fighting efficiency, etc.).

Wednesday, October 21, 1903. At sea, stood into and anchored off Guantanamo, Cuba. 6 a. m. sighted high land on the bows. Anchored at 10.32 a. m. Broke out and restored the 6-pounder magazines. Swimming party left ship at 3.45.

Thursday, October 22, 1903. At anchor off Guantanamo, Cuba. Drills, etc.

Friday, October 23, 1903. At anchor off Guantanamo, Cuba. Commanding officer inspected lighthouse and entrance to the harbor by order of the department. Drills, etc.

Saturday, October 24, 1903. At anchor off Guantanamo, Cuba. At 10.40 Cuban mail steamer left; sent mail by her.

Sunday, October 25, 1903. At anchor of Guantanamo, Cuba. The commanding officer inspected the crew and ship.

Monday, October 26, 1903. At Guantanamo, Cuba, stood out en route to Kingston, Jamaica. At 9.15 lighted fires, 11.15 got under way. Drills, etc.

Tuesday, October 27, 1903. At sea and stood into Kingston, Jamaica; 6.53 a. m., stopped both engines; took on a pilot; 7.02, went ahead full speed; stood in for anchorage in Kingston Harbor. At 8.30 stopped both engines. Fired national salute of 21 guns with the English flag at the main, returned gun for gun by the shore battery; fired salute 11 guns to the commandant of the station, returned gun for gun by the shore battery. At 9.25 anchored in Kingston Harbor. American consul visited ship; fired salute seven guns with American ensign at the fore when he left ship. The commanding officer called officially on the commandant of the naval station. Sent ashore to make arrangements for coaling.

Wednesday, October 28, 1903. At anchor off Kingston, Jamaica, and stood alongside coal dock. Took aboard 244 tons of coal and 15,000 gallons of water. Unmoored ship at 5.28 p. m. and stood out into harbor. Anchored at 6.10 p. m. in 7 fathoms.

Thursday, October 29, 1903. At anchor off Kingston, Jamaica. The commanding officer made an official call on the general commanding the military forces of Jamaica.

Friday, October 30, 1903. At anchor off Kingston, Jamaica. At 11 a. m. the commodore commanding the naval station paid an official visit aboard. At 11.15 the representative of the governor of the island called aboard.

Saturday, October 31, 1903. At Kingston, Jamaica, and making passage to Colon, Colombia. 5.15 pilot came on board. At 6 sounded to quarters (three absentees); at 6.05 got under way, and stood out of harbor.

Sunday, November 1, 1903. At sea en route to Colon, Colombia. The commanding officer inspected ship and crew. (226 miles.)

Monday, November 2, 1903. At sea and stood into Colon, Colombia. At 3 p. m. slowed and sounded with deep-sea machine, finding no bottom. At 3.05 sighted land (Manzanilla Point); at 5.25 standing into Colon Harbor, sounded to quarters. At 5.30 anchored. At 5.40 sent surgeon ashore to obtain pratique; at 6.10 surgeon returned on board with pratique. At 11.50 Colombian troopship *Cartagena* came in and anchored.

Tuesday, November 3, 1903. At anchor off Colon, Colombia. Panama Railroad steamer *City of Washington* came in. At 6 sent a boarding officer to the Colombian troopship *Cartagena*. Found her to have 500 troops and general commanding the army in command of ship and troops. Destination of troops, Panama city. At 8.20 the *Cartagena* got under way and went alongside the dock. Mustered at quarters at 9.15. At 11.15 the *Cartagena* cast off from the dock and anchored. *Yucatan* and French steamer *France* left. At 5.30 mustered and equipped the landing force. At 7.30 rigged out first cutter and sailing launch ready for lowering.

Wednesday, November 4, 1903. At anchor off Colon, Colombia, patrolling water front. Started fires in boilers C and D at 6.35 a. m. Put a slip rope on the cable. The British steamer *Orinoco* came in and went alongside dock at 6.15. Mustered crew to quarters at 9.15. Drilled divisions under arms. At 9.30 Colombian transport got under way and went alongside No. 2 dock; at 10.55 unmoored and dropped anchor in old berth. The commanding officer went ashore in answer to the United States ensign hoisted at the railroad office, returning aboard at 1.25. Called away landing parties, lowered the waist boats, hoisting steam launch and whaleboat. At 1.35 the first squad, lightly equipped with one day's rations, left the ship in the first cutter under Lieut. Commander H. M. Witzel. At 1.30 the Colombian transport got under way and stood out. At 1.40 the second squad of landing party under Midshipman J. P. Jackson left the ship. Sounded to quarters and clearing ship for action, trying engines. Under way at 1.46. Men at general quarters. Shrapnel provided for four guns. Steaming back and forth in front of town near railroad office where landing party is barricaded. Foreign residents in railroad office building and aboard ships alongside of docks. For signals see signal record book. At 5.02 officer went alongside of incoming French steamer from Cartagena but found no troops aboard. At 5.30 let go starboard anchor. Maj. Black and Lieut. Brook, United States Army, came aboard in ship's boat and offered services. At 6 p. m. Mr. Jackson came aboard to confer with the captain. The commanding officer left the ship. The commanding officer returned aboard at 6.25. Lowered waist boats and sent in for landing party. Landing party returned at 7.10.

Thursday, November 5, 1903. At anchor off Colon, Colombia, and patrolling water front. 6 a. m. officer boarded Austrian steamer from Savanilla; found no troops aboard. At 9 a. m. landing force of 30 men left the ship in command of Lieut. Commander H. M. Witzel. Took possession of and barricaded railroad office building. At 9.15 sent marines ashore with two 1-pounders and mounts. Mounted same on a flat car. Colombian troops seen maneuvering in the streets. At 9.20 hove in to 15 fathoms; at 11.10 went to general quarters; at 11.15 got up anchor and got under way. The commanding officer at the conning. Stood in close to wharves to protect the landing force and water front. Acting German consul came on board. Signals as per signal record book. At 12.15 let go starboard anchor. At 12.55 got up anchor, and got underway;

stood in to protect water front and landing force. At 1.25 let go starboard anchor. At 1.30 secured from general quarters. Signals as per signal record book. At 4 p. m. sounded to general quarters; at 4.15 got underway; at 4.20 anchored. At 5.40 sounded to general quarters; at 5.50 got underway, and stood in to protect landing force from threatened attack of Colombian troops on Royal Mail Wharf, their commanding officer having refused to embark for Cartagena, as per agreement. At 6.15 anchored; at 6.20 sighted the U. S. S. *Dixie*; at 7 got underway; at 7.05 the U. S. S. *Dixie* came in and anchored. At 7.15 anchored abreast of the U. S. S. *Dixie*, and commanding officer went on board the *Dixie*. At 7.35 the Royal Mail Steam Packet *Orinoco* went out with the 500 Colombian troops on board. Signals as per signal book. At 8.15 landing force of marines left the U. S. S. *Dixie* to relieve the landing force from this ship. At 8.45 the landing force returned on board with equipments, ammunition, and 1-pounders complete. At 9.30 got underway and shifted berth. At 9.40 anchored.

Friday, November 6, 1903. At Colon, Colombia, and at sea maneuvering along the coast. At 12.15 commanding officer of the U. S. S. *Dixie* called officially on board. Lost by the landing party, 2 rifles. Received from the *Dixie* 40,000 rounds of 6 mm. ammunition. Got underway at 8.35 p. m., and stood out on various courses. At 11 stopped engines; dead in water.

Saturday, November 7, 1903. At sea and stood into Porto Bello Harbor and anchored. Commencement lying with engines stopped 15 miles west of Manzanilla Point. At 6.10 full speed to Porto Bello, where anchored 10 a. m. Secured engines. 3.20 p. m. gun was fired on shore, and new flag of Panama was hoisted. Steamer *Alban*, flying British flag, came in; 5 p. m. sent boarding officer; at 6.30 sent boarding officer on *Alban* again for additional information.

Sunday, November 8, 1903. At anchor in harbor of Porto Bello, Colombia. Routine inspection of magazines.

Monday, November 9, 1903. At Porto Bello, and patrolling coast, and anchored off entrance to harbor. Lighted fires in boilers C and D at 6.10 a. m. At 10.53 stood over to communicate with schooner *Intrepid*, of Colon. At 11.25 overhauled the *Intrepid*; at 11.28 went full speed ahead; at 11.35 put helm hard-aport and stood back after the schooner *Intrepid*, standing into Porto Bello Harbor. Entered harbor at 12.50. The auxiliary schooner *Intrepid* entered harbor with 11 Panama troops on board, and anchored at 12.55. At 2.30 the auxiliary schooner *Intrepid* got underway, and left for Colon. At 4.57 got underway, and stood slowly out of harbor. Got up 3 rounds of common shell for each 4-inch gun and 1 box of ammunition for each pair of 6-pounders. At 5.30 anchored.

Tuesday, November 10, 1903. At anchor off entrance of Porto Bello Harbor.

Wednesday, November 11, 1903. At anchor off Porto Bello, Colombia.

Thursday, November 12, 1903. At anchor off Porto Bello, Panama (Colombia erased and Panama written over erasure). On list of punishments note Bonneau, W. P., landsman, leaving post while on duty on shore, 10 days double irons; Cochrane, F. L., landsman, drunk while on duty on shore, and losing revolver, 10 days double irons.

Friday, November 13, 1903. At Porto Bello, stood out and into Colon, Panama (Colombia erased and Panama written over erasure). At 7 a. m. sighted steamer heading northward. Steamer changed course, heading toward us; made preparations getting underway. Steamer changed course again, heading for Colon. Turned out to be U. S. naval collier *Hannibal*. Spread fires at 8.25. U. S. collier *Hannibal* came within hail; sent boat for orders. Lieut. Mainwaring, United States Marine Corps, reported aboard with ship orders. A Marine detachment being aboard the collier for the protection of Porto Bello, collier entered harbor and anchored. Went alongside collier, took in 106 tons of coal. Got underway at 5.12, full speed to Colon. At 9.35 made our number to ships in harbor. Requested permission to anchor, granted by *Atlanta*. Other signals as per Record Signal Book. At 10.14 anchored

Saturday, November 14, 1903. At Colon and making passage to Bocas del Toro, Panama. Commanding officer went aboard the *Atlanta*. Commander Merriam, United States Navy, U. S. S. *Dixie*, called aboard officially. Received aboard stores from *Atlanta* and *Dixie*. Received $4,000 in United States currency. At 11.15 the *Atlanta* got underway and stood out of harbor. Signals as per Signal Record Book. U. S. S. *Atlanta* standing in flying General Signal 458. Sent steam launch alongside, returned with dispatches. At 5.48 underway and standing out of Colon Harbor.

Sunday, November 15, 1903. At sea and anchored off Bocas del Toro, Panama. At. 9.15 mustered at quarters, followed by reading of the "Articles of War." 3.18, anchored at entrance of Bocas del Toro. Fired one blank 6-pounder to attract attention. 4.32, pilot and party of American citizens came aboard. Underway and standing in. At 5.35 let go anchor. Boarded the United Fruit Co.'s steamer *Lillie* from Philadelphia.

Monday, November 16, 1903. At anchor off Bocas del Toro, Panama. Drills.

Tuesday, November 17, 1903. At anchor off Bocas del Toro, Panama. Norwegian steamer *Fort Gaines* came in. 8 a. m., sent boarding officer on board her. The officials of Bocas del Toro made an unofficial call on the commanding officer. Target practice.

Wednesday, November 18, 1903. At anchor off Bocas del Toro. Norwegian steamer *Mount Vernon*, United Fruit Co., entered harbor. Boarded her.

Thursday, November 19, 1903. At anchor off Bocas del Toro, Panama. Inspected magazines.

Friday, November 20, 1903. At anchor off Bocas del Toro, Panama. Norwegian steamer *Belvedere* came in at 5 p. m. Boarded her.

Saturday, November 21, 1903. At anchor off Bosac del Toro, Panama. Inspected magazines.

Sunday, November 22, 1903. At anchor off Bocas del Toro, Panama. Inspected magazines. British steamer *Barnstable* came in. Boarded her.

Monday, November 23, 1903. At anchor off Bocas del Toro, Panama. Drills.

Tuesday, November 24, 1903. At anchor off Bocas del Toro, Panama. Norwegian steamer *Fort Morgan* entered harbor. Boarding officer went aboard. Inspected magazines.

Wednesday, November 25, 1903. At anchor off Bocas del Toro, Panama. At 10.40 English schooner *Elva* stood into harbor with mail and dispatches from the commander of the Caribbean Squadron at Colon, Panama, and troops as follows: Fifty men and seven officers with arms, equipment, and ammunition. Fighting efficiency drills.

Thursday, November 26, 1903. At anchor off Bocas del Toro, Panama. Norwegian steamer *Hispania* came in from New Orleans. Sent boarding officer on board.

Friday, November 27, 1903. At anchor off Bocas del Toro, and off Chiriqui Lagoon, Panama. Got underway at 8.52; at 2.45 anchored off Zapatilla Cays.

Saturday, November 28, 1903. In Chiriqui Lagoon and standing toward Bocas del Toro, Panama. 9.30 stood across Chiriqui Lagoon. 10.20 stopped both engines and sent a boat in with officer in charge to make inquiries as to local conditions. At 12.45 made out the U. S. S. *Mayflower* standing in. Signals as per signal book. Stopped engines; received despatches. At 1.45 proceeded to anchorage off Zapatilla Cays, followed by *Mayflower*. Stopped engines at 2.30. *Mayflower* anchored near by at 2.43. Lieut. Commander Gleaves, United States Navy, commander of the *Mayflower*, came aboard to confer with Commander Hubbard. At 3.15 got underway; stood out of lagoon.

Sunday, November 29, 1903. Stood into Bocas del Toro, Panama, where anchored. At 9.20 let go port anchor in Bocas del Toro Harbor. A party of ladies and gentlemen from the United States visited the ship. U. S. schooner *Intrepid* stood out of harbor. Routine inspection of magazines.

Monday, November 30, 1903. At Bocas del Toro, Panama, and en route to Colon. At 3.40 got underway and stood out of Bocas del Toro Channel.

Tuesday, December 1, 1903. At sea and stood into Colon, Panama, where anchored. At 4.30 a. m. made out lights of Colon. At dawn sighted ships at anchor. *Dixie* signalled "Send to steamer for mail." Rounded to under stern of *Mayflower*. Let go anchor at 7.45. Found following United States ships at anchor: U. S. S. *Dixie*, flying rear admiral's pennant; U. S. S. *Maine*, U. S. S. *Atlanta*, and U. S. S. *Mayflower*. At 9.15 mustered to quarters. The commanding officer called on the commander in chief of the Caribbean squadron. At 9.20 the commander of the squadron transferred his flag from the U. S. S. *Dixie* to the *Mayflower*. Midshipman J. P. Jackson received a commission as an ensign in the United States Navy. *Yucatan* sailed for New York. U. S. S. *Atlanta* went out. Received on board 100,000 rounds of ball cartridge.

Wednesday, December 2, 1903. At anchor off Colon, Panama. Commanding officer of the *Maine* made an official call on board. Commanding officer of the *Dixie* made an official call on board. *Dixie* got underway and left port. Commanding officer went on board the *Mayflower*.

Thursday, December 3, 1903. At anchor off Colon, Panama.

Friday, December 4, 1903. At anchor off Colon, Panama. U. S. S. *Bancroft* got underway. U. S. S. *Maine* went out.

Saturday, December 5, 1903. At anchor off Colon, Panama.

Sunday, December 6, 1903. At anchor off Colon, Panama.

Monday, December 7, 1903. At anchor off Colon, Panama, and stood in to coal.

Tuesday, December 8, 1903. At anchor off Colon, Panama.

Wednesday, December 9, 1903. At anchor off Colon, Panama.

Thursday, December 10, 1903. At Colon, and making passage to Bocas del Toro, Panama.

Friday, December 11, 1903. Making passage to Bocas del Toro, Panama, where anchored. Anchored at 3.11 p. m. Officer called on consular agent ashore.

Saturday, December 12, 1903. At anchor off Bocas del Toro, Panama.
Sunday, December 13, 1903. At anchor off Bocas del Toro, Panama.
Monday, December 14, 1903. At anchor off Bocas del Toro, Panama, and underway.
Tuesday, December 15, 1903. Making passage to Chiriqui Lagoon, where anchored.
Wednesday, December 16, 1903. At anchor in Chiriqui Lagoon.
Thursday, December 17, 1903. At anchor in Chiriqui Lagoon.
Friday, December 18, 1903. At anchor in Chiriqui Lagoon and at Bocas del Toro.
Saturday, December 19, 1903. At Bocas del Toro and at anchor in Chiriqui Lagoon.
Sunday, December 20, 1903. At anchor in Chiriqui Lagoon and making passage to Colon.
Monday, December 21, 1903. At sea and at anchor off Colon. At 5.50 stood into Colon Harbor. Commanding officer of the U. S. S. *Prairie* returned visit of the commanding officer.
Tuesday, December 22, 1903. At anchor off Colon, Panama. Rear Admiral Coglan transferred his flag from the *Prairie* to the *Mayflower*.
Wednesday, December 23, 1903. At Colon and making passage to Chiriqui Lagoon. U. S. S. *Bancroft* alongside of pier. U. S. S. *Olympia* came in. At 9.40 the captain went on board the flagship; returned aboard at 10.40. At 10.50 went aboard the *Olympia*; returned at 11.55. U. S. S. *Atlanta* went alongside pier at 1.40. Admiral transferred his flag from the *Mayflower* to the *Olympia*. 3.05 got underway and went within hail of the flagship. At 3.25 stood out of harbor.
Thursday, December 24, 1903. At sea and in Chiriqui Lagoon.
Friday, December 25, 1903. In Chiriqui Lagoon and at Bocas del Toro, Panama.
Saturday, December 26, 1903. At anchor off Bocas del Toro.
Sunday, December 27, 1903. At anchor off Bocas del Toro.
Monday, December 28, 1903. At anchor off Bocas del Toro.
Tuesday, December 29, 1903. At Bocas del Toro, Panama, and in Chiriqui Lagoon.
Wednesday, December 30, 1903. At anchor in Chiriqui Lagoon.
Thursday, December 31, 1903. At anchor in Chiriqui Lagoon. U. S. S. *Olympia* and U. S. S. *Prairie* came in.
Friday, January 1, 1904. At anchor in Chiriqui Lagoon.
Saturday, January 2, 1904. At anchor in Chiriqui Lagoon.
Sunday, January 3, 1904. At anchor in Chiriqui Lagoon.
Monday, January 4, 1904. At anchor in Chiriqui Lagoon.
Tuesday, January 5, 1904. At anchor in Chiriqui Lagoon.
Wednesday, January 6, 1904. At anchor in Chiriqui Lagoon.
Thursday, January 7, 1904. At anchor in Chiriqui Lagoon.
Friday, January 8, 1904. At anchor in Chiriqui Lagoon.
Saturday, January 9, 1904. In Chiriqui Lagoon and at anchor off Bocas del Toro, Panama.
Sunday, January 10, 1904. At anchor off Bocas del Toro.
Monday, January 11, 1904. At Bocas del Toro and at anchor in Chiriqui Lagoon.
Tuesday, January 12, 1904. At anchor in Chiriqui Lagoon.
Wednesday, January 13, 1904. At anchor in Chiriqui Lagoon.
Thursday, January 14, 1904. In Chiriqui Lagoon and at anchor off Bocas del Toro.
Friday, January 15, 1904. In Almirante Bay and at anchor off Bocas del Toro.
Saturday, January 16, 1904. Bocas del Toro and Almirante Bay
Sunday, January 17, 1904. At anchor off Bocas del Toro.
Monday, January 18, 1904. In Bocas del Toro and Bocas del Dragon.
Tuesday, January 19, 1904. At anchor in Bocas del Dragon.
Wednesday, January 20, 1904. In Bocas del Toro and at anchor in Chiriqui Lagoon.
Thursday, January 21, 1904. At anchor in Chiriqui Lagoon.
Friday, January 22, 1904. In Chiriqui Lagoon and making passage to St. Andrews Island.
Saturday, January 23, 1904. On passage to St. Andrews Island and Old Providence Island, Colombia.
Sunday, January 24, 1904. Old Providence Island, Colombia, and on passage to Colon, Republic of Panama.
Monday, January 25, 1904. Making passage to Colon, Republic of Panama.
Tuesday, January 26, 1904. At anchor off Colon, Republic of Panama. Commanding officer went on board the flagship.
Wednesday, January 27, 1904. At anchor off Colon and alongside dock.
Thursday, January 28, 1904. At Colon and Porto Bello and en route to Mandingo Harbor. U. S. S. *Atlanta* was at Porto Bello.
Friday, January 29, 1904. At anchor off Mandingo Harbor and en route to Caledonia Harbor.
Saturday, January 30, 1904. At anchor off Caledonia Harbor and en route for ,Colombia. The U. S. S. *Castine* was at Caledonia Harbor.

EXCERPTS FROM THE LOG BOOK OF THE U. S. S. "DIXIE," UNDER THE COMMAND OF COMMANDER FRANCIS H. DELANO, UNITED STATES NAVY.

Thursday, October 1, 1903. At the navy yard, New York. The ship went into commission at 2 p. m.

Friday, October 2, 1903. At the navy yard, New York.

Saturday, October 3, 1903. At the navy yard, New York.

Sunday, October 4, 1903. At the navy yard, New York.

Monday, October 5, 1903. At the navy yard, New York. Ship receiving engineer's stores.

Tuesday, October 6, 1903. At the navy yard, New York. Ship receiving navigation stores.

Wednesday, October 7, 1903. At the navy yard, New York. Ship receiving medical and navigation stores.

Thursday, October 8, 1903. At the navy yard, New York. Ship receiving general stores.

Friday, October 9, 1903. At the navy yard, New York. Ship receiving engineer's and construction and repair stores.

Saturday, October 10, 1903. At the navy yard, New York. Ship receiving construction and repair stores.

Sunday, October 11, 1903. At the navy yard, New York. Commander F. A. Delano, United States Navy, left the ship in obedience to an order to appear before a naval examining board at Washington, D. C.

Monday, October 12, 1903. At the navy yard, New York. Ship receiving engineer and electrical stores.

Tuesday, October 13, 1903. At the navy yard, New York. Ship receiving steam and engineer's stores.

Wednesday, October 14, 1903. At the navy yard, New York. Ship receiving steam and engineer's stores.

Thursday, October 15, 1903. At the navy yard, New York. Ship coaling. The commanding officer called officially on the commander in chief of the Atlantic station.

Friday, October 15, 1903. At the navy yard, New York. Ship coaling and taking on supplies.

Saturday, October 17, 1903. At the navy yard, New York. Ship taking on steam and engineer's supplies.

Sunday, October 18, 1903. At the navy yard, New York. Commander F. H. Delano, United States Navy, returned to the ship from special duty in Washington, D. C.

Monday, October 19, 1903. At the navy yard, New york. Ship taking on engineer and general supplies.

Tuesday, October 20, 1903. At the navy yard, New York. Ship receiving general supplies and ordnance; 20,000 rounds of ball cartridge, cal. .30; 95,000 rounds of ball cartridge, 6 mm.; 21,000 rounds of cal. .38; 5,000 rounds of cal. .45.

Wednesday, October 21, 1903. At the navy yard, New York. Ship receiving ordnance, ammunition, construction and repair, and steam and engineer's stores. At 8.30 got all the ammunition on board. Total amount, 1,833 5-inch common shells; 55 5-inch A. T. shells; 100 5-inch shrapnel; 2,002 6-pounder common shells; 2,400 1-pounder steel shells; 297 6-pounder saluting charges; 93,000 rounds of .30 caliber; 3,400 pounds of common powder.

Thursday, October 22, 1903. In Gedney Channel, entrance to New York Harbor.

Friday, October 23, 1903. At League Island, Pa., receiving stores for supplies and accounts department.

Saturday, October 24, 1903. At League Island, Pa. Draft of 104 Marines from the League Island Barracks. Supplies brought aboard the U. S. S. *Dixie* by the Marine batallion included 33 cases of arms, 18 boxes shrapnel, 200,000 rounds of ball cartridge, cal. .30. List is signed Capt. N. G. Burton, United States Marine Corps, and acting quartermaster. Commander Delano made a call on Admiral Wise. Left the navy yard and stood down the Delaware River at 3.05 p. m.

Sunday, October 25, 1903. At sea.

Monday, October 26, 1903. At sea.

Tuesday, October 27, 1903. At sea.

Wednesday, October 28, 1903. At sea.

Thursday, October 29, 1903. At sea, and at anchor off Guantanamo, Cuba. At 11.10 came to anchor off Guantanamo, Cuba.

Friday, October 30, 1903. At Guantanamo, Cuba. At 8 a. m. sent the steam launch to Caimanara. U. S. S. *Atlanta* entered harbor at 11.40.

Saturday, October 31, 1903. At Guantanamo, Cuba. Sent mail to the United States via Santiago at 7.30 a. m. Commanding officer of the *Atlanta* called officially; call returned by commanding officer. At 4.50 *Atlanta* got under way and stood out of Guantanamo. At 6 p. m. *Dixie* under steam and on course south.

Sunday, November 1, 1903. At sea, and in Port Royal, Jamaica. At 8 a. m. standing in for entrance of Kingston Harbor. At 10 a. m. came to anchor. Fired a national salute of 21 guns with English flag at the main, and a salute of 11 guns to the commandant of the naval station. Shore battery returned salutes, gun for gun. Sent officer ashore to call on the United States consul. Commanding officer called officially on the commodore commanding the naval station.

Monday, November 2, 1903. At Port Royal, Jamaica. At 6.05 got under way and went alongside of dock; moored to coal pier for purpose of coaling. British commodore commanding the naval station at Port Royal called officially on the commanding officer. At 6 p. m. knocked off coaling, having taken 104 tons, 1,747 pounds. Aide from the general commanding the forces called on the commanding officer.

Tuesday, November 3, 1903. At Port Royal, Jamaica, and at sea. At 6 a. m. commenced coaling. Commanding officer left ship to call officially on the governor commanding the Island of Jamaica, and on the major general commanding the local forces. At 3.15 stopped coaling. At 4 p. m. breasting away from dock; left steam launch at market wharf for pay clerk ashore on duty. Steam launch returned at 6.45 with pay clerk. Hoisted in steam launch and made preparations for getting under way. At 7.50 got up anchor and stood out of harbor.

Wednesday, November 4, 1903. At sea. Marine batallion drilled and instructed by companies. Mustered and inspected divisions at quarters.

Thursday, November 5, 1903. At sea and in Colon. At 9.15 sounded to general quarters. Fired all guns with one test shot each, except the 12 port, from which two shots were fired. All guns in good order. Drilled riflemen. At 6.15 p. m. sighted Manzanilla Point. At 5.30 mustered at quarters. Found the U. S. S. *Nashville* in harbor. *Nashville* got under way and steamed into hailing distance. At 7.30 anchored. Received following signals from the U. S. S. *Nashville:* At 7.15, ship's number 270. At 7.25, "Advise having battalion ready for landing immediately." At 7.30, "Situation very critical." At 7.35, by megaphone, "Situation ashore very grave; you should have your battalion ready to land immediately. I will show you where to go and will follow you in." Lowered all davit boats and embarked two companies of Marines in command of Maj. Lejeune, United States Marine Corps. Commanding officer of the *Nashville* called on the commanding officer of this vessel. Commanding officers of this vessel and of *Nashville* went ashore in the U. S. S. *Nashville's* steam launch, towing cutters with force of Marines, leaving ship at 7.55. Commanding officer returned from shore in the *Nashville's* steam launch, towing boats from this ship. Sent *Nashville's* launch, with cutter in tow, with packed knapsacks for Marine force on shore. Steamer and cutter returned. Hoisted all boats. At 10.20 sent wigwag to Maj. Lejeune: "Allow no armed force of either party to land."

Friday, November 6, 1903. At Colon. Six a. m. received signal from Marine force ashore: "All quiet ashore, Lejeune." Commanding officer left ship at 6.30 to visit Marine force and railroad officials. Sent in steam launch, with cutter, at 7.30 with breakfast for the landing party. At 9.15 sent officer in boat to bring the United States consul on board. Sent steam launch with three cutters in charge of the boatswain to bring off the Marine detachment. Boats returned with Company B a little before noon. Maj. Black, United States Corps of Engineers, called officially on the commanding officer. Signals as per Signal Record Book. *Nashville* wigwagged: "Have you received any personal baggage?" *Dixie* answered by wigwag: "No personal baggage has been received."

Saturday, November 7, 1903. At Colon. 4.45 a. m. U. S. S. *Atlanta* came in and anchored. *Atlanta* signaled to *Dixie*: "International 131." *Dixie* answered in the affirmative. Commanding officer of the *Atlanta* called officially. The commanding officer went ashore at 9.30; returned at 11.30. At noon sent the steam launch ashore with officer in charge to answer signal displayed at the railroad office, indicating that the Government officials wished to communicate on important matters. The launch returned with letter. Capt. Turner of the *Atlanta* came on board at 5 p. m. Left the ship at 5.20.

Sunday, November 8, 1903. At anchor in the harbor of Colon. At 1 p. m. sent boat ashore in answer to signal and brought off the secretary to the United States consul with a message for the commanding officer.

Monday, November 9, 1903. At anchor in the harbor of Colon. The auxiliary schooner *Intrepid* left the harbor at 6.30. At 11 the U. S. S. *Nashville* came in sight, but did not enter the harbor.

THE STORY OF PANAMA.

No. 4.

HEARINGS ON THE RAINEY RESOLUTION BEFORE THE COMMITTEE ON FOREIGN AFFAIRS OF THE HOUSE OF REPRESENTATIVES.

FEBRUARY 15, 16, AND 20, 1912.

THE STORY OF PANAMA.

AFTER RECESS.

THURSDAY, FEBRUARY 15, 1912, 2 P. M.

STATEMENT OF MR. HENRY N. HALL—Resumed.

The CHAIRMAN. You may proceed, Mr. Hall.

Mr. HALL. As soon as the cable office opened the next morning, Mr. Ehrman sent off the following message:

PANAMA, *November 4*.

SECRETARY OF STATE, *Washington:*

Cables *Nashville* received. *Nashville* notified. Troops will not be moved. Last night gunboat *Bogota* fired several shells on city. One Chinaman killed. *Bogota* threatens bombard city to-day.

EHRMAN.

There was still considerable fear among the conspirators in Panama that the Colombian troops would manage to get over from Colon, and at daybreak on the 4th all the forces the Panamans could muster were divided into two regiments, the "First Isthmian," made up of the soldiers of the old Colombia regiment, which had gone over on the previous day, and the "Second Isthmian," made up of members of the fire brigade and volunteers. They were well armed from the Colombian barracks and numbered about 1,200 men.

It was arranged that the moment the Colombian troops should leave Colon, Melendez should start an independent movement there. The following telegram was sent by him over the Panama Railroad Co.'s line, which we have seen was the sole means of communication remaining open between Colon and Panama:

PANAMA, *November 4*.

PORFIRIO MELENDEZ, *Colon:*

As soon as the troops leave for this city, you must act. Inform me of the result. The uprising here has been completely successful. Boats in the bay controlled by us. Duque wired Cotes to give you 1,000 pesos.

J. A. ARANGO.

Immediately after this had been sent, the junta met and sent off the following telegram to Porfirio Melendez:

PORFIRIO MELENDEZ, *Colon:*

Inform the chief of the troops that came from Cartagena of what took place in this city yesterday afternoon; that the people as a whole approve the movement; Gens. Tovar and Amaya are prisoners, as are all their aides, and resistance is entirely useless; that desirous of avoiding bloodshed, the junta of Government offers to provide rations and will give the passage for the return to Baranquilla, always provided they shall surrender their arms. Understand yourself with the captain of the American warship and with Col. Shaler, and communicate the result.

J. A. ARANGO.
FEDERICO BOYD.
TOMAS ARIAS.

On receipt of this message, Porfirio Melendez called on Col. Shaler, with whom he had had frequent conferences since November 1, who told him that he had received an order issued on board the U. S. S. *Nashville* by Commander Hubbard the previous evening, confirming verbal instructions he had received in the morning. This order read:

U. S. S. "NASHVILLE," *November 3*
(Colon, United States of Colombia, November 4).

SIR: The condition of affairs at Panama being such that any movement of troops in the neighborhood must inevitably produce a conflict and interrupt that transit of the Isthmus which the United States Government is pledged to maintain uninterrupted, I am obliged to prohibit the carrying of troops of either party or in either direction by your railroad, and hereby notify you that I do so prohibit it.

Yours, very respectfully, JOHN HUBBARD, *Commanding.*

Col. SHALER,
General Superintendent of the Panama Railroad Co., Colon.

After Commander Hubbard had issued this order from the *Nashville*, the United States consul at Colon, late on the evening of the 3d, had received two urgent messages from the State Department in Washington. The first was:

WASHINGTON, *November 3, 1903—8.45 p. m.*

MALMROS, *Colon:*

The troops which landed from the *Cartagena* should not proceed to Panama.

LOOMIS, *Acting.*

The second dispatch read:

WASHINGTON, *November 3, 1903—10.30 p. m.*

MALMROS, *Colon:*

If dispatch to *Nashville* has not been delivered, inform her captain immediately that he must prevent Government troops departing for Panama or taking any action which would lead to bloodshed, and must use every endeavor to preserve order on the Isthmus.

HAY.

Meantime the Colombian officials at Bogota were reposing peacefully in the faith that the United States, under its obligations in the treaty of 1846–1848, could be depended upon to uphold Colombian sovereignty on the Isthmus of Panama. Their confidence was shown in the following cable from the minister for foreign affairs to Acting Minister Herran, dated Bogota, November 2, 1903:

Congress has adjourned without legislating about the canal. Reiterate to the Secretary of State declarations in telegram of September 8. Advise him to maintain order on the Isthmus and safety of traffic.

Now, all day on November 3, Col. Torres, who had been left in command in Colon by Gen. Tovar when the latter went to Panama, and who had disembarked his Tiradores regiment, tried his best to obtain transportation for his 500 men. Three times he called on Col. Shaler, alone and in company with Gen. Cuadros, the prefect, and he also appealed to Mr. Malmros, the American vice consul; but in vain. At first Col. Shaler repeated the promise that had been made to Gen. Tovar, that the Tiradores would be taken over to Panama on the afternoon train. Then Torres was told that it was against the regulations to furnish transportation unless paid for in advance. Torres had no money, and demanded that the troops be transported for account of the Government of Colombia on credit. Mr. Malmros was obliged to admit that the railroad could not refuse this request, under the contract of concession of the company, but Col. Shaler pointed to another regulation, that requisitions for the transportation of troops for account of the Colombian Government had to be signed by the governor of the Province, Obaldia. Finally, when Torres became more insistent, he was told that there were not enough cars available, and that they would have to wait until the necessary rolling stock would be brought over from Panama.

Col. Shaler, however, told Porfirio Melendez several times that he was greatly worried because he did not see how he could avoid transporting the Colombian troops without jeopardizing the railroad's concession, and that he would have given Col. Torres a train had he not received the written orders of the United States Government to refuse the transportation.

At daybreak on the 4th of November Col. Torres renewed his effort to get his men carried over to Panama, but when he saw Col. Shaler the latter informed him that Commander Hubbard, of the U. S. S. *Nashville*, had refused to allow the railroad to transport his troops, but the general superintendent gave him no inkling of what had occurred the previous day in Panama.

Commander Hubbard, after he had given written orders to Col. Shaler not to transport Colombian troops, sent off the following cable, printed in Senate Document No. 51, Fifty-eighth Congress:

COLON, *November 4, 1903.*

SECRETARY OF THE NAVY, *Washington:*

Provisional government was established at Panama Tuesday evening; no organized opposition. Governor of Panama, Gen. Tovar, Gen. Amaya, Col. Morales, and three others of the Colombian Government troops who arrived Tuesday taken prisoners at Panama. I have prohibited transport of troops now here across the Isthmus.

HUBBARD.

When Melendez called on Col. Shaler with the message he had received from the junta the two talked the matter over, and as a result Señor Melendez went over to where Col. Torres was and engaged him in conversation; took him over to the Astor House to have a drink. There Melendez broke the news to Torres, and told him that the independence of Panama was secured by the United States, and that the American warship then in the harbor and others that were on their way were sent by arrangement with the Government of the United States. Torres was very much excited, and at first refused to believe the news; but when it was confirmed he flew into a violent passion and swore that he would kill every American in the town unless the Colombian generals were at once released.

Col. Torres at once made his way back to the wharf, where his anger was, if anything, added to when this letter from Commander Hubbard, of the *Nashville*, was handed to him [shows photograph of letter]:

U. S. S. "NASHVILLE," 3D RATE,
Colon, United States of Colombia, November 4, 1903.

To the GENERAL OFFICER COMMANDING "THE TROOPS, COLON."

SIR: The condition of affairs at Panama, I am advised, is such that a movement of the Colombian troops now at Colon to that neighborhood must bring about a conflict and threaten that free and uninterrupted transit of the Isthmus which the Government of the United States is pledged to maintain. I have therefore the honor to notify you that I have directed the superintendent of the Panama Railroad at Colon that he must not transport on his line troops either of the opposite party.

Trusting that this action on my part will meet with your cordial acquiescence, I have the honor to be, sir,

Very respectfully, yours,

JOHN HUBBARD,
Commander, U. S. Navy, Commanding.

To the General Officer Commanding "The Troops, Colon."

Determined to force the release of his superior officers, Col. Torres went to the prefect of Colon, Gen. Pedro A. Cuadros, and ordered him to go to the American consulate and tell Mr. Malmros that he was determined to burn down the town and kill every American in it if the generals were not released before 2 o'clock. Cuadros tried to dissuade Torres from taking this step, but the latter insisted, saying that he was going to take a train by force. Cuadros opposed this plan and advised Torres to take the money offered by Melendez and return with his men to Cartagena.

Torres would not listen to this proposal, and insisted that the prefect carry his message to the American consul. This was done, and as soon as Mr. Malmros had heard of the Colombian officer's intentions he sent for his vice consul, James Hyatt, and together they went to the Panama Railroad, where they saw Col. Shaler, who told them that the captain of the Colombian gunboat *Cartagena* had just asked for supplies of water and coal on a Colombian Government requisition, and that he had replied that he would not give either unless paid for in advance, as Panama was now independent and under the protectorate of the American Government.

After Malmros, Hyatt, and Shaler had discussed Torres's threat, of which Shaler had already been informed by Melendez, they decided to call Commander Hubbard ashore, which they did by a prearranged signal to the U. S. S. *Nashville* by raising an American flag over the Panama Railroad depot. They went to the wharf and within a few minutes Commander Hubbard arrived. What then occurred can best be told in Commander Hubbard's own words in his report to the Navy Department of November 8, 1903:

At 1 p. m. on November 4 I was summoned on shore by a preconcerted signal, and on landing met the United States consul, vice consul, and Col. Shaler, the general superintendent of the Panama Railroad. The consul informed me that he had received notice from the officer commanding the Colombian troops—Col. Torres—through the prefect of Colon, that if the Colombian officers, Gens. Tovar and Amaya, who had been seized in Panama on the evening of November 3 by the independents and held as prisoners, were not released by 2 o'clock p. m., he, Torres, would open fire on the town of Colon and kill every American citizen in the place, and my advice and action were requested. I advised that all the United States citizens should take refuge in the shed of the Panama Railroad Co., a stone building susceptible of being put in good shape for defense, and that I would immediately land such body of men, with extra arms for arming the citizens as the complement of the ship would permit. This was agreed to, and I immediately returned on board, arriving at 1.15 p. m. The order for landing was immediately given, and at 1.30 p. m. the boats left the ship with a party of 42 men, under the command of Lieut. Commander H. M. Witzel, with Midshipman J. P. Jackson as second in command. Time being pressing, I gave verbal orders to take the building above referred to, to put it in the best state of defense possible, and protect the lives of the citizens assembled there—not firing unless fired upon. The women and children took refuge on the German steamer *Marcomania* and Panama Railroad steamship *City of Washington*, both ready to haul out from dock if necessary. The *Nashville* got under way and patroled along the water front close in and ready to use either small arms or shrapnel fire. The Colombians surrounded the buildings of the railroad company almost immediately after we had taken possession, and for about one and a half hours their attitude was most threatening, it being seemingly their purpose to provoke an attack. Happily, our men were cool and steady and, while the tension was very great, no shot was fired.

Here are photographs showing the building placed in a state of defense [shows photographs to committee].

Just as the *Nashville* was landing her men, Commander Hubbard received the following cable from the Navy Department, Senate Documen 51 of the Fifty-eighth Congress:

WASHINGTON, *November 4, 1903.*

NASHVILLE, *Colon:*

Gunboat of Colombia shelling Panama. Send immediately battery 3-inch field gun and 6-pounder with a force of men to Panama to compel cessation of bombardment. Railroad must furnish transportation immediately.

DARLING, *Acting.*

Commander Hubbard immediately replied:

COLON, *November 4, 1903.*

SECRETARY OF THE NAVY, *Washington:*

I have landed force to protect the lives and property of American citizens against threats Colombian soldiery. I am protecting water front with ship. I can not possibly send to Panama until things are settled at Colon.

HUBBARD.

When the captain of the Colombian gunboat saw the *Nashville* weigh anchor and move in with decks cleared for action and guns trained on his ship and on the wharf, he thought that discretion was the better part of valor, and, although he had only a small supply of coal and water, he got up steam and left at full speed. Referring to her departure, Commander Hubbard says:

I did not deem it expedient to detain her, as such action would certainly in the then state of affairs have precipitated a conflict on shore which I was not prepared to meet.

The departure of the *Cartagena* frustrated the plans of the junta, which, on receipt of Melendez's letter urging that she be captured, decided that the man for this job was Gen. H. O. Jeffries, an American. He had been at once sent for by Arosemena and had arrived in Panama from the Bayano River in a little dugout, a native fishing canoe. The junta had immediately sent him over to Colon on the early morning train with Hector Valdez, the judge who sat on the rogatory commission in Panama, and certified to the proceedings I have produced here, and half a dozen heavily armed young Panamans. Their plan, which differed somewhat from that proposed by Melendez, was, as all the troops from the *Cartagena* had been landed, to board the vessel, cut the guy ropes holding her to the wharf, and after overawing the unarmed crew with their revolvers, take possession of her in the name of the Republic of Panama.

At about 3.13, Col. Torres went to the Panama Railroad building and asked to see the American officer in charge. He said that he had never made any threats and that he was well disposed toward the Americans, who he asserted were under a misapprehension as to his intentions, and he said that he wished to send the alcalde of Colon, Col. Eleazer Guerrero, to Panama to see Gen. Tovar and obtain orders from him.

This was agreed to by Melendez, who suggested that it would be better to have some other person accompany the alcalde, and he asked Joe Lefevre to go over with Guerrero as his (Melendez's) representative. Lieut. Commander Witzel requisitioned a special train, which was at once furnished by Col. Shaler, but when it was ready to start Joe Lefevre could not be found, so Torres said he would send over one of his own lieutenants to escort the alcalde. This was satisfactory to Melendez, and the safe conduct of Col. Torres's two envoys was guaranteed by the American commander.

At about 4 p. m. Maj. William Murray Black, of the United States Engineers, and Lieut. Brooke, who had been detailed at the request of the Isthmian Canal Commission to follow the work of the French at Culebra and who had knowledge of the plans of the revolutionists, arrived on a freight train and at once offered their services to Lieut. Witzel, and from then on they aided in placing the railroad building in a state of defense.

The employees of the Panama Railroad Co. and other Americans were formed into a company and armed with rifles, etc., landed from the U. S. S. *Nashville*. Maj. Black and Lieut. Brooke took command of them, and this body was afterwards known as "Black's Legion."

When Torres saw that the Americans were preparing for hostilities and fortifying the building he made a proposition to Commander Hubbard, who had come on shore, that the Colombian troops were to withdraw to Monkey Hill if the *Nashville's* forces were reembarked and the town left in possession of the Colon police till the return of the alcalde at 10.45 next morning, November 5.

Commander Hubbard then had an interview with Mr. Malmros, United Staes consul in Colon; Col. Shaler, general superintendent of the Panama Railroad, and Senor Porfirio Melendez, and, after they had advised him as to the probability of Col. Torres's good faith in the matter, he decided to accept the Colombian commander's proposition and ordered his men to return on board. Col. Torres then withdrew to Monkey Hill, where he remained until the following morning.

In Panama meanwhile the organization of the Government was proceeding apace. An examination of the national and departmental treasuries showed how wise was the precaution taken by Amador in insisting on arrangements being made with a bank before he left the United States and which in his letter to his son he says actually were made. The national treasury was empty. Worse, as a matter of fact, it was some $2,000 in debt, which had been advanced by Isaac Brandon & Bros. on the personal note of the treasurer, Senor Don Eduardo de la Guardia.

The departmental treasury, which afterwards became the National Treasury of Panama, had on its books an apparent balance of $162,350 Colombian silver, equal at the then rate of exchange (135 per cent) to $68,947 American gold. But the greater part of this money was in "documentos por legalizar"—that is, vouchers, promissory notes, advances on salaries, etc.

Exactly how much hard cash there was in the departmental treasury has never been ascertained. Albino Arosemena, who was the treasurer, maintains complete silence. Mr. John Ehrman, present head of the banking house of Ehrman & Co., the best authority on Panama banking matters, says that "No one knows how much it was, but it was not much"; and Eduardo de Ycaza, who was the paymaster for the Republic of Panama, says that when he took over the treasury on November 5 or 6 it contained only $38,000 silver. Other estimates of the amounts the treasury contained vary from $12,000 to $50,000 silver.

Be that as it may, on the night of November 3 a market cart drawn by a mule was backed up against the pavement in front of the treasury and money was taken out. This, it is said, had to be done because Gen. Reuben Varon, commander of the *Padilla*, insisted on getting $10,000 silver of the $35,000 silver promised him by Amador for delivering up the gunboat he was in command of to the revolutionists. Certain it is that on the night of November 3 the *Padilla*, while not joining the *Bogota* in its bombardment of the city, remained out in the bay, and it was only on the morning of the 4th that she came close in and raised the Panaman flag.

Mr. HARRISON. Mr. Hall, where did you get that information?

Mr. HALL. I have Mr. Prescott's statement, sir; and the evidence of two others. Every fact I have advanced here is supported by affidavits, statements, or by these documents.

Mr. DIFENDERFER. Mr. Hall, is it not a fact that you were enabled to get very much of this testimony because of the fact that those that had been interested in this treachery were boastful about it after the matter had been concluded?

Mr. HALL. Those who were immediately concerned in it—the conspirators?

Mr. DIFENDERFER. Yes.

Mr. HALL. The members of the junta have never really assisted in this investigation by direct statements of their own which fully satisfied me, with the exception of Mr. Herbert G. Prescott and Dr. Raoul Amador, the son of Dr. Amador, who turned over to the World all the papers and letters which his father left: and we were fortunate enough to obtain some papers and letters of Mr. Arango, who was also one of the conspirators; but these details as to the money mostly appear in the sworn testimony of Capt. Tascon, who was one of the officers of the Colombian forces, and from the testimony of Mr. Calderon, who was the paymaster of the Colombian battalion, and also from the treasurer of the revolution, they are the people who actually paid out the money. We have sworn testimony for every single sum of money to which I shall make any allusion.

Mr. HARRISON. I suppose all the statements were given voluntarily?

Mr. HALL. All of them were given voluntarily. I can say this: I have been personally connected with this investigation since February, 1909, and to my knowledge of all these documents I have brought here not a single document or statement has been obtained by the use of money or promises in any way, shape, or form; nor has any of it been improperly obtained. The only outlays of money made to the people whose testimony I am able to adduce here are the ordinary traveling and per diem expenses which we have had to pay witnesses brought up from the Isthmus of Panama to testify in the case of The United States *v.* The Press Publishing Co. Some of those witnesses never testified, because the case never came to trial on the real issue. The case was halted on a technicality. The indictments were quashed by Judge Hough. Afterwards the Supreme Court of the United States decided that there was no jurisdiction and threw the case out of court entirely. Therefore we were never able to introduce this sworn evidence, but all these witnesses were examined by counsel of the Press Publishing Co. They are alive and can be brought before this committee at any time, and they will swear to these facts.

Mr. HARRISON. You say that these witnesses testified before counsel representing the Press Publishing Co.?

Mr. HALL. They were examined by counsel; yes, sir.

Mr. HARRISON. Was the other side represented, or were they simply ex parte statements?

Mr. HALL. All of the evidence taken in Panama, which was taken before a commission sitting in the American consulate under letters rogatory issued to the Republic of Panama by the Circuit Court of the United States for the Southern District of New York, was, of course, taken in the presence of counsel for the United States, Mr. Knapp, Assistant Attorney General, and each witness was cross-examined by him. I have only stated here such things as could honestly be supposed to be well proven. Now, after this rogatory commission had been sent down to Panama, other statements were volunteered, and we sent down a staff correspondent to the Isthmus of Panama, and on the second trip the staff correspondent of the World made to the Isthmus of Panama he obtained additional information, such as the codes between the conspirators—between Bunau-Varilla, Arango, and Amador. These codes, of which we have photographs, and which were copied by counsel of the World from the books in which they were kept in Panama, have never been sworn to before any court, but they are obtainable and can be produced as evidence.

On the morning of November 4 the Ehrman Bank, of which United States Consul Felix Ehrman was the senior partner, had to be called upon to provide eight boxes of Colombian silver in order that the rank and file of the Colombia regiment might be given the bribe money—$50 apiece—they had been promised.

This had been done first thing in the morning. Dr. Amador had gone to the Chiriqui Barracks a little after 8 o'clock. The Colombian battalion, drawn up under Huertas, formally recognized him and promised to support the junta. He made a speech to them from written notes. He said:

Boys, at last we have carried through our splendid work. The world is astounded at our heroism. Yesterday we were but the slaves of Colombia; to-day we are free. Have no fears. Here we have the proof [holding up some sheets of paper on which was the American coat of arms] that our agent in the United States, Señor Bunau-Varilla, gave us. Panama is free. The cup of gold for Bogota has been drained; therefore the United States are aiding us. Here you have proof of their word. President Roosevelt has made good, for there, you know, are the cruisers which defend us and prevent any action by Colombia. They have worked skillfully in order to avoid shedding Colombian blood, for in no other way could the American Government aid us. Free sons of Panama, I salute you. Long live the Republic of Panama! Long live President Roosevelt! Long live the American Government!

That speech, as I have quoted it, was written down by an eye-witness of the scene.

Mr. HARRISON. Who was the man who made that speech?

Mr. HALL. Dr. Amador. I have here the original notes, which were written at the time in a book which this man kept in his pocket, and I have here his sworn statement to that effect, and everything is legally certified to by the proper authorities.

After the applause of the soldiers had subsided Dr. Amador turned to Gen. Huertas and asked him to appoint a paymaster, as they had in the treasury the funds sent from the United States to pay the soldiers. Dr. Amador said:

They sent the money by draft on the bank of Ehrman in gold, and there it was changed for us in Colombian silver.

These notes were made by Col. Calderon himself, the man who paid out the money, and this is his own sworn statement.

Huertas turned to Col. Calderon, who was standing near, and said:

Go to the national treasury and receipt as paymaster for the money in the national treasury and pay it out to those persons who present orders or due bills signed by Dr. Amador, the junta, or myself.

Calderon went to the treasury, and there received eight boxes full of silver money, which he took in a public coach to the Chiriqui Barracks, where, on seeing him enter with the money, Gen. Huertas called his men together and addressed them. We have likewise a written note of Mr. Huertas's speech. He said, in part:

Soldiers, owing to the exertion of Dr. Amador and myself we have obtained that the United States shall recompense your efforts. The money which is denied us by the Government of Bogota we have here in the treasury.

This was an allusion to the fact that during the revolution of 1901 the pay of the Colombian soldiery had fallen behind and there was an outstanding debt by the Government of Colombia to these soldiers, and it happened to be very nearly the $50 a head which was then paid to them. Huertas continued:

Col. Calderon has just brought it, and he will proceed in a few minutes to pay you. The bank of Ehrman changed the American gold we received into silver and has given it to the treasury to attend to our immediate needs. We have money. We are free. The cruisers which are here remove all our fears. Colombia may battle with the weak, but she holds her peace in the presence of the United States. The Tiradores battalion, which is in Colon with ammunition, can not withstand us. We are more numerous and have more arms. The railroad is at our orders and the port of Colon is well guarded by the cruisers of the Americans, who, in case of a fight, will land men to back us up. Do not fear. We are free and powerful. Colombia is dead. Long live independent Panama. Long live Dr. Amador. Long live the American Government.

Mr. HARRISON. How long had the cruisers been there at that time?

Mr. HALL. There were no cruisers then in Panama at all. There was only one cruiser in Colon of which Huertas could have had any knowledge, and that was the *Nashville*, which arrived just after 6 o'clock on November 2. The *Dixie* arrived on November 5.

Immediately the payment of the soldiers began, each man receiving $50 Colombian silver. The officers and others who aided the cause of independence were paid later by Senor Don Eduardo Ycaza by checks on Brandon's.

At a little before 2 o'clock all the leaders went to the solemn session of the municipal council. The authority of the junta was recognized and the following cabinet appointed by it was accepted as the new Government of Panama:

Secretary of government, Dr. Eusebio A. Morales.
Secretary of war and the navy, Dr. Nicanor de Obarrie.
Secretary of foreign affairs, Dr. Francisco V. de la Espriella.
Secretary of the treasury, Dr. Manuel L. Amador.
Secretary of justice, Dr. Carlos A. Mendoza.
Secretary of public instruction, Dr. Julie J. Fabrega.

Then the council and all present went into the Cathedral Plaza, where from the stoop of the cathedral Dr. Carlos A. Mendoza read the declaration of independence.

During the reading of the declaration of independence the following cables were sent to the State Department in Washington:

PANAMA, *November 4, 1903.*

SECRETARY OF STATE, *Washington:*

We take the liberty of bringing to the knowledge of your Government that on yesterday afternoon, in consequence of a popular and spontaneous movement of the people of this city, the independence of the Isthmus was proclaimed, and the Republic of Panama being instituted its provisional government organizes an executive board, consisting of ourselves, who are assured of the military strength necessary to carry out our determination.

JOSE AUGUSTIN ARANGO.
FEDERICO BOYD.
TOMAS ARIAS.

A circular letter was prepared by the junta and sent to all the foreign consuls in Panama.

Circular No. 1.]

REPUBLIC OF PANAMA,
Provisional Government, November 4, 1903.

SIR: We have the honor of informing you, for your knowledge and that of the Government which you represent, that on this day a political movement has taken place by which the former Department of Panama is separated from the Republic of Colombia in order to constitute a new State, under the name of "Republic of Panama," and that those who subscribe themselves have received the honor of being designated to form the junta of the provisional government of the Republic.

We beg you to kindly acknowledge receipt and accept the sentiments of consideration which it is pleasing to subscribe ourselves.

Your attentive servants,

J. A. ARANGO.
FEDERICO BOYD.
TOMAS ARIAS.

Some time before the meeting of the municipal council Mr. Ehrman had received the following cable from the State Department in Washington:

WASHINGTON, *November 4, 1902—p. m.*

EHRMAN, *Panama:*

Communicate with commander of gunboat *Bogota* and state plainly that this Government, being responsible for maintaining peace and keep transit open across the Isthmus, desires him to refrain from openly shelling the city. We shall have a naval force in Panama in two days, and are now ordering men from the *Nashville* to Panama in the interests of peace.

LOOMIS, *Acting.*

At the request of Mr. Ehrman the consular corps had already met in the morning and prepared the following protest to the commander of the *Bogota*, but the *Bogota* left before this document could be sent on board:

PANAMA, *November 4, 1903.*

The COMMANDER OF THE "BOGOTA."

SIR: The consular corps of this city considers the action of the warship *Bogota*, under your command, last night in bombarding a defenseless city without notice of any kind to the consuls is contrary to all rights and practices of civilized nations. Consequently the consular corps protests in the most solemn manner, and holds responsible for the consequences and responsibilities of this act whoever is to blame, furnishing their respective Governments with an account of the circumstances referred to.

Yours, respectfully,

FELIX EHRMAN,
United States Vice Consul General.
B. H. ROHRWEGER,
Acting British Vice Consul.
EMILE GREY,
Agent of the French Consulate.
ARTHUR KOHPOKE,
Consul of Germany, Acting Consul of Italy.
A. JESURUM, JR.,
Consul of the Netherlands.
ED. JARAMILLO AVILES,
Consul of Ecuador.
J. F. ARANGO,
Consul General of Guatemala.
FEDERICO BOYD,
Consul of Spain, Consul of Salvador.
JACOB L. MADURO,
Consul of Denmark.
B. D. FIDANQUE,
Consul of Belgium.
J. G. DUQUE,
Consul of Cuba.
B. MENDEZ,
Consul of Mexico.
PEDRO ARIAS,
Consul of Brazil.
JEROMINO DE LA OSSA,
Consul of Chile, Consul of Honduras.
JUAN VALLARINO,
Consul of Peru.

All of these consuls, with the exception of E. H. Rohrweger, acting British vice consul; Mons. Emile Grey, French consular agent, and Arthur Kohpoke, the German consul, were either active revolutionists or bound to them by close family and business ties. They were merely taking advantage of their consular appointments to protest against being shot at in their revolutionary capacity.

Just after the declaration of independence had been read, the following cable from Mr. Bunau-Varilla was handed to Dr. Amador:

WASHINGTON, *November 4—2.45 p. m.*

AMADOR, *Panama:*

Aphrodisio Colon, but if agazapados aphidian statu quo heavy or powerful ancnesis program appellant daily press formation bona fide government aftreskel every alachinar apparvero alkalinity government Britanum both sides apatelles.

BUNAU-VARILLA.

Worked out by the Amador-Lindo-Bunau-Varilla and Lieber's fifth edition codes, counting six words down in the latter, this cable reads:

Try to get hold of Colon, but if cannot control hold firm for the present statu quo four or five days execute program give earliest possible information to the daily press of the formation as to the development of government ships; will remain both sides. Will give guarantee immediately.

When the threat made by Col. Torres to burn Colon and kill every American in it was communicated to Col. Shaler he tried to get Mr. Prescott on the phone, but the latter was not at the railroad depot, so he told the telegraph operator to have Mr. Prescott notified, and the operator in Colon sent the following message to the operator in Panama:

Troops refuse proposal and say unless Tovar and Amaya are released by 2 p. m. they will burn the town and kill every American in it; that colonel wants him to get in communication with Junta and see what can be done if necessary.

This message was sent out by a railroad employee who had instructions to find Prescott. This he did near Cathedral Square, and Prescott at once went in to Amador, who declared that the only thing they could do would be to send an armed force over to Colon to assist the *Nashville's* men in preventing the outrage.

Prescott then went down to the station to tell Col. Shaler that a force would be sent over; but he was told to wait further orders, as Torres was still negotiating and had expressed a desire to send to Panama and get instructions from his superior officers in prison. Later, Mr. Prescott was notified that the envoys of the Colombian commander had left on a special train and were coming to see Gen. Tovar.

Dr. Amador at once called at police headquarters, where the Colombian generals were closely confined and had Gen. Amaya, with whom he had been on friendly terms for many years, brought down. Their interview is thus described by Gen. Amaya in his report to the Colombia minister of war on November 14, 1903:

Dr. Amador, an old friend of mine, came to see me within a few hours of my being placed in jail, and he said to me textually, "You must understand that we who started this movement are not insane; we fully appreciated the fact that in no case could we withstand all the rest of the nation, and in consequence we had to resort to means that, although painful, were indispensable. The United States has fully entered into this movement, and the Panamans are not alone, as in every event they will back up our actions. Not another Colombian soldier will ever disembark again on any of the coasts of the Isthmus, and our independence is guaranteed by that colossus." He offered me his services and said that he wished to present his respects to my chief, to whom I heard him make similar assertions, which, unfortunately, were corroborated by the increasing number of warships of that power in both seas and by the disembarkation of its forces to mock our weakness.

As described by Gen. Amaya, Dr. Amador then sent for Gen. Tovar and was even more explicit in his assertions of the participation of the United States Government in the revolution. Gen. Tovar thus describes his meeting with Dr. Amador in his report of November 20, 1903. I have here properly certified copies of both the report made by Gen. Amaya on November 14 and the report made by Gen. Tovar on November 20. The latter says in part:

The solitary confinement in which I was kept from the afternoon of the 3d was broken on the evening of the following day by the visit which Señor Manuel Amador Guerrero, principal leader of the revolutionary movement, paid me in my prison. Dr. Amador, after having spoken with Gen. Amaya, had me brought down from the room I occupied at police headquarters and informed me that events which had taken place on the previous evening were the result of a plan for a long time conceived and discussed at length in Panama and in Washington and executed under the protection and guaranty of the Government of the United States with which he personally had recently come to an understanding and from which he had received $250,000 to meet the first expenses of the new republic; that in consequence it was ridiculous to suppose that the Panamans could have successfully defied the rest of the republic, and for the same reason all resistance on my part would be quite useless; that therefore I ought to order the reembarkation of the battalion Tiradores which remained in Colon, taking advantage for this purpose of the royal mail steam packet *Orinoco*, then in that port. and thus avoiding in a spirit of humanity the shedding of blood. At the same time he informed me that there were in Colon several American warships which had come to protect the revolutionary movement. I answered Señor Amador that I would take no account of what he had just told me, as my duty and the duty of the army I commanded was sufficiently clear, and that in consequence no human force could drag from me the order that he desired. I considered my conference with him at an end and turned to be conducted back to my prison, where I learned that a similar proposition had been made to Gen. Amaya, but without success.

Now, I have no doubt in my own mind that Amador did tell Tovar that $250,000 had been sent by the Government of the United States, but all the investigations I have pursued in this matter, and all the information I have, convince me very thoroughly that the Government of the United States never supplied any money at all. The amount of money was $200,000, not $250,000; of this sum $100,000, as we have seen, was cabled over by the Credit Lyonnais for the French Canal Co. to Heidelbach, Ickleheimer & Co., and the other $100,000 was advanced by the Bowling Green Trust Co. on the securities deposited by Mr. Cromwell.

Dr. Amador returned to his fellow conspirators and reported that he had not been able to win over the generals, and it was decided to send Dr. Eusebio A. Morales to meet the envoys of Col. Torres at the station. When Col. Elezear Guerrero arrived he was at once driven by Dr. Morales to police headquarters, where he had an interview with Gen. Tovar, which the latter thus described:

A short time after Dr. Amador left, I was again conducted to the guard room of the police headquarters, and in the same room in which I had been talking with Senor Amador Guerrero I met Senor Eusebio Morales and Col. Elezear Guerrero, alcalde of Colon, who placed in my hands a note from Col. Eliseo Torres, commander of the Tiradores regiment, and a petition signed by a number of ladies of the city of Colon, both of which documents I consider it indispensable to transcribe here.

The note says as follows:

"Gen. JUAN B. TOVAR and GAMON G. AMAYA, *Panama:*

"To-day, at 1 p. m., I learned through the prefect that you had been reduced to prison, and through the same person it was proposed to me to deliver my arms and ammunition, and that means would be afforded me of returning to Cartagena with my men; but, as you must well know, neither I nor the regiment under my orders will withdraw an inch leaving you prisoners. and, therefore, although the separatist leader (Arango) conferred with me by telephone on this matter, exhorting me to accept the proposition or would be attacked at once, I told him that my troops were ready to resist any attack rather than be traitors. I am sending alcalde to confer on my behalf with the representatives of the new government in order that they may place you at liberty. The same person also carries, at my suggestion, a petition from the leading families of this city that it, the new government, may hasten your return here. It is my duty to inform you that in no case will I receive orders to do anything unless you give them to me verbally; therefore it will be useless for you to send orders in writing. I am not getting ready to face any traitor forces. I forewarn you that as a last resource we will perish in the flames of this city, but in any case you may count upon it that I shall know how to uphold the honor of my arms.

"Your affectionate faithful servant and subordinate,

"ELISEO TORRES G.

"NOTE.—Sublieut. Jiminez will accompany you on your return to this city, on which solely and exclusively depends the total loss of this city or its salvation, for if you do not come I shall proceed to act without wasting any time.

"TORRES G.

"COLON, *November 4.*"

The petition is couched in the following terms:

"Señor Gen. JUAN M. TOVAR, *Panama:*

"The undersigned native and foreign ladies, as a conflict threatens which will place in danger our lives and those of many others if it is not averted by charitable and Christian sentiments, appeal to you with every respect to beg you, taking into account the magnanimity of your heart, that you will use your decisive influence over Col. Torres, commander of the Tiradores regiment, now in this city, the honor of the call he commands being saved, will avoid the shedding of blood in this country, already drenched with it in the fearful struggle which lately took place, and greater calamities and misfortunes. From your hands we believe we shall receive this boon for which posterity itself will be duly grateful.

"Colon, November 4, 1903.

"EMILIA TARRINGTON.
"RACHEL ALBERGER.
"ADELA YOUNG.
"GERALDINE SIMMONS.
"MARIA S. LAPIERA.
"M. DE LEON.
"ETHEL DE LEON.
"ADELINA DE MARTINEZ.
"MARIA J. MARTINEZ.
"EUSABIA C. DE AMADOR," etc.

Col. Guerrero told me that he had accepted his mission because he believed that any sacrifice would be useless, and in every way he believed that the destruction of the city of Colon, planned by Col. Torres, would be no good.

He confirmed the information that there were two American warships in that port, and even told me that part of the foreign troops had been disembarked.

Gen. Tovar, however, absolutely refused to give any orders, and Col. Guerrero left him, promising to return first thing next morning.

At daybreak Señor Morales, who had taken Col. Guerrero home with him, brought the envoy back to the police headquarters to get Gen. Tovar's answer. Gen. Tovar's account of this second visit is as follows:

On the morning of the 5th Col. Guerrero returned to me, accompanied by this same Señor Morales, to receive and take back my answer to the colonel's note, but as it was quite plain from the tenor of the note itself that a written reply would be useless, I confined myself to telling these gentlemen, in order that they might convey it to the commander of the Tiradores regiment, that, being as I was a prisoner, it was impossible for me to give him verbal orders; that I was satisfied with his conduct and confident that he would always do his duty; and that in consequence I had no doubts as to the determination he would take.

The result of this interview was communicated to the junta immediately after Col. Guerrero had left for Colon, and it was decided that Dr. Federico Boyd and Señor Tomas Arias should see what they could do with Gen. Tovar. In consequence these two gentlemen called at the prison, but the reception they met with from the Colombian general was such that Dr. Boyd withdrew. In his report Gen. Tovar says:

In view of the bluntness of my refusal and the deep disgust with which I received the proposal made by the traitors, Señor Boyd withdrew, leaving me alone with Señor Arias, who assured me repeatedly of his friendship and told me how much he was pained by the separation, and he even went so far as to go to Bogota without loss of time and persuade the National Government to send a commission of influential public men to come to an understanding with those of Panama.

Not even thus could Señor Arias convince me that I ought to give the order they so greatly desired, and I turned to rejoin my comrades, filled with the hope that even then all was not lost and that even at the cost of our lives the Tiradores regiment would bravely uphold and command respect of our national Colombian honor on the shores of Colon.

At about the same time, Gen. Rafael Aizpuru, of the municipal council, called on Dr. José Angel Porras, one of the loyal Colombians, who had been arrested and was confined in the police barracks, and in the course of their conversation, as Dr. Porras commented on the fact that the separatist movement was in reality the work of only a few leaders, said:

Yes; but the Republic of Panama is an accomplished fact, as you will soon be convinced.

I can not believe it [answered Dr. Porras]. Colombia will soon call Panama to account for her temerity and ingratitude.

The Government of Colombia will not be able to do anything in the matter [was Aizpuru's answer]. Panama is under the protection of the United States; if it were not it would have recognized its helplessness and would not have attempted its freedom.

In the course of the morning United States Vice Consul General Ehrman received the circular of the junta, and at once dispatched the following cable to Washington.

PANAMA, *November 5.*

SECRETARY OF STATE, *Washington:*

Received an official circular letter from the committee of the Provisional Government, saying that on the 4th political move occurred, and the Department of Panama withdraws from the Republic of the United States of Colombia and formed the Republic of Panama. Requested to acknowledge the receipt of circular letter.

EHRMAN.

Mr. Ehrman then went to Amador's, and later both took part in a great popular demonstration in honor of Huertas. A crowd of more than a thousand persons, led by the prime movers of the independence and accompanied by the United States vice consul general, went to the barracks at Chiriqui and carried Huertas in triumph through the principal streets of the town. Huertas, seated on a chair, was carried on the shoulders of four men, under the folds of the American flag, carried by Mr. Ehrman, and the Panaman flag, carried by Dr. Amador. An enormous crowd followed, carrying hundreds of American flags which had been freely distributed both in Colon and Panama. The parade was brought to an end by a sudden downpour of rain, and Amador, the members of junta, Ehrman, and about 50 others repaired to the Central Hotel, which belongs to the Ehrmans, and there Huertas was nearly drowned in champagne, the contents of dozens of bottles being poured over him.

Commander Hubbard was kept informed almost hourly of the progress of events in Panama by Prescott and Shaler. The events that took place in Colon on the morning of the 5th are thus described by Commander Hubbard:

After the withdrawal of the Colombian forces on the evening of November 4 and the return of the *Nashville's* forces on board, as reported in my letter No. 96, there was no disturbance on shore and the night passed quietly. On the morning of the 5th I discovered that the commander of the Colombian troops had not withdrawn so far from the town as he agreed, but was occupying buildings near the outskirts of the town. I immediately inquired into the matter and learned that he had some trivial excuse for not carrying out his agreement, and also that it was his intention to occupy Colon again on the arrival of the alcalde at 10.45 a. m., unless Gen. Tovar sent word by the alcalde that he, Col. Torres, should withdraw. That Gen. Tovar had declined to give any instructions I was cognizant of, and the situation at once became quite as serious as on the day previous. I immediately landed an armed force, reoccupied the same building; also landed two 1-pounders, and mounted them on platform cars behind protection of cotton bales, and then, in company with United States consul, had an interview with Col. Torres, in the course of which I informed him that I had relanded my men because he had not kept his agreement; that I had no interest in the affairs of either party; that my attitude was strictly neutral; that the troops of neither side should be transported; that my sole purpose in landing was to protect the lives and property of American citizens, if threatened, as they had been threatened; and to maintain the free and uninterrupted transit of the Isthmus, and that purpose I should maintain by force if necessary. I also strongly advised that in the interests of peace, and to prevent the possibility of a conflict that could not but be regrettable, he should carry out his agreement of the previous evening and withdraw to Monkey Hill.

Col. Torres's only reply was that it was unhealthy at Monkey Hill, and a reiteration of his intentions, of his love of Americans, and a persistence in his intentions to occupy Colon should Gen. Tovar not give him instructions to the contrary.

On the return of the alcalde about 11 a. m., the Colombian troops marched into Colon, but did not assume the threatening demeanor of the previous day. The American women and children again went on board the *Marcomania* and *City of Washington*, and through the British vice consul I offered protection to British subjects, as directed in the department's cablegram. A copy of the British vice consul's acknowledgement is hereto appended. The *Nashville* I got under way as on the previous day and moved close to protect the water front.

Porfirio Melendez again approached Col. Torres with a view to having him reembark on the Royal Mail steam packet *Orinoco*, offering him to pay the expenses of the voyage and give him a substantial indemnity. At first Torres rejected these advances and insisted that he would burn Colon to the ground if the Colombian generals were not brought over, and that on no account would he leave them behind, even if they gave him permission to reembark.

While these negotiations were going on, the steamship *Jennings* arrived with Gen. Pompilio Guiterrez, one of Colombia's most distinguished soldiers, who had been sent on a special mission by the Government of Bogota. He had with him several Colombian officers. Melendez at once sent Juan A. Henriquez on board to explain the situation. He told Guiterrez that the independence of Panama was an accomplished fact and that overwhelming American forces were on their way and would not permit Colombia to attack the new Republic. So thoroughly convinced was Guiterrez of the futility of any effort on his part that he at first decided to remain on board, but later agreed to go with Henriquez to the Royal Mail Steam Packet Co., where he had an interview with Torres, who asked him as senior officer to take command of the Tiradores regiment; but Guiterrez refused to have anything to do with the matter or to give any orders. Commenting on his action, the Panama Star and Herald said:

The revolutionary agents were fighting with a weapon more potential than the most modern arms, and Gen. Guiterrez went away convinced of the uselessness of making any effort against them.

This left Torres a free hand in Colon, and as he still insisted that Gens. Tovar and Amaya, and their staff, be brought over from Panama, a conference was held between Col. Shaler, the United States consul, and Commander Hubbard. It was decided to have the generals brought over by Prescott from Panama.

Mr. Prescott at once sent Señor Manuel Espinosa B. to police headquarters with orders to bring the generals down to the depot. In his official report Gen. Tovar says:

At about 5 p. m. on the same day I was notified to get ready to leave with my comrades, Gens. Amaya, Angel M. and Luis Alberto Tovar, Cols. Ismael Nogurra Conde, and José M. Tovar, and Dr. Alberto Bernal Ospina, leaving in the police barracks a number of other prisoners who were not allowed to accompany us, despite their repeated entreaties.

Surrounded by a numerous escort, we were conducted to the railroad station, where a long altercation took place between the assistant superintendent of the railroad and myself, as he asserted that no troops could be carried on the trains, and that therefore it was necessary for me to give my word of honor that I would go to Colon as a prisoner and embark immediately.

I roundly refused this request, and he insisted that I should either go as a prisoner to Colon or be returned to the police barracks.

Whereupon it was proposed to surround me in the train with rebel troops which the railroad was willing to carry over. At length Mr. Prescott agreed that the escort which guarded us should be placed on the train, as his chief, Col. Shaler, had just ordered him to do so by telephone from Colon, and we were immediately taken to the car which had been prepared for us and in which our escort was placed; besides a number of other soldiers were placed on the train.

As I was entering the car I received a telegram from Col. Torres, which was handed to me by the same Mr. Prescott and which said:

"COLON, *November 5, 1903—2.15 p. m.*

"Gen. RAMON G. AMAYA, or JUNA B. TOVAR, *Panama:*

"I inform you that yesterday the cruiser *Cartagena* left, completely thwarting my plans. I am waiting your opinion as to what I ought to do. The envoy I sent you told me that you had shown a desire to abstain from sending an opinion on the matter. Again, and for the last time, I wish to have your opinion in order to fulfill orders. I have obtained permission to confer with Gen. Tovar by telephone, in order to receive his final instructions. The enemy's troops and my own are preparing for attack. Americans have entrenched and are deploying. What must I do? Await immediate reply.

"Servant, ELISEO TORRES, G."

I could not give an answer to this telegram, as I was not allowed to do so.

Acting on a countermanding order brought by the alcalde, Senor Don Francisco de la Ossa, it was decided to take us back to prison, where we arrived, escorted in the usual manner, at half-past 7.

The reason for not sending the generals over was that when Prescott had sent Espinosa off to get the generals he made up a special train with one ordinary first-class coach in front and the special car America behind. He sent C. C. Arosemena and Guillermo Andreve to get together a number of young Panamans in civilian clothes and arm them with revolvers, his intention being to go over to Colon himself in the private car with the generals and to have the first-class coach in front filled with armed men in case the generals tried any tricks. When Tovar arrived, Prescott asked him to give his word that he would not attempt to escape, but as the general's replies were not as satisfying as Prescott wished, he called Nicanor Obarrio, the new minister of war, who was standing near, and asked him to explain to Gen. Tovar that he must give his word to go over as a prisoner, as the orders received from the American Government prohibited the transportation of soldiers. This Tovar refused, and Prescott called up Col. Shaler on the telephone. Col. Shaler told Prescott that Commander Hubbard was in the office with him in the Colon depot, and Prescott heard Col. Shaler speaking to Commander Hubbard. Col. Shaler told him to put the Panama troops on the train and send the generals over under escort. This was about to be done, and the generals had already taken places in the car when Col. Shaler called up Mr. Prescott again and told him that Señor Melendez had succeeded in getting Torres to agree to embark on the *Orinoco* if he was given $8,000 and his passage paid, and that in order to expedite matters, if Prescott would get the money from the junta, he would have the amount paid from the Panama Railroad's safe, in Colon, by Wardlaw, the cashier. Telling Obarrio to hold the generals till he came back, Prescott at once took a coach and went after Dr. Amador, who was in company with Boyd and Arango, and they told him all the money they had had already been given to the troops, but that they would get the money from Brandon's. In order not to lose time, and knowing that it was safe, Mr. Prescott telephoned that it was all right; that he had the money in his possession, and Col. Shaler answered that it was all right, the money would be paid; a little later Col. Shaler again called up and said that the Colombian troops were just beginning to reembark, and Prescott told Francisco de la Ossa, the alcalde, to take the generals back to prison.

As soon as the news that the Colombian soldiers were actually leaving the Isthmus reached Arango, thus insuring the success of the independence movement, Arango wrote out this message to Prescott on one of his cards [shows photograph to committee]:

NOVEMBER 5, 1903.

MY DEAR MR. PRESCOTT: Allow me to address these lines to you in Spanish to truly express my sentiments toward you. To you in great measure the public owes its salvation from the horrors of bloody strife—to you, our constant and valorous coworker—also to brave Col. Shaler and our determined friend, Capt. Beers. To all many greetings.

Your friend, JOSE AUGUSTIN ARANGO.

P. S.—I beg that you will not fail to advise Capt. Beers.

In Colon Torres had agreed to accept the $8,000 bribe only after Col. Shaler had assured him that 5,000 American troops were on their way to the Isthmus, and pointed out the folly of his remaining, to be either killed or taken prisoner.

As to the payment of this $8,000, there is all the testimony in the world. The money was counted out by Mr. Wardlaw, the cashier of the Panama Railroad Co., and by Mr. Joseph Lefevre, who afterwards was the minister of public works of the Republic of Panama, and the money was carried out in two sacks and paid to Col Torres.

There then arose another difficulty, and as this part of the story affects one of the most distinguished officers in the American Navy, I want to surround it with every possible reservation. All the money in the Panama Railroad Co.'s safe having been given to Col. Torres, and he having agreed to go back on board the *Orinoco*, the English captain of the Royal Mail Steam Packet Co.'s ship *Orinoco* told the agent of the Royal Mail Co. in Colon that he was not going to transport all those Colombian soldiers back to Cartagena unless he was paid for it, and the agent of the Royal Mail Steam Packet Co. very naturally thought that was reasonable and went to Col. Shaler and said, "Now, how about paying for all these people we are taking back?" and Shaler said, "We have not got any money, but you take them over and it will be all right." The agent of the Royal Mail Steam Packet Co. said "No"; he could not; that that would be against all the regulations. And the testimony of the agent is that, in answer to his insistent requests, there being no money, he was given a guarantee for a sum of a little over £1,000 for passage money of the troops back to Cartagena, and that as he would not take any other signatures the guarantee was signed by Commander Hubbard, of the U. S. S. *Nashville*, and by Col. Shaler, of the Panama Railroad Co.

That does seem to me to be just what a businesslike steamship agent would insist upon. The World made great efforts, as you can imagine, to get that guarantee. We found that it had been sent over to Brandon's bank in Panama; that it had been redeemed for cash, the passages having been paid for later; that the amount was included in the account afterwards honored by J. P. Morgan & Co. out of the first $1,000,000 that was received by the Republic of Panama from the United States. But I have never seen, and I do not think anyone connected with this investigation has seen, the original guarantee with Commander Hubbard's signature attached. However, the testimony is that the agent of the Royal Mail Steam Packet Co. made a very full report on all these occurrences to his employers in London; and two years ago one of the editors of the World was in London and called on the Royal Mail Steam Packet Co. and explained the circumstances to them; that the World was being criminally prosecuted by the Government of the United States; that we were very anxious to obtain access to this report and to know if this guarantee had really been given by Commander Hubbard and Col. Shaler. The editor of the World was told that this report and this information affected the Government of the United States and could not and would not be given voluntarily by the Royal Mail Steam Packet Co.; that it was only by process of law we could obtain it. We had such a superabundance of documentary evidence of every kind that we decided it was really not worth while to go to the heavy expense of sending a rogatory commission over to London, with lawyers and all the rest of the paraphernalia, in order to get this solitary document. But Commander Hubbard is now living—he is now Admiral Hubbard. He has just returned from command of the China station, and if his memory is not entirely clear of the events that took place on the Isthmus of Panama in 1903, I think it can be easily refreshed by some of the documents we have here.

The *Orinoco* took away 2 commanders, 21 officers, 438 soldiers, and 13 women; and just before she drew out a couple of cases of champagne were sent on board for Col. Torres, with Col. Shaler's compliments.

Melendez went to the Panama Railroad offices to see the $8,000 paid over. Part of the money was given to Torres in cash in two sacks. and the rest, which he could not carry, was paid to the purser of the Royal Mail steam packet *Orinoco*, who was to give it to Torres when out at sea. When this had been done, Melendez gave Wardlaw, the cashier of the Panama Railroad Co., a draft on the junta in Panama. The money was all in American $20 gold pieces and was counted and carried out by the cashier and Mr. Joe Lefevre.

Referring to these events, Commander Hubbard reported as follows:

During the afternoon several propositions were made to Col. Torres by representatives of the new government, and he was finally persuaded by them to embark on the Royal Mail steamer *Orinoco* with all his troops and return to Cartagena. The *Orinoco* left her dock with the troops, 474 all told, at 7.35 p. m.

I beg to assure the department that I had no part whatever in the negotiations that were carried on between Col. Torres and the representatives of the provisional government.

Just as the Colombian troops were reembarking on the *Orinoco*, the U. S. S. *Dixie* arrived. As she was coming into the bay, the *Nashville* had signaled to land a party with all possible speed, and before the *Orinoco* pulled out 19 boats had been launched and about 400 marines landed.

The *Dixie* cast anchor at 7.05 and Commander Hubbard at once went on board and reported to Commander F. H. Delano, United States Navy, his superior in rank. The men from the *Nashville* were withdrawn and the American marines from the *Dixie* patrolled the town.

As soon as the Colombian troops had reembarked a crowd gathered at the house of Don Porfilio Melendez, and after nailing a Panaman flag to a long pole raised it on his house. The formal raising of the flag of the new Republic and the declaration of independence in Colon was fixed for the following day, November 6, at 10 a. m.

At the appointed time the Republic of Panama was formally proclaimed in Colon. Most of the foreign consuls, Col. Shaler, a number of officers from the U. S. S. *Dixie* and the U. S. S. *Nashville*, all the leading merchants, and a large crowd of inhabitants were present to witness the ceremony which took place at the prefecture.

Señor Ocano, the vice president of the municipal council, read a resolution passed by a majority of the board on the previous evening signifying the adhesion of the district of Colon to the Republic of Panama. Melendez then addressed the meeting, confining his remarks to the statement that the object that had brought them together was of so far-reaching a nature that comment on the events that had taken place in Panama and Colon was unnecessary. He then proceeded to read the manifesto of the junta and the declaration of independence, at the conclusion of which there were numerous cries of "Viva el Istmo!" "Viva la Republica de Panama!"

Then the new flag was brought out to be hoisted. It was handed by Melendez to Maj. William Murray Black, of the United States Army, who, in the uniform of the United States Army, himself ran it up to the top of the flagpole of the prefecture, and as he flung its folds to the breeze the police force which had been drawn up outside in the street saluted it and the crowd cheered and cried "Viva la Republica!" "Vivan los Americanos!"

You will no doubt remember that in the Senate Col. Black was very severely criticized by Senator Carmack for the part he took in this proceeding.

Mr. HARRISON. Was that a general celebration by all the natives that day?

Mr. HALL. Yes, sir; everybody came out that day. It was all over then. The Colombian troops had left the Isthmus. It was just a regular official raising of the national flag; and Col. Black, whom, we have seen, was present at the luncheon given in the month of July previous, at which the first seeds of the revolution were sown, and who afterwards had been in touch with Prescott and with Beers and knew all the details of the conspiracy, and who came in on a freight train from Culebra to assist the *Nashville* in preventing the Colombian troops from exercising their sovereignty over the Isthmus, was naturally selected, as a compliment to the Americans. to raise the flag of independence.

Mr. LEVY. That $1,000,000 which you referred to a moment ago, was that paid out of the $40,000,000?

Mr. HALL. No, sir; the $40,000,000 was paid by the United States for the property and archives of the French Panama Canal Co. I do not know who got the money. Ten million dollars was paid by the United States to the Republic of Panama. Perhaps this is a good moment to mention the fact, although I do not want to dwell upon it, that the $10,000,000 was paid in two installments, one installment of $1,000,000, which was paid in cash, and there remained to be paid $9,000,000. The $1,000,000 was paid to J. P. Morgan & Co., and out of it $643,000 was kept by the bankers to meet the drafts which had been made on them from the Isthmus for the first expenses of the revolution, including the $50,000 paid to Huertas; $200,000 was sent to the Isthmus, and about $160,000 disappeared. When Señor Hazera was secretary of the treasury of Panama, at the end of the first year of Dr. Amador's administration, in making up the report of the secretary of the treasury, Dr. Amador told him not to say anything about the $1,000,000, because they could not account for it.

When it came to the payment of the $1,000,000 to Panama, Mr. Shaw, who was Secretary of the Treasury, refused to honor the requisition sent to him by the State Department to pay any of this money unless he was first given an opinion by the Attorney General of the United States that the Spooner Act, under which the contract for the $10,000,000 had been entered into, was certified by the Attorney General as applying not to Colombia, which was mentioned in terms in the Spooner Act, but to Panama, which had been created since the Spooner Act was passed.

Mr. HARRISON. How do you know that, Mr. Hall?

Mr. HALL. I will read from the official records in the Treasury Department, certified copies of which I have here.

DEPARTMENT OF STATE,
Washington, February 24, 1904.

The SECRETARY OF THE TREASURY.

SIR: By Article XIV of the treaty of November 18, 1903, between the United States and the Republic of Panama for the construction of an interoceanic canal, to the ratification of which the Senate gave its advice and consent on the 23d instant, the United States agrees to pay to the Republic of Panama "the sum of ten million dollars in gold coin of the United States on the exchange of the ratification" of the convention.

Arrangements have been made with the Panama minister for the exchange of the ratification of the convention on Friday, the 26th instant. By direction of the Secretary of State, I have the honor to inquire whether your department is prepared, under the act of Congress approved June 28, 1902 (Stat. L., vol. 32, Pt. 1, pp. 481, et seq.), to furnish him with a draft for the sum stated to hand to the minister at the time of exchange, or wheher he shall say to the mihister that the payment will be made in a few days.

I have the honor to be, sir,
Your obedient servant,
ALVEY A. ADEE,
Acting Secretary.

The Secretary of the Treasury replied as follows:

TREASURY DEPARTMENT,
OFFICE OF THE SECRETARY.
Washington, February 24, 1904.

MY DEAR MR. SECRETARY: I am in receipt of your letter of the 24th instant, asking whether the Treasury Department is prepared to pay to the Republic of Panama the sum of $10,000,000 on Friday, the 26th instant.

In answer I beg to advise that the department is prepared to make the payment whenever the Attorney General shall give an opinion that the act approved June 28, 1902, authorizes the payment to the Republic of Panama.

The act referred to in terms directs the payment to be made to the Republic of Colombia. I call attention to this fact not for the purpose of throwing a doubt upon the subject, but to call attention to what is at least a technical variance. I prefer, in any event, not to make the payment before Monday, the 28th instant.

Yours, very truly, L. M. SHAW.

The SECRETARY OF STATE.

With your permission I will put into the appendix all the documents now in the possession of the Treasury of the United States, certified copies of which have been given to me by Mr. Franklin MacVeagh, and they can appear in the record, relating not only to the $10,000,000, but should you desire, also relating to the $40,000,000.

Mr. LEVY. How is that $10,000,000 found situated now?

Mr. HALL. I do not think there is very much of it left. Out of the $10,000,000 it was first proposed that the sum of $8,000,000 should be invested in New York real estate.

Mr. LEVY. In mortgages?

Mr. HALL. So I understand. When the first constitutional convention met in Panama—months after the recognition of the Republic by the United States—it was decided that only $6,000,000 should be invested "for posterity"; and this sum was actually invested in New York by Mr. Cromwell who was acting as general counsel for the special fiscal commission appointed for the purpose of making this investment. I do not want to go into this financial end of the story; but I will say that 875 Panama Railroad bonds were bought for $919,843.75 and $4,080,000 was invested in mortgages on New York real estate to the satisfaction of Mr. Cromwell.

Mr. LEVY. Have they still got the $6,000,000?

Mr. HALL. I understand the $6,000,000 has dwindled, but as far as I know the Republic of Panama has never published any official report from Mr. Cromwell covering his actions as fiscal agent of the Republic of Panama. A list of the original mortgages was published, but no one knows how they stand to-day. Most if not all have fallen in and the money has been reinvested by Mr. Cromwell, but there has been no official report beyond this "Informe de la Comision Fiscal Especial" in 1904.

Mr. LEVY. I understand that, but you say it was held in trust. Was there a trust agreement? How did Mr. Cromwell get the money?

Mr. HALL. There was no trust agreement, that I am aware of, sir. Mr. Cromwell was appointed fiscal agent of the Republic of Panama, with the most sweeping powers and without any bond or security to protect the Republic of Panama against loss. Mr. Cromwell conceived and, with the assistance of Mr. Roosevelt, carried out the rape of the Isthmus and the estblishment there of this little Republic. He is its general counsel; he is its fiscal agent. In after-dinner speeches on the Isthmus he has proclaimed himself a citizen of Panama; really he at one time believed that Panama belonged to him. In a letter to Dr. Amador describing a certain phase of the Cortez negotiations to which I do not wish to refer, Carlos Constantino Arosemena, minister of Panama in the United States, wrote:

Unfortunately Cromwell is convinced that he has a monopoly of everything connected with Panama, and whatever step is taken, without having first been submitted to him and having obtained his approval, is no good.

Mr. LEVY. But the point I want to make is, is there any sort of trust by which, for instance, if these mortgages were paid off to Mr. Cromwell, they could afterwards come back from Panama and say to these people who paid the money that they still had a lien, because you have paid the money to the wrong person?

Mr. HALL. I do not know, sir. That is a new point; but as you will see, a great many of these mortgages have fallen due since the time they were made, and a number of them have been paid to Mr. Cromwell, and as fiscal agent he has reinvested the money. He has never been under any bond and has never had to give any guarantee for this money.

Mr. LEVY. From what I hear, I think the amount left is about $3,000,000. I do not know how true it is.

Mr. HALL. As I stated at the beginning of this hearing, I am anxious to confine myself as nearly as possible to the legal and international aspects of the question, and not to enter into any scandal that may or may not exist in connection with the payment of the $40,000,000 to the French Panama Canal Co., or the $10,000,000 to the Republic of Panama, or minister in Panama that there was an agreement that $8,000,000 should be invested, but I understand that was a verbal agreement made between Mr. Roosevelt and Dr. Amador. I will put into the appendix a dispatch from Mr. W. W. Russell, United States minister to Panama, that I refer to.

Mr. LEVY. When you speak of real estate, you mean invested in mortgages?

Mr. HALL. Mortgages on real estate.

Mr. LEVY. Mortgages on real estate?

Mr. HALL. Yes, sir. In connection with the investment of these $6,000,000, all the details are included in the report of the special fiscal commission.

Mr. LEVY. The important thing is whether Cromwell had any power to draw that money in.

Mr. HALL. He was fiscal agent, sir, and I understand that most if not all of those mortgages have fallen due and the money has been paid in to Mr. Cromwell and reinvested by him. How I do not know.

Mr. LEVY. And if it has been paid improperly, some people in New York may still have mortgages outstanding against their property, and that is a very serious question to the people who borrowed the money and have paid it.

Mr. HALL. I am not competent to discuss that question, sir; but I will, if you so desire, append to this hearing the report of the fiscal commission which invested that $10,000,000, and also all of the documents now in the possession of the Treasury Department of the United States, copies of which Mr. Franklin MacVeagh was kind enough to furnish to the World, and which throw full light upon the reasons why Mr. Shaw refused for nearly three months to pay out the money.

Now, to go back to my story, immediately after the raising of the Panaman flag in Colon by Maj. Black, in the uniform of the United States Army, Gen. Pedro A. Cuadros, prefect of Colon, and the alcalde, Col. Elezear Guerrero, sent in the following joint letter of resignation to the junta. It lays great stress on the protection given by the American forces in Colon to the revolutionists:

SENORES JOSE AUGUSTIN ARANGO, TOMAS ARIAS, FEDERICO BOYD,
Panama.

In presence of the events which have occurred in Panama and this city, and not having the means of preventing the outrages committed against the national sovereignty, especially by those who have betrayed the Republic as well as the marked hostility shown to her by the American forces disembarked to support the betrayal, we see ourselves obliged to relinquish the authority with which we are invested and to separate ourselves from our position with the heartfelt grief of Colombians who have seen our country outraged by traitors and their foreign allies.

PEDRO A. CUADROS.
ELEZEAR GUERRERO.

A cable was also sent off by Commander Delano, of the U. S. S. *Dixie* immediately after the proclamation of the Republic of Colon. It reads:

COLON, *November 6.*

SECRETARY OF THE NAVY, *Washington:*

All quiet. Independents declare government established as Republic of Panama. Have withdrawn marines.

DELANO.

In Panama on November 6 Señor Don Eduardo Ycaza, who had been appointed paymaster by the junta, began paying off the officers and others who had assisted in the movement. There was no money left to speak of in the treasury, and all of Ycaza's payments were made by arrangement with Messrs. Isaac Brandon & Bros.

Mr. Ycaza drew checks on Brandon & Bros. when there was no money on deposit there, but Brandon honored them, and afterwards Brandon & Bros. drew on J. P. Morgan & Co., and were paid out of the first $1,000,000. In this manner he disbursed on November 6, and the days following, more than $200,000 silver, besides which the Brandons let him have $70,000 in American gold.

Most of the officers were given $10,000, although some got more Among those who got $10,000 were Capt. Luis Gil, Capt. Forget, Commander Rojas, Capt. Marco Salazar, Capt. Clodomiro Alfonso, Commander Leoncio Tascon, and Capt. Ramon Garcia. Among those who were contented with less Capt. Eduardo Perez and Capt. Jose Manuel Rodriguez seem to have been contented with $6,000 apiece. A number of "men who seemed to be officers" got more, but did not tell how much they were paid.

Money was given away with the most extreme liberality.

A simple order written on any old piece of paper and signed by Huertas was enough for the fortunate one to get the money he asked for.

Huertas was given $30,000 silver in two payments of $15,000, and $35,000 in all was paid to Gen. Ruben Varon, the commander of the *Padilla.*

Afterwards Huertas was given an additional $50,000 in American gold. Here is a photograph of him garbed in the wondrous uniform covered with gold lace on which he spent part of his bribe money. [Shows photograph to committee].

The junta meanwhile was busy getting things in shape for the promised recognition of their independence by the United States.

On the previous evening, the 5th, the junta had sent the following cable:

PANAMA, *November 5, 1903.*

SECRETARY OF STATE, *Washington:*

We notify you that we have appointed Señor Phillipe Bunau-Varilla confidential agent of the Republic of Panama, near your Government, and Dr. Francisco V. de la Espriella, minister of foreign affairs.

ARANGO.
BOYD.
TOMAS.

This was followed on the morning of the 6th by two cables, one from the junta and the other from United States Consul General Ehrman. The junta's cable read:

PANAMA, *November 6, 1903.*

SECRETARY OF STATE, *Washington:*

Colon and all the towns of the Isthmus have adhered to the declaration of independence proclaimed in this city. The authority of the Republic of Panama is obeyed throughout its territory.

ARANGO.
ARIAS.
BOYD.

Mr. Ehrman's cable said:

PANAMA, *November 6, 1903.*

SECRETARY OF STATE, *Washington:*

The situation here is peaceful. Isthmian movement has obtained, so far, success. Colon and interior Provinces have enthusiastically joined independence. Not any Colombian soldiers known on Isthmian soil at present. *Padilla* equipped to pursue *Bogota.* Bunau-Varilla has been appointed officially agent of the Republic of Panama in Washington.

EHRMAN.

The truth was that the independence had not been even heard of in important parts of the interior, and that very day, as shown by a cable from the American consul in Colon, received in the State Department at 4.50 p. m. of November 6, they were just sending an expedition to Bocas del Toro to proclaim the revolution. Bocas del Toro is the fourth most important town of the Isthmus and the center of the banana industry. The Province of Chiriqui, with its capital, David, the third most populous and important place and the center of the cattle business, held out against the independence until a letter from the provisional government warned the commander of the Colombian forces that if he did not join the revolution a white ship of the North American Navy would appear in those waters.

In the documents of the Navy Department which were not sent to Congress there is also a dispatch from one of the naval commanders stating how he went with representatives of the Government to persuade a portion of the Isthmus to recognize the Republic. I will read that dispatch into the record later.

Within an hour of the receipt of Mr. Ehrman's misleading cable Secretary of State John Hay sent the following to Mr. Ehrman:

WASHINGTON, *November 6—12.51 p. m.*

AMERICAN CONSUL, *Panama:*

The people of Panama have, by an apparently unanimous movement, dissolved their political connections with the Republic of Colombia and resumed their independence. When you are satisfied that a de facto government, republican in form and without substantial opposition from its own people, has been established in the State of Panama, you will enter into relations with it as the responsible Government of the territory and look to it for all due action to protect the persons and property of citizens of the United States and to keep open the isthmian transit, in accordance with the obligations of existing treaties governing the relations of the United States to that territory.

Communicate above to Malmros, who will be governed by these instructions in entering into relations with the local authorities.

HAY.

On receipt of this cable Mr. Ehrman telephoned over to Mr. Malmros, who sent the following cable to the State Department:

COLON, *November 6.*

SECRETARY OF STATE, *Washington:*

Tranquillity absolute in Colon. Porfilio Melendez appointed governor of this Province. Proclaimed Republic of Panama at Colon prefectura at 10 o'clock a. m. English and French consuls present. I arrived after proclamation, and upon their suggestion I told governor that presence of consuls must not be looked upon as recognition of revolutionary state by their respective Governments. Melendez sent steam launch to Bocas del Toro to proclaim independence.

MALMROS.

Before Mr. Ehrman had time to enter into any formal relations with the junta he received the following cable from the State Department:

WASHINGTON, *November 5, 1903.*

AMERICAN CONSUL GENERAL, *Panama:*

I send for your information and guidance in the execution of the instructions cabled to you to-day the text of a telegram dispatched this day to the United States minister at Bogota: "The people of the Isthmus having by an apparently unanimous movement dissolved their political connections with the Republic of Colombia and resumed their independence, and having adopted a government of their own, republican in form, with which the Government of the United States has entered into relations, the President of the United States, in accordance with the ties of friendship which have so long and so happily existed between the respective nations, most earnestly commends to the Governments of Colombia and Panama the peaceful and equitable settlement of all questions at issue between them. He holds that he is bound not merely by treaty obligations, but by the interest of civilization, to see that the peaceable traffic of the world across the Isthmus of Panama shall not longer be disturbed by constant succession of unnecessary and wasteful civil wars."

HAY.

Mr. Ehrman showed this cable to the junta, which at once sent off the following:

PANAMA, *November 6, 1903.*

SECRETARY OF STATE, *Washington:*

The Junta of Provisional Government of the Republic of Panama has appointed Senor Philippe Bunau-Varilla envoy extraordinary near your Government with full powers to conduct diplomatic and financial negotiations. Deign to receive and to heed him.

J. A. ARANGO,
ARIAS,
BOYD DE LA ESPRIELLA,
Foreign Affairs.

Mr. Ehrman then sent the following:

PANAMA, *November 6, 1903.*

SECRETARY OF STATE, *Washington:*

Philippe Bunau-Varilla has been appointed envoy extraordinary and minister plenipotentiary to the United States of America. Perfect quiet.

EHRMAN.

Now, I think that here is a good place to point out a remarkable coincidence. We have the State Department telegraphing to its agent in Bogota on the 6th of November this dispatch beginning, "The people of Panama having by an apparently unanimous consent," and ending "constant succession of unnecessary and wasteful civil wars." The same day, or, rather, the next morning, not from Washington, but in New York, Mr. Philippe Bunau-Varilla wrote to the State Department announcing that he was appointed as minister plenipotentiary of the Republic of Panama to the United States, and his letter reads:

NEW YORK, *November 7, 1903.*

His Excellency JOHN HAY,
Secretary of State, Washington:

I have the privilege and honor of notifying you that the Government of the Republic of Panama has been pleased to designate me as its envoy extraordinary and minister plenipotentiary near the Government of the United States. In selecting for its first representative at Washington a veteran servant and champion of the Panama Canal my Government has evidently sought to show that it considers a loyal and earnest devotion to the success of that most heroic conception of human genius as both a solemn duty and the essential purpose of its existence. I congratulate myself, sir, that my first official duty should be to respectfully request you to convey to His Excellency the President of the United States on behalf of the people of Panama an expression of the grateful sense of their obligation to his Government. In extending her generous hand so spontaneously to her latest born, the mother of the American nations is prosecuting her noble mission as the liberator and educator of the peoples. In spreading her protecting wings over the territory of our Republic the American eagle has sanctified it. It has rescued it from the barbarism of unnecessary and wasteful civil wars to consecrate it to the destiny assigned to it by Providence, the service of humanity and the progress of civilization.

PHILIPPE BUNAU-VARILLA.

There you have Bunau-Varilla using the very words "unnecessary and wasteful civil wars" used a few hours previously by Secretary Hay in his dispatch to the American minister at Bogota, and the coincidence is almost as remarkable as the figure of speech "rise as one man" which suggested itself to Mr. Cromwell in his conversation with Gen. Valez, to Mr. Arango in his letter to Dr. Amador, and to Mr. Roosevelt in his message to Congress.

The CHAIRMAN. Where is Bunau-Varilla now?

Mr. HALL. In Paris.

The CHAIRMAN. What does he do in Paris?

Mr. HALL. I do not know. Mr. Bunau-Varilla is said to be a wealthy man.

The CHAIRMAN. Was he wealthy before he pulled off this trick?

Mr. HALL. No, sir; I do not think so. He had some Panama Canal Co. stock. His brother, Maurice Bunau-Varilla, is a well-known newspaper man, the proprietor of Le Matin, a French newspaper.

Mr. LEVY. I never understood that Bunau-Varilla was a rich man until this Panama affair.

Mr. HALL. He is said to be a wealthy man now. I have not had access to his bank account, and I do not know the status of Mr. Bunau-Varilla's financial affairs before this matter took place. I have tried to fight as shy as possible of personalities unless it was something really essential, like, for instance, the personal resources of Dr. Amador before the revolution was pulled off and afterwards. Before the revolution Dr. Amador was a very poor man, and afterwards he was wealthy. Here is an affidavit made by Donaldo Valasco, who lives in Panama, in reference to this matter:

I, Donaldo Velasquez, a native of Colombia, living in Panama, of age, a publicist and owner of a printing establishment situated in the city of Panama, declare:

That I, being married to Doña Amanda Cervera, daughter of Ramona de la Ossa, being the youngest sister of Maria de la Ossa (wife of the late Dr. Manuel

Amador Guerrere), my relations with Dr. Amador and his family were always cordial and friendly until the latter part of the year 1904.

(2) During the six months of the year 1903 Doña Maria de la Ossa, wife of the said Dr. Manuel Amador, spoke to me of a propaganda for the independence of Panama; at first she spoke more by inuendo than by direct words, but at last she asked me what I would do if the State of Cauca (I am a Caucaño) joined with Panama for separation from the mother country. Every time I answered I am always absolutely for the great work of Bolivar—that is to say, the United States of Colombia. Little by little my relations with the Amador family grew less cordial, until at last I separated myself completely from them.

(3) I know of my own knowledge that Dr. Amador and his family in those days considered as their friends Dr. José Augustin Arango, Mr. Obaldia, and the Americans of the Panama Railroad, Messrs. Shaler, Beers, and Prescott, speaking frequently of the last three as persons of the greatest importance to the fortunes of the country. From what I heard in family conversations and from what I knew from the relations existing between them in the period prior to the independence, I consider Dr. Amador and Dr. José Augustin Arango as cofounders of the separatist movement.

(4) Dr. Amador, in company with Mr. J. Gabriel Duque, left Colon in August or September of 1903 to go to New York, and returned to Panama in the latter part of October of the same year. I know that his time in the United States was extremely occupied and that the matters that engaged his attention were many and most important, as when he left here I gave him a photographic apparatus to give to the Kodak Co. for repairs and he returned the apparatus to me without any repairs whatever, and on account of this incident I remember the journey perfectly. A few days after his arrival here it reached my ears that he had entered into an understanding with the American Government through the medium of Mr. William Nelson Cromwell and Mr. Bunau-Varilla, the conferences being held with Mr. John Hay, in those days Secretary of State, and that Dr. Amador had personally visited the House of Government in Washington.

(5) From the 1st of November of 1903 onward, I know that the participants in the separatist movement received quantities of money. Between the first and the third day of the month of November, several persons, among them Mr. Arture Cevera, sublieutenant, under the orders of Gen. Huertas, told me that Amador had brought from New York drafts for $200,000 gold to meet the first expenses of the independence. As a matter of fact in those days, which were called of independence, money was given away with extreme profusion. A simple order written on any old piece of paper signed by Huertas was enough for the fortunate one to get the money he had asked for.

(6) I am not certain of the money that Dr. Amador took for his own use; but I know that before the independence he lived off his pay as a doctor employed in the St. Thomas Hospital, and that he was in a very bad financial condition, and it was evident after the revolution that he had enough to pay his debts, to live well, and eventually to purchase the building known by the name of Bela de Ore in company with Mr. Manuel Espinosa B., paying large sums in cash.

(7) Also my information at that time was to the effect that the funds brought here by Dr. Amador were given to him by American bankers, that is to say, New York, through the intermediary of Mr. William Nelson Cromwell.

(8) Having then been elected a senator to the Colombian Congress, Dr. Jose Augustin Arango left Colon at about the middle of the year 1903, giving the impression that he was on his way to Bogota. Shortly afterwards there came to us the news that he had arrived in the city of Kingston, Jamaica, and that there he was busy holding conferences with Mr. Cromwell or his representative. Certain it is, as even is now of history, that he took no part in the sessions of the national Congress of which he was a member.

Signed in Ancon, Canal Zone of Panama, two copies of even effect and tenor, the 12th day of July, 1909.

DONALDO VELASCO.

UNITED STATES OF AMERICA, CANAL ZONE,
Circuit Court, First Judicial Circuit.

Personally appeared before me the undersigned clerk of the circuit court aforesaid, Donaldo Velasco, to me known by representation to be the person whose name is signed to the foregoing instrument, and acknowledged that he executed the same for the purposes therein contained.

Witness my hand and seal of the court this 12th day of July, 1909.

[SEAL.]

WALLIS EMERY,
Circuit Court Clerk.

There are a number of other statements bearing on Dr. Amador's finances, it being essential, not having the original draft—a record of which I believe exists on the books of the Chemical National Bank of New York and on the books of J. P. Morgan & Co., showing the payment to Dr. Amador out of the first million dollars of a sum approximating $100,000—I though it necessary to establish the facts in some other way. There is no doubt whatever that Dr. Amador was $100,000 richer after the revolution than he was before.

The CHAIRMAN. We had better stop here for to-day, Mr. Hall.

Mr. HALL. Very well, sir.

Thereupon the committee adjourned till Friday, February 16, at 10 a. m.

COMMITTEE ON FOREIGN AFFAIRS,
Friday, February 16, 1912.

The committee met at 10 o'clock a. m., Hon. William Sulzer (chairman) presiding.

STATEMENT OF MR. HENRY N. HALL—Resumed.

The CHAIRMAN. Mr. Hall, you may proceed.

Mr. HALL. On November 6, 1903, the junta sent the following cable to the Secretary of State in Washington:

PANAMA, *November 5, 1903.*

SECRETARY OF STATE, *Washington:*

The junta of provisional government of the Republic of Panama has appointed Señor Philippe Bunau Varilla envoy extraordinary near your Government, with full powers to conduct diplomatic and financial negotiations. Deign to receive and to heed him.

J. A. ARANGO,
ARIAS,
BOYD DE LA ESPRIELLA,
Foreign Affairs.

Mr. Ehrman then sent the following cable:

PANAMA, *November 6, 1903.*

SECRETARY OF STATE, *Washington:*

Philippe Bunua Varilla has been appointed envoy extraordinary and minister plenipotentiary to the United States. Perfect quiet.

EHRMAN.

On the following day Felix Ehrman entered into diplomatic negotiations with the Republic of Panama and recognized it in the following official communication to the junta:

PANAMA, *November 7.*

Senores J. A. ARANGO, TOMAS ARIAS, and FREDERICO BOYD,
Junta of the Provisional Government, present.

GENTLEMEN: As it appears that the people of Panama have, by unanimous movement, dissolved their political connection with the Republic of Colombia and resumed their independence and as there is no opposition to the Provisional Government in the city of Panama, I have to inform you that the Provisional

Government will be held responsible for the protection of the persons and property of citizens of the United States as well as to keep the Isthmian transit free, in accordance with the obligations of existing treaties relative to the Isthmian territory.

I have the honor to remain, gentlemen,

Very respectfully, FELIX EHRMAN,

United States Vice Consul General.

The U. S. S. *Boston* arrived in Panama Bay on November 7. She at once sent a gig to the railway mole, apparently for information. Soon a launch put out with Consul Ehrman on board, and after a while the little white puffs from the sides of the American warship were followed by the heavy booming of the guns saluting the representative of the United States. Gen. Huertgas, thinking the honor was meant for him, responded with the guns of the *Bovedas*. Then the little gunboat *Padilla* ran up the Stars and Stripes and in turn saluted.

There was great jubilation over the arrival of the U. S. S. *Boston*, and the public delight was intensified by the distribution broadcast through the town of copies of Mr. Ehrman's letter to the junta recognizing the Republic of Panama. The municipal council met, and, to show its appreciation of President Roosevelt's action, they determined to present him with the flag that had been raised on November 4 in the Cathedral Plaza after Mendoza had read the declaration of independence. They took this opportunity of showing their appreciation of the great assistance rendered to the independence movement by Prescott and the Panama Railroad by making the presentation through him. The following letter of the president of the municipal council was sent the same evening with the precious flag to Mr. Prescott's house:

MUNICIPAL COUNCIL OF PANAMA,

Panama, November 7, 1903.

Señor Don H. G. PRESCOTT:

The illustrious municipal council over which I have the honor and good fortune to preside, bearing in mind the spontaneous and sincere proofs of sympathy you have given in favor of the independence of the Isthmus of Panama from the rest of Colombia, is highly pleased at being able to reciprocate these proofs of sympathy by intrusting to you the honor of conveying to His Excellency the President of the United States of America the first flag of the Republic of Panama, raised on the municipal palace on the 4th day of November after we had sworn the independence of our fatherland.

May this also be a testimonial of our gratitude to you for the many favors received.

With sentiments of distinguished consideration, I have the pleasure of subscribing myself,

Your obedient servant, DEMETRIO H. BRID.

On the following morning, November 8, the junta acknowledged the recognition of the Republic of Panama by the United States, in a letter addressed to the United States vice consul general, in the follwing terms—you will find it in Senate Document No. 51, Fifty-sixth Congress:

REPUBLIC OF PANAMA,

Panama, November 8, 1903.

SIR: The junta of the provisional government, informed of your communication of yesterday, has requested me to inform you that the Republic of Panama cherishes the most sincere determination of protecting, and it has so far protected, the lives and properties of the citizens of the United States, which determination involves for the Republic a sacred and pleasing duty; and that in regard to the obligations existing on account of treaties in connection with the isthmian territories theretofore with the Republic of Colombia are now with the Republic of Panama, that has substituted the former in them and their rights.

With sentiments of the highest consideration, I beg to remain,

Your attentive servant,

F. V. DE LA ESPRIELLA,
Minister of Foreign Affairs.

The VICE CONSUL GENERAL OF THE UNITED STATES OF AMERICA.

The junta also received by cable a copy of the communication Bunau-Varilla had addressed to the State Department in Washington on the previous day on receipt of his promised appointment as minister.

You will recall how, in that communication to the State Department, Bunau-Varilla made use of the same words, "unnecessary and wasteful civil wars," which Mr. Hay also made use of in a confidential dispatch to the American minister in Bogota.

And then, the farce being ended, Amador sat down and wrote to Prescott, who had returned to Colon, the laconic little note Mr. Rainey read to you and of which I showed you a photograph.

The chief conspirator congratulates his chief aid-de-camp for the manner he behaved during the conspiration.

It was thus, that, in the words of President Roosevelt, "the people of Panama rose literally as one man." Senator Carmack was not far wrong when he said that one man was Roosevelt.

Now, in Washington, on November 7, the same day United States Vice Consul General Ehrman recognized the Republic of Panama, Secretary of State Hay gave an official statement to the correspondents of the press in the State Department. This statement was issued under the directions of President Roosevelt and said:

The action of the President is not only in the strictest accordance with the principles of justice and equity and in line with events precedents of all public policy, but it was the only course he could have taken in compliance with our treaty rights and obligations.

The hurried recognition of the Republic of Panama before even an election had been held, or a constituting assembly called, or a constitution adopted, and which then as now could not have existed a week but for the protection of the United States, was on the face of it contrary to the accepted tenets of the law of nations. It contrasts strangely with the long delay in recognizing the Republic of Portugal after it possessed a fully constituted administration which collected taxes and custom dues and maintained an army, and which had taken the place of a monarchial government.

Mr. Roosevelt's acts in connection with the creation and recognition of the Republic of Panama were not only contrary to the treaty obligations of the United States and to the accepted tenets of the laws of nations, but they were specifically in violation of fundamental principles of international law which the United States itself, as I am now about to show you, had laid down and recognizes.

That these principles laid down by the United States at the time of the civil war were violated by Mr. Roosevelt's acts in connection with the creation and the recognition of Panama will be apparent to all who are familiar with the correspondence between Secretary Seward and the Hon. Charles Francis Adams, United States minister to England in 1861. The famous note of instructions of April 10, 1861, contains the following:

You will hardly be asked by responsible statesmen abroad why has not the new administration already suppressed the revolution. Thirty-five days are a short period in which to repress a movement, etc.

Referring to the principle of secession, Mr. Seward said:

The so-called Confederate States therefore * * * are attempting what will prove a physical impossibility. Necessarily they build the structure of their new government upon the same principle by which they seek to destroy the Union, namely, the right of each individual member of the Confederacy to withdraw from it at pleasure and in peace. A government thus constituted could neither attain the consolidation necessary for stability nor guarantee any engagements it might make with creditors or other nations.

Again, Secretary Seward said:

You will in no case listen to any suggestions of compromise by this Government, under foreign auspices, with its discontented citizens. If * * * you shall unhappily find Her Majesty's Government tolerating the application of the so-called seceding States, or wavering about it, you will not leave them to suppose for a moment that they can grant that application (for recognition) and remain the friends of the United States. You may even assure them promptly in that case that if they determine to recognize they may at the same time prepare to enter into alliance with the enemies of this Republic.

The doctrine of recognition is thus laid down by Secretary of State Seward to Mr. Charles Francis Adams in these terms:

We freely admit that a nation may, and even ought, to recognize a new state which has absolutely and beyond question effected its independence and permanently established its sovereignty, and that a recognition in such a case affords no just cause of offense to the government of the country from which the new state has so detached itself. On the other hand, we insist that a nation that recognizes a revolutionary state, with a view to aid its effecting its sovereignty and independence, commits a great wrong against the nation whose integrity is thus invaded, and makes itself responsible for a just and ample redress.

There you have, in terms, the United States recognizing the principle that a "just and ample redress" is due to a nation claiming damages—in this case the Republic of Colombia—for the violation of international law in the recognition of a rebel state—in this instance Panama—and the assistance given to such rebel state to prevent the national authority—in this case Colombia—reasserting her sovereignty over it. If that paragraph had been written after the rape of the Isthmus, instead of more than 40 years before, it could not have more forcefully stated the principles on which Colombia bases her just claims for damages.

Referring to the commercial advantages which Great Britain might have hoped to have obtained from the recognition of the Confederate States, Mr. Seward said—and I do not think I go too far when I say that in 1903 Mr. Roosevelt was putting the interests of the United States above its honor, and that one of the impelling motives of the recognition of the Republic of Panama, the sole motive, in fact, was to insure the acquisition of the Canal Zone—Mr. Seward said:

The President would consider it inconsistent with his habitually high consideration for the Government and people of Great Britain to allow me to dwell longer on the merely commercial aspects of the question under discussion. Indeed, he will not for a moment believe that, upon consideration of merely financial gain, that Government would be induced to lend its aid to a revolution designed to overthrow the institutions of this country and involving ultimately the destruction of the liberties of the American people.

And further:

To recognize the independence of a new state, and so favor, possibly determine, its admission into the family of nations is the highest possible exercise of sovereign power, because it affects in any case the welfare of two nations, and often the peace of the world. In the European system this power is now seldom attempted to be exercised without invoking a consultation or congress of nations. That system has not been extended to this continent. But there is an even greater necessity for prudence in such cases in regard to American States than in regard to the nations of Europe.

At another point in the same note Mr. Seward said:

* * * The several nations of the earth constitute one great federal republic. When one of them casts its suffrage for the admission of a new member into that republic, it ought to act under a profound sense of moral obligation, and be governed by considerations as pure, disinterested, and elevated as the general interests of society and the advancement of human nature.

On May 21, 1861, Mr. Seward annunciated the position of the United States even more forcefully. He instructed Mr. Adams as follows:

You will say that by our laws, and the laws of nature, and the laws of nations, this Government has a clear right to suppress insurrection.

And further in the same dispatch:

A concession of belligerent rights is liable to be construed as a recognition of them. No one of those proceedings will pass unquestioned by the United States in this case. Hitherto recognition has been moved only on the assumption that the so-called Confederate States are de facto a self-sustaining power. Now, after long forbearance, designed to soothe discontent and avert the need of civil war, the land and naval forces of the United States have been put in motion to repress insurrection. The true character of the pretended new state is at once revealed. It is seen to be a power existing in pronunciamiento only. It has never won a field. It has obtained no forts that were not virtually betrayed into its hands or seized in breach of trust. It commands not a single port on the coast nor any highway out from its pretended capital by land. Under these circumstances Great Britain is called upon to intervene and give it body and independence by resisting our measures of suppression. British recognition would be British intervention to create within our territory a hostile state by overthrowing this Republic itself.

If that dispatch had really been written for the purposes of the Panama situation, it could hardly fit in better. At the time when Mr. Roosevelt was using the armed power of the United States to prevent Colombia from asserting her sovereignty over the Isthmus of Panama, the land and naval forces of Colombia had been put in motion to suppress rebellion, and the Republic of Panama was a power existing in pronunciamiento only.

On the same date, May 21, 1861, Mr. Adams, in a dispatch to Secretary of State Seward, giving details of his interview with Lord John Russell on May 18, reports that he asserted on behalf of the United States:

The rule was clear that whenever it became apparent that any organized form of society had advanced so far as to prove its power to defend itself and protect itself against the assaults of enemies, and at the same time to manifest a capacity to maintain binding relations with foreign nations, then a measure of recognition could not be justly objected to on either side. The case was very different when such an interference should take place prior to the establishment of the proof required, so as to bring about a result which would not probably have happened but for that external agency.

Finally, on June 19, 1910, Secretary Seward, in dispatch to Mr. Adams, after informing him that Lord Lyon's instructions contained a decision at which the British Government had arrived, to the effect that America was divided into two belligerent parties and that Great Britain assumed the attitude of a neutral between them, said:

The United States are * * * solely and exclusively sovereign within the Territories they have lawfully acquired and long possessed * * * they are living under the obligations of the law of nations and of treaties with Great Britain * * * and they insist that Great Britain shall remain their friend * * *. Great Britain by virtue of these relations is a stranger to parties and sections in this country, whether they are loyal to the United States or not, and Great Britain can neither rightfully qualify the sovereignty of the United States, nor concede nor recognize any rights or interests or power of any party, State, or section in contravention of the unbroken sovereignty of the Federal Union.

England had never guaranteed the sovereignty of the Federal Union over the Southern States. She was not preventing the United States from repressing the rebellion, nor was she lending aid to the South. It was only after the North had declared a blockade, thus specifically recognizing a state of civil war, that Lord John Russell had taken the position that America was divided into two belligerent parties, and that England assumed the attitude of a neutral. Yet the United States protested even that step. How different was the situation in 1903. The United States had guaranteed the sovereignty of Colombia over the Isthmus, and yet she was employing her armed force to prevent Colombia maintaining and exercising the rights of sovereignty it had itself guaranteed, and guaranteed in return for valuable consideration received. The United States actually recognized the rebel province as an independent nation 72 hours after the fake revolution, and Mr. Roosevelt received as minister of Panama a Frenchman, who was neither a native nor a citizen of Panama, who was directly interested in the sale of the canal to the United States, and who presented his credentials so soon after the establishment of the new Republic that it was a physical impossibility for them to be sent up from the Isthmus.

On November 8 press dispatches from Washington stated that the constitution of the new Republic was already prepared, and that in the canal treaty, which would be concluded, Panama would be given the same indemnity, $10,000,000 cash and $250,000 a year, which Colombia was to have received under the Hay-Herran treaty.

On November 7 Mr. Curtis—he, as you know, was Mr. Cromwell's partner—had an audience with the President, who asked that the company formally declare that it agreed to the application of the existing understanding to the new situation as it had been generally set forth by cable on October 21. Mr. Cromwell, having been notified by cable, immediately wrote, and, in accordance with instructions from the board of directors and the liquidator, sent on February 9 the following cable.

The original is in the Department of Justice, and this copy, which I am quoting, is from Mr. Cromwell's brief:

PARIS, *November 9, 1903.*

To the PRESIDENT OF THE UNITED STATES,
Washington, D. C.:

I am authorized to confirm the cable that I had the honor to address you on October 31 in the name of President Bo, with the unanimous approval of the board of directors, as well as of the liquidator of the old company, and to add in their name that they fully confirm the understanding that the agreement entered into on March 4 last between Your Excellency and the Compagnie Nouvelle covers and equally applies to the new situation with which you are dealing. You can have the utmost confidence in the good faith of the company, whose attitude remains the same. I am sailing on Wednesday with powers to settle any details that may have to be arranged.

WILLIAM NELSON CROMWELL,
General Counsel of La Compagnie Nouvelle du Canal de Panama.

The CHAIRMAN. What is the date of that cable?

Mr. HALL. November 9, 1903.

The CHAIRMAN. Was that sent from New York?

Mr. HALL. It was sent from Paris to President Roosevelt.

Mr. DIFENDERFER. Cromwell was in Paris at that time?

Mr. HALL. Yes, sir.

During his stay in Paris—I am quoting from Mr. Cromwell's brief in his own words—during his stay in Paris Mr. Cromwell was in constant communication with the United States, giving advice and instructions, and, having accomplished the object of his brief stay, he sailed on November 11 for the United States to be present at the conference previously arranged with the special delegates of the new Republic of Panama on their arrival in New York.

On November 9 Gen. Rafael Reyes was dispatched from Bogota with Gens. Pedro Nel Ospina, Lucas Caballero, and Jorge Holguin as special commissioners to Panama and Washington to negotiate a settlement with the Panama rebels and a new canal treaty satisfactory to the United States. Rioting began in Bogota as news of the secession was amplified, and the populace stoned the house of Lorenzo Marroquin, blaming him and his father's government for the loss of Panama.

The instructions to Gen. Reyes, as published in the Colombian Blue Book, were that he should ascertain upon what basis the United States would renew negotiations; that if modifications of the treaty were expected he should attempt to provide that Colombia's jurisdiction should be integrally preserved and that the indemnity should be augmented, but if the special commission found that it was necessary to sign the treaty as it stood in order to save Colombia's integrity it should do so, subject to ratification by Congress.

But Mr. Cromwell had already arranged with President Roosevelt that the new Republic of Panama, through its French Panama Canal Co. minister, should immediately ratify the pending Hay-Herran treaty or another treaty that would be satisfactory; and to this end he had stipulated that as soon as the fake republic was recognized by the United States it should at once send special delegates to Washington to assist Bunau-Varilla in negotiating the treaty and in arranging to finance the newly created nation.

The special delegates were Dr. Amador (later President of the Republic) and Federico Boyd, with Dr. Pablo Arosemena (now President) as counsellor. Before leaving Panama these personages had arranged by cable to meet Mr. Cromwell in New York for a conference, Mr. Cromwell being on his way at the same time from Paris to New York.

Before the return of Mr. Cromwell from Paris and before the signing of the treaty even Mr. Bunau-Varilla had taken up with J. Pierpont Morgan the finances of the new Republic. On Sunday, November 15, desiring an immediate reply, Bunau-Varilla sent the following telegram to Mr. Morgan's residence:

WASHINGTON, *November 15, 1903.*

PIERPONT MORGAN, Esq.,
219 Madison Avenue, New York City:

I beg to be excused to trouble you to-day, but am obliged to have an immediate decision on financial plan which I submitted to you and to know from you by telegraphic message addressed to me, New Willard Hotel, Washington, whether you agree or disagree with it.

I repeat as follows said plan: I would name your firm agent of the Republic of Panama in the United States in virtue of the full powers I have received from my Government for said object. You would immediately have full and exclusive power to collect from the United States Treasury any sum which would have to be delivered to the Republic of Panama, and you would have to place said sums to the credit of the Republic on the account opened in your firm and dispose of them according to the orders of my Government. You would immediately open a credit to the Republic for an amount of $300,000, of which the Government could dispose at different periods as follows:

Hundred thousand would be placed at the immediate disposition of the Republic and delivered for the account of the Republic according to the orders I shall give to your firm in the name of my Government; $50,000 would be placed at the disposition of the Republic immediately after the signature of the canal treaty and its consequent ratification by my Government; the rest, $150,000, immediately after ratification of the canal treaty by the Senate of the United States.

I add that, to limit your risk, I am willing to guarantee you personally against any loss to the extent of $100,000, and to make such guaranty effective I would have to-morrow $75,000 placed in the hands of your firm and $25,000 two or three days after, it being understood that such guaranty shall cease as soon as the account of the Republic will be credited on your books.

BUNAU-VARILLA.

The $75,000 that Mr. Bunau-Varilla wanted to place with J. P. Morgan & Co. were then with Heidelbach, Ickelheimer & Co., to whom they had been telegraphed over by President Bo.

On November 16 the Panama banking house of Isaac Brandon & Bros., which in part financed the fake republic during this period, charging no interest for its loans and having no security outside of the "credit" of the new Government, bought a $75,000 draft on Piza, Nephews & Co. from Mr. Lindo's Panama house of Piza, Lindo & Co. This draft was stamped with Piza, Nephews & Co.'s acceptance on November 23, payable at the Mechanics and Traders' Bank November 30, but was paid, according to Piza, Nephews & Co.'s books, on November 24. Thus, the Brandons received no "security," but the cash equivalent for their advances, in the form of drafts of a reputable fellow banker for the first $100,000 they contributed.

On November 16 Bunau-Varilla announced in Washington that J. P. Morgan & Co. had been appointed fiscal agents of the Republic of Panama.

The next day, November 17, Heidelbach, Ickelheimer & Co. placed with J. P. Morgan & Co. to the credit of Bunau-Varilla $75,000, thereby exhausting the original credit of $100,000 cabled by Credit Lyonnais to his account on October 26. Morgan & Co. transferred the $75,000 the same day to Piza, Nephews & Co. On the same day Heidelbach, Ickelheimer & Co. received a cable from Credit Lyonnais instructing them to pay to Bunau-Varilla, upon his application, $4,000, the same amount referred to specifically in the Amador-Bunau-Varilla code. This $4,000 was disposed of by Bunau-Varilla's bankers on November 23, by sending $1,500 to the New Willard Hotel, Washington, and $1,000 to the Waldorf-Astoria Hotel, leaving a balance of $1,500.

The Panaman special envoys arrived in New York on the steamer *City of Washington*, which reached the bar at 6.45 a. m. of November 17, 1903. Mr. Cromwell's principal agent, Roger L. Farnham, who, you will recall, brought in to the Washington correspondent of the World on June 14, 1903, the whole story of the revolution four and a half months before it occurred, went down the bay on a revenue cutter, met the delegates, and escorted them to the old Fifth Avenue Hotel, where they remained from the morning of the 17th to 3.30 o'clock in the afternoon of the 18th before taking the train for Washington. Had they gone at once to Washington, as they afterwards falsely reported to their Panaman constituents they did do, they would have arrived before Bunau-Varilla could have rushed through the treaty to the detriment of Panama.

Mr. Cromwell arrived from Paris, also on November 17, 1903, on the *Kaiser Wilhelm der Grosse*, which reached the bar at 12.12 p. m. Farnham, having taken care of the Panaman envoys, met his chief at the pier. Amador spent that night at the home of his son, Dr. Raoul A. Amador, No. 216 West One hundred and twelfth Street. The next day, November 18, 1903, occurred the "all-day" conference of which Mr. Cromwell tells in his brief. Current newspaper reports said Cromwell was closeted with the special commissioners at their hotel for an hour. Apprised of the coming of the special commissioners, who might interfere with his freedom of action, Bunau-Varilla, who already had been received informally by Secretary Hay at luncheon on the 9th, made haste with his diplomatic mission. On the 13th he had been formally received by President Roosevelt, and by the 18th—the day after the arrival of the special commissioners in New York—he was prepared to sign the treaty, and did so before the envoys reached Washington. Bunau-Varilla's signing the treaty, unsatisfactory as it was to Panama, has been from that day, and always will continue with the Panamans to be, a subject for recriminations.

Anyone by looking at the two treaties—the Hay-Herran treaty and the Hay-Bunau-Varilla treaty—will see the difference, and that Secretary Hay forced Bunau-Varilla to concede the authority of the United States in the establishment of courts of the United States in the Canal Zone, so that all the laborers might not be amenable to the laws of Panama as they were amenable to the laws of Colombia, but under the immediate authority, legal and otherwise, of the United States. And I can state on the highest possible authority that it would have been, in the opinion of the administration, impossible for the United States to have constructed the canal with the speed and efficiency with which it has been constructed if that provision had not been included in the Hay-Bunau-Varilla treaty. How deep the feeling on that matter was I think I shall be able to show to you. This hastily drawn up treaty by Hay and Bunau-Varilla gave rise to certain very serious differences between the United States and the Republic of Panama about a year later, and Mr. Taft, who was then Secretary of War, was later sent down to the Isthmus to negotiate a settlement with the Panamans and to smooth their ruffled feathers.

Dr. Morales, as we have seen, came to New York with Mr. Arias to arrange with Mr. Cromwell for the investing of the $16,000,000, and all this happened at about the same time. Obaldia was then the minister of Panama to the United States, and in order to force the Government here to accede to the wishes of the Panamans Dr. Morales, who speaks English very fluently, wrote an article for the North American Review on the secret history of the signing of the Hay-Bunau-Varilla treaty, and I think I had better read into the record certain letters in connection with that matter. We sent a staff correspondent to the Isthmus of Panama. He was present on the 28th of June, 1909. He had an interview with Dr. Morales on this point, and Dr. Morales said he would only answer questions put to him in writing. The following questions were put to him:

1. Will you kindly relate in detail the circumstances which prompted you to write for the North American Review the article on the Hay-Bunau-Varilla treaty and the reasons that led to its withdrawal?

2. Who suggested the withdrawal of the article and with whom did you consult as to the advisability of publishing it?

3. As a member of the special fiscal commission of 1904, did you have a part in the selection of Mr. William Nelson Cromwell as counsel to the commission?

Dr. Morales answered, in writing, as follows; here is his letter [shows letter to committee]:

1. In September of 1904 there was pending between Panama and the United States a diplomatic question originating in the diverse interpretations which the two countries gave to the canal treaty. In matters referring to the enforcement of the Dingley tariff in the zone, to jurisdiction over the ports of Panama and Colon, and to other points of minor importance. I, interested on behalf of my country in making known the issue to the level-headed and just people of America, published several articles in the New York newspapers, and doubtless for this reason the editor of the North American Review solicited my collaboration, asking me to prepare an article on this subject, which was to be handed to him on October 20.

Happily for Panama, President Roosevelt convinced himself of the justice of our claims and on the 18th or 19th of October addressed to Secretary Taft the celebrated letter in which he gave the latter instructions to come to the Isthmus and effect a settlement with the Panaman Government of the pending questions.

As my only aim in publishing the article already prepared for the North American Review was to favor the interests of my country, the publication no longer had any object. Furthermore, I received from Mr. Obaldia, then minister of Panama in Washington, a communication pointing out to me the profitableness of withdrawing my article, and this I gave expression to in a letter which I addressed to the editor of the Review on the 19th of October.

2. I did not consult with anybody about the publication of my article, and as to its withdrawal Mr. Obaldia alone intervened in the manner I have stated. Nevertheless, I ought to say that some distinguished persons were at my hotel to beg of me not to publish the article, thinking doubtless that it might contain revelations against President Roosevelt in connection with the independence of Panama; but it is the fact that in my work there was nothing which was not a dispassionate and calm exposition of the international question which was being debated, as is shown by the title of the article which was: "The Panama Canal treaty; its history and interpretation."

Dr. Morales later amplified this statement by giving to a representative of the World the names of the "distinguished persons" who called on him at his hotel and begged him not to publish anything about the history of the canal treaty. He said they were the late George A. Burt, formerly superintendent of the Panama Railroad, and another American whose name Dr. Morales understood to be Mr. Anson. They represented themselves, said Dr.

Morales, as the direct spokesmen for Cornelius N. Bliss, the Republican campaign collector, and his chief, George Bruce Cortelyou, Republican national chairman. They told Dr. Morales frankly that they feared an exposure of the history of the Panama revolution would defeat Mr. Roosevelt for the presidency, and declared that they were authorized to reimburse the author for his article if he would suppress it, and furthermore declared that President Roosevelt would sign any order desired for the adjustment of the differences with Panama if Dr. Morales would acquiesce.

As Dr. Morales explained in his written statement, his object was to compel the United States to recognize what the Panamans contended were their rights, but would accept no compensation, and on the following day President Roosevelt wrote his letter to Mr. Taft ordering him to go to the Isthmus and adjust the differences. Mr. Taft went to Panama accompanied by Mr. Cromwell and they had their photographs taken together [shows photographs to committee].

When the Panama commisisoners arrived in Washington, they were again met by Mr. Cromwell, who promised to obtain the ratification of the treaty signed by Bunau-Varilla. His partner, Curtis, had remained in Washington after the declaration of independence and had received assurement from Secretary of State Hay that articles 1 and 22 of the Hay-Herran treaty would be reincorporated verbatim in any treaty signed with the new Republic of Panama.

In Washington Mr. Cromwell brought about conferences between the special delegates and Senators Hanna, Fairbanks, and Kittredge, and during their entire stay in the United States Dr. Amador and Mr. Boyd conferred daily with one or several of the partners in Mr. Cromwell's firm and were guided by him in their negotiations with the United States.

Five days after the treaty was signed—November 23—Lindo gave Bunau-Varilla check No. 4507 for $25,000, dated November 23 and made on the Mechanics and Traders' Bank by the firm of Piza, Nephews & Co. Bunau-Varilla indorsed the check to Heidelbach, Ickelheimer & Co., and it was paid through the Importers and Traders' National Bank. Heidelbach, Ickelheimer & Co. on the following day transferred the $25,000, by instructions of Bunau-Varilla, to J. P. Morgan & Co., who in turn paid it over on November 25 to Mr. Lindo's firm.

Amador and Boyd on November 25 signed an agreement with the Bowling Green Trust Co. pledging the first moneys received from the United States or the customs revenues of the ports of Panama and Colon to repay a loan of $100,000 which the trust company made at 6 per cent per annum, payable in four months and renewable for four months upon payment of 3 per cent bonus. Mr. Cromwell, who had reorganized the Bowling Green Trust Co. and was its attorney and one of its directors, had secured the first loan for the new Republic. It was amply secured by $90,000 par value of Northern Pacific bonds and $10,000 par value of Baltimore & Ohio bonds, which were deposited in the name of William Griffiths, jr., whose signature was witnessed by E. B. Hill, of Mr. Cromwell's firm. Notice of failure to pay the interest was sent not to the representative of the Panama Republic, but to Mr. Cromwell. This was the financial arrangement "already made with a bank" referred to by

Dr. Amador in the letter of October 18, 1903, to his son. A commission of 3 per cent on the Bowling Green loan appears on the debit side of the books of Piza, Nephews & Co. as of December 27, but it does not appear to whom it was paid.

The $100,000 received from the Bowling Green was transferred to Piza, Nephews & Co.; $50,000 on November 27 and $50,000 on December 1. Then appears on Piza, Nephews & Co.'s books debits of $30,384.67 on December 4 for an invoice of supplies sent to the new Republic on the steamer *Allianca* and $9,932 for an invoice on the *Yucatan* December 14. On December 22 the Brandon banking house was paid $46,000 through Piza, Nephews & Co. This makes a total of $340,000 at then prevailing exchange repaid to the Brandons of the $450,000 silver which they say they lent the new Republic, without security and partly without interest. By November 30 Bunau-Varilla had served the purposes of Mr. Cromwell and was treading on his toes, so it was deemed advisable to have him removed as the Panaman minister to Washington. Accordingly Mr. Cromwell, in the name of E. A. Drake, vice president of the Panama Railroad, on November 30, 1903, sent to the Isthmus a cable in cipher, of which the following is a translation:

NEW YORK, *November 30, 1903—6.10 p. m.*

BEERS, *Panama:*

Several cables urging immediate appointment of Pablo Arosemena have been sent to the junta since Friday. We are surprised that action was not taken and suppose it is only because the minister of the Republic of Panama is trying to disturb the junta by cabling that there is great danger that Washington will make a trade with Reyes and withdraw warships and urge his retention because of his alleged influence with President Roosevelt and Senators. This is absolutely without foundation. Mr. Cromwell has direct assurances from President Roosevelt, Secretary Hay, Senator Hanna, and other Senators that there is not the slightest danger of this. Evidently the minister's pretense of influence is grossly exaggerated. We have fullest support of Mr. Cromwell and his friends who have carried every victory for past six years. Junta evidently do not know that objection exists in Washington to the minister of Republic of Panama, because he is not a Panaman, but a foreigner, and initially has displeased influential Senators regarding character of former treaty. He is recklessly involving Republic of Panama in financial and other complications that will use up important part of indemnity. Delegates here are powerless to prevent all this, as minister of Republic of Panama uses his position as minister to go over their heads. He is sacrificing the Republic's interests and may any moment commit Republic of Panama to portion of the debts of Colombia same as he signed treaty omitting many points of advantage to Republic of Panama—and which would have been granted readily—without waiting for delegates, who were to his knowledge within two hours of arrival. With discretion inform junta and cable me immediately synopsis of situation and when will junta appoint Pablo Arosemena. Answer to-day if possible.

DRAKE.

Nearly all of Mr. Cromwell's cables that were sent to Beers were signed by Mr. Drake, and sent to Beers addressed to the Panama Railroad Co. in Panama. One of the things which the World was not able to obtain in its investigation, but which this committee can obtain with the utmost ease, is the entire correspondence in cipher and in plain English that passed between the Panama Railroad Co. and Drake and Beers on the Isthmus at the time when all this was going on. The Panama Railroad Co., now belonging to the Government of the United States, certainly would not be in a position to refuse to give Congress access to its books and records, which also contain two reports made by Col. Shaler, one giving the true history of the revolution, the other prepared for publication to safeguard the company's interest in the event of failure.

Mr. Cromwell not only used Capt. Beers in his intrigue against Bunau-Varilla, but also to find out what Admiral Walker, who had been sent to the Isthmus of Panama by President Roosevelt, was doing. Here is another telegram from Drake to Capt. Beers:

> Your telegram is of utmost importance. You telegraph as soon as possible reply Walker gets from Washington, also action Junta takes on same. Subject of minister of Republic of Panama is of vital importance, and we rely on you to keep me well posted promptly and fully by cable on action Junta or anyone else regarding same.

Herbert G. Prescott, intrusted, immediately after the revolution, to transmit to President Roosevelt the first flag raised by the Republic, had forwarded it to Mr. Cromwell, and on November 30 he received the following cabled answer:

> [S. J. 26, Date, 30-11-03. No. of words, 162. From New York. Time, 7.15 p. m.]
>
> H. G. PRESCOTT, *Panama:*
>
> Inform municipal council and Junta I had honor and pleasure presenting to President Roosevelt the flag of the Republic, forwarded through you. Among other things, I remarked that while the United States would never part with its historic treasure, the Liberty Bell, which first rang out the independence of this Nation, and the reverberation of which continues to be an inspiration to all liverty-loving people, yet so fond was the gratitude and affection of the Republic of Panama to the President that they gave into his hands their most precious treasure, the sacred and historic flag, the first raised upon the declaration of independence. The president accepted the gift in most enthusiastic and grateful terms, and requested me to convey his unbounded thanks and pleasure, and to say he designs having a suitable inscription woven upon its surface to perpetuate its historic character and the grateful acts of its donors. I greet you all.
>
> WILLIAM NELSON CROMWELL.

President Roosevelt, on the 29th, in his message, confronted Congress with his dictum:

> The question now, therefore, is not by which route the Isthmian canal shall be built, for that question has been definitely and irrevocably decided. The question is simply whether or not we shall have an Isthmian canal.

In his efforts to calm the storm of criticism which was sweeping the country, Mr. Roosevelt told the Congress that the canal treaty "was entered into at the urgent solicitation of the people of Colombia," when just the contrary was the truth. He further said: "In drawing up this treaty every concession was made to the people and to the Government of Colombia. We were more than just in dealing with them." When it became evident that the treaty was hopelessly lost, Mr. Roosevelt told the Congress, "the people of Panama rose literally as one man. * * * The Colombian troops stationed on the Isthmus, who had long been unpaid, made common cause with the people of Panama, and with astonishing unanimity the new Republic was started." The truth was that the Colombian troops on the Isthmus had been paid promptly up to date, and the pay-roll vouchers and receipts, up to October, signed by Gen. Huertas and his paymaster, are on file in the War Department at Bogota. The October salaries were disbursed, but the receipts were never forwarded. There was, however, an account carried over from the last civil war, which was charged to the war indebtedness, and remains to this day upon the books of the Colombian Government unpaid.

This furnishes the only possible pretext for justification of Mr. Roosevelt's statement that the troops had been long unpaid.

Col. Tascon, second chief of the forces in Panama, who was sent by Gov. Obaldia and Huertas with his 100 loyal men into the bush just before the "revolution," says that his men were paid promptly up to date and that there was no dissatisfaction with the arrangement of the few months' arrears of the civil-war time, as the men had been paid promptly after the war and were confident that the Government eventually would be able to pay up the war debt.

In Mr. Roosevelt's message there also appears a "partial list of the disturbances on the Isthmus * * * as reported to us by our consuls" since the making of the treaty of 1846. This list, which, as admirably shown by Mr. Chamberlain, is absurdly inaccurate, is virtually the same as Mr. Cromwell's false and inaccurate data furnished to Senator Hanna and used in the conferences he arranged and directed between Amador and Boyd and Republican Party leaders in the Senate. Mr. Cromwell also prepared a thorough résumé of the "unjust wrongs" which Panama had suffered from a period of 50 years, which statement he communicated to the American Government and to Members of Congress to justify the revolution, and to help an opinion favorable to the new Republic and to a treaty with her.

On December 10 Mr. Cromwell, through Vice President Drake, cabled Capt. Beers to obtain a leave of absence from Supt. Shaler and come to the United States. Beers accordingly embarked on December 15, and for the next two months was Mr. Cromwell's assistant in Washington and New York in a campaign to undermine the influence and official position of Bunau-Varilla.

To return to Mr. Cromwell's brief; as soon as the treaty between the United States and Panama was signed, the Canal Co. asked Mr. Cromwell to obtain, if possible, a full statement defining the attitude of Panama to the canal concession. In his brief Mr. Cromwell says:

After the independence the company cabled us to obtain, if possible, formal statements defining the official attitude of the new Republic as to the concessions, the canal stock, and the question of sovereignty. We immediately took this matter up, had conferences with the special delegates for three successive days, and obtained an official, formal declaration signed by them (Nov. 27) which was addressed to us as general counsel of the company, as well as similar declarations for the railroad company.

By these official statements the Republic, as the new sovereign, confirmed all the concessions of the canal and railroad companies, and acknowledged and approved the disputed extension to 1910; it claimed for Panama the absolute succession to the sovereignty of Colombia; it demanded the appointment of a delegate to the board of directors and the appointment of agents in Panama in accordance with the concessions; and it also claimed all the assets and rights due to the Government which had granted the concession, including the Panama Canal shares.

These important documents not only officially established and confirmed the title and protected the property of the canal and railroad companies under the new Republic, but they also supplied a full answer to the later demands that Colombia made on the company in Paris in suits which were afterwards begun by Colombia.

Soon after, the Colombian Government made a formal claim on the company in Paris for the said shares, and contested the devolution of sovereignty to Panama. The company, sustained by the governmental declarations mentioned above, resisted these claims. It will be seen below that Colombia began an action in Paris in 1904 to enjoin the transfer to the United States, to establish its right to con inue to vote as owner of the canal shares, and to retain its representation on the board of the Canal Co. In its decision on this matter the cour. cited these documents as decisive factors in support of the attitude of the company in its refusal to recognize that the sovereignty of Colombia still existed.

Following this important step, we had the Republic of Panama appoint as its agent on the board of the Canal Co. Mr. Poylo, of Paris, in order to show its sovereignty, and we also had to recognize Mr. Renaudin and Mr. Shaler as agents on the Isthmus of the canal and railroad companies, respectively, under the concessions. All the documents and notices on this subject were written and filed under our supervision.

The company was thus fully protected and strengthened in its concessions and property under the new régime.

Mr. Cromwell further tells us:

On December 17 Senator Morgan introduced (in the Senate) a resolution forbidding the conclusion of the purchase from the Canal Co. until after fresh action by both Houses of Congress, as well as a resolution calling upon the Attorney General to report to Congress on the status of the negotiations between Panama and the United States in the matter of the title. On January 4 a Senator introduced a resolution in respect to a treaty with Colombia to settle the differences arising out of the action of the United States in Panama. On January 13 another Senator introduced a resolution for an investigation into the events of the revolution. On January 18 Senator Morgan introduced a resolution rejecting Article XXII, by which the transfer by the Canal Co. was authorized. On January 26 the situation was considered so grave that the group of Democratic Senators met, discussed the whole matter, and adopted resolutions in favor of an investigation and report to the Senate on the revolution by the Senate Committee on Foreign Relations. A resolution declaring that the action of the United States constituted an act of war, and that the President had no power to declare war without the consent of Congress, was also pending, as well as another resolution declaring that the action of the Government was contrary to the Spooner Act, which did not apply to the new conditions.

As fast as these resolutions were introduced we conferred with prominent Senators and presented to them arguments against these resolutions. The resolutions thus introduced had been submitted to the Colombian envoy, and corrected and approved by him. They were very fully discussed, but nevertheless they were all ultimately rejected.

The Senate Committee on Foreign Relations, however, was not willing to report the Panama treaty as signed by Bunau-Varilla. It insisted on amendments which would give the United States greater authority and more complete sanitary control over the terminal ports on the Atlantic and Pacific, and reported the treaty to the Senate on January 18 with these amendments.

Mr. Cromwell was consulted on the subject of these amendments, and strongly advised their rejection, on the ground that they would indefinitely delay the treaty, as Panama itself desired to insert, if any changes were to be made, the clauses which had been purposely omitted at the time of its signature by Bunau-Varilla, and the discussion of which had been prevented by what Mr. Cromwell calls "the rapid march of events." Later, on January 29, the committee yielded to Mr. Cromwell's wishes, reconsidered its action, and withdrew the amendments.

The treaty was put to a vote on February 23, 1904, and, after debate, was passed by the necessary two-thirds majority, but with 17 adverse votes, which were maintained to the end. The ratifications were duly exchanged on February 26, 1904.

During all this time, between November 10 and February 24, although there was no treaty with the Republic of Panama, Mr.

Roosevelt was forcefully preventing Colombia from putting down the rebellion on the Isthmus.

Immediately after the revolution, President Roosevelt abandoned all pretext of only maintaining free and uninterrupted transit across the Isthmus, and had issued orders that no Colombia forces were to be allowed to land within the limits of the State of Panama, the boundary which extended beyond the geographical limits of the Isthmus.

A large force of warships was hurried down to both the Atlantic and Pacific coasts of the Isthmus. Not only were Colombian waters patroled by American vessels, but armed parties of United States marines and sailors were landed and sent into the interior, and United States Army officers were sent into Colombia to prepare plans for capturing the seaport towns and carrying out an active campaign.

The following correspondence and official reports were not published by President Roosevelt when called upon by Congress for information.

After President Roosevelt had done these things, it naturally came to the knowledge of some of the Senators of the United States; and Senator Gorman, if I am not mistaken, introduced a resolution calling for full information as to the use of military forces in Colombia. President Roosevelt told Mr. Moody, the Secretary of the Navy, to have the war records of the departments searched in order to quote precedents for the action he was then taking. Mr. Moody gave these instructions to the superintendent of the war records, and, I am informed, the superintendent of the war records told him there was not any precedent whatever to be found in all the official correspondence of the Navy Department that could serve Mr. Roosevelt's purpose. Whereupon Mr. Roosevelt sent for the superintendent of the naval war records, Mr. Charles W. Stewart, and the newspaper men and the White House staff still remember the very great displeasure Mr. Roosevelt manifested at not being able to get what he wanted from Mr. Stewart. But Mr. Stewart did compile a complete history of the use of force by the United States, and the use of military force in Colombia, which was transmitted to the Senate of the United States by Mr. Roosevelt on February 3, 1904. In his message to the Senate Mr. Roosevelt says:

In response to the resolution of the Senate of January 22, 1904, I transmit herewith report from the Acting Secretary of the Navy, with accompanying papers. The correspondence since November 16, 1902, referred to in the letter of the Secretary of the Navy, which has not already been transmitted to the Senate, has no reference to the matters covered by the resolution and deals with military movements, and it is for that reason deemed incompatible with the public interests to make it public at this time.

Now, very far from having no reference to the matters covered by the resolution, those records in the Navy Department, which I was permitted to inspect and make copies of by the present Secretary of the Navy, deal exclusively with the events covered by the resolution.

From Admiral Glass, Acapulco, Mexico, on November, 1903, to the Secretary of the Navy, Washington:

Secret and confidential. *Marblehead* and *Concord* to Panama to-day 4 p. m. *Wyoming* will follow to-morrow afternoon. If *Boston* is to go with squadron, I will suggest department will order to rendezvous off Cape Mála, Colombia, about 6 p. m. on November 9. I have ordered *Nero* to Acapulco. I will leave sealed orders for her to proceed to Panama unless otherwise directed.

On November 10 Capt. Delano, of the U. S. S. *Dixie*, wrote to the Secretary of the Navy from Colon that in obedience to the department's cables of November 2, received on board the *Dixie* at Kingston, Jamaica, at 9.15 a. m. on November 3, he left Kingston at 4.20 p. m. the same day, but was obliged to anchor off Port Royal to await stores already contracted for, getting away from Port Royal at 7.45 p. m. *Dixie* arrived in Colon on November 5 at 7.26 p. m. Delano reports:

Found the *Nashville* in port and was informed by signal that the situation on shore was extremely critical, and advising that the battalion be landed immediately. The battalion was formed at once in heavy marching order, ready for any service. Two companies, under command of Maj. Lejeune, were embarked and left the ship before 8 p. m. and were formed on shore at 8.15.

On November 13, Admiral Glass informed the Secretary of the Navy, Washington, that:

The administration of Panama requests, through the acting American consul general, that upon the arrival of Gen. Reyes at Colon he may be received on board the American man-of-war to confer with the authorities. His presence ashore, considering the circumstances, believed to be attended with more or less danger. Shall I arrange accordingly?

In another cable of the same date he said:

After consultation with Admiral Walker I have decided to salute flag of the Republic of Panama to-morrow morning and shall call upon the head of the Government officially.

On November 16 Admiral Glass reported to the Secretary of the Navy on the employment of the forces under his command and on the condition of affairs on the Isthmus. Flagship *Marblehead* and the *Concord* arrived at Panama on the morning of the 10th. *Boston* found at anchor, having arrived on the 7th. *Wyoming* arrived on the 13th. On arrival Glass assumed functions of senior United States naval officer on the Isthmus, and communicated with the senior American naval officer present at Colon and the acting United States consul general in Panama: "I found that affairs on the Isthmus were quiet." No official news had been received from the Province of Chiriqui since the secession, but there is said to be no likelihood of any opposition from that quarter. On November 11, Glass removed the restrictions as to the moving of troops over the line of the Panama Railroad.

He reports that the garrison of Panama, under Gen. Huertas, transferred their allegiance in a body to the new government. He adds:

They are well armed with the grasses .45-caliber rifle, and are believed to have plenty of ammunition. As to the number of troops the Government of Panama could place in the field in the event of hostilities the information received varies greatly, but it is probable that while between 2,000 and 3,000 men are available, only 600 could at present be furnished with good arms. In this connection, however, it is understood that a plentiful supply of arms and ammunition has been purchased and is expected to arrive shortly.

Glass sent the *Concord* to patrol Parita Bay and prevent the landing of Colombian troops, and sent the *Boston* to patrol Cape Mala and San Miguel Bay for the same purpose. He says that on the north coast the *Atlanta* and *Nashville* have been patrolling Porto Bello and Bocas del Toro; that the *Dixie* is stationed at Colon; the *Hannibal* arrived at Colon on November 11; the *Mayflower*, flying the flag of Rear Admiral J. B. Coghlan, arrived at Colon on November 15, and the *Maine* on the following day (date of letter). Glass incloses in his letter: (10) A copy of a letter from the French consul explaining situation to masters of French vessels; (20) copy of orders sent to the U. S. S. *Concord* on November 10; (30) copy of order sent to the U. S. S. *Concord* on November 12; (40) copy of order sent to the U. S. S. *Boston* on November 12; (50) copy of order sent to the U. S. S. *Concord* on November 16; (60) instructions for the guidance of the senior officer at Colon, November 10; (70) copy of letter to the United States acting consul general in Panama removing the restrictions as to transportation of troops; (80, 90, 100, 110) copies of letters relating to the reception of Gen. Reyes; (120) copy of telegram sent to the Secretary of the Navy re affairs on the Isthmus; (130) a drawing of the new flag of Panama.

Glass's orders to the U. S. S. *Concord* of November 10, above referred to, contain the following:

In case you fall in with the *Bogota* you will inform the commanding officer that for the present no armed forces will be allowed to land within the limits of the State of Panama, and you will use any force that may be necessary to prevent such landing should it be attempted after the warning.

Admiral Glass's instructions to the senior American naval officer on November 10, transmitting the department's cable of November 9, were: "Prevent landing of men with hostile intent within limits of State of Panama," and says:

In carrying out that part of the department's instructions directing that the landing of men with hostile intent within the limits of the State of Panama be prevented, you will make such disposition of the force under your command as may be necessary and will report promptly by wire any action taken.

He adds:

Please forward to me at your earliest convenience a statement of the available landing force on board the vessels under your command.

Here we find on November 10, at the time when there was no treaty whatever with the Republic of Panama, when the minister of the Republic of Panama had not even been received at Washington, Mr. Roosevelt had abandoned entirely the idea of keeping open traffic and defending the Isthmus, and he undertook to defend the whole State of Panama, which extends right into the continent of South America.

Acting United States Consul General Felix Ehrman, by letter of November 13, 1903, to Glass, transmitted a translation of a letter received by him from the provisional government of Panama respecting Gen. Reyes's arrival, and recommended that request therein made be granted.

The letter from the provisional government was as follows:

REPUBLIC OF PANAMA, MINISTRY OF FOREIGN RELATIONS,
Panama, November 13, 1903.

SIR: I have received instructions from the junta of the provisional government to request you, as I do very ardently, that you use your good offices in order to reach the end that one of the American warships which are now situated in the port of Colon, give reception (hospedaje) to Gen. Rafael Reyes, who has announced his approximate arrival as commissioner of the Colombian Government.

The committee of the provisional government fears that Gen. Reyes might be an object of popular hostility, and not being possible to avoid it, and that in order to stop them it would be necessary to employ rigorous means, which they wish to avoid, and judge it to be more convenient that the said Gen. Reyes be transhipped immediately that he arrives from the ship which brings him to one of the warships of the American Government, in which he remains till his return.

Thanking you in advance for your good offices in this matter to which this note refers, I remain, Mr. Consul,

Very attentive, etc.,

F. V. DE LA ESPRIELLA.

FELIX EHRMAN,
Acting United States Consul General, Panama.

The other letters referring to the arrival of Gen. Reyes were one of November 14, in which Admiral Glass writes to Acting United States Consul General Ehrman that Reyes will be received on board the *Mayflower* and asks names of the Panaman commissioners.

Also Admiral Glass's orders to the senior officer present at Colon, November 14, 1903. He recites that the authorities of Panama can not allow Reyes to land, but are willing to appoint a commission to meet him for a conference on board a vessel of war of the United States at Colon. Orders an officer sent on board vessel in which Reyes arrives to apprise Reyes of conditions, and orders senior officer to call on Reyes and offer all possible facilities for the carrying out of his mission. Orders senior officer to assure Reyes of his perfect safety and freedom of action while on board any vessel of the United States Navy and that he will be received and treated with all the honors and consideration due to his rank. Instructions end:

You will bear in mind the positive instructions heretofore given that no armed force must be allowed to land within the territorial limits of Panama, and you will take any measures necessary to prevent such landing.

On November 17 Admiral Coghlan reported from Colon to the Secretary of the Navy his arrival at Colon on board the *Mayflower* on Sunday, November 15; says that Admiral Walker and Consul General Gudger left ship immediately and proceeded to Panama on a special train. Reports on *Dixie*, *Atlanta*, *Hannibal*, and *Maine*. Further reports:

On Sunday evening the Hamburg-American steamer *Scotia* came in from Cartagena. She was boarded, and among the passengers were found five peace commissioners from the State of Bolivar, sent by the governor of that State to enter into negotiations with the representatives of the Panama junta, to the end to bring about an adjustment of the affairs on the Isthmus. I was informed by the United States consul that the Panama representatives would arrive in Colon at 6 o'clock last night, and they are expected on board the *Mayflower* this morning for a conference. I will afford every facility to both parties. From what I learn on shore I think the peace overtures of the Bolivar commissioners will be rejected by the Panama adherents and the conference will come to naught. Gen. Rafael Reyes, of Bogota, is expected here on a mission similar to that of the Cartagena commissioners, and will adopt the same measures in case the Panama representatives agree to meet him in a conference. While everything is quiet here now, it is understood that there is a deep feeling prevalent against Colombia, and it is deemed advisable to have any meeting of the two parties on board a neutral vessel such as the *Mayflower*. (380 D. H.)

The next day, November 18, Admiral Coghlan wired the Secretary of the Navy:

Another small collier needed. *Castine*, *Marietta*, and *Newport* or *Bancroft* needed coast patrol. Large ships can not get close in.

And Secretary Moody replied:

Will send *Marcellus*, *Castine*, *Bancroft* soon as practicable. Take coal from shore whenever practicable.

The same day the Secretary of the Navy asked Admiral Coghlan:

Is there anything in the report that the German vessels *Scotia* and *Markomania* have been stopped by American man-of-war? Answer without delay.

And received in reply the following information:

***Markomania* en route to Cartagena stopped off Colon dropped launch and passengers, boarded in a proper manner. Was not interfered with. *Scotia* arrived about sunset three days overdue from Cartagena. *Mayflower* stood out; informed him no armed forces permitted to land. Captain of *Scotia* reporting none, vessel was not interfered with. Darkness alone prevented (rest illegible).**

This was followed by an official report as under:

NOVEMBER 19, 1903.

SECRETARY OF THE NAVY, *Washington.*

SIR: Referring to my telegram of this date in relation to the German vessels *Scotia* and *Markomania*, I submit the following:

(1) On November 13 the *Markomania* came in from Bocas del Toro bound to Cartagena and stopped off this city to land some passengers and a large launch. While so employed she was boarded by a boat from the *Dixie*. As there were no armed troops on board she was not interfered with.

(2) On November 15, after my arrival here, I learned that the Hamburg-American Line steamer was three days overdue from Cartagena, and that Gen. Rafael Reyes was en route to and expected to reach Colon the 15th to 17th.

(3) When the *Scotia*, of that line, hove in sight late in the afternoon of the 15th I had the *Mayflower* get under way and stand out to meet and speak the incoming steamer; this she did off the lighthouse, informing her that no forces would be permitted to land at Colon. The captain of the *Scotia* reporting that he had none on board, she was told everything was all right; and the *Mayflower* proceeded to her previous berth and anchored, having some difficulty in turning in front of the city. The *Scotia* was boarded in the usual way soon after the *Mayflower* spoke her by a boat from the *Dixie* and got the usual information. The *Scotia* anchored to swing, got under way to stand in for her dock, but it being too dark anchored again, so remained all night. She was not interfered with by any of our vessels.

(4) After dark I sent an officer on board the *Scotia* with my compliments to the captain, asking if Gen. Reyes was among his passengers. The captain very kindly told us that he was not, but that others claiming to be peace commissioners were. Upon hearing this I sent Commander Merriam on board to communicate with them and he arranged with them to come on board the *Mayflower*, which they very gladly and willingly did the next morning about 5.20 a. m. before the *Scotia* got under way. In the meantime the prefect of Colon had been communicated with, who said he could protect the commissioners, but would arrest them if they came on shore. I therefore kept them on board this vessel all the time.

Very respectfully, J. B. COGHLAN.

On November 21 Admiral Glass cabled to the Secretary of the Navy from Panama:

Conference Gen. Reyes with the authorities of Panama yesterday without result. He has sailed on French steamer for Port Limon, having announced his intention to proceed to Washington for the representation of Colombia's interests. Conference was requested with senior officer present at Colon, but it was rejected. General inquired in what zone the United States Government prohibits the landing of troops. Informed his orders do not permit within the limits of the State.

On the same day Admiral Coghlan also cabled to Secretary Moody as follows:

Special Commissioner Bogota Government, Reyes, tenders his sincere thanks to the President and Secretary for his gracious treatment here by our naval forces. Reyes has gone to Port Limon, Costa Rica, thence by fruit steamer to New Orleans, thence to Washington for conference with Amador (and others inf.) in the United States. Said they had ordered the Colombian forces to do

nothing hostile until further orders from them. Said Panama Government had cabled Amador to await arrival of Reyes. He expects to make amicable relations with special commissioners from Panama now in Washington.

On November 23 Admiral Glass reported to the Secretary of the Navy that on the 17th he saluted the flag of the Republic of Panama with 21 guns, which salute was returned by the Panaman gunboat *21 de Noviembre* and by the port. On same day he called officially on the head of the Government. On the 18th the members of the Panama junta returned the call and were received on board the *Marblehead* with all the honors due the head of a sovereign State. Says "this interchange of courtesies has had the best effect with the people of the Isthmus." Glass reports the Reyes visit to Colon. Says Reyes declined to go on board the *Mayflower*. Adds "the prefect of Colon having assured the superior officer present in Colon that he could afford all necessary protection to Gen. Reyes and his party, all interference with the movements of the Colombian commission was withdrawn." Says affairs on the Isthmus continue quiet. On the 18th received information that the Province of Chiriqui supports the new Government. He adds, "On the same day I received through reliable, but confidential, channels the information that the Departments of Cauca and Antioquia would secede shortly and would apply to be admitted into union with Panama * * * and that the Government (Colombian) apparently intended a land invasion of Panama." Glass reports details of patrolling both the Pacific and Atlantic coasts.

Admiral Glass attached to the above report Reyes's letter to Coghlan (Nov. 19) asking Coghlan to discuss the political situation with Ospina, dated on board the *Canada*, November 19. (Printed in the Colombian Blue Book.) To it the following footnote by Coghlan is appended:

In answer to this I simply said I was not authorized to confer on political affairs and could not meet the gentleman for that purpose; nor did I.

J. B. COGHLAN.

Also Reyes letter to Admiral Glass (Nov. 20) rehearsing Colombia's power and right to repress the rebellion of Panama, and asking in what zone the United States forbids the landing of forces. (Printed in Colombian Blue Book.)

This was answered thus:

NOVEMBER 20, 1903.

Gen. RAFAEL REYES,
Colon, Panama.

DEAR SIR: Your note of this date has been received and will be transmitted to my Government through the commander in chief of the Pacific Squadron.

In reply to the question in the last paragraph, I may say that our present orders are to prevent the landing of men with hostile intent within the limits of the State of Panama.

Very respectfully, etc., J. B. COGHLAN.

On November 21 Admiral Glass ordered the *Boston* to cruise around Parita Bay, as far to the southward and eastward as Punta Pinas and to the westward as Montijo Bay. Former instructions as to preventing the landing of troops to govern the commander's actions.

Admiral Coghlan cabled the Secretary of the Navy on November 26 that the Colombian authorities of Cartagena prevented the American consul from taking passage in the Royal Mail Steam Packet *Trent;* and that no passengers, freight, or vessels are allowed to clear for the Isthmus.

On November 30 Admiral Coghlan, from on board the *Dixie*, reported a reconnaissance by the *Nashville*, the *Mayflower*, and the *Marcellus*. Confirms his cable of the 26th, and adds:

To-day the steamer *La Plata* of the same line (Royal Mail Steam Packet) came in with the news that no passengers or freight are allowed to leave Cartagena for the Isthmus.

Secretary of the Navy Moody cabled to Admiral Glass on December 3, 1903:

Secret and confidential. United States Army officers will report to you, having been ordered by the War Department to establish advance posts for observation at Yatisa. Render all assistance in your power. Give him boat, men, marines as necessary.

These officers were Capt. A. Cloman and Maj. H. E. Haan. They reached the Isthmus in disguise, Capt. Cloman posing as Mr. S. A. Otts, a lumberman, and Maj. Haan as Mr. H. E. Howard, a mining engineer. In the naval reports they were referred to as agent No. 1 and agent No. 2. They were accompanied by Maj. Guy L. Eddie, now physician to President Taft, who went as plain G. E. Eddie, of New York, capitalist.

On the same date, December 3, the following cable was sent in duplicate to both Admirals Glass, at Panama, and Coghlan, at Colon:

War Department fears lest Colombia forces may advance on the Isthmus by land. Every effort must be made to obtain information promptly, establish of the State of Panama. In addition with the foregoing cooperate with Army outposts of marines if necessary in the interior of the Isthmus near frontier officers when desired, but hold yourself responsible for the situation. Confer with Admiral Walker, to whom the Navy Department has cabled.

The cable to Admiral Walker was to the following effect:

By the President's direction inform the department if there is any reasonable probability of Colombian forces advancing overland and, if so, if the present force is sufficient for the protection of the Isthmus, or whether additional naval force or troops desirable; whether outposts of Panama troops can be placed to obtain information early; and generally on all the necessary steps for the control, complete and uninterrupted, of the situation, with special concern for the next few weeks.

MOODY.

Admiral Walker replied on December 8:

SECRETARY OF THE NAVY, *Washington:*

A sufficient number of troops here. No probability of force advancing on Panama until after dry season has set in next month. Yesterday afternoon had consultation with the junta. Coghlan and I recommended that Glass send vessel to San Miguel Bay, taking an officer of the United States Army and some natives to reconnoiter as far as [word illegible], through which or in that vicinity advancing troops must pass. The country very wild from Atrato River to Panama, very few inhabitants except Indians. There is great hostility to strangers passing through their country. The country without food and impassable for any considerable force during wet season; very difficult at all times. Junta state that they have sent man to Chepo River, Colombia, and other importatnt points east for information. Also, I have recommended taking ship along north coast of Panama as far as Atrato River for observation. Considering the circumstances, I do not anticipate trouble for considerable time to come because of the wet season. As a precaution, I suggest holding marines now at Guantanamo for service on the Isthmus at short notice and, also, as it is stormy weather and the vessels at Colon may be forced to put to sea, the battalion when here, for sanitary and other reasons, to go into camp. Best positions, Gorgona.

WALKER.

At this time, December 7, one month after the recognition of the Republic of Panama, the Province of Chiriqui, which I alluded to yesterday, had not yet accepted the independence movement, so, on December 7, Admiral Glass sent the following instructions to the commanding officer of the *Concord:*

SIR: When the vessel under your command is in all respects ready for sea, you will sail from this port with the U. S. S. *Boston* and the Panaman gunboat *21 of Nov.* in company. On arriving in the vicinity of Pearl Islands the *Boston* will be detached to proceed on duty assigned, and you will proceed with the *Padilla* in company to David, west coast of Panama. Two officials of the Panama Government will accompany the *Concord* and the *21 of Nov.*, and you will afford them such means of communicating with the local authorities at David as are practicable. You will also, as far as seems desirable, place yourselves in communiction with the local authorities at David. On the completion of your visit to David return to this port in company with the *21 of Nov.*, visiting Montijo Bay and Rio Dulce en route for communication with persons on shore at both places should it be so desired by the Panaman officials. It is desirable to have both vessels return to Panama as soon as compatible with an effective performance of the duty assigned you.

GLASS.

When the Colombian officials, who had remained loyal, saw the gunboat of their own country, the *Padilla*, captured and called the *21st of November*, escorted by two warships of the United States Navy they probably thought they had no further reason for not recognizing the Republic of Panama: they had to recognize it. But it is to be noted here that the report of the commanding officer of the *Concord*, the same as one or two confidential reports of Commander Hubbard, of the *Nashville*, are no longer in the Navy Department. They have been transferred to the archives of the State Department.

On the same day, December 7, 1903, Glass ordered the *Boston* to proceed to San Miguel Bay—

taking as passengers three officers previously designated. On your arrival * * * near head of bay you will fit out such boats as may be necessary to take your passengers by the Tuyra River as far as Yavissa, or such place as they may select for a landing, in order to make certain observations required by the Navy Department.

Yavissa, be it noted, although under the boundary of the old department of Panama, is not on the Isthmus, but on the mainland of South America, south of the imaginary line from Cape Tiburon to Point Garachinie, which has always been accepted by all geographers and is specifically indicated in the Panama Railroad concession and Salgar-Wyse Canal contract as the line of demarcation of the Isthmus. There was no possible excuse for this advance onto the mainland, as the necessity of keeping open the transit across the Isthmus could not be pleaded in justification, and the treaty with the new Republic of Panama had not yet been ratified by the Senate.

On December 8 Secretary Moody cabled to both Admirals Glass and Coghlan:

American consul at Jamaica reports that Colombia cruisers *Cartagena* and *Pinzon* sailed December 3 from Cartagena with 15,000 men.

To which Admiral Coghlan replied:

Cartagena, *Pinzon*, for one day's run can carry at most 800 men. *Atlanta* has been sent Gulf of Darien.

President Roosevelt immediately decided to send more marines to the Isthmus. Under instructions from him, Secretary Moody cabled to Col. Barker, at Caimanera, Cuba:

After December 10 direct *Prairie* to proceed to Colon. Battalion will be landed at discretion of senior officer present on the Isthmus. Direct *Prairie* to leave sergeant's guard for duty ashore and aboard *Vixen*.

On December 9 Secretary Moody cabled to Admirals Glass and Coghlan:

It is reported that Colombian forces, 1,100 men, have been landed mouth Atrato. Verify and inform department. Are our vessels patroling coast between Colon and Atrato? The department desires to be kept informed of the state of affairs. Cable daily.

This elicited the following reply from Admiral Glass on December 10:

Instructed Coghlan Sunday send vessels to visit ports from Colon to Cape Tiburon, Colombia, to obtain information. No report yet. Will send vessel Atrato River immediately.

Again, the next day, Admiral Glass cabled:

French steamer from Cartagena brings unofficial report 450 men were sent Atrato River to make path across country. Were compelled to return on account of foul provisions. Troops from Honda were sent back from Baranquilla by order of Colombian authorities. I have extended patrol to Atrato River. Am in communication with the post at Yavissa. No indications of invasion there. American consular agent at Cali, near Beunaventura reports there is great hostility to American citizens. Mob is threatening. No violence.

Admiral Glass's orders to Admiral Coghlan of December 10 directed that one of the vessels of the Caribbean Squadron "Proceed immediately to the mouth of the Atrato River and somewhat to the eastward."

On December 11 Admiral Coghlan received a report by mail from the American consul at Cartagena to the effect that 800 Colombian soldiers with provisions had been landed the preceding week near the Atrato River. The admiral at once reported this to Washington by cable and added:

Cruiser *Cartagena* been at Cartagena December 9. Some more troops expected to follow. *Mayflower* and *Atlanta* now in that vicinity; investigation.

On receipt of this information, Secretary Moody cabled to Admiral Glass as follows:

Establish strong posts, men and marines, with artillery in the direction of Yavissa or other better position for observation only rapid transmission of information, but not for forcible interference with Colombian troops advancing by land.

Also offering to "send you one or more destroyers for dispatch vessels south coast of Panama, if desired."

To Admiral Coghlan Secretary Moody cabled:

Do not prevent Colombian forces landing in territory of Colombia.

On December 13, 1903, Admiral Glass cabled to Secretary Moody:

According to your telegram of December 11, will establish posts 100 men, several machine guns each. Yavissa and Real de Santa Maria, or in that vicinity. The *Boston* and *Concord* will go San Miguel Bay to keep up communications. I request two destroyers sent immediately; will be very valuable. Fifty men of Panama have been stationed at Real; also scouts up Tuyra River. Reports are very conflicting; the probabilities are Colombian forces landed Acanti or that vicinity. Probable destination Yavissa. See Coghlan's telegram of December 13. Referring to your instructions in relation to armed interference, what course must I pursue if Colombian force should attack very inferior Panama force.

On December 13 Admiral Coghlan reported to the Secretary of the Navy that the *Atlanta* had come in from Cape San Blas and would leave at once for Cape Tiburon and the Gulf of Darien.

The following day Admiral Glass reported to the Secretary of the Navy that the *Boston*, *Concord*, and Panaman gunboat had arrived at Panama 21st of November. No information from Yavissa. *Boston* and *Wyoming* leave for San Miguel "taking company of *Dixie's* marines to establish outposts."

Admiral Glass's orders to Lieut. W. G. Miller, United States Navy, who was to have charge of the landing party, were that upon the arrival of the *Wyoming* and the *Boston* at San Miguel Bay he was to assume command of the landing force composed as shown in the memorandum attached, and proceed up the Turra River with as little delay as possible. He was ordered to establish observation posts at the villages of Yavissa and Real de Santa Maria, but to exercise great care to prevent any conflict with Colombian troops. Any information obtained as to the movements of Colombian troops toward or in country under observation was to be reported immediately.

The memorandum of instructions for the landing party contained the following:

With the *Wyoming* and the *Boston* working together, the force to be landed from these ships will be approximately as follows: Lieut. W. G. Miller, United States Navy, commanding; Past Asst. Paymaster P. G. Kennard, United States Navy, commissary; Surg. H. C. Curl, United States Navy, surgeons; Capt. J. M. Sallady, United States Marine Corps, commanding marines; 1 junior officer from the *Boston;* 1 junior officer from *Wyoming;* 1 junior officer from the *Marblehead;* 2 section, 54 bluejackets, from the *Boston;* 1 section, 27 bluejackets, from the *Wyoming;* 1 section, 27 marines, from the *Boston;* 1 hospital apprentice from the *Wyoming;* and such messmen, special details, and ammunition party as may be necessary.

The *Boston* and *Wyoming* will each land two Colt's automatic guns with crews thoroughly able to keep the guns in working order, these men to be included in the bluejackets and marines mentioned above.

The *Dixie* company of marines, commanded by Capt. H. L. Bearse, United States Marine Corps, will be stationed as directed and will be a part of the whole landing force under the command of Lieut. W. G. Miller, United States Navy.

(The remainder of the instructions referred to medical water, commissary, ammunition, health, etc.)

In Admiral Glass's official report to Secretary of the Navy, dated Panama, December 14, 1903, he says that the Panama Government has established an outpost of 50 men at Real de Santa Maria, on the Tuyra, with scouts operating toward the Colombian frontier; also a post at Chepo. The admiral further reports that, "in accordance with the department's telegrams of the 12th and 13th, the *Boston* and *Wyoming*, with a company of marines from the *Prairie* on board, sailed for San Miguel Bay to establish observation outposts of about 100 men each at Yavissa and Real de Santa Maria." Composition of forces, orders given, etc., shown in attached correspondence. He continues:

On the 8th the *Concord*, accompanied by the Panaman gunboat *21 of November*, was dispatched, at the request of the junta, to David to communicate with the local authorities and obtain information as to the condition of affairs in that neighborhood. The commanding officer of the *Concord* reports having been received by local authorities in a most cordial manner and that the signing of the canal treaty and other acts of the Panama Government were fully approved at a "ratification meeting."

Further reports:

Until the 10th instant the vessels of the Caribbean Squadron effectively patrolled the north coast of Panama from Colon to Cape Tiburon, but * * * I directed that the patrol be extended to the mouth of the Atrato and somewhat to the eastward for the purpose of verifying the reports of the movements of Colombian troops.

(Dispatch concludes with reports on routine matters.)

On December 15 Admiral Coghlan reported to the Secretary of the Navy that the U. S. S. *Bancroft* had returned to Porto Bello with orders to patrol from there to Nombre de Dios. *Nashville* sailed December 10 for Bocas del Toro and the western end of the Isthmus. December 11 the *Mayflower* sailed for the lower end of the Gulf of Darien. The *Atlanta* arrived on the 12th from a trip from Port Gandi to San Blas Point. Found trail from San Blas to Colon. Sent *Atlanta* to visit every port and indentation of the coast which could be a possible landing place in the Gulf of Darien. *Prairie* arrived on the 13th from Guantanamo. Sent one company of marines, with four Colt automatic guns, tents, beds, etc., to La Boca, Panama, by the morning train on the 14th. *Bancroft* returned and reported finding a trail from Mandingo Harbor to Colon via Porto Bello. Camp at Empire ready to receive remainder of battalion; will be sent there to-morrow.

On the same day, December 15, the American naval patrol discovered the Colombian forces encamped at Concepcion de Titumati, in the department of Cauca, Colombia, away off the Isthmus of Panama. The events that transpired were reported by Lieut. H. P. Perrill, United States Navy, to the commanding officer of his ship, the *Atlanta*. The repeated that it was his boarding visit to the Colombian schooner *Antioquia* which led to the discovery of Colombian forces and of his subsequent visit ashore to see Gen. Ortiz, the commander of the Colombian forces at Concepcion de Titumati. Says that at 9.15 a. m. on December 15, Lieut. Perrill was ordered to board a schooner that the *Atlanta* had been following for some time. At 9.30 Perrill left the ship in company with Mr. Harold Martin, correspondent of the Associated Press, who acted as interpreter. On approaching schooner they saw she carried Colombian troops but no colors. She proved to be the *Antioquia*, in command of Gen. Novo, a Venezuelan, with a commission in the Colombian Army. He also commanded the troops on board. Novo said there were 24 men, but Perrill counted more than that on deck, and a glimpse of the hold showed many more below.

Novo avoided answering question and suggested that Lieut. Perrill should visit Gen. Ortiz on shore. Lieut. Perrill returned to the *Atlanta*, which he left again at 12.45. The *Atlanta* towed the

Antioquia at Novo's request. Perrill went ashore with Novo and was presented to Gen. Ortiz, who was courteous, but whose attitude was one of hostility, but Perrill says no overt act of unfriendliness was noticed on the part of any of the Colombians, "apparently their feeling was one of resentment against the United States generally * * *." As soon as we had landed, Gen Ortiz requested that, in view of the fact that we were in Colombian waters, I take down the American flag and put up the Colombian flag, or, at least, show the Colombian flag at the bow. This I told him that I could not do; first, because I had no Colombian flag; and, secondly, that I was bound by the law of nations to carry the flag of my own country in the boats belonging to a man of war. Perrill and his party were detained on the beach; he said, "their determination not to let us see anything being so evident that we deemed it imprudent to attempt any reconnoitering." The Colombians avoided all questions, and Gen. Ortiz himself began questioning the purpose of the ship's visit to Colombian waters, and refused to believe it was friendly. Perrill says:

He wished to enter a protest, and gave a long line of arguments, ending up with the flowery statement that the trouble between the United States, Colombia, and Panama was in the hands of Gen. Reyes, who hoped to settle it by diplomatic means, but should he fail, Colombia, though poor and bankrupt, would, in order to maintain her national honor, fight to the last man, and, if need be, to the last woman.

Perrill, not having learned anything of value, "permitted Mr. Martin, in his capacity of correspondent, to pick up whatever information he could by his own means." As Martin speaks Spanish well, he got on good terms with Gen. Novo, but was balked by Dr. A. Sanchez O'Byrne, who kept close to Novo all the time. Gen. Ortiz wrote his protest out and read it aloud. It was received with cheers. He then asked Perrill if the American warships would interfere with the movements of Colombian gunboats in Colombian waters. Perrill said he thought not, but Ortiz was not satisfied with this assurance and wrote letters to the commanding officer of the *Atlanta*, which he sent on board by Novo, who, however, was accompanied by O'Byrne. However, Martin got the following information, chiefly from Novo: (*a*) Ortiz is second in command to Reyes. (*b*) His forces are distributed from Revesa Point to Cape Tirburon and consist of about 2,000 soldiers, with equal number of laborers, which is being added daily. (*c*) The Colombian forces are stationed in camps throughout the district mentioned, and includes a small force on the Atrato to prevent transit along that "stream." Ortiz's headquarters are at Titumati, where he has 500 men, including the Tiradores, also two or three field pieces, which are mounted at advantageous points at Tomate. (*d*) Novo, next in command to Ortiz, has been in the district since the middle of November, constructing coastwise trails, locating artillery, etc. (*e*) This district is apparently intended as a base and the Colombians are strengthening their position while awaiting the Reyes's orders as to their future movements. (*f*) On the Pacific coast Gen. Bustamento is in command of the forces working toward Panama, probably with the Gulf of San Miguel as an objective point. Report concludes: "I can not too highly commend the invaluable services rendered by Mr. Martin."

The correspondence referred to in Lieut. Perrill's report is the following:

TITUMATI, *December 15, 1903.*

To the Captain of the American warship "Atlanta."

SIR: I take the liberty of asking you, for I consider it my duty to do so, to inform me what your orders from your Government may be with regard to our warships in these waters.

Noblesse oblige, God guard you.

DANIEL ORTIZ,
Commander in Chief.

This was immediately acknowledged by Capt. Turner of the U. S. S. *Atlanta* in part as follows:

Permit me to state that Colombian vessels will receive the same courteous treatment that the vessels of any other nation at peace with my Government would be accorded, and I would advise that the ships of war of the United States expect and look for the same courteous treatment that I have stated would be shown to your vessels, which includes the right to visit the waters and ports of nations with whom we are at peace without being questioned.

Gen. Ortiz then sent to the commander of the American warship *Atlanta* a formal protest against the presence of American forces in Colombian waters (published in the Colombian Blue Book). He accompanied it by the following letter:

REPUBLIC OF COLOMBIA, DEPARTMENT OF CAUCA,
OFFICE OF THE CHIEF OF STAFF OF ARMY,
Concepcion de Titumati, December 15, 1903.

To the Captain of the American warship "Atlanta."

SIR: Your answer to my question as to the attitude which will be observed by American warships toward our ships of war satisfies me fully.

Insomuch as you tell me that American ships of war are patrolling our waters without special orders so to do from your Government, I beg you to leave this port, because the waters surrounding it are part of the department of Cauca of this Republic.

I permit myself to inform you that the rebel department of Panama borders this department at Cape Tiburon. As long as war is not declared it seems to me but just and natural that American ships of war should not, as they have already done, come into the waters south of Cape Tiburon.

Should you have any occasion to confer with me, I hope your vessel will fly the Colombian flag upon approaching the coast.

God guard you.

The general in chief.

DANIEL ORTIZ.

While Lieut. Perrill was visiting Ortiz, Lieut. E. M. Manwaring, United States Marine Corps, was sent in with a second boat and reported "while the boats were ashore, we steered a short distance to the south endeavoring to open out the schooner that was behind the islands."

These events were at once reported to the Secretary of the Navy by Admiral Coghlan in the following cable, dated Colon, December 16:

Atlanta returned from the Gulf of Darien. Found about 500 men, Colombians, inland, between Tomate and Terena Island. Had been landed by Cartagena and Pinson. Gen. Ortiz commanding. Claimed to be second to Reyes. He said he had 2,000 men in district of Cauca, with equal number of laborers, and getting there by means of small boats from east shore. Headquarters, Titumati. They seemed well armed and some fieldpieces. Said that Gen. Bustamento was in command on Pacific side working toward Panama.

President Roosevelt immediately took drastic action; although the treaty with Panama had not been ratified in the Senate and opposition to it was daily coming more and more marked, he ordered Secretary Moody to send the following cable to Admiral Glass:

My telegram of the 11th December is modified so that the posts in the vicinity of Yavissa and all others established must be strong enough to resist attack. Positions once taken to be held by force if necessary. Panamans to be supported at your discretion if necessary. No force hostile to be allowed to interrupt communications with your posts advanced. Reserve ample force at Panama and Colon to subdue local disturbances likely to occur there. Is the present force sufficient to meet demands? *Dixie* will bring 400 marines. Inform the department of the state of affairs in detail, daily changes made or contemplated, and the disposition of forces at the present. Submit in general terms your (word illegible) plan if ordered to prevent invasion of the State of Panama by Colombian forces. Acknowledge.

Admiral Glass at once, December 18, sent the following order to the senior officer present at San Miguel Bay:

SIR: Referring to my letter 520 of this date, you will proceed as rapidly as possible with the establishment of posts at Yavissa and Real de Santa Maria, putting the posts in as thorough state of defense as practicable. Two boats with guns will be attached to each boat if possible. This may include steam cutters as soon as they can be utilized for that purpose.

20. These posts are to be held until further orders, and especially against any attack by Colombian forces. No hostile force must be allowed to interrupt communications between the posts and our ships in Darien Harbor.

30. The Panaman force now at Real de Santa Maria will be reenforced at once, and in case of an attack upon this by Colombia troops our force is to support them as necessary, but no hostilities against Colombian troops are to be provoked.

40. The Panaman steamer *Chuicito* will report to you to-morrow to assist in keeping up communications and transporting men and supplies. You are authorized to furnish her with coal as required while performing this duty. You are also authorized to employ native boats and schooners where the necessary service can not be performed with the facilities now at your command.

50. Keep me informed of the progress of affairs as frequently as possible and report when posts ashore are fully established with sufficient provisions on hand.

Admiral Glass cabled to the Secretary of the Navy on December 19:

Referring to your telegram of December 18, now keeping up communication between Yavisa and Darien Harbor by ships' boats. I have borrowed a small steamer from Panama; time by ships' boats 12 hours; time by steamer 6 hours. Additional steamer and native schooners can be obtained if needed. * * * The men live in tents or improvised huts; 150 tents are needed soon. I will send 100 additional marines to reinforce posts if necessary, when fully established. Four boats with rapid-fire guns on the river. Panama will send 300 men Sunday. Yavisa and Real control main rivers; no other post is considered necessary at present. Marines on the Isthmus are ample for local conditions; marines coming by *Dixie* will be employed to strengthen Darien post as expedient. *Boston* left yesterday for Darien. No other changes. Vessels patrolling north coast of Panama for information. The invasion of Panama must be by mountain passes to headwaters of rivers and hence by water to Yavisa country. Boats on these rivers are now being destroyed. Yavisa and Real maintained strongly will check movement of any probable advancing force, we controlling rivers and seacoast with present force, and coming by *Dixie* can hold Lavisa country against Colombian force in Cauca, reported 2,000 men.

He also, on the same day, wired instructions to the commanding officer of the *Wyoming*, in which he said, in part:

The *Concord* will sail this afternoon, and will deliver to you for use in the boats to be armed in river service and at the posts established on shore two .30 cal. Colt automatic guns and two 1-pounder rapid-fire guns, with a supply of ammunition. The Panaman gunboat *21 of Nov* will sail to-morrow with 300 men to reenforce the post at Real de Santa Maria. She will probably need the *Chuicito* in transporting her men, and you may give her such further assistance as is practicable. Report when our posts are ready and in a condition to re-

ceive an additional force of 100 marines for distribution as necessary between Yavisa and Real de Santa Maria. Inform me if any 3-inch field guns can be transported to our posts and used to advantage there, in the meantime landing at your discretion those of the *Boston* and *Wyoming*.

President Roosevelt had meanwhile apprised several Senators in Washington of the steps he was taking, and had encountered very strong opposition. It was at this time, in order to show that his actions on the Isthmus were justified by precedent, that he ordered Secretary Moody to have prepared in the Navy Department such papers as might be necessary to sustain the President's position.

As I have told you, however, the keeper of the war records of the Navy Department reported to Secretary Moody that there was absolutely no precedent for the orders which had been issued since the 3d of November, and the Secretary so reported to President Roosevelt, who sent for Mr. Stewart, who told the President quite plainly that he wrong, and when Mr. Roosevelt saw that there was no means by which he could justify his actions he averted the introduction of adverse resolutions in the Senate by informing the Senators that he had been misled, and would modify the instructions given to naval officers on the Isthmus.

In consequence, on December 19, Secretary Moody cabled to Admiral Glass:

Referring to my telegram of December 17, maintain points in the vicinity of Yavisa for observation only. Do not have posts beyond support of ships or launches. Withdraw your posts if liable to be attacked. It is the intention of the Government to confine active defense against hostile operations to the vicinity of the railroad line on the Isthmus and for its protection. Disregard all other instructions previous apparently conflicting with these.

In reply, Admiral Glass sent the following cable to the Navy Department on December 21:

Referring to your telegram of December 19, because it is not proposed to hold Yavisa posts against attacks will bring back marines and artillery to Panama, leaving two ships in the harbor of Darien and posts of 25 men and 2 Colt automatic guns at Yavisa and two well-armed steam launches to patrol adjacent rivers for communication with scouts at Real and transmitting news rapidly. This force ample to attain the desired object. To withdraw larger force with means available in case of possible attack would be difficult, involving danger of considerable loss. Will advise Panama Government to hold here for the present reenforcements intended for Real, as number too small without our assistance if any Colombian force approach that country.

This was accompanied by a detailed report acknowledging receipt of the department's telegrams of December 17 and December 18, Glass says that on receipt of the first he sent the U. S. S. *Boston* to Darien with orders to the senior officer present and made arrangements to send as soon as practicable an additional company of marines to Yavisa and Real de Santa Maria, to be followed as soon as advisable by the marine battalion coming on the *Dixie*. Glass says that he also suggested to the junta of Panama the sending of reenforcements to their outposts at Real, and that they promised to send 300 men immediately. Glass further reports that on receipt of the department's telegram of the 19th, however, instructing him that the posts were to be withdrawn in case of liability to attack, he withdrew the marines altogether and left only an observation post of 25 men at Yavisa and suggested to the Panaman Government to hold their reenforcements in Panama, as without American assistance at Real the Panaman forces " would be liable to capture or destruction should any large force of Colombians approach from the Atrato River or Titumati."

In consequence, on December 21, Admiral Glass ordered the commanding officer of the U. S. S. *Wyoming* to withdraw the marines, artillery, etc., from Yavisa and send them back to Panama. A post of 25 men with two .30-cal. Colt guns and two steam cutters armed with Colts or 1-pounders will be maintained at Yavisa. The remainder of the men to be returned to their ships. Lieut. Miller to remain in command at Yavisa.

The force left at Yavisa is for the purpose of obtaining information and transmitting news rapidly only, and no hostile movement is to be commenced at any time against Colombian forces appearing in the vicinity. In case an attack should seem probable, the party must fall back to the ships at Darien Harbor defending themselves, of course, in case of actual attack, etc.

Meanwhile, S. A. Cloman had made his way to Cartagena, and from there had transmitted a confidential report to the Secretary of War, who sent it to Secretary Moody. The information thus obtained was cabled to Admiral Coghlan, as follows:

DECEMBER 22, 1903.

COGHLAN, *Colon:*

Cloman. United States Army officer, reports at Cartagena two 6-inch short breech-loading rifles, Armstrong, mounted on southwest bastion in front of big yellow building, are in good condition. Two 4-inch breech-loading rifles, Armstrong, probably in store; 3,000 men at Baranquilla drilling November 27, 9,000 men about to arrive there. Two Hotchkiss machine guns, four 3-inch breech-loading rifles, field guns; and at Savanilla 30 men and two 6-pounders, mounted. Have you information additional as to the military resources of the ports named? When you visit Cartagena form your plans for its occupation in the event of hostilities, if ordered, and to blockade Savanilla. Colombian forces at Baranquilla can reach Cartagena by Magdalena River and rail route. Is the present force sufficient, with 200 marines by *Dixie*, to capture and hold position strong commanding at Cartagena until United States troops arrive. What means available for moving Colombian forces at the Atrato River?

To this Admiral Coghlan replied as follows:

COLON, *December 30, 1903.*

SECRETARY OF THE NAVY, *Washington:*

There is a camp of 5,000 men near the headwaters of the Atrato River. None have started down yet. Gen. Castro, best guerrilla in Colombia, has been sent there via Adara. If war is declared there is a suitable position southeast of La Popa, Cartagena, which could be captured and from which railroad could be commanded to a great extent, but this would place the forces under my command between two fires—Cartagena and army coming from Baranquilla. As far as railroad bridge across El Dique, half way to Magdalena River, country is quite open and getting more passable day by day. * * * With present vessels and 400 marines in *Dixie* Tierra Bomba Island could be occupied, Boca Chica kept open, shore of bay kept free of works, and city blockaded. The approach from the north open and clear for musketry fire, rendering necessary big detour through the country easily defended; at the same time, could blockade Savanilla; 30 steamers Magdalena River available for transportation of troops. * * *

COGHLAN.

Now, war had not been declared, and the United States was still at peace with the Republic of Colombia; the treaty with Panama had not been ratified by the Senate; not only had a landing force been sent into the continent of South America, but United States Army officers had been sent to seacoast towns to make observations and instructions had been sent to the Army officers to find out how they could make their plans for the capture of Cartagena.

On December 22 Admiral Coghlan reported to the Secretary of the Navy with 10 inclosures saying that the Colombian forces had been discovered south of Port Gandi, between Tomate and Tarene Islands. He admits "that Gandi people are Colombians;" says that he is in receipt of information from the prefect of Colon that the Panama junta does not lay claim to the islands of St. Andrews and Old Providence. (These are the islands referred to in the Colombian Bluebook at San Andreas de Providencia and San Luis de Providencia.)

On December 24 Capt. Colman sent some sketches to Admiral Coghlan. He also reported many 5-ton sloops and numerous canoes, from 4 to 10 men, available to the Colombian forces.

Admiral Coghlan sent a detailed report to the Secretary of the Navy, giving particulars of his visit to Cartagena in the *Olympia* to get United States Minister Beaupre and wife. Says he arrived on the morning of the 27th and saw the Colombian gunboat *Cartagena*, which had all ports open and was evidently ready for action. The *Olympia* anchored at 10 a. m. and fired a national salute with the Colombian flag at the main, which was returned by the guns on shore. Coghlan sent boat ashore for the United States consul and the United States minister, Beaupre, and the chief clerk of the consulate returned in the boat and informed that the United States vice consul was lying at the point of death. The minister was received with all his cabinet in a cordial manner. The American admiral invited the governor to visit his ship. This he promised to do at 3 p. m. The admiral took leave and at once returned to the *Olympia*, and as he left the shore the batteries fired a salute of 13 guns. He sent the steam launch in for the governor and his staff, and they arrived on board shortly after 3 p. m. After a suitable entertainment, the governor left and a salute of 17 guns, with the Colombian flag at the fore, was fired in his honor. At 4.45 the United States minister came on board with his wife, and the *Olmypia* sailed for Colon. Coghlan reports that there were "no signs of unpleasantness, ill-feeling, or unfriendliness against us."

On December 31 Admiral Coghlan cabled as follows:

SECRETARY OF THE NAVY, *Washington:*

Prairie sailed for Chiriqui for coal. (In cipher.) Shall I land marines from *Dixie*? I will require 48 hours to concentrate vessels and marines in case of operations contemplated by department cipher.

Glass wrote to the commanding officer of the *Boston* January 1, 1904, that "the Navy Department desires further and more complete information in regard to all means of transportation within the Republic of Panama and the practicability of an invasion," and orders him to send out scouting parties from Yavisa to cover the region drained by the Tuyra and Chucunaque Rivers and their tributaries.

Col. Villasmil, of the Panama Railroad, commanding the Panaman force, on the northeast coast of the Isthmus, reports to Admiral Coghlan on January 4 that he had examined thoroughly the coast from Nombre de Dios Mandingo Bay. He had small detachments stationed different points along the coast and was emphatic no trails lead inland from those parts except Nombre de Dios, confirming the reports of the *Bancroft* and other sources. Villasmil returned to Mandingo Bay in *Mayflower* the next day.

In reporting the above to the Navy Department, Admiral Coghlan adds:

Cipher to prepare plan received.

The same day, January 4, the 400 marines from Guantanamo (Caimanera), Cuba, under Lieut. Col. Elliott, also had arrived on January 23, encamped at Empire.

Admiral Glass reported to the Secretary of the Navy, January 4, on the situation in Darien, confirming cable reports. Says:

Marines encamped on the Canal Zone; are now sending out scouting parties to the eastward in the Chagres Valley and approaches.

On January 7, 1904, Admiral Glass ordered to the commanding officer of the U. S. S. *Wyoming* to make reconnaissance up the Bayano River. At El Llano to hire as guide Namiel Diego Rodriguez. Says:

You will have the use of a Panama gasoline launch that will accompany the *Wyoming* for taking such party as you may consider necessary up the Bayano River.

Also ordered the commanding officer of the *Concord* to make reconnaissance of the Rio Dulce and Parita Bay.

Capt. Colman came back to Colon and sent from Colon to the information bureau of the General Staff, on January 7, an important cable. Now, Capt Colman is the man who has rendered distinguished service as military attaché of the United States in London. He is a man of great reserve, and, in order that you may have no doubt as to what his idea of the attitude of the United States Army to the Colombian Government was, I call attention to the fact that in all of his confidential reports he refers to the Colombians as "the enemy."

Cabling from Colon to the military information bureau of the General Staff, Capt. Colman, on January 7, said:

Report confirmed enemy's scouts working along north coast inside reefs in small boats trying to win good will and assistance of Indians. Letter from white man, Carti River, December 31, says Indian Chiefs Sasarti and Carti have been to Titumati and now returned, trying to persuade Indians conceal enemy moving and assist them. Friendly Indians uneasy. All coast Indians east of Diablo River now in accord with enemy. Situation unsatisfactory, and this should be stopped quick. Boundary not fixed by west limit of Caucan claim is Miel River, and expeditions west are invasions. Guard boats should patrol inside reefs night and day this neighborhood, with posts on San Blas coast as before recommended. Believe this would stop scouting without clash as in Darien. Will remain north coast. Address, Colon. Send official check book.

Lieut. Commander Albert Gleaves reported to Admiral Coghlan on the *Mayflower's* visit to Mandingo Bay on January 11. He said, in part:

At 1.15 on January 5, the *Mayflower* got under way at Colon, having on board Col. Villasmil, of the Panama Army, 1 Panama soldier, 1 interpreter, and 3 Indian guides,

arriving at Caledonia at 10 a. m. the following day, when "Col. Villasmil, accompanied by Lieut. Poor, United States Navy, went ashore, but the attitude of the inhabitants was unfriendly and no information could be obtained." At 5 p. m. the *Mayflower* got under way, and at 10 a. m. on the following day, January 7, anchored in Mandigo Harbor, Gulf of San Blas, near the Indian village of Nellie.

Four scouting parties landed under Lieuts. Jewell, Poor, Woods, and Ensign Buchanan. Explorations extended from Point San Blas to Rio Diablo, a coast line distance of 44 miles. There were no roads, and the search for trails proved fruitless, only one from Chicumbali River to Santa Isabel, where it joins the old Matachin trail, existing. Report contains notes on river topography and continues:

The San Blas Indians, contrary to expectation, are decidedly unfriendly.

The chief of Mandingo village went on board the *Mayflower* with a party of Indians and asked Gleaves to go and see the "big chief" from Carti, who was in Mandingo.

Accompanied by Col. Villasmil, Ensign Buchanan, and First Sergt. Cottner, who speaks Spanish fluently, I went ashore and had an interview with the chief in a hut in the presence of a large number of men and boys who crowded around. The chief, whose name is Guayaquilile, and who is next in authority to the chief at Sasardi, was almost surly in his bearing and declined all overtures of friendship and proffered courtesies. He complained that sailors had frightened his women and stolen his coconuts. He said he did not understand why the ship was here, and objected to our boats entering the rivers and requested that I leave at once. He refused to give any information regarding the country or the Colombians, and in answer to my question who was the chief of the Indians, replied that "the chief of Sasardi, but that the President at Bogota was chief of all." He declined to visit the *Mayflower* for fear of being carried away. The next morning a subchief and attendants from another village came on board and were given breakfast and shown through the ship. They were friendly, but expressed the same fear for their women and their coconuts, and warned me that anyone coming ashore from the ships at night would be killed. In the afternoon I returned the call, and was received kindly, but informed by the head chief that he would not permit the boats to enter the rivers again. No explanations seemed to satisfy them.

The report continuing says that an Indian from Carti said that the chief of Sasardi was to place 300 canoes at the disposition of Gen. Ortiz to move the Colombian forces. That on January 9, Lieut. Jewell, accompanied by Col. Villasmil, visited the settlement at the mouth of the Rio Diablo, where Col. Villasmil's interpreter is personally known. The reception was gratifying, and the chief promised to notify the Panamanian Government if he heard of any move on the part of the Colombians. Comamnder Gleaves adds that the Indians are much disquieted, and the presence of the *Mayflower* had added to their alarm and excitement, and every day they grow more distinctly hostile toward us. While in the Carti River an Indian drew his bow and arrow on Ensign Buchanan, but was restrained from firing by Col. Villasmil's interpreter. Lieut. Jewell, Lieut. Poor, and Lieut. Woods were all at various times peremptorily ordered out of the river.

On the 9th one of the chiefs of the district went on board a Colon trading schooner and ordered the Panama flag hauled down, threatening to tear it. On the 15th I was informed by Col. Villasmil, who had just returned from Carti, that the restless and hostile feeling of the Indians was increasing, and that upon the *Mayflower's* departure all the Colon traders would leave the Gulf, etc.

Admiral Coghlan, in dispatches dated January 12, reports to the Secretary of the Navy that the situation remains the same. He confirms that the Government of Panama has notified him that they do not claim St. Andrews and Old Providence Islands. Says that the Colombians have not interfered with the American citizens on these islands, and that the principal American trader on St. Andrews is reported as being very friendly to Colombia.

Admiral Glass on January 11 cabled to the Secretary of the Navy reiterating information about the situation on St. Andrew Island, saying:

I have directed Coghlan to send a vessel immediately to preserve order and assure the people against any agressive movement of Colombia.

Admiral Coghlan on January 12 reported to the Secretary of the Navy by cable that there were 4,000 Colombians at Baranquilla. Says:

Castine from Caledonia Harbor reports Indians unfriendly, chief at Sasardi now wears uniform colonel Colombian force. * * * *Mayflower* returned; found Mandingo Bay Indians unfriendly. Objected strongly to explorations in their territory. From Conception Bay south to Mosquito village the Indians are friendly and say they will not permit Colombian forces or Indians to pass them.

The same day Admiral Coghlan forwarded the report of Commander Knight, of the U. S. S. *Castine*, on the attitude of the Indians in the vicinity of Caledonia Bay, Pinos Island, and Mosquito Bay. Says Indians came on board soon after the shop had anchored at Caledonia Harbor and inquired the reason of the American's visit; said that their women and children were so much alarmed that they could not sleep. Next day the chief sent off a canoe and asked Commander Knight to go ashore; this he did in company of the commanding officer of the *Bancroft* and the executive officer of the *Castine*. They found the Indian chief dressed in the uniform of a Colombian colonel; his manner was violent and almost insulting. The chief protested vigorously against our remaining and was not in the least placated by my assurances that we wished to be friendly.

The day after we anchored off Pinos Island a delegation from Navangandi village came on board and informed me that I must go away at once. The leading man of this party was said to be the chief man of the village and second only to the chief whom I had seen at Caledonia. He was less violent in manner but not less peremptory. He showed much concern about the marks we had erected for surveying, seeming to think, as I understood, that these indicated an intention to take possession of the land. When one of our officers in exploring a trail leading from Navangandi Lagoon approached the village, he was surrounded by about 30 men and noticed others approaching. They made no threats but closed about him in such a way that he thought it best to withdraw after a time. We have tried in several cases to buy fruit or fish from these people, but they refuse to deal with us on any terms. I have tried to get guides but without success. The attitude of the people is one of * * * entire unfriendliness.

On January 12 Capt. Cloman cabled the War Department:

Confidential information received only line of railway to be protected in case of invasion before ratification. Wire if true as guide for work. Information to-day, reliable source, 400 enemy occupy San Andreas Island. Send 50 yards of blue-print paper.

A copy of this cable in the Navy Department has this memo. attached:

Reply sent confirming truth of information as to railway line only to be protected in case of invasion before ratification.

H. A. G., *Secretary*.
(For the Chief of Staff).

On January 13 President Roosevelt, who had been asked by certain Senators for assurances that pending the ratification of the Hay-Bunua-Varilla treaty defense against possible hostile operations would be confined to the strategical vicinity of the railroad, ordered

Secretary Moody to prepare suitable orders, and these were drawn up and submitted in the folowing form, and after approval was cabled to Admirals Glass and Coghlan.

Vol. 1, page 243.
Strictly confidential.

JANUARY 13, 1904.

Proposed to Glass and Coghlan: It is the intention of the department that the defense against possible hostile operations shall be confined to the strategical vicinity of the railroad. Do not interfere with hostile troops except this limit, which must not extend beyond a distance necessary for the protection of the transit of the Isthmus effectively.

NOTE.—January 13. Submitted to the President and by him authorized, after full explanation of previous orders. To be held confidential.

W. H. M.

On January 13 Admiral Glass cabled to the Secretary of the Navy:

From the most reliable information obtainable at present there seems to be no doubt that a majority of the Indians on the coast of Panama between San Blas Point and Cape Tiburon are unfriendly to us and to Panama, and in the event of hostilities they will support Colombia, at least passively. Upon these conditions a small number of Colombian force can invade the Isthmus, skirting the coasts in small vessels and canoes inside reefs and shoals and entering the vicinity of headwaters of the Bayano River through Indians' country. It is not considered practicable for any large force to so operate; but if the American force does not prevent it, probably sufficient force can enter to take possession of the inland country east of the Canal Zone. There is every reason to believe that Colombian force will not attempt invasion through Yavisa country, owing to the presence of United States ships and the difficulty of this force operating there, even unopposed. If the United States policy would permit us to resist invasion, the force on Isthmian territory is ample to provide agains possible contingencies. The force at Panama would not be able, probably, to resist attack if not assisted actively between small parties very probable, and may occur very soon. The department will appreciate fully difficult position in which such contingency would place the United States forces. All quiet on this side of the Isthmus yesterday. Post has been withdrawn from Yavissa to the *Boston*, the health of the crew and men from the post improving.

Admiral Glass made all arrangements for defending the line of the Panama Railroad against any possible attack. On January 16 he cabled the Secretary of the Navy:

Making all arrangements to occupy Cruces and San Juan on Chagres River with strong force marines with artillery. At the approach of hostile force toward railroad, scouts will give ample notice. The intended occupation can be effected in two days from the base, Obispo. Distribution of the force will be as follows: Empire, 100 marines; Obispo, 600 marines; Cruces, 400 marines; San Juan, 200 marines. Train to be ready to move force on the line of railroad to threatened points in case of necessity. Will establish outpost on road to Chepoif, advisable. Marine brigade will be strengthened by marines and bluejackets from both squadrons if large hostile force approaches railroad. Coast being kept under observation constantly.

On January 25 Admiral Glass further reported that "a Panama spy," following the trail through Pucro, Paya, Tapalisa, Tartarcuna, Cuti, Baie Tuela, Titumati, and back (18 days), had got information about the Colombians, which is detailed in an appended report, which, after referring to the large number of canoes the Indians have and to the facility of invasion from Mandingo Bay to Bayano or Chagres country, adds:

As stated before, it is believed that the Panamans, unaided, could not be successful in expelling an invasion.

Glass appends a tabulated statement of the Panaman forces as follows:

(Tabulated returns of the officers and men in the Panama forces, extra rifles and ammunition and artillery in possession of the Republic. Details furnished by Minister of War of Panama, Sr. Don Nicanor de Obarrio.)

TROOPS AND ARMS OF THE REPUBLIC OF PANAMA.

On board the gunboat *3 de Noviembre* (*Padilla*): Officer, 11 armed troops, 2,000 car. ridges.

On board the gunboat *Chacuito:* One officer, 7 armed troops, and 1,000 cartridges.

At David: Four officers, 100 armed troops, 50 extra rifles, and 20,000 cartridges.

At Colon (part at San Blas): Five officers, 85 armed troops, 90 extra rifles, 100,000 cartridges.

At Bocas del Toro: Five officers, 50 armed troops, 50 extra rifles, and 10,000 cartridges.

At Darien: Thirteen officers, 92 armed troops, 30 extra rifles, and 8,000 cartridges.

At Chepo: Six officers, 99 armed troops, 45 extra rifles, and 7,960 cartridges.

At Santiago (probably Los Santos): Two officers, 25 armed troops, 34 extra rifles, and 4,000 cartridges.

At Panama: Fifty-two officers, 411 armed troops, 537 extra rifles, and 447,010 cartridges. Marginal note: "One million thirty thousand three hundred rounds of Remington have arrived."

Total: Eighty-eight officers, 861 armed troops, 836 extra rifles, and 509,970 cartridges.

POLICE FORCE AND ARMS.

At Panama: 225 policemen, 140 rifles, 20,000 cartridges.
At Chiriqui: 66 men, 130 rifles, and 6,000 cartridges.
At Los Santos: 40 men, 90 rifles, and 5,000 cartridges.
At Colon: 100 men, 100 rifles, and 2,000 cartridges.
At Bocas del Toro: 80 men, 110 rifles, and 4,000 cartridges.
At Veraguas: 40 men, 90 rifles, and 6,000 cartridges.
At Cocle: 40 men, 90 rifles, and 5,000 cartridges.
Total: 591 policemen, 750 rifles, and 48,000 cartridges.

GUNS AND AMMUNITION.

On board the *3 de Noviembre* and at Las Bovedas, Panama: One 15-pounder, with 288 rounds of ammunition; one 12½-pounder, with 19 rounds; five 6-pounders, with 3,520 rounds; five 2-pounders, with 250 rounds; one 1-pounder, without ammunition; four Colt automatic guns, with 87,600 rounds; and two Maxims, with 230,470 rounds.

Finally, on March 4, 1904, after the ratification of the Hay-Bunau treaty, and in reply to a request from Admiral Coghlan for a specific statement as to what the United States was pledged to, Secretary of the Navy Moody sent the following cable:

Replying to your cable, treaty of Panama provides for the maintenance of independence of Republic of Panama, not integrity of her soil. Do not prevent citizens of Colombia landing in Panama unless within the strategic limits of the Canal Zone and with arms and hostile intent.

The committee thereupon adjourned until Tuesday, February 20, 1912, at 10 o'clock a. m.

COMMITTEE ON FOREIGN AFFAIRS,
HOUSE OF REPRESENTATIVES,
Washington, D. C., Tuesday, February 20, 1912.

The committee met at 10 o'clock a. m., Hon. William Sulzer (chairman) presiding.

STATEMENT OF MR. HENRY N. HALL—Resumed.

The CHAIRMAN. Mr. Hall, you may resume your statement.

Mr. HALL. Mr. Chairman and gentlemen, I had intended this morning taking all of Mr. Roosevelt's messages to Congress bearing on this matter, prior to the ratification of the treaty with the Republic of Panama by the Senate of the United States; and it was my intention to show you, paragraph by paragraph, how the information on which the Senate acted was incomplete and, in many cases, misleading. But it has appeared to me, on second thought, that by so doing I should be placing myself somewhat in the attitude of a prosecutor of Mr. Roosevelt; and that is the very last thing I wish to do. I have, as you know, confined myself very carefully to presenting to you the evidence gathered by the New York World for its defense in the criminal libel suit brought against it by Mr. Roosevelt, and only such of that evidence as bears directly upon Mr. Rainey's resolution.

I have called your attention in detail to the treaty of 1846 and the negotiations which led up to that treaty. I have shown you how the treaty of 1846 was a contract under which, in exchange for valuable consideration received, the United States guaranteed the sovereignty of Colombia over the Isthmus of Panama. I have shown you the Panama Railroad contract of 1850, whereby Colombia, carrying out the provisions of the treaty of 1846, facilitated as much as she could the transit of American merchandise and American citizens over the Isthmus of Panama; and I have shown you how under that contract the reversionary right in the Panama Railroad belonged to Colombia.

I have shown you the treaty of 1857, wherein the United States for the second time specifically recognized the sovereignty of Colombia over the Isthmus. I have called your attention to the large pecuniary sacrifices Colombia made in order to obtain this guaranty of sovereignty; how in the first 10 years after the Panama Railroad was constructed $700,000,000 worth of specie and $300,000,000 worth of merchandise, upon which Colombia did not levy a single cent, were carried across the Isthmus of Panama, whereas if the differential dues had still been in force she would have collected in the neighborhood of $200,000,000. I have in some detail alluded to the Panama Railroad contract of 1867.

Mr. FLOOD. Mr. Hall, referring to the guaranty of sovereignty, do you take the position that that was a guaranty of the sovereignty of Colombia against any internal disturbance or revolution?

Mr. HALL. I think that the terms of the guaranty are perfectly clear. They are not qualified in any way, shape, or form. The treaty says that the United States will guarantee the right of sovereignty and property which New Granada has and possesses over the Isthmus of Panama, and in the absence of any limitation of that guaranty I think it is fair to assume that at the time that contract was made the parties understood it would apply to every possible eventuality.

Mr. FLOOD. And you now think that New Granada would have made a contract authorizing the United States to come in and interfere with a revolution in her own borders?

Mr. HALL. The United States was not pledged merely to maintain the free transit across the Isthmus. The freedom of transit across the Isthmus was guaranteed to the United States, and the United States assumed the obligation of maintaining that freedom of transit, and on several occasions forces of the United States were landed in Colombia in order to maintain the freedom of transit, and if any revolution or disturbance jeopardized or put in danger that freedom of transit which was guaranteed to the United States, the United States had a right to, and on several occasions did, intervene to maintain order and establish a police force, but, in the words of Mr. Cleveland, "always in maintenance of the sovereignty of Colombia."

Mr. FLOOD. For the purpose of maintaining the freedom of transit?

Mr. HALL. For the purpose of maintaining the freedom of transit, But in the note of Mr. Allan Burton, the minister at Bogota, which I read to you, it was very clearly pointed out that the treaty by no means limited the obligations of the United States to the maintenance of the freedom of transit, but extended its obligation to maintaining over the whole of the Isthmus. Now, that treaty was made at a time when the Panama Railroad was not built and when the freedom of transit applied to the whole breadth of the Isthmus, from its southernmost boundary, Cape Tiburon to Point Garachine, up to the border of Costa Rica.

I have alluded somewhat at length to the Panama Railroad contract of 1867. That is the contract which is now in force, and the United States to-day owns all the stock of the Panama Railroad Co. and have assumed all the obligations of that corporation. Under that civil contract Colombia conceded the railroad to the Panama Railroad Co. for a period of 99 years in return for payment of $1,000,000 in cash and $250,000 a year, and the railroad was to revert to Colombia at the end of the 99 years. Now, that was a civil contract, and the obligations of the Panama Railroad toward Colombia do not to me seem to be affected by the question whether there has or has not been a change of sovereignty over the territory in which the railroad happened to be built.

Then I showed you the two treaties of 1869 and 1870 entered into by the United States and the Republic of Colombia at the earnest solicitation of the United States, in which Colombia conceded to the United States everything she could possibly ask for the building of the canal. No pecuniary indemnity was demanded. The United States was given the very broadest rights and privileges to build a canal and to protect it with her own armed forces, which were not to exceed 1,000 men at any time; and all that Colombia was to get was 10 per cent of the net profits, if there were any, 12 years after the canal was opened, or after such time as the United States should have reimbursed to itself the entire cost of the canal, Colombia was to get 25 per cent of the net profits. That treaty was rejected by the Senate of the United States. The following year, in 1870, another treaty was made substantially on the same lines. This treaty was passed by the senate of Bogota, but again rejected by the Senate of the United States; and Colombia, not being able to get the United States to build the canal or to have anything to do with it, turned and gave the Panama Canal concession to Lucien Napoleon Bonaparte Wise, who sold it to De Lesseps; and then I traced very briefly the operations of the old Panama Canal company, the formation of the New Panama Canal Co. out of the ruins of the old company. I showed you how only 5 per cent of the total stock of the New Panama Canal Co. was subscribed by the public. Most of the rest of it was in the hands of men who were known as the "penitentiary" shareholders—people who had looted the old company and who maintained a control at the time they sold it over again to the United States.

Mr. FLOOD. They were required to take as much stock in the new company as they had stolen money from the old company.

Mr. HALL. Yes, sir. Criminal prosecutions against them were dropped and they were not sent to jail on condition that the money they stole from the old company was subscribed by them to the new company.

Then I showed you how Mr. William Nelson Cromwell came into this matter. The masterful man who started out to defeat legislation which was being urged in the Congress of the United States in favor of the Nicaraguan Canal; and how he claimed—and I was very careful in any statements that I made to you about Mr. Cromwell's activities to tell it to you in his own words, for which he and he alone must be responsible—how he wrote the speeches of Senators; how he wrote the minority reports of Senate committees; how he induced Senator Hanna to change the Republican platform of 1900; how he usurped the functions of Secretary Hay; how he was allowed to dictate ultimatums to Colombia by Mr. Roosevelt; how he received from his clients their thanks for communicating to them the secret instructions sent by the American Government to its diplomatic representative in Bogota. Of course, all that is on the evidence of Mr. Cromwell. He boasts how he wrote the treaty himself; how he obtained its signature by trickery; and you can clearly trace from his own brief how he planned a revolution when he saw that the treaty never would be accepted by Colombia.

Mr. FLOOD. Mr. Hall, I did not hear all the evidence. Was there any evidence that any money was used in this country except the $60,000 contributed to the Republican campaign committee in 1900?

Mr. HALL. I think it is a fair assumption that money was used. Anybody who reads the brief—and it has been published in the record in full—must arrive at that conclusion; but Mr. Cromwell does not give specific instances, and it is impossible to adduce proof of it until the United States gets possession of the archives of the New Panama Canal Co., which belong to it, for which it paid part of the $40,000,000, and which contain all of Mr. Cromwell's reports, all of his correspondence with the company, all of his accounts; and, most important of all, a list of the people to whom the $40,000,000 was ultimately distributed. I explained to you how efforts to obtain those papers had failed and how they are locked up in the vaults of the Credit Lyonnais beyond the reach of any legal agency, but I trust not beyond the reach of the Congress of the United States.

Then I showed you how, four and a half months before the revolution, after telegraphing to the New Panama Canal Co. and receiving its reply saying they approved of the plan and of its commencement of execution, on the very day Mr. Cromwell sent his telegram, he had an interview with President Roosevelt; how he had then sent his press agent to a newspaper and obtained the publication of an article forecasting in its minutest details the revolution that took place four and a half months later.

Mr. FLOOD. The accomplishments of Mr. Cromwell in getting officials to change their position on this question are based on his own testimony?

Mr. HALL. On his own testimony, sir. The many assertions he makes affecting Secretary of State Hay, who is dead, and Senator Hanna, who is dead, are matters which rest on his own authority. It is improbable, of course, knowing that the company was in possession of all his correspondence and all of his accounts that he would put forward statements he could not substantiate. Having made weekly and monthly reports to them, covering a period of six years, and having received their replies and acknowledgments, it is hardly to be believed that he would deliberately add into his brief anything he had not reported to the company at the time. Also, Mr. Cromwell's standing at the bar in New York is a very high one, and it would mean his disbarment if he were to present in an arbitration for remuneration for professional services facts which were not true. Of course I have accorded the weight of testimony to Mr. Cromwell's own written assertions.

Mr. KENDALL. Has he made those assertions elsewhere than his brief?

Mr. HALL. He has not. When some of the questions were put to him by Senator Morgan before the Senate Committee on Interoceanic Canals in the investigation in 1906, he refused to answer any questions dealing directly or indirectly with his services to the new Panama Canal Co. on the ground that they were privileged as between lawyer and client. He went so far as to put himself in contempt of the committee when called before the committee, and a special report with a list of the questions he refused to answer was published and is a matter of record.

I can put the whole of that in the appendix if you wish.

Mr. KENDALL. This brief to which you refer as containing the statements made by Mr. Cromwell is a very elaborate presentation on his part of what he insists are the services he rendered to the company in connection with the entire Isthmian question?

Mr. HALL. Yes, sir.

Mr. KENDALL. This brief was to be submitted to some board of arbitration, whose duty it was to determine what the services were worth?

Mr. HALL. Yes, sir.

Mr. FLOOD. It seems they were trying to rob him after he had done all this work for them.

Mr. HALL. He asked for a fee of $800,000, or 2 per cent on the sale price of the canal; that is, 2 per cent on the $40,000,000. A legal fee of 4,000,000 francs was an unheard of thing in Paris. The arbiters gave him 1,000,000 francs, or $200,000, and if Mr. Cromwell's brief is true, his services were remarkably cheap at the price.

Mr. FLOOD. Do you mean that that was all Mr. Cromwell got?

Mr. HALL. Oh, I would not go so far as to say that.

Mr. FLOOD. I mean, as a fee. He demanded $800,000 and got $200,000?

Mr. HALL. That is the statement made by Mr. Bunau-Varilla, who is intimate with all the affairs of the company. One of the reasons for Mr. Cromwell's dismissal on the 31st of July, 1901, from the service of the company was the company was dissatisfied with the methods he employed, the very heavy expenditures, and the promises he had made to people in the United States. It is clear from the letter of reinstatement that they had refused to approve his accounts or settle them.

Now, I have been able to show you in detail Mr. Cromwell's intrigues with the Panaman conspirators; how he fomented the revolution; how he communicated by means of cable codes, the originals of which I have presented to you; and I have also presented some of his correspondence showing beyond all doubt there was this conspiracy; and then I have shown you from the files of the Navy Department and from official documents belonging to the Government of this country, which documents were withheld from Congress by Mr. Roosevelt, that the United States not only prepared in advance, nearly three weeks in advance, for the revolution and sent the ships of war down to the Isthmus to prevent Colombia from asserting her sovereignty, but they went a great deal further and occupied the Isthmus militarily; made plans for the taking of the city of Cartagena, and actually landed a large force of marines, invading the continent of South America; that these drastic measures were modified afterwards; that to avoid criticism in the Senate it was decided only to defend the line of the railroad; and that finally, after the whole thing was over and after the treaty with Panama had been ratified by the Senate, then Mr. Roosevelt put that extraordinary interpretation upon it—that the treaty with Panama guaranteed the independence of the Republic of Panama, but did not guarantee the integrity of her territory.

I believe that the presentation I have made to you of these facts thoroughly bears out what I said it would. You will recall my assertion that the evidence gathered by the World for its defense in the Panama libel suit which I was about to present to you proved the most conclusively three things:

First. That Mr. Roosevelt and some members of his administration were cognizant of and gave their support to the preparations being made for the Panama revolution.

Mr. COOPER. Will you please name the members of the administration you think were cognizant of those preparations besides the President?

Mr. HALL. Secretary Hay undoubtedly was. There is the sworn testimony of Mr. Duque, who had a conference with Secretary Hay on the 14th of September, at which the matter was thoroughly discussed, and two of the most reputable newspaper men in Washington, one of them Mr. Cotterill, of the Associated Press—I have forgotten for the moment the name of the other man, but his name is in the record—were told by Secretary Hay more than a week before the revolution that there was going to be one. I think it is a fair assumption that other members of the cabinet were cognizant of the revolution and undoubtedly Secretary Moody, from the records of the Navy Department, when he issued the orders to the naval officers to go down there and prepare for it, must have been cognizant of it.

Mr. Cooper. Secretary Hay and Secretary Moody—any others?

Mr. Hall. Not that I have proof of, sir.

Mr. Difenderfer. You say those are all you know of?

Mr. Hall. All of the members of Mr. Roosevelt's administration, whose signatures appear attached to any documents bearing on it. I have mentioned the names of those who are brought into it by direct testimony. I do not doubt that the matter was known to other members of the administration, such as Attorney General Knox, for instance, but I do not want to say anything I can not substantiate.

Mr. Difenderfer. Was not the Secretary of War cognizant of it?

Mr. Hall. I suppose he must have been, sir, because orders were issued for the sending down of the military officers to the Isthmus and for the preparing in the second division of military information the notes on Panama which were issued at the time of the revolution, and were marked "Confidential, for the sole use of the officer to whom issued," copies of which I presented to you. But I have no record or document here bearing his signature.

The Chairman. Who was Secretary of War at that time?

Mr. Hall. I think Senator Root was, sir.

Mr. Difenderfer. Mr. Loomis was the Assistant Secretary?

Mr. Hall. Mr. Loomis was Assistant Secretary of State, and Mr. Loomis's name appears attached to a number of the telegrams in the cipher of the State Department, which were suppressed by Mr. Roosevelt when the correspondence was sent to the Senate.

Mr. Difenderfer. As a matter of fact, you believe that Mr. Loomis knew more about it than Secretary Hay, do you not?

Mr. Hall. I can not say what I believe, sir. The record does not show that. I would like to have those telegrams signed by Mr. Loomis translated. They are in the cipher of the State Department, and are going to be printed in the record. But I have always understood from everybody with whom I have talked about it that it was Mr. Loomis who was handling this matter at the State Department at that time.

Mr. Difenderfer. If those telegrams were translated, you think they would throw more light upon the situation?

Mr. Hall. I imagine they were not withheld without a reason. I do not know what they show. I have not been able to translate them myself, sir.

Mr. Cooper. In answer to my question, you first mentioned Secretary Hay and then Secretary Moody.

Mr. Hall. And Secretary Root.

Mr. Cooper. No; I asked you if there were any others, and you said "No." Then I observed Mr. Rainey speak to Mr. Difenderfer, and then he inquired specifically if the Secretary of War knew about it, and then you said you thought the Secretary of War must have known about it. Why did not that occur to you when I asked you if there were any others besides the Secretary of State and Secretary Moody? What had the Secretary of War done that now makes you think he was a party to this transaction?

Mr. Flood. He has just stated that.

Mr. Cooper. The witness knows what he said.

Mr. HALL. I am not charging—and I want to make myself quite clear on this—I am not charging in any way that a regular round-table conspiracy was entered into by all these gentlemen, although these matters were discussed at Cabinet meetings. I am saying that Mr. Roosevelt and some members of his administration were cognizant of and gave their support to the movement for a Panaman revolution. Now, there is no doubt in my mind that Mr. Moody, for instance—and, I imagine, also Mr. Root—carried out the orders of the President. That they were cognizant of these matters is a necessary assumption from the facts, in Mr. Moody's case that he signed those Navy telegrams, and in Mr. Root's case, he must have known of the orders for the preparation of the "Notes on Panama," which were marked "Confidential; for the sole use of the officer to whom issued."

Mr. COOPER. The first man you named was Secretary Hay. What did he do? What made you think that Secretary Hay knew about these things or was a party to any conspiracy?

Mr. HALL. I do not think you were present when I read from Mr. Cromwell's brief and from Mr. Duque's testimony, and from the letters and telegrams of the Colombian minister to his Government, describing in great detail, all of them, the visit that Mr. Duque paid to Mr. Hay after the appointment made by Mr. Cromwell; how Mr. Duque came down on the midnight train with Mr. Charles B. Hart, and Mr. Hart took Mr. Duque in and introduced him to Mr. Hay, and then they had an interview, at which Mr. Hay said he wanted to get all the information he could, but he would not cross the bridge until he came to it; and Mr. Duque says he was given to understand that if the Panamans did declare independence they would be protected from any acts of repression by Colombia. All of that is in the record.

Mr. COOPER. Mr. Duque is a Colombian?

Mr. HALL. No, sir; he is an American citizen who is one of the most prominent men down in Panama. He has large interests down there and is a wealthy man, the owner of the Panama lottery, of a newspaper, of an ice plant, and of a construction company.

Mr. COOPER. This American citizen, the owner of an ice plant and the Panama lottery, says that in a private conversation with the Secretary of State, Mr. Hay, he told this private citizen that the United States Government would protect Panama in any revolution that was started. You rely upon that, in part, to show that John Hay was a party to this proceeding; is that it?

Mr. HALL. In part.

Mr. COOPER. In part; that is what I wanted to know.

Mr. HALL. Mr. Cromwell in his brief gives a great many details of his conferences with Mr. Hay and the manner in which he drafted the ultimatum sent by Mr. Hay to the Government of Colombia, and the instructions sent to the American minister in Bogota; and I also rely on the fact that Mr. Hay told newspaper men here in Washington a good week before the revolution that there was going to be a revolution.

Mr. FLOOD. This revolution occurred on the 3d of November, 1903?

Mr. HALL. Yes, sir.

Mr. FLOOD. How many American troops were on the Isthmus at that time?

Mr. HALL. There were no American troops on the Isthmus of Panama on the 3d of November. There were a few marines and sailors landed from the *Nashville* on the 4th. American officers were there and were cognizant of it. Maj. Murray Black and Lieut. Brooks went down to Colon and took command of these Panama Railroad employees and formed, as I told you, "Black's legion."

Mr. FLOOD. How many warships were on both sides of the Isthmus at that time?

Mr. HALL. After the telegram I produced had been sent to Bunau-Varilla, and he had seen the Secretary of the Navy and sent back the reply that the warships would be on the Atlantic in 36 hours and the Pacific in 48 hours, 8 warships were ordered to the Isthmus.

Mr. FLOOD. How many were there on the 3d day of November?

Mr. HALL. On the 3d day of November the *Nashville* was at Colon, where the revolution only became known on the 4th. The *Dixie* arrived the following day with 400 marines that had been sent over from Jamaica, and the placing of the marines on board the *Dixie* had been ordered on October 15 by Secretary Moody.

Mr. DIFENDERFER. Referring again to Mr. Hay, do you know whether or not Mr. Hay at any time expressed disgust with this entire deal and, ostensibly on account of his health, retired from the whole thing and left it in the hands of Mr. Loomis?

Mr. HALL. I have heard that, sir, but I have not any statement, affidavit, or written record which I could produce to this committee that would substantiate it. That has been my understanding, but I really have just confined myself, as you are aware, solely to documents and statements which could be substantiated. Now, I may believe that to be true, but I do not know it.

Mr. DIFENDERFER. Have you any reason to believe that he did express his displeasure about this matter?

Mr. KENDALL. What would the reason be? What is the evidence about it, not what somebody told you?

Mr. HALL. I certainly have not got any such evidence, sir.

Mr. HARRISON. Mr. Hall, Secretary of State Hay is dead. Is this man Loomis still living?

Mr. HALL. Oh, yes sir.

Mr. HARRISON. Is he in the employment of the Government?

Mr. HALL. I think after the trouble he had in Venezuela he was made commissioner to some exposition; but I do not know. I can find out for you.

The second proposition which I said these documents would prove was that the steps taken by Mr. Roosevelt to prevent Colombia from maintaining sovereignty over the Isthmus of Panama, and to prevent the landing of Colombian troops within the State of Panama and the suppressing of the fake rebellion, were in violation of the treaty of——

Mr. FLOOD (interposing). How many Colombian troops were on the Isthmus of Panama on the 3d of November?

Mr. HALL. Five hundred had just landed from the steamship *Cartegena*. Their commander was paid $8,000 from the Panama Railroad Co. coffers, and on November 5 he took this force back to Cartagena on the steamship *Orinoco*.

Mr. FLOOD. They went back willingly after being paid?

Mr. HALL. Oh, yes; they obeyed their commander. He took them back. Then there were also 480 Colombian soldiers who were in Panama and who arrested the generals. The officers got from $6 to $3,500 each, and the men were paid $50 each, and they remained as Panaman forces. Many of them are members of the Panaman police force to-day.

Mr. FLOOD. Then Colombia has as much complaint against her own army as against the citizens of this country?

Mr. HALL. She has a great deal to complain of against her own army, I should think. But she could have landed 10,000 men on the Isthmus and restored her lawful authority if the American warships had not prevented it. So my second proposition, that these documents would prove that the steps taken by Mr. Roosevelt to prevent Colombia from maintaining her sovereignty over the Isthmus of Panama and to prevent the landing of forces—as he did—to suppress rebellion on her own territory, were in violation of the treaty of 1846. I do not think that there can be any doubt that that treaty was violated, and that Colombia was prevented from exercising her own rights of sovereignty which had been guaranteed to her. She was prevented by force from suppressing a rebellion in her own state.

Mr. FLOOD. By force of arms or by force of something besides arms?

Mr. HALL. By the force of arms; by the presence of the American war ships and the landing of marines and sailors with orders to resist the advance of any Colombian forces. That is what prevented the landing of any Colombian forces.

Mr. FLOOD. It would seem that those who did land were bought off very readily.

Mr. HALL. Those that did land were bought off, and those who were loyal were prevented by force from landing.

My third proposition was that the acts of Mr. Roosevelt in respect to the creation and recognition of the Republic of Panama were in violation, not only with treaty obligations of the United States, but also of fundamental principles of international law which have been and are recognized by the United States itself as binding upon nations in their dealings one with another; and in support of that proposition I read to you from the correspondence between Secretary Seward and Mr. Charles Francis Adams, in 1861, wherein the principles to which the United States subscribed and which it proclaimed to be binding upon all nations, are very clearly and fully set forth. Each and every one of those principles was undoubtedly violated by Mr. Roosevelt in the recognition of the Republic of Panama.

Mr. FLOOD. I was not here when you referred to that matter. Do you mean that Panama was recognized too quickly by this country?

Mr. HALL. Panama was recognized 72 hours after this fake rebellion, at a time when no elections had been held, when she had no constitutional assembly, when the news of the so-called independence had not reached any of the populous towns of the interior; and I showed you how the American war ships, a month afterward, going along the coast, were the first ones to bring the news that that territory was no longer under the domination of Colombia.

Mr. FLOOD. Before you leave this matter, did you deal in your testimony with the question of why Colombia refused to accede to the treaty that was negotiated, by which she was to receive $10,000,000?

Mr. HALL. Yes, sir. That is all in the record, and dealt with very fully, indeed.

The CHAIRMAN. Before you conclude, Mr. Hall, I would like to ask you a question or two. Under section 4 of article 35 of the treaty of 1846, between New Granada and the United States, the Government of the United States practically guaranteed the sovereignty——

Mr. HALL (interposing). Section 1 of article 35 contains the guarantee of the sovereignty, sir.

The CHAIRMAN. And section 4 also.

Mr. HALL. Section 4, if I recall, is the section which says that any citizen of either country who violates the treaty shall be held personally responsible. It was under that section that they sent down, in 1885, and hanged three Colombians who had violated the treaty by interrupting transit.

The CHAIRMAN. Mr. Hall, you have given a great deal of time and study to this entire Panama question. Have you any objection to telling us what, in your opinion, the Government of the United States should do by way of reparation to Colombia?

Mr. HALL. Mr. Flood, I think, asked me a question very much along that line the first day I was here, and I told him I was here merely to give what facts I could. So far I have spoken as a representative of the World. I came here and I was sent here by Mr. Don C. Seitz, the manager of the Press Publishing Co., at Mr. Rainey's request, to present to you this evidence which the World had gathered for its defense. The position of the World in this matter was, I think, made abundantly clear by the "Let it be without stain" editorial, printed on Saturday, January 27, after these hearings had commenced. I will quote only the last paragraph, which seems to present the matter in a very clear and lucid way:

> If Colombia has no claim to indemnity that fact will be established by a full and fair investigation. If Colombia has a claim, that claim ought to be satisfied. No other course is compatible with the honor and integrity of the American people. Whether the controversy is to be settled by a congressional investigation or referred to The Hague tribunal is a matter of detail. The important thing is that this international scandal be disposed of for all time before the canal is opened, and that no stain be left upon the American title. Congress owes that to the country, and the country owes that to itself.

I have spent many months on the Isthmus of Panama. I have seen the great work which is being carried on there.

I have seen the whole face of the Isthmus changed by the labor of American Army engineers, who are building the Panama Canal. It is the greatest piece of engineering work ever accomplished anywhere in the world, and it is being done in a manner which reflects the utmost credit upon Col. Goethals and everybody who is connected with it. The Panama Canal, the great American highway through which ships of all nations will soon carry the commerce of the world, stands for all time as a monument to the constructive genius of the American people. It is a thing to be proud of; an achievement wherein the people of this country have succeeded after others have failed. It should be without stain. It should be born into its usefulness and given to the commerce of the world without the bar sinister of rape and lawlessness.

Now, you ask me if I have any opinion personally in this matter. I know that this problem is a very delicate and a very difficult one; and if I might be permitted to express an humble opinion—if I thought that my voice might be heard in the State Department—I would want to utter a very serious and solemn warning that this controversy can not be settled in the manner in which a settlement was attempted with Señor Cortez, when the tripartite treaties were made by Señor Cortez, Mr. Arosemena, Mr. Cromwell, Mr. Root, and other high officials of the American Government. Although familiar with their every detail I have scrupulously avoided and reference to those negotiations, and I have stopped at the ratification of the treaty with the Republic of Panama without delving into the subsequent efforts made to settle this question. But no good or lasting settlement can ever come from any such negotiations as the Cortez negotiations, and I feel sure that if the circumstances surrounding those negotiations were brought to the knowledge of this committee you would feel regret that they had ever been inaugurated. Now, if it be true, as I have heard from Members of Congress and from members of this committee, that it is the plan of Mr. Knox to arrive at a settlement of this question with Colombia by means of a special commission, one arbitrator to be appointed by the United States and one to be appointed by Colombia, and in case they can not agree the President of some South American country to be appointed an umpire, I wish to say as emphatically as I can that such a proposition will never satisfy the people of Colombia. I know that even if the Government of Colombia should accept it the people will not. Colombia has good reason to want to have care of her own public men, and the people of Colombia as a whole will not be satisfied with anything except a decision by The Hague Tribunal, a tribunal that the whole world recognizes as being absolutely incorruptible.

Mr. KENDALL. Is it your idea, Mr. Hall, that if Colombia should appoint a commissioner, he would be liable to subsidy?

Mr. HALL. No, sir; I think that if Colombia were to appoint a commissioner and the United States were to appoint a commissioner, although they might agree on the facts, they would never agree on the solution. This means that the decision would rest with the umpire, and the decision of no one man would satisfy the people of Colombia. If the two arbitrators did agree there would always be the danger of accusations, however unwarranted, that one of them had been improperly interested.

Mr. KENDALL. I think, perhaps, I misunderstood you. I understood you to say that Colombia had good reason to suspect the integrity of her own public officials.

Mr. FLOOD. That is what he did say.

Mr. HALL. Colombia still has before her the recent example of Gen. Reyes. Cortez was no better. Obaldia is dead, and I will not speak of him.

Mr. KENDALL. Then, I guess I did not misunderstand you. What I was about to say was this: Would there be any more ground for confidence in the integrity of a Colombian who would have the duty of presenting the facts to a board of arbitration than in the integrity of a Colombian who was on the board of arbitration itself?

Mr. HALL. No, sir. I have no doubt that if a board of arbitration of that kind were appointed there are very many learned and able men in Colombia who would admirably present the case of their country to such a board, and others who would be capable of sitting upon it as arbitrators; but I can say, from my knowledge of the Colombian people, in the light of their past experience, that no such commission as that would satisfy the general sentiment of the country; that they would always look with suspicion upon anything less than an arbitration before The Hague.

Mr. FLOOD. Do you mean that the Colombian people do not trust any of their public men?

Mr. HALL. I would not go so far as to say that they do not trust any of their public men. But why resort to any such commission? The nations of the world have established a great tribunal at The Hague, and to it the United States is urging all nations to bring their disputes for settlement, just as private individuals bring their controversies into duly established courts of law. The Hague tribunal exists, a great and learned judge sits there to represent the United States. Much of the eclat, much of the prestige of The Hague tribunal is derived from the controversies which the United States has submitted to it. Why therefore should an exception be made in this case?

When England and the United States could settle such a long-standing quarrel as the fisheries dispute by reference to The Hague, surely the United States and Colombia ought to be able to settle their present controversy by reference to that same august tribunal.

Mr. HARRISON. Do you think that would be satisfactory to the people of Colombia?

Mr. HALL. Yes, sir; undoubtedly.

Mr. DIFENDERFER. And no one man would have any influence with The Hague?

Mr. HALL. No one man would have influence with The Hague. Secretary Knox, the other night, came down to the Press Club, and in one of the most eloquent 10-minute speeches I have ever listened to pointed out how The Hague was the tribunal to which the United States wants to see all nations submit their differences and the decisions of which will always be satisfactory to the United States. Surely the United States should be ready to practice what it preaches.

Mr. GARNER. If Secretary Knox made such a statement to the Press Club, how do you account for the fact that he does not arrange to have this matter submitted to The Hague?

Mr. HALL. Of course, I am speaking as a newspaper man, and have given you my own point of view. But let us look at it in another light, in the light in which Mr. Knox perhaps sees it. I can well understand how there may perhaps be some hesitation on Mr. Knox's part in wanting to go into a court, where England, Germany, and South America are represented, with a case to which there is no defense. Mr. Knox knows that as well as anybody, and it is perhaps too severe a test of the genuineness of his desire for universal arbitration. Mr. Knox is too good a lawyer not to want to settle a losing case out of court if he can do it, because he knows that if the case goes before The Hague tribunal the judges there will do justice, but it is unlikely that their justice will be tempered with mercy. If they found that by the acts of the United States, in violation of a solemn treaty and of the law of nations, Colombia had lost her rights of sovereignty and property over the Isthmus, they might, very possibly would, award Colombia the intrinsic value of the Isthmus.

Mr. FLOOD. What is the intrinsic value of the Isthmus?

Mr. HALL. I do not know what the intrinsic value of the Isthmus is, and it seems to me that this element of uncertainty is one of the reasons which cause the United States to hesitate to present this matter to The Hague. The question of national honor is not really involved in this, as I see it, except that the United States is in honor bound to give Colombia her day in court. The policy of ignoring Colombia's claims, and leaving unanswered her demands for arbitration, must be abandoned as inconsistent with the dignity of the United States. That, I believe, is the attitude of the vast majority of thoughtful men, and of American people as a whole. The Congress and people of the United States never had any part in this spoliation. The acts complained of are Mr. Roosevelt's own acts. He did not give information to Congress about them, or rather, what information he did give was incomplete and misleading. He himself is on record as saying:

> I am interested in the Panama Canal because I started it. If I had followed traditional conservative methods I would have submitted a dignified state paper of probably 200 pages to Congress, and the debate on it would have been going on yet; but I took the Canal Zone and let Congress debate; and while——

Mr. FLOOD (interposing). That was the flamboyant speech he made out in California?

Mr. HALL. Yes; and in which for once he told the truth.

Mr. GARNER. You think there are two reasons why Secretary Knox does not take this to The Hague Tribunal at the present time; first, that he is trying to settle it direct, and, second, he is afraid to go to The Hague Tribunal for fear the result would injure our trade with South America countries?

Mr. HALL. No, sir. It would help, not hurt trade.

Mr. GARNER. Now your proposition is that we shall ask Mr. Knox to go to The Hague in order that an indemnity may be found against the United States, or rather that its honor may be maintained throughout the world.

Mr. HALL. I will say this, sir: If this matter could have been settled diplomatically—and that is what the nations of this earth keep state departments for—it ought to have been settled long ago by direct negotiations with Colombia. There is a clause in the treaty with Panama of 1904 which would appear to offer a loophole for settlement. It says that Panama shall transfer to the United States all rights that she has acquired or may in the future acquire from Colombia. That is because the treaty of 1904 was probably written by a corporation lawyer instead of being written by a statesman, and he was very anxious at some future time to get a clear title to the Panama Railroad Co. under a civil contract; he knew perfectly well that the railroad contract was a civil contract and that Panama could give no title to it unless that title was transferred by Columbia to Panama, and that was one of the bases of the Cortez negotiations, that Colombia was to recognize the sovereignty and title of Panama.

Mr. COOPER. You say that treaty was written by a corporation lawyer? Who was Secretary of State in 1904?

Mr. HALL. Secretary Hay, sir; but I think Mr. Cromwell drafted the treaty.

Mr. KENDALL. Your opinion is that if this controversy was to be submitted to The Hague for adjudication it incontestably would be found that the United States is responsible for all of the territory which secured its independence from Colombia?

Mr. HALL. Yes, sir; when the matter of the boundary between Panama and Colombia came up for negotiation the Colombian minister told the State Department that this was not a question of international law, but of fact, just what territory the United States will employ force to prevent Colombia reasserting her sovereignty over.

Mr. KENDALL. Your opinion is that the United States would be found by The Hague Tribunal to be responsible for all of the territory which it permitted to be alienated from Colombia?

Mr. HALL. Yes; the territory over which the United States prevented and prevents Colombia from reasserting her sovereignty.

Mr. KENDALL. What do you think the value of that would be as determined by The Hague Tribunal?

Mr. HALL. I have not an idea; sir. If you agree upon the facts, and the only question was the determination of the amount of indemnity to be paid, and the matter was submitted to The Hague, the Supreme Court of the United States, or to any board of arbitration in the world, I can not imagine for a moment how they could give Colombia less than the value of what she has lost.

Mr. HARRISON. Have you any knowledge or information which leads you to think the State Department is trying to fix up this matter directly with the Republic of Colombia?

Mr. HALL. All the information I have is that the requests of Colombia for an arbitration of this matter have always been left unanswered.

Mr. FLOOD. You just stated that you thought Secretary Knox was trying to settle this matter by diplomatic negotiations, but that is not consistent with the letter of the Colombian minister and your statement that he did not even answer the requests for arbitration.

Mr. HALL. Pardon me, sir. I did not say he was trying to settle it by diplomatic negotiations. I said I thought it ought to have been settled long ago by diplomatic negotiations; but as I understand the plan of the State Department—and my information comes from Members of Congress who ought to be well informed about these matters—it is, instead of going to The Hague, to have the matter referred to some less august tribunal, some sort of a commission with one arbiter appointed by each country and the President of some South American Republic to act as umpire.

Mr. CLINE. Who suggested that?

Mr. HALL. I do not know, but I am told that is the suggestion that is being spoken of as the one that Mr. Knox would probably make if he went to Colombia; but it is quite certain that the people of Colombia would not want——

The CHAIRMAN (interposing). Suppose this committee should report legislation to pay the United States of Colombia a lump sum of money, do you think they would accept it in full settlement for any claims she may have against the United States?

Mr. HALL. I do not think it is so much money that Colombia wants; that is the idea I have gathered from speaking with the different Colombian ministers who have been here, Minister Borda, notably, and others. Mr. Borda had a plan which I believe was presented to the President for the settlement of this matter on the basis of the resumption of sovereignty by Colombia over the whole of the Isthmus and then Colombia agreeing to a servitude in perpetuity of whatever territory the United States judged to be necessary for the canal, no indemnity to be given for such servitude, but the Republic of Colombia to be reinstated in all her rights and receive the $250,000 a year secured to her by the Panama Railroad contract of 1867.

Mr. COOPER. If Colombia is going to take that, why was she not willing to accept $10,000,000 in cash?

Mr. HALL. Colombia never refused to accept $10,000,000 in cash at any time.

Mr. COOPER. I understand she practically refused to accept $10,000,000 under the Hay-Herran treaty.

Mr. HALL. That was a very different thing. She refused to ratify the Hay-Herran treaty for many excellent reasons, but not because of the $10,000,000 or because she was not satisfied with the $10,000,000 from the United States.

Mr. FLOOD. She wanted $25,000,000 from us.

Mr. HALL. No, sir; if there is one thing that is clearer than any other, and if there is any one thing in the whole controversy which is beyond dispute it is that the statement put out so industriously here that the Republic of Colombia was trying to blackmail the United States or hold up the United States for more money is a fabrication out of the whole cloth.

Mr. FLOOD. Did not her ministers unanimously reject the treaty providing for the payment of $10,000,000?

Mr. HALL. The Senate of Colombia rejected it, not because the payment was unsatisfactory, but for other reasons.

Mr. FLOOD. Did they not suggest that $20,000,000 would be an amount that would be satisfactory to them?

Mr. HALL. No, sir; I have searched the records of the Colombian Senate, and there was not one single amendment introduced in the Colombian Senate during the discussion of that treaty which in any way, shape, or form bore upon the amount of indemnity to be paid by the United States.

Mr. CLINE. That was a part of the conspiracy, was it not, to get the Colombian Senate to refuse to accept the terms of that treaty?

Mr. FOSTER. Was not this the real situation: That this was in 1903, and the concessions of the new company expired in 1904, and Colombia thought that in 1904, when those concessions to the new French company would have expired, she would be enabled to get not only the $10,000,000 for permitting the United States to use the Canal Zone, but a large portion of the $40,000,000 which we paid to the French Government for the buildings there and the work that had been done? Is not that, in a nutshell, practically the situation?

Mr. HALL. The concession was to expire in 1910, not 1904. It is stated in the final instructions of the Colombian Government to Minister Concha——

Mr. FLOOD (interposing). The statement made in this committee about January, 1904, was that in addition to the attempt to hold the matter up until this charter expired, some time in the year 1904, by which Colombia would probably get a part of the $40,000,000, she demanded more than $10,000,000 from this Government as the purchase price of the strip of land on which the canal is built, and I heard the amount suggested as being $20,000,000 or $25,000,000; I never looked into it at all, but I did not hear the matter questioned at that time.

Mr. HALL. The Government of Colombia did not reject the Hay-Herran treaty because she was not satisfied with the $10,000,000. She did want to amend it; she wanted to amend article 1, which said that the Republic of Colombia authorized the New Panama Canal Co. to transfer their concessions to the United States, and she wanted to amend that by the addition of the words "After the new canal company and the railroad company shall have come to a previous equitable arrangement with Colombia." That is to say, Colombia did not want to lose the $250,000 a year she was getting for the Panama Railroad Co. and did not want to lose her reversionary right in the Panama Railroad Co., which was given to her under the contract of 1867, and for that reason Colombia insisted that there should first be a settlement; that before doing anything with the United States there should be a settlement with the canal company and the railroad company.

Mr. GARNER. If I understand it, your whole discussion here has been to convince the committee that it should make an investigation in order to determine how Panama was acquired or, rather, whether or not the Colombian Government should have its day in court at The Hague. Now, if I understand your statement at this time, it is that Mr. Knox, the Secretary of State, is now making an effort to settle this matter directly with the Colombian Government, and, if that is so, do you not think it would be advisable for us to wait and find out what success he is going to have in that direction before we go into such an investigation, and especially in view of your conclusive statement that we convict ourselves when we put ourselves in The Hague court?

Mr. HALL. I have no doubt that the case, if it went to The Hague court, would be decided against the United States; I think everybody who has given the matter any thought or any attention knows that; but I did not say, and I have no authority to say, that Mr. Knox is making any kind of direct negotiations with Colombia at the present time. I said that, in my opinion, it should have been settled across the table long ago. It has not been settled. It ought to be settled before the canal is opened, and settled at The Hague; but Mr. Knox does not seem willing to take it there, if we are to judge his intentions by the letter from him to the Colombian minister, which appeared in the papers recently, and in which he says that his requests for arbitration have been left unanswered.

The CHAIRMAN. If you have concluded your statement the committee will go into executive session.

Mr. HALL. I wish to thank you gentlemen very much——

Mr. COOPER (interposing). May I ask one question? Mr. Hall, I observed in the newspaper articles first published that Charles P. Taft, the President's brother, was named specifically as one of the parties to the conspiracy which was charged and that he was one of the beneficiaries, and so forth.

Mr. HALL. Yes, sir.

Mr. COOPER. I have not observed, during your remarks, that you named him at all—is that true?

Mr. HALL. I have not named him, as there was no reason whatever for naming him, and I can say that when you read the record you will see a statement of how his name got into the papers; investigation has shown that Mr. Taft had absolutely nothing whatever to do, directly or indirectly, with the sale of the New Panama Canal Co. to the United States.

Mr. COOPER. Over and over again, however, in various papers throughout the Middle West and elsewhere his name was coupled with that of Mr. Cromwell as being particeps criminis, and I presume I have received altogether 100 letters from constituents touching upon that very accusation, and I never could quite understand why a man who is entirely innocent of all complicity could have been so specifically informed against.

Mr. HALL. The reason for Mr. Taft's name being brought into this is very clearly set forth in the statement which I presented to the committee of how the World came to publish the article of October 3, 1908, in which Mr. Taft's name was mentioned.

Mr. COOPER. I did not refer to the World particularly, but I referred to the newspapers generally.

Mr. HALL. Well, they all copied their articles from the story which appeared in the World. Mr. Taft owes this undeserved notoriety to Mr. Cromwell and to Mr. Cromwell alone. It was Mr. Cromwell's own press agent, Jonas Whitley, formerly a reporter on the World, who came into the World office one evening and told the managing editor that the World was about to print a Panama news article that was entirely false. The managing editor knew nothing about it, so he inquired at the city editor's desk. He was told that the World had no Panama article of any sort or description, but that it had been trying to verify a report of a complaint made by Mr. Cromwell to the district attorney, and had been unable to do so. Mr. Whitley had voluntarily related the substance of the complaint. He said that the persons who were alleged to be trying to blackmail Mr. Cromwell pretended that Charles P. Taft and Douglas Robinson were members of a syndicate interested in the sale of the Panama Canal, and these persons threatened to exploit the story for political purposes unless Mr. Cromwell bought them off.

Mr. COOPER. Is Douglas Robinson a brother-in-law of ex-President Roosevelt?

Mr. HALL. Yes, sir.

Mr. COOPER. And he was also absolutely innocent?

Mr. HALL. I have no proof here to substantiate the charge that Douglas Robinson was connected with the revolution in any way, shape, or form. A synopsis of Mr. Whitley's account of the Cromwell complaint was then dictated to a stenographer, and the typewritten copy was turned over to Mr. Whitley to revise. This manuscript is still in possession of the World. It shows that Mr. Whitley scratched out the name of Charles P. Taft and substituted the name of Henry W. Taft. Then he erased the name of Henry W. Taft and restored the name of Charles P. Taft. The story was published the next morning with a statement that Mr. Cromwell made over the telephone that night in which he denied the accusations in the most sweeping terms. That is how Charles P. Taft's name got into this thing, and there was no more reason for bringing his name into it than there was for bringing mine.

Mr. COOPER. And is that the way the name of Douglas Robinson got into it?

Mr. HALL. Yes, sir.

Mr. COOPER. Then his name ought to be stricken out the same as Mr. Taft's.

The CHAIRMAN. Is that all?

Mr. HALL. I wish to thank you, Mr. Chairman, and I do thank you and all the members of this committee for the very kind and courteous attention you have given to my statement. I have not spoken here as the advocate of Colombia, nor as the prosecutor of Mr. Roosevelt. I have endeavored fairly and impartially to place the truth before you as I saw it from the documents gathered by the World. To that end I have employed whatsoever of ability I possess, and the experience gained in more than 20 years of active newspaper work. I trust you will arrive at a just and satisfactory solution of this momentous question. I sincerely hope you will find some way of settling a difference with Colombia which ought to be settled, because the United States is losing in South American trade to-day very nearly as much as it is spending on the construction of the Panama Canal, and you are paying for the Panama Canal once in cash and once in trade. But apart from sordid or commercial interests, there are other and higher reasons why this controversy ought to be settled. I firmly believe that "righteousness alone exalteth a nation," and that to-day, as never before in the history of the world, with nations even more than with individuals, honesty is the best policy. Truth, justice, honor, demand that Colombia's claims be satisfied; and the Congress and people of this country owe it to themselves to satisfy those claims in a manner consistent with the dignity of the United States, and in keeping with its glorious traditions.

The committee thereupon proceeded to the consideration of executive business.

EXHIBIT E.

PAYMENT TO PANAMA.

DOCUMENTS IN TREASURY DEPARTMENT, ETC., RELATING TO PAYMENT OF $10,000,000 TO REPUBLIC OF PANAMA.

WASHINGTON, *June 6, 1910.*

To the honorable the SECRETARY OF THE TREASURY,
Washington, D. C.

SIR: I have the honor to request that you furnish me with a copy of the report made by Messrs. J. P. Morgan & Co., as fiscal agents of the United States, in the matter of the payment of the $40,000,000 of the Panama Canal purchase.

I also have the honor to apply for permission to inspect the records and documents in the possession of the Treasury Department bearing upon this matter and upon the payment of the $10,000,000 to the Republic of Panama.

In order to avoid any misunderstanding, I beg to say that the request made some time ago through Mr. Dunlap, the Washington correspondent of the World, was simply for an exact account of the figures that the transaction covered in the turning over of the $40,000,000 by Secretary Shaw to J. P. Morgan & Co., as fiscal agents, early in May, 1904. This was a request for the amounts of money checked out from the various United States depositories and turned over to the subtreasury to make up the $40,000,000 which the Treasury was to turn over to Mr. Morgan. When this information was given us, it was in exact figures, and on receiving it the managing editor wrote to Mr. Dunlap that it was satisfactorily done. That recommendation covered the one single transaction. What I am now asking for is the report made by Messrs. Morgan & Co., as fiscal agents of the United States, in this matter. This report has not, as far as I am aware, been published; and in reference to it and to the other documents I desire to inspect, I beg to recall that President Roosevelt wrote (message to Congress, Dec. 15, 1908; letter to Mr. Foulke, Dec. 1, 1908), as follows:

"All of these documents which possessed any importance as illustrating any feature of the transaction have already been made public. There remains a great mass of documents of little or no importance which the administration is entirely willing to have published, but which, because of their mass and pointlessness, nobody has ever cared to publish. If you or Mr. Smith or Mr. Booth Tarkington or Mr. George Ade—in short, if any reputatble man—will come on here, he shall have free access to these documents and can look over everything himself."

Should you grant me the permission hereby applied for, I shall, of course, make the inspection at times convenient to the Department of the Treasury and in company with a representative of the department. The papers will be carefully handled and replaced, and any extracts or copies made from them will be made in duplicate and one of the duplicates, initialed by me, left with the department, and by reference identifying the papers or books from which the extract or copy was taken. The above being the conditions imposed by the War Department for an inspection of what records they have bearing on the matter.

Awaiting the honor of a favorable reply, I beg to subscribe myself, Mr. Secretary,

Your obedient servant, ——— ———.

June 18, 1910.

To the honorable the Secretary of the Treasury,
Washington, D. C.

Sir: I have the honor to request that you furnish me with certified copies of the documents bearing upon the payment of the $40.000,000 to the Panama Canal companies in the spring of 1904, which I picked out from the files placed at my disposal by Dr. Miller, Chief of the Bureau of Bookkeeping and Warrants, under instructions from you through Mr. Bailey.

I also beg that you will be so good as to add to the above certified copies of the two receipts turned in by Morgan, and showing that 128,600,000 francs were paid through the Bank of France, to Monsieur Pierre Gautron, liquidator of the old Panama Canal company, and 77,400,000 through the Bank of France to Messrs. Marius Bo and Georges Martin for the New Panama Canal Co.

Permit me, Mr. Secretary, to express my very great appreciation for the courtesy shown me by employees of the Treasury Department; and, again thanking you,

I beg to subscribe myself, your obedient servant,

——— ———.

I, Henry Noble Hall, a staff correspondent of the New York World, residing at 220 West Twenty-first Street, in the city of New York, in the United States of America, make oath and declare as follows:

That on the 15th day of December, in the year 1908, Mr. Theodore Roosevelt, then President of the United States, in a message to the Congress of the United States, made grave charges against the New York World and its editor and proprietor, Mr. Joseph Pulitzer, in connection with a series of articles published in the New York World respecting the Panama Canal purchase and the Panama revolution.

That, as President of the United States, Mr. Roosevelt in terms charged that "the stories are scurrilous and libelous in character and false in every particular"; that the statements "are false in every particular from beginning to end"; that "the wickedness of the slanders is only surpassed by their fatuity"; that the stories were so utterly baseless that "they represent in part merely material collected for campaign purposes and in part stories originally concocted with a view of possible blackmail."

That President Roosevelt forwarded to Congress with the message above referred to and as part of the same message a number of documents bearing upon the payment of $40,000,000 to the French Panama Canal Co. and upon the payment of $10,000,000 to the Republic of Panama, and a letter written by him to Mr. Foulk under date of December 1, 1908, in which he says:

"All of these documents that possessed any importance as illustrating any feature of the transaction have already been made public. There remains a great mass of documents of little or no importance which the administration is entirely willing to have published, but which, because of their mass and pointlessness, nobody has ever cared to publish. Any reputable man can have full access to these documents. If you or Mr. Smith or Mr. Booth Tarkington or Mr. George Ade—in short, if any reputable man—will come on here he shall have free access to these documents and can look over everything for himself."

That the New York World and Mr. Joseph Pulitzer, in order to establish the truth and arrive at the real facts, instructed me to inquire into and report upon this matter.

That under date of June 6, 1910, I made application to the honorable the Secretary of the Treasury for permission to inspect the records and documents in the possession of the Treasury Department bearing upon these matters and to make any extracts or copies therefrom that might assist me in arriving at the truth.

That under date of June 10, 1910, Mr. R. O. Bailey, private secretary to the honorable the Secretary of the Treasury, wrote, informing me that I would "be permitted to inspect the said accounts by applying to the department in person";

That by virtue of this authority the records and documents in the possession of the Treasury Department bearing upon this matter were placed at my disposal by Dr. Miller, Chief of the Bureau of Bookkeeping and Warrants, and that I made notes of their contents; and that from the documents dealing with the payment of $40,000,000 to the French canal companies, I laid aside, for the purpose of obtaining copies thereof, the requisition of the Auditor of the State and Other Departments of May 9, 1904, for $40,000,000; the letter of President Roosevelt of May 6, 1904, directing payment of the $40,000,000; the letter of May 6, 1904, from the Secretary of the Treasury to the Auditor of the State and Other Departments; the appointment of Messrs. J. P. Morgan & Co. as special disbursing agents of the United States Treasury, and their acceptance of the same, both dated May 9, 1904; the letter of assistant treasurer at New York to the Secretary of the Treasurer concerning the deposit by Morgan & Co. of $25,000,000 security; the letter of the Attorney-General of September 20, 1904, transmitting, at the request of the Auditor of the State and Other Departments, copies of an agreement between the United States and the French Panama Canal companies; and a letter to Messrs. J. P. Morgan & Co. and their reply; and copies of said documents; and two letters from J. P. Morgan & Co. to Hamilton Fish, assistant treasurer at New York, one of May 26, 1904, as a sample of the method of reporting progress of the payment, and one of June 27, 1904, advising of the final payment of the $40,000,000;

That, at the request of the chief clerk of the Treasury Department, I made formal application, under date of June 18, in writing, for certified copies of the above-mentioned documents and also for certified copies of the two receipts turned in by Morgan & Co., and showing that 128,600,000 francs was paid through the Bank of France to Monsieur Pierre Gautron, liquidator of the old Panama Canal company, and 77,400,000 francs through the Bank of France to Messrs. Marius Bo and George Martin for the new Panama Canal company;

That, under Rule IX of the Regulations of the Treasury Department, I solemnly affirm and declare that the New York World and Mr. Joseph Pulitzer desire the above-mentioned certified copies of the original public records now in the Treasury Department for the purpose of establishing the true facts in connection with the above-mentioned transactions; and

That I am duly authorized to make said application for and on behalf of the New York World and Mr. Joseph Pulitzer.

——— ———.

STATE OF NEW YORK,
City and County of New York, ss:

Before me personally appeared, this 23d day of June, 1910, Henry Noble Hall, to me known and known to me to be the person who signed the above affidavit, who swears that the foregoing statements are true.

——— ———,
Notary Public.

I, Robert Hunt Lyman, assistant managing editor of the New York World, of No. 204 West Seventieth Street, New York City, do hereby certify that Henry Noble Hall, a staff correspondent of the New York World, is the duly authorized representative of the New York World entrusted with the assignment of securing the facts relative to the purchase of the Panama Canal, etc., as indicated in the attached affidavit made by him in New York on this day.

——— ———.

Dated the 23d day of June, 1910.

STATE OF NEW YORK,
City and County of New York, ss:

Before me personally appeared this 23d day of June, 1910, Robert Hunt Lyman, to me known and known to me to be the person who executed the above affidavit, who swears that the foregoing statement is true.

——— ———,
Notary Public.

TREASURY DEPARTMENT,
Washington, August 26, 1910.

Mr. HENRY N. HALL,
Washington Bureau, New York World, Washington, D. C.

SIR: Replying to the request contained in your letter of June 18, 1910, supported by your affidavit, dated August 10, 1910, there are transmitted herewith certified copies of certain additional documents relating to the Panama Canal payments.

The reply of the Secretary of State to a letter from the Secretary of the Treasury to the Secretary of State, dated February 24, 1904, and the opinion of the Attorney General on certain phases of the subject can not be located on the files of the Treasury Department.

By direction of the Secretary.

Respectfully,

A. PIATT ANDREW,
Assistant Secretary.

UNITED STATES OF AMERICA,
TREASURY DEPARTMENT,
August 26, 1910.

Pursuant to section 882 of the Revised Statutes I hereby certify that the annexed letters relating to the Panama Canal payments in 1904 are true copies of the originals which are on file in this department.

In witness whereof, I have hereunto set my hand, and caused the seal of the Treasury Department to be affixed, on the day and year first above written.

[SEAL.]

A. PIATT ANDREW,
Assistant Secretary of the Treasury.

WASHINGTON, *December 16, 1903.*

The honorable the SECRETARY OF THE TREASURY.

SIR: I have the honor to inclose for your information copy of a note from the minister of Panama at this capital in which he advised the department that Messrs. J. P. Morgan & Co., of New York, have been appointed financial agents of the Republic of Panama for one year, with the full and exclusive power to collect for the account of that Republic any sum the Government of the United States may have to pay to Panama for any cause whatsoever.

I have the honor to be, sir, your obedient servant,

ALVEY A. ADEE, *Acting Secretary.*

LEGACION DE LA REPUBLICA DE PANAMA, EN WASHINGTON,
Washington, D. C., December 10, 1903.

His Excellency JOHN HAY,
Secretary of State, Washington.

SIR: I think it is necessary, in view of the ratification of the Canal treaty by the Government of the Republic of Panama, and in view of the steps taken by His Excellency the President of the United States for the ratification by the Government of the United States, to inform you of the name of the banking house that has been designated by the financial agents of the Republic of Panama in the United States.

I have therefore the honor, sir, to notify you, and through you his excellency the Secretary of the Treasury, that by letter dated November 17, 1903, and in virtue of the full power given me by my Government in fiscal questions, I have named the firm of J. P. Morgan & Co. the financial agents of the Republic of Panama for one year, with the full and exclusive power to collect for the account of the Republic of Panama any sum the Government of the United States may have to pay the Republic of Panama for any cause whatsoever.

It goes without saying that the Government of the Republic of Panama will notify the Government of the United States in due time, and previously to the collection by Messrs. J. P. Morgan & Co., the amount that the Government of the Republic intends to withdraw from the United States Treasury on the sums placed to its disposition according to the conventions in force.

I am, sir, with great respect, your obedient servant,

P. BUNEAU VARILLA.

DEPARTMENT OF STATE,
Washington, February 24, 1904.

The honorable the SECRETARY OF THE TREASURY.

SIR: By Article XIV of the treaty of November 18, 1903, between the United States and the Republic of Panama for the construction of an interoceanic canal, to the ratification of which the Senate gave its advice and consent on the 23d instant, the United States agrees to pay to the Republic of Panama "the sum of $10,000,000 in gold coin of the United States on the exchange of the ratification of the convention."

Arrangements have been made with the Panama minister for the exchange of the ratification of the convention on Friday, the 26th instant. By direction of the Secretary of State, I have the honor to inquire whether your department is prepared, under the act of Congress approved June 28, 1902 (Stat. L., vol. 32, pt. 1, pp. 481 et seq.), to furnish him with a draft for the sum stated to hand to the minister at the time of exchange, or whether he shall say to the minister that the payment will be made in a few days.

I have the honor to be, sir, your obedient servant,

ALVEY A. ADEE,
Acting Secretary.

TREASURY DEPARTMENT,
OFFICE OF THE SECRETARY,
Washington, February 24, 1904.

MY DEAR MR. SECRETARY: I am in receipt of your letter of the 24th instant, asking whether the Treasury Department is prepared to pay to the Republic of Panama the sum of $10,000,000 on Friday, the 26th instant.

In answer, I beg to advise that the department is prepared to make the payment whenever the Attorney General shall give an opinion that the act approved June 28, 1902, authorizes the payment to the Republic of Panama.

The act referred to in terms directs the payment to be made to the Republic of Colombia. I call attention to this fact, not for the purpose of throwing a doubt upon the subject, but to call attention to what is at least a technical variance. I prefer, in any event, not to make the payment before Monday, the 28th instant.

Yours, very truly,
L. M. SHAW.

The honorable the SECRETARY OF STATE.

TREASURY DEPARTMENT,
OFFICE OF THE SECRETARY,
Washington, March 2, 1904.

MY DEAR MR. SECRETARY: On December 16, 1903, the Acting Secretary of State, Mr. Adee, wrote me that the minister of Panama had advised the department that Messrs. J. P. Morgan & Co., of New York, had been appointed financial agents, with full and exclusive power to collect for the account of that Republic any sum the Government of the United States may have to pay to Panama for any cause whatsoever. Possibly the letter from the minister, a copy of which was inclosed, is sufficient authority for the payment to Mr. Morgan. I did not have the letter in mind at our interview yesterday.

Very truly, yours,

L. M. SHAW.

The honorable the SECRETARY OF STATE.

[Personal and confidential.]

TREASURY DEPARTMENT,
OFFICE OF THE SECRETARY,
Washington, March 3, 1904.

MY DEAR MR. SECRETARY: I am prepared this morning to draw a Treasury warrant for the money to be paid to Panama under the provisions of the canal treaty. Shall I make it payable to you or to J. P. Morgan & Co., and shall I draw it in one warrant for $10,000,000, or 10 warrants of $1,000,000 each? I shall be very glad to arrange the transaction in a way most satisfactory to all concerned.

Very truly, yours, L. M. SHAW.

Hon. JOHN HAY,
Secretry of State.

DEPARTMENT OF STATE,
Washington, March 3, 1904.

DEAR MR. SECRETARY: I think the draft might better be made payable to J. P. Morgan & Co., financial agents of the Republic of Panama, and the warrant may as well be for the whole $10,000,000. The Panama minister, who has just this moment left me, thinks he would prefer to telegraph his Government for positive authority to receive the money and deposit it with Morgan, and has probably done so; but, if you think proper, you can make out the warrant for the entire sum and place it in my hands for delivery to the proper person, and if he does not receive it immediately it can be deposited in the safe of the Department of State until delivered.

Very sincerely, yours, JOHN HAY.

The Hon. L. M. SHAW,
Secretary of the Treasury.

DEPARTMENT OF STATE,
Washington, April 26, 1904.

The honorable the SECRETARY OF THE TREASURY.

SIR: It would oblige the Government of the Republic of Panama if this Government, as a special favor, would make payment of the $10,000,000 due the Panama Government by virtue of the Isthmian Canal treaty in the following manner:

One million to be paid to J. P. Morgan & Co., the financial agents of the Republic of Panama, and the rest to be held until the arrival of the newly appointed minister, who leaves for Washington by the first steamer in June.

If you prefer to name payment of the entire sum at once, I would suggest that you give me two drafts on the Treasury, payable to me on account of the Republic of Panama, one being for the sum of one million and the other for nine millions. In that case I could deposit with J. P. Morgan & Co. the one million and retain the check for nine millions until called for by the minister of Panama. If, however, you should for any reason prefer to pay the one million now and retain the nine millions until the arrival of the minister, that course will be equally satisfactory to this department.

I am, sir, very sincerely, yours, JOHN HAY.

TREASURY DEPARTMENT,
OFFICE OF THE SECRETARY,
Washington, April 29, 1904.

MY DEAR SIR: I have the honor to transmit herewith Treasury settlement warrant No. 4674, payable to the Republic of Panama, J. Pierpont Morgan & Co., financial agents, for $1,000,000.

Very truly, yours,

L. M. SHAW.

The honorable the SECRETARY OF STATE.

DEPARTMENT OF STATE,
Washington, April 29, 1904.

The honorable the SECRETARY OF THE TREASURY.

SIR: I have the honor to request that payment of $1,000,000 be made to Messrs. J. Pierpont Morgan & Co., the financial agents of the Republic of Panama, New York City, in part payment of the amount now due the Republic of Panama under the provisions of an act to provide for the temporary government of the Canal Zone at Panama, approved April 28, 1904, the remainder of the appropriation of $10,000,000 to be held until the arrival here of the new minister from the Republic of Panama, who is expected to arrive in June next.

Please mail to my address the warrant issued in favor of J. Pierpont Morgan & Co.

I am, sir, your obedient servant, JOHN HAY.

WHITE HOUSE, *April 29, 1904.*

Approved.

THEODORE ROOSEVELT.

[Indorsement.]

TREASURY DEPARTMENT, *April 29, 1904.*

Respectfully referred to the Auditor for State and other departments for statement of account in favor of the Republic of Panama in the sum of $10,000,000, in pursuance of treaty stipulations and in accordance with the provisions of an act of Congress "to provide for the construction of a canal connecting the waters of the Atlantic and Pacific Oceans," approved June 28, 1902, as amended by an act "to provide for the temporary government of the Canal Zone at Panama, the protection of the canal works, and for other purposes," approved April 28, 1904; a warrant for $1,000,000 to be issued to the Republic of Panama, J. Pierpont Morgan & Co., financial agents, New York, and delivered to the Secretary of State, and the balance to remain subject to future directions, as indicated herein.

L. M. SHAW, *Secretary.*

DEPARTMENT OF STATE,
Washington, May 19, 1904.

The honorable the SECRETARY OF THE TREASURY.

SIR: Referring to my letter of this morning requesting that a warrant be issued in favor of the Panama Government through its fiscal agents, J. P. Morgan & Co., for the payment of $9,000,000 due the Panama Government, I am directed by the President to ask that this warrant be executed and forwarded immediately to this department.

I have the honor to be, sir, your obedient servant,

FRANCIS B. LOOMIS,
Acting Secretary.

DEPARTMENT OF STATE,
Washington, May 19, 1904.

The honorable the SECRETARY OF THE TREASURY.

SIR: I have the honor to request that payment of $9,000,000 be made to Messrs. J. Pierpont Morgan & Co., the fiscal agents of the Republic of Panama, New York City, the warrant to be drawn to the order of the Republic of Panama, J. P. Morgan & Co., fiscal agents, the same being the balance due the Republic of Panama, under the provisions of an act to provide for the temporary government of the Canal Zone at Panama, approved April 28, 1904.

I am, sir, your obedient servant,

FRANCIS B. LOOMIS,
Acting Secretary of State.

WHITE HOUSE, *May 19, 1904.*

Approved:

THEODORE ROOSEVELT.

Please deliver the warrant to Mr. Morrison of this department.

[Department of Justice. File No. 10,963. Inclosed in Department of Justice envelope which bears among other indications: "Copy of proposed opinion to Secretary of State on payment of $10,000,000 to Panama."]

DEPARTMENT OF JUSTICE,
Washington, February 26, 1904.

The SECRETARY OF STATE, *Washington, D. C.*

SIR: In answer to your request for an opinion to be given to the Secretary of the Treasury or to yourself as to whether he can pay to the Republic of Panama the ten millions of dollars stipulated for in the treaty about to be ratified, or whether I think further legislation by Congress is required, I have to say:

Section 2 of the act to provide for the construction of an Isthmian Canal authorizes the President, when he shall have arranged to secure a satisfactory title to the property of the new Panama Canal Co., and shall have obtained by treaty control of the necessary territory from the Republic of Colombia, to pay for the property of the company $40,000,000, and to the Republic of Colombia such sum as shall have been agreed upon, the money being thereby appropriated for these purposes.

In view of this section and of the treaty about to be ratified I do not think that further legislation is necessary and I regard such legislation as inadvisable.

The treaty provides for payment to Panama "on the exchange of the ratifications of this convention." I do not understand this to mean that actual payment must be made at the moment of the exchange of ratifications and as part of such exchange; but if the representatives of Panama insist that it shall be, it is possible to postpone for a few days such exchange.

The arrangement to secure a satisfactory title may require a few days to complete.

Respectfully,

——— ———,
Acting Attorney General.

[Confidential dispatch from W. W. Russell, United States minister to Panama, to Mr. Hay, Secretary of State.]

PANAMA, *May 24, 1904.*

SIR: I have the honor to inform you that in accordance with your cabled instructions of the 20th instant, which instructions were read both to the president and to the minister of foreign affairs and copies left with each, I now have the honor to inclose a copy with translation of the reply to said cable handed to me by the secretary of foreign affairs.

[Translation.]

The secretary of government of the Republic of Panama has the honor to inform the honorable chargé d'affaires ad interim of the United States of

America, that the President of the Republic has been advised of the contents of the cablegram which he was pleased to deliver to him personally, dated yesterday, and signed by his excellency the Acting Secretary of State, in which cablegram the Government of the United States of America sets forth divers opinions in relation to the naming of Messrs. J. P. Morgan & Co. as financial agents of the Republic, and concerning request made by my Government to the United States to delay the payment of the balance of nine millions due according to the canal treaty between the two Governments until the arrival at Washington of the special commissioners named by Panama to receive and invest the said millions; and concluding with the resolve to pay over the said sum to the above-mentioned J. P. Morgan & Co., because this action was considered more convenient by the Government of the United States.

In the face of these positive declarations, which have since become accomplished facts, there remains to the President of the Republic no other course but to accept the situation.

Likewise the Republic of Panama has been advised of the desire of the Government of the United States that my Government should carry out the confidential and spontaneous declaration made by the junta of the provisional government that not less than eight million of dollars should be invested in a secure manner in order to secure the finances of the Republic. This declaration the President would have carried out had not the national convention, as a sovereign body, in actual session, reduced the before-mentioned sum to six millions in accordance with article 138 of the constitution.

[Department of Justice. File 10963. No. 37152.]

SULLIVAN & CROMWELL,
New York, May 24, 1904.

Hon. P. C. KNOX,
Attorney General,
Department of Justice, Washington, D. C.

MY DEAR SIR: I thank you for your prompt reference of this subject to the Isthmian Canal Commission, for report upon the facts of the case, and I have already received a note from the chairman of the commission officially taking up the matter. I know that the company will be gratified at the promptness with which this matter has received attention.

The Panama Fiscal Commission will arrive here to-night or to-morrow. Mr. Perkins and I have been in close conference upon the subject and are in full sympathy with the sound advice you gave me on Friday.

These matters may call me to Washington within a few days, when I will call upon you; but I again beg leave to repeat that I am at your call by telephone or telegram upon any subject whatever concerning the canal company, the railroad company, or other Isthmian matters,

Yours, truly,

WM. NELSON CROMWELL,
General Counsel.

[Department of Justice. File 10963-02. No. 37151.]

SULLIVAN & CROMWELL,
New York, May 26, 1904.

MY DEAR MR. ATTORNEY GENERAL: I confirm the telegram which I sent you as follows:

"Bearing in mind your good advice at our conference last Friday, I think it will interest you to know that the Republic of Panama, by official decree of the 17th instant, appointed me counsel to the special fiscal commission, which arrived yesterday and was to-day organized in my office, which it has made its headquarters. It shall be my endeavor to discharge our duties to the Republic in such manner as to justify the full confidence of the Government."

I have fully explained to the commission the reasons of state which influenced the Government in making payment to the fiscal agent of the balance of $9,000,000.

The commission have formally organized under the title of "Special Fiscal Commission of the Republic of Panama," with offices in this building, and we have commenced our duties.

I shall bear in mind the wise words of the President and yourself upon this subject.

Faithfully, yours, WM. NELSON CROMWELL.

EXHIBIT F.

WILLIAM NELSON CROMWELL.

EXTRACTS FROM THE HEARINGS HAD BEFORE THE COMMITTEE ON INTEROCEANIC CANALS RELATIVE TO THE REFUSAL OF WILLIAM NELSON CROMWELL TO ANSWER CERTAIN QUESTIONS.

[Senate document No. 457, Fifty-ninth Congress, first session.]

On his motion to require the witness, William Nelson Cromwell, to answer each and every one of the questions set forth in Exhibit A, hereto attached, the undersigned, a member of the Committee on Interoceanic Canals, respectfully submits to the committee the following as the ground of his motion:

On the questions of law that arise on the facts herein set forth, the undersigned submits the following:

[Memorandum.]

AS TO PRIVILEGE OF COUNSEL NOT TO TESTIFY WHEN CALLED AS A WITNESS.

(1) The privilege of counsel in regard to not testifying as to matters occurring between a client and himself is based on the policy of the law to protect inviolate communications made by a client to his attorney in order to get the benefit of legal assistance. The privilege is that of the client, not of the attorney. While the attorney is not required or permitted to reveal communications, verbal or written, made by the client to him, nor to produce documents belonging to his client, he is not exempted from the obligation of testifying as to his own acts. The privilege is strictly limited to cases coming within the principle on which it is based. There is no element of "confidential communication" in the acts done by an attorney in executing the business of his client. If the nature of the employment of the attorney requires him to communicate to others the business of the client and to conduct negotiations to prepare documents of a public nature, such as charters of incorporation, obviously the element of confidence is eliminated.

(2) Neither does the principle apply to acts done by an attorney in the conduct of a business in which he is interested. The papers submitted show that the witness repeatedly refused to answer questions as to acts done by him, propositions submitted to others, character of documents prepared, and as to the distribution of documents thereto. These acts can not be brought within the principle of the ———— granted in cases of "privileged communications."

The following cases show how strictly the rule is limited in its application:

(3) The fact that a witness is one of the attorneys in the case is no ground for refusal to testify unless the question asked tends directly to elicit some disclosure of a privileged communication between attorney and client.

(Amer. Ency. of Law, vol. 23, p. 58.)

(4) As the privilege has a tendency to prevent the full disclosure of the truth, it should be limited to cases which are strictly within the principles of the policy which gave birth to it.

Satterlee *v.* Bliss, 36 Cal., 489.
Turner's Appeal, 72 Conn., 305.
Goltra *v.* Wolcott, 14 Ill., 89.
Gower *v.* Emery, 18 Me., 79.
Hatton *v.* Robinson, 14 Pick., 416.
Beeson *v.* Beeson, 9 Pa. St., 279.

"The appellant is under a mistake in supposing that an attorney or counsel is privileged of answering as to everything which comes to his knowledge while he is acting as attorney or counsel. The privilege only extends to information derived from his client as such, either by oral communications or from books or papers shown him by his client or placed in his hands in his character of attorney or counsel. Information derived from other persons or sources, although such information is obtained while acting as attorney or counsel, is not privileged."

Spenceley *v.* Schulenburgh, 7 East, 357.
Crosby *v.* Berger, 11 Paige, 377.
Stoney *v.* McNeill, 18 Am. Dec., 666.

(5) It is not sufficient for the attorney in invoking the privilege to state that the information came somehow to him while acting for the client, nor that it came from some particular third person (not an agent) for the benefit of the client.

(4 Wigmore on Evidence, sec. 2317.)

(6) The privilege does not extend to every fact which the attorney may learn in the course of his employment. There is a difference in principle between communications made by the client and acts done by him in the presence of the attorney. It may be, and undoubtedly is, sound policy to close the attorney's mouth in relation to the former, while in many cases it would be grossly immoral to do so in relation to the latter.

(Coveney *v.* Tannahill, 1 Hill, 33.)

(7) The right of an attorney to refuse to disclose matters with which he has become acquainted in the course of his employment as such does not extend to matters of fact which he knows by any other means than confidential communication with his client, though if he had not been employed as attorney he might not have known them.

(Weeks on Attorneys at Law, sec. 179.)

(8) There is no privilege where the attorney is himself a party to the transaction or agreement which he is called upon to disclose.

Am. Enc. of Law, vol. 23, p. 76.
Jeans *v.* Fridenberg, 3 Pa. L. J. Rep., 199.
Ethier *v.* Homier, 18 L. C. Jur., 83.
Weeks on Attorneys at Law, sec. 179, p. 375.
Rochester *v.* Bank, 5 How. Pr., 259, 261.
Brown *v.* Foster, 1 Hurl. & N., 736.

In general a strict construction is the proper one, especially in those cases where attorneys combine the occupation of real estate and insurance brokers or act also as executive officers of a corporate business.

(4 Wigmore on Evidence, sec. 2297.)

It is also respectfully submitted that the statements and bearing of the witness on his examination show that his attempt to conceal the facts as to which the questions were propounded to him was not in fact based upon his alleged privilege, or that of the New Panama Canal Co., of withholding those facts from exposure because they were confidential communications between attorney and client, or because a knowledge of them was obtained while the witness was acting as counsel for the Panama Canal Co., but the alleged privilege was resorted to for the purpose of concealing his acts and his dealings conducted on his own account. The refusal of the witness to answer questions because they were impertinent or irrelevant or were not within the purview of the subject that the committee had the power to examine are set forth in Exhibit A, hereto, and need not be restated in this motion.

As to the limitation of time, insisted upon in his objections, within which the investigation by the committee is limited, it is insisted that there is no such limitation in the resolution of the Senate. That inquiry is required to be as broad and as searching as is necessary to show the conduct and character of any person engaged in the employment of the Government in connection with its operations in carrying on the construction of the Panama Canal. The President in his message and the Senate in its response thereto did not undertake to limit the inquiry into the conduct of William Nelson Cromwell or any other person or as to the qualifications and fitness for such employment to a period of time since the canal work and property and the property of the Panama Railroad Co. was turned over to the United States.

This was the first point the witness presented in his statement to the committee. He had thought it over and came prepared to resist any question as to his acts prior to that date in connecton with the Panama Canal Co. There is no statute of limitation on any proper inquiry into the character and qualification of any person who holds a fiduciary relation toward the Government of the

United States. In the case of this witness such relations are and have been so numerous and important in connection with the entire history of the Panama Canal that his conduct and his character are parts of that history, and it is impossible to separate him from it at any designated period of time. But it is unquestionable, as a rule of law, that the witness, having been called to testify as to his own conduct and that of other persons in connection with matters relating to the Panama Canal that include the question of his fitness for the places he now holds, like a party testifying in his own defense, or to support his own cause, is subject to examination as to all matters that bear upon the subject even in a remote degree.

The witness Cromwell, whose refusal to answer questions set forth in the paper hereto attached, marked "Exhibit A," was duly sworn to make true answers to such questions as should be propounded to him by the committee of the Senate on Interoceanic Canals, or by any member thereof, and was examined on the 26th, 27th, and 28th days of February and on the 1st and 2d days of March, 1906, and on May 9 and 11.

His personal knowledge of the matters to which the subjoined questions related that were put to him was not denied by him. The facts disclosed by him on his statements before the committee show his intimate acquaintance with the conduct of the affairs and business transactions of the New Panama Canal Co. and its connection with the old or former Panama Canal Co., to which it became the successor, and with the business and affairs of the Panama Railroad companies since 1893.

The old company had purchased about 69,000 shares of the 70,000 shares of the stock of the Panama Railroad Co., of the face value of $100 each, and turned over these shares and the concession from Colombia, of railroad and other privileges and property it owned, to the New Panama Canal Co., which was created and organized under decrees of a court in France, to take over the concessions and property of the old company under an agreement to complete the canal at Panama.

The railroad company thus placed within the control and direction of the New Panama Canal Co. was chartered by the laws of the State of New York, to build, own, and operate a railroad in the State of Panama, then a Province of Colombia, on a line or route extending across the Isthmus, from the waters of the Atlantic to the waters of the Pacific Ocean, under concessions from the Republic of Colombia.

In view of the general and intimate knowledge of the history and transactions of the old and new canal companies, having been general counsel of the Panama Railroad Co. since 1893, which office he still holds, and of the New Panama Canal Co., which office he still holds; and having been a stockholder and director of the railroad company since 1893, both of which relations still continue; and having been general counsel of the Republic of Panama, representing it in a diplomatic sense in making agreements with the President of the United States while he still held his offices and relations above stated; and being the fiscal agent of the Republic of Panama in control of certain large investments in bonds and stocks held in the United States; and being the counsel of the legation of Panama to the United States, all of which offices and appointments he still holds; and being the confidential adviser and informant of the Secretary of War and of the President of the United States in very important affairs relating to the Panama Railroad and the conduct of all the operations of the Government in the Canal Zone connected with the organization of the forces and the qualification of appointees for doing the work of construction, sanitation, and preparation; and having been actively engaged, at the request of this Government, in making agreements with the Government of Panama for changes in the postal affairs of the United States and Panama; and in enacting a tariff law for the Canal Zone; and in arranging with bankers of Panama for supplying coin for the payment of officers, clerks, and laborers who were doing service in Panama for the United States; and in making agreements with Panama in reference to supplying food for persons so employed; and in many other matters disclosed in Cromwell's testimony, it was the right of the undersigned to question the witness, as the witness, as a witness produced by the Government, as to his knowledge of the affairs with which he was familiar.

The resolution of the Senate, under which the committee is taking testimony, is as follows:

"*Resolved*, That the Committee on Interoceanic Canals or any subcommittee thereof be, and are hereby, authorized and directed to investigate all matters relating to the Panama Canal and the government of the Canal Zone and the management of the Panama Railroad Company, to send for persons and papers and to administer oaths and employ a stenographer to report such hearings; and that the committee be authorized to sit during the sessions or recess of the Senate, and that all expenses thereof be paid out of the contingen fund of the Senate."

This resolution is broad and also specific. It seems needless to discuss the point that every question asked Cromwell is covered by the resolution of the Senate. This action of the Senate was taken in response to the message of the President of January 8, 1906, in which he says:

"The zeal, intelligence, and efficient public service of the Isthmian Commission and its subordinates are noteworthy. I want the fullest, most exhaustive, and most searching investigation of any act of theirs, and if any one of them is ever shown to have done wrong, his punishment shall be exemplary."

This is more than a request. It is a demand and a challenge. Mr. Wallace was called as a witness and proceeded to give his testimony on all points that the committee thought relevant to his conduct as chief engineer, as to which he had been severely criticized in an interview of the Secretary of War, published in the newspapers. In his explanation Wallace made statements respecting the conduct of Cromwell toward him in his official and personal conduct, relating to the canal. Cromwell in his deposition contradicted statements made by Wallace and presented letters and made statements with the evident purpose of impeaching the testimony of Wallace.

This effort at impeachment brought the conduct of Cromwell and his character into question, especially in his connection with the Panama Railroad and the Panama Canal Co., and the questions asked him that he refused to answer were in point as to his character for honesty and for truth and veracity, and were relevant, on that ground, to the inquiry that the Senate instructed the committee to conduct.

In answer to the questions 51 to 54 in the exhibit hereto attached Cromwell states the fact that he was the sole negotiator, representing the canal company in the sale of its property to the United States in 1904, and that said contract included the prior negotiation which was conducted in 1902. The minute books of the railroad company show two instances of unjust and covinous conduct in which Cromwell participated, by which the United States was deprived of several hundred thousand dollars. One of these transactions was in declaring and paying dividends to the stockholders of the railroad company in excess of the receipts for the preceding fiscal year, and the other was in relation to the repairs on two ships, whereby a heavy debt was imposed unjustly upon the United States in the purchase of the railroad, all of which is shown by the records of the hearings before this committee and need not be repeated on this motion.

Other matters relating to the ambidextrous and fraudulent dealing of Cromwell with Colombia and with the Government of the United States, in his double capacity of general counsel for the Panama Canal Co. and of the Panama Railroad Co., are strongly suggested and indicated by the statements of himself and others that are set forth in these hearings. It is those matters and his participation in the Hay-Varilla treaty that he attempts to conceal by his refusal to answer questions propounded to him on his examination, under the false pretense that his duty to his alleged client—the Panama Canal Co.—requires him to make such refusal.

The facts that appear in the record invalidate these excuses and will be hereinafter more fully stated in this motion, which is that the witness Cromwell be required by the committee to answer the questions set forth in the exhibit hereto. The witness now holds the official relation to the United States of stockholder and director in the Panama Railroad Co. and member of the executive committee of the board of directors and also that of general counsel of said company.

The importance of this railroad to the work of constructing the canal and in providing it with almost the entire material and supplies for that work, and in transporting commerce between the Atlantic and Pacific Oceans, is so great that it could scarcely be overstated, and if Cromwell is an unfit person to share in such powers as belong to the official relations he holds to the Panama Railroad, he being a subordinate of the Isthmian Commission, he should be removed, which would be the "exemplary punishment" that the President desires shall be visited upon such persons.

In this view of his necessary qualifications for the high fiduciary employment he holds under the Government, his character for honesty and integrity, especially in respect of his dealings with the Panama Railroad and the Panama Canal Co., is open to inquiry. Questions propounded to him as a witness, even if they impute delinquency, when character or conduct is the subject of inquiry, afford him the opportunity of vindication by his own testimony. If the answers should incriminate him, he can not refuse to answer, for the law protects him with ample safeguards against punishments unless perjury is committed in giving the answers.

Cromwell, in his meager and incautious statement of facts that seemed to add to his personal consequence and veracity in being concerned in transactions of national importance, made statements that committed him to personal dealings in respect of the property and concessions of the Panama Canal Co., on his own account and for his own benefit. When the consciousness of the effect of these disclosures was felt by him he attempted to take shelter under his alleged privileges as a lawyer, and became defiant, insulting, and recalcitrant as a witness, and his behavior under examination was that of a person detected in falsehood, who evaded and refused to answer any question asked him that tended to contradict or to explain the facts he had incautiously admitted.

His demeanor as a witness, as is shown by the record, was such as to repel confidence in his integrity.

Was he interested personally in the property and business of the New Panama Canal Co.?

In 1893 the witness Cromwell purchased shares of the stock in the Panama Railroad Co. and was appointed its general counsel, and was made a director. It was then owned, as to a majority of its stock, amounting to about 98 per cent thereof, by the New Panama Canal Co., and Cromwell was made a director at the request of M. Boyard, who was the general agent of the New Panama Canal Co. in the United States.

In 1896 Cromwell was appointed by the New Panama Canal Co. its general counsel in the United States and in Colombia. He is now a director in the railroad company and is its general counsel, and is still the general counsel of the New Panama Canal Co.

The stock of the Panama Railroad Co., acquired by the old Panama Railroad Co., was capitalized at $7,000,000 and had cost that company over $18,000,000. It was transferred by a receiver of the old company, by the order of the French court, under a conveyance in escrow, which made the railroad inalienable by the new company. It contained a provision to the effect that the new company would pay to the receiver of the old company $5,000,000 for the stock and property of the railroad company in the event that the new company, for any cause, should fail to complete the Panama Canal. The decree went into effect on October 4, 1894, and is as follows:

"The present company (the new company) shall be the owner of the property and rights granted and contributed from the date of its formal organization, except as hereinafter provided with respect to the Panama Railroad. * * *

"Third. The rights of every nature in the Panama Railroad belonging to the estate in liquidation and contributed by M. Gautron under section 4 of this article shall become the property of the present company from and after the stockholders' meeting, provided by article 75 hereof, without any pecuniary compensation, but upon the expressed condition that the canal be constructed within the time fixed by the agreement of concession. Upon default in completion within such time, said right shall revert to the estate in liquidation.

"If, contrary to all expectation, the meeting in question should not take the necessary action for the completion of the canal, or if the course of action adopted by the meeting can not be carried out, the said rights in the railroad shall remain the property of the present company (the new company); but it shall pay into the estate in liquidation the sum of 20,000,000 francs by way of indemnity, and a share of profits set apart or the estate in liquidation shall be half the profits of the present company, without other deductions than those provided in sections 2 and 3 article 53 hereof.

"Accordingly said rights shall remain inalienable in the hands of the new company until either the payment of said sum of 20,000,000 francs or the entire completion of the canal."

M. Gautron was the liquidator of the old company.

This arrangement had the effect, and it must have been so intended, to prevent Colombia from the confiscation of the railroad stock and property, in the event of the failure of the New Panama Canal Co. to work out and comply with the wise concessions granted by Colombia to the old Panama Canal Co., to execute which the New Panama Canal Co. was created and was pledged by its contract with the receiver of the old Panama Canal Co.

This property, so held under the conveyance in escrow, was to become a perfect title in the new company and without compensation when it should complete the canal under the concessions from Colombia and was to be paid for at the price of $5,000,000 to the receiver of the old company if the canal should not be completed by the new company. This transaction unified the interests of the New Panama Canal Co. with that of the stockholders of the railroad company in the question of the success or failure of the New Panama Canal Co. to complete the canal. In the event of the completion of the canal, the new canal company was to have the railroad without charge. If it failed to complete the canal, it was to have the railroad, that had cost the old company $18,000,000, on payment of $5,000,000 to the liquidation of the old company, and that would be a profit of $13,000,000 to the stockholders of the new company.

These conditions have occurred: The canal has not been completed, and the stockholders of the New Panama Canal Co. have been paid $16,000,000 for all they owned on the Isthmus, including the railroad, and the old Panama Canal Co. has been paid $24,000,000 for all the rest of the property by the United States. Of the results of the transaction, between $3,000,000 and $4,000,000 remain in the treasury of the New Panama Canal Co., and, according to Cromwell's statement, awaiting its distribution, and to that fund Cromwell says he is looking for his compensation for work done for the canal companies. His interest in that fund must be owing, in part at least, to his demands as a stockholder in the railroad.

If the canal, for any cause, should not be completed according to the concessions, it was stipulated in the decree that chartered the New Panama Canal Co. that the railroad company, chartered in New York, should have the property that had cost the old company $18,000,000 for the stock, besides all betterments and very costly improvements, and the lines of steamers bought by the new company, and all dividends which were earned by the company while the canal company controlled it, for the upset price of $5,000,000. These net dividends amounted in —— years to the sum of ————.

These facts, which are of record and have been officially reported to the Government of the United States and are of record in France, and have never been questioned or contradicted by the witness, Cromwell, as to their existence or as to the verity of any of these reports, show that the witness had a direct and personal interest in all that was done, or would be done, by the railroad company, of which he was both a stockholder and a director. And he had a direct personal interest in the contract of the old Panama Canal Co. with the New Panama Canal Co. relating to the completion of the canal by the new company.

He was not a stockholder in either of the canal companies, but he held a more advantageous position as the general counsel of both the New Panama Canal Co. and of the railroad company, and a still more personal and advantageous position as stockholder and director of the Panama Railroad.

During the years from 1893 to 1904 Cromwell was a stockholder and director of the Panama Railroad Co., which during all that period was held in the almost exclusive ownership and in the irresistible power of control over all its operations by the New Panama Canal Co., of which he was the general counsel in the United States.

It was a profitable deal that Cromwell was making out of the ownership of railroad stock, and its value in selling the canal, besides his heavy retainer, amounting to $200,000 in 10 years.

There was nothing done by him or his law partner, as general counsel, in any litigation for the canal company. They conducted no legal business in any court or before any tribunal for the New Panama Canal Co. It was all advice, influence, contrivance, and no judicial trial or controversy was in contemplation, nor did any ever take place.

It was an engagement to conduct diplomacy, promotion, and management; and in all he did or advised or influenced he was taking care of his personal interest.

He swears that "my law firm of Sullivan & Cromwell have been the general counsel of the Panama Railroad Co. for over 12 years, and of the Panama Canal Co. for 9 years" (p. 1041).

In his statement as to his employment by the New French Panama Canal Co. he swears that his employment was by Mr. Whalen, who was vice president of the Panama Railroad Co. It was in June, 1896. It was verbal, and no record of it was ever made. It was made in New York City. Cromwell was then a stockholder and director in the Panama Railroad Co., to which he was invited by Bayard, another agent of the Panama Canal Co., and the contract had been made by which the Panama Railroad was taken over by the New Panama Railroad Co. from the receiver of the old company, which owned all the 70,000 shares of $100 each, except 1,100 which were held by Cromwell and other private persons. The employment of Cromwell by Whalen, vice president of the Panama Canal Co., was an employment to take care of his own interests in both companies, as well as the interests of the New Panama Canal Co. The receiver of the old company, with the sanction of the French courts, had made such a disposition of the railroad to the new company that Cromwell, as a stockholder and director of the railroad company, was unified in his personal interests with the New Panama Canal Co., and was tied to that company beyond his power of resistance, even if he had objected to the combination of interests that the French courts had decreed.

His only way to escape that involvement was to sell his stock in the railroad company. Instead of doing that, he held onto it and continued as a director of the railroad company and its general counsel, at a salary of $3,500 per annum.

In the election of directors the New Panama Canal Co. voted its stock, through its proxy, as the United States is now doing, and its actual power to control every act of the railroad company was in the proportion of 1,100 to 5,900 shares, the whole stock being 70,000 shares. The control of the railroad was full and complete in the New Panama Canal Co., and Cromwell, as stockholder, director, and general counsel, was as completely identified with the Panama Canal Co. as if he had been a stockholder in it since 1896. When, in 1896, his law firm was employed as general counsel for the New Panama Canal Co., Cromwell had added to his income $25,000 per annum, paid by the New Panama Canal Co. Add to this his salary of $3,500 per annum, paid nominally by the railroad company, but in fact by the canal company, as owner and operator of the Panama Railroad Co., and his dividends on the stock held by him in the railroad company, and his income, all of which was taxed upon the railroad, for there were no earnings from any other source, amounted to not less than $30,000 per annum.

The purpose of his employment was distinctly aside from his services as a lawyer or legal adviser. In the legal acceptance of the character of legal counsel, Cromwell was his own lawyer, because of his personal interest in the property and in its exploitation. The New Panama Canal Co., although it had stipulated with the receiver of the old company and with the French court that it would provide the money to complete the canal, and its principal stockholders had received condonation of fines and forfeitures and of penitentiary punishments from the French Government for robberies committed on the old company in further consideration of their agreement to complete the canal, and although 5,000,000 francs of the paid-up stock of the New Panama Canal Co. was given to Colombia for a prolongation of her concessions from 1893 to 1904—a term of 10 years—and for her acceptance of the transfer of the property of the old company to the new company, including the Panama Railroad, yet the new company never raised a dollar by selling stock or by loan or subscription to complete a canal that had already cost the old company $260,000,000 and was not one-third finished.

The purpose of the employment of Cromwell as general counsel was not to assist the New Panama Canal Co. in working out its contract with Colombia to build a canal, but to get the consent of Colombia to sell-or dispose of the canal to the United States or to an American syndicate on terms that would be advantageous to the stockholders of the New Panama Canal Co. They had gained emancipation from penitentiaries and remittances of fines by making a promise to France and Colombia that they would complete the canal, and Cromwell was employed to get the consent of the Government of Colombia for a condonation of their breach of faith and of their express promises, and a further protection against the forfeiture of their charter, in which the people of Colombia had a vital interest and an intense national feeling of wrong and injustice, and their consent to extending the concessions from 1904 to 1910. This was in process of accomplishment in 1898–1900.

The plan was to induce the president of Colombia to cut off reversionary interests of the people of the state under the canal concessions by postponing the right of forfeiture, and to defy the power of congress and the people to prevent it.

When Cromwell saw the purpose of the inquiry into his conduct in this transaction he took shelter behind his alleged protection as a lawyer of the Panama Canal Co. He did not seek this shelter until it could not screen him, he having disclosed the fact that he was acting as an agent to drive a bargain with Colombia, in which he had a personal interest as owner of railroad stock and as a director of the Panama Railroad.

On page 1083 of his deposition Cromwell swears, in answer to questions as follows:

"Senator MORGAN. Did you have any powers to be operated and executed up here (the United States) in respect of Colombia, of the sort I have been mentioning?

"Mr. CROMWELL. The only subject with which I had any connection with Colombia was in regard to its permission for a transfer of the canal to the United States. The concession, you remember, Senator, prohibited the transfer to any foreign government without the permission of Colombia.

"Senator MORGAN. That was all you had to deal with?

"Mr. CROMWELL. It was prohibited, and my effort was to secure that consent.

"Senator MORGAN. I wish you would be careful to recollect about that and then state again, after recollection, whether that was all the power you had down there.

"Mr. CROMWELL. Down where?

"Senator MORGAN. In Colombia. That all the power you had down there was in dealing with the question of the transfer of the canal to the United States.

"Mr. CROMWELL. I think that is the only subject, Senator.

"Senator MORGAN. Was that subject defined in any letter of instructions to you from the canal company?

"Mr. CROMWELL. What subject?

"Senator MORGAN. The one you just answered about. You know the question: now answer it, please.

"Mr. CROMWELL. I do not recall any specific letter on that subject, Senator.

"Senator MORGAN. Was it defined in any resolution of the board of directors of the Panama Canal Co.?

"Mr. CROMWELL. I do not know.

"Senator MORGAN. You do not know?

"Mr. CROMWELL. No, sir.

"Senator MORGAN. And you have never known?

"Mr. CROMWELL. I never have known."

Cromwell, on page 1081 of the hearings, had stated and defined the nature and extent of his employment by the New Panama Canal Co., for service in Colombia, as follows:

"Senator MORGAN. You were to represent the company in Colombia and in the United States?

"Mr. CROMWELL. Yes, sir.

"Senator MORGAN. In what matters were you to represent the company?

"Mr. CROMWELL. In its general interests.

"Senator MORGAN. Without limitation or qualification?

"Mr. CROMWELL. Such as would arise. I had no specifications.

"Senator MORGAN. Did you have charge of any diplomatic relations with Colombia?

"Mr. CROMWELL. In behalf of the canal company?

"Senator MORGAN. Yes.

"Mr. CROMWELL. Whatever negotiations were to be conducted I had charge of in behalf of the company.

"Senator MORGAN. Was that embraced in your retainer?

"Mr. CROMWELL. Yes, sir.

"Senator MORGAN. At the time it was made?

"Mr. CROMWELL. Oh, no; it grew up.

"Senator MORGAN. Nothing was said of it at the time you were retained?

"Mr. CROMWELL. Well, nothing was thought about it then, probably. It had not arisen."

On the foregoing statements of the witness it is perfectly clear that his employment by the New Panama Canal Co., for services in Colombia, was tha of an agent to accomplish the object of obtaining from the Government its consent for the transfer to the United States of the rights and privileges held by that company for building and owning a canal at Panama under the Wyse concession, and that his powers gave him the full and discretionary right to negotiate with that Government. He regarded his powers as being diplomatic, or such as a government would intrust to its minister. His powers were those of a negotiator and purchasing agent for the Panama Canal Co.

In such an employment for such services there was no hing that even resembles the relations of attorney and client as to the confidence between them that the law shields from exposure.

The following s atement of the witness, in his testimony, is presented to show what he did in the United States to accomplish and effect his service to the Panama Canal Co., toward procuring the consent of Colombia, that he Panama Canal Co. might sell its canal concessions and property, which included the Panama Railroad, to the United States.

The powers of Cromwell, as the agent of the Panama Canal Co., and the proof that they are not of the class of privileged communications between attorneys and their clients, are conclusively shown by the way in which he used and employed his authority in the exploitation, in the United States, of the plan of the canal company to sell its concessions from Colombia and its property to the United States or to a syndicate or to a corporation chartered in the State of New Jersey under the name of "The New Panama Canal Co. of America."

The further statement of facts is as follows:

On page 1080 of the hearings before the committee, after stating that his retainer by the canal company was general and verbal and that no record was made of it, he was asked:

"Have you ever had a power of attorney from the company?" He answered: "No general power; no, sir. I remember that they once gave me a power to conclude some agreements with the Secretary of State here, which I filed with the Secretary of State." He then stated that this was about 1893 and that he had received no other power of attorney from the company.

The questions asked the witness, No. 21 to No. 39, both inclusive, relate to Cromwell's correspondence with Secretary Hay, dated November 28, 1898, and December 5. 1898. and December 21, 1898, which are herein copied. His refusal to answer these questions is manifestly without any shadow of protection under any professional confidence, and the testimony of Lampré that follows question 39 shows that the Panama Canal Co., in its official action, had spread upon its minutes the history of the transaction that Cromwell was attempting to conceal under the pretense of sheltering his client from the exposure of its professional confidences.

Questions 40 to 48, inclusive, relate to a paper mentioned in the deposition of Lampré, and another paper as to which Cromwell had been previously interrogated, in Nos. 8, 9, 10, 11, 12, 13, 14, 15, and 16. The paper set forth and inquired about in these questions proves conclusively that Cromwell, in his dealings with the canal company and with the people in the United States, was acting for himself under the authority of a personal contract with the New Panama Canal Co. to create a syndicate in the United States to take over the concessions from Colombia, and the railroad property and the property of the old company turned over to the New Panama Canal Co. and Americanize it. That paper was dated November 21, 1899. The extension of the concession by Sanclemente, President of Colombia, was not completed, by his decree, until April, 1900, after Congress had rejected it in November, 1898, as Cromwell informed Mr. Hay in his letters of December 5 and 21, 1898. These letters and the papers dated November 19, 1899, show conclusively that Cromwell was conducting this entire transaction on his personal account, under a contract with the New Panama Canal Co., and, in his examination before the committee, he set up the false pretense that he was acting solely under the shelter of his professional confidence and privilege as counsel for the Panama Canal Co.

The power to conclude some arrangement with the United States Secretary of State, of which he testified, was probably Cromwell's earliest employment in the work of "Americanizing the canal," as this project is called. The corresponding work of gaining the consent of Colombia to the sale of this concession and its property was conducted simultaneously with the Government of Colombia, but under a concealment of the purpose from the people of Colombia, under the guise of obtaining the extensions of the concessions for the alleged purpose of gaining time to complete the canal, the real purpose being to cut Colombia off from its power to annual the concessions under legal proceedings for declaring their forfeiture.

It was the effort to compel the disclosure of this fraud upon the people of Colombia that Cromwell attempted to prevent by taking shelter under his alleged privilege as a lawyer, and in refusing to make any disclosure of anything he did and of any facts that became known to him in his dealings in respect of the New Panama Canal Co. in the United States and in Colombia.

His contemporaneous transactions with and his overtures to the President and to Congress about that transfer of the concessions made to Wyse by Colombia still more clearly show that his employment by the New Panama Canal Co. was not such as created the relations of client and attorney. It was, at most, that of agent and principal in conducting a special enterprise not in any way connected with proceedings in any court or with legal advice, or with any litigation. His general employment was that of a broker to purchase and sell certain properties on account of the Panama Canal Co., in which he had a personal interest, secured by the contract of November 21, 1899, under which he acted alone for his personal interests, expecting to realize great profits and to become possessed of great power and éclat.

Cromwell's first known movement toward Americanizing the Panama Canal was on November 28, 1898, when he wrote the Secretary of State, Mr. Hay, to notify him of a letter from M. Bonnardel, president of the canal company; M. Hutin, director general, was detained on the sea by rough weather, and on his arrival he and Hutin would call on Mr. Hay to explain Panama Canal matters. The letter of Bonnardel was dated November 18, 1898.

The letter of Cromwell to Mr. Hay, dated November 28, 1898, was as follows:

Mr. Cromwell to Mr. Hay.

DEAR SIR: Referring to the interview which you accorded me on Friday last, and your gracious assurance that you would give audience to the director general of the New Panama Canal Co. and ourselves in connection with the presentation to the President of the communication which the New Panama Canal Co. is about to make to the Government, I beg leave to advise you that by reason of the severe prevailing storm *La Touraine* was delayed in arrival until to-day, and that we shall therefore not be able to translate the documents and prepare them for presentation before Wednesday.

I will advise you further of our coming, keeping in mind the preference which you indicated, that the hour of conference be about 11 o'clock in the forenoon.

I have the honor to be, etc.,

WM. NELSON CROMWELL,
American Counsel for New Panama Canal Co.

This letter was followed by a telegram and a letter, both dated December 5, 1898, from Cromwell to Mr. Hay, as follows:

[Telegram.]

Mr. Cromwell to Mr. Hay.

Am writing you to-day concerning the cable from Consul General Hart, published Saturday. It is evident that the limited purpose and nature of the measure referred to is not fully reported from Bogota, and is given under significance.

WM. NELSON CROMWELL,
Counsel New Panama Canal Co.

Mr. Cromwell to Mr. Hay.

MY DEAR SIR: I beg leave to confirm the telegram which I sent you at 10.45 this morning, as per inclosure.

Upon my return I learned through Director General Hutin (who had preceded me to New York) that the measure which had just been acted on by one branch only of the Colombian Congress was a bill to authorize the executive to negotiate the terms of and to conclude a further prorogation of six years from 1904 for the completion of the canal under a communication which the company had addressed to the Government, in the form of which I inclose you a translation.

You will note that the company specifically stated to the Government that the prorogation was not a matter of absolute necessity, but was desirable in the interest of commerce and navigation, to enable even a deeper cut to be made (and which would reduce the number of locks to four), but which reduction would, of course, require more time than the plan adopted.

You will note that the bill proposed to confer power upon the executive, and this happened to arise under extraordinary political conditions in Bogota. As you have probably been advised through official channels, a serious difference has recently been existing between the House of Representatives of Colombia and the President, the House having passed formal resolution declaring the office of President vacant and refusing to recognize the qualification of the President before the supreme court.

We therefore construe the action of the House of Representatives as only a part of the strife between the House and the President and not a declaration of the policy of the nation or the Congress in respect of the Panama Canal, and as not evidencing hostility to the company itself. We are more confirmed in this belief because of the uniform consideration and cordiality displayed by the Congress and the Government to the New Panama Canal Co., which we have no doubt their minister at Washington would fully confirm to you.

Our company has not the least apprehension regarding any prorogation of its concessions it may consider necessary in the future.

I have, etc., your obedient servant,

WM. NELSON CROMWELL,
Counsel New Panama Canal Co.

These writings show that Cromwell was, at and before their date, at work in Colombia to get a further prolongation of the Wyse concession; that the bill had failed to pass the Congress of Colombia; and that it had declared the office of San Clements, as President, vacant. This letter, on its face, is an attempt to conceal the truth of the situation in Colombia, but closes with an assurance to Mr. Hay that the company would finally get the concession.

On the 21st of December, 1898, Cromwell informed Mr. Hay that San Clements had signed the concession.

It is public history that Colombia was embroiled in civil war immediately after it dissolved by its own adjournment. Cromwell knew it, and referred to it in his letter of December 5, 1898.

On the 21st of December, 1898, Cromwell wrote the following letter to Mr. Hay:

NEW YORK, *December 21, 1898.*

MY DEAR SIR: Further to my letter of December 5, 1898, receipt of which was acknowledged by your favor of the 8th instant, I beg leave to say that we are advised by our counsel at Bogota that the official minutes of the session of the House of Representatives declare that the bill concerning the extension of the New Panama Canal Co. has not been acted upon for lack of time. We, however, yesterday received further cable advising us that the Government had granted the extension, subject to the approval of the next Congress, and I note from this morning's Herald that similar advises have been received by the press.

It is the opinion of the Government executives and of ourselves that power to give such extension is already located in the Government by the terms of the original concession, but the formality of ratification will be requested in due course, and of its being granted we have not the remotest apprehension.

You will thus see that my confidence in the attitude of Colombia, as indicated in my last note, has been fully and quickly confirmed.

Faithfully, yours,

WM. NELSON CROMWELL,
General Counsel New Panama Canal Co.

On the 6th of May, 1898, Cromwell was at the meeting of the executive committee of the Panama Railroad Co. and participated in passing a resolution under which that company agreed to purchase from the Panama Canal Co. the use of certain lands in the vicinity of the La Boca terminal for $20,000, to be reduced to $14,000 in the event of the failure of the canal company to obtain from Colombia the extension of its concessions from 1904 to 1910, and Cromwell, who was then the general counsel of the Panama Canal Co. and of the railroad company, was instructed to prepare the papers. Thus the two companies were concerting measures to avoid the forfeiture of the concession to the canal company, which, at that time, was so uncertain of success that the price of the property was reduced from $20,000 to $14,000 if the prolongation of the concession should fail. This fact proves Cromwell's knowledge of the efforts that were being made to prevent Colombia from declaring the forfeiture of the Wyse concessions and also of the concerted action of the two companies in their dealings with Colombia.

It is not intended on this motion to go into the recital of the entire history of Cromwell's dealings with the Panama Canal Co. or with the Panama Railroad, but only to recite herein such facts as show the relevancy of the questions that he has refused to answer; but all the facts stated in said record that show his connection with either of said companies or subjects were referred to in support of this motion.

JOHN T. MORGAN.

APPENDIX A.

1.

[Page 1142.]

Senator MORGAN. What was the first work that you did in America for the Panama Canal Co.?

Mr. CROMWELL. I must beg to be excused, Senator, from the pursuit of that subject, as that is a professional confidence.

Senator MORGAN. Is the fact that you had lawsuits, or gave advice, or anything of that sort a professional secret?

Mr. CROMWELL. In respect of the business of the Panama Canal Co., our relations are professional and confidential, and I must beg to be excused from relating their business.

2.

[Page 1143.]

Senator MORGAN. What was the principal work that you first did for the Panama Canal Co. in America?

Mr. CROMWELL. I do not recall what I did at any time in their affairs, and if I did I should not feel at liberty to state their business.

3.

Senator MORGAN. Did you conduct any business for them in America?

Mr. CROMWELL. I beg to be excused from a reply to that.

4.

Senator MORGAN. What was your salary as general counsel of that company?

Mr. CROMWELL. I beg to be excused from reply.

Senator MORGAN. You do not propose to tell anything about what you did or what you received from that company?

Mr. CROMWELL. I do not consider myself at liberty to discuss the professional relations of a client.

5.

Senator MORGAN. You have mentioned already that you received $200,000 from them, and that it was in installments, not annually exactly, but as you called for them. You have mentioned that fact. Was that a professional confidence?

Mr. CROMWELL. I have mentioned it, sir, out of good nature, perhaps.

Senator MORGAN. Was that in payment for work that you did in the United States?

Mr. CROMWELL. I beg to be excused from replying. My service was general and broad, and covered trips to Europe and——

Senator MORGAN. Were they paying you for your personal influence upon the United States or the people of the United States and the Congress of the United States, or were they paying you for professional services,

Mr. CROMWELL. For professional services.

Senator MORGAN. Exclusively?

Mr. CROMWELL. Yes, sir.

Senator MORGAN. And, although you stated that you received $200,000 from them, you decline to state any business that you did for them at all?

Mr. CROMWELL. I do.

Senator MORGAN. And you cover that under a professional confidence?

Mr. CROMWELL. I do; and also because I think this committee has no power to go into such subjects; but that I do not pass upon.

6.

[Page. 1144.]

Senator MORGAN. Was your business in anywise connected with the lobbying of measures of the Panama Railroad Co. through Congress?

Mr. CROMWELL. No, sir.

Senator MORGAN. Or advocating them before committees of Congress?

Mr. CROMWELL. I have appeared before committees of Congress.

Senator MORGAN. At the instance of that company?

Mr. CROMWELL. Yes, sir; as counsel for the company.

7.

Senator MORGAN. That is one thing that we have got, anyway. Were you paid for that? Have you been, to any extent, and what?

Mr. CROMWELL. I can not differentiate, Senator, and I must decline to go further into that subject. I have rendered no bill for individual services.

Senator MOTRGAN. I did not suppose that you had rendered any bill, and I did not ask if you had. I asked whether or not you had been paid for the service in whole or in part?

[Page 1145.]

Mr. CROMWELL. I decline to proceed further into the discussion of that topic.

8.

Senator MORGAN. What arguments or propositions or offers did you make as the counsel of the Panama Canal Co. to other persons besides those you addressed to the President of the United States, to the Secretary of State, and to the chairman of the Committee on Interstate and Foreign Commerce of the House?

[Page 1146.]

Mr. CROMWELL. I decline to answer, on the ground that it is a professional confidence.

Senator MORGAN. Do you decline to answer in explanation of what you have stated in those written communications?

Mr. CROMWELL. I do.

Senator MORGAN. You do?

Mr. CROMWELL. Yes, sir.

Senator MORGAN. You will give no explanation of them?

Mr. CROMWELL. I will not.

9.

Senator MORGAN. You seem disposed to treat the subject with contempt. I do not understand that. You had a contract with the Panama Canal Co. which bears date November 21, 1899. Do you recall that contract?

Mr. CROMWELL. What contract?

Senator MORGAN. The contract made with the canal company on November 21, 1899.

Mr. CROMWELL. I do not recall any contract, Senator.

Senator MORGAN. Do you recall any power of attorney or authorization that they gave to you of that date?

Mr. CROMWELL. I do not recall it by its date; no, sir. There may have been some instrument that passed at that time, but the date does not identify it to me.

Senator MORGAN. I will read the first part of it to you to see whether you recall it [reading]:

"Mr. William Nelson Cromwell is exclusively empowered under the formal agreement with the board of directors of the Compagnie Neuvelis du Canal de Panama (New Panama Canal Co., of France) to effect, with an American syndicate, the Americanization of the Panama Canal Co. under the following basis."

Do you recall that?

Mr. CROMWELL. I recall that there was a proposal of that kind.

[Page 1147.]

Senator MORGAN. That was not made with you as general counsel, was it?

Mr. CROMWELL. Yes, sir.

Senator MORGAN. Is that a professional secret?

Mr. CROMWELL. Yes, sir.

Senator MORGAN. Unfortunately I shall have to reveal it for you. I will read it [reading]:

Americanization of the Panama Canal.—The Panama Canal Co. of America.

"Mr. William Nelson Cromwell is exclusively empowered under the formal agreement with the board of directors of the Compagnie Nouvelis du Canal de Panama (New Panama Canal Co., of France) to effect with an American syndicate the Americanization of the Panama Canal Co. under the following basis:

I. American Co.—A new corporation shall be organized under the laws of the State of New York, or New Jersey, or Delaware, under the name of "The Panama Canal Co. of America" (or other title), which company shall have for its principal object the completion, maintenance, and operation of the Panama Canal, and any other object that may tend to the realization of that purpose, as well as such other objects that may be set forth in the articles of incorporation.

The articles of incorporation shall prescribe that at least three-fourths in number of the entire board of directors shall be citizens of the United States, and that the principal office of the company shall be located in the United States.

II. Capitalization.—Preferred stock, 600,000 shares of $100 each, $60,000,000.

(*a*) Entitled to preference over the common stock in dividends which may be declared in any year to the extent of 5 per cent; and also entitled to participate pro rata with the common stock in all dividends which may be declared in any year in excess of 5 per cent upon the preferred stock and 5 per cent upon the common stock.

(*b*) Entitled to preference over the common stock, to the extent of the par value thereof, upon liquidation of the company.

Common stock, 450,000 shares of $100 each, $45,000,000.

The common stock subject to the aforesaid preferences in respect of the preferred stock is entitled to the dividends which may be declared in any year to the extent of 5 per cent; and also is entitled to participate pro rata with the preferred stock in all dividends which may be declared in any year in excess of 5 per cent upon the preferred stock and 5 per cent upon the stock.

III. Both classes of stock shall have like voting powers.—The American company, in consideration of $100,000,000 (of which $55,000,000 shall be paid in such preferred stock and $45,000,000 in such common stock), will purchase and acquire from Mr. Cromwell, or his nominees:

(*a*) The Panama Canal and concessions (and all existing deposits under such concessions), including all the canal works, plant, machinery, buildings, and all other real and personal fixed and movable property upon the Isthmus of Panama belonging to the Compagnie Nouvelle du Canal de Panama (the French company), or in which the latter may be interested; all plans, surveys, reports, data, and records pertaining to the canal; also all lands ceded gratuitously by the Colombian Government under paragraphs 7 and 8 of Article I of the concessions necessary for the requirement of the construction and operation of the

[Page 1148.]

canal. (The subsidy lands granted by Article IV of the concessions and not upon the line of the canal are exempted from this transaction.)

(*b*) The American company will also acquire the rights of every nature belonging to the French company in the 68,534 shares of stock (out of the total issue of 70,000) of the Panama Railroad Co., a corporation created in 1849 under special act of the Legislature of the State of New York.

These railroad shares are to become the absolute property of the American company, upon the completion of the canal, without any further payment whatever. In the meantime they will continue to be held in trust (as at present is the case is respect of the French company) to abide the fulfillment of said condition.

(*c*) The American company also shall receive $5,000,000 in cash as a part of this transaction.

(*d*) The American company also will have $5,000,000 preferred stock remaining in its hands for future sale.

IV. Absolute title to property and freedom from mortgage sale.—The title of the American company to the property and concessions so to be acquired shall be absolute (subject to said provisions as to said Panama Railroad Co. stock); and such property and concessions shall be free and clear of any mortgage or other lien.

All money payments and deposits (amounting to many millions of francs) required by the concessions to be made to the Republic of Colombia have been made to date and the concessions are in full force. A large portion of the canal works is already constructed, and it is not doubted that the period (October, 1904) fixed by the concessions for the entire completion of the canal will be extended by Colombia in due course (as on each previous occasion) for such further period as may be found necessary, and that Colombia will thus continue to further the undertaking which is of such vast concern to its national and commercial welfare.

V. Provision for completion of canal by bond issue.—The board of directors shall be empowered to create, issue, and sell bonds, secured by mortgage or mortgages upon all the canal property, concessions, etc., of the American company, acquired and to be acquired; and also to determine the amount of such bond issues, the rate of interest upon such bonds, and the conditions and price of issue. To comply with the requirements of the charter of the French company, there shall be accorded to the shareholders and bondholders of the "Universal Interoceanic Canal Co., in Liquidation" (the original French company), a right of preference to subscribe for one-half in amount of such bonds.

VI. Twenty-two million five hundred thousand dollars common-stock trust.—Agreeably to the requirements of the syndicate, a trust shall be established by Mr. Cromwell or his nominees, in respect of $22,500,000 par value of the shares of the common stock acquired by him or them, or in respect of trust certificates for such shares. The shares or trust certificates (and all dividends thereon) embraced in said trust (*a*) may be disposed of by the trustees for the best interests of the said certificate holders or shareholders and of the other stockholders of the American company, at such time and in such manner, under such conditions, and to such ends as they may deem advisable; and (*b*) upon the termination of the trust the shares or trust certificates and moneys then in hand shall be distributed for the best interests of such certificate holders or shareholders and the other stockholders of the American company, at such time, in such manner, under such conditions, and to such ends as the trustees may deem advisable; and in the meantime such share or trust certificates may, by the trustees, be voted for the election of such board of directors of the American company and for such acts and measures as they may deem to the best interests of the syndicate and of the stockholders of the American company.

The trustees shall be five in number; a majority shall be citizens of the United States; of said trustees, two citizens of the United States shall be designated in the first instance by the advisory committee, and the vacancies in respect of two such memberships shall be filled by the holders (acting by and through a majority in interest) of the shares of the trust certificates purchased by the syndicate.

This trust shall continue until 10 years after the opening of the canal to commerce, unless sooner terminated pursuant to the terms of the contract or trust covering the subject.

VII. Guaranty to American syndicate of full minority representation in directory of American company.—Agreeably to the requirements of the syndicate, provision shall be made whereby the holders of the shares or trust certificates purchased by the syndicate shall be entitled to designate and cause to be elected the full minority (to wit, one less than a majority) of the members composing the board of directors of the American company, until 10 years after the opening of the canal to commerce, unless such right be sooner terminated pursuant to the terms of the contract or trust covering the subject. Such minority shall, in the first instance, be designated by the advisory committee, and thereafter by such holders of shares or trust certificates, acting by and through a majority in interest of such holders; and all nominees of such holders or advisory board committee shall be citizens of the United States.

VIII. Execution of plan.—It is understood that the articles of incorporation, by-laws, trust deeds, contracts, and other instruments requisite for the accomplishment of the plan are necessarily subject to the approval of the French company, upon the acceptance by it of stock in payment from Mr. Cromwell or his nominees; and it is also recognized that the unique character of the enterprise, the international interests involved, and the special circumstance of the case require that plenary and discretion and power be possessed by Mr. Cromwell to effect the Americanization of the canal.

It is therefore understood and agreed that Mr. Cromwell may proceed to negotiate, determine, and agree upon all plans, terms, agreements, conditions, questions, and details which he may deem necessary and advisable in respect of the purposes herein generally indicated, including the terms and provisions of all trusts and agreements which he may deem advisable to have established or made; the articles of incorporation and by-laws of the American company, which may include adequate provisions for the redemption and retirement of the capital stock, any merger, consolidation, reincorporation, dissolution, or other disposition, arrangement, or rearrangement of all or any of the property capitalization and concerns of the company upon any consideration approved by the board of directors and the holders of the specified proportion (not less than two-thirds) of the capital stock of the company outstanding at the time being, all titles, property, and transfers, all stock issues and trust certificate issues, and every other subject or matter which he may consider to be involved in the execution of the plan, and his action in any such regard shall be and become part hereof as if herein set forth; and, further, that he and any member of the advisory committee and counsel, like others, may become a subscriber to the syndicate agreement and be eligible to any trusteeship or directorate, and may occupy any official or personal relation to said enterprise without accountability for any benefit derived therefrom.

[Page 1150.]

All the terms and provisions of this plan may be carried out by contracts, trusts, or other legal method, and certificates for shares of such stock or negotiable certificates of trust or other evidence of interest (daily registered with a trust company in the city of New York) shall be issued and delivered by the syndicate subscribers.

IX. Advisory committee and counsel.—Messrs. ——— ———, ——— ——— are constituted an advisory committee of the syndicate subscribers with the professional assistance of Messrs. Sullivan & Cromwell and Mr. ——— ———, as counsel, to possess and exercise the powers specified in Division VI and VII hereof and to advise with Mr. Cromwell in the execution of the plan. The reasonable charges and expenses of said committee shall be discharged by the trustees of the stock trust to be created under Division VI hereof.

Dated November 21, 1899.

Americanization of the Panama Canal—Syndicate subscription agreement, $5,000,000.

Referring to the foregoing plan, we, the undersigned, each for himself and not for the other, in consideration of $1 to each of us in hand paid by William

Nelson Cromwell, the receipt whereof is hereby acknowledged, and of our mutual subscriptions, do hereby severally subscribe for, and do agree with said William Nelson Cromwell to purchase and from him to take—

One hundred dollars par value of the preferred capital stock, or, at his option, negotiable preferred-stock trust certificates for all or any part thereof; and $200 par value of the common capital stock, or, at his option, negotiable common-stock trust certificates for all or any part thereof, issued in respect of capital stock of the American corporation to be created under the foregoing plan.

For each $100 in money to the amount set opposite our respective names, and to pay for the same upon the call of the said William Nelson Cromwell, provided such call be not made prior to February 1, 1900, and 15 days' notice be given of such call.

Payments shall be made to ——— Trust Co., in the city of New York, and shall by it be paid over to the American company upon the order of Mr. Cromwell against the receipt of such trust company from him for account of the subscribers of the stock or trust certificates purchased by them hereunder.

It is understood and agreed that this agreement shall not be binding unless subscriptions be made and allotted to the full amount of $5,000,000, and that owing to the special circumstances of the case, and in the interests of all, Mr. Cromwell shall have the right and power to reject or to reduce any subscrip-

[Page 1151.]

tion hereunder at any time before final allotment by him, and also that he may deliver certificates for the shares of such stock or trust certificates to any extent within the respective classes of preferred and common stock or trust certificates that he may find desirable.

This agreement shall bind, and is for the benefit of the parties hereto and their respective executors, administrators, survivors, and assigns, and may be executed in several parts or copies with the same force and effect as if all the subscription agreements were to be one part or one copy thereof.

Dated November 21, 1899.

10.

Senator MORGAN. Did you prepare that paper?

Mr. CROMWELL. I decline to answer.

Senator MORGAN. On what ground?

Mr. CROMWELL. On the ground that it is a professional communication.

11.

[Page 1152.]

Senator MORGAN. I will read this first paragraph again:

"Mr. William Nelson Cromwell is exclusively empowered under the formal agreement with the board of directors of the Compagnie Nouvelle du Canal de Panama (New Panama Canal Co., of France) to effect, with an American syndicate, the Americanization of the Panama Canal Co., under the following basis."

Mr. CROMWELL. That was a fruitless suggestion of the company, which came to naught, and under which I acted as their counsel solely. For that reason I decline to enter into a discussion of it, any more than I would into any other affair of theirs.

Senator MORGAN. You put it upon the ground that it was a professional arrangement with that company?

Mr. CROMWELL. Yes, sir.

Senator MORGAN. Well, if so, why do you stipulate in this proposition that William Nelson Cromwell shall receive the fees that were coming in consequence of any legal services?

Mr. CROMWELL. It does not say so.

Senator MORGAN. Well, what does it say, then? I will see.

The CHAIRMAN. Is that paper signed? I did not hear any signatures read. Are there any signatures attached to that paper?

Senator MORGAN. No, sir; there are no signatures to it, and none needed, when a party swears that he executed such a contract.

Mr. CROMWELL. It is not a contract; it is an abortive project.

12.

Mr. CROMWELL. Nothing was ever done under it.

Senator KITTREDGE. Senator Morgan, have you asked the one question that you desired to ask before answering the question that I suggested?

Senator MORGAN. I had read that to him, and he had made a statement in regard to it.

Have you a copy of the "agreement with the board of directors of the New Panama Canal Co. to effect with an American syndicate the Americanization of the Panama Canal Co. upon the following basis"?

Have you a copy of that agreement?

Mr. CROMWELL. I beg to be excused from pursuing that subject, because it involves confidential and professional relations. I do not wish to be impolite,

[Page 1153.]

and I do not wish to be constantly making the statement that may seem a little harsh; but I say, once and for all, that all these matters are confidential.

13.

[Page 1154.]

Senator MORGAN. Did you obtain an act of incorporation in New York or New Jersey for the purpose of carrying this agreement into effect?

Mr. CROMWELL. I decline to answer, for the same reason.

14.

[Page 1157.]

Senator MORGAN. Mr. Cromwell, yesterday in speaking of a paper that is in the record, concluding on page 1150 of this testimony, you say of that paper:

"It is not a contract. It is a power of attorney to me, as general counsel of the company, written in my name, to accompany broad plans which the board of directors considered. It never matured into anything. It never was consummated, either by subscription or by assent, and it is obsolete and an impracticable thing—proved so to be. It has no life or force of being, did not exist, and never has existed, and is as dead as a doornail."

Was it ever signed?

Mr. CROMWELL. I will make, Senator, the same reply I have heretofore.

Senator MORGAN. What is that?

Mr. CROMWELL. That the whole subject is covered by the seal of professional confidence.

Senator MORGAN. How long would that professional lockjaw last—from the time you were first employed down to this date?

Mr. CROMWELL. It exists now.

Senator MORGAN. When did it begin?

Mr. CROMWELL. It began with my employment, and continues now.

Senator MORGAN. When was that? When was the employment?

Mr. CROMWELL. When was my employment by the New Panama Canal Co.?

Senator MORGAN. Yes, sir.

Mr. CROMWELL. In 1896.

Senator MORGAN. And this is 1906. You apply that cloture to all questions asked of you in regard to all of your transactions from that time to this in connection with that company, do you?

Mr. CROMWELL. I do, sir.

[Page 1158.]

Senator MORGAN. Yes; and you refuse to state anything that you have done in connection with their business from 1896 down to 1906?

Mr. CROMWELL. I refuse to state.

By direction, the stenographer read aloud the last question.

Mr. CROMWELL. I will reply to specific questions, Senator; I can not reply to general questions.

Senator MORGAN. I understood you to say broadly that you would not answer any question that was connected with the business that you were engaged in for the Isthmian Canal Co.

Mr. CROMWELL. You mean for the New Panama Canal Co.?
Senator MORGAN. I mean the New Panama Canal Co., or in that connection. You do?
Mr. CROMWELL. I do so state.
Senator MORGAN. That seems to be broad enough. I do not see how it can be any broader. Now, was all the business that you have transacted in connection with that company from that date—1896 to 1906—professional?
Mr. CROMWELL. Yes, sir.

15.

Senator MORGAN. Was this contract you made with them professional?
Mr. CROMWELL. That is not a contract.
Senator MORGAN. What is it?
Mr. CROMWELL. It speaks for itself.
Senator MORGAN. What do you call it?
Mr. CROMWELL. I do not choose to call it anything.
Senator MORGAN. You have called it something. You called it an abortion yesterday, did you not?
Mr. CROMWELL. I did not.
Senator MORGAN. Well, the record states that you did.
Mr. CROMWELL. The record states that you stated so. I did not. I said it was "abortive."
Senator MORGAN. "Abortive"—oh, yes; we change to the adjective phrase.
Mr. CROMWELL. You used the phrase; I did not.
Senator MORGAN. In what sense do you use that word "abortive"?
Mr. CROMWELL. I do not care to make any further explanation of it, Senator.
Senator MORGAN. Do you use it to show that it was never executed—I mean that the papers were never signed?
Mr. CROMWELL. I do not care to make any further explanation of it.
Senator MORGAN. Or do you use it to show that it was never carried out?
Mr. CROMWELL. I make the same reply.
Senator MORGAN. What efforts did you make to carry it out?
Mr. CROMWELL. I make the same reply.
Senator MORGAN. To whom did you submit it for the purpose of carrying it into effect?
Mr. CROMWELL. I make the same reply.
Senator MORGAN. What person not connected in any way with the Panama Canal did you submit that to in order to carry it into effect—to get them to cooperate with you in your effort?
Mr. CROMWELL. I make the same reply, Senator.
Senator MORGAN. It is called a plan for the "Americanization" of the canal. What does that mean? What is the meaning of that word "Americanization"?
Mr. CROMWELL. I have no explanation to make, Senator.
Senator MORGAN. Do you know?
Mr. CROMWELL. I have no explanation to make, sir.
Senator MORGAN. Do you know?
Mr. CROMWELL. I have no explanation to make. If I have any knowledge, it is knowledge acquired in my professional capacity.
Senator MORGAN. Have you any knowledge——
Mr. CROMWELL. I have no knowledge.
Senator MORGAN (continuing). In regard to that subject—why it should be called a plan for the Americanization of the canal?
Mr. CROMWELL. Whatever knowledge I have acquired upon that subject I have acquired in a professional capacity.
Senator MORGAN. Did you not originate that phrase yourself?
Mr. CROMWELL. Whatever duty I performed in the subject was done in a professional capacity.
Senator MORGAN. Did you not project the plan of Americanizing the canal through that syndicate agreement?
Mr. CROMWELL. I decline to answer for the same reason.

16.

Senator MORGAN. What was done by any other person, within your knowledge, not connected with the canal company, to carry that contract into effect?
Mr. CROMWELL. I make the same reply.

Senator MORGAN. To whom did you distribute copies of that contract and project for the purpose of getting them to assist in it by subscriptions?

Mr. CROMWELL. I make the same reply.

Senator MORGAN. Did you submit it to anybody?

Mr. CROMWELL. I make the same reply.

Senator MORGAN. What was your purpose in projecting and attempting to execute that contract?

Mr. CROMWELL. I make the same reply.

17.

Senator MORGAN. You got a corporation created in New Jersey, did you not?

Mr. CROMWELL. I make the same reply.

Senator MORGAN. You are a subscribing witness to that act of incorporation?

Mr. CROMWELL. I make the same reply, sir.

Senator MORGAN. Did you prepare it?

Mr. CROMWELL. I make the same reply, sir.

Senator MORGAN. The records of the government in New Jersey show that you obtained that corporation, and that you are a subscribing witness to it. Why did you not object to making that communication to the world at that time, if it was professional?

Mr. CROMWELL. I make the same reply, sir.

Senator MORGAN. Having made it, why do you object to testifying in regard to it?

Mr. CROMWELL. I make the same reply, sir.

Senator MORGAN. You are not shutting out any information by these facts that I know of.

Senator KITTREDGE. Why do you ask the question of the witness?

18.

[Page 1160.]

Mr. Cromwell, did you have any part in any conference with Bunau-Varilla, or in any conference with Mr. Hay, or in any conference with any of the authorities of the Republic of Panama, in negotiating the treaty called the Hay-Varilla treaty?

Mr. CROMWELL. I make the same reply.

Senator MORGAN. What is that reply?

Mr. CROMWELL. That all my service in every respect was as counsel of the New Panama Canal Co. and covered by the obligation of professional confidence.

19.

[Page 1177.]

Senator SIMMONS. I may have misunderstood you, but I understood you to say yesterday that you did not receive any compensation as an attorney from the Republic of Panama.

Mr. CROMWELL. That is true, sir.

Senator SIMMONS. For what consideration were you representing them as fiscal agent in making this transaction?

Mr. CROMWELL. What do you mean by "what consideration?"

Senator SIMMONS. I mean what was the inducement to you to represent them? You got no money for it; you were not employed as counsel; you were

[Page 1178.]

not paid as fiscal agent. What was the inducement or consideration to you to perform that service for the Republic of Panama?

Mr. CROMWELL. The broad instinct of good nature, which has prompted me to do so much work for that cause, Senator, and the other consideration that I have more money than I need, unfortunately.

Senator MORGAN. Did that broad instinct of good nature lead you also to take out of the act of incorporation which is here on page 23 of the report of the Committee on Interoceanic Canals, made to the Senate, Fifty-sixth

Congress, first session, to which I will call your attention, and to which you were a subscribing witness?

Mr. CROMWELL. Are you still harping on our daughter, going back to that subject? She is an old maid by this time, and I think we had better get her married to somebody. [Laughter.]

Senator MORGAN. She is a harp of many strings, I discover. [Laughter.] So you must excuse me if I want to know her better.

I read from this report of the Committee on Interoceanic Canals that I have referred to. [Reading:]

Ship canals in the Isthmus of Darien.

May 21, 1900.—Ordered to be printed.

Mr. Morgan, from the Committee on Interoceanic Canals, submitted the following supplemental report (to accompany H. R. 2538):

The Committee on Interoceanic Canals report the following certified copies of charters of corporations of New Jersey relating to ship canals in the Isthmus of Darien, and request that the same be printed as a document for the use of the Senate:

Certificate of corporation of Panama Canal Co. of America.

UNITED STATES OF AMERICA,
State of New Jersey:

We, the undersigned, hereby do associate ourselves into a corporation, under and by virtue of the provisions of an act of the Legislature of the State of New Jersey entitled "An act concerning corporations (revision of 1896)," and the several acts amendatory thereof and supplemental thereto, for the purposes hereinafter named, and do make this our certificate of incorporation.

First. The name of the corporation is Panama Canal Company of America.

Second. The location of the principal office of the corporation in the State of New Jersey is at 76 Montgomery Street, in Jersey City, in the county of Hudson, and the name of the agent therein and in charge thereof, upon whom process against this corporation may be served, is William Brinkerhoff.

Third. The objects for which the corporation is formed are as follows:

To acquire, by purchase or otherwise, the maritime ship canal of the Compagnie Nouvelle du Canal de Panama and the railway across the Isthmus of Panama between the Atlantic Ocean and the Pacific Ocean; to construct, exploit, complete, equip, repair, and enlarge; to operate, manage, maintain, and control said canal and railway and the various enterprises connected therewith;

[Page 1179.]

to collect tolls and revenues therefrom, and to use and enjoy the same.

To acquire, by purchase or otherwise, and to construct, operate, exploit, manage, and control lines of railway along or in the vicinity of such canal.

To acquire, by purchase or otherwise, and to construct, operate, and exploit, manage, and control cable lines, telegraph lines, and telephone lines along and to connect with such canal and such railway or railways, and in and along the shores of the oceans, seas, gulfs, and bays at, near, or to connect with such canals or railways.

To acquire, by purchase, lease, or otherwise, and to construct, maintain, operate, manage, and control, and to sell, let, pledge, or otherwise dispose of ships, boats, and other vessels of every kind and nature, and propelled by any power; to acquire concessions, grants, privileges, or licenses for the establishment and working of lines of steamships or sailing vesels, and to establish and to maintain lines or regular services of steamships or other vessels between any parts of the world, and generally to carry on the business of shipowners, and to enter into contracts for the carriage of mails, passengers, goods, and merchandise by any means, either by its own vessels, railways, and conveyances, or by the vessels, conveyances, and railways of others; and to collect, use, and enjoy revenues therefrom.

To construct, purchase, or otherwise acquire, and to own, equip, maintain, use, and manage wharves, warehouses, piers, docks, buildings, or works capable of being advantageously used in connection with the canal, shipping, carrying, or other business of the company; and to charge and collect dues and rentals for the use thereof.

To construct, purchase, or otherwise acquire, and to own, equip, improve, work, develop, manage, and control public works and conveniences of all kinds, including railways, docks, harbors, lighthouses, piers, wharves, canals, conduits, locks, reservoirs, irrigation works, tunnels, bridges, viaducts, embankments, buildings, structures, and any and all other works of internal improvement or public utility.

To enter into any arrangement with any governments or authorities, national, State, municipal, local, or otherwise, that may seem conducive to the company's objects or any of them, and to obtain from any such government or authority any and all rights, privileges, grants, and concessions which the company may think it desirable to obtain and to carry out, exercise, and comply with any such arrangements, rights, privileges, and concessions, including the construction of any and all internal improvements of any and every nature.

To issue shares, stock, debentures, debenture stock, bonds, and other obligations; to subscribe for, to acquire, to invest in, and to hold and control the stocks, shares, bonds, debentures, debenture stock, and securities of any government, national, State, or municipal, and of any canal, railway, or other corporation, private or public, and to exercise all the rights, powers, and privileges of ownership thereof; to vary the investments of the company; to mortgage, pledge, or charge all or any part of the property, concessions, rights, and franchises of this company, acquired and to be acquired; to make advances upon, hold in trust, sell, or dispose of, and otherwise deal with any of the investments or securities aforesaid, or to act as agent for others for any of the above or the like purposes.

[Page 1180.]

In general, to carry on any other business in connection therewith, with all the powers conferred by the aforesaid acts of the legislature of the State of New Jersey and acts amendatory thereof and supplemental thereto.

The corporation shall also have power to conduct its business in all its branches, to have one or more offices, to hold meetings of the directoirs, to keep its books (except the stock and transfer books), and to hold, purchase, mortgage, lease, and convey real and personal property without the State of New Jersey and in any and all the other States, the Territories, the District of Columbia, and the colonies, dependencies, and possessions of the United States of America, and upon the Isthmus of Panama, and in the United States of Colombia, and in any and all other foreign countries.

The objects in this article specified shall not be limited or restricted by reference to nor inference from the terms of any other article, clause, paragraph, or provision in this certificate contained.

Fourth. The amount of the total authorized capital stock of the corporation is $30,000,000; the number of shares into which the capital stock is divided is 300,000 shares, consisting of 50,000 shares of first preferred stock, 150,000 shares of second preferred stock, and 100,000 shares of common stock, and the par value of each share is $100. The amount of capital stock with which it will commence business is $5,000, consisting of 24 shares of first preferred stock, 9 shares of second preferred stock, and 17 shares of common stock.

From time to time the first preferred stock, the second preferred stock, and the common stock shall be issued in such amounts and proportions as shall be determined by the board of directors and as may be permitted by law.

From time to time the capital stock and each class of the capital stock of the corporation may be increased as permitted by law in such amounts as may be determined by the board of directors and authorized by the holders of two-thirds in amount of each class of the capital stock then issued and outstanding.

The holders of the first preferred stock shall be entitled, out of any and all surplus or net profits, to receive noncumulative dividends whenever the same shall be declared set apart for or paid upon any other stock of the corporation.

In each and every fiscal year for which full dividends shall have set apart for or paid upon all of the first preferred stock, the holders of the second preferred stock shall be entitled, out of any and all surplus or net profits, to receive noncumulative dividends, whenever the same shall be declared by the board of directors, at the rate of but not exceeding 8 per cent per annum for such fiscal year; such dividend to be paid before any dividend for such fiscal year shall be declared, set apart for, or paid upon the common stock.

In addition thereto, in the event of the dissolution or liquidation of the corporation, the holders of the first preferred stock shall be entitled to receive the par value of their preferred shares before anything shall be paid upon the second preferred stock or upon the common stock out of the assets of the corporation; and the holders of the second preferred stock shall be entitled to receive the par value of their preferred shares before anything shall be paid upon the common stock out of the assets of the corporation.

[Page 1181.]

The common stock shall be subject to the prior rights of the first preferred stock and the second preferred stock, as above declared. If, after providing for the payment of full dividends for any fiscal year on the first preferred stock and the second preferred stock, there shall remain any surplus or net profits, such remaining surplus or net profits shall be applicable to the payment of dividends at the rate of 4 per cent per annum upon the common stock whenever the same shall be declared by the board of directors; and out of and to the extent of any such remaining surplus or net profits, after the close of any such fiscal year, the board of directors may pay dividends for such fiscal year at the rate of 4 per cent per annum upon the common stock, but not until after said preferential dividends for such fiscal year upon the first preferred stock and the second preferred stock shall have been actually paid or provided and set apart.

After dividends for any such fiscal year shall have been paid at the rate of 5 per cent upon the first preferred stock and at the rate of 8 per cent per annum upon the second preferred stock, and at the rate of 4 per cent upon the common stock, and any and all other dividends from any remaining net profits which may be declared by the board of directors shall be declared and paid equally in respect of each and every share of the first preferred stock and the common stock of the corporation.

At all meetings of the stockholders of the company the holders of the first preferred stock shall be entitled to one and four-tenths votes (in person or by proxy) for each share of such first preferred stock; and the holders of such second preferred stock and of such common stock shall be entitled to one vote (in person or by proxy) for each share of such second preferred and for each share of such common stock.

With the consent of any holder thereof, any and all of the first preferred stock and any and all of the second preferred stock shall be subject to redemption, and may be redeemed at not less than the par thereof and accrued interest, upon the 1st day of January in any year, at the principal office of the corporation, at Jersey City, N. J. On or before the 1st day of November next preceding such date for redemption, notice of intention so to redeem shall be given as follows: Printed notice addressed to each several record holder of such preferred stock who shall have caused his address to be recorded upon the books of the corporation shall be mailed to him at such address, and also shall be published once in each week for the eight weeks, beginning of such 1st day of November, in one newspaper published in the city of New York and in one newspaper published in the city of Paris, which notice shall invite tenders of such preferred stock for retirement.

To provide wholly or in part for such redemption and retirement of such preferred stock, from time to time the corporation, by its board of directors, and in the discretion of the board, may create and may issue common stock in an aggregate amount equal to the amount of such preferred stock so redeemed and retired; and from time to time, upon the redemption and retirement of such preferred stock, certificates may be issued and delivered for corresponding amounts of common stock, which shall be deemed to be, and shall be, full paid and nonassessable if issued either for money or in exchange for a corresponding amount of such preferred stock.

[Page 1182.]

Fifth. The names and post-office addresses of the incorporators and the number of shares subscribed for by each (the aggregate of such subscriptions being the amount of the capital stock with which the company commences business) are as follows:

Name.	Post-office address.	Number of shares.		
		First preferred stock.	Second preferred stock.	Common stock.
William P. Chapman, Jr.	310 West Forty-fifth Street, New York City, N. Y.	8	3	6
Henry W. Clark	329 West Seventy-fourth Street, New York City, N. Y.	8	3	6
Francis D. Pollack	Summit, N. J.	8	3	5

Sixth. The duration of the corporation shall be perpetual.

Seventh. The corporation may use and apply its surplus earnings or accumulated profits, authorized to be reserved as a working capital, to the purchase or acquisition of property and to the purchase and acquisition of its own capital stock, from time to time, to such extent and in such manner and upon such terms as its board of directors shall determine; and neither the property nor the capital stock so purchased and acquired, nor any of its capital stock taken in payment or satisfaction of any debt due to the corporation, shall be regarded as profits for the purposes of declaration or payment of dividends, unless otherwise determined by a majority in interest of all the stockholders.

The board of directors, by resolution adopted by a majority of the whole board, may designate five or more directors to constitute an executive committee, which committee, to the extent provided in said resolution or in the by-laws of the corporation, shall have and may exercise all the delegable powers of the board of directors in the management of the business affairs of the corporation.

The board of directors, by resolution adopted by a majority of the whole board, may designate a special committee of the board, consisting of directors resident in France; and such special committee shall possess and exercise such powers and perform such duties as may be delegated to it from time to time by the board of directors or by the by-laws of the corporation.

The board of directors, from time to time, shall determine whether and to what extent and at what times and places and under what conditions and regulations the accounts and books of the corporation, or any of them, shall be open to the inspection of the stockholders, and no stockholder shall have any right of inspecting any account or book or document of the corporation, except as conferred by statute or authorized by the board of directors or by a resolution of the stockholders.

The board of directors shall have power to make and to alter by-laws, but without prejudice to the power of the stockholders in general meeting to alter or repeal the same.

The corporation in its by-laws may prescribe the number necessary to constitute a quorum of the board of directors, which number, unless otherwise required by law, may be less than a majority of the whole number.

[Page 1183.]

The board of directors, without any assent or vote of stockholders, shall have power to create, issue, and sell bonds of the corporation, and to authorize and cause to be executed mortgage and liens upon the real property and the personal property, concessions, and franchises of the company (acquired and to be acquired) to secure the payment of the principal and interest of any such bonds, and also to determine the amount of such bond issue or issues, the rate of interest upon such bonds, and the conditions and price of issue, the holders of all the stock of the corporation at any time outstanding hereby expressly consenting to and approving of any and all bonds and mortgages so authorized, but in the event of the acquisition of the canal of the Campagnie Nouvelle du Canal de Panama there shall be accorded to the shareholders and bondholders of the Campagnie Universelle du Canal Interoceanique de Panama in liquidation a right of preference to subscribe for one-half in amount of such bonds whenever offered for sale.

In witness whereof we have hereunto set our hands and seals the 27th day of December, 1899.

William P. Chapman, Jr. [L. S.]
Henry W. Clark. [L. S.]
Francis D. Pollak. [L. S.]

Signed, sealed, and delivered in the presence of—
Wm. Nelson Cromwell.
Francis Lynde Stetson.

State of New York, *County of New York*, *ss:*

Be it remembered that on this 27th day of December, 1899, before the undersigned, a duly authorized commissioner of deeds for the State of New Jersey, in and for the State and county aforesaid, personally appeared William P. Chapman, Jr., Henry W. Clark, and Francis D. Pollak, who I am satisfied are the persons named in and who executed the foregoing certificate of incorporation, and I having first made known to them the contents thereof, they did acknowledge that they signed, sealed, and delivered the same as their voluntary act and deed.

In witness whereof I have hereunto set my hand and affixed my official seal as such commissioner for New Jersey on the date aforesaid.

[SEAL.] CHARLES EDGAR MILLS,
Commissioner of Deeds for the State of New Jersey in New York.

The Interoceanic Canal Company.

This is to certify that the undersigned do hereby associate themselves into a corporation under and by virtue of the provisions of an act of the Legislature of the State of New Jersey, entitled "An act concerning corporations" (revision of 1896), and the several supplements thereto and acts amendatory thereof, and do severally agree to take the number of shares of capital stock set opposite their respective names:

First. The name of the corporation is the Interoceanic Canal Company.

[Page 1184.]

Second. The location of the principal office in the State of New Jersey is at No. 83 Montgomery Street, in the city of Jersey City, county of Hudson. Said office is to be registered with the New Jersey Title Guarantee and Trust Company. The name of the agent therein and in charge thereof, upon whom process against this corporation may be served, is "The New Jersey Title Guarantee and Trust Company."

Third. The objects for which this corporation is formed are:

To survey, locate, excavate, construct, enlarge, extend, use, maintain, own, and operate a maritime canal and its accessories between the Atlantic and Pacific Oceans through the territory of Nicaraugua or any other territory in Central or South America.

To acquire the concessions granted, or heretofore granted, by any government for the construction and operation of a maritime canal and its accessories between the Atlantic and Pacific Oceans in Central or South America; and the corporation shall have all the rights, prerogatives, and powers necessary to fulfill the duties and obligations imposed, and to enjoy the privileges conferred upon it by such concessions; and the corporation shall have the power to formulate rules and regulations for the construction, management, care, protection, improvement, use, and operation of the canal and its accessories and appurtenances, and for the collection of its tolls, and may modify such rules and regulations at its discretion.

To survey, locate, construct, purchase, lease, maintain, own, and operate roads, railways with any motive power for the carriage of passengers and freight, navigation lines by boats or steamers, and any other means of transportation, and telegraph, cable, and telephone lines in such place or places as the company may deem necessary or convenient for the construction and surveys of the canal and its appurtenances and for the more advantageous maintenance and operation thereof.

To acquire, hold, deal with, and dispose of as to the company may seem proper all spaces of lands and waters that may be necessary or convenient for the construction, extension, enlargement, maintenance, repair, protection, use, and enjoyment of the canal and its accessories, including all spaces required for the deposit of materials from excavations and cuttings for the overflow arising from lakes, lagoons, and streams, and from dams in rivers, and from all deflections and rectifications of streams, and for ports and extensions thereof, and for docks, dikes, piers, basins, sluices, weirs, locks, guard gates, reservoirs, embankments, walls, and drainage and discharge channels, for lights, lighthouses, beacons, buildings, storehouses, machine shops, hospitals, shipyards, deposits of coal, wood, and materials, and including all land traversed or submerged by overflow or by surplus waters, and for whatever purpose may be necessary or convenient; also to acquire, hold, colonize, deal with, and dispose of all lands and rights in land and real property which it may from time to time acquire.

To levy and collect transit, navigation, tonnage, light, lighthouse, anchorage, and port dues, towage, lighterage, storage, wharfage, pilotage, hospital, quarantine, and all other similar charges, from steamers, ships, vessels, and boats of all

[Page 1185.]

kinds, and from passengers, merchandise, and cargo of all kinds, for which purpose the corporation may at its pleasure establish and modify its tariffs.

To have and exercise all the rights and privileges enjoyed by mining enterprises, lumber companies, manufacturing companies of all kinds, importing and exporting companies and in general all mercantile companies; and also to have and exercise all the rights and privileges enjoyed by enterprises which have for their object the establishment of shipyards, dry docks, warehouse business, the purchase, storage, and sale of coal, the organization of express companies, agricultural pursuits, and fishing.

To buy and sell and otherwise deal in real estate.

To operate hotels and boarding houses, and hospitals, and stores for the sale of provisions, clothing, and every kind of merchandise.

To supply water from the canal and its appurtenances to persons, firms, or corporations that may desire it for irrigation, supply of towns, motive power, or for any other purpose, and to fix and collect dues for these services.

To establish in countries foreign to the United States, and in accordance with terms of concessions granted by the governments of such countries, a police force duly organized for the protection of life and property and preservation or order along the route of the canal.

To survey, locate, construct, purchase, lease, maintain, own, and operate railways, telegraph, cable, and telephone lines, roads, and lines of navigation by boats or steamers and other means of transportation anywhere outside the State of New Jersey.

To purchase, hold, sell, assign, transfer, mortgage, pledge, or otherwise dispose of the shares of the capital stock or any bonds, securities, or evidences of indebtedness created by any other corporations of the State of New Jersey or of any other State or foreign country, and while owner of said stock to exercise all the rights, powers, and privileges of ownership, including the right to vote thereon.

To build, construct, and repair railroads, water, gas, or electric works, tunnels, bridges, viaducts, canals, hotels, wharves, piers and any like works of internal improvement or public use or utility outside the State of New Jersey.

To make and enter into contracts of every sort and kind with any individual, firm, association, corporation, private, public, or municipal, body politic, or with any government, national, State, Territorial, or colonial.

The corporation shall have power to conduct its business in all its branches in any State or country, or have one or more offices, and unlimitedly to hold, purchase, mortgage, and convey real and personal property in the State of New Jersey and in all other States and in all foreign countries.

Fourth. The total authorized capital stock of this corporation is $100,000,000, divided into 1,000,000 shares of the par value of $100 each.

Fifth. The names and post-office addresses of the incorporators and the number of shares subscribed for by each, the aggregate of such subscriptions being

[Page 1186.]

the amount of capital stock with which the company will commence business, are as follows:

Name.	Post-office address.	Number shares.
William B. Crowell	Jersey City, N. J.	10
Levi B. Gillchrest	do	10
James M. V. Rooney	do	10
James J. Traynor	do	10
George W. Bell	do	10
Charles B. Cadley	do	10
Richard D. Purcell	do	10

Sixth. The board of directors may by resolution provide that any government, upon becoming and while continuing to be a stockholder in this corporation, may have the right of naming one or more members of the board of directors of the corporation, which director or directors shall have all the rights, privileges, and powers conferred upon any director by this certificate of incorporation by the laws of the State of New Jersey or by the by-laws of this corporation. The board of directors shall have power, without the assent or vote of the stockholders, to make, alter, amend, and repeal by-laws for the corporation, but the by-laws shall always provide for notice of the objects of any special meeting of stockholders, and the by-laws shall require an annual meeting of the stockholders to be held at the principal office of the corporation in the State of New Jersey on the first Tuesday of May in each and every year at 12 o'clock noon, and no change in the time of holding the said annual meeting of the stockholders shall be made except by amendment made to said by-laws by the stockholders at any one of such annual meetings or at a special meeting called for such purpose upon notice to the stockholders at least fifteen days before day fixed by such by-laws for such a meeting.

The directors shall have power to fix the amount to be reserved as working capital, to authorize and cause to be executed to any amount bonds or other obligations of the corporations and mortgages and liens upon the property of the corporation, or any part thereof, and whether then owned or afterwards acquired, and from time to time to sell, assign, transfer, or otherwise dispose of any or all of its property; but no sale of all of its property shall be made except upon the vote of the holders of a majority of the stock. The board of directors from time to time shall determine whether and to what extent and at what time and places and under what conditions and regulations the accounts and books of the corporation or any of them shall be opened to the inspection of the stockholders, and no stockholder shall have any right of inspecting any account, or book, or document of the corporation except as conferred by statute or authorized by the board of directors or by a resolution of the stockholders.

The directors shall have power to hold their meetings, to have one or more offices, and to keep the books of the corporation (except the stock and transfer of books) outside of the State of New Jersey and at such places as may from time to time be designated by them.

The number of directors of this corporation upon its organization shall be five, but thereafter the directors can increase or diminish the number by power of the provisions contained in the by-laws.

[Page 1187.]

The directors shall be divided as equally as may be into three classes. The seats of directors of the first class shall be vacated at the expiration of the first year, of the second class at the expiration of the second year, and of the third class at the expiration of the third year, so that one-third may be chosen every year.

The board of directors, by resolution passed by a majority of the whole board, may designate three or more directors to constitute an executive committee, to the extent provided in said resolution or in the by-laws of the corporation, shall have and may exercise the power of the board of directors in the management of the business and affairs of the corporation, and shall have power to authorize the seal of the corporation to be affixed to all papers which may require it.

The board of directors may in like manner designate one of their number to be a managing director, who may possess and exercise all such of the powers of the corporation as may be conferred upon him by the said board by resolution or by the by-laws of the company.

Seventh. The period of existence of this corporation is to be perpetual.

In witness whereof we have hereunto set our hands and seals this 31st day of March, A. D. 1900.

William B. Crowell. [L. S.]
Levi B. Gilchrest, [L. S.]
James M. V. Rooney. [L. S.]
James J. Traynor. [L. S.]
George W. Bell. [L. S.]
Charles P. Cadley. [L. S.]
R. D. Purcell. [L. S.]

Signed, sealed, and delivered in the presence of—
Joseph Garrison.

STATE OF NEW YORK,
City and County of New York, ss:

Be it remembered that on the 21st day of March, A. D., 1900, before me, a master in chancery of New Jersey, personally appeared William B. Crowell, Levi B. Gilchrest, John M. V. Rooney, James J. Traynor, George W. Bell, Charles P. Cadley, Richard D. Purcell, who I am satisfied are the persons named in and who executed the foregoing certificate, and I having first made known to them the contents thereof, they did each acknowledge that they signed, sealed, and delivered the same as their voluntary act and deed.

JOSEPH GARRISON,
Master in Chancery of New Jersey.

Senator MORGAN. Was that the same broad, philanthropic or patriotic sentiment that caused you to take out that charter?

Mr. CROMWELL. Senator, I have declined to answer so often that I think I had better get a phonograph to repeat it to you.

Senator MORGAN. If you will be good enough to remember that you are under oath, and a witness——

Mr. CROMWELL. I remember both, sir.

Senator MORGAN (continuing). And answer the questions; we will get along better.

Mr. CROMWELL. I remember both, sir; and I repeat the answer again.

Senator MORGAN. What is the answer?

[Page 1188.]

Mr. CROMWELL. That I decline to answer, on the ground that it is a privileged communication.

Senator MORGAN. Why was it privileged?

Mr. CROMWELL. That is my answer, sir.

Senator MORGAN. Why was it privileged? State how and why.

Mr. CROMWELL. I have already answered, sir; and I shall answer no further.

Senator MORGAN. You have not answered that question. It has never been put to you before.

How and why is that a privileged matter or question?

Mr. CROMWELL. Because it arises in the course of my employment as general counsel of the New Panama Canal Co.

Senator MORGAN. And you refuse, therefore, to acknowledge or to state anything about your being a subscribing witness to that incorporation charter, which is printed in the laws of New Jersey?

Mr. CROMWELL. I decline, for the same reason.

20.

[Page 1216.]

Senator MORGAN. Who was your correspondent down there?

Mr. CROMWELL. I had nothing to do with that subject.

Senator MORGAN. Who was your correspondent down there?

Mr. CROMWELL. I must beg to be excused, if you are going to go into the matter of my professional relations to the canal company.

Senator MORGAN. Your professional relations appear and disappear so rapidly

[Page 1217.]

that I never know when I am touching on them. [Laughter.]

Mr. CROMWELL. You are a good lawyer, and you ought to knew without being told.

Senator MORGAN. I am not as good a lawyer as it requires to ascertain when a man's professional obligations bounce up and stop the ship, and then again when they sink out of sight, as he wants to progress with his voyage. I can not understand that. I am not that sort of a lawyer.

Mr. CROMWELL. You are so many sorts of a lawyer that I should think you would be equal to any such emergency.

21.

[Page 1219.]

Senator MORGAN. Do you recall that letter?

Mr. CROMWELL. This is a part of the professional service which I have performed to the Panama Canal Co., and I beg to be excused from interrogation concerning it.

Senator MORGAN. We can not excuse you; at least, I can not. I will ask you the question, do you remember the letter?

Mr. CROMWELL. I beg to be excused from any interrogation regarding any business——

Senator MORGAN. You can not exactly put a gag in the mouth of a Senator at this committee table and refuse him permission to ask you a question. I ask you the question and I ask you to answer.

By request, the stenographer read the pending question, as follows:

[Page 1220.]

"Do you remember the letter?"

Mr. CROMWELL. The letter speaks for itself. It is a matter of public record. I have no comment to make upon it.

Senator MORGAN. Do you remember it?

Mr. CROMWELL. I do.

Senator MORGAN. From what sources did you get that very important information contained in those letters?

Mr. CROMWELL. I respectfully beg to be excused from any statement or discussion of the affairs of my clients.

Senator MORGAN. Did that letter contain the truth as you understood it?

Mr. CROMWELL. I respectfully beg to be excused from a discussion of the affairs of my clients.

Senator MORGAN. I did not ask if it contained falsehood. Do you want to be excused from telling the truth about it?

Mr. CROMWELL. I beg to be excused from a discussion of the affairs of my clients.

Senator MORGAN. You decline to say whether that letter contains the truth as you understood it?

Mr. CROMWELL. I decline to be drawn into a discussion of the affairs of my clients.

Senator MORGAN. You have already spoken of that concession. That has been mentioned here in your testimony this morning.

Mr. CROMWELL. That is a part of the record titles of the Panama Canal Co. and part of the records of the Government of the United States, and I very properly referred to it.

Senator MORGAN. Having made the disclosure of your knowledge of the fact that that concession was then under negotiation and what was given for it, etc., I ask you, on the basis of that disclosure, to explain to this committee fully the whole transaction.

Mr. CROMWELL. The statement which I have made to you is no disclosure. The statement I have made to you concerning the extension is a matter of record in the opinions of the Attorney General and upon file in the archives of the Government of the United States passing the title of the New Panama Canal Co.

Senator MORGAN. If so, give your recollection of what those records contain.

Mr. CROMWELL. The information I have given you this morning is based upon the opinions which have been passed by the Attorney General, and which are a part of the archives of this Government. They are not confidential communications, and for that reason, and for that reason alone, have I stated them to you.

Senator MORGAN. Will you state your recollection of what those records contain?

Mr. CROMWELL. The opinion of the Attorney General?

Senator MORGAN. As you have given it there, and as you have given it here, and as it is recorded, and as you have sworn to it. As you have refused to state what you know, I want to know if you refuse to state what you recollect of the contents of those records?

Mr. CROMWELL. Senator, I respectfully decline to be drawn into a discussion involving confidential relations.

Senator MORGAN. I am not attempting, nor have I any privilege of discussing anything with you. It is my duty, as an officer of the Government of the United States and as a Member of the Senate and as a member of this com-

[Page 1221.]

mittee, to ask you questions to bring out information material to the inquiry in this matter, and not to discuss it. I ask you the questions to get the information that you evidently have, and I ask whether you will disclose it?

Mr. CROMWELL. I repeat my answer, sir.

22.

Senator MORGAN. There was a telegram mentioned in this letter as having been sent by you to Mr. Hay, Secretary of State: "I beg leave to confirm the telegram which I sent you at 10.45 this morning, as per inclosure." What was that telegram?

Mr. CROMWELL. I respectfully beg to be excused, for the same reason.

Senator MORGAN. Well, there was an inclosure in that letter, was there not?

Mr. CROMWELL. I repeat my answer.

Senator MORGAN. You refuse to state?

Mr. CROMWELL. I do.

Senator MORGAN. Did you write that letter?

Mr. CROMWELL. I did.

Senator MORGAN. And there was an inclosure in it?

Mr. CROMWELL. I decline to state.

Senator MORGAN. Will you give the substance of that inclosure?

Mr. CROMWELL. I decline to answer.

Senator MORGAN. You refuse to answer?

Mr. CROMWELL. I do refuse to answer.

23.

Senator MORGAN. Yes. I do not propose to stop this——

Mr. CROMWELL. Whatever was inclosed is a matter of public record, and you can get it at the State Department.

Senator MORGAN. It might not suit the convenience of the committee to get the public records in this matter, and as you know it, why can you not state it?

Mr. CROMWELL. I am under the obligations of professional duty, as you are under certain obligations which you consider.

Senator MORGAN. Is it true, Mr. Cromwell, that you are now under a professional obligation to refuse to state the contents of this letter or of the telegram inclosed in it?

Mr. CROMWELL. It is.

Senator MORGAN. Is that true?

Mr. CROMWELL. It is, and you ought to know it, as a lawyer.

24.

Senator MORGAN. You did not know that a war was about to break out? Did you know what the quarrel was between the President of Colombia and the Panama Canal Co. at that time?

Mr. CROMWELL. I respectfully decline to answer.

25.

[Page 1222.]

Senator MORGAN. Had the Panama Canal Co. then made an overture or a request of the Colombian Government for this concession from October 31, 1904, to October 31, 1910?

Mr. CROMWELL. I respectfully decline to answer.

26.

Senator MORGAN. Was that subject pending before the Government of Colombia at the time of the date of this letter?

Mr. CROMWELL. I respectfully decline to answer.
Senator MORGAN. You refuse to answer?
Mr. CROMWELL. I do.

27.

Senator MORGAN. You put that on the ground of professional confidence?
Mr. CROMWELL. I do.
Senator MORGAN. You know the fact, whether it was or not?
Mr. CROMWELL. I do not say whether I knew the fact or not.
Senator MORGAN. What is that?
Mr. CROMWELL. I have not said that I knew the fact.
Senator MORGAN. Well, do you know the fact?
Mr. CROMWELL. I decline to answer.

28.

[Page 1223.]

Senator MORGAN. Who submitted that agreement with the Panama Canal Co. to the Congress of Colombia?
Mr. CROMWELL. I respectfully decline to answer.
Senator MORGAN. It was submitted.
Mr. CROMWELL. You stated it so.
Senator MORGAN. What do you say about it?
Mr. CROMWELL. I decline to answer.
Senator MORGAN. But you have already informed Mr. Hay that it was submitted.
Mr. CROMWELL. The record speaks for itself, Senator.
Senator MORGAN. Is that your letter?
Mr. CROMWELL. It is.
Senator MORGAN. You wrote it?
Mr. CROMWELL. I did.
Senator MORGAN. Is it true?
Mr. CROMWELL. Well, Senator, you ought to have the courtesy, if you have not the judgment, to know that I would not write a letter that was not true.
Senator MORGAN. It is not that point, at all. I want to know whether you stated at that time what you knew to be the fact?
Mr. CROMWELL. I decline to be drawn into a discussion of my relations to my clients.
By request, the stenographer repeated the pending question.
Mr. CROMWELL. I repeat that I decline to be drawn into a discussion of business involving my clients.
Senator MORGAN. You refuse to answer that question?
Mr. CROMWELL. I do, sir, for the same reason.

29.

[Page 1229.]

Senator MORGAN. On yesterday, Mr. Cromwell, I read you a letter from Mr. Bonnardel, president of the board of directors, dated the 18th of November, 1898, which has gone into the record. Previously there had been incorporated in the record your letter signed "William Nelson Cromwell, counsel New Panama Co.," addressed to Mr. Hay, Secretary of State, upon which I desire to ask you some questions. You declined on yesterday to state what was the inclosure in that letter. Do you still decline?
Mr. CROMWELL. The letter speaks for itself, Senator. I decline to make further comment upon it.
Senator MORGAN. That inclosure was a part of the letter?
Mr. CROMWELL. The letter speaks for itself, and I decline to make further comment upon it.
Senator MORGAN. Was that inclosure a part of that letter?
Mr. CROMWELL. The letter speaks for itself, and I must beg to be excused from further explanation.
Senator MORGAN. Do you remember the contents of that inclosure?
Mr. CROMWELL. The letter speaks for itself.
Senator MORGAN. No; the letter does not speak about your memory.

Mr. CROMWELL. I respectfully decline to go into the discussion of either the letter, its contents, or any inclosures.

Senator MORGAN. You decline, then, to state whether you recollect the contents of that inclosure?

Mr. CROMWELL. I do, sir; for the reason that it is part of my professional duty.

Senator MORGAN. To do what—to conceal everything that comes into your hands?

Mr. CROMWELL. It is part of my professional duty to observe the confidences of my client in the professional work in which I am engaged.

30.

Senator MORGAN. Did you observe the confidence of your client in communicating that paper to the Secretary of State?

Mr. CROMWELL. It speaks for itself; it is a matter of public record.

Senator MORGAN. Well, but did you?

Mr. CROMWELL. It speaks for itself; it is a matter of public record.

Senator MORGAN. Mr. Cromwell, you may think that you are concealing the truth by these refusals, but you are not.

Mr. CROMWELL. I do not think anything of the kind; nor do I think that you are conducting your examination properly.

31.

What decision of the Government of Panama is it that is included in the statement that I will read to you:

"Upon my return I learned through Director General Hutin, who had preceded me to New York, that the measure which had just been acted on by one branch only of the Colombian Congress was a bill to authorize the Executive to negotiate the terms of and to conclude a further prorogation of six years from 1904 for the completion of the canal, under a communication which the company

[Page 1230.]

had addressed to the Government, in the form of which I inclose you a translation."

What was the action of the Colombian Congress to which you referred?

Mr. CROMWELL. For the reason stated I respectfully decline to answer.

32.

Senator MORGAN. You inclosed a translation, did you, of that order—that action?

Mr. CROMWELL. The letter speaks for itself, Senator. It is on the files of the State Department. You can get it if you want it, with any inclosures.

Senator MORGAN. I want your recollection of it, Mr. Cromwell.

Mr. CROMWELL. There is no secrecy about it.

Senator MORGAN. I want your recollection of it. State it.

Mr. CROMWELL. I decline to discuss the subject for the reasons I have stated.

Mr. MORGAN. You decline, then, to state what was the translation that you sent to Mr. Hay of the paper referred to?

Mr. CROMWELL. I do. The public records will give you the information, if you want it.

33.

Senator MORGAN. Do you not know that the Congress of Colombia rejected and refused to ratify the proposition made to it by the Panama Canal Co. at that time for a prorogation or prolongation of the concession from October 31, 1904, to October 31, 1910?

Mr. CROMWELL. I decline to state for the reson given.

Senator MORGAN. Do you know that personally?

Mr. CROMWELL. I decline to state for the reason given, sir.

Senator MORGAN. Is all your knowledge—your personal, outside knowledge, that you acquired as any other citizen—at the bidding of your company?

Mr. CROMWELL. I decline to answer further than I have answered.

34.

Senator MORGAN (reading):

"You will note that the company specifically stated to the Government that the prorogation was not a matter of absolute necessity, but was desirable in the interests of commerce and navigation to enable an even deeper cut to be made and which would reduce the number of locks to four, but which reduction would, of course, require more time than the plan adopted."

What did you mean by a cut there?

Mr. CROMWELL. I decline to discuss the subject for the reason I have stated.

Senator MORGAN. You propose, then, to be merely recalcitrant?

35.

[Page 1231.]

Senator MORGAN. Well, you made the statement. If the confidence existed, so that you can not now reveal it to the committee of the Senate, why did it not exist at the time that you revealed it to the Secretary of State?

Mr. CROMWELL. Senator, my answer is complete and should be convincing to you that any reference by way of explanation or exposition of any correspondence that I have had is professional. The fact of the correspondence is official is true; it is on the record; you can get it. There you should get it.

36.

Senator MORGAN. You further say to Mr. Hay: "You will note that the bill proposed to confer power upon the Executive, and this happened to arise under extraordinary political conditions in Bogota." What were they?

Mr. CROMWELL. I decline to state, for the reasons I have mentioned.

Senator MORGAN. Are extraordinary political conditions in Bogota part of your professional confidences with your company?

Mr. CROMWELL. Any information I acquired is within the scope of that duty.

Senator MORGAN. So that if the Panama Canal Co. had employed you to do any work that was contrary to the welfare and interests of the United States, you would feel that you would be obliged to conceal it?

Mr. CROMWELL. I decline to answer such hypothetical and impertinent questions.

Senator MORGAN. Hypothetical and impertinent, both?

Mr. CROMWELL. Both.

Senator MORGAN. Well, I have to submit to your very unusual and indecent interruptions, because the committee seems to be disposed to compel me to.

Mr. CROMWELL. It is no more unusual or indecent than yours.

37.

[Page 1232.]

Senator MORGAN. I will read that entire paragraph again, so as to get the precise language of it (reading):

'You will note that this bill proposes to confer power upon the Executive, and this happened to arise under extraordinary political conditions in Bogota. As you have probably been advised through official channels, a serious difference has recently been existing between the House of Representatives of Colombia and the President, the House having passed formal resolutions declaring the office of President vacant and refusing to recognize the qualification of the President before the supreme court."

Did you get that statement that you made to Mr. Hay as a professional confidence from the New Panama Canal Co.?

Mr. CROMWELL. It is embraced, sir, within the scope of my professional duty.

Senator MORGAN. You revealed it to Mr. Hay; you decline to reveal it again to the committee?

Mr. CROMWELL. It is revealed in the letter, Senator.

Senator MORGAN. Very good. Do you decline to state now, as a fact within your knowledge at that time, that the House had refused to recognize the qualification of the President before the supreme court, and that they had declared his office vacant?

Mr. CROMWELL. I decline to make further discussion of the letter, Senator, because the letter explains itself.

Senator MORGAN. Is that a professional confidence, that you shall not make a further explanation of this letter?

Mr. CROMWELL. Yes, sir.

Senator MORGAN. It is?

Mr. CROMWELL. It is.

Senator MORGAN. You swear to that?

Mr. CROMWELL. I do.

38.

[Page 1233.]

Senator MORGAN. In what part of your duties as attorney was that professional confidence provided for?

Mr. CROMWELL. Within the general scope of my professional duties, sir.

Senator MORGAN. What was that?

Mr. CROMWELL. I can describe it no more particularly than that.

Senator MORGAN (reading):

"We therefore construe the action of the House of Representatives as only a part of the strife between the House and the President, and not a declaration of the policy of the Nation or the Congress in respect of the Panama Canal, and as not evidencing hostility to the company itself."

On what basis did you make that construction?

Mr. CROMWELL. I have to repeat my former answer, Senator.

Senator MORGAN. You do not have to do it unless you want to swear to it.

Mr. CROMWELL. I beg your pardon. I mean I do repeat my former answer.

Senator MORGAN. And you therefore decline to inform the committee the basis of fact upon which you made that statement to Mr. Hay?

Mr. CROMWELL. I do, sir, respectfully, for the reasons given.

39.

Senator MORGAN (reading):

"Our company has not the least apprehension regarding any prorogation of its concessions it may consider necessary in the future."

What removed your apprehensions in regard to the prorogation of its concessions?

Mr. CROMWELL. I make the same reply, Senator.

Senator MORGAN. If the Panama Canal Co. has, through its secretary, Mr. Lampré—you know Mr. Lampré, do you?

Mr. CROMWELL. Yes, sir.

Senator MORGAN (continuing). If that company has, through Mr. Lampré, uncovered this whole subject in his deposition before this committee on a previous occasion, do you still feel bound to withhold all information you possess in regard to the same subject?

Mr. CROMWELL. I do, Senator.

40.

Senator MORGAN. Well, I will read that to you, or I will get my friend on my right here to read it. because I am in quite a poor condition of health this morning. Just read it right along, question and answer, right through.

Senator Taliaferro, as requested, thereupon read as follows:

"The examination of Mr. Lampré then went on, as follows:

"The CHAIRMAN. Now, Mr. Lampré, that letter to the President of the United States does not contain any proposition?

"M. LAMPRÉ. No; not at that time; no, sir.

"The CHAIRMAN. Why was it written?

"M. LAMPRÉ. Because, to my recollection, it was contemplated at the time that something ought to be done in the way of a reorganization of the company. It appeared at the time that the Nicaragua concession was under discussion; that the rivalry of such a canal might be a great danger to the Panama Canal, and we thought at the time, as far as I can remember—it is rather old, it is three years ago—we thought at the time that we had to lay the whole subject before the President in order to ascertain and to see under what condition we might, if necessary, Americanize our corporation and build the canal in partner-

[Page 1234.]

ship with the American interests. That is my recollection."

Senator MORGAN. One minute. You observe that the words "Americanize the corporation" are there. Was that paper that was read to you the other day, containing a statement of what had taken place by the Panama Canal Co. in regard to the Americanization of the canal, the result of the action spoken of there?

Mr. CROMWELL. I do not know, Senator.

Senator MORGAN. You have no information on that subject?

Mr. CROMWELL. No, sir.

Senator MORGAN. Although the paper handed to you recites it?

Mr. CROMWELL. It recites a different subject, sir.

Senator MORGAN. Sir?

Mr. CROMWELL. It recites a different subject at a different time.

Senator MORGAN. A different subject at a different time?

Mr. CROMWELL. Yes, sir.

Senator MORGAN. Read on, if you please.

Senator Taliaferro, as requested, read as follows:

"The CHAIRMAN. With the American Government?

"M. LAMPRÉ. Well, I suppose private or public American interests. I think at the time it was contemplated to have a private corporation.

"The CHAIRMAN. You had money enough then on hand or in prospect to build the canal?

"M. LAMPRÉ. We had not in cash money enough.

"The CHAIRMAN. You had good credit, though?

"M. LAMPRÉ. Yes; I think we had, but still——

"The CHAIRMAN. You were confident, then, that you could complete the canal?

"M. LAMPRÉ. We were confident; but still, as you know, there was the rivalry of the Nicaragua Canal.

"The CHAIRMAN. And it was the rivalry of the Nicaragua route that caused this paper to be printed?

"M. LAMPRÉ. Yes, sir; exactly.

"The CHAIRMAN. Was it argued at the time the letter was written that the United States was about to take or had taken action in favor of the Nicaragua route?

"M. LAMPRÉ. I forget whether it was at that time.

"The CHAIRMAN. We can ascertain that by reference. Was this letter discussed and the authority given to send it to the President at a meeting of the board of directors of the New Panama Canal Co.?

"M. LAMPRÉ. Yes; it is in accordance with the resolution of the board.

"The CHAIRMAN. The letter says that the board of directors is composed of gentlemen in an independent position.

"M. LAMPRÉ. Yes, sir.

"The CHAIRMAN. They must have been interested in and identified with large affairs in Paris?

"M. LAMPRÉ. So they were, and are still at the present time.

"The CHAIRMAN. Of a financial character?

"M. LAMPRÉ. Yes, sir.

"The CHAIRMAN. Was it not the fact that the new board was composed of gentlemen who took over the property on speculation?

[Page 1235.]

"M. LAMPRÉ. At the time or now?

'The CHAIRMAN. At the time it was consummated.

"M. LAMPRÉ. For speculation? No, sir.

"The CHAIRMAN. They took it over with the intention of completing the canal

"M. LAMPRÉ. Quite so. They were honest and straightforward in the intention. I must be positive on the subject.

"The CHAIRMAN. They are still able to do it, are they not?

"M. LAMPRÉ. Oh, yes, sir.

"The CHAIRMAN. The French people are still able to do it?

"M. LAMPRÉ. They might.

"The CHAIRMAN. They paid the indemnity to Germany without any trouble, and we thought that the most marvelous act ever performed.

"M. LAMPRÉ. I think we have enough cash in France.
"The CHAIRMAN. You have plenty there to do it?
"M. LAMPRÉ. Yes, sir.
"The CHAIRMAN. Why are you trying to sell this canal enterprise for $40,000,000 when your people are able to build it and have so much involved in it?
"M. LAMPRÉ. That is quite a different question, in my opinion. We have plenty of cash in France to build it, but the rivalry with the Nicaragua route and the possibility of the Congress of the United States passing a resolution for the construction of the Nicaragua Canal has frightened the people there, and so we thought it best to seek some kind of a combination here to build the canal, then with the assistance of the United States, and now to let the canal go to the United States if they will have it.
"The CHAIRMAN. Your first proposition was to build the canal and realize out of it what you expected to do?
"M. LAMPRÉ. Exactly.
"The CHAIRMAN. That was your first idea?
"M. LAMPRÉ. Exactly.
"The CHAIRMAN. That was the idea on which that letter was written?
"M. LAMPRÉ. Exactly, sir.
"The CHAIRMAN. Then if you could not do that, to prevent the building of it on the Nicaragua route?
"M. LAMPRÉ. We did not intend preventing anything, but we thought the Panama route in our opinion the best.
"The CHAIRMAN. Was it not the purpose of this movement to compel the United States to build on your ground or not build at all?
"M. LAMPRÉ. To compel?
"The CHAIRMAN. Yes.
"M. LAMPRÉ. We had no mind to compel anybody.
"The CHAIRMAN. I do not mean by force of arms.
"M. LAMPRÉ. Our opinion was that the United States Government, or Congress, passing upon a resolution for the construction of the Nicaragua Canal would place us in great difficulty to raise the money in France. So we thought that we might as well lay the whole subject before the United States.
"Senator MITCHELL. May I ask a question right there?
"The CHAIRMAN. Certainly.

[Page 1236.]

"Senator MITCHELL. Suppose the United States should decline the offer which has been made by your company, and suppose, furthermore, Congress should go on and authorize the construction of the Nicaragua Canal, do you think that the Panama Canal would then be completed?
"M. LAMPRÉ. It might be.
"Senator MITCHELL. What is your best judgment on that point? What is your opinion?
"M. LAMPRÉ. It might be. We might raise the money still in France.
"The CHAIRMAN. Just in that connection I will ask you if you have made efforts to raise in France to complete the canal?
"M. LAMPRÉ. No; for we have no bondholders and not any bonded indebtedness at all.
"The CHAIRMAN. I do not mean that. Have you asked for subscriptions?
"M. LAMPRÉ. No; we have not.
"The CHAIRMAN. You have not invited the French people to subscribe at all?
"M. LAMPRÉ. No; we have not, because we thought it best, under the circumstances, not to go before the public, being given the possibility of the construction of the Nicaragua Canal by the United States.
"The CHAIRMAN. In this letter to the President it is stated that the assets of the company exceed in value $100,000,000.
"M. LAMPRÉ. Yes, sir.
"The CHAIRMAN. That the property is free from incumbrance; that the title is unquestionable; that the company has no other debts than the monthly pay rolls; that it has no mortgages or bonded indebtedness, and its cash reserve is largely in excess of its actual needs.
"M. LAMPRÉ. Yes, sir.

"The CHAIRMAN. So this statement of the great strength and confidence of the Panama Canal Co. was sent to the President to inspire him with like confidence in the success of the Panama Canal and to convince him and Congress and our people that it would be a fatal competition to the Nicaragua Canal?

"M. LAMPRÉ. Well, I do not know, sir. I do not know what was at the time in the mind of the board. I can not answer that question. I do not know what they aimed at. I think it was only putting the whole subject before the President in the light in which it stood and showing how it stood.

"The CHAIRMAN. Or was it the purpose then to prepare the United States to become the purchasers of the Panama Canal?

"M. LAMPRÉ. At that time?

"The CHAIRMAN. At that time.

"M. LAMPRÉ. I do not know at the time what it was.

"The CHAIRMAN. You do not know when that idea originated?

"M. LAMPRÉ. No.

"The CHAIRMAN. What was the actual purpose and object of the letter to the President of the United States and the letters and telegrams to Cromwell, attorney, given with the message of the President of February 20, 1900? What was the actual purpose and object of the letter to the President of the United States

[Page. 1237.]

of the 18th day of November, 1898?

"M. LAMPRÉ. As far as I can recollect, the purpose was to lay the whole subject before the United States, and at the time we stated that should the United States abandon the idea of constructing the Nicaragua Canal we were ready to reorganize under the laws of this country and to organize an American corporation to complete the Panama Canal, which we thought the best route, and still think the best route. That is why we laid the whole subject before the United States at the time.

"The CHAIRMAN. In addition to this cheerful picture of the resources of the company, these letters boast of the conciliation of Colombia and that the entire feasibility and practicability of completing the canal is established by the members of two commissions who were the most distinguished men in their professions. Why did not a canal that was so well fortified in its appeal to public confidence obtain the money to complete it by subscriptions among the French people, who had already sunk $250,000,000 in it and only had the ditch, the buildings, the machinery, and the material on hand to show for this expenditure?

"M. LAMPRÉ. Just as I told you, Senator, on account of the contemplated building by the United States of the Nicaragua Canal."

41.

Senator MORGAN. Do you know anything at all of the transaction mentioned by Mr. Lampré in his testimony?

Mr. CROMWELL. Of what transaction, Senator?

Senator MORGAN. That which has just been read.

Mr. CROMWELL. The word "transaction" that you employ is a little uncertain to me, that is all.

Senator MORGAN. Well, do you know anything of the matter contained in the statement of Mr. Lampré which has just been read?

Mr. CROMWELL. As it is involved in the general scope of my professional duty, I must beg to be excused from further explanation.

Senator MORGAN. Here, then, Mr. Cromwell, is the secretary of the company under oath before this committee disclosing these facts. Do you pretend to have a professional confidence with that company that prevents you from making a statement in regard to those facts?

Mr. CROMWELL. The secretary had no such obligation. He was the secretary of the company and disclosed the facts, as he had a right to do and did do. That does not affect my duty.

Senator MORGAN. The secretary, then, you state, had the right to disclose them because he was not under a professional obligation?

Mr. CROMWELL. Yes, sir.

Senator MORGAN. You were not the counsel of the Panama Canal Co. in France, as you have stated here under oath two or three times?

Mr. Cromwell. I was not their general counsel in France, although when I visited there almost annually I advised them in my professional capacity, of course.

Senator Morgan. Not being the counsel of the company in France, and this disclosure having been made on oath by the secretary of the company, do you still insist that your professional relations to the Panama company compel you to refuse to make any statement in regard to the statement Mr. Lampré has made before this committee and which has just been read in your hearing?

[Page 1238.]

Mr. Cromwell. I do, Senator; because my relations are entirely distinct from those of Mr. Lampré.

Senator Morgan. What is the distinction?

Mr. Cromwell. He is the secretary of the company, an officer of the company, and gave his testimony fully. My relation is entirely different, sir.

Senator Morgan. Mr. Lampré states here, in respect of why the letter was written:

"Because, to my recollection, it was contemplated at the time that something ought to be done in the way of reorganization of the company. It appeared at the time that the Nicaragua concession was under discussion that the rivalry of such a canal might be a great danger to the Panama Canal; and we thought at the time, as far as I can remember—it is rather old; it is three years ago—we thought at the time that we had to lay the whole subject before the President in order to ascertain and to see under what conditions we might, if necessary, Americanize our corporation and build the canal in partnership with the American interests."

Do you not know, as a matter of fact contained in the records of the Panama Canal Co. in Paris, that a resolution was entered into by them to carry into effect this project of the Americanization of the canal?

Mr. Cromwell. Whatever information I have upon the subject, Senator, is comprised within the scope of my professional duty.

42.

Senator Morgan. Are the records and your knowledge of the records in Paris a matter of professional secrecy?

Mr. Cromwell. A matter of professional secrecy, Senator.

Senator Morgan. Confidence?

Mr. Cromwell. Yes, sir.

Senator Morgan. Did you not know, and do you not know, that that company came to the resolution that that canal was to be Americanized if practicable?

Mr. Cromwell. I repeat my answer, Senator.

Senator Morgan. Do you contradict anything that Mr. Lampré has stated in his sworn testimony before this committee?

Mr. Cromwell. I am not at liberty to speak about it, sir.

43.

[Page 1239.]

Senator Morgan. The plan that Mr. Lampré has revealed here was to take the canal out of the reach of Colombia, Americanize it, and make it an American institution. Do you know of any plan or project on the part of the canal company to carry that into effect?

Mr. Cromwell. I beg to be excused, Senator, for the reasons I have stated.

Senator Morgan. Excused from what?

Mr. Cromwell. From discussion of the subject.

By request, the stenographer read aloud the pending question, as follows:

"The plan that Mr. Lampré revealed here was to take the canal out of the reach of Colombia, Americanize it, and make it an American institution. Do you know of any plan or project on the part of the canal company to carry that into effect?"

Senator Morgan. What is your answer?

Mr. Cromwell. My answer is the same—that my professional relations would prohibit me from discussion of it, Senator.

44

Senator MORGAN. I will ask you whether that paper that was read in your hearing the other day, and that has gone into the record of the committee, the record of this examination, which recited the fact that you had been exclusively intrusted with the execution of the plan for the Americanization of the canal—whether that instrument, just prepared, and prepared by you, was intended to execute that order of the canal company?

Mr. CROMWELL. I decline to answer for the same reasons, sir.

Senator MORGAN. Have you any knowledge on the subject?

Mr. CROMWELL. I decline to state, sir, for the same reason.

Senator MORGAN. You decline to state whether you have any knowledge on the subject?

Mr. CROMWELL. Yes, sir; I mean I decline to discuss the subject, which involves my client's relations.

45.

Senator MORGAN. Did you not prepare that paper under a contract with the French company—the Panama Canal Co.—with you individually, giving you the exclusive right to control that subject in the United States? And did you not submit it to different persons in the United States?

Mr. CROMWELL. I have already answered that question the other day, and I beg leave to repeat it, sir, with the greatest respect to yourself.

46.

[Page 1240.]

By direction the stenographer read aloud the pending question, as follows:

"That contract confers upon Nelson G. Cromwell exclusive privileges and large remuneration for carrying a plan into effect. Was that the same plan of which Lampré was speaking?

Mr. CROMWELL. I beg to be excused from a discussion of the subject, which involves——

Senator MORGAN. Well, I can not excuse you. Do you refuse?

Mr. CROMWELL. I do refuse, Senator, for the reasons stated.

47.

Senator MORGAN. A while ago, in your testimony, you spoke about this same matter to which I have just referred, and said that what Lampré was speaking of referred to a different matter from this paper of yours about the Americanization of the canal. What different matter was it?

Mr. CROMWELL. My impression was that that related to the proposal that had been made to the Committee on Rivers and Harbors of the House of Representatives, in which it was proposed to Americanize the company.

Senator MORGAN. What proposition was that? Who made that proposition?

Mr. CROMWELL. That was made by the New Panama Canal Co., through its president and myself.

Senator MORGAN. Were you present at the time?

Mr. CROMWELL. Yes, sir.

Senator MORGAN. Did you assist in it?

Mr. CROMWELL. Yes, sir.

Senator MORGAN. That was a plan for the Americanization of the canal?

Mr. CROMWELL. Yes, sir. That was a proposal of a plan. It is on record.

Senator MORGAN. You proposed that to the committee of the House?

Mr. CROMWELL. Yes, sir; it is in the record.

Senator MORGAN. In what did that differ from this plan I have called your attention to and have recited in the record?

Mr. CROMWELL. I can not, Senator, enter into a description and definition of the differences, because that of itself involves the relations to my clients; that is all. I referred to the naked fact that such a proposal was made.

Senator MORGAN. The difference between the two plans involves the confidential relations between you and your clients?

[Page 1241.]

Mr. Cromwell. Yes, sir; it does.

Senator Morgan. How can we determine that unless you state what the differences were? This committee will shield you if you are entitled to protection.

Mr. Cromwell. I can answer no more definitely, Senator. I am trying to aid you all I can within the scope of my duties.

48.

Senator Morgan. I was trying to refresh your memory by reading Lampré's deposition. You state that the plan that he refers to here was not the plan that you had been questioned about before?

Mr. Cromwell. I frankly am not distinct in my memory about the two subjects.

Senator Morgan. I am trying to refresh it by bringing the paper to you and reading it to you, and you refused to make any statement about that paper at all?

Mr. Cromwell. Yes, sir.

Senator Morgan. Is that the paper in regard to which you refused to make a statement?

Mr. Cromwell. Yes, sir.

Senator Morgan. So there was a paper about which you refused to make a statement. Now, what was that paper?

Mr. Cromwell. The paper you have already presented, Senator.

Senator Morgan. The paper that I presented here and carried into the record?

Mr. Cromwell. Yes, sir.

[Page 1242.]

Senator Morgan. So you admit, then, that there was such a paper?

Mr. Cromwell. I do not admit the paper in the sense of an admission.

Senator Morgan. Well, why do you state it, then—just because you can not get out of it?

Mr. Cromwell. Because it is a fact; just because you have mentioned it, and I am referring to the topic to which you allude.

Senator Morgan. Well, I will assume, on the facts you have stated, that there were two papers, and that Mr. Lampré has described one of them in a sense, to a certain extent, and that the other, so far as you are concerned, has received no identification or description. Now, I want you, from the best of your recollection, to describe that other paper which Mr. Lampré did not describe.

Mr. Cromwell. I respectfully decline, Senator, for the reasons I have stated.

Senator Morgan. You will not answer that question?

Mr. Cromwell. For the reasons I have stated, sir.

Senator Morgan. You refuse to answer the question?

Mr. Cromwell. For the reasons I have stated, I do refuse, Senator.

49.

[Page 3059.]

Senator Morgan. Mr. Cromwell, when we last had the pleasure of your company here for examination we had gotten down to the date of 1898, and were referring to a letter written by you on December 21, 1898, addressed to Mr. Hay, in which you say [reading]:

"It is the opinion of the Government executives and of ourselves that power to give such extension is already located in the Government by the terms of the original concession, but the formality of ratification will be requested in due course, and of its being granted we have not the remotest apprehension.

"You will thus see that my confidence in the attitude of Colombia, as indicated in my last note, has been fully and quickly confirmed."

What does that relate to?

Mr. Cromwell. It speaks for itself, Senator. I have already answered upon that subject.

Senator Morgan. That is not an answer to my question, Mr. Cromwell. I ask you, upon your personal knowledge and oath, What does that relate to?

Mr. Cromwell. I repeat that it speaks for itself, and refers to the proposal for the extension of the concession of the Panama Canal.

Senator MORGAN. Which concession?
Mr. CROMWELL. The concession of the company; the extension of the original concession of 1878.
Senator MORGAN. That was the extension from 1904 to 1910?
Mr. CROMWELL. The one which was subsequently granted, in April, 1900.
Senator MORGAN. Extending from 1904 to 1910?
Mr. CROMWELL. Yes, sir.
Senator MORGAN You had knowledge of that transaction?
Mr CROMWELL. I had such knowledge as I have indicated in the letter.
Senator MORGAN. No more?
Mr. CROMWELL. I had more.
Senator MORGAN. What is it?
Mr. CROMWELL. It is confidential.

50.

[Page 3060.]

Senator MORGAN. You refuse to state it?
Mr. CROMWELL. I do.
Senator MORGAN. You refuse, then, to make any statement in regard to your knowledge of the transaction referred to in that letter?
Mr. CROMWELL. I do.
Senator MORGAN. You gave the transaction to Mr. Hay. Did you explain to him, also, further in oral conversation with him anything about it?
Mr. CROMWELL. I decline to make further explanation than I have, sir.
Senator MORGAN. Do you decline to answer that question?
Mr. CROMWELL. I do, sir.
Senator MORGAN. Well, do you decline on the ground that you were the counsel of the Panama Canal Co.?
Mr. CROMWELL. I do; and also upon the ground that it is not germane to the inquiry of this committee.
Senator MORGAN. Well, its being germane I do not think is a question that a witness has a right to decide. You put it upon both grounds?
Mr. CROMWELL. I do.
Senator MORGAN. Do you put it on the ground that you were also counsel of the Panama Railroad Co.?
Mr. CROMWELL. I do not.
Senator MORGAN. You do not? Well, we will go back to that, then. You do not consider that, as counsel of the Panama Railroad Co., you are under any obligation to withhold any facts from the United States Government that you received from that company as counsel?
Mr. CROMWELL. I do not care to answer such a question. When you put me a question I will answer it.
Senator MORGAN. Well, that is the question I put to you.
Mr. CROMWELL. When you put a pertinent question to me I will answer it—not hypothetical questions.
Senator MORGAN. Probably, Mr. Cromwell, you overrate either your capacity or your standing if you think that you have the right to decide upon the pertinency of any question that is asked you at this board.
Mr. CROMWELL. I think I must decide whether it is pertinent. Upon my responsibility I must decide. You may decide upon your responsibility.
Senator MORGAN. You do decide that it is not pertinent?
Mr. CROMWELL. Upon my responsibility I do so decide.
Senator MORGAN. You decide that it is not pertinent?
Mr. CROMWELL. Yes, sir.
Senator MORGAN. And that is one of the reasons you have for not answering it?
Mr. CROMWELL. It is.
Senator MORGAN. You have no reason such as that there is some obligation resting on you as counsel of the Panama Railroad Co. that prohibits you from answering?
Mr. CROMWELL. I again state, Senator, that I will not reply to hypothetical questions. If you will be good enough to address me a question which is pertinent, I shall be glad to give you my conclusions upon it.
Senator MORGAN. As the counsel of the Panama Canal Co., do you refuse to answer any question that you believe is covered by the protection of your clients against your making any disclosures?

51.

[Page 3031.]

Mr. CROMWELL. The question you present is hypothetical, and I decline to answer hypothetical questions.

52.

[Page 3136.]

Senator MORGAN. Turn back in that letter and repeat that remark "as you negotiated," etc. What was that?

Mr. CROMWELL (reading): "As you negotiated the sale of the property of the New Panama Canal Co. to the Government and have been general counsel"——

Senator MORGAN. Is that a fact; did you do that?

Mr. CROMWELL. I assisted in the negotiation.

Senator MORGAN. Did you do it by yourself?

Mr. CROMWELL. Yes, sir.

Senator MORGAN. In what capacity?

Mr. CROMWELL. As general counsel of the Panama Canal Co.

Senator MORGAN. That was the sale, now, of the property of the Panama Canal Co., of every kind and character, to the United States that you negotiated?

Mr. CROMWELL. It was the sale as the offer of the Canal Co. describes; a sale of the totality of the property on the Isthmus.

Senator MORGAN. The totality?

Mr. CROMWELL. Yes, sir.

53.

[Page 3137.]

Senator MORGAN. I never did know what totality meant, unless it meant it all. Did it mean anything less than all?

Mr. CROMWELL. The totality of its property on the Isthmus, which comprised its physical properties there, and I construed it liberally to mean also the shares of the Panama Railroad Co., although it did not describe the shares.

Senator MORGAN. How about the concessions?

Mr. CROMWELL. It included the concessions.

Senator MORGAN. All of them?

Mr. CROMWELL. All of them.

Senator MORGAN. From Colombia to Panama?

Mr. CROMWELL. All the then existing concessions from Colombia to Panama.

Senator MORGAN. And all that had passed from Colombia to Panama by the resurrection—or insurrection——

Mr. CROMWELL. Resurrection is just the word, Senator.

Senator MORGAN. I do not know what word to use, precisely, in——

Mr. CROMWELL. I think resurrection is a very apt word.

Senator MORGAN. The "transformation." I will put it that way.

Mr. CROMWELL. Inspiration.

Senator MORGAN. Well, it included all that?

Mr. CROMWELL. The offer of the canal company, sir, was dated January 9-11, 1902, at which time Colombia was sovereign of the Isthmus.

Senator MORGAN. Was that the contract, that you speak of now, in 1902, that was made with the United States?

Mr. CROMWELL. The offer of the canal company to the United States dated January 9-11, 1902.

Senator MORGAN. But that is not the one under which we took the property?

Mr. CROMWELL. It was in pursuance of that that we took the property.

Senator MORGAN. How in pursuance of it?

Mr. CROMWELL. In consummation of it.

Senator MORGAN. In consummation?

Mr. CROMWELL. Yes.

Senator MORGAN. Then, that offer of 1902 and the later offer were parts of the same transaction, and the one was in consummation of the other?

Mr. CROMWELL. Yes, sir.

Senator MORGAN. That is the fact?

Mr. CROMWELL. Yes, sir. May I proceed now?

Senator MORGAN. Not exactly just yet. Now, Mr. Cromwell, you negotiated that one of 1902, also?

Mr. CROMWELL. No, sir.

Senator MORGAN. You had no part in that?

Mr. CROMWELL. No; that offer originated in Paris.

Senator MORGAN. I did not ask you where it originated. I want to know whether you had any part in the negotiation?

Mr. CROMWELL. I must respectfully decline to discuss the affairs of the canal company when I get into the field of negotiations.

Senator MORGAN. We have come to another pitfall in which you take cover in the midst of a statement, in the midst of a sentence.

Mr. CROMWELL. We come to the principle of law and of privilege to which I have referred.

54.

[Page 3138.]

Senator MORGAN. We will test that privilege somewhere or other that will have some authority to it.

Mr. CROMWELL. I hope so, Senator. Then you will learn more law than you know now.

Senator MORGAN. I want to know, Mr. Cromwell, and I will ask you the question again: Did you participate in that negotiation of the proposition, the offer, and the contract, which I believe was not finally closed at that time, between the New Panama Canal Co. and the United States?

Mr. CROMWELL. I respectfully decline to enter into a discussion——

Senator MORGAN. You already stated that you did it.

Mr. CROMWELL. I decline to enter into a discussion of it.

Senator MORGAN. I am not discussing anything with you; I am asking you questions.

Mr. CROMWELL. I refuse to answer, sir.

Senator MORGAN. You refuse to answer?

Mr. CROMWELL. Yes, sir.

Senator MORGAN. Very good. Whatever you did—you state that you did something—did you do that as the employed counsel of the Panama Canal Co.?

Mr. CROMWELL. I have already answered that question many times.

Senator MORGAN. Will you please answer it again?

Mr. CROMWELL. I do, by refusing.

Senator MORGAN. Were you acting in any sense in your own right?

Mr. CROMWELL. I again decline to answer.

Senator MORGAN. You refuse to state whether you had any interest in the transaction personally?

Mr. CROMWELL. I refuse to discuss it any further than I have.

Senator MORGAN. You are not discussing it. I am asking you a question, and I want an answer.

Mr. CROMWELL. I make the same answer.

Senator MORGAN. What is the same answer?

Mr. CROMWELL. That I refuse to reply.

EXHIBIT G.

MR. ROOSEVELT'S PANAMA MESSAGES.

MESSAGE COMMUNICATED TO THE TWO HOUSES OF CONGRESS AT THE BEGINNING OF THE SECOND SESSION OF THE FIFTY-SEVENTH CONGRESS.

To the Senate and House of Representatives:

We still continue in a period of unbounded prosperity. This prosperity is not the creature of law, but undoubtedly the laws under which we work have been instrumental in creating the conditions which made it possible, and by unwise legislation it would be easy enough to destroy it. There will undoubtedly be periods of depression. The wave will recede, but the tide will advance. This Nation is seated on a continent flanked by two great oceans. It is composed of men the descendants of pioneers, or, in a sense, pioneers themselves; of men winnowed out from among the nations of the Old World by the energy, boldness, and love of adventure found in their own eager hearts. Such a nation so placed will surely wrest success from fortune.

As a people we have played a large part in the world, and we are bent upon making our future even larger than the past. In particular, the events of the last four years have definitely decided that, for woe or for weal, our place must be great among the nations. We may either fail greatly or succeed greatly; but we can not avoid the endeavor from which either great failure or great success must come. Even if we would, we can not play a small part. If we should try, all that would follow would be that we should play a large part ignobly and shamefully.

* * * * * * *

The Congress has wisely provided that we shall build at once an isthmian canal, if possible, at Panama. The Attorney General reports that we can undoubtedly acquire good title from the French Panama Canal Co. Negotiations are now pending with Colombia to secure her assent to our building the canal. This canal will be one of the greatest engineering feats of the twentieth century; a greater engineering feat than has yet been accomplished during the history of mankind. The work should be carried out as a continuing policy without regard to change of administration; and it should be begun under circumstance which will make it a matter of pride for all administrations to contine the policy.

The canal will be of great benefit to America, and of importance to all the world. It will be of advantage to us industrially and also as improving our military position. It will be of advantage to the countries of tropical America. It is earnestly to be hoped that all of these countries will do as some of them have already done with signal success, and will invite to their shores commerce and improve their material conditions by recognizing that stability and order are the prerequisites of successful development. No independent nation in America need have the slightest fear of aggression from the United States. It behooves each one to maintain order within its own borders and to discharge its just obligations to foreigners. When this is done, they can rest assured that, be they strong or weak, they have nothing to dread from outside interference. More and more the increasing interdependence and complexity of international political and economic relations render it incumbent on all civilized and orderly powers to insist on the proper policing of the world.

* * * * * * *

Through a wise provision of the Congress at its last session the White House, which had become disfigured by incongruous additions and changes, has now been restored to what it was planned to be by Washington. In making the restorations the utmost care has been exercised to come as near as possible to the early plans and to supplement these plans by a careful study of such buildings as that of the University of Virginia, which was built by Jefferson. The White House is the property of the Nation, and so far as is compatible with living therein it should be kept as it originally was, for the same reasons that we keep Mount Vernon as it originally was. The stately simplicity of its architecture is an expression of the character of the period in which it was built, and is in accord with the purposes it was designed to serve. It is a good thing to preserve such buildings as historic monuments which keep alive our sense of continuity with the Nation's past.

The reports of the several executive departments are submitted to the Congress with this communication.

WHITE HOUSE, *December 2, 1902.*

MESSAGE COMMUNICATED TO THE TWO HOUSES OF CONGRESS AT THE BEGINNING OF THE SECOND SESSION OF THE FIFTY-EIGHTH CONGRESS.

To the Senate and House of Representatives:

The country is to be congratulated on the amount of substantial achievement which has marked the past year, both as regards our foreign and as regards our domestic policy.

* * * * * * *

By the act of June 28, 1902, the Congress authorized the President to enter into *treaty with Colombia* for the building of the canal across the Isthmus of

Panama; it being provided that in the event of failure to secure such treaty after the lapse of a reasonable time, recourse should be had to building a canal through Nicaragua. It has not been necessary to consider this alternative, as I am enabled to lay before the Senate a treaty providing for the building of the canal across the Isthmus of Panama. This was the route which commended itself to the deliberate judgment of the Congress, and we can now acquire by treaty the right to construct the canal over this route. The question now, therefore, is not by which route the Isthmian Canal shall be built, for that question has been definitely and irrevocably decided. The question is simply whether or not we shall have an Isthmian Canal.

When the Congress directed that we should take the Panama route under treaty with Colombia, the essence of the condition, of course, referred not to the Government which controlled that route, but to the route itself; to the territory across which the route lay, not to the name which for the moment the territory bore on the map. The purpose of the law was to authorize the President to make a treaty with the power in actual control of the Isthmus of Panama. This purpose has been fulfilled.

In the year 1846 this Government entered into a treaty with New Granada, the predecessor upon the Isthmus of the Republic of Colombia and of the present Republic of Panama, by which treaty it was provided that the Government and citizens of the United States should always have free and open right of way or transit across the Isthmus of Panama by any modes of communication that might be constructed, while in return our Government guaranteed the perfect neutrality of the above-mentioned Isthmus with the view that the free transit from the one to the other sea might not be interrupted or embarrassed. The treaty vested in the United States *a substantial property right carried out of the rights of sovereignty and property which New Granada then had and possessed over the said territory*. The name of New Granada has passed away and its territory has been divided. Its successor, the Government of Colombia, has ceased to own any property in the Isthmus. A new Republic, that of Panama, which was at one time a sovereign state, and at another time a mere department of the successive confederations known as New Granada and Colombia, has now succeeded to the rights which first one and then the other formerly exercised over the Isthmus. But as long as the Isthmus endures, the mere geographical fact of its existence, and the peculiar interest therein which is required by our position, perpetuate the solemn contract which binds the holders of the territory to respect our right to freedom of transit across it, and binds us in return to safeguard for the Isthmus and the world the exercise of that inestimable privilege. The true interpretation of the obligations upon which the United States entered in this treaty of 1846 has been given repeatedly in the utterances of Presidents and Secretaries of State. Secretary Cass, in 1858, officially stated the position of this Government as follows:

"The progress of events has rendered the interoceanic route across the narrow portion of Central America vastly important to the commercial world, and especially to the United States, whose possessions extend along the Atlantic and Pacific coasts and demand the speediest and easiest modes of communication. While the rights of sovereignty of the States occupying this region should always be respected, we shall expect that these rights be exercised in a spirit befitting the occasion and the wants and circumstances that have arisen. Sovereignty has its duties as well as its rights, and none of these local governments, even if administered with more regard to the just demands of other nations than they have been, would be permitted, in a spirit of eastern isolation, to close the gates of intercourse on the great highways of the world, and justify the act by the pretension that these avenues of trade and travel belong to them, and that they choose to shut them, or, what is almost equivalent, to encumber them with such unjust relations as would prevent their general use."

Seven years later, in 1865, Mr. Seward in different communications took the following position:

"The United States have taken and will take no interest in any question of internal revolution in the State of Panama or any State of the United States of Colombia, but will maintain a perfect neutrality in connection with such domestic altercations. The United States will, nevertheless, hold themselves ready to protect the transit trade across the Isthmus against invasion of either domestic or foreign disturbers of the peace of the State of Panama. * * * Neither the text nor the spirit of the stipulation in that article by which the United States engages to preserve the neutrality of the Isthmus of Panama imposes an obligation on this Government to comply with the requisition [of the President of the United States of Colombia for a force to protect the Isthmus of Panama from a body of insurgents of that country]. The purpose of the stipulation was to guarantee the Isthmus against seizure or invasion by a foreign power only."

Attorney General Speed, under date of November 7, 1865, advised Secretary Seward as follows:

"From this treaty it can not be supposed that New Granada invited the United States to become a party to the intestine troubles of that Government, nor did the United States become bound to take sides in the domestic broils of New Granada. The United States did guarantee New Granada in the sovereignty and property over the territory. This was as against other and foreign governments."

For 400 years, ever since shortly after the discovery of this hemisphere, the canal across the Isthmus has been planned. For two score years it has been worked at. When made, it is to last for the ages. It is to alter the geography of a continent and the trade routes of the world. We have shown by every treaty we have negotiated or attempted to negotiate with the peoples in control of the Isthmus and with foreign nations in reference thereto our consistent good faith in observing our obligations—on the one hand to the peoples of the Isthmus, and on the other hand to the civilized world, whose commercial rights we are safeguarding and guaranteeing by our action. We have done our duty to others in letter and in spirit, and we have shown the utmost forbearance in exacting our own rights.

Last spring, under the act above referred to, a treaty concluded between the representatives of the Republic of Colombia and of our Government was ratified by the Senate. This treaty was entered into at the urgent solicitation of the people of Colombia and after a body of experts appointed by our Government especially to go into the matter of the routes across the Isthmus had pronounced unanimously in favor of the Panama route. In drawing up this treaty every concession was made to the people and to the Government of Colombia. We were more than just in dealing with them. Our generosity was such as to make it a serious question whether we had not gone too far in their interest at the expense of our own, for in our scrupulous desire to pay all possible heed, not merely to the real, but even to the fancied rights of our weaker neighbor, who already owed so much to our protection and forbearance, we yielded in all possible ways to her desires in drawing up the treaty. Nevertheless, the Government of Colombia not merely repudiated the treaty, but repudiated it in such manner as to make it evident by the time the Colombian Congress adjourned that not the scantiest hope remained of ever getting a satisfactory treaty from them. The Government of Colombia made the treaty, and yet when the Colombian Congress was called to ratify it the vote against ratification was unanimous. It does not appear that the Government made any real effort to secure ratification.

Immediately after the adjournment of the Congress a revolution broke out in Panama. The people of Panama had long been discontented with the Republic of Colombia, and they had been kept quiet only by the prospect of the conclusion of the treaty, which was to them a matter of vital concern. When it became evident that the treaty was hopelessly lost, the people of Panama rose literally as one man. Not a shot was fired by a single man on the Isthmus in the interest of the Colombian Government. Not a life was lost in the accomplishment of the revolution. The Colombian troops stationed on the Isthmus, who had long been unpaid, made common cause with the people of Panama, and with astonishing unanimity the new Republic was started. The duty of the United States in the premises was clear. In strict accordance with the principles laid down by Secretaries Cass and Seward in the official documents above quoted, the United States gave notice that it would permit the landing of no expeditionary force, the arrival of which would mean chaos and destruction along the line of the railroad and of the proposed canal, and an interruption of transit as an inevitable consequence. The de facto Government of Panama was recognized in the following telegram to Mr. Ehrman:

"The people of Panama have, by apparently unanimous movement, dissolved their political connection with the Republic of Colombia and resumed their independence. When you are satisfied that a de facto government, republican in form and without substantial opposition from its own people, has been established in the State of Panama, you will enter into relations with it as the responsible government of the territory, and look to it for all due action to protect the persons and property of citizens of the United States, and to keep open the isthmian transit, in accordance with the obligations of existing treaties governing the relations of the United States to that territory."

The Government of Colombia was notified of our action by the following telegram to Mr. Beaupré:

"The people of Panama having, by an apparently unanimous movement, dissolved their political connection with the Republic of Colombia and resumed their independence, and having adopted a Government of their own, republican in form, with which the Government of the United States of America has entered into relations, the President of the United States, in accordance with the ties of friendship which have so long and so happily existed between the respective nations, most earnestly commends to the Governments of Colombia and of Panama the peaceful and equitable settlement of all questions at issue between them. He holds that he is bound not merely by treaty obligations, but by the interests of civilization, to see that the peaceful traffic of the world across the Isthmus of Panama shall not longer be disturbed by a constant succession of unnecessary and wasteful civil wars."

When these events happened, 57 years had elapsed since the United States had entered into its treaty with New Granada. During that time the Governments of New Granada and of its successor, Colombia, have been in a constant state of flux. The following is a partial list of the disturbances on the Isthmus of Panama during the period in question as reported to us by our consuls. It is not possible to give a complete list, and some of the reports that speak of "revolutions" must mean unsuccessful revolutions.

May 22, 1850. Outbreak; two Americans killed. War vessel demanded to quell outbreak.

October, 1850. Revolutionary plot to bring about independence of the Isthmus.

July 22, 1851. Revolution in four southern Provinces.

November 14, 1851. Outbreak at Chagres. Man-of-war requested for Chagres.

June 27, 1853. Insurrection at Bogota, and consequent disturbance on Isthmus. War vessel demanded.

May 23, 1854. Political disturbances; war vessel requested.

June 28, 1854. Attempted revolution.

October 24, 1854. Independence of Isthmus demanded by provincial legislature.

April, 1856. Riot and massacre of Americans.

May 4, 1856. Riot.

May 18, 1856. Riot.

June 3, 1856. Riot.

October 2, 1856. Conflict between two native parties. United States forces landed.

December 18, 1858. Attempted secession of Panama.

April, 1859. Riots.

September, 1860. Outbreak.

October 4, 1860. Landing of United States forces in consequence.

May 23, 1861. Intervention of the United States forces required by intendente.

October 2, 1861. Insurrection and civil war.

April 4, 1862. Measures to prevent rebels crossing Isthmus.

June 13, 1862. Mosquera's troops refused admittance to Panama.

March, 1865. Revolution and United States troops landed.

August, 1865. Riots; unsuccessful attempt to invade Panama.

March, 1866. Unsuccessful revolution.

April, 1867. Attempt to overthrow Government.

August, 1867. Attempt at revolution.

July 5, 1868. Revolution; provisional government inaugurated.

August 29, 1868. Revolution; provisional government overthrown.

April, 1871. Revolution; followed apparently by counter-revolution.

April, 1873. Revolution and civil war which lasted to October, 1875.

August, 1876. Civil war which lasted until April, 1877.

July, 1878. Rebellion.

December, 1878. Revolt.

April, 1879. Revolution.

June, 1879. Revolution.

March, 1883. Riot.

May, 1883. Riot.

June, 1884. Revolutionary attempt.

December, 1884. Revolutionary attempt.

January, 1885. Revolutionary disturbances.

March, 1885. Revolution.
April, 1887. Disturbance on Panama Railroad.
November, 1887. Disturbance on line of canal.
January, 1889. Riot.
January, 1895. Revolution which lasted until April.
March, 1895. Incendiary attempt.
October, 1899. Revolution.
February, 1900, to July, 1900. Revolution.
January, 1901. Revolution.
July, 1901. Revolutionary disturbances.
September, 1901. City of Colon taken by rebels.
March, 1902. Revolutionary disturbances.
July, 1902. Revolution.

The above is only a partial list of the revolutions, rebellions, insurrections, riots, and other outbreaks that have occurred during the period in question; yet they number 53 for the 57 years. It will be noted that one of them lasted for nearly three years before it was quelled; another for nearly a year. In short, the experience of over half a century has shown Colombia to be utterly incapable of keeping order on the Isthmus. Only the active interference of the United States has enabled her to preserve so much as a semblance of sovereignty. Had it not been for the exercise by the United States of the police power in her interest, her connection with the Isthmus would have been sundered long ago. In 1856, in 1860, in 1873, in 1885, in 1901, and again in 1902, sailors and marines from United States warships were forced to land in order to patrol the Isthmus, to protect life and property, and to see that the transit across the Isthmus was kept open. In 1861, in 1862, in 1885, and in 1900, the Colombian Government asked that the United States Government would land troops to protect its interests and maintain order on the Isthmus. Perhaps the most extraordinary request is that which has just been received and which runs as follows:

"Knowing that revolution has already commenced in Panama [an eminent Colombian] says that if the Government of the United States will land troops to preserve Colombian sovereignty, and the transit, if requested by Colombian chargé d'affaires, this Government will declare martial law, and, by virtue of vested constitutional authority, when public order is disturbed, will approve by decree the ratification of the canal treaty as signed; or, if the Government of the United States prefers, will call extra session of the congress—with new and friendly members—next May to approve the treaty. [An eminent Colombian] has the perfect confidence of vice president, he says, and if it became necessary will go to the Isthmus or send representative there to adjust matters along above lines to the satisfaction of the people there."

This dispatch is noteworthy from two standpoints. Its offer of immediately guaranteeing the treaty to us is in sharp contrast with the positive and contemptuous refusal of the congress which has just closed its sessions to consider favorably such a treaty; it shows that the Government which made the treaty really had absolute control over the situation, but did not choose to exercise this control. The dispatch further calls on us to restore order and secure Colombian supremacy in the Isthmus from which the Colombian Government has just by its action decided to bar us by preventing the construction of the canal.

The control in the interest of the commerce and traffic of the whole civilized world of the means of undisturbed transit across the Isthmus of Panama, has become of transcendent importance to the United States. We have repeatedly exercised this control by intervening in the course of domestic dissension, and by protecting the territory from foreign invasion. In 1853 Mr. Everett assured the Peruvian minister that we should not hesitate to maintain the neutrality of the Isthmus in the case of war between Peru and Colombia. In 1864 Colombia, which has always been vigilant to avail itself of its privileges conferred by the treaty, expressed its expectation that in the event of war between Peru and Spain the United States would carry into effect the guaranty of neutrality. There have been few administrations of the State Department in which this treaty has not, either by the one side or the other, been used as a basis of more or less important demands. It was said by Mr. Fish in 1871 that the Department of State had reason to believe that an attack upon Colombian sovereignty on the Isthmus had, on several occasions, been averted by warning from this Government. In 1886, when Colombia was under the menace of hostilities from Italy in the Cerruti case, Mr. Bayard expressed the serious concern that the United States could not but feel that a European power should resort to force against a sister Republic of this hemisphere, as to the sovereign and uninterrupted use of a part of whose territory we are guarantors under the solemn faith of a treaty.

The above recital of facts establishes beyond question: First, that the United States has for over half a century patiently and in good faith carried out its obligations under the treaty of 1846; second, that when for the first time it became possible for Colombia to do anything in requital of the services thus repeatedly rendered to it for 57 years by the United States, the Colombian Government peremptorily and offensively refused thus to do its part, even though to do so would have been to its advantage and immeasurably to the advantage of the State of Panama, at that time under its jurisdiction; third, that throughout this period revolutions, riots, and factional disturbances of every kind have occurred one after the other in almost uninterrupted succession, some of them lasting for months and even for years, while the central government was unable to put them down or to make peace with the rebels; fourth, that these disturbances instead of showing any sign of abating have tended to grow more numerous and more serious in the immediate past; fifth, that the control of Colombia over the Isthmus of Panama could not be maintained without the armed intervention and assistance of the United States. In other words, the Government of Colombia, through wholly unable to maintain order on the Isthmus, has nevertheless declined to ratify a treaty the conclusion of which opened the only chance to secure its own stability and to guarantee permanent peace on, and the construction of a canal across the Isthmus.

Under such circumstances the Government of the United States would have been guilty of folly and weakness, amounting in their sum to a crime against the Nation, had it acted otherwise than it did when the revolution of November 3 last took place in Panama. This great enterprise of building the interoceanic canal can not be held up to gratify the whims, or out of respect to the governmental impotence, or to the even more sinister and evil political peculiarities of people who, though they dwell afar off, yet, against the wish of the actual dwellers on the Isthmus, assert an unreal supremacy over the territory. The possession of a territory fraught with such peculiar capacities as the Isthmus in question carries with it obligations to mankind. The course of events has shown that this canal can not be built by private enterprise, or by any other nation than our own; therefore it must be built by the United States.

Every effort has been made by the Government of the United States to persuade Colombia to follow a course which was essentially not only to our interests and to the interests of the world, but to the interests of Colombia itself. These efforts have failed; and Colombia, by her persistence in repulsing the advances that have been made, has forced us, for the sake of our own honor, and of the interest and well-being, not merely of our own people, but of the people of the Isthmus of Panama and the people of the civilized countries of the world, to take decisive steps to bring to an end a condition of affairs which had become intolerable. The new Republic of Panama immediately offered to negotiate a treaty with us. This treaty I herewith submit. By it our interests are better safeguarded than in the treaty with Colombia which was ratified by the Senate at its last session. It is better in its terms than the treaties offered to us by the Republics of Nicaragua and Costa Rica. At last the right to begin this great undertaking is made available. Panama has done her part. All that remains is for the American Congress to do its part and forthwith this Republic will enter upon the execution of a project colossal in its size and of well-nigh incalculable possibilities for the good of this country and the nations of mankind.

By the provisions of the treaty the United States guarantees and will maintain the independence of the Republic of Panama. There is granted to the United States in perpetuity the use, occupation, and control of a strip 10 miles wide and extending 3 nautical miles into the sea at either terminal, with all lands lying outside of the zone necessary for the ocnstruction of the canal or for its auxiliary works, and with the islands in the Bay of Panama. The cities of Panama and Colon are not embraced in the Canal Zone, but the United States assumes their sanitation and, in case of need, the maintenance of order therein; the United States enjoys within the granted limits all the rights, power, and authority which it would possess were it the sovereign of the territory to the exclusion of the exercise of sovereign rights by the Republic. All railway and canal property rights belonging to Panama and needed for the canal pass to the United States, including any property of the respective companies in the cities of Panama and Colon; the works, property, and personnel of the canal and railways are exempted from taxation as well in the cities of Panama and Colon as in the Canal Zone and its dependencies. Free immigration of the personnel and importation of supplies for the construction and operation of the canal are granted. Provision is made for the use of military force and the building of fortifications by the United States for the protection of the transit. In other details, particularly as to the acquisition of the interests of the New Panama Canal Co. and the Panama Railway by the United States and the condemnation of private property for the uses of the canal, the stipulations of the Hay-Herran treaty are closely followed, while the compensation to be given for these enlarged grants remains the same, being ten millions of dollars, payable on exchange of ratification; and, beginning nine years from that date, an annual payment of $250,000 during the life of the convention.

WHITE HOUSE, *December 7, 1903.*

MESSAGE COMMUNICATED TO THE TWO HOUSES OF CONGRESS ON JANUARY 4, 1904.

To the Senate and House of Representatives:

I lay before the Congress for its information a statement of my action up to this time in executing the act entitled "An act to provide for the construction of a canal connecting the waters of the Atlantic and Pacific Oceans," approved June 28, 1902.

By the said act the President was authorized to secure for the United States the property of the Panama Canal Co. and the perpetual control of a strip 6 miles wide across the Isthmus of Panama. It was further provided that "should the President be unable to obtain for the United States a satisfactory title to the property of the New Panama Canal Co. and the control of the necessary territory of the Republic of Colombia * * * within a reasonable time and upon reasonable terms, then the President" should endeavor to provide for a canal by the Nicaragua route. The language quoted defines with exactness and precision what was to be done, and what as a matter of fact has been done. The President was authorized to go to the Nicaragua route only if within a reasonable time he could not obtain "control of the necessary territory of the Republic of Colombia." This control has now been obtained; the provision of the act has been complied with; it is no longer possible under existing legislation to go to the Nicaragua route as an alternative.

This act marked the climax of the effort on the part of the United States to secure, so far as legislation was concerned, an interoceanic canal across the Isthmus. The effort to secure a treaty for this purpose with one of the Central American Republics did not stand on the same footing with the effort to secure a treaty under any ordinary conditions. The proper position for the United States to assume in reference to this canal, and therefore to the governments of the Isthmus, had been clearly set forth by Secretary Cass in 1858. In my annual message I have already quoted what Secretary Cass said; but I repeat the quotation here, because the principle it states is fundamental:

"While the rights of sovereignty of the States occupying this region (Central America) should always be respected, we shall expect that these rights be exercised in a spirit befitting the occasion and the wants and circumstances that have arisen. Sovereignty has its duties as well as its rights, and none of these local governments, even if administered with more regard to the just demands of other nations than they have been, would be permitted, in a spirit of eastern isolation, to close the gates of intercourse on the great highways of the world, and justify the act by the pretension that these avenues of trade and travel belong to them and that they choose to shut them, or, what is almost equivalent, to encumber them with such unjust relations as would prevent their general use."

The principle thus enunciated by Secretary Cass was sound then and it is sound now. The United States has taken the position that no other Government is to build the canal. In 1889, when France proposed to come to the aid of the French Panama Co. by guaranteeing their bonds, the Senate of the United States in executive session, with only some three votes dissenting passed a resolution as follows:

"That the Government of the United States will look with serious concern and disapproval upon any connection of any European Government with the construction or control of any ship canal across the Isthmus of Darien or across

Central America, and must regard any such connection or control as injurious to the just rights and interests of the United States and as a menace to their welfare."

Under the Hay-Pauncefote treaty it was explicitly provided that the United States should control, police, and protect the canal which was to built, keeping it open for the vessels of all nations on equal terms. The United States thus assumed the position of guarantor of the canal and of its peaceful use by all the world. The guaranty included, as a matter of course, the building of the canal. The enterprise was recognized as responding to an international need; and it would be the veriest travesty on right and justice to treat the Governments in possession of the Isthmus as having the right, in the language of Mr. Cass, "to close the gates of intercourse on the great highways of the world, and justify the act by the pretension that these avenues of trade and travel belong to them and that they choose to shut them."

When this Government submitted to Colombia the Hay-Herran treaty three things were, therefore, already settled.

One was that the canal should be built. The time for delay, the time for permitting the attempt to be made by private enterprise, the time for permitting any Government of antisocial spirit and of imperfect development to bar the work was past. The United States had assumed, in connection with the canal, certain responsibilities, not only to its own people, but to the civilized world, which imperatively demanded that there should no longer be delay in beginning the work.

Second. While it was settled that the canal should be built without unnecessary or improper delay, it was no less clearly shown to be our purpose to deal not merely in a spirit of justice but in a spirit of generosity with the people through whose land we might build it. The Hay-Herran treaty, if it erred at all, erred in the direction of an overgenerosity toward the Colombian Government. In our anxiety to be fair we had gone to the very verge in yielding to a weak nation's demands what that nation was helplessly unable to enforce from us against our will. The only criticisms made upon the administration for the terms of the Hay-Herran treaty were for having granted too much to Colombia, not for failure to grant enough. Neither in the Congress nor in the public press, at the time that this treaty was formulated, was there complaint that it did not in the fullest and amplest manner guarantee to Colombia everything that she could by any color of title demand.

Nor is the fact to be lost sight of that the rejected treaty, while generously responding to the pecuniary demands of Colombia, in other respects merely provided for the construction of the canal in conformity with the express requirements of the act of the Congress of June 28, 1902. By that act, as heretofore quoted, the President was authorized to acquire from Colombia, for the purposes of the canal, "perpetual control" of a certain strip of land; and it was expressly required that the "control" thus to be obtained should include "jurisdiction" to make police and sanitary regulations and to establish such judicial tribunals as might be agreed on for their enforcement. These were conditions precedent prescribed by the Congress; and for their fulfillment suitable stipulations were embodied in the treaty. It has been stated in public prints that Colombia objected to these stipulations on the ground that they involved a relinquishment of her "sovereignty"; but, in the light of what has taken place, this alleged objection must be considered as an afterthought. In reality the treaty, instead of requiring a cession of Colombia's sovereignty over the canal strip, expressly acknowledged, confirmed, and preserved her sovereignty over it. The treaty in this respect simply proceeded on the lines on which all the negotiations leading up to the present situation have been conducted. In those negotiations the exercise by the United States, subject to the paramount rights of the local sovereign, of a substantial control over the canal and the immediately adjacent territory, has been treated as a fundamental part of any arrangement that might be made. It has formed an essential feature of all our plans, and its necessity is fully recognized in the Hay-Pauncefote treaty. The Congress, in providing that such control should be secured, adopted no new principle, but only incorporated in its legislation a condition the importance and propriety of which were universally recognized. During all the years of negotiation and discussion that preceded the conclusion of the Hay-Herran treaty, Colombia never intimated that the requirement by the United States of control over the canal strip would render unattainable the construction of a canal by way of the Isthmus of Panama; nor were we advised, during the months when legislation of 1902 was pending before the

Congress, that the terms which it embodied would render negotiations with Colombia impracticable. It is plain that no nation could construct and guarantee the neutrality of the canal with a less degree of control than was stipulated for in the Hay-Herran treaty. A refusal to grant such degree of control was necessarily a refusal to make any practicable treaty at all. Such refusal therefore squarely raised the question whether Colombia was entitled to bar the transit of the world's traffic across the Isthmus.

That the canal itself was eagerly demanded by the people of the locality through which it was to pass, and that the people of this locality no less eagerly longed for its construction under American control, are shown by the unanimity of action in the new Panama Republic. Furthermore, Colombia, after having rejected the treaty in spite of our protests and warnings when it was in her power to accept it, has since shown the utmost eagerness to accept the same treaty if only the status quo could be restored. One of the men standing highest in the official circles of Colombia, on November 6, addressed the American minister at Bogota, saying that if the Government of the United States would land troops to preserve Colombian sovereignty and the transit, the Colombian Government would "declare martial law; and, by virtue of vested constitutional authority, when public order is disturbed, [would] approve by decree the ratification of the canal treaty as signed; or, if the Government of the United States prefers, [would] call extra session of the Congress—with new and friendly members—next May to approve the treaty." Having these facts in view, there is no shadow of question that the Government of the United States proposed a treaty which was not merely just, but generous to Colombia; which our people regarded as erring, if at all, on the side of overgenerosity; which was hailed with delight by the people of the immediate locality through which the canal was to pass, who were most concerned as to the new order of things, and which the Colombian authorities now recognize as being so good that they are willing to promise its unconditional ratification if only we will desert those who have shown themselves our friends and restore to those who have shown themselves unfriendly the power to undo what they did. I pass by the question as to what assurance we have that they would now keep their pledge and not again refuse to ratify the treaty if they had the power; for, of course, I will not for one moment discuss the possibility of the United States committing an act of such baseness as to abandon the new Republic of Panama.

Third. Finally the Congress definitely settled where the canal was to be built. It was provided that a treaty should be made for building the canal across the Isthmus of Panama; and if, after reasonable time, it proved impossible to secure such treaty, that then we should go to Nicaragua. The treaty has been made; for it needs no argument to show that the intent of the Congress was to insure a canal across Panama, and that whether the Republic granting the title was called New Granada, Colombia, or Panama mattered not one whit. As events turned out, the question of "reasonable time" did not enter into the matter at all. Although, as the months went by, it became increasingly improbable that the Colombian Congress would ratify the treaty or take steps which would be equivalent thereto, yet all chance for such action on their part did not vanish until the Congress closed at the end of October; and within three days thereafter the revolution in Panama had broken out. Panama became an independent State, and the control of the territory necessary for building the canal then became obtainable. The condition under which alone we could have gone to Nicaragua thereby became impossible of fulfillment. If the pending treaty with Panama should not be ratified by the Senate this would not alter the fact that we could not go to Nicaragua. The Congress has decided the route, and there is no alternative under existing legislation.

When in August it began to appear probable that the Colombian Legislature would not ratify the treaty it became incumbent upon me to consider well what the situation was and to be ready to advise the Congress as to what were the various alternatives of action open to us. There were several possibilities. One was that Colombia would at the last moment see the unwisdom of her position. That there might be nothing omitted, Secretary Hay, through the minister at Bogota, repeatedly warned Colombia that grave consequences might follow from her rejection of the treaty. Although it was a constantly diminishing chance, yet the possibility of ratification did not wholly pass away until the close of the session of the Colombian Congress.

A second alternative was that by the close of the session on the last day of October, without the ratification of the treaty by Colombia and without any steps taken by Panama, the American Congress on assembling early in November would be confronted with a situation in which there had been a failure to come to terms as to building the canal along the Panama route, and yet there had not been a lapse of a reasonable time—using the word reasonable in any proper sense—such as would justify the administration going to the Nicaragua route. This situation seemed on the whole the most likely, and as a matter of fact I had made the original draft of my message to the Congress with a view to its existence.

It was the opinion of eminent international jurists that in view of the fact that the great design of our guaranty under the treaty of 1846 was to dedicate the isthmus to the purposes of interoceanic transit, and above all to secure the construction of an interoceanic canal, Colombia could not under existing conditions refuse to enter into a proper arrangement with the United States to that end without violating the spirit and substantially repudiating the obligations of a treaty the full benefits of which she had enjoyed for over 50 years. My intention was to consult the Congress as to whether under such circumstances it would not be proper to announce that the canal was to be dug forthwith; that we would give the terms that we had offered and no others; and that if such terms were not agreed to we would enter into an arrangement with Panama direct, or take what other steps were needful in order to begin the enterprise.

A third possibility was that the people of the isthmus, who had formerly constituted an independent state, and who until recently were united to Colombia only by a loose tie of federal relationship, might take the protection of their own vital interests into their own hands, reassert their former rights, declare their independence upon just grounds, and establish a government competent and willing to do its share in this great work for civilization. This third possibility is what actually occurred. Everyone knew that it was a possibility, but it was not until toward the end of October that it appeared to be an imminent probability. Although the administration, of course, had special means of knowledge, no such means were necessary in order to appreciate the possibility, and toward the end the likelihood, of such a revolutionary outbreak and of its success. It was a matter of common notoriety. Quotations from the daily papers could be indefinitely multiplied to show this state of affairs; a very few will suffice. From Costa Rica, on August 31, a special was sent to the Washington Post, running as follows:

"SAN JOSE, COSTA RICA, *August 31.*

"Travelers from Panama report the Isthmus alive with fires of a new revolution. It is inspired, it is believed, by men who, in Panama and Colon, have systematically engendered the pro-American feeling to secure the building of the Isthmian Canal by the United States.

"The Indians have risen, and the late followers of Gen. Benjamin Herrera are mustering in the mountain villages, preparatory to joining in an organized revolt caused by the rejection of the canal treaty.

"Hundreds of stacks of arms, confiscated by the Colombian Government at the close of the late revolution, have reappeared from some mysterious source, and thousands of rifles that look suspiciously like the Mausers the United States captured in Cuba are issuing to the gathering forces from central points of distribution. With the arms goes ammunition, fresh from factories, showing the movement is not spasmodic, but is carefully planned.

* * * * * * *

"The Government forces in Panama and Colon, numbering less than 1,500 men, are reported to be a little more than friendly to the revolutionary spirit. They have been ill paid since the revolution closed and their only hope of prompt payment is another war.

"Gen. Huertes, commander of the forces, who is ostensibly loyal to the Bogota Government, is said to be secretly friendly to the proposed revolution. At least, all his personal friends are open in denunciation of the Bogota Government and the failure of the Colombian Congress to ratify the canal treaty.

"The consensus of opinion gathered from late arrivals from the Isthmus is that the revolution is coming, and that it will succeed."

A special dispatch to the Washington Post, under date of New York, September 1, runs as follows:

"B. G. Duque, editor and proprietor of the Panama Star and Herald, a resident of the Isthmus during the past 27 years, who arrived to-day in New York, declared that if the canal treaty fell through a revolution would be likely to follow.

"'There is a very strong feeling in Panama,' said Mr. Duque, 'that Colombia, in negotiating the sale of a canal concession in Panama, is looking for profits that might just as well go to Panama herself.

"'The Colombian Government, only the other day, suppressed a newspaper that dared to speak of independence for Panama. Awhile ago there was a secret plan afoot to cut loose from Colombia and seek the protection of the United States.'"

In the New York Herald of September 10 the following statement appeared:

"Representatives of strong interests on the Isthmus of Panama, who make their headquarters in this city, are considering a plan of action to be undertaken in cooperation with men of similar views in Panama and Colon to bring about a revolution and from an independent government in Panama opposed to that in Bogota.

"There is much indignation on the Isthmus on account of the failure of the canal treaty, which is ascribed to the authorities at Bogota. This opinion is believed to be shared by a majority of the Isthmians of all shades of political belief, and they think it is to their best interest for a new republic to be formed on the Isthmus, which may negotiate directly with the United States a new treaty which will permit the digging of the Panama Canal under favorable conditions."

In the New York Times, under date of September 13, there appeared from Bogota the following statement:

"A proposal made by Señor Perez y Sotos to ask the executive to appoint an antisecessionist governor in Panama has been approved by the senate. Speakers in the senate said that Señor Obaldía, who was recently appointed governor of Panama and who is favorable to a canal treaty, was a menace to the national integrity. Senator Marroquín protested against the action of the senate.

"President Marroquín succeeded later in calming the Congressmen. It appears that he was able to give them satisfactory reasons for Gov. Obaldía's appointment. He appears to realize the imminent peril of the Isthmus of Panama declaring its independence.

"Señor Deroux, representative for a Panama constituency, recently delivered a sensational speech in the House. Among other things he said:

"'In Panama the bishops, governors, magistrates, military chiefs, and their subordinates have been and are foreign to the department. It seems that the Government, with surprising tenacity, wishes to exclude the Isthmus from all participation in public affairs. As regards international dangers in the Isthmus, all I can say is that if these dangers exist they are due to the conduct of the National Government, which is in the direction of reaction.

"'If the Colombian Government will not take action with a view to preventing disaster, the responsibility will rest with it alone.'"

In the New York Herald of October 26 it was reported that a revolutionary expedition of about 70 men had actually landed on the Isthmus. In the Washington Post of October 29 it was reported from Panama that in view of the impending trouble on the Isthmus the Bogota Government had gathered troops in sufficient numbers to at once put down an attempt at secession. In the New York Herald of Octover 30 it was announced from Panama that Bogota was hurrying troops to the Isthmus to put down the projected revolt. In the New York Herald of November 2 it was announced that in Bogota the Congress had indorsed the energetic measures taken to meet the situation on the Isthmus and that 6,000 men were about to be sent thither.

Quotations like the above could be multiplied indefinitely. Suffice it to say that it was notorious that revolutionary trouble of a serious nature was impending upon the Isthmus. But it was not necessary to rely exclusively upon such general means of information. On October 15 Commander Hubbard, of the Navy, notified the Navy Department that though things were quiet on the Isthmus a revolution had broken out in the State of Cauca. On October 16, at the request of Lieut. Gen. Young, I saw Capt. C. B. Humphrey and Lieut. Grayson Mallet-Prevost Murphy, who had just returned from a four-month tour through the northern portions of Venezuela and Colombia. They stopped in Panama on their return in the latter part of September. At the time they were sent down there had been no thought of their going to Panama, and their visit to the Isthmus was but an unpremeditated incident of their return journey; nor had they been spoken to by anyone at Washington regarding the possibility of a revolt. Until they landed at Colon they had no knowledge that a revolution was impending, save what they had gained from the newspapers. What they saw in Panama so impressed them that they reported thereon to Lieut. Gen. Young, according to his memorandum—

"that while on the Isthmus they became dissatisfied beyond question that, owing largely to the dissatisfaction because of the failure of Colombia to ratify the Hay-Herran treaty, a revolutionary party was in course of organization, having for its object the separation of the State of Panama from Colombia, the leader being Dr. Richard Arango, a former governor of Panama; that when they were on the Isthmus arms and ammunition were being smuggled into the city of Colon in piano boxes, merchandise crates, etc., the small arms received being principally the Gras French rifle, the Remington, and the Mauser; that nearly every citizen in Panama had some sort of rifle or gun in his possession, with ammunition therefor; that in the city of Panama there had been organized a fire brigade which was really intended for a revolutionary military organization; that there were representatives of the revolutionary organization at all important points on the Isthmus; that in Panama, Colon, and the other principal places of the Isthmus police forces had been organized which were in reality revolutionary forces; that the people on the Isthmus seemed to be unanimous in their sentiment against the Bogota Government, and their disgust over the failure of that Government to ratify the treaty providing for the construction of the canal, and that a revolution might be expected immediately upon the adjournment of the Colombian Congress without ratification of the treaty."

Lieut. Gen. Young regarded their report as of such importance as to make it advisable that I should personally see these officers. They told me what they had already reported to the lieutenant general, adding that on the Isthmus the excitement was seething, and that the Colombian troops were reported to be disaffected. In response to a question of mine they informed me that it was the general belief that the revolution might break out at any moment, and if it did not happen before, would doubtless take place immediately after the closing of the Colombian Congress (at the end of October) if the canal treaty were not ratified. They were certain that the revolution would occur, and before leaving the Isthmus had made their own reckoning as to the time, which they had set down as being probably from three to four weeks after their leaving. The reason they set this as the probable inside limit of time was that they reckoned that it would be at least three or four weeks—say, not until October 20—before a sufficient quantity of arms and munitions would have been landed.

In view of all these facts I directed the Navy Department to issue instructions such as would insure our having ships within easy reach of the Isthmus in the event of need arising. Orders were given on October 19 to the *Boston* to proceed to San Juan del Sur, Nicaragua; to the *Dixie* to prepare to sail from League Island; and to the *Atlanta* to proceed to Guantanamo. On October 30 the *Nashville* was ordered to proceed to Colon. On November 2, when, the Colombian Congress having adjourned, it was evident that the outbreak was imminent, and when it was announced that both sides were making ready forces whose meeting would mean bloodshed and disorder, the Colombian troops having been embarked on vessels, the following instructions were sent to the commanders of the *Boston*, *Nashville*, and *Dixie:*

"Maintain free and uninterrupted transit. If interruption is threatened by armed force, occupy the line of railroad. Prevent landing of any armed force with hostile intent, either Government or insurgent, at any point within 50 miles of Panama. Government force reported approaching the Isthmus in vessels. Prevent their landing if, in your judgment, the landing would precipitate a conflict."

These orders were delivered in pursuance of the policy on which our Government had repeatedly acted. This policy was exhibited in the following orders, given under somewhat similar circumstances last year, and the year before, and the year beofre that. The first two telegrams are from the Department of State to the consul at Panama:

"JULY 25, 1900.

"You are directed to protest against any act of hostility which may involve or imperil the safe and peaceful transit of persons or property across the Isthmus of Panama. The bombardment of Panama would have this effect, and the United States must insist upon the neutrality of the Isthmus as guaranteed by the treaty."

"NOVEMBER 20, 1901.

"Notify all parties molesting or interfering with free transit across the Isthmus that such interference must cease and that the United States will prevent the interruption of traffic upon the railroad. Consult with captain of the *Iowa*, who will be instructed to land marines, if necessary, for the protection of the railroad, in accordance with the treaty rights and obligations of the United States. Desirable to avoid bloodshed, if possible."

The next three telegrams are from and to the Secretary of the Navy:

"SEPTEMBER 12, 1902.

"'RANGER,' *Panama:*

"United States guarantees perfect neutrality of Isthmus and that a free transit from sea to sea be not interrupted or embarrassed. * * * Any transportation of troops which might contravene these provisions of treaty should not be sanctioned by you nor should use of road be permitted which might convert the line of transit into theater of hostility.

"MOODY."

"COLON, *September 20, 1902.*

"SECRETARY NAVY, *Washington:*

"Everything is conceded. The United States guards and guarantees traffic and the line of transit. To-day I permitted the exchange of Colombia troops from Panama to Colon, about 1,000 men each way, the troops without arms in train guarded by American naval force in the same manner as other passengers; arms and ammunition in separate train, guarded aslo by naval force in the same manner as other freight.

"MCLEAN."

"PANAMA, *October 3, 1902.*

"SECRETARY NAVY, *Washington, D. C.:*

"Have sent this communication to the American consul at Panama:

"'Inform governor while trains running under United States protection I must decline transportation any combatants, ammunition, arms, which might cause interruption traffic or convert line of transit into theater hostilities.'

"CASEY."

On November 3 Commander Hubbard responded to the above-quoted telegram of November 2, 1903, saying that before the telegram had been received 400 Colombian troops from Cartagena had landed at Colon; that there had been no revolution on the Isthmus, but that the situation was most critical if the revolutionary leaders should act. On this same date the Associated Press in Washington received a bulletin stating that a revolutionary outbreak had occurred. When this was brought to the attention of the Assistant Secretary of State, Mr. Loomis, he prepared the following cablegram to the consul general at Panama and the consul at Colon:

"Uprising on Isthmus reported. Keep department promptly and fully informed."

Before this telegram was sent, however, one was received from Consul Malmros, at Colon, running as follows:

"Revolution imminent. Government force on the Isthmus about 500 men. Their official promised support revolution. Fire department, Panama, 441, are well organized and favor revolution. Government vessel, *Cartagena*, with about 400 men, arrived early to-day with new commander in chief, Tobar. Was not expected until November 10. Tobar's arrival is not probable to stop revolution."

This cablegram was received at 2.35 p. m., and at 3.40 p. m. Mr. Loomis sent the telegram which he had already prepared to both Panama and Colon. Apprently, however, the consul general at Panama had not received the information embodied in the Associated Press bulletin, upon which the Assistant Secretary of State based his dispatch; for his answer was that there was no uprising, although the situation was critical, this answer being received at 8.15 p. m. Immediately afterwards he sent another dispatch, which was received at 9.50 p. m., saying that the uprising had occurred, and had been successful, with no bloodshed. The Colombian gunboat *Bogota* next day began to shell the city of Panama, with the result of killing one Chinaman. The consul general was directed to notify her to stop firing. Meanwhile, on November 4, Commander Hubbard notified the department that he had landed a force to protect the lives and property of American citizens against the threats of the Colombian soldiery.

Before any step whatever had been taken by the United States troops to restore order, the commander of the newly landed Colombian troops had indulged in wanton and violent threats against American citizens, which created serious apprehension As Commander Hubbard reported in his letter November 5, this officer and his troops practically began war against the United States, and only the forbearance and coolness of our officers and men prevented bloodshed The letter of Commander Hubbard is of such interest that it deserves quotation in full, and runs as follows:

U. S. S. "NASHVILLE," THIRD RATE,
Colon, U. S. Colombia, November 5, 1903.

SIR: Pending a complete report of the occurrences of the last three days in Colon, Colombia, I most respectfully invite the department's attention to those of the date of Wednesday, November 4, which amounted to practically the making of war against the United States by the officer in command of the Colombian troops in Colon. At 1 o'clock p. m. on that date I was summoned on shore by a preconcerted signal, and on landing met the United States consul, vice consul, and Col. Shaler, the general superintendet of the Panama Railroad. The consul informed me that he had received notice from the officer commanding the Colombian troops, Col. Torres, through the prefect of Colon, to the effect that if the Colombian officers, Gens. Tobal and Amaya, who had been seized in Panama on the evening of the 3d of November by the independents and held as prisoners, were not released by 2 o'clock p. m., he, Torres, would open fire on the town of Colon and kill every United States citizen in the place, and my advice and action were requested. I advised that all the United States citizens should take refuge in the shed of the Panama Railroad Co., a stone building susceptible of being put into good state for defense, and that I would immediately land such body of men, with extra arms for arming the citizens, as the complement of the ship would permit. This was agreed to and I immediately returned on board, arriving at 1.15 p. m. The order for landing was immediately given, and at 1.30 p. m. the boats left the ship with a party of 42 men under the command of Lieut Commander H. M. Witzel, with Midshipman J. P. Jackson as second in command. Time being pressed I gave verbal order to Mr. Witzel to take the building above referred to, to put it into the best state of defense possible, and protect the lives of the citizens assembled there—not firing unless fired upon. The women and children took refuge on the German steamer *Marcomania* and Panama Railroad steamer *City of Washington*, both ready to haul out from dock if necessary. The *Nashville* I got under way and patrolled with her along the water front close in and ready to use either small arm or shrapnel fire. The Colombians surrounded the building of the railroad company almost immediately after we had taken possession, and for about one and a half hours their attitude was most threatening, it being seemingly their purpose to provoke an attack. Happily our men were cool and steady, and while the tension was very great no shot was fired. At about 3.15 p. m. Col. Torres came into the building for an interview and expressed himself as most friendly to Americans, claiming that the whole affair was a misapprehension and that he would like to send the alcalde of Colon to Panama to see Gen. Tobal and have him direct the discontinuance of the show of force. A special train was furnished and safe conduct guaranteed. At about 5.30 p. m. Col. Torres made the proposition of withdrawing his troops to Monkey Hill, if I would withdraw the *Nashville's* force and leave the town in possession of the police until the return of the alcalde on the morning of the 5th. After an interview with the United States consul and Col. Shaler as to the probability of good faith in the matter, I decided to accept the proposition and brought my men on board, the disparity in numbers between my force and that of the Colombians, nearly 10 to 1, making me desirous of avoiding a conflict so long as the object in view, the protection of American citizens, was not imperilled.

I am positive that the determined attitude of our men, their coolness and evident intention of standing their ground, had a most salutary and decisive effect on the immediate situation and was the initial step in the ultimate abandoning of Colon by these troops and their return to Cartagena the following day. Lieut. Commander Witzel is entitled to much praise for his admirable work in command on the spot.

I feel that I can not sufficiently strongly represent to the department the grossness of this outrage and the insult to our dignity, even apart from the savagery of the threat.

Very respectfully,

JOHN HUBBARD,
Commander, United States Navy, Commanding.

The SECRETARY OF THE NAVY,
Navy Department, Washington, D. C.

In his letter of November 8 Commander Hubbard sets forth the facts more in detail:

U. S. S. "NASHVILLE," THIRD RATE,
Porto Bello, United States of Colombia, November 8, 1903.

SIR: 1. I have the honor to make the following report of the occurrences which took place at Colon and Panama in the interval between the arrival of the *Nashville* at Colon on the evening of November 2, 1903, and the evening of November 5, 1903, when, by the arrival of the U. S. S. *Dixie* at Colon, I was relieved as senior officer by Commander F. H. Delano, United States Navy.

2. At the time of the arrival of the *Nashville* at Colon at 5.30 p. m. on November 2 everything on the Isthmus was quiet. There was talk of proclaiming the independence of Panama, but no definite action had been taken and there had been no disturbance of peace and order. At daylight on the morning of November 3 it was found that a vessel which had come in during the night was the Colombian gunboat *Cartagena*, carrying between 400 and 500 troops. I had her boarded and learned that these troops were for the garrison at Panama. Inasmuch as the Independent Party had not acted and the Government of Colombia was at the time in undisputed control of the Province of Panama, I did not feel, in the absence of any instructions, that I was justified in preventing the landing of these troops, and at 8.30 o'clock they were disembarked. The commanding officers, Generals Amaya and Tobal, with four others, immediately went over to Panama to make arrangements for receiving and quartering their troops, leaving the command in charge of an officer whom I later learned to be Col. Torres. The department's message, addressed to the care of the United States consul, I received at 10.30 a. m.; it was delivered to one of the ship's boats while I was at the consul's, and not to the consul, as addressed. The message was said to have been received at the cable office at 9.30 a. m. Immediately on deciphering the message I went on shore to see what arrangements the railroad company had made for the transportation of these troops to Panama, and learned that the company would not transport them except on request of the governor of Panama, and that the prefect of Colon and the officer left in command of the troops had been so notified by the general superintendent of the Panama Railroad Co. I remained at the company's office until it was sure that no action on my part would be needed to prevent the transportation of the troops that afternoon, when I returned on board and cabled the department the situation of affairs. At about 5.30 p. m. I again went on shore and received notice from the general superintendent of the railroad that he had received the request for the transportation of the troops, and that they would leave on the 8 a. m. train on the following day. I immediately went to see the general superintendent, and learned that it had just been announced that a provisional government had been established at Panama; that Gens. Amaya and Tobal, the governor of Panama, and four officers, who had gone to Panama in the morning, had been seized and were held as prisoners; that they had an organized force of 1,500 troops and wished the Government troops in Colon to be sent over. This I declined to permit, and verbally prohibited the general superintendent from giving transportation to the troops of either party.

It being then late in the evening, I sent early in the morning of November 4 written notification to the general superintendent of the Panama Railroad, to the prefect of Colon, and to the officer left in command of the Colombian troops, later ascertained to be Col. Torres, that I had prohibited the transportation of troops in either direction in order to preserve the free and uninterrupted transit of the Isthmus. Copies of these letters are hereto appended; also copy of my notification to the consul. Except to a few people, nothing was known in Colon of the proceedings in Panama until the arrival of the train at 10.45 on the morning of the 4th. Some propositions were, I was later told, made to Col. Torres by the representatives of the new Government at Colon, with a view to inducing him to reembark in the *Cartagena* and return to the port of

Cartagena, and it was in answer to this proposition that Col. Torres made the threat and took the action reported in my letter No. 96, of November 5, 1903. The *Cartagena* left the port just after the threat was made, and I did not deem it expedient to attempt to detain her, as such action would certainly, in the then state of affairs, have precipitated a conflict on shore, which I was not prepared to meet. It is my understanding that she returned to Cartagena. After the withdrawal of the Colombian troops on the evening of November 4 and the return of the *Nashville's* force on board, as reported in my letter No. 96, there was no disturbance on shore and the night passed quietly. On the morning of the 5th I discovered that the commander of the Colombian troops had not withdrawn so far from the town as he had agreed, but was occupying buildings near the outskirts of the town. I immediately inquired into the matter and learned that he had some trivial excuse for not carrying out his agreement, and also that it was his intention to occupy Colon again on the arrival of the alcalde due at 10.45 a. m., unless Gen. Tobal sent word by the alcalde that he, Col. Torres, should withdraw. That Gen. Tobal had declined to give any instructions I was cognizant of, and the situation at once became quite as serious as on the day previous. I immediately landed an armed force, reoccupied the same building; also landed two 1-pounders and mounted them on platform cars behind protection of cotton bales, and then in company with the United States consul had an interview with Col. Torres, in the course of which I informed him that I had relanded my men because he had not kept his agreement; that I had no interest in the affairs of either party; that my attitude was strictly neutral; that the troops of neither side should be transported; that my sole purpose in landing was to protect the lives and property of American citizens if threatened, as they had been threatened, and to maintain the free and uninterrupted transit of the Isthmus, and that purpose I should maintain by force if necessary. I also strongly advised that in the interests of peace and to prevent the possibility of a conflict that could not but be regrettable he should carry out his agreement of the previous evening and withdraw to Monkey Hill.

Col. Torres's only reply was that it was unhealthy at Monkey Hill, a reiteration of his love of Americans, and persistence in his intention to occupy Colon should Gen. Tobal not give him directions to the contrary.

On the return of the alcalde at about 11 a. m. the Colombian troops marched into Colon, but did not assume the threatening demeanor of the previous day. The American women and children again went on board the *Marcomania* and *City of Washington*, and through the British vice consul I offered protection to British subjects, as directed in the department's cablegram. A copy of the Britisih vice consul's acknowledgment is hereto appended. The *Nashville* I got under way as on the previous day and moved close in to protect the water front. During the afternoon several propositions were made to Col. Torres by the representatives of the new Government, and he was finally persuaded by them to embark on the Royal Mail steamer *Orinoco* with all his troops and return to Cartagena. The *Orinoco* left her dock with the troops—474 all told—at 7.35 p. m. The *Dixie* arrived and anchored at 7.05 p. m., when I went on board and acquainted the commanding officer with the situation. A portion of the marine battalion was landed and the *Nashville's* force withdrawn.

3. On the evening of November 4 Maj. William M. Black and Lieut. Mark Brooke, Corps of Engineers, United States Army, came to Colon from Culebra and volunteered their services, which were accepted, and they rendered very efficient help on the following day.

4. I beg to assure the department that I had no part whatever in the negotiations that were carried on between Col. Torres and the representatives of the Provisional Government; that I landed an armed force only when the lives of American citizens were threatened, and withdrew this force as soon as there seemed to be no grounds for further apprehension of injury to American lives or property; that I relanded an armed force because of the failure of Col. Torres to carry out his agreement to withdraw and announced intention of returning, and that my attitude throughout was strictly neutral as between the two parties, my only purpose being to protect the lives and property of American citizens and to preserve the free and uninterrupted transit of the Isthmus.

Very respectfully,

JOHN HUBBARD,
Commander, United States Navy, Commanding.

The SECRETARY OF THE NAVY,
Bureau of Navigation, Navy Department, Washington, D. C.

This plain official account of the occurrences of November 4 shows that, instead of there having been too much prevision by the American Government for the maintenance of order and the protection of life and property on the Isthmus, the orders for the movement of the American warships had been too long delayed; so long, in fact, that there were but 42 marines and sailors available to land and protect the lives of American men and women. It was only the coolness and gallantry with which this little band of men wearing the American uniform faced ten times their number of armed foes, bent on carrying out the atrocious threat of the Colombian commander, that prevented a murderous catastrophe. At Panama, when the revolution broke out, there was no American man-of-war and no American troops or sailors. At Colon, Commander Hubbard acted with entire impartiality toward both sides, preventing any movement, whether by the Colombians or the Panamans, which would tend to produce bloodshed. On November 9 he prevented a body of the revolutionists from landing at Colon. Throughout he behaved in the most creditable manner. In the New York Evening Post, under date of Panama, December 8, there is an article from a special correspondent which sets forth in detail the unbearable oppression of the Colombian Government in Panama. In this article is an interesting interview with a native Panaman, which runs in part as follows:

* * * "We looked upon the building of the canal as matter of life or death to us. We wanted that because it meant, with the United States in control of it, peace and prosperity for us. President Marroquin appointed an Isthmian to be governor of Panama; and we looked upon that as of happy augury. Soon we heard that the canal treaty was not likely to be approved at Bogota; next, we heard that our Isthmian governor, Obaldia, who had scarcely assumed power, was to be superseded by a soldier from Bogota. * * *

"Notwithstanding all that Colombia has drained us of in the way of revenues, she did not bridge for us a single river, nor make a single roadway, nor erect a single college where our children could be educated, nor do anything at all to advance our industries. * * * Well, when the new generals came we seized them, arrested them, and the town of Panama was in joy. Not a protest was made, except the shots fired from the Colombian gunboat *Bogota*, which killed one Chinese lying in his bed. We were willing to encounter the Colombian troops at Colon and fight it out; but the commander of the United States cruiser *Nashville* forbade Superintendent Shaler to allow the railroad to transport troops for either party. That is our story."

I call especial attention to the concluding portion of this interview which states the willingness of the Panama people to fight the Colombian troops and the refusal of Commander Hubbard to permit them to use the railroal and therefore to get into a position where the fight could take place. It thus clearly appears that the fact that there was no bloodshed on the Isthmus was directly due—and only due—to the prompt and firm enforcement by the United States of its traditional policy. During the past 40 years revolutions and attempts at revolution have succeeded one another with monotonous regularity on the Isthmus, and again and again United States sailors and marines have been landed as they were landed in this instance and under similar instructions to protect the transit. One of these revolutions resulted in three years of warfare; and the aggregate of bloodshed and misery caused by them has been incalculable. The fact that in this last revolution not a life was lost save that of the man killed by the shells of the Colombian gunboat, and no property destroyed, was due to the action which I have described. We, in effect, policed the Isthmus in the interest of its inhabitants and of our own national needs, and for the good of the entire civilized world. Failure to act as the administration acted would have meant great waste of life, great suffering, great destruction of property, all of which was avoided by the firmness and prudence with which Commander Hubbard carried out his orders and prevented either party from attacking the other. Our action was for the peace both of Colombia and of Panama. It is earnestly to be hoped that there will be no unwise conduct on our part which may encourage Colombia to embark on a war which can not result in her regaining control of the Isthmus, but which may cause much bloodshed and suffering.

I hesitate to refer to the injurious insinuations which have been made of complicity by this Government in the revolutionary movement in Panama. They are as destitute of foundation as of propriety. The only excuse for my mentioning them is the fear lest unthinking persons might mistake for acquiescence the silence of mere self-respect. I think proper to say, therefore, that no one connected with this Government had any part in preparing, inciting, or encouraging the late revolution on the Isthmust of Panama, and that save from the reports of our military and naval officers, given above, no one connected with this Government had any previous knowledge of the revolution except such as was accessible to any person of ordinary intelligence who read the newspapers and kept up a current acquaintance with public affairs.

By the unanimous action of its people, without the firing of a shot—with a unanimity hardly before recorded in any similar case—the people of Panama declared themselves an independent Republic. Their recognition by this Government was based upon a state of facts in no way dependent for its justification upon our action in ordinary cases. I have not denied, nor do I wish to deny either the validity or the propriety of the general rule that a new State should not be recognized as independent till it has shown its ability to maintain its independence. This rule is derived from the principle of non-intervention, and as a corollary of that principle has generally been observed by the United States. But, like the principles from which it is deducted, the rule is subject to exceptions; and there are in my opinion clear and imperative reasons why a departure from it was justified and even required in the present instance. These reasons embrace, first, our treaty rights; second, our national interests and safety; and, third, the interests of collective civilization.

I have already adverted to the treaty of 1846, by the thirty-fifth article of which the United States secured the right to a free and open transit across the Isthmus of Panama, and to that end agreed to guarantee to New Granada her rights of sovereignty and property over that territory. This article is sometimes discussed as if the latter guaranty constituted its sole object and bound the Unitcd tSates to protect the sovereignty of New Granada against domestic revolution. Nothing, however, could be more eroneous than this supposition. That our wise and patriotic ancestors, with all their dread of entangling alliances, would have entered into a treaty with New Granada solely or even primarily for the purpose of enabling that remnant of the original Republic of Columbia, then resolved into the States of New Granada, Venezuela, and Ecuador, to continue from Bogota to rule over the Isthmus of Panama, is a conception that would in itself be incredible, even if the contrary did not clearly appear. It is true that since the treaty was made the United States has again and again been obliged forcibly to intervene for the preservation of order and the maintenance of an open transit, and that this intervention has usually operated to the advantage of the titular Government of Colombia, but it is equally true that the United States in intervening, with or without Colombia's consent, for the protection of the transit, has disclaimed any duty to defend the Colombian Government against domestic insurrection or against the erection of an independent government on the Isthmus of Panama. The attacks against which the United States engaged to protect New Granadian sovereignty were those of foreign powers; but this engagement was only a means to the accomplishment of a yet more important end. The great design of the article was to assure the dedication of the Isthmus to the purposes of free and unobstructed interoceanic transit, the cosummation of which would be found in an interoceanic canal. To the accomplishment of this object the Government of the United States had for years directed its diplomacy. It occupied a place in the instructions to our delegates to the Panama Congress during the administration of John Quincy Adams. It formed the subject of a resolution of the Senate in 1835, and of the House of Representatives in 1839. In 1846 its importance had become still more apparent by reason of the Mexican War. If the treaty of 1846 did not in terms bind New Granada to grant reasonable concessions for the construction of means of interoceánic communication, it was only because it was not imagined that such concessions would ever be withheld. As it was expressly agreed that the United States, in consideration of its onerous guaranty of New Granadian sovereignty, should possess the right of free and open transit on any modes of communication that might be constructed, the obvious intent of the treaty rendered it unnecessary, if not superfluous, in terms to stipulate that permission for the construction of such modes of communication should not be denied.

Long before the conclusion of the Hay-Herran treaty the course of events hao shown that a canal to connect the Atlantic and Pacific oceans must be built by the United States or not at all. Experience had demonstrated that private enterprise was utterly inadequate for the purpose; and a fixed policy, declared by the United States on many memorable occasions, and supported by the practically unanimous voice of American opinion, had rendered it morally impossible that the work should be undertaken by European powers, either singly or in combination. Such were the universally recognized conditions on which the legislation of the Congress was based, and on which the la.e negotiations with Colombia were begun and concluded. Nevertheless, when the well-considered agreement was rejected by Colombia and the revolution on the Isthmus ensued, one of Colombia's first acts was to invoke the intervention of the United States; nor does her invitation appear to have been confined to this Government alone. By a telegram from Mr. Beaupré, our minister at Bogota, of the 7 h of November last, we were informed that Gen. Reyes would soon leave Panama invested with full powers; that he had telegraphed the President of Mexico to ask the Government of the United States and all countries represented at the Pan-American Conference "to aid Colombia to preserve her integrity"; and that he had requested that the Government of the United States should meanwhile "preserve the neutrality and transit of the Isthmus" and should "not recognize the new Government." In another telegram from Mr. Beaupré, which was sent later in the day, this Government was asked whe.her it would take action "to maintain Colombian right and sovereignty on the Isthmus, in accordance with Article 35 [of] the treaty of 1846" in case the Colombian Government should be "entirely unable to suppress the secession movement there." Here was a direct solicitation to the United States to intervene for the purpose of suppression, contrary to the treaty of 1846, as this Government has uniformly construed it, a new revolt against Colombia's authority brought about by her own refusal to permit the fulfillment of the great design for which that treaty was made. It was under these circumstances that the United States, instead of using its forces to destroy those who sought to make the engagements of the treaty a reality, recognized them as the proper custodians of the sovereignty of the Isthmus.

This recognition was, in the second place, further justified by the highest considerations of our national interests and safety. In all the range of our international relations, I do not hesitate to affirm that there is nothing of greater or more pressing importance than the construction of an interoceanic canal. Long acknowledged to be essential to our commercial development, it has become, as the result of the recent extension of our territorial dominion, more than ever essential to our national self-defense. In transmitting to the Senate the treaty of 1846, President Polk pointed out as the principal reason for its ratification that the passage of the Isthmus, which it was designed to secure, "would relieve us from a long and dangerous navigation of more than 9,000 miles around Cape Horn, and render our communication with our own possessions on the northwest coast of America comparatively easy and speedy." The events of the past five years have given to this consideration an importance immeasurably greater than it possessed in 1846. In the light of our present situation, the establishment of easy and speedy communication by sea between the Atlantic and the Pacific presents itself not simply as something to be desired, but as an object to be positively and promptly attained. Reasons of convenience have been superseded by reasons of vital necessity, which do not admit of indefinite delays.

To such delays the rejection by Colombia of the Hay-Herran treaty directly exposed us. As proof of this fact I need only refer to the program outlined in the report of the majority of the Panama Canal Committee, read in the Colombian Senate on the 14th of Occtober last. In this report, which recommended that the discussion of a law to authorize the Government to enter upon the new negotiations should be indefinitely postponed, it is proposed that the consideration of the subject should be deferred till October 31, 1904, when the next Colombian Congress should have met in ordinary session. By that time, as the report goes on to say, the extension of time granted to the New Panama Canal Co. by treaty in 1893 would have expired, and the new Congress would be in a position to take up the question whether the company had not, in spite of further extensions that had been granted by legislative acts, forfeited all its property and rights. "When that time arrives," the report significantly declares, "the Republic, without any impediment, will be able to contract, and will be in more clear, more definite, and more advantageous possession, both legally and materially." The naked meaning of this report is that Colombia proposed to wait until, by the enforcement of a forfeiture repugnant to the ideas of justice which obtain in every civilized nation, the property and rights of the New Panama Canal Co. could be confiscated.

Such is the scheme to which it was proposed that the United States should be invited to become a party. The construction of the canal was to be relegated to the indefinite future, while Colombia was, by reason of her own delay, to be placed in the "more advantageous" position of claiming not merely the compensation to be paid by the United States for the privilege of completing the canal, but also the 40,000,000 authorized by the act of 1902 to be paid for the property of the New Panama Canal Co. That the attempt to carry out this scheme would have brought Colombia into conflict with the Government of France can not be doubted; nor could the United States have counted upon immunity from the consequences of the attempt, even apart from the indefinite delays to which the construction of the canal was to be subjected. On the first appearance of danger to Colombia this Government would have been summoned to interpose, in order to give the effect to the guaranties of the treaty of 1846; and all this in support of a plan which, while characterized in its first stage by the wanton disregard of our own highest interests, was fitly to end in further injury to the citizens of a friendly nation, whose enormous losses in their generous efforts to pierce the Isthmus have become a matter of history.

In the third place, I confidently maintain that the recognition of the Republic of Panama was an act justified by the interests of collective civilization. If ever a Government could be said to have received a mandate from civilization to effect an object the accomplishment of which was demanded in the interest of mankind, the United States holds that position with regard to the interoceanic canal. Since our purpose to build the canal was definitely announced, there have come from all quarters assurances of approval and encouragement, in which even Colombia herself at one time participated; and to general assurances were added specific acts and declarations. In order that no obstacle might stand in our way Great Britain renounced important rights under the Clayton-Bulwer treaty and agreed to its abrogation, receiving in return nothing but our honorable pledge to build the canal and protect it as an open highway. It was in view of this pledge, and of the proposed enactment by the Congress of the United States of legislation to give it immediate effect, that the second Pan-American conference, at the City of Mexico, on January 22, 1902, adopted the following resolution:

"The Republics assembled at the International Conference of Mexico applaud the purpose of the United States Government to construct an interoceanic canal and acknowledge that this work will not only be worthy of the greatness of the American people, but also in the highest sense a work of civilization and to the greatest degree beneficial to the development of commerce between the American States and the other countries of the world."

Among those who signed this resolution on behalf of their respective Governments was Gen. Reyes, the delegate of Colombia. Little could it have been foreseen that two years later the Colombian Government, led astray by false allurements of selfish advantage, and forgetful alike of its international obligations and of the duties and responsibilities of sovereignty, would thwart the efforts of the United States to enter upon and complete a work which the nations of America, reechoing the sentiment of the nations of Europe, had pronounced to be not only "worthy of the greatness of the American people," but also "in the highest sense a work of civilization."

That our position as the mandatory of civilization has been by no means misconceived is shown by the promptitude with which the powers have, one after another, followed our lead in recognizing Panama as an independent State. Our action in recognizing the new Republic has been followed by like recognition on the part of France, Germany, Denmark, Russia, Sweden and Norway, Nicaragua, Peru, China, Cuba, Great Britain, Italy, Costa Rica, Japan, and Austria-Hungary.

In view of the manifold considerations of treaty right and obligation, of national interest and safety, and of collective civilization by which our Government was constrained to act, I am at a loss to comprehend the attitude of those who can discern in the recognition of the Republic of Panama only a general approval of the principle of "revolution" by which a given government is overturned or one portion of a country separated from another. Only the amplest justification can warrant a revolutionary movement of either kind. But there is no fixed rule which can be applied to all such movements. Each case must be judged on its own merits. There have been many revolutionary movements, many movements for the dismemberment of countries, which were evil, tried by any standard. But in my opinion no disinterested and fair-minded observer acquainted with the circumstances can fail to feel that Panama had the amplest justification for separation from Colombia under the conditions existing, and, moreover, that its action was in the highest degree beneficial to the interests of the entire civilized world by securing the immediate opportunity for the building of the interoceanic canal. It would be well for those who are pessimistic as to our action in peacefully recognizing the Republic of Panama, while we lawfully protected the transit from invasion and disturbance, to recall what has been done in Cuba, where we intervened even by force on general grounds of national interest and duty. When we interfered it was freely prophesied that we intended to keep Cuba and administer it for our own interests. The result has demonstrated in singularly conclusive fashion the falsity of these prophesies. Cuba is now an independent Republic. We governed it in its own interests for a few years, till it was able to stand alone, and then started it upon its career of self-government and independence, granting it all necessary aid. We have received from Cuba a grant of two naval stations, so situated that they in no possible way menace the liberty of the island, and yet serve as important defenses for the Cuban people, as well as for our own people, against possible foreign attack. The people of Cuba have been immeasurably benefited by our interference in their behalf, and our own gain has been great. So will it be with Panama. The people of the Isthmus, and, as I firmly believe, of the adjacent parts of Central and South America, will be greatly benefited by the building of the canal and the guaranty of peace and order along its line; and hand in hand with the benefit to them will go the benefit to us and to mankind. By our prompt and decisive action, not only have our interests and those of the world at large been conserved, but we have forestalled complications which were likely to be fruitful in loss to ourselves and in bloodshed and suffering to the people of the Isthmus.

Instead of using our forces, as we were invited by Colombia to do, for the twofold purpose of defeating our own rights and interests and the interests of the civilized world, and of compelling the submission of the people of the Isthmus to those whom they regarded as oppressors, we shall, as in duty bound, keep the transit open and prevent its invasion. Meanwhile, the only question now before us is that of the ratification of the treaty. For it is to be remembered that a failure to ratify the treaty will not undo what has been done, will not restore Panama to Colombia, and will not alter our obligation to keep the transit open across the Isthmus, and to prevent any outside power from menacing this transit.

It seems to have been assumed in certain quarters that the proposition that the obligations of article 35 of the treaty of 1846 are to be considered as adhering to and following the sovereignty of the Isthmus, so long as that sovereignty is not absorbed by the United States, rests upon some novel theory. No assumption could be further from the fact. It is by no means true that a state in declaring its independence rids itself of all the treaty obligations entered into by the parent government. It is a mere coincidence that this question was once raised in a case involving the obligations of Colombia as an independent state under a treaty which Spain had made with the United States many years before Spanish-American independence. In that case Mr. John Quincy Adams, Secretary of State, in an instruction to Mr. Anderson, our minister to Colombia, of May 27, 1823, said:

"By a treaty between the United States and Spain, concluded at a time when Colombia was a part of the Spanish dominions, * * * the principle that free ships make free goods was expressly recognized and established. It is asserted that by her declaration of independence Colombia has been entirely released from all the obligations by which, as a part of the Spanish nation, she was bound to other nations. This principle is not tenable. To all the engagements of Spain with other nations, affecting their rights and interests, Colombia, so far as she was affected by them, remains bound in honor and in justice. The stipulation now referred to is of that character."

The principle thus asserted by Mr. Adams was afterwards sustained by an international commission in respect to the precise stipulation to which he referred; and a similar position was taken by the United States with regard to the binding obligation upon the independent State of Texas of commercial stipulations embodied in prior treaties between the United States and Mexico when Texas formed a part of the latter country. But in the present case it is unnecessary to go so far. Even if it be admitted that prior treaties of a political and commercial complexion generally do not bind a new state formed by separation, it is undeniable that stipulations having a local application to the territory embraced in the new state continue in force and are binding upon the new sovereign. Thus it is on all hands conceded that treaties relating to boundaries and to rights of navigation continue in force without regard to changes in government or in sovereignty. This principle obviously applies to that part of the treaty of 1846 which relates to the Isthmus of Panama.

In conclusion let me repeat that the question actually before this Government is not that of the recognition of Panama as an independent Republic. That is already an accomplished fact. The question, and the only question, is whether or not we shall build an isthmian canal.

I transmit herewith copies of the latest notes from the minister of the Republic of Panama to this Government, and of certain notes which have passed between the special envoy of the Republic of Colombia and this Government.

WHITE HOUSE, *January 4, 1904.*

EXHIBIT H.

PROTEST OF COLOMBIA.

PROTEST OF COLOMBIA AGAINST THE TREATY BETWEEN PANAMA AND THE UNITED STATES.

MINISTRY OF FOREIGN RELATIONS,
Bogota, April 12, 1904.

To the Hon. ALBAN G. SNYDER,
Chargé d'Affaires of the United States in Colombia.

SIR: In a note which I addressed to your honorable legation on the 12th of November last, concerning the Separatist rebellion on the Isthmus of Panama, I forecasted that, in some way or other, the treaty of 1846 would be violated. I transmitted, through his excellency Mr. Beaupré, to the United States Government, an exposition of the circumstances which would arise if that compact were infringed or violated, feeling confident that the United States Government would act with justice toward the Government of Colombia in accordance with the stipulation contained in the said treaty and with a due regard to international rights.

The stipulation referred to is contained in clause 5 of article 35 of the treaty, and reads as follows:

"If any of the articles contained in the treaty are violated or infringed, it is expressly stipulated that neither of the two contracting parties shall order or authorize acts of reprisal nor shall declare war against the other for acts of an insulting or damaging character until the offended party shall have previously presented a statement of the alleged injuries, supported by absolute proofs, and demanded justice and satisfaction; and in the event of these being denied, such denial would be judged to constitute a violation of international law and right."

Your excellency's Government has not only dealt unjustly toward the Government of Colombia in violating the treaty of 1846 and international rights, but has also infringed the provisions of the said treaty in the following manner:

1. By formally recognizing, as an independent Republic, the revolutionary department of Panama.

2. By officially receiving as a minister plenipotentiary an agent of the Revolutionists.

3. By Admiral Coghlan's notification to the general in chief of the Atlantic army of Colombia that he had received instructions not to permit the landing of Colombian troops on the Isthmus.

4. By the notification, in a special dispatch to the Colombian minister in Washington, that the treaty concluded with the Secessionists (although the same had not yet received the sanction of the United States Senate) made it obligatory on the United States to maintain the independence of the Isthmus and the preservation of peace and order, and pointing out the serious consequences that would follow an invasion of the Isthmus of Panama by Colombian troops; also that it appeared to the United States that the time had arrived for closing the chapter of the civil war on the Isthmus.

5. By reiterating the statements contained in the former note of the 30th December in which it was expressed that the formal attitude of the American

Government would be indicated and governed according to circumstances and that that Government would be sorry to be provoked into assuming an hostile attitude.

6. By celebrating a treaty with the revolutionary Government of Panama for the opening of an interoceanic canal through the Isthmus.

7. By the guarantee given in the aforesaid treaty assuring the independence of the Isthmus in direct contravention of the treaty made by the United States with Colombia guaranteeing the latter her property in and sovereignty over the same territory.

To further demonstrate that the attitude assumed by the United States Government toward the Secessionists was not in conformity with the terms of the treaty of 1846 and with international rights is wholly unnecessary. The accomplished facts are in such open contradiction to the terms of the treaty and to the principles of right that any additional reasoning on the subject would be superfluous.

Neither in the act of independence of the city of Panama nor in the manifesto of the assembly called "the Government" do the rebels say that the Isthmus has ever been an independent State; but, that Panama, in separating herself from Spain, spontaneously linked her fate with that of the Republic of Colombia.

From the act of independence of the 28th November, 1821, I copy the following:

1. Panama, spontaneously and in conformity with the unanimous vote of her people, declares herself free from and independent of the Spanish Govrenment.

2. The territory of the Provinces of the Isthmus belong to the Republic of Colombia and shall be represented in Congress by its deputies.

It is therefore clearly seen that the Provinces of the Isthmus were formed without the intervention or consent of the viceroy of Santafé. Notwithstanding this historical fact the United States informed me, through its legation, on the 11th November last, that the people of Panama had reassumed their independence, intending thereby to suggest the erroneous idea that the Isthmus had been once an independent State.

The United States Government, in the treaty agreed upon with the agent of the revolutionists for the opening of the canal, besides guaranteeing the independence of the Isthmus, accepted the stipulations I mention below, which are extracted from the treaty and have been published by the newspapers of the United States.

Article 2 of the treaty grants to the United States dominion over a zone of 5 miles on either side of the canal and over an extension of 3 nautical miles at each end of the canal, together with the lands necessary for the construction and conservation of the canal and its dependencies. The same article also grants to the United States the perpetual use and occupation of and dominion over all the islands lying in the bay of Panama called Perico, Naos, Flamenco, and Culebra.

By article 3 Panama grants to the United States the right to exercise over the zone mentioned in article 2 the same power and authority that the United States would have had if that country had possessed the right of sovereignty over the Isthmus, to the exclusion of the exercise of this right and power by Panama.

By article 4 the Republic of Panama grants to the United States the perpetual use of the rivers, streams, lakes, and other navigable bodies of water within its limits which may be necessary for the construction and maintenance of the canal and its sanitation.

In effect, article 5 cedes perpetually to the United States the monopoly of any system of communication over the Isthmus by a canal or by railways.

These concessions are equivalent to an alienation or grant to the United States of all the territory to which they refer.

This compact was agreed upon a few days after the initiation of the Separatist rebellion, which latter had not even been properly organized to indicate that it was the outcome of popular feeling. And to this hurried and precipitate act must be added, as I have already said, the putting into force of the compact guaranteeing the independence of Panama before the same was ratified or perfected.

These incidents will doubtless convey to the mind of every one the idea that the United States acted in this way so that under her open and unconcealed military protection the Isthmus might gain its independence, the object, of course, being to obtain those advantages under the treaty above referred to which are substantially in excess of those offered by Colombia, for it is undeniable that the concessions made by the so-called Republic of Panama to the United States ensures to the latter complete dominion and government over the zone and other lands and territorial waters. This deduction would not have been so tenable if the compact had not been celebrated at the commencement of the insurrection.

If the existence of this compact and the fact that Colombian troops were not permitted to land on the Isthmus are no sufficient to prove what I have above stated, strong confirmatory evidence is found in certain diplomatic documents which I proceed to cite.

On the 13th June, 1903, his excellency the minister of the United States presented me with the following memorandum:

"I have received instructions by cable from my Government that from all appearances the Government of Colombia evidently does not appreciate the gravity of the situation. The negotiations with respect to the Panama Canal were initiated by Colombia and were energetically solicited of my Government for several years. The propositions presented by Colombia, with some small modifications, were finally accepted by us. In virtue of this convention our Congress revoked their former decision and determined that interoceanic transit should be by way of Panama. If Colombia now unduly and without reason rejects the treaty, it will retard its ratification, and the friendly relations existing between the two countries will be so seriously compromised that our Congress, during next winter, might take steps for which every friend of Colombia will be sorry."

In his note to me of the 5th August, Minister Beaupré said:

"In virtue of the official data in my possession, I can affirm that the circumstances which have taken place in all the negotiations with respect to the canal treaty are of such a nature as to fully warrant the United States considering any modification of the conditions stipulated in the treaty a violation of the compact which would produce the greatest complications in the friendly relations which, up to the present, exist between the two countries."

To the above-quoted memorandum and note and to several other notes from the United States legation I replied, maintaining the right of our Congress to modify or reject the treaty without such an act being construed as contrary or opposed to previous negotiations or in the nature of a violation of the promises made by my Government.

My reasoning, although based on the constitution of this country and on international rights, unhappily had not the effect of altering the trend of the intentions forecasted against Colombia in the documents above mentioned—intentions that have taken practical form in the initiation of very grave measures with the qualification, however, that these measures have not originated with the Senate but with the Executive power of the United States.

It is of the greatest importance to correctly appreciate and understand the procedure of the two Governments in the matter of the canal, and to recall some past incidents intimately related to the last serious events that have lessened the integrity and sovereignty of this Republic.

On the 14th of January, 1869, there was signed by the plenipotentiaries of Colombia and the United States, at Bogota, a treaty for the excavation of a canal through the Isthmus of Panama joining the Atlantic and Pacific Oceans.

Article 8 of that agreement reads as follows:

"The United States of Colombia shall conserve and retain its political sovereignty and jurisdiction over the canal and adjacent territory, and not only will she permit, but shall guarantee to the United States of America, in conformity with the constitution and laws on force in Colombia, the peaceful enjoyment government, direction, and management of the canal as before stipulated."

Before this treaty was submitted to the Congress of Colombia for ratification there was substituted for it another treaty dated the 26th January, 1870, article 10 of which is as follows:

"As soon as the canal, with its dependencies and annexes, is constructed, the power of inspection, possession, direction, and management of the same shall vest in the United States of America, and the same shall be exercised by that Government without any foreign interference; but the United States shall not exercise jurisdiction or authority in any manner soever over the territory or its population. The United States of Colombia shall conserve and retain its political sovereignty and jurisdiction over the canal and adjacent territory; but it shall guarantee and permit to the United States of America, conformably with the constitution and laws in force in Colombia, the peaceful enjoyment, the administration, direction, and management of the canal as already stated. This guaranty shall not, however, differ in any respect from that usually conceded under the laws of the Republic of Colombia to persons and interests in Colombian territory; and in order to insure the greatest possible security to the canal undertaking an extraordinary public force will be provided, the cost of which shall be borne by the said undertaking."

This compact was not ratified owing to the Colombian Congress making some modifications which the Executive power of the United States refused to accept; but in both drafts agreed upon and signed by the United States minister the United States Government accepted the provision that Colombia should retain and preserve its full and complete sovereignty and jurisdiction over the canal and the territory adjacent. It was not until the last convention was subscribed to in Washington on the 22d January, 1903, that owing to the persistent demands of the United States—a course first suggested by the chief of the Isthmian Canal Commission—it was agreed to establish mixed and American tribunals in the Canal Zone for the trial of civil and criminal cases, and the provision was made for conceding, for periods of 100 years at a time, the said zone and the canal works to the exclusive will and control of the Government of the United States.

This radical change of views on the part of the United States placed the Publicists of Colombia on the alert and had the effect of bringing about the nonratification of the treaty, especially as the compensation offered was insufficient in view of the fact that Colombia surrendered her right of taking possession, without any indemnification, of the canal works, the lands, the buildings, the furniture, machinery, and materials which would have come to her, at the latest, within six years, as it was well known that it was impossible for the French company to complete and terminate their agreement; also in view of the fact that the landed and other property, together with the large number of shares in the Panama Railroad Co. held by the French company, all of which the United States was going to acquire for $40,000,000, Colombia had every expectation of obtaining. The small sum of $10,000,000 was offered Colombia by the United States without consideration being had for the true value of the property which Colombia was surrendering, but was offered in accordance with article 25 of the treaty, which provides that pecuniary indemnification shall be paid Colombia "as price or compensation for the right of use of the zone granted in this convention by Colombia to the United States for the construction of the canal and for the rights of property in the Panama Railroad and the annuity of $250,000 gold which the said railroad pays to Colombia, and also as compensation for any other rights and privileges granted to the United States and in consideration of the increased expenditure in the public administration of the Department of Panama caused by the construction of the canal."

Colombia, in order to facilitate the negotiations, had agreed that article 25 of the treaty should be drawn up in the above form notwithstanding that the $10,000,000 would be insufficient compensation for all the property and other valuable benefits which she renounced. The sum offered, as a fact, did not represent any indemnification for the use of the zone and the islands of Culebra, Naos, Perico, and Flamenco. The agreement, although it was opposed to her interests, was entered into by Colombia because she had considered the matter and had decided not to oppose in any way the execution of the great work needed in the interests of navigation and trade of the whole world and she, therefore, granted the most liberal concessions compatible with her integrity and sovereignty.

The annual rental of $250,000 (which Colombia was to receive from the United States and which would not begin until the expiration of nine years) was to take the place and be in the stead of that which for 60 years the Panama Railroad Co. had agreed to pay to Colombia, and it should not, therefore, appear or be counted as forming part of the compensation to be paid by the United States to Colombia.

Allow me, your excellency, to recall to your attention, certain past occurrences which induced the Colombian Government to expect from the United States a different course of action to that which it followed in regard to the Separatist movement on the Isthmus.

In replying to a note from the chargé d'affaires of Colombia, in which the latter proposed to the then United States Secretary of State, on the 30th March, 1820, that the United States should supply a certain quantity of arms, it being mentioned as a reason for this request that the nations of New Grenada and Venezuela had been united by a law passed by the sovereign congress at the unanimous desire of the people of both countries and were forming a sovereign State, free and independent, under the name of the Republic of Colombia with a provisional constitution and representative Government, His Excellency John Quincy Adams said:

"Whereas the First Magistrate of the Nation had observed, and continues to observe the principle of impartial neutrality in this war, he considers inviolable his obligation to abstain from supplying to one of the two parties in the contest which is being carried on any help that, in similar circumstances, would be denied to the other party. Such is the law of neutrality. This position can not be deviated from, according to the principles of the Constitution of the United States excepting only by an act of Congress."

Your excellency will observe that although 10 years had elapsed since New Grenada and Venezuela had proclaimed their independence and they were still struggling for the same, yet the Government of the United States recognized that the law of neutrality forbade the supply to one of the belligerents of any help that, in similar circumstances, would be denied to the other. Your excellency will also observe that, contrary to this rule, your Government promptly recognized the independence of the Isthmus so as to harass Colombia and put into force and operation a compact, not approved or ratified by the Senate, guaranteeing the maintenance of that independence.

In the message of the State Department to Congress, dated the 14th July, 1860, the following passage is found respecting the commercial relations existing between the United States and Spanish-American countries: "With many of them we have established relations by particular treaties. The treaty of 1846 between the United States and New Grenada contains stipulations of guarantee for the neutrality of certain parts of the Isthmus in the territory of Colombia and for the protection of the rights of sovereignity and of property belonging to the nation. That treaty, therefore, constitutes a true and genuine alliance of protection between the United States and that Republic."

In a note dated 30th April, 1866, Mr. Seward, referring to the sovereignty and independence of Colombia on the Isthmus, said that "if those great interests were to be at any time attacked by any power, internal or external, the United States would be ready, in conjunction with the Colombian Government, its ally, to defend them."

On the 24th June, 1881, Mr. Secretary Blaine addressed an important note to Mr. Lowell, United States minister in London, from which I extract the following:

"In 1846 a memorable and important treaty was signed between the United States of America and the Republic of New Grenada (now States of Colombia). By article 35, in exchange for certain concessions to the United States, we guarantee 'positively and effectively' the complete neutrality of the Isthmus and of all ways of interoceanic communication which might be established on it and the protection and maintenance of free transit from one ocean to the other, and we bind ourselves as well to guarantee the rights of sovereignty of the United States of Colombia over the territory of the Isthmus comprised within the limits of the State of Panama.

"According to the judgment of the President, this guaranty by the United States of America does not require the adhesion, acquiescence, or support of other powers. On more than one occasion has the United States Government had to carry into force and effect its guaranty of neutrality, and nothing at this moment can be seen to warrant a doubt that this nation will fail to comply with or leave unfulfilled its guaranty and obligations.

"There has never existed the least doubt, on the part of the United States, regarding the object of the obligation undertaken or respecting the free transit of the commerce of the world through the canal or the protection of the territorial rights of Colombia against aggression of any kind * * * neither has there ever been cause to discuss the advantages (resulting, naturally, from its geographical position and from its political relations with the Western Continent) which were obtained by the United States from Colombia, the nation which owned the territory, in exchange for this important and extensive guaranty." (Foreign Relations of the United States, 1881, pp. 537, 538.)

With reference to the same subject, Mr. Blaine transmitted to Mr. Dichman, United States minister in Bogotá, on the same day (24th June, 1881) the following dispatch:

"Your letter numbered 269, of 9th ultimo, informs me of the confidential rumors which reached your ear, viz, that Colombia is endeavoring to obtain from the European powers a declaration in common of the neutrality of the Isthmus of Panama and of the sovereignty of Colombia over that territory.

"Like rumors have reached me from various sources, and these reveal a tendency on the part of several maritime powers to consider the propriety of uniting in order to offer such a guaranty. In these circumstances I have prepared circular instructions for the representatives of the United States in Europe, in which I have directed them, in case they are of opinion that such a proposition is likely to assume a tangible form, to call the attention of the respective Governments to which they are accredited to the opinion of the President that the existing guaranties entered into under the treaty of 1846 between the United States and Colombia are complete and sufficient and do not require additional reenforcement from any other power.

"I am not yet prepared to communicate this dispatch in extenso to the Colombian Government; but if the excitement which was produced by the return of Mr. Santo Domingo Vila to Bogotá (which went so far as to demand your recall) has subsided, giving place to better sentiments and manifesting a return of confidence, you can, if the opportunity offers, inform the secretary for foreign affairs of the measures adopted by this Government for the purpose of preventing the realization of the suspected intent of the European powers of offering a common guaranty, the same being considered unnecessary and offensive alike to Colombia and the United States." (Foreign Relations, 1881, pp. 356, and 357.)

The declarations made in the preceding letter produced in this country the belief that our territorial rights on the Isthmus of Panama would be protected by the United States "against all aggression," and that the guaranty offered by that Government did not require the cooperation, acquiescence, or support of any other power, especially as the United States had offered a complete and sufficient guaranty that did not require reenforcement from any other power.

This guaranty was stipulated in a special clause of the treaty of peace, friendship, navigation, and commerce of 1846. And whether this guarantee be considered solely as a clause of this compact, or as a treaty of guarantee, or as an alliance of protection, it undeniably is a solemn engagement or obligation which absolutely binds the United States, but which now has been wholly departed from and ignored. Such a procedure on the part of the guarantor will be correctly judged by history, that supreme judge on earth of men and nations.

The plenipotentiaries of North Germany, Austro-Hungary, Great Britain, Italy, Russia, and Turkey declared "that they recognized as an essential principle of international right that no power could be freed from the obligations of a treaty, or modify or vary its terms in any other manner but by and with the consent of the contracting parties obtained by means of an amicable agreement." (Addition to Protocol the Fifth, 12th Jan., 1871.)

By the interpretation now given to article 35 of the treaty of 1846 by the Government of the United States, it is freed, on its own mere notion and by its own will, and without the consent of Colombia, from the obligation guaranteeing the property and sovereignty of this Republic on the Isthmus; and it arrogates to itself the right and power of thus proceeding—a course of action diametrically opposed to that obligation and one constituting a violation of the essential principle of public rights expressly recognized by the above-named powers. Under the aegis of this principle Colombia considered her rights shielded and protected as in an impregnable bulwark as I recently declared before the Senate when fears were being entertained that a Separatist movement was in course of development on the Isthmus.

This confidence on the part of Colombia was not only founded on the principle mentioned but was based also on the terms of the treaty and on the note of Mr. Blaine and of that of the 5th August, 1903, addressed to me by the minister of the United States, in which amongst other very important matters, the following occurs:

"It is regrettable that in the report of the committee of the Senate reference is made to the necessity of having the treaty of 1846–1848 declared effective—a suggestion almost involving a doubt of the good faith and intentions of the United States in complying with the terms of the same. I must assure your excellency that unless the treaty is denounced in accordance with the clause which provides the manner of effecting such, my Government is not capable of violating it neither in letter nor in spirit; nor should Colombia fear that in case the present treaty be ratified that the Government of the United States would neglect complying with the clauses which guarantee her sovereignty as they are framed in much more precise and solemn terms than those of 1846."

I referred to the foregoing extracts in the Senate and at the same time affirmed my belief that, unless the treaty was denounced, the possession and sovereignty of Colombia on the Isthmus of Panama were not exposed to any danger whatever.

The declaration of the Representatives of the United States and article 4 of the law of the United States of the 28th of June, 1902, which authorizes the construction of the Nicaraguan Canal if the negotiations with Colombia were not effected (the text of which law was communicated to this Government), justified completely the confident attitude of the latter notwithstanding certain signs, among which were the writings of the press of the United States and other countries which, in some instances, were in favor of, and, in others, against the revolutionary movement in Panama, because the promises of the minister and the provisions of the law absolutely deprived of any show of authority the rumors and fears then current on the matter.

If Mr. Beaupré had not made the above quoted very definite and decisive declaration, and had the Government of the United States not formally communicated to Colombia the text of the law of 28th June, 1902, the Government of this Republic would most assuredly have adopted such precautionary measures as would effectually have checked the revolutionary movement, and the events which took place on the Isthmus on the 3d November, 1903, and afterwards would never have occurred.

The Government of the United States has used its military strength on the Isthmus in order to favor and insure the independence of Panama. This being undoubtedly so, the question that arises is: What will the future fate of the independence and integrity of the Republics of Central and South America? The logical answer is that they will be at the will and mercy of the powerful and, for them, irresistible Republic of the North.

The interoceanic canal will modify the conditions of navigation between the two seas, but the execution of its excavation in a zone under the dominion of the United States will result in the destruction of Latin-American solidarity, whilst the official ties which bind the Department of Panama to the Republic of Colombia will be wholly and absolutely ruptured, and those of trust and confraternity, which have linked together the inhabitants of this hemisphere, will be weakened. I make these very necessary and pertinent observations as Colombia has suffered severely by the application of the new régime which appears like a threat to the integrity, autonomy, and consolidation of the Republics of this continent. It is expected that the people of the United States, notwithstanding the treaty which guaranttes the independence of Panama, will not consent to the establishment of such a régime, and that the solution of the incident which has actually occurred between the two countries will be found in the reintegration of Colombia and the consolidation of the bonds of friendship which should exist between the people of the New World so as to give an impulse to the development of progress on the foundation of order and right.

Amongst the documents transmitted by the Colombian legation in Washington to this ministry were the messages of the President of the United States to the Senate dated, respectively, the 7th December, 1903, and the 4th January, 1904, both of which relate to the canal and the separatist movement in Panama. In both messages I find statements made and opinions of much gravity expressed which it is my duty to take into respectful consideration, as they directly concern this Republic. It is not my intention to analyze each of these statements and opinions, but I propose making a brief comment on the most important of them, so that it may not be supposed that Colombia accepts or recognizes them as authentic, as they are all, or in part, entirely at variance with her traditions and history, and because silence would be taken to mean the acceptance of principles and doctrines contrary to those universally acknowledged and accepted as the prime factors in the maintenance of national integrity and sovereignty and of the letter and spirit of public treaties.

The treaty of 1846 does not vest in the United States any substantial right of property in the Isthmus of Panama which would lessen those rights of property and sovereignty which New Granada (now Colombia) had (and Colombia now possesses) in and over the said territory. According to the universally admitted principles of "public rights," national territory can not be transferred without a compact or sale, and in the above referred to treaty there is no agreement or stipulation of such a nature, neither is there any provision authorizing such sale which, if effected, would be in direct contradiction to the terms of that diplomatic document.

In the synopsis presented with the message of the President of the United States to the Senate on the 7th December last, it is stated that according to the reports of the United States consuls, 53 revolutionary outbreaks have occurred on the Isthmus in 57 years, 19 of which are made to appear as attempts at incendiarism, revolts, or insurrections. As a fact, however, these were mere incidents which by no stretch of imagination, could properly be called revolutions—incidents, which, under other names, have occurred frequently in the most advanced and civilized countries in the New and Old Worlds. Of the remaining 34 ebullitions against public order 8 only affected the whole country and 28 were strictly local and of very short duration, the majority of them taking place during the Federal régime which began on the Isthmus in 1855 and ended in 1886.

The revolution that took place in 1899 lasted for three years, but the same has been counted as four separate outbreaks, occurring in the years 1899, 1900, 1901, and 1902, thereby quadrupling the one event.

Notwithstanding the revolts that occurred during the existence of the treaty of 1846 the interoceanic transit was very rarely interrupted, and these interruptions were only for a short time. It must also be remembered that long periods of time elapsed without any interruption occurring at all.

It is true that the presence of the ships of the United States and the landing of the troops of that country (although this was of very rare occurrence and without the necessity presenting itself for the troops being obliged to fight) have contributed toward preserving the free and uninterrupted transit of the Isthmus which was precisely the object of article 35 of the treaty and for which service Colombia granted the United States sufficient compensation. It is notorious that during the 57 years such a compact has been in force Colombia has been able to fulfill her duties and obligations and peace has been maintained on the Isthmus.

To merely guarantee the preservation of order on the Isthmus is not alone sufficient to warrant the United States assuring to Panama her independence, but the United States should absolutely impose its sovereignty on the Isthmus, for it is well known that nearly all the revolutionary movements which have affected that department have been organized and carried out by the Isthmians themselves and have been of an exclusively political character. Autonomy alone will not make for the accomplishment of constant peace on the Isthmus, as has been proven by the history of the peoples of this continent; but notwithstanding their revolutions their commerce has prospered and their civilization has advanced.

Doubtless foreseeing the need of providing for the maintenance of peace on the Isthmus the convention between Panama and the United States contained provisions to that effect in article 7 thereof which is as follows:

"The United States shall have the same right and authority to maintain public order in case the Government of Panama can not maintain the same in Panama and Colon."

Let me quote another provision of the same compact contained in article 21 thereof:

"If at any time the need should arise to employ armed force for the security and protection of the canal, ships in its use, railways or other enterprises, the United States shall have the right to employ with discretion its police or its naval forces and establish fortifications to accomplish such an end."

In accordance with the above-quoted articles the constitution of the so-called Republic of Panama contained the following provision in article 131:

"The Government of the United States of America can intervene or mediate in any part of the Republic of Panama so as to reestablish public order and uphold the constitution provided that that power has, by a treaty, assumed the obligation of guaranteeing the independence and sovereignty of this Republic."

In virtue of this article and of the two other preceding ones the autonomy of Panama is entirely illusory.

Incontestable proofs that Colombia has not been opposed to free transit across the Isthmus or to the Isthmus being made of general use for the traffic of the world are to be found in the facts that there has been constructed, under contract with Colombia, about one-third part of the canal, and that a French company is answerable, under bonds, for its delivery, completed, in 1910. As I said on a former occasion: "Colombia has declared the free transit of passengers and merchandise across the Isthmus and has rigidly maintained the same for more than half a century, placing in this manner her territory and her authority at the service of the trade of the world. And further, that, from its foundation, the Republic has, by means of legislative acts and various negotiations, demonstrated its strong desire to facilitate in every way the opening of the Isthmian Canal which was one of the many points of discussion in the Congress of the Republics of the American Continent convened by Bolivar in 1826."

"The United States has decided that no other Government but its own shall construct the canal." This declaration, as also that made by the Government of your excellency that the construction of the canal can not be delayed, and that the Nicaraguan Canal would not be constructed, established a political doctrine which, logically, conduced to disown Colombian sovereignty on the Isthmus, the treaty of 1846, and the prescriptions of international right respecting the recognition of new States or powers.

In the Hay-Pauncefote convention it was stipulated that the canal could be constructed under the auspices of the United States; but from this can not be deduced any right for the construction of such an undertaking without the consent of the government of the territory previously agreed upon, consideration being had to the convenience of the universal traffic and to the interests of such government. And in the case of Colombia with so much more reason because she has never attempted in any way to harass or exclude the worldwide traffic of the Isthmus, but, on the contrary, she has always striven to facilitate the same by means of negotiations, some of which, however, have not been carried into effect through causes over which Colombia had no control.

The offer of the United States minister by one of the men occupying the highest position in the official circles of Colombia respecting the approval and ratification of the Herrán-Hay treaty by an act of the legislature or by a new and complacent congress did not reach or attain to the proportion of a governmental act. Had it reached this, then the administration would have fulfilled its promise if such could have been effected by thoroughly constitutional and legal means.

As I have stated already, the Government of Colombia could not attach importance to the reports of the press concerning the formation and development of the Separatist movement because, as I declared in the Senate, such a movement could not be feared seeing that the treaty of 1846 was in force and Colombia being absolutely confident that the United States would faithfully fulfill its obligations under that compact. In these circumstances the Department of Panama could not have obtained her independence without the support of some very powerful nation.

In view of the friendly relations that had subsisted between the two Governments it was obligatory upon the United States to have informed the Colombian Government that, according to information received from its agents, a revolution was imminent in Panama, the movement having for its object the disintegration of the Republic of Colombia, and that measures had been taken for having its warships near by so as to be able easily to reach the Isthmus when the revolution broke out.

Instead of this friendly proceeding, however, the United States despatched the following order to the commanders of the *Boston*, *Nashville*, and *Dixie:*

"Maintain free and without interruption the transit. If you are threatened to be interrupted by armed force you are to occupy the railroad line. Prevent the landing of any armed force with hostile intentions, whether it belongs to the Government or to the revolutionists, appearing at any point within a zone of 50 miles from Panama. Get information of the Government forces that are now on their way to the Isthmus. Prevent them landing if, in your judgment, their presence will precipitate a conflict."

These orders are not in accordance with the precedents established by the United States, which never, in former revolutions, impeded or prevented the landing of the troops of the Government of Colombia nor the transit of them by the railroad as appears by the orders transcribed in the message of the President of the United States of the 7th December, 1903, to the Senate, which orders were issued by the United States in the years 1900, 1901, and 1902, in which that Government indicated that it was only disposed to take measures to prevent the transit being interrupted or be put in danger or the railroad line being converted into a theater of war.

In September, 1858, it was agreed between the then minister of New Granada, Gen. Herrán, and the United States Secretary of State, Gen. Casey, that, in future, when the forces of the United States were passing over the Isthmus they should be disarmed and travel like private individuals "without the enjoyment of those privileges usually accorded to troops passing through foreign territory and who are not subject to local jurisdiction." In 1885 the United States despatched troops to Panama and notwithstanding the fact that the railroad was undefended and that one of the revolutionary parties went to the extreme length of placing in prison the person of the United States consul in Colon, that Government did not pretend to execute acts of authority or of jurisdiction, and on the demand of Mr. Becerra, Colombian Minister in Washington, for an explanation as to the reason for the detention on board the United States cruiser *Galena* of two of the incendiaries of Colon an order was immediately issued by Mr. Bayard, Secretary of State, for the delivery of the prisoners to the local authorities.

In giving an account of the conference that took place in the Department of State in Washington on the 4th November, 1902, regarding the negotiations for the canal treaty, Dr. Concha, the Colombian minister, said, in relation to the events which took place on the Isthmus in September and October of the same year: "Mr. Hay referred directly and spontaneously to the attitude assumed by Admiral Casey in those events, and added that he had addressed to the United States minister in Bogota a note directing him to signify to the Colombian minister of foreign affairs the cordial friendship of the Unted States Government and the wish of the latter to avoid any act or procedure which would offend the dignity of Colombia or lessen her rights as an independent nation; that in this connection the United States Government had addressed by cable communications to Admiral Casey to the end that he should regulate and adjust his proceedings in accordance with the feelings and spirit of his Government, and that the aspect of matters had very much changed on the Isthmus, and that at present there was complete harmony on that territory between the authorities of both nations."

In my note of 19th November, 1903, addressed to your honorable legation, the following occurs:

"The recognition as a State by one power of a department whose aim and intention is the separation from the nation to which it belongs neither justifies nor legalizes the intervention of that power in the struggle which a separatist movement might produce. And although in this present emergency of affairs the United States has wholly neglected to fulfill its obligation under the treaty of 1846 to guarantee the prosperity of Colombia in and its sovereignty over the Isthmus and insists in maintaining such an attitude, it was at least expected by Columbia that the United States would remain neutral and abstain from recognizing the rebels as belligerents."

I quote the preceding paragraph so that it may be remembered that the Government of Colombia has made no demand on the United States for the submission of the rebels because it refused to permit the landing of Colombian troops sent to effect such submission.

The commander of the United States fleet addressed, on the 4th November, an official letter to the commander of the battalion Tiradores, which is as follows:

"I have information that the situation in Panama is such that any movement effected by the Colombian troops, stationed in Colon, toward that neighborhood, will provoke a conflict and threaten the free and uninterrupted transit of the Isthmus, which latter the Government of the United States is compelled by treaty obligations to maintain. I have therefore the honor to inform you that I have directed the superintendent of the Panama Railroad in Colon not to permit the transportation of the Colombian troops or those of the opposite party. Hoping that this action on my part will receive your cordial assent,

"I have the honor to be, very respectfully,

"JOHN HUBBART.
"*Commander of the United States Fleet.*"

According to the information supplied by Gen. Tobar this order was carried out in respect of Colombian troops; the commander in chief of the Panama army and other military officers were conveyed by the railroad and were escorted by the soldiers of the rebels. These had the railroad placed at their services constantly. It is also known that the superintendent of the Panama Railroad refused to transport the battalion Tiradores from Colon to Panama with the assent, of course, of Commander Hubbart, who, as will be seen from his note, had assumed supreme authority in regard to the conveyance of the military over the Isthmus by railroad.

In the statements made by the colonel of the Tiradores to the commander in chief of the army in Cartagena, there is to be found evidence of the facts that on the 4th and 5th November, 1903, troops and artillery men landed in Colon from the United States fleet; that these forces were stationed in the railway offices and that they constructed trenches; that the colonel having communicated with the United States consul on the subject, that official replied by asking the colonel to remove his forces from the town, and that one of the causes which determined the return to Cartagena of the battalion was the threatening attitude of the United States troops and their officers.

On the 8th November, Mr. Manuel Amador Guerrero, the then chief of the Separatist movement and at present President of the so-called Republic of Panama, visited the general in chief of the Atlantic army of Colombia, who was confined in prison at Panama. Mr. Guerrero, at that interview, confessed to the general in chief that the events which had occurred were the result of a plan well matured, lengthily discussed in Panama and in Washington, and executed under the protection and guarantee of the United States Government, with which Government he, personally, had come to an understanding and from which he had received two and a half millions of dollars to be employed in defraying the initial expenses of the new Republic; that there were several American warships at Colon ready to protect the revolutionary movement, all resistance against which would be futile. and, in conclusion, suggested that the general, actuated by a spirit of humanity, should order the reembarkation of the battalion Tiradores.

Messrs. Tomas Arias and Federico Boyd, members of the Junta of Government, made similar statements.

I have been informed that Mr. Amador Guerrero has contradicted Gen. Tobar's statements, but it is not known whether Messrs. Arias and Boyd have done the same either in respect of Gen. Tobar's statements or in respect of those made by Gen. Amaya, chief of staff of the Atlantic army, who was also in prison in Panama.

Although it is alleged by the United States Executive that the presence in Isthmian waters of the United States fleet did not lend support to the revolutionists it can not for a moment be doubted that the presence of that fleet encouraged the revolutionists, and that the action of the commanders of the fleet had the effect of paralyzing the effects of the Colombian authorities in meeting the rebels.

That the citizens of Panama were desirous of proceeding to Colon for the purpose of attacking and expelling the Colombian troops from that town is a circumstance not mentioned by Commander Hubbart in his dispatches and was only brought to light in an article which appeared in the New York Evening Post. If, therefore, this object was not accomplished it was from no lack of will to do so, but only because it was considered unnecessary in view of the attitude assumed by the United States in preventing the reoccupation of the Isthmus by Colombian troops—an attitude that has been persistently maintained and one that has been declared in the following terms: "It is almost wished that, on our part, there shall not be any imprudent conduct that would cause Colombia to become engaged in a war that can not result in the restitution of her dominion on the Isthmus, but would cost much blood and suffering." It is only because the United States has undertaken the defense of the rebels that Colombia has not by force of arms attempted to regain her dominion on the Isthmus. This she could easily have accomplished, as her military forces are notoriously greater than those of the small Department of Panama.

The action of the people was not in any way unanimous. In this regard, as in many others, the Government of the United States has been erroneously informed. Natural-born Isthmians, certainly the most important section of the community, have not acquiesced in the act of secession, and among these are such prominent and reputable citizens as Messrs. José Marcelino Hurtado, ex-minister plenipotentiary; Senator D. Juan B. Pérez y Soto; Representative Oscar Terân; Belisario Porras; Carlos Vallarino; and Alejandro V. Orillac. Dr. Pablo Arosemena, ex-Colombian secretary of state, explained in the press that he was not a party to the separatist movement, but he accepted it as he thought it irrevocable. The people of Colon did not know that on the night of the 3d November a revolutionary movement was being effectuated in Panama. So it was with the majority of the inhabitants of the Isthmus. It seems, however, that afterwards they all accepted the situation for the same reason assigned by Dr. Arosemena.

Against the supposed unanimity on the subject of the revolution is there the fact that a large number of the Isthmians of high position signified through the press their opposition to the ratification of the Herran-Hay treaty and joined in the issue of leaflets throughout the city of Panama expressive of this opposition.

The Government of the United States admits that in recognizing the independence of Panama it has acted against the generally recognized rule of not recognizing the independence of a new State until the same has demonstrated its ability to maintain its independence; but the United States justifies its procedure in this case for the following three reasons:

First, the rights acquired under treaty; second, its national interests and security; third, the collective interests of civilization.

The United States pretends to derive its rights from that part of article 35 of the treaty of 1846, which says:

"The Government of New Granada guarantees to the Government of the United States that the right of way or transit across the Isthmus of Panama by any means of communication which now or in future may exist will be free and expeditious for the citizens and the Government of the United States, and for the transportation of any articles or products, manufactures or merchandise of legitimate trade belonging to the citizens of the United States; and the citizens of the United States shall not be called upon to pay any charges or fees for the passage of their merchandise through any canal or railroad that might be constructed by the Government of New Granada or with its authority but those which, in similar circumstances, are imposed or charged on the citizens of New Granada; that products, manufactures, or merchandise of the United States which pass in any direction from one sea to another, for the purpose of exportation to any foreign country, shall not be subjected to any import duty, and if the same shall have been paid, the amount so paid shall be returned; and that the citizens of the United States, in passing through the Isthmus, shall not be subjected to any other duty, fees, or tax but those to which the citizens of New Granada are liable."

The United States Government interpreted the above provision in the sense that if the Treaty of 1846 did not compel, in terms, New Granada to grant concessions for the construction of interoceanic means of communication it was only because the United States did not at the time the treaty was drawn up force New Granada to do so; but that as it was expressly stipulated that the Government of the United States, in return for its guarantee of the sovereignty of New Granada, would enjoy the right of free and expeditious transit by any way of communication that might be constructed, the very clear intention of the treaty made unnecessary if not superfluous stipulation in specific terms that permission would not be denied the United States for the construction of such way of communication.

This interpretation is not in accordance with the general rules guiding the intelligent construction of treaties. There is no rule which authorizes the contention that a compact expresses or means anything beyond what has been expressly stipulated in it, and it is perfectly clear that what the Government of New Granada guaranteed to the United States was but the right of transit over the Isthmus of Panama by any means of communication then existing or which in future might exist, and that there should be no imposition upon the citizens of the United States or upon their merchandise passing over the Isthmus, by any road or canal that might be constructed by New Granada or under its authority, of any other duty or tax but that imposed upon citizens of New Granada. Here, of course, reference is made to a canal which might be constructed by New Granada (now Colombia) or under its authority; but in no part of the treaty is it shown that the construction of the canal was the cardinal idea or intention of the treaty and much less that the Government of Colombia could not deny the United States the privilege of constructing it.

The peculiar interpretation placed upon the article of the treaty above referred to by the United States gives to that Government power to make additions to the treaty. In these circumstances Colombia is forced to declare that she utterly repudiates the contention of the United States Government that it was superfluous to express, in terms, any concession intended to be granted by the treaty, and she also declares that the interpretation given by the United States to the said treaty is in every way unjustifiable and introduces a system of deduction and implicit promises which is at variance with international practice, with the will and intention of the contracting parties and with those universally accepted rules and principles which make public treaties the basic law of all civilized nations.

The importance of the Isthmus is to be found in its geographical position, and the Colombian Government has for many years been struggling to accomplish the betterment of the transit, so as to obtain easy and expeditious means of transport by railways and an interoceanic canal.

The Colombian Government having received notice that the Government of the United States would not permit the landing of Colombian troops on the Isthmus, I, personally, asked Mr. Beaupré to put the following question to his Government:

First. If the United States, which had several warships at Colon and Panama, would prevent Colombia landing her troops for combat in those ports and on the railway line, if necessary?

Second. If, in the event of Colombia being able to check the development of the Separatist movement, the United States Government would be disposed to assist her action so as to maintain the property and sovereignty of Colombia on the Isthmus in accordance with the provisions of article 35 of the treaty of 1846?

It was clearly foreseen by the Colombian Government that it could not check the Separatist movement because the United States would place obstacles in the way of doing so; this being the case, it was the clear duty of the United States to itself oppose the movement and restore order in consonance with its treaty obligations.

The doctrine advanced as a second reason for the recognition by the United States of the so-called Republic of Panama, viz, that such recognition was imposed upon the United States by a supreme consideration for the interests and security of that Government is not based upon any known principle of public right. Besides, if in the fulfillment of a treaty the interests and security of one of the contracting parties are challenged such party has the right to denounce the treaty but not to proceed in a sense contrary to the express stipulations of the compact. If the United States, in conformity with subclause 3 of article 35 of the treaty of 1846 had notified to Colombia its wish for a redrafting, or alteration, or modification of such treaty in regard to its guaranty, Colombia once informed of the danger that was threatened, would have made provisions to avoid it by means of other and new negotiations for the construction of the canal.

The existing treaty was and is an insuperable obstacle in the way of the United States proceeding exclusively in protection of its own interests and security; but if even this compact had not existed the procedure adopted by the United States to prevent Colombia employing its forces to suppress the revolution can not be justified but on the principle of a strong nation dominating a weaker one. This, however, is in open contradiction to the principles of liberty and autonomy which the great North American people always professed to defend and protect.

The policy that establishes the practice of strong powers modifying or changing the limits of a country by reason of interest or convenience or for the alleged necessity of territorial expansion is founded only on the conception or principle that the territorial expansion of a nation rises above and is altogether superior to the quality of justice.

The alleged necessity for building the canal is not so pressing that it could not be delayed, and to demonstrate this I shall transcribe article 24 of the Herrán-Hay treaty.

"ARTICLE 24. The United States Government undertakes to complete the preliminary works of the canal in the shortest possible time, and within two years, counted from the date of the exchange of ratification of this treaty, shall begin the effective construction of the same, which shall be open for the purposes of commerce between the two seas 12 years after the 2 years mentioned. In case, however, difficulties and obstacles, at present unforeseen, arise in the construction of the canal and in consideration of the good faith of the United States Government as shown by the amount expended on the work, and judging from the nature of the difficulties met with, the Colombian Government shall extend the time stipulated in this article for 12 years more for the termination of the construction of the canal.

"But if at any time the United States should determine to construct a tide-level canal, in such case the term shall be extended to 10 years longer."

A work which requires 2 years for preliminary operations, 12 years for its construction, 12 more if difficulties are encountered, and 10 more if it be constructed on the tide-level principle—making a total of 36 years—is certainly not of such urgent necessity that would not admit a delay of a few months pending the adjustment of new negotiations with the real and legitimate Government of the country through which it is to be constructed.

The report of a committee of the Colombian Senate, presented to that body on the 14th of October, contains, inter alia, the recommendation that before

Colombia negotiates any treaty with the United States for the construction of the canal she should wait until the expiration of the period of prolongation granted to the French company. This recommendation did not, however, receive the approval of the Senate. It is true that the Senate did not authorize the Government to enter into any new negotiations concerning the canal, but I can inform your excellency that if such authorization was withheld it was, very probably, because the Senate considered that the executive power had, under the Colombian Constitution, authority to make treaties, but that it was not relieved of the obligation of submitting such treaties for the approval of Congress.

In view of the possession by the executive of the authority above referred to I addressed, on the 8th September, to our chargé d'affaires in Washington the following cable message:

"'Confidentially communicate to the State Department that whether the proposal presented to the Senate relative to new negotiations concerning the canal treaty be adopted or not, the Colombian Government shall propose to the United States Government to reopen negotiations upon bases which it judges acceptable to the Congresss of next July."

There is not in existence a single act or thing to indicate that the Government intended to declare null and void the prolongation of the period for the construction of the canal to 1910 conceded to the French company; and Congress not only did not dictate or suggest this, but the report of the Senate committee contained a recommendation that a law be passed approving of the contract granting the concession of the prolongation. This recommendation received unanimous approval in the first debate thereon, but no definite or final action was taken in regard to the passing of such a law up to the time the session of Congress terminated. But it was, nevertheless, clearly demonstrated that the sense of this Chamber was favorable to the validity of the concession of prolongation.

The third reason assigned by the United States for recognizing the so-called Republic of Panama is that such recognition was an act performed in the interests of civilization.

Civilization stands for or represents the intelectual, moral, and material progress of the world. The first two rule and govern the conduct of nations and without which the nations would be engaged in perpetual warfare. If for the furtherance of material interests intelectuality and morality are ignored, or the obligations under public contracts are unobserved the fundamental bases of modern civilization are undermined and we retrograde and return to that condition which, in ancient times, such as during the reign of Roman Caesars, took the form of domination by right of conquest.

It is not believed that the people of the United States, or their Government, desire to associate themselves with such an unjustifiable course of action merely for the sake of expediting by a few months the construction of the canal when such an undertaking, by its very nature, requires a long period of time to be carried out; and when such construction, too, should be with the consent of the true and legitimate government of the country in accordance with those principles of right upon which the civilization of the world is founded.

The action of several of the powers of Europe and America in following the example of the United States in recognizing the independence of the so-called Republic of Panama is considered by the Government of Colombia solely due to the fact of the United States having recognized such independence and sustained the same by force and not because the creation of the new Republic would expedite the construction of the Canal; so much so at if the United States would withdraw its recognition of, and protection from, Panama those nations, I am sure, would regard very quietly and without surprise the reincorporation of the Department of Panama with the Republic of Colombia.

The opinion expressed in the message of the President of the United States to Congress that any disinterested and judicious observer could not but admit that Panama was fully justified in separating from Colombia is itself an act of interference or intervention in the domestic affairs of a foreign State—an act, as is admitted in another part of the message, very exceptional, and only justified by the exceptional nature of the case. But this act of intervention or interference by the United States is not included or comprehended in those cases in which the international right of intervention is admitted; and the conduct of a government, however censurable it might be (the conduct of Colombia does not admit of or merit reproach) so long as it does not lessen or threaten the rights of other sovereign powers, does not give to any power the right of intervention in its affairs. (Heffter, Derecho International de la Europa, p. 95 to 98. Berlin, 1873.)

The conduct of Colombia has neither threatened nor lessened the acquired rights of the United States which power could not even adduce by way of a reason for its action that it had suffered by its being contiguous to Colombia.

The Isthmus of Panama enjoyed peace up to the 3d of November, 1903, and it is highly probable that the rebels would have come to an understanding in Colon with Gen. Reyes and so have avoided the effusion of blood if the United States had not intervened to prevent the landing of Colombian troops; therefore the procedure of the United States can not even be said to have been dictated by reasons of humanity.

If the recognition of Panama as an independent Republic is considered by the United States an accomplished fact, and as such irrevocable, without stopping to demonstrate the illegality of this theory, I contend that the recognition of the independence of Panama by the United States and other powers does not annul the rights of Colombian sovereignty over the Isthmus, and that this Republic does not admit the principle that such recognition is irrevocable.

Gen. Rafael Reyes, special Colombian envoy, presented, in the name of the Government and people of Colombia, on the 23d December last, to the United States Department of State, a statement of the injuries inflicted on Colombia. In the reply which Mr. Secretary Hay gave to this there are several additional statements to those already made in the messages of the President which I must take into consideration and which, in defence of the rights of Colombia, call for some observations.

Mr. Hay maintains that treaties, save when they relate to private rights, and unless the contrary is stipulated, are obligations on the contracting parties from the date they are signed, and that the exchange of ratifications confirm the treaties from the date they are so ratified. "This rule," he says, "necessarily implies that the two Governments, between whom the treay is celebraed, through their duly authorized representatives, are under the obligations, pending its ratification, not only not to oppose such ratification, but also to do nothing that is in contravention to its stipulations."

This doctrine that treaties are obligations which are in force, enirely or in part, before they are ratified in conformity with the laws of the respective countries between which they have been celebrated, gives rise to reflections regarding the extraordinary obligation laid on Colombia by the United States. Whaton in his "International Rights," volume 1, page 289, expresses himself thus:

"The civil constitution of each particular State determines in whom is vested the power to ratify treaties negotiated and concluded wih foreign powers. In absolute monarchies this prerogative is vested in the sovereign who confirms the acts of his plenipotentiaries by his definite sanction. In certain limited or constitutional monarchies the consent of the legislature of the nation is, in some cases, asked for. In some Republics, like that of the United States of America, the opinion and consent of the Senate are necessary and essential to legalize and make valid the act of the Executive Chief of the State who pledges the national faith in that form. Consequently, in all these cases, the condition is implied in all negotiations with foreign powers that treaties concluded by the executive power are subject to ratification in the manner prescribed by the fundamental laws of the State."

In the Herrán-Hay treaty it was expressly reserved in article 28 that the same should be ratified in conformity with the laws of the United States and Colombia. This recognition of the fact that ratification was of the essence of the whole proceeding has been observed from the most ancient times down to the present day, and if the United States otherwise interprets this doctrine of international right, such interpretation does not bind the other powers which recognize the principle that "the constitution of each particular State determines in whom is vested the power to ratify treaties negotiated and concluded with foreign powers, thereby constituting it the guardian of the nation." This principle is that generally observed and adopted, in substance, by such accredited expositors of international law as Vattel, Klüber, G. F. Martens, Despagnet, Vergé, and Pradier-Fodéré. The executive power in Colombia can not perfect international compacts because the Constitution confers on Congress the power of approving or disapproving of public treaties.

The Government of Colombia not only did not oppose the ratification of the treaty relating to the construction of the canal, but it convened an extraordinary meeting of Congress for the express object of considering the same and the compact was submitted to the Senate during the first days of the session. The regulations of the Senate prescribed that in the first debate the propriety of legislating upon any subject proposed for legislation should be discussed. In the first debate after the treaty was submitted I spoke lengthily, emphasizing the great importance of the negotiations and denying the accusations which had been formulated against the Government for having celebrated such a compact. My speech concluded as follows:

"His excellency the vice president of the Republic has requested me to furnish this honorable Senate with these explanations. It had been clearly proven that the initiation of the treaty was due to, and had been actuated by, the highest motives; that the negotiations had been conducted with ability and judgment, and that if the conditions of the compact did not wholly accord with the desire and wish of the people of Colombia it was only because the other high contracting party would not accede to propositions more advantageous. In a word, the Government of Colombia had proceeded in this very important matter with the greatest circumspection and had been inspired by a feeling of the purest patriotism."

This speech affords irrefragable proof that the Government did not oppose the ratification of the treaty; and it is with regret that I now recall the fact that I directed attention to the memorandum and other communications presented to me by Mr. Beaupré pointing out the injurious effect which the disapproval by the Senate of the treaty would produce in the relations between the United States and Colombia, and that any modifications made by the Colombian Senate to the treaty would be considered as a violation thereof by the United States. The Senate did not consider the treaty at the first debate thereon and for that reason this Government was not afforded the opportunity of explaining its provisions. There was not, therefore, anything in the nature of opposition in the conduct of the Government in respect of the treaty.

On the 10th June, 1903, Mr. Beaupré addressed to this department a note detailing the objections that his Government had made to the notes that had passed between the Colombian Minister of the Interior, the new canal company, and the Panama Railroad Co., in which these companies had been informed that in order to legally transfer their contracts to the United States the permission of the Colombian Government to do so was necessary.

In my reply to Mr. Beaupré, dated the 27th of the same month, I called attention to the dates of the notes which the Department of the Interior had addressed to those companies, viz, the 25th and 27th December, 1902, respectively, and that the date of the treaty agreed upon by plenipotentiaries in Washington for the construction of the canal was the 22d January, 1903. A comparison of these dates shows that the condition imposed by Colombia upon these companies was communicated to them about a month before the treaty had been subscribed to. After this had been signed the Department of the Interior did not interfere further in the matter, and as the explanations on this point made by me to the United States legation preceded by four months the Separatist movement and as my note was very promptly published, it is plain that the pretended exigencies of the situation neither called for nor excused the initiation and execution of such a movement.

The Colombian Government did not suddenly discover after the convention had been subscribed to that it contained stipulations subversive of the sovereignty of the Republic in the zone set apart for the construction of the canal. Ever since the Government of the United States submitted the projected traty notice was taken of these stipulations, notwithstanding which, however, the minister in Washington, charged with the duty of negotiating the treaty, was ordered to sign the same, the object of the Colombian Government being to facilitate and assure the execution of the great work in the hope that in the end Congress might be induced to make such declarations or to take such measures as would cure the constitutional defects which, in our judgment, marred the compact.

Simply changing the name of a country neither alters nor modifies the situation of its frontiers and less even if, as in the case of the country which took the name of New Granada in November, 1831, those frontiers or boundaries have been fixed by the Constitution.

If, as was said by Mr. Secretary Fish in a note dated May 27, 1871, the principal object of New Granada (now Colombia) in celebrating the treaty of 1846 was the conservation and maintenance of the sovereignty of the country against foreign aggression, the recognition of the independence of Panama by the United States created a situation of affairs which compels the United States to prevent the so-called Republic attacking the property and sovereignty of Colombia on the Isthmus, because by virtue of such recognition such attacks must be regarded as being made by a foreign power; and, if instead of preventing those attacks, the United States favor and support the destruction of Colombia's sovereignty in that department of the Republic, such a proceeding can not otherwise be regarded but as being in direct antagonism to the letter, the spirit, and the intelligence of the treaty as construed by Mr. Fish.

From the above observations the insurmountable logical conclusion is arrived at that the United States can not assume toward Panama the obligations under the treaty of 1846, because the property and sovereignty of that department and the property and sovereignty of Colombia over the same department of Panama have been set aside and ignored simultaneously, in consequence of which the Isthmus has not acquired a title to enjoy those rights or is it subject to the obligations of the said treaty.

On the other hand, the doctrine of Hall is not applicable to the point in question, because Colombia had not contracted the obligation to permit the United States to construct the canal, a work which in no way is similar to laying out the bed of a river, which was cited as an example. For the same reason the opinion of Rivier is not applicable, as article 35 of the treaty of 1846 does not refer to limits, or streams of water, or ways of communication which did not then, or at present exist. The interpretation given to the above compact by the Government of the United States does not coincide with the doctrine above quoted, and the United States can not arrange with the de facto government of the Isthmus for the performance of those duties which it had contracted with Colombia to perform.

The Government of Colombia dissents from the opinion held by the United States that its claims are of a purely political nature; and holds that special circumstances place those claims in the category of those of a judicial character.

The claims of Colombia are:

First. The violation, on the part of the United States Government, of the Treaty of 1846.

According to the doctrine propounded by Piédelièvre in his "Public International Rights," Vol. II, page 76, questions of this kind are of a judicial character and susceptible of being arbitrated with the greater reason because from them others are derived, such, for example, as the great damage caused to this Republic, which is incontestably of the same character.

Second. The violation of the neutrality laws established by international right.

In regard to claims founded on a violation of neutrality, the United States contributed very largely towards establishing the precedent that I now proceed to mention. I refer to the claims generally known as the "Alabama claims," in which Great Britain had so completely neglected to fulfill the obligations of neutrality imposed upon her by the Rights of Nations as to afford the United States ample and just cause for declaring war. Lord Russell denied the legality of these claims and peremptorily refused to submit the same to arbitration in 1865, but Mr. Secretary Seward persisted in the suggestion of arbitration as being a prudent and honorable course to be followed by both nations. Upon the invitation of the British Government negotiations were reopened with the result that on May 8, 1871, a treaty was concluded between the two nations under which the Alabama claims were submitted to a tribunal of arbitrators.

Article 6 of this treaty provided that the questions to be submitted to the arbitrators should be governed by three rules, proposed by the United States, regarding neutrality, notwithstanding the fact that the same article contained the following:

"Her Britannic Majesty has charged her high commissioners and envoys plenipotentiary to declare that the Government does not admit that the preceding rules are to be considered as expositions of the principle of the rights of nations in force at the time the United States made the claims mentioned in article 1; but that, in order to prove her wish to strengthen the amicable relations existing between the two countries and to provide useful measures for the future, the Government of Her Majesty consents to have the questions which these claims have given rise to decided on the understanding that the arbitrators shall bear in mind that the English Government has no intention of departing from the principle enunciated in the preceding rules."

The high contracting parties agreed to observe these rules in their reciprocal dealings in future and to bring them to the notice of the other maritime powers and invite them to adopt and adhere to the same.

The doctrine laid down in these three rules received the confirmation of the Institute of International Rights, which body adopted the following resolution.

"The three rules of the treaty of Washington, dated 8th May, 1871, are but the application of the recognized principles of the rights of nations; that a neutral state desirous of remaining at peace and in friendship with the belligerents was bound to abstain from taking any part whatever in a war toward lending military aid to one or both of the belligerents, and was also bound to exercise such due vigilance in its territory that no act could be construed into constituting one of cooperation in the war."

The Colombian Government, supported by such an authoritative precedent, invokes the proper authorities of the United States and of the Institute of National Rights to rule that acts which constitute a violation of neutrality fall within the category of those matters which should be referred to arbitration for settlement.

Third. The celebration of a contract with the so-called Republic of Panama for the opening of the interoceanic canal notwithstanding that at the time there was in existence a treaty of peace, friendship, navigation, and commerce between New Grenada (now Colombia) and the United States of America.

The Government of the United States gave to article 35 of that treaty a construction which the Government of Colombia judged to be contrary to the rules of interpretation generally admitted and usually applied in dealing with such cases before arbitral tribunals and propounded by Klüber in his "Rights of Nations," page 85, as follows:

"When a public treaty is framed in a doubtful sense it can not receive authentic interpretation without a declaration by the contracting parties or by those who have appealed to arbitation. The same preliminary question of discerning what really is meant when expressed in a doubtful sense can not be decided except by a similar convention."

In the present case the matter turned, in the first instance, on the preliminary question as to whether the sense of the treaty was doubtful or not; although I am bound to say that the opinion of Colombia on the point was clear and complete and the same had been unanimously agreed upon by both Governments, but which agreement has now been departed from by the United States.

The chargé d'affaires of Colombia in Washington informed me by cable that the Senate of the United States had approved the treaty with Panama respecting the construction of the canal. That treaty, as I have already said, contains in its first clause the obligation of the United States to maintain the independence of Panama—a clause which declares to the world that Panama can not exist independently of Colombia without the military support of the United States.

As the above-referred-to treaty is in direct opposition to that of 1846 made between Colombia and the United States, let us suppose—a supposition admitted by the United States, but denied by Colombia—that Panama is an independent nation; the coexistence therefore of these two treaties justifies the application of the doctrine propounded by Vattel that "treaties can not be made contrary to those existing"—a doctrine exemplified by G. F. Martens in his "Rights of Nations," page 167, Volume I, in these terms: "When two treaties are concluded with different nations, if incompatible, the older of the two should be preferred, and indemnification should be given to the nation whose treaty has been set aside if the collision could have been foreseen or prevented." If the Isthmus of Panama was really a Republic the United States, which must have been aware of the collision that would occur, is under obligation to grant an indemnity because it can not fairly evade the fulfillment of the terms of the treaty of 1846. If the justice of this doctrine is not admitted the practice would obtain that a nation, acting as judge in its own cause, could evade the fulfilment of its treaty obligations merely by contracting with the insurrectionary section of the country with which it has made treaties, or with a third power—a practice which would result in ending the guarantees of public treaties which safeguard national rights.

The Government of Colombia considers that the treaty for the construction of the canal which the United States has concluded with the de facto government established in the Colombian Department of Panama is in violation of that celebrated with this Republic in 1846, and protests against the validity of the same and demands the observance of the obligations of the said treaty of 1846, especially that portion which obliges the United States of America to guarantee the property of Colombia in and its sovereignty over the Isthmus of Panama.

I have the honor to refer to the presidential messages and to the notes of Mr. Secretary Hay addressed to Gen. Reyes confirming the declarations of his Government and his own arguments, because the approval of the treaty with Panama by the Senate and the ratification and exchange of that treaty were acts performed posterior to the date on which Gen. Reyes was absent from the United States, and also because of the observations I have made vigorously advocating the adoption of a mode which would be honorable to both parties and be at once an equitable and conciliatory means of arriving at a solution of our differences—a mode which would harmonize with the wish often expressed by the United States of doing nothing to the prejudice of this Republic.

I also have the honor to return my most sincere thanks to the United States Government for the tender of its good offices to amicably arrange matters between Colombia and Panama—an offer made, doubtless, in the belief that this Government would accept as definitive the situation created by the Separatist rebellion on the Isthmus.

Once more I reiterate to your excellency the assurances of my distinguished consideration.

LUIS CARLOS RICO.

EXHIBIT I.

DEMANDS FOR ARBITRATION.

CORRESPONDENCE BETWEEN SECRETARY ROOT AND SEÑOR DON DIEGO MENDOZA IN 1906, PROTEST OF SEÑOR BORDA IN 1910, AND SECRETARY KNOX'S PLEA FOR ARBITRATION BEFORE THE NATIONAL PRESS CLUB.

LEGATION OF COLOMBIA,
Washington, D. C., October 21, 1905.

SIR: The undersigned, representative of the weak Republic of Colombia, deems this an opportune moment to turn to you, as representative of the most powerful republic of modern times, with the request for a just, equitable, and complete diplomatic adjustment of the differences which have arisen between the two nations; or, if this should not be practicable, or, if once brought about, it should fail to produce satisfactory results for both or either of the parties, the undersigned would request that a convention be signed which should submit such differences to some form of arbitration honorable for both countries. The undersigned has all the more reason to hope for a favorable response to his proposition because the questions pending between Colombia and the United States are of exactly the same nature as those to which the numerous arbitration treaties relate which have been concluded by your Government with many other nations, both great and small, within less than a year. These said treaties, as you know very well, were submitted by the President to the Senate on December 14, 1904, and, with slight amendments which do not affect in the least the propositions of the undersigned, were all ratified almost unanimously by the Senate of the United States; so that the branches of your Government which have the authority to conclude treaties were in happy accord concerning the suitability of settling by arbitration the controversies mentioned in those treaties. The text of these treaties embraces "the differences of a legal nature which may arise, or which relate to the interpretation of the treaties, existing between the contracting parties, and which it has been impossible to settle through diplomacy;" the only exceptions are those which may "affect the vital interests, the independence, or the honor of the nation, or which may compromise the rights of third parties."

The request which the undersigned hereby makes for the conclusion of an arbitration convention between your country and his—in case the proposed diplomatic adjustment should fail—is exactly comprised within the provisions cited. The differences which have arisen, as he will have the honor to explain further on, are of a legal character; refer to the interpretation of a treaty in force between the two contracting parties; do not in anywise affect the vital interests, the independence, or the honor of the United States, and do not compromise the interests of third parties. Inasmuch as all the reclamations against the United States which the Republic of Colombia desires to have submitted to an impartial court of arbitration for settlement are differences of a legal nature between the two countries, involving, on the one hand, the correct meaning of the law of nations, and, on the other, the exact interpretation of the treaty of 1846, existing between the two countries, it can not be claimed on any grounds that they affect the vital interests, or the independence, or the honor of the United States, and much less can it be claimed that they impair the rights of third parties.

The request of the undersigned being clearly and precisely within the very course of the international policy of the United States, both as regards direct diplomatic adjustments, of which several cases could be cited, and as regards arbitration, which latter is palpably demonstrated in the various treaties presented recently by the President to the Senate (Dec. 14, 1904), and in these respects ratified by that body, the undersigned can not bring himself to believe that it is really necessary to adduce any more arguments in asking you to accede to his proposition. If other reasons were necessary, they could be found in the long and honorable history of the United States, which has so persistently advocated and fostered the peaceful and honorable adjustment of difficulties through direct diplomacy and arbitration as the best means of deciding controversies between nations. The upholding of this great and noble cause originated, in fact, as you know, with the creation of the Government of your country and found its most recent confirmation in the treaties submitted to the Senate last year, and to which reference has already been made. The undersigned takes the liberty, nevertheless, of calling to your attention the following memorable words of President Roosevelt in his inaugural address:

"Much has been conceded to us, and much, therefore, is justly expected of us. We have duties to fulfill toward others, as well as toward ourselves, and we can not neglect either. We have come to be a great nation, obliged from the very fact of our greatness to maintain relations with the other nations of the earth, and we must conduct ourselves as becomes a people with such great responsibilities. Toward all other nations, both great and small, our duty must be to cherish cordial and sincere friendship. We must prove, not only by our words but also by our actions, that we are ardently desirous of winning their good will by acting toward them with a spirit of just and generous respect for all their rights. But justice and generosity in nations, just as in individuals, have greater significance when exercised, not by the weak but by the powerful."

A just and generous respect for her right to have the questions pending between Colombia and the United States equitably adjusted by diplomatic means, or, failing the latter, submitted to the decision of an impartial court, is exactly what Colombia, the weak State, demands to-day of the United States, the powerful Nation; and, cherishing the assurance that such a diplomatic arrangement or such arbitration will be granted, the undersigned takes the liberty of setting forth, as clearly and succinctly as possible, the nature of the differences between the two nations. The undersigned feels no need of stating that his words will be guided by a spirit of the greatest moderation.

The general treaty of peace, amity, navigation, and commerce of 1846 between New Granada, now the Republic of Colombia, and the United States established the rights and the obligations of the two contracting parties. The undersigned will not tire you now with an analysis of the principal stipulations of the treaty, but will confine himself to saying that certain concessions which were then considered of great value to your nation were granted in exchange for what was deemed valuable protection for Colombia. This protection, for the purposes of this note, may be said to be comprised in article 35 of the treaty, and especially in the following clause: "And in order to secure to themselves the tranquil and constant enjoyment of these advantages and as an especial compensation for the said advantages and for the favors they have acquired by the fourth, fifth, and sixth articles of this treaty, the United States guarantee positively and efficaciously to New Granada"—now the Republic of Colombia—"by the present stipulation, the perfect neutrality of the before-mentioned isthmus, with a view that the free transit from the one to the other sea may not be interrupted or embarrassed in any future time while this treaty exists; and in consequence the United States also guarantee, in the same manner, the rights of sovereignty and property which New Granada"—now the Republic of Colombia—"has and possesses over said territory."

During the full vigor of this treaty between the United States and Colombia the following facts occurred, as Colombia believes, although you may refute them or view them in a different light:

1. In September and October, 1903, the Government of the United States promised certain interests located on the Isthmus of Panama, as well as per-

sons interested in the French Canal Co., that the United States would prevent the Republic of Colombia from combating any disturbance which might arise on the Isthmus.

2. In fulfillment of these promises, war vessels of the United States were sent both to Panama and to Colon in October and during the first days of November, 1903.

3. On November 2, 1903, the commanders of said war vessels received the following telegrams, sent by the Department of State through the Navy Department, as is believed:

"(*a*) Keep the transit free and uninterrupted. Should there be a threat of interruption by armed force, occupy the railroad line; prevent the landing of any armed force having hostile intentions, whether of the Government or insurgent, at Colon, Portobelo, or any other point. Prevent landing if in your judgment it might precipitate a conflict.

"(*b*) In case of doubt regarding the intentions of any armed force, occupy Ancon Hill and fortify it with artillery."

4. At 3.40 p. m. of November 3, 1903, Mr. Loomis, Assistant Secretary of State, acting, sent the following telegram to the person in charge of the United States consulate in Panama: "We are informed that there has been an uprising on the Isthmus; keep this department informed of everything without delay." The consul of the United States answered on the same day: "The uprising has not occurred yet; it is announced that it will take place this evening. The situation is critical."

5. At 8.45 p. m. of the same day, November 3, 1903, the following telegram, signed "Loomis, acting," was delivered to the person in charge of the United States consulate in Panama: "The troops which landed from Cartagena must not continue to Panama"; and by virtue of this telegram, the officer commanding the American warship *Nashville* gave orders to the Panama Railroad Co. not to transport troops of the Colombian Government to the city of Panama.

6. At 10.30 p. m. of the same day, November 3, 1903, another telegraphic dispatch from the State Department was sent to the American consul in Panama, reading as follows: "If the cablegram to the *Nashville*"—one of the said war vessels—"has not been delivered, inform her captain immediately that he must prevent the Government troops from continuing on to Panama or from assuming an attitude which might result in bloodshed, and that he must make every effort to maintain order on the Isthmus."

7 On the same day, November 3, 1903, the following telegram was transmitted from Colon to the Secretary of the Navy by the commander of one of the aforementioned war vessels stationed there: "I acknowledge the receipt of your telegram of November 2. Before receiving it there were landed here this morning by the Colombian Government about 400 men from Cartagena. There is no revolution on the Isthmus nor any disturbance. The railroad company has refused to transport these troops unless the governor of Panama requires it. The demand has not been made. It is possible that the movement to proclaim independence may take place in Panama this evening. * * *" (Here there is missing a part of the dispatch as printed.)

8. At 9.50 p. m. of the same date, November 3, 1903, the Department of State received from the vice consul of the United States in Panama the following telegram: "The revolt took place this evening at 6; there has been no bloodshed. The officers of the army and navy have been reduced to prison. The government will be organized this evening and will be composed of three consuls and a cabinet. The soldiers have been exchanged. It is believed that a similar movement will take place in Colon. Up to the present order has prevailed. The situation is serious. Four hundred soldiers landed in Colon to-day from Barranquilla."

On the same day, November 3, 1903, Gen. Tovar arrived at Colon with the battalion of sharpshooters of the Colombian Army, a force more than sufficient to repress the aforementioned uprising.

9. At 11.18 p. m. of the same day, November 3, 1903, Mr. Loomis, Assistant Secretary of State, acting, telegraphed to the vice consul of the United States in Panama: "The telegraphic dispatch sent to the *Nashville* at Colon may not have been delivered. See, therefore, that the following dispatch is transmitted to the *Nashville* immediately: '*Nashville*, Colon: In the interests of peace make every effort in order to prevent the troops of the Government at Colon from continuing to Panama. Transit on the Isthmus must be kept open and order

maintained. Acknowledge receipt. (Signed) Darling, acting.' Obtain a special train if it should be necessary. Act with speed."

10. On the following day, November 4, 1903, Hubbard, commander of one of the war vessels stationed at the time at Colon, addressed the Secretary of the Navy as follows: "Government troops now at Colon. I have prohibited the movement of troops in either direction. There has been no interruption of transit yet. I shall make every effort to preserve peace and order."

11. On the same day, November 4, 1903, the American consul in Panama received the following communication: "We have the honor to inform you, for your own knowledge and that of the Government which you represent, that on this very date there has taken place a movement by which the old Department of Panama has separated from the Republic of Colombia, with the object of constituting a new State by the name of 'Republic of Panama,' and that the undersigned have had the honor of being designated to form the committee of the Provisional Government of the Republic."

12. Two days later—that is, November 6, 1903—the Secretary of State telegraphed to the vice consul in Panama in the following terms: "The people of Panama by an apparently unanimous movement, have severed their political bonds with the Republic of Colombia and have resumed their independence. As soon as you are convinced that a de facto government, republican in form and without substantial opposition on the part of its own people, has been established on the Isthmus of Panama, you will enter into relations with it as the responsible government of the territory, and you will address to it a request that it take the measures necessary for the protection of the persons and property of citizens of the United States, and that it keep open the transit on the Isthmus in accordance with the obligations of the existing treaties which govern the relations of the United States with that territory."

13. On the same date, November 6, 1903, the commander of one of the war vessels communicated as follows to the Secretary of the Navy: "I arrived yesterday afternoon; I landed forces. The situation is as follows: A little before landing, the Colombian troops had departed on the steamer *Orinoco* for Cartagena. The independent party is in possession of Colon, of Panama, and of the railroad line. The *Nashville* withdrew her forces."

14. On the following day, November 7, 1903, the vice consul of the United States sent the following note to the so-called committee which represented the would-be revolution: "Inasmuch as the people of Panama, by a unanimous movement, have broken their political bonds with the Republic of Colombia and resumed their independence, and as there is no opposition to the provisional government in the State of Panama, I hereby inform you that the provisional government will be held responsible for the protection of the persons and property of the citizens of the United States, as well as for the maintenance of free transit on the Isthmus, in accordance with the stipulations of the treaties in force regarding the territory of the said Isthmus."

15. On the following day, November 8, 1903, a telegram was sent to the Secretary of the Navy by the commander of one of the American war vessels, as follows: "Everything quiet; traffic uninterrupted; the telegram in which I was ordered to interfere was received." On that same day the vice consul of the United States in Panama stated, in a telegram to the Secretary of State, as follows: "The Colombian troops were reembarked for Cartagena by the *Royal Mail*. It is believed that the *Bogáto* is at Buenaventura. Peace Reigns."

16. Four days later, on November 11, 1903, the minister of the United States in Bogota informed the Colombian Republic that the Government of the United States had entered into relations with the so-called new Republic of Panama.

17. Two days aferwards, on November 13, 1903, the Government of the United States officially received Mr. Bunau-Varilla, a French citizen interested in the French Canal Co., as minister plenipotentiary of Panama.

18. On the following day, November 14, 1903, the minister of the United States in Bogota notified the Colombian Republic as follows: "I have just received instructions from my Government by cable to notify you that it does not deem it suitable to permit Colombian troops to land on the Isthmus, because this would precipitate civil war and would indefinitely interrupt the free transit which my Government is obligated to protect."

19. Gen. Reyes, commander at that time of the Colombian forces sent to repress the so-called rebellion on the Isthmus—which troops were more than sufficient for the purpose—had announced to Vice Admiral Coghlan, commander of one of the United States war vessels, his intention to embark his troops and

to proceed to Panama in order to restore order there; and the vice admiral, in reply, notified him that his orders were to prevent the landing of troops with hostile designs within the limits of the State of Panama.

20. On November 18, 1903, the Secretary of State of the United States and the said Bunau-Varilla signed a treaty, the purpose of which was to arrange a compact between the United States and the so-called Republic of Panama. By article 1 of this treaty the United States expressly and positively guarantee and obligate themselves to uphold the independence of the so-called Republic of Panama.

The foregoing recital, taken principally from the official records as they were transmitted by the President to the Senate when the treaty between the United States and the so-called Republic of Panama was being discussed in that body, amply justifies, in the opinion of the undersigned, the following conclusions, in which you may not perhaps agree with him:

(*a*) The well-known favorable attitude of the United States toward a rebellious uprising in the Department of Panama was the determining cause of the revolt, and to this extent it was a violation of the express stipulations of the treaty of 1846.

(*b*) The United States, by means of their armed forces, prevented the Republic of Colombia from repressing the aforesaid rebellion and so preserving the integrity of her national territory, this being also in violation of the positive stipulations of the treaty.

(*c*) The United States recognized with undue haste the so-called Republic of Panama, to the detriment of the rights and interests of the Republic of Colombia, and this recognition annulled the express stipulations of the treaty of 1846 and disregarded the principles established by the law of nations.

(*d*) The United States guaranteed to maintain by force the separation of Panama from the Republic of Colombia, not only against the explicit stipulations of the treaty of 1846, but, also, and in view of the time at which this obligation was contracted, in violation of the duties of neutrals under the law of nations.

I therefore take the liberty of again calling your attention to the fact that each of these injuries which Colombia maintains was inflicted on her by the United States assumes the character of a controversy of a legal nature, or of a difference regarding the correct interpretation of the treaty existing between the two contracting parties. In the opinion of the Government of the undersigned, these acts of the United States were the sole and only cause of the dismemberment of the Republic of Colombia, of the loss to her of the valuable and important department of Panama, and of the loss of her rights in contracts, one referring to the Isthmian Canal, in course of construction, and the other to the Panama Railroad, already constructed across that department.

The undersigned does not flatter himself that you will be disposed to admit the justice of these reclamations. On the contrary, he supposes that they will be denied by you. If this should be the case, it appears to be clear that the only practicable means of adjustment, honorable for both countries, would be to submit them to the decision of an impartial court of arbitration. On the other hand, if your Government were disposed to admit the justice of Colombia's reclamations [complaints], a path would be happily opened toward a prompt and satisfactory adjustment by direct diplomacy.

The undersigned is aware that it is not his place to point out the manner in which this court should be constituted before knowing your views on the matter; however, as a mere hint at the facility with which it might be formed, he ventures to respectfully suggest that each country should without delay appoint a distinguished jurist of its own nationality to represent it, and that the selection of the umpire be made by the chief magistrate of an absolutely disinterested nation.

It does not appear necessary to remind you that if such a court is constituted and the United States have committed no injury against the Republic of Colombia, their conduct will be fully vindicated. At all events, the worst that could happen to the United States would be a decision that they had inflicted an injury on a weak sister Republic while seeking what they thought to be of universal benefit and the exaction from the United States of the appropriate indemnity. In either case the result would be a settlement of all controversies between the two Republics and a resumption of the cordial and friendly relations which always existed between them before the occurrences on the Isthmus above enumerated.

To conclude, the refusal of so great and powerful a Nation as the United States to consent to enter into negotiations, of one nature or another, with a weak nation unable to obtain reparation by arm would, as its only result, convince the weaker nation that the United States do not wish to give her the justice due her or to submit their conduct to a judicial investigation and to arbitration. This refusal would certainly have only the most unfortunate influence on the citizens of the weak nation, denied justice because too weak to have any hope of sustaining its claim by force; and, inversely, if your Government maintains its uninterrupted tradition of doing justice to others, regardless of their lack of strength, as your Chief Magistrate so emphatically expressed it recently in the following terms: "We must be scrupulous in our respect for the rights of the weak," then the consequences will undoubtedly be highly salutary, not only as an efficacious means of allaying all resentment in the Colombian mind, but of removing all apprehension in the minds of the weak peoples who inhabit the Western Hemisphere.

For all of the reasons hereinbefore set forth, the undersigned earnestly entreats you to consider favorably the petition he makes to you for a direct adjustment or for the constitution of a court of arbitration to decide the differences between the two countries, and in either manner you will add one more to the illustrious cases in which your great Nation has favored the cause of justice and of international arbitration.

The undersigned embraces this opportunity to express to the Hon. Mr. Elihu Root, Secretary of State, the assurances of his highest consideration.

Diego Mendoza.

The Secretary of State to the Colombian Minister.

No. 10.] Department of State,
Washington, February 10, 1906.

Sir: I had the honor to receive, by personal delivery, the note which you addressed to me under date of the 21st of October last, proposing that the United States shall join with Colombia, in the event of diplomatic adjustment failing, in submitting to international arbitration the questions presented by your Government growing out of the separation of Panama from the Republic of Colombia.

The nature of this proposition, which has been made and answered before, and the allegations and arguments now put forward in its support, have demanded renewed, careful, and protracted consideration on the part of the President and his constitutional advisers, in order that the reply should conform to the spirit of perfect amity which has ever controlled and should control the relationship of the United States to the Republic of Colombia.

Your note renews the proposal of arbitration as an alternative resort if a prompt and satisfactory adjustment by direct diplomacy be not attainable; but I do not find therein any clear indication of the nature of the contemplated diplomatic settlement. You present an elaborate recital of the grievances which Colombia believes to have been inflicted upon her by the alleged conduct and acts of the United States in regard to Isthmian affairs, and you sum up the 20 enumerated specifications of injuries under 4 conclusions, without suggesting the diplomatic remedy which, in the judgment of your Government, would be appropriate. You merely intimate that if the Government of the United States were disposed to admit the justice of your complaints a path would be happily opened toward a prompt and satisfactory settlement by diplomacy, and in the same breath you assume that their justice will be denied, in which event you declare that it appears to be clear that the only practicable means of adjustment, honorable for both countries, would be to submit their differences to the decision of an impartial court of arbitration. It may not have been your intention to exclude legitimate discussion touching the merits of the alleged complaints, but the language and tenor of your note seem to require either the complete admission of their justice as a condition to seeking a diplomatic adjustment or the appearance of the United States as a defendant before the bar of an arbitral court to meet the grave charges formulated by Colombia.

It gives me pleasure to assure you of my entire agreement with the sentiments which you express so eloquently in favor of the settlement of international disputes by arbitration. I hope the time will never come—I do not believe that it will ever come—when the United States is not in accord with these sentiments and does not respond to them in its action. Beyond the very able expression of these views, however, I find in your note no statement of grievance or of reasons why there should now be an arbitration between Colombia and the United States which were not in substance and with great ability presented by Gen. Reyes in his letters of December 23, 1903,[1] January 6, 1904,[1] and January 11, 1904,[1] and finally and conclusively answered by Mr. Hay on the 5th,[1] 9th,[1] and 13th[1] days of January, 1904. Upon the most painstaking review of the facts and of the positions then taken by my predecessor, I find no just ground for departing from the conclusions which he reached. It is needless to repeat the views then expressed.

There is one consideration, however, which Mr. Hay was not at liberty to present at that time because the treaty between the United States and Panama had not then received the approval of the Senate of the United States and had not been ratified, although it had been signed by the plenipotentiaries of the two Governments. That treaty has since been ratified by the consent of the Senate and both Houses of Congress have concurred in appropriating the money necessary to give the treaty effect; upon its ratification, the force of the treaty related back to the 18th of the preceding November, when it was signed. The executive and legislative branches of our Government have thus united to create, in the most solemn and binding form, a guaranty by the people of the United States of the independence of the people of Panama.

The real gravamen of your complaint is this espousal of the cause of Panama by the people of the United States. No arbitration could deal with the real rights and wrongs of the parties concerned unless it were to pass upon the question whether the cause thus espoused was just—whether the people of Panama were exercising their just rights in declaring and maintaining their independence of Colombian rule. We assert and maintain the affirmative upon that question. We assert that the ancient State of Panama, independent in its origin and by nature and history a separate political community, was confederated with the other States of Colombia upon terms which preserved and continued its separate sovereignty; that it never surrendered that sovereignty; that in the year 1885 the compact which bound it to the other States of Colombia was broken and terminated by Colombia, and the Isthmus was subjugated by force; that it was held under foreign domination to which it had never consented; and that it was justly entitled to assert its sovereignty and demand its independence from a rule which was unlawful, oppressive, and tyrannical. We can not ask the people of Panama to consent that this right of theirs, which is vital to their political existence, shall be submitted to the decision of any arbitrator. Nor are we willing to permt any arbitrator to determine the political policy of the United States in following its sense of right and justice by espousing the cause of this weak people against the stronger Government of Colombia, which had so long held them in unlawful subjection.

There is one other subject contained in your note which I can not permit to pass without notice. You repeat the charge that the Government of the United States took a collusive part in fomenting or inciting the uprising upon the Isthmus of Panama which ultimately resulted in the revolution. I regret that you should see fit to thus renew an aspersion upon the honor and good faith of the United States, in the face of the positive and final denial of the fact contained in Mr. Hay's letter of January 5, 1904. You must be well aware that the universally recognized limitations upon the subjects proper for arbitration forbid that the United States should submit such a question to arbitration. In view of your own recognition of this established limitation, I have been unable to discover any justification for the renewal of this unfounded assertion.

Accept, Mr. Minister, the renewed assurances of my highest consideration.

ELIHU ROOT.

The Colombian Minister to the Secretary of State.

THE ROCHAMBEAU,
Washington, April 6, 1906.

SIR: Both your favor of the 10th of last February and the note of the 12th, correcting mistakes as to dates made in the former and signed by Mr. Adee, were received at this legation in due time.

---

[1] Printed in S. Doc. No. 95, 58th Cong., 2d sess.

The nature and importance of the matter dealt with in this correspondence compel me once again to draw your kind attention, and through you that of the President and his advisers, to the pending difficulty between my country and the United States. I do so the more gladly because your communication contains new points which seem to open the way for an honorable settlement of my country's claim. I dare to hope, therefore, that my present communication will accomplish this happy result, following, as it does, the line of your suggestion, and removing, as I feel confident, certain misconceptions which apparently still exist notwithstanding the "careful and protracted consideration" which you inform me was given to my former one by the President and his constitutional advisers, and by yourself.

At the outset, allow me to say I am sorry to learn that the President and his advisers have concluded from my note that I meant to cast aspersions upon the honor and good faith of the United States. An honorable settlement of a controversy, such as I suggested, can not with reason be proposed to one considered as lacking in honor and good faith. My purpose was to state—and I thought I had made it perfectly plain—that the honor and good faith of the United States could not possibly be impaired by accepting either of the propositions suggested by me.

It is my purpose to consider in this communication only facts about which there is no question, and to leave out of thought entirely all matters about which there may be an erroneous opinion, either in the United States or in Colombia. There can in this case be no possible ground for supposing that I mean to cast aspersions upon the honor of the United States.

The particular claim of Colombia has been stated several times in the various communications from my country, but not so definitely perhaps as might be desired. The very nature of the claim itself prevents this. I am availing myself, however, of the wise suggestion contained in your communication; and before proceeding to a consideration of the facts on which the claim of Colombia is based, and of the possible methods of its adjustment in a way honorable to both our countries, I will now make as definite and distinct a statement of Colombia's claim as the nature of the damage inflicted on her will permit.

As a result of certain acts admitted to have been done by the United States, and which have heretofore been made a part of the public records of the United States, one of Colombia's members—the department of Panama—has been cut off or severed from her body and erected into what the United States calls and has recognized as an independent nation. The circumstances under which this was done, in view of the treaty of 1846 between the United Sta es and Colombia, and in view of certain principles of international law to which the United Sta es has assented, obligate the United States to compensate Colombia for this loss, in so far as money can compensate for such a loss.

To facilitate our arriving at an agreement as to the justice of this, my country's claim, I wish to review with the Presiden and his constitutional advisers, the events leading up thereto—events which are well known, but which must be carefully and connectedly considered in order that we may see clearly what justice demands.

As has been well said in the correspondence issuing from the Department of State of the United States, Providence seems o have designed the Isthmus of Panama as a highway for mankind between the two great oceans which lave the eastern and western shores of our continen .

During the great upheaval which freed the American continents from the political errors which had fastened themselves on Europe, the people of the United States introduced into human government the true political principles. Almost immediately thereafter Colombia founded her nationality, and the territory of Panama became a part of Colombia's body. It was but natural that Colombia and the United States should desire to carry out the designs of Providence as respects Panama, and that an agreement should be concluded between them, with a view (1) to insure the use of the Isthmus of Panama as a highway, open at all times to the people of the United States, and (2) to preserve and maintain forever the possession of this Isthmus by Colombia.

This having been accomplished by the treaty of 1846, various efforts were made by Colombia to improve the method of transit across the Isthmus, such as granting to an American company a franchise for the construc ion of the Panama Railroad. When this communication was deemed insufficient, Colombia negotiated several contracts for the construction of the Panama Canal, and later granted extensions of time to the concessionaries of the work. Among these efforts to improve the transit across the Isthmus must be mentioned the negotiations which Colombia entered into with the United States in 1869 for the conclusion of a treaty under which the United States should construct there a ship canal. The Senate of the United States failed and refused to ratify this treaty, signed by the Presidents of Colombia and of the United States, and duly ratified by the Colombian Congress.

The hope of my country, and indeed of the whole world, was thus disappointed by the act of the United States Senate; but this hope was by no means destroyed. It was inevitable that in the course of time the Isthmus of Panama should be devoted "to the use for which Providence seemed to have designed it," and in the presence of difficulties encountered by the French company in completing this work, negotiations were renewed with a view to placing the United States in a position to carry out the great enterprise. After much effort the treaty of the 22d January, 1903, known as the Herran-Hay treaty, was agreed upon by the Presidents of the two countries, and then ratified by the United States Senate; but it failed to obtain the approval of the Colombian Congress, thus meeting with the same fate which befell the treaty of 1869, with a reversal of the situation, however, in that the Colombian Congress, instead of the United States Senate, caused the failure at this time.

It is necessary that I should allude here to some of the causes which contributed to the failure or defeat of the treaty of January 22, 1903.

The United States, by an act commonly called the "Spooner Act," greatly increased the difficulties inherent in the negotiation of treaties by governments whose constitutions require legislative approval of every treaty negotiated by the executive department. This Spooner Act instructed the President of the United States to proceed with the construction of an isthmian canal by the Nicaragua route, unless he could secure from Colombia within defined time the right to construct the canal through the Isthmus of Panama upon terms satisfactory to the United States.

Perhaps it is not proper for me to inquire into the underlying reasons of this act, so I only say incidentally that after its passage the United States received from the Panama Canal Co., at the price of $40,000,000, property for which that company had previously demanded $150,000,000. But whatever its motives, this act necessitated the approval of the Herran-Hay treaty by the Colombian Congress without the least amendment and within a specified time or this new attempt to provide for the construction of the canal by the United States would be abortive, unless, indeed, the Spooner Act should be amended or repealed by the United States.

The minister of the United States resident at Bogota was not unmindful of this effect of the Spooner Act, for he notifies the Government of Colombia that the Herran-Hay treaty had to be approved by the Colombian Congress immediately and without the least amendment. If the Spooner Act had not been on the statute books of the United States, the minister of the United States at Bogota would have had no ground on which to stand while making this declaration, even had it been made in the most friendly and judicious manner, because the constitution of Colombia, as well as that of the United States, contemplates the amendment, by the legislative branch of the Government, of any treaty previously negotiated by the executive department before it can become operative, in case an amendment seems desirable in the judgment of the legislature. While it is true that the Spooner Act did not, and could not, abrogate the constitution of Colombia in any particular, still, in its practical operation, this act of the United States prevented the proper exercise of the constitutional right and duty of every member of the Colombian Congress to propose any amendment which might seem to him advisable, in order that the interests and welfare of Colombia might be perfectly protected in the treaty granting this important concession. This arose from the fact that the date fixed by the Spooner Act for proceeding to construct the canal by the way of Nicaragua was so near at hand when the Herran-Hay treaty came up for discussion in the Colombian Congress that there was no possibility of bringing the United States Senate and the Colombian Congress into agreement upon any amendment to that treaty which might be suggested by the Colombian Congress, even if the Presidents of Colombia and of the United States should have given assent to the same.

It is manifest, therefore, that the Spooner Act greatly increased the difficulties necessarily involved in the negotiation of a treaty between governments constituted as are those of Colombia and the United States, in a matter of such magnitude, large even for so great a nation as the United States.

Here, then, was the situation in August, 1903. After half a century of desire by Colombia that there should be a canal through the Isthmus of Panama.

constructed by the United States under a concession from Colombia, the United States was still without authority to accomplish this great work.

First, because the constitution of Colombia and that of the United States alike require legislative approval of treaties negotiated by the executive departments of the Government. But for this difficulty the efforts of our two countries would before now have resulted in the construction of the canal through Panama by the United States under a concession from Colombia.

Second, because of the refusal of the United States Senate to ratify the treaty of 1869.

Third, because the Colombian Congress did not ratify the Herran-Hay treaty, under conditions whose difficulties were increased by the act of the United States necessitating ratification of this treaty without the least amendment as soon as it came before the Colombian Congress.

The adjournment of the Colombian Congress, after its refusal to ratify the Herran-Hay treaty, brought the Executive of the United States face to face with the Spooner Act and seemed to necessitate the construction of the canal through Nicaragua, which was considered the wrong route, or else the securing of an amendment to this act in order that the United States might continue negotiations with Colombia.

Confronted by this situation, the President of the United States was formulating in a message to Congress the thought that there did or should exist some means whereby the United States could dedicate the Isthmus of Panama to the use most necessary for the general welfare of the people of all nations—that is, for an interoceanic canal—a sort of international eminent domain, perhaps.

Colombia does not profess this doctrine and does not see how it can be practiced in international affairs prior to the establishment of an authority superior to the sovereign nations in whose name it could be invoked. The mere fact, however, that the President of the United States was formulating the thought of finding some way to dedicate the Isthmus to canal purposes other than by agreement upon the terms and price of concession with the sovereign having title to the same seems to call for a pause in this recital of events long enough to remark that what subsequently happened was very like a concrete application of this doctrine to Colombia, but without compensation for the territory taken—a so-called "new nation," which was preserved from the day of its birth and guaranteed permanently in its life by the powerful arm of the United States, serving as the means in the absence of an international body having proper authority.

While the President of the United States was at work upon this thought of some means of "dedicating the Isthmus of Panama to the use for which Providence seems to have designed it," other than by treaty with Colombia, the independence of Panama was declared. The executive department of the United States Government immediately issued orders to the United States Navy to prevent the landing of any Colombian troops in Panama—Colombia's own territory—with a view to the reduction of Panama to submission. The United States Navy obeyed the instructions thus given by the executive department of the United States Government. The only possible way for a Colombian army to reach Panama was by water, owing to the topography of Panama. All the waterway between Colombia and Panama was occupied by war ships of the United States Navy. It was impossible, therefore, for Colombia to reach Panama with an armed force, because of the presence and action of the war vessels of the United States. Consequently the effect of this lifting up of the powerful hand of the United States was to prevent Colombia from maintaining her sovereignty over Panama, and thus Panama was severed from the body of Colombia.

The action which brought about this result was taken by the executive department of the United States Government, on the supposition that it was not in violation of any principles of international law by which the United States had bound itself to act, and was not contrary to the provisions of the treaty of 1846, then in force between Colombia and the United States. On the contrary, it was asserted by the United States that this action was lawful and necessary for the faithful performance of the duties imposed upon the United States by the treaty of 1846, and, indeed, was demanded in order to promote the general welfare not only of the people of both North and South America, but of all civilized nations.

Colombia does not for a moment lose sight of the fact that, during a long period, the United States has shared with her in the desire to see a canal constructed through Panama for the promotion of the general welfare of all nations, nor does she overlook the fact that there were special reasons why it would be of particular value to the United States to have this canal constructed and operated by the United States. Disregarding the particular interests of the United States for constructing and operating the canal, and looking solely to the promotion of the general welfare of all nations by the timely construction of the canal, at the proper place and in the proper way, it is apparent that the rights of Colombia—the sovereign of Panama—should be carefully respected in securing the concession for the canal; for only in this way could the canal be constructed so as to promote the general interest of all nations without doing an injury to any nation. Without in any way reflecting upon the motives of the United States in the course which was pursued when the independence of Panama was declared, it is proper to inquire whether the executive department of the United States Government was correct in its belief that it had a right to take the action which it is admitted was taken, after the declaration of the independence of Panama, and which prevented Colombia from maintaining her sovereignty over the Isthmus; also whether the acts performed by the United States were contrary to the obligations which the United States was under by reason of the provisions in the treaty of 1846, or by reason of certain principles of international law which the United States has declared as binding upon nations and to the observation of which it has held other nations.

When the independence of Panama was declared, the treaty of 1846 between Colombia and the United States was in full force, and our two countries are and ever have been in perfect accord upon this point, namely, that this treaty bound the United States to preserve Colombia's sovereignty over Panama against menace or destruction from foreign nations.

Upon the declaration of independence of Panama, a grave question arose, namely, Did the treaty of 1846 bind the United States to preserve Colombia's sovereignty over Panama against menace from every danger whatsoever, regardless of its origin, even from internal violence, rebellion, or revolution, or at least to take no action that would hinder Colombia in such case? Colombia, in the face of the Panama crisis, called upon the United States, as an obligation imposed by the treaty of 1846, to take no steps that would embarrass her suppressing the rebellion and maintaining her sovereignty over the Isthmus. The United States, on the other hand, without an exchange of one word with Colombia on this subject, announced an interpretation of the treaty of 1846 not theretofore formulated; that is, that Colombia, in whose behalf the protection clause in this treaty was inserted, had granted to the United States the right to take steps which would prevent Colombia from suppressing within her own territory a rebellion which, if successful, would destroy her sovereignty over the Isthmus of Panama.

Colombia declares that the United States has in this respect misinterpreted the treaty of 1846.

It is an admitted fact that under this construction of the treaty of 1846 the United States has so acted as to cause the loss of Panama to Colombia. Thus, by the admitted acts of the United States Colombia has been deprived of that very member of her body which the United States had agreed to preserve to her forever.

If the acts of the United States were lawful and right, this loss must fall upon Colombia. If, on the other hand, this loss was wrongfully occasioned by acts of the United States done in violation of the provisions of the treaty by which the United States has obligated itself, or in violation of principles of international law to which the United States has assented, then the United States is lawfully bound to compensate Colombia for the damage thus done to her.

The United States formulated the construction of the treaty of 1846, by which this loss was occasioned to Colombia in the face of a great emergency, when it appeared to the United States that any other course would cause the permanent loss of all hope of locating the Isthmian Canal at the proper place, and would "frustrate forever" the policy in regard to the Isthmus of Panama to which both of our countries had long adhered, and which was for the welfare of the people of all nations. Without emphasizing the fact, I desire to state in passing that the Government of the United States took too gloomy a view of the situation. There is higher authority than Abraham Lincoln, one of the great Presidents of the United States, for believing that "nothing is settled till it is settled right," and therefore both Colombia and the United States could have rested in the conviction that a firm adherence to the principles involved in due time would have brought our Governments into agreement upon the terms of a treaty for the construction of a canal through Panama, despite any appearance to the contrary. The very secession of Panama altered the conditions in Colombia to such an extent that the United States would have received the canal concession from Colombia if the United States had only remained inactive while Colombia was reducing Panama to submission. But leaving this entirely out of view, as not being a matter of accomplished fact, the condition to-day is this: The canal concession has been secured by the United States, and that member of my country's body which the United States had agreed to preserve to Colombia forever has been lost, and this by the act of the United States, done under a construction of the treaty of 1846 not heretofore announced, and formulated by the United States in the face of this emergency. In the clear light of the present day, and freed from fear of losing the canal concession, the United States can be expected to see that the people and the Government of Colombia never agreed by the treaty of 1846 that the United States, while complying with its terms, might lawfully cause the loss to Colombia of the very thing for which Colombia entered into that treaty.

The treaty could not possibly give the United States any such right unless the mind of Colombia and of the United States came into agreement upon that point. Is it possible to believe that any national entity would ever enter into an agreement with another for the preservation of a member of its own body, and by the very terms of the agreement authorize the severance of that member by the act of the party that was binding itself to preserve said member?

Certainly the United States, on reconsideration of this matter in the light of these facts, can see that Colombia never agreed by the treaty of 1846 that the United States might lawfully commit such acts, under the provisions of that treaty, as to cause the loss to Colombia of her sovereignty over the Isthmus of Panama. When the United States does see this it will recognize its duty to compensate Colombia for the loss occasioned by its admitted acts done under a misconception of the rights supposed—in an emergency—to have arisen from the treaty of 1846.

The damage done to Colombia by admitted and published acts of the United States is the value of the Department of Panama. The amount of damage thus caused to Colombia and for which the United States is lawfully responsible has not been stated in exact figures, for the reason that the exact amount can not easily be stated. The lost member was very valubale, being the strategic point of the whole Western Hemisphere. Liability for this loss being conceded by the United States, the estimation of the amount of damage could be either by direct negotiation or by a committee of experts appointed by our two Governments.

If the United States desires, I can submit an amount as approximating the value of the lost member of Colombia, upon the payment of which my country would feel compensated, in so far as money can compensate for such a loss. Or we can now proceed to the appointment of a joint commission, charged with the duty of determining in justice and in equity the amount of compensation to which Colombia is entitled from the United States by virtue of this loss; that is to say, the value of Panama, including not only the value of territory but that of the railroad, of the contract with the French company, and so forth.

Though the acts of the United States which severed Panama from the body of Colombia were done by the executive department of the United States Government, the Senate of the United States, as you inform me, subsequently ratified a treaty which the President and the Department of State had negotiated with Panama, whereby the independence of Panama was guaranteed by the United States and whereby the United States received from Panama a concession to construct a canal through Panama; and, still later, the House of Representatives of the United States joined with the Senate of the United States in making an appropriation of money to be expended in Panama under a canal concession granted to the United States by Panama as an independent nation. By the act of the Senate the severance of Panama from Colombia is made permanent, to the extent that the United States can by its act accomplish this, and the state of things thus created has been accepted by joint action of the Senate and House of Representatives of the United States. The Panama incident may seem, therefore, to be closed, but this is not true, at least so far as Colombia is concerned, and can not be closed until Colombia is compensated or has an opportunity to plead her cause before an impartial court of arbitration.

Having acted in an emergency, when it appeared to the United States that a work most necessary for the general welfare of the whole world was in jeopardy, and in such a way as to insure the execution of this work without delay and at a place and upon terms entirely satisfactory to the Government of the United

States, it is but natural that the executive department of the United States Government and all the members of the Congress of the United States who were called upon to take part in this action, should consider carefully, in the light of all the facts which bear upon the history of the relations of our two Governments in regard to Panama, whether in this emergency any damage was done which the United States ought to repair, according to the highest sense of justice and right.

As the question of impairing the honor of the United States has been brought into discussion, I may be permitted to remark that the honor of every act is coeval with the act itself. It is, therefore, impossible for the honor of an individual or of a nation to be tarnished by an agreement to do what is eventually recognized to be right, independently of the question as to whether an act previously done was either right or wrong. Indeed, the enlightened opinion of the whole world is agreed upon this, that even when a wrong action has been taken, conscieusly or unconsciously, that which will most redound to the honor of any party thereto is to correct the same. Therefore, whether the acts of the United States done in the Panama emergency were right or wrong, whether they were in accordance with the provisions of the treaty of 1846 and of recognized principles of international law or contrary thereto, the honor of the United States would be enhanced by consenting to arbitrate the claim of Colombia, in the event that the United States can not see, in the light of the facts set forth in this communication, that it is in duty bound to compensate Colombia.

In this connection, I feel sure that the United States will not forget that the Government of Great Britain refused at first to arbitrate the claim of the United States for damages done by the *Alabama*, asserting that to arbitrate that claim would impair the honor of the British Government. Throughout the whole world, and particularly in the United States, it is now recognized that the arbitration of the *Alabama* claims by Great Britain and the United States set the tide of the past century in favor of the arbitration of disputes between nations and that the reconsideration of this decision by the Government of Great Britain and the reference of the *Alabama* claims to arbitration is one of the greatest honors achieved by the British Government, although the decision of the arbitrators was against Great Britain. A similar honor can now be achieved by the consent of the United States to arbitrate the claim of my Government during that administration of the United States under which this claim arose.

And, in order to facilitate so happy a decision by the Government of the United States, in case it can not yet see that it is lawfully bound to compensate Colombia, I propose on behalf of Colombia that the United States and Colombia forthwith enter into a convention for the purpose of securing an impartial judgment upon the following strictly legal questions:

1. Did the treaty of 1846 obligate the United States to maintain the sovereignty of Colombia over the Isthmus of Panama against menace or attack from any foreign power and against internal disturbances that might jeopardize said sovereignty?

2. Did the treaty of 1846 obligate the United States to refrain from taking steps which would hinder Colombia in maintaining her sovereignty over Panama by suppressing rebellion, revolution, secession, or internal disorder?

3. Did the treaty of 1846 grant to the United States the right to take those steps which it is admitted were taken by the United States to prevent the landing of troops in Panama and the suppression of the rebellion?

4. Did the treaty of 1846 leave the United States free lawfully to take the steps which it is admitted by the United States were taken as regards Panama?

5. Did these acts of the United States, which it is admitted were taken, prevent Colombia from taking the steps necessary to suppress the rebellion and maintain her sovereignty over the Isthmus?

6. Were the admitted acts of the United States in respect to Panama in violation of principles of international law which have been recognized by the United States as binding upon nations in their dealings with each other?

7. What damage, if any, has been occasioned to Columbia by acts of the United States which are admitted by the United States, and which may be adjudged as having been in violation of obligations imposed upon the United States by the treaty of 1846 or by principles of international law to which the United States has assented?

The foregoing questions are all of a purely legal character, arising upon the proper interpretation of a treaty and the proper application to undisputed facts of well-recognized principles of international law. They are therefore identical in kind with the questions included in the treaties recently negotiated by the United States with nine governments and almost unanimously ratified by the Senate of the United States as to said questions which are recognized the world over as eminently suitable for judicial determination. Nevertheless, to provide against all possible misconception of the scope of the arbitration proposed, Colombia will gladly add to the convention, if the United States so desires, a clause providing that the jurisdiction of the arbitrators shall not be construed as extending to the point of passing upon the political policy of the United States, further than to determine whether the policy pursued by the United States, as respects Panama was outside of the limits within which the United States had bound itself to remain, either by the treaty of 1846 or by principles of international law to which the United States has assented.

I am led to suggest this because it appears from your communication that my proposition was supposed to imply the reference of the political policy of the United States to the judgment of arbitrators, for you say: "Nor are we willing to permit any arbitrator to determine the political policy of the United States in following its sense of right and justice by espousing the cause of this weak people (Panama) against the stronger Government of Colombia, which has so long held them in unlawful subjection."

The erroneous supposition that I propose permitting an arbitrator to determine the political policy of the United States has been removed by my suggestion that the Arbitral Convention expressly forbids this by limiting the jurisdiction of the arbitrators to deciding whether the acts of the United States in 1903 were contrary to provisions of the treaty concluded in 1846 or contrary to principles of international law for violation of which the United States has held other nations accountable.

I need make no further allusion, therefore, to the question of the public policy of the United States, but I am compelled to reply to the charge contained in this paragraph of your communication, and to another clause where you say: "That the ancient State of Panama, independent in its origin, and by nature and history a separate political community, was confederated with the other States of Colombia upon terms which preserved and continued its separate sovreignty; that in the year 1885 the compact which bound it to the other States of Colombia was broken and terminated by Colombia, and the Isthmus was subjugated by force; that it was held under foreign domination to which it had never consented, and that it was justly entitled to assert its sovereignty and demand its independence from a rule which was unlawful, oppressive, and tyrannical."

I must say in reply that the question between Colombia and the United States is not whether Panama was justly entitled to assert independence, but whether the United States was under obligation, by treaty or by principles of international law, not to do the things which it is admitted were done by the United States after the declaration of Panama's independence was made.

Permit me to say further that these allegations come as a surprise to my country, in view of certain public records of the United States, which I must now recall to your attention on account of these allegations.

In regard to the alleged "separate sovereignty" of Panama, it seems to me that you can hardly mean what the language would seem to imply, remembering that in 1846 the United States bound itself to preserve the sovereignty of Colombia over the Isthmus of Panama forever, and in view of the further facts that in 1869, and again in 1903, the United States negotiated with Colombia, as sovereign of Panama, for valuable concessions, in order to construct an isthmian canal through Panama.

These acts could not have occurred if Panama had been a separate sovereignty, or had been so regarded by the United States.

As for the allegation of oppressive or tyrannical conduct toward Panama by the Government of Colombia, permit me to call to your attention the fact that not once since the United States bound itself to maintain forever the sovereignty of Colombia over Panama has the United States intimated to Colombia that her rule in Panama was oppressive, tyrannical, or unlawful; nor has the United States or any other government ever made representations to Colombia on account of injuries to its interests, or the interests of its citizens in Panama, caused by unlawful, oppressive, or tyrannical conduct toward Panama by the Government of Colombia.

Were it proper for us to disclose the political relation between Colombia and Panama prior to the 2d of November, 1903, or the internal affairs of Colombia,

I could set forth many facts, capable of easy proof, which would show that the allegations into which you have been led are contrary to the facts of the history of my country.

In addition to the foregoing allusion to facts of record in the United States I may say that, owing to the nature of republican institutions, under which Colombia has lived ever since she achieved her independence, through her own efforts, Colombia has been governed by the vote of the people. There has been no disparity in the rights enjoyed by any of the several members of Colombia's body. All the States or Departments constituting the nation have always had equal rights. It is true that political struggles have occurred in Colombia which resulted in civil strife, even as in all other nations with whose history Colombia is acquainted; but never has Panama or any other State or Department of Colombia endeavored to sever its relations with the rest of Colombia, or even protested against any act of the Government as being against its welfare and designed for the special interest of other parts of the national body. Such civil wars as have occurred in Colombia came from struggles between parties having representatives in all parts of the nation. The sacrifices imposed upon the nation by these struggles and the efforts made to work our way through them have been undergone and shared alike by all parts of the nation.

The citizens of Colombia in Panama took part in the struggles on both sides, and in the outcome Panama shared equally in the benefits with all the other parts of the nation, but, in several particulars of an economical, political, and vital character, was burdened less with the evil consequences than were the others. For instance, Colombia generally had to suffer the evils of a paper currency, whereas the people of Panama, throughout the whole crisis and afterwards, continued by the act of Colombia, to enjoy the benefit of specie currency, though paper currency was made, by the act of the Colombian Congress, the only lawful currency in all other parts of the Republic.

Taking the most unfavorable view possible of the refusal of the Colombian Congress to sanction the Herran-Hay treaty, it was only a repetition of the act done in 1869 by the United States Senate. During almost every session of every double-chambered national legislature measures most necessary to the national welfare fail for want of agreement by the two bodies whose assent must be secured, and consequently go over until unity of action can be obtained. The thing which so imperiled the vital interests of the people of Panama was not the refusal of the Colombian Congress to ratify the Herran-Hay treaty without amendment, but the existence of the Spooner Act of the United States, which operated to prevent free and full discussion of and final agreement upon a treaty for the construction of the canal, after the exercise of their constitutional rights by all parties charged by law with a responsibility in regard thereto. But for this act the people of Panama could have counted upon the conclusion of a treaty during subsequent sessions of the Congresses of the two countries. Otherwise, republican government must be admitted to be a failure. Moreover, what was there to prevent the United States from amending or repealing this act if actual conditions called for this, in the interest of the United States, of Panama, of Colombia, and of other nations?

I can not escape, however, from the feeling that consideration of the internal government of Colombia and of the relation of Panama to Colombia prior to the 2d of November, 1903, can only serve to confuse the issue, for the arbitrators in the case which Colombia proposes to submit could not inquire into the internal government or the foreign policy of either Colombia or the United States, but only into the questions submitted, questions which are purely of law, upon acts all of which are admitted. The accuracy or the inaccuracy of the statements made by us in this discussion of the history of Colombia could not be passed upon in the arbitration which I propose, and does not have to be decided by us in making a direct settlement, for the sole question is: Did the United States act contrary to the treaty of 1846 or to principles of international law assented to by the United States?

I beg of you, therefore, to assure the President and his constitutional advisers that I have not intended to propose that the United States submit its public policy to the decision of any arbitrator, and that you will put out of mind all matters which do not affect the claim which is made by my country or the method proposed for its honorable settlement, either by compensation of Colombia or the arbitration of her claim.

Having endeavored to confine myself in this communication to facts about which there is no dispute and which must be considered first by ourselves in arriving at a direct settlement of Colombia's claim, and then by any court of arbitration to which this claim may be referred, if a direct settlement is not made, I trust that you will assist me to clear away all other questions and to bring to the attention of the President and his constitutional advisers only such questions as will promote an honorable settlement of this unhappy contention at the earliest possible moment.

In former communications received from the Department of State of the United States, it was stated that the actions of the United States sprang from motives of the friendliest kind toward Colombia, and were taken in order faithfully to perform the duties imposed upon the United States by the treaty of 1846.

I note the fact that in your communication it is stated for the first time, on behalf of your Government, that the United States espoused the cause of Panama, the language being:

"Now, are we willing to permit any arbitrator to determine the political policy of the United States in following its sense of right and justice by espousing the cause of this weak people against the stronger Government of Colombia, which had so long held them in unlawful subjection?"

As my country must suffer a continuous injury until the United States determines either to compensate Colombia or to arbitrate this claim, and as a considerable time has already elapsed since the events complained of, I take the liberty of expressing the hope that the President and his constitutional advisers will give the earliest possible reconsideration to my country's claim, in the light of the facts and arguments thereon set forth in this communication, and will submit the same to the Senate and to the House of Representatives of the United States in order that the members of these two honorable bodies may determine the course which it is proper for them to take under existing conditions.

After the most painstaking review of the situation I find myself convinced that considerations not only of absolute but of practical justice, as well as of honor and of the general welfare of our two countries, our two continents, and, indeed, of the whole world, call for the compensation of Colombia for her loss or the arbitration of her claim, and I feel confident that the Government of the United States will be glad to accede to one or the other of these honorable proposals, now that all question of casting aspersions upon the honor of the United States has been removed from this correspondence.

If the United States does not feel called upon to compensate Colombia without recourse to arbitration, I propose that the questions herein stated be referred to an impartial court of arbitration constituted in accordance with the provisions of the treaty of The Hague, adopted by the United States and by 25 other nations after most careful consideration. But if for any reason the United States would prefer a court of arbitration constituted in any other way, Colombia will consent to any method suggested by the United States which will assure the selection of competent and impartial arbitrators to determine this unhappy contention.

With assurances of high personal regard and of liveliest hopes for the success of our mutual efforts for a settlement of this controversy which will be honorable to all parties, I beg to remain,

Your Excellency's obedient servant, DIEGO MENDOZA.

COLOMBIA'S PROTEST.

MARCH 28, 1911.

To His Excellency P. C. KNOX,
Secretary of State, Washington, D. C.

MR. SECRETARY: In order to place on record and to establish the proof of the facts asserted by Colombia in the course of the negotiations which have been carried on, and I trust will continue, between the two Governments in connection with the events that took place in Panama in November, 1903, from the consequences of which Colombia is still suffering, I have the honor to set forth in this note an article published in the Washington Post, No. 12706, of the 24th instant.

"I took the Canal Zone."—T. R. Otherwise, he avers, Congress would still be debating subject.

BERKELEY, CAL., *March 23.*

Speaking at the annual charter-day exercises in the Greek Theater of the University of California to-day, Theodore Roosevelt said:

"I am interested in the Panama Canal because I started it. If I had followed traditional conservative methods I would have submitted a dignified state paper of probably 200 pages to the Congress, and the debate would have been going on yet.

"But I took the Canal Zone and let the Congress debate, and while the debate goes on, the canal does also."

This article, upon which the press of the country comments with severity to-day, contains a public, deliberate, and spontaneous declaration by the ex-President of the United States, Mr. Theodore Roosevelt, made in the presence of a most respectable body of young students in a State destined more than any other to establish close and commercial relations with Colombia.

I send your excellency the article referred to for what it may be worth as an historical or legal record or document, or rather as the spontaneous confession of a man who, having been President of the United States at the time of the accession of Panama, to-day boasts of having committed an act of the most far-reaching gravity against the country I have the honor to represent and which the latter has left to the justice of this nation—the inheritor of the highest traditions of loyalty and honor.

As the fact whereof Mr. Roosevelt to-day boasts is the act committed by him in 1903, which at that time he described to Congress as "the greatest triumph of diplomacy in the century," and against which Colombia protested as being an act of war at a time when the two nations were at peace, and a flagrant violation of the public good faith of the United States pledged in the treaty signed in 1846 and ratified in 1848, I deem myself forced to renew to your excellency, respectfully but firmly, that protest in the name of the nation gratuitously, deeply, and unexpectedly offended and injured.

It is a pleasure for the Colombian minister to place on record here that this renewal of the protest against the events of 1903 does not affect, nor could it affect, the relations of Colombia with the present Government of the United States, far less the high esteem in which she holds the spirit of justice that presides over all its acts. The hope that the dignity and rights of Colombia will some day be fully satisfied is precisely based upon those qualities of honesty and loyalty which distinguishes the head of this great Republic, Mr. Taft. This hope is confirmed by the assurance which I have received that the Army of the United States has not been moved,[1] nor will it be moved, with the object of impairing the autonomy or the territorial rights of the Latin-American Republics, and that in any case the President of the United States will always await, as his duty and his honor demand, and with the calm becoming his high office, the decision of the National Congress.

With sentiments of the highest consideration, I have the honor to subscribe myself, Mr. Secretary, your respectful and obedient servant,

FRANCISCO DE P. BORDA,
Envoy Extraordinary and Minister Plenipotentiary from the Republic of Colombia to the United States.

To His Excellency the SECRETARY OF STATE OF THE UNITED STATES,
Washington, D. C.

SECRETARY KNOX'S SPEECH.

If by appearing before this all-star audience there arises an implication that I claim to be the sole proprietor of a thoroughbred hobby I must challenge my own title to the honor you have done me. The subject to which my mind most frequently recurs, which I believe is the definition of a hobby, is one

[1] Referring to the mobilization of American troops in connection with the Mexican revolution.

which has engrossed some of the greatest and noblest minds, and it can fairly be said at present to be most conspicuously and practically championed by the distinguished Chief whom I have the honor now to serve; my own relations to it being that of trying to be useful to one who is more useful in the great task of endeavoring, as far as possible, to bring about the peace of the world.

The subject is inspiring to me because I conceive the peace of the world to be a condition of the world in which the fabulous sums that are expended for war will be employed for the improvement of humanity and the advancement of the arts of peace; a condition in which battleships and bayonets will be converted into stationary engines and harrow teeth, and the genius and science now constructively employed upon devices for the destruction of human life will be engaged in studying the physics of the air and the chemistry of the soil, so that a man will surely reap where he has sown and the harvest will be multiplied a hundredfold.

Peace among nations is a status depending for its existence upon the recognition of each other's rights and a willingness to be just. A great statesman declared that "the respect for the rights of others is peace." Respect for the rights of others involves a willingness to submit the question of their existence to judicial determination where they can not be conceded.

What the United States is pressing upon the world through the proposed Permanent Court of Arbital Justice and the pending treaties with Great Britain and France is that differences as to national rights shall be determined according to the principles of justice.

The treaties are the concrete expression of the three great nations concerned of their intention to do justice where a wrong has been inflicted or a right withheld by referring their differences to The Hague Court or some other tribunal. They are first steps toward the goal of peaceful adjustment of all international differences, not by a mere arbitration but by a final judicial judgment in a permanent international court of justice to which all nations will habitually resort.

The solemn assertion of highly civilized nations that war is not to be resorted to as a means for settling their future differences obliges them to provide other means to that end, and unerringly points to the speedy establishment of a permanent court to which nations may submit their differences with confidence. And when they agree, as between themselves, to refer to judicial decision all their justiciable differences the foundations of a permanent court of justice are already laid.

It has been suggested that the treaties with Great Britain and France should contain a provision that we should, in addition to agreeing to arbitrate the differences between the parties to the treaties, likewise agree to arbitrate differences with other nations not parties to the treaties. This is exactly what the United States has proposed to the world in the identic note inviting the nations to join in establishing a permanent court of arbitral justice, and a first and long step toward this end would be for the more powerful nations to set the example by agreements between themselves such as those now receiving the consideration of the Senate, and such as my good friend, the German Ambassador, and myself had begun to negotiate when halted by unexpected objections in the Senate to the treaties already negotiated, and some protests outside the Senate, which recalls the spirit that led to the burning in effigy of John Jay because of the arbitration clause in the Treaty of Ghent.

It is to be hoped that the broader proposition, initiated by the United States, and which has been most favorably received by the powers, will not be wrecked by the United States refusing to accept the principle involved in the pending treaties.

The creation of an international court of justice will not destroy the usefulness of the pending treaties. There will still remain that large class of nonjusticiable differences which, under the terms of the treaties, are to be referred to a commission for investigation, consideration, and advice.

The establishment of such a court has been one of the aspirations of all the centuries. As I have said on a previous occasion, "The idea is as old as the Roman altar of peace or the temple of Claudius or Vespasian." Its realization will be the fruition and crystallization of the thought and ideals of the governments and statesmen of all ages, and the glory of its achievements, like a mantle descending from on high, will be ample enough to enfold all who have contributed to its accomplishment.

EXHIBIT K.

COMPILATION OF FACTS.

VERIFICATION OF MR. CROMWELL'S STATEMENTS AS FOUND IN OFFICIAL RECORDS, PRIVATE DOCUMENTS, CONTEMPORANEOUS PRESS DISPATCHES, AND AFFIDAVITS AND STATEMENTS OF INDIVIDUALS, WITH SOME CHAPTERS OF PANAMA HISTORY WHICH MR. CROMWELL DID NOT RELATE, BY EARL HARDING, A STAFF CORRESPONDENT OF THE WORLD.

How William Nelson Cromwell initiated the Panama Canal negotiations, made tools of the diplomats of both the United States and Colombia, and used the "big stick" of Mr. Roosevelt to protect the profits of his speculating clients—Cromwellian origin of the Spooner amendment, and Senator Spooner's denial thereof—Senator Hanna's deceptions and equivocations in his speech to the Senate, written by Cromwell—The $60,000 contribution to the Republican campaign fund of 1900, after Cromwell was permitted to amend the canal plank in the national platform—Proposals for the dismemberment of Colombia made by the State Department in 1902—Corruption of the Colombian Government with American money, and the deal with Gen. Reyes—Secret conferences of Roosevelt and Cromwell with emissaries of the Panama rebels before the "revolution"—Falsehoods in the State papers of President Roosevelt and Secretary Hay, and fatal flaws in Mr. Cromwell's alibi.

"This (Panama) was the route which commended itself to the deliberate judgment of the congress."—Roosevelt's message to Congress, December 7, 1903.

"The Canal negotiations were initiated by Colombia, and were energetically pressed upon this Government for several years."—The Beaupre-Hay-Roosevelt-Cromwell ultimatum, delivered to the Colombian minister for foreign affairs, June 13, 1903.

"The treaty (Hay-Herran) was entered into at the urgent solicitation of the people of Colombia."—Roosevelt's message to Congress, December 7, 1903.

The diplomatic negotiations to bring about the sale of the Panama Canal to the United States were initiated, not by Colombia, but by the French Canal Co.'s lawyer and lobbyist, William Nelson Cromwell; not "at the urgent solicitation of the people of Colombia," as Mr. Roosevelt says, but as Mr. Cromwell boasts, they were carried on at his own urgent solicitation, and generally under his own direction.

The lawyer-lobbyist of the Panama Canal Co. admits using Colombian diplomacy as his cat's-paw for the first time in March, 1897, a year and three months after his employment as general counsel of the New Panama Canal Co.

Thanks to the activities of the Cromwell lobby, the Nicaragua bills in both Senate and House failed to reach a vote before Congress adjourned, March 4, 1897. But Mr. McKinley, upon his inauguration, called an extra session for March 15, the Nicaragua bills were immediately reintroduced, and the new Secretary of State, Mr. Sherman, who had just stepped from the position of chairman of the Senate Committee on Foreign Affairs, gave them his active support. The friends of Nicaragua, seeing that their bills could not reach a vote in a session so occupied by the tariff discussion, concentrated their efforts on providing for a new investigation and created the Nicaragua Canal Commission, commonly referred to as the first Walker commission. The members were Rear Admiral John G. Walker, Col. Peter C. Hains, and Prof. Lewis M. Haupt.

Mr. Cromwell at this time, as he says, had become imbued with the idea "that the negative policy which had been pursued hitherto must be abandoned, since it would be utterly insufficient to combat the dangers which menaced the company on every side, and that the sole hope for its salvation lay in the adoption of a plan of action upon bases which Mr. Cromwell suggested, different, open, audacious, agressive." Mr. Cromwell set forth this plan in a letter to the canal company, February 2, 1897, in which he advises "a vigorous campaign of publicity, enlightenment, and opposition." In this letter Mr. Cromwell said: "It is no longer a bankrupt company which is your competitor, it is the nation itself. How to turn the nation away from this design becomes the new and serious problem." Mr. Cromwell reiterated this advice on the 9th, 10th, and 13th of February in letters and telegrams, and again elaborated his plan and policy in a letter dated March 20, 1897, when he urged upon the canal company "that the Colombian Government and the Panama Co. ought to bring officially to the knowledge of the United States the existence of the Panama Canal concession * * * and recall to it the clauses of the treaty of 1848 between the United States and Colombia. * * * Colombia, as well as the Panama Canal Co., ought to wake up. * * * It ought to notify its minister immediately and by cable to present a note containing the grounds which we indicate and cooperate with us earnestly and at once."

"The company," says Mr. Cromwell, "immediately authorized the adoption of the part of this program that had to do with the intervention of Colombia," and he at once set about to make Colombia's diplomacy his servant. How he accomplished this is best told in his own words:

"Confronted by the unlooked-for circumstances of the extra session and the active negotiations between the United States and Nicaragua that Secretary Sherman had set on foot, we conceived the idea of inducing Colombia itself to intervene in order to validate its rights according to the terms of the treaty of 1846–1848 between New Granada (now Colombia) and the United States and to protect the rights of the Panama Canal Co. as purchaser of the concession which had been granted by Colombia on the basis of this treaty. The idea thus conceived by us was presented to the company, which approved it at once; and in consequence, we immediately spoke of it to the representative of Colombia in the United States (Mr. Rengifo), chargé d'affaires in Washington, and a series of conferences followed, in which we made a full explanation of the new situation of the canal company, discussed the treaty of 1848, and furnished arguments in support of these views.

"We prepared an official protest and presented it to the representative of Colombia and, after discussion, it was accepted by him and presented to the Government of the United States. This step produced its effect and the attention of the United States was drawn to the matter of the Panama Canal through important diplomatic channels. This arrested the attention of the Government and advantageously introduced the Panama Canal as an element which must be considered in the solution of pending problems; until then it had been completely neglected."

At the next session of Congress, 1897–98, action on Nicaragua, fortunately for Mr. Cromwell, was prevented by the absorbing preparations for the War with Spain. By the summer of 1898 popular clamor for the interoceanic canal had become so pronounced that he had no difficulty in bringing his client around to sanctioning his entire program for an "open, audacious, aggressive" campaign of argument, enlightenment, and publicity;" and in August, 1898, this campaign was opened with the organization of Mr. Cromwell's press bureau. Here we find Mr. Cromwell's next admission of the usefulness of his Colombian diplomatic connections. He mentions that "at our request" the Colombian Legation in Washington sent to the press and to the State Department an official denial of the accuracy of a report from Bogota concerning refusal to extend the French Canal Co.'s concession. Then there is a long jump in Mr. Cromwell's story before we come to his next admitted manipulation of that office.

December 2, 1898, Mr. Cromwell induced the Panama Canal Co. to present to President McKinley a statement, dated in Paris, November 18, 1898, of the alleged condition and prospects of its enterprise—a statement which Mr. Morgan, of Alabama, denounced in the United States Senate as misleading and false in many details, and whose apparent innocence was "only the veneer of its crafty diplomacy." At the same time Mr. Cromwell presented the report of the French company's "international technical commission," which had just been published. Mr. Cromwell's press bureau flooded the country with copies of this report and of the statement to President McKinley, but Mr. Cromwell complains, "not one newspaper would voluntarily reproduce them, and we could not get them publicity that was so necessary at this time except as paid advertisements."

Gen. Abbot and Mr. ——— Corthell, a distinguished engineer, both especially employed, so Mr. Cromwell says, for his press bureau, had been busy preparing Panama literature. Mr. Cromwell says he offered one of Gen. Abbot's articles on the Panama Canal to "one of the great magazines of the country, and this politely refused to publish it. We later procured its publication, but in a less important magazine."

Mr. Cromwell was at this time urging his client to save its life by making an offer of outright sale to the United States, but the Frenchmen could not see the danger. The Nicaragua bills were reintroduced in both House and Senate, and propelled by the canal enthusiasm which had been engendered by the voyage of the Oregon around Cape Horn in the Spanish War times, they were fast approaching passage, backed up by the recommendation in President McKinley's message of December 5, 1898, that the Nicaragua canal be built. The Senate passed the bill by 48 votes against 6, on January 21, 1899.

Mr. Cromwell foresaw early and inevitable defeat in the Senate and so advised his client on January 6. Then he set about to force the Panama project before the House. Mr. Cromwell says: "We resolved to adopt an audacious and aggressive plan of exposition. We demanded a hearing under circumstances that made a refusal impossible," and public hearings were granted by Representative Hepburn on the 17th, 18th, and 19th of January. Using the words of Senator Morgan, Mr. Cromwell "took charge of the French forces as general in chief, legal counsel, diplomatic functionary, orator, and witness for the Panama Canal Co.," and both he and his partner, Curtis, "broke in with their statements when it was found necessary." One of their principal witnesses was Gen. Henry L. Abbot, who had been one of the American members of the reorganized French Canal Co.'s "international technical commission," but was at the time of his appearance before the House committee on the pay roll of the Panama Canal Co.

Foreseeing that the Nicaragua bill would pass the House and that the cause of Panama would be lost forever, in spite of the testimony he had brought before the House committee, Mr. Cromwell says that "in this desperate situation we conceived the plan of obtaining the appointment of a new canal commission with a view to examining the Panama Canal, as well as all the other routes." Then having, "by personal interviews and arguments," won over Speaker Reed, "Uncle Joe" Cannon, Representative Burton, and other Republican leaders to agree to this program, Mr. Cromwell tells the French arbitrators that he was able to get a bill passed creating the Isthmian Canal Commission (the second Walker Commission), "not only on account of the universal confidence which these members inspired, but also on account of their position and their great power in virtue of the parliamentary procedure of the Chamber." Mr. Cromwell would lead the French arbitrators to believe that he roped in Speaker Reed because "fortunately Mr. Curtis, who was a native of the same State as the Speaker, enjoyed his confidence."

The Nicaragua forces, led by Senator Morgan, at this juncture resorted to a flanking movement that threatened new disaster. They tacked the whole Nicaragua bill onto the rivers and harbors bill from the House, and passed it through the Senate by a vote of 50 to 3, on February 25, 1899. To meet this situation Mr. Cromwell says he conceived his "Americanization" scheme and induced M. Hutin, director general of the Panama Canal Co., to permit him to propose it officially to the United States.

Naively and condescendingly, in this proposal, Mr. Cromwell made his French client say that it would be willing to reincorporate in the United States under American law, but reserving the right to complete its enterprise with its own resources (bankrupt mendicant that it was!) and would grant to the United States the privilege of acquiring an interest in the stock ownership and a voice in its directorate.

Cromwell and Curtis saw Chairman Burton, of the House Rivers and Harbors Committee, on this proposition and secured a hearing on February 27, 1899, and Cromwell and Hutin presented it formally in writing to President McKinley on February 28, 1899.

The rivers and harbors bill, with the Senate amendment adopting the Nicaragua Canal project, went to conference. Representative Burton, directing the House conferees, stood by Mr. Cromwell's guns until the Senate, fearing to jeopardize the rivers and harbors bill, yielded in the last hours of the Congress, and on March 3, 1899, the law creating the second Walker Commission was finally passed.

"It was thus," says Mr. Cromwell, "that the imminent disaster was avoided and that the examination of the Canal of Panama was assured. * * * We believe ourselves justified in declaring that but for our labors this new commission would not have been formed, and the Nicaragua bill would have been adopted."

And Mr. Roosevelt says that the Panama route "commended itself to the deliberate judgment of the Congress."

Mr. Cromwell calls the attention of the arbitrators to his having made a study of the records of all the American engineers who might be candidates for this new canal commission, and to a letter he wrote to President McKinley, March 11, 1899, in which, so he tells the arbitrators, he confirmed the proposal to "Americanize" the French company. But he does not ask the arbitrators to notice and duly reward him for his insolent suggestion in this letter that Mr.

McKinley should not appoint Admiral Walker, Col. Hains, and Prof. Haupt, on the new commission because they had made one report in favor of Nicaragua, nor does he mention Mr. McKinley's answer to his insolence in naming all three of them in spite of his request. Mr. Cromwell does say: "Our first consideration was the composition of the commission itself * * * we prepared a list from which we judged the President could make a choice, in case he should ask for suggestions. We went to Washington and had interviews with Secretary Hay and President McKinley, to whom we declared our sole desire was to obtain an impartial commission. We refused to propose the appointment of anybody, but upon the demand of the President we furnished him the list of possible engineers which we had prepared. Later, when the commission was named, it was ascertained that the greater number of the engineer members of the commission were comprised in the list thus furnished."

The members of this second Walker Commission were Rear Admiral John G. Walker, United States Navy, president; Samuel Pasco, ex-Senator from Florida; George S. Morison, Lieut. Col. Oswald H. Ernst, and Col. Peter C. Hains, Corps of Engineers, United States Army; Prof. Lewis M. Haupt; Prof. William H. Burr; and Alfred Noble; and Prof. Emory R. Johnson, of the University of Pennsylvania.

The commission was organized June 15, 1899, and sailed for Paris on August 9, 1899. Their intention from the first, according to Mr. Cromwell, was to begin their investigations on the Isthmus of Panama, but there they would be within the zone of discussion and influence of the Nicaragua idea, so Mr. Cromwell claims credit before the French arbitrators for leading the commissioners to overturn all their plans and start in on the French company's books and maps in Paris, where he would "with the object of influencing its decision" (so Mr. Cromwell says) produce before the commission the distinguished English, French, German, and Russian engineers who had served on the French company's "international technical commission," and who were, of course, committed to the Panama route. Mr. Cromwell says he advised the company by cable when he had brought the Walker Commission to this decision, so that the company could be ready to receive the Americans in Paris.

Needless to say, Mr. Cromwell, "ubiquitous and ever present," as Senator Morgan described him, now qualified as an engineering expert, hastened to Paris, and "was present every day throughout this period."

After the Walker Commission left Paris, Mr. Cromwell says he remained several weeks conferring with officials of the company upon "the general business of the company, including its financial condition, its future, and its general plans; upon the subject of the organization of syndicates; upon the offer of sale which the Government of the United States had invited it to make; the possibility of obtaining from English, German, American, and other sources the capital desired for continuation of the work, and the divers eventualities that must be foreseen in view of the Isthmian Canal Commission's report, whether this were favorable or unfavorable."

It appears from this that, besides his syndicate schemes, which are described at length elsewhere, Mr. Cromwell had in mind other plans besides his patriotic and altruistic idea of giving the United States the "best possible" canal; he was willing to dicker with foreign capital to defeat the aim of his own country to secure a canal owned and controlled by the United States—reference to his own story will show that he was secretly working for a neutral canal, because Colombia demanded a neutral canal, and only by appeasing Colombia could he unload the French bankrupt on his own Government. Furthermore, even if the Walker Commission should report against Panama, he had no idea of giving up his fight.

The Walker Commission, after its return from Paris, and later from Panama, made the first proposal for acquiring the Panama route, by letter of April 16, 1900, wherein Admiral Walker formerly asked the French company on what terms it would sell its property and concession to the United States. The French company hesitated to sell, and on November 26, 1900, replied to Admiral Walker's inquiry of April 10, 1900, renewing the Cromwell proposal to reincorporate in the United States and permit the American Government to acquire representation in the company. The Walker Commission accordingly made its preliminary report November 30, 1900, favorable to Nicaragua, and setting forth that the French company had made no proposition whereby the United States could obtain ownership and control of Panama.

Mr. Cromwell tells in his story how he used the pending Hay-Pauncefote negotiations to stave off adoption of the Nicaragua route by the Congress of

1900–1. He was still, however, unable to induce his client to make an offer of absolute sale, so he turned again to Colombia to serve him in supplying an international diplomatic expedient.

"One part of our plan," says Mr. Cromwell, "consisted in getting Colombia to send to Washington a minister competent to take up the canal matter, and it was upon our urgent advice that the company gave instructions to its agent in Bogota to suggest this idea to the Colombian Government."

Mr. Cromwell then tells how he induced the Colombian consul general in New York, Mr. Arturo de Brigard, who was in charge of Colombia's diplomatic affairs in the United States in the absence of a legation representative in Washington, to cable to President Marroquin, of Colombia, "an urgent message to this effect, on December 3, 1900." Word came back from President Marroquin that Dr. Martinez-Silva, one of Colombia's foremost public men, then minister for foreign affairs, would be sent as minister to Washington. Mr. Cromwell proceeds:

"At our request, and after we had convinced him of the urgency of the matter, the consul general sent to Secretary Hay an official message, with which he transmitted a copy of President Marroquin's telegram, notifying him of the appointment of Mr. Silva, the minister, as envoy extraordinary charged with negotiating with the United States on the subject of Panama.

"Having succeeded in this respect, we took advantage of the fact to impress upon Secretary Hay that the negotiations between the United States, Nicaragua, and Costa Rica should not be concluded before the arrival of Minister Silva and before the Canal Co. had had an opportunity to enter into negotiations with him.

"Minister Silva reached New York in the middle of February, 1901, and his first call was upon Mr. Cromwell in our office; then began a series of conferences between the minister and ourselves which extended over several months, and of which we shall give the substance.

"Thanks to our conference with Mr. Silva, we early discovered that the canal concession would in any event necessarily be forfeited in 1910, by reason of the manifest impossibility of the company finishing the canal by that date, and that, in consequence, Colombia considered that in this matter it was her interest which ruled and which should be taken into consideration first of all; that the opinion of Colombia was opposed to a cession to a foreign Government, but the Government then in power was inclined to consider such an outcome, on the condition that it be based on conditions sufficiently advantageous to Colombia."

Mr. Cromwell, after telling how he explained all phases of the situation to Minister Silva, adds:

"Mr. Silva, convinced by our explanation and our arguments, agreed to them in principle, and in the course of an official call he paid upon Secretary Hay on March 13, 1901, informed the latter of his willingness to facilitate the plans of the United States if the conditions were of a nature to satisfy Colombia.

"This action of ours introduced a new element into the canal situation; that is to say, an official act of presence by Colombia, and a possible opportunity for the United States to acquire the Panama Canal, an opportunity suggested by the entrance of Colombia into the affair.

"We gave widest publicity to this incident. It had the effect of demonstrating more clearly to the public understanding the possibility of the United States acquiring the Panama Canal."

Mr. Cromwell says that for three months he or his partner, Mr. Hill, assisted in the negotiations between Admiral Walker, Minister Silva, and the president of the canal company, Mr. Hutin. The result of these conferences he summarizes as follows:

"(1) The Colombian minister consented that the company make an offer of sale to the United States, and Colombia announced to the United States that it was disposed to permit the United States to acquire the rights of the canal company, on condition that arrangements and treaties, the conditions of which should satisfy Colombia, should be concluded between Colombia and the United States.

"(2) In consequence, the canal company informed the minister of Colombia and the Isthmian Canal Commission that it would consent (upon the basis of such consent on the part of Colombia) to the cession of its concession to the Government of the United States, at a price which was not fixed but which should be decided by amicable agreement or by arbitration; and that over and above the purchase price of its property there should be added an indemnity for the eventual profits which its concessions would have put the company in a position to realize if it had constructed the canal."

Here we have the real genesis of the canal negotiations which "were initiated by Colombia"; this was the method of "urgent solicitation of the people of Colombia" cited by Mr. Roosevelt in his explanation to Congress of his dismemberment of a friendly nation.

Although Colombia sent a minister to negotiate for a canal treaty at the suggestion and instigation of Mr. Cromwell, it thought that it was entering into the bargaining with the United States with its eyes open. "It is very probable," said the Colombian foreign minister in his letter of instructions to Minister Silva, dated January 12, 1901, "that the American Government will make extraordinary demands of you, of which you will naturally give opportune advice to this Government, using the cable, so that in the most delicate cases you may operate with special authorization from the Government."

Minister Silva, as we have seen from Mr. Cromwell's story, called at once on Mr. Cromwell when he landed in New York. Thereupon Mr. Cromwell's first move was to try to unload on the Colombian Government part of the expense of his publicity campaign, and to utilize the new minister as an assistant to Roger Farnham, Cromwell's chief press agent. Less than three weeks after Minister Silva arrived he wrote to his Government, under date of March 7, 1901:

"At present what must be done * * * is to open an active press campaign for the purpose of changing public opinion, which is so decidedly in favor of Nicaragua, and to work directly on the men who dominate Congress and who manage the executive centers of politics. I am already taking measures for this, being advised by men who understand it; but I notify you that from now on this will need money. If the Government is not disposed to spend it, little or nothing can be accomplished."

Minister Silva's first reports to his Government indicate clearly the definite purpose of Colombia not to yield her sovereignty over the canal strip. He pinned his hopes then upon England's rejecting the American amendments to the Hay-Pauncefote treaty. He says in his letter of February 21, 1901:

"If England retracts all of her former policies and submits to the United States, we are out of the fight, and the Panama enterprise will be dead."

The Hay-Pauncefote treaty, then pending, introduced the clauses of the Constantinople convention neutralizing the Suez Canal, and the amedments proposed by the United States made reservations providing for American control of the canal in the interests of the national defense. Minister Silva considered his negotiations hopeless if England permitted America to control the canal absolutely, because Colombia would not cede her sovereignty and the United States would then turn to Nicaragua on account of her willingness to cede anything demanded. In his next letter Minister Silva, pursuing this discussion, tells his Government: "We will take hold of the skirts of the coat of John Bull and will see where we come out, but we will come out on the other side with splendor and profit."

In the diplomatic correspondence of this time we find light on the antecedents of another phase of the Panama affair which has caused endless dispute—the threat of Colombia to repudiate the extension of the canal company's concession to 1910. The Colombian Congress, having refused the extension, the late Dr. Nicolas Esguerra, one of the most celebrated international lawyers of South America, was sent to Paris as a special commissioner for Colombia to negotiate with the canal company. In Esguerra's absence, and without his approval, Carlos Calderon-Reyes, then minister of finance, a nephew of General Rafael Reyes, whose infamy later appears, granted the extension from October 31, 1904, to October 31, 1910.

In a letter to his Government of February 28, 1901, Minister Silva questions the legality of this extension, and suggests that the question be studied carefully with a view to refunding the 5,000,000 francs which the canal company paid for the extension, and terminating the concession in 1904. "It would be a terrific outrage," says Minister Silva, "if the Republic should have to sacrifice itself by recognizing the validity of that infamous contract, the work which was not based on necessities of war, but on secret thievery, and assisted by a cynical lie that Mr. Esguerra had recommended the granting of the extension. I have at hand the original communications which prove the contrary."

When the canal negotiations reached their critical stage in the summer of 1903, efforts were made to lead the American public to believe that Colombia, purely as an afterthought and without justification, considered and discussed—although it did not act upon—the suggestion of canceling this extension.

Mr. Cromwell was at this time still trying to induce his client to authorize his long-desired proposal of outright sale to the United States. Minister Silva was able to assist him by writing to President Hutin, of the canal company, April 29, 1901, in part as follows:

"To facilitate this (Isthmian Canal) commission in obtaining the means of presenting a complete report it would be proper that you, as representing the New Panama Canal Co., should tell me, at least in general terms, what are the bases, given the previous consent of the Government of Colombia, upon which the company would be disposed to transfer its concession to the Government of the United States."

President Hutin complied in part with this request, and at the same time called the attention of the Colombian minister to the restrictions in the canal company's concession under which "it could not, without the previous consent of Colombia, answer the questions which were put to it, nor the propositions which were made to it. By every means in our power," continued M. Hutin in this letter, "we have sought to bring about the necessary intervention of your Government. Your presence and your action, as authorized representative of the Colombian Government at Washington, establish the proper situation in which our company should be placed in order to discuss the questions presented by the Government of the United States."

Here again is the genesis of the canal negotiation clearly and officially stated: The American Government, through the Walker Commission, presented questions to the canal company which the canal company could not answer until it brought about, through Mr. Cromwell, the sending of a Colombian minister to Washington to authorize the negotiations.

President Hutin went on to state officially to Minister Silva that the company would transfer its concession to the United States if Colombia were willing, but he named no price. Nor was the Walker Commission able to get any definite price set by the canal company until a few days before it made its report the following November. Admiral Walker and Senator Pasco, for the canal commission, submitted to Minister Silva, on May 9, 1901, a memorandum of 18 points to be considered in the negotiations with Colombia, and on June 3, 1901, Minister Silva replied to the commission that he had submitted the memorandum to his Government and asked for instructions. This effectually tied up the report of the canal commission, which was exactly what Mr. Cromwell was seeking to accomplish through divers strategies.

Mr. Cromwell continued meantime, in season and out, insistently to urge the canal company to give the United States a definite price on its tottering concession, its streak of rust and scarcely begun ditch across the Isthmus, its antiquated buildings, useless machinery, and its heritage of scandal. His anxiety to induce them to sell, coupled with his syndicate operations, aroused finally the suspicion of his French employers until they became satisfied that he was trying to salvage the corpse of his own client, and on July 1, 1901, they dismissed him. President Hutin here took up and attempted to carry on without Mr. Cromwell's guidance the negotiations in the United States.

Until fall nothing definite was accomplished in the negotiations which continued between Minister Silva and the canal commission, but in the diplomatic notes of this period we learn something of the attitude of Colombia, especially toward the Isthmus of Panama. In Minister Silva's report to his Government of June 25, 1901, this appears:

"In studying the question of the canal and the Panamans, the Government of Bogota should take very much into consideration the particular interests of the inhabitants of Panama. For them the canal is a matter of life or death. It is possible that in the interior of Colombia this is regarded with relative indifference, but it would be the height of cruelty and short-sightedness to sacrifice the interests of an entire department to ideas such as have been proclaimed, or to mere fantasies. Interests so sacred and valuable, which represent the future of an entire people, can not be made the material of a political game. What can Colombia do, therefore, in benefit of the Isthmus? With what right can it offer opposition to provision by that section of the country for its primary necessities even should it reach the point of seeking annexation to the United States?"

Admiral Walker finally succeeded in pinning down the French Canal Co. to an offer to sell for $10,141,500 on November 4, 1901, and on November 16, 1901, the canal commission made its report to the President recommending the adoption of the Nicaragua route.

December 21, 1901, came the meeting of the Panama Canal Co. shareholders in Paris, followed by the resignation of Hutin and the substitution of Marius Bô, president of Credit Lyonnais, as president of the canal company.

January 4, 1902, five days before the Nicaragua bill passed the House by a vote of 309 to 2, President Bô cabled to Washington the offer to sell for $40,000,000.

The canal commission was pressing Minister Silva for a satisfactory answer as to the position of Columbia, and on January 8, 1902, Minister Silva wrote to his Government a long letter which he dispatched to Bogota by special diplomatic courier. In part he said:

"I have not told the representative here of the French company on what conditions the permission to transfer the concession would be granted, but it appears to me strictly just that they (the New Panama Canal Co.) should give a good sum to the Government of Columbia as, if permission is denied them, they will lose everything. Besides, as the company took advantage of the straitened circumstances of the Government to obtain an extension of six years, which is really what they are going to sell for $40,000,000, I do not think it would be contrary to what is equitable if we exact from them $2,000,000 more, in addition to the $1,000,000 which they paid (for the six years extension."

January 9, 1902, the House of Representatives passed the Hepburn bill for construction of the Nicaragua Canal, with only two dissenting votes, refusing to consider the Panama Canal Co.'s $40,000,000 offer. Mr. Roosevelt then called the members of the canal commission individually to the White House, and on January 16, 1902, the commission was reassembled and the supplementary report, recommending the Panama route at the price now offered, was presented. The motion to adopt this report was made in the meeting of the commission by George S. Morison, who was on intimate terms with Mr. Cromwell. (Morison first sent Ella Rawls Reader to Cromwell for counsel.)

Minister Silva having cabled his Government the offer of the Panama Co. to sell to the United States for $40,000,000, it was decided at Bogota to send another Minister, Dr. Jose Vicente Concha, to complete the negotiations. No reasons for this change appears in the Colombian diplomatic correspondence, excepting Minister's Silva's complant that he lacked definite instructions and his statement that if his Government did not repose sufficient confidence in him he was entirely willing to resign. Mr. Cromwell's explanation is that Dr. Silva was accused by his Government of having exceeded his powers in authorizing the negotiations between the canal company and the United States, and that he was too friendly to American inteerests. From subsequent events it appears also that Dr. Silva was too considerate of the welfare of the Department of Panama to meet the approval of the corrupt Marroquin administration. His successor, Dr. Concha, was a much different type of man and diplomat. Concha was erratically brilliant, though boorishly bitter in his antipathy toward North Americans. Mr. Cromwell describes the characteristics and equipment of Minister Concha as follows:

"Although brilliant, highly intellectual, and a former member of the cabinet, he was not only without acquaintance with the English language, but also absolutely without experience of the world outside of Colombia, for he never before had been out of his own country, nor had he seen the Isthmus of Panama. He took no part in the official life of Washington, and held himself apart from all those who were connected with the canal matter, whom he looked upon with distrust."

Noted in his own country for his capriciousness and his fiery temper, Dr. Concha was just the man to scatter thorns in Mr. Cromwell's diplomatic path.

In his official instructions, issued on January 22, 1902, Minister Concha was enjoined to obtain "the final adoption of the Isthmus of Panama for the opening of the Interoceanic Canal on the best terms for Colombia, without affecting the integrity of its territory or its national sovereigny." He was also authorized to confer with the Washington diplomatic corps to obtain an international control of the Panama Canal and a guarantee of its neutrality by all the powers. Concha's instructions further read: "If you obtain this international arrangement you will proceed to denounce the treaty of 1846 with the United States." Concha's supplemental instructions, issued in Bogota January 27, 1902, required his exacting not less than $20,000,000 from the canal company for Colombia's permission to transfer its concession, for the following reasons:

"1. Because Colombia's consent is essential, as without its consent the transfer would be void, and if made without its consent the French company, in penalty, would lose its rights;

"2. Because Colombia, by consenting to the transfer of the concession, would lose its expectation of acquiring the Panama Railroad at the expiration of the concession. This railroad was bought by the canal company for 93,000,000 francs ($18,600,000), and at the opening of the canal that would be lost, and

"3. Because in the new contract it is proposed that Colombia should renounce the participation it is now entitled to in the future earnings of the canal, which may amount to a million dollars a year."

This was the situation when Mr. Cromwell, through the intervention of Senator Hanna and others, was reinstated as general counsel, on January 27, 1902, and resumed his lobbying in Washington. The news of his reinstatement was conveyed to Mr. Cromwell by Philippe Bunau-Varilla, who was then in Washington, in the following telegram:

WASHINGTON, *January 27, 1902—10.20 a. m.*

CROMWELL,
Care Sullivan & Cromwell,
49 Wall Street, New York City.

Your affair was settled this morning Paris according to my recommendation, which I had to renew yesterday with great force. Felicitations.

BUNAU-VARILLA.

To which Mr. Cromwell replied:

NEW YORK, *January 27, 1902.*
(Received 2.15 p. m.)

PHILIPPE BUNAU-VARILLA,
New Willard, Washington, D. C.:

Many thanks for your kind message; when will confirmation be received by me? I returned from Washington Friday filled with deep concern. Not an hour is to be lost, and I will prepare to act at once. Expect important movement in our favor this morning and will give you details.

WM. NELSON CROMWELL.

Mr. Cromwell does not make clear in his story what was this "important movement in our favor" which he was expecting on the morning of January 27, 1902. He did not include these Bunau-Varilla telegrams in his little book. He had, however, been keeping busy all the time he was officially disconnected with the canal company's affairs. On the very day Mr. Cromwell received notice of his reinstatement Senator Scott, of West Virginia, introduced a joint resolution to appropriate $15,000 and create a special board to investigate the practicability of the Darien Canal route. Whether it was intended as an aid to Mr. Cromwell or was not, the Scott resolution served to divert attention from Nicaragua, which was all grist for the lobbyist's mill. And on the very next day, January 28, 1902, Mr. Spooner, of Wisconsin, submitted an amendment intended to be proposed by him to the Nicaragua bill which had passed the House, and it was ordered printed. This amendment, substituting the Panama for the Nicaragua route, was the basis of the Spooner law, under which the Panama Canal is being built.

The World can not say whether the "important movement in our favor" which Mr. Cromwell was expecting on the morning of January 27, 1902, was the Darien resolution of Senator Scott, which was introduced that day, or the Spooner amendment, which was submitted 24 hours later. Senator Spooner protested in the Senate, June 12, 1902, that he not only wrote the amendment that bore his name but devised it. Nevertheless, in a telegram which reached the French Canal Co. on January 31, 1902, Mr. Cromwell said:

"I have formulated a general plan of campaign * * * I have inspired a new bill which adopts our project and which sends to the President for decision all questions relative to titles and to the new treaty to be concluded with Colombia * * * I am working to have this bill passed by the two Chambers. My next step will be to obtain from Colombia precise and satisfactory conditions for the treaty with our Government."

Discussing the situation at the time he resumed his activities, Mr. Cromwell says that it was Colombia's plan to compel the canal company to pay heavily for permission to transfer its concession, or possibly to treat as void the extension of the concession to 1910 and obtain all of the pecuniary advantages for itself. Mr. Cromwell adds:

"Hence the necessity to frustrate the scheme of the Colombian Government against the company and to lead it (Colombia) to make a proposition to the United States became of supreme and vital importance."

We find further enlightenment on the genesis of these diplomatic negotiations which Mr. Roosevelt says were "initiated by Colombia" in the following excerpt from Mr. Cromwell's work:

"Neither of the Governments wanted to act, and yet, without some agreement between them the company's offer (to sell for $40,000,000) could not even receive consideration. So Mr. Cromwell, in person and without assistance, opened negotiations with the minister and impressed him with the necessity for a proposition as the basis of a treaty between Colombia and the United States, a proposition that must include the consent of Colombia to the cession" (of the canal concession).

This was before Dr. Concha's arrival and while Minister Silva was still in charge. Minister Silva finally did prepare a draft of a proposed treaty, which was not, however, presented to the State Department because Mr. Cromwell, as he relates, first read it and said its terms would be utterly unacceptable to the United States. Minister Silva proposed a 200-year lease of a canal zone at $600,000 a year, in addition to the $250,000 a year which the Panama Railroad was paying for its concession, and the eventual purchase of the railroad by the United States. Minister Silva said that even this proposal was much more generous than the attitude of his Government justified.

The Senate committee, of which Senator Morgan was chairman, was about to bring the Nicaragua bill to a vote and Mr. Cromwell found that, in order to stave off action, it would be necessary to get some formal proposition before the Government, so again he appealed to his friend Silva to draw up a fuller draft of his proposition, which he did. Mr. Cromwell says he "edited and corrected" this second draft, but just as Silva was about to present it to Secretary Hay he received his recall, and with the arrival of Concha came more trouble for Cromwell.

Dr. Concha, adopting quite naturally the "manana" tactics of his country, set himself down placidly in New York to let Uncle Sam and the canal company fret and wait. Meantime the Colombian Government, through its consul general in Paris, served notice on the canal company before the meeting of stockholders, February 28, 1902, to ratify the proposal of sale to the United States, that it could not make the transfer without Colombia's consent. Mr. Cromwell was much worried, because this action in Paris and the attitude of the new Colombian minister in refusing to proceed to Washington, present his credentials, and take up the treaty negotiations gave Congress the impression that Colombia was hostile. At Mr. Cromwell's behest Dr. Silva, who was remaining in Washington until Dr. Concha would consent to take his post, "continued with telegram and letter to urge Minister Concha, then in New York, to hurry his arrival in Washington," but all to no effect. Then Mr. Cromwell sent Facundo Mutis Duran, a Panaman, who for years had been local attorney under Cromwell on the Isthmus, to plead with the new minister. Concha received Mutis Duran with indifference. Mr. Cromwell then came from Washington to New York and himself called on Concha and spent all day of March 7, 1902, convincing him that Nicaragua would win out unless Colombia changed her attitude. As a result Concha consented to write to Mr. Cromwell stating that the notification to the Paris stockholders' meeting was not an indication that Colombia opposed the transfer of the concession, and that he would soon take up negotiating of a canal treaty. Thus again the situation was saved by the negotiations "initiated by Colombia."

While passing this period of disquietude and brain-fagging labor of Mr. Cromwell's it is interesting to note in the Colombian diplomatic correspondence two letters of Bunau-Varilla, one of February 7, 1902, to Minister Silva, the other of March 22, 1902, to Minister Concha, urging adoption of the same ideas Mr. Cromwell was endeavoring to have the Colombian Government accept. The incident is noteworthy only in view of the claims later made in the attempts to establish an alibi for the Panama lobbyist, that Bunau-Varilla and Cromwell were enemies.

But in spite of Bunau-Varilla and Mutis Duran and Silva and any other influences that Mr. Cromwell may have tried to bring to bear upon Minister Concha, neither the Colombian representative nor Secretary Hay would take any step toward negotiating a treaty, and "to save the situation" Mr. Cromwell "again personally took the initiative." And before the obstreperous Concha knew he had been caught, he, too, was eating straw in Mr. Cromwell's stable and performing in the biggest ring of Mr. Cromwell's diplomatic circus. Witnesseth Mr. Cromwell's unblushing tale.

"We overcame Minister Concha's repugnance of any discussion with an American, above all with a representative of the canal company, and at last we were asked by him to prepare any draft of a treaty that he might decide to propose. Mr. Cromwell devoted almost every day of the following month to discussion with the minister, at the latter's residence, and advised the minister as to all questions at issue, and he himself prepared the text of the draft of a treaty."

This was the forerunner of the treaty entered into, according to Mr. Roosevelt, "at the urgent solicitation of the people of Colombia."

The drafting of this treaty was no easy task, if we may believe Mr. Cromwell's narrative. "Little by little, in the course of the conferences which succeeded each other for weeks at a time," his story goes, "Mr. Cromwell led the minister to pledge himself as to different bases for a proposition, but until March 24, 1902, the best pecuniary conditions that Minister Concha cared to propose were $7,500,000 in cash and $600,000 a year beginning 15 years after the completion of the canal * * * and a limited lease."

Knowing that the United States would insist upon a perpetual lease, Mr. Cromwell says he devised the compromise of a lease renewable for 100-year periods. Mr. Cromwell's own narrative continues:

"Mr. Cromwell succeeded in obtaining the assent of Mr. Hay and Minister Concha to this proposition as necessary to constitute an element of the treaty. In all of these negotiations we were thinking especially of obtaining, as the object of prime importance in the negotiation, the assent of Colombia to the cession to the United States; and we inserted in the draft of the treaty a clause to this effect (Article I), and to it we obtained the consent of Minister Concha. Although that was a long step toward a definite proposition so essential to the interests of the company, the heavy pecuniary exactions, if maintained, would be fatal."

Therefore, Mr. Cromwell again sent Silva and Mutis Duran to labor with Concha, "but their efforts were fruitless."

The situation now, to use Mr. Cromwell's words, was "gravely perilous and disquieting." Minister Concha had not even seen the Secretary of State nor given him any assurances of the possibility of reaching an agreement, and Cromwell's allies, Hanna, Kittredge, Millard, and Pritchard, constituting the minority of the Senate committee that was holding out against the Nicaragua bill, lacked any basis for a minority report unless Mr. Cromwell could negotiate a satisfactory diplomatic excuse. If he permitted a treaty to be proposed with the exhorbitant pecuniary demands of Colombia it would kill the Panama project at once. Concha, so Mr. Cromwell says, confided to him that he was thinking of giving up his post and returning to Colombia without making any offer at all.

Here Mr. Cromwell's ingenuity came to the rescue, so he relates, with the suggestion to leave the amount of the annuity to Colombia to be determined later by arbitration. Mr. Cromwell's scheme of arbitration proves beyond question his patriotic watchfulness of his country's interests. He proposed that the United States and Colombia should each appoint two arbitrators, and if they could not agree—which, of course, they never could—they were to call in the then President of the Tribunal of The Hague. Thus Mr. Cromwell proposed to leave the amount the United States should pay to the future determination of a foreigner whose sympathies and interests would not be those of America. Nevertheless, such an expedient served Mr. Cromwell's temporary purpose to skid his negotiations over an apparently insurmountable obstacle.

With this suggestion incorporated, "Mr. Cromwell persuaded him (Concha) to sign the proposition and send it immediately to the Secretary of State; arranged for an interview for this purpose, and accompanied the minister to make the official presentation of it to the Secretary of State on March 31, 1902." Mr. Cromwell adds:

"This marked an important step toward the acceptance of the company's offer. It accomplished our purpose, which was to make the consent of Colombia enter into the domain of international relations and to supply the indisputable basis for obtaining the support of the Senate."

Later, when the Big Stick is swung to prevent Colombia's refusing this consent to transfer the canal concession, we see with what shrewdness Mr. Cromwell was insisting, thus early in his game, upon placing the consent within "the domain of international relations," in order to obtain for his client the protection of the United States in resisting Colombia's exactions.

Colombia's distrust of the United States found expression even in this first draft of a treaty. In articles 3 and 4 Colombia deemed it necessary for its own protection to compel the United States specifically to renew its guarantees under the existing treaty of 1846–1848, as follows:

"Article 3. All the stipulations contained in article 35 of the treaty of 1846–1848 between the contracting parties shall continue and apply in full force to the cities of Panama and Colon and to the accessory community lands within the said zone, and the territory thereon shall be neutral territory, and the United States shall continue to guarantee the neutrality thereof and the sovereignty of Colombia thereover, in conformity with the above-mentioned article 35 of the said treaty.

"Article 4. The rights and privileges guaranteed to the United States by the terms of his convention shall not affect the sovereignty of the Republic of Colombia over the territory within whose boundaries such rights and privileges are to be exercised.

"The United States freely acknowledges and recognizes this sovereignty and disavows any intention to impair it in anyway whatever or to increase its territory at the expense of Colombia or of any of the sister republics in Central or South America, but, on the contrary, it desires to strengthen the power of the republics on this continent and to promote, develop, and maintain their prosperity and independence."

Minister Concha's distrust is further reflected in the following extracts from his letter to the Colombian Foreign Minister, written April 1, 1902:

"The first thing that comes to one's mind in this respect, and especially on account of the present political situation of the Isthmus, is the imminent danger that there may take place a secession movement in that part of the Republic, either spontaneously or by reason of indirect suggestions of foreign interests, which would be a source of incalculable evils for the Republic. The opinion which prevails in the Department of Panama (Concha had never been in Panama, and his informants were Mr. Cromwell and Mr. Cromwell's Panaman employee, Mutis Duran) is very clear and decidedly in favor of the concession of the canal to the United States at any cost whatever; every day there is made clearer in all political parties on the Isthmus a sentiment of aversion, not to say of repulsion, to the Central Government; American influence, its language and its customs, are continually making headway in that region, and if an open resistance was opposed to the opinion predominating in the said department, a conflict would be precipitated which, on the contrary, would be avoided if a power, such as the United States, not only guaranteed the integrity of our territory, but also satisfied the by no means unreasonable desires of that portion of Colombia.

"But should the doors of our national territory be closed in hostility to the United States, it would in retaliation denounce, as the press has already suggested, the treaty of 1846, and once the undertakings of this treaty are removed, it (the United States) will view with complacency the events which will then take place in Panama, in order to occupy at once our territory, at the first interruption of the railroad service, or to embrace whatever tendency there may be toward separation whereby they will bring about a lesion of Colombian sovereignty of far greater consequence than any limitation to which the Republic may subject itself in the use of a given zone of its territory."

In a cable to his Government April 10, 1902, Minister Concha announced the failure of his efforts to bring about European intervention to neutralize the canal, at least so far as France was concerned. "The French ambassador," said Concha, "has informed me that his Government has prohibited his intervening in the affair of the Panama Canal." Concha added sarcastically in his cable: "What kind of a power is this that proceeds evasively and leaves the Government of the United States to be the arbitrator?" A day later Concha confirmed this cable and added that the Washington representatives of all the powers had taken the same position as the French ambassador.

Mr. Cromwell, meantime, "continued the negotiations for the purpose of obtaining the modifications of the Colombian proposition deemed necessary to get the approval of Congress." He acted, according to his own version, as the "sole intermediary for communications" between Secretary Hay and Minister Concha; he "edited the divers clauses several times over," until "about the middle of April we had brought about amendments to the proposition of March 31, which received the approval of the President and the Secretary of State. Among the important points of the protocol was the vital point of the consent of Colombia to the cession to the United States (Art. I)." How valuable this strategy was considered by Mr. Cromwell's client is shown by the following excerpt from President Bo's letter of April 16, 1902, thanking and complimenting Mr. Cromwell for his successful diplomacy:

"We especially appreciate the first article of the protocol by which Colombia gives our company the right to sell its property to the United States, which, in fact, abrogates articles 21 and 22 of our contracts of concession, which were opposed to us, and will permit us to resist the pecuniary pretensions of Colombia, to which we are absolutely determined."

Mr. Cromwell gives us this further light on the history of these diplomatic negotiations which Mr. Roosevelt said were "initiated by Colombia":

"As the result of these supplementary negotiations we drew up a new draft of the treaty (which is known under the name of the Hay-Concha convention of April 18, 1902), and had it officially transmitted to the Secretary of State by Minister Concha."

With this victory of diplomacy Mr. Cromwell did not, however, find himself out of the woods. His faithful friends, the minority of the Senate committee, insisted, even after President Roosevelt transmitted the Hay-Concha treaty to the Senate, upon having proof that the stockholders of the Panama Canal Co. would ratify the offer of sale for $40,000,000. This had not been obtained at the Paris meeting of February 28, 1902, because Colombia had served notice that the concession could not be transferred without permission. The company feared to call another meeting because Colombia might renew its warning at just the time when the treaty was under discussion in the Senate, and thereby cause the death blow to the Panama project.

To meet this emergency Mr. Cromwell says he conceived the idea of obtaining "from at least a majority of the shareholders of the company the written signatures of formal consent to the sale, with a definite pledge to ratify this sale at any general meeting convoked in the future for this purpose." These consents and pledges, Mr. Cromwell says, were obtained by the company and forwarded to him, and he was successful in inducing his friends in the Senate to accept this assurance in lieu of ratification by the shareholders.

According to Mr. Cromwell's story, this obtaining of the signatures of "at least a majority" of the 8,000 shareholders was accomplished some time between April 18, 1902, and the filing of the Hanna minority report at the end of May. The presence in Paris of Cromwell's partner, Curtis, at the end of April is noted in Mr. Cromwell's book. Mr. Curtis's name has always been connected with the reports of operations in France of the American syndicate in buying up the stock which the 8,000 Frenchmen were supposed to own when the United States bought the canal.

The next step was Mr. Cromwell's professed drafting of the Hanna minority report in favor of the "inspired" Spooner bill. "This report," Mr. Cromwell says, "after full consideration, was corrected, adopted, and signed by this minority." Mr. Cromwell had several hundred copies of it printed and distributed them to each Member of Congress, members of the Cabinet, and "also assured them circulation through other influential channels." Mr. Cromwell adds: "We annexed (to the Hanna report) a recapitulation drawn by us of the existing claims, concessions, etc., of the Maritime Canal Co. and of the Nicaragua Construction Co." as an argument against the Nicaragua route. Furthermore, the "minority adopted also textually and annexed to its report our opinion on the subject of the titles of the (Panama) company, its concessions, its power to cede, etc., and also gave to this opinion the seal of official use and approval." Mr. Cromwell adds that at least two of his firm were occupied during several weeks in compiling this minority report and securing its adoption.

One of Mr. Cromwell's distinguished services for which he laid claim to remuneration was the manufacturing of what Senator Morgan described in opening the Canal debate in the Senate, June 4, 1902, as a "cloud of volcanic smoke and ashes which the opponents of the measure outside of the Senate have brought as a funeral pall to place over its bier."

Mr. Cromwell had been preparing for several months an earthquake argument when Mount Pelee on May 8, 1902, conveniently erupted. He at once converted the catastrophe into his own advertising purposes, as did he also a report of an alleged eruption of Mount Momotombo, and an earthquake at Lake Managua on the Nicaragua route. Mr. Cromwell also made capital for Panama out of reports of Prof. Angelo Heilprin, the celebrated archaeologist of Philadelphia, whom he had hired to visit Nicaragua and Panama and write of the volcanic character of these regions. Prof. Heilprin's articles were quoted extensively in the "Hanna minority report." The history of Prof. Heilprin's employment is given by Mr. Cromwell as follows:

"The volcanic character of the region across which the Nicaragua route passed was utilized by us constantly as an argument against the choice of this way. Previously we had obtained the services of a distinguished savant, whose name is known all over America as that of a recognized expert on these subjects, who visited the countries of Nicaragua and Panama, and who later wrote articles upon this aspect of the question setting forth the dangers to which the Nicaragua route was exposed for this reason."

Mr. Cromwell also had prepared and printed maps graphically illustrating the earthquake zones, and had them sent to all the Senators. "These maps made prominent the fact," says Mr. Cromwell, "that volcanic eruptions characterized Central America, including Nicarague and Costa Rica, and that no volcanoes existed within 200 miles of the Panama route."

Mr. Cromwell's friend on the Isthmian Canal Commission, Mr. George S. Morison, also assisted in the earthquake campaign. The Hanna minority report quotes from a lecture delivered by Mr. Morison before the Contemporary Club, of Bridgeport, May 20, 1902:

"I do not believe that in the whole world there exists a location in which a repetition of the Martinique disaster is more probable than directly on Lake Nicaragua."

Another authority quoted in Mr. Cromwell's Hanna minority report was a dispatch from New Orleans, May 28, 1902, to a New York newspaper (Sun) stating that "passengers arriving from Guatemala brought this account of the Nicaragua earthquake and the activity of the Nicaragua volcanoes," etc. When Senator Morgan opened the canal debate on June 4, 1902, he quoted this dispatch and an editorial from the same paper, which he said had been manufactured concerning himself without foundation in truth. On this account Senator Morgan said he had inquired officially of the Nicaraguan minister, who cabled to his Government and received on June 3, 1902, the following reply:

"The news published about recent eruptions of volcanoes and earthquakes in Nicaragua entirely baseless."

Senator Morgan also read a letter from Secretary of State Hay of May 29, 1902, inclosing a dispatch from William Lawrence Merry, American Minister to Costa Rico, stating, under date of May 17, 1902, that "during the very serious seismic disturbances that have occurred on the west coast of the American continent and in the West India islands, the line of the proposed Nicaragua Canal and its vicinity has been exempt from this phenomena," and that "at Panama and on what is called the 'Spanish main,' earthquakes have recently been frequent and in some locations severe." Senator Morgan also read a letter directed to himself by Minister Merry, May 24, 1902, confirming the information he had communicated to the Secretary of State. Senator Morgan aso quoted the testimony of various witnesses before the Senate Committee to disprove the Cromwell—or what was then supposed to be the minority—argument. His remarks show clearly that he suspected the earthquake dispatch to the New York paper was originated in Cromwell's press bureau.

As an additional authority on the earthquake bugaboo, Mr. Cromwell's Hanna minority report quoted "a recent article" by Gen. Henry L. Abbot, with an elaborate tabulation of seismic disturbances in Central America. Gen. Abbot was also on Mr. Cromwell's staff. Originally he was one of the American members of the international technical commission of the New Panama Canal Co., and was retained by the company and brought from Paris to testify against the Hepburn Nicaraguan bill, and also before the Senate committee.

It is thus seen that Mr. Cromwell not only "inspired" (according to his own story) the Spooner bill and wrote the Hanna minority report in support thereof, but that he also employed the principal expert witnesses whose testimony was cited therein, if he did not actually, through his press bureau, as Senator Morgan suspected, manufacture the earthquake news which was "played up" in the Hanna report.

It is only necessary to read in the Congressional Record the report of the Senate debates on the substitution of the Spooner Panama amendment for the Hepburn Nicaraguan bill, June 4–19, 1902, to verify the accuracy of Mr. Cromwell's claims to the French arbitrators. Mr. Cromwell says:

"During all the time of this struggle two, at least, of the members of our firm, with other assistants, were in constant conference with the Senators and helped them to reply to the arguments advanced against Panama in the course of the debate, giving information in support of this project, as well as furnishing arguments and information in replies to the arguments advanced in favor of Nicaragua; calling on Senators and presenting arguments to them * * * and by all possible means increasing and strengthening the support of Panama. As fast as the discussion progressed we pased in review every detail of the debate and all the changes in the affair, which were the object of advice and suggestion on our part."

One of Mr. Cromwell's signal services was the attempt to refute the argument against adoption of the Panama route that it would be impossible for sailing vessels, on account of the calms prevailing in the Gulf of Panama, and not so advantageous as Nicaragua because of the greater distance between American ports on the Atlantic and Pacific via the Panama route. "At our suggestion," says Mr. Cromwell in his tale, "Senator Hanna authorized us to obtain" the testimony of the shipowners and captains of vessels as to which route they would prefer to use. Twenty-eight questions were submitted to some 80 men, ranking from fourth officers to captains, and their names, rank, and ship, in a tabulated statement that is a delight to the printer, were all read into the Congressional Record by Senator Hanna, together with a summary of their answers. The questions which Mr. Cromwell says he drew up and sent out purported to be based on the conditions specified for the two canals by the Walker Commission, but they were, as a matter of fact, grossly misleading, and upon Cromwell's false hypotheses the questions were answered. Senator Perkins, of California, replying to Senator Hanna, said:

"When we consider the nature of the data on which the questions were based not much wonder may be felt at the character of the answers, for the data in the two most important cases were misleading. In fact, the proposition placed before the captains is so widely misleading that the answers that they gave on the comparative difficulties of navigation have no material bearing on the conditions as they will exist when the canal is constructed."

The two propositions which Senator Perkins protested especially as misleading were (1) the curvature of the canals, which was falsely stated to be "three times sharper" on Nicaragua than on Panama; Senator Perkins showed that this exaggerated by 25 per cent the relative curvatures reported by the canal commission; and (2) that sailing vessels, if towed 140 miles out of Panama Bay, would be outside the belt of calms. Senator Perkins cited the evidence to prove that this, also, was a false hypothesis.

Mr. Cromwell says of the earthquake argument and the seamen's answers that they "constituted a splendid basis for the operations, a basis without which the best friends of Panama would not have been disposed to continue to uphold the cause of Panama, which would have resulted in a victory for Nicaragua."

Senator Perkins thought Senator Hanna himself had drafted these hypothetical questions, and consequently that their hypotheses were "unintentionally" misleading, but Senator Morgan said in closing the canal debate that he thought he detected Cromwell's "fine Italian hand" in these very questions—and he lacked Mr. Cromwell's boasting confession to guide him to this opinion.

Senator Mitchell, of Oregon, likewise scented the lobbyist's taint upon Mr. Hanna's speech while he was in the midst of it, and interrupted him after Mr. Hanna had read the eighteenth question to the seamen and their summarized answer to inquire where the testimony came from; whether through the Senate committee or otherwise? Nearly two columns of the Congressional Record (pp. 6384-5, vol. 35, pt. 7, 57th Cong., 1st sess.) are burdened with the colloquy between Senators Hanna and Mitchell in the Oregon Senator's vain endeavor to learn the source of this testimony. Senator Hanna kept evading: he reiterated that the questions were put to the men in writing and were answered in writing. Senator Mitchell pressed his inquiry until Senator Hanna retreated to the following (in the light of Mr. Cromwell's confession) equivocation:

"Mr. MITCHELL. Does the statement which the Senator is reading give the name of the person who asked the questions?

"Mr. HANNA. No; it does not give the name of the person who asked the questions. It was not confined to one person. I used whatever means of acquaintance I have in vessel circles. I have had a great deal of such experience, and I know of many of those people myself personally. I have written letters to vessel owners and vessel captains, and I have asked the companies who sail these big ships to give me the facts, and in writing in answer to written questions the facts are given in writing by the men who navigate their ships."

Then Senator Harris of Kansas took a hand in Mr. Hanna's discomfiture. Quoting again from the Congressional Record:

"Mr. HARRIS. I should like to know whether the Senator will say now who is the person who propounded the proposition that the curvature in one canal is three times as sharp as it is in the other.

"Mr. HANNA. That is a pretty sharp question.

"Mr. HARRIS. But it is easily answered, Mr. President, if the Senator desires to answer it.

"Mr. HANNA. Well, I decline to answer further. I have not got down to such details as that."

Senator Hanna proceeded then to read Mr. Cromwell's remaining 10 questions and answers, and, in discussing them at length, made this further equivocation:

"Knowing that, and appreciating fully the dangers and delays in the operation of a canal like this, and not wishing to claim a standing here as an expert, I took advantage of my acquaintance with those connected with the great maritime interests of this country to obtain these facts, not with a view of producing evidence to gain a simple point, but to submit them to my colleagues as facts, vouched for by myself as correctly taken, and in written form open to your examination."

Knowing that Mr. Cromwell, upon his own suggestion and with the consent of Mr. Hanna, procured the answers of the 80 seamen, addressed direct to the Ohio Senator, and having Mr. Cromwell's word for how closely he was directing the Senate debate, another series of questions and answers which Mr. Hanna read into the Congressional Record falls under suspicion. They appear in Senator Hanna's closing speech of June 18, 1902, in refutation of arguments of various advocates of the Nicaragua route. There were 11 of these interrogatories, addressed to members of the Isthmian Canal Commission, of whom all made written reply to Senator Hanna, excepting Prof. Emery R. Johnson and Prof. Lewis M. Haupt. It does not appear from the record whether these members were interrogated. These 11 questions, which Senator Hanna said he prepared himself, are not claimed by Mr. Cromwell in his interesting document as services which he performed for the New Panama Canal Co. Nevertheless the manner of presenting their answers is nearly identical with the system of Mr. Cromwell's marshaling the 80 seamen's replies to his 28 questions.

So keenly alive to Cromwell's activities was Senator Morgan that on the last day of the canal debate he openly accused Cromwell of having written the "Hanna minority report," and the accusation went unchallenged.

From Mr. Cromwell's own boasts, and statements made to the World by an intimate friend of the late Senator Hanna, the suspicion of Cromwellian taint rests upon nearly every speech made in the Senate in favor of the Spooner amendment. In his account of his supervision of the final debate in the Senate Mr. Cromwell makes to the French arbitrators this false statement:

"All the members present in the Senate participated in the debates, and a great many among them made long speeches which had been prepared in advance."

Only 17 Senators made speeches, and very few outside their number so much as interrogated those who participated in the debates. The alignment was:

For Nicaragua—Morgan of Alabama, Mitchell of Oregon, Harris of Kansas, Turner of Washington, Perkins of California, Stewart of Nevada, Hawley of Connecticut, Pettus of Alabama, Clark of Montana.

For Panama—Hanna of Ohio, Fairbanks of Indiana, Cullom of Illinois, Kittredge of South Dakota, Gallinger of New Hampshire, Spooner of Wisconsin, Teller of Colorado, Allison of Iowa.

The four most formidable and carefully prepared speeches in favor of Panama were made by Hanna, Kittredge, Gallinger, and Cullom. A close political friend of the Ohio Senator has admitted (Senator Dick to Mrs. Annis Riley Hale) that Cromwell wrote Hanna's speech, if not in its entirety, at least in greater part. Even to the subheads, which appear in the Congressional Record in approved newspaper fashion, the Hanna speech is a strong testimonial to the efficiency of Mr. Cromwell's bureau of seismography, engineering, editorial advertising, diplomacy, legislation, and law. Mr. Hanna spoke from manuscript. The speeches of Kittredge, Gallinger, and Cullom also appear carefully subheaded, while on the Nicaragua side this style of editing appears in the Record only in Senator Mitchell's address.

Both Senators Hanna and Kittredge, who were Mr. Cromwell's most valuable allies, emphasized that Colombia had consented, in the Concha draft of a treaty (drafted by Mr. Cromwell), to the transfer of the canal concession to the United

States—the consent which Mr. Cromwell, for his own ends, had labored to bring within the realm of diplomatic negotiations and international relations.

Senators Kittredge and Cullom both called attention to and quoted from Cromwell's letter to Secretary Hay, which accompanied Concha's draft of a treaty, March 31, 1902. Mr. Cullom, by the way, made a speech in favor of the Nicaragua route in the Senate in 1894.

Senator Gallinger quoted at length from Gen. Henry L. Abbot in support of the earthquake bugaboo, but left it for Senator Morgan to direct attention to Gen. Abbot's being on the Panama Canal Co.'s pay roll. Senator Gallinger's answers to some of Senator Morgan's arguments cause one now reading the Congressional Record to refer queryingly to Mr. Cromwell's story where he tells of "furnishing arguments and information in replies to the arguments advanced in favor of Nicaragua." In like manner one wonders whence sprang Seator Kittredge's answers to the arguments of Senator Turner, who spoke for Nicaragua. And still the allies of Mr. Cromwell in the Senate attacked the Nicaragua forces with the charge that the witnesses who had appeared in behalf of that route were partisan and prejudiced.

Senator Gallinger read into the Record an entire article in the Medical News of January 4, 1902, on "Sanitary Aspects of the Panama and Nicaragua Canal," by Dr. George A. Soper, Ph. D., of New York. If this article was not originally inspired by Mr. Cromwell's press bureau it was about the only authority cited in the whole debate that did not bear the Cromwell brand.

Senators Spooner and Fairbanks appear to have spoken in extemporaneous debate. They confined themselves mainly to legal phases of the canal negotiations. Nothing in their speeches indicates that they were acting merely as chartered phonographs for the Panama lobby. Both vigorously condemned Prof. Lewis M. Haupt for abandoning his championship of the Nicaragua route. They did not consider legitimate his excuse that he signed the supplemental report in favor of Panama in order to make the report of the Isthmian Canal Commission unanimous. It was not publicly known at that time, however, that the chairman of the commission, Admiral Walker, had called Prof. Haupt out of the commission's meeting and pleaded with him to sign the report, stating that President Roosevelt demanded a unanimous report because he feared a divided report would be used by the transcontinental railroad lobby to prevent any canal legislation; and no one said in the Senate in defense of Prof. Haupt that he signed the report on this account and stipulated his reasons in the minutes of the commission. Neither was it publicly known then—because Mr. Cromwell hadn't yet written his confessions—that it was Mr. Cromwell's Panama lobby, not the transcontinental railroad's (unless Mr. Cromwell's lobby was serving both the French canal and the transcontinental interests at the same time and collecting fees from both sides) that had blocked canal legislation for years.

Nor was it known at this time that Mr. Cromwell, in 1900, after he had been permitted to amend the Republican platform in the interest of the Panama route, had contributed $60.000 to the Republican national committee, of which Senator Hanna was chairman—$60,000 which Mr. Cromwell later charged up as a "necessary expense" to the New Panama Canal Co. and asked that company to pay. Consequently when Senator Hanna presented the Hanna minority report there was no suspicion, save in the minds of such men as Senator Morgan, that Cromwell had drafted it, nor that he had written Senator Hanna's speech. To none, save those like Senator Morgan who suspected the hypocrisy, was there significance when Senator Hanna, opening the Panama battle on June 5, 1902, said to his fellow Senators:

"In the report of the minority of the committee, after careful study, research, and preparation, we have put before the members of this body a report which I believe covers every question in point, and were I to have my choice as a matter of argument, I would prefer to read that report. Therefore I can only urge upon all Senators to take my advice and read it carefully." (P. 6317, pt. 6, vol. 35, Congressional Record, 57th Cong., 1st sess.)

Doubtless very nearly all of Mr. Hanna's colleagues who followed him in deserting Nicaragua for Panama believed that the rugged and honest Ohio Senator, and not the crafty Panama lobbyist, was speaking when Senator Hanna said:

"I repeat—and I repeat it with pride as an American citizen—that the inspiration of this great work does not come from any selfish or narrow motive. * * *

"I wish to have it understood * * * that those of us who have joined in the minority report (Hanna, Pritchard, Millard, and Kittredge) have merely sought to give to this body the result of our judgment as to what is for the best interest of our country—the whole country." (P. 6387, pt. 7, vol. 35. Congressional Record, 57th Cong., 1st sess.)

Again Senator Hanna assured his colleagues:

"There is no politics, there is no sectionalism, there is no partisanship in this project."

And again he declared:

"I am anxious that every man before he votes upon this question shall decide it for himself in view of all the conditions and environments, because the country expects us collectively and individually to do the best thing for its interests."

Perhaps not curiously Senator Hanna let slip this testimonial in support of Mr. Cromwell's later claim that it was his lobby and his press agency that foisted Panama upon the United States:

"Mr. President, that (the Panama offer to sell for $40,000,000) brought into this question an entirely new factor, a feature that never was considered for one moment in the debate in the House. But through the discussion in the newspapers and the gossip in the corridors members of that body come to know something about it and that something new was coming" (p. 6379), which led Senator Morgan to remark (p. 6662):

"It seems not to have come through the door of the sheep cote, but by some back way. * * * That is not surprising, for in this effort to build a canal for the American people something new has all the time been coming, and up to this last intervention by cable, of this mighty sacrifice to prevent Congress from destroying the country by building the Nicaragua Canal, these new obstructions have not failed to arrive in time to prevent Congress from this reckless delinquency."

Senator Morgan was suspicious of the origin of the Spooner amendment, reported favorably with the "Hanna minority report." Speaking on the order of business on June 11, 1902 (p. 6609), the Alabama Senator referred to it as "the amendment accredited to the Senator from Wisconsin." On June 12, 1902 (p. 6657), he again referred to it as "the amendment that has been offered here in his name." Senator Spooner at once demanded to know of the Senator from Alabama: "Does he mean that I am not the author of it?"

"Mr. MORGAN. I am satisfied the Senator wrote it.

"Mr. SPOONER. And the Senator was the author of it.

"Mr. MORGAN. Of course. (Oh, senatorial courtesy!)

"Mr. SPOONER. And not only wrote it, but devised it."

The World does not propose here to go over the ground of the canal debate as to the respective merits of Panama and Nicaragua. It neither seeks nor suggests reopening that question. But it is necessary to cite at some length the debate of Senator Morgan to show how clearly and precisely the United States was warned against Cromwell and his Panama scheme.

Opening the final debate in the Senate June 4, 1902, Senator Morgan said:

"In this $40,000,000 gift to a corporation of France, under the guise of a purchase of property that inevitable bankruptcy induces them to sacrifice in order to divert the proceeds from their honest creditors into their own pockets, there is much circumspection necessary if we would not disparage the fair name of the United States by greedily seizing a proffered bauble, gilded with fine gold, but full of corruption" (p. 6278).

Directing his sarcastic shafts aginst the Cromwell press agency, whence came the pamphlets which flooded the Senate, Senator Morgan told, on June 14, 1902, of having found on his desk a copy of the pamphlet, "Comparative Characteristics (construction and operation) of Panama and Nicaragua," by Philippe Bunau-Varilla, formerly chief engineer of the Panama Canal, later minister from the Republic of Panama, Senator Morgan proceeded:

"I have seen nothing so elegant in letterpress and illustration, unless it is the edition of the report of the minority of the Committee on Interoceanic Canals, placed upon our desks, which is handsome enough to be the repository of the argument of the first-class New York railroad lawyer, whose opinion is added to that report to give it the weight of his approval. I refer to Mr. Cromwell, who, it is said, has saved many a wrecked railroad company through his great skill as professional osteopathist—legal bonesetter for railroad companies—as to some of which he is credited with having broken their homes a second time, to the great increase of his reputation and income.

* * * * * * *

"He (Bunau-Varilla) is also a stockholder in the (Panama Canal) company, and was finding great fault with M. Hutin as to his management. Hutin was too stiff and deliberate. Mr. Philippe Bunau-Varilla wanted small investment and quick returns.

"If, added to his other labors, he had a part in engineering the slump in the price of the property from $109,000,000 to $40,000,000, of which $2,000,000 is for maps and literature, with 10 per cent added for omissions and contingencies (estimate of the Isthmian Canal Commission), it would be sad to think that his masterpiece of deception should not be paid for out of the map-and-literature fund that we are invited to tax our people to pay by passing the Spooner substitute before the Senate.

"But I suppose it is none of our business who is to get the $40,000,000 when we get rid of it. We appear to be out for a sharp bargain, and will be satisfied if we can get the property and escape responsibility for the application of the funds by the alleged trustee with whom we are dealing" (p. 6795).

On June 17, 1902, Senator Morgan trained his batteries on Cromwell. After outlining the manner in which President McKinley served notice on Great Brtain by negotiating protocols with Nicaragua and Costa Rica, December 1900, while the Hay-Pauncefote discussion was still pending, Mr. Morgan said:

"There were still other embarrassments that he (President McKinley) encountered. The chief of these was the artful, persistent, and intrusive overtures and supplications of the Panama Canal Co., assisted by its powerful allies, the Transcontinental railroads. The entire group, in one solid agreement, which included all the railroads from the Canadian Pacific to the Panama Railroad, brought all their power to bear upon the President, and have never ceased their opposition to these agreements. He stood firm while life lasted.

"Further on in my observations I will trace the insidious course of the Panama Canal Co., that never pursued any course which did not leave in its trail the marks of disaster and the stain of discredit. Mr. McKinley knew its odious history as well as any man that lived, and he despised it as thoroughly. * * * He had studied the report of the committee of which Hon. John R. Fellows was the chairman, dated March 3, 1893, made to the House, of which Mr. McKinley was then a member, and he knew the story of peculation and bribery and of the monopolistic agreements of the Panama Canal Co., laid bare in that document. * * *

"That was while De Lesseps was in the full tide of his glory and was permitting hundreds of millions of French money to be squandered in corrupt contracts. And it was during the time that the American committee of the Panama Canal Co. were the dispensers of French money in Washington. Mr. McKinley had even been worried and badgered by Cromwell and other agents of that company by letters thrust upon him that I will presently read to the Senate.

* * * * * * *

"He knew of the report of the Senate Committee on Interoceanic Canals, of May 16, 1900, of which the Senator from Ohio (Hanna) was a member, and that the committee denounced the Panama Canal Co. in the terms which I will now quote and in other censures of like character. That committee reported thus:

"This manifest purpose of this company to interfere with legislation by asking the President to inform Congress of a state of facts, as alleged, of which Congress is 'presumably without knowledge,' is an insult to the intelligence of Congress. It is an insolent invitation to the President to control the action of Congress so that they shall not act upon bills reported by committees in both Houses. * * *

"It is a spectacle that is, happily, without precedent, that this foreign corporation, acting in a foreign country and without any recognition even of the honesty of its dealings, while it has all the time been the subject of distrust by our Government, should ask the President to 'advise the Congress of the facts of the case' for the purpose of opposing Congress in declaring and enforcing the public policy of our people and Government.

"A bill that the House had agreed to consider on the 1st and 2d days of May, 1900, is severely censured by this speculating corporation, because its passage would destroy the hope of that company of unloading a failing enterprise upon the United States under its proposal of February 28, 1899, which is again renewed in this letter.

"Aside from the fact that said proposal contains suggestions that provide for the robbery of the stockholders of the 'old company' and the violation of the decrees of the courts of France, it proposes a direct violation of the statutes of Colombia, enacted in granting the concessions to that company, and a breach of our treaty of 1846 with Colombia, which binds us to guarantee the sovereignty of that territory over the State of Panama.

"The President has never answered said overture, nor has he responded to the suggestions and requests contained in the letter from Sullivan & Cromwell of April 30, 1900, but the Secretary of State has sent that letter to the chairman of the Committee on Interoceanic Canals * * *" (p. 6922).

Further on in Senator Morgan's address of June 17, 1902, we find:

"The most humiliating and repulsive feature of this entire situation to the people of the United States is the direct, constant, and offensive intrusion of the Panama Canal Co. into the legislation of Congress, the hearings of committees, the deliberations of canal commissions, and the frequent presentation of letters of advice and remonstrance to the Secretary of State and to the President, rebuking the conduct of the House of Representatives and its ignorance.

"The accusation of the ignorance of the House of Representatives has been so harped upon by the agents of the Panama Canal Co. that it has grown into a bad habit, into which the Senator from Ohio (Mr. Hanna) has fallen, inadvertently, of course."

Senator Morgan had reference to Mr. Hanna's statement, on June 9, 1902, that "When the Hepburn bill passed the House of Representatives I do not believe there were 25 men in that body who had ever read that report (of the Isthmian Canal Commission), brief as it was, and scores of them have told me since that they knew nothing about it, except that they were voting for what they supposed to be a canal." Senator Morgan condemned this statement of Senator Hanna's as manifestly inaccurate and unjust to the coordinate legislative body.

Continue Senator Morgan's attack on Cromwell and his company:

"Two leading characters have had charge of this campaign of false pretenses and misrepresentations—M. Hutin and Mr. Cromwell, who is general counsel for this company, and has a large experience in the hospital treatment of infirm corporations.

* * * * * * *

"He (Hutin) was in bad shape to face the storm that came upon him when the House passed the second Hepburn bill, now before the Senate. When it broke upon him he stood by the $109,000,000, which was the value of the canal and railroad property as it had been appraised, and refusing to join the set that intended to capture the $40,000,000 for their own purposes, they turned him out of office and determined to become voluntary bankrupts, but to reserve the $40,000,000 from their schedule of their assets.

"M. Hutin disappeared when his scheme failed, but Mr. Cromwell followed the sinking ship and kept a sharp lookout for the salvage.

* * * * * * *

"The only hope left to the New Panama Canal Co. was to sell out to the Government.

"To accomplish this feat was the loved task of Mr. Cromwell. This new movement, which was made indispensable by the flat refusal of the French people to be a second time victimized, required adroit manipulation, and no one was so adroit as Mr. Cromwell.

"He also had a keen appreciation of the humor of the little Sunday-school girl who, being asked to recite a Bible story, said: 'The Bible does not tell stories. It tells the truth. It says that a lie is an abomination unto the Lord and an ever-present help in time of need.'

"Mr. Cromwell opened his campaign of deception as to facts and concealment as to motives by giving to the President information of the excellent condition and bright prospects of the New Panama Canal Co." (p. 6927).

Senator Morgan then read into the record Mr. Cromwell's first letter to President McKinley, November 18, 1898, of which he said: "No description of this letter would do justice to its apparent innocence, which is only the veneer of its crafty diplomacy. There is nothing like it that I have ever seen in any lawyer's brief before."

Cromwell, said Senator Morgan, proceeded to magnify this missive to President McKinley into the importance of a great state paper and its presentation into the dignity of a solemn state function. Senator Morgan then proceeds:

"What was the alleged purpose of all this parade? Only to give information of the splendid condition and happy prospects of the New Panama Canal Co.? * * * Why did he venture on the gratuitous falsehood that this company became 'the sole owner of all the canal works, plant, material, concessions, and other property of the old company,' and that 'the title of the undersigned is therefore unquestionable and has been recognized by the Government of Colombia'? Both of these statements were false. But what interest could the united statements serve if it was not the purpose of Cromwell, when the letter was written, to dispose of the canal property to the United States?"

Senator Morgan answered his own question thus:

"Cromwell knew that otherwise Mr. Hay could have no interest in this spectacular advertisement of the canal.

"Why should he add the false statement that 'the condition of the new company is equally satisfactory; that the company has no mortgage of bonded indebtedness; the property is free from all encumbrances; the company has no other debts than monthly pay rolls; its cash reserve is largely in excess of its actual needs?'

"These statements are apparently so gratuitous and so foreign to any interest of the United States in the subject that the presentation of them would be a ridiculous parade of boastful nonsense if there was no other design except to give information to the United States.

"The covert meaning of this approach to the President is found in the last paragraph of his diplomatic epistle, as follows:

"'The undersigned company also invites your attention to the provisions of its concession, particularly Articles V and VI, which reserves all rights to the United States secured by treaty with the Republic of Colombia signed in 1846 and ratified in 1848.'"

Senator Morgan then introduced another letter of Cromwell's, directed to Secretary Hay, December 5, 1898, concerning the propagation of the company's concession in Bogota, which he said made plain what Cromwell was driving at. Senator Morgan proceeded.

"The canal company fancied that it saw in this revolt (the civil war in Colombia, precipitated largely by the canal company's efforts to get its concession extended), which is still flagrant, the opportunity to turn over the canal to the United States, so that in protecting the canal it would be protecting its own property.

"It was a bold movement of the reckless lawyer to involve the United States in a war, if need be, to get rid of this property by selling it, or an interest in it, to the United States. This ugly device was received in silence by Mr. McKinley, and Mr. Cromwell was thrown upon his ingenuity to arrange another coup.

* * * * * * *

"But to follow Mr. Cromwell. When he found that he could not inveigle the United States into the dishonorable scheme of capturing the canal and railroad, because we had engaged to protect them, and that to own them would be the easiest way to protect them, the canal company then broke up the peace and unity of the Colombian Government, as I have shown from admissions in his own (Cromwell's December 5, 1898) letter, by buying the consent of the President to sign an extension of the concession that Congress had refused to ratify. There is where that Government went to pieces; that is the rock on which it broke, and it stays there yet.

"The French people were still unwilling, notwithstanding this extension, to put any more money into the canal, and he again approached the President of the United States with a proposition for the joint ownership of stock in the New York or New Jersey corporation under the title of the New Panama Canal Co. of America.

"To accomplish this project it was becoming, in his opinion, to boast more loudly than ever of the wealth and power of his company and also to make a side lick at its rival, the Maritime Canal Co. That letter carries its own interpretation, and it will be seen, as it is read, that it is the last bid of a desperate gambler in corporation stocks."

Senator Morgan then read into the Congressional Record the proposal of Cromwell and the New Panama Canal Co. to the President, February 28, 1899—Cromwell's proposal to "Americanize" the French bankrupt and permit the United States to acquire an interest in it—and then Cromwell's letter of March

11, 1899, asking the President to appoint no one on the new Isthmian Canal Commission who had previously declared himself in favor of Nicaragua. President McKinley proceeded to reappoint all three members of the first Walker Commission. "That," said Senator Morgan, "was his way of answering such insolence."

Next, Senator Morgan read the testimony of Gen. Abbot and further correspondence of Cromwell's. The Congressional Record proceeds:

"Mr. MORGAN. Mr. President, these statements establish positively that all the movements of Mr. Cromwell, from the beginning of his conduct of the affairs of the company in the United States, were directed to the purpose of defeating the Nicaraguan Canal movement, whether by the Government or by the Maritime Canal Co. If the Nicaraguan Canal could be defeated, the way was open to the Panama Canal, and, in any event, they had a paying property in the Panama Railroad.

* * * * * * *

"The later letters, which I have just read, show that when Cromwell failed to ensnare the President with his New Jersey corporation scheme, he attacked the lion in his den and made direct and almost open war on the Nicaragua Canal bill.

* * * * * * *

"On the 18th of January, 1899, the House committee, of which Mr. Hepburn was chairman, began a full and searching examination of the whole subject of the canal.

"Mr. William Nelson Cromwell was the first witness to be examined, and he took charge of the French forces as general in chief, legal counsel, diplomatic functionary, orator, and witness for the Panama Canal Co.

* * * * * * *

"Mr. Cromwell was assisted by Mr. Curtis in conducting the examinations, and both broke in with their statements when it was found necessary.

* * * * * * *

"In the meantime, on December 1, 1900, President McKinley had entered into agreements with Costa Rica and Nicaragua which he knew would close the controversy and shut off Mr. Cromwell's intrusions into legislation relating to the canal.

"The President passed to his new and greater estate believing that he had settled the canal question, if Congress would authorize the President to acquire the right to do so from Nicaragua and Costa Rica.

"He understood the reasons for the choice he made as well as any man who has survived him, having been fully informed by Mr. Cromwell and other agents of the Panama Canal Co. as to every fact and plea and finesse and misrepresentation they had to make. It is a shameful reflection on Mr. McKinley to say that he did not have the opportunity to understand the Panama route when he chose the Nicaragua route.

"But what respect has Mr. Cromwell, or anyone who is opposed to any canal, for the decision made by Mr. McKinley, when the occasion is again presented for further delay and final defeat of the will of the American people at the behest of the great railroads?"

Senator Morgan then pictured Cromwell taking up his new "rôle of chief negotiator for Colombia, in formulating the draft of the proposed convention," and referred to Cromwell's explanatory letter which accompanied the Concha treaty draft as "attended with a disgusting cajolery and sycophancy that only too well indicates that it is intended to mislead Congress."

Of Cromwell's course in his diplomatic campaign Senator Morgan said: "I refer only to what the record discloses of his action. I would not dare to follow him when he is not on the surface." The record proceeds:

"Mr. Cromwell's final appearance, in the open, in his letter of indorsement and explanation appended to the report of the minority of the committee. (The "Hanna Minority Report.") Why was he not called before the committee, as Mr. Pasco was, to swear to his opinions, if they are so important? It is plain enough for common comprehension that Mr. Cromwell could not afford to appear to support his attack upon the Nicaragua route.

"The friends of Nicaragua could not call him as a witness without indorsing him, and could not compel him to disclose professional secrets to the disadvantage of his clients.

"The Cromwellian phase of the situation is not likely to commend the Panama Canal Co. or its ditch to the favor of the American people.

"Mr. President, I have shown the circumstances under which this matter has been brought before the Congress and before the Senate to-day, and I have shown how the discerning eye of the President and of the chairman of the Committee on Interstate and Foreign Commerce of the House saw through this pretender, trapped him as he came along wih his cajolery and his seductive offers, and how they have disregarded him.

"But it seems, Mr. President, that we can not shake him off. I presume he is in the gallery now listening to me. He has been here all the time during this debate.

* * * * * * *

"We have no business committing the honor of this country to any such transaction. Senators may find in acts of friendship that they think they owe to leading Senators or others in this country some excuse for accepting such a situation, but I have no such responsibilities and no such inducements to lead me from what I consider to be the path of duty" (pp. 6928–6983).

On the closing day of the debate, June 19, 1902, Senator Morgan offered this apology: "I can not neglect Mr. Cromwell, because he will not permit it. He is now obliged to figure wherever there is a chance to appear at all." He read into the record the greater part of Cromwell's letter to Secretary Hay, which supplemented and explained his draft of the proposed Concha treaty, March 31, 1902, and called attention to Mr. Cromwell's misrepresentation of the reason for the recall of Concha's predecessor, Dr. Silva. Cromwell's praise of the Isthmian Canal Commission in this letter caused Senator Morgan to exclaim:

"This is the man who put in the protest against Walker and Haupt and Hains because they had been on a previous commission and reported against him, now coming in with this fulsome eulogiums upon them—nearly as enthusiastic as some I have heard pronounced in the Senate—so nearly alike that they sound to me like quotations. This is the standard eulogium crystallized in the beautiful language of the Hon. Mr. Cromwell, general counsel of the Panama Canal Co.

"I trace this man back—other Senators, I know, have not had time to observe it—back to the beginning of this whole business. He has not failed to appear anywhere in this whole affair; and after this convention (Hay-Concha) was submitted here, he finds his way to the rear end of the report of the minority of the committee, and they quote his letter. Of course he wrote it; and, Mr. President, there is so much in the balance of that minority report of the committee that is just like it that I have dreadful fears that Mr. Cromwell wrote pretty nigh the whole report. I am sure that Mr. Cromwell never appeared before the committee—he would have been received with delight there—for the purpose of undergoing the test of a cross-examination, and before he got through it I think he would have shrunk a little in his magnitude, to say the least of it.

"I have discharged my obligation to show the conduct of this marplot to the Senate, distasteful as has been this public duty, and I shall take no further notice of him. Whoever has the unhappy task of conducting diplomatic negotiations with the new Panama Canal Co. on behalf of the United States will have to encounter the audacity of the diplomat who in the name of that company is the joint negotiator for Colombia with Señor Concha, and it is my duty to give warning. That will be the first event of its kind in all history, and the weight of the distinction is likely to overburden any other than a very hardened man. I warn that distinguished citizen, whoever he may be, to beware of Mr. Cromwell."

Twice in Senator Morgan's argument we find the warning that Colombia had no Congress to ratify the canal treaty, as the country had been plunged in civil war largely through the fight over the extension of the Panama Canal Co.'s franchise. On the last day of the debate Mr. Morgan said: "It is certain, on the face of the transaction, that we will not be able to acquire a title to the Panama Canal from Colombia unless we take hold of affairs in that Republic with a strong hand and end the civil war there." Whether of prescience or intuition, this warning of the Alabama Senator proved to be even a prophecy. Before two months had elapsed the shadow of the Big Stick had fallen across Colombia, and the Roosevelt administration was engaged in diplomatic intrigues there and in Washington to bring about peace and was exacting as the price for its "friendly offices" a treaty which would release the international gamblers' stakes.

Senator Mallory, of Florida, made two efforts to put a curb on the administration by limiting the "reasonable" time given to President Roosevelt, under the Spooner law, in which to conclude a deal with Colombia. He first proposed to place this limit at six months. His amendment was defeated, 44 to 31. He next proposed a year's limit, and this amendment was lost by 30 to 35. Had it carried, Mr. Roosevelt would have been driven to the Nicaragua route as events in Colombia developed, unless history had shaped its course in other ways.

The deciding vote on the substitution of the Spooner amendment recommended by the "Hanna minority report" was 42 to 34, with 12 Senators not voting. Fourteen Senators who had voted for the Nicaragua route when the Senate passed the Nicaragua Canal bill, January 21, 1899, by a vote of 48 to 6, voted with the Panama forces. These 14 are indicated by the (*) in the vote on the substitution of the Spooner amendment June 19, 1902:

Yeas, 42 (for Panama).—Aldrich, Allison(*), Bard, Beveridge, Burnham, Burrows(*), Burton, Clark of Wyoming, Cullom(*), Deboe, Dietrich, Dryden, Fairbanks(*), Foraker, Foster of Washington, Frye(*), Gallinger(*), Gamble, Hale, Hanna(*), Hansborough(*), Hoar(*), Jones of Arkansas(*), Jones of Nevada, Kean, Kittredge, Lodge(*), McComas, McCumber, McMillan(*), Mason, Millard, Platt of Connecticut, Pritchard, Proctor(*), Quarles, Scott, Spooner(*), Teller, Warren, Wellington, Wetmore.

Nays, 34 (for Nicaragua).—Bacon, Bailey, Bate, Berry, Blackburn, Carmack, Clapp, Clark of Montana, Clay, Cockrell, Culberson, Daniel, Dubois, Foster of Louisiana, Harris, Hawley, Heitfeld, McLaurin of Mississippi, Mallory, Martin, Mitchell, Morgan, Nelson, Patterson, Penrose, Perkins, Pettus, Platt of New York, Quay, Simmons, Stewart, Taliaferro, Turner, Vest.

Not voting, 12.—Depew, Dillingham, Dolliver, Elkins, Gibson, Kearns, McEnery, McLaurin of South Carolina, Money, Rawlins, Simon, Tillman.

Senator Depew was absent, but had a general pair with Senator McEnery, who announced that if voting he would vote "Nay."

Senator Hanna announced that Senator Rawlins had released him from his general pair on the canal vote.

Senator Dolliver, who was absent, was paired with Senator Money, who would otherwise have voted, he announced, "Nay," while Senator Dolliver would have voted "Yea."

Senator Tillman was absent, but paired with Senator Dillingham. Senator Berry announced that if Senator Tillman had been present he would have voted "Nay." Senator Dillingham, if voting, would have voted "Yea."

Senator Elkins expressed himself in the debate in favor of the Darien or San Blas route. The Congressional Record gives no explanation of his not voting, nor of the failure to vote of Senators Gibson, Kearns, McLaurin of South Carolina, and Simon, nor why Senator Rawlins, having released Senator Hanna from his pair, did not yote.

The conference committees of the two houses—Senators Morgan, Hanna, and Kittredge; Representatives Hepburn, Fletcher, and Davey—struggled over the disagreement until June 25, 1902, when the House members surrendered to the ultimatum of Panama or no canal legislation whatever. In vain the House conferees pleaded even to limit the time for making a treaty with Colombia; the Senate members were adamant. Mr. Cromwell says:

"At each step of this critical combat we were consulted by Senators Hanna and Kittredge, who were among the conferees, * * * and we had an exchange of views with them on each question."

The conference committee reported to the House on June 25, 1902, recommending concurrence in the Senate's substitution of the Spooner amendment for the original Hepburn Nicaragua bill, which the House had passed, 309 to 2, on January 9, 1902. The conference report was adopted by a vote of 260 to 8, with 80 Members "not voting."

Representative Burton, of Ohio, was the only Member to raise his voice in favor of the Panama route. Every other Member of the House who advocated adoption of the Spooner substitute followed the general line of Representative Hepburn's argument, which was epitomized in these few words:

"If I had thought it was possible to secure other legislation than this, I would not have consented to the action I now recommend. I consented to it because I believe that at this time it is this or nothing."

Representative Mann said:

"I confess I do not know whether their (the Panama people's) success is due to the fact that they have the better route or to the fact that they had a skilled lobby and made some powerful friends in this country with wide influence. * * * Under the bill which is now to become a law, the Panama Canal route is worth $40,000,000 to sell to this country. It is possible that if it were not sold to this country it might be worth as much as $4,000,000 to entice some money out of gullible people in France, but it is quite certain that except for these two purposes it is not worth 40 cents." (P. 7740, vol. 35, pt. 8.)

To this record Mr. Cromwell adds his villainous boast:

"We are more than justified in saying that without our labors this (surrender of the House) would not have been obtained, the offer of the company would have been rejected, and the Nicaragua route would have been chosen."

And thus, quoting the message of Mr. Roosevelt to Congress December 7, 1903, "This was the route which commended itself to the deliberate judgment of the Congress!"

President Roosevelt signed the Spooner bill on June 28, 1902, whereupon Mr. Cromwell says, "We prepared a revision of the treaty and submitted it to Secretary Hay, at his request"—the same old treaty he had drafted and proposed in the name of Minister Concha. With this as a basis, if we may believe Mr. Cromwell's boastings, "we finally arrived at an understanding with Secretary Hay and the President on the subject of what would seem acceptable to the Senate."

Doubtless on the part of Mr. Roosevelt this understanding with the President was an exchange of "purely formal courtesies," since Mr. Roosevelt has declared that he met Mr. Cromwell only a few times solely for this purpose during the canal negotiations.

The amendments thus agreed upon by Cromwell, Roosevelt, and Hay were transmitted by Secretary Hay to Minister Concha, through Cromwell, as always. Concha and Hay didn't meet, Mr. Cromwell says, except "to exchange the final documents."

The Colombian Blue Book of 1904 contains a letter of Minister Concha to his Government, dated July 11, 1902, reporting that on July 9, 1902, he had received through an "unofficial source" (Mr. Cromwell says he was always this source) the American draft of the treaty as Secretary Hay (or rather Cromwell) had amended the original Concha (or rather Cromwell) proposal. Minister Concha added:

"The Secretary of State before a formal presentation of his amendments has desired to feel out the opinion of the undersigned concerning the changes referred to, but I have expressed no opinion in this matter, pending instructions from your excellency, which were asked for by cable sent yesterday."

The Colombian Government replied by cable July 17, 1902: "Do not break off negotiations. Refer to Congress." In a letter explaining to Minister Concha the order to refer the negotiations to Congress, the Colombian Foreign Minister said that the concessions demanded in the American amendments were of a character that could be passed upon only by the Congress.

Minister Concha's correspondence with his Government, from early in June, 1902, indicates that he was anticipating demands by the United States that would be unacceptable. He considered that in the proposals made in March and April of that year he had offered all that Colombia would be willing to concede, and he was determined, as he notified his Government June 20, 1902, to oppose any amendments looking toward the diminution of Colombian sovereignty or affecting the proposed neutrality of the canal. In this attitude he was supported by his Government in a letter from the Minister for Foreign Affairs, dated July 31, 1902. In this letter the Colombian Foreign Office also approved Concha's suggestion that they should agree upon a new cable code, Minister Concha having warned his Government that he had reasons for suspecting that the Colombian secret code was in possession of the American State Department.

Mr. Cromwell now transferred the field of his activities from lobbying, legislation, and diplomacy to law, and on July 24, 1902, went to Paris to assist the Special Assistant Attorney General for the United States in reaching the conclusion that the Panama Canal Co. could deliver a valid title. Meanwhile Farnham, having no more earthquake articles to place in the magazines, was left in charge of Minister Concha in Washington, and Mr. Hill, one of the members of Mr. Cromwell's firm, made frequent trips thither to assist the chief press agent. They made "frequent reports by cable to our partner (Mr. Cromwell) in Paris." So says Mr. Cromwell. Attorney General Knox himself went over later to Paris, and Mr. Cromwell having satisfied him as to the title, they all came back together, the last of September.

Upon his return Mr. Cromwell "encountered new complications and a complete and radical change of attitude" on the part of Minister Concha who "openly manifested his hostility to the United States Government and abstained from calling upon Secretary Hay, and even from communicating with him."

Mr. Cromwell neglected to relate why Minister Concha had changed his attitude; we have to seek elsewhere for the story of the brandishing of the Big Stick in Colombia for the purpose of ending the civil war in order that a Congress might be assembled to ratify the pending treaty.

During the summer of 1902 Mr. Carlos Lievano, representing the revolutionary (Liberal) party of Colombia' conferred several times with Charles Burdett Hart, then American minister to Bogota, with the motive of obtaining American intervention to terminate the disastrous three-years' civil war favorably to the Liberals, who had defeated the forces of the conservative government of President Jose Manuel Marroquin everywhere excepting in Panama, and were there on the point of final victory with an army of 7.000 against a Government force of less than 2,000. Mr. Lievano held out to the American minister the argument that humanity demanded that the struggle should be ended, Colombia already having lost 80,000 men; and that furthermore, if the Liberal party, constituting a recognized majority of the people of Colombia, came into power it would be in a position to negotiate forthwith the desired canal treaty. Mr. Lievano was elated when Minister Hart finally told him that the proposed intervention could be arranged; that he had received his instructions from Washington and that at last the time had arrived when they (the American minister and the Liberal representative) might combine to find means of disrupting the Marroquin Government, to which Mr. Hart was the accredited minister.

Three days later, Mr. Lievano declares, he returned to Mr. Hart and was told, in effect, "It's all off; there's no revolution." Upon asking the minister why, Mr. Lievano was told: "You know we have to build the canal." The Liberal representative protested and demanded to know the reason for this reversal of policy, and was told that Lorenzo Marroquin, son and political manager of the aged President, and Aristides Fernandez had come to the American minister and sought intervention to end the war in behalf of the Conservative forces, and in consideration for the promised intervention had pledged the Marroquin Government to enter into a satisfactory canal treaty with the United States. Lorenzo Marroquin declared under oath in October, 1909, that he and Fernandez did confer with the American minister to bring about the American intervention on the Isthmus, resulting in the signing of the treaty of peace of November 21, 1902, aboard the American battleship *Wisconsin*.

Gen. Lucas Caballero, who signed the treaty of the *Wisconsin* in behalf of the Liberals, declares that the American naval officers openly threatened future intervention by the American Government to assist the Panamans to win their independence—or the outright annexation of Panama by the United States—if the conflict was not ended, and that this was one of the reasons why the Liberals agreed to the abandonment of a successful war.

The Liberal leaders recognized the serious intent of the Roosevelt administration because of the open advances previously made in Washington. The revolutionary headquarters had been for some time in New York, in charge of Gen. Vargas Santos and Dr. Modesto Garces, a Colombian lawyer, who was the emissary of the revolutionists in several conferences at the State Department, whither he had been sent to try to obtain American intervention for the Liberals. On July 31 or August 1, 1902, Dr. Garces returned from one of these missions to Washington and reported that the American Government evidently desired to bring about the independence of Panama, and that David Jayne Hill, then Acting Secretary of State, had suggested that intervention might be arranged with this in view. Dr. Garces thereupon wrote out in Spanish the rough draft of an interrogatory which he said Acting Secretary Hill had suggested should be sent to the State Depatment, signed by Gen. Vargas Santos, general in chief of the revolutionary forces, who was then in New York purchasing arms and securing financial assistance. In substance this proposed memorandum asked:

"What would be the attitude of the United States in the event that the revolutionary forces should declare the independence of the Cauca and Panama?"

This memorandum was submitted to Gen. Vargas Santos, who refused to sign it or to become in any way a party to a proposal to dismember his own country. The original memorandum of Dr. Garces is now in possession of Gen. Celso Rodriguez, of Bogota, one of the chief lieutenants of Gen. Vargas Santos. Dr. Garces is dead.

The American naval officers landed marines on the Isthmus and virtually disarmed the fighting forces by preventing transportation of troops on the line of the Panama Railroad. Thus "neutrality" was enforced in order to maintain free and uninterrupted transit on the railroad, notwithstanding it was notorious that the Panama Railroad had been aiding the revolutionists by moving their munitions and refusing transportation to the established Government. Freight tags of the railroad taken from revolutionary ordnance transported in contravention of this "neutrality" were exhibits in a suit which the late Gov. Alban, of Panama, was preparing before his death to institute against the Panama Railroad.

Thus the Roosevelt administration displayed "our purpose to deal not merely in a spirit of justice but in a spirit of generosity with the people through whose land we might build it" (the canal); thus early was foreshadowed the design which Mr. Roosevelt frankly admitted in his message to Congress, January 4, 1904, "to announce * * * that if such terms were not agreed to we would enter into an arrangement with Panama direct, or take what other steps were needful in order to begin the enterprise."

Whatever exchanges there were on this subject were carefully suppressed by the Colombian Government when Gen. Reyes, during his administration as President, published what purports to be the complete diplomatic correspondence concerning the canal negotiations. This was after Reyes had arrived at an understanding with Cromwell, as set forth in Mr. Cromwell's book.

August 9, 1902, President Marroquin cabled Minister Concha:

"In order to render the amendments to memorandum presentable to our Congress, demand ten millions cash and annuity of six hundred thousand after 14 years."

August 13, 1902, the Colombian foreign minister wrote to Concha that as the drawbacks to the use of the cable were clearly insuperable, the Colombian Government had decided that the negotiations with the United States should not be broken off, but that everything must be submitted to the decision of the Congress. Minister Concha was notified that in a recent conference in the Foreign Office the Bogota agent of the Panama Canal Company had been told that Colombia would demand of the company the full par value of the 50,000 shares of canal stock which the Government owned as one of the conditions of consent to the transfer.

August 14, 1902, the Colombian foreign minister cabled Concha:

"Special messenger on the 13th instant carries registered instructions Panama Canal."

These instructions were suppressed.

The thumbprints of Cromwell appear in the Colombian "Blue Book" in a letter to Minister Concha from Enrique Cortes, one of the Reyes coterie, who later appears as Mr. Cromwell's ally when he becomes Colombian minister to Washington several years later. Writing from Cazenovia, N. Y., August 27, 1902, Cortes informs the minister that he assisted Concha's predecessor, Dr. Silva, "in the preparation of the bases of the treaty, in which also took part Dr. Facundo Mutis-Duran, as representative of Panama, and Mr. Cromwell." Cortes refers to the American Nation as "knowing what it wants, and able—should occasion arise—to obtain by the force of its strong right arm what it desires."

In this letter Cortes uses the identical expression employed by Mr. Cromwell a year later, when the Panama Canal lobbyist assures Gen. Pedro Velez, of Colombia, that the United States could never be guilty of designing the dismemberment of Colombia, because the United States is "a gentleman among the nations." This phrase, as well as the general line of argument pursued by Cortes, points strongly to Cromwell as the real author of this letter. Cortes recites the dealings of the United States with Spain, Cuba, China, and the Philippines, and continues:

"If Colombia tries to be extortionate we shall expose ourselves to loosening the wrath of the Colossus, and then, alas for us! This wrath of the Colossus, which, once its patience is exhausted, ended in a few short months the power of Spain in America, could sweep away in the twinkling of an eye our sovereignty in the Isthmus. The imminence of this danger and the impossibility of Colombia's maintaining her integrity have been made more than apparent, palpable by the events of the civil war on the Isthmus."

Cortes goes on to say that the negotiations now proceeding will "crystallize the final say in the American Government, and that Colombia will act wisely in giving its simple and full approval." In reference to the suggestion in Colombia of forfeiting the canal company's concession in 1904, Mr. Cortes says that, besides delaying the negotiations two years, it might provoke in the United States "an outburst of indignation that would culminate in the annexation of the Isthmus of Panama to the American Union."

This, Cortes points out, would be a simple and profitable negotiation for the United States, which would then give the French company its $40,000,000 and retain unaltered the friendship of its traditional ally, France; effect a saving of the amount it would have to pay to Colombia, and become the absolute owner of the Isthmus as well as of the canal. Mr. Cortes ends: "Our line of conduct can not be other than to approve without delay—and blindfolded—whatever the American Government has arranged with the Colombian legation. Danger is in delay."

August 25, 1902, the Colombian Government cabled Minister Concha: "Tell the American Government that the Colombian Government accepts in principle the last amendments presented. Await instructions which left beginning of August. Ratification by Congress is necessary. In order to convoke it there only lacks the pacification of Panama."

The pacification of Panama by the "strong hand" that Senator Morgan suggested in June, 1902, was very shortly to be begun. News of the surrender of the Government forces to the revolutionists at Aguadulce, Panama, after a month's siege, reached the United States on September 8, 1902, and was confirmed a few days later. September 12, 1902, the Secretary of the Navy cabled to the commander of the Ranger, at Panama, not to permit transportation of troops that would convert the Panama Railroad into a theater of hostilities; September 14, 1902, the Panther sailed with 320 United States Marines and four rapid-fire guns from League Island Navy Yard; September 18, 1902, the Cincinnati, which arrived at Colon on the 16th, landed marines and put them aboard the Panama Railroad trains.

Minister Concha did not work in with the pacification plans of his Government, which, having made a secret deal to save its own life, viewed with complacence the intervention on the Isthmus. In a cable to Concha on September 20, 1902, the Colombian Government notified him of the sending of an army to the Isthmus, and added:

"Now is the time to demand from the Government of the United States of America the execution of the treaty of 1846 to assure the transit from Panama to Colon."

September 22, 1902, Concha was informed by cable by his Government:

"We are ignorant of the nature of the intervention of the United States of America. All that we demand is execution of article 35 of the treaty of 1846, as has already been done in analogous circumstances."

And on the same day Concha cabled to Bogota:

"I to-day presented to the Secretary of State a memorandum reestablishing truth of events in Panama, without making any comments, reserving the right of my Government to make such declarations as it judges fit."

September 24, 1902, the governor of Panama cabled to President Marroquin:

"Americans have disembarked troops in the city of Panama. Concha tells me that he will protest appeal to force. Should occasion arise, prevent him."

September 25, 1902, the Marroquin Government cabled to Concha:

"Abstain from treating of the matter of the American intervention in Panama. Minister of foreign affairs will do so here."

Minister Concha protested vehemently to his Government. On October 3, 1902, he cabled to his Government that the governor of Panama had asked him to protest against the order of the Americal admiral prohibiting transportation of war munitions or troops on the Panama Railroad—a service which the railroad was bound by its concession to perform. Concha said he replied that he had been forbidden to intervene, and added:

"For the fourth time I resign from this legation. Order secretary to take charge."

Concha's Government replied, October 7, 1902:

"Your resignation unpatriotic and inadmissible."

On the day Concha cabled his fourth resignation he wrote to his Government in part:

"The recent events culminating in the armed intervention of the United States modify from the ground up the negotiations now in progress. The commander of the American forces has assumed de facto the supreme authority in that part of the Isthmus not occupied by the rebels; our Colombian troops are disarmed by those of the United States, their officers travel in the custody of the Americans, even the governor himself is escorted like a viceroy; the American commander notifies the Government employees and the rebels alike of what he will or will not permit in the region he occupies; and lastly, the minister of the Republic in Washington, when he announces that he has asked for details necessary to formulate such protest as international law and the most elementary national dignity demand, has silence peremptorily imposed upon him by the Chief Executive of Colombia and her minister of foreign affairs. Between a power which thus imposes its strength, and a Government which does not know how to or does not care to defend its national sovereignty, treaties can not be consummated, the law of diplomacy gives way to that of conquest, and all discussion ceases between two nations on a footing of equality, and there remains but one to dictate its laws, which the other must accept and obey. In the presence of this new position, for this and other reasons, the undersigned considers his labors in defense of the rights of the Republic at an end."

Up to this time the bargain with Gen. Reyes seems not to have been made, for on October 8, 1902, Concha cabled to his Government:

"Gen. Reyes telegraphs me thus: 'Attitude American admiral in Panama will prevent approbation by Congress of canal treaty; obliges you protest; demand passports.' We, all the Colombians not forgetful of our mother country, think as Reyes."

A year later Gen. Reyes was acting as first friend and secret informant of the American minister in Bogota, and for reasons which Mr. Roosevelt or someone in the State Department can best explain, it was deemed advisable to expurgate his name from the Beaupre correspondence Mr. Roosevelt transmitted to Congress.

October 9, 1902, the Colombian Government cabled Minister Concha:

"Do not demand passports. Matter admiral is being dealt with direct with Hart."

Hart was then American minister in Bogota.

October 23, 1902, Concha wrote to his Government that his convictions would not permit him to sign the pending treaty with the American Government, because it was then violating in Panama the treaty of 1846. He recited the grievances expressed in his letter of October 2, 1902, and again insisted that his resignation be accepted.

October 25, 1902, Concha cabled to his Government:

"It is impossible to advance the negotiations of the Panama Canal while there still exists the order prohibiting my discussion of the intervention of the treaty of 1846–1848, an essential part of the future treaty. * * * I think that prolongation of occupation of the Isthmus by the forces of the United States is unjustifiable, as all danger has disappeared. Silence of the Government of Colombia will cause loss of the Republic."

Concha then addressed Secretary Hay, October 26, 1902, informing him that he had received final supplementary instructions for concluding the canal negotiations. The letter continues:

"The instructions to which I refer were dated in Bogota on the 9th of September last, prior to the acts committed in the department of Panama by officers of the Navy of the United States, acts which imply on the part of the Government of your excellency a new interpretation of the treaty existing between the two countries, an interpretation regarding which I am not at present allowed to express any opinion whatever—this prohibition coming directly from the minister of foreign affairs in Bogota, as your excellency knows—but which will perforce affect substantially the pending convention in which article 35 of that treaty is incorporated and developed.

"In view of the preceding, your excellency will recognize the impossibility of my fulfilling the instructions received; consequently I have addressed my Government by cable so that they may determine what steps will be most appropriate. * * * *

"My object in addressing your excellency on this occasion is principally to make manifest the good will and frankness of intention of my Government in the pending negotiations, because after overcoming considerable difficulties arising from disturbers of public peace in the country, it has reached the point of sending to its representative instructions necessary to complete the treaty which should be submitted to the legislative corps within a short time; and if to-day an unforeseen delay should arise in the progress of the matter my Government has no responsibility therefor."

Since Mr. Roosevelt cites the American intervention of 1902 as a justifying precedent for his prevention of Colombia's reasserting her sovereignty over the

Isthmus after he and Mr. Cromwell, a year later, manufactured the Panama "revolution," it is well to pause here long enough to hear still more of the other side of the argument. While Roosevelt was making his "precedent" Minister Concha was attacking it in a letter to his Government, dated October 30, 1902, in part as follows:

"That the interpretation given to the treaty of 1846, by the acts which American forces are to-day in Panama, is new appears to be indisputable.

"When for the first time the United States used the right of transit via the Isthmus, which is guaranteed them by the existing treaty, it was with the simple object of sending troops to Oregon and California; that was effected by disembarking them and sending them across the Isthmus without having given any previous notice to the authorities; for that our secretary of foreign affairs presented a protest in Washington through the legation, and in a conference in September of 1858 between the Granadian minister, Gen. Herran, and the Secretary of State, Gen. Casey, it was agreed that in future whenever it was necessary to send American forces through the territory of the Isthmus they would come unarmed and as groups of private individuals 'without enjoying the exemptions which are customary when troops pass through foreign territory, but, on the contrary, being subject to the territorial jurisdiction exactly like all other strangers.' This agreement was punctually fulfilled during the American war of secession on the occasion when forces of the Government of the United States were sent to the Pacific. To-day, so advanced is the interpretation, that American forces are disembarked in Panama to disarm those of the sovereign of the territory. Whatever more extensive comment might be made on this point would be redundant.

"In 'Foreign Relations of the United States,' 1885, pages 239 to 251, there is found the correspondence exchanged between the legation of Colombia in Washington and the Department of State. Therein will be see clearly that when in that year the United States sent forces to Panama, in spite of the fact that the established Government there had practically disappeared, that the railroad line was without defense, and that when contending bands had reached the extreme of imprisoning the American consul the United States never pretended to execute acts of authority or jurisdiction; on the contrary, when Capt. Kane, commander of the cruiser *Galena*, arrested two of the incendiaries in Colon and stated in a telegram, which he made public, that he would not deliver them to the authorities in Panama, because they would be allowed to escape, a slight protest on the part of the minister of Colombia, Mr. Vecerra, was sufficient to cause the Secretary of State, Mr. Bayard, in a note of April 6 of the same year, to give satisfactory explanations of the case and decide that the prisoners should be delivered to the authorities of the country.

"To-day no one with the slightest particle of reason could compare the solitary act of Capt. Kane in a condition of total anarchy—in which it was difficult, not only for a foreigner, but for the people of the country themselves, to locate the legitimate authorities—with the repeated acts, first of Capt. McLean, and afterwards of Admiral Casey, in very different circumstances, when the transit has not been interrupted, when the Colombian authorities have means and forces sufficient to fulfill their duties, and when the American officers not only have ignored the prerogatives of the Colombians, but have humiliated them, dictating orders, by their acts preventing fulfillment of Colombia's obligations and authorizing the railroad to violate a perfect civil contract by which it is bound to transport troops, employees, and munitions of the Government.

"And this is not all. The American Government has detained the troops of the Colombian Government in their march; it has prevented the opportune arrival at their destination of an abundance of elements of war which arrived from abroad at Colon for the campaign of the Pacific; it has attacked and interfered with the disembarkation of Colombian troops from the cruiser *Cartagena* in the Atlantic, and has exercised the right of visit on board the Colombian war vessel in the Bay of Panama; with all of which the marines of the United States in the name of their Government have outraged and ignored the same sovereignty which by a solemn, public treaty not only should they respect themselves, but should compel all others to respect.

"The acts briefly enumerated have commanded the public and solemn joint approbation of the State and Navy Departments of the American Government, which assert that these acts are the legitimate development of article 35 of the treaty of 1846.

"Suppressing, therefore, all other considerations for the object of this note, it is clear that if the practical interpretation of the treaty is that series of acts the interpretation is new. and was not known by the minister of Colombia when he prepared the memorandum of the 21st of April (1902) for the canal negotiations, nor was it known either by the minister of foreign affairs when he dictated definite instructions on the 9th of September last.

"The memorandum of April above referred to, basis of the canal negotiations, from its very title demonstrates the intimate connection that exists between it and the treaty of 1846, because it expresses that this is the development of the latter, and in article 3 it is stated that: 'All dispositions of article 35 of the treaty of 1846–1848 celebrated between the contracting parties will continue in force and will be applied in all their force to the cities of Panama and Colon and the accessory islands situated within the said zone and the territory comprised within them will be neutral, and the Government of the United States will continue to guarantee that neutrality and the sovereignty of Colombia in accordance with article 35.' "

October 29, 1902, Concha cabled his Government the substance of the foregoing letter to Secretary Hay, and added: "The State Department replied today that there was no new interpretation, and that the United States would adopt the Nicaragua route if the treaty was not signed before the American Congress meets in December."

Secretary Hay also transmitted this ultimatum respecting adoption of the Nicaragua route to the Colombian Government through the American minister in Bogota, and Minister Concha received cable instructions to continue the canal negotiations.

Concha accordingly sought an audience with Secretary Hay on November 4, 1902, and, pursuant to his instructions demanded that article 23, as he had drafted it in April, and as Secretary Hay had accepted it, should be reinstated instead of the modified article 23 which Secretary Hay had proposed in July. Concha contended that his original draft was the correct interpretation of American rights to intervene on the Isthmus under the treaty of 1846.

Concerning the negotiations at this time Mr. Cromwell claims credit for having induced Minister Concha not to resign, and adds:

"Minister Concha * * * yielded, and promised to take up the treaty, but on the condition that the negotiations be confined in the first place to the question of sovereignty. In consequence, on November 5 (November 4 is correct) Concha submitted the question of sovereignty to Mr. Hay. The latter sent for Mr. Cromwell and detailed conferences ensued. Finally the President authorized Mr. Hay to yield. It was an important point, because unless the principle of sovereignty were granted the negotiations could have no result."

And still Mr. Roosevelt said in his message to Congress January 4, 1904:

"It has been stated in public prints that Colombia objected to these stipulations on the ground that they involved a relinquishment of her 'sovereignty;' but in the light of what has taken place this alleged objection must be considered as an afterthought."

An "afterthought" of a year before.

How President Roosevelt "authorized Mr. Hay to yield" this "important point" of sovereignty is shown in a letter of Secretary Hay to Minister Concha November 18, 1902, in which is the following:

"The President has considered with much attention whether he may admit the amendment that you consider so important for your country—substitution of the first article 23 for the last article 23. Desirous of manifesting in unquestionable manner the good will of this Nation toward Colombia, the President authorized me to say that if all the other stipulations are accepted to the satisfaction of the United States he will consent to the substitution of article 23 as it appears in the first instrument for the same article in the draft of July 18, 1902, but that not otherwise will he give his acquiescence."

Mr. Cromwell says that "at the request of Mr. Hay" he drew up the revision of the treaty which Secretary Hay transmitted to Minister Concha on November 18, 1902. On the theory that Colombia would yield, the revision admitted none of the demands Concha had made in his proposed seven amendments, except his original draft of article 23. What Mr. Roosevelt was willing to concede is seen best by comparing the respective drafts:

"*Article 23.* (Hay's draft of July 18, 1902).—If it shall become necessary at any time, in order to enforce the guaranty of neutrality and of freedom from blockade and from the exercise of rights or acts of war, within said zone or within 3 marine miles of either end thereof, assumed by the United States in the treaty entered into by it with Great Britain on November 18, 1901, or in order efficiently to discharge the performance of the obligations to Colombia embodied herein, or in order promptly and efficiently to insure the safety and protection of the canal and dependencies, or of the ships, cargoes, and persons using the same, or of the railways and other works on the said zone or appertaining thereto, the United States shall have the right to employ such of its armed forces to that end as may be necessary, according to the circumstances of the case, withdrawing, however, said forces, in whole or in part so soon as the necessity for their presence has ceased. Said Government shall give immediate advices to Colombia of the measures adopted for the purposes stated."

"*Article 23.* (Concha's draft of Apr. 18, 1902, which Roosevelt ordered accepted).—If it should become necessary at any time to employ armed forces for the safety or protection of the canal, or of the ships that make use of the same, or the railways and other works, the Republic of Colombia agrees to provide the forces necessary for such purpose, according to the circumstances of the case, but if the Government of Colombia can not effectively comply with this obligation, then, with the consent of or at the request of Colombia, or of her minister at Washington, or of the local authorities, civil or military, the United States shall employ such force as may be necessary for that sole purpose; and as soon as the necessity shall have ceased will withdraw the forces so employed. Under exceptional circumstances, however, on account of unforeseen or imminent danger to said canal, railways, and other works, or to the lives and property of the persons employed upon the canal, railways, and other works, the Government of the United States is authorized to act in the interest of their protection, without the necessity of obtaining the consent beforehand of the Government of Colombia; and it shall give immediate advice of the measures adopted for the purpose stated; and as soon as sufficient Colombian forces shall arrive to attend to the indicated purpose, those of the United States shall retire."

Transmitting a memorandum of his conference with Secretary Hay, Minister Concha reported to his Government by letter of November 4, 1902, that Secretary Hay voluntarily brought up the subject of interpretation of the treaty of 1846 and said that he could not give any reply as to what recognition should be given to such interpretation in the canal treaty without conferring with President Roosevelt.

Discussing article 23 in a letter to Secretary Hay, November 11, 1902, Minister Concha said, in part:

"In article 23, which your excellency expressly accepted with the rest of the memorandum in the note which you sent to the legation on the 21st of last April, it appears that even if Colombia concedes to the United States a certain extension of authority in the Isthmus, should the canal treaty be perfected, by so doing it does not renounce, nor could it renounce, inherent faculties of exercising sovereignty of the Republic; * * * without abdicating the elemental right of transporting her officials, her troops, her elements of war, etc., within her own boundaries without any limitation whatever, as is set forth in article 17 of the same memorandum; nor could Colombia agree to have her authorities at any time deprived of the exercise of their legal functions.

"The fact that your excellency accepted in the mentioned official note of April 21 the articles of which we are treating, shows well that the explanation there given to the Government of the United States is the correct understanding of the treaty of 1846, an understanding which my Government deems it necessary to have put in statute form in a solemn manner, maintaining and ratifying it for the future. The article proposed by your excellency, instead of the one above mentioned, might give rise to Colombia's being incapacitated, on some occasion, from exercising her power of maintaining order in her territory, or might give rise to contradictions or discussions which could be usefully avoided."

November 6, 1902, Concha cabled his Government that the State Department had not yet answered to his demands made on the 4th, and added: "Whatever it (Hay's answer) may be, I will not sign any treaty during the American occupation of the Isthmus."

November 7, 1902, Concha again tendered his resignation by letter, in which he reiterated that under no circumstances would he sign a treaty with the United States so long as it troops, "against every principle of right and justice, and in violation of a public word of honor, continue to trample under foot Colombian territory, and to exercise thereon a usurped jurisdiction."

At this point in the chronology we find in Mr. Cromwell's story: "Minister Concha, forced now to reveal his intentions fully, drew up and presented, first to us and later to Mr. Hay (Nov. 11), seven amendments to the projected treaty." The seven appear in the Colombian Blue Book, together with Minister Concha's note, but Mr. Cromwell sets forth in his story only the one amendment vital to his client. This proposed that the first article of the treaty, dealing with Colombia's consent to the transfer of the canal concession to the United States, should state specifically that such consent should be governed by agreements previously to be entered into between Colombia and the canal and railroad companis. This, Mr. Cromwell says, "would oblige the (canal) company to pay an enormous tribute in cash or to see the treaty fail if the company did not yield to the exigencies of Colombia."

The value to Mr. Cromwell's client of his having made the consent of Colombia "enter into the domain of international relations" begins now to appear. Concerning the proposal of Colombia that she should deal with her concessionaries in her own way when it came to consenting to the transfer of their rights to the United States, and Mr. Hay's answer thereto, Mr. Cromwell says:

"This was a vital and fundamental point for the company, and Mr. Cromwell put all his energies into combatting the acceptance of this amendment. He conferred frequently with Secretary Hay about the matter, and at his request explained to him all the scope of the amendment, as well as the relations between the parties. He demonstrated to him that it would be disadvantageous to consent to this amendment. The result of these conferences and these arguments was that Secretary Hay announced himself as in accord with our views, and in his official reply to Minister Concha he rejected the amendment."

Mr. Hay's answer, as it appears in his official note, was: "The United States considers this suggestion wholly inadmissible."

To whom, in fact, was this suggestion "inadmissible"—the United States, or Mr. Cromwell and his speculative friends, whose profits would thereby be claimed in part or in entirety by Colombia? Was it "disadvantageous" to the United States to allow Colombia to dictate terms, just or unjust, to the bankrupt concessionaire that had failed repeatedly to execute its contract? Was there anything in the Spooner law—under which President Roosevelt and Secretary Hay were supposed to be proceeding—whereby they were enjoined to protect from the demands of the Colombian Government the $40,000,000 allotted to the French canal company?

November 14, 1902, President Marroquin cabled to Concha: "Congress meets 1st of March. Ask all possible advantages in respect to article 23. In any case sign the treaty, to save our responsibility. The Congress of Colombia must decide definitely."

November 15, 1902, Minister Concha wrote to his Government, expressing his pleasure with the situation in which he had placed Secretary Hay. In part his letter follows:

"Although Mr. Hay is very clever, the dilemma that faces him can not but cause him some little mortification; he must either accept article 23 of the memorandum of April as a correct interpretation of the treaty of 1846, and then he implicitly recognizes that the occurrences in Panama are violations of this treaty, or he must assert that article 23 is not the correct interpretation of the treaty, thereby throwing to the ground his note of April, in which he accepted the memorandum. Of course this would be but a wish of Hay for one having jaws as powerful as this Uncle of ours, and he can settle it all with a single crunch. * * * The desire to make themselves appear as the nation most respectful of the rights of others forces these gentlemen to toy a little with their prey before devouring it, although when all is said and done they will do so in one way or the other. The outbursts of the press, of which you will learn when you receive this, and the more or less hidden threats which appear every day in the papers, emanating from Mr. Hay himself or from Cromwell, who is a rat, and is very active in fomenting this and other fusses, have not given them the result they hoped for. * * *"

So firmly convinced was Dr. Concha of the uselessness of continuing negotiations while American forces occupied the Isthmus, that he said in this letter of November 15, 1902: "I must repeat to you that I believe my presence here is not only useless, it is improper."

Novmber 18, 1902, Secretary Hay submitted to Minister Concha the Cromwell revision of the treaty, with the compromise on article 23, as heretofore related. It was proposed to settle the question of Colombia's indemnity from the United

States by payment of $7,000,000 and an annuity of $100,000, or $10,000,000, and an annuity of $10,000. Secretary Hay suggested in his note that Dr. Concha's Government should no longer delay, indicating which alternative it would choose.

November 19, 1902, Concha cabled the Bogota Foreign Office: "The Department of State in Washington answered me regarding the matter of the Panama Canal in the form of an ultimatum. * * * Denies increase of the amount of indemnity; sustains change in the counter memorandum of July 18; does not permit the canal company to celebrate a previous arrangement with the Government of Colombia, but pretends that the treaty constitutes permission for cession of the rights to the Government of the United States without other conditions; denies the return to Colombia of Government lands; does not accept indicated termination of period (of lease). * * * I do not believe the treaty is admissible in this form. * * * Communication of the State Department does not admit of new objection."

In another cable on November 19, 1902, Concha notified his Government:

"I can not conscientiously agree to treaty last proposed by State Department in Washington, as it sacrifices Colombia without even the excuse of a pecuniary advantage, because she will receive less than she now gets from the Panama Railroad alone," ($250,000 a year).

He added that his determination to leave his post was irrevocable.

November 22, 1902, Minister Concha replied to Secretary Hay at great length, setting forth Colombia's objections to the treaty as Mr. Hay had submitted it. Respecting the refusal of the United States to admit Colombia's right to exact conditions from the canal and railroad companies before transferring their concessions, Dr. Concha said, in part:

"Limited as is the time during which the companies will enjoy the usufruct from these properties, it is clear that if these have a great price, it pertains to Colombia, and there is no reason or motive for its being paid to the companies or that its owner shall cede it gratuitously. Already Colombia has exercised an act of exceptional liberality in extending to the canal company the period of construction of the works, the only effect of which has been that the latter is now in a position possibly to recover a part of its capital, which, without this circumstance, would have passed to Colombia within a few months.

"The undersigned does not demand nor suggest that the United States shall intervene in the questions that are to be discussed between the Government of Colombia and the said companies, but he does present these questions so that there may be clearly seen the equity with which Colombia proceeds in her petitions. At present, if there is lacking any example of her liberality in concessions of land, it will be sufficient to demonstrate the increase of the Canal Zone from the 200 meters conceded to the company to the 5,000 meters offered to the United States.

"The preceding reasons serve in part, also, to demonstrate the necessity that exists that the Government of Colombia shall celebrate a special contract with the companies which are to cede their rights; but to them we add, that the treaty between Colombia and the United States can not have the judicial faculties of adjusting or cancelling the bonds which exist between the Republic of Colombia and those companies, bonds arising from perfect contracts which can not be undone, in conformity with the principles of universal jurisprudence, because one of the parties celebrates a pact concerning the same material with a third party, which in this case would be the United States. Thus, as these latter must enter into a contract to acquire the rights of the companies themselves, this negotiation could not be included in the treaty that has to be celebrated between the two countries, any more than the resolution of the obligations between Colombia and the companies. Of any other manner, the result would be that Colombia, relinquishing all of her rights in relation to these antities, or depriving herself of the means of making them effective, would leave in force her obligations to them. The very payment of the preferred shares of the canal company, possessed by Colombia would have no guarantee if a special contract was omitted, especially as in the reform proposed by the Department of State to article 1 of the memorandum of April, it is expressly stated that the United States will not contract any obligation in that respect ('No obligation under this provision is imposed upon or assumed by the United States').

"No matter how sincere and earnest may be the desire of the Colombian Government to remove the difficulties from the negotiations, it could not, without causing irreparable damage to interets of the Colombian people, withdraw the conditions which have been expressed regarding article 1."

Disgusted by the attitude of his own Government, and his revulsion against Americans roused to a passion, Dr. Concha cabled to Bogota on November 28, 1902, that Dr. Tomas Herran, secretary, would take his place as chargé d'affaires and the same day, without waiting for his letters of recall, Dr. Concha left Washington. He did not even take leave of the State Department. His last official act before leaving was to transmit to Bogota the Cromwell-Hay draft of the treaty of November 18, 1902, which he refused to sign.

Dr. Herran entered upon his work with the following instructions cabled December 11, 1902, from Bogota:

"Do all you can to get $10,000,000 cash and $600,000 yearly payment, and all possible advantages as per former instructions. Demand a written declaration from the United States Government that it will not make any better terms, if such be the case, and sign the treaty with the indispensable stipulation that it be subjected to whatever the Colombian Congress decides."

At this time, to quote Mr. Cromwell, "Secretary Hay considered that his duty was to continue the negotiations with Nicaragua and Costa Rica," but "the President took the responsibility of granting a new and brief delay and abstained from making remarks upon the matter in his message."

Dr. Herran gave his Government a more truthful account of the juggling of Roosevelt's message in a letter dated December 19, 1902, in which he said that he had been told confidentially that the President in the first draft of his message had discussed the inactivity of Colombia and had proposed demanding an answer by January 5, 1903. Herran added that his confidential informant (presumably Cromwell) told him that "at the instance of various members of the Cabinet and several Senators, this part of the message was suppressed and was replaced by the colorless paragraph on Colombia." The "colorless paragraph," or rather paragraphs, on the canal in Mr. Roosevelt's message of December 2, 1902, follow:

"The Congress has wisely provided that we shall build at once an Isthmian Canal, if possible at Panama. The Attorney General reports that we can undoubtedly acquire good title from the French Panama Canal Co. Negotiations are now pending with Colombia to secure her assent to our building the canal. This canal will be one of the greatest engineering feats of the twentieth century; a greater engineering feat than has yet been accomplished during the history of mankind. The work should be carried out as a continuing policy without regard to change of administration; and it should be begun under circumstances which will make it a matter of pride for all administrations to continue the policy.

"The canal will be of great benefit to America, and of importance to all the world. It will be of advantage to us industrially and also as improving our military position. It will be of advantage to the countries of tropical America. It is earnestly to be hoped that all of these countries will do as some of them have already done with signal success, and will invite to their shores commerce and improve their material conditions by recognizing that stability and order are the prerequisites of successful development. No independent nation in America need have the slightest fear of aggression from the United States. It behooves each one to maintain order within its own borders and to discharge its just obligations to foreigners. When this is done they can rest assured that, be they strong or weak, they will have nothing to dread from outside interference. More and more the increasing interdependence and complexity of international, political, and economic relations render it incumbent on all civilized and orderly powers to insist on the proper policing of the world."

Dr. Herran, to quote Mr. Cromwell, "maintained intimate and confidential relations with us." On this account, so he says, he knew what were Herran's instructions. Mr. Cromwell's story proceeds:

"The United States continued firmly to oppose the Concha amendments and the increase of indemnities. We understood that unless the parties were brought into accord the negotiations must fail and the consequences of this would be disastrous. At least two of our partners were absorbed by this affair in conference with Chargé d'Affaires Herran, Secretary Hay, and others. Mr. Cromwell urged Mr. Hay to increase the annuity, and on December 12, after a long conference with him, the latter, after a conference with the President, authorized us to promise Minister Herran an increase of annuity payable by the United States from $10.000 to $100,000 a year."

Again corroborating Mr. Cromwell the Colombian Blue Book presents Dr. Harran's cable to his Government, December 13, 1902:

"Government of the United States, after various discussions, offers maximum $10,000,000 cash and afterwards an annuity of $100,000. I think this is unacceptable, but await orders of the Colombian Government."

In his letter of December 19, 1902, in addition to reporting to his Government the change in Roosevelt's message, whereby further delay was granted, Dr. Herran said:

"Besides this deferred ultimatum another danger threatens us. Mr. Shelby M. Cullom, Senator from Illinois and chairman of the Committee on Foreign Relations, maintains that in case Colombia does not lend itself to a satisfactory agreement the Government of the United States can come to an understanding with the Canal Co. direct, passing over the head of Colombia and expropriating part of our territory, justifying this on the ground of universal public utility, and leaving the compensation due to Colombia to be decided upon later. * * * President Roosevelt is a determined partisan of the Panama route, and in view of his impetuous and violent disposition it is to be feared that the scheme of Senator Cullom is not distasteful to him."

How accurate was Dr. Herran's conception appears later when President Roosevelt calls Senator Cullom to Oyster Bay to discuss his scheme, and later when Mr. Roosevelt admits in his message to Congress, January 4, 1904, that he entertained this very purpose.

His fears more fully confirmed, Dr. Herran cabled to his Government, December 25, 1902: "Probable that State Department will present ultimatum January 5."

December 31, 1902, the Colombian Government cabled Herran: "We await with impatience ultimatum announced, so as to decide whether you shall sign."

Instead of the ultimatum which Dr. Herran was expecting, he received the following letter:

DEPARTMENT OF STATE,
Washington, December 30, 1902.

ESTEEMED MR. MINISTER: I regret appearing to importune you, but to-day it is absolutely necessary that I report to the President regarding the condition of our negotiations. Will you have the kindness to let me know as briefly as possible what I should say.

JOHN HAY.

December 31, 1902, Dr. Herran replied to Secretary Hay:

"MY DEAR SIR: In answer to your letter of yesterday I hasten to inform you that, although I immediately telegraphed to Bogota synopsis of our last conference, I have not yet received instructions that enable me to resolve in a satisfactory manner the difficulty that exists regarding the annuity to be authorized to Colombia.

"The instructions according to which I am proceeding fix that annuity in $600,000; considering that this sum is a just equivalent of the rent which Colombia should receive in view of the stipulation of the projected treaty.

"The discrepancy between the sum offered and the sum demanded is so great that it does not appear as if we can arrive at an advantageous agreement; but, as before the annuity shall begin several years must elapse, possibly the present difficulty can be overcome by deferring determination of the annuity for a future contract between the two Governments."

Mr. Cromwell in his own story says that Secretary Hay "prepared to close the negotiations, and so informed us. * * * Such action, although fully justified, would have a disastrous effect and would involve as a consequence the selection of Nicaragua, and we conferred personally with Secretary Hay on January 2, 1903, and also wrote him beseeching him not to send his ultimatum." As a result of this "beseeching" and more "urgent pleadings" in another long conference on Januray 3, 1903, Mr. Cromwell says "Secretary Hay consented to put off his ultimatum for a brief time." Mr. Cromwell adds that "we immediately devoted one whole day to a conference with Minister Herran, and we collaborated in preparing a cablegram to Bogota urgently demanding wider powers in the negotiations, but these instructions did not arrive." If such a cablegram as Mr. Cromwell describes was sent by Dr. Herran it was suppressed when Gen. Reyes compiled the "Blue Book."

Mr. Cromwell here neglected to relate or to claim responsibility for a further concession which appears in the following cable of Herran to his Government, January 3, 1903:

"Final proposition of American Government ten millions cash and one hundred thousand annually after nine years. They add stipulation that once Panama Canal is open the two Governments can negotiate an equitable increase of the annuity. This cablegram is urgent, because the Congress will make a definite decision soon."

In a letter to his Government, Dr. Herran confirmed this cable and supplied a copy of Secretary Hay's proposal as follows (translation):

"*Stipulation proposed by Secretary Hay January 3, 1903.*

"It is agreed that when the canal shall have been finished, if the circumstances appear to justify an increase in the annuity above stipulated ($100,000), the two Governments, by mutual initiative, may discuss the point by diplomatic negotiations."

How such diplomacy as this could have originated outside of Mr. Cromwell's private Department of State is quite as inconceivable as that he should have been, as in all else, the initiator and should have forgotten to claim credit—and pay—for it. Mr. Cromwell says he did induce Secretary Hay to increase the annuity to $100,000, but says nothing of the plan to negotiate a later increase.

Again comes up the usefulness of having brought "within the domain of international relations" the question of Colombia's permitting the canal company to transfer its concession. Let Mr. Cromwell tell:

"In the meanwhile (Jan. 3) the United States minister at Bogota, Mr. Hart, informed Secretary Hay by cable that the Colombian Government was determined to demand an indemnity from the canal company before ratifying a treaty. We immediately had conferences with Secretary Hay and the President (purely 'formal exchange of courtesies,' of course!) to combat Colombia's attitude.

"At one of these interviews Secretary Hay told us that President Roosevelt had informed him that he would approve the Nicaragua and Costa Rica treaties and send them to the Senate for ratification if Colombia did not act promptly, and Secretary Hay authorized us to repeat these words to Minister Herran, which we did at once."

Advising his Government by mail on January 8, 1903, Dr. Herran wrote in part:

"The President shows that he is determined to terminate negotiations for the construction of the interoceanic canal, whether it be by Panama or by Nicaragua, before the 4th of March, the date on which the present Congress will close its meetings. He is a decided partisan of the Panama route, but he does not reject that of Nicaragua, and probably will adopt the latter in case he does not quickly arrive at a satisfactory arrangement with Colombia.

"Another alternative presented to us is the adoption of the treacherous project of Senator Cullom—expropriation of the coveted zone in Panama—invoking therefor 'universal public utility' and offering to pay Colombia the value of the territory so usurped in accordance with appraisal by experts. This contingency appears to me very improbable, but I do not venture to qualify it as being absolutely impossible.

Dr. Herran's "confidence in us" and the "intimate and confidential relations," of which Mr. Cromwell advised the French arbitrators, had passed behind a cloud of distrust by this time, if we may judge from Dr. Herran's letter to his Government, January 9, 1903, in which he said:

"In the initial period of our work here, when it was necessary to gain adherents to the Panama route, in competition with that of Nicaragua, the agents of the Panama Canal Co. were very useful allies, especially Mr. William Nelson Cromwell, the clever lawyer of the company, a man of indefatigable activity and great influence. So long as the interests of Colombia and the canal company were identical, this powerful cooperation was most useful, but now these interests are no longer common and I am working independently of our former allies. Now that the Panama route has been preferred, the agents of the company, in order to clinch the negotiations they have begun with the United States, are doing all they can to have the treaty signed, no matter what the cost to Colombia. Mr. Philippe Bunau-Varilla is trying to intervene officiously in this affair and I know that he has been sending cables to the Colombian Government. This gentleman is an important shareholder of the canal company, but he holds no official position in it; his activity is entirely on his own account and "he represents solely his own interests."

January 10, 1903, President Marroquin and Foreign Minister Paul stated by cable that they supposed the Concha amendments had been accepted by the United States. They instructed Dr. Herran to try to get better pecuniary terms and some reduction in the delay to elapse before the annuity payments begin. "If this is not possible and you see that by the delay everything may be lost, sign the treaty," is the final instruction. Herran did not receive this cable until January 16, when immediately he showed it to Cromwell.

On the same day, January 16, 1903, so Mr. Cromwell says, he was told by Secretary Hay that Minister Hart had cabled from Bogota that Colombia would not accept the conditions imposed by the United States and that she had instructed Herran to hold out for all the Concha amendments. Mr. Cromwell then sets forth in his story the ultimatum to Colombia sent by cable to Minister Hart. This ultimatum was communicated also to Dr. Herran in the following letter from Secretary Hay, dated January 16, 1903:

"DEAR MR. HERRAN: I must inform you that by telegram to-day I have told our minister in Bogota that if the Government persists in its present attitude it will make impossible future negotiations."

Dr. Herran acknowledged with thanks the receipt of this note from Secretary Hay, but added no comment. Mr. Cromwell then goes on with his story:

"Senator Morgan and others were every day renewing their urging to the President and Secretary of State for the termination of the negotiations with Colombia and the selection of the Nicaragua route.

"The Bogota Government maintained its obstinate, indifferent and exacting attitude, both toward the United States and the canal company * * * It was evident to all that unless the negotiations reached a climax at once, the President would be not only within his rights in abandoning them because of Colombia's attitude, but would also be obliged to do so by virtue of the very provisions of the Spooner law which provided an alternative and granted him only a reasonable delay to conclude this treaty."

"It is no exaggeration," confided Mr. Cromwell, to the arbitrators, "to say we were almost in despair," and that "under these critical conditions we were busy for several successive days developing our arguments with the chargé d'affaires of Colombia, examining with him the instructions that had been given, and discussing different plans to bring him to an agreement * * * We were holding continuous sessions with Mr. Herran and at last we persuaded him to assume the responsibility and abandon all the Concha amendments."

Mr. Cromwell was not, however, "out of the deadlock as to the pecuniary clauses," but "we continued our efforts to persuade him (Herran), and again Mr. Cromwell found a solution" by inducing Dr. Herran to sign an agreement to submit the question of the amount of the annuity to a commission with the president of The Hauge Tribunal as arbiter Cromwell says: "We immediately presented this note to Secretary Hay and the President, urging them to approve it," and "after long conferences we were authorized to announce to Mr. Herran that his proposition would be accepted, unless a definite sum could be fixed by argument, which was preferred."

So Mr. Cromwell, guarding patriotically the interests of his country, for a second time induced the President and Secretary of State to commit the question of future payment—a question eventually involving hundreds of millions of dollars—to the arbitrament of a foreigner of unknown tendencies and sympathies.

January 20, 1903, Dr. Herran cabled to the Colombian Minister of Foreign Affairs: "The Department of State in Washington considers as an ultimatum the draft of November 18, and will return the observations of Concha. Discussion of the annuity continues without obtaining any further concession than that stated in my cable of the 3d. Should it be necessary I will sign treaty as per your cable of January 10."

January 22, 1903, Dr. Herran wrote to the Colombian Minister of Foreign Affairs, referring to Secretary Hay's amendments of November 28, 1902, which he says were not at that time explicitly stated to be an ultimatum, and notes that Dr. Concha on the 22d of November, 1902, replied to Secretary Hay rejecting many of the stipulations. Dr. Herran states that Secretary Hay did not even acknowledge receipt of this reply of Dr. Concha, and says that then "the negotiations were suspended if not broken off." Dr. Herran reviews the negotiations and adds: "Meanwhile I have taken up this question with several Senators and, availing myself of an excellent intermediary, with the President himself, * * * I have given the President to know that even if I was authorized to do so I would not accept the annuity of $100,000. I understand that to-day or to-morrow a formal ultimatum will be presented to me with the annuity doubled or a little more. If this happens, I will accept in compliance with the orders contained in your cable of the 10th of this month. Moreover, my acceptation will be given in conformity with your orders and instructions your excellency has communicated to me." These orders reserved the acceptance of the treaty to the decision of the Colombian Congress.

In the "Blue Book" of Colombian diplomatic correspondence, it appears that nothing more was cabled or written until January 23, 1903, when Herran cabled to the foreign minister in Bogota: "I signed to-day treaty accepting ultimatum ten millions and two hundred and fifty thousand dollars annuity." Mr. Cromwell supplies the following:

"Having made this progress (inducing Herran to sign the arbitration stipulation, thus putting off the ultimatum of the United States), we proposed a transaction on the basis of $250,000 a year. * * * The United States, however, had not displayed the least inclination to exceed the figure of $100,000. At last Mr. Herran yielded to our urging and authorized us to offer Mr. Hay a transaction on the basis of $250,000. Although the success was great, it still remains to induce the United States to increase the indemnity to acceptance of this figure."

Mr. Cromwell, if we may take his own words for it, by "arguments and persuasions" induced Secretary Hay to authorize the transaction, provided Herran would accept the other terms of the treaty. Mr. Cromwell then made "a supreme effort" and "brought him (Herran) to an understanding;" then "rapidly corrected the draft of the treaty," took it and Dr. Herran to Secretary Hay's house on the night of January 22, 1903, and was the sole witness there to the signing by Hay and Herran of this celebrated treaty, thus completing this stage in the negotiations which Mr. Roosevelt says were "initiated by Colombia."

Mr. Cromwell neglects to state that he was assisted in bringing Herran to an "understanding" by the following ultimatum:

DEPARTMENT OF STATE,
Washington, January 22, 1903.

ESTEEMED MR. HERRAN: I am commanded by the President to say to you that the reasonable time that the statute accords for the conclusion of negotiations with Colombia for the excavation of a canal on the Isthmus has expired, and he has authorized me to sign with you the treaty of which I had the honor to give you a draft, with the modification that the sum of $100,000 fixed therein as the annual payment be increased to $250.000. I am not authorized to consider or discuss any other change.

With sentiments of high consideration, etc., JOHN HAY.

Mr. Cromwell takes to himself for the conclusion of these diplomatic negotiations the following credit:

"It is not through vanity, but simply because it is absolutely necessary to state the fact, so as to point out the true significance of this service, that it is worthy of notice here that the entire negotiation of the treaty with Colombia was conducted by Mr. Cromwell."

Modestly, behind parentheses, in his brief, Mr. Cromwell calls to the judicial attention of the arbitrators of his fee the significant fact that—

("The pen with which the Secretary and the chargé d'affaires signed this treaty is one of the previous souvenirs of this incident; the Secretary made a present of it to Mr. Cromwell as a token of the part which he had taken in the negotiations that had been so long, and apparently so hopeless.")

Before passing from his labors as diplomat, in negotiating the Hay-Herran treaty, to those of lobbyist, in securing its ratification by the United States Senate, Mr. Cromwell impresses upon the French arbitrators "as a historical detail which shows by what a narrow margin we succeeded," that "a few hours after the signing of the treaty Mr. Herran received a peremptory cablegram from his Government directing him to suspend all negotiations until he should receive new instructions," and that, "thanks to strongest pressure, we succeeded in having the treaty concluded to avoid this very possibility which we had feared."

The cable ordering Herran not to sign this treaty—which Mr. Roosevelt told Congress had been "entered into at the urgent solicitation of the people of Columbia"—was carefully suppressed by the Marroquin-Reyes gang of politicians when they gave out the "Blue Book" of diplomatic correspondence to explain to the people of Colombia how they had caused the loss of Panama. From another source the World procured this cable, which follows:

[Translation.]

BOGOTA, *January 24, 1903.*

COLOMBIAN MINISTER, *Washington:*

Do not sign canal treaty. You will receive instructions in letter of to-day.

MARROQUIN.

The letter of instructions referred to in Marroquin's cable also was suppressed.

It is interesting to note that although the situation was so desperate, as pictured by Mr. Cromwell in his claim for fees, his assurance was so great that on January 21, 1903—the day before Secretary Hay delivered his ultimatum by order of President Roosevelt, and the day before Cromwell led Herran to Hay's house to sign the treaty—he felt so sure of the outcome that "we wrote to the company announcing to it the happy conclusion of the treaty."

Dr. Herran's reports to his Government on the signing of the treaty, and his reasons for doing so, follow:

[Cable.]

WASHINGTON, *January 22, 1903.*

FOREIGN AFFAIRS, *Bogota:*

Treaty signed to-day, accepting ultimatum ten millions and two hundred and fifty thousand dollars annuity.

HERRAN.

[Letter.]

WASHINGTON, *January 29, 1903.*

HIS EXCELLENCY THE MINISTER OF FOREIGN AFFAIRS,
Dr. FELIPE F. PAUL, *Bogota:*

On the evening of the 22d of this month, after having dispatched the letter which I directed to your excellency on that date, I received the ultimatum, a copy of which I inclose.

The same evening I had an interview with the Secretary of State, in his house, and there signed the treaty, accepting the ultimate conditions of his final proposal. This matter did not admit of any further postponement, and I was obliged to take one of the two courses that presented themselves, either to accept a treaty which does not satisfy us, or abandon all hope that the interoceanic canal will be opened through Colombian territory. Being guided by the categorical orders which your excellency has communicated to me and reiterated respecting the acceptance of an ultimatum in such a case as actually has presented itself, I decided upon the first alternative. It is now incumbent on the Colombian Congress finally to resolve this important matter, as without its acceptance the treaty signed has no value, and the Congress is entirely at liberty to approve or reject it.

To the many difficulties that have surrounded me in the course of these arduous negotiations have been added additional embarrassments caused by recent cables from the American Minister in Bogota and the agent of the canal company. Both asserted and reiterated that the Colombian Government had ordered me to accept the ultimatum that would be presented to me, even if the annuity of $100,000 were not increased. This was communicated to me by the Secretary of State. I answered that the information furnished him was not trustworthy, and added that I should persist in my resolution to reject so small an annuity. This reply resulted in the ultimatum which is inclosed, in which the annuity is increased to $250,000. For the reasons that I already have pointed out, I accepted this final proposition, although I did not give it my approval.

TOMAS HERRAN.

January 23, 1903, the day after it was signed, President Roosevelt sent the Hay-Herran convention to the Senate, and until March 17, 1903, Mr. Cromwell was busy lobbying it to ratification. We leave the recounting of these exploits to Mr. Cromwell's own shameless confession, and follow his trail "in the domain of international relations," whereby now he had securely intrenched his client.

The option given to the United States by the New Panama Canal Co. expired on March 4, 1903. Mr. Cromwell says Secretary Hay told him that the extension of the option must be made without any pledges on the part of the United States, which would be unsatisfactory to the company, as Mr. Cromwell feared any change in the form of the option would cause legal complications in France, or with Columbia. So he proposed that the United States accept an extension of the option, "under the sole reservation of the ratification of the Colombian treaty and of the legal formalities, and so give to the affair the character of a conditional pledge instead of extending the option, without obtaining a pledge." Mr. Cromwell says he devoted himself to this subject for two weeks, with conferences with Secretary Hay and the President, the Attorney General, and his friendly Senators, and finally induced the United States to accept. Attorney General Knox accordingly wrote a formal acceptance of the extension of the option, with the conditions desired by Mr. Cromwell, on February 17, 1903.

But Mr. Cromwell wanted more, so he wrote asking Mr. Knox to confirm an interpretation of the option, which he set forth as follows: "(1) That the phrase in your cablegram 'properties, etc., in Paris' means only the plans and records in Paris, as it is stated in the company's cable of January 11, 1902; (2) that the company takes no obligation to obtain a modification of Articles XXI and XXII of the contract of concession."

Under this option the "records" turned over eventually to the United States never did include the financial records whereby the actual ownership of the canal stock could be traced. The second clause Mr. Cromwell sought to have interpreted affected the transfer of the concession which Mr. Cromwell was seeking to accomplish without paying tribute to Colombia.

Attorney General Knox declined to enter into any interpretation at this time, so Mr. Cromwell maintained silence for a fortnight, and on March 3, 1903, sent a formal ratification of the agreement. Mr. Cromwell calls the attention of the arbitrators to his having kept the United States waiting for this answer until he was assured that Mr. Roosevelt would call the extra session which was to ratify the treaty. The call was issued March 2, 1903, after Mr. Cromwell, according to his story, had held "constant conferences with Senator Hanna and other party leaders during this critical period," and "urgently demanded an extraordinary session to assure action upon the treaty."

Recounting the advantages of his strategy, in securing the acceptance of the extended option in the form he desired, Mr. Cromwell says: "It also gave the company a great advantage in its resistance to the exactions of Colombia." From this time on we see Mr. Cromwell and his brood of speculators huddling closer and closer under the wing of the American eagle, and the advantage of having brought the question of transfer of the canal concession within the "domain of international relations" can not escape notice.

The Colombian Blue Book for this period is strangely barren of correspondence. Gen. Reyes permitted to creep into it, however, one significant letter from Jose Pablo Uribe, then Colombian Minister to France, dated Paris, February 7, 1903. It was addressed to the Colombian Minister for Foreign Affairs, Bogota, in part as follows:

"In the journal of quotations of the Paris Bourse there has been published a notice of the syndicate of bankers (corresponding to the board of governors of the stock exchange), announcing that they will admit to purchase and sale only the shares of the New Panama Canal Co. marked with the numbers from 1 to 600,000. This action excludes the shares of the Government of Colombia, which are those numbered from 600,001 to 650,000, and can not be negotiated as are the others; naturally this measure serves as a pretext for depreciating their value, which should be the same as the others.

"We clearly see the intention to impede the sale of the shares that belong to Colombia, or the idea of buying them cheap.

"Possibly they figure that in this way Colombia will accelerate the signing and ratification of the treaties referring to the canal, so that they may, with greater facility, have this value (collateral) for negotiation. In this there is an error, because it is not the way to compel us to do that which is desired by the speculators, nor do I think that this measure is adjustable to the law and practice in such matters."

March 25, 1903, reporting by letter to his Government on the final debate in the American Senate before ratification of the canal treaty, Dr. Herran said in part:

"Those interested in the transcontinental railway companies of this country are giving powerful aid to this Senator (Mr. Morgan, of Alabama) and it is probable that they will send to Bogota a commission well equipped to foment and invigorate the opposition that is being organized in our Congress against the treaty that has been celebrated.

"It was with much difficulty that approbation of the treaty was obtained here without modification; even our best friends, among whom were Senator Spooner, of Wisconsin, Hanna and Foraker, of Ohio, considered certain amendments indispensable. At last, however, they understood, as did the President, that the proposed amendments would probably frustrate approbation of the treaty in Colombia. The powerful influences which could be brought into the game, nevertheless, gave as a result the success which we obtained."

The canal and railroad companies had been formally notified by the Colombian Government in February, 1903 (notifications dated in December, 1902), to send representatives to Bogota to be present when Congress met and negotiate for the transfer of their concessions, and this purpose, of which Mr. Cromwell had been apprised, made him all the more determined to force into the treaty the stipulation in Article I that Colombia consented to the transfer. It will be recalled that Concha refused to admit this stipulation, and that Herran did so only when Mr. Cromwell convinced him that the United States would end the negotiations and only in view of Secretary Hay's answer to Concha's amendment thereto that "The United States considers this suggestion wholly inadmissible." In this connection we find Mr. Cromwell boasting "we have also treated of the refusal of the United States to accede to this amendment (of Concha's requiring special agreement between the companies and Colombia), due to our repeated arguments and objections."

Mr. Cromwell says that as early as January 3, 1903, Minister Hart cabled to Secretary Hay that Colombia was counting on demanding an indemnity from the canal company, and that "on January 9, 1903, Secretary Hay informed us that he knew positively that the delay which had overtaken the negotiations and the attitude of Colombia were due to the refusal of the Panama Canal Co. to negotiate for the consent of Colombia to pay the tribute which Colombia had resolved to exact before concluding the treaty."

Scarcely had the treaty been ratified when the State Department set its machinery in motion to protect the canal speculators from the exactions of Colombia. The first move of the State Department, so far as the published correspondence shows, was the following cable from Secretary Hay to the American minister in Bogota:

"April 7, 1904.

"Referring to the requests of Colombia to canal and railroad companies for appointment of agents to negotiate cancellation of present concessions, et cetera, if the subject arises, inform the Colombian Government that the treaty covers entire matter, and any change would be in violation of Spooner law and not permissible."

The diplomatic correspondence sent to the United Senate shows that from this time on the "Big Stick" was swung incessantly in support of the ridiculous proposition that the exaction of an indemnity from the canal company by Colombia was in violation of the Spooner law!

Mr. Beaupre was keeping the State Department well advised, and according to Mr. Cromwell, "Secretary Hay communicated to us as fast as they were received" all news of this danger threatening the company in Bogota.

April 24, 1903, Mr. Beaupre deemed it best, although the subject had not arisen, to sound the Colombian minister of foreign affairs upon the intentions to exact payment from the canal company to transfer the concession, and he so notified Secretary Hay by letter of this date.

Long before this Mr. Cromwell had recognized "that the only means of escaping from these demands * * * and of saving the company from the payment of a tribute of many millions of francs was to convince the American Government that it must refuse to consent to any amendment * * * as Colombia was demanding." So before Mr. Beaupre's letter reached the State Department, Mr. Cromwell had had "numerous conferences with Secretary Hay, Senators Hanna, Spooner, and Kittredge, Representative Burton, and other leaders in Congress, and on certain occasions with the President"; and had induced the American Government to accept Mr. Cromwell's view "that Colombia had already morally pledged herself to consent and that her consent ought to be imposed upon her as being exacted by international good faith."

Accordingly Mr. Hay, under date of April 28, 1903, wrote to Mr. Beaupre instructions concerning which Mr. Cromwell says: "Secretary Hay honored us with his confidence in permitting us to collaborate with him in preparing these instructions." So intimate were the relations between the diplomatic bureau of 49 Wall Street and the State Department that Mr. Cromwell "sent a copy of these instructions (supposed secret diplomatic correspondence) to the Company, which expressed its appreciation in the following cable:

"'MAY 14, 1903.

"'We have received Mr. Hay's letter of instructions to the United States minister at Bogota, which satisfies us and for this we thank you.'"

So plainly does Secretary Hay's letter to Mr. Beaupre bear the imprint of Cromwellian argument and style that the Panama lobbyist's boast of being Mr. Hay's collaborator in its preparation is indeed modest. The instructions read as though Mr. Cromwell had drafted them himself. In part this letter to the American minister follows:

"Such action on the part of Colombia or on that of the companies would be inconsistent with the agreements already made between this Government and this canal company, with the act of June 28, 1902, under the authority of which the treaty was made, and with the express terms of the treaty itself.

"By the act of June 28, 1902, the President was authorized to acquire, at a cost not exceeding $40,000,000, the 'rights, privileges, franchises, and concessions,' and other property of the New Panama Canal Co., and an agreement to that end was made by him with the company. It was, of course, known to the President, to the company, and to the Government of Colombia that, by articles 21 and 22 of the Salgar-Wyse concession of 1878, the company could not transfer to the United States its 'rights, privileges, franchises, and concessions' without the consent of Colombia. Therefore, and before entering upon any dealings with the New Panama Canal Co., the present treaty with Colombia was negotiated and signed."

Long before the canal treaty was negotiated or signed, the United States, through the Isthmian Canal Commission, had entered upon dealings with the New Panama Canal Co., formally asking hat company to name a price at which it would transfer these "rights, privileges, franchises, and concessions," and the Spooner law had been passed, because the United States held that company's option to sell for $40,000,000.

The Hay-Cromwell instructions to the American minister continue:

"The first article of that treaty provides as follows:

"The Government of Colombia authorizes the New Panama Canal Co. to sell and transfer to the United States its rights, privileges, properties, and concessions, as well as the Panama Railroad and all the shares or parts of shares of said company.

"The authorization thus given, it will be observed, covers expressly the 'rights, privileges * * * and concessions' of the company, as well as its other property.

"Colombia now, by these notices, indicates a purpose not only of disregarding the authorization thus explicitly given * * * but to destroy a great part of the subject matter to which it refers. She states an intention of requiring the company to cancel all obligations of Colombia to it, and thus to deprive the United States of the rights, privileges, and concessions which she has expressly authorized the company to transfer to them and which the canal company has contracted to sell and convey to the United States.

"This Government can not approve such a transaction either by Colombia or by the company. * * * The Government of Colombia initiated the negotiations, and it can not be conceived that it should now disclaim its own propositions, nor can this Government acquiesce in such a course. * * * It is not necessary here to consider the question of good faith toward the canal company which would be raised by new exactions of that company at this time."

The canal company had been given repeated notice of these "new exactions," and, as Mr. Cromwell's confessions show, was preparing to use the "big stick" to resist them. Mr. Hay's letter proceeds:

"The foregoing considerations, however, though sufficient in themselves to justify this Government in declining to recognize any right of the Republic of Colombia to limit the consent given by Article I of the treaty by any terms or conditions of any kind, are less important than others arising from the actual negotiations attending the making of the treaty. These other considerations render it impossible that any such new limitations should even be considered, and give any attempt by Colombia in that direction the character of a serious departure from the agreement reached between the Executive Governments of the two nations."

Mr. Hay then sets forth as "these other considerations" the supposed Colombian origin of the treaty, which Mr. Cromwell, however, admits having negotiated himself, and cites Colombia's consent in the treaty to the transfer of the canal concession, which Mr. Cromwell cajoled or bullied Minister Concha into including in the first draft of March 31, 1902. Mr. Hay declares that Concha assented to this proposal until November 11, 1902, when he proposed amendment of Article I, which the United States rejected as "wholly inadmissible." And here is what Mr. Cromwell had been playing for in getting the question of consent brought "within the domain of international relations." The Hay-Cromwell instructions continue:

"The consent of Colombia to the sale of the canal company's property and concessions to the United States is a matter of agreement between the two nations. It has not been granted by Colombia to the company alone, but also to the United States. To that agreement neither the canal nor the railroad company is or can be a party; nor can the United States permit its international compacts to be dependent in any degree upon the action of any private corporation. Such a course would be consistent neither with the dignity of either nation nor with their interests. To make the effectiveness of the agreement between Colombia and the United States depend upon the willingness of the canal company to enter into arrangements with Colombia of a character satisfactory to that country would not only give that company an influence which it can never be permitted to exercise in the diplomatic affairs and international relations of this country but would enable it to control the acquisition by the United States of the rights granted by Colombia and the enjoyment by Colombia of the equivalent advantages secured to her by the United States."

From the very first the Hay-Herran treaty was opposed by public sentiment in Colombia. March 30, 1903, Mr. Beaupre, who had succeeded Hart as minister, reported by letter to Secretary Hay that "without question public opinion is strongly against its ratification," and that "it is apparent lately that the French Canal Co. is to take a decided interest in securing the ratification of the convention, and that its influence to that end will be of much importance."

April 15, 1903, Mr. Beaupre advised Secretary Hay that "from approbation to suspicion and from suspicion to decided opposition have been the phases of change in public sentiment during the last month," and that "this fact is clear, that if the proposed convention were to be submitted to the free opinion of the people it would not pass."

May 4, 1903, a letter of Mr. Beaupre to Secretary Hay represents Alexander Mancini, agent of the French Canal Co. at Bogota, as being emphatically of the opinion "that the Congress will refuse to ratify the convention and that he (Mancini) has written to his company to that effect." Thus early was Mr. Cromwell given reason for his abiding faith, which he avows repeatedly in his own story, that the canal treaty would be rejected and that it would be necessary to make a revolution in Panama.

The diplomatic correspondence of Colombia during this period was suppressed, and there appears in the "Blue Book" nothing between April 8, 1903, and August 13, 1903, when the treaty was rejected, excepting a note from the former Colombian minister to Washington, Dr. Concha, on July 7, 1903, when he wrote to President Marroquin:

"It would be well in the course of the debates to rectify the error into which some papers have fallen that Colombia proposed the negotiation to the American Government, when, on the contrary, it was the Isthmian Canal Commission, presided over by Admiral Walker, which began the discussion of the matter with Dr. Silva."

May 7, 1903, Mr. Beaupre notified the State Department by cable that the Colombian Congress had been called to meet June 20, 1903. On the same day by letter he makes the first reference which appears in the published diplomatic correspondence of the United States to the secession of Panama. "The probabilities," says Mr. Beaupre, "are that when the measure is presented to Congress there will be a lengthy debate and an adverse report. Then the representatives of the coast departments of the Cauca, Panama, and Bolivar will ask for a reconsideration and urge a ratification of the convention as the only means of preventing a secession of those departments and the attempt to constitute of their territories an independent republic. The debate will be resumed, and in the end the friends of the Government and of confirmation will prevail."

May 12, 1903, Mr. Beaupre transmitted to the State Department translation of an extract from an article written by Dr. Juan B. Perez y Sota, who had been elected a Senator from the Department of Panama, as indicative of the popular feeling against the Hay-Herran convention. In this article the Panama senator said:

"The Herran treaty will be rejected, and rejected by a unanimous vote, in both chambers. * * * The insult, however, which Herran had cast upon the Colombian name will never be wiped out. The gallows would be a small punishment for a criminal of this class."

June 2, 1903, Secretary Hay wrote to Mr. Beaupre: "You should, when the time seems opportune, in so far as you discreetly and properly may, exert your influence in favor of ratification. It is also expected that you will know what hostile influences, if any, are at work against the ratification of the treaty and whether or not there is opposition to it from European sources. The situation is seemingly a grave one, but the department has confidence that you will rise to the full measure of its requirements."

Mr. Cromwell tells of his receiving a detailed report from Charles Burdett Hart upon his return from Bogota May 30, 1903, and his sending Farnham to see Hart in Virginia later in the summer. Hart came from Bogota at this time, having been permitted to return to Colombia to remove his belongings and resign after answering charges filed against him by the Colombian Government. Hart's son was engaged in business in Bogota with the son of J. Gabriel Duque, owner of the Panama lottery and the Panama Star and Herald. Here was another close link between Panama and the diplomatic offices of Hay and Cromwell. While ex-Minister Hart was advising Cromwell, the younger Duque was lobbying in Bogota for the ratification of the treaty.

Mr. Cromwell says that on June 2, 1903, Secretary Hay received from Mr. Beaupre a cable saying that Colombia "was determined to compel the company to make a heavy payment, without which no ratification." If such a cable was transmitted, it was suppressed when the diplomatic correspondence was called for by the Senate.

Mr. Cromwell's next diplomatic maneuver was devising the Beaupre ultimatum, cabled from Washington June 9, 1903, and delivered to Dr. Luis Carlos Rico, Colombian minister for foreign affairs, June 13, 1903. Mr. Cromwell says he proposed this step to Secretary Hay because of the manifest intention of the Colombian Congress, which had been called to meet June 20, to exact an indemnity from the canal company. Mr. Cromwell thought it would serve his purpose "to have the American Government announce to the Colombian Government in advance of the meeting of its Congress, and with absolute frankness and firmness, that the United States had been led to adopt the Panama route and to make its engagements with the canal company, relying on Colombia's propositions for a treaty and upon the consent that was compromised in these propositions."

Then Mr. Cromwell puts the Beaupre ultimatum up to Mr. Roosevelt's responsibility as follows:

"The Secretary accepted these views and submitted them to the President, who a few days later sent for Mr. Cromwell for an audience on the matter, and after deliberation directed that instructions be sent to Colombia, which was done by Secretary Hay in a message, in which it was said: * * *"

Mr. Cromwell appears to have given to the French arbitrators his own original rough draft of the ultimatum, for his version, although a verbatim quotation of the most important phrases of the official text does not contain all of the following cable as Secretary Hay sent it to Minister Beaupre:

"The Colombian Government apparently does not appreciate the gravity of the situation. The canal negotiations were initiated by Colombia and were energetically pressed upon this Government for several years. The propositions presented by Colombia, with slight modifications, were finally accepted by us. In virtue of this agreement our Congress reversed its previous judgment and decided upon the Panama route. If Colombia should now reject the treaty or unduly delay its ratification the friendly understanding between the two countries would be so seriously compromised that action might be taken by the Congress next winter which every friend of Colombia would regret. Confidential. Communicate substance of this verbally to the minister of foreign affairs. If he desires it, give him a copy in form of memorandum."

The Colombian foreign minister asked for the memorandum and Minister Beaupre delivered to him the Hay cable verbatim.

June 18, 1903, Dr. Rice answered the ultimatum. He cited the long delay and the narrow margin by which the treaty had been ratified by the United States Senate. "And if it had been rejected," the Colombian foreign minister wrote, "it would have been without any diminution of the right of Colombia, just as its rejection here will be without any diminution of any right of the United States." Answering the argument that Colombia was bound to complete the negotiations because she had initiated them (a statement which is untrue) Dr. Rice said:

"Having proposed a negotiation does not necessarily imply that it is to be approved, either in whole or in part, by the legislative body of the country that began it." As a notable example Dr. Rice cited the United States' rejection of the convention abrogating the Clayton-Bulwer treaty after the project had been proposed by the United States, because it would not accept the British amendments. The foreign minister indicated that Colombia did not consider as within the bounds of possibility the seizure of Panama, which Mr. Roosevelt had confessed he did contemplate. On this point the answer to the ultimatum says: "The Colombian Government has derived the correct conclusion that the only results that can affect adversely the interests of this nation, if their Congress should reject the project of the treaty, is that the Government of the United States will cease negotiations and adopt the Nicaragua route."

"When is there such an undue delay in the ratification of a treaty which will tend to cause a serious compromise in the friendly relations with the contracting party," asks the Colombian foreign minister. "In this country there would be an undue delay if, the ratification having been ordered by the law, the executive power should show a disposition to disregard it with the evident purpose of causing injury to his own country or the other nation interested in the pact."

After citing interference in Cuba and in Venezuela as proof of America's "determination to procure and preserve the independence, sovereignty, and integrity of the American nations," the foreign minister concludes his reply to the ultimatum in the following paragraph:

"If the Congress, using its inherent prerogative of national sovereignty, rejects the pact in question because, in their judgment it is not for the benefit of the Republic, it will be, I am sure, with much regret that it can not comply with the desires of the Government and the Congress of the United States; but feeling confident for the reasons of justice that by this act it will not have altered in any particular the friendly relations which fortunately exist between the two Republics, and to the preservation of which Colombia attaches the highest importance."

Mr. Cromwell says that after this ultimatum was devised by him and approved by President Roosevelt he conferred with Dr. Herran, who "sent his Government a message by cable backing up Secretary Hay." Mr. Cromwell says that Dr. Herran "inserted in his cable the declaration to his Government that he was convinced that if the treaty was not ratified soon Panama would secede and would conclude the treaty itself."

If Dr. Herran did send such a warning to his Government it was suppressed when the Colombian diplomatic correspondence was published.

July 5, 1903, Mr. Beaupre cabled to Secretary Hay that a part of the ultimatum had been read in a secret session of the Senate, that it had created a sensation, and was "construed by many as a threat of direct retaliation against Colombia in case the treaty is not ratified. This and the statement of just-arrived members of Congress from Panama that this department would revolt if the treaty is not ratified, caused alarm, and the effect is favorable."

This threat of retaliation in the Beaupré ultimatum probably did more than any other diplomatic blunder to incense the hot-tempered Colombians who already believed that the United States was seeking to drive a canal bargain to its own advantage without reference to the welfare of Colombia. Mr. Cromwell takes cognizance of the effect of the ultimatum in the following paragraph:

"It was this attitude taken by the American Government under the circumstances which we have just set forth that furnished the basis and the jusification for the subsequent events of which the consequences were so transcendent."

July 9, 1903, Mr. Beaupré cabled confidentially to Secretary Hay that Gen. Reyes suggested that the treaty could not be ratified without two amendments, providing that the canal company should pay $10,000,000 for permission to transfer its concession, and increasing the indemnity to be paid by the United States from $10,000,000 to $15,000,000.

This is the first of the correspondence sent to the Senate by Mr. Roosevelt (S. Doc. No. 51, 58th Cong., 2d sess), in which, for reasons unstated, the name of Reyes was suppressed in four instances. When, in 1904, this correspondence was republished in "Foreign Relations of the United States, 1903," from the same plates, the letters and cables in which Reyes's name had been indicated with "(———)" were reset, and his name given.

July 11, 1903, Mr. Beaupré cabled to Secretary Hay: "I think strong intimation from you, through Colombian minister or this legation, that unnecessary delay should be avoided would be effective."

July 13, 1903, Secretary Hay replied by cable: "Any amendment whatever or unnecessary delay in the ratification of the treaty would greatly imperil its consummation."

During this period Mr. Cromwell was busy, as he had to visé "all the cablegrams and other messages between Secretary Hay, Minister Herran, and ourselves." He also was utilizing the interest and zeal of the Panamans to arouse active support for the treaty. Showing how closely he kept in touch with the situation, he says: "We kept them constantly informed as to the state of affairs; they, on their side, kept us fully informed upon the state of affairs on the Isthmus; we maintained the closest intimacy with them, and they relied much upon our advice."

Although Mr. Cromwell was receiving cable reports from his agent in Bogota, as well as through the American minister, on the progress of the treaty in the Colombian Congress, and although "he examined and passed judgment upon reports" of the committees of Congress in Bogota, he was satisfied, even before Congress met, that the treaty would be rejected and was making his plans for the revolution which would bring about the separation of Panama. Witness his own story:

"In fact, as we have explained, Minister Herran himself had cabled in June to his Government that this (separation of Panama) would be the probable result. We ourselves had not then and did not have later, any doubt of the result, and this rendered us more attentive in order that the vast interests which were confided to us, might not be imperiled or complicated."

Mr. Cromwell's favorite expression, which he uses several times in his confession, is that he was preparing to resolve the situation "in some other satisfactory manner."

How generally it was recognized in Washington that the Roosevelt administration was a menace to the territorial integrity of Colombia is indicated by a letter written from Washington, July 6, 1903, by Gen. Pedro Velez R., of Barranquilla, Colombia, to his brother, Luis Velez R., then governor of the Department of Bolivar. So impressed was Gov. Velez that he sent the following telegram to President Marroquin, to the ministers of foreign affairs and war, and to the president of the Colombian Senate:

"Pedro Velez R., now in the United States, writes, in effect, as follows under date of July 6:

"'The position of our country is looked upon here with many misgivings. Some people believe that if the treaty is not ratified the American Government will take possession of the canal works by force; others believe that a revolution will be fomented in Panama, the independence of which will be recognized. It is asserted by newspaper men that a deputation has come from Panama to arrive at an understanding with the Washington Government and to find out if the latter will support the independence; that this Government has made inquiries in Europe as to whether the Governments there would object in case it recognized the independence and negotiated for the construction of the canal immediately afterwards, and that the answers were favorable. He (Pedro Velez) considers it urgent to send and maintain sufficient forces in the principal centers of population in Panama to repress any uprising and also to hold in readiness considerable reinforcements in Bolivar so as not to attract too much attention. The American Government is absolutely considering the Nicaragua route. Consider it my duty inform Government.

"'LUIS VELEZ R., *Governor*.'"

Before leaving the United States, Gen. Pedro Velez R., went to talk over the situation with Mr. Cromwell, and was assured by him, in Mr. Cromwell's office, on July 20, 1903, "that the United States never followed a crooked policy: that perhaps from a lack of refinement, only acquired by nations of very ancient civilization, it had not displayed and did not then display that deep and wily diplomacy, but little sincere at times, of which some European nations can boast," but that the American Government was "open and honest, respectful of its obligations," as witness Cuba, and that "the American Government wished to be a gentleman among the nations." Mr. Cromwell also assured Gen. Velez that "if ever the day came when an administration in the United States should depart from this line of conduct, the American people would rise as one man to bring back to the paths of honesty and rigteousness the disloyal men who had been misled to break with the antecedents and the irrevocable desires of the nation."

But while Mr. Cromwell was impressing his hypocritical platitudes upon the Colombian visitor he was rushing preparations to resolve the situation "in some other satisfactory manner." To this end it had been arranged that Jose Augustin Arango, attorney and lobbyist of the Panama Railroad Co., and a Senator from the Department of Panama, should meet Mr. Cromwell or his representative in Kingston, Jamaica, before proceeding to Bogota to the opening of Congress on June 20, 1903. At the last moment, according to the present recollection of his family, Senator Arango received a cable canceling this appointment.

It is, to say the least, an interesting coincidence that just when Mr. Cromwell became convinced that it would be necessary to resolve the situation "in some other satisfactory manner" his client cabled from Paris, June 13, 1903: "Are completely in accord with you on your program and we are pleased; commencement execution;" also on June 19: "We hope that the step taken will produce decisive effect."

Possibly there is significance in the fact that in the same month Capt. Chauncey B. Humphrey, Twenty-second Infantry, instructor in drawing at West Point, and Second Lieut. Grayson Mallet-Prevost Murphy, graduated from West Point June 11, 1902, and assigned to the Seventeenth Infantry, United States Army, was sent as military spies on a "four months' tour through the northern portions of Venezuela and Colombia." (Roosevelt's message January 4, 1904.)

The movements of Arango in the early part of the summer of 1903 are difficult to trace. Various persons in Panama are positive that he was absent for some time, and they were given to understand that he left for the Congress at Bogota, but were told afterward that he went to Kingston to keep the appointment, either to discuss a lobbying campaign in favor of the ratification of the treaty at Bogota or to plan the revolution. There is, however, no record discoverable of his having been in Kingston. In his own account Arango wrote that he commissioned Capt. James R. Beers, freight agent and port captain for the Panama Railroad at its western terminus, "a man of sane and clear views, of absolute probity and honor," and possessed of the confidence of William Nelson Cromwell, to go to New York. Beers left early in June, while Arango, according to his own published story, remained in Panama "to foment discontent and nurse hopes," instead of going to Bogota to exert his influence as a Senator to secure the ratification of the pending treaty.

That the object of Capt. Beers was to see whether he could enlist the active support of William Nelson Cromwell for a revolution in order to declare the independence of the Department of Panama was well known to his most intimate associates on the Isthmus before his departure. It was also known to these, especially to Herbert G. Prescott, assistant superintendent of the Panama Railroad, who was within the inner circle of the conspiracy, that Capt. Beers went as the authorized spokesman of Arango and a very few of Arango's relatives and friends. In an effort to protect Mr. Cromwell and give to the world the impression that the secession was a "spontaneous" movement, Arango suppressed Cromwell's name altogether in his "Data for a History of the Independence," published in El Heraldo del Istmo December 15, 1905, and referred to him only as "the responsible person who, through Capt. Beers, had opened the road to our hopes and thus stimulated the sending of a representative of the committee." Later Arango published the same "Data for a History," expurgated of much tell-tale information, in pamphlet form. This Arango story has long been one of the thorns in Mr. Cromwell's flesh—if he is not impenetrable. In this interesting pamphlet—the nearest to a complete and truthful account of the independence ever published in Panama or elsewhere until now—Senator Arango says he refused to assist in the work of the Colombian Congress, "because I had complete conviction that the Herran-Hay treaty * * * would be rejected; consequently I saw only one means of saving the Isthmus from the ruin toward which it was trending—our separation from Colombia."

Arango's emissary, Capt. Beers, in his subordinate executive position with the Panama Railroad commanded the respect and confidence of his employers and the unbounded friendship of the natives of Panama, but he lacked altogether the influence with "persons in high position" with which Arango clothed him in his "Data for a History," excepting his acquaintance with Cromwell. The secret codes which have come into the possession of the World fully corroborate the statements of certain of Capt. Beers's associates that "the friends who there would cooperate with us," and the "persons of high position and influence" referred to in Arango's pamphlet were none other than Cromwell and Cromwell alone.

While Capt. Beers was in the States the absentee senator, Arango, was not laboring in vain "to foment discontent." On a Sunday late in July, just before Capt. Beers's return from New York, Ramon, jr., and Pedro Arias gave a luncheon at their country home outside the city of Panama to 26 or 28 guests, Americans and Panamans. If this gathering was not planned deliberately to sound the opinion of leading Americans and natives it accomplished this end of obtaining expressions of their views as to the future of the canal negotiations and the possibilities of a revolution. This luncheon recorded the first public discussion of revolutionary plans on the Isthmus; torrential libations were poured, and speeches were made in favor of free Panama.

Hezekiah A. Gudger, then American consul general in Panama, now chief justice of the supreme court of the Canal Zone, was among the speakers. Judge Gudger doesn't remember what he said; in fact, no one's memory was very clear after the last inning, and J. Gabriel Duque, proprietor of the Panama Star and Herald and one of the guests, didn't report the speeches nor even mention in his paper this noteworthy social event. Among the other guests were Herbert G. Prescott, assistant superintendent of the Panama Railroad, in charge of transportation; Maj. (now Col.) William Murray Black, United States Army, Engineer Corps, in charge of inspection of canal excavation by the French Canal Co. in behalf of the Isthmian Canal Commission; Lieut. Mark Brooke, United States Army, Engineer Corps, assistant to Maj. Black; Austin C. Harper, of Phillipsburg, Pa., an American civilian engineer under Maj. Black; Carlos Constantino Arosemena, later secretary of the revolutionary committee; Gen. Ruben Varon, Colombian "admiral," who was bought by the Panama rebels with a bribe of $35,000 silver; Mr. Arango; and others.

The date of this luncheon at the Arias House is strangely fixed in Col. Black's diary, which the World brought into court under subpœna, as July 28, 1903, which was a Tuesday. The host and several guests fix the day positively as Sunday. This and other entries in the book lead one to suspect that Col. Black "wrote up" his diary when his memory was none too fresh; possibly after the revolution, or after he was criticized publicly by the late Senator Carmack, of Tennessee, for having, in United States Army uniform, raised the Panaman flag of independence in Colon on November 6.

But to return to the home office of diplomacy and revolution:

Before Capt. Beers left New York, Mr. Cromwell furnished him a cable code book, with additions and special instructions for its use written in the blank pages in the back of the book. Mr. Cromwell doubtless never expected this to be shown to others, but it was, and when Beers exhibited the code upon his return to the Isthmus, August 4, 1903, he told his friends that Mr. Cromwell could be depended upon to "go the limit" with them in their revolutionary project.

On the Sunday following his emissary's return, Arango gave a luncheon at his country house in honor of Capt. Beers. Only a half dozen or so of Arango's most intimate friends were invited, with only two Americans, Prescott and Beers. Before the luncheon Beers had made his report to each conspirator, and at the table he did not go into these details again, except to say that the plan for the revolution could be carried out successfully, and that they could depend on Cromwell not only to assist them himself but to obtain other assistance which he had promised to secure for the movement.

From this Sunday the propaganda was pushed in earnest, and frequent conferences were held in the office of Arango, attorney and land agent of the Panama Railroad, or in the adjoining office of Dr. Manuel Amador Guerrero, intimate friend of Arango and physician to the railroad. Amador had been taken into the plot by Arango during Beers's absence in the States, had been told of Beers's mission, and had entered with enthusiasm into the conspiracy.

At the outset Amador promised that Arango should be the first president of of the projected Republic, and Arango in turn put Amador forward as leading man in the revolutionary farce, while he, the faithful Senator, shifted scenery for the great stage director in Wall Street. Beers, with the Cromwell code, occupied the important post of prompter. Already the scenery was painted.

the press agent and director had taken counsel, and it had been settled that the curtain raiser should be put on November 3, 1903—election day—when the American papers would be crowded with political news and a revolution in Panama might attract the minimum of attention in the United States. Here Mr. Cromwell displayed his ability not only to obtain publicity but also to avoid it when disadvantageous. Roger Farnham, his chief press agent, said boastfully to a newspaper acquaintance (Samuel G. Blythe) on July 4, 1903, that there would be a revolution and secession of Panama on election day.

Taking up again the diplomatic thread in Bogota we find Minister Beaupre cabling to Secretary Hay, July 13, 1903, for instructions and recommending that another intimation be sent by the State Department for Mr. Beaupre's use upon the obstinate Colombians. This cable was not delivered in Washington until July 27, 1903. Meantime, Beaupre had been gathering information respecting the "foreign influence" of which so much has been made in the apologies for the administration's attitude toward Colombia in these negotiations. July 21, 1903, Mr. Beaupre wrote to Secretary Hay as follows:

"At times I have thought, from the tone of the conversation of certain opponents, that foreign hostile influences were at work, but I have never been able to be certain of this. If there be opposition from this source it is of too secret a nature to be discovered, and can not therefore be particularly effective. On the whole I am inclined to believe that no direct hostile influence is being used here, but that if any exists it comes through Colombian legations or consulates in Europe.

"I have certain, but private, information that Dr. Uricoechea, a member of the special Senate committee, heretofore referred to (a committee to consider and amend the canal convention), and who lived a great many years in Germany, called on Baron Grunau, the German chargé d'affaires, to inquire what would be the attitude of the German Government in case of trouble arising out of the matter, and whether it would be willing to undertake or aid the construction of the canal in case the treaty with the United States should not be ratified. Baron Grunau replied that he had no instructions bearing upon the subject, but that he was of a positive opinion that, considering how desirous his Government was at the present moment to remain on friendly terms with the United States, it would not take any steps with reference to the construction of the canal or to any controversy growing out of the present negotiations; that he would, however, submit the matter to his Government."

So much for Germany's alleged activity in the canal negotiations, of which much has been made by the Roosevelt apologists. The published diplomatic correspondence of Colombia and the United States shows no better foundation than this for the reports of German activity in the canal matter.

Mr. Beaupre adds in this letter that a Colombia congressman called on the English minister with a similar inquiry and was told that his Government thoroughly considered the question at the time of the modifications to the Clayton-Bulwer treaty, and that in view of the safeguards provided in the Hay-Pauncefote arrangement "was therefore willing now to leave the United States quite free as regards any further negotiations with reference to the construction of a canal."

July 21, 1903, the Colombian minister for foreign affairs interrogated Minister Beaupre as to the meaning of his note of April 24, 1903, when Mr. Beaupre transmitted in a letter the cabled instructions of April 7, 1903, when Secretary Hay told him to inform the Colombian Government, if the subject arose, that any change in the Hay-Herran treaty affecting the clause granting permission to transfer the concessions "would be in violation of the Spooner law and therefore not permissible." The foreign minister now wished to know whether any other amendments to the treaty would be regarded by the American Government as violations of the Spooner law. To this Mr. Beaupre responded, on July 22, 1903, with the following argument:

"I have the honor to say to your excellency that with the approval by the United States Senate of the treaty between Colombia and the United States, signed on the 22d of January, 1903, the Spooner law, which authorized the making of that treaty, was fully complied with, in the opinion of the Senate, so far as the Panama route was concerned. * * * Hence, the said law went out of active existence with reference to Panama and can only again become a subject of discussion, and then in reference to the Nicaragua route, in the event of the rejection of the treaty by Colombia. * * * I consider it my duty to inform your excellency that I have no reason to believe that my Government will consider or discuss any modifications whatever to the treaty as it stands. * * * It would seem that the treaty itself, as the official interpretation of the law, can not be modified at all without violating that law."

The cables between Bogota and Washington were badly delayed, and on July 29, 1903, Acting Secretary of State Loomis cabled Mr. Beaupré: "Would like information as to present situation." Receiving no reply, Secretary Hay sent another cable, reiterating the views which Mr. Cromwell, in the interest of his client, had forced upon the administration. Mr. Hay's cable in full follows:

"Instructions heretofore sent to you show the great danger of amending the treaty. This Government has no right or competence to covenant with Colombia to impose new financial obligations upon canal company, and the President would not submit to our Senate any amendment in that sense, but would treat it as avoiding the negotiations and bringing about a failure to conclude a satisfactory treaty with Colombia. No additional payment by the United States can hope for approval by United States Senate, while any amendment whatever requiring reconsideration by that body would most certainly imperil its consummation. You are at liberty to make discreet unofficial use of your instructions in the proper quarters. The Colombian Government and Congress should realize the grave risk of ruining the negotiations by improvident amendment."

August 5, 1903, Mr. Beaupré cabled: "From conversation with prominent Senators, I believe the Government does not consider my opinions as final or authoritative. I beg for an emphatic statement from you or instructions, under my telegram of July 15. There is much danger that the treaty will be amended."

August 5, 1903, was a day of anxiety for Minister Beaupré. His cables, which Mr. Cromwell says were always placed by Secretary Hay at the disposition of the lawyer lobbyist of the Panama Canal Co., for this one day alone cost the United States $992.20, at regular tariff rates now in force. In one $600 message, which did not reach Washington until August 12, 1903, Mr. Beaupré transmitted a summary of the report of the Senate committee, recommending nine amendments to the treaty. Another cable of this date transmits the substance of Mr. Beaupré's note which he addressed to the Colombian minister of foreign affairs. In this note, dated August 5, 1903, Mr. Beaupré said to the Colombian Government:

" * * * It is clear that the committee's proposed modification of Article I (so as to provide that the canal company should pay Colombia for the privilege of transferring its concession to the United States) is alone tantamount to an absolute rejection of the treaty. I feel it my duty to reiterate the opinion I have before expressed to your excellency, that my Government will not consider or discuss such an amendment at all."

Mr. Beaupré cited as the next serious objection a proposed amendment of the form of the tribunals for the Canal Zone, and said that "the other modifications, though not equally serious in principle," were so inconsequential to Colombia that she should not place them in the way of approval of the treaty. By Mr. Beaupré's letter it is seen that he interpreted his instructions as giving first importance to the protection of the canal speculaors' $40,000,000 from the demands of Colombia. His letter to the Colombian foreign minister contains also the following:

"If the present modifications of the committee constitute really the final decision that is likely to be arrived at by the Congress of Colombia, the matter should be voted without any delay, and so give at least a slight opportunity to my Government to consider the matter before the expiration of the time for exchange of raitfications provided in the treaty. Less than this can not be expected by my Government, which in good faith signed the pending treaty more than six months ago, and promptly ratified it without amendment."

In his zeal to force upon Colombia the policy which Mr. Cromwell, in the interest of his client, had induced President Roosevelt and Secretary Hay to adopt, Minister Beaupré permitted himself to misstate the facts in his official representations. If the United States did "in good faith sign the pending treaty," it did not "promptly ratify it," and this Mr. Beaupré well knew. The treaty was signed January 22, 1903, when the American Senate was in session, and so anxious was Mr. Roosevelt to have it ratified that he transmitted it to the Senate the next day. Mr. Cromwell heads a chapter of his story, "Prolonged and bitter struggle over the ratification of the treaty in the Senate of the United States." He describes the tactics of the Nicaragua party in attempting to overwhelm the treaty with amendments. Senator Morgan submitted more than 60, against which Mr. Cromwell says he supplied arguments for his senatorial allies. Senator Cullom made the principal speech in favor of its ratification. Notwithstanding "personal interviews with many influential Senators," and his "giving the Senators all the assistance possible in the course of the debates," Mr. Cromwell found "the opposition was so vigorous and the discussion so prolonged that the session of Congress closed without action on the subject of the treaty."

Yet we find no record of Colombia's having threatened the United States, either through its foreign office or its minister in Washington, with retaliation because the treaty was impeded or in danger of modification; Secretary Hay was not warned that the American Senate did not "appreciate the gravity of the situation" and was putting in jeopardy the friendly relations between the two countries. Dr. Herran simply notified his Government by cable as follows:

February 22. "Obstruction of minority in Senate hampers approval of treaty, causing Government anxiety."

February 25. "Tenacious opposition to treaty in Senate continues. Many substantial modifications proposed, which again makes situation critical."

March 1. "Opposition to treaty continues; will probably prevent its approval this session, but I believe the President will at once call a special session."

March 3. "Opposition to the treaty continues; Senate sessions terminating, but to-day it will be convened in extra sesssion to resolve urgent and important matters that are pending. We fight against introducing many substantial modifications of the treaty."

March 12 (Colombian Government to Herran). "Persist in abstaining from acceptance of modifications of the treaty. Report frequently by cable in code as to course of the matter in the Senate."

March 17. "The Senate discusses modifications of the treaty regarding absolute jurisdiction of the United States and an annual rental during only 60 years. I reject all modifications. Situation difficult, but we hope for success. The President of the United States is amenable; I will comply with orders contained in cable of the 12th."

March 18. "Senate has approved treaty without amendment."

There is no other correspondence; there were no intimations, no threats because the Senate of the United States dared to debate a treaty which its own Government had negotiated, and to delay ratifying it for nearly two months. Fifty-four days elapsed between submission of the treaty by President Roosevelt and its ratification by the American Senate, and fifty-four days between the convening of the special session of the Colombian Congress and the treaty's rejection by its Senate.

With this comparison between the diplomatic attitude of the two countries we return to Mr. Beaupre and his Cromwell-inspired threats. In his letter of August 5, 1903, Mr. Beaupre adds to his misstatement that the United States "promptly ratified" the treaty:

"I take this opportunity to respectfully reiterate what I have before expressed to Your Excellency, that if Colombia really desires to maintain the present friendly relations existing between the two countries, * * * the pending treaty should be ratified exactly in its present form, without any modifications whatever. I say this from a deep conviction that my Government will not in any case accept amendments."

Later in the same day Secretary Hay's cabled instructions of July 31, 1903, reached the Bogota legation, and Mr. Beaupre wrote another note to the Colombian foreign minister in which he said that he had received such definite instructions from his Government as to enable him not only fully to confirm but to amplify materially all his previous notes. Mr. Beaupre said in part:

"I may say that the antecedent circumstances of the whole negotiation of the canal treaty, from official information in the hands of my Government, are of such a nature as to fully warrant the United States in considering any modification of the terms of the treaty as practically a breach of faith on the part of the Government of Colombia, such as may involve the very greatest complications in the friendly relations which have hitherto existed between the two countries."

Mr. Beaupre concludes this amazing diplomatic threat with the following assurance concerning the treaty of 1846–1848, in which treaty Mr. Roosevelt found his alleged justification for ordering the United States Navy to uphold Mr. Cromwell's revolution:

"It is to be regretted that the reference to the necessity for the practical reenactment of the treaty of 1846–1848 in the (Colombian) Senate committee's report should constitute almost a doubt as to the good faith of the intention of the United States in its compliance therewith. I must assure Your Excellency that unless that treaty be denounced in accordance with its own provisions my Government is not capable of violating it, either in letter or spirit; nor should there be any fear on the part of Colombia that if ratified the clauses guaranteeing her sovereignty in the pending treaty, couched as they are in still more precise and solemn terms than those of 1846, will ever be disregarded in the slightest degree by the Government of the United States."

Both of Mr. Beaupre's notes of August 5, 1903, were read in secret sessions of the Colombian Senate and served to intensify the resentment which had been rising ever since the reading of his celebrated ultimatum of June 13, 1903.

August 6, 1903, Mr. Beaupre cabled to Secretary Hay:

"Confidential. Note reference to treaty 1846 in the committee report. Colombia dreads above all things newspaper-reported intention of the United States to denounce the treaty in the event of rejecting canal treaty. I have as additional confirmation the statement of my dispatch No. 49, June 15.

Mr. Beaupré's dispatch, No. 49, of June 15, 1903, is one which Mr. Roosevelt failed to transmit to the Senate of the United States. Presumably publicity was not "compatible with the interests of the public service."

Augus 11, 1903, the day before the rejection of the treaty, Foreign Minister Rico in a long letter replied to Mr. Beaupré's various threats and warnings. In part he said:

"In the opinion of the Colombian Government the view expressed by your excellency's Government that the circumstances attending the whole negotiation of the canal treaty are of such a nature as would fully authorize the United States in considering as a violation of the pact any modification whatever of the conditions of the treaty is not compatible with diplomatic usages nor with the express stipulations of article 28 of the same convention. (Article 28 provides for exchange of ratifications by the Congresses of the two countries.)

"In fact, plenipotentiaries in concluding public treaties propose and accept conditions with the purpose of facilitating the negotiations, which is not final except by means of ratification, which in republics is vested in the executive power, with the concurrence, direct or indirect, of some other high power of state.

"Your excellency tells me that when the canal convention was presented to the Senate of the United States it met there the most violent opposition; that not only were the strongest efforts made to reject it as a whole, but that many amendments more or less important were proposed for immediate discussion, and that the final and definite victory was only attained after the most strenuous efforts on the part of the friends of the administration, convinced as they were that it ought to be ratified without any alteraion.

"The course of the honorable Senators who proposed the modifications make it clear that they used their constitutional rights in proposing changes in the conditions of the pact without any reason to consider that the Government of the United States was bound to approve the treaty without modification, as has been claimed in regard to the Government of Colombia.

"I suppose that your excellency's Government has never denied to the Senate the right to introduce modifications in the international pacts, and that this right has the same legal force as that of approving or disapproving public treaties, and I understand that the Senate has exercised its right to propose modifications not only in this case but also in others, as I pointed out to your excellency in my contra memorandum of June 18 in connection with the project of convention dated November 28, 1902, between the United States and Great Britain for the abrogation of the Clayton-Bulwer treaty of 1850."

Dr. Rico in this letter reiterates Colombia's confidence "that justice and equity govern the course of the United States in its relations with all powers," and his own belief that the United States must recognize the right of the Columbian Congress not only to propose modifications in the treaty but even to reejct it, and that exercise of that right "can not in any manner entail complications great or small in the relations of the two countries, which, it is to be hoped, will continue on the same equal footing and in the same good understanding which has happily existed until now."

August 12, 1903, came the rejection of the treaty by unanimous vote of the Colombian Senate. Senator (later governor) Obaldia, of Panama, avoided voting. Minister Beaupré had made it so plain by his threats and warnings, all of which were read to the Senate, that the United States would accept no amendment of the treaty that it was decided to reject it entirely. The principal argument was made by Gen. Pedro Nel Ospina, of Antioquia, who contended that the treaty was in violation of the Colombian constitution, which he proposed amending in order that the treaty could be passed as demanded by the United States.

News of the rejection was cabled on August 12, by Minister Beaupre to the State Department, but was not received in Washington until August 15. But the State Department did receive on the 12th Mr. Beaupre's cable of August 5, 1903, announcing the report of the committee recommending nine amendments to the treaty. The most objectionable of these proposed amendments, as heretofore indicated, were those to compel Mr. Cromwell's client to pay part of its $40,000,000 to the Colombian Government for permission to transfer its concession, and altering the form of tribunals proposed for the Canal Zone. Nothing in these nine amendments suggested any change in the amount of indemnity the United States itself should pay to the canal company or to Colombia. It was simply the blow aimed at the canal speculators' profits which Mr. Cromwell had so long anticipated. Receipt of this cable was not announced at the State Department until the following day, when press despatches brought news of the committee's mutilation of the treaty.

And now appears the justification of Dr. Herran's fears, expressed in his letter of December 19, 1902, that President Roosevelt's "impetuous and violent disposition" might lead him to adopt the scheme of Senator Cullom to seize Panama "on the ground of universal public utility." Without waiting for news of the action of the Colombian Senate on its committee's report amending the treaty, and without knowing that the treaty had been rejected, Mr. Roosevelt sent for Senator Cullom, chairman of the Senate Committee on Foreign Relations. Mr. Cullom went to Oyster Bay on Friday, August 14, 1903, accompanied by his son-in-law, William Barrett Ridgely, then Controller of the Currency. Secretary Hitchcock and T. E. Burns, of Minneapolis, were also of the luncheon party this day at Sagamore Hill. Aside, the President discussed with Senator Cullom the canal situation. The conference was reported the next morning in the New York Herald under the following heading, two columns wide in large type on its front page:

"We might make canal treaty with Panama" (Senator Cullom). Illinois statesman, after a talk with President, says latter may take new step if Bogota blocks the way. But would not foment any rebellion."

The Herald's report says, in part:

"One might expect from a statement previously made by the President to the effect that he considered either canal route practicable, and from the two reports of the Isthmian Canal Commission, one of which favored Nicaragua and the other Panama, that the administration, as soon as the Colombian Congress killed the treaty by amending it, would be willing to follow out the act of Congress under which the canal is to be built and turn to Nicaragua.

"No such intention can yet be discovered. The administration is still wedded to the Panama route. It does not yet seem willing to go so far as to invade Panama, as soon as Colombia acts adversely, and with an armed force to protect the workmen, proceed to dig the canal, but there has been significant talk in administration circles of getting around the matter in some other way.

"This intention, which is not clearly defined, was voiced this evening by Senator Cullom in an interview soon after he left Sagamore Hill."

The Herald quotes Senator Cullom as saying that he considers the outlook for the treaty not encouraging, but that even in the event of Colombia's sending the treaty back mutilated with amendments, Mr. Cullom did "not think we are ready to abandon Panama yet; not by any means."

"But if the United States is being held up for greater payments than it is willing to make, how can the canal be built without the treaty?" asked the simple-minded correspondent. Senator Cullom is quoted as replying—and the correspondent was not, of record, added to the Ananias Club:

"Well, we might make another treaty—not with Colombia, but with Panama."

The report of the interview continues:

"But Panama is not a sovereign State, and is only a department of Colombia."

"Intimations have been made that there is a great discontent on the Isthmus over the action of the Congress of the Central Government, and Panama might break away and set up a government which we could treat with," was the reply.

"Is the United States prepared to encourage such a schism in a South American Republic?"

"No; I suppose not. But this country wants to build that canal and build it now. It needs it for its own defense, and it is needed by the whole world. The treaty is blocked by a country that has been treated well by us, and there are very weighty considerations which make us feel that at all hazards this great work should be undertaken at the earliest possible minute."

"Senator Cullom's talk would indicate that, if Colombia amends the treaty so that it is not acceptable to the United States, the subject may be treated in an entirely new way by the President in his message to Congress."

On the day the State Department gave out information concerning the proposed amendment of the treaty in Bogota, the New York Herald's Washington correspondent telegraphed his paper, August 13, 1903:

"Mr. Beaupre, the American minister at Bogota, has cabled the State Department discouraging news about the canal treaty. The cablegram says that amendments to the treaty have been recommended, and the minister believes one of the principal amendments, which provides for an increase in the purchase price for the canal concession, will probably be adopted."

Other newspapers were led into making the same misstatement. Mr. Beaupre's $600 cable of August 5, 1903, which reached the State Department the day before this distressing though false information was handed to the Washington correspondents, contained absolutely no basis for such a statement or surmise. Mr. Beaupre's cable set out the proposed amendments seriatim. The part of the cable referring to this subject was as follows:

"Second. In article 1 the condition shall be introduced that the Panama Railroad & Canal Co. shall be obliged beforehand to make arrangements with the Colombian Government in which the conditions shall be established under which that Government will grant consent necessary to enable these companies to transfer their rights to the United States."

And still the State Department permitted the impression to go abroad through the press, without contradiction, that Colombia was attempting to hold up the United States for more money!

Mr. Beaupre's cable of August 12, 1903, announcing rejection of the canal treaty by the Colombian Senate reached Washington on the 15th, but the State Department held back the news until confronted with press dispatches, which did not get through until the 17th. The New York Herald's Washington correspondent then telegraphed his paper that, while the acting minister of Colombia, Dr. Herran, had about abandoned hope, "there is a reluctance on the part of the State Department to yield to what appears to be the inevitable and admit all hope is gone for a canal treaty with Colombia. This attitude of the administration—for there is no reason to believe that it is not dictated by the President himself—is difficult of explanation in view of the explicit and mandatory provision of the Spooner Canal Act, empowering the President to turn at once to Nicaragua and Costa Rica if he is unable to successfully negotiate with Colombia."

On August 14, 1903, the day Senator Cullom dropped the suggestion that "We might make another treaty, not with Colombia, but with Panama," Mr. Cromwell became very active at the State Department. The New York Herald's dispatch of August 14, 1903, says:

"Alarmed at the gravity of the situation at Bogota, William Nelson Cromwell, counsel for the Panama Canal Co., made two calls at the State Department to-day to see Acting Secretary Loomis and Mr. Adee, the Third Assistant Secretary. In a last effort to save the treaty from annihilation by amendment, Mr. Cromwell and Dr. Herran are sending detailed cables to Bogota reiterating that the United States insists upon the treaty's ratification without amendment."

Curiously enough Mr. Cromwell's own narrative becomes meager of details after his client cabled from Paris June 13, 1903:

"Are completely in accord with you on your program and we are pleased beginning execution."

He neglected to call attention to these conferences with Herran, these cables to Bogota, these visits, as frequent as twice a day, to the State Department. Two pages in his story cover the interval between the rejection of the treaty August 12, 1903, which he dismisses with one sentence, and his departure to Paris, October 15, 1903.

"We were deeply worried," confesses Mr. Cromwell in his recital. "Another crisis had arrived. What could be done? As before, the company itself could give us no direct assistance. It encouraged us, however, by cabling us as follows:

"'PARIS, *August 17, 1903.*

"'Have received your three cables. We hope that present difficulties will be surmounted, thanks to your efforts.'

"And again, on August 25, 1903, Mr. Cromwell says the company wrote him from Paris:

"'It is still a little difficult to see by what road we shall attain our end; but there is no reason that makes it permissible to admit that we can lose the fruit of your long and successful efforts.'"

Already Mr. Cromwell had determined "by what road we shall attain our end." No revolution in Panama could be successful if the governor, appointed by the national administration, were efficient and loyal. The first necessary step was to bring about the removal of the governor of the department, and to install in his place one who would close his eyes to secessionist preparations and join in the movement when it was made. Such a man was Jose Domingo de Obaldia, one of the senators from the department, and an outspoken advocate of the treaty, although he, as one of the committee, signed the report amending the treaty, thereby killing it. In spite of private and public warnings and pleadings, President Marroquin, who was but a puppet in the hands of his son, Lorenzo, agreed late in August to name Obaldia governor, and offered Mutis-Duran, the governor of Panama, a place in the cabinet of Bogota. Whether Obaldia was cognizant of the source of the influences brought to bear to secure his appointment as governor may never be known. Since 1903 the charge has repeatedly been made in Colombia and in Panama that American money was sent to Bogota for this purpose. Dr. Indelacio Camacho, of Bogota, who spent several months before his death investigating these charges, declared that he saw in Barranquilla, Colombia, a photograph of a draft or check by which part of this alleged corruption fund was transferred.

President Marroquin's excuse for appointing an avowed secessionist as governor of Panama, in face of a threatened revolution, was that Obaldia had agreed to cooperate to elect Gen. Rafael Reyes as Marroquin's successor and assure a Congress that would pass the canal treaty at the next session. At the same time Gov. Velez, of the Department of Bolivar, who had warned his Government in July, 1903, that the United States might seize Panama and that troops should be held ready to suppress any uprising, was rewarded for his loyalty, and that of his brother, who was visiting the United States, by being removed. The governor of the adjoining Department of Magdalena also was replaced, so that the three neighboring Departments of Panama, Bolivar, and Magdalena were ruled by men pledged to the Reyes program, which turned out to be a program of self-expoltation at the expense of the nation.

Minister Beaupré announced by cable of August 30, 1903, to the State Department, two days before the appointment was officially made, that Gov. Obaldia had been named; and on the following day cabled:

"I had an interview with Senator Obaldia to-day. He informed me that he is willing to remain so long as there is hope for the treaty, but he is convinced that there is none and will leave, therefore, on the sixth proximo. Confirms Gen. Reyes's statement concerning presidential candidate, and says that the next Senate was made certain for the treaty; * * * that in accepting the governorship of Panama he told the President that in case that the department found it necessary to revolt to secure canal he would stand by Panama; but he added that if the Government of the United States will wait for the next session of Congress canal can be secured without a revolution. * * * Confidential. My opinion is that nothing satisfactory can be expected from this Congress."

Here was Mr. Roosevelt's warrant for seizing Panama; it would mean waiting a year for favorable action on the treaty in order to secure the canal without a revolution.

Mr. Beaupré's cable of August 30, 1903, concerning Obaldia and a revolution reached the State Department September 12, 1903. On September 10, 1903, Senator Perez y Soto, of Panama, made an attack in the Colombian Senate which Minister Beaupré considered so important that he cabled to the State Department:

"Fierce attack to-day in the Senate upon the appointment of Obaldia as governor of Panama. The appointment is regarded as being the forerunner of separation. Of several senators who spoke, only the son of the President defended the action of the Government. A resolution passed by almost unanimous vote, which is equivalent vote of censure against the Government."

Amplifying this telegram Mr. Beaupré wrote to Secretary Hay:

"Senator Obaldia's separatist tendencies are well known, and he is reported to have said that, should the canal treaty not pass, the department of Panama would declare its independence, and would be right in doing so. That these are his opinions, there is, of course, no doubt, as I stated in my telegram to the department of August 30, 1903."

Meantime Mr. Roosevelt had been discussing the uglier and shorter means to his end—openly seizing the canal strip and fighting Colombia if she dared to protest with arms. The New York Herald correspondent at the Summer Capital telegraphed from Oyster Bay under date of August 28, 1903:

"Public sentiment may yet be called on to determine whether the United States shall take action which would lead to war with a sister Republic over the right to complete the Panama Canal.

"A step which might lead to war with the Unied States of Colombia is one of the contingencies discussed by representatives of the Administration in seeking to find some way out of the difficulty arising through the failure of the Colombian Congress to ratify the Panama Canal treaty without amendments.

"The canal question was the chief reason why Secretary of State Hay came here to see the President to-day. * * * President Roosevelt and Secretary Hay regard the treaty as probably dead. They take little interest in the dispatches from Minister Beaupre at Bogota, which purport to detail efforts being made by the Colombians to 'save the treaty' by amending it.

"The United States long ago informed the little Republic that if any amendments were made to the treaty they would not be acceptable to this Government.' It is impossible for this Government to recede from 'this statement soberly made, and to consider talk of negotiating a new treaty which would give Colombia greater advantages and an annuity of $500.000 instead of $250,000, which some of the Colombians demand. This demand is termed blackmail.'"

It is interesting here to note that, while the Administration was misleading the press and the American public to believe that Colombia was seeking to "blackmail" the United States by demanding more money for the canal, the only official proposal to this date was the report of the Colombian senate committee transmitted by Mr. Beaupre's cable of August 5, 1903, received in the State Department August 12, 1903. The only amendment affecting monetary considerations provided that "the Panama Canal and Railroad Cos. shall previously enter into a agreement with the Colombian Government, setting forth certain conditions, which the Colombian Government shall give the necessary consent that such companies may transfer their rights to the United States." This affected the canal speculators' profits, not the price the United States was to pay.

Furthermore, the Administration had been informed before this conference of Roosevelt and Hay by Dr. Herran of the receipt from his Government of the following cable, which had also been published in Panama:

BOGOTA, *August 13, 1903.*

COLOMBIAN MINISTER, *Washington.*

Senate unanimously disapproved canal treaty; among other reasons advanced in the debate being the diminished sovereignty and the companies not having previously arranged for transfer of their concessions. All the notes of the American minister against the introduction of amendments and his memorandum (the Beaupre-Cromwell ultimatum of June 13) on the possible rejection of the treaty or delay in its exchange contributed to its rejection. It is considered probable that Congress will fix the bases for renewing the negotiations.

RICO, *Foreign Minister.*

Furthermore, the administration before this conference of Mr. Roosevelt and Mr. Hay at Oyster Bay had received in the dispatches from Mr. Beaupre repeated assurances that the rejection of the treaty was not, in all probability, final. On August 23, 1903, Mr. Beaupre's cable of the 17th had arrived, stating:

"The President (of Colombia) informs me that Congress will pass law authorizing him to continue and finish negotiations for canal; but what conditions will be specified he can not state at the present moment."

Before this Oyster Bay council of war, Dr. Herran had received from his Government on August 21, 1903, ad by its order had communicated to Secretary Hay the following cable, dated in Bogota, August 16, 1903:

"The Senate, considering that the people of Colombia desire to maintain the most cordial relations with the United States and that completion of the canal is of the greatest importance for universal American commerce, have named a commission of three Senators to study the manner of satisfying the desire of digging the canal, harmonizing legal and national interests."

And before this Oyster Bay council of war Secretary Hay had cabled to Minister Beaupre, on August 24, 1903:

"The President (Roosevelt) will make no engagement as to his actions on the canal matter, but I regard it as improbable that any definite action will be taken within two weeks."

On the day of the Roosevelt-Hay conference the following cable from Mr. Beaupre, dated August 24, 1903, reached the State Department:

"Nothing has been done, and very little satisfactory action, this depending upon the attitude of the Government of the United States, which is waited for in great anxiety. The report of the committee prepared."

Reverting to the Herald's report of the Roosevelt-Hay council of August 28, 1903:

"The conference of the President and Secretary Hay was to map out a plan to be pursued in view of the admitted failure of the treaty. There are three alternatives for the administration, and none will be taken until after full consultation with leaders in Congress.

"The first is to ignore Colombia, proceed to construct the canal under the treaty with New Granada of 1846, fight Colombia if she objects, and create the independent government of Panama out of the present State of Panama. This would give the United States what would be expected to be a short and inexpensive war, but would insure a permanent settlement of the question of the sovereignty of a canal zone across the Isthmus of Panama.

"The second alternative is that the President shall act in accordance with the provisions of the Spooner law, and, having failed to make a treaty of a satisfactory kind with Colombia, turn to the Nicaragua route.

"The third course is to delay this great work until something transpires to make Colombia see light, and then negotiate for another treaty. * * *

"It will doubtless be a surprise to the public that a course which is sure to involve the country with war with a South American Republic is one of the methods of procedure being soberly contemplated by the United States. * * *

"The position taken by those who are now advising extreme action by the United States is that the State Department has met Colombia more than half-way, and that her statesmen are trifling with this Government and seeking to blackmail it in a matter of great importance to the security of the United States.

"Persons interested in getting the $40,000,000 for the Panama Canal Co. are of course eager that this Government shall go ahead and seize the property, even though it leads to war."

August 29, 1903, the day after the Roosevelt-Hay council of war, Secretary Hay cabled to Minister Beaupre as follows:

"The President is bound by the Isthmian Canal statute, commonly called the Spooner law. By its provision he is given a reasonable time to arrange a satisfactory treaty with Colombia. When, in his judgment, the reasonable time has expired and he has not been able to make a satisfactory arrangement as to the Panama route he will then proceed to carry into effect the alternative of the statute. Meantime the President will enter into no engagement restraining his freedom of action under the statute."

We are at the end of August, 1903; Mr. Cromwell has managed to keep public attention fixed on his diplomatic circus. His revolutionary side-show tent has sprung up silently overnight without attracting attention. The flap is spiked down; no barker, no press agent is in sight; but it is time to peep under the wings, for the dress rehearsal is on.

Jose Agustin Arango, the land agent, lobbyist, and local lawyer for the Panama Ralroad; Capt. James R. Beers, an Amercan, freight agent and port captain; and Dr. Manuel Amador Guerrero, the company's physician, all of them directly dependent upon Mr. Cromwell's favor, formed the nucleus of the revolutionary conspiracy in Panama. Beers, who had returned on August 4, 1903, with Mr. Cromwell's code book and instructions, was keeping his principal fully informed by cable and by letter, and time was ripe to put to the front a native Panaman who should appear as the Moses or the George Washington.

Chief of the advisers to the conspiracy was Herbert G. Prescott, the most popular American on the Isthmus, married there, and on account of his family ties and his position as assistant superintendent of the Panama Railroad, intrusted with all that the conspirators were doing. For appearance's sake, Prescott, as well as Beers, kept in the background, for this was to be an uprising of outraged Panaman patriots.

Arango states in his booklet that before sending Capt. Beers to New York he consulted only his sons and sons-in-law, and that after the plot was well outlined he did not, for diplomatic reasons, admit any of his family to the "Patriots' revolutionary committee," but depended upon them as a family counsel for his own guidance and support. The "Patriots' committee" was composed at first of Arango, Amador, and Carlos Constantino Arosemena, later minister to Washington. To this committee were added, by the end of August, Nicanr A. de Obarrio, Ricardo Arias, Federico Boyd, Tomas Arias, and Manuel Espinosa B.

Amador, according to Arango's story, expressed a desire "to be one of the commissioners to be sent to the United States for the work that was necessary there." To allay suspicion, Dr. Amador wrote to his son, Dr. Raoul A. Amador, then acting assistant surgeon in the United States Army, stationed at Fort Revere, Mass., instructing him to send a cable: "I am sick; come." This the younger Amador did before his father embarked from Colon on the Panama Railroad Steamship Co.'s steamer *Seguranca*, August 26, 1903, for New York. Ricardo Arias, who was designated as another commissioner to accompany Dr. Amador, was obliged at the last moment to remain in Panama and Amador was intrusted alone with the mission.

The purpose of Dr. Amador's mission was (1) to confirm to the satisfaction of the native Panamans the promises of assistance brought back from Mr. Cromwell by Capt. Beers and obtain the aid of the other forces which Cromwell told Beers he could enlist for the movement; (2) to secure assurance, if possible, directly from the American Secretary of State or the President, that the revolution would be supported by the armed forces of the United States, and that the infant republic, once born, would be promptly clothed with recognition, bottle fed from the United States Treasury, and protected by American warships and soldiers from a spanking by Colombia; and (3) to secure the resources, in money and arms, necessary for the movement.

Before Amador's departure the conspirators drafted a cable code which reveals clearly what were their plans and purposes. It was in two sections, headed "From there to here" and "From here to there." Not a single name was mentioned, but in the code "X" stood for John Hay, Secretary of State; "W" was William Nelson Cromwell, and "Ministro" referred to the Colombian chargé d'affaires, Dr. Tomas Herran. "B" appears also once in the code, but the World is unable to state authoritatively whether "B" was Capt. Beers, Minister Beaupre, or some other interested person. In the code to be used by Ámador in cabling from New York there were 30 expressions, providing for all manner of contingencies, even for Cromwell's turning out to be only a boastful liar. Sixteen code messages were provided for the revolutionists to cable to Amador. The code word in each case was to be a numeral.

The World presents these illuminating state documents, translated and with the names substituted for the letters, as per the key, in their entirety.

FROM HERE TO THERE.

(For Amador's advices from New York to Panama.)

I. Have not been satisfied with Hay in my first conference.

II. Have had my first conference with Hay, and I found him determined to support the movement effectively.

III. Have not been able to talk to Hay personally, only through a third person; I believe that everything will turn out in line with our desires.

IV. Hay is determined to aid us in every way, and has asked me for exact details of what we need to insure success.

V. My agent is going with me, fully authorized to settle everything there.

VI. Cromwell has behaved very well, and has facilitated my interviews with important men who are disposed to cooperate.

VII. You can hurry up matters, as everything here goes well.

VIII. I am satisfied with the result and can assure success.
IX. Minister Herran has suspected something and is watching.
X. Have not been able to obtain assurances of support in the form in which I demanded it.
XI. Delay of Cromwell in introducing me to Hay makes me suspect that all he has said has been imagination and that he knows nothing.
XII. It appears that Hay will not decide anything definitely until he has received advices from the commissioner who is there (in Panama).
XIII. I understand that Hay does not wish to pledge himself to anything until he sees the result of the operation there (in Panama).
XIV. The people from whom I expected support have attached little importance to my mission.
XV. Those who are decided can do nothing practical for lack of necessary means.
XVI. I have convinced myself that Hay is in favor of the rival route, and for that reason will do nothing in support of our plan.
XVII. News that has arrived from there (Panama) on facilitating the construction of the canal has caused opinion here to shift in regard to our plan.
XVIII. The pretensions manifested in the new draft of an agreement (treaty) render all negotiations between the two Governments impossible, and for this reason I have again resumed conferences.
XIX. The new commissioner is expected here to negotiate. On this depends my future movements.
XX. I consider that I can do nothing practical here now, and for this reason I have decided to take passage for home.
XXI. Await my letter which I write to-day.
XXII. Here it is thought best to adopt a different plan in order to obtain a favorable result for the construction of the work.
XXIII. Cromwell is determined to go the limit, but the means at his disposal are not sufficient to insure success.
XXIV. Hay, Cromwell, and myself are studying a general plan of procedure.
XXV. The commissioner there (in Panama) is an agent of Cromwell's, of which fact Hay is ignorant.
XXVI. I wish to know if anything has been advanced there (in Panama) and can I fix date here to proceed.
XXVII. Delay in getting a satisfactory reply obliges me to maintain silence.
XXVIII. B communicates here (New York) that the contract can be satisfactorily arranged.
XXIX. I have considered it prudent to leave the Capital (Washington), and continue negotiations from here (New York) by correspondence.
XXX. I await letters from there (Panama) in reply to mine, in order to bring matters to a close.

FROM THERE TO HERE.

(For the conspirators' advices from Panama to Amador in New York).

Forty. The situation here is the same as when you left, in every respect.
Fifty. The object of your trip is suspected here and in consequence you must be circumspect.
Sixty. New military commander expected here shortly.
Seventy. Letters received. All is well. You can proceed.
Eighty. We write at length on variation of plan, as the one outlined has certain drawbacks.
Ninety. We accept indications contained in cable.
One hundred. Cable received. Go ahead.
Two hundred. Forces coming from Bolivar will arrive shortly.
Three hundred. Forces coming from Cauca will arrive here soon.
Four hundred. From Bogota they ask what has been done in the matter.
Five hundred. The matter is being much talked about. In consequence much precaution is necessary in acting.
Six hundred. Newspapers of there (Panama) give account of object of your journey.
Seven hundred. Strong opinion shown in favor of the plan, but this may hamper its realization.
Eight hundred. Here nothing has been done awaiting what you have to communicate.

Nine hundred. Without our being able to tell how, the Government has discovered the secret and is on the watch.

One thousand. We must have the resources asked for to proceed with probabilities of success.

From this cable code it is manifest that—

1. Panama looked, not to itself, but to the United States, to William Nelson Cromwell, and Secretary of State Hay for the "general plan of procedure;" in fact for all the sinews of war, material and moral; success depended entirely upon the attitude of Washington and the financial assistance furnished in New York.

2. There was a mysterious "commissioner" on the Isthmus; the Panamans suspected he was a secret agent of Cromwell and that Secretary Hay was ignorant of this supposed connection.

3. They believed respecting Cromwell (a) that he might be bluffing and that all he had told Capt. Beers might have been from his imagination; (b) that Cromwell would be ready, as reported by Beers, to "go the limit," but that he might lack resources to carry the revolution through successfully.

4. They feared that Secretary Hay might already be committed to the Nicaragua route.

5. They were prepared for a turn in the negotiations (a) by shifting of opinion in the United States on account of developments "facilitating the construction of the canal;" (b) by "pretensions" in the draft of a new treaty at Bogota which would render further negotiations with Colombia impossible and require a revolution; (c) the sending of a new minister from Colombia to reopen canal negotiations—a step which Colombia did propose and which the United States rejected; and (d) that, as a last hope, the negotiations might be brought to a satisfactory conclusion, in which event no revolution.

6. They expected Amador to conduct his negotiations for American assistance in the dismemberment of Colombia right in the shadow of the Capitol at Washington.

7. They were already aware of the plan to send a new military commander and soldiers from the interior, and they feared discovery of their plot by the Government.

8. Some one in Bogota, evidently working toward their same ends, might inquire as to the progress made; therefore Colombian treason was not confined to the Isthmus.

9. They feared that if public opinion on the Isthmus should manifest itself strongly in favor of the plan it might hamper its own realization—there where they "rose as one man."

Thus provided with means of secret communication—a copy of the code being left with Arango, Boyd, and Arias—Dr. Amador embarked for New York. An indication of the financial condition of the "Patriots' committee" of, if not of its own poverty, at any rate of its determination that the Americans should pay the costs of the movement, is the fact that Amador was not supplied with even enough money to pay the expenses of his trip. This he had to borrow later in New York on his personal credit from Joshua Lindo, a Panaman banker. Fortunately, Dr. Amador was a good poker player and on the voyage won from his fellow passengers enough to tide him over several days.

Sailing on the *Seguranca* with Dr. Amador were J. Gabriel Duque, proprietor of the Panama Lottery and the Panama Star and Herald, and Tracy Robinson, both American citizens, old and influential residents of the Isthmus. Mr. Duque looks back now with pride to his having been the "goat" of the *Seguranca's* poker party, thus making him the first contributor to the expenses of the separation.

"Dr. Amador bade me good-by at the pier in New York," says Mr. Duque, "and I never suspected that he was on any other mission than to see his sick son, as he told me then. I did not see him again until he returned to Panama." Mr. Robinson says he was likewise without Dr. Amador's confidence. From the steamer Dr. Amador went to the Hotel Endicott, Columbus Avenue and Eighty-first Street, where he registered on September 1, 1903. He retained room No. 152–C from his arrival till departure for Panama on October 20, 1903.

Mr. Duque insists to this day that he came to New York on one of his customary business trips, and that he had no appointment to see Mr. Cromwell about manufacturing a republic. But upon arriving at the exporting office of Andreas & Co. Mr. Duque met Roger L. Farnham, man Friday of the Panama Canal lobbyist, who told Mr. Duque that Mr. Cromwell wished to see him, and together Farnham and Duque went to No. 49 Wall Street. Mr. Duque had met Mr. Cromwell two or three years before this time, but had no intimate acquaintance.

Mr. Cromwell told Mr. Duque that there was no prospect of favorable action on the pending treaty by the Colombian Congress, and that the department of Panama should make a revolution and declare its independence. He asked Mr. Duque whether the leading men of Panama would or could furnish the necessary funds for a revolution, and Mr. Duque replied that he did not think so. Cromwell said that if Mr. Duque would advance the necessary $100,000 he, Cromwell, would furnish the security for such a loan, to be repaid after independence, and that if Mr. Duque would make the Republic of Panama he, Cromwell, would make Duque its first president.

Mr. Cromwell, after thoroughly discussing the situation in Panama and Bogota, said that Secretary of State Hay wished to confer with Mr. Duque in Washington. He made an appointment accordingly and gave Mr. Duque a note of introduction to the Secretary of State.

Mr. Duque was not positive how Mr. Cromwell made this engagement, but was led at the time to believe that Mr. Cromwell simply called the State Department on the long-distance telephone.

Now we come to a fair sample of the craft of the fox of Wall Street in covering his tracks by wading streams and jumping over chicken coops.

Farnham cautioned Mr. Duque not to remain over night in Washington, and suggested that, in order to avoid registering at a hotel and leaving a record of his visit, he take the night train from New York, arriving in Washington at 7 o'clock in the morning, see Mr. Hay and come promptly away. This suggestion Mr. Duque followed.

Before leaving New York, however, he met Charles Burdett Hart, former American minister to Bogota, in the office of Andreas & Co., and Hart said he would introduce Mr. Duque to Secretary Hay. They therefore journeyed to Washington together on the night of September 2, 1903, and after breakfasting at Harvey's went to the Department of State at half past 9 o'clock and waited until the arrival of Secretary Hay about 10 a. m. Hart then presented Mr. Duque, and shortly afterwards left them in a conference which lasted until between 12 and 1 o'clock.

In this conference the Secretary of State made no promise of direct assistance to the revolutionists of Panama, saying that he would not cross that bridge until he got to it, but he did say distinctly that the United States would build the Panama Canal and that it did not purpose to permit Colombia's standing in the way. Mr. Duque's recollection is furthermore clear and distinct of another statement by Secretary Hay, that should the revolutionists take possession of the cities of Colon and Panama they could depend upon the United States to prohibit Colombia's landing troops to attack them and disturb the "free and uninterrupted transit" which the American Government was bound by treaty with Colombia to maintain. This assurance Mr. Duque communicated to his friends in Panama before the 3d of November.

If this was not encouraging a revolution, what was it? And what was it but encouraging a revolution for the American Secretary of State to ask Mr. Duque, as representative of a plot against the Colombian Government, to remain in Washington or return to confer with the President when Mr. Roosevelt should come back from Oyster Bay the day after Labor Day? This was Mr. Hay's proposal, but it was impossible of acceptance because Mr. Duque had arranged to sail on September 7, 1903.

Having conferred two hours and more, during which he says Mr. Hay tried his best to pump him of all the information he possessed relative to the situation in Panama and Bogota, Mr. Duque left the State Department to call on his friend Dr. Herran, the Colombian chargé d'affaires. So highly did Mr. Duque prize the counsel of Mr. Cromwell's man Friday that he avoided even appearing in a public dining room in Washington at midday, and went without luncheon altogether.

Mr. Duque, although a Cuban by birth and an American citizen by adoption, had the kindliest feelings for Colombia; his son had prospered in business in Bogota and married into one of the foremost families of that capital, and Mr. Duque had no desire to see the bonds between Panama and the national Government severed. His intentions, therefore, were of the best when he went to Dr. Herran, thinking that a friendly warning might be communicated to Bogota in time to be effective. He told Dr. Herran that if the treaty was not ratified Panama would revolt and Colombia would lose everything.

According to Mr. Cromwell this was no news to Herran, who had communicated the same warning to his Government in June, 1903. The day after Duque's visit, Dr. Herran sent his Government the following cable:

"Revolutionary agents of Panama here. Yesterday the editor of the Estrella de Panama had a long conference with the Secretary of State. If treaty is not approved by September 22 (date Hay-Herran treaty expired by limitation), it is probable that there will be a revolution with American support.

On the same day that he sent this cable to Bogota, September 4, 1903, Dr. Herran wrote to the Colombian consul general in New York, Arturo de Brigard:

"Yesterday Mr. J. G. Duque, editor and proprietor of the Star and Herald, had a long interview with the Secretary of State, and I understand that the plan for a revolution which he brought with him has been well received by the Government here, and it is most probable that in the event that the canal treaty is not approved before the 22d of this month there will be a revolutionary Separatist movement on the Isthmus with the powerful support of this country.

"Besides Duque, there have come from Panama the following persons, and some of them, if not all, are compromised on this projected revolution: Tracy Robinson, G. Lewis, Amador, Arosemena. It appears that the headquarters of the revolution in New York is in the offices of Andreas & Co., whose address you know.

"The canal and Panama railroad companies are deeply implicated in this matter.

"Duque will return to Panama on Tuesday next.

"I have already informed our Government of this matter by cable, but you may perhaps be able to discover something more with the information I give you.

"The situation is exceedingly critical, and I fear we shall not be able to ward off the blow which threatens us if the treaty is not approved in time and without substantial modifications."

Dr. Herran immediately put detectives on the track of Amador and wrote to Mr. Cromwell and to the canal company in Paris, warning them that Colombia would hold them responsible for any secessionist plot on the Isthmus.

In a letter to his Government confirming his cable of September 4, 1903, and amplifying the information concerning Duque's interview with Secretary Hay, Dr. Herran wrote:

"As long as our Government preserves its authority in the cities of Panama and Colon, American intervention will contribute powerfully to preventing the realization of the revolutionary plans; but in the event that the conspiracy should succeed in taking possession of the city of Panama, recapture of that place would be exceedingly difficult, because, probably, our forces would not be able to use the railroad, nor would they be permitted to begin in the terminal cities operations which would suspend or obstruct traffic. This is the indirect aid which the conspirators hope for."

Mr. Duque, upon his return from Washington to New York, did not see Mr. Cromwell, but again conferred in the office of Andreas & Co. with Farnham, who spoke for Cromwell in all their conferences. He reported that he had been unable to obtain any positive assurances from Secretary Hay other than that the rebels would be protected in their possession of the two principal towns of the seceding Department.

Colombia can plead no lack of warning of what might be expected from the United States; it has only to thank the venal perfidy of its own Marroquin-Reyes Government, corrupted by American influences or American money. Only men purposely blind could have failed or refused to act on such advices and warnings as the following:

[Cable.]

BOGOTA, *August 29, 1903.*

COLOMBIAN MINISTER, *Washington:*

Please inform me by cable and in code what effect the rejection of the treaty has produced on the Government of the United States.

RICO.

[Cable.]

WASHINGTON, *September 6, 1903.*

FOREIGN MINISTER, *Bogota:*

Disapproval of treaty has produced a bad impression, but the Government of the United States awaits a favorable reaction before September 22. Otherwise it is probable that the President of the United States will assume a hostile attitude.

HERRAN.

[Cable.]

BOGOTA, *September 10, 1903.*

COLOMBIAN MINISTER, *Washington:*

Tell me in what hostile attitude will consist.

RICO.

[Cable.]

WASHINGTON, *September 15, 1903.*

FOREIGN MINISTER, *Bogota:*

Hostile attitude will consist in favoring indirectly a revolution in Panama.

HERRAN.

Dr. Herran explained his statement respecting the probable hostile attitude of President Roosevelt in the following paragraph of a letter to the Colombian foreign minister, written in Washington September 11, 1903:

"The warning that I gave relative to the probable future attitude of the President is founded on threatening statements which he has uttered in private conversations and which by indirect means have come to my knowledge. Special reference is made to the promptness with which the independence of our Department of Panama will be recognized. President Roosevelt is a decided partisan of the Panama route and hopes to begin excavation of the canal during his administration. Your excellency already knows the vehement character of the President, and you are aware of the persistence and decision with which he pursues anything to which he may be committed. These considerations have led me to give credit and importance to the threatening expressions attributed to him."

We must now go back to September 1, 1903, and pick up the trail of Dr. Manuel Amador Guerrero from his revolutionary headquarters in the Hotel Endicott. Like Arango, Amador possessed an ambition to perpetuate his name in history, and from his original manuscript, written within a year of his death in 1909, it has been possible to forge many of the missing links in this story of conspiracy. Amador, after his service as first President of the Republic, realized how necessary it was "for the honor of Panama" as well as for that of his "friends of the north" to suppress certain facts and to distort others. This manuscript, which was never published, is in Dr. Amador's own handwriting, and was edited most carefully by him. Its misstatements, its contradictions of truths recorded in some of his confidential correspondence during the days of the conspiracy, its careful editing out of statements damaging to his friend Roosevelt, as well as all that is expressed between the lines, make this manuscript a rare contribution to history. But all that Dr. Amador wrote or said for publication, and even much that he told his fellow conspirators, should be considered in the light of the confidences which he kept, even to his death. During his long last illness Dr. Amador was asked to tell the real story of the independence. Referring to this request, he said to his son, Dr. Raoul A. Amador:

"I am a dying man and beyond need of the help or friendship even of the American Government; but my children here (meaning the Panaman people) some day may need the good will of the great people of the north, and if I should tell all I know the United States would discover that we do not keep our political secrets and would no longer trust us. Therefore, I am not going to tell all that I know of our history."

As an employee of the Panama Railroad, Dr. Amador reported, after his arrival on September 1, 1903, to the company's offices in New York, and with the vice president, E. A. Drake, went to call on Mr. Cromwell. He presented a letter to Mr. Cromwell from Jose Augustin Arango. Dr. Amador in his manuscript describes the meeting this way:

"The first interview was most cordial, and Mr. Cromwell made me a thousand offers in the direction of assisting us. But nothing could be done, he said, except when the Herran-Hay treaty has been absolutely rejected, for in the end we believe it will be approved in spite of the great opposition of the houses of Congress. Vain were my efforts to convince Mr. Cromwell that no hope whatever should be entertained, and we continued the appointment to go on discussing the matter on the following day."

Here is the first palpable misstatement in Dr. Amador's unpublished history, for Mr. Cromwell was conferring at this same time with Duque, telling him that the treaty was dead, that Panama should make a revolution, offering security if Duque would finance the movement, and arranging for Duque to go by night to the State Department to discuss revolutionary plans with Secretary Hay. Furthermore, we have Mr. Cromwell's own word for it that neither in June nor at any subsequent time did he have any doubt of the unsuccessful outcome of the treaty negotiations.

Arango in his history describes Amador's first meeting with Cromwell as follows:

"At the beginning Dr. Amador Guerrero found no difficulty in the way of his mission, because the initial interview with the responsible person who, through Capt. Beers, had opened the road to our hopes and thus stimulated the sending of a representative of the committee, caused the first news which we received to be very satisfactory. Later came an unexpected and unfortunate incident which, for the moment, discouraged Dr. Amador Guerrero, who, as a consequence, sent us a cablegram containing the word 'disappointed' and, after various fruitless efforts, advised us that he would shortly leave New York to return here. We prevented this by begging him to remain there and write us details."

Arango attributed this "unexpected and unfortunate incident" to Mr. Duque's blunder in going from Secretary Hay's office to warn Dr. Herran that Colombia stood in danger of losing Panama, and Herran's consequent warning to Cromwell and the canal company. Arango's history continues:

"This (warning of Herran) influenced so unfavorably the soul of the responsible gentleman with whom our representative had come to an understanding, that he evaded from that time, on various occasions, a meeting with Dr. Amador, and there was produced a notable change in his conduct. This was sorrowfully obeserved by Amador Guerrero at the time, and was only explained when later our friend of North America said that it was caused by the indiscretion above set forth, which inspired him with a great fear. Not knowing our commissioner, he supposed that the latter might be guilty of indiscretion and compromise him in an adventure of doubtful outcome."

Dr. Amador's manuscript washes Cromwell's hands of the revolutionary conspiracy in this fashion, parenthetical phrases having been crossed out by Amador:

"After the first two satisfactory conferences with Mr. Cromwell I noticed that he excused himself (although he was in his office and did not give fulfillment to the appointments which I made with him—I obliged him to receive me) from discussion of the matter. On my insisting he received me, and I told him plainly that I was pained to see that he had changed his course, and that consequently I would do the same thing. I took leave of him and had no further news of him except several weeks after the 3d of November in New York. I understand that, cowed by the threats of the Colombian minister, he had shaped his course for Europe."

For the interest, if not the accuracy and completeness of history, it is unfortunate that Mr. Cromwell did "not judge it necessary to enter into the details of the events of this period"—August 12 to November 3, 1903. We might, if these events were given their true Cromwellian proportions, have even more brilliant sidelights on the method in Mr. Cromwell's mad scramble to disavow connection with the Panaman conspirators.

It is true that Mr. Cromwell did go through the formality of shooing Dr. Amador out of his office; there were witnesses to prove it; and doubtless Mr. Cromwell was frightened, for men who know him best, under trying circumstances, know him to be an arrant coward when the fight is going against him.

It is true that on September 10, 1903, Mr. Cromwell did cable to Col. James R. Shaler, superintendent of the Panama Railroad on the Isthmus, as follows:

"While there may be no real foundation for newspaper statements of possible revolution at Panama, I advise and request that you take extra and every precaution to strictly perform our obligations to Colombia under concession and instruct officials and employees to be careful, as heretofore, not to participate in any movements or hostilities whatever, and that you make at once your attitude known to Government officials there, and make careful record of your acts in this regard, in order to prevent even a pretext for complaint or claims by Bogota or Panama Governments; also take every precaution to protect the property in your care from possible damage or interruption of service.

"CROMWELL, *General Counsel*."

Earlier in the summer a notice of like tenor had been posted in the railroad offices in Panama for the protection of the company's interests. Both Col.

Shaler and Capt. Beers had been to New York and received instructions direct from Mr. Cromwell. They considered that the sincerity of Mr. Cromwell's cabled instructions of September 10, 1903, was in keeping with that of his statement therein that "there may be no real foundation for newspaper statements of possible revolution"—the same revolution which Mr. Cromwell had been promoting and discussing with them himself! They had reason to believe that Cromwell had sent the cable solely for the purpose of protecting the company in the event that the revolution should fail; they well knew that he didn't want it to fail, and consequently they acted as they did, and they were neither reprimanded nor discharged therefor. In this relation there is the following significant sentence in Mr. Cromwell's own story:

"The protection of the concessions and the property of the company against confiscation or difficulties on the part of Colombia presented a subject which exacted and obtained from us vigilance, care, and energetic services."

Further on Mr. Cromwell says:

"The canal and railroad companies * * * were publicly accused of encouraging and aiding the revolutionary movements; and it was only too evident that Colombia would seize on the least indication of such a fact to confiscate and take possession of their property, or to make them suffer serious complications. We exercised incessant care, and in September, seeing that a tempest was approaching, we cabled to all the officials on the Isthmus explicit instructions to be careful to avoid furnishing a cause of forfeiture or seizure, which was supplemented by personal interviews which we had with the general superintendent of the railroad, who came to New York partly to confer with us about the situation on the Isthmus."

In respect to his personal interview with the general superintendent in New York, Mr. Cromwell's statement is untrue. Col. Shaler, the general superintendent, returned to the Isthmus from New York on July 28, 1903. The incident upon which Mr. Cromwell bases his statement was the visit of Herbert G. Prescott, the assistant superintendent. The facts were these:

Mr. Prescott came up on his regular leave of absence, without any suggestion that it was partly or wholly to confer respecting the revolutionary situation. On the same boat came Hezekiah A. Gudger, the American consul general in Panama, who made a speech at the first luncheon where independence of Panama was publicly discussed, in July, 1903. They arrived in New York on the steamer *Saratoga* on September 8, 1903, and after luncheon at Miller's Hotel went to the offices of the Panama Railroad, where Judge Gudger said he wished to make a call before leaving that night for his home in Asheville, N. C. At the railroad offices they met Cromwell, and while Gudger had a long conference in an inner office with him Prescott remained outside with Vice President Drake.

Judge Gudger declares that neither he nor Mr. Cromwell discussed the revolutionary situation. On the other hand, Prescott was talking nothing but revolution to Vice President Drake. He knew that Capt. Beers's cables to Cromwell were transmitted through Drake, so he freely discussed the plans. Drake's attitude was plainly favorable to secession, which he believed was the only solution for the problems confronting Panama and the canal and railroad companies. Drake mentioned the first official warning which had been sent down to the Isthmus and posted and asked Prescott if he had seen it. He spoke of it only in a casual and perfunctory manner. Gudger was engaged so long in his conference that when he left Cromwell asked Prescott to come to his law office the following morning at 10 o'clock, there being no more time for conferences that evening.

Arriving at Cromwell's office, as per appointment, Prescott was met by Roger L. Farnham, who said Mr. Cromwell was busy. In a few minutes Edward B. Hill, one of Cromwell's firm, came out and invited Prescott into his office after Farnham had introduced them. Hill talked very frankly. He said that the Panamanians must be fools if they expected the United States to give them any guarantee before the revolution took place; that they must make the movement themselves, but that they surely could understand that once they had established their independence the United States would never permit Colombian troops to land to attack them, as there was precedent for such a course. Hill also called Prescott's attention to the order to the employees on the Isthmus and said that of course the railroad could not afford to take any chances of forfeiting its concession in the event of the movement failing. Neither Hill nor Drake gave Prescott any official instructions concerning the revolutionary situation. Hill asked Prescott's opinion as to whether the Panamans had enough "sand" to carry the movement out successfully, and Prescott replied that he did not believe they would take such risks unless they felt sure of protection from the United States, as otherwise the Colombian troops would overrun them.

During this conversation, which lasted from 10 o'clock until nearly noon, Farnham came in and out of Hill's office several times, joined freely in the discussion, asked many questions, and expressed his desire to go to the Isthmus and help pull off the revolution himself. No reason was offered for Cromwell's failure to keep the appointment, and supposing that Cromwell was occupied, and having no reason of his own to confer with him, Prescott left when Hill was through.

Cromwell's attention was called several times to Prescott's being in Hill's office, but he excused himself from seeing him. Prescott had committed himself to the cause of the revolution in his conversation with Drake. Whether Drake had communicated this fact to Cromwell overnight is not known. But at any rate there was no necessity for Cromwell to see him after what Drake had learned, and Cromwell was "playing safe." If the revolution failed, and it became necessary to use the State Department to collect the Panama Railroad's claims against the Colombian Government for forfeiture of its concession, Cromwell could swear—and so could Prescott—that the general counsel had not conferred with him nor suggested that he assist the rebels.

We are now come to the point where we are asked to believe that Mr. Cromwell, his soul possessed of terror, washed his hands of the revolutionary conspiracy, shunned it thereafter as he would a plague, and fled away to Europe, taking no part in promoting, financing, or making successful the fake "revolution" in Panama; that he left the fat he had fried so assiduously for seven long, lean years to fall, if it might, in the fire, without so much as knowing what hand might be near to save it or what hostile breath might smother or fan to uncontrolled fury the seditious sparks he had nursed into a revolutionary flame; that he, who had managed thus far to rescue the bankrupt French canal from every situation where "for the company it was a matter of life or death"; he who had proposed plans "different, open, audacious, aggressive"; who had been reinstated as general counsel with the admonition that he must not use "methods as dangerous as they are unlawful"; he who "had not then (June, 1903) and did not have later any doubt of the result"—being Panama's secession—that this same master lobbyist, Cromwell, his political ambition unsatisfied, his $800,000 fee unpaid and uncollectible if this revolution failed, abandoned his client's interests—and his own—to the hands of Providence!

Philippe Bunau-Varilla, discredited French speculator, one of the "penitentiary crowd," as were known in France the penalized shareholders who helped rob and wreck the old canal company, now appears upon the scene. We have crossed his trail in Dr. Herran's describing him "interfering officiously" in the canal negotiations. The World has quoted Mr. William Nelson Cromwell's telegram, in which he thanked this same Bunau-Varilla profusely for having assisted in securing his reinstatement as general counsel a year and a half before this time. Now Bunau-Varilla comes from Paris, on the 23d of September, 1903, some two weeks after Amador has sent his cable "Disappointed" to the Isthmus—or just in the time needed for Mr. Cromwell, seeing that he must get under cover after Herran's warnings, to cable his cry from Macedonia to Paris and for that worthy engineer-speculator and would-be diplomat to take the first steamer to America.

Whether there was or was not an understanding between Mr. Cromwell and M. Philippe Bunau-Varilla is more or less inconsequential. The circumstantial evidence points strongly to Mr. Cromwell's having sent, directly or indirectly, for this able proxy. If there was no understanding, as both these gentlemen state, at any rate there remain some questions to be answered.

Why did Bunau-Varilla arrive so opportunely in New York three weeks after Cromwell had told Amador that he could not, himself, be seen assisting the revolutionists?

Why did Amador seek Bunau-Varilla at the Waldorf-Astoria Hotel on the very night of his arrival, and why do the stories told by Amador, Bunau-Varilla, and the man who says he introduced them differ by two weeks on the date of this meeting?

Why did Amador lie and lead every man who has attempted to chronicle these events to misstate the facts concerning the hope on which was built the Panama Republic?

Why did he conceal the truth even from his fellow conspirators and lead them, not only as in Arango's case to write the story falsely, but with other "patriots" to swear in court to statements which were false?

Amador's own written version of his meeting Bunau-Varilla says:

"The vacations of Secretary Hay appeared to me to be lasting a century, when, one night, Mr. J. J. Lindo, of Piza, Nephews & Co., who was aware of all that was taking place, said to me: 'Why don't you see if Bunau-Varilla can do something?' 'Where shall I meet him,' I said—'in Paris?' 'Nothing of the sort,' he said to me; 'he has just arrrived and is at the Waldorf-Astoria.' For me, who knew the energy of B. V. and his interest in bringing to a head the canal undertaking, this gave me such renewed strength that from then on I augured the most complete success of my business. Mr. Lindo left me at 10 p. m. in the Endicott, and I forthwith went to see Bunau-Varilla at the Waldorf-Astoria. At 11 p. m. this gentleman was not in the hotel, and I left my card giving him an appointment for the following day at his residence (apartment). I found him in my first conference so enthusiastic that I gave him a memorandum of what in Panama we needed in order to proclaim and uphold our independence."

Amador here commits himself to having first discussed Bunau-Varilla with Lindo at the Endicott; Mr. Lindo declares it was in his office at No. 18 Broadway, when Amador came, despairingly, to bid him good-by and say he was going back to Panama, having failed to arrange anything. Mr. Lindo even points out the chair in which Amador sat.

Amador says they met when Bunau-Varilla had "just arrived," and Bunau-Varilla arrived at the Waldorf on September 23, 1903; Bunau-Varilla corroborates this story, but Mr. Lindo fixes his bringing together of Amador and Bunau-Varilla not longer than 5 to 10 days before Amador's departure for the Isthmus, which was October 20, 1903. Amador's own story tends to corroborate Mr. Lindo, for he says: "After some three days of conferences everything was arranged to my satisfaction, and I so informed my friends, announcing to them my early return and giving them complete assurance of the triumph of our project."

Arango's "Data for a History," written when the desirability of hiding the real story of the independence, so far as Americans were concerned therein, had not been impressed upon Panama, says:

"The setback (Cromwell's alleged refusal to help) to Amador Guerrero was prejudicial to our cause; he found himself obliged to set a date for his return if in the meantime something unexpected did not happen. In the interim he received a suggestion from a good friend of Panama, Mr. Joshua Lindo, of the commercial house of Piza, Nephews & Co., to the effect that Bunau-Varilla, at that time in the Hotel Waldorf-Astoria, was very favorably inclined toward the canal treaty and could do much for us, etc."

Thus reanimated, without delay Amador Guerrero went to the hotel mentioned but found that Bunau-Varilla was away; finally he saw the latter gentleman, and after various interviews they agreed upon a plan which should be adopted and which would give as a result the satisfying of our agent. He then cabled us the word "hopes."

Arango in his original story solemnly avowed that all his data departed not from the strict truth. His family declare now that if his account of Amador's visit to the States is untrue—as it is—then Amador deliberately misled him.

And finally we have the administration-O. K'd version of the Amador-Bunau-Varilla negotiations in Mr. Willis Fletcher Johnson's "Four Centuries of the Panama Canal," dedicated to William Howard Taft and frontised with Mr. Taft's portrait. This version was furnished to Mr. Johnson by Dr. Amador in Panama when Mr. Johnson visited the Isthmus as Secretary Taft's guest. Mr. Cromwell also is acknowledged gratefully as a contributor to the information this book contains. Mr. Johnson says:

"On reaching New York Dr. Amador first called upon Mr. William Nelson Cromwell, the counsel for the Panama Railroad Co. and for the French Panama Canal Co., who, of course, was deeply interested in securing the ratification of the treaty. To him he broached the plan of the revolutionists, and of him solicited aid. Mr. Cromwell, despite his earnest desire to see the United States secure the canal route and enter upon the undertaking, was strongly disinclined toward anything like a forcible revolution. He told Dr. Amador frankly that he could not and would not have anything to do with the scheme, and warned him that, in his opinion, the United States would not countenance anything of the sort."

Mr. Johnson then tells of the sending of the cable "disappointed" and at the same time of Mr. Cromwell's departure for Europe. "Disappointed" was cabled before September 7, 1903, and Mr. Cromwell went to Europe on October 15, 1903. This is not meant to asperse Mr. Johnson; he never aspired to be a "muckraker"; he simply accepted without question what Cromwell, Amador, and the administration told him as facts. His narrative continues:

"More for sake of consolation in sympathetic talk than in hope of material advantage, he (Amador) went, immediately after his last call at Mr. Cromwell's, to the office of a Panaman friend and sympathizer, Joshua Lindo, of the firm of Piza, Nephews & Co., in New York. To him he related the failure of his errand and bewailed the apparent hopelessness of the Panaman cause.

"'There is one man would help us, I am sure,' he said, 'and that is Bunau-Varilla. But he is in Paris, and I can not go thither and see him in time to do anything. It would then be too late.'

"While the two were speaking of him and deploring his absence from America at that critical time, the telephone in the office rang. Señor Lindo answered the call, and then uttered an ejaculation of amazement and delight.

"'Santa Maria! Amador!' he cried, turning to his guest, 'it's Bunau-Varilla, now!'

"It was quite true. The French engineer had just arrived in New York from Paris, and had telephoned down to the office from his hotel to ask what had been happening at Panama and at Washington while he was on shipboard. Dr. Amador sprang to the telephone:

"'Is that really you, Bunau-Varilla? For heaven's sake, wait right there until I come up!'

"Within half an hour they were closeted together, and M. Bunau-Varilla was committing himself to the revolutionary cause."

What a pretty fairy story! Further on, a little way, we find this:

"Raised from despair to exultant confidence by his interview with M. Bunau-Varilla, Dr. Amador cabled to the junta at Panama the one word 'Esperanzas,' 'hopes.'"

We have set forth the principal versions, all in accord, as to the central facts of the story long ago agreed upon, which in brief is:

That Amador came to New York, saw Cromwell, and that Cromwell, frightened by the warnings of Dr. Herran, refused to have anything to do with the revolution and went to Europe, whereupon Amador cabled "Disappointed"; that he then was put in touch with Bunau-Varilla, purely by accident, through Joshua Lindo, whereupon he cabled "Hopes"; and that Bunau-Varilla, alone and with no understanding between himself and Cromwell, took up the revolutionary propaganda where Cromwell had dropped it.

All very good, if it were not built on a lie; and all very good at that—for the Roosevelt-Cromwell purpose—"had not Cromwell's man in Panama been an ass and left so much evidence uncovered," as one of the Roosevelt-Cromwell gumshoe brigade expressed himself in confidential disgust.

This lie about the source that inspired Amador's "hopes" is the keystone to the whole structure of falsehood and deception upon which the heretofore-accepted history of the Panama Republic is written.

The Roosevelt prosecution depended upon this lie to help convict the World of "libeling the American Government" when testimony was taken by a rogatory commission sent at the World's expense to Panama in June, 1909. All the surviving members of the "patriots' revolutionary committee" who were called to testify swore to the truth of this historic falsehood. Confronted later by proof that their stories were untrue, the friends of the late Dr. Amador threw up their hands in real or simulated astonishment and declared that Amador lied to them.

And why should Amador lie to his fellow conspirators, even at the time when failure of the plot would put his own and his friends' necks in the noose? Why did he tell them that Bunau-Varilla's roseate promises in his first interview inspired his cable "hopes," when Bunau-Varilla was still in Paris and did not reach New York until two weeks after this cable was sent? Why lie as to what Bunau-Varilla did if Bunau-Varilla alone accomplished all that Amador tried to lead his friends to believe he did unless Amador was lying under instructions, and for the purpose of concealing some one else's responsibility or criminality or malfeasance?

Irrefutable proof that Amador did lie appears in the following letter written in Spanish by Arango to Amador in New York, the original handwritten manuscript of which came into the World's possession in the summer of 1909:

[Translation from Spanish.]

PANAMA, *September 14, 1903.*

MY DEAR FRIEND: As to-morrow, Tuesday, the *Seguranca* should arrive at Colon (sailed from New York Sept. 8) I trust that during the day we shall receive your expected letter which will give us the explanation of your discouraging cablegram "Disappointed; await letters." Since then we have received the cable saying "Hope" and ——— nothing more; so that we are in a position of fearful expectancy, as we are ignorant of what has happened to you over there, and of the reasons for the profound silence which Mr. Cromwell maintains.

Tired of so much incertitude, we decided to send the following cables to that gentleman; they are as yet unanswered, but which we trust he will give attention and reply to within two or three days:

On September 10, in cipher:

"Confidential. Regret Capt. Beers letters and cables are not replied. Opportunity now excellent to secure success provided United States promply recognizes our independence under conditions with our agent there, who is fully authorized to contract for us. Should Congress concede contract, although improbable, will be through fear of our attitude. Congress controlled by enemies of contract. Answer by wire in cipher through Beers. Tell our agent that to use all caution possible must send his cables through Beers, not to use Brandon again. Arango."

On the 12th of September, also in cipher:

"Our position being critical we must have immediate answer to act promptly or abandon business."

The recommendation made to you in the first cable set out above, not to use Brandon, is because your cable "Disappointed" was made quasi public, and I suspect that the other one also has been known to several persons, which doubtless comes from the cable having been known to young Brandon and by him communicated to Gustave Leeman, who must have divulged it; but be that as it may, it is better for you to communicate through Capt. Beers, even when using Arias's or Boyd's cipher.

You already know of the change of governor; and this afternoon there arrived in Colon Gen. Baron (Varon), bringing news that Obaldia and Sarria are already in Barranquilla with 15 officers and officials, which is explained by the fact that as Sarria is on bad terms with Huertas, he has asked to be allowed to bring fresh officials, which is a contretemps for us, even if everything can be arranged. Anyhow we shall see if "they burn our bread in the door of the oven."

The opportunity which is being lost is a brilliant one—here the whole country will rise as one man. Since you left the desire for independence with a protectorate has greatly increased. Everyone in town and country ask for it openly. It would be a pity to lose this brilliant opportunity.

I suppose that Maria and your son Manuel will give you general news, therefore I have only referred to urgent matters which are incumbent upon me.

Against my custom I am writing this in plain language and without reserve, confident that you will tear up this letter as soon as you have read it and taken note of its contents.

I can think of nothing more to say and take leave, wishing that our efforts may not be fruitless.

Your unswerving friend, J. A. ARANGO.

Relatives of Arango, being shown this letter, tried to save the situation by suggesting that Arango unintentionally wrote "September 14" where he should have dated his letter in October. The context of the letter, especially that part about Obaldia's arrival disproves this hopeless assumption many times over. Obaldia reached Panama September 18, 1903. Finally the Arango family representatives had to express the conclusion that Amador, on his return from New York, had deceived even Arango, who had put him forward as the leader of the independence.

In another important particular in which the testimony given in Panama before the World's commission is at variance with the facts, the Panamans now excuse their misstatements by saying Amador deceived them. This is in the accounts of his movements in New York and his visits to Washington. The surviving members of the "patriots' revolutionary committee" declare that Amador reported upon his return from New York that he had not been to Washington, and that he did not see Secretary Hay nor President Roosevelt. Ricardo Arias, examined by the World's counsel on June 12, 1909, testified:

"Q. Did he (Amador) go to Washington on that trip (to the United States before the revolution)?—A. He did not.

"Q. Did he not see President Roosevelt?—A. He did not see President Roosevelt.

"Q. So any negotiations he may have had with the American Government he must have had through what men?—A. He had no actual negotiations with the United States Government.

"Q. That is directly, you mean?—A. Directly or indirectly; no, sir."

Frederico Boyd, who became one of the three members of the Provisional Government after the revolution, testified:

"Q. (By United States attorney.) You never received any assurance from any official of the United States or from any other place; is that a fact?—A. No. Our representative, Dr. Amador, didn't even go to Washington because the inquiries he had made—he didn't think he would be either received or satisfactorily——"

The truth is that Amador went to Washington at least twice. If he denied this to his fellow conspirators upon his return to Panama, as they testified and still declare is true, he deceived them at whose suggestion? By his deception he nearly lost the support of several of his most influential followers, who confess that they would have dropped out of the movement had that been possible, because Amador said he had no assurances from Washington except what Bunau-Varilla had promised after going there alone.

But Amador, after the revolution, did tell various persons that he went to Washington himself. He did not tell them that he went with William Nelson Cromwell in a compartment of the Congressional Limited train from New York; that Cromwell on his trip drafted the manifesto of independence for the proposed Republic of Panama; that they, like Duque, when advised by Cromwell's man, Farnham, avoided going to a Washington hotel, where a record of their visit would be left, but went to the White House near midnight and remained in conference with Roosevelt until nearly daylight, in time to catch a morning train back to New York. Yet this is the report of Amador's visit which was received by the late United States Senator John T. Morgan, of Alabama, on the morning Amador is alleged to have come away from the White House.

F. F. Whittekin, of Medellin, Colombia, an American civil engineer, furnishes partial corroboration of this statement. He was told of the Cromwell-Amador trip to Washington on the following day by the conductor of the Congressional Limited train on which they traveled.

Amador also told Arango, in the presence of Arango's son-in-law, Ernesto T. Lefevre, of Panama, that he went to Washington with Bunau-Varilla and was kept waiting in a hotel lobby until nearly midnight while Bunau-Varilla was at the White House. He also made the statement to Dr. Eusebio A. Morales, later secretary of state of the new Republic, that he had been to Washington.

To Prescott, in New York, on October 7, 1903, Amador said that he had been to Washington alone, but had been unable to accomplish anything definite, but was going to be taken down by Bunau-Varilla the next day and was sure of getting all the promises he required.

Still further, there is the following account of Amador's movements by Mr. Johnson, the administration historian, and which Mr. Johnson verifies as having come to him direct from Amador's lips.

"He then presently (after meeting Bunau-Varilla and cabling 'Hope' to Panama) revisited Washington and sought a conference with the Secretary of State. * * * His aim was to learn what the United States would do in case of a revolution on the Isthmus. * * * The replies given by Mr. Hay were diplomatically discreet and guarded. * * * Dr. Amador made only a few calls at the State Department. * * * He was then told, kindly but firmly and plainly, that, as he was confessedly and notoriously the would-be organizer of a revolution against a power with which the United States was at peace, any further visits at that office would not be proper. At that, he gracefully took his leave, with the proverbial 'mingled emotions.' He had received no direct encouragement or promise of aid, but, on the other hand, he had been assured of the benevolent neutrality of the United States, and that, he thought, would be sufficient for the purpose. * * * He at once returned to Panama to complete preparations for the revolution and to report to his associates the result of his mission."

Dr. Amador's own account of his negotiations suppresses altogether the visits to Washington. He carefully crossed out even the statement that Bunau-Varilla had been there. After telling of Mr. Cromwell's shaping his course for Europe, Amador says:

"I was not downcast by this failure, for I expected to meet just such deceptions in the arduous task that had been entrusted to me."

Dr. Amador's manuscript continues:

"In a trip I made to Boston to see my son, who was doctored at Fort River (Fort Revere), I wrote, with the assistance of the latter, a letter to Mr. Gudger, with whom I maintained excellent relations. Its object was to ask him for a letter of introduction to Secretary Hay, in which he would tell him how far he could believe me in an important matter I was to speak to him about. The letter came so splendid that I myself would not have been able to say more than my good friend said to the honorable Secretary: but the latter was on his vacation (a friend advised me), and I preferred to wait until he came to Washington in order to speak to him about the matter."

Dr. Amador even preferred not to mention the friend who advised him to wait until Hay should return from his vacation, so he crossed that out. Consul General (now Judge) Gudger says that he wrote this letter of introduction without so much as suspecting why Amador desired to see Secretary Hay.

Dr. Amador's manuscript, after describing his first meeting with Bunau-Varilla, continues, with the parenthetical phrases crossed out:

"He (left for Washington and) gave me an appointment for two days later and called me to a conference (and told me), giving me to know that, although he had not obtained the pecuniary resources which I desired, he did have resources offered to him which insured the success of the matter once we had struck the blow in Colon and Panama. I wanted to make and did make clear certain doubtful points, and I satisfied myself that it was intended to limit the independence of Colon, Panama, and the zone necessary for the canal undertaking, to which I opposed myself energetically."

It is well to note that Amador says nothing anywhere about the $100,000 which Bunau-Varilla pretends to have advanced out of his own pocket to finance the revolution. Amador says that Bunau-Varilla "had not obtained the pecuniary resources which I desired," but that "he did have resources offered to him which insured the success," etc. If Bunau-Varilla had had $100,000 of his own to advance, would this have been his statement on October 20, 1903? It sounds more as though the $100,000 which Crédit Lyonnais cabled three days after Mr. Cromwell's arrival in Paris was the "resources offered to him."

In the foregoing statement Dr. Amador tells another untruth. He wrote to his son on October 18, 1903, a confidential letter in which he describes the proposed plan to declare independent only the strip which his American friends desired for their own purposes, and says of it: "The plan, I believe, is a good one." Upon his return to Panama Dr. Amador argued in favor of this plan against the opposition of his fellow conspirators. Continue Amador's story, with the telltale parenthetical elisions:

"After several conferences and (two trips of B. V. to Washington) some three days of conferences everything was arranged to my satisfaction, and I so informed my friends, announcing to them my early return and giving them complete assurance of the triumph of our project.

"All being ready for my departure for Panama on October 20, I had a long discussion with Bunau-Varilla about certain conditions which he wished to exact from me, and I ended with the understanding that we should not touch upon this point till later.

"I arrived in Colon and Panama on the 27th of October, and my friends, very satisfied, gave me an appointment that I might unfold the plan to them. On the carrying out of the appointment, lack of confidence prevailed among them, with rare exceptions, as they believed I would show them some secret treaty with a sovereign, and that nothing remained for us to do but to found our Republic."

The conditions which Bunau-Varilla discussed on October 20, 1903, related to his request to be appointed first minister of the new Republic in Washington. Amador, for reasons which might be made clear by the hidden history of the understanding which he had with the person who really inspired his "hope," opposed Bunau-Varilla's aspirations, because he desired himself to be the first minister. It was only through the insistence of Arango, as one of the provisional government established after the revolution, that Bunau-Varilla received his appointment.

Attempting to conceal the facts, the story has been generally told, and is so related in Mr. Johnson's "Four Centuries of the Panama Canal," that Amador had opportunity to send only the two cables, "Disappointed" and "Hope." The admission that this is not true was carefully expurgated when Arango published in pamphlet form his "Data for a History of the Independence," which originally appeared in El Heraldo del Istmo. The Arango story says: "I cabled, by agreement with my companions, that in future all advices by wire, as well as his letters, should come through Capt. Beers, because it was dangerous to continue as theretofore." Then is stricken out in the revised edition the following, which in the original stood in a paragraph by itself:

"He proceeded in accordance with these instructions, and we had the assurance that the conspirators would be kept informed of all developments."

Going back now to the movements of Mr. Prescott, assistant superintendent of the Panama Railroad, we find considerable enlightenment on the deceptions of Amador. About a week after his arrival in New York, Prescott went to the Hotel Endicott, having learned at the railroad or in Mr. Cromwell's office that this was the revolutionary agent's headquarters. Finding that Dr. Amador was out, he left his card, but Amador later called on him at Miller's Hotel. Prescott later saw Amador on two different occasions at the Endicott and at the latter of these two interviews he informed Amador of the date of his proposed sailing for Panama on October 7, 1903. At the first interview at the Endicott, Amador told Prescott that he had been in Washington himself but had accomplished nothing definite; that Duque had upset everything by his indiscreet talk with Tomas Herran, the Colombian chargé d'affaires, who, Amador said, was having him watched. Prescott noticed that Amador was much more reserved than he had been when they discussed the revolutionary plan together in Panama. At this time Cromwell, according to the story which Amador told to other persons, had taken fright and refused any assistance, but Amador told no such tale to Prescott. It was unnecessary to deceive him. He said nothing to Prescott about being in despair and about to return to the Isthmus unsuccessful. Quite the contrary, he told Prescott that, while things were not progressing so rapidly as he wished, he was accomplishing the object of his mission. At the last interview in the Hotel Endicott he said he expected to complete arrangements in a week or so. He said nothing at this time about Bunau-Varilla, who had then been in town for more than a week and who was supposed to be, according to the official version, already the sole backer of the revolution.

On October 7, 1903, Amador came to the pier to see Prescott off for Panama. His reserve seemed to have been broken, and Prescott believed at the time that Amador was informing him quite freely. Then for the first time Amador mentiond to Prescott Cromwell's attack of chills, but it was not the exaggerated story which it was deemed advisable later to give to the public. Dr. Amador did not say that Cromwell had driven him out of the office. He said he had been to Cromwell's office only a few days before this and had been told that Cromwell was out. Incredulous, he sat down to wait, and Cromwell soon came out of his private office thinking that Amador had gone. Amador told Prescott that he said to Mr. Cromwell "Your clerk must have made a mistake." He told Prescott that while Mr. Cromwell appeared to be unwilling to assist in the revolution, he had just met, on the night before, coming to the pier, the man who would accomplish everything the Panamanians desired and that this man, Bunau-Varilla, would take him to Washington on the following day and obtain the hoped-for promises of American assistance. Amador told Prescott to communicate to the friends on the Isthmus this news; to tell them that Bunau-Varilla would arrange everything satisfactorily, including the finances; that they might expect Amador down on the next steamer, and that they should be prepared to make the movement shortly after he arrived in Panama.

For better perspective it is necessary now to look to Panama and Bogota, and even to Paris.

We left the situation in Bogota at the end of August, 1903, when Minister Beaupre was cabling to Washington the news of Obaldia's appointment as governor of Panama, two days before it was made, and announcing Obaldia's statement that "if the Government of the United States will wait for the next session of Congress (summer of 1904) canal can be secured without a revolution."

After the rejection of the treaty, due to the Cromwell-Roosevelt-Hay-Beaupre ultimatum and the various threats and demands for ratification without amendment in any form, the Colombian Senate appointed a special committee to devise a canal program satisfactory to Colombia and within that country's constitutional limitations, and acceptable to the United States. This committee's report had been prepared but not presented. Mr. Beaupre obtained and cabled to the State Department September 5, 1903, a synopsis of this committee's report, but the cable did not reach Washington until September 11.

This report proposed a project of law, which passed first debate, but went no further. It was the only definite expression of Colombia's desire to "blackmail" the United States. It expressed the views of Colombia's leading statesmen on the terms under which they believed the canal treaty should be negotiated. The rejection of the Hay-Herran treaty by the Senate was approved in this project, and President Marroquin was authorized to negotiate a new treaty without subsequent ratification, subject only to limitations set forth in the proposed law. The monetary limits were:

The Panama Canal Co. would be permitted to transfer its concession and receive cancellation of the 50,000 shares of canal stock owned by Colombia upon payment of $10,000,000 to the Colombian Government.

The Panama Railroad Co. would be permitted to transfer its concession if it agreed to continue the payment of its $250,000 annual subsidy to Colombia until expiration of its concession in 1967, when the United States might exercise the privileges of purchasing the railroad at arbitrators' price from Colombia, to which the property would revert by terms of the concession.

The United States should pay $150,000 a year rental until 1967, and after that $400,000 a year for use of the canal; lease to be renewable every 100 years at 25 per cent increase over the last period.

The United States should pay Colombia $20,000,000 for the concession upon ratification of the canal treaty.

The chairman of the committee appointed to prepare this project of law for second debate became ill and delayed action. Another senator finally was appointed in his place and this committee proposed indefinitely postponing consideration of the bill, thus leaving the Government free to begin negotiations anew, subject to ratification by Congress. This is what was eventually done.

Meantime Minister Beaupre was keeping the State Department fully advised by cable and letter. In a letter of Mr. Beaupre's to Secretary Hay on September 25, 1903, we find this interesting sidelight on affairs in Bogota:

"It is a positive fact that some of the most prominent senators avoided me because of the charge frequently made that bribery was being resorted to by the United States and the consequent fear that if seen in conversation with the American minister they would be under suspicion. This was admitted to me after the rejection of the treaty."

In this letter Mr. Beaupre complained bitterly of the unreliability of the information obtainable and the many lies told him.

Gov. Obaldia left Bogota September 3, 1903, and, arriving in Panama, took up his duties on the 18th. He made his home in the house of Dr. Amador, the revolutionary conspirator, and proceeded to be ignorant of the conspiracy.

Just at this time we find the first trace of the presence of Mr. Roosevelt's military spies on the Isthmus. Capt. Chauncey B. Humphrey, Twenty-second Infantry, United States Army, and Second Lieut. Grayson Mallet-Prevost Murphy, Seventeenth Infantry, United States Army, registered at the Hotel Central, Panama, as "C. B. Humphrey, New York," and "G. Mallet-Prevost Murphy, New York." They remained at the hotel from September 16 to 20, 1903. Capt. Humphrey, a son of Gen. Charles F. Humphrey, then Quartermaster General, United States Army, was instructor in drawing at West Point. Lieut. Murphy was graduated from West Point June 11, 1903, a few days before being dispatched with Capt. Humphrey on this expedition. Returning from Panama, they arrived in New York on the Red D Liner *Caracas* on October 12, 1903. This steamer sailed from Laguayra September 30, 1903, and from Curacao October 5, 1903. Mr. Roosevelt, in his message to Congress January 4, 1904, says of this expedition:

"On October 16, at the request of Lieut. Gen. Young, I saw Capt. C. B. Humphrey and Lieut. Grayson Mallet-Prevost Murphy, who had just returned from a four months' tour through the northern portions of Venezuela and Colombia. They stopped in Panama on their return the latter part of September. At the time they were sent down there had been no thought of their going to Panama, and their visit to the Isthmus was but an unpremeditated incident of their return journey; nor had they been spoken to by anyone at Washington regarding the possibility of a revolt. Until they landed at Colon they had no knowledge that a revolution was intended save what they had gained from the newspapers. What they saw in Panama so impressed them that they reported thereon to Lieut. Gen. Young, according to his memorandum:

"'That while on the Isthmus they became satisfied beyond question that, owing largely to the dissatisfaction because of the failure of Colombia to ratify the Hay-Herran treaty, a revolutionary party was in course of organization, having for its object separation of the State of Panama from Colombia, the leader being Dr. Richard Arango, a former governor of Panama; that when they were on the Isthmus arms and ammunition were being smuggled into the city of Colon in piano boxes, merchandise crates, etc., the small arms received being principally the Gras French rifle, the Remington, and the Mauser; that nearly every citizen in Panama had some sort of rifle or gun in his possession, with ammunition therefor; that in the city of Panama there had been organized a fire brigade which was really intended for a revolutionary military organization; that there were representatives of the revolutionary organization at all important points on the Isthmus; that in Panama, Colon, and the other principal places of the Isthmus police forces had been organized which were in reality revolutionary forces; that the people on the Isthmus seemed to be unanimous in their sentiment against the Bogota Government, and their disgust over the failure of the Government to ratify the treaty providing for the construction of the canal; and that a revolution might be expected immediately upon the adjournment of the Colombian Congress without ratification of the treaty.'

"Lieut. Gen. Young regarded their report as of such importance as to make it advisable that I should personally see these officers. They told me what they had already reported to the lieutenant general, adding that on the Isthmus the excitement was seething, and that the Colombian troops were reported to be disaffected. In response to a question of mine they informed me that it was the general belief that the revolution might break out at any moment, and if it did not happen before, would doubtless take place immediately after the closing of the Colombian Congress (at the end of October), if the canal treaty were not ratified. They were certain that the revolution would occur and before leaving the Isthmus had made their own reckoning as to time, which they had set down as being probably from three to four weeks after their leaving. The reason they set this as the probable inside limit of time was that they reckoned that it would be at least three or four weeks—say not until October 20—before sufficient quantity of arms and munitions would have been landed."

If the visit of these young officers to the Isthmus "was but an unpremeditated incident of their return journey," why did they return in the roundabout way by Curacao? If they had not been spoken to by anyone at Washington regarding the possibility of a revolt, why their amazing initiative in acquiring the wealth of detailed military information, part of which is contained in Document No. 217, War Department, Office Chief of Staff, a book of 286 pages bearing the stamp of the Government Printing Office of November, 1903, under the heading "No. 1, Notes on Panama"? This document was marked "Confidential. For the sole use of the officer to whom issued."

Before quoting some of the observations made by Capt. Humphrey in his report on his entirely "unpremeditated" expedition into the rebellious department of a Government with which the United States was then on friendly terms, conducting supposedly honorable diplomatic negotiations, it might be well to note that Capt. Humphrey's father, on September 15 and September 17, 1903, while his son was in Panama, came up from Washington and occupied rooms adjoining that of Dr. Amador, the revolutionary conspirator, in the Hotel Endicott, New York. Gen. Humphrey after his retirement as Quartermaster General became the recognized lobbyist in Washington of the Du Pont powder crowd, whose earlier connection with Mr. Cromwell's efforts is noted in the financial chapter of this story.

Where Capt. Humphrey and Lieut. Murphy spent their time from June to October in their "tour through the northern portions of Venezuela and Colombia" was not volunteered to Congress by President Roosevelt; neither did he say why they were sent there. The extracts from Capt. Humphrey's report published in the "Confidential Notes on Panama" contain an astonishing wealth of information concerning interior points in Panama which never could have been obtained in the four days these military spies remained at the Hotel Central, in Panama city.

"About 40 miles southeast of the city of Panama is a fine anchorage for a fleet of at least 10 large vessels" is the first quotation from Capt. Humphrey's report, found on page 143 of the "Notes on Panama."

The next extract refers to "Ports, breakwaters, etc." Of Colon, Capt. Humphrey said in part: "No timber exists in the vicinity of Colon, yet a small amount of large pine timber could be found in the railroad yard. Small boats could be landed along the shore about one-half mile south of the wharves. The anchorage in the harbor off Colon is sufficiently large for almost any number of vessels."

Concerning the fortification of Panama City, Capt. Humphrey's report says: "The harbor at La Boca (at the mouth of the canal) and the harbor of Panama might be commanded perfectly by artillery placed on the hills between the two places. La Boca is also commanded by a hill to the east, shown in the charts, about 1,000 yards away."

On the military possibilities at Colon, Capt. Humphrey reported as follows: "The other chief buildings are the stations and the storehouses of the railroad and steamship companies. These could be used as excellent barracks for troops to the number of 1,200."

After enumerating the sources of supplies Capt. Humphrey's report continues:

"The buildings which may be used as barracks for troops have already been mentioned. Near Colon there are really no suitable locations for camps, the country being generally too swampy about the city. The climate is hot; the rainfall during the rainy season is very heavy

"Troops should not be landed from ships in Colon for any length of time before operations were to begin. It would be preferable to keep them aboard ship. * * *

"There is an old frame building, covered with galvanized iron, two stories in height, about 50 by 70, along the railroad in the southern part of the town which was used as a railroad station, but it is now occupied by about 75 Colombian troops.

"The railroad trains all have good, energetic American conductors and engineers."

On page 162 of Notes on Panama we find quoted from Capt. Humphrey's report:

"Panama is a city of about 30,000 inhabitants. * * * A garrison of about 450 well-drilled Colombian troops is stationed in the cuartel in the 'Plaza des Armas,' in the city of Panama. These troops, commanded by a Colombian general, drill according to Upton's tactics and use the same bugle calls as those used by the United States Army."

Notes on Panama describes all the roads and trails of the Isthmus in great detail, the main authority being the report of the Intercontinental Railway Commission. Capt. Humphrey's report is called upon for the following detail:

"The country between Panama and 'Panama Viejo' (Old Panama) is very rolling and grown with grass, affording fine pasturage for cattle. Along this road the country would also afford excellent camping facilities for large bodies of troops. The water supply of Panama at the present time is very poor, the only good water being stored in cisterns in the city. Water is also drawn from wells along the railroad near the city, but this is exceedingly impure."

The next contribution in the Notes on Panama by Capt. Humphrey is a reproduction of his map of La Boca, the mouth of the canal, and Ancon Hill, which Admiral Glass, on November 2, 1903, was ordered by cable to "occupy strongly with artillery" if necessary to prevent the landing Colombian forces.

Among the data accumulated by these two young Army officers on their "unpremeditated" and incidental sojourn on the Isthmus was an estimate of the number of mules that "may be obtained in numbers and in localities and in one week's notice, as follows: Pedregal, 100; Puerto Mutis, 30; Mensable, 50; Aguadulce, 50; Chepo, 10; Chorrera, 10; Panama, 50."

All of the forementioned settlements outside of Panama are far in the interior, without means of communication, and no reliable information could have been obtained therefrom without going there.

One feature alone of Capt. Humphrey's "unpremeditated" investigations in Panama must have consumed a week's time. The resulting detailed information is set forth in Notes on Panama, pages 186–189. It is a report on each of the 25 stations between Panama and Colon on the railroad. Distance from Panama, population, topographical features, and capacity of sidetrack at each station are given. Typographical sketches of several of the principal stations are reproduced in the War Department handbook for the campaign on the Isthmus. Concluding this section of his report, Capt. Humphrey says:

"About 2 miles south of Colon, along the railroad, is a small station of five or six frame houses, near the foot of a small hill about 150 feet in height, known as 'Monkey Hill.' Artillery placed here would command all approaches to Colon from the south. It would also command the city of Colon and, were the artillery of sufficient power, would command both the harbors of Manzanilla and Limon Bay.

"The north entrance to the canal is located about one-half mile west of 'Monkey Hill' and can be plainly seen from the top of the hill. All along the railroad and canal line between Colon and Panama the country is overgrown with a dense underbrush, rendering communication along the trails very difficult. There is no wagon road or cart road across the Isthmus, only a narrow trail 2 feet wide, with low-hanging vines and underbrush overhead, quite impracticable during the rainy season for travel. There is absolutely no land communication either from Colon or Panama, along the neck of the Isthmus, with the interior of Colombia. The only communication had with Bogota or the interior of Colombia from the State of Panama is by steamship from Buenaventura Harbor on the west coast of Colombia to Panama, while the only communication on the Atlantic side is by steamship from either Cartagena or Savanilla.

"There is at present communication from Porto Bello Harbor across the Isthmus with Panama by means of the old Spanish mule trail. This trail was at one time in very good condition, having been paved with cobblestones by the Spanish, but it is now in very bad repair, and during the rainy season almost impassable for mules and horses."

November—when the Roosevelt-Cromwell revolution was to be pulled off—is in the rainy season.

Porto Bello, being at the Atlantic end of the old trail from Panama City, was duly kept in mind when blockading orders were sent to the American fleet, as we shall soon see.

The compiler of "Notes on Panama," Capt. H. C. Hale, of the General Staff, illustrated his guidebook with photographs of numerous topographical field maps of the various towns and villages along the line of the Panama Railroad. The latest time-table of the railroad is printed in full, and there are complete statistical data of political divisions, populaton, telegraphs, and distances from place to place. The last observation quoted from Capt. Humphrey's report is as follows:

"An advance across the Isthmus from Colon toward Panama would be, of course, easiest by the rairoad line, as the trails are all generally very difficult and overgrown with brush. There is a telegraph and telephone line which runs across the Isthmus along the railroad. The railroad is ballasted with rock nearly the whole distance from Colon to Panama. Light artillery could be taken along the railroad on trains or could be taken along the railroad track, when necessary amount of boards or planks would have to be carried to lay over the bridges. Three equipped men on foot could march abreast along the railroad line.

"There is water communication from the mouth of the Chagres River to Gatun, which has already been spoken of.

"The railroad is generally straight, with no more than the ordinary number of curves. Vegetation on both sides of the track grows most luxuriantly, there being a great many bamboo and banana trees.

"There are several hills which could be occupied to prevent advance along the line. The railroad is quite well equipped with plenty of rolling stock. There are about 65 bridges, principally steel, the most important and longest crossing the Chagres River at Gatun.

"About 150 small cart mules and horses could be obtained in the city of Panama; about 75 pack mules could be obtained in Chorrera, while not more than 50 or 60 animals could be obtained in the city of Colon.

"Guns mounted upon a point near the lighthouse in the city of Colon could protect both harbors against a hostile fleet. Fresh water is obtainable at Colon for vessels, but is of poor quality.

"About one-half mile west of the city of Panama is a large hill about 600 feet in height (Ancon). On the northeast side of this hill are located large hospital buildings of the French Canal Co. This hospital has 18 wards, each ward having 40 beds, and has very modern equipment. The drainage system.

however, is not very well arranged, and at present the sanitary condition of the hospital is not good Modern artillery could be placed upon this hill and command the city of Panama and both the harbors; also the anchorage near the island of Culebra. Other hospitals are the Hospital de Estranjeros, having room for 75 patients, and the Hospital of Santo Tomas, with 11 nurses, Sisters of Charity.

"The other points where troops could be landed near Colon on the Atlantic side of the Isthmus are Portobelo Harbor, Manzanillo or Limon Bay, at Boca del Toro, or, in favorable weather, at the mouth of the Chagres River. The only place where troops could be landed on the south side of the Isthmus is at the harbor of Panama or La Boca, or at the mouth of the Camito River, near Chorrera."

The Isthmus is strangely devoid of information as to the operations and presence of these military spies. It is remembered that Humphrey and Murphy traveled as civilians, and the purpose of their sojourn was known only to the representatives of the American Government. Whether they, like other United States Army officers on the Isthmus, posed as mining engineers and timber-concession hunters, under assumed names, is not known. Whether they did what they did without instructions, and whether, as Mr. Roosevelt told the Senate, "their visit to the Isthmus was but an unpremeditated incident of their return journey," must be left to the sanity of the reader to determine, in the light of other events of this period which Mr. Cromwell and others have not deemed it necessary or advisable to relate.

Curiously enough, on the very day Capt. Humphrey and his assistant landed in the United States to report the result of their four months' secret making of war against a friendly country, there appeared in the Outlook an article by John D. Long, former Secretary of the Navy, telling of Mr. Roosevelt's desire, while Assistant Secretary of the Navy, to pursue a similar policy before the War with Spain. Mr. Long said:

"His (Roosevelt's) activity was characteristic. He was zealous in the work of putting the Navy in condition for the apprehended struggle.

"His ardor sometimes went faster than the President or the department appreciated. Just before the war he, as well as some naval officers, was anxious to send a squadron across the ocean to sink the ships and torpedo-boat destroyers of the Spanish fleet while we were yet at peace with Spain."

The memorandum of Lieut. Gen. Young, quoted in Mr. Roosevelt's message of January 4, 1904, contains statements requiring illumination before we return from Panama to the intrigue in Washington and New York.

"When they (Capt. Humphrey and Lieut. Murphy) were on the Isthmus, arms and ammunition were being smuggled into the city of Colon in piano boxes, merchandise crates, etc."

This official report, quoted by Mr. Roosevelt, corroborates the statement of Dr. Federico Lopez Pomareda, Colombian consul at Kingston, Jamaica, that in the summer of 1903 he was offered by a mysterious agent a $3,000 bribe if he would issue manifests for shipments of arms as pianos to the port of Colon. It was represented to him that the movement was another revolution in Colombia, and that the arms were to be sent to the interior from Panama. He refused to listen to the offer, and as early as September 18, 1903, reported officially to his Government that a secession plot was well organized, and that Kingston was being made the base of communication between the United States and Panama.

Still, the witnesses called to testify in Panama swore that no money was supplied before the revolution, and that the arms on which they depended in the event of being compelled to fight for their independence were none other than those in the barracks belonging to the Colombian Government, and that none were imported.

Lieut. Gen. Young's memorandum says:

"That there were representatives of the revolutionary organization at all important points on the Isthmus; that in Panama, Colon, and the other principal places of the Isthmus police forces had been organized which were in reality revolutionary forces; that the people on the Isthmus seemed to be unanimous in their sentiment against the Bogota Government; * * * that a revolution might be expected immediately upon the adjournment of the Colombian Congress without ratification of the treaty."

There were no representatives of the revolutionary organization at any points on the Isthmus outside the city of Panama when Capt. Humphrey and Lieut. Murphy were on the Isthmus, nor even when they were reporting to Mr. Roosevelt in the White House three weks later. The so-called "patriots' revolutionary committee," fearful of making any decisive move until Amador should return from Washington and New York, was waiting for cable advices through Mr. Cromwell's personal representative, Capt. Beers, before attempting to start any revolutionary movement. Porfirio Melendez, who was intrusted with organizing and leading the movement in Colon, was not taken into the conspiracy until November 1, 1903. As to the villages of the interior, Arango's original story, from which the following paragraph was carefully expurgated when he put it out in pamphlet form, tells the real situation:

"Mr. Ramon Valdes Lopez was commisioned by Dr. Amador Guerrero (after his return from the United States on October 27), by agreement with the committee, to go to the interior and be ready; that when he had once received notice that the movement (revolution) had been effected, he should proceed to propagate the idea of independence in those provinces, which he did in satisfactory fulfillment of the program agreed upon."

Mr. Roosevelt says further in his message of January 4, 1904:

"Lieut. Gen. Young regarded their (Capt. Humphrey and Lieut. Murphy's) report as of such importance as to make it advisable that I should personally see these officers. They told me what they had already reported to the lieutenant general, adding that on the Isthmus the excitement was seething, and that the Colombian troops were reported to be disaffected. * * * They were certain that the revolution would occur, and before leaving the Isthmus had made their own reckoning as to the time, which they had set down as probably being from three to four weeks after their leaving. The reason they set this as the probable inside limit of time was that they reckoned that it would be at least three or four weeks—say not until October 20—before a sufficient quantity of arms would have been landed."

The secret cable code betwen Amador and Bunau-Varilla and Joshua Lindo, which will soon come into our story in its entirety, tends strongly to corroborate the testimony of various Panamans that, so far as they knew, no arms, except 50 revolvers, were bought by Amador or his agent, Bunau-Varilla. If they did arrive in Panama, they must have been furnished by other agencies of whose existence the military spies of the United States had knowledge when they reported to the White House.

Of the multiplicity of reports concerning the shipment of arms for the revolution, the most definite was published by the New York Tribune on November 5, 1903, stating that several weeks before the revolution 4,000 stands of arms and a quantity of ammunition had been shipped from Morgan City, La., 50 miles below New Orleans, on a lumber schooner bound for a Mexican port; that at an agreed point in the Gulf the war munitions had been transferred to another schooner and landed on St. Andrews Island (San Andres), a Colombian possession off the coast of Nicaragua about 100 miles, and thence sent ashore in small boats to the Department of Panama. Another report has persistently coupled a United States warship with the transportation of these arms to St. Andrews.

The auxiliary cruiser *Dixie*, which arrived at Colon with United States marines with such "intelligent anticipation," was recommissioned at League Island Navy Yard on October 1, 1903, two days after the *Nashville* put out for St. Andrews Island from Pensacola, Fla.

Revolutionary supplies actually did reach St. Andrews and 3,000 Marlin carbines were seized there immediately after the revolt in Panama, by a Colombian expedition sent from Cartagena under command of Dr. M. Lara Cordoba to prevent the execution of the plan to have this island secede along with Panama. Dr. Cordoba was in Panama in October, 1903, and heard of the plot concerning St. Andrews Island as early as October 13, 1903, after the arrival of the *Nashville*, under command of Capt. John Hubbard, and he hastened to Cartagena and warned the governor of his department, Insignares, who had been appointed by Marroquin at the same time Obaldia was made governor of Panama. Insignares refused to act, and not until after the revolution had taken place in Panama was Cordoba sent with a battalion to protect St. Andrews. Dr. Cordoba, in a letter, says:

"Ten days later there arrived an American man-of-war; the purpose of its officers was to bring about uprising among the people of San Andres, as I learned from the priest, Father Livingston, who had been told this by the commander. I put the priest in jail for having communicated with the ship in spite of a decree of prohibition. I had gathered from among the inhabitants of the island, who are Jamaicans and of other foreign nationalities, 3,000 Marlin carbines, which proves that they (the inhabitants) had been won."

In the New York Herald's Navy notes, telegraphed under date of October 12, 1903, from Washington, appeared the following:

"Commander John Hubbard, commanding the gunboat *Nashville*, which arrived yesterday at Colon, telegraphed the Navy Department that all is quiet at St. Andrews Island, a Colombian possession off the coast of Nicaragua, where it was reported certain American workmen had been interfered with. The *Neshville* was sent there from Pensacola.

In the correspondence transmitted to Congress by Mr. Roosevelt is the following translation of a cable of Commander Hubbard to the Navy Department, dated Colon, October 15, 1903:

"Report is current to the effect that a revolution has broken out in the State of Cauca. Everything is quiet on the Isthmus, unless a change takes place. On this account there is no necessity to remain here. Do not think it necessary to visit St. Andrew's Island."

In Colon it was observed that a boat from the *Nashville* landed mail both for the American consulate and the Panama Railroad Co.

October 14. 1903. Dr. Herran wrote to Arturo de Brigand, Colombian consul general in New York:

"A new trouble, brought on by Andreas & Co., threatens us. You having refused them permission to ship their 24,000 cartridges or bullets, they have brought about diplomatic reclamations through their lawyer, John Henry Mann, of 76 William Street, New York, and yesterday the Secretary of State, Mr. John Hay, sent me an official note on this matter. If the cartridges which Andreas & Co. wish to ship are not forbidden to be imported into Colombia, I think it would be very risky to refuse them the permission they ask for, although it would be well to give timely warning of the shipment to the civil and military authorities in Panama. It would be very well for us to put an end to this matter and thus avoid a serious claim which would bring with it a demand for payment of damages, etc. In existing circumstances questions of this kind are especially serious."

Having some light now on Mr. Roosevelt's methods in secretly committing acts of war in the territory of the friendly nation with which he was at the same time conducting diplomatic negotiations, we may view with broader comprehension the events immediately preceding the Panama revolution.

October 1, 1903: The *Dixie* was recommissioned.

October 7: Dr. Amador met Herbert G. Prescott, assistant superintendent of the Panama Railroad, at the pier of the Panama Railroad Steamship Co., in New York, and saw him embark for Panama. Amador told Prescott that he had just met Bunau-Varilla the night before, and that Bunau-Varilla was going to take him to Washington the following day and obtain all the promises of assistance the Panamans desired. He asked Prescott to tell the other conspirators that everything would be arranged in a few days, and that he expected to take the next week's boat for Panama, prepared to make the revolution soon after his arrival.

October 7: The New York Herald's Washington correspondent telegraphed his paper:

"William Nelson Cromwell * * * called on President Roosevelt to-day. * * * Mr. Cromwell declared this afternoon: 'The Panama Canal will be built, and by the United States Government.' He would not say what new development had made this possible."

October 10: President Roosevelt wrote to Dr. Albert Shaw, editor of the American Review of Reviews, who had been forecasting with the accuracy of an inspired prophet the events soon to take place in Panama:

"I cast aside the proposition made at this time to foment the secession of Panama. * * * Privately, I feel free to say to you that I should be delighted if Panama were an independent State, or if it made itself so at this moment; but for me to say so publicly would amount to an instigation of a revolt, and therefore I can not say it."

October 10: Beaupre wrote to Secretary Hay:

"Monsieur Mancini (the Panama Canal Co.'s agent in Bogota) informs me * * * moreover, that some time before the rejection of the Hay-Herran treaty he wrote to Mr. Cromwell, informing him that in all probability an attempt would be made to override the rights of the French company to call in question the validity of the extension of time (of the canal concession) granted to it. To this he received no reply beyond the mere acknowledgment of his message, and his only instructions have been not to move in the matter at all. He therefore concludes, so he told me, that the United States Government and the French company have arrived at some satisfactory understanding."

October 13: William Nelson Cromwell wrote a letter to President Roosevelt, to which Cromwell refers in a cable to Roosevelt from Paris, October 31, 1903. This letter, as well as the conference at the White House on October 7, 1903, appears to have been in relation to Mr. Cromwell's inducing Mr. Roosevelt "to extend the conditional agreement while awaiting new negotiations with Colombia, or until such time as it should be possible to resolve the new situation in some other satisfactory manner."

October 13: Dr. Amador saw Bunau-Varilla at night at the Waldorf-Astoria, and, according to Bunau-Varilla's statement, demurred to Bunau-Varilla's proposal, then outlined for the first time, to confine the revolution to the Canal Zone. Bunau-Varilla says Amador called the next morning and agreed to the plan.

October 14: The State Department received Mr. Beaupre's cables of October 9 and 10, forecasting an unfavorable report on the Senate committee in Bogota.

October 15: "Happenings in Washington, Bogota, and Panama made it 9 and 10, forecasting an unfavorable report of the Senate committee in Bogota. sailed for Paris on October 15, to confer rapidly and return."—Mr. Cromwell's confessions.

October 16: Mr. Roosevelt received in person the reports of the military spies, who, as an "unpremeditated incident of their return journey," had reported every detail that might be useful in a campaign on the Isthmus, even to the best positions for artillery to command Panama and Colon, and the number of mules that might be procured in far-interior villages.

October 16: "As a consequence of Gov. Obaldia's quieting dispatches, the fears formerly felt in Bogota regarding a secession of the Isthmus has been entirely dissipated, and public opinion is now assured that no further danger is threatened."—New York Herald dispatch from Bogota.

The bank account of the American minister in Bogota for this period shows that the Herald correspondent, Luis Halberstadt, from time to time received checks for various amoun's ranging up to $30. In 1909 the then secretary of the American legation in Bogota stated that he had paid Halberstadt $25 to spy on a representative of the World, and that he had long been in the pay of the American minister.

October 17: Capt. Humphrey and Lieut. Murphy, having reported in person to President Roosevelt on the 16 h, it was found advisable to detail military attachés to the American legation in Bogota. Capt. Sidney A. Cloman, whose detail to the military information division had been announced on September 16, 1903, and Capt. William G. Haan were assigned, though only Cloman's detail appeared in the press dispatches from Washington. The reason for Cloman's assignment to Bogota announced at the State Department was that the United States was going to pursue a new policy and send Army men to all the American legations in South America to forearm this country with military information on account of the activity of Germany there and i's evident purpose to oppose us in enforcing the Monroe doctrine. Notice of the return of Capt. Humphrey and Lieut. Murphy inconveniently found its way into the papers, and a Washington dispatch explained that they had been exploring northern Venezuela to this purpose, estimating carefully the sized army that country could put in the field to back up the United States in a crisis, and that these officers "also went to Panama and studied it from a soldier's point of view."

October 17: Bunau-Varilla says that on this day he gave full instructions to Amador and told him to sail on the first boat, October 20, for Panama, and pull off the revolution not later than November 3.

October 17: Dr. Raoul A. Amador, son of the revolutionary conspirator, was refused a leave of absence from Fort Revere, Mass., where he was acting assistant surgeon in the United States Army. He wro'e to his father in New York and also telegraphed, saying that on this account it was impossible for him to come to New York as per his father's request.

October 18: Dr. Amador wrote from the Hotel Endicott, in answer to his son Raoul's letter and telegram. Aside from personal affairs, the let'er, of which the World obtained the original, said:

"The object of your coming was for you to see Bunau-Varilla, to whom I have talked of you. He says that if all turns out well you will have a good position on the medical (sanitary) commission, which is the first that will begin the (canal) work; that my name is in the office of Hay, and that certainly nothing will be denied you.

"The plan appears to me good. A portion of the Isthmus will be declared independent, on which the United States will not permit forces of Colombia to arrive to attack us. They will convoke an assembly, which will invest with authority a minister who will be named by the new Government to make a treaty without necessity of later ratification by that assembly. The treaty, being approved by both parties, the new Republic will already be protected by the United States, and they will add the other settlements which were not forming part of that Republic, and which will also remain under the protection of the United States.

"The movement will be delayed a few days; we want to have here the minister that they are going to name, so that when the movement has been made he will be named by cable and will occupy himself with the treaty. In 30 days everything will be concluded.

"We have cer.ain resources on the movement being made, and this has already been arranged with a bank.

"As soon as everything is arranged I will tell B. V. to occupy himself about you. He says that if you do not want to go he will look for a position here in New York. He is a man of great influence. * * * Your affectionate father, Amador."

The foregoing letter of Dr. Amador to his son was one of the exhibits introduced by the World in Panama, which caused the remark by one of the horde of secret agents that "Cromwell's man on the Isthmus was an ass and left too much evidence uncovered." From this letter it is apparent that—

1. Bunau-Varilla was in Secretary Hay's office, notwithstanding his efforts later to make it appear that when he went to Washington he saw neither the President nor the Secretary of State, but secured the dispatching of American warships to Panama simply "by spreading from the New Willard Hotel a report that was not 15 minutes in reaching the White House." Wayne MacVeagh, former Attorney General of the United States, and brother of President Taft's Secretary of the Treasury, saw Bunau-Varilla with Acting Secretary of State Loomis before the Panama revolution.

2. The plan was cut and dried to take only that part of Panama which Mr. Roosevelt and Mr. Cromwell wanted for their purpose, and prevent, by use of the armed power of the United States, the reassertion of Colombia's sovereignty over it. Anticipating protests and possible complications, it was decided to have Panama's diplomatic representatve on the ground so that the canal treaty could be rushed through and ratified by the minister without further authorization.

3. The finances of the revolution, at least in part, had "already been arranged with a bank."

Young Dr. Amador was given the choice of a place on the sanitary commission, or the Panaman consular post in New York. As soon as he received his father's letter of October 18, 1903, he resigned, in order that he might be in New York to accept at once the consular post, which he chose. His resignation not being accepted, he deserted on November 1, 1903, and came to New York. Finding Bunau-Varilla absent in Washington, young Dr. Amador, afraid to confide in any other person, walked the streets the 2d and 3d of November, nervously watching the newspaper bulletin boards for announcement of the revolution.

October 18: The State Department received Minister Beaupré's cable of the 15th stating that the Colombian Senate committee had proposed a project of law to ratify the extension of the canal concession. Minister Beaupré added that the tone of the committee's report "gives to understand that Colombia would greatly benefit by canceling of the extension" of the concession, thereby coming into full possession of the canal company's property within another year, and becoming free to negotiate for its sale direct to the United States.

October 19: The State Department received the following message from Minister Beaupré, dated October 17:

"Have received information, confidentially, that there was a meeting of the cabinet yesterday to discuss the question of renewing canal negotiations with the United States, and that the adjournment of Congress "will be followed by the mission of special envoy to Washington for that purpose. The President's message dissolving Congress will be delivered probably before 30th instant."

October 19: "Orders were given on October 19 to the *Boston* to proceed to San Juan del Sur, Nicaragua; to the *Dixie* to prepare to sail from League

Island; and to the *Atlanta* to proceed to Guantanamo."—Mr. Roosevelt's message, January 4, 1903.

Several days before this it was announced at the Navy Department that the Pacific Coast Fleet had been ordered to Acapulco, Mexico, for tactical drill, and reference to the Washington Navy reports shows that the fleet had been moving gradually southward for a month or more.

October 20: Dr. Amador sailed from New York for Panama. He was provided with cable codes, of which the World was given the originals in Panama, where again "Cromwell's man was an ass." Following are the translations from Spanish of these codes, complete:

CODE WITH LINDO.

(In Dr. Amador's handwriting.)

The plan is accepted; minister will start — abete.
Ask Bunau-Varilla for the $4,000 — abbot.
Ask Bunau-Varilla for the balance up to 100,000 — ably.
Send the 50 revolvers, not very large ones, with 1,500 cartridges; must behandy but not small Smith & Wesson's — abode.
Meet minister on the wharf — abrupt.
Pablo Arosemena — accuse.
J. A. Arango — absurd.
Tomas Arias — accent.
Federico Boyd — account.
They do not accept the plan — accord.
I have received of B. V. the 4,000 — adult.
I have received from B. V. the balance up to 100,000 — advent.
The minister will negotiate loan — adept.
This word in your cable to Maduro means that it is for me — obscure.
Cables with this word are for B. V. transmit them (to him) — fate.
Minister sailed from Colon the 3 — three.
Minister sailed from Colon the 10 — ten.
Minister sailed from Colon the 17 — seventeen.
Minister sailed from Colon the 24 — twenty-four.
Minister sailed from Colon the 1st of December — first.
Code of Liebert (Lieber).

Read the sixth word, counting that of the cable as the first.

ADDITION TO CODE WITH LINDO.

(In Dr. Amador's handwriting on the back of a sheet of letterhead of the Hotel Endicott.)

Send 500 Remington rifles and 500,000 cartridges — sorry.
Movement delayed for lack of arms — truble.
Movement delayed for six days — sin truble.
B. V. agrees to the delay — O. K.

(The following was written and crossed out by Amador:)

For the 100,000 loan they charge 5 per cent–10 per cent — 5–10 per cent.

CODE WITH (JONES) BUNAU-VARILLA.

(Heading written in ink in the handwriting of Jose Augustin Arango.)

(Typewritten by some one who did not know Spanish, and evidently copied from Amador's manuscript.)

Tomorrow at daybreak the movement will take place — Galveston.
We have great hopes of good result — Mobile.
The movement is effected with good success without casualties — safe.
The movement is effected with losses of life of small importance — serious.
The movement is effected with losses of life of grave importance — grave.
From 1 to 10 killed or wounded — Belgium.
From 10 to 20 killed or wounded — France.
From 40 to 80 killed or wouded — Turkey.
More than 80 killed or wounded — Russia.
We have taken several Colombian warships — take.

Warship *Bogota*	wood.
Warship *Padilla*	crowd.
Warship *Boyaca*	female.
Warship *Chucuito*	small.
They have left for the Cauca	south.
Rendered useless	spoiled.
They are in Buenaventura, or absent from Panama	laugh.
We have news of the arrival of Colombian forces	news.
The Pacific	good.
The Atlantic	bad.
One day	word.
Two days	ton.
Three days	weight.
Four days	heavy.
Five days	powerful.
All the friends approve plan and we are proceeding to carry it out	sad.
Enthusiasm	faithful.
Discouragement	great.
Met troops disembarking, or disembarked	tradition.
One hundred	rabbit.
One hundred and fifty	cat.
Two hundred	lion.
More than 200	tiger.
The great number of troops prevents us making the movement	elephant.
This cable is for Jones New York	fate.
This cable is for Smith Panama	obscure.
Tell me if anything had happened which obliges them not to follow plans agreed upon	content.
Nothing has occurred which necessitates modification	boy.
Something has happened which compels abandonment of all idea of movement	heaven.
We have issued the declaration of independence with the six declarations without changing a word	London.
Repeat your cable where occurs the word X, in order to be perfectly certain	plus X.
I repeat the word X, which is perfectly correct	X plus.
I think it is extremely dangerous to refuse that which the United States desires	India.
I think that to arrive at our ends it is necessary to show some resistance	Japan.
It is impossible to resist longer; you accept	China.
Here is that which they desire to change	Mongolia.
I think these changes extremely advantageous and that they should be accepted	Indochina.
I think these changes acceptable	Manchuria.
I think it can not be accepted	Liberia.
Accept everything that you think just	Arabia.
Do not be worried by the delay, all is well	Canada.

(Added in Amador's handwriting.)

The movement will take place within	United.
Days	River.
One	Kentucky.
Two	Ohio.
Three	Mississippi.
Four	Hudson.
Five	Missouri.

Amador's codes indicate that—

1. Amador had not agreed when he left New York that Bunau-Varilla should be the minister from Panama. This is corroborated by statements of members of the "patriots' committee" in Panama that Amador desired this place himself.

2. There was an understanding about a specific $4,000 for a purpose which Mr. Lindo does not explain. This, or some other $4,000, was cabled to Bunau-Varilla's New York bankers on November 17, 1903, by Credit Lyonnais. The $100,000 in the code is the sum which Lindo and various other Panamans declare Bunau-Varilla promised to contribute to the revolution, and of which they

say he only gave $25,000; Mrs. Amador, widow of the revolutionary leader, corroborates the World's information that this was the price Bunau-Varilla was willing to pay to be named Panama's first minister to the United States. It was testified before the World's rogatory commission in Panama that Bunau-Varilla never contributed more than half of the sum he had promised. Mr. Lindo declares that when he, authorized by Amador, called on Bunau-Varilla after the revolution to make good his promise, Bunau-Varilla said he could not do so, but finally advanced $25,000, which he secured upon Mr. Lindo's signing his note for that amount. Bunau-Varilla says he gave the $100,000 gladly, as he was a "man of large affairs," and what was $100,000 to him? New York, however, saw little evidence of Bunau-Varilla's large estate. While he retained his $5-a-day room at the Waldorf-Astoria as his diplomatic headquarters, where his wife also was registered on October 8, 1903, he moved his family on October 31 to the modest and moderate-priced New Amsterdam Hotel in Fourth Avenue, where he registered with Mme. Bunau-Varilla and Mlle. Herzog, a guest. He kept his family there until his diplomatic mission ended in January, 1904.

3. Amador and Bunau-Varilla anticipated borrowing $100,000 in New York and having to pay 5 to 10 per cent interest therefor, but abandoned this idea.

4. Amador anticipated the need of 50 revolvers and 500 rifles, but Lindo says he was sent none until after the Republic of Panama was established and feared invasion from Colombia. Amador was seemingly ignorant of the arms which Mr. Roosevelt's military spies reported as being shipped into the country in piano boxes and feared that the movement would fail for lack of munitions.

5. Fighting, with possible casualties, was anticipated, though they had hopes of a bloodless independence.

6. As early as October 20 Amador had reason to expect the arrival of Colombian forces, which might be encountered disembarking or disembarked, and he recognized the possibility of their great number making impossible the revolution.

7. The movement was planned originally to take place at dawn instead of sunset.

8. The declaration of independence of the Republic of Panama was written in New York or Washingon.

9. The Panama rebels recognized their dependence upon the United States to the extent that they knew it might be "extremely dangerous to refuse that which the United States desires," but thought it would be well to "show some resistance."

10. The plan, entirely in embryo when Amador came from Panama, was so well cut and dried before he left on October 20 that several code expressions referred to possible changes to be proposed.

"Smith" and "Jones" were the code names of Amador and Bunau-Varilla, respectively. All cables to Bunau-Varilla were addressed to "Tower," the cable address in New York of Joshua Lindo, and by him were transmitted to Amador's agent, while those to Amador were directed to Capt. Beers, in Panama.

Besides the declaration of independence, Dr. Amador took with him to Panama when he sailed from New York on October 20, 1903, a flag for the proposed republic, designed and made by Mme. Bunau-Varilla. For greater safety Amador carried the flag wrapped around his waist beneath his clothing and the declaration of independence and other valuable papers he deposited in the purser's safe. The purser was George K. Beers, son of Cromwell's agent on the Isthmus.

October 20: The following cable was transmitted from Washington to Minister Beaupre at Bogota:

"Have been designated military attaché Colombia. Please obtain customs courtesies baggage Capt. Sidney A. Cloman, General Staff; Capt. William G. Haan, General Staff. Sail New York 24th.

"S. A. CLOMAN, *Military Attaché*."

Nothing more was heard of the new policy of obtaining military information in South America. Capts. Cloman and Haan did not arrive at Bogota, so far as the roster of the legation shows, although the names of clerks, secretaries, ministers, and military attachés appear thereon. Shortly after the outbreak in Panama three officers appeared on the Isthmus, Capt. Cloman disguised as "S. A. Otts, lumberman," and Capt. Haan as "H. E. Howard, mining man," both of New York. They were accompanied by Maj. Guy L. Edie, now physician to President Taft, who passed as plain "Mr. G. E. Edie, of New York."

October 20: On the same day that Dr. Amador left New York, and the day after Mr. Roosevelt had ordered warships to proceed within striking distance of Panama and Colon, the American minister to Colombia wrote the following letter to the Secretary of State:

No. 185.] LEGATION OF THE UNITED STATES,
Bogota, October 20, 1903.

SIR: I have the honor to inform you that it would be of great utility and satisfaction to me to be kept posted as to the course of events on the Isthmus, and, if not inconsistent with the rules, I would be glad to have it arranged so that our consular officers at Panama and Colon could send me copies of their dispatches to the department on the political situation, and that the consul general at Panama could telegraph me whenever anything of unusual importance occurs.

I am, sir, your obedient servant, A. M. BEAUPRE.

October 21: The *Nashville*, having sailed from Colon October 18, arrived at Caimanera (Guantanamo, Cuba).

October 21: Minister Beaupre wrote to Secretary Hay:

"I have the honor to inform you that there is no disguising the alarm existing as to the possible action of the Government of the United States should the feeling of disaffection undoubtedly existing in the Department of Panama find expression in overt acts. The alarm took the form of a heated debate in the Senate yesterday, when the Government was again attacked for the appointment of Señor Obaldia as governor of Panama. The reply elicited from the minister for foreign affairs was rather significant. He read an extract from the treaty of 1846, in which the United States guaranteed Colombian sovereignty on the Isthmus, and assured the Senate that, in case of an insurrection in the Department of Panama, the United States would be bound to support the Government."

October 22: Secretary Hay cabled to Minister Beaupre:

"Referring to your telegram, 17th, if you find disposition on the part of Colombia to ask terms more favorable to Colombia than those heretofore negotiated you may intimate orally, but not in writing, that it will be useless to send a special envoy."

October 22: The *Dixie* sailed from New York for League Island Navy Yard to load marines for the campaign on the Isthmus.

October 23: Mr. Cromwell arrived in Paris. According to his own story, he discussed and explained to the administrators, the director, and the liquidator of the old and new canal companies "the situation in Bogota, that in Washington, and that in Panama, as well as the proposition he had made to the President."

October 24: The State Department received Minister Beaupre's cable of October 22, stating that the Colombian Congress appeared to him to be playing a waiting game, and that the minister for foreign affairs had informed him that at its next meeting the cabinet would consider a proposal to send a new minister and a special commission of three prominent men to renew canal negotiations.

October 24: The *Dixie*, having secretly loaded 450 marines and munitions of war, sailed from League Island Navy Yard, Philadelphia, with her announced destination Guantanamo, Cuba. The official Army and Navy Journal reported her next stop at Kingston, Jamaica, whence she proceeded under rush orders to Colon. The New York Herald's Washington correspondent telegraphed his paper on October 30, under the heading of "Movements of Navy vessels," "The *Dixie* is at Guantanamo." But in the Herald's cable reports of arrivals and departures at foreign ports, the presence of the *Dixie* at Guantanamo or Caimanera was not noted. The secret order under which the 450 marines were embarked at League Island has never been published, either in the Army and Navy Journal or in the official reports of the Navy Department.

October 25: Governor Obaldia, furthering a revolutionary scheme to divide the Colombian garrison and remove from Panama 100 men under Col. Tascon, a loyal Colombian who, the conspirators feared, could not be bribed to join the revolution, telegraphed to the governor of Cauca: "Nicaraguan invasion has disembarked north of Veraguas; command of Federico Barrera. I have sent forces to attack them. * * * Bolivar [and] Magdalena tranquil."

The report of this fake "invasion" was cabled at great length the same day to the New York Herald by its Isthmian correspondent, Samuel Boyd, brother of Federico Boyd, of the "Patriots' revolutionary committee." The Bogota foreign office, in alarm, cabled to Dr. Herran in Washington for information concerning the "invasion," and what attitude the American Government would assume.

October 25: President Roosevelt, within the shadow of the peace cross on Mount St. Albans, Washington, addressed a missionary meeting. Pleading for aggressive Christianity he said it was faint praise to say a man is harmless; he should be not only harmless as a dove, but wise as a serpent. "In our civil life," the President continued, "although we need that the average public servant shall have far more than honesty, yet all other qualities go for nothing, or for worse than nothing, unless honesty underlies them—not only the honesty that keeps its skirts technically clean, but the honesty that is such according to the spirit as well as the letter of the law."

October 26: Three days after Mr. Cromwell's arrival in Paris the Credit Lyonnais, by cable to Heidelbach, Ickelheimer & Co., of New York, opened in favor of Bunau-Varilla a credit of $100,000. The president of Credit Lyonnais was Marius Bo, also president of the New Panama Canal Co. and Cromwell's chief instrument in France in its manipulation. Bo's election as president of the canal company, December 24, 1901, was followed the next month by Mr. Cromwell's reinstatement as general counsel. Later Cromwell appears in the United States as attorney for Credit Lyonnais.

October 27: Dr. Amador arrived at Colon in the morning and was met at the pier by Herbert G. Prescott, assistant superintendent of the Panama Railroad. He told Prescott that Bunau-Varilla had promised to have American warships on hand to protect Panama from Colombia, and expressed implicit confidence in the outcome of the revolutionary project. That night in Panama he reported to his fellow conspirators, who were disappointed because Amador had not brought back "some secret treaty with a sovereign." Amador told his fellow conspirators that he had not been to Washington; that Mr. Cromwell had failed them; that Bunau-Varilla was their sole dependence; and that no money was promised until after the blow was struck, when Bunau-Varilla would give them $100,000. At least this is the story the surviving conspirators now tell.

October 28: The *Nashville*, Commander John Hubbard, sailed from Kingston, Jamaica, under sealed orders (officially verified at the Navy Department). In his message of January 4, 1904, Mr. Roosevelt says: "On October 30 the *Nashville* was ordered to proceed to Colon." Colon being only 48 hours' steaming from Kingston, if the *Nashville* sailed on the 28th she had ample time either to call at the island of St. Andrews or cruise down the Panama coast toward Colombia and keep a lookout for any Colombian warships coming with soldiers to suppress the revolution, and still arrive, as she did, at Colon on the night of November 2.

October 28: Dr. Herran wrote to his Government, in part, as follows:

"In the event that Colombia should abstain from reopening negotiations, and in case our demands should not be considered acceptable, I judge that negotiations will be definitely terminated and that the French Canal Co. will immediately give added impulse to its work with the assistance of a powerful American syndicate which will be partly owner of the enterprise. In this manner there will be no necessity for official action on the part of Colombia or of the United States * * *. Mr. William Nelson Cromwell, with general power of attorney for the Panama Canal Co. in this country, is at present in Paris conferring with the directors of that enterprise. I have been informed that he is occupied in organizing the American syndicate to which I have made reference."

October 29: Minister Beaupre cabled to Secretary Hay at 1 o'clock p. m.:

"Please give instructions to consul general at Panama keep me advised by cable matters of consequence. Canal situation unchanged."

October 29: Dr. Amador cabled from Panama to "Tower" (Joshua Lindo's cable address), New York: "Fate news bad powerful tiger urge vapor Colon." Translated by the Amador-Bunau-Varilla code, this cable reads:

"This cable for Bunau-Varilla. We have news of the arrival of Colombian forces by the Atlantic in five days, more than 200. Urge warship for Colon."

Mr. Lindo delivered this cable in person to Bunau-Varilla at the Waldorf-Astoria Hotel, and Bunau-Varilla went at once to Washington. Returning, he stopped at Baltimore to cable the assurance, "Thirty-six hours Atlantic, 48

Pacific," being the number of hours before American warships might be expected on the Atlantic and Pacific sides of the Isthmus.

October 29: The State Department received, at 10.15 p. m., Minister Beaupre's cable of October 27, announcing that the Colombian Congress would adjourn on October 31, probably without action on the renewal of treaty negotiations.

October 29: Answering a cable inquiry from his Government respecting the report of the fake "invasion" of the Isthmus which Gov. Obaldia had sent to Bogota, Dr. Herran cabled: "The Government of the United States is unaware of the character of the invasion of the Isthmus. The Secretary of State declared to me to-day that the Government of the United States will only intervene to maintain traffic."

October 30: Secretary Hay cabled to Minister Beaupre: "You may avail yourself of leave of absence under authorization cabled to you July 9." The only other reference to Mr. Beaupre's leave, found in the published diplomatic correspondence, is the following paragraph in Mr. Beaupre's letter to the State Department, under date of September 5: "I think my previous reports have given the department a very good idea of the situation, but there are some phases of it which I should like to discuss personally when I next visit the United States. This will be in March of next year, I think, if I can get the department's permission, and circumstances permit of it."

On the day of the "revolution" in Panama—November 3, 1903—the New York Evening Telegram published the following dispatch from its Washington correspondent:

"As a mark of the United States' dissatisfaction with the attitude of Colombia in regard to the Panama Canal, the United States minister, Mr. Beaupre, has been withdrawn from Bogota. Ostensibly he is coming home for his official annual leave of 60 days, but it is learned at the State Department that unless canal negotiations are resumed with favorable prospects within that time the leave will be extended by Secretary Hay, and he will be withheld from his post.

"Notwithstanding all this show of frank dissatisfaction, the administration shows no outward sign of obeying the mandate of Congress to turn to the Nicaragua route."

October 31: William Nelson Cromwell cabled from Paris to President Roosevelt that he was authorized, in the name of the president of the canal company (Marius Bo, also president of Credit Lyonnais, which had cabled $100,000 to finance the independence of Panama), and in the name of other canal officials, "to give you and the Government of the United States the assurance of loyal adherence, which they firmly maintain, and to express to you their entire confidence in the outcome of your masterly policy. I have received plenary power to complete all details on my coming return."

October 31: Minister Beaupre cabled to the State Department:

"Congress adjourned to-day. No action has been taken upon the last report concerning the canal. Therefore nothing more than the vote of August 12, rejecting treaty, done. The people here in great anxiety over conflicting reports of secession movements in the Cauca and Panama."

October 31: The Panama Railroad officials, in league with the native conspirators, refused coal to the Colombian warships in Panama, thus preventing their leaving for Buenaventura to bring troops.

November 1: Mr. Beaupre cabled:

"The Government issued manifesto to the nation to-day, severely criticising acts of Congress. * * * With regard to canal, states that Colombian chargé d'affaires has been instructed to inform the Government of the United States that the Colombian Government would consider new negotiations, which, it is believed, will be accepted by the next session of Congress. Therefore, if the Government of the United States still desires to open canal, which, it is presumed that it does, as neither by act nor word has it shown any other intention, it is to be hoped that the great work will be carried out in the end through Colombian territory. I took the opportunity of informal visit to the President yesterday to inform him of substance your cipher telegram, October 22." (That no special mission need be sent if Colombia demanded better terms.)

November 1: Amador received Bunau-Varilla's cable, sent from Baltimore, where Bunau-Varilla stopped off on his way from Washington to New York, assuring the conspirators that American warships would be at Colon in 36 hours and at Panama in 48.

November 1: The first steps were taken in Panama to organize the revolutionary movement in Colon and points in the interior.

November 2: The *Nashville*, as per Bunau-Varilla's promise, arrived at Colon at 5.30 p. m.

November 2: By direction of President Roosevelt, Acting Secretary of the Navy Darling cabled to the commander of the *Nashville*, care of the American consul at Colon, and to the commander of the *Dixie* at Kingston:

"Maintain free and uninterrupted transit. If interruption threatened by armed force, occupy the line of railroad. Prevent landing of any armed force with hostile intent, either Government or insurgent, either at Colon, Porto Bello, or other point. Send copy of instructions to the senior officer present at Panama upon arrival of *Boston*. Have sent copy of instructions and have telegraphed *Dixie* to proceed with all possible dispatch from Kingston to Colon. Government forced reported approaching the Isthmus in vessels. Prevent their landing, if in your judgment this would precipitate conflict. Acknowledgment is required."

And to the commanders of the *Marblehead* at Acapulco, Mexico, and the *Boston* at San Juan del Sur, Nicaragua:

"Proceed with all possible dispatch to Panama. Telegraph in cipher your departure. Maintain free and uninterrupted transit. Prevent landing of any armed force, either Government or insurgent, with hostile intent at any point within 50 miles of Panama. If doubtful as to the intention of any armed force, occupy Ancon Hill strongly with artillery. If the *Wyoming* would delay *Concord* and *Marblehead*, her disposition must be left to your discretion. Government force reported approaching the Isthmus in vessels. Prevent their landing, if in your judgment landing would precipitate a conflict."

November 2: Before these orders were delivered to the commanders of the American warships the Colombian troops, 500 strong, under command of Gens. Juan B. Tovar and Ramon G. Amaya, arrived at Colon aboard the Colombian gunboat *Cartagena* at 11.30 p. m.

In setting forth the orders issued to the Navy on November 2, 1903, Mr. Roosevelt is not exactly accurate in his statement in his message to Congress January 4, 1904 (S. Doc. No. 53, 58th Cong., 2d sess.). He says:

"On November 2, when, the Colombian Congress having adjourned, it was evident that both sides were making ready forces whose meeting would mean bloodshed and disorder, the Colombian troops having been embarked on vessels, the following instructions were sent to the commanders of the *Boston*, *Nashville*, and *Dixie:*

"'Maintain free and uninterrupted transit. If interruption is threatened by armed force, occupy the line of railroad. Prevent landing of any armed force with hostile intent, either Government or insurgent, at any point within 50 miles of Panama. Government force reported approaching the Isthmus in vessels. Prevent their landing, if in your judgment the landing would precipitate a conflict.'

"These orders were delivered in pursuance of the policy on which our Government had repeatedly acted."

The foregoing comprises part of the order sent to the *Nashville* and *Dixie* on the Atlantic side, and part of the order sent to the *Marblehead* at Acapulco, and the *Boston* at San Juan del Sur, on the Pacific. Neither order was reproduced in full by Mr. Roosevelt in his messasge. Mr. Roosevelt omitted from the hybrid order in his message that part in the order to the *Nashville* and *Dixie* referring to landing at "Porto Bello, or other point," and also the most significant words, which were in the order to the *Marblehead* and *Boston*, as the orders appear in Foreign Relations, 1903, and Senate Document No. 51, Fifty-eighth Congress, second session, as follows:

"If doubtful as to the intention of any armed force, occupy Ancon Hill strongly with artillery."

The possibilities of fortifying Ancon Hill had been reported by the two military spies who were called to the White House by Mr. Roosevelt on October 16. See their report and Mr. Roosevelt's message.)

The order to prevent landing of Colombian troops at Porto Bello, 20 miles east of Colon, meant, in effect, blockading the entire Atlantic seaboard of Panama, since that port was the only one outside of Colon where a landing could be effected and a march commenced against the city of Panama. Capt. Humphrey noted in his report the existence of an old trail from Porto Bello to Panama city, and this report was within Mr. Roosevelt's knowledge, if not in his hands, when the blockading order was issued.

Meantime the Colombian officials at Bogota were reposing peacefully in the faith that the United States, under its obligations in the treaty of 1846–1848, could be depended upon to uphold Colombian sovereignty in the Isthmus of Panama. Their confidence was shown in the following cable from the minister for foreign affairs to Acting Minister Herran, dated Bogota, November 2, 1903:

"Congress has adjourned without legislating about the canal. Reiterate to the Secretary of State declarations in telegram of September 8. Advise him to maintain order on the Isthmus and safety of traffic."

November 3: The revolutionary farce, booked in the early summer for election day, was duly put upon the boards, as had been announced on July 4 by Mr. Cromwell's press agent. The plans could not have been better laid to escape with the minimum of publicity. In the course of the day the Associated Press received a cable from its correspondent in Colon, and some of the afternoon papers in the United States considered it sufficiently important to print the dispatch, which follows:

"COLON, COLOMBIA, *November 3.*

"It is rumored here that startling developments, pointing to the independence of the Isthmus, are on foot. Everything, however, is quiet here.

"The United States gunboat *Nashville* arrived here late last evening.

"The Colombian gunboat *Cartagena* arrived here this morning from Savanilla with several hundred troops on board."

This dispatch was the only inkling of the pending revolution permitted to get out of Panama until after the blow had been struck on the evening of the 3d, so carefully had the conspirators understood themselves with the native newspaper correspondents. In Colon this was looked after by the superintendent of the Panama Railroad, Col. James R. Shaler, who personally cautioned the newspaper representatives there before the end of October to be careful what they sent to the United States.

Whn the House of Representatives asked President Roosevelt for "all correspondence and other official documents relating to the recent revolution," the following uncalled-for explanation was sent as a preface to the cables exchanged between the State Department and the consulates in Panama:

"A press bulletin having announced an outbreak on the Isthmus, the following cablegram was sent both to the consulate general at Panama and the consulate at Colon:

DEPARTMENT OF STATE,
Washington, November 3, 1903.
(Sent 3.40 p. m.)

Uprising on Isthmus reported. Keep department promptly and fully informed.

LOOMIS, *Acting.*

But when Mr. Loomis sent this cable to the Isthmus the State Department already had received, one hour and five minutes earlier, the following cable from the American consul at Colon, far more enlightening on the revolutionary situation than the "press bulletin," which the administration cited as the excuse for its action:

COLON, *November 3, 1903.*
(Received 2.35 p. m.)

Revolution imminent. Government force on the Isthmus about 500 men. Their official promised support revolution. Fire department Panama, 441, are well organized and favor revolution. Government vessel *Cartagena*, with about 400 men, arrived early to-day with new commander in chief, Tobar. Was not expected until November 10. Tobar's arrival is not probable to stop revolution.

MALMROS.

This cable shows how intimately the United States consul, Oscar Malmros, who is now dead, was in touch with the revolutionists, being informed even of the understanding with Gen. Huertas, who sold his loyalty and that of his battalion. Late in October, 1903, Consul Malmros said to a friend in Colon (J. W. Humphreys, editor of the Colon Telegram and correspondent of the New York Sun in 1903): "These fellows have asked us to recognize them, but we have told them they must fight for their independence."

No positive news of the revolutionary conspiracy was allowed to reach the American press until late on the night of November 3, when the Metropolitan morning papers were going to press with their first editions. Editors sweating over election tables were called on at the last minute to make room for announcement of the birth of a republic. In some papers the news found a minor position on the front page, but in most cases it was "buried" with election returns and attracted little attention on the morning of November 4.

The news that did come from the Isthmus was written to suit the purposes of the revolutionists. Samuel Boyd, correspondent of the New York Herald, brother of Federico Boyd, of the "Patriots' revolutionary committee," cabled his paper very briefly, stating that "There were 3,000 armed men in the uprising." There were not to exceed 1,200. Ernesto T. Lefevre, son-in-law of Jose Agustin Arango, of the "Patriots' committee," supplied the Associated Press with information equally devoid of the real facts. After the Colombian soldiers had been paid their bribes and the "Patriots" came in for their share of the canal millions, the useful correspondents were duly recognized, along with the American officials of the railroad and others whose assistance enabled the Republic to be born.

All of this time the guiding hand of Mr. Cromwell was on the helm. According to his own story, "During his stay in Paris Mr. Cromwell was in constant communication with the United States, giving his advice and instructions."

On the morning of November 4, 1903, his assistants in New York held council and telegraphed to Washington formally requesting the American Government to use whatever means might be necessary to protect the property of the Panama Railroad Co., an American corporation. The press dispatches from Washington announced that this request had been made, and Mr. Cromwell, in his story, gives the statement substantial verification. Nevertheless, after the prosecution of the Roosevelt libel suit was dismissed in the Federal court in New York, Roger Farnham declared (March 1, 1910, to Sam Williams) that he went to Secretary Hay two months before the revolution and asked that warships be sent to Panama to protect the property of the canal and railroad companies, and that again, shortly before the revolution, Mr. Hill, of Cromwell's firm, asked for naval protection, and was assured by Acting Secretary Loomis that no damage would be permitted, though Farnham said Loomis did not immediately order the ships sent.

On the morning of November 6, 1903, preceding the formal recognition of Panama's independence that day by President Roosevelt, the World said in an editorial:

"It is natural that we should take a deep interest in the country of the proposed canal and our treaty rights there. Anything further, any taking sides or casting of obstacles in the way of Colombia's retaining her territory, would be an invasion of a sister nation's rights, for which our excusable irritation at the Bogota Senate for failing to pass the canal treaty would furnish no excuse whatever."

November 6: At 11.55 a. m. the Sta e Department received official notice from Felix Ehrman, Panaman banker and the acting American consul general in Panama, that Bunau-Varilla had been appointed confidential agent of the new Republic at Washington, and that "Colon and interior Provinces have enthusiastically joined independence."

The truth was that the independence had not been even heard of in important par.s of the interior, and that very day, as shown by a cable from the American consul in Colon, received in the State Department at 4.50 p. m. of November 6, they were just sending an expedition to Bocas del Toro to proclaim the revolution. Bocas del Toro is the fourth most important town of the Isthmus, and the center of the banana industry. The Province of Chiriqui, with its capital, David, the third most populous and important place, and the center of the cattle business, held out against the independence until a letter from the Provisional Government warned the commander of the Colombian forces that if he did not join the revolution a white ship of the North Americans would appear in those waters.

November 6: At 12.51 p. m. Secretary Hay dispatched the cable to the American consuls in Panama announcing that "the people of Panama have, by an apparently unanimous movement, dissolved their political connection with the Republic of Colombia, and resumed their independence," and instruc ing the consular representative to enter into relations with the new Government. At the same time Secretary Hay cabled Minister Beaupre in Bogota to notify Colombia that the United Sta.es had recognized the revolutionists. The hour of sending this cable is not indicated, but it was repeated for the information and guidance of the acting consul general in Panama at 2.45 p. m. of November 6.

November 6: Bunau-Varilla, having received by cable his appointment as minister, appears to have delivered to Joshua J. Lindo, of the firm of Piza, Nephews & Co., No. 18 Broadway, New York, a check for $25,000. This left him a balance of $75,000 in the account of $100,000 which Credit Lyonnais had opened by cable to his credit with Heidelbach, Ickelheimer & Co., on October 26, 1903. On the same day in Panama, Mr. Lindo's Isthmian firm of Piza, Lindo & Co. sold to Isaac Brandon & Bros. bills of exchange for $17,000 and $8,000 against New York. Meantime the Brandon banking house in Panama had advanced funds to the revolutionary committee on the morning of November 4 to meet the immediate needs for bribing the Colombian soldiers.

This $25,000 transaction is the first recorded after the making of the independence, and the Panamans wish to have it believed that it was the first money secured for the movement from any source. On the other hand, Dr. Amador's confidential note to his son, written a fortnight before the movement, said the financial arrangements already had been made in a bank. Then, too, Mr. Lindo contradicts the record by declaring that Bunau-Varilla never gave to the revolution the amounts he claims, and that the only sum which Bunau-Varilla did contribute—$25,000—was at a later date and secured by Lindo's signing Bunau-Varilla's note for that amount. Federico Boyd, who testified that he was one of the four authors of the independence, swore that the first $100,000 for the cause was procured by Bunau-Varilla from J. P. Morgan & Co. on the day of the revolution on Bunau-Varilla's personal guaranty. Boyd swore that Bunau-Varilla had been guaranteed reimbursement by a letter given to him by Dr. Amador before the revolution.

November 7: Mr. Cromwell's partner, William J. Curtis, "had an audience with the President, who demanded that the company declare formally that it consented to the application of the existing agreement to the new situation as it had been generally set forth by cable on October 31"—the cable in which Mr. Cromwell expressed, in behalf of the canal company, "entire confidence in the outcome" of Mr. Roosevelt's "masterly policy."

November 7: Bunau-Varilla telegraphed from New York to Secretary Hay, formally notifying him of his appointment as minister and making the following frank acknowledgment of the Rooseveltian parentage of the Republic of Panama:

"In extending her generous hand so spontaneously to her latest born, the mother of the American nations is prosecuting her noble mission as the liberator and the educator of the peoples. In spreading her protecting wings over the territory of our Republic the American Eagle has sanctified it."

And yet the treaty by which the United States was to guarantee the sovereignty of the new Republic had not been drafted—unless, like the declaration of independence of the Republic of Panama, it had been written before the fake revolution. Bunau-Varilla and Secretary Hay could have held no meetings up to this time in their official capacities to negotiate the treaty. Is this not an admission that it was agreed before the "revolution" that the American Eagle would "spread her protecting wings" over the proposed Republic?

November 7: Secretary Hay issued a statement in which he said: "The action of the President is not only in the strictest accordance with the principles of justice and equity and in line with the best precedents of our public policy, but it was the only course he could have taken in compliance with our treaty rights and obligations."

November 8: Press dispatches from Washington stated that the constitution of the new Republic was already prepared, and that in the canal treaty which would be concluded Panama would be given the same indemnity—$10,000,000 cash and $250,000 a year—which Colombia was to have received under the Hay-Herran treaty.

November 9: Having been advised by cable—after Mr. Curtis's conference with President Roosevelt November 7—that there must be a formal stipulation, Mr. Cromwell cabled from Paris to the President that he could "have the most absolute confidence in the good faith of the company, whose attitude remains the same."

November 9: Gen. Rafael Reyes was dispatched from Bogota with Gens. Pedro Nel Ospina, Lucas Caballero, and Jorge Holguin as special commissioners to Panama and Washington to negotiate a settlement with the Panama rebels and a new canal treaty satisfactory to the United States. Rioting began in Bogota as news of the secession was amplified, and the populace stoned the house of Lorenzo Marroquin, blaming him and his father's government for the loss of Panama.

The instructions to Gen. Reyes, as published in the Colombian "Blue Book," were that he should ascertain upon what bases the United States would renew negotiations; that if modifications of the treaty were expected, he should attempt to provide that Colombia's jurisdiction should be integrally preserved and that the indemnity should be augmented; but if the special commission found that it was necessary to sign the treaty as it stood in order to save Colombia's integrity, it should do so, subject to ratification by Congress.

November 10: Dr. Amador and Federico Boyd ,as special commissioners to assist Bunau-Varilla in negotiating the treaty and in arranging to finance the Republic until it could receive its canal millions, left Panama for New York. On the following day Mr. Cromwell, according to his own story, "having accomplished the object of his brief stay" in Paris, "embarked for the United States on November 11, to be present at the conference previously arranged with the special delegates of the new Republic of Panama upon their arrival in New York."

Apprised of the coming of the special commissioners, who might interfere with his freedom of action, Bunau-Varilla, who already had been received informally by Secretary Hay at luncheon on the 9th, made haste with his diplomatic mission. On the 13th he was formally received by President Roosevelt, and by the 18th—the day after the arrival of the special commissioners in New York—he was prepared to sign the treaty, and did so before the envoys reached Washington.

Bunau-Varilla's signing the treaty, unsatisfactory as it was to Panama, has been from that day, and always will continue with the Panamans to be, a subject for recriminations. Within a year it was necessary for President Roosevelt to send Secretary Taft to Panama to adjust differences and pacify the new Republic, which complained bitterly that it had been betrayed by its alien minister and led into a very disadvantageous canal bargain.

Many lies have been told about the relations of the special commissioners and Bunau-Varilla and their responsibility for this bargain. The special commissioners reported upon their return to Panama that they went immediately to Washington upon their disembarking in New York and were shocked to learn that Bunau-Varilla had signed with Secretary Hay while they were on the train between New York and Washington. Called to testify before the World's rogatory commission in Panama in June, 1900. Federico Boyd swore to this same misstatement. With Mr. Cromwell's confessions, as well as the public records in his possession, the World's counsel went over this ground again and again, attempting to compel Mr. Boyd to tell the truth, but without success. Boyd declared and reiterated under oath that the special commissioners made no appointment with Mr. Cromwell; that they did not know he was returning from Europe; that they did not see him nor confer with him in New York; that they went immediately to Washington and found that Bunau-Varilla had signed the treaty behind their backs. Not until Mr. Cromwell met them, while stopping at the same hotel in Washington, testified Mr. Boyd, did they get into communication with him.

But Mr. Cromwell, in his account to the French arbitrators, says:

"Before leaving Panama those persons (Amador and Boyd) had arranged by cable to meet Mr. Cromwell in New York for a conference, Mr. Cromwell being on his way at the same time from Paris to New York. They arrived before him, but awaited his arrival in New York a few hours later, on November 18 (November 17 is correct). An important conference, which lasted a whole day, followed. * * * At their request we met these persons in Washington to help them in taking up pending questions."

Mr. Boyd's testimony, which was corroborated by other Panaman witnesses, was intended to bolster up the old story that Mr. Cromwell ran away to Europe at the critical time, left his Panaman friends to face the consequences of a possible failure of the revolution which he had fomented, and failed altogether to keep his promise to finance the independence. In order to clear his skirts it was necessary to make it appear that Amador and his compatriot, Boyd, were angry with Cromwell when they came to New York and did not have anything to do with him. Mr. Boyd would not admit that his testimony was false, even when confronted with Mr. Cromwell's own confession and the cited records to prove that what he testified was untrue. He insisted that Mr. Cromwell lied to the French arbitrators, and that the hotel and shipping records in New York must be incorrect.

The facts are that the Panaman special envoys arrived in New York on the steamer *City of Washington*, which reached the bar at 6.45 a. m. of November 17, 1903. Cromwell's Man Friday, Farnham, went down the bay on a revenue cutter, met them and escorted them to the old Fifth Avenue Hotel, where they remained from the morning of the 17th to 3.30 o'clock in the afternoon of the 18th before taking the train for Washington. Had they gone at once to Washington, as they afterwards falsely reported to their Panaman constituents they did do, and as Boyd swore they did, they would have arrived before Bunau-Varilla could have rushed through the treaty to the detriment of Panama.

Mr. Cromwell arrived from Paris also on November 17, 1903, on the *Kaiser Wilhelm der Grosse*, which reached the bar at 12.12 p. m. Farnham, having taken care of the Panaman envoys, met his chief at the pier. Amador spent that night at the home of his son, Dr. Raoul A. Amador, No. 216 West One hundred and twelfth Street. The next day, November 18, 1903, occurred the "all-day" conference of which Mr. Cromwell tells in his book. Current newspaper reports said Cromwell was closeted with the special commissioners at their hotel for an hour. He and Mr. Boyd were quoted as saying that his call was purely social; simply to congratulate the patriots.

Mr. Cromwell says in his own story that, in order to secure the ratification of the Hay-Bunau-Varilla treaty he "brought about conferences between the special delegates and Senators Hanna, Fairbanks, Kittredge, Platt, and other Members of Congress"—the same friends who stood by him in turning Congress from Nicaragua to Panama—and that during their stay in Washington Amador and Boyd "conferred daily with one or several of our partners, asked and followed our counsel and advice as to all phases of the unique situation, which had thus been recently created. I may be mentioned that these relations have been maintained even to the present day."

Before the return of Mr. Cromwell from Paris, Bunau-Varilla had taken up with J. Pierpont Morgan the finances of the new Republic. On Sunday, November 15, desiring an immediate reply, Bunau-Varilla sent the following telegram to Mr. Morgan's residence:

WASHINGTON, *November 15, 1093.*

PIERPONT MORGAN, Esq.,
219 Madison Avenue, New York City:

I beg to be excused to trouble you to-day, but am obliged to have an immediate decision on financial plan which I submitted to you and to know from you by telegraphic message addressed to me, New Willard Hotel, Washington, whether you agree or disagree with it.

I repeat as follows said plan: I would name your firm agent of the Republic of Panama in the United States in virtue of the full powers I have received from my Government for said object. You would immediately have full and exclusive power to collect from the United States Treasury any sum which would have to be delivered to the Republic of Panama, and you would have to place said sums to the credit of the Republic on the account opened in your firm and dispose of them according to the orders of my Government. You would immediately open a credit to the Republic for an amount of $300,000, of which the Government could dispose at different periods as follows:

Hundred thousand would be placed at the immediate disposition of the Republic and delivered for the account of the Republic according to the orders I shall give to your firm in the name of my Government; $50,000 would be placed at the disposal of the Republic immediately after the signature of the canal treaty and its consequent ratification by my Government; the rest, $150,000, immediately after ratification of the canal treaty by the Senate of the United States.

I add that, to limit your risk, I am willing to guarantee you personally against any loss to the extent of $100,000, and to make such guarantee effective I would have to-morrow $75,000 placed with the hands of your firm and twenty-five thousand two or three days after, it being understood that such guarantee shall cease as soon as the account of the Republic will be credited on your books.

BUNAU-VARILLA.

November 16: The Panama banking house of Isaac Brandon & Bros., which claims the credit for having nourished the infant Republic during its suckling period, charging no interest for its loans and having no security in this philanthropy outside of the "credit" of the new Government, bought a $75,000 draft on Piza, Nephews & Co. from Mr. Lindo's Panama house of Piza, Lindo & Co. This draft was stamped with Piza, Nephews & Co.'s acceptance on November 23, payable at the Mechanics & Traders' Bank, November 30, but was paid, according to Piza, Nephews & Co.'s books, on November 24. Thus the Brandons received no "security," but the cash equivalent for their advances, in the form of drafts of a reputable fellow banker, for the first $100,000 they contributed.

November 16: Bunau-Varill announced in Washington that J. P. Morgan & Co. had been appointed fiscal agents of the Republic of Panama.

November 17: Heidelbach, Ickelheimer & Co. placed with J. P. Morgan & Co., to the credit of Bunau-Varilla, $75,000, thereby exhausting the original credit of $100,000 cabled by Crédit Lyonnais to his account on October 26. Morgan & Co. transferred the $75,000 the same day to Piza, Nephews & Co. On the same day Heidelbach, Ickelheimer & Co. received a cable from Crédit Lyonnais instructing them to pay to Bunau-Varilla, upon his application, $4.000, the same amount referred to specifically in the Amador-Bunau-Varilla code. This $4,000 was disposed by Bunau-Varilla's bankers on November 23 by sending $1.500 to the New Willard Hotel, Washington, and $1.000 to the Waldorf-Astoria Hotel, leaving a balance of $1,500.

November 23: According to Joshua J. Lindo's story, on November 23 Bunau-Varilla, who had pleaded that he was not able to make good the promise to give $100,000 to the revolution, arranged with Lindo to sign his note for $25,000, whereupon Lindo gave Bunau-Varilla check No. 4507 for $25,000, dated November 23, and made on the Mechanics & Traders' Bank by the firm of Piza. Nephews & Co. Bunau-Varilla indorsed the check to Heidelbach, Ickelheimer & Co., and it was paid through the Importers & Traders' National Bank. Heidelbach, Ickelheimer & Co., on the following day, transferred the $25,000. by instruction of Bunau-Varilla, to J. P. Morgan & Co., who in turn paid it over on November 25 to Mr. Lindo's firm.

November 25: Amador and Boyd signed an agreement with the Bowling Green Trust Co., pledging the first moneys received from the United States, or the customs revenues of the ports of Panama and Colon, to repay a loan of $100,000, which the trust comapny made at 6 per cent per annum, payable in four months, and renewable for four months, upon payment of 3 per cent bonus. Mr. Boyd, on the witness stand in Panama, swore that Amador arranged this loan, having been introduced by Mr. Brandon, and that no security was given. Mr. Brandon says he had nothing to do with it. Mr. Cromwell, who had reorganized the Bowling Green Trust Co., and was its attorney and one of its directors, takes the credit before the French arbitrators for having secured this loan for the new Republic. It was amply secured by $90,000 par value of Northern Pacific bonds and $10,000 par value of Baltimore & Ohio bonds, which were deposited in the name of William Griffiths, jr., whose signature was witnessed by E. B. Hill, of Mr. Cromwell's firm. Notice of failure to pay the interest was sent, not to the representative of the Panama Republic, but to Mr. Cromwell. (Authority of Thomas S. Fuller, who inspected correspondence and documents in trust company.)

The financial arrangements for the revolution "already made with a bank," as referred to by Dr. Amador in the letter of October 18, 1903, to his son, are believed by the younger Dr. Amador to have been made also in the Bowling Green. Mr. Lindo has referred to the second Bowling Green loan in speaking of the $100,000 secured by Amador and Boyd on Mr. Cromwell's bonds on November 25, but does not state what was the first Bowling Green loan or when it was made.

A commission of 3 per cent on the Bowling Green loan appears on the debit side of the books of Piza, Nephews & Co. as of December 27, but it does not appear to whom it was paid.

The $100,000 received from the Bowling Green was transferred to Piza, Nephews & Co., $50,000 on November 27 and $50.000 on December 1. Then appears on Piza, Nephews & Co.'s books debits of $30,384.67 on December 4 for an invoice of supplies sent to the new Republic on the steamer *Alliance*, and $9,932 for an invoice on the *Yucatan*, December 14. On December 22 the Brandon banking house was paid $46.000 through Piza, Nephews & Co. This makes a total of $340.000, at then prevailing exchange, repaid to the Brandons of the $450,000 silver which they say they lent the new Republic without security and partly without interest.

November 30: Bunau-Varilla by this time had served the purposes of Mr. Cromwell and was treading on his toes, so it was deemed advisable to have him removed as the Panaman minister to Washington. Accordingly Mr. Cromwell, in the name of E. A. Drake, vice president of the Panama Railroad, on November 30, 1903, sent to the Isthmus a cable in cipher, of which the following is a translation:

NEW YORK, *November 30, 1903—6.10 p. m.*

BEERS, *Panama:*

Several cables urging immediate appointment of Pablo Arosemena have been sent to the junta since Friday. We are surprised that action has not been taken and suppose it is only because the minister of the Republic of Panama is trying to disturb the junta by cabling that there is great danger that Washington will make a trade with Reyes and withdraw warships and urge his retention because of his alleged influence with President Roosevelt and Senators. This is absolutely without foundation. Mr. Cromwell has direct assurances from President Roosevelt, Secretary Hay, Senator Hanna, and other Senators that there is not the slightest danger of this. Evidently the minister's pretense of influence is grossly exaggerated. We have fullest support of Mr. Cromwell and his friends, who have carried every victory for past six years. Junta evidently do not know that objection exists in Washington to the minister of Republic of Panama because he is not a Panaman, but a foreigner, and initially has displeased influential Senators regarding character of former treaty. He is recklessly involving Republic of Panama in financial and other complications that will use up important part of indemnity. Delegates here are powerless to prevent all this, as minister of Republic of Panama uses his position as minister to go over their heads. He is sacrificing the Republic's interests and may any moment commit Republic of Panama to portion of the debts of Colombia, same as he signed treaty omitting many points of advantage to Republic of Panama—and which would have been granted readily—without waiting for delegates who were to his knowledge within two hours of arrival, with discretion. In form junta and cable me immediately synopsis of situation and when will junta appoint Pablo Arosemena. Answer to-day if possible.

DRAKE.

Later, when the scheme suits his own purposes, Mr. Cromwell secretly becomes the negotiator for all three Governments and the author of the tripartite treaty—still unratified by Colombia—whereby Panama proposes to pay Colombia $2,500,000 toward the foreign debt. But in 1903 such a suggestion is grounds for removal of Bunau-Varilla.

Although at one time Mr. Cromwell considered it advisable to ignore Capt. Beers and decline to reimburse him for several hundred dollars of cable tolls Beers had paid out of his own pocket, leaving that to the Panama Railroad Co. finally to pay; at this time Beers was most useful in supplying Cromwell with information. Another cable, of which the date is missing, was sent soon after Admiral Walker went to the Isthmus, in November, by Mr. Drake to Capt. Beers, as follows:

"Your telegram received; is of utmost importance. You telegraph as soon as possible reply Walker gets from Washington; also action junta takes on same. Subject of minister of Republic of Panama is of vital importance, and we rely on you to keep me well posted promptly and fully by cable on action junta or anyone else regarding same." (Cable unsigned, but Prescott recalls it as translation of message from Drake to Beers.)

November 30: Herbert G. Prescott, intrusted immediately after the revolution to transmit to President Roosevelt the first flag raised by the Republic, had forwarded it to Mr. Cromwell, and on November 30 he received the following cabled answer, costing somebody $81 to gratify Mr. Cromwell's vanity:

[S. J. 26 Date, 30–11–03. Number of words, 162. From New York. Time, 7.15 p. m.]

H. G. PRESCOTT, *Panama:*

Inform municipal council and junta I had honor and pleasure presenting to President Roosevelt the flag of the Republic forwarded through you. Among other things, I remarked that while the United States would never part with its historic treasure, the Liberty Bell, which first rang out the independence of this Nation, and the reverberation of which continues to be an inspiration to all liberty-loving people, yet so fond was the gratitude and affection of the Republic of Panama to the President that they gave into his hands their most precious treasure—the sacred and historic flag, the first raised upon the declaration of independence. The President accepted the gift in most enthusiastic and grateful terms, and requested me to convey his unbounded thanks and pleasure, and to say he designs having a suitable inscription woven upon its surface to perpetuate its historic character and the grateful acts of its donors. I greet you all.

WILLIAM NELSON CROMWELL.

December 9: President Roosevelt in his message confronted Congress with his dictum: "The question now, therefore, is not by which route the Isthmian Canal shall be built, for that question has been definitely and irrevocably decided. The question is simply whether or not we shall have an Isthmian Canal."

In his efforts to calm the storm of criticism which was sweeping the country. Mr. Roosevelt told the Congress that the canal treaty "was entered into at the urgent solicitation of the people of Colombia," when just the contrary was the truth. He further said: "In drawing up this treaty every concession was made to the people and to the Government of Colombia. We were more than just in dealing with them."

"When it became evident that the treaty was hopelessly lost," Mr. Roosevelt told the Congress, "the people of Panama rose literally as one man. * * * The Colombian troops stationed on the Isthmus, who had long been unpaid, made common cause with the people of Panama, and with astonishing unanimity the new Republic was started."

The truth was that the Colombian troops on the Isthmus had been paid promptly up to date, and the pay roll vouchers and receipts up to October, signed by Gen. Huertas and his paymaster, are on file in the war department at Bogota. The October salaries were disbursed, but the receipts were never forwarded. There was, however, an account carried over from the last civil war which was charged to the war indebtedness and remains to this day upon the books of the Colombian Government unpaid. This furnishes the only possible pretext for justification of Mr. Roosevelt's statement that the troops had been long unpaid. Even this was not the explanation advanced by Mr. Roosevelt's little brothers in Panama when the World had them on the witness stand. They swore that the bribe money paid to the Colombian troops wasn't bribery at all but simply the payment of salary immediately in arrears. Col. Tascon, second chief of the forces in Panama, who was sent by Gov. Obaldia, and Huertas, with his 100 loyal men, into the bush just before the "revolution," testified that the men were paid promptly up to date and that there was no dissatisfaction with the arrangement of the few months' arrears of the civil-war time, as the men had been paid promptly after the war and were confident that the Government eventually would be able to pay up the war debt.

In Mr. Roosevelt's message there also appears a "partial list of the disturbances on the Isthmus, * * * as reported to us by our consuls" since the making of the treaty of 1846. This list was attacked by Colombian historians, and so completely riddled for its inaccuracies that one involuntarily associates it with Mr. Cromwell's false and inaccurate data furnished to Senator Hanna, and with Cromwell's declaration to the French arbitrators that his firm "arranged and directed" conferences between Amador and Boyd and Republican Party leaders in the Senate, and that "we prepared a thorough résumé of the unjust wrongs from which Panama had suffered for a period of 50 years, a statement which we communicated to the officials of the Government and to the Members of Congress to justify the revolution, and we created an opinion favorable to the new Republic and to a treaty of allegiance with her."

December 10: Mr. Cromwell, through Vice President Drake, cabled Capt. Beers to obtain a leave of absence from Superintendent Shaler and come to the United States. Beers accordingly embarked on December 15 and for the next two months was Mr. Cromwell's assistant in Washington and New York in a campaign to undermine the influence and official position of Bunau-Varilla.

Capt. Beers had not been promoting a revolution without hope or promise of reward, but was interested in plans which had been under discussion even before the creation of the Republic for the exploitation of its territory and resources in connection with the profits which were expected from construction of the canal by private contract.

One expectation was that the United States could be induced to abandon the steamship business of the Panama Railroad, and the promised reward for Capt. Beers's faithful aid in pulling off the "revolution" was that he should be the general manager on the Isthmus of the transportation line which Mr. Cromwell should organize. It will be recalled that, in his annual report for 1904, Maj. Gen. George W. Davis, United States Army, retired, governor of the Canal Zone and member of the Isthmian Canal Commission, recommended strongly that the United States abandon the steamship line and leave the business to private enterprise. It was Gen. Davis who recommended also that the United States buy the outstanding shares of the Panama Railroad Co.'s stock held by individuals, and that for this work Mr. Cromwell was specially commissioned by Secretary Taft.

Capt. Beers, under the direction of Cromwell, wrote to 8 or 10 of his friends on the Isthmus urging them to exert their influence to secure Bunau-Varilla's removal and the appointment of Pablo Arosemena as minister to Washington. In these letters, all of similar tenor, Capt. Beers said that he was having daily conferences with Mr. Cromwell. In reference to the financial scheme he said, in a letter to his friend, Herbert G. Prescott, assistant superintendent of the Panama Railroad: "I am of the opinion that Mr. Cromwell has several enterprises in view for the Isthmus, in which you and our Panama friends will be considered. I can not at this writing give you any details, but if I should not return by the *Allianca* will be able to write you fully in regard to the same."

One of the business ventures whereby Mr. Cromwell's friends were to be rewarded for their participation in the revolution was in transferring the Panama gambling concession. A few years before, Gov. Alban, of Panama, granted the concession to the American consul general, Hezekiah A. Gudger, who transferred it to Pratt & Seymour, Americans, for a fee which Prescott and John Popham, a Central American railroad builder, declare was $5,000. Prescott, Beers, and Jesse Hyatt, American vice consul at Colon, arranged immediately after the revolution to obtain the gambling concession in their own names and sell it back to Pratt & Seymour for $60,000. They considered this would be quite as legitimate as for the American consul general to act as a broker in the same transaction. Unfortunately for the triumvirate of Americans, Uncle Sam "intimated" that it desired no public gambling concession to corrupt canal diggers, and consequently no concession was granted by the new Republic.

The public utilities corporation in the city of Panama, manufacturing light and ice, was a smaller issue. Mr. Cromwell invested $45,000 in that, becoming the largest individual stockholder. It has been immensely profitable.

A land and lumber syndicate also was projected, but did not take definite form until 1908, when an attempt was made to grab all the Atlantic watershed of the republic in the names of Jonas Whitley, of Mr. Cromwell's press agency; Vice President Drake, of the Panama Railroad; and another supposed "capitalist." Farnham took the contract for the timber grab to the Isthmus and attempted to put through the deal. The late Dr. Amador publicly accused Farnham of attempting to bribe him, as the first president of the republic, to sign this concession, promising that he and all his family should be made rich thereby.

The other important source of revenue in prospect was the handling of Panama's $10,000,000. To get this prize into his office it was necessary to remove the influence of Bunau-Varilla. In this he was successful, and Bunau-Varilla was replaced by J. A. Arango. How Mr. Cromwell got himself appointed fiscal agent and how he has administered Panama's funds, pretending that he did so because of his love for Panama, and at the same time taking enormous profits for himself and his friends, is a chapter in itself.

Going back now to Gen. Rafael Reyes and his committee of Colombian generals, dispatched from Bogota on November 9: News of Reyes's appointment was received in Panama with enthusiastic celebrations, for the reason, given by the correspondent of the Associated Press, who was one of the revolutionary conspirators, that it was "looked upon as assuring the independence of the Isthmian territory."

Arriving at Barranquilla, on the Colombian coast, Gen. Reyes issued a decree prohibiting the recruiting and mobilization of troops to retake Panama. Colombia by this time was seething with war spirit, and in every town in the country men were volunteering to march overland to subdue the rebellious department. To meet such an attack United States Army officers, disguised, penetrated all of the southern end of the Isthmus exploring and mapping rivers and trails; and a United States warship patrolled the San Blas coast, and in one of its scouting expeditions penetrated what was then recognized as Colombian territory.

November 19: The Reyes commission reached Colon, but was denied permission to proceed to Panama. A committee of Panamans met them on the 20th and rejected all offers of settlement.

November 22: From Port Limon, Costa Rica, en route to New Orleans, Reyes cabled to Central and South American Republics in the hope of arousing sentiment and enlisting aid to oppose the policy of the United States.

At Port Limon, where Colombians, exiled from Panama after the revolution, were stranded, Reyes was visited aboard ship by two Colombians (Calderon and Del Valle; see their affidavits) who, before realizing the extent of the revolutionary conspiracy, had been in the confidence of Amador and Huertas and had abstracted from Dr. Amador's archives three letters addressed to Amador by Secretary Hay before November 3. These letters, with a list of Colombian soldiers who had been bribed, they delivered to Reyes, who suppressed them. From this time on the tone of Reyes's dispatches to his Government is noticeably changed.

November 28: Reyes and his commission reached Washington, via New Orleans, and he cabled his Government:

"All armed conflict with Americans should be avoided. Do not occupy territory of Panama, including Isle of Pines. Forty war vessels will meet in Panaman waters; they will look for an opportunity to make war through Cali, Medellin, to Bogota. By agreement with an attorney Holguin goes to-day to Paris. Send him the credentials requested. Situation is bad.

"REYES."

Gen. Reyes very quickly saw that his advantage would come through playing with the American administration. He at once affronted Grover Cleveland, who had agreed to preside at a mass meeting in Carnegie Hall, New York, to protest against the breaking of faith with Colombia, and who was ready to lead a delegation to Washington to voice directly to Mr. Roosevelt public disapproval of the policy that had been adopted. Through a committee of Colombians in New York who were preparing the demonstration Reyes curtly notified Mr. Cleveland that he desired no interference with his diplomatic mission.

The Colombian Government from Bogota demanded that the commission should make a campaign through the American press and arouse public opinion. Reyes made it appear in his financial accounts that this campaign was carried out. To his fellow commissioners he talked about a mysterious Mr. Morgate, whom he said he had employed because of his great ability and influence, to make a campaign through the press and among the Senators, and on February 9, 1904, just before he was leaving for Europe, Reyes signed an order to pay "Mr. W. Morgate" $20,100 American gold for such services. This order is on file in the court of accounts in Bogota, together with a voucher for receipt of the sum, dated February 10. From the original documents, which the World photographed in Bogota, it appears that Reyes, with the same pen and the same ink, signed both the order to pay and the receipt, forging, or manufacturing, the signature "W. Morgate." There was not, nor has there been since Gen. Reyes's mission, any press agent or lobbyist, or so far as it is possible to discover, any other person in Washington of that name. Certain it is, according to the other members of the commission, that no one performed for Colombia any services of the nature whatsoever.

The attorney for the Reyes mission was Mr. Wayne MacVeagh, former Attorney General of the United States in President Cleveland's Cabinet. He accepted the duty of counseling the Colombian Government with the stipulation that he should be paid no fee; that he would take no case against his own Government, and that what he did do, he did because he believed that the honor of his own country demanded that a great international wrong should be righted. Mr. MacVeagh continued to fight Colombia's case on international legal grounds until he became convinced that Reyes was simply "trading" with the Roosevelt administration, when he gave up in disgust.

While at Colon the Reyes mission was informed by Admiral Coghlan that the United States would not permit Colombia to land troops anywhere on the Isthmus.

December 8: Under cabled instructions from his Government, Reyes inquired of Secretary Hay: "What attitude would be assumed by the Government of the United States in the event which may take place of Colombian troops or forces under the Colombian flag making their appearance on the Isthmus, or attempting a landing on that territory, for the defense of the sovereignty and integrity of Colombia, and respecting the railroad line and the terminal points in accordance with the stipulation of the treaty of 1846, which my country is ever ready to observe."

Receiving an indefinite reply, Gen. Reyes again, on December 29, 1903, pressed Secretary Hay for a prompt categorical answer as to "whether military action of the Government of Colombia to subjugate the Panama rebels would be held by the Government of the United States to be a declaration of war."

December 30: Secretary Hay replied, reiterating his former answer that "the Government of the United States would regard with grave concern any invasion of the territory of Panama by Colombian troops," because already the treaty whereby the United States was to guarantee Panama sovereignty had been signed, although not ratified by the Senate, and its signing entailed moral obligation to protect the new Republic.

The statement of Colombia's grievances, prepared under the counsel of Mr. MacVeagh, was presented to Secretary Hay by Gen. Reyes on December 23, 1903.

January 5, 1904: Severely criticizing Gen. Reyes for citing newspaper reports as bases for accusations, Mr. Hay declared, in his answer to the statement of grievances:

"Any charge that this Government or any responsible member of it held intercourse, whether official or unofficial, with agents of revolution in Colombia is utterly without justification.

"Equally so is the insinuation that any action of this Government prior to the revolution in Panama was the result of complicity with the plans of the revolutionists. This department sees fit to make these denials, and it makes them finally.

"The origin of the Republic of Panama and the reasons for its independent existence may be traced in certain acts of the Government of Colombia, which are matters of official record."

Secretary Hay then cited the various diplomatic representations of Colombian ministers to Washington in the early stages of the canal negotiations—the representations which Mr. Cromwell had caused to be made by the ministers whom he had caused to be sent to the United States. Then Mr. Hay made the following misstatement:

"After the Spooner Act was approved negotiations were duly initiated by Colombia."

The Spooner Act was approved June 28, 1902. Already Mr. Hay had the draft of the Concha treaty, made by Mr. Cromwell, and the first step after the approval of the Spooner bill was the revising of the draft by Cromwell, at Secretary Hay's request, and its presentation to Minister Concha by Secretary Hay, "unofficially" through Cromwell on July 9, 1902.

Further on Mr. Hay said that "before entering upon any dealings with the New Panama Canal Co." the Government of the United States negotiated and concluded the convention with Colombia. The Government entered upon dealings with the New Panama Canal Co. as early as April 10, 1900, when the Isthmian Canal Commission formally asked for a price on the canal, and the Government held the Canal Co.'s option when the Spooner bill was introduced.

Without any reference to Mr. Cromwell's being responsible for bringing the question of transfer of the canal concession "within the domain of international relations," Mr. Hay reminded Colombia that in Article I of the treaty as proposed by Minister Concha on March 31, 1902, consent to the transfer was formally given.

January 6: Gen. Reyes, in a letter to Secretary Hay, prefered formal and specific charges against the United States, among them being "That it is known, from sworn statements, that the garrisons of Panama and Colon were bought with gold brought from the United States toward the end of October by the Panama revolutionists." Two years after the revolution Jose Agustin Arango declared in confidence to Gen. Carlos Vallarino (see his affidavit) that when Dr. Amador Guerrero came back from the United States in October, 1903, he brought with him the funds supplied by Mr. Cromwell to finance the revolution.

January 9: Replying to Reyes, Secretary Hay said:

"I do not consider that this Government is called upon to take notice of your statement as to the sources from which the revolutionary government obtained its funds. As this Government had no participation in the preparation of the revolution, it has no concern with the details of its history."

January 4: Mr. Roosevelt sent his special message to Congress, defending his Panama policy. His flat denial of complicity in the Panama revolution was generally accepted and was sufficient to turn the tide that had been setting against the ratification of the Hay-Bunau-Varilla treaty since publication of the correspondence of the State and Navy Departments. The House of Representatives, by resolution of November 9, 1903, had called for "all correspondence and other official documents" relating to the revolution if not, in Mr. Roosevelt's judgment, "incompatible with the interests of the public service" to make them public. This was supplied in part on November 16, and a second lot was sent on December 18. Mr. Roosevelt did not, however, transmit all of the correspondence. In the cables exchanged between the State Department and Minister Beaupre several bearing on Panama were not included. (Comparison of the published cables and the cipher dispatches in possession of the World show that at least 11 were withheld.) A bundle of correspondence was marked by Mr. Roosevelt, "Not to be sent to Congress—T. R.," and was put away in the secret archives of the State Department.

In his message of January 4, 1904, Mr. Roosevelt reiterated that "it is no longer possible, under existing legislation, to go to the Nicaragua route as an alternative."

Flatly contradicting both himself and Secretary Hay as to the origin of the canal negotiations, Mr. Roosevelt said:

"When this Government submitted to Colombia the Hey-Herran treaty three things were, therefore, already settled."

And again Mr. Roosevelt declared:

"Having these facts in view, there is no shadow of question that the Government of the United States proposed a treaty which was not merely just but generous to Colombia."

Mr. Roosevelt saw fit to quote at great length from newspaper reports to uphold his own position before Congress, while at the same time Secretary of State Hay was censuring Gen. Reyes for citing press dispatches to sustain his charges against Mr. Roosevelt.

Denying complicity in the revolution, Mr. Roosevelt said:

"I hesitate to refer to the injurious insinuations which have been made of complicity by this Government in the revolutionary movement in Panama. They are as destitute of foundation as of propriety. The only excuse for my mentioning them is the fear lest unthinking persons might mistake for acquiescence the silence of mere self-respect. I think proper to say, therefore, that no one connected with this Government had any part in preparing, inciting, or encouraging the late revolution on the Isthmus of Panama, and that save from the reports of our military and naval officers given above, no one connected with this Government had any previous knowledge of the revolution, except such as was accessible to any person of ordinary intelligence who read the newspapers and kept up a current acquaintance with public affairs."

Mr. Roosevelt told the Congress that the people of Panama "with a unanimity hardly before recorded in any similar case" declared their independence; he accused Colombia of scheming to annul the canal company's extension and take all of the $40,000,000 for itself, and concluded his message with his oft-reiterated dictum "that the question actually before this Government is not that of the recognition of Panama as an independent Republic; that is already an accomplished fact. The question, and the only question, is whether or not we shall build an Isthmian Canal."

Even the World, editorially, accepted the statements of Mr. Roosevelt as truthful, and said that his message "makes out a very good case for our Government."

January 17: The World published the first account of the financial motive of the separation of Panama, of the operations of a syndicate of New York and Paris bankers, of the negotiations of Amador and Duque in Washington, of Bunau-Varilla's arrangements for the warships and his cables to the Isthmus, promising that they would arrive on time to protect the revolutionists. The facts were brought to the World by Jonas Whitley, of Mr. Cromwell's staff of press agents, and the World holds Mr. Whitley's receipt for $100 for the "tip." Mr. Whitley did not mention Mr. Cromwell as the instigator, of the revolution, nor did he tell the most incriminating facts concerning the complicity of the Roosevelt administration. But in its esential truth, that the revolution was "a stock jobbers' plan to make millions," the story was accurate. It did not contain the names of the American speculators nor suggest that American politicians or statesmen were compromised. The World was not, consequently, denounced as a libeler and villifier of the American people for making this publication. Bunau-Varilla, who was made by Whitley to appear as the master plotter in the conspiracy, believed that Cromwell inspired the story and furnished Whitley with the framework of fact, dressed with enough fiction to conceal Cromwell's own handiwork.

February 9: Capt. Beers sailed for Panama, after having held his "daily conferences" in Washington with Mr. Cromwell, where he was maintained at the New Willard Hotel at Mr. Cromwell's expense. We must turn to Cromwell's narrative to the French arbitrators for an explanation, as follows:

"Having failed in his mission, Gen. Reyes left Washington and came to New York. Through the intermediary of mutual friends he and Mr. Cromwell met for a series of conferences, which had ultimately a great deal of importance, and in the course of which a warm friendship was created, a friendship which still lasts."

Mr. Cromwell and Gen. Reyes's "mutual friends" at this time included J. Pierpont Morgan and Theodore Roosevelt. Reyes, before the Panama revolution, came through the United States on his way between Bogota and his former diplomatic post in Mexico. His fame as a soldier and explorer caused him to receive an invitation to meet the strenuous President, and they swapped tales of adventure. On the same trip, in May, 1903, Reyes, instead of going direct from New York to Colombia, stopped off at Cuba and conferred with J. Pierpont Morgan, who was yachting there.

Mr. Cromwell, in his relation, tells of the compromise between the United States, Colombia, and Panama which he says he proposed and adds:

"We do not consider ourselves free to describe here the details of these conferences, but we may mention that Gen. Reyes gave them such serious consideration and encouragement that we immediately sent to the Isthmus Capt. Beers, of the Panama Railroad Co., who was charged to explain the plan to the Panama Government, which promptly authorized its consideration."

Mr. Cromwell says he advised the canal company of this compromise plan on February 3, 1904, by cable. This was the beginning of Reyes's power. His election as President of Colombia followed the same year, and during the period when he was despoiling his country of millions, before his flight to Europe, he was in close communication with Cromwell. Mr. Cromwell modestly tells the French arbitrators that he brought about the acceptance of his compromise proposition, but he omitted the details, elsewhere related, of his sharing in Reyes's plunder.

February 13: The convention of the Republic of Panama adopted the national constitution.

February 23: Dr. Manuel Amador Guerrero was inaugurated the first President of the Republic of Panama. On the same day, in celebration of that event, President Amador's son, Dr. Raoul A. Amador, gave a luncheon at the Waldorf-Astoria Hotel to the men in New York to whom he and his father considered the new Republic most indebted. Their names appeared on the menu card in the following order: William Nelson Cromwell, George H. Sullivan, E. B. Hill, William J. Curtis, R. L. Farnham, E. A. Drake, Charles Paine, R. L. Walker, S. Deming, Dr. M. J. Echeverria.

Cromwell, Sullivan, Hill, Curtis, and Farnham were of Mr. Cromwell's staff; Drake, Paine, Walker, and Deming were officers, directors, or employees of the Panama Railroad. Dr. Echeverria was the only Panama guest. In his office in New York, Dr. Amador spent much of his time between his trips back and forth to Washington, negotiating for American support of the revolution. The World introduced this menu in evidence in Panama after the surviving members of the "patriots' committee" had sworn in Mr. Roosevelt's libel suit that the revolution received no assistance from the Panama Railroad nor from Mr. Cromwell.

February 23: The Senate, accelerated by Mr. Cromwell's lobbying, voted to ratify the Hay-Bunau-Varilla treaty, and ratifications were exchanged on February 26.

March 30: The Wilson suit to restrain the Secretary of the Treasury from paying the $40,000,000 was instituted in Washington, based on the ground that the Spooner law did not apply to a treaty with Panama.

March 31: The civil tribunal of the Seine decided in favor of the canal company the suit brought by the Colombian Government to enjoin the transfer of the canal to the United States.

April 30: It is was announced in press dispatches from Washington that President Roosevelt had made peace with the house of Morgan, and had agreed to the selection of J. P. Morgan & Co. as disbursing agents for the $40,000,000. Mr. Cromwell says in his account that he procured their appointment in order to transfer the $40,000,000 directly into the Bank of France, where it could not be reached by creditors of the canal company.

May 3: The cabinet meeting confirmed the selection of Morgan & Co. as disbursing agents of the United States. On the same day Mr. Morgan left Paris after having agreed with Mr. Cromwell on the details of the method of transfer.

May 4: A check was issued of the following tenor:

New York, *May 4, 1904.*

Morgan, Harjes & Co., *Paris:*

Pay to the order of Philippe Buna-Varilla five hundred and fifteen thousand francs.

No. 31537. J. P. Morgan & Co.

Thus Bunau-Varilla, on the face of the transaction, appears to have received back the $100,000 which was deposited with J. P. Morgan & Co., according to the records of Heidelbach, Ickelheimer & Co., $75,000 on November 17, 1903, and $25,000 on November 24, and originally cabled from Credit Lyonnais, October 26, 1903.

May 4: Physical possession of the canal property on the Isthmus was delivered to the United States.

May 5: Secretary of the Treasury Leslie M. Shaw conferred with various bankers at the New York subtreasury concerning the financial operations. The security of Morgan & Co., as disbursing agents, was agreed upon.

May 7: The Treasury warrant for $40,000,000 was signed in Washington by Secretary Shaw.

May 9: Secretary Shaw, having in person brought the warrant to New York, delivered it to Charles Steele, of J. P. Morgan & Co.

May 13: President Amador signed law No. 48 of 1904, of the National Assembly of Panama, whereby the financial transactions of the revolution were concealed. This law legalized in lump sums the expenditures up to and including June 30, 1904, as follows.

Liquidated accounts of the extinct department of Panama up to and including Nov. 3, 1903	$400,000
Expenditures of the junta, or provisional government, between Nov. 4, 1903, and Feb. 20, 1904, when the first President was inaugurated	1,200,000
Expenditures of the organized government between Feb. 21 and June 30, 1904	1,400,000
Total, in Panaman silver	3,000,000
American gold equivalent at then prevailing exchange	1,365,000

J. Gabriel Duque, proprietor of the Panama Star and Herald, declares that the accounts showing how this money was disbursed were burned by agreement in a secret session of the national assembly. All efforts to obtain an accounting of the entire sum have failed. Ernesto T. Lefevre, correspondent of the Associated Press in Panama and son-in-law and executor of the late Jose Agustin Arango, admits having in his custody all of the original vouchers signed by Arango, as one of the junta. He refuses to permit their inspection, frankly stating that the persons who would thereby be compromised would cause his ruin politically if he did so.

In the Official Gazette of the new Republic, which first appeared on November 14, 1903, there is no account of the operations of the treasury general of the Republic for November, 1903. The first accounting published was for December, and that did not appear until March 10, 1904. From the court of accounts of Panama, after long delays and various refusals, the World obtained a certified statement of the operations of the treasury general of the Republic for the period not included in the public accountings. This shows:

Balance in the treasury of the old Department of Panama, Nov. 1, 1903	$162,330.45

The president of the court of accounts assured the World that the books do not show whether this balance consisted of cash or documents, but from preceding records it is clear that the greater part of this balançe was "documentos por legalizar y avances varios" and that there was little actual cash.

The certified account shows:

Expenditures from Nov. 1 to 3, inclusive	$22,629.65
Leaving a balance Nov. 3, 1903	139,812.70
Receipts, Nov. 4 to 30, inclusive	53,553.40
Expenditures from Nov. 4 to 30, 1903, inclusive	4,819.15
Balance in treasury Nov. 30, 1903	188,546.95

This certified accounting gives the lie to all the pretensions of the Panamans that the first costs of the revolution were paid out of the funds found in the treasury when the rebels took possession. The treasury balance of $188,546.95 at the end of November agrees with the balance reported in the public accounting for the beginning of December. This accounting shows:

Treasury balance Dec. 31, 1903	$161,486.80

But this apparent balance, as shown in the published accounting, consisted in only $4,158.15 actual cash and $157,328.65 of paper.

It is apparent from these figures alone—and there is ample corroboration for the statement—that the first costs of the revolution were not paid out of the treasury, excepting the $22,629.65 which would cover the sums disbursed on the night of November 3, when a cart was backed up to the treasury and the money taken out to pay the Colombian "admiral," Ruben Varon, the first installment on his $35,000 bribe.

In the certified accounting the expenditures for November, amounting to a total of $27,448.80, are not classified. The published accountings for the remaining seven months of the period for which the expenditures were legalized by the National Assembly in lump sums show the following apportionment:

	For the Army.	Other expenses of Government.	Actual cash balances
December, 1903	$103,997.65	$23,808.35	$4,158.13
January, 1904	204,506.70	13,681.55	1,688.10
February, 1904	95,954.20	31,859.20	11,470.00
March, 1904	217,051.15	115,028.20	....
April, 1904	71,579.50	104,829.60	....
May, 1904	132,224.30	106,264.50	11,060.60
June, 1904	14,927.00	34,461.30	31,857.86
Total	840,240.50	429,932.70	....

The equipment of the army had cost virtually nothing, since the arms, according to Panaman accounts, had all been taken from the Colombian garrisons. According to Mr. Roosevelt's military spies, the arms came from abroad before the revolution, and may have been paid for after the independence with part of the money appearing on the accounts as expenditures for the military.

It is certain that the "patriots" received their reward, and no one in Panama questions that a good share of it came out of the funds that appear on the public accountings as having gone to the army. After the "patriots" were rewarded, the expenditures for the military arm of this great Republic fell off suddenly from $100,000 or $200,000 a month to $14,927 in June, 1904, and $11,504 in July, instead of costing twice as much as the rest of the Government.

Gen. Esteban Huertas, for selling himself and his soldiers, was paid $30,000 silver soon after the revolution. Then, on May 30, 1904, President Amador approved law No. 60, placing at Huertas' disposal within 30 days $50,000 gold, ostensibly for a trip to the United States, France, and Germany, "on special mission to study the military organizations of those countries." Accompanied by a party of the parasites who preyed upon his generosity, he went as far as England, and came back to enjoy what he and his friends had not squandered of the reward for his treason.

The American officials of the Panama Railroad, likewise "patriots" in the Panaman sense, received their pay in the spring of 1904, in sums approximating $15,000 to $25,000 silver per "patriot." Considering their services, which were the principal factor, aside from warships and money, in giving the Panamans their independence and opportunity for "graft," the American railroad men were underpaid. Native "patriots" whose assistance on the 3d, 4th, and 5th of November did not approach in usefulness that of the Panama Railroad men, were paid as much, or more, if current accounts in Panama are not incorrect.

Simple addition of the total expenditures of the treasury general of the Republic for the period during which expenditures of $3,000,000 were legalized gives some idea of the extent of the "graft." The public accountings show expenditures for all purposes up to June 30, 1904, of $1,255,963.35. Add to this the $27,448.80 shown in the court of accounts for the missing month of November, 1903, and the $734,245.25 in obligations to be legalized at the end of June, and the total outgo accounted for is $2,017,657.40, against expenditures legalized of $3,000,000.

Present-day officials of the Republic, while making no explanation of where the money went, point out that the operations of the "treasury general of the Republic," as reported in 1904, did not include the provincial treasuries outside the Province of Panama. This could not, however, account for the missing $982,342.60. Who got it?

When Isadoro Hazera, minister of finance, prepared his first comprehensive report to the national assembly for 1908, he was instructed by the late President Amador not to attempt to straighten out the tangle. Dr. Amador remarked that the less said the better concerning the first million of the $10,000,000 paid to Panama for the canal concession. Of this first $1,000,000, it appears from the statement Mr. Cromwell submitted to the Senate committee, February 26, 1906, that $622,615.52 went to pay drafts on J. P. Morgan & Co. (P. 1043, S. Doc. No. 407, 59th Cong., 2d sess.—the Morgan hearings.) The remaining $377,384.48 of the first $1,000,000 approximates the sum unaccounted for by the treasury reports of Panama.

None of the loans which the Brandon banking firm says it made to the revolutionists in November appears in the accountings for that month or for December. The total receipts from all sources, including import duties and the lottery for December, 1903, are given as $99,155.85.

The account for January, 1904, shows the following item under receipts:

"Received of Isaac Brandon & Bros. the value of the loan of $100,000, American gold, made by Messrs. J. P. Morgan & Co., and the Brohring Grem Fruit & Co. (Bowling Green Trust Co.) to the Government of the Republic as follows:

	Silver.
$25,000 at 145 per cent premium	$61,250
$75,000 at 137 per cent premium	177,750
	239,000

In the account of the treasury operations for February, 1904, appears the receipt of $103,500 silver from the Brandons, "the value of one telegraphic draft for $46,000 American gold, which was sold at a premium of 125 per cent." There is also a loan from the Brandons of $11,000 silver.

The March account shows loans from Brandons for $100,000 and $20,000 silver, and the receipt from them of $183,000 silver from the balance of a loan of $90,000 American gold.

April shows another loan from the Brandons of $82,000 silver.

The May account shows $36,222.50 silver from J. P. Morgan & Co. in small drafts drawn in favor of various Panaman merchants; also advances of $10,000 and $40,000 silver on loans from the Brandons, and $104,441 silver, which they delivered to the Army.

The June account shows $107,000 silver received from a draft of $50,000 gold by J. P. Morgan & Co., payable to Gen. Huertas; and two other drafts against the same firm, one payable to J. A. Arango, netting $5,356.35 silver, and one payable to O. Holde, netting $34,500.35 silver. A loan of $10,000 gold from Brandons to the Junta, made on January 20, 1904, and another for $25,000 silver, made January 25, by the Junta, appear in the June account; also a current loan from the Brandons for $50,000 silver.

In the July accounting appear $200,000 gold received from J. P. Morgan & Co., a Morgan draft in favor of Gov. J. D. Obaldia for $8,566.66 gold, and five Morgan drafts payable to various Panaman merchants for sums aggregating $25,550 gold.

After July the founders of the Republic deemed it inadvisable to publish treasury statements, although they had been for many years a feature of the Official Gazette of the Department of Panama.

Mr. Roosevelt's fear of exposure of his alliance with Harriman and the corporate source of his campaign funds in 1904, which caused him to call Judge Alton B. Parker publicly a liar, was not the only ghost that stalked his political house. He feared even more the laying bare of his Panama record, even to the point of paying political blackmail to the Panamans. His alarm became a panic when Dr. Eusebio A. Morales, one of the Panaman commissioners who was assisting Mr. Cromwell in carrying out the advice of Mr. Roosevelt to invest the canal millions in America, opened fire through the New York newspapers. The Panamans, disappointed and angered by the interpretations placed upon the canal treaty by the United States, were clamoring against the application of the Dingley tariff rates to the Canal Zone, and were generally dissatisfied with the bargain made for them behind their backs by Bunau-Varilla. We will let Dr. Morales introduce the story as he put it in writing, with a brief preface.

When the World's rogatory commission arrived in Panama, Dr. Morales, who was secretary of public instruction of the Republic, was about to return to the capital from a tour of inspection of the rural schools. Immediately the late President Obaldia sent him a message suggesting that he continue his trip until further notice. At the same time Gen. Estaban Huertas departed from Panama for the interior, and Gen. Herbert O. Jeffries, a third witness the World very much desired to examine, received a card from Obaldia suggesting that it would be convenient if he should visit his hacienda in the interior and remain until he heard of developments. A representative of the World later went into the interior and saw Jeffries, and upon his return to Panama found Dr. Morales at his post. Under the Panaman procedure a member of the cabinet can not be subpœnaed, but he is obliged to answer interrogatories in writing, and they were presented June 28, 1909. The first two questions were:

"1. Will you kindly relate in detail the circumstances which prompted you to write for the North American Review the article on the Hay-Bunau-Varilla treaty and the reasons that led to its withdrawal?

"2. Who suggested the withdrawal of the article, and with whom did you consult as to the advisability of publishing it?

Dr. Morales replied June 29, 1909, as follows:

"1. In September of 1904 there was pending between Panama and the United States a diplomatic question originating in the diverse interpretations which the two countries gave to the canal treaty, in matters referring to the enforcement of the Dingley tariff in the zone, to jurisdiction over the ports of Panama and Colon, and to other points of minor importance. I, interested on behalf of my country in making known the issue to the level-headed and just people of America, published several articles in the New York newspapers, and doubtless for this reason the editor of the North American Review solicited my collaboration, asking me to prepare an article on this subject, which was to be handed to him on October 20.

"Happily for Panama, President Roosevelt convinced himself of the justice of our claims, and on the 18th or 19th of October addressed to Secretary Taft the celebrated letter in which he gave the latter instructions to come to the Isthmus and effect a settlement with the Panaman Government of the pending questions.

"As my only aim in publishing the article already prepared for the North American Review was to favor the interests of my country, the publication no longer had any object. Furthermore, I received from Mr. Obaldia, then minister of Panama in Washington, a communication pointing out to me the profitableness of withdrawing my article, and this I gave expression to in a letter which I addressed to the editor of the Review on the 19th of October.

"2. I did not consult with anybody about the publication of my article, and as to its withdrawal, Mr. Obaldia alone intervened in the manner I have stated. Nevertheless, I ought to say that some distinguished persons were at my hotel to beg of me not to publish the article, thinking, doubtless, that it might contain revelations against President Roosevelt in connection with the independence of Panama; but it is the fact that in my work there was nothing which was not a dispassionate and calm exposition of the international question which was being debated, as is shown by the title of the article, which was: 'The Panama Canal treaty; its history and interpretation.'"

Dr. Morales later amplified this statement by giving to a representative of the World the names of the "distinguished persons" who called on him at his hotel and begged him not to publish anything about the history of the canal treaty. He said they were the late George A. Burt, formerly superintendent of the Panama Railroad, and another American whose name Mr. Morales understood to be Mr. Anson. They represented themselves, said Dr. Morales, as the direct spokesmen for Cornelius N. Bliss, the Republican campaign collector, and his chief, George Bruce Cortelyou, Republican national chairman. They told Dr. Morales frankly that they feared an exposure of the history of the Panama revolution would defeat Mr. Roosevelt for the Presidency, and declared that they were authorized to reimburse the author for his article if he would suppress it, and further declared that President Roosevelt would sign any order desired for the adjustment of the differences with Panama if Dr. Morales would acquiesce.

As Dr. Morales explained in his written statement, his object was to compel the United States to recognize the rights which the Panamans contended were their due, so he consented to withdraw his article, but would accept no compensation, and on the following day President Roosevelt wrote his letter to Secretary Taft ordering him to go to the Isthmus and adjust the differences. Secretary Taft went to Panama accompanied by Mr. Cromwell, and together they were feted as Panama's two best friends. Arm in arm with two of the belles of Panama, Cromwell and Taft had their photographs taken together. (See photograph.) They were so inseparable that the chief engineer of the canal could find no opportunity to confer privately with the Secretary of War during all the trip from New York nor while Taft was on the Isthmus.

At the banquet to Secretary Taft in the Hotel Central, Panama, December 1. 1904. Mr. Cromwell made a characteristically flamboyant speech, starting off by declaring himself a citizen of Panama. At the next meeting of the municipal council of the city of Panama, December 29, 1904, Mr. Cromwell was voted, because of his great services to the Republic, a meritorious son (hijo benemerito) of the city.

In his speech at the banquet to Taft, Mr. Cromwell started off with this rare specimen of "orating":

"Mr. President and fellow citizens of Panama, what must have been the emotions of the Roman soldiers as, after years of absence in foreign wars, they reentered the capital city following their victorious generals, and bearing the trophies of their valor and the symbols of fresh conquests?

"All the weary marches, the pain of wounds, the sacrifices and privations of battle were forgotten in the glad acclaim of welcoming hosts, the flower-strewn paths, the glory of their empire.

"Does not this suggest something of the sentiments which possess me, an humble soldier in the Panama cause, as I come to greet you after the years which have separated us while I have been battling at the front for the canal—the hope of the Isthmus, and upon the fate of which, indeed, hung its very existence?"

O